BRAHMAND
WORLD DEFENCE UPDATE 2022

Editorial Advisory Board:
Dr. Sanjeev Kumar Joshi
Col. JP Uniyal (Retd.)
Cmde. RK Agnihotri (Retd.)
Gr. Cpt. (Retd.) M.K. Srivastava
Praveen Pathak

Editorial Team:
Miranda M Newmai
Ritu Mousumi Tripathy
Suman Chowdhury

Digital Edition: Sunil Kumar Choudhary and Anup Kumar

Last Updated till 31st December, 2021

DISCLAIMER:
- The data has been obtained from the open domain. Photos and illustrations for which no specific credit is given are understood to be in the public domain.
- The boundaries of the Countries shown in the maps and illustrations in this book are for representational purposes only. Readers are suggested to verify its authenticity and correctness.
- The data presented in this book should not be taken to reflect either the views or the policy of the editor's organisation to which they belong to or employed.
- The publisher, editors and their Organisation will not at all be responsible in respect of anything and the consequences of anything done or omitted to be done by any person in reliance upon the contents of this Book.
- Assessment of strategic issues by editorial staff is based on collection of general facts available via news and current events and hence shall not be held responsible for any inadvertent/ authentication errors. Any omissions or corrections brought to our attention will be remedied in future editions.

ACKNOWLEDGMENTS:
The data and images for the Country Reports have been obtained from the Ministry of Defence/ Official websites of various Countries, Armed Forces of various Countries, CIA World Fact Book and US Dept. of State website, US Department of Defence Annual Reports, published source materials of various Defence Manufacturers in the World Wide Web, besides other sources.

BRAHMAND WORLD DEFENCE UPDATE 2022

Foreword

Dr. G. Satheesh Reddy
Secretary, Department of Defence R&D
& Chairman, DRDO, Govt. of India

PENTAGON PRESS LLP

Brahmand World Defence Update 2022

ISBN 978-93-90095-53-7

First Published in 2022

Copyright © BrahMos Aerospace

Published by
PENTAGON PRESS LLP
206, Peacock Lane, Shahpur Jat,
New Delhi-110049
Phones: 011-26491568
Telefax: 011-26490600
email: rajan@pentagonpress.in
website: www.pentagonpress.in

All rights reserved. No part of this publication may be reproduced, stored in a retrieval system or transmitted in any form or by any means, electronic, mechanical, photocopying, recording or otherwise without the written permission of the copyright Owner.

Design and layout: Heena Sodhi

Printed at Aegean Offset Printers, Greater Noida, U.P.

डॉ जी. सतीश रेड्डी
FNAE, HFCSI, FRIN (London), FMACANUD (Russia), FAeSI, FRAeS (UK),
HFPMAI, FSSWR, FIET (UK), FIE, FAPAS, FIETE, AFAIAA (USA)

Dr G. Satheesh Reddy
FNAE, HFCSI, FRIN (London), FMACANUD (Russia), FAeSI, FRAeS (UK),
HFPMAI, FSSWR, FIET (UK), FIE, FAPAS, FIETE, AFAIAA (USA)

भारत सरकार
Government of India

एक कदम स्वच्छता की ओर

सचिव, रक्षा अनुसंधान तथा विकास विभाग
एवं
अध्यक्ष, डीआरडीओ

Secretary, Department of Defence R&D
&
Chairman, DRDO

FOREWORD

Rapid technological advancements coupled with geopolitical and geo-economic shifts are set to re-shape the global order. Challenges to our national security are mounting and have escalated into an extremely complex affair. The ever changing scenario of uncertainties and fluidities in the global and near regional security landscape complicates the evaluation and identification of threat a difficult proposition. Need for a strong, capable and completely self-reliant military in such a perspective needs no emphasis.

Future warfare will be characterised by Artificial Intelligence, Machine Learning, EW, Robotics and Space. This paradigm shift from the conventional war has changed India's strategic defence environment in proportions unfathomed. The right approach in the present scenario would be to seize the initiative, resort to prevent and manage crisis before it explodes and lessen the opportunity for the adversaries to create and enhance instability. Towards this, a strong, highly capable and self-reliant defence technology development is the need of the hour. Self-sufficiency in defence will be the sole constituent towards achieving strategic independence and military superiority.

The self-reliance model adopted by our country has been characterised by establishing and expanding the indigenous base for design, development and manufacturing in the field of military technology. Over the past few decades the indigenous defence technology has taken a quantum jump towards self-reliance and the contribution of defence R&D towards self-reliance in defence technology is immense. Design, development and now seamless production of indigenous weapons like ballistic missiles, supersonic and subsonic cruise missiles, new generation missiles, surface to air and air to surface missiles, Anti-Satellite missions are testimony to the growing Indian capabilities in defence sector. The production order of "LCA Tejas" and "MBT Arjun" form indications of India's resolve to indigenous development. A marked increase in the defence exports by Indian industry and government's encouragement to defence exports has set the ball rolling for an evolved ecosystem.

In pursuance of "Atmanirbharata" the defence technology study groups play an important role. 'Brahmand World Defence Update' year book which is an initiative of BrahMos Aerospace, provides a comprehensive, detailed and accurate assessment of geopolitical and strategic aspects of 113 countries spread across the world with special emphasis to defence. The book portraits a comprehensive review of economy, international disputes, defence with special emphasis to Army, Navy, Air Force, defence expenditure, major procurements and defence production and R&D.

Considering their significance due to their strategic and geo-political existence in correlation to India, 33 countries have been selected from each region with special emphasis on their threat perception, geographical importance, international and strategic relations, defence R&D, defence expenditure and production.

This book provides an authoritative source for reference and an impartial and independent and trusted source for strategic and defence intelligence. I am sure the book will serve as an authentic source of information and resource for any defence organisation in the country.

An initiative of BrahMos Aerospace, the book is extremely useful for defence forces, R&D organisations and production units across the globe. I am confident that it will serve as an indispensible reference guide for defence establishments, R&D institutions, weapons manufacturers and analysts alike. The volume promises to provide potential market entry strategies and business opportunities centering on latest hardware acquisitions in the defence industry.

(Dr. G. Satheesh Reddy)

PREFACE

Brahmand World Defence Update 2022 is a comprehensive, incisive and objective assessment of present day global military order. The yearbook presents an up-to-date compilation of military data of 113 countries including their weapons inventory, arms procurement/ upgrade, defence budget and core conflict areas.

Of the 113 countries, the book has incorporated detailed strategic information on 33 important countries selected from each continent/ region with a special thrust on their geopolitical importance, strategic relations, threat perception, defence capabilities and defence budget trends.

Coming out in its eleventh edition, Brahmand World Defence Update 2022 has included a special chapter on **'Counter-Terrorism & National Security'** aspects of six major nations – **Germany, India, Israel, Russia, UK and the USA.**

Terrorism and terror-related violence has emerged as one of the deadliest threats to global peace, stability and security in 21st century. Many nations across the world today are grappling with terrorist and extremist-induced hostility and violence. The yearbook, while shedding light on the growing menace of terrorism, armed militancy/ insurgency and extremism that has endangered national security and sovereignty, has also highlighted counter-terrorism and counter-insurgency endeavours undertaken by each nation's Government to fight this deadly threat.

Like all its previous editions, Brahmand World Defence Update 2022 has presented a complete overview of latest military developments and trends across the globe. Moreover, the yearbook has provided potential market entry strategies and business opportunities in the worldwide defence & aerospace sector by highlighting latest military acquisitions/ trends/ developments and by identifying top-notch companies involved in international arms trade.

COUNTER-TERRORISM & NATIONAL SECURITY

Terrorism poses a serious threat to international peace and security. It is a menace that does not recognise borders and affect countries and people irrespective of their geographical location.

Terrorism encompasses a range of complex threats including organised terrorism in conflict zones, foreign terrorist fighters and the emergence of radicalised 'lone wolves'. Terrorists regularly change their tactic and seek sophisticated means of attack such as chemical, biological, radiological, nuclear and explosive weapons, and cyber attacks.

In the rapidly evolving threat environment, countering terrorism has become a national security priority. Different countries have adopted counter terrorism measures, developing coordinated strategies and approaches to fight this haunting danger. Counter-terrorism or anti-terrorism, incorporates military tactics, techniques, and strategy that government, military, law enforcement, business, and intelligence agencies use to combat or prevent terrorism.

The global fight against terrorism requires the development of national counter-terrorism strategies that seek to prevent acts of terrorism, prosecute those responsible for such criminal acts, and promote and protect human rights and the rule of law. It has been noted that setting priorities is a must and match resources to a range of evolving national security challenges, to develop more sophisticated capabilities and enhanced security measures, to be vigilant using intelligence as key instrument.

In addition, through international cooperation and information sharing, by fusing foreign and domestic counter terrorism information and providing terrorism analysis, the world's police can better understand their methods, motives and financing that will help in identifying and arrest suspects. Some examples of measures being taken to counter terrorism include monitoring potential terrorists, identifying individuals who may be becoming radicalised and provides at-risk people and buildings with additional security.

The Brahmand World Defence Update 2022 has highlighted some important countries and their counter-terrorism efforts in this regard – **Germany, India, Israel, Russia, United States of America** and **the United Kingdom.** The yearbook has tried to present a brief description of the terror attacks that these countries have faced, their encounters and experiences and significant measures that are being taken to effectively counter terrorism in the future.

CONTENTS

COUNTRY NAME	PAGE NO.	COUNTRY NAME	PAGE NO.	COUNTRY NAME	PAGE NO.
A		Colombia	80	**I**	
Afghanistan	1	Croatia	82	**India**	**134**
Albania	2	**Cuba**	**85**	Indonesia	161
Algeria	**3**	Cyprus	89	**Iran**	**164**
Argentina	**8**	Czech Republic	91	Iraq	170
Armenia	14			**Israel**	**172**
Australia	**16**	**D**		**Italy**	**181**
Austria	21	Democratic Republic of Congo	93		
Azerbaijan	23	Denmark	94	**J**	
		Dominican Republic	96	**Japan**	**186**
B				Jordan	194
Bahrain	25	**E**			
Bangladesh	27	Ecuador	98	**K**	
Belarus	30	**Egypt**	**100**	Kazakhstan	197
Belgium	32	Estonia	106	Kenya	199
Bolivia	33	Ethiopia	108	Kosovo	200
Bosnia and Herzegovina	35			Kuwait	202
Botswana	37	**F**		Kyrgyzstan	203
Brazil	**38**	Fiji	109		
Brunei	45	Finland	110	**L**	
Bulgaria	47	**France**	**113**	Laos	205
				Lebanon	206
C		**G**		Libya	208
Cambodia	49	Georgia	120	Luxembourg	209
Cameroon	51	**Germany**	**121**		
Canada	**53**	Ghana	129	**M**	
Chile	**59**	Greece	131	**Malaysia**	**211**
China	**63**			Mexico	217

COUNTRY NAME	PAGE NO.	COUNTRY NAME	PAGE NO.	COUNTRY NAME	PAGE NO.
Mongolia	220	Singapore	299	**Y**	
Morocco	221	Slovakia	301	Yemen	411
Myanmar	224	**South Africa**	**303**		
		South Korea	**309**	**Z**	
N		South Sudan	316	Zambia	413
Nepal	226	Spain	317	Zimbabwe	414
Netherlands	227	Sri Lanka	319		
New Zealand	231	Sudan	321	**Abbreviations**	**417**
Niger	234	**Sweden**	**323**		
Nigeria	235	Switzerland	329		
North Korea	**237**	Syria	331		
Norway	242				
		T			
O		Taiwan	333		
Oman	245	Tajikistan	339		
		Tanzania	341		
P		**Thailand**	**342**		
Pakistan	**247**	Tunisia	350		
Peru	255	**Turkey**	**352**		
Philippines	**258**	Turkmenistan	359		
Poland	263				
Portugal	266	**U**			
		Uganda	361		
Q		Ukraine	362		
Qatar	**268**	United Arab Emirates	365		
		United Kingdom	**367**		
R		**United States of America**	**378**		
Republic of Congo	273	Uruguay	397		
Romania	274	Uzbekistan	399		
Russia	**277**				
		V			
S		**Venezuela**	**400**		
Saudi Arabia	**289**	**Vietnam**	**406**		
Serbia	297				

AFGHANISTAN
(Capital: Kabul)

INTRODUCTION
Area: 652,230 sq km
Population: 37,466,414 (July 2021 est.)
Coastline: 0 km (Landlocked)
Maritime claims: None

KEY POLITICAL PERSONS

PRIME MINISTER: Mohammad Hasan Akhund (acting)

DEPUTY PRIME MINISTER: Abdul Ghani Baradar ((acting)

KEY DEFENCE PERSONS

DEFENCE MINISTER: Mohammad Yaqoob (acting)

CHIEF OF STAFF: Qari Fasihuddin

ECONOMY

AAfghanistan is a landlocked country and dependent on foreign aid for its economic development. The country is known for producing some of the finest fruits, especially apples, apricots, cherries, figs, grapes, melons, sweet mulberries, peaches, and pomegranates. The economy was reportedly rising steadily in the last decade with substantial improvements in development programmes. However, economic growth has suffered after recovering from the 2018 drought and expiring international financial commitments, and the COVID-19 pandemic and recent political developments have further pushed Afghanistan into economic crisis. According to the World Bank, inflation accelerated gradually over the first half of 2021. Prices for basic household goods, including food and fuel, increased substantially as the Taliban captured border posts and key transit hubs, disrupting supply chains. Inflation further accelerated following the Taliban takeover.

GDP (official exchange rate): $20.24 billion (2017 est.)

Real Growth Rate (GDP): 2.7% (2017 est.), 2.2% (2016 est.)

Industries: Small-scale production of bricks, textiles, soap, furniture, shoes, fertilizer, apparel, food products, non-alcoholic beverages, mineral water, cement; handwoven carpets; natural gas, coal, copper.

Total Exports: $1.48 billion (2020 est.), $1.52 billion (2019 est.)

Export Commodities: Gold, grapes, opium, fruits and nuts, insect resins, cotton, handwoven carpets, soapstone, scrap metal (2019)

Major Markets: United Arab Emirates 45%, Pakistan 24%, India 22%, China 1% (2019)

Total Imports: $6.98 billion (2020 est.), $7.37 billion (2019 est.)

Import Commodities: Wheat flours, broadcasting equipment, refined petroleum, rolled tobacco, aircraft parts, synthetic fabrics (2019)

Major Suppliers: United Arab Emirates 23%, Pakistan 17%, India 13%, China 9%, United States 9%, Uzbekistan 7%, Kazakhstan 6% (2019)

INTERNATIONAL DISPUTES

◆ Afghan, Coalition, and Pakistan military meet periodically to clarify the alignment of the boundary on the ground and on maps and since 2014 have met to discuss collaboration on the Taliban insurgency and counterterrorism efforts.

◆ Afghan and Iranian commissioners have discussed boundary monument densification and resurvey; Iran protests Afghanistan's restricting flow of dammed Helmand River tributaries during drought.

◆ Pakistan has sent troops across and built fences along some remote tribal areas of its treaty-defined Durand Line border with Afghanistan which serve as bases for foreign terrorists and other illegal activities.

◆ Russia remains concerned about the smuggling of poppy derivatives from Afghanistan through Central Asian countries.

DEFENCE

Islamic Emirate Army

The Afghan armed forces originated in 1709. The "Islamic Army of Afghanistan" was created in 1997 after the Taliban first took power in Afghanistan. The army was, however, dissolved in 2001 after the Taliban were deposed from power following the United States invasion of Afghanistan. With the formation of the Afghan Interim Administration, new military units were created trained by NATO-member states. On 01 December 2002, a new ground force – the Afghan National Army (ANA) - was created with the issue of a decree by former President Hamid Karzai, along with an Army Air Corps as an integral part of the Army. The Islamic Republic armed forces was effectively dissolved and the "Islamic Army of Afghanistan" was officially re-established on 08 November 2021 after the Taliban's victory in the war in Afghanistan on 15 August 2021 following the recapture of Kabul and the collapse of the United States backed Islamic Republic of Afghanistan and its Afghan National Army as a whole. The "Islamic Emirate Army" is the combined Army and Air Force of the Taliban run Islamic Emirate of Afghanistan. The active personnel is reportedly 85,000–200,000 (2021).

Ground Forces: The Taliban reportedly maintains at least two elite units under its command – the Badri 313 Battalion and the Red Unit. Currently the Islamic Emirate Army is subdivided into eight corps, mostly superseding the previous corps of the Afghan National Army. Data on its military equipment is not available but it has been reported that the Army relies heavily on captured hardware from the defeated Afghan

National Army. Approximately 2,000 vehicles fell into Taliban hands after the Fall of Kabul, including the Humvee, M1117 Guardian, MaxxPro MRAP and Oshkosh ATV.

Air Force:
Currently no detail information is available about the Air Force. However, it has been reported that after the re-establishment of the Islamic Emirate of Afghanistan, the Taliban has acquired: UH-60 Black Hawks, Mil Mi-24s, Mil Mi-8s/Mil Mi-17s, A-29 Super Tucanos, Cessna 208s, and C-130 Hercules, captured from the Afghan Air Force.

Defence Expenditure
Total defence spending: $204 million (2018), $191 million (2017)

Defence spending in terms of GDP: 1.2% of GDP (2019)

Defence Production and R&D
Afghanistan has not been able to develop its defence capabilities having been experiencing decades of conflict. The country has been relying on the United States and other countries to provide financial support for its military and development work.

Defence Procurement
Afghanistan does not have any procurement policy as of now.

CONTACT DETAILS
Ministry of Defence
Pule-Mahmood Khan, PD 2, 1001, Kabul, Afghanistan
Email: info@mod.gov.af
https://mod.gov.af/en

ALBANIA
(Capital: Tirana)

INTRODUCTION
Area: 28,748 sq km
Population: 3,088,385 (July 2021 est.)
Coastline: 362 km
Maritime claims: Territorial sea: 12nm
Continental shelf: 200m depth or to the depth of exploitation

KEY POLITICAL PERSONS

PRESIDENT & COMMANDER-IN-CHIEF: Ilir Meta

PRIME MINISTER: Edi Rama

KEY DEFENCE PERSONS

MINISTER OF DEFENCE: Niko Peleshi

CHIEF OF GENERAL STAFF: Maj. Gen. Bajram Begaj

COMMANDER OF LAND FORCE: Brig. Gen. Arben Kingji

COMMANDER OF NAVAL FORCE: Brig. Gen. Ilir Xhebexhia

ECONOMY
Once a closed economy during the country's Communist regime, Albania has transitioned into a modern open-market economy. Since 2014, Albania's economy has steadily improved and economic growth reached 3.8% in 2017. However, close trade, remittance, and banking sector ties with Greece and Italy make Albania vulnerable to spillover effects of possible debt crises and weak growth in the euro zone. Remittances, a significant catalyst for economic growth, declined from 12-15% of GDP before the 2008 financial crisis to 5.8% of GDP in 2015. The agricultural sector, which accounts for almost half of employment but only about one-fifth of GDP, is limited primarily to small family operations and subsistence farming, because of a lack of modern equipment, unclear property rights, and the prevalence of small, inefficient plots of land. Inward FDI has increased significantly in recent years as the government has embarked on an ambitious programme to improve the business climate through fiscal and legislative reforms. Albania's three-year IMF programme, an extended fund facility arrangement, was successfully concluded in February 2017. The Government has strengthened tax collection amid moderate public wage and pension increases in an effort to reduce budget deficit. The country continues to face high public debt, exceeding its former statutory limit of 60% of GDP in 2013 and reaching 72% in 2016. Hit by the Coronavirus pandemic, the Albanian economy saw a 3.31% drop in GDP in 2020.

GDP (official exchange rate): $15.273 billion (2019 est.)

Real Growth Rate (GDP): 2.24% (2019 est.); 4.07% (2018 est.)

Industries: Food; footwear, apparel and clothing; lumber, oil, cement, chemicals, mining, basic metals, hydropower

Total Exports: $900.7 million (2017 est.); $789.1 million (2016 est.)

Export Commodities: Leather footwear and parts, crude petroleum, iron alloys, clothing, electricity, perfumes (2019)

Major Markets: Italy 45%, Spain 8%, Germany 6%, Greece 5%, France 4%, China 4% (2019)

Total Imports: $4.103 billion (2017 est.); $3.671 billion (2016 est.)

Import Commodities: Refined petroleum, cars, tanned hides, packaged medical supplies, footwear parts (2019)

Major Suppliers: Italy 28%, Greece 12%, China 11%, Turkey 9%, Germany 5% (2019)

INTERNATIONAL DISPUTES

◆ Albania has no known international disputes.

DEFENCE

ARMY

Personnel: 8000+

Equipment

Category	Name	In Service
APC	M113	130
ATGW	HN-5 Manpad	
	HJ-8	

New Procurements/ Upgrades

◆ The US Government has donated 37 mine-resistant ambush protected vehicles (MRAPs) to the Albanian Armed Forces.

◆ 248 High Mobility Multipurpose Wheeled Vehicles (Humvees) donated by the US as part of a $12 million aid package are being progressively inducted in the Army.

◆ The NATO-standard M4 carbine assault rifles are being procured to replace the AK-47 rifles.

NAVY

Personnel: 1,500

Equipment

Category	Name	In Service
Patrol vessel	Damen Stan 4207	4
Patrol boat	Shanghai II class	2
	Small patrol boat	17
Mine sweeper	Minesweeper	2

...continued

Category	Name	In Service
Auxiliary ship	Diving vessel	2
	Floating dock	1
	Torpedo ship	7

New Procurements/ Upgrades

No major procurement plans are under consideration at present.

AIR FORCE

Personnel: 1,400

Equipment

Category	Name	In Service
Helicopter	A-109	1
	AB-205	7
	AB-206C	7
	Bo-105E4	6
	AS-532 Cougar	4
	EC145	1 (VIP transport)+ 2 (utility)

New Procurements/ Upgrades

◆ The Air Force would be receiving three Sikorsky UH-60 Black Hawk medium-lift utility helicopters as part of a military aid package announced by the US in 2019.

◆ Funds worth €8 million (US$9.5 million) have been earmarked for the procurement of Bayraktar TB2 UAVs from Turkey.

Defence Expenditure

Defence spending in terms of GDP: 1.5% (2021)

Major suppliers of defence equipment to Albania in the past have been China, Soviet Russia, Turkey, Germany and Italy. The country is presently getting weapons and equipment mostly from the US as part of military aid.

Defence Production and R&D

There are no military research and development facilities in Albania. The country has no immediate plans to take up defence production.

Defence Procurement

The European country has procured naval patrol craft, helicopters and other weapons and equipment to strengthen its military which is undergoing comprehensive modernisation, including revision in structures and procedures to meet future challenges as a NATO member. Under the reforms drive, Albania is disposing its obsolete weapons and equipment while refurbishing the existing inventory. The Government has set a plan to gradually reduce the size of its armed forces by 3%. All military reforms are being carried out as per NATO standards. In 2018, the North Atlantic Council – the principal political decision-making body of NATO – approved a plan to build in Albania their first Air Base in the Western Balkans. In partnership with the Government of Albania, NATO has invested over €50 million in the first phase of modernization of the Kucova Air Base of the Albanian Air Force.

CONTACT DETAILS

Ministry of Defence
Dibra Street
Tirana, Albania
Tel: +355 (04) 2226601 / 2226602 / 2226603
Email: informimi_mm@mod.gov.al
www.mod.gov.al

Armed Forces
Email: fakset@aaf.mil.al

STRATEGIC INFORMATION
ALGERIA
(Capital: Algiers)

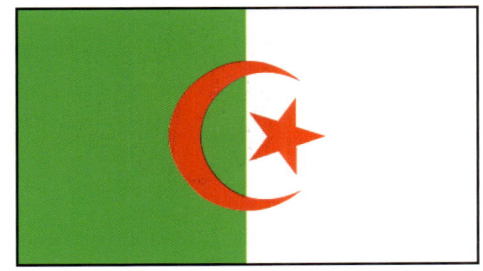

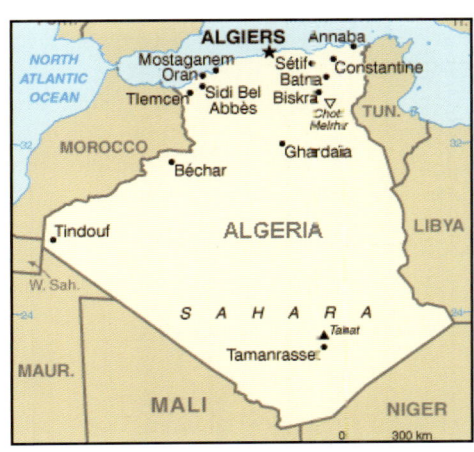

INTRODUCTION

Area: 2,381,740 sq km
Population: 43,576,691 (July 2021 est.)
Coastline: 998 km
Maritime claims: Territorial sea: 12 nm
Contiguous zone: 24 nm
Exclusive fishing zone: 32-52 nm

GEOPOLITICAL IMPORTANCE

The largest country in the African continent, Algeria acts as a gateway between Africa and Europe. The North African country is bordered by Libya and Tunisia in the East, Morocco and Western Sahara in the West, and Mauritania, Mali, and Niger in the South. The Mediterranean Sea is in its north. The Sahara Desert covers around 85% of the country's landmass and is mostly uninhabited. From a geostrategic perspective, Algeria has gained prominence with the discovery of huge amounts of oil and natural gas mostly in the Saharan desert in the 1950s. The African country today is a leading energy supplier, mainly to the European nations. It is the third biggest supplier of natural gas to the European Union.

POLITICAL OVERVIEW

After being ruled by France for over a century, Algeria gained independence in 1962 which was achieved following a bitter fight for freedom. The freedom struggle was led by the National Liberation Front (FLN) which came to power post-independence and ruled Algeria as a one-party socialist state until the late 1980s. The FLN had military affiliations which led to military interventions in the political dispensation of the country. In 1989, the country's Constitution was amended to introduce a multi-party system. The election of current President Abdelaziz Bouteflika in 1999 marked a new beginning as he contained civil unrest and also ended the dominance of the military in the country's political system. Constitutional amendments further increased Presidential powers in the political dispensation, thereby ending the Army's direct intervention in the system. Presently, Algeria functions as a presidential republic where the President is both head of the state and head of the government even though internal unrest persists and is dealt with strictly.

Former President Bouteflika, who secured his fourth term in office after general elections were held in the country in April 2014, was forced to step down in April 2019 following countrywide protests over his years-long rule. Even as Abdelkader Bensalah took charge as interim President following the political and constitutional uncertainty in the country, the Algerian Army, led by Chief of Staff Lt. Gen. Ahmed Gaed Salah, remained a major player in Algerian politics until recently. (The powerful Army General died on December 23, 2019.) After Presidential elections were held in the country in December 2019, Abdelmadjid Tebboune emerged as the new leader and was appointed President. In July 2021, President Tebboune appointed a new Government.

KEY POLITICAL PERSONS

PRESIDENT, DEFENCE MINISTER & COMMANDER-IN-CHIEF: Abdelmadjid Tebboune

PRIME MINISTER: Ayman Benabderrahmane

ECONOMY

Algeria's moderately-growing economy, the fourth largest in Africa, is highly dependent on oil and natural gas exports. The largest share of its revenue comes from exporting hydrocarbons which accounts for nearly 95% of the country's total exports and 30% of its GDP. Algeria has the 10th-largest reserves of natural gas in the world and is the sixth-largest gas exporter. It ranks 16th in oil reserves. After liberalising its economy partially in the 1990s, Algeria witnessed a spurt in economic growth compared to its post-independence socialist phase. Hydrocarbon exports also enabled the country maintain macroeconomic stability and earn large foreign currency reserves. However, with lower oil prices since 2014, Algeria's foreign exchange reserves have declined by more than half and its oil stabilization fund has decreased from about $20 billion at the end of 2013 to about $7 billion in 2017, which is the statutory minimum. The country has passed an energy law in 2019-end, and investors are still awaiting publication of regulations to decide whether to come to Algeria or not.

Algeria has struggled to develop non-hydrocarbon industries because of heavy regulation and an emphasis on state-driven growth. Investment has not been diversified into other sectors of the State-controlled economy except energy. The country is gradually introducing economic reforms as it seeks to become a member of the World Trade Organisation (WTO). Of late, Algeria has been grappling with corruption, youth unemployment and inequality which remained at the root of massive countrywide protests in 2019. In 2020, the COVID-19 outbreak slowed down consumption and investment, while falling oil prices cut into fiscal and export revenues of Algeria. The new Government has been facing the difficult tasks of maintaining macroeconomic stability, while responding to the public health crisis and also pursuing structural reforms.

GDP (official exchange rate): $169.912 billion (2019 est.)

Real Growth Rate (GDP): 1.4% (2017 est.); 3.2% (2016 est.)

Industries: Petroleum, natural gas, light industries, mining, electrical, petrochemical, food processing

Natural Gas - Proved Reserves: 4.504 trillion cu m (1 January 2018 est.)

Crude Oil - Proved Reserves: 12.2 billion bbl (1 January 2018 est.)

Total Exports: $34.37 billion (2017 est.); $29.06 billion (2016 est.)

Export Commodities: Crude petroleum, natural gas, refined petroleum, fertilizers, ammonia (2019)

Major Markets: Italy 13%, France 13%, Spain 12%, United States 7%, United Kingdom 7%, India 5%, South Korea 5% (2019)

Total Imports: $48.54 billion (2017 est.); $49.43 billion (2016 est.)

Import Commodities: Refined petroleum, wheat, packaged medical supplies, milk, vehicle parts (2019)

Major Suppliers: China 18%, France 14%, Italy 8%, Spain 8%, Germany 5%, Turkey 5% (2019)

DEFENCE & SECURITY

The African country does not face direct military threat from any country, barring few of its neighbouring states with whom it is locked in territorial disputes. Nevertheless, Algeria maintains quite a large and well-equipped military force to counter any domestic or external threat. The country's armed forces, called the People's National Army (PNA), constitute the land, naval and air forces along with an air defence command. Algeria's unusual geographic features, with about 80% of its area being desert, steppes, wasteland and mountains, pose a challenge for its armed forces to secure its borders and defend it from external aggression.

The armed forces of Algeria are equipped mostly with Soviet-era military hardware and weapons. They have received training in the then Soviet Union during the PNA's initial phase of modernisation. The PNA has also relied mostly on Soviet military doctrine which emphasised on large-scale, combined-arms warfare and operational warfare. Of late, China has emerged a major military supplier to Algeria.

The Algerian military is primarily engaged in containing domestic social unrest and Islamist armed conflict that have marred the nation since the early 1990s. The North African country is presently undergoing a phase of political uncertainty amidst a looming economic crisis. Of late, the country has also deployed a large number of its military troops across its border regions to quell the unrest emanating from terrorism and organised crime even as major terror groups are becoming active either within Algeria or on its border regions with Morocco, Tunisia, Mauritania, Mali, Niger and Libya.

KEY DEFENCE PERSONS

CHIEF OF STAFF OF PEOPLE'S NATIONAL ARMY: Lt. Gen. Said Chanegriha

COMMANDER OF ARMY: Maj. Gen. Ammar Atamnia

COMMANDER OF NAVY (Acting): Maj. Gen. Ben Maddah Mahfouz

COMMANDER OF AIR FORCE: Maj. Gen. Mahmoud Laraba

Internal Conflict

Internal problems and unrests have plagued Algeria more than its external threats and have often taken dangerous proportions. For over last two decades, Algeria has been affected by an Islamist armed conflict which has taken the form of terrorism by non-state armed groups. The armed conflict that erupted between radical Islamist militants and the country's military following a scrapped general election won by an Islamist party in 1992, has resulted in the death of over 100,000 civilians. The violence, mostly carried out as a guerrilla warfare movement, has given way to organised crime like robbery, abduction, extortion and killings in later years. While the Algerian Government has contained the decades-long civil war to a large extent, nevertheless incidents of violence and internal unrest still continue to affect the country. The recent spurt in terror-related activities within the country as also along its border regions has further exacerbated Algeria's internal security issues.

External Conflict

Algeria has no major external conflict areas barring border dispute with its neighbour, Morocco. Its longstanding border dispute with another neighbour, Tunisia, has been resolved in 1993 and the two countries have also signed an agreement in 2011 to demarcate more exactly their maritime border.

Morocco: The two African neighbours are entangled in dispute over a sparsely-populated Western Sahara Desert region. Algeria, like several other countries, is opposed to Morocco's control over Western Sahara – a former Spanish colony, which was annexed by Morocco in 1975. The 1,601-km border between Morocco and Algeria, that includes a 42-km stretch alongside the disputed Western Sahara region, has remained shut since 1994 over the issue. The stalemate over the disputed territory has continued between the Polisario movement, which demands independence and has got strong support from Algeria, and the Moroccan government's offer to grant autonomy to the region. The Polisario Front continues to receive military hardware from Algeria to resist any attempts by Morocco to annexe the Western Sahara region, like it attempted in 1976. Recently, the Moroccan king has called for direct talks with Algeria to resolve the long-standing dispute. Algeria, meanwhile, has reportedly started building a new army base on the Moroccan border. The move comes after the Moroccan Government in May 2020 announced plans to build "a small military base intended to accommodate troops" near its eastern border with Algeria. Meanwhile, the Algerian Government in August 2021 announced to cut diplomatic ties with Morocco, accusing the latter of "hostile actions", following months of resurgent tensions between the two neighbouring nations.

THREAT PERSPECTIVE

Algeria, like the rest of the North African countries, does not face any direct external military threat, although its relations with neighbouring state Morocco continue to remain tense. Algeria is primarily engaged in resolving its internal problems, terrorism being a major threat in recent times. The country, however, has never attempted to get involved in a military conflict with any of its neighbours.

STRATEGIC RELATIONS

Russia: As the most important strategic ally, Russia has provided military, technical as well as economic assistance to Algeria since the time of its freedom movement in the 1960s. The African country has received majority of its military assets from the then Soviet Union. Algerian armed forces have also been imparted training by Russian military institutions. To further strengthen this cooperation, the two countries signed a strategic partnership agreement in 2001 with a thrust on strengthening bilateral defence cooperation, particularly in expanding long-term arms trade and exchanges between their armed forces. Bilateral relations between the two countries remain strongest in the military sphere as also in the economic and energy spheres.

EU: The proximity of oil and energy-rich Algeria to Europe makes the African country a crucial strategic ally of the entire European Union which largely relies on Algerian hydrocarbons supplies. From economic aspect, Algeria has offered the European countries to explore investment opportunities, especially in its manufacturing sector and research & development area. The EU has also supported Algeria's bid to become a member of the World Trade Organisation. Some European countries, including France, Italy and Spain, have also supplied military equipment to the North African nation in the past.

China: In recent years, China and Algeria have explored ways to develop bilateral strategic partnership alongside their growing political, economic and trade ties. The two sides have bolstered their bilateral ties following the comprehensive strategic partnership established in 2014. China has emerged as one of the major military suppliers to Algeria in recent times. Even as Algeria's defence expenditure is growing, it has acquired Chinese equipment and platforms, including missiles, artillery pieces, corvettes and UAVs, as part of its military modernization drive.

MULTILATERAL ALLIANCES

Maghreb: The Maghreb is a region of Northwest Africa constituting of Algeria, Morocco, Tunisia, Libya and Mauritania. To strengthen regional cooperation, the Maghreb nations in 1989 formed the Arab Maghreb Union. The Union was formed to enhance regional cooperation in the economic, political and defence spheres while safeguarding national interests of each country. However, Algeria's internal troubles and strained Algeria-Morocco relations have hindered the growth of Arab Maghreb Union as a regional powerhouse.

Arab League: Algeria, though geographically separated from the Middle East, yet shares a cultural identity with the Arab-Islamic nations. To affirm this affinity, the African country joined the League of Arab States immediately after its independence in 1962. The Arab League or League of Arab States is a regional organisation of Arab countries in North and Northeast Africa, and Southwest Asia (Middle East). The 22-member Arab League functions with a goal to strengthen relations among member nations and enhance cooperation to safeguard their freedom and sovereignty, and to stand united for Arab interests.

DEFENCE CAPABILITIES

ARMY: The land force of Algeria, with an active strength of over one lakh personnel, is the second largest Army in North Africa after Egypt. It operates with the mission to defend and protect national sovereignty in coordination with other forces of the nation. The Algerian Army possesses a large number of Soviet-era weapons most of which have been obsolete now and are in the process of being phased out.

Personnel: 107,000 (Reserve: 150,000)

Equipment

Category	Name	In Service
MBT	T-90	372
	T-72	280
	T-62	280+
	T-54/ 55	275
IFV	BMP-1	300
	BMP-2, BMP-2M	700+
	BMP-3	100
	BTR-50, BTR-60, BTR-80	500+
APC/ Armoured Car	Panhard AML-60	50
	BRDM-2	115
	Fuchs	980
Artillery	122mm SP and 152mm towed	500+
	SU-85	5
	2S1 122mm SP	145
	2S3 152mm SP	40+
	ISU 152mm SP	10+
	Norinco 155mm towed	
	Norinco PLZ45 155mm SP	
Mortar	120mm + 160mm	400
MLRS	BM-21 (120mm)	48
	BM-14/ 16 (140mm)	50
	BM-24 (240mm)	25+
SSM	FROG-4	18
ATGW	Sagger	
	Milan	
	Spigot	
	100mm MT-12	

...continued

Category	Name	In Service
AA Gun	14.5mm ZPU-2/ 4	100
	23mm Zu-23	60
	23mm ZSU-23-4 Shilka SP	200
	M1939 37mm	100
	57mm S60	65+
	85mm KS12	30+
SAM	SA-7/14/16 (MANPAD)	150+
	SA-6	40
	SA-8	24
	SA-9	20
	SA-13	30
	2S6M Tunguska	24
	Pantsir S1-E	40+

New Procurements/Upgrades

◆ Local production and assembly of Fuchs armoured personnel carriers in partnership with Germany's Rheinmetall Defence is going on. Algeria plans to procure 980 such APCs. Rheinmetall is assembling over 1,000 Fuchs APCs in Algeria under a deal finalised in 2014.

◆ Production of Boxer IFVs under license in Algeria is being planned. The new IFVs will replace the Army's BTR-60 and BTR-80 armoured platforms.

◆ Delivery of upgraded BMP-1 IFVs by Russia's KBP Instrument Design Bureau is going on.

◆ The Buk-M2E air defence missile systems received from Russia have been deployed in service.

◆ 22 SA-22 Pantsir-S mobile air defence systems are on order from Russia since 2010.

◆ Norinco SR5 guided multiple rocket launch systems have been acquired from China.

◆ Russia has supplied the TOS-1A self-propelled multiple rocket launchers.

NAVY: The Algerian naval force is tasked with safeguarding the maritime territory of the country. The missions of the Navy include: surveillance and safety of maritime approaches; national maritime space defence; protection of national interests at sea; coastal defence and littoral protection; different kinds of public service missions at sea. The Algerian Navy is equipped with a sizable number of frigates, corvettes, submarines and other support vessels to defend the country's nearly 1,000-km long coastline.

Major naval bases: Algiers, Annaba, Mers al-Kebir, Skikda, Jijel

Personnel: 6,600

Equipment

Category	Name	In Service
Submarine	El Hadj Slimane class (Russian 877 Kilo-class)	4
	Project 636 (Improved Kilo-class)	2
Frigate	Murat Reis (Koni Type)	3
	Meko class	2
Corvette	Ras Hamidou class (Nanuchka II type)	3
	Djebel Chenoua class	3
	C28A	3
Missile Boat	Osa Class I and II	6
Gun Boat	Kebir class	15
Inshore patrol boat	El Yadek class	6
Training vessel	Shanghai class	6
Amphibious Ship	Kalaat class LST	2
	Kalaat Beni-Abbes LPD	1
	Soviet Pilnochny B class	1
Mine Hunter	T-43 class	1
Minesweeper	El-Kasseh class	2
Survey vessel		1
ASM	SA-N-4 Gecko	
	SS-N-2C Styx	
	RBU-6000 rocket	
	KH-35 batteries (coastal defence)	4
	C-802A	

Naval Aviation

Category	Name	In Service	On Order
Helicopter	AW101	6	
	Super Lynx 300	4	6

New Procurements/Upgrades

◆ Two Project 636M Varshavyanka-class (improved Kilo-class) diesel-electric submarines have been commissioned into service in January 2019. Algeria had signed a contract with Russia's Admiralty Shipyards in 2014 to acquire the new platforms. With the latest acquisition, the total number of submarines in the Algerian Navy has gone up to six.

◆ China has bagged a contract to build a 96-metre long corvette (likely the Pattani or Type 056 class) for the Algerian Navy. The platform is scheduled to be delivered in 2022.

◆ Two Meko-200 class frigates built by Germany's ThyssenKrupp Marine Systems have been commissioned in service 2016 - 2017. South Africa's Denel-made Umkhonto air defence systems are being installed on the warships.

◆ The Navy has contracted Russia's United Shipbuilding Corporation to build two Project 20382 Tiger-class corvettes. Construction of the platforms is going on.

◆ Russia's Severnaya Verf shipyard has been contracted to upgrade two Algerian warships – the Nanuchka II class corvette and a Koni II class frigate – both procured from Russia and in service with Algerian Navy since the 1980s.

◆ Two Kalaat class landing ships (LSTs) have joined service after being refurbished by Spanish shipbuilder Navantia.

◆ The second mine counter-measures vessel, El-Kasseh 2, has been commissioned into service in 2020. A third such platform is under construction.

AIR FORCE: The Algerian Air Force is entrusted with the tasks of defending the country's air space, carrying out surveillance and monitoring, coordinating with the other two wings of the military and supplying military transport and cargo airlift. The Air Force is replete mostly with Soviet-era fighter and surveillance aircraft. It also possesses US, Russian and European transport planes. The country has started modernising the air force by acquiring new combat aircraft such as the MiG-29 and Sukhoi-30, trainer jets, and is also inducting advanced attack helicopters. The old inventory of aircraft and helicopters are being upgraded and some, like the MiG-21 fighters, have been phased out from service.

Personnel: 12,000

Major air bases: Ain-Beida, Bousfer, Umm Bawaki

Equipment

Category	Name	In Service
Fighter/Trainer	Su-30MKA	55
	MiG-29S	30
	MiG-29UB	5
	MiG-25PDS	10
	MiG-25U	2
	L-39 Albatros	30+
	Yak-130	16
Ground attack	Su-24MK	30+
Reconnaissance	MiG-25RB	3
	Su-24 MR	4
Transport	C-130H/H-30	12
	C-295	5
	SE-210	3
	An-12	4
	PC-6	2
	IL-76	3

...continued

Category	Name	In Service
Refuelling	IL-78	4
VIP transport	F27-400	2
	F27-600	1
	Falcon 20	1
	Gulfstream III	3
Helicopter (attack)	Mi-24 D/V & Mk3	50
	Mi-171	39
	Mi-28 NE (On order)	42
Helicopter (transport, utility)	Mi-6	2
	Mi-4	4
	Mi-2	28
	Mi-8	45
	Mi-26T2 (On order)	6
	Bell 206 L3	3
	AS-355N Ecureuil	8
	PLZ-W3A Sokol	7
	Ka-32	5
Utility aircraft	Super King Air	2
	Zlin 142/ 143/ 242	50
Maritime patrol	Commander 650 AR	1
UAV	Seeker	
AA gun	85 mm KS 12	38
	100 mm KS19	54
SAM	SA-2	28
	SA-3, SA-6	20
	S-300 PMU-2	4 battalions (250+ missiles)

New Procurements/Upgrades

◆ An order has reportedly been placed with Russia in 2019 for 16 more of the Su-30MKA fighter platforms along with 14 MiG-29M/M2 fighters.

◆ 12 Sukhoi Su-34 fighter bombers are on order from Russia. The platforms are replacing the Soviet-era MiG-25 fighters. Delivery is expected in 2021 – 2022.

◆ Purchase of Su-35 multi-role fighters from Russia is under consideration.

◆ Delivery of Mi-28N attack helicopter is going on. A total of 42 Mi-28N attack helicopters and six Mi-26T2 heavy transport helicopters have been ordered from Russia under a deal worth $2.7 billion. The deal also entails upgrading the existing fleet of Mi-171 helicopters to the Mi-171Sh standard.

◆ Procurement of at least three A330 multi-role tanker transport aircraft from Airbus is under consideration.

◆ Plans are on to buy up to six C-17 Globemaster heavy-lift transport aircraft from the US.

◆ Delivery of four more batteries of S-300 PMU2 air defence system is going on.

◆ The CH-3 and CH-4 UAVs have reportedly been acquired from China.

Defence Production

The defence sector in Algeria is at a nascent stage and the country is looking for the development of a firm domestic defence industrial base. The Government has set up few defence manufacturing companies in recent years to produce armoured vehicles, electronics equipment and other ammunitions. The T-90 MBTs contract Algeria has inked with Russia also entails local production of the main battle tanks in the country. German firm Rheinmetall Defence's announcement to locally assemble Fuchs APCs in Algeria has also given a fillip to the domestic defence manufacturing industry. In March 2019, Italian company Leonardo and the Algerian Defence Ministry announced plans to set up a helicopter facility in the North African country. The joint venture will include local helicopter assembly, support and training at an Algerian facility. The new facility will assemble, sell and support several helicopter platforms, primarily to meet Algeria's national requirements, while also focusing on the international export market.

Defence Procurement

Algeria has imported majority of its defence equipment from the erstwhile Soviet Union, including tanks, aircraft and missiles. While Russia still remains the top-most military supplier of the North African nation, Germany has emerged as another leading exporter of military platforms and equipment to Algiers. In recent years, China and some European countries too have supplied military hardware to Algeria. The country is also making efforts to indigenously produce defence systems for its armed forces.

DEFENCE BUDGET

Defence expenditure in Algeria has increased manifold in the last two decades and according to some estimates, it is the top-most military spender in the entire African continent. Algeria became the first country in Africa having a defence budget of over US$10 billion in 2014-15. It ranks 20th in the world in military spending. Modernisation of its armed forces and acquisition of new military platforms and equipment have led to a significant rise in Algeria's annual defence expenditure in recent times.

Estimated defence spending: US$10.3 billion (2020)

Defence spending in terms of GDP: 3.4%

CONCLUSION

The resource-rich Algeria has faced frequent

internal unrest for the past three decades and is also fighting armed extremism and terrorism. The country has not been directly engaged in any external military conflict. However, the ongoing turmoil in neighbouring Libya has continued to affect Algeria militarily as well as economically and even threatened Algiers' own political stability in the longer run. The primary focus area for Algeria has been to contain domestic unrest and secure internal peace and stability while safeguarding its territorial integrity. With its oil-rich economy growing, Algeria in recent times has emerged as one of the most lucrative markets in the African continent for military hardware supplies.

CONTACT DETAILS
Ministry of National Defence
B.P 184, Alger Gare, Algiers
Tel: 021711515
Email: contact-mdn@mdn.dz

STRATEGIC INFORMATION
ARGENTINA
(Capital: Buenos Aires)

INTRODUCTION
Area: 2,780,400 sq km
Population: 45,864,941 (July 2021 est.)
Coastline: 4,989 km
Maritime claims: Territorial sea: 12 nm
Contiguous zone: 24 nm
Exclusive Economic Zone: 200 nm
Continental shelf: 200 nm or to the edge of the continental margin

GEOPOLITICAL IMPORTANCE
The second largest country in South America in terms of size and population, Argentina shares its land border with Bolivia and Paraguay in the north, Brazil and Uruguay in the east and Chile in the west. The Atlantic Ocean lies to its east. As a leading economic and military power in the Latin American region, Argentina is replete with vast natural resources. It wielded great influence during the early twentieth century by remaining one of the richest countries in the world and the richest in the Southern hemisphere. However, years of oppressive military rule coupled with corruption and a policy of economic protectionism has resulted in Argentina's burgeoning financial crisis, rising level of unemployment and poverty in present times. The country now intends to steadily gain back its lost military strength and emerge as a powerful player in the Latin American region.

POLITICAL OVERVIEW
The Constitution defines Argentina as a Federal Republic where the President is both the head of the State and head of the Government. The Executive branch of the Government is headed by the President elected for a period of four years. The Legislative power is vested with a bicameral legislature, Argentine National Congress, consisting of the Senate (upper house) and Chamber of Deputies (lower house). The judiciary functions independently with the highest federal court being the Supreme Court. Argentina, however, has witnessed military coups several times and alternated between civilian and military dispensations in the past. The last military rule in the country spanned from 1976 to 1983. Argentina embraced democracy in 1983 following restoration of the constitutional system.

KEY POLITICAL PERSONS

PRESIDENT & COMMANDER-IN-CHIEF: Alberto Fernandez

VICE PRESIDENT: Cristina Fernandez de Kirchner

ECONOMY
Argentina's economy consisting of agriculture and a diverse industry with rich, abundant natural resources is the third largest in Latin America. It is a leading food exporter in the international market and also gains from a brimming tourism industry. The economic graph of the country has been quite volatile wherein high economic growth has been alternated by severe recessions. Once a brimming economy, Argentina witnessed financial downfall and grappled

with recession, fiscal and current account deficits, high inflation, capital flight and mounting external debt in the most part of 20th century. The financial crisis continued till 2002 when the country defaulted on its debt, its GDP declined by nearly 20% in four years, unemployment reached 25%, and the peso (national currency) sharply depreciated. It was a period of complete economic meltdown for the Latin American country. It was only in 2003 onwards that the economy bounced back after new financial measures were implemented, including commodity exports, nationalisation of a number of entities and infusion of money into social development programmes. The good phase continued till 2008, but the global economic meltdown in that year once again put the Argentine economy backwards, with the GDP shrinking to a meagre 0.8% in 2009. The economy however rebounded strongly in 2010, but slowed again in 2011 even as the government continued to rely on expansionary fiscal and monetary policies. The government then expanded state intervention in the economy throughout 2012. During 2014, the government continued its expansionary fiscal and monetary policies and foreign exchange and imports controls. In July 2014, Argentina and China agreed on an $11 billion currency swap; the Argentine Central Bank received the equivalent of $3.2 billion in Chinese yuan, which it counts as international reserves.

In 2017, Argentina's economy emerged from recession with a GDP growth of nearly 3%. After years of international isolation, Argentina took up several international leadership roles in 2017, including hosting the World Economic Forum in Latin America and the World Trade Organization Ministerial Conference. In 2018, it also held the annual presidency position of the G-20 grouping. Recessionary pressures, however, continued to haunt the economy again from 2018 to 2020.

Battered by the Coronavirus pandemic, Argentina's economy contracted by around 12% in 2020. The Government and economists forecast a growth of 8.3% for the year 2021 following steady resumption of activities and easing up of lockdown measures in the country.

GDP (official exchange rate): $447.46 billion (2019 est.)

Real Growth Rate (GDP): -2.03% (2019 est.); -2.53% (2018 est.)

Industries: Food processing, motor vehicles, consumer durables, textiles, chemicals and petrochemicals, printing, metallurgy, steel

Total Exports: $82.98 billion (2019 est.); $76.14 billion (2018 est.)

Export Commodities: Soybean products, corn, delivery trucks, wheat, frozen meat, gold (2019)

Major Markets: Brazil 16%, China 11%, United States 7%, Chile 5% (2019)

Total Imports: $72.16 billion (2019 est.); $89.08 billion (2018 est.)

Import Commodities: Cars, refined petroleum, vehicle parts, natural gas, soybeans (2019)

Major Suppliers: Brazil 21%, China 18%, US 14%, Germany 6% (2019)

DEFENCE & SECURITY

As a major country in the Latin American region, Argentina has exerted power and dominance over other smaller nations in the continent. Once it competed with Brazil for regional leadership in most part of 20th century. In the current geostrategic scenario, Argentina has pursued a policy of common defence cooperation strategy with its neighbours by expanding its regional ties and a cooperative approach towards international security. The country has been a major contributor in several international peacekeeping missions led by the United Nations. It also regularly participates in global security forums.

Argentina does not face any major internal disturbances. Being a part of the 'Southern Cone', it also does not face any external threat from a hostile power. Any prospect of a major inter-state conflict in the continent has also largely dissipated in recent years as a result of greater economic and security integration among the states.

At the international level, its long-standing conflict with the United Kingdom over the Falkland Islands (called 'The Malvinas' by Argentina) in the South Atlantic Ocean has resulted in frictions between the two nations from time to time. The centuries-old dispute over the chain of islands has once again flared up after over three decades of the Falklands War which took place in 1982. The archipelago, located near Argentina, is a self-governing British Overseas Territory with the UK looking after the region's foreign affairs and defence and maintains military presence in the islands by deploying fighter jets, warships and troops. Argentina, claiming sovereignty over the islands, has decided to bolster up its military by acquiring new weapons and platforms. The large-scale military modernisation drive is believed to be aimed at containing Britain's oil drilling plans off the disputed Islands' coast. The two countries are also engaged in territorial spat over the South Georgia and the South Sandwich Islands in the South Atlantic Ocean.

Argentina maintains a strong, well-organised military force consisting of the Army, Navy and Air Force. The armed forces are dedicated to protect national sovereignty and maintain territorial integrity while also carrying out international peacekeeping and humanitarian missions. They also stand for the country's continuous presence in the Antarctica.

KEY DEFENCE PERSONS

DEFENCE MINISTER: Jorge Taiana

CHIEF OF JOINT STAFF OF ARMED FORCES: Gen. Juan Martin Paleo

CHIEF OF STAFF OF ARMY: Lt. Gen. Agustin Humberto Cejas

CHIEF OF STAFF OF NAVY: Adm. Julio Horacio Guardia

CHIEF OF STAFF OF AIR FORCE: Brig. Xavier Julian Isaac

Internal Conflict

Argentina grapples with the problems of human trafficking, contraband smuggling, illegal immigration from porous borders with neighbouring Bolivia and Paraguay, organised crime and terrorism within the country.

External Conflict

Argentina is not engaged in armed conflict with any country at present, but in the past it has fought a full-scale war with the United Kingdom over territorial sovereignty of the Falkland Islands in the South Atlantic Ocean. The chain of islands, in close proximity to Argentina which it calls 'The Malvinas', is presently administered by Britain as one of its overseas territories. The island hosts a small population, mostly of British origin.

The dispute over the Falklands dates back to 1833 when Britain reasserted control over the archipelago off Argentina's southeast coast. Argentina has staked claim over the territory which it says it inherited from the Spanish crown in the early 1800s. The two countries have fought a bitter war over the Falklands in 1982. In recent times, the dispute has once again triggered tension between the two sides. While Britain, with plans to drill oil in the island territory, has deployed its military in the South Atlantic, Argentina, on its part, has introduced new rules requiring all ships travelling to the Falklands through its waters to have a permit. Argentina has also raised the issue in the United Nations. A referendum in the self-governing Islands in 2013 resulted in more than 99 percent of voters favouring to remain a British Overseas Territory.

Argentina and UK are also sparring over the South Georgia and the South Sandwich

Islands in South Atlantic Ocean. Another territorial dispute between the two countries includes a sizable landmass of Antarctica, parts of which are also claimed by Chile. The two countries have made efforts to enhance their bilateral relations in recent years but without much success.

THREAT PERSPECTIVE

UK: The major military threat Argentina faces today is that from the United Kingdom over the Falkland Islands dispute. As tensions mount in recent times over sovereignty claims involving the chain of islands having an area of 12,200 square kilometres, Britain has rallied its warships and weapons by conducting military exercises at regular intervals and also started drilling oil in the contested maritime region. The Falklands War in 1982 had resulted in Britain reaffirming its control over the territory after Argentina surrendered. Argentina, on its part, has decided to modernise and empower its military by acquiring new weapons and platforms to counter any possible threat from the UK even while intermittently claiming its sovereignty rights over the disputed islands region.

STRATEGIC RELATIONS

Chile: Once hostile to each other for most part of the 19th and 20th century over territorial claims, Argentina and Chile today enjoy relatively warm relations ranging from trade and commerce to defence and strategy. The two neighbours resolved their territorial disputes by signing the Treaty of Peace and Friendship in 1984 which was superseded by the Maipu Treaty of Integration and Cooperation in 2009. The two countries conduct joint military exercises at regular intervals.

Brazil: The two South American countries share close relations spanning from trade and economy to education, culture, defence and strategy. Strategic partnership between Argentina and Brazil began to revive in the 1990s. In 1988, the two sides inked the landmark Treaty for Integration, Cooperation and Development covering politics, trade, investment, education, defence, technology and space among other aspects. This historic treaty later paved the way for the creation of the regional bloc – the Southern Cone Common Market (MERCOSUR) – three years later. Today, Argentina and Brazil are jointly working on a number of military programmes, including the Embraer KC-390 military transport aircraft and the UNASUR 1 basic jet trainer. In 2019, Brazil agreed to transfer four of its Tupi-class submarines (non-operational in Brazilian Navy) to the Argentine Navy which is grappling with a dwindling underwater fleet.

US: Argentina has shared strong economic and strategic ties with the US since the 1980s, especially after it transited from military dictatorship to democracy. The former supported and assisted the US during the Gulf War in 1990 following which it was accorded the status of major non-NATO ally of the US in the Latin American region in 1999. Argentina has been greatly influenced by American military strategy and planning in the past. The US has supplied majority of defence equipment to the Argentine military.

China: Argentina and China share strong bilateral trade ties. China is Argentina's third-largest trading partner after the MERCOSUR bloc and the European Union, and is one of its main destinations for food exports. In 2014, the two countries elevated their relationship to strategic level with China pledging to invest hugely in building infrastructure including hydroelectric power, ships and railways for Argentina. The two countries, of late, have also explored cooperation in the nuclear sector with China proposing to build nuclear reactors for Argentina. Beijing also continues to supply military technology to Buenos Aires. In 2011, the two sides signed a deal to build the Chinese Z-11 light helicopters in Argentina under license, and mass production of the platform for the Argentine military began in 2013. They are also discussing other military deals, including licence-production of OPVs for the Argentine Navy and APCs for the Army in Argentina. China has also offered to sell its JF-17 fighter aircraft (jointly produced with Pakistan) to Argentina.

Russia: Bilateral relationship between Argentina and Russia has mostly revolved around political and economic spheres. In the military sphere, Russia plans to supply helicopters and transport aircraft to Argentina. It also plans to install a GLONASS monitoring station in Argentina. In 2014, the two sides signed an inter-governmental agreement on cooperation in the use of nuclear energy. Under the deal, Russian atomic energy corporation Rosatom has proposed to construct two new nuclear power units in Argentina. An MoU in this regard was inked between the two sides in 2018 which could allow the Russian state's atomic agency Rosatom search for uranium in the South American nation, with a reported potential investment of US$250 million. In April 2015, the two countries also announced increasing military collaboration during the then Argentine President Cristina Fernandez's Moscow visit.

MULTILATERAL ALLIANCES

MERCOSUR: As a founding member of the MERCOSUR regional trading bloc along with Brazil, Uruguay and Paraguay, Argentina has made efforts towards greater economic, social and political integration among the South American nations. The MERCOSUR, founded in 1991, later included Venezuela as a full member. The regional block, modelled on the European Union (EU), however, has faced differences among member nations over several issues, including adopting a common currency and trade policy.

UNASUR: The Union of South American Nations (UNASUR), founded in December 2004, is a regional grouping formed by 12 South American countries that are united by shared history, religion, common culture and language. Over the years, UNASUR has made many significant achievements including in the sphere of security and defence, democratic stability, reducing crime, energy and financial integration, and institution building in the Latin American region. Its endeavours have also resulted in resolving the constitutional crises in Ecuador and Paraguay, and settled the dispute between Venezuela and Colombia. Being a part of the group, Argentina has benefited by partnering with member nations, especially Brazil, in joint military projects.

ECLAC: The Economic Commission for Latin America and the Caribbean (ECLAC) is a United Nations-led regional commission with the primary goal to encourage economic cooperation. It includes 44 member states – 20 in Latin America, 13 in the Caribbean and 11 from outside the region. Argentina is a member state.

DEFENCE CAPABILITIES

ARMY: The land forces of Argentina, called the Ejército Argentino, is organised into three divisions and one Army Rapid Deployment Force. The Army operates with the primary mission of safeguarding the sovereignty and territorial integrity of the country and its citizens. The Argentine Army operates with the purpose to "defend the interests of the nation, contributing to its scientific, technological, economic and social development, and cooperate to achieve the general welfare of its inhabitants." A fully professional force, it also contributes to international peacekeeping missions led by the United Nations. In its present status, the Argentine Army lacks manpower, modern equipment and infrastructure for combat missions. Budgetary constrains have restricted it from being entirely modernized.

Personnel: 50,000+

Equipment

Category	Name	In Service
MBT	TAM (Tanque Argentino Mediano)	230
Light Tank	AMX-13 (being withdrawn)	30
	SK-105 Kurassier	110
	Patagon	4
APC/MICV/IFV	TAM (VCTP-VCTM-VCPC)	160
	AMX (VCTP-VCDT-VCPC)	30
	M-113	288
	M-557	18
	Guarani 6x6	14
	VLEGA Gaucho (light infantry vehicle)	
Artillery	155mm AMX F-3	24
	155mm VCA-TAM	17
	155mm CITEFA Model 77 (L33)	109
	105mm Oto Melara M56	70
	105mm M-101 howitzer	60
	155mm M114	48
Mortar	120mm Thompson-Brandt	300
	81mm Thompson-Brandt	350
	60mm Thompson-Brandt	300
MRL	127 mm SAPBA-1	2
	105 mm Pampero	4
ATGW	Mathogo	
	BGM-71 TOW	
ATW	105 mm Model 1968	150
	89 mm Instalaza M65	
	M72 LAW	385
SAM	Strela-2/ Strela-2M	
	Roland	3
AA gun	40mm Bofors L-70	
	35mm K-63 (Skyguard) twin	8
	30mm HS 831	20
	20mm GAM-BO1	200

Army Aviation

Category	Name	In Service
Helicopter	AS.332L Super Puma	3
	UH1H Iroquois (being upgraded to Huey II version)	40+
	SA-315B Lama	2
	Bell 205, 206	4+5
Fixed wing aircraft	OV1D MOHAWK	7
	C-212-200	3
	Merlin IIIB/IV A	4
	Twin Otter	2
	Beechcraft B-80 Queen Air	1
	Sabreliner 75A	1

...continued

Category	Name	In Service
Fixed wing aircraft	Cessna 207	4
	T-41 Mescalero	5

New Procurements/ Upgrades

◆ Modernisation of the entire fleet of TAM MBTs, announced in 2010, is going on. Delivery of upgraded tanks has started.

◆ The US State Department in July 2020 has approved a possible Foreign Military Sale of a total of 27 M1126 Stryker Infantry Carrier Vehicles and related equipment to the Argentine Army for an estimated cost of $100 million.

◆ Plans are on to acquire over 100 of the Chinese VN1 wheeled APCs and licence-produce them domestically.

◆ The entire inventory of M-113A1 APCs is being progressively upgraded to A2 standard.

◆ Delivery of 20 LVC CP-30 multiple rocket launcher systems is going on. The MRL is capable of firing the 105mm Pampero and the 127mm SAPBA-1 rockets.

◆ RBS 70NG anti-aircraft missiles will be procured for which funds have been allocated in 2018.

NAVY: The Argentine Navy (Armada Argentina) operates with the primary mission to "ready, train and support the means of naval power in the nation to help ensure effective and efficient employment under the joint action." Its secondary missions include participation in peace operations and / or multinational coalitions under mandate of International Organisations, search & rescue, supporting the activity in Antarctica, and humanitarian assistance among other tasks. To achieve efficiency and effectiveness of maritime missions, the Navy has built up C4IS capabilities along with amphibious and underwater prowess. However, the Armada Argentina is in a parlous state at present as majority of its warships are not operational. Budgetary constraints continue to plague the maritime fleet's maintenance and modernisation.

Major naval bases: Puerto Belgrano, Mar del Plata, Espora, Rio Grande, Zarate

Personnel: 20,000+

Equipment

Category	Name	In Service
Destroyer	Almirante Brown (Meko 360H2)	4
Submarine	Salta (Type 209/ 1200)	1
Frigate	Drummond (Type A 69)	1 (2 in reserve)
	Espora (Meko 140)	6

...continued

Category	Name	In Service
Patrol Vessel	Punta Mogotes class	2
	Intrépida class (FAC)	2
	Baradero class	4
	La Adroit (Gowind) class	1 (+3 on order)
Mine hunter	Neuquen	2
Amphibious Force	Hercules	1
	LCVP Landing Craft	16
	LCM 6	4
Auxiliary ship	Survey and Research ships	4

Naval Aviation

Category	Name	In Service
Maritime patrol aircraft	King Air 200M Cormoran	4
	S-2T Turbo Tracker	4
	P3B Orion	4
Helicopter	S-61 Sea King D-4	5
	Aérospatiale SA 316 Alouette III	5
	Agusta ASH-3H Sea King	2
	Bell 205 UH-1H	6
	Eurocopter AS 555MN Fennec	3
Trainer	EMB-326GB	7
	Beechcraft T-34C-1 Mentor	9

Marines

Category	Name	In Service
APC/MICV/IFV	ERC-90	12
	LVTP-7	11
	LARC-5	13
	Panhard VCR/TT	24
	Hummers	24
Artillery	105mm Oto Melara	12
	155mm M114	6
Mortar	81mm	20
SAM	RBS-70	6
AA gun	40mm L70	4

New Procurements/ Upgrades

◆ An MoU has been inked with Brazil in 2019 for the transfer of two of Brazilian Navy's Tupi-class (Type 209) submarines to Argentina. The platforms would join the Argentine Navy after refurbishment. The deal includes a potential future transfer of two more such platforms from Brazil to Argentina in future.

◆ The Navy's only submarine platform Santa Cruz (S-41), one of the two German-built Type TR 1700 conventional platforms acquired in the 1980s, has become dysfunctional after plans to upgrade the platform have reportedly been shelved.

◆ Four 1,800 tonne offshore patrol vessels

- are on order from German shipbuilder Fassmer with construction expected to start soon in an Argentine shipyard.
- ◆ Discussion is going on with China to acquire five 1,800-ton P-18N corvettes, which will serve the Argentine Navy as "Malvinas" class OPVs.
- ◆ Four La Adroit-class offshore patrol vessels are being acquired from France under a government-to-government deal worth $324 million signed in 2018. The first platform has been commissioned into service in December 2019. The remaining three are slated for delivery between 2021 and 2023.
- ◆ Negotiation is going on with France to acquire three retired A 69 class corvettes. The corvettes are of the same class as the Drummond-class of platforms presently operational in the Argentine Navy. The platforms were acquired from France in the 1980s.
- ◆ Five refurbished French Dassault-built Super Etendard combat aircraft have been delivered in 2019 with their commissioning expected by 2022. The Defence Ministry in 2017 had approved the acquisition of the second-hand platforms from French Navy at a cost of $15.03 million.
- ◆ Four Lockheed Martin-built P-3C Orion maritime patrol aircraft (retired from US Navy) have been acquired in 2019 under a deal signed with the US Government. The P-3Cs would be upgraded under a $78 million package approved by the US State Dept. They will replace the P-3B Orion MPAs of Argentine Navy.
- ◆ The Naval Aviation Command has issued an operational requirement to carry out modernisation of its T-34C1 Turbo Mentor jet trainers. The Navy has initiated work with state-owned Fábrica Argentina de Aviones SA (FAdeA) to upgrade the aircraft.

AIR FORCE: The Air Force of Argentina, called the Fuerza Aérea Argentina (FAA), operates with the primary objective of defending the national air space and protecting national interests, including in Antarctica. It contributes to UN peacekeeping missions. Once reckoned as a strong force, the FAA has lost its prowess following the Falklands War in 1982. Today, it is grappling with obsolete and inadequate air platforms and equipment which has limited its combat capability. While the older-generation frontline fighters (French Mirage) have been retired, acquisition of new warplanes as their replacement is pending owing to budgetary constraints and political indecisiveness. The Air Force is urgently needing supersonic fighters' fleet for which negotiations are going on with a number of countries but no final decision has been taken yet. The FAA's extensive modernisation plans have been hindered due to financial and political issues. The Government is planning to reorganise the Air Force and its units by streamlining personnel and reshuffling their rank and file.

Major air bases: El Palomar, Tandil, Moreno (Buenos Aires), Parana (Entre Rios Province), Reconquista (Santa Fe Province), El Plumerillo (Mendoza Province), Villa Reynolds (San Luis Province), Comodoro Rivadavia (Chubut Province)

Personnel: 13,000+

Equipment

Category	Name	In Service
Fighters/ Attack/ Reconnaissance	A-4AR Fightinghawk	2
	FMA IA 58 Pucará	31
Transport/ Tanker	Fokker F-28 Fellowship 1000C	7
	KC-130/ C-130 Hercules	2+5
	KC-390	6 (on order)
	DHC-6 Twin Otter	9
	Saab 340B	4 (+1 on order)
Trainer, Light Attack	Beech T-34A mentor	29
	EMB-312 Tucano	20+
	IA-63 Pampa II & III	8 + 6 (34 more Pampa III on order)
	T-6C Texan II	6 (+18 on order)
	P2002JF	8
Helicopter	Bell 212 Twin Huey	7
	Bell 412EP	6
	Bell UH-1H Iroquois	
	Aérospatiale SA-315B Lama	2
	Hughes 500D Defender	10
	Hughes 369	1
UAV	Cabure	
Weapon	R 530 (AAM)	
	R 550 Magic	

New Procurements/ Upgrades

- ◆ No official decision has been announced yet on the procurement of new supersonic fighter jets fleet as a replacement for the FAA's now-retired Mirage III fighters. Acquisition of new fighters' fleet has been under active consideration for past three years with the Air Force evaluating several aircraft, including China's JF-17 and Russia's MiG-29 and MiG-35 platforms. India's LCA Tejas fighter could also be a possible contender for the proposed acquisition, as stated by the Argentine Air Force Chief in a news report.
- ◆ The Government has announced to bring up to 12 of the Air Force's A-4AR Fightinghawks back into operational service for at least five years. The Lockheed-built fighters were set for retirement by 2018 and were to be replaced by new fighters. The Government has postponed the new acquisition plan.
- ◆ Delivery of T-6C Texan II turboprop trainer/ light attack aircraft is going on since 2017. The US State Department in August 2016 had approved Foreign Military Sale of up to 24 Texan II platforms to Argentina.
- ◆ Delivery of IA-63 Pampa III aircraft being built by the state-owned FAdeA is going on. The FAdeA has been contracted to supply the Argentine Air Force with a total of 40 new Pampa III jet trainer/ light attack aircraft which are an upgraded variant of the Pampa II platform.
- ◆ Plans are on to upgrade the IA-58 Pucara light strike aircraft into IA-58H configuration.
- ◆ The sole Learjet 35A aircraft is being modified by the Avcon Industries of Argentina for electronic attack configuration.
- ◆ Eight P2002JF single seat jet trainers have been leased from Italy's Tecnam in 2016.
- ◆ Plans are on to procure six KC-390 military transport aircraft being built by Brazilian aircraft maker Embraer. The new platforms would replace the C-130 Hercules transporters of the FAA.
- ◆ Three upgraded Hercules C-130 military transport aircraft have joined service as of 2018. Argentina is upgrading all five of the Lockheed Martin-built transporters under US Foreign Military Sales programme. The remaining two aircraft are expected to be delivered in 2021 - 2022. The upgrades will extend the service life of the C-130s for about 20 years.
- ◆ The Air Force is planning to acquire new medium transport aircraft to replace the Fokker F-27s which retired in 2016. Purchase of Airbus Military C-295s or Alenia C-27J Spartan is under consideration.
- ◆ Purchase of an additional SAAB 340B transport aircraft for the Air Force has been announced.
- ◆ A new basic trainer aircraft, designated IA-100, is being developed domestically.
- ◆ Out of the nine Twin Otter aircraft being refurbished by Canada's Viking Air Limited under a $15 million contract, four have been delivered.
- ◆ An MoU has been signed for the procurement of 12 Airbus Helicopters H125 platforms as a replacement for the SA315B Lama choppers. The new choppers will be used for SAR and other non-military missions.

- Development of a new indigenously-built medium altitude long-endurance UAV, Vigia 2A, is going on.
- The 2018 budget has made provision for procurement of RBS 70NG anti-aircraft missiles for FAA.

Major Armaments Developers & Producers

Once home to a brimming, well-diversified defence industry to meet the requirements of its armed forces, Argentina has yet again initiated steps in recent times to revive the domestic defence industry which faced shutdown following privatisation and lack of political attention after the country's transition from military dictatorship to democracy. The country is also encouraging foreign investors to invest in its defence sector with an emphasis on technology transfer and partnership in military programmes. Some major military manufacturers in the country include the following:

Fabrica Militar de Armas Portatiles (FMAP) in Rosario, Santa Fe, produces a wide range of small arms and ammunition.

Fabricaciones Militares (FM) in Rio Tercero, Cordoba is a manufacturer of heavy infantry weapons, including anti-tank weapons and light mortars.

Instituto de Investigaciones Cientificos y Technicas de las Feurzas Armadas or The Institute for Scientific and Technological Research for the Defense (CITEFA) in Buenos Aires operates as federal research and development agency. It has developed artillery guns, multiple rocket launchers, anti-tank missiles among others.

The **Rio Santiago** is Argentina's leading shipyard and has built several major ships for the Navy.

Tandanor is the country's largest shipyard based in Buenos Aires. It has been entrusted with the task of building the four new 1,800 ton offshore patrol vessels for the Argentine Navy.

The Fabrica Argentina de Aviones (FAdeA) is the leading aircraft manufacturer of Argentina. Operating as a subsidiary of US defence major Lockheed Martin until March 2009, the FAdeA was nationalised in August 2009 and now operates as a fully state-owned aviation company. It is presently producing the IA-73 'Pampa' turboprop trainer jet for joint purchase by members of the Union of South American Nations (UNASUR). Plans are also on to develop a light strike version of the plane, to be called 'Pampa NG'. The company is also upgrading the IA-58 Pucara ground attack fighter jets of the Argentine Air Force. It is building a prototype of the Chinese-built CZ-11 helicopter, known locally as "Pampero."

DEFENCE DEALS

Joint Venture Programmes

Argentina has joined hands with a number of South American countries to co-develop military platforms and systems. It is partnering with China to produce a light utility helicopter and also planning to co-develop OPVs and armoured vehicles for its military.

Brazil

KC-390: Argentina's FAdeA has partnered with Brazil's Embraer in the development and production of the Brazilian KC-390 military transport aircraft. The FAdeA is supplying structural parts for the new airplane which was unveiled in Sao Paulo in October 2014. As an industrial partner in the programme along with the Czech Republic and Portugal, Argentina has pledged to buy six KC-390s for its air force.

Gaucho infantry vehicle: The two countries jointly developed and produced the Gaucho light infantry vehicle in the 2000s. While Brazil developed the engine and gearboxes for the wheeled all-terrain vehicle, Argentina designed its tubular frame and independent suspension. Presently, the vehicle is in service with the Argentine Army.

China

CZ-W11 helicopter: Partnering with China's National Aero-Technology Import and Export Corporation, Argentina has successfully developed and produced the CZ-W11 ultra-light helicopter for its military. The new platform is undergoing flight tests and is expected to be inducted in the Argentine military in near future.

Italy

The two countries have signed an agreement in 2017 under which Italy's Leonardo company will invest in Argentina's aviation major Fabrica Argentina de Aviones (FAdeA) to build the required infrastructure and know-how for the manufacturing of aircraft parts for both civilian and military markets at the Argentinian factory.

UNASUR

Unasur 1: Seven South American countries, including Argentina, have partnered to develop a new basic trainer. The new trainer jet is called 'Unasur 1' which is an adaptation of the acronym for the Union of South American Nations (UNASUR). The multinational aviation project was announced in April 2013. Besides Argentina, the other partner nations in the project include Brazil, Ecuador, Venezuela, Chile, Colombia and Uruguay – all members of the UNASUR. The 'Unasur 1' will be developed with a 1,590-kg maximum take-off weight and a flying speed of 388-km/h. It will feature a piston engine for primary training and a turbine engine for basic and primary training.

Arms Import & Export

Argentina has acquired most of its military equipment from the US in recent past. It has also bought arms from Brazil, France, Germany and Spain. Presently, defence import sources for the country is diversifying to include China and Russia from which new military equipment are being procured.

While military exports by the South American country was nil so far, in July 2019, Argentina clinched a deal with Guatemala to sell two IA-63 Pampa III jet trainers to the Guatemalan Air Force. The deal is worth US$ 28 million. The Pampa III trainer jets, built by Argentina's state-owned Fabrica Argentina de Aviones (FadeA), are also being delivered to the Argentine Air Force. Guatemala has become the first export customer for the Pampa III. Argentina has been making efforts to sell the indigenously-built jet trainers to other countries in the Latin American region. The country's moribund domestic defence industry is being revived to take part in joint defence projects with few other countries, mostly from the Latin American region, with export plans. Of late, Argentina has intensified efforts to build indigenous unmanned aerial vehicles (UAVs) as well.

DEFENCE BUDGET

Annual defence spending by Argentina presently remains at about 1% of GDP. Between 2004 and 2013, the country spent around 0.8% of GDP on defence. The Government is planning a 50% increase in defence spending but has left open-ended the amount that will eventually go into the military regeneration programme. Defence expenditure is largely driven by modernisation plans, participation in peacekeeping missions and a dispute with the UK over sovereignty of the Falkland Islands. But a major share of total defence spending goes towards personnel costs. The country's defence budget was US$ 5.7 billion in 2014; US$ 5.9 billion in 2015; US$ 4.6 billion in 2016; and US$ 6 billion in 2017.

Argentina is expected to spend a total of $42.3 billion between 2018 and 2022, with an averaging GDP of 1.1%. Its annual military budget is estimated to reach $10.5 billion by 2022, according to a report compiled by a global think-tank.

CONCLUSION

All major countries in South America are focused on steady defence modernisation and strengthening of their overall military capability, mainly to tackle internal security issues and safeguard territorial integrity even while protecting the vast natural resources in and around their vicinity. While Brazil is marching ahead in this race, Argentina has initiated steps to catch up. The military build-up of Argentina is primarily aimed at preparing it to face any immediate or imminent threat from Britain over the longstanding Falkland Islands dispute. Hence, a number of new acquisitions as well as modernisation programmes are on the cards. However, continuing economic woes has hindered any immediate action in this regard. Presently, the foremost defence priority areas for Argentina are the Falklands region and the Argentine Antarctica in addition to protection of national sovereignty and territorial integrity.

CONTACT DETAILS
Ministry of Defence
Azopardo 250,
C1107ADB, Buenos Aires
Tel: (+5411) 4346-8800
Email: info@mindef.gov.ar
www.mindef.gov.ar

ARMENIA
(Capital: Yerevan)

INTRODUCTION
Area: 29,743 sq. km
Population: 3,011,609 (July 2021 est.)
Coastline: 0 km (landlocked)
Maritime claims: None

KEY POLITICAL PERSONS

PRESIDENT & SUPREME COMMANDER IN CHIEF: Armen Sarkissian

PRIME MINISTER: Nikol Pashinyan

KEY DEFENCE PERSONS

DEFENCE MINISTER: Davit Tonoyan

CHIEF OF STAFF: Lt. Gen. Artak Matevosi Davtyan

ECONOMY

Armenia has transitioned from a Soviet central planning system economy and government to the modern era. In the early phase of the transition the country experienced challenges but it had managed to turn things around. From the industrial sector Armenia has switched to small-scale agriculture. The government has put in place prudent fiscal and monetary policies, liberal trade and foreign exchange regimes, and sustained growth, ambitious reforms, and external inflows of capital and remittances have created a market-oriented environment in the Armenian economy. New sectors, such as precious stone processing and jewellery making, information and communication technology, and even tourism are beginning to supplement more traditional sectors such as agriculture in the economy. The government relies heavily on loans from the World Bank, the International Monetary Fund (IMF), the Asian Development Bank (ADB), and Russia. Armenia joined Russia in the Eurasian Economic Union upon the bloc's launch in January 2015 and the WTO in January 2003. In March 2017 an EU-Armenia Comprehensive and Enhanced Partnership Agreement was initiated. Armenia's economy recorded a growth of 7.6 per cent in 2019. In 2020, the Covid-19 pandemic has aggravated the economic situation in the country and the war between Armenia and Azerbaijan is deepening the current economic recession.

GDP (official exchange growth): $13.694 billion (2019 est.)

Real Growth Rate (GDP): 7.5% (2017 est.), 0.3% (2016 est.)

Industries: Brandy, mining, diamond processing, metal-cutting machine tools, forging and pressing machines, electric motors, knitted wear, hosiery, shoes, silk fabric, chemicals, trucks, instruments, microelectronics, jewelry, software, food processing.

Total Exports: $3.82 billion (2020 est.), $5.64 billion (2019 est.)

Export Commodities: Copper ore, gold, tobacco, liquors, iron alloys (2019)

Major Markets: Russia 22%, Switzerland 20%, China 7%, Bulgaria 6%, Iraq 5%, Serbia 5%, Netherlands 5%, Germany 5% (2019)

Total Imports: $5 billion (2020 est.), $7.47 billion (2019 est.)

Import Commodities: Copper ore, gold, tobacco, liquors, iron alloys (2019)

Major Suppliers: Russia 29%, China 10%, Georgia 8%, Iran 6%, Turkey 5% (2019)

INTERNATIONAL DISPUTES

◆ The dispute over the break-away Nagorno-Karabakh region and the Armenian military occupation of surrounding lands in Azerbaijan remains the primary focus of regional instability; residents have evacuated the former Soviet-era small ethnic enclaves in Armenia and Azerbaijan.

◆ Turkish authorities have complained that blasting from quarries in Armenia might be damaging the medieval ruins of Ani, on the other side of the Arpacay valley.

- In 2009, Swiss mediators facilitated an accord re-establishing diplomatic ties between Armenia and Turkey, but neither side has ratified the agreement and the rapprochement effort has faltered.
- Local border forces struggle to control the illegal transit of goods and people across the porous, undemarcated Armenian, Azerbaijani, and Georgian borders.
- Ethnic Armenian groups in the Javakheti region of Georgia seek greater autonomy from the Georgian Government.

DEFENCE

Armenia, one of the constituent republics of the erstwhile Soviet Union, has developed its armed forces into a professional, well trained, and well-equipped military. The government has released a strategic document entitled "2018-2024 Modernisation Programme for the Armenian Armed Forces" designed to provide strategic guidance to the Armed Forces to hone and enhance their military prowess. The document released in 2018 touches on a wide range of spheres, including military diplomacy, good operative governance, military-industry upgrades and arms procurement policy while raising the moral resiliency of Armenian troops and preparing them for the challenges of modern warfare. The Armed Forces comprised of the Army, the Air Force and Air Defence. Being a landlocked country, Armenia has no Navy. The General Staff is responsible for operational command of the Armenian Military. The Army is functionally divided into Active and Reserve Forces. The Active Forces mainly have peacekeeping and defensive duties while the Reserve Forces consists of Enhancement Forces, Territorial Defence Forces, and Training Grounds. They deal with planning and reservist preparation, armaments and equipment storage, training of formations for active forces rotation or increase in personnel.

The de-facto independent region of Nagorno-Karabakh maintains its own armed forces – Nagorno-Karabakh Defence Army – under central command and military structure distinct from the Armenian Army. The Armed Forces of Armenia is constitutionally a conscript force. The Armenian Army is equipped with the S-300 surface-to-air missile. The country has acquired state-of-the-art Russian-made Iskander missile systems and showcased the BUK-M2 air defence system during a military parade.

ARMY
Personnel: 40,783

Equipment

Category	Name	In Service
MBT	T-90	1
	T-72	144
	T-54/55	
AIFV/APC	BMP-1/2	173
	BRM-1K	
	BTR-60/-70/80	
	MT-LB	
Artillery	D30 122mm	69
	D-20	62
	D-1	
	2A36 152mm (towed)	
	2S1 122mm	10
	2S3 152 mm (SP)	28
Mortar	M120 120mm	12
SSM	Scud-B	
	9M79 Tochka-U	8+
MLR	BM-21 122mm	47
	WM80	4
	Smerch 300mm	
ATGW	9P148	8
	9P149	14

New procurements/Upgrades
No major procurements plans are under consideration at present.

AIR FORCE
Personnel: 2000+

Equipment

Category	Name	In service
Fighter	Su-30SM	4
	Su-25	15
Transport	IL-76	3
Trainer	L-39	10
Helicopter	Mi-24P	8
	Mi-24K	2
	Mi-24R	2
	Mi-8MT	10
	Mi-9	2
	Mi-2	7
AA gun	ZSU-23-4	
	ZSU-23	
Weapon	SA-2	
	SA-3	
	SA-4	
	S-60	3
	S-300	
	Iskander-E	

New procurements/Upgrades
- Armenia has reportedly shown a keen interest in acquiring Russia's cutting-edge Ka-52M and Mi-28NE attack helicopters.
- New anti-tank missiles/rockets, air-defence systems and other equipment are being acquired from Russia.

Defence Expenditure
Total defence spending: $711 million (2022), $1.385 billion (2020)
Estimated defence spending in terms of GDP: 5.5% (2020)

Defence Production and R&D
Armenia is understood to be self-sufficient in the arms industry sectors such as: apparel, light weapons, drones, and optoelectronic. Indigenously developed small arms are getting immense exposure as well. The assembly of Kalashnikov AK-103 assault rifles under licence in Armenia has commenced at the new Neutron GAM facility which is expected to produce up to 50,000 rifles per year. Armenia has set up certified centres and joint ventures for the repair and maintenance of weapons and military equipment with assistance from Russia. The two countries have signed an agreement on military and technical cooperation. Under this programme a new military-technical research institute will be set up to identify needs and priorities for development of the country's defence capabilities.

Defence Procurement
The conflict between Armenia and Azerbaijan over the status of Nagorno-Karabakh has triggered an arms race between the two states with the Government of Armenia increasing its defence budget. The country has acquired the Russian Iskander-E short-range ballistic missiles and Buk surface-to-air missiles. Armenia has also purchased four advanced Su-30SM air superiority fighters from Russia.

CONTACT DETAILS

Ministry of Defence
5 Bagrevand St, Yerevan 0044, Armenia
Telephone: + 37410 294699
E-mail: modpress@mil.am, press@mil.am
http://www.mil.am/en

STRATEGIC INFORMATION
AUSTRALIA
(Capital: Canberra)

INTRODUCTION

Area: 7,741,220 sq km

Population: 25,809,973 (July 2021 est.)

Coastline: 25,760 km

Maritime claims: Territorial sea: 12 nm

Contiguous zone: 24 nm

Exclusive Economic Zone: 200 nm

Continental shelf: 200 nm or to the edge of the continental margin

GEOPOLITICAL IMPORTANCE

The Commonwealth of Australia is a country in the Southern Hemisphere comprising the mainland of the Australian continent, the island of Tasmania and numerous smaller islands in the Indian and Pacific Oceans. Australia, one of the largest countries on Earth, shares maritime borders with Indonesia, East Timor and Papua New Guinea to the North, the Solomon Islands, Vanuatu and New Caledonia to the North-East and New Zealand to the South-East. The largest country in Oceania, Australia, has emerged as a maritime nation in the making and is an important player in the Asia-Pacific region. Australia seeks an Indo-Pacific that is stable and prosperous. It is committed to a range of measures to strengthen Australia's partnerships with other Indo-Pacific nations. The country's strategic positioning at the confluence of the Indian and Pacific Oceans will contribute immensely to the regional developments and stability in Asia.

POLITICAL OVERVIEW

The Commonwealth of Australia is both a representative democracy and a constitutional monarchy with Queen Elizabeth II as Australia's head of state. The Parliament consists of the Queen, represented by the Governor-General, and two Houses – the Senate and the House of Representatives. The Parliament passes legislation. Proposed laws have to be agreed to by both Houses of Parliament to become law. The two Houses have equal powers, except that there are restrictions on the power of the Senate to introduce or directly amend some kinds of financial legislation.

Queen Elizabeth II's constitutional function is to appoint the governor-general, and in doing this the Queen acts as advised by the Australian prime minister. The Governor-General has a wide range of powers exercised under the authority of the Australian constitution. The functions and roles of the governor-general include appointing ambassadors, ministers and judges, giving Royal Assent to legislation, issuing writs for elections and bestowing honours. The governor-general is also commander-in-chief of the Australian Defence Force (ADF). The Prime Minister is the head of the government. The Cabinet, consisting of senior ministers, presided over by the prime minister, is the government's pre-eminent policy-making body. Major policy and legislative proposals are decided by the cabinet. Ministers are selected by the prime minister. The ministers are responsible for particular areas of administration within a major department or may be in charge of a small department. The prime minister also appoints parliamentary secretaries to assist or represent ministers in their administrative responsibilities.

The Judiciary is the legal arm of the Australian Government. The Constitution vests the judicial power of the Commonwealth – the power to interpret laws and to judge whether they apply in individual cases – in the High Court and other federal courts. The High Court is established by the constitution. Other federal courts are created by legislation of the Parliament. Judges are appointed by the governor-general acting on the advice of the prime minister and cabinet.

KEY POLITICAL PERSONS

HEAD OF STATE: Queen Elizabeth II

GOVERNOR GENERAL & COMMANDER-IN-CHIEF: Gen. David Hurley

PRIME MINISTER: Scott Morrison

ECONOMY

The Australian economy is one of the world's largest mixed market economies Australia's very open market with minimal restrictions on imports of goods and services has increased productivity, stimulated growth and made the economy more flexible and dynamic. Australia is a significant exporter of natural resources, energy, and food. It's abundant and diverse natural resources attract high levels of foreign investment and include extensive reserves of coal, iron, copper, gold, natural gas, uranium, and renewable energy sources. The country's largest export markets are Japan, China, South Korea, India and the US. Australia plays an active role in the WTO, APEC, the G20 and other trade related forums. Australia is one of the wealthiest Asia–Pacific nations and has enjoyed more than two decades of economic expansion. As of June 2021, the country's GDP was estimated at A$1.98 trillion.

GDP (official exchange rate): $1,390,790,000,000 (2019 est.)

Real Growth Rate (GDP): 1.84% (2019 est.), 2.77% (2018 est.)

Industries: Mining, industrial and transportation equipment, food processing, chemicals, steel.

Total Exports: $299.04 billion (2020 est.), $342.43 billion (2019 est.)

Export Commodities: Iron ore, coal, natural gas, gold, aluminum oxide (2019)

Major Markets: China 39%, Japan 15%, South Korea 7%, India 5% (2019)

Total Imports: $249.07 billion (2020 est.), $295.46 billion (2019 est.)

Import Commodities: Refined petroleum, cars, crude petroleum, broadcasting equipment, delivery trucks (2019)

Major Suppliers: China 25%, United States 12%, Japan 7%, Germany 5%, Thailand 5% (2019)

DEFENCE & SECURITY

The prime task of the Australian Defence Forces (ADF) is defending the country's sea lanes and infrastructure, Australia's security, stability and cohesion of its immediate neighbourhood, which the country share with Indonesia, Papua New Guinea, East Timor, New Zealand and the South Pacific island states. The ADF contributes to the whole-of-government effort to protect the Australian borders through Operation RESOLUTE. At any one time, up to 600 personnel at sea, in the air and on the land, are working to protect Australia's borders and offshore maritime interests. Externally, the ADF is engaged in the stability of the wider Asia-Pacific region and particularly Southeast Asia – assisting countries in the region to respond to threats to their security. While the Royal Australian Air Force (RAAF) provides air and space power, the Royal Australian Navy (RAN) provides maritime forces that contribute to the ADF's capacity to defend Australia, contribute to regional security, support global interests, shape the strategic environment and protect national interests. Cyber security is one of the highest national security priorities for the government. The Government has committed itself to take concrete action to combat terrorism which continues to pose a serious security challenge. The government has set up a strategy to counter violent extremism in Australia.

KEY DEFENCE PERSONS

MINISTER FOR DEFENCE: Peter Dutton

CHIEF OF THE DEFENCE FORCE: Gen. Angus Campbell

CHIEF OF ARMY: Lt. Gen. Rick Burr

CHIEF OF NAVY: Vice Adm. Michael Noonan

CHIEF OF AIR FORCE: Air Vice-Marshal Joe 'Vinny' Iervasi

Internal Conflict

Australia faces the threat of a domestic strike by transnational terrorists against innocent civilians. A number of non-state armed groups are reportedly active on Australian territory. Australians involved with violent extremist groups overseas who return home also present long-term challenges. The National Counter-Terrorism Plan is maintained by the Australia-New Zealand Counter-Terrorism Committee. It outlines the responsibilities, authorities and the mechanisms to prevent acts of terrorism within Australia and to manage the consequences if they do occur. The country has signed memorandums of understanding on counter-terrorism with Indonesia, the Philippines, Malaysia, and Thailand. The agreements promote increased bilateral co-operation between intelligence and law enforcement agencies and defence officials of Australia and the signatory countries.

External Conflict

◆ In 2007, Australia and Timor-Leste agreed to a 50-year development zone and revenue sharing arrangement and deferred a maritime boundary.

◆ Australia asserts land and maritime claims to Antarctica.

◆ Australia's 2004 submission to the Commission on the Limits of the Continental Shelf extends its continental margins over 3.37 million square kilometres, expanding its seabed roughly 30 percent beyond its claimed EEZ. All borders between Indonesia and Australia have been agreed upon bilaterally, but a 1997 treaty that would settle the last of their maritime and EEZ boundary has yet to be ratified by Indonesia's legislature.

◆ Indonesian groups challenge Australia's claim to Ashmore Reef; Australia closed parts of the Ashmore and Cartier reserve to Indonesian traditional fishing.

THREAT PERSPECTIVE

Terrorism: Australia continues to face persistent threat of terrorism, espionage, foreign interference, including cyber security threats. The Government is working closely with state, territory, and local governments, as well as the private sector and the community, in building an effective, nation-wide counter-terrorism capability, and by contributing to regional and global efforts to counter-terrorism. The Australian Security Intelligence Organisation's 2019 annual report has found that "Islamist extremism" remained the principal source of terrorist threat for Australia. The ADF maintains two elite Tactical Assault Groups, the Special Operations Engineer Regiment as well as a high readiness group in each Army Reserve brigade and the 1st Commando Regiment to meet its counter-terrorism responsibilities. Other threats include challenges from slow economic growth, social and governance challenges, population growth and climate change in the South Pacific region contributes to Australia's instability.

Cyber threat: The cyber threat to Australia represents a real and present risk to the Australian Defence Force's (ADF) war fighting capability, and national security and economic prosperity both in peacetime and during armed conflict.

STRATEGIC RELATIONS

Australia shares enduring relationships with United States and United Kingdom and growing ties with New Zealand, Indonesia and Japan in pursuing common strategic and defence interests, particularly in countering global and regional terrorist threats. Australia enjoys close and productive relations with China and India and also has valuable long-standing defence ties with Malaysia, Singapore, Thailand, the Philippines and Papua New Guinea, and developing further ties with many other countries in the Asia-Pacific.

United States: Australia shares a close relationship with the United States leaders. Their relationship is further strengthened by the ANZUS treaty and the Australia – United States Free Trade Agreement. The militaries of both the countries have fought together in every significant conflict. The US-Australia Force Posture Agreement signed at the annual Australia-United States Ministerial consultations (AUSMIN) in August 2014 has paved the way for even closer defence and security cooperation between the two nations. Australia was the first nation to back the U.S campaign against the Islamic State of Iraq and al-Sham (ISIS). The two nations work closely with like-minded partners in regional and global forums, including the G20, East Asia Summit, World Trade Organisation and United Nations. They maintain a strong relationship, characterised by cultural similarities and robust bilateral arrangements.

China: Australia and China are actively engaged economically, cultural and politically which spans different organisations such as APEC, East Asia Summit and the G20. China is Australia's largest trading partner. Further strengthening and deepening their economic relationship is a major priority for both countries, with both governments committed to sustaining the impressive trade and investment performance achieved in the past two decades. The two countries have agreed on an unspecified programme of enhanced military cooperation, including exchanges, training and service-to-service engagement

India: Defence cooperation between India and Australia has expanded significantly in recent years with the signing of MoU on defence cooperation as well as a Joint Declaration on Security Co-operation. The two nations continue to build relations between the defence forces through regular personnel and training exchanges. The two nations have decided to enhance their maritime cooperation and in 2015 established a bilateral naval exercise (AUSINDEX). India is Australia's seventh-largest trading partner and the fifth-largest export market. Recent visits by Indian and Australian prime ministers, such as Tony Abbott's visit in 2014, and later the same year Narendra Modi's visit to Australia and Malcolm Turnbull's visit in 2017 have continued to progress the relationship.

Japan: Australia and Japan have established good bilateral relationships based on mutually complementary economic relations. The two countries have strengthened their political and security cooperation which has made them a strategic partner in the Asia-Pacific region. They have been stepping up engagement between carrying out drills such as Exercise Talisman Saber, Yama Sakura and others. In a latest development, the leaders of the two countries held talks and have reached a basic agreement on a bilateral defence pact that would allow their troops to work more closely, as the two US allies seek to bolster their ties to counter China's growing assertiveness in the Asia-Pacific region. Japan is a vital and long-standing export market for Australian business.

Singapore: Australia and Singapore have signed a "Comprehensive Strategic Partnership" to boost their bilateral relationships. The two nations have agreed to deepen their economic ties, expand defence cooperation and strengthen people-to-people ties. In the area of defence, they have agreed to undertake a broad range of measures to boost ties, including elevating a signature joint bilateral military exercise; enhancing personnel exchanges; boosting intelligence and information-sharing and also to jointly develop a multi-billion military training areas and facilities in Australia. They will also work together on defence science and technology to develop combat systems/command, control, communications, computers and intelligence integration; and cognitive/human systems integration.

Vietnam: Australia and Vietnam have expanded their relations into strategic partnership. In 2017, the intent to sign a new strategic partnership was finalised during the APEC summit in Vietnam. The Foreign and Defence ministers of the two countries will now meet annually for bilateral talks. According to Australian Department of Foreign Affairs and Trade, Vietnam is Australia's fourteenth largest trading partner (2019) and Australia is estimated to be Vietnam's fourteenth largest trading partner (2018). Total two-way goods trade for 2019 was $12.2 billion. Total two-way services trade for 2019 was $3.4 billion.

DEFENCE CAPABILITIES

The Australian military is an all-volunteer force in which both women and men can enlist. The Australian Defence Force (ADF) comprised of the Australian Army, the Royal Australian Navy (RAN), and the Royal Australian Air Force (RAAF). The role of Commander-in-Chief is vested in the Governor-General, who appoints a Chief of the Defence Force from one of the armed services on the advice of the government. The Chief of Defence (CDF) commands the ADF.

The future defence force is being trained to be more capable of conducting independent combat operations and taking a step in this direction, the government is firming up defences intelligence, surveillance and reconnaissance capabilities to provide the forces with comprehensive situational awareness. Projects are being undertaken to better equip the defence force to face growing unease in the Asia-Pacific region due to military build-up, including disputes over the South China Sea. The land force is being armed with new personal equipment and a new generation of armoured combat reconnaissance and infantry fighting vehicles, as well as new combat engineering equipment while the Navy's maritime capability is being enhanced, the Air Force's has added the new F-35 JSF aircraft to its existing fleet.

The Government of Australia has released 2020 Defence Strategic Update, setting three new strategic objectives to guide all defence planning, including force structure, force generation, international engagement and operations: To shape Australia's strategic environment; to deter actions against Australia's interests; and to respond with credible military force, when required. Towards this, the government has decided to provide the armed forces with total funding of around $575 billion over the next ten years which includes approximately $270 billion investment in defence capability to 2029-30.

ARMY: The Australian Army is mainly a light infantry force commanded by the Chief of Army. They are part of a Joint Force to deter and defeat armed attacks on the country, contribute to stability and security, take part in military contingencies in the Indo-Pacific region and also contribute to military contingencies in support of global security. In step with the Army's Robotic and Autonomous Systems (RAS) Strategy, released in October 2018, the Army is working on further developing its robotic systems and artificial intelligence (AI). The Army has been using unmanned aircraft for intelligence, surveillance, and reconnaissance (ISR), and specialist tracked robots for bomb disposal.

The Army's operational headquarters, Land Command, is located at Victoria Barracks in Sydney.

Personnel: 30,000

Equipment

Category	Name	In Service	On Order
MBT	M1A1IM Abrams	62	87
APC	M113AS4	431	
APC	ASLAV (Piranha 8X8)	257	
APC	Bushmaster	1153	
Artillery	105 mm M2A2	240	
Artillery	M777A2	54	
Mortar	81 mm F2	296	
Anti-Tank GW	Javelin	92	
ATK weapon	M3 Carl Gustaf		
Weapon	Bofors RBS-70 (upgraded) (with MK3 Bolide missiles)	35	

New Procurements/Upgrades

◆ The ADF's new fleet of Hawkei protected mobility vehicles – light (PMV-L) - has achieved initial operational capability (IOC). The PMV-L is being procured under the Project Land 121 Phase 4 to replace the Australian Army's Land Rovers.

◆ The Hanwha Defence Australia (HDA) has been chosen to build 30 self-propelled howitzers for the ADF. The self-propelled howitzers will be built in the Geelong region.

◆ Rheinmetall has delivered 25 of the 211

Boxer 8×8 combat reconnaissance vehicles (CRVs) for the Army. According to the company, 131 of the total 211 vehicles will be the CRV variant. The remaining 186 will be assembled at Rheinmetall Defence Australia's Military Vehicle Centre of Excellence (MILVEHCOE) facility in Australia.

◆ The Australian Army and the ADF are set to acquire the Rafael Spike LR2 missile system under the Lethality System project (Land 159). The missile system will serve as the army's Long Range Direct Fire Support Weapon capability.

◆ Kongsberg Defence Australia, with support from 16 Regiment, Royal Australian Artillery and Raytheon Australia have successfully conducted fitment checks for the first National Advanced Surface to Air Missile System (NASAMS) Fire Distribution Centre (FDC) shelter on a HX40M truck. The ADF will purchase two versions of NASAMS, one with a trailer-mounted six-cell launcher and one with four missiles fitted to a Hawkei armoured 4×4 vehicle.

◆ Praesidium Global is developing an unmanned ground vehicles (UGV) called Mission Adaptable Platform System (MAPS), a medium-sized semi-autonomous platform, for the Army.

◆ The Army has begun trials on "stealth" e-bikes for battlefield information gathering. The bicycle comes as a detachable part of the Boxer combat reconnaissance vehicle and helps it in sighting routes.

Army Aviation
Equipment

Category	Name	In Service
Helicopter	S-70A Blackhawk	35
	CH-47D Chinook	7
	CH-47F Chinook	10
	MRH-90	45
	ARH Tiger	22
UAV	RQ 7B Shadow 200	
	ScanEagle	

NAVY: The Royal Australian Navy (RAN) is one of the largest and most sophisticated naval forces in the Pacific region, with a significant presence in the Indian Ocean and worldwide operations in support of military campaigns and peacekeeping missions. The Navy provides maritime forces that contribute to the ADF's capacity to defend Australia, contribute to regional security, support global interests, shape the strategic environment and protect national interests. The RAN is commanded through Naval Headquarters in Canberra. The professional head is the Chief of Navy, who holds the rank of Vice-Admiral. Australia has embarked on one of the most extensive and ambitious shipbuilding programmes to modernise its Navy. One of the most significant investments in military capability – the Future Frigate programme – the Hunter class frigate is being built to replace the current fleet of Anzac-class ships. The frigates will be primarily used for anti-submarine warfare (ASW). The submarine fleet will be increased from six to 12 to replace the Collins class. The surface naval capability will include three Hobart Class Air Warfare Destroyers (AWD), more capable offshore patrol vessels, new manned and unmanned aircraft and a new large-hulled multi-purpose patrol vessel, the Australian Defence Vessel Ocean Protector. The ADF's capacity for amphibious operations will be strengthened by the introduction of new weapons and equipment.

Major naval bases: Canberra ACT, Sydney NSW, Garden Island WA, Nowra NSW, Jervis Bay NSW, Westernport VTC, Cairns QLD, Darwin NT, HMAS Creswell, HMAS Penguin, HMAS Cerberus, HMAS Albatross, HMAS Coonawarra.

Personnel: 16,000+

Equipment

Category	Name	In Service
Submarine	Collins class	6
Destroyer	Nuship Sydney	1
	HMAS Brisbane	1
	HMAS Hobart	1
Frigate	Anzac class	8
	Adelaide class	4
Mine warfare force	Huon class	6
	MSA	2
	CDT	2
Replenishment ship	HMAS Success	1
	HMAS Sirius	1
Patrol Vessel	Cape-class	2
	Armidale class	13
Amphibious Force	HMAS Adelaide III LHD	1
	HMAS Canberra III LHD	1
	Tobruk class LSH	1
	Choules LSD	1
Survey Vessel	Leeuwin class	2
	Paluma class	4

New Procurements/Upgrades

◆ The RAN will receive two new multi-purpose sea lift and replenishment vessels and up to eight mine countermeasures and tactical hydrographic vessels, to be based on the Arafura-class offshore patrol vessels now under construction in local shipyards.

◆ The under construction Global Combat Ship 'Australia' to be officially called the Hunter class will replace the Anzac Frigates. The first batch of three ships of the class will carry the names – HMAS Flinders (II), Hunter and Tasman.

◆ Austal Australia has launched the first of six Evolved Cape-class patrol boats. The first-of-class vessel bearing the hull number '314' is expected to be commissioned in 2022. Austal has commenced construction of the five other boats already, and they are in varying states of construction. All are supposed to be delivered by mid-2023.

Naval Aviation
Equipment

Category	Name	In Service
Helicopter	Sikorsky S-70B-2 Seahawk	14
	MH-60R Romeo	14
	Squirrel AS-350B squirrel	13
	Agusta A109E	3
	MRH-90 Taipan	47
UAV	ScanEagle	

New Procurements/Upgrades

◆ The US Department of State has approved a potential Foreign Military Sales deal for RAN of 12 additional Sikorsky MH-60R Seahawk submarine-hunting helicopters for an estimated $985 million.

AIR FORCE: The Royal Australian Air Force (RAAF) provides air and space power for Australia's security. The RAAF, with its headquarters in Canberra, is the second-oldest independent and permanent air force in the world after Britain's Royal Air Force. The Air Force has an outstanding record of achievement, across the spectrum of conflict from strike, surveillance or humanitarian support. The RAAF is working on a strategy to turn the air force in to fifth-generation Air Force. A fifth-generation Air Force will provide the joint and networked effects necessary to prevail against the increasingly complex and lethal threats of warfare in the Information Age. The Air Force Strategy 2017-2027 outlines five areas to enable the change – Joint War fighting Capability People Capability, Communication and Information Systems, Infrastructure and International Engagement.

Major air bases: The Russell Offices complex in Canberra contains the administrative headquarters of the Australian Defence Force and is home to Air Force Headquarters.

Northern: Darwin, Tindal
Queensland: Townsville, Amberley, Scherger

South Australia: Edinburgh, Woomera Range Complex
Victoria: East Sale, Williams
Western Australia: Pearce, Learmonth, Curtin
Overseas: Butterworth (Malaysia)
Personnel: 14,447

Equipment

Category	Name	In Service	On Order
Fighter	F/A-18F Super Hornet	24	
	F-35 Lightning II	44	28
	EA-18G Growler	12	
Recon-naissance/ AEW&C	E-7A Wedgetails	6	
	C-27J Spartan	10	
	C-17 Globemaster III	8	
Transport/ Tanker	C-130J Super Hercules	12	
	Bombardier Challenger 604	3	
	Boeing 737 BBJ	2	
	King Air 350	8	
	KC-30A (A30 MRTT)	7	
	Hawk 127	33 (up-graded)	
	PC-21 turboprop	49	
Trainer	PC-9/A	60	
	AP-3C Orion	18	
	Poseidon P-8A	12	
Patrol	Triton (HALE)	3	
	Poseidon P-8A	12	
UAV/UAS	Triton (HALE)	3	7

New Procurements/Upgrades

◆ The RAAF has formally bid farewell to its F/A-18A/B fighter jet, often referred to as the Classic Hornet, after more than three decades of service.

◆ The RAAF has received its 44th F-35A 5th-gen fighter jet from the United States. The latest delivery included three aircraft, added to the 77th Squadron of RAAF. All 72 aircraft are expected to be fully operational by 2023.

◆ Boeing Defence Australia (BDA) has signed a contract worth $442.8m to upgrade the E-7A Wedgetail aircraft with the addition of advanced combat identification sensors, tactical data links, and communication and encryption systems. The upgrade work is expected to be completed by 2022.

◆ The DoD plans to purchase Lockheed Martin AGM-158C long-range anti-ship missile, which would become the country's next air-launched maritime strike weapon under Project Air 3023 Phase 1.

◆ Australia is seeking replacement fleets for the Air Force's C-130J-30 Hercules, Airbus KC-30A multi role tanker transport aircraft, Boeing E-7A Wedgetail airborne early warning and control planes and EA-18G Growler electronic attack platforms.

◆ The US has cleared Australia to buy one EA-18G Growler to replace the aircraft damaged beyond repair at Nellis in 2018.

Major Armament Producers

The Capability Acquisition and Sustainment Group (CASG) is responsible for meeting the ADF's military equipment and supply requirements as identified by Defence and approved by Government and it is the key delivery agency for Defence capability. Australian defence firms design, manufacture and maintain quality military equipment capable of operating in extreme conditions such as high heat and humidity and cold Antarctic waters. Specialist products include command and control systems, multi-sensor data fusion, signal processing, underwater systems, phased array radar, navigation and positioning aids, logistics support systems and self-monitoring propulsion systems. Specialist services include ship-building, construction and repair of major weapons, systems integration and the provision of land, maritime and air services to support peacetime and operational defence requirements. The defence firms have supplied Australia's defence forces with sophisticated capability solutions for deployments in Iraq, Afghanistan, the Solomon Islands, South-East Asia and East Timor. CEA Technologies are the producers of top-level radar equipment, including the Active Phased Array Radar used by the RAN. It has exported to the US, Europe and the Middle East. Shipbuilder Austral which builds multi-mission surface warfare combatants also supply its Littoral Combat Ships for the US Navy. Many US defence companies have large presences in Australia, including Boeing, Lockheed Martin, Rockwell Collins, Northrop Grumman, and Raytheon.

DEFENCE DEALS

Joint Venture Programmes

The Australian government and French state-owned submarine builder Naval Group have signed a strategic partnership agreement (SPA) on February 11, 2020 for the production of 12 Shortfin Barracuda Block 1A submarines, christened Attack-class, a diesel-electric derivative of the Barracuda-class nuclear attack submarine (SSN), under the Royal Australian Navy's SEA 1000 Future Submarine Programme (FSM). The two countries concluded an intergovernmental agreement (IGA) for the construction of 12 Attack-class boats in December 2016. Australia's Shortfin Barracuda will be 97 metres (318 feet) long and weight 4,500 metric tons (5,000 US tons).

AUKUS: Australia has formally embarked on a development programme to equip its naval forces with nuclear submarines after signing an agreement in September 2021 with Britain and the United States after announcing the formation of a defence alliance, - Australia, United Kingdom, United States (AUKUS). The alliance will initially build a class of nuclear-propelled submarines and also work together in the Indo-Pacific region, where the rise of China is seen as an increasing threat, and develop wider technologies. As a result of this new alliance, Australia has ended the contract given to France in 2016 to build 12 diesel electric-powered submarines to replace its existing Collins submarine fleet.

Arms Export

The Australian Government has introduced a new Defence Export Strategy with the strategic goal to achieve greater export success and build a stronger, more sustainable and more globally competitive Australian defence industry and to support Australia's Defence capability needs. The government's aim is to achieve the following five objectives by 2028 - strengthen the partnership between the Government and industry to pursue defence export opportunities, enable greater innovation and productivity in the defence industry to deliver world-leading defence capabilities, maintain the capability edge of the ADF and leverage defence capability development for export opportunities. The US, UK, Canada and New Zealand will be Australia's top priority markets. The government also plans to expand its market to Europe, Asia and the Middle East. Australia maintains a significant sector of industry involved in the manufacture and sale of armaments and military equipment. Arms exports from the country includes aircraft, armoured vehicles, artillery, radar systems, missiles, and ships and related goods. One of Australia's biggest export successes has been the Thales' Bushmaster.

Arms Import

In 2020, arms imports for Australia was 1,658 million US dollars, according to a media report. Though Australia arms imports fluctuated substantially in recent years, it tended to increase through 1971 – 2020 period ending at 1,658 million US dollars in 2020, it has stated. The country jumped from being the fourth-highest weapons importer in 2017, to the world's second biggest military purchaser in 2018, according to a report by Stockholm International Peace Research Institute (SIPRI). The arms import and spending on military equipment have surged in line with Australia's ambitious targets to update the armed forces' fleet of fighter jets, submarines, frigates and armoured vehicles. In recent years, Australia has bought combat helicopters from France, German armoured personnel carriers, radar systems from Sweden, Howitzer artillery guns from Britain, air-refuelling tanker aircraft from Spain, as well as fighter aircraft, helicopters, military transport aircraft, Shadow drones, Hellfire anti-tank and Sidewinder air-to-air-missiles from the US. New acquisitions include the MQ-4CTriton remotely-piloted aircraft, under the AIR 7000 programme.

DEFENCE BUDGET

Total defence spending: A$44.6 billion (2021-22), A$2.3 billion (2019)

Estimated defence spending in terms of GDP: 2.0%

The Government has committed to grow the Defence budget to two per cent of GDP in the 2020–21 financial year. The new 2020 Defence Strategic Update and 2020 Force Structure Plan is a 10 year funding model with a 20 year outlook that continues to provide Defence and defence industry with the planning certainty required to support the ongoing development and delivery of critical Defence capability. The Government plans to invest $270 billion over the next 10 years to upgrade the capability and potency of the ADF. According to a MoD statement, this includes investing in more lethal and long-range capabilities to hold adversary forces and infrastructure at risk, including longer-range strike weapons, offensive cyber capabilities and area denial capabilities. The government will invest $1.4 billion over the next decade to enhance the cyber security capabilities. The investment known as the Cyber Enhanced Situational Awareness and Response (CESAR) package, has been designed to boost protection and cyber resilience for all Australians, from individuals and small businesses through to the providers of critical services.

CONCLUSION

The ADF is in the midst of modernisation programme. With the release of the 2016 Defence White Paper, the Government has committed to the largest ever defence acquisition programme. The naval shipbuilding programme is continuing to develop the Royal Australian Navy of the future, while creating a strong and sustainable Australian naval shipbuilding industry. The 5th generation F-35 Joint Strike Fighter programme, along with the acquisition of EA-18G Growlers and P-8A Poseidon maritime surveillance aircraft, will give the Royal Australian Air Force unprecedented capability to combat future threats. Besides the purchase of a fleet of new Combat Reconnaissance Vehicles to protect the troops, the Government has committed to build new capabilities to strengthen the Defence Force. Australia has the unique advantage of being an island continent, solely occupied by one sovereign nation and it is one of the major political and economic powers in Southeast Asia. An ADF with higher levels of preparedness will be able to better respond to strategic developments that threaten Australia's interests where the Government requires a military response.

CONTACT DETAILS
The Department of Defence
Russell Offices
Department of Defence,
Canberra ACT 2600
Australia
Tel: +61-6-265-9111
email: dsc@defence.gov.au
www.defence.gov.au

AUSTRIA
(Capital: Vienna)

INTRODUCTION

Area: 83,871 sq km
Population: 8,884,864 (July 2021 est.)
Coastline: 0 (Landlocked)
Maritime claims: None

KEY POLITICAL PERSONS

PRESIDENT & COMMANDER-IN-CHIEF: Alexander Van der Bellen

FEDERAL CHANCELLOR: Alexander Schallenberg

KEY DEFENCE PERSONS

MINISTER OF DEFENCE: Klaudia Tanner

CHIEF OF DEFENCE STAFF: Gen. Robert Brieger

ECONOMY

Led by large service and industrial sectors and a highly-developed agricultural sector, Austria is one of the leading market economies of Europe. Historically tied to the German economy, Austria has established closer ties with other European economies as well after becoming a member of the European Union in 1995 and expanded its growth potential. Austria's economic growth strengthened in 2017, with a 2.9% increase in GDP. The country's exports, accounting for around 60% of GDP, were up 8.2% in 2017. Unemployment rate fell by 0.3% to

5.5%, which is low by European standards, but still at its second highest rate since the end of World War II, driven by an increased number of refugees and EU migrants entering the labour market. Austria's fiscal position compares favourably with other euro-zone countries. Several external risks, such as Austrian banks' exposure to Central and Eastern Europe, the refugee crisis, and continued unrest in Russia/Ukraine, eased in 2017, but are still a factor for the country's economy. The impact of Coronavirus pandemic has shrunk the Austrian economy and the IMF has projected a GDP growth rate of 3.5% for the country in 2021.

GDP (official exchange rate): $445.025 billion (2019 est.)

Real Growth Rate (GDP): 1.42% (2019 est.); 2.58% (2018 est.)

Industries: Construction, machinery, vehicles and parts, food, metals, chemicals, lumber and paper, electronics, tourism

Total Exports: $270.8 billion (2019 est.); $263.1 billion (2018 est.)

Export Commodities: Cars, packaged medical supplies, vehicle parts, medical vaccines/cultures, flavoured water (2019)

Major Markets: Germany 28%, United States 7%, Italy 6%, Switzerland 5% (2019)

Total Imports: $253.2 billion (2019 est.); $247.2 billion (2018 est.)

Import Commodities: Cars, vehicle parts, broadcasting equipment, refined petroleum, packaged medical supplies (2019)

Major Suppliers: Germany 39%, Italy 7%, Czech Republic 5% (2019)

INTERNATIONAL DISPUTES

Austria has no known international dispute, barring its opposition to the Temelin nuclear power plant built by the Czech Republic near the Austrian border.

DEFENCE

ARMY

Personnel: 15,000+

Equipment

Category	Name	In Service
MBT	Leopard 2A4	34
APC, IFV	Ulan	112
	Pandur I	71
	Dingo 2 (protected vehicle)	30+
	Iveco LMV	150
Artillery	M-109A5OE 155mm	30
Mortar	L16 81 mm	424 (total)
	M-2/M-30 107 mm	
	M-60	
	M-86 120mm	

...continued

Category	Name	In Service
ATGW	Bill 1	285
UAV	Tracker	6

New Procurements/ Upgrades

◆ 34 additional Pandur APCs are being procured under a contract awarded to General Dynamics European Land Systems in December 2016. Deliveries are scheduled to be completed by 2021 - 2022. The Army is also upgrading its entire fleet of existing Pandurs.

◆ First batch of four BvS10 armoured vehicles (APCs) has been delivered by BAE Systems in February 2019. Austria has ordered a total of 32 BvS10 platforms under a deal inked in 2016.

AIR FORCE

Personnel: 3,000

Equipment

Category	Name	In Service
Fighter/Attack	Eurofighter Typhoon	15
Transport	C-130K Hercules	3
	Skyvan 3M	2
	PC-6B	10
Helicopter	S-70 Black Hawk	9 (+3 on order)
	Bell OH-58B Kiowa	11
	AB-212	23 (being upgraded)
	SA-316 Alouette III	21
Trainer	Pilatus PC-7	12
Air Defence System	Mistral SAM	24
	35mm twin anti-aircraft gun (ZFlAK 85)	25
	20mm Fliegerabwehr-kanone 65/68 (anti-aircraft gun)	
	Skyguard 98	30

New Procurements/ Upgrades

◆ The Austrian Govt. in 2017 announced to retire the Air Force's entire fleet of Eurofighter Typhoons from 2020 onwards over increasing maintenance costs. The Govt. is considering acquisition of new, single-engine supersonic fighters (15 single-seat, 3 double-seat) to replace the Typhoons. Indonesia has put forth an offer to buy the Typhoon jets from Austria and the Austrian Govt. has agreed to the proposal.

◆ A deal has been inked with US firm Ace Aeronautics in 2019 to procure three additional UH-60A Black Hawk (S-70) utility helicopters at a cost of US$50 million. Upgrade of nine other Black Hawks in operational use has been cleared with a US$54 million contract awarded to Ace Aeronautics in June 2017. The company will upgrade the helicopter's flight decks.

◆ 18 Leonardo AW169M helicopters would be procured to replace the Alouette III light utility helicopters, the MoD has announced in September 2020. Delivery of the new platforms would start from 2022 onwards.

Defence Expenditure

Austria has one of the lowest defence budgets among the European Union nations. Its main defence suppliers include Germany, Italy and few other European countries.

Total defence spending: €3.3 billion (2021)
Defence spending in terms of GDP: 0.72% (2019)

Defence Production and R&D

The country's defence industry is primarily producing armoured vehicles, aerospace, ammunition, electronics and naval systems. The indigenous Pandur II armoured fighting vehicle has been sold to countries like Czech Republic and Portugal. Some of the defence equipment have also been sold in Africa, Middle East and few European countries.

Defence Procurement & Future Plans

Defence procurement in Austria has not been very robust as it has been hindered by low defence expenditure. The country has initiated reforms which are directed towards reducing its armed forces personnel strength and diverting the funds to acquire new defence equipment. Following a referendum in January 2013, Austria decided to retain military conscription.

In 2014, the Defence Ministry announced major restructuring plans for the Austrian military to meet the falling defence expenses. Under the plans, a large number of the Army's equipment, including MBTs, armoured vehicles, artillery and other weapons have been retired or sold. The restructuring also involved curtailment of a number of military positions, around 1,400, which were gradually cut via retirements and a recruitment freeze. Several military stations have also been shut down.

CONTACT DETAILS

Ministry of Defence
Rossauer Lande 1
A-1090 Vienna
Tel: 050201-0
www.bundesheer.at

AZERBAIJAN
(Capital: Baku)

INTRODUCTION
Area: 86,600 sq km
Population: 10,282,283 (July 2021 est.)
Coastline: Landlocked (713km coastline on the Caspian Sea)
Maritime claims: None

KEY POLITICAL PERSONS

PRESIDENT & SUPREME COMMANDER-IN-CHIEF: Ilham Aliyev

PRIME MINISTER: Ali Asadov

KEY DEFENCE PERSONS

DEFENCE MINISTER: Col. Gen. Zakir Hasanov.

CHIEF OF THE GENERAL STAFF: Lt. Gen. Karim Valiyev

COMMANDER OF THE LAND FORCES: Maj. Gen. Anvar Efendiyev

CHIEF OF NAVY: Rear Adm. Subhan Bekirov

CHIEF OF AIR FORCE: Lt. Gen. Ramiz Tahirov

ECONOMY

Post the Soviet era, Azerbaijan has transitioned to a more market-based economy. A strategic roadmap was launched for medium-and long-term goals for reforms and sustained development. The country has begun making progress on economic reform. Oil remains the most prominent product with cotton, natural gas and agriculture products contributing to its economic growth. Oil exports through the Baku-Tbilisi-Ceyhan Pipeline, the Baku-Novorossiysk, and the Baku-Supsa pipelines has boost the economy. In 2018, real GDP expanded by 1.4 percent supported by stable oil production and a modest acceleration in domestic demand, according to the World Bank. It has expanded trade with Turkey and Europe and is seeking new markets for non-oil/gas exports – mainly in the agricultural sector – with Gulf Cooperation Council member countries, the US, and others.

GDP (official exchange rate): $48.104 billion (2019 est.)

Real Growth Rate (GDP): 0.1% (2017 est.), -3.1% (2016 est.)

Industries: Petroleum and petroleum products, natural gas, oilfield equipment; steel, iron ore; cement; chemicals and petrochemicals; textiles.

Total Exports: $15.21 billion (2020 est.), $23.63 billion (2019 est.)

Export Commodities: Crude petroleum, natural gas, refined petroleum, tomatoes, gold (2019)

Major Markets: Italy 28%, Turkey 15%, Israel 7%, Germany 5%, India 5% (2017)

Total Imports: $15.54 billion (2020 est.), $17.71 billion (2019 est.)

Import Commodities: Gold, cars, refined petroleum, wheat, packaged medical supplies (2019)

Major Suppliers: United Kingdom 17%, Russia 17%, Turkey 12%, China 6% (2019)

INTERNATIONAL DISPUTES

◆ Azerbaijan, Kazakhstan, and Russia ratified the Caspian seabed delimitation treaties based on equidistance, while Iran continues to insist on a one-fifth slice of the sea

◆ The dispute over the break-away Nagorno-Karabakh region and the Armenian military occupation of surrounding lands in Azerbaijan remains the primary focus of regional instability.

◆ Residents have evacuated the former Soviet-era small ethnic enclaves in Armenia and Azerbaijan; local border forces struggle to control the illegal transit of goods and people across the porous, undemarcated Armenian, Azerbaijani, and Georgian borders.

◆ Bilateral talks continue with Turkmenistan on dividing the seabed and contested oilfields in the middle of the Caspian.

DEFENCE

After getting its independence on 28 May 1918, the People's Republic of Azerbaijan enacted a resolution to create an armed force of its own. The first army troops were established by 26 June 1918 and the process for formation of the modern regular army began in 1994. The armed force comprised of the Land Forces, the Air and Air Defence Force, and the Navy. The Azerbaijani army is known as the most powerful in the South Caucasus region. The armed force is equipped with modern main battle tanks, combat armoured vehicles, air defence systems, aircraft, helicopters, anti-tank guided missiles, artillery systems, detection equipment and unmanned aerial vehicles. Azerbaijan's conflict with Armenia over Nagorno-Karabakh has compelled the country to significantly increase its defence spending and strengthen its defence industrial base. In the last decade, the country has built a number of defence-manufacturing facilities and its domestic defence innovation has raised Azerbaijan's profile in the global arms market. The defence industry has emerged as an autonomous entity with a growing defence production capability.

ARMY
Personnel: 57,135

Equipment

Category	Name	In Service
MBT	T-90	52
	T-72	376
	T-55 (reserved)	35
AIFV/APC	Tufan MARP	
	Sandcat	100
	BMP-1	26
	BMP-2	39
	BMP-3	56
	BRM-1K	4
	BTR-60/-70/-80	24
	BTR-82A	70+
	MT-LB	196
	Matador	15
	Marauder	15
Artillery	LORA	
	152-mm DANA	36
	D30 122mm	254
	D20 152mm	24
	M46 130mm	36
	2A36 152mm towed	16
	2S19 MSTA-S 152mm SP	18
	2S1 122mm SP	66
	2S7 203mm SP	12
	2S3 152mm SP	16
Mortar	120mm (including 18 SP)	267
	Vena SP	18
	NONA-S	18
MRL	Polonez B-200BM	10
	RM-70 122MM	30
	BM-21 122mm	44
	9A52 Smerch 300mm	12
	IMI LYNX 122mm	
	Grad-LAR	16
	160mm	
	306mm	
	TOS-1A Buratino	18
SSM	9K79 Tochka (3 launchers)	
ATGW	Kornet	
	Spike	
	9M123 Khrizantema	800

New Procurements/Upgrades
No major procurement plans are under consideration at present.

NAVY
Personnel: 1,786

Equipment

Category	Name	In Service
Submarine (midget)	Triton-2M	
Mine warfare force	Sonya class	1
Light forces	Petya-2 class	1
	Vodnik	1
	S201	6
Patrol boat	S301 class	6
	Israeli Saar-72	2
	S301 class	6
Landing ship	Polnochny class	4
Miscellaneous	Hydrographic ship	3

New Procurements/Upgrades
No major procurement plans are under consideration at present.

AIR FORCE
Personnel: 7,944

Equipment

Category	Name	In Service
Fighter	Mig-29	12
	MiG-29UB	3
	Su-24	34
	Su-25	5
Trainer/ Transport	L-29	28
	Super Mushshak	10
	L-39 Albatros	
	Ilyushin Il-76	2
Helicopter	Mi-17-1B	34
	Mi-8	11
	Mi-24G	24
	Mi-35M	24
	Bell 412	2
	Bell 407	1
SAM	S-300 Favorit	
	BUK-MB	
	SA-2/-3/-4/-5	
	T-38 Stilletos	
	LORA	50
UAV	Searcher	
	Heron	
	Orbiter 2/3/4	
	Hunter/ Aerostar	
	Hermes 450/900	27+2
	Harop	
	Skystriker	100

New Procurements/Upgrades
◆ Azerbaijan has signed a deal with Ukraine to purchase of 10 AN-178 military transport planes.
◆ The MoD has ordered more than 100 Zerbe drones.
◆ An agreement has been signed with Israel to buy the Iron Dome missile defence system.
◆ A contract worth $13 million has been singed to acquire the Israeli Orbiter 1K UAV.

Defence Expenditure
Total defence expenditure: $2.267 billion (2020), $1.8 billion (2019)
Estimated defence spending in terms of GDP: 5.4% (2020)

A media report quoting Azerbaijan's Finance Ministry forecasts said the country's defence and security expenses will amount to $2.64 billion in 2022. The defence and security expenses for the next four years are projected to be $2.64 billion for 2022, $2.69 billion for 2023, $2.74 billion for 2024 and $2.79 billion for 2025.

Defence production and R & D
Azerbaijan is building up its own capabilities to produce new weaponry. According to the statistics of the Ministry of Defence Industry, Azerbaijan today offers different kind of domestically produced weaponry, including vehicles, rifles, mines, and other military equipment. Azerbaijan exports weapons to more than ten foreign countries including Turkey, Georgia, Iraq, Pakistan and Jordan. The country produces 1100 different weapons which includes vehicles, rifles, mines, and other military equipment. UAV production is one the most dynamic and strategic branches of Azerbaijan's defence industry. In 2017, Azerbaijan unveiled its first domestically developed Mine-Resistant Ambush-Protected vehicle "Tufan" (Storm) armoured military vehicle which will be produce in four varieties – medical evacuation, air-defence/anti-armour, anti-riot and a basic armoured personnel carrier (APC). The MoD is developing the Zarba-1K, a local derivative of the Israeli-produced Aeronautics Orbiter 1K. Azerbaijan has established joint ventures with various foreign defence companies. Azerbaijan has signed an agreement with Iran, Turkey, Germany and Belarus on defence industry cooperation. Azerbaijan is working together with defence industries of Ukraine, Belarus and Pakistan.

Defence Procurement
Azerbaijan has been diversifying its arms inventory with cutting-edge weapons and equipment from new suppliers although it is heavily investing in its own domestic military

industry. Azerbaijan has recently procured a series of assets from traditional suppliers, including LORA ballistic missiles, Spear-Mk.2 mortars, Spike-ER anti-tank rockets, Hermes-900 surveillance drones, Sky-Striker autonomous long-range loitering munitions, and Sky-Capture advanced radars (EL/M-2106-ATAR) from Israel; the Polonez tactical missile complex, 2A36-Giatsint-B howitzers, and the Groza-S electronic-warfare (EW) system from Belarus; İHTAR anti-drone system and SOM-B1 cruise missiles from Turkey; NTW-20 anti-materiel sniper rifles from South Africa; and BTR-82A modernised combat vehicles from Russia. According to the Stockholm Peace Research Institute (SIPRI), In 2017 and 2018, Azerbaijan imported arms and ammunition worth $ 615 million – 285 million and 330 million dollars – respectively. In the recent past, the purchases from Turkey reportedly included drones, rocket launchers, ammunition.

CONTACT DETAILS
Ministry of Defence
Parliament AV-E 3,
Baku, Azerbaijan, AZ1073
Tel.:/Fax: + (994 12) 539 24 53
www.mdi.gov.az
E-mail: info@mdi.gov.az

BAHRAIN
(Capital: Manama)

INTRODUCTION
Area: 760 sq km
Population: 1,526,929 (July 2021 est.)
Coastline: 161 km
Maritime claims: Territorial sea: 12 nm
Contiguous zone: 24 nm
Continental shelf: extending to boundaries to be determined

KEY POLITICAL PERSONS

HEAD OF STATE & SUPREME COMMANDER: King Hamad bin Isa Al-Khalifa

CROWN PRINCE, DEPUTY SUPREME COMMANDER & PRIME MINISTER: Prince Salman bin Hamad Al Khalifa

KEY DEFENCE PERSONS

MINISTER OF STATE FOR DEFENCE AFFAIRS: Maj. Gen. Abdulla Hassan Al Nuaimi

COMMANDER-IN-CHIEF OF THE BAHRAIN DEFENCE FORCE (BDF): Field Marshal Sheikh Khalifa bin Ahmed Al Khalifa

CHIEF OF STAFF OF DEFENCE FORCE: Lt. Gen. Dhiyab bin Saqr Al-Nuaimi

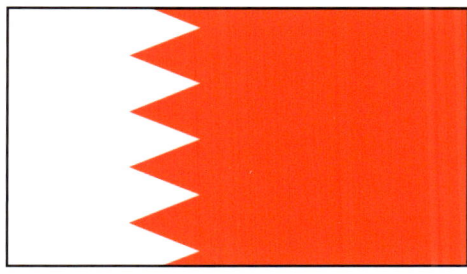

ECONOMY
Bahrain's economy strength is based on its rich oil and natural gas. More than 80% of Bahrain's budget revenues comprises mainly of oil. Other major economic activities are production of aluminium - Bahrain's second biggest export after oil and gas –finance, and construction. Bahrain implemented a Free Trade Agreement (FTA) with the US in August 2006 and also plans to implement VAT by 2018-end. Due to its relatively limited energy reserves, Bahrain has been diversifying its economy away from oil and gas production and is seeking to attract foreign investment and businesses. US exports to Bahrain include machinery, aircraft, vehicles, and agricultural products. Bahrain's economy shrank by 8.9% in 2nd quarter amid COVID-19 pandemic restrictions.

GDP (official exchange rate): $69.65 billion (2020), $73.95 billion (2019)
Real Growth Rate (GDP): 2.49% (2019 est.), 13.89% (2018 est.)
Industries: Petroleum processing and refining, aluminium smelting, iron palletisation, fertilizers, Islamic and offshore banking, insurance, ship repairing, tourism
Oil - proved reserves: 124.6 million bbl (1 January 2018 est.)
Natural gas - proved reserves: 92.03 billion cu m (1 January 2018 est.)
Total Exports: $30.1 billion (2018 est.), $26.762 billion (2017 est.)
Export Commodities: Refined petroleum, aluminum and plating, crude petroleum, iron ore, gold (2019)
Major Markets: United Arab Emirates 31%, Saudi Arabia 12%, Japan 8%, United States 8% (2019)
Total Imports: $27.19 billion (2018 est.), $22.132 billion (2017 est.)
Import Commodities: Cars, iron ore, jewelry, gold, gas turbines (2019)
Major Suppliers: United Arab Emirates 27%, China 11%, Saudi Arabia 7%, United States 5%, Brazil 5%, Japan 5%, India 5% (2019)

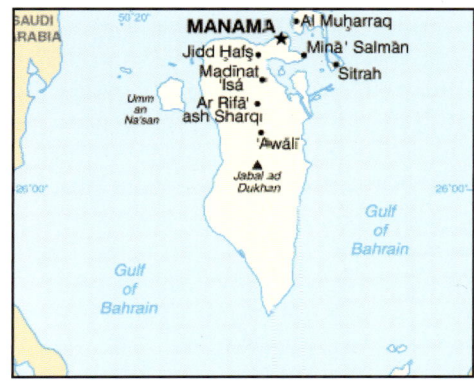

INTERNATIONAL DISPUTES
Bahrain has no known international disputes. The Government of Bahrain (GOB) is a member of the Global Coalition to Defeat ISIS and supported US government counterterrorism efforts.

DEFENCE
ARMY
Personnel: 7,500
Equipment

Category	Name	In Service
MBT	M60 A3 Patton	150+
APC/MICV/IFV	YPR-765	20+
	M-113 A2	100
	AT-105 Saxon	10
	Panhard M3	100+
	AML-90	20
Artillery	M110 203mm self-propelled	10+
	M-198 A1 155mm	15+
	L-118 105mm	
Mortar	81 mm	150+
	120 mm	
Anti Tank GW	BGM-71C TOW	1500+
	Javelin	50

...continued

Category	Name	In Service
RCL Gun	120 mm Mobat	
SAM	RBS 70	150+
	FIM-92A Stinger	300+
	Crotale	
	MIM-23 Hawk	5+
MRL	M270 MLRS	5+
	SR5	

New Procurements/ Upgrades

◆ The US Army has awarded Raytheon Company a USD551 million contract to begin production of the combat-proven Patriot air and missile defence system for the Kingdom of Bahrain. The contract was awarded on January 31, 2020.

◆ The US State Department has approved a possible Foreign Military Sale to Bahrain of various Patriot missile systems and related support and equipment for an estimated cost of USD2.478 billion. The DSCA delivered the required certification notifying Congress of this possible sale in March 2019. The Government of Bahrain has requested to buy 60 Patriot Advanced Capability-3 (PAC-3) Missile Segment Enhancement (MSE) missiles, 36 Patriot MIM-104E Guidance Enhanced Missiles (GEM-T) missiles with canisters, 9 M903 Launching Stations (LS), 5 Antenna Mast Groups (AMG), 3 Electrical Power Plants (EPP) III, 2 AN/MPQ-65 Radar Sets (RS), and 2 AN/MSQ-132 Engagement Control Stations (ECS). Also included is communications equipment, tools and test equipment, range and test programs, support equipment, prime movers, generators, publications and technical documentation, training equipment, spare and repair parts, personnel training, Technical Assistance Field Team (TAFT), US Government and contractor technical, engineering, and logistics support services, Systems Integration and Checkout (SICO), field office support, and other related elements of logistics and programme support.

◆ The US State Department has approved a possible Foreign Military Sale to Bahrain of Guided Multiple Launch Rocket System Unitary Rocket Pods and Army Tactical Missiles System (ATACMS) Unitary missiles for an estimated cost of USD 300 million. The Kingdom of Bahrain has requested to buy 120 Guided Multiple Launch Rocket System (GMLRS) M31 Unitary Rocket Pods, 6 rockets per pod for a total of 720; and 110 Army Tactical Missiles System (ATACMS) M57 T2K Unitary missiles. Also included are publications, personnel training and training equipment, software development, US Government and contractor engineering, technical and logistics support services; and other related elements of logistical and program support.

◆ The US State Department has approved a possible Foreign Military Sale to Bahrain of 28 TOW Improved Target Acquisition Systems (ITAS), and related equipment, for an estimated cost of USD 80 million.

NAVY

Personnel: 1,000 (including Coast Guard)

Equipment

Category	Name	In Service
Frigate	Sabha Class Frigate	1
Corvette	Al Manama class	2
Missile Patrol Craft	Al Fateh Class	4
	Al Riffa class	2
	Al Jarim Class	2
Landing craft	42mt landing craft	4
SSM	Harpoon	
SAM	SM-1MR	

Naval Aviation

Category	Name	In Service
Aircraft	SA 365F DAUPHINs	2
	BO-105s	2

New Procurements/ Upgrades

◆ The US State Department has approved a possible Foreign Military Sale to Bahrain to refurbish the Oliver Hazard Perry Class ship, ex ROBERT G. BRADLEY (FFG 49) with support for an estimated cost of USD150 million. The Defence Security Cooperation Agency (DSCA) delivered the required certification notifying Congress of this possible sale on October 22, 2019. The Government of Bahrain has requested refurbishment of the Oliver Hazard Perry Class ship, ex ROBERT G. BRADLEY (FFG 49), spares, support, training, publications, and other related elements of logistics and programme support.

◆ The US State Department has approved USD 70 million worth of items and services for the upgrades of Royal Bahrain Navy frigate RBNS Sabha. The approved sale includes engineering, technical, and logistics services, documentation, and modification material for US Navy supplied systems and equipment.

◆ The US State Department has approved a possible Foreign Military Sale to Bahrain of items and services in support of Follow-On Technical Support (FOTS) for the Royal Bahrain Navy Ship SABHA (FFG-90) for an estimated cost of USD 70 million.

AIR FORCE

Personnel: 1,500

Equipment

Category	Name	In Service
Fighter aircraft	F-16C	10+
	F-5 E	5+
Helicopter	AH-1E/F Cobra	20
	AB-212	15+
	UH-60M	10
Trainer aircraft	F-5F	5
	F-16D	5
	Hawk-129	5
	T67 M260	3
	TAH-1P	5+
	Bo 105	4

New Procurements/ Upgrades

◆ US Army Corps of Engineers Transatlantic Middle East District issued an USD8.4 million contract modification in support of the Kingdom of Bahrain's purchase of 16 F-16V Block 70 aircraft. The case covers the purchase, fielding, and support of the F-16V Block 70 aircraft, including studies, design and construction advisory services for facilities and infrastructure.

◆ The Transatlantic Middle East District (TAM) (Middle East District, US Army Corps of Engineers) has awarded military contract for design of Royal Bahrain Air Force F-16 facilities.

◆ Bell Textron Inc., Fort Worth, Texas, is awarded an USD8,941,785 contract to produce, deliver, install and integrate, in country, a fully assembled AH-1Z flight training device for the government of Bahrain.

◆ The US State Department has approved a possible Foreign Military Sale to Bahrain of various weapons to support its F-16 Block 70/F-16V aircraft fleet for an estimated cost of USD750 million. The DSCA delivered the required certification notifying Congress of this possible sale in May 2019. The Government of Bahrain has requested to buy 32 AIM-120C-7 AMRAAM missiles; 1 AIM-120C-7 AMRAAM guidance section; 32 AIM-9X missiles; 20 AGM-84 Block II Harpoon missiles; 2 ATM-84L-1 Block II Harpoon missiles; 40 AGM-154 Joint Standoff Weapon (JSOW) All-Up-Rounds; 50 AGM-88B High-Speed Anti-Radiation Missiles (HARM); 4 AGM-88 HARM training missiles; 100 GBU-39 250 lb Small Diameter Bomb (SDB-1) All-Up-Rounds; 400 MAU-209 C/B Computer Control Groups (GBU-10, -12); 80 MAU-210 Enhanced Computer Control Groups (GBU-49, -50); 340 MXU-650 Air Foil Group (GBU-12, -49); 140 MXU-651 Air Foil Groups (GBU-10, -50); 70 KMU-557 GBU-31 tail kits (GBU-31 JDAM, GBU-56 JDAM); 120 KMU-572 tail kits (GBU-38, -54); 100 DSU-38 proximity sensors (GBU-54); 462 MK-82 or BLU-111 500 lb Bomb Bodies (Supporting GBU-12, GBU-38, GBU-49, GBU-54); 210 BLU-109/BLU-117 or MK-84 2000 lb Bomb Bodies; (Supporting GBU-10, GBU-31, GBU-50, GBU-56); 10 practice BLU-109/BLU-117; 670 FMU-152 fuses (supporting GBU-10, -12, -31, -38; -49, -50, -54, & -56) plus many more other related items and support systems.

◆ Bahrain Defence Force (BDF) has announced the signing of a USD 3.8 billion deal with Lockheed Martin to buy 16 upgraded F-16 fighters. The deal was concluded on the second day of the Bahrain International Defence Exhibition and Conference (BIDEC 2017) in October 2017.

◆ The Royal Bahraini Air Force has ordered 19 Sniper ATPs for the F-16 Block 70 platform from Lockheed Martin. Sniper ATP detects and automatically tracks small targets at long ranges, and can support all laser- and GPS-guided weapons against multiple fixed and moving targets.

◆ The US State Department has approved a possible Foreign Military Sale to Bahrain of AH-1Z attack helicopters for an estimated cost of USD 911.4 million.

Defence Expenditure

Total defence spending: $1.400 billion (2020 approx.)

Defence spending in terms of GDP: 4.2% of GDP (2020 est.), 3.7% of GDP (2019)

United States has been the key military supplier to Manama whose military spending is fuelled by the threat from neighbouring Iran. Among other regional and global organisations, Bahrain is a member of the United Nations, International Monetary Fund, World Bank, and World Trade Organisation. The US State Department has approved a possible Foreign Military Sale to Bahrain of General Purpose (GP) and Penetrator Warhead bomb bodies for an estimated cost of USD 45 million. Bahrain has doubled its defence spending. Bahraini has ordered defence imports worth USD 80 million in 2016. US assistance enables Bahrain to continue to obtain the equipment and training it needs to provide for its own defence and to operate alongside US air and naval forces. US assistance also strengthens Bahrain's interoperability for regional security and counterterrorism cooperation; boosts Bahrain's maritime defences. According to US Dept of State data, Bahrain plays a key role in the regional security architecture and is a vital US partner in defence initiatives. Bahrain hosts the US Navy's Fifth Fleet and US Naval Forces Central Command, and participates in US-led military coalitions, including the Global Coalition to Defeat ISIS. Bahraini forces have supported the International Security Assistance Force in Afghanistan, providing perimeter security at a military base. Bahrain was the first Arab state to lead a Coalition Task Force patrolling the Gulf region and has supported the coalition counter-piracy mission with a deployment of its flagship. In August 2019, Bahrain was the first country in the Gulf region to announce publicly that it had joined the US-led International Maritime Security Construct to promote freedom of navigation in the region.

Defence Production and R&D

Bahrain has not stretched its defence production facilities and it produces very less equipments. The nation had unveiled its first military armoured vehicle 'Faisal' in 2009. Bahrain Defence Force's technical maintenance unit designed and assembled the vehicle, with the aid of a European company with experience in this field. The Bahrain Ship Repairing & Engineering Company (BASREC) and the Arab Shipbuilding & Repair Yard (ASRY) have both received contracts from the US Navy to repair and overhaul warships in recent years.

Defence Procurement

The Government of Bahrain plays a key role in the Gulf's security architecture and is an important member of the US-led anti-ISIL coalition. US assistance enables Bahrain to continue to obtain the equipment and training it needs to provide for its own defence and to operate alongside U.S. air and naval forces. The army's modernisation and expansion plans have been helped by the willingness of NATO states to cascade surplus equipment. The US has been the dominant supplier of military equipment to Bahrain. The nation also receives a large section of military equipment aid both from Iraq and Iran. Bahrain was the first Arab state to lead a Coalition Task Force patrolling the Gulf and has supported the coalition counter-piracy mission with a deployment of its flagship. The US designated Bahrain a Major Non-NATO Ally in 2002. Bahrain's small size, central location among Gulf countries, economic dependence on Saudi Arabia, and proximity to Iran require it to play a delicate balancing act in foreign affairs among its larger neighbours, as per NAVSEA website.

CONTACT DETAILS
Defence Forces HQ
C/o Ministry of Defence
P.O Box 245, HQ Bahrain
West Rifa's, Bahrain
Tel: +973-665599

BANGLADESH
(Capital: Dhaka)

INTRODUCTION

Area: 148,460 sq km
Population: 164,098,818 (July 2021 est.)
Coastline: 580 km
Maritime claims: Territorial sea: 12 nm
Contiguous Zone: 18 nm
Exclusive Economic Zone: 200 nm
Continental shelf: up to the outer limits of the continental margin

KEY POLITICAL PERSONS

PRESIDENT:
Abdul Hamid

PRIME MINISTER & DEFENCE MINISTER: Sheikh Hasina

KEY DEFENCE PERSONS

SECRETARY, MINISTRY OF DEFENCE: Md. Abu Hena Mostofa Kamal

CHIEF OF ARMY STAFF: Gen. S M Shafiuddin Ahmed

CHIEF OF NAVAL STAFF: Adm. M. Shaheen Iqbal

CHIEF OF AIR STAFF: Air Chief Marshal Sheikh Abdul Hannan

ECONOMY

The developing market economy of Bangladesh has registered an annual GDP growth of 6-7% in the past few years. While the service sector contributes majority share of GDP, the agriculture sector, employing around 45% of the population, makes up for around 20%. The country mainly produces rice. Poor infrastructure, over population, corruption coupled with political instability has hindered Bangaldesh's growth trajectory. Garment exports, the backbone of Bangladesh's industrial sector, accounted for more than 80% of total exports and surpassed $25 billion in FY 2016-17. Steady export growth in the garment sector, combined with $13 billion in remittances from overseas Bangladeshis, contributed to Bangladesh's rising foreign exchange reserves in FY 2016-17. Recent improvements to energy infrastructure, including the start of liquefied natural gas imports in 2018, represent a major step forward in resolving a key growth bottleneck. The country managed to chart a GDP growth of 5.24% in 2019-20 despite the Coronavirus pandemic. Riding on robust manufacturing and exports, the economy continued the growth trajectory in FY 2020-21. The IMF has projected a GDP growth of 4.4% in 2021 and 7.9% in 2022 for Bangladesh.

GDP (official exchange rate): $329.54 billion (2020 est.)

Real Growth Rate (GDP): 7.4% (2017 est.); 7.2% (2016 est.)

Industries: Jute, cotton, garments, paper, leather, fertilizer, iron and steel, cement, petroleum products, tobacco, pharmaceuticals, ceramics, tea, salt, sugar, edible oils, soap and detergent, fabricated metal products, electricity, natural gas

Natural Gas - Proved Reserves: 185.8 billion cu m (1 January 2018 est.)

Crude Oil - Proved Reserves: 28 million bbl (1 January 2018 est.)

Total Exports: $33.05 billion (2019 est.); $29.79 billion (2018 est.)

Export Commodities: Clothing, knitwear, leather footwear (2019)

Major Markets: United States 15%, Germany 14%, United Kingdom 8%, Spain 7%, France 7% (2019)

Total Imports: $44.8 billion (2019 est.); $45.7 billion (2018 est.)

Import Commodities: Refined petroleum, cotton, natural gas, scrap iron, wheat (2019)

Major Suppliers: China 31%, India 15%, Singapore 5% (2019)

INTERNATIONAL DISPUTES

◆ On 7 June 2015, India and Bangladesh signed a historic agreement to simplify their 4,000-km land border and clarify the identities of 52,000 living in enclaves, over four decades after the two neighbours first tried to untangle complex territorial rights set down in 1713. Under the deal, signed in the presence of Prime Minister Narendra Modi and his Bangladeshi counterpart Sheikh Hasina in Dhaka, the two countries have decided to swap 200 tiny enclaves, most of them close to the official border.

◆ On 14 May 2012, the International Tribunal for the Law of the Sea (ITLOS) delivered its judgment in the dispute concerning delimitation of the maritime boundary between Bangladesh and Myanmar. The tribunal decided on an adjusted equidistance line as the boundary between the two countries.

DEFENCE

ARMY

Personnel: 150,000+

Equipment

Category	Name	In Service
MBT	MBT-2000	44
	T-59/ T-69	350
	T-62 (light tank)	40
APC	MT-LB	19
	BTR-80, BTR-70	100+
	FAHD	60
	RN-64	
Artillery	M56A1/ L10A1 105mm	150+
	Type 83	110
	D30 122mm	14
	Type 59-1 130mm	62
	Tiger T-300 (300mm MRLS)	18
Mortar	29A1 81mm	11
	Type-57/87/M32 82mm	477
	Type 52 120mm	23
RCL	M40 106mm	246
SAM	HN-5A Manpad	8
	QW-2s	43
AA Gun	Type 55/74 37mm	114
	Type 4 59 57mm	34
Air Defence Missile	FM-90	

Army Aviation

Category	Name	In Service
Aircraft	Cessna 152	4
	Cessna 208B	1
	CASA CN 235-300	1 (+1 on order)
	C295W	1
Helicopter	Eurocopter AS365 Dauphin	2
	Bell 206	2

New Procurements/Upgrades

◆ A total of 44 MBT-2000 tanks and three armoured recovery vehicles have been procured from China.

◆ Plans are on to upgrade the entire fleet of the Chinese-built T-59 MBTs with new engine, improved guns and other systems and transform them as modern combat platform. Bangladesh has upgraded some of the platforms locally.

◆ Acquisition of new 155mm light-weight towed howitzers is under consideration.

◆ An undisclosed number (reportedly 18) of the TRG-300 'Tiger' missile / multiple rocket launcher systems (MRLS) acquired from Turkey's Rokestan has been inducted in service in June 2021.

TRG-300 'Tiger' missile / multiple rocket launcher systems (Image credit: Rokestan website)

- One CASA CN 235-300 transport aircraft on order from Airbus.
- Acquisition of RQ-12A Wasp AE micro unmanned aerial systems (UAS) is under consideration from US's AeroVironment.

NAVY

Personnel: 15,000+

Equipment

Category	Name	In Service
Submarine	Type 035G	2
Frigate	Bangabandhu (Ulsan class)	1
	Osman (modified Type 053H1)	1
	Type 053H2	2
	Type 053H3	2
	Hamilton-class cutter	2
Corvette	Castle class	2
	Durjoy class	4
	C13B (Type 056)	4
Light Force	Kapatakhaya class OPV	5
	Padma class Patrol vessel	5 (+5 being built)
	Madhumati Patrol boat	1
	Nirbhoy	1
	Salam/Barkat class	2
	Karanphuli class	2
	Type 021 class missile FAC	4
	Durbar class	5
	Shaheed Daulat class gun FAC	4
	Titas class	4
Hydro-graphic Survey ship	Darshak class	2
	Agradoot class	1
Mine Warfare Force	Shapla class mine-sweepers	
	Sagar minesweepers	1

...continued

Category	Name	In Service
Amphibious Force	Shah Poran class LCU	2
	LCT	3
	LCVP	3

Naval Aviation

Category	Name	In Service
Aircraft	Dornier 228 NG	2 (+2 on order)
Helicopter	AW-109 Power	2
	Z-9C	5

New Procurements/Upgrades

- Two Chinese Type 053H3 (Jiangwei II class) guided missile frigates (decommissioned from PLA Navy) have been delivered in December 2019.
- China has handed over the final two C13B (Type 056) class corvettes in March 2019, thereby completing the order for four such platforms. The first two platforms were commissioned into service in 2016.
- The US-based firm Metal Shark has delivered five patrol boats in 2019.
- A tender has been issued for the procurement of two new maritime helicopters to carry out anti-submarine warfare (ASW), anti-surface warfare (ASuW), over-the-horizon targeting, maritime search and rescue, medical evacuation and special forces missions.
- Two additional Dornier Do 228 aircraft have been ordered in 2017 from Russia's Ruag Corporation for maritime patrol operations. The first of the two Dornier 228-212 aircraft operational in the BAF is undergoing repair and maintenance in Germany since 2019.

AIR FORCE

Personnel: 14,000

Equipment

Category	Name	In Service
Fighter Aircraft	F-7M	12
	F-7BG/ F-7BGI	32
	MiG-29	8
	L-39 ZA Albatross	8
Transport	C-130J	5
	C-130B	4 (being retired)
	An-32	3 (being upgraded)
Helicopter	Mi-17	20
	Mi-171Sh	16 (+5 on order)
	Bell 212	11
	Bell 206L	2
	AW139	2
Trainer	Yak-130	13
	T-37B	12

...continued

Category	Name	In Service
Trainer	PT-6	12 (On order)
	Mushahk	10
	K-8W Karakoram	15

New Procurements/ Upgrades

- A tender has been issued in 2017 for the procurement of eight new multi-role combat aircraft (MRCA) with option for more such platforms in future.
- Eight new K-8W Karakoram jet trainers have been received from China in October 2020 under an intergovernmental deal signed in 2018.
- A locally upgraded F-7 fighter aircraft has been delivered to the Air Force in 2018. The F-7 platforms have been procured from China.
- Ukraine is upgrading three An-32 transport aircraft of BAF.
- All five C-130J Hercules tactical transport aircraft, acquired from the UK Royal Air Force (surplus units), have been delivered in 2020. The platforms have been acquired under Government-to-Government deal finalised with the UK in 2018-19. The C-130Js would replace the C-130B transporters.
- Five more Mi-171Sh multi-role helicopters are on order with a contract signed with Russia's Rosoboronexport in June 2017.
- Acquisition of new attack helicopters is under active consideration with Boeing's Apache AH-64E platform reportedly being a leading contender for the likely purchase.
- Procurement of a medium-altitude long-endurance (MALE) UAV for ISR operations is under consideration.

Defence Budget

Defence budget: Tk376.91 crore (US$ 4.09 billion – proposed for 2021-22); Tk348.42 crore (2020-21)

Estimated defence spending in terms of GDP: 1.5%

Defence Production and R&D

Indigenous defence industrial base of Bangladesh is steadily gaining ground with assistance from China. While some of the domestic firms are producing small arms and ammunition, its shipyards have also attained the capability of building large patrol craft besides undertaking repair and overhaul work of naval vessels. The Government-owned Khulna Shipyard has built OPVs and also plans to build new corvettes for the Bangladesh Navy. In January 2020, the Bangladesh MoD inked an MoU with Netherlands' Damen

Shipyards and Australia's Gentium Solutions to establish and develop a shipbuilding and ship repair industry in Bangladesh. The deal aims at building ships in Bangladesh for Bangladesh as well as for the international export market. Bangladesh has also locally overhauled Chinese-built battle tank and fighter platforms recently.

Defence Procurement

Bangladesh has acquired defence hardware worth Taka 15,000 crore ($2 billion) since 2010 as part of its initiatives to modernise its armed forces. The South Asian country in recent years has procured over 2,000 armoured vehicles, third-generation tanks and APCs for its Army; over two dozen maritime platforms including submarines, frigates, corvettes, patrol craft, helicopters and missiles for the Navy; fourth-generation fighter jets, trainer aircraft and transporters for its Air Force among other equipment. The recent acquisition of two Chinese-built submarines has bolstered the country's naval prowess to a great extent. Signing of new deals for the acquisition of trainer jets, transport aircraft, multi-role helicopters also indicate Bangladesh's growing military capabilities in present times. All the new acquisitions are being made under a comprehensive military modernisation drive.

CONTACT DETAILS
Ministry of Defence
Ganabhaban Complex,
Sher-E-Bangla Nagar
Dhaka-1207
www.mod.gov.bd

BELARUS
(Capital: Minsk)

INTRODUCTION
Area: 207,600 sq km
Population: 9,441,842 (July 2021 est.)
Coastline: 0 km (landlocked)
Maritime claims: None

KEY POLITICAL PERSONS

PRESIDENT: Aleksandr Lukashenko

PRIME MINISTER: Roman Golovchenkoh

KEY DEFENCE PERSONS

DEFENCE MINISTER: Lt. Gen Viktor Khrenin

CHIEF OF THE GENERAL STAFF: Maj. Gen. Viktor Gulevich

COMMANDER OF THE AIR FORCE & AIR DEFENCE: Maj. Gen. Igor Golub

COMMANDER OF THE SPECIAL OPERATIONS FORCES: Maj. Gen. Vadim Denisenko

ECONOMY

Belarus pursues a socially-oriented market economy. As a result of this policy, administrative controls over prices and currency exchange rates were introduced. Restructuring of the economic system has been very slow, and the small private sector is marginalised. The National Strategy for the Sustainable Social and Economic Development of Belarus aims to ensure high standards of living and enabling environment for harmonious personality development. Belarus's economy stagnated between 2012 and 2016 due to falling global prices on key Belarusian export commodities. In 2017 GDP grew by 2.4 percent. In 2018, the expansion continued with GDP growth at 5.6 percent with the main contributions from industry and domestic trade due to strong domestic demand growth. The major branches of the Belarusian economy include the manufacturing industry, agriculture, construction, trade, transport, information and communication technologies. According to a media report, from January to September 2021, the economy of Belarus grew by 2.7% compared to the same period in 2020.

GDP (official exchange rate): $63.168 billion (2019 est.)

Real Growth Rate (GDP): 1.22% (2019 est.), 3.17% (2018 est.)

Industries: Metal-cutting machine tools, tractors, trucks, earth-movers, s and other household appliances.

Total Exports: $37.04 billion (2020 est.), $41.97 billion (2019 est.)

Export Commodities: Refined petroleum, fertilizers, cheese, delivery trucks, crude petroleum (2019)

Major Markets: Russia 42%, Ukraine 13%, United Kingdom 7% (2019)

Total Imports: $35.16 billion (2020 est.), $42.38 billion (2019 est.)

Import Commodities: Crude petroleum, natural gas, cars and vehicle parts, packaged medicines, broadcasting equipment (2019)

Major Suppliers: Russia 57%, China 7%, Poland 5%, Germany 5%, Ukraine 5% (2019)

INTERNATIONAL DISPUTES

◆ Boundary demarcated with Latvia and Lithuania.

◆ As a member state that forms part of the EU's external border, Poland has implemented strict Schengen border rules to restrict illegal immigration and trade along its border with Belarus.

DEFENCE

Belarus has conducted military reforms which have reshaped its armed forces as a relatively effective force. The armed forces of Belarus consist of the Ground Forces, the Air and Air Defence Forces and the Special Operation Forces. Being a landlocked country, Belarus has no Navy. The Belarusian Army comprised of the Mechanised Formations, Rocket Troops and Artillery, Army Air Defences, Special Troops, as well as Logistics and Maintenance units. The Air Force and Air Defence (AFAD) is designed to defend critical facilities and military forces from air attacks, destroy enemy military industrial installations and troops and support the Belarusian Army. The Special Operations Forces are military units which are organised, trained and equipped to perform special missions for achieving political, military, economic and psychological goals. They can conduct an operation independently or join forces with the Armed Forces, the Internal Troops and other services of the Belarusian Interior Ministry, State Border Committee and State Security Committee. Belarus has a military-technical cooperation with Russia.

ARMY

Personnel: 9,896

Equipment

Category	Name	In Service
MBT	T-72	532
	T-80	18
AIFV/APC	BTR 82/A	
	BMP-2	932
	BMP-1	96
	BMD-1	97
	BTR-70	39
	BTR-80	153
	MT-LB	50
Artillery	2A36 152mm	50
	2A65 152mm towed	136
	2S1 122mm	177
	2S19 152mm	13
	2S3 152mm	148
	2S5 152mm	119
	D-20 152mm	22
	2S9 120mm SP	50
	D-30 130mm	46
Mortar	120mm 2S12	65
SSM	OTR-21 Tochka	36

...continued

Category	Name	In Service
MRL	RPO-A Shmel	
	Shmel-M	
	122mm BM-21	186
	300mm 9A52	36
	220mm 9P140	74
	Palanez 300mm	2+
ATGM	9P148	275
	9P149	80
SAM	S-300	
	Tor-M2E	

New Procurements/Upgrades

◆ The Belarus Army has received the first batch of BTR-82A armoured personnel carriers (APCs). The military has also received two BREM-K wheeled armoured recovery vehicles based on the BTR-80.

AIR FORCE & AIR DEFENCE FORCE

Personnel: 11,93

Equipment

Category	Name	In Service
Fighter	Su-30SM	2
	Yak-130 Mitten	12
	Mig-29	35
	Su-25	24
Transport	An-26	3
	IL-76	3
	Mi-26	7
Trainer	L-39	10
Helicopter	Mi-8MTV-5	12+
	Mi-24	17
	Mi-8	26
SAM	S-300	
	TOR M2	3 batteries
UAV/UAS	Burevestnik-MB	
	Busel-MB, Berkut-3	
	Kvadro-1600, Soaring Tube, Grach octocopter	

New Procurements/Upgrades

◆ The Defence Ministry has placed an order for at least 12 Su-30SM fighter jets.

Defence Expenditure

Total defence spending: $785 million (2020), $774 million (2019)

Estimated defence spending in terms of GDP: 1.3% (2020)

Defence Production and R&D

Belarus is at the final stage of developing its own Kvadro-1400 strike drone. The unmanned aerial platform will be capable of spotting, identifying and striking light armoured and un-amoured enemy targets. The country has produced long-range MRLS Polonez proving its capability to manufacture high-precision weapons system. The country's defence industry is on a mission to develop more missile systems to boost its military's strike capabilities as well as combat unmanned aerial vehicles to reinforce its air force. Belarusian companies have built the weaponised multi-copter unmanned aircraft systems (UASs) - Kvadro-1600, Soaring Tube, Grach octocopter. Belarus has also rolled out the Berkut-3 UAV. The new combat reconnaissance/patrol vehicle Kayman became one of its most celebrated products.

The State Military Industrial Committee is in charge of Belarus' military-technical policy, regulating and controlling the following spheres. The Committee coordinates activities of several companies which are licensed to develop, produce, improve and maintain military products. Military products developed by these companies include unmanned aircraft systems, multiple launch rocket systems, lightly-armoured vehicles and vehicles for carrying weapons systems, radar systems, automation systems, as well as reconnaissance, electronic warfare, and communications systems.

Defence Procurement

As part of the military modernisation over the period 2021-2025, Belarus plans to procure a number of high-tech weapons from Russia including four Mi-35 helicopters, Su-30MS aircraft, BTR-82A APCs. This is alongside the procurement of electronic warfare and communications equipment. Other military equipment purchased from Russia included the multi-purpose Mi-8MTV5 helicopters, Yak-130 trainer jets, and second-hand S-300PS and new Tor-M2 SAM systems. Minsk has also purchased arms from Ukraine and China.

CONTACT DETAILS

Ministry of Defence
1, Kommunisticheskaya St., Minsk, 220034, Belarus
Tel/Fax: +375-17-2971581
E-mail: modmai@mod.mil.by
Website: http://www.mil.by/en/

BELGIUM
(Capital: Brussels)

INTRODUCTION

Area: 30,528 sq km

Population: 11,778,842 (July 2021 est.)

Coastline: 66.5 km

Maritime claims: Territorial sea: 12 nm

Contiguous zone: 24 nm

Exclusive Economic Zone: Geographic coordinates define outer limit

Continental shelf: Median line with neighbours

KEY POLITICAL PERSONS

CHIEF OF STATE & COMMANDER-IN-CHIEF: King Philippe

PRIME MINISTER: Alexander De Croo

KEY DEFENCE PERSONS

MINISTER OF DEFENCE: Ludivine Dedonder

CHIEF OF DEFENCE STAFF: Adm. Michel Hofman

LAND COMPONENT COMMANDER: Maj. Gen. Pierre Gerard

MARITIME COMPONENT COMMANDER: Adm. Jan De Beurme

AIR COMPONENT COMMANDER: Maj. Gen. Thierry Dupont

ECONOMY

The modern, well-developed economy of Belgium has benefited from a robust infrastructure, mainly transport network and diversified industrial base. The country, though lacks in natural resources, imports raw material and semi-finished goods, re-processes them and exports to other countries. Belgian economy is well integrated with other European economies. The country's service sector contributes a majority share of its GDP followed by the industrial sector. Belgium's GDP grew by 1.7% in 2017. In 2017, Belgium approved a tax reform plan to ease corporate rates from 33% to 29% by 2018 and down to 25% by 2020. The tax plan also included benefits for innovation and SMEs, intended to spur competitiveness and private investment. In the wake of the deadly Coronavirus outbreak, the Belgian economy was projected to contract by around 8% in 2020.

GDP (official exchange rate): $533.02 billion (2019 est.)

Real Growth Rate (GDP): 1.41% (2019 est.); 1.49% (2018 est.)

Industries: Engineering and metal products, motor vehicle assembly, transportation equipment, scientific instruments, processed food and beverages, chemicals, base metals, textiles, glass, petroleum

Total Exports: $474.2 billion (2019 est.); $469.4 billion (2018 est.)

Export Commodities: Cars and vehicle parts, refined petroleum, packaged medicines, medical cultures/vaccines, diamonds, natural gas (2019)

Major Markets: Germany 17%, France 14%, Netherlands 13%, United Kingdom 8%, United States 6%, Italy 5% (2019)

Total Import: $473.1 billion (2019 est.); $469.5 billion (2018 est.)

Import Commodities: Raw materials, machinery and equipment, chemicals, raw diamonds, pharmaceuticals, foodstuffs, transportation equipment, oil product

Major Suppliers: Netherlands 16%, Germany 13%, France 10%, United States 8%, Ireland 5%, China 5% (2019)

INTERNATIONAL DISPUTES

◆ Belgium has no known international disputes. The country is one of the founding members of North Atlantic Treaty Organisation (NATO) which is headquartered at its capital Brussels.

DEFENCE

ARMY

Personnel: 12,000

Equipment

Category	Name	In Service
APC	Mowag Piranha III	242
	Pandur	60
	Dingo 2	220
Armoured Car	IVECO Light Multirole Vehicle	440
Artillery	LG1 Mark II 105 mm towed howitzer	14
Mortar	120mm 120 RT	48
	81 mm M1	39
	60 mm M19	50+
ATGW	Milan	
Helicopter	NH-90 TTH	4 (to be retired)

New Procurements/Upgrades

◆ Procurement of 60 Jaguar AFVs and 382 Griffon multi-role light combat vehicles at an estimated cost of €1.1 billion (US$1.23 billion) has been approved in 2017. The platforms are under development in France.

The two vehicle types will replace the Piranha and Dingo armoured vehicles currently operational in the Army. The new platforms will enter service between 2025 and 2030.

NAVY

Personnel: 1,400+

Equipment

Category	Name	In Service
Frigate	F930 Leopold I	1
	F931 Louise-Marie	1
Patrol vessel	P902 Liberation (river patrol vessel)	1
Minesweeper	Tripartite class	6
Auxiliary ship	A962 Belgica (oceanographic research vessel)	1
	960 Godetia (command & logistic support ship)	1
	A999 Barbara (hovercraft)	1
Helicopter	SA316B Alouette III	3
	NH-90 NFH	4

New Procurements/Upgrades

◆ Acquisition of two new frigates has been finalised. The acquisition will be made jointly with Netherlands at an estimated cost of around €4 billion. Netherlands will also acquire two frigates as per the agreement finalized in 2016. Commissioning of the first platform into the Belgian Navy is scheduled for 2027. The new frigates will replace the existing two M-class frigates – Leopold I and Louise-Marie.

◆ Six new minehunters would be acquired to replace the existing ones. The Belgium Naval & Robotics consortium has won a contract to build the platforms. Delivery is scheduled for 2023.

◆ Twenty nine MK54 lightweight torpedoes are being procured from the US under FMS route to replace the MK46 torpedoes.

AIR FORCE

Personnel: 5,000+

Equipment

Category	Name	In Service
Fighter/Attack	F-16A/B Falcon	54
Transport/Surveillance	Falcon 20E-5	2
	Falcon 900B	1
	Embraer ERJ 135LR	2
	Embraer ERJ 145LR	2
	C-130H	11
	Airbus A400M	3 (+4 on order)
Helicopter	Agusta AW109	20
AAM	AIM-9X-2 Sidewinder	
UAV	MQ-9B SkyGuardian	4 (on order)
	RQ-5 Hunter	12

New Procurements/Upgrades

◆ The Government has selected Lockheed Martin-built F-35A Joint Strike Fighter (JSF) variant as the Belgian Air Force's next-generation fighter platform which will replace the aging fleet of F-16 jets. The new fighters would be procured at an estimated cost of €4 billion. Initial deliveries are expected to start in 2023.

◆ Seven Airbus A400M heavy transport aircraft are on order to replace the C-130H planes. Delivery has started and slated for completion by 2023. (One of the seven A400Ms would be jointly operated with the Luxembourg Air Force.)

◆ The Government has decided to allocate €258 million for the acquisition of one Airbus A330 MRTT (Multi Role Tanker Transport) aircraft which would be operated by the European Union and NATO member nations.

◆ Delivery of AIM-9X-2 Sidewinder air-to-air missiles from the US under foreign military sales deal is going on.

◆ In March 2019, the US State Department approved the sale of four MQ-9B SkyGuardian UAVs and related equipment to the Belgian Air Force at an estimated cost of $600 million. US's General Atomics has received contracts to build and deliver the unmanned platforms which are slated for induction by 2023. They would replace the Israel-built RQ-5 Hunter drones.

Defence Expenditure

Total defence spending: €4.75 billion (2020)

Defence spending in terms of GDP: 1.1% (2020)

Major suppliers of defence equipment to Belgium include Netherlands, Germany and other European countries. Some Middle East and Latin American countries have bought defence equipment from Belgium.

Defence Production and R&D

Belgium's defence industry is engaged in the production of small arms, ammunition, and military electronics equipment.

Defence Procurement

A Governmental Committee under a Strategic Defence Plan approved in December 2015 had proposed to maintain a military manpower of 25,000 active personnel by 2030. The plan also called for €9.2 billion to be spent on major equipment investment programmes for the Army, Navy and Air Force. These would include 34 new combat aircraft, two frigates, six mine-hunters and six drones. All new acquisitions are to be made by 2030. Belgium has announced plans to sign contracts worth nearly €10 billion on a number of military acquisition programmes.

CONTACT DETAILS
Ministry of Defence
Quartier Reine Elisabeth
Block 4, Rue d'Evere 11140 Evere
Brussels
www.mil.be/nl/

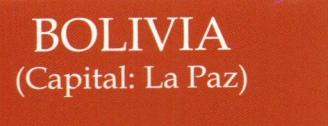

BOLIVIA
(Capital: La Paz)

INTRODUCTION

Area: 1,098,581 sq km
Population: 11,758,869 (July 2021 est.)
Coastline: 0 km (landlocked)
Maritime claims: None

KEY POLITICAL PERSONS

PRESIDENT: Luis Arce

VICE PRESIDENT-ELECT: David Choquehuanca

KEY DEFENCE PERSONS

DEFENCE MINISTER: Edmundo Novillo

COMMANDER GENERAL OF ARMY: Brig. Gen. Hugo Eduardo Arandia López

COMMANDER GENERAL OF NAVY: Adm. Francis Efrain Franck Salazar

COMMANDER GENERAL OF AIR FORCE: Maj. Brig. Marcelo Juan Heredia Cuba

ECONOMY

Bolivia is a resource rich country with strong growth attributed to captive markets for natural gas exports - to Brazil and Argentina. High commodity prices between 2010 and 2014 sustained rapid growth and large trade surpluses with GDP growing 6.8% in 2013 and 5.4% in 2014. Lower GDP growth rate came into effect in 2015 and 2016 to 4.9% and 4.3% respectively due to global decline in oil prices. The Government of Bolivia approved the 2016-2020 National Economic and Social Development Plan. Bolivia is generally open to foreign direct investment. An investment promotion law adopted in 2014 guarantees equal treatment for national and foreign firms, but specifies that public investment has slight higher edge over private investment and that the Bolivian government will determine which sectors require private investment. The negative economic impact of the COVID-19 pandemic has affected Bolivia due to restrictions.

GDP (official exchange rate): $92.59 billion (2020), $100.45 billion (2019 est.)

Real Growth Rate (GDP): 2.22% (2019 est.), 4.23% (2018 est.)

Industries: Mining, smelting, electricity, petroleum, food and beverages, handicrafts, clothing, jewellery

Oil - proved reserves: 211.5 million bbl (1 January 2018 est.)

Natural gas - proved reserves: 295.9 billion cu m (1 January 2018 est.)

Total Exports: $7.55 billion (2020 est.), $10.26 billion (2019 est.)

Export Commodities: Natural gas, gold, zinc, soybean oil and soy products, tin, silver, lead (2019)

Major Markets: Argentina 16%, Brazil 15%, United Arab Emirates 12%, India 10%, United States 6%, South Korea 5%, Peru 5%, Colombia 5% (2019)

Total Imports: $8.27 billion (2020 est.), $11.95 billion (2019 est.)

Import Commodities: Cars, refined petroleum, delivery trucks, iron, buses (2019)

Major Suppliers: Brazil 22%, Chile 15%, China 13%, Peru 11%, Argentina 8%, United States 7% (2017)

INTERNATIONAL DISPUTES

Chile and Peru rebuff Bolivia's reactivated claim to restore the Atacama corridor, ceded to Chile in 1884, but Chile offers instead unrestricted but not sovereign maritime access through Chile for Bolivian natural gas.

DEFENCE

ARMY

Personnel: 37,000

Equipment

Category	Name	In Service
MBT	SK-105 Kurassiers	30+
APC/ MICV/IFV	EE-9 Cascavel	20+
	M113	50+
	EE-11 Urutu	20+
	M9 Half-track	20
	Mowag Roland	20
	V100 Commandos	10+

...continued

Category	Name	In Service
Artillery	M1 75mm pack Howitzers	30+
	M101 105mm	
	122mm Type 54	15
Mortar	M29 81mm	200+
	M120 120mm	
	M30 107mm	
RCL	90mm	50
	160mm	20+
AA Gun	2x37mm Type 65	10+
	2x20mm Oerlikon K20	50+
SAM	HN-5 MANPAD	40+

Army Aviation

Category	Name	In Service
Aircraft	Beechcraft King Air C90	1
	CASA C-212 Aviocar	2
	Cessna 206 Stationair	4
	Cessna 421B Golden Eagle	1
	Emb810 Seneca	1

New Procurements/ Upgrades

◆ The Bolivian defence ministry has ordered radar systems from Thales for military and civil use.

NAVY

Personnel: 5,000 (including 1,000 Marines)

Equipment

Category	Name	In Service
Patrol Craft	PR-51 Class	1
	Capitan Bretel	5+
	Lake	4
	Boston Whaler	30+
Other Ship	Piranha assault boats Mk.1	50+
	Tankers	2
	Transport vessel	1
Aircraft	Cessna 206 Stationair	1
	Cessna 402	1

New Procurements/ Upgrades

No major procurement plans are under consideration at present.

The Marine corps of the Bolivian Naval Force maintains a similar number of troops including premilitares.

AIR FORCE

Personnel: 8,000

Equipment

Category	Name	In Service
Aircraft	K-8 Attack/Trainer	5+
	Canadair CT-33 Attack/Trainer	10+
	Pilatus PC-7 Attack/Trainer	3
	Foxtrot 4	2
	Robinson R44 Trainer	5+
	Learjet 25	2
	Z 242L	2
Helicopter	AS350 Utility	2
	Alouette SA 316	1
	AS332 Cougar	1
	EC145	2+
	UH-1H	10+
Transport	C-130B	3
	Jetstream 31	2
	King Air 90/200/350	5
	Xian MA60	On order
UAV	RemoEye-006	1

New Procurements/ Upgrades
No major procurement plans are under consideration at present.

Defence Expenditure
Total defence spending: $650 million (2018 approx.)
Defence spending in terms of GDP: 1.3% of GDP (2020 est.), 1.4% of GDP (2019)
Foreign suppliers: Venezuela, Brazil, United States, Austria, China, South Korea, Russia, Peru, Argentina, Turkey & Mexico.

Defence Production and R&D
The country has plans to manufacture small-arms ammunition, explosives, light vehicles and light vessels. Several small local, government owned shipyards have been constructed to assembly, design and produce small, aluminium river boats. A boat building yard is constructed at Puntiti, Cochabamba. 'Kojak' a buggy-type light attack vehicle has been made by Bolivian army's logistics battalion.

One scout version is equipped with a MAG and an Instalanza or RPG-7V. There is an anti-tank guided weapon version armed with two HJ-8A missiles. Construction has been limited to about 10 of the scout version and at least three of the anti-tank version, with a total requirement of up to 60 vehicles.

Aviotec Ltd. is the only company to produces light aircraft and helicopters for the local and US export market. Russian and Bolivian Defence Ministers Sergei Shoigu and Reimi Ferrera have signed an agreement on military cooperation. Bolivian defence industry receives aircraft repair and maintenance assistance from Russian government situated at the department of Cochabamba as part of an engagement policy with Bolivia.

Defence Procurement
The military plays an important role in Bolivia. In 2018, the Bolivian government is requesting a 3.7% increase compared to 2017 defence spending. The Bolivian defence ministry has made a new modernise plan for its forces, which includes the establishment of a Supply, Replacement and Equipment Fund (FARE), which will draw from multiple taxes to fund procurement. Bolivian Defence Minister Walker San Miguel had introduced the 15-point plan in January 2010. Bolivian Navy has procured second-hand equipments for its commercial and civilian section from the US or South American civil markets and its naval inventory is relatively adequate within its present limited operational parameters. The nation receives various new materials from China, Venezuela, Brazil and Argentina. Various helicopters, training aircraft, armour and logistical support equipment are donated to the nation. Bolivia has already received a credit line for up to USD100 million worth of weapons and logistical equipment from Russia in 2009. Bolivia has also signed a 20-year military cooperation agreement with Russia, which may allow Bolivia's credit line to be increased up to USD 300 million in coming years. The Bolivian government awarded USD 216 million worth contract to the French company Thales to install a system of 13 radars for military defence and air traffic control in order to effectively combat drug trafficking and contraband.

CONTACT DETAILS
Ministry of National Defence
Av. Pedro Salazar esquina 20 de Octubre Plaza Avaroa
2502 La Paz, Bolivia
Tel: +59122379240, 377131, 371186
Fax: +59122377135, Telex: entel 2320

Armed Forces HQ
Gran Quartel General de Miraflores La Plz Bolivia
Tel: +59122370120, 378180 through 82
Telex: 5384 comanfab

BOSNIA AND HERZEGOVINA
(Capital: Sarajevo)

INTRODUCTION
Area: 51,197 sq km
Population: 3,824,782 (July 2021 est.)
Coastline: 20 km
Maritime claims: None

KEY POLITICAL PERSONS

PRESIDENCY MEMBER (Serb): Milorad Dodik

PRESIDENCY MEMBER (Croat): Zeljko Komsic

PRESIDENCY MEMBER (Bosniak): Sefik Dzaferovic

KEY DEFENCE PERSONS

MINISTER OF DEFENCE: Sifet Podzic

CHIEF OF GENERAL STAFF: Lt. Gen. Senad Masovic

ECONOMY

The inter-ethnic warfare in Bosnia and Herzegovina has hindered its continuous economic growth with production levels plummeting and unemployment rate soaring from time to time. The economy relies heavily on the export of metals, energy, textiles, and furniture as well as on remittances and foreign aid. It receives substantial amounts of reconstruction assistance and humanitarian aid from the international community and relies heavily on West Europe for trade and credit. Bosnia and Herzegovina's private sector is growing slowly, but foreign investment has dropped sharply since 2007. High unemployment remains the most serious macroeconomic problem. . The country's top economic priorities include acceleration of integration into the EU; strengthening the fiscal system; public administration reform; World Trade Organization membership; and securing economic growth by fostering a dynamic, competitive private sector. Bosnia's GDP contracted by 4.3% in 2020 due to the Coronavirus pandemic. Unemployment rates also increased sharply. The economy is expected to chart a growth of 2.8% in 2021, according to projections made by the World Bank.

GDP (official exchange rate): $20.078 billion (2019 est.)

Real Growth Rate (GDP): 3% (2017 est.); 3.2% (2016 est.)

Industries: Steel, coal, iron ore, lead, zinc, manganese, bauxite, aluminium, motor vehicle assembly, textiles, tobacco products, wooden furniture, ammunition, domestic appliances, oil refining

Total Exports: $8.84 billion (2019 est.); $8.91 billion (2018 est.)

Export Commodities: Electricity, seating, leather shoes, furniture, insulated wiring (2019)

Major Markets: Germany 14%, Italy 12%, Croatia 11%, Serbia 11%, Austria 9%, Slovenia 8% (2019)

Total Imports: $12.5 billion (2019 est.); $12.4 billion (2018 est.)

Import Commodities: Refined petroleum, cars, packaged medicines, coal, electricity (2019)

Major Suppliers: Croatia 15%, Serbia 13%, Germany 10%, Italy 9%, Slovenia 7%, China 6% (2019)

INTERNATIONAL DISPUTES

Sections along the Drina River remain in dispute between Bosnia and Herzegovina and Serbia.

DEFENCE

ARMY

Personnel: 10,000+

Equipment

Category	Name	In Service
MBT	M60A3	45
	AMX-30B2	32
	M-84	16
	T-55	150 (in reserve)
Armoured vehicle	M113A2/A3	150
	BVP M-80	90
	BOV	50+
	M1145 HMMWV	25
	AMX 10P	35
	IVECO	
ATGM	AT-4 Spigot	
	AT-3 Sagger	
	HJ-8	
MRL	BM-21 Grad	29
	M-63	5
	M-77	7
Howitzer	D-30	86 (+35 in reserve)
Helicopter	UH-1H	2
	Mi-8	4
	Mi-17	3
	Soko Gazelle Gama	3

New Procurements/Upgrades

No major procurement plans are under consideration at present.

AIR FORCE

Personnel: 2,500+

Equipment

Category	Name	In Service
Trainer	Lola Utva 75	9
Utility Helicopter	UH-1H	14
	Mi-8/17	14
	Soko Gazelle Gama	4

...continued

Category	Name	In Service
Helicopter	Mi-34	1
MANPAD & SAM	FIM-92 Stinger	50
	9K38 Igla	20
	Bofors 40mm L/70	Two batteries
	ZU-23-2, AAA	150
	9K31 Strela-1	15
	2K12 Kub	
	P-40 radar	12

New Procurements/Upgrades

No major procurement plans are under consideration at present.

Defence Expenditure

Total defence spending: $0.18 billion (2019)

Estimated defence spending in terms of GDP: 1.13%

Military suppliers to Bosnia and Herzegovina are Russia, US, China, Turkey, Italy and Germany.

Defence Production and R&D

While in the past, Bosnia and Herzegovina has produced and exported ammunitions and other equipment to a number of countries including the US, presently it does not have any facilities to manufacture defence equipment. Some ammunition plants in the country are currently producing explosives for military and commercial purposes. The country is now working on reviving its defence industry and enter the international arms market.

Defence Procurement

No major procurement plans are under consideration by the Government at present. While the focus would be to phase out the existing inventory of obsolete weapons and artillery, the unified Armed Forces is set to adopt a light infantry-based force model mainly for international operations along with disaster relief missions, combating terrorism and other organised crime within the country. The all-volunteer force will constitute of 10,000 professional military personnel and 5,000 reserve force.

CONTACT DETAILS

Ministry of Defence
Hamdije Kresevljakovica 98
71 000 Sarajevo, BiH
Phone: +387 33 285 800
E-mail: info@mod.gov.ba
www.mod.gov.ba/

BOTSWANA
(Capital: Gaborone)

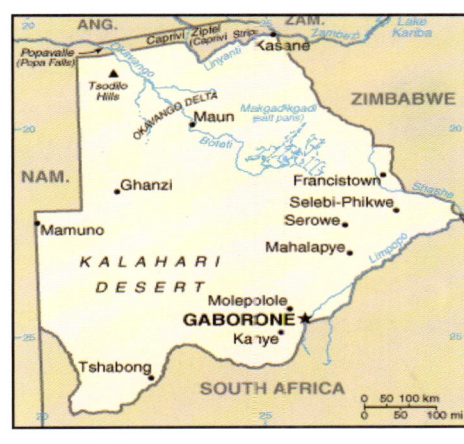

INTRODUCTION
Area: 581,730 sq km
Population: 2,350,667 (July 2021 est.)
Coastline: 0 km (Landlocked)
Maritime claims: None

KEY POLITICAL PERSONS

PRESIDENT:
Mokgweetsi Eric Masisi

VICE PRESIDENT:
Slumber Tsogwane

KEY DEFENCE PERSONS

MINISTER OF DEFENCE:
Kagiso Mmusi

COMMANDER OF THE DEFENCE FORCES: Lt. Gen. Placid Segokgo

ECONOMY

Botswana is one of the world's fastest growing economies today averaging 5% per annum in the past decade. The country's significant diamond wealth, good governance, coupled with prudent economic management, has reportedly made it an upper middle-income country. In 2017, Diamond exports increased to the highest levels since 2013 at about 22 million carats of output, driving Botswana's economic growth to about 4.5% and increasing foreign exchange reserves to about 45% of GDP. Tourism is the secondary earner of foreign exchange and many Botswana engage in subsistence farming and cattle raising. The Government has announced a stimulus plan to boost the economy through projects in agricultural production, construction, manufacturing, and tourism development. Tourism accounts for almost 12% of GDP.

GDP (official exchange rate): $18.335 billion (2019 est.)
Real Growth Rate (GDP): 2.4% (2017 est.), 4.3% (2016 est.)
Industries: Diamonds, copper, nickel, salt, soda ash, potash, coal, iron ore, silver; beef processing; textiles
Total Exports: $6.16 billion (2019 est.), $7.53 billion (2018 est.)
Export Commodities: Diamonds, insulated wiring, gold, beef, carbonates (2019)
Major Markets: India 21%, Belgium 19%, United Arab Emirates 19%, South Africa 9%, Israel 7%, Hong Kong 6%, Singapore 5% (2019)
Total Imports: $7.44 billion (2019 est.), $7.31 billion (2018 est.)
Import Commodities: Diamonds, refined petroleum, cars, delivery trucks, electricity (2019)
Major Suppliers: South Africa 58%, Namibia 9%, Canada 7% (2019)

INTERNATIONAL DISPUTES
Botswana has no known international disputes.

DEFENCE
The Botswana Defence Force (BDF) was established in 1977 by an Act of Parliament. The President is the Commander-in-Chief of the Defence Force. The Defence Council is responsible for the control, direction and general superintendence of the Defence Force. The BDF consists of the Ground Forces Command, Air Arm and Defence Logistics Command. The country has no Navy. The military doctrine is to maintain a small tactical, trained force capable of defending itself, and also for rapid deployment anywhere in the continent. The BDF is acquiring new equipment which includes fighter, trainer aircraft, aerial defence systems, tanks and armoured personnel carriers. It is developing a mechanised capability with light tanks and other armoured vehicles. Although a landlocked country, Botswana has a number of waterways hence, the Army has a marine unit with patrol boats and river craft. The BDF is carrying out its defence modernisation programme acquiring new equipment such as fighter/trainer aircraft, aerial defence systems, tanks and armoured personnel carriers. The National Development Plan 11 runs from 2017 to 2023.

ARMY
Personnel: 10,000+

Equipment

Category	Name	In Service
Tank	SK-105 Kurassier (light)	52
	Scorpion (light)	24
Armoured Vehicle	Piranha IIIC	45
Artillery	105mm light guns towed	36
	Soltam 155mm towed	12
	Aerostar SA 120mm (MLR)	20
	Carl Gustav 84mm RCL	30
ATGW	Milan, Tow	
Mortar	81 mm	
SAM	Javelin	
	SA 7	

New Procurements/Upgrades
◆ BDF plans to buy K2 Black Panther tanks from South Korea.

AIR ARM COMMAND
Personnel: 2,500

Equipment

Category	Name	In Service
Fighter	CF-5A	9
	CF-5D	3
Transport/ liaison	C-130B	3
	CN-235	2
	C-212	2
	BN-2 Islander	10
	Cessna O2	5
Trainer	Pilatus PC-7 Mk II	5

...continued

Category	Name	In Service
Helicopter	Bell 412	4
	AS.350 Ecureuil	4
VIP transport	Gulfstream IV	1
	King Air 200	1
	Bell 412	1
UAV	Hermes 450	

New Procurements/Upgrades
◆ The BDF plans to buy Korea Aerospace Industries (KAI) T-50 Golden Eagle supersonic trainer.

Defence Expenditure
Total defence spending: $546 million (2020), $516 million (2019)
Defence spending in terms of GDP: 2.8 % (2019)

Defence Production and R&D
Botswana has no defence industry base. There are some repair facilities for the maintenance of the combat vehicle. The Indian Air Force (IAF) imparts training to the BDF. The professionalism and contribution made by the IAF Training Team has been acknowledged and appreciated by the Government of Botswana. There have been regular exchanges of high military officials between the two countries. A large segment of BDF officers also received training from the United States.

Defence Procurement
The BDF is expected to continue with the acquisition of new equipment, specifically fighter/trainer aircraft, aerial defence systems, tanks and armoured personnel carriers to boost its defence capability. Botswana has reportedly expressed interest in a dozen second hand Saab Gripens or Korea Aerospace Industries FA-50s. The fighter jet acquisition is the latest in the country's defence modernisation effort. Botswana has purchased €304.2 million worth of military hardware from France in 2016, including MICA-VL and Mistral missiles. Other procurements include a $179 million deal for 45 Piranha 3 armoured vehicles from Swiss company GDELS-Mowag.

CONTACT DETAILS
Ministry of Defence Justice and Security
Private Bag 00384, Gaborone
TEL:(+267)3698200/300
FAX:(+267)3933034
TOLLFREE:0800 600 971
Email Public Relations: mdjs@gov.bw
Public Relations TEL:3973977
www.gov.bw

STRATEGIC INFORMATION
BRAZIL
(Capital: Brasilia)

INTRODUCTION
Area: 8,515,770 sq km
Population: 213,445,417 (July 2021 est.)
Coastline: 7,491 km
Maritime claims: Territorial sea: 12 nm
Contiguous zone: 24 nm
Exclusive Economic Zone: 200 nm
Continental shelf: 200 nm or to edge of the continental margin

GEOPOLITICAL IMPORTANCE
Brazil is the largest country in the South America region bounded by the Atlantic Ocean on the east. The country is bordered on the north by Venezuela, Guyana, Suriname and the French overseas region of French Guiana; on the northwest by Colombia; on the west by Bolivia and Peru; Colombia to the northwest; on the southwest by Argentina and Paraguay and on the south by Uruguay. Brazil borders all other South American countries except Chile and Ecuador. Semi arid along northeast coast, mountains, hills, and rolling plains in the southwest, including Mato Grosso with Midwestern savannahs; the country has world's largest wetland area and coastal lowland. It also encompasses a number of oceanic archipelagos, such as Fernando de Noronha, Rocas Atoll, Saint Peter and Paul Rocks, and Trindade and Martim Vaz.

POLITICAL OVERVIEW
The Federal Republic of Brazil is one of the world's largest democracies. The political and administrative organisation of Brazil comprises the federal government, the states, the federal district and the municipalities. The form of government is that of a democratic republic, with a presidential system. The President appoints the Ministers of State, who assist in government. Executive power is exercised by the President, advised by a cabinet. Legislative power is vested upon the National Congress, a two-chamber legislature comprising the Federal Senate and the Chamber of Deputies. Judicial power is exercised by the judiciary, consisting of the Supreme Federal Court, the Superior Court of Justice and other Superior Courts, the National Justice Council and the regional federal courts. The Federal Constitution is the supreme law of Brazil.

KEY POLITICAL PERSONS

PRESIDENT: Jair Messias Bolsonaro

VICE PRESIDENT: Antonio Hamilton Martins Mourão

ECONOMY
Brazil is the world's twelfth-largest economy and the United States is Brazil's second-largest trading partner. Two-way trade in goods and services was USD104.3 billion

(USD66.9 billion in goods and $37.4 billion in services) in 2019, but declined to USD77.3 billion during the pandemic in 2020. The government also boosted infrastructure projects, such as oil and natural gas auctions, in part to raise revenues. Brazil is a member of diverse economic organizations, such as Mercosur, Unasul, G8+5, G20, WTO, Paris Club and the Cairns Group. Brazil is still recovering from the worst economic recession in its history. Economic recovery has been slow. In 2017 and 2018, the economy grew at a small pace of 1.1% a year. Due to the ongoing COVID-19 lockdown restrictions, Brazil's economy has been hit badly. Industry, household consumption and government spending has reduced a lot due to the pandemic measures, as per news reports. The United States is Brazil's second-largest export market. The primary products are crude oil, aircraft, iron and steel, and machinery.

GDP (official exchange rate): $2.9 trillion (2020 est.), $3.1 trillion (2019 est.)

Real Growth Rate (GDP): 1.13% (2019 est.), 1.2% (2018 est.)

Industries: Textiles, shoes, chemicals, cement, lumber, iron ore, tin, steel, aircraft, motor vehicles and parts, other machinery and equipment

Oil - proved reserves: 12.63 billion bbl (1 January 2018 est.)

Natural gas - proved reserves: 377.4 billion cu m (1 January 2018 est.)

Total Exports: $239.18 billion (2020 est.), $260.07 billion (2019 est.)

Export Commodities: Soybeans, crude petroleum, iron, corn, wood pulp products (2019)

Major Markets: China 28%, United States 13% (2019)

Total Imports: $227.44 billion (2020 est.), $269.02 billion (2019 est.)

Import Commodities: Refined petroleum, vehicle parts, crude petroleum, integrated circuits, pesticides (2019)

Major Suppliers: China 21%, United States 18%, Germany 6%, Argentina 6% (2019)

DEFENCE & SECURITY

Brazil constitutes the largest armed force in Latin America. It consists of the Brazilian Army (Exercito Brasileiro), the Brazilian Navy (Marinha do Brasil), the Brazilian Marine Corps & Brazilian Naval Aviation (Corpo de Fuzileiros Navais), and the Brazilian Air Force (Forca Aerea Brasileira). The functions of military institutions are to ensure the integrity of the national territory; defend Brazilian natural, industrial and technological interests and resources; protect citizens and assets of the country; guarantee the sovereignty of the nation. Brazil has an established national security strategy to modernise the country and populate the vast central and western areas of Brazil. The Brazilian National Defence Policy is primarily directed by the Brazilian Constitution. Brazil's national defence policy is outlined in the National Defence Policy, the National Mobilization Policy and the National Defence Strategy. The country's armed forces have been participating in various UN peacekeeping operations such as the United Nations Stabilisation Mission (MINUSTAH) in Haiti. The National Defence Strategy establishes guidelines for the adequate preparation and training of the Armed Forces, in order to guarantee the country's security both in times of peace and in crisis situations. It has also been developed to meet the Military Command's equipment needs, reorganising the defence industry so that the most advanced technologies are under national control. The five Brazilian strategic areas are: Amazon, Midwest, Prata river Basin, Central Brazil, and the Northeast. The Amazon is the Brazilian top priority strategic area. The armed forces have expanded their presence in the Amazon under the Northern Corridor (Calha Norte) programme, with the aim of protecting its natural resources from any action coming from outside the region.

KEY DEFENCE PERSONS

MINISTER OF DEFENCE: Walter Souza Braga Netto

CHIEF OF JOINT STAFF OF THE ARMED FORCES (EMCFA): Army Gen. Laerte de Souza Santos

CHIEF OF ARMY: Gen. Paulo Sérgio Nogueira De Oliveira

CHIEF OF NAVY: Adm. Almir Garnier Santos

CHIEF OF AIR FORCE: Lt. Brig. Carlos de Almeida Baptista Júnior

Internal Conflict

Brazil has been involved in numerous armed actions inside its territory and also along its borders with its neighbours. Currently, Brazil has good relationships with all of its South American neighbours, and hasn't been to war with any of them since the 19th century. Brazil's main internal security concern is violent crime. The crime rate remains high in most urban centres, including the cities of Brasilia, Rio de Janeiro and Sao Paulo, and is also growing in rural areas (Favela the slum in Rio de Janeiro, Brazil) within those states. Individuals with ties to criminal entities and traffickers operate along all the Brazilian borders. These organizations are involved in the trafficking of illicit goods and drugs. The border reinforcements are part of Operation Agatha which the government initiated on their country's borders with Bolivia, Argentina, Paraguay and Uruguay. Operation Agatha seeks to combat trans-border and environmental crimes along the borders of the Western Amazon region. Brazilian Navy and Air Force are also deployed on a larger scale and working directly in the operation. In previous stages of the operation, Brazil seized more than 2.3 tonnes of illicit drugs, along with 302 boats used by traffickers and has also confiscated 60 firearms and other weapons. It also destroyed various clandestine airstrips. According to an UNHCR report, the communities formerly controlled by drug dealers are now in the hands of militias. These militias are made up of police officers, prison guards and firefighters and control up to a third of favelas in Rio de Janeiro. The militias are still active and a security threat in the region. But these criminal gangs operating in Brazil are not normally considered as non-state armed groups.

External Conflict

Brazil hasn't had its territory invaded since year 1865 during the Paraguayan War. Also, Brazil has no contested territorial disputes with any of its neighbours. Few as mentioned is given below:

◆ Uncontested boundary dispute between Brazil and Uruguay over Braziliera/Brasiliera Island in the Quarai/Cuareim River leaves the tri-point with Argentina in question.

◆ Smuggling of firearms and narcotics

continues to be an issue along the Uruguay-Brazil border.

◆ Colombian-organised illegal narcotics and paramilitary activities penetrate Brazil's border region with Venezuela.

Brazil faces external security threats in the form of drug-trafficking, arms smuggling and guerrilla activity mostly volatile in the regions of Amazon. Colombia's FARC, a leftist insurgency, finances itself largely through illicit activities, which are often located along the Brazilian border. On 27 June 2017, FARC ceased to be an armed group, disarming itself and handing over its weapons to the United Nations, but there are still many dissident FARC guerrillas involved in drug trafficking operations. Brazil is expanding its border security. The country will increase the number of security personnel along the Bolivian, Peruvian and Colombian borders. The move is focused on curbing out illegal arms and drugs trafficking along Brazil's 16,000 kilometre border.

THREAT PERSPECTIVE

Brazil is by far the largest country in Latin America and enjoys generally good relations with its ten South American neighbours. Brazil has resolved all its border-related disputes peacefully and generally do not interfere in the affairs of other countries. Currently, there is no immediate or concrete threat to the country but border security and sovereignty concerns continues to be a driving factor for Brazil to have a foolproof national security strategy which is important to protect the country's aquifers, its strategic minerals, its biodiversity, oil and gas.

Brazil has some concerns with regard to the triple frontier area. The Tri-Border Area of Argentina, Brazil, and Paraguay has long been used for arms smuggling, money laundering, and other illicit purposes which are all potential funding sources for terror outfits. Brazil has therefore focused their efforts in the areas of Sao Paulo; the Tri-Border Areas of Brazil, Argentina, and Paraguay, and Brazil, Peru, and Colombia; and along the Colombian and Venezuelan borders in order to counter terrorist threats as also safeguard its territory from any terrorist attacks. The country is a member of the Financial Action Task Force (FATF) and the Financial Action Task Force on Money Laundering in South America.

STRATEGIC RELATIONS

US: The United States and Brazil are working together on key global, multilateral, and regional issues. Both the countries have traditionally enjoyed cooperative, active relations encompassing a broad political, economic and military agenda. The military ties between Brazil and US have increased in recent years mainly in the areas of defence, counterterrorism and counternarcotics. Brazilian and US personnel have worked together following the Haiti earthquake. The Brazilian troops have also participated in a number of UN missions around the world. In April 2010, the United States and Brazil signed a Defence Cooperation Agreement designed to promote cooperation in areas such as research and development, technology security, and acquisition of defence products and services. This was followed by a General Security of Military Information Agreement, signed in November 2010, which will facilitate the sharing of classified defence and military information. Additional areas of defence cooperation include information exchanges, combined military training, and joint military exercises. Since 2015, Brazil and the US have engaged through the Defence Industry Dialogue (DID) to increase bilateral trade and investment in the defence sector, improve the regulatory and bureaucratic environment for US and Brazilian defence firms, and enhance understanding of US export control policies to increase opportunities for technology transfer and exchange. In June 2019, US President designated Brazil as a Major Non-NATO Ally of the United States. Brazil's main imports from the United States are aircraft, machinery, petroleum products, electronics, and optical and medical instruments. The United States is Brazil's second-largest export market. The primary products are crude oil, aircraft, iron and steel, and machinery. US Cyber Command and US Southern Command are working closely with their Brazilian counterparts to strengthen cyber defences. USAID and the Government of Brazil work together to promote development in other countries, particularly in Africa and Latin America, through trilateral technical assistance. The constructive dialogue between Brazil and the United States benefits from the existence of various cooperation mechanisms such as Defence Cooperation Dialogue, US-Brazil Permanent Forum on Security, US-Brazil Commission on Economic and Trade Relations, etc.

India: Brazil and India are members of the BRICS group of emerging powers (along with China, Russia and South Africa) and Brasilia views its multi-faceted partnership with New Delhi, including in the defence field, as a "strategic priority". Both countries are having excellent bilateral cooperation in the area of defence, particularly in the joint development of high-tech military aircraft. Both Brazil and India have co-operated in the multilateral level on issues such as international trade and development, environment, reform of the UN and the UNSC expansion. Brazil and India are also involved in the IBSA initiative. The strategic partnership established in 2006 between India and Brazil has deepened with both countries cooperating closely in such as BRICS, BASIC, G-20, G-4, IBSA, International Solar Alliance, Biofuture Platform and in the larger multilateral bodies such as the UN, WTO, UNESCO and WIPO. India's strategic partnership with Brazil continued to intensify in 2019. Bilateral trade between India and Brazil was at USD8.2 billion in 2018-19. This included USD3.8 billion as Indian exports to Brazil and USD4.4 million as imports by India from Brazil. Major Indian exports to Brazil include agrochemical, synthetic yarns, auto components and parts, pharmaceuticals and petroleum products. Brazilian exports to India include crude oil, gold, vegetable oil, sugar and bulk mineral and ores. An MoU on cooperation in the area of Cyber Security between CERT-In and its counterpart agency was signed in January 2020. India and Brazil also cooperate in cyber issues at BRICS and IBSA.

China: China has been a major source of investment and Brazil's leading trading partner since 2009. Brazil and China collaborate on successful bilateral projects in such fields as space, nanotechnology, renewable energy, among others. Brazil and China share a healthy relation in the field of strategic alliance development. As one of the BRICs countries, Brazil has a very good relationship with China and it always welcomes investments as well as products from China. Brazil considers China an important trade partner. The ties between the two armies have also grown stronger through mutual visits and personnel training. China became Brazil's largest trading partner in 2009. Chinese exports to Brazil collapsed in July 2016 in the latest dramatic sign of the deepening recession in Latin America's biggest economy. The two sides had close military-to-military exchanges and cooperation.

Russia: Brazil shares an important alliance with the Russian Federation, with partnerships in areas such as space and military technologies, and telecommunications. Both the countries have seen a significant improvement in recent years, by increasing commercial trade and cooperation in military and technology areas. The participation of Brazilian research institutions in the Russian satellite navigation system, GLONASS, emphases bilateral aerospacial partnership. Brazil is the largest host of the GLONASS system outside Russia. Russia is one of

Brazil's largest trading partners. Bilateral trade flow amounts to USD5 billion annually. Bilateral trade between Brazil and Russia is highly concentrated in agrobusiness-related products.

Argentina: Brazil and Argentina are both close and share strong integration and partnership between each other. Both the countries are engaged in several joint venture projects in the military field, such as the Gaucho armoured vehicle and the Embraer KC-390 military transport aircraft. Argentina and Brazil have close cooperation in the field of space science. Brazil has been a strong supporter of the Argentine claim over the Falkland Islands. Both account for each other's largest export and import market. Argentine foreign policy has given special emphasis in deepening the strategic alliance with Brazil in all its aspects. Brazil accounts for Argentina's largest export and import market. The construction of a political relationship of trust and cooperation with Argentina contributes to the establishment of a regional space of peace and cooperation. Together, Brazil and Argentina account for about two thirds of the territory, population and GDP of South America.

Multilateral Alliances: Brazil is a member of international organisations including the United Nations, Organization of American States, Inter-American Development Bank, G-20, International Monetary Fund, World Bank, and the World Trade Organisation. Brazil traditionally has been a leader in the inter-American community, and is a member of the sub-regional MERCOSUR and UNASUR groups. Brazil is a founding member of the OAS and the Inter-American Treaty of Reciprocal Assistance (Rio Treaty).

DEFENCE CAPABILITIES

ARMY: The Army's mission is to preserve and guarantee the defence of Brazil. The Brazilian Army has fought in several international conflicts, mostly in South America during the 19th century. In the 20th century it participated on the Allied side in World War I and World War II, as well as in UN peacekeeping missions. The Brazilian Army is trying to renew its equipment and making a redistribution of its barracks in all the Brazilian Regions, prioritising the Amazon. The Brazilian Army is creating an Expeditionary Force (F EXPD) to provide permanent support for the country's participation in foreign missions.

Personnel: 215,000

Equipment

Category	Name	In Service
MBT	Leopard 1A5	250 (30 reserve)
	Leopard 1A1	127
	M60 Patton A3 TTS	90
APC/ MICV/ IFV	EE-9 Cascavel (6x6)	400 (To be replaced by VBR-MR 8×8)
	EE-11 Urutu (6x6)	220 (To be replaced by VBTP-MR)
	VBTP-MR Guarani (6x6)	240+ (More on order)
	M113-BR/A2	580+ (To be upgraded)
	M577A2	100+
	AV-VBL	20+
	Iveco LMV 4x4	30+ (More on order)
Artillery	M114A1 155mm howitzer	80+
	M109 155mm self-propelled	76
	M109 155mm	20+
	L118 105 mm howitzer	50
	M101 105 mm howitzer	300+
	Oerlikon 35mm	30+
	M992	
Mortar	M30 107 mm	217
	120 mm	100+
MRL	Astros 2020	38 launchers vehicles
RCL	Carl Gustav 84 mm	300
Anti Tank GW	Eryx 136 mm	12
	AT4 84 mm	1,500
	ALAC 84 mm	(2,000 on order)
	MSS-1.2 130 mm	(400 on order)
	MILAN	20
SAM	RBS 70	16
	Pantsir-S1	(1 battery on order)
	9K38 Igla SA24	24
	9K38 Igla SA18	120
AA Gun	40 mm, 35 mm, 57 mm, 90 mm	240
	Gepard 1A2	30+

Army Aviation

Category	Name	In Service
Helicopter	EC-725 Caracal	15
	AS532 Cougar	8
	HM-1 Pantera	30
	AS550	33
	UH-60L	4
UAV	FT-100, FT-200	

New Procurements/ Upgrades

◆ Iveco Defence Vehicles delivered 500th Guarani and LMV-BRV batch to Brazilian Army, thus ending the contract for the acquisition of the 1st lot (32 units) of the new "Viatura Blindada Multitarefa, Leve de Rodas" (VBMT-LR 4x4). LMV-BR Project The LMV-BR project began in 2015 when Iveco Defence Vehicles won the tender for the delivery of 186 units to the Brazilian Army.

◆ Collins Aerospace has been selected by the Brazilian Army to provide its High Frequency (HF) Cellular communications system as part of the Brazilian Army Border Surveillance and Monitoring Strategic Programme (SISFRON) to improve communications capabilities for forces operating in the Amazon region.

◆ Aircraft Propeller Service, LLC has signed a major contract with the Brazilian Army to overhaul approximately 300 Airbus Helicopter main and tail rotor servo actuators for Fennec AS350/550 and Panther AS365 aircraft. The Brazilian Army fleet, currently consisting of 97 Helicopters (34 Panther AS365, 35 Fennec AS350/550, 4 Black Hawk S70, 8 Cougar AS532 and 16 Super Puma H225M) is the largest fleet of helicopters among all Latin America countries for both civil and military operators.

◆ Saab has signed a contract with the Brazilian Army for deliveries of RBS 70 NG – the latest generation of the RBS 70 man-portable air defence system. In addition to the RBS 70 NG system, the order also includes training systems, camouflage systems and other associated equipment. This is the Brazilian Army's first order of the latest RBS 70 NG version and marks a significant upgrade to their air defence capability. The RBS 70 NG offers a day/night capability, unjammable laser guidance and an automatic target tracker that ensures the missile hits its target.

◆ General Dynamics European Land Systems has signed a contract with the Brazilian Army Commission for the production and delivery of its Improved Ribbon Bridge (IRB). In addition to the Improved Ribbon Bridge, the company will deliver trucks, bridge adapter pallets, a bridge erection boat, as well as Integrated Logistics Support (ILS).

NAVY: The Brazilian Navy is the largest navy in Latin America. It is equipped with a 32,800-tonne aircraft carrier, the NAe São Paulo (formerly Foch of the French Navy), British-built frigates, locally built corvettes, coastal diesel-electric submarines and many other river and coastal patrol craft, among other vehicles. The main branches of the Brazilian Navy are: Naval Operations Command, Surface Fleet Command, Submarine Fleet Command, Naval Aviation Command, 1st Fleet Division Command, 2nd Fleet Division Command & Marine Corps General Command.

Naval Bases: Val de Cães, Almte. Ary Parreiras, Natal, Ladário Fluvial, Rio Negro, Rio Grande, Almte. Castro e Silva, Ilha das Flores, Ilha do Governador, Rio Meriti, Navy Arsenal of Rio de Janeiro, Rio de Janeiro, Aratu.

Personnel: 75,000 (including Marines)

Equipment

Category	Name	In Service
Submarine	Type 209 class	5
	Scorpene class	1
Frigate	Brasil class (Training)	1
	Niteroi class (Multi-purpose)	5
	Type 22 (Anti-submarine)	2
Corvette	Inhauma class	2
Patrol Vessel	Amazonas class	3
	Imperial Marinheiro class	1
	Macae class	2
	Grajau class	12
	Bracui class	4
	Roraima class	3
	Pedro Teixeira class	1
	Piratini class	6
Amphibious Force	Round Table class	2
	Mattoso Maia class	1
	Foudre class	1
	Ocean class	1
Minesweeper	Aratu class	5
Auxiliary ship		12
Missile	Exocet ASM, MAN-1-SUP ASM, MAN-1-SUB ASM, Aspide SAM, Sea Wolf SAM, Simbad SAM	

Naval Aviation

Category	Name	In Service
Fighter/Attack	A-4 Skyhawk	3+
Tanker	KC-2/C-1 Trader	(4 on order)
Helicopter	S-70B	6 (2 on order)
	Westland Lynx	10
	EC725	7
	AS332	5
	AS355	9
	AS350	19
Trainer	A-4 Skyhawk	2
	Bell-206	10+

...continued

Category	Name	In Service
UAV	FT-100 Horus	1
Weapon	AIM-9H Sidewinder, MAA-1A/1B Piranha, Sea Skua, Python, Derby	

Marines

Category	Name	In Service
APC/MICV/IFV	SK-105 Kurassier	15+
	M113	25+
	AV-VBL 4x4	3
	AAV7A1	52
	Piranha IIIC 8X8	20+
Artillery	M114A1	6
	L118 105 mm	18
	ASTROS II	6
	120 mm	
	M29 A1 81 mm	100
	Bofors 40 mm	6
Missile	Mistral	24
	RBS 70	12
	Pantsir-S1	
UAV	Carcara	42
	Horus FT-100	1

New Procurements/ Upgrades

◆ Airbus Helicopters has delivered the first H225M in naval combat configuration to the Brazilian Navy. Stationed at the naval base in São Pedro d'Aldeia, the aircraft will boost the Brazilian Navy's mission capabilities including anti-surface warfare and maritime surveillance.

◆ The Brazilian submarine Álvaro Alberto is a nuclear-powered attack submarine under construction for the Brazilian Navy by the Brazilian state-owned naval company ICN.

◆ The Brazilian Navy has signed a contract worth £133 million with BAE Systems for the supply of three Ocean Patrol Vessels and ancillary support services.

◆ The Águas Azuis Consortium, formed by thyssenkrupp Marine Systems, Embraer Defense & Security and Atech have been selected by Brazilian Navy to build the Tamandaré Class Corvettes (Tamandaré Corvettes Class Programme). With four corvettes scheduled for delivery between 2024 and 2028, the Navy will now have new Escort Ships to counter possible threats, ensure the protection of maritime traffic, and control the Brazilian jurisdictional waters and exclusive economic zone, which together form the so-called Blue Amazon.

◆ Naval solutions companies, Saab and Damen Schelde Naval Shipbuilding, have come together to compete for the project that will supply four Tamandaré Class Corvettes (CCT) for the Brazilian Navy. Saab will provide the complete combat system including the world leading Saab 9LV Combat Management System (CMS) if the proposal is chosen by the Brazilian Navy. The Saab 9LV is known for its flexibility and easy integration of third-party modules as well as high performance mission equipment. Damen will be responsible for supplying the ship Sigma 10514, an off-the-shelf product that will be adapted according to the requirements of the client, a Saab statement said. The companies are proposing a large technology transfer programme, in addition to partnerships with local companies, benefiting the Brazilian defence industry.

Brazilian nuclear submarine Alvaro Alberto. (Image Credit: Brazilian Navy)

AIR FORCE: The Brazilian Air Force is the aerospace branch of the Brazilian armed forces and is managed by the "Aeronautics Command" (Comando da Aeronáutica - COMAer). The COMAer was created in 1999, and replaced the Ministry of Aeronautics. Now, the COMAer is one of the three armed forces assigned to the Ministry of Defence (Ministério da Defesa). The COMAer is led by the "Aeronautics Commander" (Comandante da Aeronáutica). He is nominated by the President and reports directly to the Minister of Defence.

Air Bases: Anápolis, Belém, Boa Vista, Brasília, Campo Grande, Canoas, Florianópolis, Fortaleza, São Paulo, Manaus, Natal, Porto Velho, Recife, Galeão, Santa Cruz, Afonsos, Salvador, Santa Maria, Santos, Campo de Provas Brigadeiro Velloso.

Personnel: 70,000

Equipment

Category	Name	In Service
Fighter/attack/Reconnaissance aircraft	F-5EM	40
	A-1/A-1M	45
	A-29A	30
	F-39E	On order
	E-99 AWACS	4
	R-99	4
	Learjet 35	5
	EMB 110	3
	EMB 110	10
	P-3AM	7

...continued

Category	Name	In Service
Transport Aircraft/ air refuelling	KC-130H/M	3
	KC-767	(on order)
	EMB 120	20
	EMB 110	50
	C-130E/H/M	12
	CASA C-295	10+ (More on order)
	Cessna 208	20+
	KC-390	4 (More on order)
Helicopter	UH-1H	15+
	Bell 206	1
	EC725	5
	AS332	5
	UH-60L/M	12
	Mi-35	10
Trainer	AMX-T	8
	A-29B	40+
	EMB 312	100+
	F-5FM	2
	F 39F	On order
UAV	Hermes 450	4
	Hermes 900	1
SAM	9K38 Igla	10+ (More on order)
AAM	MAA-1A Piranha, MAA-1B Piranha, A-Darter, Derby, Python-3, Python-4	
Anti-Ship missile	AGM-84 Harpoon, MAN-1	
Anti-tank missile	9M120 Ataka-V, 9K114 Shturm	

New Procurements/ Upgrades

◆ Embraer delivered the fourth C-390 Millennium multi-mission medium airlifter to the Brazilian Air Force. Total 28 on order.

◆ Gripen E has entered serial delivery phase for Brazilian and Swedish Air Forces. Saab held a high-level meeting in Nov 2021 with authorities from Brazil and Sweden to present the first six serial production Gripen E aircraft, which have left the factory and entered the delivery phase.

◆ First T-27 Tucano aircraft of the Brazilian Air Force (FAB) is in the final stage of the modernisation process. The plane is used in the instructional flights of the Cadets of the Air Force Academy (AFA), located in Pirassununga (SP).

◆ The Brazilian Air Force received 13 C-295, designated C-105A Amazonas, to replace the ageing DHC-5/C-115 Buffalo transports. Additional orders are to bring the total number up to 15 by 2020.

◆ The first Saab F-39E Gripen fighter arrived in Brazil in Sept 2020. This F-39E Gripen is a test unit equipped with instruments for the continuation of the test campaign, which started in August 2019 in Sweden. Brazil has signed a contract of 28 single and 8 two-seated Gripen E fighters. A part of the first Gripen ordered for the Brazilian Air Force will be built in Sweden while the remainder will be built in Brazil. Brazilian industry will be responsible for developing a big part of the Brazilian – unique techniques of the Gripen system, such as the all-new dual seat version. Brazil will be the sixth country to fly the Gripen and recently Saab handed over the first Gripen E to the Brazilian Minister of Defence. In 2021, deliveries to the Brazilian Air force will begin.

◆ Brazilian Air Force plans to buy 28 KC-390 military cargo aircraft and initial logistical support from Embraer. Embraer delivered the first multi-mission airlift KC-390 to the Brazilian Air Force (FAB) in Sept 2019 at a ceremony held at Anápolis Air Base. The KC-390 was developed as a joint project between the Brazilian Air Force and Embraer.

Nuclear Weapons Programme

Brazil has never developed either chemical or biological weapons. In the 1980s, Brazil began a secret nuclear weapons programme in response to Argentina's programme, under the military regime and was supplied with nuclear materials and equipment by US, France and West Germany. However, with the decline of military rule, Brazil also ended the weapons of mass destruction and acceded to the Nuclear Non-Proliferation Treaty in 1998. Brazil has also ratified the Geneva Protocol on 28 August 1970, the Biological Weapons Convention on 27 February 1973, and the Chemical Weapons Convention on 13 March 1996.

Nevertheless, the country still possesses the key technologies needed to produce nuclear weapons. Brazil's nuclear capabilities are the most advanced in Latin America. Reports indicate that Brazil has the capabilities, technological knowhow and is in a position to produce nuclear weapons within a short period. Angra Nuclear Power Plant is Brazil's sole nuclear power plant which consists of Angra I and Angra II. Angra III is currently under construction

The Brazilian Navy is currently developing a nuclear submarine fleet. In 2008, France agreed to transfer technology to Brazil for the joint development of the nuclear submarine hull. On the other hand, Brazil which has signed many treaties has also declared itself a nuclear-weapon-free zone by signing the Treaty of Tlatelolco in 1967. The country is fighting against the nuclear proliferation by being an active participant in the International Atomic Energy Agency and the Nuclear Suppliers Group. Brazil is also the founding member of Brazilian–Argentine Agency for Accounting and Control of Nuclear Materials. The safeguards agency plays an active role in the verification of the peaceful use of nuclear materials that could be used, either directly or indirectly, for the manufacture of weapons of mass destruction.

Major Armaments Producers

Domestic suppliers: Embraer, Avibras, NUCLEP, CBC, IMBEL, Taurus, Helibras, EMGEPRON, Agrale, Mectron, Aero Bravo, Iveco Brazil, MAN Latin America, Odebrecht, Indústria Aeronáutica Neiva, Troller, INACE, Usiminas, XMobots

Foreign suppliers: United States, France, Germany, Spain, Colombia, Russia, Israel, United Kingdom, Sweden, Italy

Brazil has the potential to once again take centre stage in this international market - which moves around USD 1.5 trillion per year. Brazil has firm defence R&D facilities for the development of the aircrafts, artillery, missiles infantry weapons, submarines and space research. The country has joint ventures with Italy for the development of the multirole aircraft. According to reports in Export.Gov of US Department of Commerce, Brazil has been one of the top 10 export destinations for U.S. aerospace products over many years.

Major defence development by Brazil:

◆ SS-80 long range artillery rocket (300mm)

◆ MAA-1 piranha air to air missile

◆ AV-SF-70 Skyfire 70mm rocket launcher which is also supplied to many nations

◆ Tupi class submarines

Aircraft/ helicopter/ aerospace equipment manufacturers

◆ Helibras or Helicópteros do Brasil S.A: Helicopters of Brazil, Inc. is a Brazil-based helicopter manufacturer which is a wholly owned subsidiary of Eurocopter, a division of EADS.

◆ Aero Bravo: It is a Brazilian aircraft manufacturer founded in 1993 in Belo Horizonte. The firm manufactures light aircraft of its own design and under license.

◆ Indústria Aeronáutica Neiva: It is a subsidiary of Embraer which produces airplanes and aircraft components. Its main product is the Embraer EMB 202 Ipanema, the most employed agricultural aircraft in Brazil.

- **Advanced Composites Solutions (ACS):** The company constructs light aircraft. ACS is the production of the ACS-100 Sora, a two seat light sport aircraft. ACS is also involved in the development and integration of Unmanned Aircraft Systems through its subsidiary Flight Solutions.
- **Embraer:** Embraer S.A. (BM&F Bovespa: EMBR3 / NYSE: ERJ) is a giant aerospace conglomerate of Brazil that produces commercial, military, and executive aircraft and provides aeronautical services. Currently, Embraer imports approximately 56% of its components from North America, mostly from the United States.

The Brazilian Aerospace and Defence industry is a strong segment in the country's economy presenting an impressive growth and worldwide projection. EMBRAER leads this industry and as recognised as one of the four major aerospace manufacturers of commercial aircraft and with a growing presence in the defence and business aviation markets.

ABIMDE- Brazilian Defence and Security Industries Association, congregates the companies that manufacture army stuff, with the objective to sponsor, promote and represent their common interests and objectives, aiming at the social and economic enlargement of the country.

Brazil's Industrial Defence Base (IDB) focuses on the participation of state and private companies in various stages of research, development, production, distribution and maintenance of strategic defence products - goods and services. The IDB depends on the joint and harmonious work of the productive sector, mainly concentrated in the private sector, with the development sector, in charge of the State. The Ministry of Defence works to promote conditions that allow the leverage of the Brazilian Defence Industrial Base, enabling the national industry in the sector to gain autonomy in strategic technologies for the country. Two initiatives in this direction are the establishment of the Articulation and Defence Equipment Plan (PAED) and the advent of the Defence Industrial Defence Base Law. In addition to establishing a regulatory framework for the sector, the standard reduces the cost of production of companies legally classified as strategic and establishes incentives for the development of technologies indispensable to Brazil, according to the Ministry of Defence, Brazil.

DEFENCE DEALS

Joint Venture Programmes

Brazilian defence firm Embraer and Israel's AEL Sistemas, a subsidiary of Elbit Systems, have formed a joint venture company, Harpia Sistemas, to develop, produce and market unmanned aerial vehicles (UAVs). The two defence firms had announced their partnership to jointly develop, produce and market UAVs and related components. The Brazilian Air Force has signed a contract worth 1.4 million reals with Denel do Brasil to prepare facilities in the industrial park in the city of Sao José dos Campos in the state of Sao Paulo for the production of A-Darter missiles. This new technology, the result of a joint development between Brazil and South Africa, has already reached the end of the test phase, and is ready to move into the next phase, large-scale production. This missile will equip the modernised version of the A-1 fighter aircraft as well as the future F-X2 fighter aircraft. The production of the new missile will involve several Brazilian companies, including Mectron, Avibras and Opto Electronics, which have benefited from a transfer of technology in areas such as optics, navigation, sensors and image processing. Jaragua launched a joint venture with the Italian firm Oto Melara to produce cannons in Brazil and set up a maintenance centre for Latin America.

Arms Import

The US State Department has approved a possible Foreign Military Sale to the Government of Brazil of MK 54 Lightweight Torpedoes and related equipment for an estimated cost of USD70 million. The Government of Brazil has requested to buy 22 MK 54 conversion kits - to convert MK 46 Mod 5 A(S) torpedoes to MK 54 Mod 0 lightweight torpedoes. Also included are torpedo containers, Recoverable Exercise Torpedoes (REXTORP) with containers, Fleet Exercise Section (FES) and fuel tanks, air launch accessories for rotary wing, torpedo spare parts, propellant, lanyard start assembly suspensions bands, thermal batteries, training, publications, support and test equipment.

ST Kinetics, arm of ST Engineering has won a contract worth USD 20.9 million from the Brazilian Navy for the supply of 5 units of 40mm L70 naval gun and an associated Integrated Logistics Support (ILS) package. The contract was signed between the Brazilian Navy and Allied Ordnance of Singapore (Pte) Ltd (AOS), a wholly owned subsidiary of ST Kinetics. Brazil has also an agreement with Colombia, valued at 10 million dollars, for the purchase of patrol vessels to monitor the Amazon region.

Arms Export

Brazilian Defence Industrial Base (IDB) exports reached USD 1.5 billion in the year 2021 in categories composed of aircraft, ships, cyber, radar, secure communication systems, weapons, among other high-tech items.

Brazil has witnessed several new developments in its aerospace industry as well as in other defence sectors. The Brazilian helicopter manufacturer, Helibras recently won the contract to assemble a number of Eurocopter EC 725 Super Cougars in its new facility at Itajubá.

Saab AB announced that they will be investing in the Brazilian aero-structure integrator Akaer.

Brazil in March 2020 signed a defence agreement with the United States enabling joint development of military capabilities. A bilateral agreement was signed on Research Development, Test & Evaluation (RDT&E) Projects. The agreement will help both the countries to jointly work on projects in the area of defence.

DEFENCE BUDGET

Total defence spending: $26 billion (2019 approx.)

Estimated defence spending in terms of GDP: 1.3% of GDP (2020 est.), 1.5% of GDP (2019)

Brazil's 2020 federal budget proposal for the defence sector is approximately USD 397.5 billion. The National Defence Strategy (NDS) continues to be the guide for the medium and long-term planning for the defence sector in Brazil. The three strategic sectors highlighted in the NDS are: nuclear, cyber, and space, as well as promoting the development and strengthening of the Brazilian defence industry. Major Brazilian Defence Strategic projects include: the Submarine Development Program (PROSUB) and the Navy Nuclear Program (PNM) coordinated by the Brazilian Navy; the Guarani Armoured wheeled vehicles, the Integrated Border Monitoring System (SISFRON) and Cyber Defence coordinated by the Brazilian Army; and the KC-390 aircraft, the Gripen AM-X aircraft modernization, and Space System Strategic Program coordinated by the Brazilian Air Force, according to the International Trade Administration US Department of Commerce.

Brazil's national defence policy is outlined in the National Defence Policy, the National Mobilisation Policy and the National Defence Strategy. According to a report by SIPRI, Brazil at present spends about 1.6% of GDP on defence; other countries, including Russia and the United States, spend more than 4%.

Brazil is planning to spend closer to 2% of GDP on defence in the coming years in order to help the defence industry of the country that could supply the weapons and equipment necessary to fulfil the government's defence goals. From 22 billion USD, 3.34% of GDP, 5.6 billion is included for defence procurement (approx. data). Most of the weapon systems in service with Brazilian armed forces are of US or EU origin. Russian weaponry is limited up to SAMs and recently ordered Mi-35 attack helicopter. The defence ministry had recently approved [law n°] MP 544/ 11 which creates a special tax regime for the national defence industry. The law is aligned with the Greater Brazil Plan, which aims to increase the competitiveness of domestic industry. In 2008, Brazil's Ministry of Defence released the National Strategy of Defence (NSD), a strategic review of the country's defence posture and objectives. The NSD emphasises the development of a robust domestic defence industrial capability to both compete with external markets in order to increase their production scale and create the technological capacity to gradually rule out the need to purchase imported services and products.

ABIMDE, which groups 170 companies, hopes to invest USD 120 billion over the long term, planning boost annual export sales from USD 1.7 billion to USD 4 billion. The government is also planning to increase the exports of its locally made defence products by shifting the focus more on its industrial and manufacturing sectors.

The Brazilian Armed Forces have long-term development, construction and acquisition plans that include: weapons, escort ship platforms, transport ships, offshore patrol vessels, tugs and hydrographic/oceanographic ships, UAVs, long range radars, helicopters, tactical radio communication systems, and spare parts and components, among others, according to Export.Gov, the US Department of Commerce's International Trade Administration report.

CONCLUSION

Brazil's armed forces are the second largest in the Americas, after the United States, and the largest in Latin America. Brazil Defence Ministry shows its participation in international forum through peace missions, initiatives with other federal agencies, international cooperation, bilateral partnerships and agreements, etc. Brazil's international relations are based on Article 4 of the Federal Constitution, which establishes non-intervention, self-determination, international cooperation and the peaceful settlement of conflicts as the guiding principles of Brazil's relationship with other countries and multilateral organisations. Brazil's emerging economic growth has led the country to embark on a more ambitious and long term defence plan to modernise its armed forces and also to build a strong domestic defence industry over the next ten years. Brazil maintains a stable and friendly relationship with neighbouring countries and has never engaged in armed conflict with any other nation. The country is vast and geographically diverse and is home to the Amazon River and rainforests. Brazil has large reserves of many natural resources and has recently discovered substantial oil reserves. Brazil's armed forces with no serious external or internal threats, are searching for a new role. They are expanding their presence in the Amazon under the Northern Corridor (Calha Norte) programme. The country's defence procurements are largely focused on the protection of such resources, including the Amazon system from illegal mining, deforestation and drugs and arms trafficking. The defence ministry focuses on providing its domestic industry with technology procured from foreign OEMs (original equipment manufacturers). The technology procured has assisted the development of the domestic aeronautical sector and continues to provide the Brazilian defence forces with attack helicopters, light attack aircrafts and air cargo transport systems. The recent government incentives to modernise the forces and develop a strong, export-oriented military industrial complex has helped Brazil's defence industry to gain momentum and focus more on invest and growth.

CONTACT DETAILS
Ministry of Defence
Esplanada dos Ministérios Bloco Q
CEP 70049-900 Brasília,
Distrito Federal, Brazil
Tel: (+55 61) 33 12 40 00
Websites: www.defesa.gov.br
www.exercito.gov.br/, www.mar.mil.br/
www.fab.mil.br/

BRUNEI
(Capital: Bandar Seri Begawan)

INTRODUCTION
Area: 5,770 Sq Km
Population: 6,919,180 (July 2021 est.)
Coastline: 161 km
Maritime claims: Territorial sea: 12 nm
Exclusive Economic Zone: 200 nm or to median line

KEY POLITICAL PERSONS

PRIME MINISTER & DEFENCE MINISTER: Sultan Hassanal Bolkiah

KEY DEFENCE PERSONS

COMMANDER OF ARMED FORCES: Maj. Gen. Hamzah bin Haji Sahat

CHIEF OF THE LAND FORCE: Brig. Gen. Muhammad Haszaimi bin Bol Hassan

CHIEF OF ROYAL BRUNEI NAVY: First Adm. Spry bin Haji Serudi

CHIEF OF ROYAL BRUNEI AIR FORCE: Brig. Gen. Mohd Sharif bin Dato Paduka Haji Ibrahim

ECONOMY

Brunei is an energy-rich nation with added focus on innovative technology & creative industry, business services, tourism and downstream oil & gas industry. The country enjoys convenient access to the Southeast Asian markets, with neighbours such as Vietnam, Thailand, Singapore, Malaysia, Philippines and Indonesia located nearby. Its deep water port, Muara Port, has 13 shipping lines and is connected to 15 ports in the region. Brunei Darussalam is also a signee to several other trade agreements with its ASEAN neighbours and East Asian trading partners such as China, Japan and South Korea. It also has comprehensive trade ties with countries in the Middle East such as Bahrain, Kuwait, Oman and Qatar. All this facilitates business and entrepreneurial ventures within the country. Crude oil and natural gas production account for approximately 65% of GDP and 95% of exports. Per capita GDP is among the highest in the world. Brunei's trade increased in 2016 and 2017. Brunei was a member of the P-4, the four founding members of the Trans-Pacific Partnership trade agreement (TPP) and is also a negotiating partner of the Regional Comprehensive Economic Partnership (RCEP). Brunei has increasingly and actively sought out foreign direct investment in an effort to diversify away from its oil and gas dependence and developed various incentives for new industries and economic activities in order to create a more attractive marketplace for investors. Brunei's non-petroleum industries include manufacturing, construction, agriculture, forestry, fishing, and services.

GDP (official exchange rate): $27.23 billion (2020), $26.91 billion (2019 est.)

Real Growth Rate (GDP): 1.3% (2017 est.), -2.5% (2016 est.)

Industries: Petroleum, petroleum refining, liquefied natural gas, construction, agriculture, aquaculture, transportation

Oil - proved reserves: 1.1 billion bbl (1 January 2018 est.)

Natural gas - proved reserves: 260.5 billion cu m (1 January 2018 est.)

Total Exports: $7.83 billion (2019 est.), $7.04 billion (2018 est.)

Export Commodities: Natural gas, crude petroleum, refined petroleum, industrial alcohols, industrial hydrocarbons (2019)

Major Markets: Japan 34%, Australia 12%, Singapore 10%, India 8%, Malaysia 8%, Thailand 7%, China 6%, South Korea 5% (2019)

Total Imports: $6.81 billion (2019), $5.68 billion (2018 est.)

Import Commodities: Crude petroleum, refined petroleum, cars, tug boats, valves (2019)

Major Suppliers: Singapore 18%, China 14%, Malaysia 12%, Nigeria 5%, United Arab Emirates 5%, United States 5% (2019)

INTERNATIONAL DISPUTES

◆ According to Letters of Exchange signed in 2009, Malaysia in 2010 ceded two hydrocarbon concession blocks to Brunei in exchange for Brunei's sultan dropping claims to the Limbang corridor, which divides Brunei.

◆ Brunei claims a maritime boundary extending as far as a median with Vietnam, thus asserting an implicit claim to Louisa Reef.

DEFENCE

ARMY
Personnel: 4,500

Equipment

Category	Name	In Service
Light Tank	FV101 Scorpion	10+
APC	FNSS AIFV	5+
	M113	50+
	V150 Commando	50+
	AIFV	40
	VAB	30
	Anoa	30+
Artillery	155 mm	
	L16	20
	L118 105 mm	10
Mortar	M81 80 mm	50+
RCL	M-67 90 mm	
	M40 106 mm	70+

New Procurements/Upgrades

No major procurement plans are under consideration at present.

NAVY
Personnel: 1,000

Equipment

Category	Name	In service
Patrol vessel (Offshore and Inshore)	Waspada Class	3
	Perwira Class	3
	Ijhtihad class	4
	Darussalam Class	4
Amphibious Force	Serasa class	2
	Teraban class	2
Assault Boat	Fast assault boat	20+

New Procurements/Upgrades

◆ The new joint venture, named Muara Maritime Services, between Brunei government-owned holding company Darussalam Assets and Lürssen will perform full service support for the entire Royal Brunei Navy's fleet, including the PV 80 Offshore Patrol Vessel, which is a similar design to the Royal Australian Navy OPV in the SEA 1180 programme. The sustainment contract includes maintenance, repair and overhaul services as well as spare part supply and warehousing services. The contract between the government of Brunei represented by the Ministry of Defence and Muara Maritime Services was signed on 6 March 2019 in the presence of the Minister of Defence II, the Minister at the Prime Minister's Office and Minister of Finance and Economy II, the Acting Commander of the Royal Brunei Armed Forces, Peter Lürssen and other dignitaries in Brunei. The sustainment contract is for an initial period of ten years.

AIR FORCE
Personnel: 1000

Equipment

Category	Name	In Service
Fighter	FA-50	On order
Transport	CN-235	1 (more on order)
	C-130J	On order
Trainer	Pilatus PC-7	4
	Bell 206	2
Helicopter	UH-60	10
	Bell 214ST	1
	Bo-105	5+
	S-70A	5+
	S-70i	(12 on order)

Air Defence

Two squadrons are for air defence and are equipped with 10 Rapier and Mistral SAM systems.

The Royal Brunei Armed Forces relies primarily upon helicopters to deploy its forces for border security, to perform coastal surveillance missions, for disaster response missions, and for law enforcement support. The Air Force possesses one troop transport fixed-wing plane, flight training aircraft, and a number of rotary wing aircraft.

New Procurements/Upgrades
- Brunei has expressed interest in the FA-50.
- Sikorsky Aircraft, a subsidiary of United Technologies Corp. formally signed a contract with the Brunei Ministry of Defence to provide 12 S-70i BLACK HAWK helicopters with associated spare parts, training and ground support equipment. The contract contains an option for 10 additional helicopters.

Defence Expenditure
A major share of military budget is spent on payment for the weapon system and their maintenance.

Total defence spending: $370 million (2018)

Estimated defence spending in terms of GDP: 3.7% of GDP (2020 est.), 3.3% of GDP (2019)

Foreign Suppliers: Australia, Belgium, Canada, France, Germany, Indonesia, Italy, Netherlands, Singapore, Sweden, United Kingdom, United States

The Ministry of Defence has been allocated a budget of BND$451,790,210.00 for the new fiscal year (2017/2018) during the third day of the 13th Legislative Council Session in March 2017. Central to the defence budget is the continued focus in adopting the best dynamic approach in aligning the Ministry's strategic objectives towards enhancing the protection of national interests such as territorial integrity and sovereignty, economic development, social harmony, national philosophy, as well as in contributing to regional and global peace. The overall national budget for the new fiscal year stands at BND$5.3 billion.

Trade between the United States and Brunei in 2016 totalled USD628 million. Aircraft procured by Brunei from the United States in recent years include Sikorsky Black Hawk S70i helicopters and Boeing 787 Dreamliners.

Defence Production and R&D
TThere is no major defence R&D policy formed by state majority of the defence budget is being spend on the procurement of new systems. The Centre of Science and Technology Research and Development (CSTRAD) and Royal Brunei Technical Services (RBTS) are responsible for the R&D, assessment, and selection of defence technology solutions for Royal Brunei Armed Forces. CSTRAD was formed with the sole focus of conducting defence research and development through the application of science and technology in order to provide suitable leading edge technology solutions for the Royal Brunei Armed Forces' capabilities development and force modernisation. RBTS is a wholly-owned government company in Brunei Darussalam. RBTS is the leading acquisition management and systems management service provider in the country.

Defence Procurement
Brunei Army/Navy/Air Force have not done any major procurements in recent years.

CONTACT DETAILS
Ministry of Defence - MINDEF,
Directorate of Logistics - DOL
Kementerian Pertahanan
Bolkiah Garrisen, 3510 Negara, Brunei
Tel: (+673 2) 38 63 33
(+673 2) 38 23 60
Fax: (+673 2) 38 68 08
(+673 2) 33 70 72
E-mail: dirlog_mindef@brunet.bn

Public Relations Unit
Ministry of Defence
Bolkiah Garrison BB3510
Brunei Darussalam
Tel: +6732-2386371 / 2386372 / 2386373
Fax: +673-2381934 / +673-2383277
Email: pru@mindef.gov.bn
www.mindef.gov.bn

BULGARIA
(Capital: Sofia)

INTRODUCTION
Area: 110,879 sq km
Population: 6,919,180 (July 2021 est.)
Coastline: 354 km
Maritime claims: Territorial sea: 12 nm
Contiguous zone: 24 nm
Exclusive Economic Zone: 200 nm

KEY POLITICAL PERSONS

PRESIDENT: Roumen Radev

PRIME MINISTER: Kiril Petkov

KEY DEFENCE PERSONS

DEFENCE MINISTER: Georgi Panayotov

CHIEF OF DEFENCE: Adm. Emil Eftimov

COMMANDER OF LAND FORCES: Maj. Gen. Mihail Dimitrov Popov

COMMANDER OF NAVY: Rear Adm. Kyril Mikhaylov

COMMANDER OF AIR FORCE: Maj. Gen. Dimitar Petrov

ECONOMY

Bulgaria has undergone a significant transformation changing from a highly centralised planned economy to a more liberal, market-driven economy. The Bulgarian economy has experienced rapid growth in recent years as a result of the advancement of structural reforms. The strongest sectors contributing to the economy are energy, mining, metallurgy, machine building, agriculture and tourism. The global economic crisis of 2008, and the pandemic-induced crisis in 2020 undid some of the gains achieved during the high-growth period. The Bulgarian economy has experienced significant growth (416%), starting from $13.15 billion (nominal, 2000) and reaching estimated gross domestic product (GDP) of $67.9 billion (nominal, 2019 est.), according to media reports. Bulgaria is a member of the European Union (EU), World Trade Organization (WTO), Organisation for Security and Co-operation in Europe (OSCE) and Organisation of the Black Sea Economic Cooperation (BSEC).

GDP (official exchange rate): $68.49 billion (2019 est.)

Real Growth Rate (GDP): 3.39% (2019 est.), 3.2% (2018 est.)

Industries: Electricity, gas, water; food, beverages, tobacco; machinery and equipment, automotive parts, base metals, chemical products, coke, refined petroleum, nuclear fuel; outsourcing centres.

Total Exports: $39.27 billion (2020 est.), $44.04 billion (2019 est.)

Export Commodities: Refined petroleum, packaged medicines, copper, wheat, electricity (2019)

Major Markets: Germany 16%, Romania 8%, Italy 7%, Turkey 7%, Greece 6% (2019)

Total Imports: $38.07 billion (2020 est.), $41.84 billion (2019 est.)

Import Commodities: Crude petroleum, copper, cars, packaged medicines, refined petroleum (2019)

Major Suppliers: Germany 11%, Russia 9%, Italy 7%, Romania 7%, Turkey 7% (2019)

INTERNATIONAL DISPUTES

Bulgaria has no known international disputes.

DEFENCE

The Bulgarian Government is pursuing the ambitious goal of bolstering the operational capabilities of the Bulgarian Armed Forces and meeting the country's collective defence commitments. The Programme for the Development of the Defence Capabilities of the Armed Forces of the Republic of Bulgaria 2020 has been adopted by the National Assembly in 2010. The programme envisages the establishment of the Special Operations Forces as a separate military unit within the Bulgarian Army. According to the programme, the Armed Forces will maintain the size of 37,000 during peacetime and not more than 40,000 personnel during wartime. The defence capabilities of the Armed Forces are being developed as a set of the following elements: doctrines and concepts; organisational structures; training; materiel; command and control; personnel; infrastructure and interoperability.

The Land Forces of Bulgaria are functionally divided into Deployable and Reserve Forces. The Forces are in the process of continued restructuring since 2004. Under the most recent reform, brigades were reduced to regiments, while several garrisons and brigades were disbanded. The Bulgarian Air Force is one of the oldest air forces in Europe and the world. The Navy has traditionally been the smallest component of the Bulgarian military. In response to the growing threats in cyberspace, there are plans to develop cyber defence capabilities in the Armed Forces. On 31 October 2018, the Bulgarian parliament passed the Cyber Security Act.

ARMY

Personnel: 14,480

Equipment

Category	Name	In Service
MBT	T-72	90
AIFV/APC	BMP-23	70
	BMP-1	90
	BTR-60C	20
	MT-LB	100
Artillery	D20 152mm towed howitzer	24
	2S1 122mm SP howitzer	48
MRL	BM-21 122mm	24

...continued

Category	Name	In Service
ATGW	9P148 Konkurs	18
	AT-5 Spandrel	
SAM	SA-8	24

New Procurements/Upgrades

No major procurement plans are under consideration at present.

NAVY

Personnel: 3,610

Equipment

Category	Name	In Service
Frigate	Drazki class (ex-Belgian Wielingen class)	3
	Smeli (ex-USSR KONI class)	1
Patrol craft	Reshitelni ex-USSR Pauk class	2
Light forces	Mulniya missile FAC	1
Mine warfare force	Tsibar mine hunter (ex-Belgian Tripartite type)	1
	ex-USSR Sonya class minesweeper	3
	ex-USSR Vanya class	2
Landing craft	Vidra class LCU	1
Auxiliaries	AOTL	2
	ARS	1
	YDT	2
	AGSC	2
	ADG/AX	1

Naval Aviation: Three AS.565MB Panther helicopters.

New Procurements/Upgrades

◆ Germany's NVL Group has started construction of the Bulgarian Navy's Multipurpose Modular Patrol Vessels (MMPV) project. The vessels are being built at MTG Dolphin in Varna. Delivery of the first vessel is scheduled for 2025, and the second vessel in 2026.

AIR FORCE

Personnel: 6,840

Equipment

Category	Name	In Service
Fighter	Su-25K/KB	14
	MiG-29A	12
	MiG-29UB	4
	MiG-21Bis	2 (in reserve)
	MiG-21UM	1
Transport	C-27J	3
	An-30	1

...continued

Category	Name	In Service
Transport	PC-12M	1
	An-2T	1
	L-410	2
Trainer	L-39	6
	PC-9M	6
Helicopter	Mi-24D/V	6
	AS.532AL	12
	Mi-17	6
	Bell 206	6
SAM	S-300	
	S75-Dvina	
	S-125 Pechora	
	S-200	
	2K12 KUB	

New Procurements/Upgrades

◆ Russia has completed the delivery of components for MiG-29 fighter jets ahead of schedule. In January 2020, Bulgaria's defence ministry signed a $4.68 million/4.04 million euro contract with MiG Corporation for buying equipment for its MiG-29s.

◆ Bulgaria has signed up for eight F-16C/D Block 70 fighters in July 2019. The government has released a letter of request (LOR) for a letter of offer and acceptance (LOA) for a second batch of eight F-16 Block 70 multi role fighters.

◆ Bulgaria plans to purchase AMRAAM missile from the US.

Defence Expenditure

Total defence spending: $1.253 billion (2021), $2.179 billion (2019)

Defence spending in terms of GDP: 1.56% (2021)

Defence Production and R&D

Bulgaria has a large indigenous defence industry. The defence industry comprised of two parts with the first under the control of the Ministry of Industry. The sub-group - Metalchim – deals with arms and ammunition. The second is under the control of the Ministry of Defence (MoD) and comprises the TEREM enterprise, dealing with repair works and defence equipment manufacturing. Defence production exports are mainly undertaken by the MoD and four defence trade agencies – Kintex, Teraton, Arimex and Elmet Engineering. Bulgaria is ranked as a "medium" small arms exporter according to the Small Arms Survey.

Defence Procurement

The Government has approved three major projects worth around 1.2 billion euro to modernise the Bulgarian Navy and Air Force. For the Navy, the government has started the Multipurpose Modular Patrol Vessels (MMPV) project and it has decided to purchase 8 F-16 jets (6 single-seat and 2 two-seat fighters) to replace the ageing fleet of MiG-29 jets of the Air Force. The agreement includes supply of munitions for the jets, Sidewinder AIM 9X Block II missiles, and a multifunctional information distribution system joint tactical radio system (MIDS JTRS).

CONTACT DETAILS
Ministry of Defence
3, Dyakon Ignatiy Street, 1000 Sofia
Phone: +359 2 92 20 922
Fax: +359 2 987 96 93
e-mail: presscntr@mod.bg
www.md.government.bg/en/

CAMBODIA
(Capital: Phnom Penh)

INTRODUCTION

Area: 181,035 sq km
Population: 17,304,363 (July 2021 est.)
Coastline: 443 Km
Maritime claims: Territorial sea: 12 nm
Contiguous zone: 24 nm
Exclusive Economic Zone: 200 nm
Continental shelf: 200 nm

KEY POLITICAL PERSONS

HEAD OF STATE & COMMANDER-IN-CHIEF: King Norodom Sihamoni

PRIME MINISTER: Hun Sen

KEY DEFENCE PERSONS

MINISTER OF DEFENCE: Gen. Tea Banh

ARMY CHIEF: Gen. Hun Manet

NAVY CHIEF: Vice Adm. Tea Vinh

AIR FORCE CHIEF: Lt. Gen. Soeung Samnang

ECONOMY

Cambodia remains one of the poorest countries in Asia. The country has experienced strong economic growth over the last decade. Cambodia has become the last ASEAN's Member in April 1999. The tourism, garment, construction and real estate, and agriculture sectors accounted for the bulk of growth. Manufacturing output is concentrated in the garment sector, which dominates Cambodia's exports, especially to the US and the European Union. The Cambodian Government has been working with bilateral and multilateral donors, including the Asian Development Bank, the World Bank, the World Trade Organisation and IMF, to address the country's many pressing needs. Textile exports accounted for 68% of total exports in 2017. The COVID-19 pandemic has affected badly Cambodia's main drivers of economic growth- tourism, manufacturing exports, and construction.

GDP (official exchange rate): $70.08 billion (2020), $72.36 billion (2019 est.)

Real Growth Rate (GDP): 6.9% (2017 est.), 7% (2016 est.)

Industries: Tourism, garments, construction, rice milling, fishing, wood and wood products, rubber, cement, gem mining, textiles

Total Exports: $19.4 billion (2020 est.), $21.07 billion (2019 est.)

Export Commodities: Clothing, precious metal scraps, trunks/cases, gold, leather footwear (2019)

Major Markets: United States 21%, Singapore 8%, Thailand 8%, Germany 7%, Japan 6%, China 5%, Canada 5%, United Kingdom 5% (2019)

Total Imports: $23.12 billion (2020 est.), $25.52 billion (2019 est.)

Import Commodities: Refined petroleum, clothing, gold, cars, flavored water (2019)

Major Suppliers: China 27%, Thailand 25%, Vietnam 15%, Singapore 8% (2019)

INTERNATIONAL DISPUTES

◆ Cambodia is concerned about Laos' extensive upstream dam construction

◆ Cambodia and Thailand dispute sections of boundary. In 2011 Thailand and Cambodia resorted to arms in the dispute over the location of the boundary on the precipice surmounted by Preah Vihear temple ruins, awarded to Cambodia by ICJ decision in 1962 and part of a planned UN World Heritage site.

◆ Cambodia accuses Vietnam of a wide variety of illicit cross-border activities. Progress continuing on a joint development area with Vietnam is hampered by an unresolved dispute over sovereignty of offshore islands.

DEFENCE

ARMY
Personnel: 90,000

Equipment

Category	Name	In Service
MBT	T-55	200+
	Type 62/63	100+
	Type 59	150+
	PT-76	30
APC/MICV/IFV	BRDM-2	20+
	BTR-60	200+
	BMP-1	80+
	OT-64	40
	M113	25
Artillery	76 mm (Zis-3)	15+
	100 mm (T-12)	20
	122 mm Type 81	50+
	130 mm M-46	80+
	R-70	50
	107 mm Type 63	150+
Mortar	160mm	
	81mm	
MRL	122 mm BM-21	
ATW	100mm & 82mm B-10	
AA gun	37mm Type 65/74	80+
	23mm ZU-23-2	80+
	57mm S-60	80+
	14.5mm ZPU-1/-2/-4	90
	12.7mm	
MANPADS	SA-7	
	HN-5	
	FN-12/16	

New Procurements/ Upgrades

◆ China and Cambodia signed new defence cooperation agreement in 2018. China has provided military vehicles and transport trucks for Cambodia Armed Forces.

◆ Royal Cambodian Armed Forces and China's People's Liberation Army have signed new defence agreement in 2019. Through this agreement, China will continue to assist and support the building and development of Cambodia's defence sector.

NAVY
Personnel: 3000 (Marines included)

Equipment

Category	Name	In Service
Patrol Craft	Stenka class	4
	Koh Chlam class	2
	Zhuk class	2
	Shmel class	2
	T4 class	2
River patrol Craft	Riverine patrol craft	3

New Procurements/ Upgrades
No major procurement plans are under consideration at present.

AIR FORCE
Personnel: 1000

Equipment

Category	Name	In Service
Aircraft	L-39ZA Albatros	
Transport	MA60	1
	An-24	1
	Y-12	2
	A320	1
Helicopter	Mi-17	5
	Mi-8	4
	Mi-26	2
	Harbin Z-9	8
	AS355	1

New Procurements/ Upgrades
No major procurement plans are under consideration at present.

Royal Gendarmerie of Cambodia: The Royal Gendarmerie of Cambodia is a paramilitary unit deployed in all provinces to keep law and order and internal security in Cambodia.

Defence Expenditure

Total defence spending: $600 million (2021 approx.)

Defence spending in terms of GDP: 2.5% of GDP (2020 est.), 2.3% of GDP (2019 est.) The European Union (EU) signed an agreement with the government to provide Cambodia with radiation detection equipment and counterterrorism technology to detect illicit trafficking or criminal use of nuclear and radiological materials at the country's border checkpoints. The deal will see radiation detection equipment and alarm communication systems get installed at the New River Port in Phnom Penh and both Phnom Penh and Siem Reap International Airports.

Defence Production and R&D
Cambodia has some repair facilities for the maintenance of combat vehicles. The nation does not possess any defence industry base for producing equipment.

Defence Procurement
Cambodia has bought 100 tanks and armoured vehicles from Eastern Europe to improve the nation's military capacity.

CONTACT DETAILS
Ministry of National Defence
Jodomim Road is located at
Meas Por Commune
Khan 7 Makara, Phnom Penh
Kingdom of Cambodia
Phone / Fax: +855 (23) 883274
E-mail: generalsec@mod.gov.kh
www.mod.gov.kh

Royal Cambodian Marines embark aboard the amphibious dock landing ship USS Tortuga (LSD 46) in 2010.

CAMEROON
(Capital: Yaounde)

INTRODUCTION
Area: 475,440 sq km
Population: 28,524,175 (July 2021 est.)
Coastline: 402 km
Maritime claims: Territorial sea: 12 nm
Contiguous zone: 24 nm

KEY POLITICAL PERSONS

PRESIDENT & COMMANDER-IN-CHIEF: Paul Biya

PRIME MINISTER: Joseph Dion Ngute

KEY DEFENCE PERSONS

MINISTER DELEGATE AT THE PRESIDENCY IN CHARGE OF DEFENCE: Joseph Beti Assomo

CHIEF OF DEFENCE STAFF: Maj. Gen. Rene Claude Meka

CHIEF OF STAFF OF THE ARMY: Maj. Gen. Baba Souley

CHIEF OF STAFF OF THE NAVY: Rear Adm. Jean Mendoua

CHIEF OF STAFF OF THE AIR FORCE: Brig. Gen. John Calvin Momha

ECONOMY

Cameroon is a lower middle-income country and has one of the best-endowed primary commodity economies in sub-Saharan Africa. Cameroon is endowed with modest oil resources and favourable agricultural conditions alongwith significant natural resources, including oil and gas, high-value timber species, minerals, and agricultural products such as coffee, cotton, cocoa, maize, and cassava. International oil and cocoa prices have a significant impact on the economy. Cameroon continues to seek foreign investment to improve its inadequate infrastructure. Cameroon is currently the

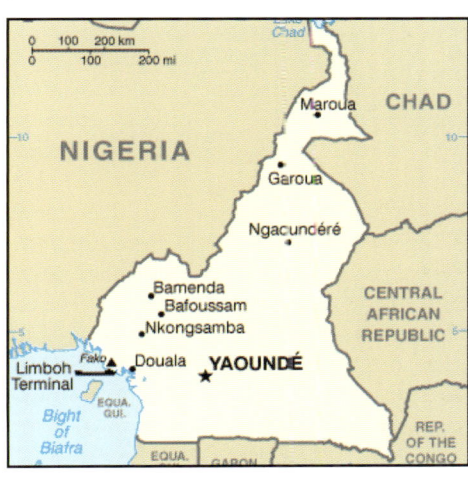

United States' 124th largest goods trading partner with $41 million in total (two way) goods trade during 2016. The IMF has announced a $56 million new disbursement for Cameroon to address the impact of the COVID-19 pandemic. The new emergency disbursement will help Cameroon meet its urgent balance of payments and fiscal needs.

GDP (official exchange rate): $94.94 billion (2020), $94.25 billion (2019 est.)

Real Growth Rate (GDP): 3.5% (2017), 4.6% (2016 est.)

Industries: Petroleum production and refining, aluminum production, food processing, light consumer goods, textiles, lumber, ship repair

Natural gas - proved reserves: 135.1 billion cu m (1 January 2018 est.)

Oil - proved reserves: 200 million bbl (1 January 2018 est.)

Total Exports: $7.73 billion (2019 est.), $7.3 billion (2018 est.)

Export Commodities: Crude petroleum, cocoa beans, lumber, gold, natural gas, bananas (2019)

Major Markets: China 17%, Netherlands 14%, Italy 9%, United Arab Emirates 8%, India 7%, United States 6%, Belgium 6%, Spain 5%, France 5% (2019)

Total Imports: $9.09 billion (2019 est.), $8.42 billion (2018 est.)

Import Commodities: Crude petroleum, scrap vessels, rice, special purpose ships, packaged medicines (2019)

Major Suppliers: China 28%, Nigeria 15%, France 9%, Belgium 6% (2019)

INTERNATIONAL DISPUTES

◆ The Ambazonia Defence Forces (ADF) are a military organisation that fights for the independence of Ambazonia, a self-declared independent state in the Anglophone region of Southern Cameroons, Cameroon. The ADF has been fighting a guerrilla war against the Cameroonian Armed Forces in the Anglophone part of the country since September 2017.

◆ The United States has handed over six peacekeeping security vehicles to the Cameroonian armed forces in order to help combat Boko Haram, a terrorist organisation originating in Nigeria. U.S. security assistance strengthens Cameroon's ability to contain Boko Haram and ISIS-West Africa, assists maritime security in the Gulf of Guinea, contributes to regional stability, strengthens military justice, and protects human rights.

◆ Sovereignty dispute between Equatorial Guinea and Cameroon over an island at the mouth of the Ntem River.

◆ Joint Border Commission with Nigeria reviewed a 2002 ICJ ruling on the entire boundary and bilaterally resolved differences, including a June 2006 Greentree Agreement that immediately ceded sovereignty of the Bakassi Peninsula to Cameroon with a full phase-out of Nigerian control and repatriation of residents in 2008.

◆ Cameroon and Nigeria agreed on maritime delimitation in March 2008.

In 2019, Cameroon experienced a resurgence of terrorist activity in the Far North Region.

DEFENCE

ARMY

Personnel: 25,000

Equipment

Category	Name	In Service
APC/ MICV/ IFV	M-8	10+
	FERRET	5+
	VBL M-11	4
	COMMANDO V-150	30+
	M-3 halftrack	7
Artillery	M101 105 mm	15
	SOLTAM 155 mm	4
	M116	5
MRL	122mm	15+
Anti Tank GW	MILAN	5
	HOT	5

...continued

Category	Name	In Service
AA Gun	Type 63 37 mm	15+
	35 mm twin	15+
	Type 58 14.5 mm	15+

New Procurements/ Upgrades

◆ Russia and Cameroon have signed a defence cooperation agreement aimed at boosting Cameroon's military as it combats Boko Haram militants. Russia will provide military equipment, training of Cameroonian military personnel and humanitarian aid to refugees and internally displaced people affected by the Boko Haram conflict.

◆ China is providing funds to Cameroon for military assistance which will include military equipment, etc.

NAVY

Personnel: 2,000

Equipment

Category	Name	In Service
Patrol Vessel	BAKASSI class (P48S type)	1
	L'AUDACIEUX class missile FAC (P48 type)	1
	ALFRED MOTTO class	1
	Swiftship	15+
	Boston Whaler	3
Auxiliary Craft	LCM	2
	7m RHIB	2

New Procurements/ Upgrades

No major procurement plans are under consideration at present.

AIR FORCE

Personnel: 1000

Equipment

Category	Name	In Service
Combat	Atlas Impala	5+
	MB-326	5
	Dassault/Dornier Alpha Jets	5+
Transport/ Utility	C-130 Hercules	3
	IAI Arava 202	1
	Piper PA-23 Aztec	1
	Gulfstream III	1
	CN-235	1
Training	Humbert Tetras	5+
	Dassault/Dornier Alpha Jets	5+
Helicopter	SA 330 Puma	1
	Alouette II	1
	Mi-17	2
	Bell 206	
	Bell 412	

Cameroon's President in Sept 2018 said that Boko Haram has been defeated in the country, the first such announcement since he declared war on the extremist group four years ago. Cameroon became the first country outside of Nigeria to launch coordinated air strikes against Boko Haram.

New Procurements/ Upgrades

No major procurement plans are under consideration at present.

The Gendarmerie is a paramilitary force composed of about 9,000 soldiers as of 2016. It performs both law enforcement and national security responsibilities across the country.

Defence Expenditure

Total defence spending: $340 million (est.)

Estimated defence spending in terms of GDP: 1% of GDP (2020 est.), 1.1% of GDP (2019)

Foreign Suppliers: India, China, Pakistan and France.

Cameroon's military expenditure is fluctuating in recent years and is on the decline curve in 2017-2018. Cameroon's government has tabled a 2016 budget of 4,200 billion CFA francs (USD 6.9 billion), up 13.5% on last year. Cameroon has increased its defence budget as it attempts to deal with Boko Haram militants carrying out raids in its territory. Cameroon is part of an 8,700-strong task force including troops from Chad, Niger, Nigeria and Benin that has pledged to destroy Boko Haram.

Defence Production and R&D

Cameroon does not undertake any defence production activities.

Defence Procurement

Cameroon Army and Air Force have not done any major procurement in recent years. The Cameroon Navy on the other hand, has modernised and increased its capabilities with the acquisition of a number of small Rodman patrol craft and the retirement of some small older craft.

CONTACT DETAILS

Ministry of Defence

PO Box 1162

Yaoundé, Cameroon

Tel: (+237 2) 222 69 20

(+237 2) 222 19 31

(+237 2) 223 40 45

STRATEGIC INFORMATION
CANADA
(Capital: Ottawa)

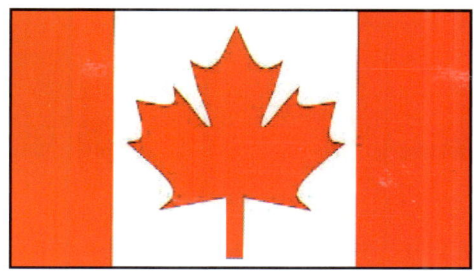

INTRODUCTION

Area: 9,984,670 sq km
Population: 37,943,231 (July 2021 est.)
Coastline: 202,080 km
Maritime claims: Territorial sea: 12 nm
Contiguous zone: 24 nm
Exclusive Economic Zone: 200 nm
Continental shelf: 200 nm or to the edge of the continental margin

GEOPOLITICAL IMPORTANCE

Canada is a North American country consisting of ten provinces and three territories. Located in the northern part of the continent, it extends from the Atlantic Ocean in the East to the Pacific Ocean in the West and northward into the Arctic Ocean. It is the world's second largest country by total area, after Russia. Canada's common border with the United States to the South and northwest is the longest in the world. With the opening of the Arctic Ocean for sea trade Canada forms a part of the Arctic Council and is gradually investing in that region.

POLITICAL OVERVIEW

Canada is a federal state that is governed as a parliamentary democracy and a constitutional monarchy with Queen Elizabeth II as its head of state. The Queen's representative, the Governor General of Canada, carries out most of the federal royal duties in Canada. Canada has three levels of government: federal, provincial or territorial and municipal (city). The Prime Minister heads the federal government based in Ottawa. It deals with national and international matters. A Premier leads each province and territory. The provincial and territorial governments have the power to change their laws and manage their own public lands. Mayors lead municipal governments. Municipal governments run cities, towns or districts (municipalities). Across the country, band councils govern First Nations communities. Band councils are similar to municipal governments. Band members elect the band council, which makes decisions that affect their local community. Parliament has three parts: the Sovereign (Queen or King), the Senate and the House of Commons.

KEY POLITICAL PERSONS

HEAD OF STATE & COMMANDER-IN-CHIEF: Queen Elizabeth II

GOVERNOR GENERAL: Mary May Simon

PRIME MINISTER: Justin Trudeau

ECONOMY

According to the Department of Finance Canada, the Government posted a budgetary deficit of USD14.0 billion for the fiscal year ended March 31, 2019, compared to an estimated deficit of USD14.9 billion in the March 2019 budget. Revenues increased by USD21.0 billion, or 6.7 per cent, from 2017–18. Programme expenses increased by USD14.6 billion, or 4.7 per cent, reflecting increases in all major categories of expenses. Public debt charges were up USD1.4 billion, or 6.3 per cent. Canada's total government net debt-to-GDP ratio continues to be the lowest among the Group of Seven (G7) countries and less than half the G7 average. Canada has a large oil and natural gas sector with the majority of crude oil production. It is also the fourth largest exporter of natural gas. Canada is the largest foreign supplier of oil, natural gas, and electricity for the United States. Canada's economy posted strong growth in 2017 at 3%. Canada has the fourth highest total estimated value of natural resources. Canada is a member of the APEC, NAFTA, G7, G20, OECD and WTO. COVID-19 has deeply impacted the economy of Canada in 2020 and led the country towards recession though it is slowing gearing back to normalising the economic activity with fiscal stimulus, around the country. Canada's tourism and air travel sectors are the worst hit.

GDP (official exchange rate): USD1.742 trillion (2020 est.), USD1.842 trillion (2019 est.)

Real Growth Rate (GDP): 1.66% (2019 est.), 2.02% (2018 est.)

Industries: Transportation equipment, chemicals, processed and unprocessed minerals, food products, wood and paper products, fish products, petroleum, natural gas

Oil - proved reserves: 170.5 billion bbl (1 January 2018 est.)

Natural gas - proved reserves: 2.056 trillion cu m (1 January 2018 est.)

Total Exports: $477.31 billion (2020 est.), $555.83 billion (2019 est.)

Export Commodities: Crude petroleum, cars and vehicle parts, gold, refined petroleum, natural gas (2019)

Major Markets: US 73% (2019)

Total Imports: $510.29 billion (2020 est.), $583.6 billion (2019 est.)

Import Commodities: Cars and vehicle parts, delivery trucks, crude petroleum, refined petroleum (2019)

Major Suppliers: US 57%, China 11%, Mexico 5% (2019)

DEFENCE & SECURITY

The Department of National Defence (DND) is the department within the government of Canada with responsibility for all matters concerning the defence of Canada. In addition to the civilian components of the department, this also includes Canada's military, known as the Canadian Forces. DND is led by the Minister of National Defence and is headquartered at National Defence Headquarters (NDHQ) in Ottawa. The Canadian Forces (CF) are the unified armed forces of Canada and consists of the sea, land, and air environmental commands called the: Royal Canadian Navy (RCN), Canadian Army, and Royal Canadian Air Force (RCAF), which together are overseen by the Armed Forces Council, chaired by the Chief of the Defence Staff.

The Commander-in-Chief is the Canadian monarch, Elizabeth II, represented by the governor general. Canada's First Defence Strategy is to increase personnel levels to 70,000 active and 30,000 reserves sometime in the next 20 years. The Canada First Defence Strategy (CFDS) entails military recruitment, procurement and improvement strategy of the Canadian government to enhance the overall effectiveness of the Canadian Forces. The strategy also aims to enforce Arctic sovereignty with the Royal Canadian Mounted Police and the Canadian Coast Guard. The purpose of the Canada First Defence Strategy is to give Canada a modern military with clearly defined missions and capabilities. The strategy focuses on many key military functions and operations and on improving the equipment and fleets that the Canadian Forces operates. The Canadian Armed Forces (CAF) has personnel deployed across Canada and around the world, with approximately 2000 personnel deployed on more than 20 different operations.

KEY DEFENCE PERSONS

MINISTER OF DEFENCE:
Anita Anand

CHIEF OF THE DEFENCE STAFF:
Gen. Wayne D. Eyre

COMMANDER OF THE ARMY:
Maj. Gen. M.H. St-Louis (Acting)

COMMANDER OF THE NAVY: Vice Adm. C.A. Baines

COMMANDER OF THE AIR FORCE: Lt. Gen. A.D. Meinzinger

COMMANDER FOR JOINT OPERATIONS COMMAND:
Vice Adm. Bob Auchterlonie

Internal Conflict

Terrorism: Terrorism in Canada primarily consists of fundraising for terrorist attacks outside of the country. It includes fundraising, lobbying through front organisations, providing support for terrorist operations, procuring weapons and material, coercing and manipulating immigrant communities in Canada, facilitating transit to and from the US and other countries, and other illegal activities. According to the Department of Public Safety and Emergency Preparedness, Canada's terrorist threat environment remains stable. The principal terrorist threat to Canada continues to stem from individuals or groups who are inspired by violent ideologies and terrorist groups, such as Daesh or al-Qaida (AQ). Canada also remains concerned about threats posed by those who harbour right-wing extremist views and individuals who support terrorist groups.

External Conflict

◆ Canada has managed maritime boundary disputes with the US at Dixon Entrance, Beaufort Sea, Strait of Juan de Fuca, and the Gulf of Maine, including the disputed Machias Seal Island and North Rock.

◆ Canada and the United States dispute regarding the division of the Beaufort Sea and the status of the Northwest Passage is being resolved deliberately and both are cooperating on the survey of Arctic continental self.

◆ US works closely with Canada to intensify security measures for monitoring and controlling legal and illegal movement of people, transport, and commodities across the international border.

◆ Sovereignty dispute with Denmark over Hans Island in the Kennedy Channel between Ellesmere Island and Greenland.

◆ Commencing the collection of technical evidence for submission to the Commission on the Limits of the Continental Shelf in support of claims for continental shelf beyond 200 nautical miles from its declared baselines in the Arctic, as stipulated in Article 76, paragraph 8, of the United Nations Convention on the Law of the Sea.

War on Terrorism: Canada joined the United States in the war on terror after the attacks on the World Trade Centre and Pentagon. Adopted by Canada's Parliament following the attacks of September 11, 2001, the Anti-Terrorism Act (ATA) amended the Criminal Code, the Official Secrets Act, the Canada Evidence Act, the Proceeds of Crime (Money Laundering) Act and a number of other Acts. It also enacted the Charities Registration (Security Information) Act. It was not a stand-alone Act, but rather an amending statute, as per Canada's Dept. of Justice. Amendments came in the form of Bill S-7, the Combating Terrorism Act, 2012 and Bill C-51, the Anti-Terrorism Act, 2015.

Afghanistan War: Canada's goal is to help Afghans rebuild Afghanistan into a viable country that is better governed, more stable and secure, and never again a safe haven for terrorists. Canadians have assisted in improving security, diplomacy, human rights and development. After 11 September 2001 attacks, Canada announced that it will contribute air, land and sea forces to Operation Enduring Freedom. In 2011, Canada terminated its combat mission in Kandahar province. Further on 15 December 2011, the last troops returned to Canada from Kandahar after completing the military operations in Kandahar Province as part of Mission Transition Task Force (MTTF). Canada's participation is in the NATO Training Mission–Afghanistan (NTM-A), which delivers training and professional development support to the national security forces of Afghanistan: the Afghan National Army (ANA), the Afghan Air Force (AAF), and the Afghan National Police (ANP). The last few soldiers left Afghanistan in 2014, ending Canada's military presence in the country.

Iraq War: Canada did not join the invading coalition, but still participated in the conflict in Iraq, joining a number of non-belligerent nations in helping to rebuild the country post-invasion. This included the training of Iraqi police and army officers. Canadian Special Forces troops in northern Iraq were involved in several with Islamic State extremists. In 2015, Prime Minister Justin Trudeau announced the withdrawal of Canada's fighter aircraft from the fight against ISIL, but their surveillance and transport and refuelling aircraft would remain in the area. In 2016, Canada announced a strategy to respond to the crises in Iraq and Syria and their impact on the region. Canada is committing more than USD2 billion over three years toward security, stabilization, and humanitarian and development assistance, a significant portion of which is focused on Iraq. For the period 2016 to 2019, Canada has committed over USD265 million in assistance projects to Iraq, as per Govt. of Canada website.

NATO: Canada was a founding member of the Alliance and has remained as a member since its inception. NATO is a major contributor to international peace and security and is the cornerstone of Canadian security and defence policy. The Canadian

Armed Forces are among the most engaged, agile, deployable and responsive armed forces within NATO. Canada has contributed to every NATO operation. Canadian troops have been involved in NATO-led mission in Afghanistan, ISAF. The Canadian Forces have also participated in NATO-led missions in Libya and Syria.

THREAT PERSPECTIVE

Although Canada has not often been targeted specifically for a terrorist attack, it is vulnerable to terrorism. Graduates of terrorist training camps in countries such as Afghanistan and Pakistan reside in Canada or continue to seek access to Canada. To effectively combat terrorist activities, enhanced participation in joint initiatives and the sharing of information have become critical. Also crucial is the growing collaboration between agencies that seek to prevent attacks and those seeking evidence to support prosecution. Canada's National Terrorism Threat Level (NTTL) is a tool that government officials, including law enforcement agencies, may use to identify risks and vulnerabilities from threats, and in turn determine what responses may be needed to prevent or mitigate a violent act of terrorism in Canada. It also helps ensure a common understanding of the general terrorist threat to Canada. The Kanishka Project provides research on terrorism-related issues affecting Canada, such as preventing and countering violent extremism.

STRATEGIC RELATIONS

United States: Canada and the United States are currently the world's largest trading partners, share the world's longest border, and have significant interoperability within the defence sphere. American defence arrangements with Canada are more extensive than with any other country. The Permanent Joint Board of Defence, established in 1940, provides policy-level consultation on bilateral defence matters. US defence arrangements with Canada are more extensive than with any other country. The United States and Canada share North Atlantic Treaty Organisation (NATO) mutual security commitments, and US and Canadian military forces cooperate on continental defence within the framework of the binational North American Aerospace Defence Command (NORAD). Canada has been involved in international responses to the threats from Daesh/ISIS/ISIL in Syria and Iraq, and is a member of the Global Coalition to Counter Daesh. Canada is the second-largest trading partner of the United States. The United States-Mexico-Canada Agreement (USMCA) entered into force on July 1, 2020, replacing NAFTA as the free trade agreement for North America. The United States is Canada's largest foreign investor by far. The United States provides no foreign assistance to Canada. Both have one of the world's largest investment relationships.

India: Indo-Canadian relations are the longstanding bilateral relations between India and Canada. Being fellow members of the Commonwealth of Nations, Canada and India share high commissioners rather than ambassadors. Canada and India maintain a dialogue on regional security and global strategic issues of common interest through the annual Canada-India Strategic Dialogue and through regular meetings of the Canada-India Joint Working Group on Counter-Terrorism, as well as annual Foreign Policy Consultations. Canada and India maintain a bilateral dialogue on anti-terrorism, including an annual meeting of the Canada-India Strategic Dialogue, as well as regular meetings of the aforementioned Canada-India Working Group on Counter-Terrorism. India and Canada are working together to enhance defence cooperation in fields of counter terrorism, cold climate warfare, peace keeping and naval cooperation. India is Canada's 9th largest export market, and 10th largest trading partner. Canadian investment in India has been in telecommunications, environment, energy and mining. Indian investment in Canada is in the information technology, software and natural resources sectors.

Japan: Canada and Japan are partners in numerous international groups and organizations including the G7, G20, Asia-Pacific Economic Cooperation, the Comprehensive and Progressive Agreement for Trans-Pacific Partnership, Asian Development Bank, International Monetary Fund, Association of Southeast Asian Nations and Organisation for Economic Co-operation and Development. Japan and Canada have been in good relations and have frequent high-level exchanges. Japan and Canada have been cooperating in many fields. The Japan-Canada/ Canada Japan Inter-Parliamentary Friendship Group meets every year. Talks between the two governments include peace and security, housing, fisheries, finance, and telecommunications.

Multilateral Alliances: Canada is a member of the United Nations, NATO, WTO, G7, G20, Organisation for Security and Cooperation in Europe, Organisation for Economic Cooperation and Development, Organisation of American States, and Asia-Pacific Economic Cooperation forum.

DEFENCE CAPABILITIES

ARMY: The Canadian Army is the land component of the combined Canadian Forces. Canada's Army is the largest section of the Canadian Forces. The Regular Force has three Mechanized Brigade Groups composed of units stationed in Western Canada, Ontario, Quebec and Atlantic Canada. The Army is equipped with the latest in modern weapons.

Major Army bases: Edmonton, Alberta; Shilo, Manitoba; Petawawa, Ontario; Kingston, Ontario; Montreal, Quebec; Valcartier, Quebec; Gagetown, New Brunswick and numerous training facilities.

Personnel: 23,000

Equipment

Category	Name	In Service
MBT	Leopard 2A4/2A4M	50+
	Leopard 2A6M	15+
APC/IFV	M113A3/MTVL	100+
	Cougar	30+
	Husky (Mine Cleaning)	4
	LAV 6.0	500+
	TLAV	
	Coyote Reconnaissance Vehicle	50+
	Buffalo A2 (Mine cleaning)	10
	Bison	175+
Artillery	105 mm LG1 Mark II	20
	105 mm C3 Close Support Gun	90
	155 mm M777 Ultra Light Howitzer	30+
	81 mm L16	
Anti-Tank GW	BGM-71 TOW with ITAS	30+
	Spike	
Recoilless rifle	Carl Gustav M2 & M3	
SAM	ADAT	withdrawn
UAV	RQ-21 Blackjack	6
	IAI Heron	
	RQ-11 Raven	
UGV	Telerob Explosive Ordnance Disposal and observation robot, Multiagent tactical sentry, Remotely Operated Mechanical Explosive Clearance System	

New Procurements/ Upgrades

◆ Newcon Optik has been awarded Department of National Defence (DND) supply contract for its state-of-the-art handheld LRM 3500M laser rangefinder monocular. The initial delivery of rangefinders will provide FOO/JTACs with advanced mission capability requirements and will serve as an additional sensor platform for

Canada's Integrated Soldier System Suite.

◆ General Dynamics Mission Systems-Canada announced that it was awarded three contracts - valued at USD621.5 million - by the Government of Canada to support the Land Command, Control, Communications, Computers, Intelligence, Surveillance and Reconnaissance (C4ISR) system for the Canadian Army. The three contracts include: Engineering and Integration, Software Support and Cyber Security Engineering Support.

◆ Kongsberg Defence & Aerospace has signed a contract with General Dynamics Land Systems - Canada for delivery of the PROTECTOR Remote Weapon Stations (RWS) to the Canadian Army valued 500 MNOK.

◆ The US State Department has approved a possible Foreign Military Sale to Canada of 152 MIDS-JTRS (5) with support for an estimated cost of USD44 million.

NAVY: The Royal Canadian Navy (RCN) is the naval force of Canada. The Canadian Navy fleet has destroyers, frigates, replenishment ships submarines and maritime coastal defence vessels, plus auxiliary and support vessels. Canada's warships, submarines, and coastal defence vessels are divided more or less evenly between the Atlantic and Pacific coasts. They serve a number of roles; from major international operations, sovereignty operations and patrols, to single ship support of multinational deployments. The Naval Reserve, headquartered in Québec City, is made up of 24 Naval Reserve Divisions located across Canada. The Royal Canadian Navy's Atlantic Fleet is known as Maritime Forces Atlantic (MARLANT). The Royal Canadian Navy's Pacific Fleet is known as Maritime Forces Pacific or MARPAC.

Personnel: 12,000

Equipment

Category	Name	In Service
Destroyer	Iroquois Class DDG	retired
Submarine	Victoria Class	4
Frigate	Halifax Class FFG	12
Patrol Vessel	Kingston Class	12
Training vessel	Orca Class	8
Auxiliary ship	Queenston class	(2-3 Planned)
	Harry DeWolf-class OPV	6 (Planned)
Weapon	Mk 141 Harpoon (SSM), Mk 41(GMVLS), Phalanx 20mm (CIWS), Mk 32 Torpedo, Bofors SAK 57 mm	

Naval Aviation

Category	Name	In Service
Helicopter	CH-124 SeaKing (ASW)	Retired

New Procurements/ Upgrades

◆ The US State Department has approved a possible Foreign Military Sale to the Government of Canada of AEGIS Combat System and related equipment for an estimated cost of USD1.7 billion.

◆ The Government of Canada has awarded a performance-based contract to Seaspan's Vancouver Shipyards for the full construction of two joint support ships (JSS). Valued at USD2.4 billion (including taxes), this contract will allow the transition to full-rate construction of the first ship.

◆ The Government of Canada and Irving Shipbuilding Inc. have identified Lockheed Martin Canada Inc. as the preferred bidder to provide the design and design team for the Royal Canadian Navy's future Canadian Surface Combatants.

◆ The US State Department has approved a possible Foreign Military Sale to Canada of 425 MK 54 lightweight torpedoes with support for an estimated cost of USD387 million.

◆ The Royal Canadian Navy's second Arctic and Offshore Patrol Ship (AOPS), the future HMCS Margaret Brooke, was launched on Nov. 10, 2019, at Halifax Shipyard. The launch of the second of six AOPS for the Royal Canadian Navy marks a significant milestone for Canada's National Shipbuilding Strategy (NSS) and the revitalization of the Royal Canadian Navy's combatant fleet. The future HMCS Margaret Brooke joins Canada's lead AOPS, the future HMCS Harry DeWolf, pier side at Halifax Shipyard.

◆ QinetiQ has been awarded a CUSD51m (c£30m) contract to deliver unmanned aircraft systems (UAS) that will drive enhanced situational awareness for the Canadian Armed Forces. The contract will be delivered from QinetiQ's state-of-the-art unmanned vehicle manufacturing and operational facilities in Medicine Hat, Alberta. The system, based on the UMS SKELDAR V-200 UAS, will be equipped with a number of sensors including an Active Electronically Scanned Array (AESA) radar and Electro-optic infrared (EO/IR) camera.

◆ Irving Shipbuilding has successfully delivered the HMCS Harry DeWolf to the Royal Canadian Navy, the first Arctic and Offshore Patrol Ship (AOPS) built under Canada's National Shipbuilding Strategy. Thales delivered innovative in-service support for new AOPS vessel in partnership with Royal Canadian Navy.

AIR FORCE: The Royal Canadian Air Force (RCAF) is responsible for all aircraft operations in the Canadian Forces, enforcing the security of Canada's airspace and providing aircraft to support the missions of Royal Canadian Navy and Canadian Army. The RCAF is a partner with the United States Air Force in protecting continental airspace under the North American Aerospace Defence Command (NORAD). The RCAF also provides all primary air resources to the National Search and Rescue Programme.

Personnel: 12,000

Equipment

Category	Name	In Service
Fighters/ attack/ Reconnaissance	CF-188 Hornet	70+
Transport	BE-350 King Air	
	CC-130J Hercules	
	CC-138 Twin Otter	
	CC-144 Challenger	
	CC-150 Polaris	
	CC-177 Globemaster III	
Helicopter	CH-124A Sea King	20
	CH-146 Griffon	70
	CH-149 Cormorant	10+
	CH-147F Chinook	5
Trainer	Bell 412CF	
	C-90B King Air	
	CH-139 Jet Ranger	
	CT-142 Dash-8	
	CT-155 Hawk	
	CT-156 Harvard II	
	Grob-G120A	
Maritime Patrol	CH-148 Cyclone	
	CP-140 Aurora	
Missile	AGM-65G Maverick (AGM), AIM-120 (AAM), AIM-9 (AAM), AIM-7 (AAM)	
UAV	Elbit Skylark, IAI Heron, RQ-20PUMA, Insitu ScanEagle	

New Procurements/ Upgrades

◆ The US State Department has approved a possible Foreign Military Sale to the Government of Canada of C-17 Sustainment and related equipment for an estimated cost of USD275 million.

◆ The US State Department has approved a possible Foreign Military Sale to the Government of Canada of 50 Sidewinder AIM-9X Block II Tactical missiles and related equipment for an estimated cost of USD862.3 million.

◆ Saab, Lockheed Martin and Boeing

have submitted bids to the Government of Canada for advanced fighter aircraft contract to replace the Royal Canadian Air Force's existing fleet of CF-18 fighters. The Future Fighter Capability Project (FFCP) plans to procure 88 advanced jets, associated equipment and weapons, with set-up of training and sustainment services.

◆ The US State Department has approved a possible Foreign Military Sale to Canada of three King Air 350ER (extended range) aircraft with customer unique post-modifications for Intelligence, Surveillance and Reconnaissance (ISR) operations for an estimated cost of USD 300 million.

◆ The US State Department has approved a possible Foreign Military Sale to Canada for AIM-120D Advanced Medium Range Air-to-Air Missiles (AMRAAM) for an estimated cost of USD 140 million.

◆ Contract with Australian Govt. to receive 18 F-18 fighter jets and associated spare parts from the Royal Australian Air Force.

◆ The US State Department has approved a possible Foreign Military Sale to Canada of 152 MIDS-JTRS (5) with support for an estimated cost of USD44 million. Also included are spare cables and MIDS batteries; Link-16 mobile racks; diagnostic support tools; technical documentation; training and engineering technical support; and other related elements of logistics and programme support.

◆ Minister of National Defence, Canada announced a USD9.2-million contract award to EllisDon Construction Services Inc., of Edmonton, Alta., for the design of a new fighter jet facility at 4 Wing Cold Lake, one of two main operating bases for Canada's future fighter aircraft. A second facility and contract award is also planned for 3 Wing Bagotville. Combined, this infrastructure will support the long-term maintenance and operation of 88 new aircraft being procured for the Royal Canadian Air Force (RCAF) through the Future Fighter Capability Project (FFCP).

◆ The US State Department has approved a possible Foreign Military Sale to the Government of Canada of Standard Missile 2 (SM-2) Block IIIC missiles and related equipment for an estimated cost of USD500 million.

Major Armaments Producers L-3 Communications MAS, CAE Meggitt Training Systems Canada, Colt Canada, Textron Systems Canada, Kongsberg Protech Systems, Canada, Rheinmetall Defence Canada, Irving Shipbuilding Inc., General Dynamics Land Systems Canada, Raytheon Canada Limited, Seaspan Marine Corporation, Thales Canada, Boeing Canada

Defence Production and R&D

Canada's defence industry develops, maintains, and produces a range of equipment, including aircraft, combat vehicles, naval vessels, and associated components. Defence Research and Development Canada (DRDC) is an agency of the Canadian Department of National Defence that responds to the scientific and technological needs of the Canadian Forces. Defence R&D Canada has an annual budget of USD 350 million. DRDC is organised around nine research centres located across the country with headquarters in Ottawa. Each research centre focuses on a particular set of scientific and operational requirements. DRDC supports innovation and S&T as an engine for generating solutions. DRDC accesses knowledge, builds networks and leverages capacity across a broad range of partners, nationally and internationally creating innovative partnerships for new solutions to challenging problems.

General Dynamics Canada has been awarded a contract to develop and demonstrate an automated computer-network defence capability to enhance the security of the Canadian Department of National Defence's (DND) networks. The ARMOUR project, conceptualised by Defence Research and Development Canada (DRDC), will develop and integrate advanced scientific and technological solutions to the increasingly challenging and complex problem of defending DND networks, protecting their mission-critical information. ARMOUR will integrate leading-edge network cyber assessment tools to proactively deal with cyber vulnerabilities and mitigate attacks in real time, as well as automatically generate optimised courses of action for potential future threats. Demonstrations will be used to validate the functionality of the resulting system.

DEFENCE DEALS

Arms Export

A key priority of Canada's foreign policy is the maintenance of peace and security. The Government of Canada guarantees that Canadian military exports are not prejudicial to peace, security or stability in any region of the world or within any country. Canadian Arms Sales are governed by the country's Export and Imports Permits Act. Sales with the United States are also specifically regulated by the 1959 Defence Production Sharing Arrangement. Canada jumped from fifteenth to twelfth largest exporter of military hardware in the world. The country exports to several governments engaged in human rights violations, like the Philippines, Israel, Saudi Arabia, China, Libya and Tunisia. Between 2006 and 2009 Canada exported some USD 1.4 billion worth of military gear, according to the Report on the Export of Military Goods from Canada for 2007-2009, published by the Department of Foreign Affairs. Canada has become the world's second-largest exporter of defence equipment to the Middle East after United States.

DEFENCE BUDGET

Total defence spending: USD 23 billion (2021 est.)

Estimated defence spending in terms of GDP: 1.42% of GDP (2020 est.), 1.29% of GDP (2019)

Canada stands as the 14th largest spenders in the NATO group. After the release in 2017 of the Strong, Secure, Engaged (SSE) Defence Policy, the Department of National Defence (DND), Canada released its 2018 Defence Investment Plan. The document identifies projects and outlines projected capital spending of USD82.5 billion on an accrual basis (USD 126 billion on a cash basis,) operating expenditures of USD 218.9 billion, and sustainment costs of USD 81.3 billion over a 20-year period. Further, DND projects annual cash defence spending to grow from USD 14.5 billion in 2016-17 to USD 25.2 billion in 2026-27, with a total defence spending projected to reach USD 426.7 billion in 2038 (on a cash basis). DND has increased its spending authority, allowing the department to contract projects valued up to USUSD3.9 million without the need to go through Public Services and Procurement Canada, as per Export.Gov of US Department of Commerce and Canada's Strong, Secure and Engaged (SSE) Defence Policy document.

Budgetary planning summary for Core Responsibilities and Internal Services (dollars)

Core Responsibilities and Internal Services	2021–22 Planned spending	2022-23 Planned Spending
Operations	684,035,922	688,988,747
Ready Forces	9,972,852,765	10,096,532,908
Defence Team	3,554,626,936	3,591,485,901
Future Force Design	768,019,319	779,337,759
Procurement of Capabilities	4,741,325,826	4,310,164,815
Sustainable Bases, Information Technology Systems and Infrastructure	3,829,653,614	3,899,491,700

...continued

Sub-Total	23,550,574,382	23,366,001,830
Internal Services	744,630,785	761,153,272
Total	24,295,205,167	24,127,155,102

Core Responsibilities and Internal Services	2022–23 Planned spending
Operations	703,688,999
Ready Forces	10,296,558,574
Defence Team	3,681,978,625
Future Force Design	795,850,417
Procurement of Capabilities	3,538,411,344
Sustainable Bases, Information Technology Systems and Infrastructure	3,952,624,573
Sub-Total	22,969,112,532
Internal Services	781,495,899
Total	23,750,608,431

(Source: Vice-Chief of the Defence Staff Group / Assistant Deputy Minister (Finance) / Chief Financial Officer Group (CFO). Department of National Defence and Canadian Armed Forces 2021-22 Departmental Plan)

Year	USD (Millions)
2014	18,172
2015	18,689
2016	17,708
2017	23,700
2018	22,399
2019*	22,572
2020*	23,595
2021*	26,523

(*Figures for 2020 and 2021 are estimates.)
Source: Defence Expenditure of NATO Countries (2014-2021), NATO Press Release.

Defence Procurement

The activities of the Canadian Forces and the Department of National Defence (DND), like those of every other federal government organisation, are carried out within a framework of legislation that is approved and overseen by Parliament. The Canadian Forces and the Department of National Defence have complementary roles to play in providing advice and support to the Minister of National Defence and in implementing the decisions of the Government on the defence of Canada and of Canadian interests at home and abroad. In broad terms:

◆ The Deputy Minister has responsibility for policy, resources, interdepartmental coordination and international defence relations; and

◆ The Chief of the Defence Staff has responsibility for command, control and administration of the Canadian Forces and military strategy, plans and requirements.

The Government of Canada is delivering on its Canada First commitment to strengthen Canada's multi-role, combat-capable defence force. The Department of National Defence is purchasing equipment and related support services for the Canadian Forces. Effective defence procurement is vital to ensuring the CAF is equipped and ready to fulfill the important missions required to protect and defend Canada and Canadians. Procurement and contracting require significant planning and management to ensure goods and services are acquired and supported in a responsible manner. The Defence Team will reinvest in core capabilities and invest in new areas that will allow the CAF to succeed in meeting Canada's defence needs.

Key equipment acquisition projects in FY 2021-22 include: Manned airborne intelligence, surveillance and reconnaissance; Canadian Surface Combatant; Arctic and Offshore Patrol Ship; Joint Support Ship; Fixed-wing Search and Rescue Aircraft Replacement Project; Future Fighter Capability Project; Remotely Piloted Aircraft System; Strategic Tanker Transport Capability; Logistics Vehicle Modernisation; Armoured Combat Support Vehicle; CP-140 Aurora Incremental Modernisation Project; Interim Fighter Capability Project; Hornet Extension Project; CH-148 Cyclone Project; and Victoria-class Modernisation.

CONCLUSION

A strong and modern military, designed specifically to meet Canada's security and foreign policy needs, serves Canada's pride and Canada's interests. Defending Canadians from threats to their safety and well-being is a critical role for government. To deliver on this core responsibility, the Government commits itself to rebuild the Canadian Forces into a first-class, modern military. Canadian defence policy today is based on the Canada First Defence Strategy. Based on that strategy, the Canadian military is oriented and being equipped to carry out six core missions within Canada, in North America and globally. Canada needs and benefits from combat-capable maritime, land and air forces able to fulfil a broad range of missions and tasks. While Canada faces no direct conventional military threat, there remain direct and indirect threats to the national security which includes drugs, organised crime, illegal immigration, terrorism and the uncertainty caused by the growing proliferation of missiles carrying weapons of mass destruction, according to Canadian Forces. The force development plans and mission projections for the Canadian Forces (CF) and the ongoing Revolution in Military Affairs (RMA) have far-reaching implications for the future role of Canada's Military Intelligence also. Till now, approximately 41,000 Canadian forces personnel have served in the Afghanistan mission; USD 7.5 billion have been spent on combat operations. Since the Korean War, it was the forces' first combat experience. These experiences in Afghanistan and in other operations, such as counter-piracy missions off the Horn of Africa, have had an important impact on the armed forces. The Canadian Armed Forces conducts training and presence operations while seeking to improve mobility and enhance surveillance capabilities in Canada's North. The Canadian Forces are a vital instrument of national defence and sovereignty and a key implement for the achievement of Canadian national goals at home and abroad. Canadian government is tasked to ensure that Canada's military forces are well-funded, equipped to the highest standards, and recruited and trained to fight alongside the best, against the best. The Canadian Joint Operations Command (CJOC) conducts operations at home, across North America, and around the world. A changed security environment demands that the Canadian Armed Forces enhances its ability to operate in the Arctic region.

CONTACT DETAILS
Department of National Defence
Maj. Gen. George R. Pearkes Bldg
101 Colonel By drive
Ottawa, Ontario K1A 0K2, Canada
Tel: +1-613-995-2534
Fax: +1-613-992-4739
www.forces.gc.ca
(Government Procurement Agency)
Public Works & Government Services Canada
16A1, 102 Corporate Communications, Portage III
E-mail: questions@pwgsc.gc.ca
Tel: +1-800-622-6232-1
Defence Research and Development Canada
www.drdc-rddc.gc.ca
Partnering with Defence R&D Canada
corp.bdo-bda@drdc-rddc.gc.ca
Defence R&D Canada Contacts Abroad
Canadian Defence Liaison Staff (Washington)
wshdc-outpack@dfait-maeci.gc.ca
Canadian Defence Liaison Staff (London)
ldn@dfait-maeci.gc.ca
Canadian Defence Liaison Staff (Paris)
paris@dfait-maeci.gc.ca

STRATEGIC INFORMATION
CHILE
(Capital: Santiago)

INTRODUCTION

Area: 756,102 sq km
Population: 18,307,925 (July 2021 est.)
Coastline: 6,435 km
Maritime claims: Territorial sea: 12 nm
Contiguous zone: 24 nm
Exclusive Economic Zone: 200 nm
Continental shelf: 200/350 nm

GEOPOLITICAL IMPORTANCE

Chile is one of South America's most stable and prosperous nations recognised as an emerging economy and a key regional player. The country lies on a long, narrow strip of land between the Andes Mountains to the East and the Pacific Ocean to the West. To the North is the Atacama Desert, the driest desert in the world, and to the South are the ice-fields and glaciers of Chilean Patagonia. Chile shares frontiers with Argentina, Peru and Bolivia. Its distinctive shape – 4,300 kilometres long and on average 175 kilometres wide – makes it the longest country in the world, North to South, with the fifth lengthiest coastline at over 78 thousand kilometres. Its territory includes the Pacific Islands of Juan Fernández, Salas y Gómez, Desventuradas, and Easter Island in Oceania. Chile belongs to a number of organisations, including the United Nations, Organisation of American States, Community of Democracies, Asia-Pacific Economic Cooperation forum, Organisation for Economic Cooperation and Development, International Monetary Fund, World Bank, and World Trade Organisation. Chile is also a member of the Pacific Alliance, Union of South American Nations (UNASUR), and Community of Latin American and Caribbean States (CELAC).

POLITICAL OVERVIEW

Chile is a republic with Executive, Legislative and Judicial branches. The executive branch consists of the president and the legislative branch. The president is both head of state and head of government. The president appoints the cabinet and he has the authority to remove the commander-in-chief of the armed forces. The president who is elected by popular vote for a single four-year term cannot run for office for two consecutive terms. The Legislative power is vested in both the government and the two chambers of the National Congress. The parliament or the national congress consists of a Senate – the Upper House with its 50 members to serve eight-year terms and the Chamber of Deputies – the lower house with 155 members to serve for four-years. The Judicial branch consists of the Constitutional Tribunal, the Supreme Court, the Court of Appeals and Military courts. The judiciary is independent of the executive and the legislature of Chile. Chile eliminated the binomial electoral system through its 2015 electoral reforms, shifting the electoral format toward proportional representation giving smaller political parties better opportunity of winning seats in the National Congress without having to join one of the two major political parties in the country.

KEY POLITICAL PERSONS

PRESIDENT:
Gabriel Boric

MINISTER OF FOREIGN AFFAIRS:
Roberto Ampuero Espinoza

ECONOMY

Chile has a market-oriented economy characterized by a high level of foreign trade. Exports of goods account for approximately one-third of GDP, with commodities making up some 60% of total exports. Copper is Chile's top export and provides 20% of government revenue. The service sector has reportedly grown fast and consistently due to the rapid development of communication and information technology also non-mining activities, particularly wholesale trade, commercial services and manufacturing. According to reports, violent protests late in 2019 to early 2020 with calls for the State to broaden the social safety net, has had a negative impact on economic growth. The

GDP growth had fallen by 1.9% in 2014 and 2.1% in 2015, as a result of the slowdown in the mining sector and the decline in copper prices and private consumption followed by the COVID-19 pandemic which further plunged the economy into the worst recession in decades. GDP contracted 6.0 percent in 2020, according to the World Bank. The Chilean economy is expected to fare better than expected in 2021. Chile is the first in Latin America to join the Organisation for Economic Cooperation and Development (OECD). It has 26 trade agreements covering 60 countries including agreements with the EU, Mercosur, China, India, South Korea, and Mexico.

GDP (official exchange rate): $282.655 billion (2019 est.)

Real Growth Rate (GDP): 1.03% (2019 est.), 4% (2018 est.)

Industries: Copper, lithium, other minerals, foodstuffs, fish processing, iron and steel, wood and wood products, transport equipment, cement, textiles.

Total Exports: $79.8 billion (2020 est.), $78.02 billion (2019 est.)

Export Commodities: Copper, wood pulp, fish fillets, pitted fruits, wine (2019)

Major Markets: China 32%, United States

14%, Japan 9%, South Korea 7% (2019)

Total Imports: $66.43 billion (2020 est.), $80.17 billion (2019 est.)

Import Commodities: Refined petroleum, crude petroleum, cars, broadcasting equipment, delivery trucks (2019)

Major Suppliers: China 24%, United States 20%, Brazil 8%, Germany 5%, Argentina 5% (2019)

DEFENCE & SECURITY

The main objectives of the well-equipped military of Chile is to secure the country from external threats; protect the country against terrorism, drug traffickers, and organised crime; and to provide quick and effective responses to natural disasters. Chile collaborates with the United States on security issues related to drug trafficking, with Bolivia in counter-narcotics operations on their shared border and it has a joint military force with Argentina trained in humanitarian work. Besides joining international humanitarian and peacekeeping operations, such as the UN mission in Haiti, Chile has signed other defence bilateral and multilateral defence agreements worldwide. Security problems such as drug trafficking, organised crime and piracy has been brought under the broad umbrella of national defence in the National Defence and Security Strategy (ENSYD) released by the government. The Carabineros and Policia de Investigaciones have been tasked with safeguarding internal security. The Carabineros, although a part of the armed forces, has now come under the Ministry of the Interior Ministerio del Interior from the Ministry of Defence Ministerio de Defensa Nacional.

KEY DEFENCE PERSONS

DEFENCE MINISTER: Baldo Prokurica

CHIEF OF THE JOINT CHIEFS OF STAFF: Vice Admiral Rodrigo Alvarez Aguirre

CHIEF OF ARMY: Gen. Ricardo Martinez Menanteau

CHIEF OF NAVY: Admiral Julio Leiva Molina

CHIEF OF AIR FORCE: Lt. Gen. Arturo Merino Nunez

Internal Conflict

For hundreds of years the indigenous Mapuche people have occupied southern regions of South America as their ancestral land. The Mapuche people in Chile have been fighting for the restoration of their ancestral lands for centuries. They have demanded the return of their ancestral territory, jurisdictional autonomy and cultural identity. The Mapuche have waged violent campaigns to win back their land. Protests have ranged from marches, hunger strikes and the occupation of public buildings to the setting up of road blocks, the occupation of disputed land, arson and the sabotage of machinery and equipment. Mapuche activists have continued to stepped up their attacks also targeting agricultural or forestry companies. The Coordinadora Arauco-Malleco (CAM) formed in 1998 is an organisation of the Mapuche people dedicated to the recovery of former Mapuche lands. Vast swathes of Mapuche territory were reportedly handed to wealthy business families. Following Chile's return to democracy, the government said it would hand back some of the land to the Mapuche but progress has been minimal. President Sebastian Pinera, who returned to power in 2017, has vowed to prioritise solving the centuries-old conflict with the Mapuche.

External Conflict

Chile and Peru rebuff Bolivia's reactivated claim to restore the Atacama corridor, ceded to Chile in 1884, but Chile has offered instead unrestricted but not sovereign maritime access through Chile to Bolivian natural gas; Chile rejects Peru's unilateral legislation to change its latitudinal maritime boundary with Chile to an equidistance line with a southwestern axis favouring Peru; in October 2007, Peru took its maritime complaint with Chile to the ICJ; territorial claim in Antarctica (Chilean Antarctic Territory) partially overlaps Argentine and British claims; the joint boundary commission, established by Chile and Argentina in 2001, has yet to map and demarcate the delimited boundary in the inhospitable Andean Southern Ice Field (Campo de Hielo Sur).

THREAT PERSPECTIVE

Chile faces threats from the globalisation of terrorism, from the ever-increasing drug trade, organised crime, civil attacks, and arms proliferation. Chile's shared borders with cocaine producing countries Peru and Bolivia makes it vulnerable to the threat of drug trafficking. Territorial issues continue to fester among Chile, Argentina, Bolivia, and Peru and the internal instability in neighbouring countries also poses a threat to Chile.

STRATEGIC RELATIONS

India: : India and Chile's bilateral relations have strengthened over the years with the exchange of high-level visits. They have signed Agreements and MoUs covering different fields of cooperation such as defence, outer space among others. There has been a steady increase in exchanges between the Armed Forces of the two countries. Chile is the fifth largest trading partner of India in the Latin American region. India has offered to train Chilean armed forces in the country's premier defence institutions including courses in mountain warfare and peacekeeping. They have decided to further explore opportunities for cooperation in the defence field including jointly manufacturing defence equipment under the Make in India programme.

United States: Chile is one of the United States' strongest partners in Latin America. Chile has political, economic and trade relations with US. Both countries are working with like-minded partners to promote stability and security regionally and globally. They have committed to collaborate on technological innovation in fields such as military medical research or the development of drones. The United States is Chile's second-largest trading partner, and the largest foreign investor in Chile. The United States and Chile have had a Free Trade Agreement (FTA) since 2004 that allows the duty free export to Chile of 100% of U.S. consumer and industrial goods. Bilateral trade in goods and services between the United States and Chile were worth approximately $31.1 billion in 2020

China: Chile and China have a strategic relationship with exchanges and co-operation at high levels in various fields. Chile was the first South American country to establish diplomatic ties with China and also the first country from the region to sign an FTA with China. In 2019, Chile became the first country in South America to update its trade agreement with China. The signing of

Chile – China FTA has brought about an important increase in bilateral trade. China remained Chile's largest trading partner and largest export destination. The two nations maintained close coordination at the United Nations, APEC and other international organisations and multilateral mechanisms. Military-to-military cooperation have increased between the two countries.

Canada: Canada and Chile continue to expand their bilateral defence collaboration, which has grown in scope and intensity in recent years, particularly since the signing of MoU on Defence Cooperation in April 2012. The two nations share many common defence goals, including the desire to increase the coherence and effectiveness of the Inter-American Defence Board. Both countries seek to cooperate in dealing with hemispheric defence and security issues, and to contribute to the enhancement of security. To that end, Armed Forces from Canada and Chile have successfully initiated trilateral defence cooperation to support capacity-building in Central America. The two countries work together in support of regional trade integration in the context of the Trans-Pacific Partnership negotiations.

Australia: Chile maintains good bilateral relations with Australia. Both nations are members of the Asia-Pacific Economic Cooperation, Cairns Group and the OECD. In 2017, Australia launched Free Trade negotiations with Chile. Chile is Australia's third-largest trading partner in Latin America. Australia is the sixth largest foreign investor in Chile, with investments totalling over $6.34 billion AUS.

DEFENCE CAPABILITIES

Chile possesses the most modern and capable armed forces in Latin America. The Armed Forces are subject to civilian control exercised by the President through the Minister of Defence. The President appoints service chiefs to four-years term and has the authority to remove them. The Joint Chief of Staff is the sole authority in charge of planning the use of armed forces, as well as training. He is also responsible for Chilean troops in international operations, and in the case of natural disasters or emergencies. The Chilean national police 'Carabineros' are incorporated into the Defence Ministry. Military service is obligatory in Chile. The country is strengthening its armed forces with enhanced capabilities, equipment, technology and training. The government has signed and brought into force a new law replacing the older Copper Law system for funding military procurement.

ARMY (Ejercito de Chile): The Chilean army is organised into six divisions, a special operations brigade and an air brigade. Its main mission is to ensure national sovereignty, maintain the territorial integrity and protect the people, institutions and vital resources of the country in the face of any external threat or aggression. A recent order has allowed women to serve in all combat and front-line units of the Chilean Army. The new order allows women into the infantry and armoured units, areas that had been limited to men only.

Personnel: 33,529 (includes conscripts)

Equipment

Category	Name	In Service
MBT	Leopard 2A4	131
	Leopard 1V	20
APC/IFV	M-113A2 (including derivative versions)	477
	Piranha (6X6,8X8)	179
	Marder	173
	YPR-765	18
Artillery	Soltam M86/M71 155mm	48
	M56 105mm pack howitzer	104
	M101 105mm	89
	M109A3 155mm SP	36
Mortar	81 mm	744
	120mm	276
	120mm SP	78
RCL	M40A1 106mm	221
	Carl Gustav	243
Anti-Tank GW	Spike	62
Weapon	Mistral (SAM)	12
	AIM-9D Sidewinder (SAM)	

Army Aviation

Category	Name	In Service
Aircraft	CN-235	3
	C-212-300	2
	Cessna C-208 Caravan	3
	Cessna 680	1
Helicopter	H215M	10
	AS.532AL Cougar	9
	AS.330L Puma	4
	AS.350B	3
	AS.355F	1
	MD-530F (attack)	9

New Procurements/Upgrades

No major procurement plans are under consideration at present.

NAVY (Armada de Chile): The presence of the long coast in Chile has led to formation of the Chilean Navy. The Navy is responsible for protecting more than 4,300 km of coastline and 4.5 million square kilometres of maritime territory, including the Exclusive Economic Zone (EEZ) and the Continental Shelf. In addition to defending against external attacks, the Navy protects the nation from such threats as drug trafficking, piracy, and terrorism. It also maintains security, promotes national development and supports national interests abroad.

Major naval bases: Pacific zone: Iquique, Easter Island, Valparaíso, Talcahuano, Puerto Montt. Atlantic zone: Strait of Magellan: Punta Arenas, in the Beagle Channel: Puerto Williams. Antarctica: Captain Arturo Prat Base.

Personnel: 26,000 (includes conscripts)

Equipment

Category	Name	In service
Submarine	Thomson class (type 209)	2
	O'Higgins class (Scorpene type)	2
Frigate	Adelaide class	2
	Almirante Latorre class	2
	Almirante Cochrane class	3
	Almirante Williams	1
	Almirante Blanco Encalada	2
Patrol vessel	Cabo Odger	
	Marinero Fuentealba	
	Piloto Sibbald	
	Aspirante Isaza	
	Contramaestre Ortiz	
	Casma class missile FPB	3
	Piloto Pardo class OPV	4
	Contramastre Micalvi OPC	6
Amphibious Force	Sargento Aldea LSDH	1
	Batral – type LST	2
	LSM	1
Auxiliaries	Fleet oilers	2
	Transport ship	1
	Oceanographic ship	1
	Icebreaker	1
	Buoy ship	1
	Training ship	1

Marines

Personnel: 2,125

Equipment

Category	Name	In Service
Light Tank	Scorpion	15
Armoured Car	Mowag	25
	HMMWV	8

...continued

Category	Name	In Service
Artillery	KH-178 105mm Howitzer	4
	G-5 155mm towed howitzer	14
Mortar	M29 81 mm	8
ASM/SSM	Trailer mounted MM38 Exocet missile	2

Naval Aviation
Personnel: 574

Category	Name	In Service
Aircraft	C-295 ASW	2
	P68 Observer 2 aircraft	7
	P-3ACH Orion	3
	C-295 Persuader	3
	CASA 212	3
	P-111	1
	Cessna O-2A Skymaster	7
Helicopter	Bo-105	5
	HH-65 Dauphin	4
	PC-7	7
	SA.365F Dauphin II	4
	AS.532SC Cougar	5

New Procurements/Upgrades
◆ The Navy has contracted shipbuilder ASMAR to build a new ice breaking vessel. The ship, Antarctica I, will replace the Navy's current icebreaker Oscar Viel.

AIR FORCE Fuerza Aerea de Chile (FACh)) is considered to be one of the most professional and capable air arms in Latin America. The country's defence modernisation programme has benefited the FACh and moulded its inventory into an effective and balanced force. The Service has five air brigades headquartered in Iquique, Antofagasta, Santiago, Puerto Montt, and Punta Arenas. Its mission is to defend the country through the control and use of the air space, the participation in surface warfare and support to the national and friendly forces.

Major air bases: Los Condores, El Bosque, Pudahuel, Quintero, El Tepual, Chabunco, Cerro Moreno and Santiago. The Air Force also operates an airbase on King George Island, Antarctica and at Quintero, near Valparaiso.

Personnel: 8,143 (including 349 conscripts)
Equipment

Category	Name	In Service
Fighter/Light attack aircraft	F-16 MLU/A/B	34
	F-16 C/D	10
	F-5E/F	14
	A-29 Super Tucano	6

...continued

Category	Name	In Service
Transport / Air refuelling/ tanker	KC-130R	2
	Beech 99A	2
	Beech 200 King Air	1
	Boeing 737-300/500	2
	Boeing 707 AEW	1
	Boeing 767-300 ER	1
	C-212	3
	C-130H/B	3
	Citation CJ-1	3
	KC-135E Stratotankers	3
	O2-OAa	6
Trainer	A-29 super tucano	12
	T-36 Pillan	19
	T-35 Pillan	7
	A-36 Halcon	8
VIP transport	BK-117	1
	Gulfstream IV	1
	C-130 Hercules	3
Helicopter	Sikorsky UH-60 S-70i	3
	UH-1H	18
	DHC-6 Twin Otter	12
	Bo.105 CB-4	1
	Bell 412	9
	Bell 206 B/B2	3
UAV	Hermes 900	3
Weapon	AIM-7 Sparrow (AAM)	
	AIM-9 Sidewinder (AAM)	
	IRIS-T(AAM)	
	AIM-120 AMRAAM (AAM)	
	Python-4(AAM)	
	AGM-45 Shrike (AGM)	
	AGM-65 Maverick (AGM)	
	AGM-88 HARM (AGM)	
	AGM-84 Harpoon	
	AGM-119 Penguin	

Air Defence
The Air Defence operates AAA systems (Miguel FCS), Blowpipe, Mistral SAMs and Mygale system. Each Mygale has Samantha truck-mounted radar and three ASPIC truck-mounted four-cell launchers for Mistral missiles.

DEFENCE PRODUCTION AND R&D

Chile is a major regional producer of defence equipment including small arms and ammunition; infantry support weapons, armoured and soft-skinned vehicles, ballistic rocket systems, vessels, command and control systems, aircraft and artillery. However, it depends largely on imports for its armed forces modernisation plans. Chilean state-owned companies continue to dominate as military suppliers and, in the maintenance, and repair of existing systems. It has developed the capability for manufacturing vehicles, ships, aircraft, and ammunition. Key opportunities identified for defence industry include fighter aircraft, landing platform dock (LPD)-type amphibious assault ships, lighter armoured vehicles such as MRAPs, 8×8 armoured personnel carriers and 4×4 armoured security vehicles, AV-8B Harrier aircraft, unmanned aerial vehicles (UAVs) and light attack and reconnaissance aircraft.

Major Armament Producers
FAMAE (Fábricas and Maestranzas del Ejército) is a government-owned weapons producer. The Company specializes in research projects and weapon system modernisation. It is responsible for modifying and maintaining the tanks, aircraft and other military devices that reach the Chilean Army.

ENAER (Empresa Nacional de Aeronáutica), the national aeronautics company design and builds military aircraft, including basic trainers and light jet fighters.

ASMAR shipyard is one of the region's largest and most capable naval production and overhaul facilities, having produced naval vessels up to 2,000 tonnes.

DTS Technology Development and Systems Ltd., specializes in information technology, electronics and telecommunications, providing solutions for the military, specifically for the Air Force of Chile, through the development of major military projects in areas of Command and Control and Electronic Warfare.

DESA is a system integrator located specializing in real time systems focused at defence applications – ground and naval fire control systems, command and controls systems, tactical network etc.

Linktronic is involved in the design and production of high technology electronic equipment with particular emphasis on Air and Coastal Surveillance Radars, Defence Systems and Computers.

Detroit Chile is a Chile-based company engaged in the marine operations, as well as the production of engines.

SISDEF Ltd. develops systems engineering solutions for defence, security and marine and industry.

The largest import trading partners are currently the US, Spain, Germany and the

Netherlands. Foreign Original Equipment Manufacturer (OEMs) enters the market through defence exhibitions, joint ventures and direct commercial sales.

Foreign suppliers: Australia, Brazil, Canada, Colombia, France, Germany, Israel, Italy, Russia, Spain, Sweden, Taiwan, United Kingdom, United States.

DEFENCE DEALS

Joint Venture Programmes

The Chilean Ministry of Defence encourages joint ventures and technology-sharing agreements to enable domestic firms to enhance their capabilities and also promote diplomatic relations between the countries. Chile has signed a Declaration of Intent with Brazil for participation in the development of the new KC-390 military transport aircraft, carried out by the Brazilian aerospace firm Embraer.

Arms Imports

Chile is one of Latin America's largest arms importers. As part of its military modernisation programme Chile has made various acquisitions such as F-16s fighters, Embraer EMB-314 Super Tucano trainers, 412EP tactical helicopters, Hermes 900 UAV and Cirrus SR22T intelligence, surveillance and reconnaissance (ISR) aircraft, and KC-135E Stratotanker aircraft, surplus aircraft from the Netherlands as part of the Amstel I and II programmes. The arms import also included medium transport aircraft and helicopters, Scorpene class diesel-electric submarines from France, Leopard I-V tanks from Germany, Type 23 frigates from the UK.

DEFENCE BUDGET

Total defence spending: $5.04 billion (2020), $4.25 Billion (2018)

Defence spending in terms of GDP: 1.9 % (2020)

In September 2019 Chile partially replaced the Copper Law with new legislation. The new funding system for arms acquisitions and other military investment is composed of a Multi-year Fund for Strategic Defence Capacities and a Strategic Contingency Fund.

CONCLUSION

Chile today is one of South America's most stable and prosperous nations and the Chilean Armed Forces the most advanced military force in the region. Chile fully implements the principle of international cooperation and has developed an intense multilateral diplomacy by actively participating in the United Nations missions related to peace and security in the world. The country actively participates in combined forces exercises in third world countries to prevent disruption to global security.

CONTACT DETAILS
Ministry of National Defence
Zenteno 45 4 Floor
OIRS: +56 2 2937 9900
E-mail: mdn@defensa.cl
www.defensa.cl

STRATEGIC INFORMATION
CHINA
(Capital: Beijing)

INTRODUCTION

Area: 9,596,960 sq km
Population: 1,397,897,720 (July 2021 est.)
Coastline: 14,500 km
Maritime claims: Territorial sea: 12 nm
Contiguous zone: 24 nm
Exclusive Economy Zone: 200 nm
Continental shelf: 200 nm or to the edge of the continental margin

GEOPOLITICAL IMPORTANCE

China is a major Asian power that occupies large landmass and ranks third in the world in terms of land area. It is bordered by 14 countries that include India, Pakistan, Afghanistan, Nepal, Bhutan, North Korea, Russia, Tajikistan, Kazakhstan, Kyrgyzstan, Laos, Mongolia, Vietnam and Myanmar. Surrounded by Korea Bay, Yellow Sea, East China Sea and South China Sea, China has a widely varied terrain ranging from mountains and deserts to plateaus and sea coasts. It is a more enclosed state than any other major power in the world. From geostrategic standpoint, China occupies and plays an important role in Asia, especially in East Asia,

South Asia and Southeast Asia. The vast size of the country along with its huge population has made China a rapidly rising market economy and the second largest economy in the world after that of the US in terms of GDP. China is predicted to replace the US as the world's largest economy in GDP terms by 2030 or even before. The country's rapid financial rise has given way to swift expansion of its geostrategic ambitions and increasing military influence, not only in the Asian continent, but at the global sphere as well.

POLITICAL OVERVIEW

The People's Republic of China (PRC) functions as a single-party socialist republic. It is ruled by the Communist Party of China (CPC) which is the only political party in the country and influences the state and society. The unitary government led by the CPC controls the state, military and media. State power within the People's Republic of China is exercised through the CPC, the Central Peo-ple's Government and their provincial and local counterparts. The

unicameral legislature of the country, called the National People's Congress (NPC), is controlled by the Communist Party. The PRC heralded a new regime in March 2013 when Xi Jinping took charge as the President and Chairman of the powerful Central Military Commission (CMC) and Li Keqiang became the Prime Minister of the country. In April 2016, President Xi assumed the designation of Commander-in-Chief of the "Joint Battle Command Centre" of the CMC.

In yet another significant development in 2018, the Communist Party of China (CPC) cleared the way for President Xi to stay in power "indefinitely" by approving the removal of the two-term limit on Presidency through a Constitutional amendment. The move paved the way for Xi Jinping to remain the head of state even after 2023. In November 2021, the ruling CPC, during a high-profile conclave, adopted a "landmark resolution" of the party's major achievements in the last 100 years and also cleared the decks for a record third term for President Xi in 2024 and possibly beyond.

KEY POLITICAL PERSONS

PRESIDENT & CHAIRMAN OF CENTRAL MILITARY COMMISSION: Xi Jinping

VICE PRESIDENT: Wang Qishan

PRIME MINISTER: Li Keqiang

ECONOMY

China is a leading economic power in 21st century world. Until 2013, it was the second largest economy in the world after the US. Measured on purchasing power parity (PPP) basis that adjusts for price differences, China in 2017 stood as the largest economy in the world, surpassing the US in 2014 for the first time in modern history. From 2013 to 2017, China had one of the fastest growing economies in the world, averaging slightly more than 7% real growth per year. The country also became the world's largest exporter in 2010, and the largest trading nation in 2013. Still, China's per capita income remains below the world average.

Being the world's most populous nation, China's market economy has witnessed rapid growth after the country braced up for reforms and adopted an open market system in the 1980s that attracted large-scale foreign investments. China is the world's second-largest oil consumer – an important factor in driving the country to meet its energy needs by expanding its geopolitical and military footprint all across the world. On the whole, the Chinese economy has gained prominence over the past decades and is significantly influencing the global economic sphere in present times. The country is a member of leading international financial institutions including the World Bank, International Monetary Fund (IMF), World Trade Organisation (WTO), Asia-Pacific Economic Cooperation (APEC) and the G-20. It has also become a part of the G-8+5 international group of powerful economies.

Facing a gradual slowdown in its overall economic growth in the past few years, China has taken several stimulus measures, including huge investments in infrastructure and other government projects as well as funding its banking sector with fresh liquidity to revive the economy. The country is attempting a transition from an export-led economy to a consumer and services-led economy.

The government's 13th Five-Year Plan, unveiled in March 2016, emphasized the need to increase innovation and boost domestic consumption to make the economy less dependent on government investment, exports, and heavy industry. Chinese leaders in 2010 pledged to double the country's GDP by 2020, and the 13th Five Year Plan included annual economic growth targets of at least 6.5% through 2020 to achieve that goal.

However, amidst a global economic slowdown and an escalating US-China trade war, it was the outbreak of the deadly Coronavirus pandemic in the Chinese city of Wuhan in 2019 which put a sudden brake on China's galloping economy and also shattered the entire world economy. Nevertheless, Beijing charted quick recovery from the negative impacts of the COVID-19 health crisis.

China was the only economy in the world to have averted a contraction in 2020 with its GDP recording an expansion of 2.3%. While the Chinese Government has set a target to achieve a GDP growth of 6% in 2021, fresh Covid outbreaks reported in the country may put a dent over the same.

In October 2020, top Chinese leaders met to discuss the 14th five-year plan for 2021-25, and a medium-term strategy named 'Vision 2035' which aims at making the country "a modern socialist power in the economic, technological and other fields by 2035." During the key conclave of the ruling CPC, the country also finalised plans to build "a fully modern military" on par with the US by 2027.

GDP (official exchange rate): $14.32 trillion (2019)

Real Growth Rate (GDP): 6.14% (2019 est.); 6.75% (2018 est.)

Industries: World leader in gross value of industrial output; mining and ore processing, iron, steel, aluminium, and other metals, coal; machine building; armaments; textiles and apparel; petroleum; cement; chemicals; fertilizers; consumer products, including footwear, toys, and electronics; food processing; transportation equipment, including automobiles, rail cars and locomotives, ships, and aircraft; telecommunications equipment, commercial space launch vehicles, satellites

Natural Gas - Proved Reserves: 5.44 trillion cu m (1 January 2018 est.)

Crude Oil - Proved Reserves: 25.63 billion bbl (1 January 2018 est.)

Total Exports: $2.49 trillion (2018 est.); $2.21 trillion (2016 est.)

Export Commodities: Broadcasting equipment, computers, integrated circuits, office machinery and parts, telephones (2019)

Major Markets: United States 17%, Hong Kong 10%, Japan 6% (2019)

Total Imports: $2.14 trillion (2018 est.); $1.74 trillion (2016 est.)

Import Commodities: Crude petroleum, integrated circuits, iron, natural gas, cars, gold (2019)

Major Suppliers: South Korea 9%, Japan 8%, Australia 7%, Germany 7%, US 7%, Taiwan 6% (2019)

DEFENCE & SECURITY

China is a powerful Asian country. It has evolved as a leading regional and global military power in 21st century. Safeguarding its territorial integrity while maintaining domestic and regional stability has driven the country towards a rapid expansion of its military might. While strongly defending its territory, China has also adopted an assertive policy over strategic issues in the Asian continent. The military organisation of the country, called the People's Liberation Army (PLA), is controlled by the Central Military Commission (CMC) which is the supreme defence policy making body. The Chairman of the CMC is the Commander-in-Chief of the PLA. The active forces of PLA consist of the Army, Navy, Air Force, PLA Rocket Force (erstwhile Second Artillery Corps), military schools and national defence scientific research institutions.

China has rapidly modernised its armed forces in the aftermath of the two Gulf Wars fought in 1990 and 2003. Once following "limited local war" strategy evolved from Mao Zedong's "protracted people's war", the PLA of today has adopted the "people's war under hi-tech conditions" tactics as part of its modernisation drive that began in 1993. The new warfare tactics rely more on advanced technology than on troops. The "people's war" strategy, based on large-scale land and guerrilla warfare methods, was designed to confront mainly Japan and the erstwhile Soviet Union. However, the doctrine became redundant following disintegration of Soviet Union in 1991. Shifting away from such warfare methodology to a modern, hi-tech condition was necessitated with the rise of the US as the supreme world power.

Of late, the PLA has followed the doctrine of "active defence" relying on state-of-the-art military hardware, modern high-tech weapons, precision guided munitions, sophisticated command & control systems coupled with a strict military training regime and large-scale use of information technology. The new military doctrine along with structural changes in its armed forces, development of pre-emptive strike capability, change in warfare methodology, C4I2SR, ground, sea and airspace-based surveillance and information technology have gained importance in present-day Chinese armed forces. By acquiring advanced military capabilities, China has steadily transformed its posture to that of an aggressive power. The country has ramped up efforts to build and deploy strategically critical missile systems capable of not only defending its territory but also launch offensive strikes against potential enemy installations. Advanced and extensive researches have been undertaken in the past decades to develop anti-ship ballistic missile system (ASBM), ballistic missile defence (BMD) capabilities and even anti-satellite weapons (ASW) to carry out space warfare. All these powerful weapons have been developed as part of China's "anti-access and area-denial" (A2AD) strategy. In 2010, China for the first time conducted a ground-based mid-course interceptor missile test which demonstrated its capability to track down and destroy mid-course ballistic missiles, with many defence experts believing that the country was nearing to achieve BMD capability. In January 2013, PRC conducted another such test to exhibit that it was increasing its potential in missile interception capabilities. The test was followed by another one in 2014 during which a land-based mid-course missile interceptor successfully traced, tracked and destroyed a ballistic missile flying in outer space. In February 2018, Beijing announced yet another successful test firing of its ground-based mid-course anti-missile interceptor system.

Back in 2007, the country had also tested a ground-based direct-ascent anti-satellite (ASAT) weapon to destroy one of its defunct weather satellites, proving its capability to attack satellites and space assets in low-Earth orbit. The successful ASAT mission demonstrated China's prowess to launch space warfare missions and was viewed by many countries as a serious threat to their vital space-based systems. In May 2013, Beijing launched a rocket into space which later re-entered Earth's atmosphere above the Indian Ocean. According to military experts, the test was a new interceptor weapon that could be used to destroy satellites in orbit. Another test of a similar weapon, designated Dong Neng-3 (DN-3), was conducted in October 2015.

In yet another new military technical breakthrough in January 2014, China test flew a hypersonic glide vehicle (HGV) capable of cruising at a top speed of Mach 10. The HGV test, marking a step beyond China's ASBM programme, featured a slower, shorter-range manoeuvrable re-entry vehicle (RV). The ultra high-speed vehicle was launched into space by an intercontinental ballistic missile. A second test flight of the new system was carried out in August 2014 followed by one more test reported in December 2014. In June 2015, the Chinese Defence Ministry confirmed the fourth test of hypersonic nuclear delivery vehicle followed by a second test that year in August 2015 and yet another test in November 2015, which was the sixth test launch of the new weapon. The glider vehicle was tested again in April 2016. In October 2017, China for the first time publicly revealed the images of the hypersonic vehicle along with a hypersonic wind tunnel that is being used for testing the HGV. The country continued to undertake more tests involving hypersonic technology in 2018. The most recent test of the HGV was conducted in July - August 2021, in which "the glide vehicle launched by China fired the projectile over the South China Sea while moving at five times the speed of sound," US media reported citing intelligence sources. The Chinese officials, however, said that the test involved a "routine spacecraft" to check its "re-usability."

According to reports, Beijing is pursuing at least two separate HGV programmes – namely the Xing Kong-2 HGV (likely tested once in August 2018) and the DF-ZF HGV (reportedly mounted with the DF-17 MRBM and tested at least eight times since Jan 2014).

Another frontier that has come to occupy centre-stage in China's overall military strategy is the strengthening of its asymmetric warfare capabilities involving cyberspace. China has accelerated its activities in cyberspace domain by developing newer capabilities to not only defend its information technology network but even launch offensive operations against its adversaries. Acknowledging the potentiality of information technology in military arena which can have wider implications from both tactical as well strategic perspectives, China has swiftly built up its information warfare capability to launch computer network-based war that could paralyse and upset the entire civilian and military apparatus of a country by taking control of its information & information-based systems. Development of electronic countermeasure weapons, cyber espionage and carrying out attacks on internet network are becoming potential tools for China to launch cyberspace-based operations.

One of the most vital aspects of modern Chinese military build-up is the rapid growth of its maritime power. As the country expands its economic horizons and realises the increased importance of sea lanes as vital trading routes, it is adopting a strategy of "sea control" and "sea denial" to ascertain its supremacy over water resources within its territory and beyond. The country's navy has focused on strengthening its anti-surface, anti-submarine and anti-air warfare capabilities while building up a credible at-sea nuclear deterrent.

The PLA's air power too has taken significant strides in the present century by deploying new-generation stealth warplanes/ bombers, combat helicopters, drones, long-range transporters, refuelling tankers along with advanced weapon systems to carry out integrated operations alongside the Army and Navy. According to a Pentagon report, China's air force is "pursuing modernisation on a scale unprecedented in its history and is rapidly closing the gap with Western air forces across a broad spectrum of capabilities including aircraft, command and control, jammers, electronic warfare and data-links." The steady enhancement and expansion of PLA's military aviation capabilities is clearly marked by the fact that the country announced the establishment of an air defence identification zone (ADIZ) over a swath of the disputed East China Sea in December 2013. The move was aimed at putting the Air Force at the forefront in the eventuality of a war and thereby supporting the country's expanded maritime power projection. In recent past, China has also invoked its right to set up an ADIZ in the hotly disputed South China Sea region, more so after an International Court ruled in favour of the Philippines over a disputed region in the SCS.

China also announced to optimize the size and structure of its army, while also focusing on optimizing the function and institution settings of the Central Military Commission. In September 2015, Beijing announced that its 2.3 million strong People's Liberation Army – the world's largest ground force – would be cut by 3,00,000 troops. A 2017 report further stated that number of troops in the PLA Ground Forces (PLAGF) would be reduced to less than one million in the coming years even as the troops strength of PLA Navy, PLA Strategic Support Force and PLA Rocket Force would be increased while the PLA Air Force's active service personnel would remain the same. The PLAGF has subsequently been reduced over the years.

In yet another sweeping reform carried out in 2015, Beijing integrated the PLA area commands overseeing two neighbouring countries – India and Pakistan, thereby junking its Soviet-era model for a US-style joint command structure to fortify the ruling Communist Party's control. Of the seven military area commands – at Beijing, Nanjing, Chengdu, Jinan, Shenyang, Lanzhou and Guangzhou – the Chengdu military command was in charge of security along India's Eastern sector in the Tibet region including Arunachal Pradesh while the Lanzhou military command looked after the Western sector, including the Kashmir region and Pakistan. As per the new strategic zone plan unveiled by President Xi, both the Chengdu and Lanzhou have been integrated into a strategic command region, making it perhaps the biggest areas for the PLA. The overhaul is aimed at moving away from an army-centric system towards a Western-style Joint Command in which the Army, Navy and Air Force are equally represented.

Beijing has also announced to strengthen the joint operational command authority under the CMC, and the theatre joint operation command system. All these transformations are steadily being implemented.

In early 2016, the PLA was reformed again so as to include five new Theatre Commands by replacing the seven previously existing Military Regions. The Defence Ministry announced that the new Theatre Commands – North, South, East, West and Central – under the administration of the CMC, would be based on the functions and structure of the military regions (MRs) they replaced, with improved mechanisms for command and logistics. The PLA would establish a Transitional Work Office to ensure a smooth transition from the old MRs to the new Theatre Commands. As part of the overall military reforms initiated by President Xi Jinping, who also heads the decision-making Central Military Commission (CMC) and also assumed the role of Commander-in-Chief of the Joint Battle Command Centre of the CMC in 2016, the PLA has dissolved the four existing general headquarters and instead set up 15 new organisations including the Headquarters of the Joint Force. The restructuring of the CMC has been done to consolidate its authority and further centralise the structure of the People's Liberation Army. All the reforms have been announced to transform the PLA into a leaner fighting force with improved joint operations capability.

The urge to grow economically and militarily has driven China to exert its influence in and around the resource-rich areas of Asia-Pacific region, particularly in the South China Sea and East China Sea which are the major trading routes and are also believed to treasure huge amounts of oil and natural gas along with fishing and mineral resources. The Asian giant has intensified efforts to expand its footprint in the SCS, ECS and recently, even in the Indian Ocean Region (IOR) by building up new harbours and other infrastructural setups, thereby adding to the worry of the neighbouring littoral states which are at loggerheads with Beijing. In the coming decades, the PLAN is likely to bolster its presence in the IOR significantly by deploying one or more aircraft carrier battle groups (CBGs) and building more naval bases, according to military analysts. China's growing power projection and aggressive stance over regional and littoral issues has alarmed the international community even though Beijing maintains that it follows a "non-offensive strategy" with a "need to expand" while safeguarding its "rights and interests". The growing territorial disputes in the Asia-Pacific region, with China being at the centre, have not only flared up regional tensions but intensified arms race at an alarming pace, thereby inviting global attention and concern. Moreover, the highly secretive military plans and pursuits by the Communist China have cast a blurred picture of the country's real ambitions and intentions in the longer run.

In July 2019, the country released its latest Defence White Paper which, among other aspects assessed the PLA's progress on modernisation and military reforms. It emphasised on "fully transforming the PLA into a world-class force by the mid-21st century," while focusing more on "mechanization", "informationization" and greatly bolstering their "strategic capabilities". The report also states the official stance of Beijing and its response to the evolving strategic realities of the Asia-Pacific and beyond. Besides, it puts light on a number of key military weapons and platforms that have been commissioned into service of late.

The previous Defence White Paper was released in 2015.

KEY DEFENCE PERSONS

VICE CHAIRMAN OF CENTRAL MILITARY COMMISSION: Gen. Zhang Youxia

VICE CHAIRMAN OF CENTRAL MILITARY COMMISSION: Gen. Xu Qiliang

DEFENCE MINISTER: Gen. Wei Fenghe

CHIEF OF JOINT STAFF DEPARTMENT OF CMC: Gen. Li Zuocheng

COMMANDER OF PLA GROUND FORCE: Gen. Liu Zhenli

COMMANDER OF PLA NAVY: Adm. Dong Jun

COMMANDER OF PLA AIR FORCE: Gen. Chang Dingqiu

Internal Conflict

The major internal areas of concern for China have been the separatists from Tibet, Muslim Uighurs in Xinjiang and Mongolians in Inner Mongolia. The Uighur Muslims issue continues to draw global attention over China's unbridled human rights violations in the Xinjiang province, mass incarceration of Uighurs in the so-called "re-education" camps and the razing of mosques and other historical places in the region. Nearly a million ethnic minority Uighurs along with Kazakhs and others have been confined into the camps for over the past three years, according to recent media reports. The recent developments in Afghanistan wherein the Taliban took complete control of the Islamic country after the withdrawal of US troops is predicted to have a direct bearing on China's Xinjiang province due to its proximity to the strife-torn nation.

In 2019, mass protests by the residents of Hong Kong over a controversial extradition law (later revoked) promulgated by the Chinese Government led to largescale civilian unrest in the autonomously-ruled Hong Kong region. The massive protests subsequently turned violent, resulting in loss of lives and destruction of public property due to frequent clashes between the civilians and law enforcement authorities.

External Conflict

China continues to assert its economic and military supremacy while projecting itself as a major power in the 21st century world-order. While its dominance in the entire Asian continent is visible, including in the energy-rich Central Asian region where it has made rapid forays by establishing strong trade and economic ties, and clinching new deals for oil and gas, the primary areas of contention in the Asia-Pacific region where Beijing is a party include the resource-rich waters of South China Sea (SCS) and East China Sea (ECS). The SCS, a major shipping lane, is believed to be rich in oil and gas reserves. It is claimed by several littoral states including Brunei, Malaysia, the Philippines, Taiwan and Vietnam. A group of uninhabited islands in the ECS has also become a major source of regional tension between China and Japan in recent times. Meanwhile, China has steadily gained access into the strategic waters of Indian Ocean Region (IOR) in recent times, thereby heightening India's security concerns.

Territorial disputes: : China is engaged in border disputes, both land and maritime, with many of its neighbouring nations in the Asia-Pacific region. The aggressive posturing by Beijing has increased in recent times which has further escalated regional tensions in the wider Asian continent. The continuing unilateral attempts by Beijing to change the disputed territorial regions to its favour have been aimed at consolidating its political and strategic positions across Asia.

On 23 October, 2021, China's national legislature, the National People's Congress (NPC), adopted a new law "on the protection and exploitation of its land border areas" even while asserting that sovereignty and territorial integrity of the country were "sacred and inviolable". The new law would be operational from January 1, 2022.

India: The two neighbours, sharing a land boundary of 4,057-km, are locked in a long-standing dispute over the Himalayan border region and even fought a brief war over the same in 1962. The border dispute between the two big Asian countries which historically roots back to 19th century when India was under British rule, has mainly involved two areas – the northeast border areas of Kashmir that includes the Aksai Chin region lying in the northern section of India on China's south-western border; and the North-East Frontier Agency (NEFA, which later became the Union Territory of Arunachal Pradesh) in the north-eastern portion of India, on China's southern border. While the China-administered Aksai Chin region in the Karakoram Mountains covering an area of around 43,000-sq kms is claimed by India as a part of its state of Jammu & Kashmir, China has been a claimant of India's north-eastern state Arunachal Pradesh, covering an area of around 90,000-sq km.

Even as India has regarded the McMahon Line (in Arunachal region) as the effective Sino-Indian boundary which was agreed to by Britain and the then independent state of Tibet as part of the Shimla Accord inked in 1914, the same has been disputed by the Chinese government time and again. The Chinese administration, on the other hand, has recognised the Line of Actual Control (LAC) as the demarcation line that separates the Indian-controlled territory from Chinese-controlled territory. (The term LAC was first used by Chinese Prime Minister Zhou Enlai to Indian Prime Minister Jawaharlal Nehru in 1959.) India rejected the concept of (Chinese propagated) LAC in both 1959 and 1962.

While India considers the LAC to be 3,488 km long, China considers it to be only around 2,000 km. The LAC is divided into three sectors: the eastern sector spanning Arunachal Pradesh and Sikkim; the middle sector in Uttarakhand and Himachal Pradesh; and the western sector in Ladakh. The area of contention in the ongoing dispute between the two neighbours is the western sector covering Ladakh.

India's repeated attempts to clarify the LAC has been rejected by the Chinese government. Mutual agreements reached by the Indian and Chinese sides in the 1990s to the still-unsettled LAC was necessitated to maintain peace and tranquility along the undemarcated border regions, pending a final resolution of the dispute.

In June 2020, a major conflict over territorial control flared up between the two large neighbours involving the Line of Actual Control, leading to a violent face-off between the Indian and Chinese troops at the Galwan valley in India's eastern Ladakh region. The acrimonious confrontation resulted in both sides' militaries suffering casualties. High-level military and diplomatic talks are presently going on to settle the long-standing boundary dispute even as both sides have massively deployed their troops along the LAC for any possible confrontation. While Beijing and New Delhi have taken few steps to disengage, military and diplomatic engagements at frequent intervals have not yielded any substantive results.

On the maritime front, the Brahmaputra River, one of the major rivers in Asia that flows through India, China and Bangladesh, has remained another source of Sino-India conflict for decades. The river that originates in Tibet and enters India in the state of Arunachal Pradesh is an important source of irrigation, trade and transportation. Attempts by China to build a number of dams on the riverbed to divert its water for irrigating a large landmass covering the Gobi Desert have caused frictions between Beijing and New Delhi.

Both neighbours, from time to time, have asserted to resolve all their border disputes amicably. Even though negotiations and high-level talks have been going on between them for over two decades now to settle the long-standing border issues, no concrete results have been achieved over the same.

Bhutan: China stakes claim over a total of 764-sq km of Bhutanese land covering the north-west (269-sq km) and central parts (495-sq km) of the country. The north-west part constitutes Doklam, Sinchulung, Dramana and Shakhatoe in Samste, Haa and Paro districts. The central parts are the Pasamlung and the Jakarlung valley in Wangdue Phodrang district of Bhutan. In June 2017, the dispute over the Doklam region became an international focal point after Chinese soldiers attempted to unilaterally change the status quo by trying to build a high mountain road in the area which falls between India and China on a Bhutanese plateau. The Bhutanese Government termed the Chinese move a "direct violation" of agreements reached in 1988 and 1998 to maintain peace and refrain from unilateral action in the disputed area pending a final border settlement. The Doklam plateau being of great strategic importance to India's security led New Delhi to directly intervene in the matter by sending its troops to prevent the Chinese side from any road construction activity in the region. The standoff between Indian troops and Chinese troops over the disputed border region continued for nearly three months. In August 2017, both sides announced to withdraw from the area.

On October 14, 2021, China signed a Memorandum of Understanding (MoU) with Bhutan on a "three-step roadmap" to expedite negotiations to resolve their boundary dispute. Both sides have been holding boundary negotiations since 1984, but without any tangible results.

Japan: China and Japan are claiming a group of uninhabited islands in the East China Sea which has become a major irritant in their bilateral relations in recent times, leading to frequent skirmishes. Both China and Taiwan lay claim over the islands, which are part of what Japan calls the Senkaku, and China calls the Diaoyu group. The dispute flared up further after Japan's decision in September

2012 to buy the chain of islands from a private Japanese family which the country recognised as its "owner". Tokyo's decision to "nationalise" the islands resulted in China dispatching a number of its naval vessels to enter the disputed waters to conduct patrol. Chinese aircraft also stepped up activity over the region. Both Asian powers have scrambled their military planes against each other several times to project dominance over the disputed areas. China has continued to send its Coast Guard and other ships to sail near the islands' waters, despite Japanese opposition over the same. Japan also strongly protested China's move to send for the first time a drone aircraft to patrol over the region in 2017. Tokyo has alleged that China is escalating the situation unilaterally in the disputed territory. Meanwhile, Japan's Maritime Self-Defense Force in October 2019 conducted "goodwill exercises" with the Chinese Navy for the first time in eight years, amidst signs of warming ties between the two Asian powers. Leaders of the two countries met during the G-20 summit held in Osaka, Japan in June 2019 where Tokyo invited the Chinese President for a state visit in early 2020. The visit, however, was put off in the wake of the Coronavirus pandemic. It would have been the first state visit by China's top leadership to Japan in over a decade.

Vietnam: While land border conflict between China and Vietnam has been resolved, territorial water dispute between the two neighbours over a number of islands in the South China Sea, in particular the Spratly Islands and Paracel Islands, has resulted in regional tension. The Vietnamese Navy has conducted military drills in the region and held military training exchanges with the US Navy in a sign of renewing its defence ties with Washington to counter Chinese assertiveness over the SCS. Recent Chinese moves to explore the disputed waters of SCS for oil and gas reserves have led to intensified maritime confrontations between the two sides. Beijing has also started constructing lighthouses in the Spratly Islands. Vietnam has continued to bolster its overall military might, especially its naval power, to efficiently and effectively protect its sovereignty and deal with any threat from an increasingly assertive China.

Philippines: The resource-rich South China Sea is again at the centre of China-Philippines territorial spat. The Philippines is locked in a tense dispute with China over the Scarborough Shoal – a group of islets in the South China Sea. Even as the Chinese ships took control of the islets in 2012, China in 2014 announced plans to begin regular patrols of the South China Sea, known in Manila as the West Philippines Sea. The Philippines, which had earlier expressed its intent to reinvigorate its military ties with the US over the dispute, and signed deals to buy new fighter aircraft, military helicopters and ex-US warships that could be used in the maritime disputes against Beijing, however, has taken a sudden U-turn, apparently miffed at Washington's failure to help protect Manila's maritime rights in the SCS. There has been a major shift in Philippines' policy towards the US in recent past, including scaling down of joint military exercises between the two allies. Meanwhile, in another recent development in July 2016, an international tribunal backed by the United Nations ruled in favour of the Philippines in the South China Sea maritime dispute, while stating that China had no legal basis to assert its rights over the resources within its unilaterally declared "nine-dash line," which extended hundreds of miles to the south and east of its island province of Hainan and covered some 90% of the disputed waters. Immediately after the verdict, China released a White Paper denouncing the verdict while insisting that Beijing had claims over the strategic region "for 2,000 years." Relations between Manila and Beijing nosedived yet again after a Chinese fishing trawler hit and sank a Filipino boat in June 2019 in the contested waters of SCS. The Presidents of the two countries have met on and off to ward off any potential military conflict over the disputed territory.

Malaysia: A small group of islands in the Spratlys in South China Sea is the area of contention between Malaysia, China and few other littoral states in the region. China's sovereignty claims over the entire South China Sea have further accentuated the multi-national dispute. While Malaysia has pushed for non-militarisation of the South China Sea region, it has at the same time felt the need to strengthen its defence capability to deal with any potential military flare off in the region.

THREAT PERSPECTIVE

US: While from political and military perspective, China has achieved its strategic goals by strongly defending its territory and often asserting it beyond the internationally-demarcated areas, the most pertinent threat it faces today is that from the United States. The presence of US Navy submarines, aircraft carriers and other large warships in the Pacific Rim area has been the cause of constant bickering between China and the US as Beijing sees it as American hegemony and intrusion in the Asia-Pacific region. The US's interventions in Taiwan and in the contested maritime regions of the SCS and ECS have also made Beijing belligerent. The autonomously-administered Taiwan, which China claims as part of its territory and intends to unify it with the mainland even by force if needed as part of its "One-China" principle, has been the foremost reason for US-China confrontations. The US's military support to Taiwan has remained a contentious issue between the two leading world powers. China has vehemently opposed any kind of US military sales to the island state for it fears that this could empower Taiwan against China. Besides, the strong military relations the US enjoys especially with Japan and South Korea have further intensified the race to assert supremacy in the region. The ever-growing US-India relations in recent years has also made China jittery.

With the intent to retain its supremacy, the US under the then President Barack Obama announced its grand "Pivot to Asia" policy which included a major strategic shift by Washington towards the highly-tensed Asia-Pacific region. The "Pivot to Asia" involved coordinated efforts to boost US defence, diplomatic, and economic ties with the Asia-Pacific countries, especially the ones locked in bitter territorial spat with Beijing. The US administration had also decided to deploy 60 percent of its naval assets, including as many as six aircraft carriers, in the area. However, the grand policy could not take off as successfully as it was conceived. Amidst all the flip-flops at Washington's end, China remains undeterred and continues to be aggressive in and around the Asian continent, especially in the disputed territories involving many of its neighbours.

Japan: The two Asian powers consider each other a threat in the continent. Tokyo, which once regarded the erstwhile Soviet Union as its main adversary, has shifted focus towards its economically and militarily growing neighbour China. Japan is home to US military bases and some 55,000 US troops are currently stationed in the country. It also conducts regular military drills with the US. Strongly supported by Washington, Japan has significantly strengthened its overall military capability, especially its air and naval power, over the last two decades. While it is making its ground forces more mobile for quick response against any contingency, especially in southwest Japan, its navy has deployed the US-supplied Aegis air defence systems to defend the country, and the warplanes in the air force have been armed with advanced weapons, including air-to-air missiles. Japan is adding more teeth to its naval and air prowess by acquiring new class of submarines, destroyers, helicopter carriers, advanced combat jets, spy planes and related equipment. It is also in race alongside China and Russia to develop a new stealth fighter jet to ascertain its air supremacy in the Pacific. Amidst the ongoing maritime skirmishes in the Asian-Pacific region, Japan has added a large warship – a helicopter carrier – in its naval fleet. The 19,500-ton warship, named Izumo, is the largest warship in Japan's possession after World War II. The Sino-Japan relationship ebbed to its lowest point in recent past over the Senkaku/Diaoyu Islands with fighter planes and naval vessels from two sides confronting each other head-on many times. Of late, bilateral meetings involving the top leadership of the two countries appear to have sobered past tensions, at least from the outset.

Taiwan: China perceives the military rise of Taiwan with American backing as another major threat against it. The autonomously-ruled island state, which China claims as part of its own territory, has embarked on an ambitious military modernisation plan. Taiwan's major defence acquisition plans include frigates, new-age fighters, combat helicopters along with Patriot air defence systems from the US and new indigenously-built anti-ship missiles, stealth warships and submarines among others. The country is also developing new-class of missile boats and stealth corvettes in addition to anti-ship cruise missiles to safeguard territorial sovereignty. The US has also cleared the sale of major military platforms and equipment, including fighter aircraft, anti-ship missiles, drones etc. for Taiwan.

India: China is the world's third largest country in terms of geographical area and the most populous nation; India, the seventh largest in terms of landmass and second in terms of population. Hence, the two countries occupy centre-stage in the Asian continent. With their rapid economic rise along with military progress, India and China are playing a crucial role in the 21st century world-order.

An air of misgiving and mutual competitiveness has prevailed over bilateral relationship between the two Asian neighbours having two completely separate political setups, policies and ideologies. With its deep-seated roots in democracy and transparent policies, India has followed the strategy of peaceful coexistence with all its neighbours while favouring an all-round development of the region. The Communist China, on the other hand, has followed strict internal controls and secretive, opaque policies in several spheres, including in its foreign and military dealings. The 7th Defence White Paper of China released in 2011 listed Tibet as one of its three core areas. The Tibet Autonomous Region (TAR) has been at the heart of centuries-old Sino-Indian contentious border relations. At a time when China has taken an aggressive stance over its territorial claims in Asia, it has not spared the Indian state of Arunachal Pradesh, especially the Tawang district having historical affiliations with Tibet, and reasserted its claim over it from time to time. China views India as a major rival to its 'rising power' status in the Asian continent. At the global front, Beijing has maintained an ambivalent position over India's aspiration to become a permanent member of the United Nations Security Council (UNSC). In recent times, New Delhi's repeated efforts of becoming a member of the Nuclear Suppliers Group (NSG) has also been scuttled by Beijing. Even as New Delhi has reinvigorated its defence ties with Washington and also with Tokyo, China has felt unease over the same.

The gradual reshaping of the 'Indo-Pacific' region and increasing importance being given to its development for mutual cooperation, navigation and conducting global trade while maintaining strategic autonomy has also led to the formation of the QUAD coalition involving India, US, Australia and Japan. China has expressed its strong reservation over this new formation.

From military perspective, after the 1962 Sino-India war, India has gone on to massively bolster its military capability – a move being cautiously but warily watched by China. India's growing maritime prowess, in particular its Navy's 'Blue Water' ambitions, has troubled China which too is pursuing similar aspirations in the present century. Rising Indian defence spending and acquisition of most advanced weapon systems and platforms has raised Chinese eyebrows and even found mention in its Defence White Papers.

China views India as its main rival in the wider Indo-Pacific region. It has acknowledged the ramifications of an economically and strategically growing India in the entire Asian continent. Even as New Delhi is making cautious approach to keep any kind of confrontation with Beijing at bay and diplomatic efforts continue to instil mutual trust between the two sides, India, at the same time, has not shied away from adding newer capabilities to its armed forces to counter any "surprising and unexpected move" from its militarily growing Western neighbour. Acquisition of new land platforms, naval platforms including destroyers, frigates, submarines, aircraft carriers, and advanced air platforms such as multi-role fighters, strategic transporters, combat drones in addition to new ballistic and cruise missile systems and other top-of-the-line military assets have enormously galvanised the Indian Armed Forces in recent times to face any possible hostility from China.

Vietnam: Sharing a complex and troubled relationship with China (despite having similar ideologies and forms of Government), Hanoi has been entangled in a bitter maritime dispute with Beijing in the South China Sea over the Spratly Islands and the Paracel Islands. Even while diplomatic relations with Beijing continue (the two nations marked the 70th anniversary of official diplomatic ties in 2020), Vietnam at the same time has endeavoured to bolster its military capabilities, especially its naval power, to safeguard its maritime sovereignty and integrity in the SCS amidst China's increasing belligerence and hostility over the disputed territories.

South Korea: Though South Korea considers North Korea as its major military threat, Seoul is also expanding its air and naval power to counter a rising China in the Asia-Pacific. The country has progressively inducted new KDX-class of warships equipped with US-made Aegis air defence systems and also acquiring new submarines. Procurement of new-generation stealth fighters, Unmanned Aerial Vehicles and missile systems too are going on. In yet another recent development, deployment of the US Terminal High Altitude Area Defense (THAAD) system in Seoul has angered China which has vehemently opposed any such deployment.

STRATEGIC RELATIONS

Pakistan: China has attached great importance to its strategic ties with Pakistan and consequently, established strong military relations by supplying weapons and armament to Islamabad. The two countries have become "all-weather allies" and expanded the ambit of their bilateral cooperation. Both have been working on joint production of defence weapons and equipment which they intend to sell in the international arms market. Pakistan's nuclear weapons programme is assisted by China. Chinese PLA is working in Pak-occupied-Kashmir (PoK) to construct a new road from China's Xinjiang province to a part of Gwadar – a port being built in Balochistan province of Pakistan. The port, located at the peak of Arabian Sea and the entrance of Persian Gulf, will provide a key transit route to China to enter and strengthen its foothold in the Middle East. Beijing has also taken over operational control of the strategically located port and decided to deploy its naval ships along with those of Pakistan's to safeguard the port. The port would be connected with China's western province of Xinjiang through rail and road links under Beijing's ambitious, multi-billion dollar China-Pakistan Economic

Corridor (CPEC) project which entails other infrastructural developments in the region in a phased manner. The CPEC is the flagship project under the larger Belt-and-Road (BRI) initiative of Beijing. Meanwhile, China has also extended space cooperation with Pakistan and has been launching satellites for it.

Iran: Not quite open in its military dealings with other nations, China has maintained secret alliance with Iran by supplying weapons and military hardware, especially ballistic and cruise missile technology to Tehran. Among the other Middle Eastern countries, Iran is believed to have received maximum Chinese assistance in missiles and related technology.

North Korea: The secret strategic tie-up between China and North Korea has involved development of missiles and nuclear arsenal. The former has supplied an unknown number of cruise missiles and related technology to the DPRK along with training in rocket engine design, reverse engineering, small warhead design, airframe expertise and other assistance.

Myanmar: China, Myanmar relations date back to 1949 when the latter became one of the first countries to recognise the sovereignty of the People's Republic of China. Though bilateral relation witnessed a downward turn in later years, it again assumed importance in 1988 when Myanmar faced international sanctions following a crackdown on pro-democracy protests. China during that phase supplied arms and aid to the country. The two neighbours today share good trade relations and China is engaged in several infrastructural development projects in Myanmar. China has realised the strategic importance of Myanmar to gain access into the Indian Ocean Region (IOR) and accordingly focused on improving political, diplomatic as well as military ties with Nay Pyi Taw. In a recent significant development, China inaugurated its rail link to Myanmar. The project is part of Beijing's sea-road-rail link under the wider one-belt-one-road (OBOR) programme. The new link connects China's Chengdu region with Lincang which is opposite Chin Shwe Haw, a town in Myanmar's North East. Myanmar's cities of Mandalay, Lashio and Hsenwi will now have rail connectivity with other intersecting points with China.

From military perspective, China and Myanmar held their first major naval drill in 2017. Beijing has supplied battle tanks, fighter jets, naval craft and other weapons to Myanmar. In fact, China has emerged as the biggest supplier of military hardware to Myanmar, accounting for nearly 61% of weapons imported by Myanmar between 2014 and 2018. The Chinese military presence in Myanmar's Coco Islands, located in close proximity to India's Andaman Islands, has often been reported but denied by both Beijing and Nay Pyi Taw. In January 2020, Chinese President Xi Jinping during his maiden visit to Myanmar, pledged to elevate China's ties with Myanmar to a "new level". The development of Myanmar's Kyaukphyu port at a cost of US$ 1.3-million was reportedly discussed along with other infrastructure projects during the high-level talks. The development of the Kyaukphyu port would provide China a stepping stone into the Indian Ocean region. Meanwhile, Beijing has also proposed the CMEC model (China-Myanmar Economic Corridor in lines of the CPEC with Pakistan as part of the larger BRI project) to connect China's Yunnan province with far-away regions of Myanmar.

Russia: China has overtly depended on Soviet-era military technology and weapons supplies in the past. China and Russia have shared strong bilateral trade relations since long and Moscow is a leading oil supplier to Beijing. The fast evolving geopolitical equations of 21st century has brought the two powerful nations closer. Beijing and Moscow are renewing and strengthening their strategic alliance in order to consolidate their respective positions in the wider Asia-Pacific region. Both the nations are influential members in the multilateral Shanghai Cooperation Organisation (SCO) forum. Recently, the two sides have held joint military exercises and are viewing issues, both regional and global, in a united manner. In May 2014, Moscow and Beijing signed a 30-year, $400 billion landmark deal to pipe natural gas from Russia's Far East to China. The deal was clinched amidst worsening relations between Russia and the Western countries over the Ukraine crisis. In June 2019, Chinese President Xi Jinping made a state visit to Russia to meet President Vladimir Putin during which the two sides pledged to elevate bilateral relations to "comprehensive strategic partnership" in "a new era of friendship". Russia was set to deliver the remaining S-400 air defence systems to China in 2020, but reportedly suspended the deliveries in the backdrop of the Coronavirus pandemic.

Israel: China and Israel have pledged to strengthen bilateral military ties in recent times. China shares close ties with Israel's defence industry and has received sophisticated defence technology from it in the past. Israel-China military relations date back to the 1970s. Beijing has developed one of its most modern fighter jets, the J-10, from an Israeli design.

Indonesia: With an aim to expand its reach in its extended neighbourhood, China in the past few years has made efforts to renew its ties with Indonesia. While the two countries share political, economic and cultural relations, China has been making efforts to expand it further so as to include strategic alliance with Indonesia. The two Asian countries have pledged to boost their military technical cooperation and expand it further by including joint military exercises, training and maritime security missions as well as defence production. Indonesia has also expressed interest in acquiring naval patrol ships from Beijing.

Saudi Arabia: In 2016, China and Saudi Arabia upgraded their relationship into a "comprehensive strategic partnership." China is the world's biggest importer of Saudi oil. China bought $46 billion worth of products from Saudi Arabia in 2018, a year in which overall bilateral trade increased by 33 percent to $63 billion.

Thailand: Of late, China has significantly bolstered its strategic and military ties with its Southeast Asian neighbour Thailand which occupies an important geographic position in the continent. Bilateral relation between the two countries is growing stronger with cooperation in the fields of infrastructure, energy and trade. China also supplies military equipment to Thailand. In 2017, the Thai Government approved a deal with China to procure submarines for the Royal Thai Navy. In yet another major military pact inked in 2019, the Thai Navy would acquire an amphibious transport dock from Beijing. The two sides have been conducting joint military exercises at regular intervals. They have worked jointly on developing multiple rocket launcher systems in the past. Discussions about a joint military production facility is also going on.

Seychelles: China's relations with the island country in the Indian Ocean over the last three decades were confined to political, social and cultural spheres. China is now exploring new ways to expand its defence and strategic cooperation with the island nation keeping in mind its prominent geographic position in the IOR.

Sri Lanka: China has strengthened its ties with Sri Lanka in recent times. The two countries have upgraded their relationship to strategic level. The renewed ties include military exchanges, including submarine dockings at the Lankan ports, besides trade and economic relations. China has also been investing in infrastructure development projects in the South Asian island nation. China has also agreed to provide defence technology as well as training to the Lankan army personnel. Sri Lanka, on its part, has committed to join the multi-billion dollar

Maritime Silk Road (MSR) project initiated by China. The leasing of Sri Lanka's Hambantota port to China and development of the Colombo port city with Chinese funds and assistance bear resonance to China's increasing influence over the Island nation in the Indian Ocean region. Meanwhile, Beijing has also funded and built the first new rail line in Sri Lanka under the flagship BRI (Belt & Road) project. It has also agreed to support Colombo in developing capabilities in satellite communication, space technology and maritime industries. In November 2012, China launched Sri Lanka's first communications satellite, SupremeSAT-I. In 2019, Beijing gifted a Type 053 frigate to the Lankan Navy, thereby further deepening its defence ties with Colombo.

Bangladesh: China has firmed up its relations with Bangladesh of late, thereby swiftly expanding its strategic foothold in South Asia. The two countries' militaries have pledged to strengthen defence ties. Bangladesh has received massive military aid, military training, technology and equipment from China in recent years. The two countries signed the defence cooperation agreement in 2002 and 2004 to strengthen their strategic ties. In 2016, Bangladesh acquired two Type 035G attack submarines from China. Dhaka is also receiving other major naval, land, air platforms and weapon systems from Beijing under recently signed military deals.

Nepal: Beijing has swiftly expanded its ties with Kathmandu of late by providing financial and other aid to the tiny Himalayan Kingdom. China aims to rope in Nepal for its ambitious Belt and Road project and has proposed to build the Trans-Himalayan Connectivity network (THCN) which aims to connect Nepal and China through Tibet. In another major development, China announced to provide military aid worth $21 million to the Nepalese Army in October 2019. The aid included unspecified "disaster relief materials" to the Army over the next three years. The announcement came after President Xi Jinping's visit to Kathmandu on October 12, 2019 – the first such trip by a Chinese President to Nepal in over two decades. In August 2020, the two nations marked the 65th anniversary of the establishment of diplomatic relations between them.

Djibouti: China has emerged as a new strategic partner of Djibouti, the tiny country in the Horn of Africa. The two countries have agreed to establish strategic partnership to strengthen all-round cooperation. In a recent development, Beijing has set up a naval logistics base in Djibouti under a 10-year agreement signed with that country. It has also dispatched PLA personnel to guard the overseas base. The new military base in the Indian Ocean, situated near the strategic maritime choke-point connecting the Red Sea to the Gulf of Aden, assumes significance amidst China's growing strategic expansion. Beijing also plans to increase the number of its marine corps from 20,000 to one lakh as part of plans to deploy them overseas for the first time, including at the Djibouti base. The expansion is planned to protect China's maritime lifelines and its growing interests overseas.

MULTILATERAL ALLIANCES

SCO: The Shanghai Cooperation Organisation (SCO), established in 2001, with China, Russia, Kazakhstan, Kyrgyzstan, Tajikistan and Uzbekistan as its founder members, has emerged as a potential strategic block in Asia. China played an instrumental role in setting up the multilateral organisation. The group has accorded observer status to Afghanistan, Iran, Mongolia and Belarus, while six other countries (Sri Lanka, Nepal, Cambodia, Turkey, Armenia and Azerbaijan) have been granted the dialogue partner status at the organisation. India and Pakistan joined the group as full-time members in 2017. While emphasising on political and economic coordination among its member nations, the alliance has also focused on strategic and security issues in the Asian continent. Many analysts view the SCO as a potential rival block to Western alliances, especially the US-led NATO in the long run.

BRICS: The forum was established in 2006 with Brazil, Russia, India and China (BRIC) as its members. South Africa later joined the block in 2010. The alliance has primarily focused on political, economic and financial cooperation among the member nations.

APEC: The Asia-Pacific Economic Cooperation (APEC) came into existence in 1989 to promote trade and economic cooperation among the Asia-Pacific nations. China joined the forum in 1991. The 21-member nation APEC has solely focused on free and open trade and investment, promoting and accelerating regional economic integration and encouraging economic and technical cooperation among the member countries to build a dynamic and harmonious Asia-Pacific region.

DEFENCE CAPABILITIES

ARMY: The People's Liberation Army (PLA), once pegged as the largest active standing army in the world, has steadily been reduced to less than one million active personnel. Currently, the PLA Ground Force (PLAGF) has an estimated strength of around one million active troops (9,70,000 appx.) and an additional around 800,000 as reserve force. The reserve forces have been placed under the centralised and unified command of the Communist Party of China and the Central Military Commission (both headed by the country's all-powerful President) since July 2020 in order to build a "world-class" Army. The Chinese ground forces were previously deployed in seven Military Regions (MR) across China based at Shenyang, Beijing, Jinan, Nanjing, Guangzhou, Chengdu and Lanzhou. In 2016, the country announced major military reforms under which five new Theatre Commands – the Eastern, Western, Southern, Northern and Central – were established to focus on joint combat and modern warfare (Amidst the ongoing border conflict with India, China appointed Lt. Gen. Xu Qiling [Vice Chairman of the Central Military Commission] as the new commander of the PLA Army's Western Theatre Command in 2020. Lt. Gen. Qiling was subsequently promoted to the General rank in 2021. The Western Theatre Command oversees the borders with India.)

Beijing has also set up two new leading organs – the PLA Rocket Force (PLARF) and PLA Strategic Support Force (PLASSF) – as part of building up a modern military. While the Rocket Force has replaced the Second Artillery Force (SAF) "to strengthen nuclear deterrence and nuclear counter-attack capabilities, intensify the construction of medium and long-range precision strike power, and reinforce the strategic check-and-balance capability," the Strategic Support Force (SSF) has been set up as a new type of command force primarily to maintain national security and as an important growth point of PLA's combat capabilities. It has been designed "to leverage synergies and facilitate integration across Chinese capabilities for space, cyberspace, and the electromagnetic spectrum." In future conflict situations, it is the PLA-SSF which would be integral to PLA's plans to fight and win "informationized" warfare.

The PLA Ground Force has continuously been restructured to deal with future land warfare operations and also to move from regional defence to trans-regional mobility. The PLAGF has accelerated the development of army aviation troops, light mechanised units and special operations forces. It has also expedited work on digitalized units, gradually making the units smaller, modular and multi-functional in organization so as to enhance their capabilities for air-ground integrated operations, long-distance manoeuvres, rapid assaults and special operations. Induction of advanced battle tanks, armoured vehicles, howitzers, attack/ utility helicopters, unmanned air platforms, guns, other small arms along with the integration of information systems with weapons and platforms have been going on to strengthen the PLA Army.

Personnel: Arouond 1 million (+0.8 million reserve force)

Equipment

Category	Name	In Service
MBT	Type 99A, A2	800+
	Type 96B	
	Type 98G	250
	Type 96, 96A, 96G	2500+
	Type 69/79	300+
	Type 59D/D1	
	Type 54/55	
Light Tank	Type 63/63A	800
	ZTD-05	200+
	Type 15	
IFV/AIFV/ APC/ATV	Type 97	50+
	Type 89	300
	Type 63	2000
	ZBL-08	100
	ZBL-09	100
	ZBD-05/ ZTD-05 (Type 05)	1000
	ZBD-04 (Type 04)	200
	ZBD-03 (Type 03)	40
	Type 90/92	600+
	Type 86	600+
	Type 85	
	Norinco VP-4 (Lynx)	
Artillery	Type 05 155mm SP	100
	AH4 155mm lightweight howitzer	
	PLZ-45 155mn SP	80+
	Type 89 122mm SP	500
	Type 83 152mm SP	500+
	U/I ARTY 130mm SP	
	WZ-551 122mm SP	
	Type 85 122mm SP	
	Type 70 122mm SP	200
	Type 54 122mm SP	
	WZ-551 105mm SP	
	Type 88 155mm towed	150
	Type 66 152mm	1,400
	Type 54 152mm	
	Type 59-1 130mm field gun	1,000
	Type 83 122mm	
	Type 60 122mm	
	Type 54 122mm	6,000
Mortar	YW-381 120mm SP	
	WZ-551 120mm SP	
MLRS	PHL03 300mm	
	WS-1/2/3/6 SP	
	A-100 300mm	

...continued

Category	Name	In Service
MLRS	Type 83 273 mm SP	
	Type 82 130 mm, Truck	
	Type 70 130 mm, APC	
	Type 63 130 mm, Truck	
	Type 90,122 mm, Truck	
	Type 89,122 mm, APC	
	Type 83 122 mm, Truck	
	Type 81,122 mm Truck	
AT Gun	120mm/125mm SP	
	Type 86, 120 mm SP	
ATGM	HJ-8	
	HJ-9	24
	HJ-10	
	HJ-11	
	HJ-12	
AA gun	Type 59, 100mm radar, towed	
	Type 56, 85mm, radar, towed	
	Type 59, 57mm radar/ optic, towed	
	Type 88, Twin-37mm optic, tracked	
	Type 63, Twin 37mm optic, towed	
	Type 90, Twin 35mm optic, tracked	55+
	Type 87, Twin 25mm optic, tracked	
SAM	HQ-17, HQ-17A	
	HQ-16A	
	HQ-7/7B	
	HQ-64, LY-60	
	HQ-6	
	QW-1/QW-2 (MANPADs)	
SSM (conventional)	DF-11	~200
	DF-15	~100
	DF-21 (CSS-5)	~100
	DF-31	15
	DH-10	300+
	HY-2	
	HY-4	

Army Aviation

Category	Name	In Service	On Order
Helicopter	HC-120 (EC120)	100+	
	Mi-17	20	
	Mi-171, Mi-171E	50	34
	Mi-17-V5	35	
	Mi-6	2	
	S-70 (Black Hawk)	19	
	Z-9 (utility)	64	
	Z-8A/B (to be retired)	12	

...continued

Category	Name	In Service	On Order
Helicopter	Z-9A, Z-9WZ, Z-9WA & other variants (attack)	250+	
	Z-10 (attack)	50+	
	Z-18A (transport)		
	Z-19 (reconnaissance/ attack)	10+	
	Z-20 (medium-lift utility)		
UAV	CH-1		
	GJ-2 (Wing Loomg II)		
	ASN-15		
	ASN-105		
	ASN-104		

New Procurements/Upgrades

◆ The Type 96B third-generation MBT is replacing the Type 59 and Type 69 tanks.

◆ The Type 15 light tank, built by NORINCO, has been been inducted in service.

◆ New tracked AIFVs are being commissioned. A new variant of ZBD-04/04A IFV is being inducted.

◆ A new lightweight 122-mm wheeled howitzer has been commissioned.

◆ HQ-17 tracked and HQ-17A wheeled variants of surface-to-air missiles are progressively being inducted.

◆ The Z-10 attack helicopter is being progressively inducted in all PLAGF aviation units.

◆ Limited number of Z-20, a new medium-lift utility helicopter built by Harbin Co., has been inducted.

◆ Z-18A – a new transport helicopter built by CAIG, has been inducted.

◆ A new 125mm cannon, termed as the world's fastest anti-tank gun, has been delivered to the Army for trial. The gun is likely to be used for the next generation of Chinese main battle tanks.

◆ NORINCO-built SH-11 self-propelled howitzer has been inducted.

◆ A new (laser guided) vehicle-mounted howitzer, "PCL-181" (155mm), has been deployed in the Tibet region.

◆ AR500C vertical take-off and landing UAV/ helicopter built by AVIC has been introduced into service. It is reported to be China's first unmanned helicopter drone designed to fly in plateau areas and capable of firing and conducting reconnaissance operations from high altitude.

NAVY: The People's Liberation Army Navy

(PLAN), which was once a subordinate force to the PLA Ground Force and played a limited role during the Cold-war era, has metamorphosed into a major naval power in the world today. Numerically, the PLAN has become the largest naval force globally, having in possession of a battle fleet of approximately 350 surface and sub-surface platforms.

China began modernising its naval forces in the 1990s with an aim to build up a robust "Blue Water Navy" that would take up operations far and beyond its territorial waters. The Navy is being rapidly modernised to follow the strategy of "open water defence" – a shift from its earlier strategy of "offshore defence." The massive modernisation programme, involving acquisition and deployment of a large number of frigates, corvettes, destroyers, submarines, aircraft carriers, naval combat jets, helicopters and manned/ unmanned aircraft and (possibly) unmanned underwater platforms along with a broad range of weapons, especially ballistic and cruise missiles, has established China as a major maritime power in 21st century. The PLAN currently possesses over 100 destroyers and frigates, and more than 70 submarines, both nuclear and conventional even as it is advancing to induct several new-generation submarines into its fleet in the coming years. Induction of a Soviet-era aircraft carrier in 2012 majorly bolstered the PLAN's maritime capabilities. Meanwhile, Beijing has also swiftly built and commissioned its first indigenously-made aircraft carrier 'Shandong' in 2019 even as it has advanced in developing a second indigenous carrier with planned induction by 2022.

The country is pursuing the ambitious goal to build aircraft carrier battle groups (CBGs) and deploy them in the strategically vital South China Sea and East China Sea to deter the presence of US naval forces as well as other regional powers. Development and progressive induction of other support ships is also going on to expand China's global maritime power projection capabilities.

The last military White Paper released in May 2015 called for a greater role for the PLA Navy in particular by emphasising the maritime domain as one of four "critical security domains" where China must increase its capabilities. The White Paper stated the following: In line with the strategic requirement of offshore waters defence and open seas protection, the PLA Navy will gradually shift its focus from "offshore waters defence" to the combination of "offshore waters defence" with "open seas protection," and build a combined, multi-functional and efficient marine combat force structure. The PLAN will enhance its capabilities for strategic deterrence and counter-attack, maritime manoeuvres, joint operations at sea, comprehensive defence and comprehensive support. The latest Defence White Paper of 2019 mentions about "moderate increase" in the active force strength of the PLAN.

Accordingly, China has built the most diverse and powerful naval force in the entire Asian continent to stake claim over the resource-rich ECS and SCS while expanding its strategic outreach beyond its territorial waters. With an intent to secure strategic oil routes in the Arabian Sea and Indian Ocean, and lay claim over vital energy resources all across Asia and beyond, Beijing has also opened its first overseas naval logistics base in Djibouti even as it plans to set up more such military bases in other countries in the foreseeable future. The PLAN also conducts complex multi-discipline warfare trainings throughout the year besides taking part in multilateral naval exercises. It has steadily expanded its outreach by operating in the Mediterranean even while increasing its intelligence collection deployments in the Western Pacific. The PLAN has also gone on to deploy submarines and other strategic naval assets in the Indian Ocean Region (IOR) in recent times.

Of late, the Chinese Navy has also fulfilled a long-held dream of gaining access to the "First Island Chain" in the Pacific Ocean. The "First Island Chain" refers to the first major archipelagos off the East Asian continental mainland, including the Japanese archipelago, Ryukyu Islands, Taiwan and the northern Philippines. The Chinese naval vessels have sailed through these major East Asian archipelagos which are closely guarded by the US and Japan. The PLA Navy, for the first time, also showcased its fleet of nuclear submarines during a military exercise in the West Pacific in October 2013.

The People's Liberation Army Navy is divided into three fleets – the East China Sea (Beihai) fleet, the South China Sea (Nanhai) fleet and the North China Sea (Donghai) fleet headquartered at Qingdao, Zhanjiang and Ningbo respectively. Each fleet has under its command fleet aviation, support bases, flotillas, maritime garrison commands, aviation divisions and marine brigades. In terms of equipment and war operational responsibilities, the PLAN is composed of submarine, surface vessel, naval aviation, Marine Corps and coastal defence arms.

Major naval bases: Lushun, Huludao, Qingdao, Shanghai, Zhoushan, Wenzhou, Xiamen, Guangzhou, Zhanjiang, Yulin, Yalong, Luda, Dalian, Hong Kong, Whampoa

Personnel: 240,000+

Equipment

Category	Name	In Service	On Order
Aircraft Carrier	Liaoning (STOBAR)	1	
	Shandong / Type 001A class (indigenously built)	1	1 (more likely to be built)
Training Ship	ATS Shichang (multi-role aviation)	1	
Destroyer	Luhai-class (Type 051B)	1	
	Luyang I class (Type 052B)	2	
	Luyang II class (Type 052C)	6	
	Luyang III class (Type 052D)	20	5
	Type 055	3	5
Submarine	SSBN Jin class (Type 094/ 094A)	6	
	SSBN Xia class (Type 092)	1	
	SSB Qing (Type 032)	1	
	SSN Shang (Type 093/093A/ 093B/093G)	2	4
	SSN Han (Type 091)	2	
	SSN Type 095		14
	SS Kilo class (Project 877EKM & 636)	2 + 10	
	SS Song class (Type 039/039G)	13	
	SS Yuan class (Type039A, B, C, AG/ Type 041)	17	5+
	SS Ming class (Type 035)	15	
Frigate/ Corvette	Jiangkai (Type 054)	6	2
	Jiangkai II (Type 054A)	31	
	Jianghu class (Type 053)	6	
	Jiangwei II class (Type 053H3)	10	
	Jiangdao (Type 056/56-A)	72	
Patrol Boat	Houbei class (Type 022)	70+	
	Houjian (Type 037II)	4	
	Houxin class (Type 037IG)	25	
	Hainan (Type 037)	40 (being phased out)	
	Shanghai III class (Type 062I) gunboat	10+	

...continued

Category	Name	In Service	On Order
LPD	Yuzhao (Type 071)	5	3
LHD			2+
LCAC	Jingsah II/Yuyi class (Type 726)	30	
	Zubr class	5	
LCM	Yuchin class (reserve) (Type 068/ 069)	30	
LCU	Yunnan class (Type 067)		
LST	Yuting II (Type 072A)	15	
	Yuting (Type 072 II/ III)	15+	
	Yukan (Type 072)	3	
LSM	Yuhai class (Type 074/ 074A)	14	
	Yudao class (Type 073II/ 073III)		
	Yunshu class (Type 073A)		
APA	Qiongsha class (attack/ transport)	4	
AH	Shichang (multi-role aviation)	2	
Patrol Hydrofoil	Huchuan class	20	
Mine sweeper/ Mine hunter	Wolei / Bulieijian class (minelayer)	1	
	Wochi class (Type 81/81-A)	10	
	Wozang-class (Type 082B)	5	
	Type 010 (Sov T-43) (in reserve)	40	
	Lianyun class (minesweeper-coastal)	50+	
Auxiliary ship	Type 901 (fast combat supply ship)	2	
	Fuchi-class (Type 903/ 903A) replenishment ship	8	
	Oiler/ Cargo	50	
	Type 908 replenishment ship	1	
	Survey (Ocean/ Hydro) Ship	35+ 3	13
	Hospital ship	4	
	Ocean Going Training ship Qi Jiguang	1	
	Reconnaissance / Surveillance/ Intelligence	20+	
	Space Event ship (Yuan Wang class)	7	

...continued

Category	Name	In Service	On Order
Weapons	ASM C802A C602 C704 C705		
	SAM HQ-61 HQ-7 HQ-9 HQ-16 Shtil		
	Torpedo Yu-1/Yu-1A Yu-2, Yu-3 Yu-4, Yu-6 53-65KE		

New Procurements/ Upgrades

◆ The first domestically-built aircraft carrier, Type 001A (Shandong), commissioning into service in December 2019, has completed its first operational deployment in 2021. Development of a second indigenous carrier platform is advancing and it is expected to be launched in 2022. The PLAN intends to operate at least six aircraft carriers.

◆ The country's first aircraft carrier group, formed around aircraft carrier Liaoning, reached initial operational capability (IOC) in 2018. Other naval platforms in the carrier group include a Type 052D class destroyer, three Type 052C class destroyers, and two Type 054A class frigates.

◆ Type 095, a new variant of the Type 093 Shang-class nuclear-powered submarine (SSN), is under development to replace the older generation of Han-class SSNs. The new improved submarines would feature vertical launch system and may be able to carry the YJ-18 anti-ship cruise missiles. A total of 14 such platforms are being planned to be inducted in coming years. The first Han-class platform retired in 2016 with the remaining two likely to be retired soon.

◆ Yuan-class (Type 039A/Type 041) SSKs with AIP technology are being progressively inducted.

◆ Two more advanced Jin-class (Type 094A) SSBNs have likely been inducted, taking their total number to six. Each SSBN is designed to carry up to 12 JL-2 SLBMs having an estimated range of over 8,000-km. The new subs with the long-range missiles will give China its first credible sea-based nuclear deterrent capability.

◆ The Type-096 class SSBN, currently under development, is expected to become the PLAN's next-generation missile submarine. Based on the Type-094 class SSBN, the Type-096 class is likely to be armed with the longer range JL-3 ballistic missiles, the first test of which was conducted in 2018. The PLA Navy may deploy as many as eight Type-096 class submarines in the coming years.

◆ At least three Type 055 large guided missile destroyers have been commissioned into service since 2020. The 10,000-ton class powerful warship, built indigenously, is capable of carrying over 100 anti-ship, anti-air and ship-to-land cruise missiles. A total of eight such platforms are likely to be inducted over the years. The Type 055 class of warships could possibly be used to escort the PLAN's indigenous aircraft carriers.

◆ More number of Type 052D (Luyang III class) guided missile destroyers are progressively being inducted into service. The 25th platform of the class was unveiled in September 2020. The warships, being built as an advancement over the Type-52C class of DDGs, are capable of launching HQ-9B air-defence missiles along with anti-ship and anti-submarine missiles.

◆ The sole Luhai class (Type 051B) destroyer has completed a major modernisation programme and is now equipped with HHQ-16 SAMs, YJ-12 anti-ship missiles and Type 1130 CIWS, replacing the older weapon systems. The warship's air and surface search radars have also been upgraded.

◆ Commissioning of the final batch of Type 056A "Jiangdao" class of stealth corvettes is completed in 2021, taking their total number to 72. The new warships flaunt a sleek design and are replacing the Type 037 patrol boats. They would primarily be deployed on escort missions and for anti-submarine warfare operations.

◆ The Yuzhao-class (Type 071) landing platform docks (LPDs) are being commissioned. A total of eight such platforms would be inducted.

◆ Type 075 class of LHD (landing helicopter docks) are being inducted. While the first platform has been commissioned, two others are at different stages of development/ sea trial. The new class of amphibious assault ships, reportedly capable of carrying at least 30 armed helicopters, is the biggest-ever such platform being built for the PLAN.

◆ The second Type 901 fast combat supply ship has entered service in 2018-end. The first platform was commissioned in 2017. The new supply ships, pegged as Asia's largest, will form part of the Chinese aircraft carrier fleet.

◆ At least five Type 815A sophisticated electronic reconnaissance (ELINT) ships, capable of conducting all-weather, round-the-clock observation on multiple targets, have been commissioned over the years.

Marine Forces

Personnel: 30,000 (Plans are on to increase the number to 100,000 and deploy them in overseas bases)

Equipment

Category	Name	In Service
MBT	Type 63A	150+
	Type 60	
APC	Type 63	60
Artillery	Type 83, 122mm	
	Type 54, 122mm	
MLRS	Type 63, 107mm	
ATGW	HJ-73	
	HJ-8	
SAM	HN-5	
	JL-2	

Naval Aviation

Personnel: 30,000+

Equipment

Category	Name	In Service	On Order
Bomber/ Anti-ship strike	Su-30Mk2	40+	
	H-6/ H-6J	50	
	H-6G		
	JH-7/JH-7A/B	50+	
	J-10A/B	30+	
Fighter/ Ground attack	J-15	24	
	J-11B/BS	50	
	J-7	30	
	Q-5	40+	
	J-8	40+	
Maritime Patrol/ ISR/ ASW	Be-6	10	
	SH-5	6	
	Y-8X		
	Gaoxin-6		
AEWCS	KJ-500, KJ-600		
Trainer	JL-9, JJ-9		
	JL-10	12	
Helicopter	Z-8 Super Frelon	12	
	Z-9	50	
	Z-20F		
	Ka-27	3	
	Ka-28	15	
Transport	Y-7		40+
	Y-8		
Amphibious	AG-600		17

New Procurements/ Upgrades

◆ Gaoxin-6, an anti-submarine aircraft developed and manufactured by Aviation Industry Corp of China and based on the Y-8 transport plane, has been commissioned into service and deployed with the PLAN's North Sea Fleet.

◆ China has formed its first aircraft carrier-borne aviation force under the PLAN. The force comprises carrier-borne fighter jets, jet trainers and ship-borne helicopters to carry out anti-submarine, rescue and vigilance tasks.

◆ Development of J-31 (FC-31) stealth fighter is progressing. The new platform, being developed for both PLAN and PLA Air Force, is likely to replace the Navy's J-15 carrier-borne fighters in future. The indigenously built J-15s have faced technical glitches and some have crashed during flight trials. The PLAN may now consider adopting the J-20 stealth fighters (deployed in the PLAAF) for carrier-borne operations, according to media reports.

◆ H-6G bomber – a new electronic warfare aircraft configuration – has been deployed with the PLAN's South China Sea fleet. The aircraft is a modified variant of H-6 strategic bomber.

◆ KJ-600 – a new naval airborne early warning and control (AEW&C) aircraft designed to operate from the PLAN's aircraft carriers – is undergoing flight trials.

◆ A new variant of the KJ-500 airborne early warning and control (AEW&C) aircraft fitted with aerial refuelling probe has been commissioned into the PLAN's aviation wing.

◆ The first regiment of JL-10H advanced jet trainers/ light attack aircraft has been commissioned into service. The JL-10H is the naval variant of L-15 advanced jet trainer.

◆ A new anti-submarine warfare helicopter, designated Z-18 (F & J), is undergoing flight tests. The rotorcraft has been developed from the Z-8 platform which is a derivative of French SA-321 Super Frelon.

◆ Naval variant of Z-20 multi-role rotorcraft, designated Z-20F, is under development. It is likely to be used for amphibious roles.

◆ The AG-600 large amphibious aircraft has successfully undergone its maiden flight over sea in July 2020. The aircraft undertook its maiden successful flight in December 2017, followed by a high-speed glide test on water in 2018. The indigenously built platform was officially unveiled by AVIC in 2016. Pegged as the world's largest amphibious aircraft, the AG-600 is designed for passenger transport, maritime patrol, and search & rescue missions among other military and non-military tasks.

◆ A new medium altitude long endurance (MALE) UAV, HK-5000G, has been unveiled in 2018. The drone could be deployed on the PLAN's aircraft carriers.

◆ Blowfish I – a new vertical take-off and landing (VTOL) UAV has entered service.

◆ A new amphibious drone boat, named "Marine Lizard", has successfully been tested in 2019. The new platform – a trimaran propelled by diesel-powered hydrojet – is world's first armed amphibious drone boat.

COAST GUARD: In the wake of rising maritime disputes with a number of its neighbours, China, in July 2013 operationalised a new, unified Coast Guard, enabling it to be armed with weapons. The previous configuration of the coast guard attached it to the police, fisheries law enforcement and Customs' anti-smuggling maritime police. The new China Coast Guard (CCG) has integrated the functions of marine surveillance with the existing coast guard. The new agency is now dealing with conflicts in the disputed waters as per Chinese law and the divisions that were previously not allowed to be equipped with weapons, are now armed. The CCG reportedly has 11 squadrons and more than 16,000 personnel. The CCG is rapidly inducting new vessels, including patrol ships and cutters, to ramp up its capabilities.

In 2018, China decided to transfer the Coast Guard's command to the country's military. The Coast Guard was previously administered by the State Oceanic Administration. With the latest change, the CCG has come under direct administration of China's Central Military Commission (CMC) and is more involved in military drills and daily exercises with the PLA Navy.

AIR FORCE: The People's Liberation Army Air Force (PLAAF), which was primarily tasked to defend the country by carrying out air defence missions and provide protection to the PLA ground forces, has rapidly evolved as a modern, aggressive air power capable of conducting offensive aerial missions against targets even beyond its territory.

The PLA Air Force's modernisation programme began in the 1990s when China acquired fourth-generation fighter aircraft capability along with support aircraft and advanced weapons. The country's robust economic growth further propelled its defence indigenisation efforts which included development of a range of modern air platforms such as new trainer jets, combat helicopters, advanced stealth fighters, unmanned aerial systems, early warning and electronic warfare support aircraft, transport aircraft and airborne early warning systems among others. Since 2012, the PLA Air Force has made increasing efforts to bolster its overall capabilities by acquiring whole new range of modern air platforms and related assets. In the wake of the continuing territorial disputes in the South China Sea and East China Sea regions, the PLA Air Force has continued to conduct military exercises involving a wide variety of its aircraft including strategic bombers, fighter jets, early warning aircraft and refuelling aircraft. It also conducts regular aerial patrols over the East China Sea Air Defence Identification Zone (ADIZ) set up in 2013.

According to the 2015 defence White Paper released by the Chinese Defence Ministry, the PLAAF has shifted its strategy from "territorial air defence" to a strategy of both "offense and defence". Besides, it is also focused on building up an air-space defence force structure that can meet the requirements of "informationized" operations. The PLAAF would enhance its capabilities for strategic early warning, air strike, air and missile defence, information countermeasures, airborne operations, strategic projection and comprehensive support, the 2015 White Paper had stated.

The PLAAF is primarily composed of aviation, ground air defence, radar, airborne and electronic countermeasures (ECM) arms. It is made up of air teams, regiments (airports and air stations), divisions, and regional air forces (air armies). In terms of equipment and war operational responsibilities, it mainly consists of air units, anti-aircraft units, surface-to-air missile units, paratroops and radar units.

Major air bases: Shahezhen, Xijiao, Datong, Zunhua, Chengdu, Jing Hong/Gasa, Luliang, Jiugucheng, Luyang and Zhengzhou. China also has operational airfields, around 14, in Tibet Autonomous Region, including at Lhasa, Kashgar, Korla, Yankaw, Hotan, Hoping, Cherchen (Qiemo) and Gardzong. Other major airfields in the region include Bangda, Shiquanhe, Bayixincun and Kongka. The PLAAF has also swiftly activated more airfields in the TAR.

Personnel: 400,000+

Equipment

Category	Name	In Service	On Order
Fighter/ Ground attack/ Interceptor aircraft	J-20	50+	100+
	J-16	150+	
	Su-27SK	60	
	Su-30MKK, Su-30 MKK2	105+100	
	Su-35	24	
	J-11B/BS	300+	
	J-16	24	
	J-7	250	
	J-8	160+	
	J-8II	60	
	Q-5	50+	
	J-10A, B, C	100+	200+

Category	Name	In Service	On Order
Bomber	H-6/ 6H/ 6M	120	
	H-6K	40	
	JH-7A/B	100+	
Surveillance/ Reconnaissance aircraft	Y-9G	7	
	JZ-6/7/8	100	
	HZ-5, HZ-7	40	
AWACS, AEW&C	KJ-2000	6	
	KJ-200	5	
	KJ-500		
ELINT/ SIGINT aircraft	Tu-154M/D	4	
	Y-8JB/ Y-9JB	8	
Transport, Tanker aircraft	Y-20	5	50+
	Y-12	8	
	Y-11	15	
	Y-9	50	
	Y-8	40	
	Y-7	40	
	Il-76MD	20+	
Air-refuelling aircraft	HY-6	12	
	Il-78	4	
Trainer aircraft	Su-27UBK	40+	
	Hongdu L-15 Falcon		
	CJ-6		
	JL-8	10	40
	JL-9	30+	
	JL-10		
Helicopter	Mi-8	40+	
	Mi-17		
	Mi-171/ Mi-171E	160+	
	Z-8	30+	
	Z-9 (A/B & W)	40+	
	Z-11, Z-19 (attack)		
	As332 Super Puma (VIP transport)	6	
UAV	Wing Loong I, II		
	BZK-005		
	CH-4		
	WZ-8		
SAM	HQ-9, HQ-7, HQ-22		
	S-300	6 regiments	
	S-400		On order (deliveries going on)
LACM, AShM	KD-20, KD-88, YJ-12, KD-63		

Category	Name	In Service	On Order
Anti-radiation missile	YJ-91		
AAM	PL-2, PL-5, PL-7, PL-8, PL-9, PL-11, PL-12		

New Procurements/Upgrades

◆ The new J-20 advanced stealth fighters are progressively being inducted. J-20 was officially commissioned in 2017 and put into combat service in 2018.

◆ J-11D, a new variant of J-11 fighter, is under development. The new warplane, being built by Shenyang Aircraft Corporation, features a phased-array radar and an air refuelling system and is armed with PL-10 air-to-air missile.

◆ The J-16 multi-role attack aircraft are being inducted since 2016. The new combat platform is believed to be a derivative of the Russian Su-30MKK fighter. It has been designed for both the PLA Air Force and Navy.

◆ Russia has completed delivery of all 24 Su-35 super-manoeuvrable fighters to PLAAF in 2019. The platforms were delivered under a $2 billion deal inked with Moscow in November 2015.

◆ Acquisition of Sukhoi Su-57 stealth fighters from Russia is under consideration.

◆ Induction of advanced H-6K strategic bombers has started. The new bombers, with extended range, are capable of carrying long-range cruise missiles. New modified variants of the bomber also feature nose-mounted refuelling probe.

◆ A new strategic bomber, designated H-20, with long-range strike capability is under development.

◆ The new KJ-500 airborne early warning and control (AEW&C) aircraft has started entering service. The platform is based on the Shaanxi Y-9 four-turboprop transport aircraft. Development of another improved variant, the third-generation KJ-3000 AEWC, has also started.

◆ The L-15 advance jet trainer has completed development phase and entered series production. PLAAF has commissioned limited number of L-15s so far. An armed variant of the jet trainer is also likely to be inducted. The new supersonic training and light attack jet has been developed to train the pilots of China's fourth-gen warplanes, including the J-10, J-11 and JF-17.

◆ More number of Y-20 military transport aircraft are joining service after the first platform was inducted in 2016. The indigenously-built large military transport plane made its maiden test flight in 2013. Bearing resemblance with the US' C-17 Globe master and Russia's Il-76 freighter aircraft, the Y-20 is China's largest home-grown military transport plane. The aircraft can also be configured for airborne early warning & control (AEW&C) operations.

◆ An agreement has been signed with Ukraine's Antonov to jointly develop An-225 strategic airlifter.

◆ A new variant of Z-11 attack helicopter which was unveiled in 2016 and designated Z-11WB, is likely to be inducted by 2022.

◆ The Z-20 multi-role helicopter is likely being inducted for transport and other roles.

◆ Wing Loong II – a new variant of Wing Loong UAV – has been inducted.

◆ The CH-4 medium altitude long-range unmanned combat aerial vehicle (UCAV) has entered service. A new, improved variant, CH-4C, is also under development.

◆ The first set of Russian-made S-400 Triumf advanced interceptor-based air defence system was delivered in July 2018. Russian media (TASS news agency) reported delivery of the second batch of the weapon systems in January 2020 (however, there was no official confirmation of the same). Later news reports stated that delivery of the remaining S-400 long-range anti-aircraft missiles, expected to be completed by 2020, had been "suspended" in the wake of the Coronavirus pandemic.

◆ Development of a new air-launched ballistic missile (ALBM) is under progress. The new weapon will reportedly arm the latest variant of H-6 strategic bomber, dubbed "H-6N". The new bomber was publicly unveiled in October 2019. According to some reports in 2020, the new bomber could possibly be armed with China's hypersonic weapon, work on which is progressing.

STRATEGIC FORCE COMMAND: The strategic force command or the strategic missile force was created to control China's ground-based strategic missile arsenal, including its nuclear ballistic and conventional missiles. Previously called the PLA Second Artillery Force (PLASAF), it was renamed as the PLA Rocket Force (PLARF) as part of largescale military reforms announced in 2016.

The PLARF has been upgraded into a "full-fledged" new service on par with the PLA Army, Air Force and Navy, indicating that it now has several arms and special troops besides having academies, research institutes and logistic support system under its command. As the core force of China's strategic deterrence, the PLARF, unlike the erstwhile PLASAF, is likely to be in command of all three legs of China's nuclear triad and could deploy its nuclear assets on land, sea and air in the coming years. The new force thus could eventually emerge as the first independent service with land, sea and air nuclear forces in the world. The PLARF is also expected to separate its nuclear and conventional wings. While the nuclear missiles would be responsible for strategic nuclear deterrence, the conventional arsenal would be used in the first round of strikes. The PLARF now focuses on nuclear deterrence and nuclear counter-attack capabilities; intensify the construction of medium and long-range precision strike weapons; and reinforce the strategic check-and-balance capability of the country. According to the 2019 Defence White Paper, the active force strength in the PLARF has been "moderately increased". The PLARF "has organized force-on-force evaluation-oriented training and training based on operational plans at brigade and regiment levels, strengthened training for joint strikes, and completed regular exercises," the Defence White Paper notes. Besides bolstering its overall arsenal by adding a wide range of sophisticated ballistic and cruise missiles, the PLARF has also continued to conduct new weapon tests at frequent intervals.

SPACE FORCE COMMAND: Acquisition of advanced space-based technology for civil and military purposes has played a crucial role in China's steady ascent as a rising power, outperforming its other Asian counterparts, including Japan and India. China has avidly pursued the goal to reach outer space and exploit its potential for carrying out both civilian as well as military operations. It has also emphasised on the need to effectively integrate its air and space prowess for launching offensive and defensive operations. From orbiting a large number of communications, navigation, surveillance and reconnaissance satellite systems to developing and testing an anti-satellite (ASAT) weapon, China has taken giant strides in its space capabilities in the 21st century. The successful ASAT test in January 2007, indeed, made China the first country to hit down a satellite in outer space and raised global concern over unleashing a future arms race in space. Such space-based capabilities of China have been affiliated with its Central Military Command which controls and overviews the country's space programme. Beijing has also placed in orbit a significant number of satellites dedicated for military roles.

The PRC has also successfully put in place an independent satellite navigation network consisting a constellation of indigenously-built 'Beidou' or Compass navigation satellites. The robust navigation network was completed in June 2020 when China successfully placed in orbit the 55th and final satellite (30th Beidou-3 configuration) of the network. The Beidou is now one of the four global navigation networks operational alongside that of the US' GPS, Russia's GLONASS and the European Union's Galileo.

The Beidou project, formally initiated in 1994, began serving China in 2000 and the Asia-Pacific region in 2012-end. The robust network has been put to service with both civilian and military roles. The satellites in the network have been developed in Beidou-1, Beidou-2 and Beidou-3 configurations.

Major Armaments Producers

Land equipment manufacturers
China North Industries Group (Norinco) is a leading producer of most of China's battle tanks, armoured vehicles and other armament.

Shipbuilders/ naval equipment manufacturers
China State Shipbuilding Corporation (CSSC) is a leading shipbuilding conglomerate consisting of shipyards, naval equipment manufacturers and research institutes.

China Shipbuilding Industry Corporation (CSIC) is another major shipbuilding conglomerate mainly involved in warships design, development, repairing of domestic and foreign naval vessels. In 2016, the conglomerate announced a plan to consolidate some of its shipbuilding activities in a bid to boost efficiencies. In 2019, the Chinese Government approved the merger of CSIC with CSSC.

Dalian Shipbuilding Industry Company (DSIC) is the largest shipbuilding company of China operating under CSIC.

Guangzhou Shipyard International (GSI) operates under CSSC. It is the largest modern integrated shipbuilding facility in Southern China.

Jiangnan Shipyard located in Shanghai, designs, develops and repairs both military and civilian ships.

Aerospace equipment manufacturers
China Aerospace Science and Technology Corporation (CASTC) is

the leading missile weaponry manufacturer.

China Changfeng Mechanics and Electronics Technology Academy works under CASTC to design, develop and produce air and missile defence systems.

China Aviation Industry Corporation (CAIC) is the aircraft manufacturing consortium. It has been split into two groups – AVIC I which is primarily producing fighters, bombers and other large aircraft, and AVIC I II which is manufacturing trainer jets, transport aircraft, helicopters and other small planes.

Chengdu Aircraft Industrial Corporation (CAC) is the manufacturer and supplier of combat jets and aircraft parts.

Changhe Aircraft Industries Corporation is a helicopter manufacturer.

China National Aeroengine Corporation (CAREC) is an aero engines' producer for manned aircraft.

China National Aerotechnology Import–Export Corporation (CATIC) is a leading trading agency that deals with the import and export of defence products.

Harbin Aircraft Manufacturing Corporation (HAMC) manufactures helicopters. It operates under the Harbin Aircraft Industries Group that produces helicopter, light and general-purpose aircraft, and regional aircraft in China.

Shenyang Aircraft Corporation (SAC) is a civilian and military aircraft manufacturer.

DEFENCE DEALS

Joint Venture Programmes

Pakistan

Al-Khalid (MBT-2000): China and Pakistan jointly developed the main battle tank in the 1990s. The MBTs are operational in the Pakistan Army.

Hongdu JL-8 jet trainer: The Hongdu Aviation Industry Corporation (HAIC) of China and Pakistan Aeronautical Complex (PAC) have jointly developed the Hongdu JL-8 (export variant Karakorum-8 or K-8) basic two-seat jet trainer with light attack capabilities.

JF-17 Thunder (FC-1) fighter: China has developed the multi-role fighter aircraft jointly with Pakistan. The Pakistan Air Force has inducted the fighters. The two partner countries have also been working to export the jet to other countries. Nigeria has acquired the JF-17 fighters for its Air Force in 2021.

Indonesia

Missile: Indonesia and China have agreed to strengthen their defence cooperation, including joint production of C-702 missiles.

The two countries signed an MoU in 2011 that stipulates joint military procurement by both countries in a government-to-government plan and a technological transfer with regard to certain types of weapons production, as well as joint-development and joint-marketing of certain types of military weapons.

Thailand

MRLS: Thailand and China have worked jointly to develop multiple rocket launchers with guidance system. The two sides signed an agreement in 2012 under which the Thai Defence Technology Institute, with China's help, developed the multiple rocket launchers called "DTI-1G (Guided)" which has a greater range than similar existing systems. In an earlier joint deal, the two countries had developed the DTI-1 system, having a range between 60 and 180 km. The new DTI-1G system has been put into service with the Royal Thai Army in 2015-16.

Arms Export

China has almost doubled its weapons exports in the past few years and emerged as one of the world's top five largest arms exporters, the others in the list being the US, Russia, France and Germany. China's arms sales account for nearly 6% of the global share. Pakistan remains the top-most receiver of Chinese defence hardware. Beijing has also exported arms and weapons to several other countries including Iran, Libya, Saudi Arabia and Kuwait in the Middle East; Algeria, Egypt and Nigeria in Africa; Thailand, Indonesia, Bangladesh, Malaysia, Myanmar, North Korea and Sri Lanka in Asia; Argentina, Ecuador, Venezuela and Bolivia in South America among others. It has also made efforts to establish bilateral military-technical collaborations with Indonesia, Israel, Brazil, Switzerland and some other Latin American countries.

Recent major defence export deals clinched by Beijing include supply of submarines to Bangladesh, Pakistan and Thailand. It is also building four littoral mission ships for Malaysia (two platforms delivered as of 2021) while delivering main battle tanks to Thailand. Algeria has also emerged as another major market for Chinese weapons and platforms.

China's domestic shipbuilders have unveiled a slew of new submarine design concepts aimed at the export market. Chinese aerospace companies too have exported a large number of UAVs to a number of foreign customers in recent years even as newer drone variants have been unveiled for the export market. In 2018, China delivered an Y-8 military transport aircraft to Kazakhstan, thus marking its entry into the Commonwealth of Independent States (CIS) region. It has also reportedly delivered the HQ-9 air-defence system (FD-2000) to Uzbekistan in November 2018. Beijing has forayed into the European arms market as well by clinching a major deal with Serbia recently to deliver the Wing Loong combat drones. The first platforms have been delivered to Serbia in 2020.

A recently released report by the global military think-tank SIPRI has placed China as the world's second-biggest arms producer, behind the US and ahead of Russia. The report has taken into account the data available on the weapons production and exports by four major Chinese companies between 2015 and 2017. The companies include the Aviation Industry Corporation of China (AVIC), China North Industries Group Corporation (NORINCO), China Electronics Technology Group Corporation (CETC) and China South Industries Group Corporation (CSGC). Over the past 12 years, China has imported arms and weapons worth over $16 billion across the globe, a SIPRI report estimates.

Arms Import

While in the past, China has relied heavily on Russian technology for building majority of its defence equipment including aircraft, missiles and naval vessels, the country, in the last two decades, has vociferously attempted to be self-reliant in military sphere. Before the imposition of international arms embargo as a result of the Tiananmen Square crackdown in 1989, China was also importing weapons from France, Germany, Canada, UK, Israel and Egypt. The country was the world's top arms importer until 2009, but subsequently developed a robust domestic defence industry to meet its Armed Forces requirements as well as for export in the international arms market. Between 2011 and 2015, China's arms imports fell 25% compared with the previous five-year period, signalling growing confidence in the country's home-grown weaponry.

With an agenda of modernising and strengthening its armed forces by inducting indigenous platforms, weapons and systems, Beijing has focused on new technological innovations and breakthroughs and successfully produced a wide range of new-generation military hardware, even though many of such products find their origin either in the Western or Russian designs and technology. China is still importing some of the critical defence hardware, including aircraft engines, even as it intends to achieve complete self-reliance in military production in near future. Recently, it signed major defence contracts with Russia to acquire the S-400 air defence missile system and Su-35 fighter platform.

DEFENCE BUDGET

China is the top-most defence spender in Asia and ranks second in the global chart after the US. The country's defence budget maintained a double-digit growth for over two decades till 2015. In 2012, the defence budget of the Asian giant crossed $100 billion mark for the first time. Keeping pace with its rapid economic rise, China has been spending a visible share of its GDP – officially around 1.4% – on military developments, though according to defence analysts, the allocation could be as high as 3% as the country's defence budget does not include military R&D spending. An all-round military modernisation that includes development of new-generation fighter aircraft, large transport aircraft, combat helicopters, unmanned aerial systems, submarines, warships, aircraft carriers, new weapons and other systems along with existing military hardware upgrade, military training and human resource development have led to a sharp rise in China's annual defence budget. The military budget announced for 2017-18 was 1.044 trillion yuan ($151.43 billion) which was an increase of 7% over previous year's allocation. For 2018-19 period, Beijing allocated 1.11 trillion yuan ($175 billion) on defence. The amount was an increase of 8.1% over previous year's allocation. For 2019-20, the Government announced a budget of 1.19 trillion yuan (around US$177.61 billion) towards defence. The amount was an increase of 7.5% over previous year's spending. For 2020-21, the country announced a defence budget worth 1.27 trillion yuan (US$179 billion) – an increase of 6.6% over the last year's allocation.

The defence allocation for 2021 - 2022 is 1.35 trillion yuan (US$209 billion) – a slight increase (of 6.8%) over previous year's budget (at 6.6%). With this, China's defence budget crossed the US$200 billion mark for the first time even as Beijing has announced grandiose plans to build up a powerful military at par with that of the US by 2027.

Year	Allocation	% of GDP	% increase over previous year
2021	Yuan 1.35 trillion ($209 billion)	1.3	6.8
2020	Yuan 1.27 trillion ($179 bln)	1.3	6.6
2019	Yuan 1.19 trillion ($177.6 bln)	1.3	7.5
2018	Yuan 1.11 trillion ($175 bln)	1.5	8.1
2017	Yuan 1.04 trillion ($152 bln)	1.3	7
2016	Yuan 954 billion ($146 bln)		7.6
2015	Yuan 886.9 billion ($142 bln)	1.34	10.1
2014	Yuan 808.2 billion ($132 bln)	1.31	12.2
2013	Yuan 720.2 billion ($117 bln)	1.3	10.7
2012	Yuan 670 billion ($106 bln)	1.28	11.2
2011	Yuan 601 billion ($91.5 bln)	1.4	12.7

CONCLUSION

While evolving as a global economic powerhouse, China has simultaneously pursued large-scale, comprehensive military modernisation agenda to rapidly ramp up its force projection capabilities in 21st century. The country has laid down an ambitious roadmap to make rapid military strides by 2027 (to be at par with the US military) and win "informationised" wars by 2050. By aggressively flexing its military muscles, China appears to be posing a serious security challenge to several Asian powers, including India and Japan, and also to the US in the foreseeable future. Its "anti-access/ area-denial" (A2AD) strategy to keep "other" countries away from vital natural resources of the Asia-Pacific region has raised concern among the global community.

With its military resurgence and increasingly belligerent posture over territorial and regional issues, China has been aggressively attempting to steadily tilt the delicate balance of power in the entire Asian continent in its favour. By challenging and countering the US presence in the Asia-Pacific and asserting its supremacy in the waters of South China and East China Seas, the Asian nation has gone loud and clear in stating that it would confront any challenge to maintain its territorial sovereignty even while dictating terms in the region and beyond to safeguard its economic, strategic and all other interests.

Moreover, amidst the tightening global financial conditions and moderating international trade, the highly ambitious "Belt and Road" initiative (BRI) unveiled by Beijing which aims at reviving the ancient Silk Road trade route by building a grand new Silk Road and linking it with Asia, Africa, the Middle East and Europe, holds the possibility to reshape China and bolster its global power stature in a significant way over the coming years. In November 2020, the China-initiated Regional Comprehensive Economic Partnership (RCEP) programme also took shape with 14 countries spanning across the Asia-Pacific region signing the deal including Japan, South Korea, Australia and New Zealand, along with the 10 members of the ASEAN bloc besides China itself. Signed after eight long years of negotiations, the RCEP has emerged as the world's largest trading bloc, aimed at boosting the member nations' economic growth and prosperity.

Meanwhile, the deadly Coronavirus pandemic that originated in the Chinese city of Wuhan in late 2019 and rapidly spread to the entire world by early 2020, has not only resulted in massive economic downturns, but now poses even a greater challenge to drastically alter the wider strategic stability and change regional as well as global power equations in the ensuing future. In addition to all the above, the recent chaotic developments in Afghanistan following the withdrawal of America and the Taliban taking control of the Islamic country, may have long-term ramifications for regional security and stability, including that for China.

H-6K Bomber of PLA Air Force

CONTACT DETAILS
Ministry of Defence
No. 34, Fuchengmenwai Street
Xicheng District
Beijing, China
Email: mod@mod.gov.cn
www.eng.mod.gov.cn/

COLOMBIA
(Capital: Bogota)

INTRODUCTION
Area: 1,138,914 sq km
Population: 50,355,650 (July 2021 est.)
Coastline: 3,208 km (Caribbean Sea 1,760 km, North Pacific Ocean 1,448 km)
Maritime claims: Territorial sea: 12 nm
Exclusive Economic Zone: 200 nm
Continental shelf: 200 m depth or to the depth of exploitation

KEY POLITICAL PERSONS

PRESIDENT & COMMANDER-IN-CHIEF: Iván Duque Márquez

VICE PRESIDENT: Marta Lucía Ramírez

KEY DEFENCE PERSONS

MINISTER OF DEFENCE: Diego Andrés Molano Aponte

GENERAL COMMANDER OF THE ARMED FORCES: Gen. Luis Fernando Navarro Jiménez

CHIEF OF ARMY: Gen. Eduardo Enrique Zapateiro Altamiranda

CHIEF OF NAVY: Vice Adm. Gabriel Alfonso Pérez Garcés

CHIEF OF AIR FORCE: Gen. Ramsés Rueda Rueda

ECONOMY
Colombia is Latin America's fourth largest oil producer and the world's fourth largest coal producer, third largest coffee exporter, and second largest cut flowers exporter. Colombia's economy slowed in 2017 because of falling world market prices for oil and lower domestic oil production. Colombia has been a member of the Andean Community, which constitutes a free trade agreement with Bolivia, Ecuador, and Peru. Colombia has various FTAs with individual countries or associations. After slowing down to 1.4 percent in 2017, economic growth accelerated to 3 percent in the first half of 2019, driven by robust private consumption and stronger investment. It is expected to accelerate further to 3.6 percent in 2020. Higher profitability in the oil sector is expected to incentivize investments in exploitation and exploration. According to the Colombian government, the country's economic activity shrank by 16-17% in the second quarter of 2020 due to COVID-19 pandemic restrictions.

GDP (official exchange rate): $683.94 billion (2020), $734.22 billion (2019 est.)

Real Growth Rate (GDP): 3.26% (2019 est.), 2.51% (2018 est.)

Industries: Textiles, food processing, oil, clothing and footwear, beverages, chemicals, cement; gold, coal, emeralds

Oil - proved reserves: 1.665 billion bbl (1 January 2018 est.)

Natural gas - proved reserves: 113.9 billion cu m (1 January 2018 est.)

Total Exports: $39.14 billion (2020 est.), $52.96 billion (2019 est.)

Export Commodities: Crude petroleum, coal, refined petroleum, coffee, gold (2019)

Major Markets: United States 31%, China 11%, Panama 6%, Ecuador 5% (2019)

Total Imports: $51.56 billion (2020 est.), $65.83 billion (2019 est.)

Import Commodities: Refined petroleum, cars, broadcasting equipment, packaged medicines, corn (2019)

Major suppliers: United States 27%, China 20%, Mexico 7%, Brazil 6% (2019)

INTERNATIONAL DISPUTES
◆ In December 2007, the ICJ allocated San Andres, Providencia and Santa Catalina islands to Colombia under a 1928 Treaty but did not rule on 82 degrees W meridian as the maritime boundary with Nicaragua. It has managed a dispute with Venezuela over maritime boundary and Venezuelan-administered Los Monjes Islands near the Gulf of Venezuela.

◆ Managed dispute with Venezuela over maritime boundary and Venezuelan-administered Los Monjes Islands near the Gulf of Venezuela.

◆ Colombia, Honduras, Nicaragua, Jamaica and the US assert various claims to Bajo Nuevo and Serranilla Bank.

◆ The Colombian government and the FARC rebels signed a historic ceasefire deal in 2016, bringing them closer to ending more than five decades of conflict. As of December 2019, roughly 13,000 FARC ex-combatants continue to participate in the reintegration process based on the 2016 peace accord.

DEFENCE
ARMY
Personnel: 235,000

Equipment

Category	Name	In Service
APC/MICV/IFV	EE-9 Cascavel	170
	EE-11 Urutu	80+
	M8 Greyhound	5
	M113	100+
	M1117	30
	BTR-80	20

...continued

Category	Name	In Service
APC/MICV/IFV	RG-31 Nyala	
	ISBI	10+
RCL Gun	106mm M40	50+
Artillery	M116 howitzer	50+
	M101 howitzer	50+
	105 mm GIAT LG1	20
Mortar	81mm	100+
	120 mm	100+
	155 mm	
	60 mm	
	M30	50+
Anti-Tank GW	BGM-71 TOW	15
	Nimrod	
	Spike	
AA Gun	M1A1 40mm	30
	Bofors 40mm/L70	25+

Army Aviation

Category	Name	In Service
Aircraft	Commander 1000	2
	Beechcraft King Air 90	1
	Convair 580	1
	Piper PA-31 Navajo	2
	Rockwell 685 Commander	2
	An-32	2
	CASA C-212 Aviocar	5
	Piper PA-34 Seneca	5
Helicopter	UH-1H	30
	Bell Huey II	20+
	Kaman K-MAX	5
	Mil Mi-17	20+
	UH-60L	50+
UAV	RQ-11 Raven	

New Procurements/ Upgrades

◆ US handed over 60 training helicopters to Colombia to safeguard national security. The total case value is more than USD1.5 million; each helicopter costs about USD25,000. The delivery of the TH-67 aircraft to Colombia will certify Colombia as the premier rotary wing training facility in the region offering high-quality primary and advanced flight training to partner nations. USASAC and US Southern Command in this regard.

◆ The Colombian Army has contracted Sikorsky Aircraft to buy two additional S-70i BLACK HAWK helicopters. They will augment five S-70i helicopters in the Special Forces of the Colombian Army's Air Assault Division. The Colombian Army has already inducted five new Sikorsky S-70i multi-mission helicopters into its fleet of BLACK HAWK aircraft.

◆ The government is negotiating for the procurement of the at least 50 Leclerc Main Battle Tanks (MBTs) and support vehicles that are surplus from French Army.

NAVY

Personnel: 45,000 (including about 22,000 marines)

Equipment

Category	Name	In Service
Submarine	Type 209/1200	2
	Type SX-506	2
Frigate	Almirante Padilla class	4
Corvette	Donghae class	1
Offshore Patrol Vessel	Fassmer-80	3
	Auxiliary vessels	10+
	Boston Whaler Patrol craft	15
	Riverine support patrol vessel	5+

Naval Aviation

Category	Name	In Service
Aircraft	Cessna 208 Caravan	2
	Aero Commander 690	5
	C-212-100	1
	Cessna 208	2
	Super King Air	1
	CN-235-200	3
	Piper PA-28 Cherokee	3
	Piper PA-34 Seneca	4
Helicopter	MBB Bo 105 CB	2
	AS 555 Fennec	2
	Bell UH-1N Twin Huey	5
	Bell 412	

New Procurements/ Upgrades

◆ LRAD has been awarded a contract by the Colombian Navy to deliver 300X systems in support of its coastal defence patrol boats.

◆ The 209 class submarines of the Colombian Navy will be installing state-of-the-art sighting systems from Cassidian Optronics. The Colombian Navy has now ordered a SERO 250 search periscope from Cassidian Optronics for a 209 Class submarine.

◆ Two existing U209/1200 Class submarines, ARC Pijao and ARC Tayrona, are being modernised at the state-owned ship at Cartagena. These will be joined by another two German U206A submarines.

◆ The ARC is working on additional medium and long-term defence programmes, including the development and acquisition of a number of Coastal Patrol Vessels (Fassmer CPV-40), and the research & development of an indigenous corvette or frigate-class vessel, planned towards 2018-2020, as per reports.

AIR FORCE

Personnel: 14,000

Equipment

Category	Name	In Service
Fighter	IAI Kfir	20+
	EMB 314	20+
	OV-10	5
	AC-47T	5
	A-37	5+
Trainer	T-41D	10
	T-34M	10
	T-37B/C	10+
	AT-27	10+
	T-90 Calima	2
Tanker/Transport	707-373C	1
	KC-767	1
	C-212-300	3
	CASA CN-235-200	3
	CASA C-295M	4
	EMB 110P1A	2
	Arava	1
	C-130 Hercules	5+
	PA-23 Aztec	1
	PA-31T Cheyenne	1
	PA-34 Seneca	3
	Cessna 208	1
Helicopter	Bell 205	20+
	Bell 212 Twin Huey	10+
	MD 500 Defender	10+
	UH-60 Black Hawk	50+
	Bell 206	30
Reconnaissance and Intelligence	SA 2-37	5
	C-26A	5
	Citation SR-560	5+
	Cessna 208	5
	Super King Air 300	3

New Procurements/ Upgrades

◆ Sweden has signed a defence cooperation agreement with Colombia. Saab, on the other hand, is hopefully interested in selling Gripen fighter aircraft to Colombia.

◆ Colombian Air Force has acquired AESA Radars for Kfirs.

Defence Expenditure

Total defence spending: $10 billion (2018 approx.)

Defence spending in terms of GDP: 3% of GDP (2020 est.), 3.2% of GDP (2019)

Domestic suppliers: INDUMIL (arms and ammo), CIAC (aviation), CODALTEC (digital), and COTECMAR (naval).

Foreign suppliers: United States, Israel,

Brazil, South Africa, Spain, Russia, Belgium, Germany, France, United Kingdom, Sweden, Canada.

According to the International Trade Administration, US Department of Commerce, the Colombian Defence Ministry has a budget of approximately USD 10.4 billion, which is equivalent to roughly 12 percent of the total Colombian budget for 2021. According to an online report by the US Commercial Service of the US Department of Commerce, Colombia's defence budget decreased slightly in 2019 to a total of USD10.5 billion. Of this total, USD438 million is earmarked for purchases of equipment and hardware. Additionally, Colombia's Armed Forces continue to transform into a traditional force that protects national sovereignty from external threats, instead of fighting an internal conflict against armed guerrilla groups. The demobilised guerrilla group FARC has converted itself into small political party that has had no official army since the peace deal was signed in 2017. Colombia will continue to be a major defence equipment importer via state-owned entities and local manufacturing entities such as: INDUMIL (manufacturer of Galil rifles, Cordoba pistol, ammunition and explosives), COTECMAR (currently manufacturing patrol vessels under Fassmer's license and LPR 40s), CIAC (Manufacturer of aircraft parts and the T-90 Calima), CODALTEC (simulator manufacturer and software developer), INDUMIL (arms and ammo), CIAC (aviation), CODALTEC (digital), and COTECMAR (naval).

Defence Production and R&D

Grupo Social y Empresarial de Defensa - GSED (Social and Entrepreneurial Defence Group) is the organisation built by the Colombian Defence ministry by involving 18 of the State-run enterprises and institutions that were defence-oriented. GSED has become the second largest Colombian State-run conglomerates, employing over 8,900 people by 2010. Colombia has produced a number of wheeled APC prototypes, armoured cars, river patrol boats, tugs, medium-sized river support ships, light aircrafts, mortars and so on. The GSED companies were involved in several high-tech research and development contracts, including developing sensors and data links, unmanned aerial vehicles (UAVs), 70-mm rockets, and mine-resistant boots for infantrymen and mine detection systems. In 2006, the Corporacón de Ciencia y Tecnología de la Industria Naval, Marítima y Fluvial (COTECMAR), reported sales of $39 million. By 2009 these sales had gone up to $106 million. This included major work on 39 of the Navy's boats and ships. The manufacturing of BTR-80 APC's has also started in the COTECMAR inventory.

Defence Procurement

Former Colombian President Uribe had announced the launch of the Democracy Consolidation Plan in 2007, which is an armed forces expansion and modernisation plan funded by some $3.73 billion obtained from a new tax elaborated by his administration and applied to a number of high performing Colombian enterprises. The defence ministry has also negotiated for the procurement of the at least 50 Leclerc Main Battle Tanks (MBTs) and support vehicles that are surplus from French Army, in February 2010. At present, a wide variety of equipment is on order from France, Germany, Israel and Russia in addition to US defence aid under bilateral anti-drug support programmes.

CONTACT DETAILS

Ministry of National Defence
Carrera 54 No. 26 - 25 CAN,
Bogotá - Colombia PBX (57-1)
315 0111 - 018000 913022

Defence Forces HQ
Centro Administrativo Nacional
Avenida Eldorado, Carrera 52
Santa Fe de Bogota, D.C
Tel: +5712669300

CROATIA
(Capital: Zagreb)

INTRODUCTION

Area: 56,594 sq km
Population: 4,208,973 (July 2021 est.)
Coastline: 5,835 km (mainland 1,777 km, islands 4,058 km)
Maritime claims: Territorial sea: 12 nm
Continental shelf: 200 m depth or to the depth of exploitation

KEY POLITICAL PERSONS

PRESIDENT & COMMANDER-IN-CHIEF: Zoran Milanovic

KEY DEFENCE PERSONS

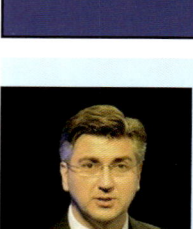
PRIME MINISTER: Andrej Plenkovic

MINISTER OF DEFENCE: Mario Banozic

CHIEF OF GENERAL STAFF: Adm. Robert Hranj

COMMANDER OF ARMY: Col. Gen. Boris Seric

COMMANDER OF NAVY: Commodore Ivo Raffanelli

COMMANDER OF AIR FORCE: Brig. Gen. Michael Krizanec

ECONOMY

Croatia is a member of the European Union. Croatia's economy began to improve between 2000-2007, with moderate GDP growth focusing more on tourism and credit-driven consumer spending. Tourism is one of the main pillars of the Croatian economy, comprising 19.6% of Croatia's GDP. Croatia entered the EU on July 1, 2013, and is now subject to EU trade agreements. Croatia is working to become a regional energy hub by 2019-2020. The government projects Croatia will adopt the Euro by 2024. Croatia is a strong democracy with a market-oriented economy, but retains significant state control or involvement in a number of industries. The Croatian Government has made progress on robust economic reforms, and says it intends to further consolidate public spending, improve the business climate, and foster economic growth. Croatia is an active member in United Nations, North Atlantic Treaty Organisation, Euro-Atlantic Partnership Council, Organisation for Security and Cooperation in Europe, International Monetary Fund, World Bank, and World Trade Organisation. Croatia also is an observer to the Organisation of American States. Croatia's economy has been affected severely triggered by COVID-19 pandemic and it has the reversed the economic gains of last five years. There is hope that the economic recovery will gain momentum in 2021.

GDP (official exchange rate): $107.11 billion (2020 est.), $116.89 billion (2019 est.)

Real Growth Rate (GDP): 2.94% (2019 est.), 2.7% (2018 est.)

Industries: Chemicals and plastics, machine tools, fabricated metal, electronics, pig iron and rolled steel products, aluminium, paper, wood products, construction materials, textiles, shipbuilding, petroleum and petroleum refining, food and beverages, tourism

Oil - proved reserves: 71 million bbl (1 January 2018 est.)

Natural gas - proved reserves: 24.92 billion cu m (1 January 2018 est.)

Total Exports: $23.66 billion (2020 est.), $31.07 billion (2019 est.)

Export Commodities: Refined petroleum, packaged medicines, cars, medical cultures/vaccines, lumber (2019)

Major Markets: Italy 13%, Germany 13%, Slovenia 10%, Bosnia and Herzegovina 9%, Austria 6%, Serbia 5% (2019)

Total Imports: $27.59 billion (2020 est.), $31.39 billion (2019 est.)

Import Commodities: Crude petroleum, cars, refined petroleum, packaged medicines, electricity (2019)

Major Suppliers: Italy 14%, Germany 14%, Slovenia 11%, Hungary 7%, Austria 6% (2019)

INTERNATIONAL DISPUTES

◆ Dispute remains with Bosnia and Herzegovina over several small sections of the boundary related to maritime access that hinders ratification of the 1999 border agreement.

◆ The Croatia-Slovenia land and maritime boundary agreement, which would have ceded most of Pirin Bay and maritime access to Slovenia and several villages to Croatia, remains unratified and in dispute.

◆ Slovenia has objected to Croatia's claim of an exclusive economic zone in the Adriatic Sea.

◆ In 2009, however Croatia and Slovenia signed a binding international arbitration agreement to define their disputed land and maritime borders, which led to Slovenia lifting its objections to Croatia joining the EU. Slovenia continues to impose a hard border Schengen regime with Croatia.

◆ Croatia has participated in NATO operations including the International Security Assistance Force and subsequently to the Resolute Security Force in Afghanistan, the Kosovo Force, and Operation Unified Protector in Libya, and United Nations peacekeeping missions in Lebanon, Cyprus, India and Pakistan, the Western Sahara, and the Golan Heights.

DEFENCE
ARMY
Personnel: 10,000

Equipment

Category	Name	In Service
MBT	M-84A4 Sniper	50+
	M-84D	(under development)
	M-95 Degman	4

...continued

Category	Name	In Service
APC/MICV/IFV	BVP M-80A	100+
	Patria AMV	100+
	Iveco LMV	10
	M1151	50+
	M-ATV	110+
	RG-33	32+
	International MaxxPro MRAP	30
Artillery	105mm M56	40
	122mm D-30 RH M94	30+
	130mm M-46H-1	30
	152mm M84	15
	CITER 155mm L33 Gun	5+
	155mm M114	15+
	Panzerhaubitze 2000	12+
	122mm 2S1 Gvozdika SP	5+
Mortar	60mm M57	50+
	82mm M96	50+
	120mm M75	40+
MRL	128mm RAK-12	8
	122m APR-40	30+
	122mm M-96 Tajfun	4
	122mm M-91 Vulkan	8
Anti-Tank GW	Spike ER	On order
	9K115-2 Metis-M	50+
	9K111 Fagot	100+
	RL90 M95, AT4 RPGs	
	9K11 Malyutka	200
AA Gun	BOV 20/3 SPAAG	50+
	L/70	5+
SAM	10CROA1	10
	9K38 Igla	60
	Strela 2	300+

New Procurements/ Upgrades

◆ Contracts worth 313 million kuna for the procurement of equipment for the army were signed with 34 Croatian companies at the Defence Ministry.

◆ The US State Department has approved a possible Foreign Military Sale to the Government of Croatia of refurbishment/modernisation and support for 76 M2A2 Operation Desert Storm (ODS) Bradley Fighting vehicles and related equipment for an estimated cost of USD757 million.

NAVY
Personnel: 1500

Equipment

Category	Name	In Service
Patrol boat	Mirna class	4

...continued

Category	Name	In Service
Missile boat	Kralj class	2
	Helsinki class	2
	Koncar class	1
Landing craft	Silba class	2
	Type 11	2
	Type 22	1
	Type 21	1
Minehunter	Korcula class	1
Weapon	RBS-15	30+
	MOL Mobile anti-ship missile launchers with RBS-15 (Coastal batteries)	3

New Procurements/ Upgrades

No major procurement plans are under consideration at present.

AIR FORCE AND AIR DEFENCE

Personnel: 1500

Equipment

Category	Name	In Service
Fighters/attack/Reconnaissance	MiG-21bis	8+
	MiG-21UM	4
Transport/Tanker	An-32B	2
Helicopter	Mi-171Sh	10
	OH-58D	10+
	Mi-8T	10+
	Bell 206B-3	5+
Trainer	Pilatus PC-9M	20
	242L	5
UAV	Skylark I	5+
	Hermes 450	2

New Procurements/ Upgrades

◆ Croatia signed a deal with Dassault Aviation to buy 12 French Rafale fighter jets worth nearly USD1.2 billion. The state-to-state contract mainly covers the transfer of 12 Rafale fighters from the French Air Force along with their equipment, as well as a training service for the Croatian Air Force. The logistics support contract covers all support resources, including additional spare parts for these aircraft, over a three-year period.

◆ The US State Department has approved a possible Foreign Military Sale to Croatia of two UH-60M Black Hawk helicopters and related equipment for an estimated cost of USD115 million. The Government of Croatia has requested a possible sale of 2 UH-60M Black Hawk Helicopters in standard USG configuration with designated unique equipment and Government Furnished Equipment (GFE), up to 9 each T700-GE-70 ID engines, and up to 9 each H-764GU/Embedded Global Positioning/Inertial Navigation (EGI). Also included are Communication Security equipment including an AN/APX-123A Identification Friend or Foe (IFF) transponder, AN/ARC-201D RT-1478D, and AN/ARC-231 RT-1808A radios, aircraft warranty, air worthiness support, calibration services, spare and repair parts, support equipment, communication equipment, weapons, ammunition, night vision devices, publications and technical documentation, personnel training and training devices, site surveys, tool and test equipment, U.S. Government and contractor technical and logistics support services, and other related elements of logistical and programme support.

Defence Expenditure

Total defence spending: USD1 billion (2020 est.)

Estimated defence spending in terms of GDP: 1.83% of GDP (2020 est.), 1.65% of GDP (2019)

Year	USD (Millions)
2014	1,064
2015	883
2016	837
2017	924
2018	966
2019*	1,002
2020*	1,031
2021*	1,846

*(*Figures for 2020 and 2021 are estimates.)*
Source: Defence Expenditure of NATO Countries (2014-2021), NATO Press Release.

Croatia currently allocates between 1.7 and 1.75 percent of its GDP for defence.

Domestic suppliers: Đuro Đaković (armoured vehicles), Brodosplit (naval vessels), HS Produkt (small arms).

Foreign suppliers: Belgium, Czech Republic, Finland, Germany, Israel, Italy, Norway, Russia, Switzerland, Sweden, United States.

According to Croatian MoD, the funds allocated in the 2021 budget totalled HRK 4.801.780,350 HRK, of which 2.275.478,960 were allocated for the material purposes. The 2021 Procurement Plan includes 865 procurement items worth ca 1.2 billion HRK. In 2019, the defence budget was USD1.045 billion or 1.7% of GDP, representing a yearly increase of 10.1%. The economic downturn caused by the COVID-19 pandemic decreased the defence budget in absolute numbers in 2020, however the percentage of GDP remained at 1.7%. In 2021, the Croatian government decided to purchase 12 used Dassault Rafales F-3R from the French government. The first jets are expected to arrive in 2024 to replace the outdated MiGs. According to the Govt. of Republic of Croatia news release in Dec 2019, Croatia plans to increase its defence budget to 2% of GDP by 2024 and to allocate 20% of the defence budget for equipment and modernisation. According to the plan, Croatia should set aside 1.74% of GDP for defence in 2020, 1.79% in 2021, about 1.86% in 2022 and 2023, and about 2% in 2024. Also, it should earmark 9.74% of the defence budget for modernisation and equipment in 2020, 12.92% in 2021, 17.98% in 2022, 19.66% in 2023 and 20% in 2024. Croatia's current defence budget is 1.68% of GDP and only 6.73% goes on equipment and modernisation, the least in NATO, but the purchase of Black Hawk helicopters raises that to almost 10%. In nominal amounts, the defence budget should be HRK 7.19 billion in 2020 and HRK 9.4 billion in 2024. The allocation for equipment and modernisation would rise from HRK 700 million in 2020 to HRK 1.88 billion in 2024. The funds would be used to procure a squadron of fighter jets and Black Hawk helicopters, for the development of special operation capabilities, to procure Bradley vehicles, and to upgrade Patria vehicles with additional weapons. Another goal is to develop a mechanised brigade according to NATO standards.

Croatia and US has signed USD5 million agreement to launch Cyber Security Operations Centre in Zagreb in 2020. In support of Croatia's efforts to upgrade its defence capabilities, the United States is providing $4.2 million in special assistance for the establishment of the Croatian military's new Cyber Security Operations Centre and mobile Cyber Incident Response Team, while the Government of Croatia is also contributing funds. A range of complementary US-funded programmes will facilitate the advancement of Croatia's Cyber Command with equipment, training, and technology needed to prevent cyber intrusions and defend the Croatian military and the Ministry of Defence (MoD) networks, as per US Embassy in Croatia.

In just the last 10 years, Croatia has received over USD700 million from the United States in support of Croatia's military modernisation and capability development. This funding facilitated the procurement of a range of high-end equipment including Blackhawk and Kiowa helicopters, Mine Resistant Ambush Protected Vehicles, water purification systems, night vision devices, and communications technology, as per US Embassy in Croatia news.

Defence Production and R&D

Croatia has a relatively well-developed arms industry that is highly competitive internationally, with significant annual arms exports. Kraljevica Shipyard is a shipbuilder at Kraljevica, on the Adriatic coast of Croatia. The shipyard was founded in 1729 and is claimed to be the oldest continuously operational shipyard in the world. The government of Croatia has repeatedly attempted to privatise the shipyard, most recently in November 2010. In 2008, the Croatian government announced that five of the country's shipyards would be privatised, in accordance with EU regulations for gaining membership. According to the new ten year plan of the Croatian Armed Forces (The Croatian Armed Forces Long-Term Development Plan 2006-2015), the defence force will develop and cooperate with expert scientific and research institutions in Croatia and abroad as well as with the producers of military equipment and weaponry. The Institute of Defence Research and Defence Systems Development will be responsible for research and development of the armed forces' needs. The Institute for Research and Development of Defence Systems (IROS) is where the needs of national defence and security meet the scientific and technological potentials of the Republic of Croatia. The Institute is organised as an administrative unit of the Ministry of Defence which carries out, coordinates and guides scientific activity in the field of defence systems as well as scientific-research and development activities in other fields which are important for the Croatian Armed Forces. The Institute carries out research activities in the field of defence and security, as well as in the interdisciplinary fields of advanced defence technologies, defence systems, management of human resources and many others.

Defence Procurement

Domestic production and procurement remains a top most priority with the Croatian government. The country has established a series of defence procurement priorities for each branch of service. At present, the ongoing procurement is in line with the reforms in progress. Croatia Army/Navy/Air Force has not done any major procurement last year.

CONTACT DETAILS

Ministry of Defence of the Republic of Croatia
Phone: +385 (1) 4567-111
e-mail: infor@morh.hr
Trg kralja Petra Krešimira IV br. 1
10 000 Zagreb

Public Relations and Information Department
Sarajevska cesta 7 (building no. 15)
10 000 Zagreb
Tel.: +385 (1) 4832-433,
Fax: +385 (1) 4832-905
E-mail: infor@morh.hr

Institute for Research and Development of Defence Systems (IROS)
Ilica 256b, HR-10000 Zagreb, Croatia
Telephone: + 385 1 37 84 690
Fax: + 385 1 37 84 878
E-mail: lea.gradecak@morh.hr
http://iros.morh.hr/en

STRATEGIC INFORMATION
CUBA
(Capital: Havana)

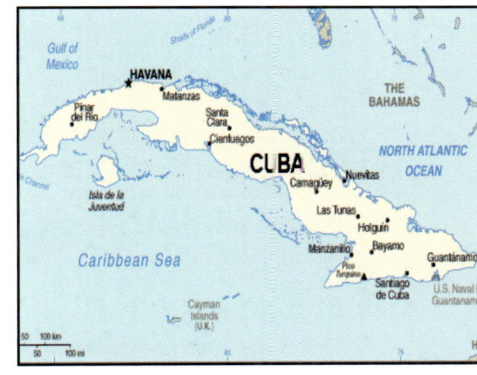

INTRODUCTION

Area: 110,860 sq km
Population: 11,032,343 (July 2021 est.)
Coastline: 3,735 km
Maritime claims: Territorial sea: 12 nm
Contiguous zone: 24 nm

GEOPOLITICAL IMPORTANCE

Cuba (the Republic of Cuba) is the most populous and largest island nation in the Caribbean. It is situated between the Caribbean Sea and the North Atlantic Ocean. United States (150 km) and the Bahamas lies to the north of Cuba, Mexico is to the west, the Cayman Islands and Jamaica are to the south, and Haiti and the Dominican Republic are to the southeast. Isla de la Juventud is the main island of Cuba which includes several archipelagos.

POLITICAL OVERVIEW

Cuba is constitutionally defined as a "socialist state guided by the principles of José Julián Martí Pérez, and the political ideas of Vladimir Lenin, Friedrich Engels, and Karl Marx." The constitution describes the Communist Party of Cuba as the "leading force of society and of the state". Cuban government has the executive power and is represented by the Council of State and the Council of Ministers. Cuba has an elected national legislature, the National Assembly of People's Power. The People's Supreme Court is the highest judicial body. The President of Cuba, who is also elected by the Assembly, serves for five years and there is no limit to the number of terms of office. Fidel Castro, who has stepped down in 2008 as Cuba's President, has run the country for 49 years, since 1959 when the communist revolutionary came to power after leading the successful Cuban Revolution. Under his leadership Cuba was converted into a one-party socialist state, with industry and business being nationalised under state ownership and socialist reforms implemented in all areas of society. He adopted Marxism-Leninism as his guiding ideology. By following the path of communism and support from Soviet Union Fidel Castro transformed Cuba economically and socially. With the collapse of the Soviet Union in 1991, Castro had to struggle while Cuba was led into its economic "Special Period". In order to come out of the economic decline Castro formed many alliances with Latin American countries. Subsequently, Cuba under his rule made impressive domestic strides which include universal free healthcare and a much-admired education system, which has produced doctors for the developing world, but the economic growth is still poor. In 2006, amidst failing health, Castro transferred his responsibilities to Vice-President Raul Castro, who then became President in 2008. With the passage of the 2019 Cuban Constitution, the head of the Council of State will be transferred from the President of Cuba to the President of the National Assembly. The First Secretary of the Central Committee of the Communist Party of is the de facto leader of Cuba. Miguel Díaz-Canel, who has been President of Cuba since 2019, was elected First Secretary of the Communist Party on 19 April 2021.

KEY POLITICAL PERSONS

PRESIDENT & COMMANDER-IN-CHIEF: Miguel Díaz-Canel Bermúdez

FIRST VICE PRESIDENT: Salvador Valdés Mesa

ECONOMY

The economy of Cuba is centrally planned and controlled by the Government of Cuba. It follows socialist principles in terms of production and employment. The government controls labour force, capital investment and sets most prices and rations goods. The Cuban sugar economy is the principal agricultural economy in Cuba. Its economy is dominated by the exports of sugar, tobacco, coffee and skilled labour. Tourism in Cuba attracts over 2 million people a year, and is one of the main sources of revenue for the island. Cuban cigars rolled from tobacco leaves remain one of the country's leading exports. Since 2016, Cuba has attributed slowed economic growth in part to problems with petroleum product deliveries from Venezuela. Recently, US has eased the trade embargo (sanctions which were imposed by US on Cuba since 1962) lifting some travel restrictions and allowing Cuban Americans to send unlimited remittances back home and has also granted a special permit for sending a weekly shipment of humanitarian aid to the Communist-run island. Although economic sanctions remain in place, the United States is the largest provider of food and agricultural products to Cuba, with exports of those goods valued at USD220.5 million in 2018. The United States is also a significant supplier of humanitarian goods to Cuba, including medicines and medical products, with total value of all exports to Cuba of USD275.9 million in 2018, as per US State Department. The ongoing COVID-19 has affected the economic situation badly due to the restrictions in the lockdown and dismal foreign tourists though the pandemic situation seems to be under control. The shortages of basic essential goods are also hurting the already crisis-ridden Cuban economy, as per media reports.

GDP (official exchange rate): $137 billion (2017 est.), $134.8 billion (2016 est.)

Real Growth Rate (GDP): 1.6% (2017 est.), 0.5% (2016 est.)

Industries: Petroleum, nickel, cobalt, pharmaceuticals, tobacco, construction, steel, cement, agricultural machinery, sugar

Oil - proved reserves: 124 million bbl (1 January 2018 est.)

Natural gas - proved reserves: 70.79 billion cu m (1 January 2018 est.)

Total Exports: $2.63 billion (2017 est.), $2.546 billion (2016 est.)

Export Commodities: Cigars, raw sugar, nickel products, rum, zinc (2019)

Major Markets: China 38%, Spain 11%, Netherlands 5%, Germany 5% (2019)

Total Imports: $11.06 billion (2017 est.), $10.28 billion (2016 est.)

Import Commodities: Poultry meat, wheat, soybean products, corn, concentrated milk (2019)

Major Suppliers: Spain 19%, China 15%, Italy 6%, Canada 5%, Russia 5%, United States 5%, Brazil 5% (2019)

DEFENCE & SECURITY

The Cuban Revolutionary Armed Forces (Fuerzas Armadas Revolucionarias - FAR) comprises of Revolutionary Army (Ejercito Revolucionario, ER, which includes Territorial Militia Troops (Milicia de Tropas de Territoriales, MTT)); Revolutionary Navy (Marina de Guerra Revolucionaria, MGR, which includes Marine Corps); Revolutionary Air and Air Defence Forces (Defensas Anti-Aereas y Fuerza Aerea Revolucionaria, DAAFAR); and Youth Labour Army (Ejercito Juvenil del Trabajo, EJT). The military, intelligence and internal security forces are managed by the Ministry of the Revolutionary Armed Forces (MINFAR) and Ministry of Interior (MININT). The armed forces is the most powerful and influential institution in Cuba with top military generals playing crucial roles in the functioning of the entire system. The Cuban military is currently prepared for two major missions: the defence of Cuba against foreign aggression and the provision of internal security.

KEY DEFENCE PERSONS

MINISTER OF THE REVOLUTIONARY ARMED FORCES: Corps Gen. Álvaro López Miera

Internal Conflict

Currently there are no reports of non-state armed groups or private military companies in Cuba.

External Conflict

There is currently no armed conflict involving Cuba.

THREAT PERSPECTIVE

USA: Cuba and the United States restored diplomatic relations on July 20, 2015, which had been severed in 1961 during the Cold War. The countries' respective "interests sections" in one another's capitals were upgraded to embassies on July 20, 2015. US stated that the country is ready for dialogue and lifting the trade embargo completely if Cuba has political change such as institution of democratic reforms and improving human rights. In 2012, Cuban President Raul Castro said that his government is willing to mend differences with the US government and sit down to discuss anything, as long as it is a conversation between equals. In 2014, President Obama announced plans to restore diplomatic relations in major policy shift. Obama said the United States will open an embassy in Cuba and relax some of the restrictions on commerce and travel between the United States and Cuba. Cuba and the United States belong to a number of the same international organisations, including the United Nations and the World Trade Organisation, but usually take opposing positions on international issues. In 2015, Cuba attended the Summit of the Americas for the first time. In 2016, President Barack Obama visited Cuba, the first by a sitting president in over 80 years. In 2017, US President said that he was suspending the policy for unconditional sanctions relief for Cuba, though he was hoping for a better agreement between both the countries. Although economic sanctions remain in place, the United States is the largest provider of food and agricultural products to Cuba. US Naval Base at US Naval Base at Guantanamo Bay is leased to US and only mutual agreement or US abandonment of the facility can terminate the lease Bay is leased to US.

STRATEGIC RELATIONS

Russia: After 1959, Cuba was increasingly dependent on former Soviet Bloc for economic and military aid. Castro regime built a strong armed force with the help of Soviet equipment and military support. With changing times and new governance, the relations improved between Russia and Cuba. The two governments also signed many economic agreements for increasing joint cooperation with each other including sending huge amount of humanitarian aid to Cuba. Russia has also offered Cuba its space technology and would help the latter build its own space centre. An agreement has also been signed in 2009 to explore Cuba's offshore oil deposits, which are believed to be substantial. Russia is also in talks with Cuba to set up naval bases there. Both the countries currently maintain very strong diplomatic relationship. The relations have also been substantially enhanced in the Russian-Cuban military cooperation which has reached a new level. In July 2014, Vladimir Putin also visited Cuba, where he said about his decision to wipe clean 90% of the island's USD35 billion debt to Moscow and announced deals to invest in Cuba's offshore oil industry. The Russian Defence Ministry is considering of renewing Russia's presence in the bases in Cuba, according to media reports. Moscow is planning to renew its commercial, military and political ties with the island in recent years.

Venezuela: Cuba shares a very warm and significant relationship with Venezuela. Both the governments have taken positive steps to promote investment as well as technical and educational cooperation between the two countries. Cuba and Venezuela have signed many agreements to work together in the area of oil, energy, electricity, agriculture, service, medical, infrastructure, and business joint ventures. Close military ties with Cuba are also helping Venezuela to transform its military as Cuba has decades of experience in military equipment, training & strategy, guerrilla warfare and in counter insurgency operations.

Bolivia: Relationship between Bolivia and Cuba has increased considerably, and Cuba has sent doctors and teachers to Bolivia. Both the countries have also signed agreements on bilateral cooperation and mutual judicial assistance. Bolivia and Cuba had series of visits last year to boost bilateral military relations and continuous exchange between the armed forces. Cuba and Bolivia have enhanced their bilateral relations significantly, and the two countries have signed a number of cooperative agreements, mostly in the fields of health and education.

China: With the decline of support from former Soviet Union, Cuba had to look for new major allies. China emerged as a new key partner for Cuba thus lifting its diminishing economy. The relations continued to grow between the two countries with focus on trade, credits and investments. China is Cuba's second largest trading partner after Venezuela. Cuba is China's largest trading partner in the Caribbean region. China and Cuba have signed many agreements for easing bilateral trade such as opening factories producing local goods, selling wide range of Chinese-made items from bicycles to locomotives and developing oil resources with the aim of providing a boost to Cuba's national infrastructure. Both the countries have recently agreed to promote relations between the two armed forces. Cuba is willing to enhance exchanges with the Chinese military and strengthen bilateral cooperation in personnel training and other areas. China is also working with Cuba to strengthen friendship and enhance cooperation for the sake of national unity and territorial integrity. Cuba and China in August 2016 signed new agreements aimed at deepening bilateral cooperation in a number of fields. Chinese-built floating dry dock delivered to Cuba in 2019. Cuba and China authorities also signed a cooperation agreement with the aim of creating an artificial intelligence centre on the island. Both the countries also did trade promotions and investment related participation through various platforms such as China International Fair for Investment and Trade, China Import and Export Fair, Havana International Fair and Cuba-China Business Council.

India: India-Cuba relations have been traditionally warm and friendly. India was amongst the first countries to recognise Cuba after the 1959 Revolution. Both countries have maintained close contacts with each other in various international fora, such as the UN, NAM, WTO, etc. India supports resolutions in the UN General Assembly calling for lifting of US sanctions against Cuba. Cuba shares India's views on democratising UN and expansion of the UN Security Council. It also holds the reform of the UN Security Council as central to the overall reform process. Cuba supports India's inclusion as a permanent member in the restructured UN Security Council. In 2018, President of India announced India's offer of USD75 million LoC for 100 MW solar power project in Cuba. An additional 10 slots under ITEC programmes for Cuba was also announced. Bilateral assistance through Indian Technical & Economic Cooperation (ITEC) has increased in the last few years. ITEC programmes are popular and Cuba's utilization is near total. Bilateral trade between India and Cuba stands at USD38.81 million. The main items of Indian export to Cuba are pharmaceutical products, organic chemicals, plastic products, medical equipment, textile products, metal products, mineral oil products and tools. Imports from Cuba primarily comprise of pharmaceutical and tobacco products, as per Indian Embassy in Cuba.

Organisation of American States (OAS): Cuba, despite being a founding member, was excluded from participation in the OAS in January 1962. Cuba was technically still a member but was barred from sending representatives to the OAS. Later in June 2009, the Ministers of Foreign Affairs of the Americas present for the OAS's 39th General Assembly passed a vote to annul Cuba's suspension from the OAS. The 2009 resolution states that the participation of the Republic of Cuba in the OAS will be the result of a process of dialogue initiated at the request of the Government of Cuba, and in accordance with the practices, purposes, and principles of the OAS. Cuba, though welcomed the decision as a historically significant, the country has confirmed that it will not return to the OAS. The move was published in an editorial by Granma, official newspaper of the Central Committee of the Cuban Communist Party

Multilateral Alliances: Cuba is a founding member of the Bolivarian Alliance for the Peoples of Our America (ALBA), which is an international cooperation organisation based on the idea of social, political, and economic integration between the countries of Latin America and the Caribbean. Cuba is also a member of United Nations (UN) but is not contributing personnel to UN peacekeeping operations. The country is also a member of the Non-Aligned Movement (NAM) and the Association of Caribbean States (ACS). Ties between the nations of the Caribbean Community (CARICOM) and Cuba have remained cordial.

DEFENCE CAPABILITIES

ARMY: Revolutionary Army (Ejercito Revolucionario, ER) consists primarily of armour and artillery units. There are three armies: the eastern, central, and western. The army composed of ground units structured into brigades, regiments and infantry, tank, artillery and air defence battalions, the battalions of regular troops and the Territorial Troops Militia.

Personnel: 40,000

Equipment

Category	Name	In Service
MBT	T-62	300+
	T-54/55	500+
	PT-76	30
	T34 (coastal defence)	300+
APC/ MICV/ IFV	BRDM-1	45
	BRDM-1	100+
	BMP-1	100+
	BTR 40/ 50/ 60/ 152	
	76 mm	
	85 mm	
	122 mm	1000+
	130 mm	
	152 mm	
Mortar	82mm M-41/ 43	800+
	120 mm M-38/ 43	
MRL	122mm BM-21	100+
	BM-14	
	FROG - 4/ 7	50+
RCL	57mm	
Anti Tank GW	AT-1, AT-3	
	9K111	
	D-44, T-12	
	SU-100 (tank destroyer)	100+
AA Gun	ZU-23-2	
	ZPU-4	
	ZSU-23-4	
	ZSU-57-2	
	S-60	
	M-1939	
SAM	SA-6	10
	SA-7	
	SA-8	10
	SA-9	50
	SA-13	40
	SA-14	
	SA-16	
	S-75	140
	S-125	50+

New Procurements/ Upgrades

No major procurement plans are under consideration at present.

NAVY: Revolutionary Navy (Marina de Guerra Revolucionaria) is the naval force of Cuba.

Personnel: 3,000

Equipment

Category	Name	In Service
Submarine	Delfin class (midget)	4
Frigate	Rio Damuji class	2
Corvette	Soviet PAUK type	1

...continued

Category	Name	In Service
Light Force	OSA I-II missile FAC	6
Mine warfare force	Yevgenya class inshore	5
	Sonya coastal	3
Patrol boat	Pauk II	1
SSM	P-15 Termit (Coastal defence)	

Naval Aviation

Category	Name	In Service
Aircraft	Ka-28	4
	Mi-4	4
	MiG-29	6

New Procurements/ Upgrades

No major procurement plans are under consideration at present.

AIR FORCE: Revolutionary Air and Air Defence Forces (Defensas Anti-Aereas y Fuerza Aerea Revolucionaria, DAAFAR) is the air force of Cuba.

Active Naval & Air bases: Cabanas, Holguin, Havana – Playa Baracoa Airport, Havana- Jose Marti International Airport, La Coloma Airport.

Personnel: 8,000

Equipment

Category	Name	In Service
Fighter/ Attack/ Bomber	MiG-21	12
	MiG-23	24
	MiG-29	3
Transport/ Tanker	An-26	2
Trainer	Aero L-39	25
Helicopter	Mi-8/17	10
	Mi-35	4

New Procurements/ Upgrades

No major procurement plans are under consideration at present.

Major Armament Producers

Domestic suppliers: Union de Industrias Militares

Foreign suppliers: Russia, China, North Korea, Kazakhstan, Mongolia, Spain, Soviet Union (Former)

Union of Military Industry (Unión de Industria Militar - UIM), started in the year 1998, is the small industry owned by the Cuban government and run by the military of the country. The main task of the organisation is to provide repair, maintenance and upgrade for the military equipments. The organisation is made up of seven research and development centres, 12 military-industrial enterprises and two scientific technological centres. Marta Abreu de Las Villas Central University at Villa Clara; Doctor Carlos J. Finlay Central Military Hospital; José Martí Military Technical Institute and Simulator Research and Development Centre (SIMPRO) are the research centers involved in UIM. There are 12 military-industrial enterprises. There is some limited production of infantry weapons, such as AKM assault rifles, automatic grenade launchers and RPGs, munitions, land mines and support equipment.

The military-industrial complex works for the repair of the weaponry and technology for the ground, air and naval units of the Revolutionary Armed Forces. They are also involved in the modernisation of the forces in order to keep pace with the world technological development. The organisation has series of factories devoted for production of light weapons for infantry, ammunition, mines and other equipment of diverse nature. There are also large workshops, repair bases specialising in tanks, artillery, aviation, navy, radio communications, transport, radars, missile systems, metallurgical products and others.

DEFENCE DEALS

Cuba and Russia signed a new defence technology agreement in 2016 to increase cooperation and help modernise Cuba's armed forces until 2020. The deal was signed at Russian-Cuban intergovernmental commission in Havana in 2016. Historically, the two countries have enjoyed close military, diplomatic, and cultural ties and the majority of Cuba's military equipment has come from the former Soviet Union. Even after the Soviet Union's collapse, successive Russian governments have maintained close relations with Cuba. The bilateral cooperation agreement also includes advice on implementing a programme of planning for the development of the Armed Forces and all the logistics related to the technical maintenance of Cuba's military equipment.

Cuba used to receive huge support in the form of military and financial aid from former USSR. The support was supplied to all the three branches of armed forces. After 1990s, Cuban military power was sharply reduced by the loss of Soviet subsidies. Cuba was totally dependent on indigenous production for the maintenance of existing inventory. In terms of development, Cuban defence industry is only capable of producing small arms like the AKM, RPG-7V and sniper rifles, plus munitions which includes large maintenance and repair capabilities. The army unit of Cuban Revolutionary

Armed Forces is equipped with all Russian-made equipment, but most of the weaponry has crossed their time limit and are ageing. There is also shortage of workable spare parts and the country lacks hard currency to buy more specially materials for the tanks, motor transport, and costly munitions anti-tank, anti-aircraft, towed and self-propelled artillery stocks. The scenario has compelled Cuban government to stretch itself to other resources available and strengthening relations with nations believing in their ideology. In Sept 2012, a Cuban senior general agreed to further deepen military cooperation with China during a visit to Beijing. He said that Cuba was willing to enhance exchanges with the Chinese military and strengthen bilateral cooperation in personnel training and other areas. Cuba already share strong relationship with Venezuela.

DEFENCE BUDGET

Total defence spending: Exact defence expenditure figures are unavailable.

Estimated defence spending in terms of GDP: 2.9% of GDP (2018 est.), 2.9% of GDP (2017 est.)

The accurate statistics of Cuban defence budget is not disclosed by the country since 2003. The last estimated budget of the nation was said to be $1.9 billion for 2009. Since 2001, military budgets may have increased by up to 400 per cent compared to the dark days of the mid-1990s. Cuban military was deprived of logistic support, arms and ammunitions and financial aid since the disintegration of USSR. The defence expenditure before was around $1.4 billion but later dropped to $600 million following the collapse of Soviet Union. This sudden change had a deep impact in the economy and the state of Cuban military equipment. The Cuban army at present remains well trained and professional in nature. However, lack of replacement parts for its existing equipment has increasingly affected operational capabilities. The increase in defence expenditure since 2001 which was very low in the 90s is due to the broadening of horizons of the armed forces and also participating in the commercial markets. Cuba in order to increase the funding of its military operations and controlling the economy is concentrating more on tourism, agriculture which includes sugarcane productions, trade and other varied activities.

CONCLUSION

The armed forces have long been the most powerful institution in Cuba. The military controls maximum percentage of the economy through the management of hundreds of enterprises in key economic sectors. Fidel Castro with a rebel armed forces led Cuba's communist revolution to victory in 1959. But with the collapse of Soviet Union in 1991, Castro's rule was severely tested as it went through major downgrade in terms of military and financial aid. It led to a period of huge economic crisis which is known in Cuba as the Special Period. However, the period radically transformed Cuban society and the economy, as it necessitated the successful introduction of sustainable agriculture, decreased use of automobiles, and revamped industry, health, and diet throughout the country. Cuba which was comparatively isolated in the 1990s, has renewed its bilateral cooperation with several South American countries, most notably Venezuela and Bolivia. The country has also developed a growing relationship with the People's Republic of China and Russia. Cuba's armed force, though facing severe shortages of fuel and replacement of parts for its existing equipment, still has the capabilities to give strong resistance to any regional power. In 2006, the power was transferred from Fidel Castro to Raul Castro and with that many changes took place in the political arena of the country including foreign relations. Raul Castro's reforms include the right to buy and sell private property, but so far there has been no migratory reform. The process of reform might have stepped up a gear but is moving in snail pace. With much developments going on all around the region, transition is inevitable in Cuba. The Cuban Revolutionary Armed Forces which controls most of Cuban economy will play a key role in the transition. FAR has long been the strong, influential and competent institution in Cuba. The military, with a strong revolutionary tradition, still plays a pivotal role as a decisive power in the functioning of the country. The current administration has significant challenges to deal with including striking a balance between improving of economy and maintaining political and military control. In 2017, Cuba signed the UN treaty on the Prohibition of Nuclear Weapons.

CONTACT DETAILS
Ministry of the Revolutionary Armed Forces
Plaza de la Revolucion
Havana, Cuba
Tel: +537-511151
http://www.cubagob.cu/

CYPRUS
(Capital: Nicosia)

INTRODUCTION

Area: 9,251 sq km
Population: 1,281,506 (July 2021 est.)
Coastline: 648 km
Maritime claims: Territorial sea: 12 nm
Contiguous zone: 24 nm
Continental shelf: 200 m depth or to the depth of exploitation

KEY POLITICAL PERSONS

PRESIDENT: Nikos Anastasiadis

KEY DEFENCE PERSONS

DEFENCE MINISTER: Charalambos Petrides

CHIEF OF THE NATIONAL GUARD: Lt. Gen. Dimokritos Zervakis

COMMANDER OF THE NAVY: Capt. Charalambous Charalambo

COMMANDER OF THE AIR FORCE: Brig. Gen. Pattihis Gabriel

ECONOMY

The economy of the government-controlled Cyprus has shifted from agriculture to an open, free-market, service-based economy. The economy is dominated by services which accounted for 82.79% of gross valued added in 2019, while industry accounted for 8%, construction 7% and agriculture and forestry and fishing 2.3%. After the banking crisis of 2013, the economy bounced back swiftly returning to growth in 2015, investment grade rating in 2018 and recording annual average real GDP growth of 5.4 % in 2016 to 19. The government has introduced a series of measures to attract investment through modernising legislation, promoting development projects, diversifying tourism, introducing tax incentives and speeding up licensing procedures. The discovery of natural gas resources has increased the strategic potential of the island. The economy of Turkish-occupied Northern Cyprus mainly revolves around the agricultural sector and government service. It is about one-fifth the size of the economy of the government-controlled area and GDP per capita is around half.

GDP (official exchange rate): $24.946 billion (2019 est.)

Real Growth Rate (GDP): 3.08% (2019 est.), 5.25% (2018 est.)

Industries: Tourism, food and beverage processing, cement and gypsum, ship repair and refurbishment, textiles, light chemicals, metal products, wood, paper, stone and clay products.

Total Exports: $16.1 billion (2020 est.), $17.92 billion (2019 est.)

Export Commodities: Ships, refined petroleum, packaged medicines, cheese, crude petroleum (2019)

Major Markets: India 9%, Greece 9%, Libya 8%, United Kingdom 7% (2019)

Total Imports: $17.58 billion (2020 est.), $18.2 billion (2019 est.)

Import Commodities: Refined petroleum, ships, cars, coal tar oil, packaged medicines (2019)

Major Suppliers: Greece 16%, Italy 10%, Turkey 8%, Russia 5%, Germany 5%, United Kingdom 5%, China 5% (2019)

INTERNATIONAL DISPUTES

◆ Hostilities in 1974 divided the island into two de facto autonomous entities, the internationally recognised Cypriot Government and a Turkish-Cypriot community (north Cyprus). The 1,000-strong UN Peacekeeping Force in Cyprus (UNFICYP) has served in Cyprus since 1964 and maintains the buffer zone between North and South.

◆ On 1 May 2004, Cyprus entered the EU still divided, with the EU's body of legislation and standards (acquis communitaire) suspended in the North.

◆ Turkey protests Cypriot Government creating hydrocarbon blocks and maritime boundary with Lebanon in March 2007

DEFENCE

CYPRIOT NATIONAL GUARD

The National Guard of Cyprus also known as the Greek Cypriot National Guard or simply National Guard, is the joint arms military force of the Republic of Cyprus. The National Guard was established in 1964 as a force composed predominantly of ethnic Greeks, following the 1963-1964 breakdown of social and political relations between Greek and Turkish Cypriots on the island of Cyprus. The National Guard consists of Air, Land, Sea and Special Forces. Military service is mandatory for males. The Turkish military has occupied the Northern part of the island since the Turkish invasion of Cyprus in 1974.

Personnel: 12,000 (50,000 reserve)

Equipment

Category	Name	In Service
MBT	T-80U/UK	82
	AMX-30	52
AIFV/APC	BMP-3	43
	VAB	126
	Leonidas Is	168
	EE-9 Cascavel	67
Artillery	F1 155mm towed	12
	F3 155mm SP	12
	Zuzana 155mm SP	12
	M56 105mm	72
	100mm AT guns	20
MRL	M-68 128mm towed	18
	BM-21 122mm	4
Mortar	RT61 120mm	112
ATGW	Milan	45
	Hot	70

New Procurements/Upgrades

No major procurement plans are under consideration at present.

Air Service

Category	Name	In Service
Helicopter	Mi-35P	11
	SA-342 Gazelle/Hot	4
	AW139 (SAR)	3
SAM	Skyguard/ Aspide system	12
	Mistral	30
	SA-10	
	TOR-M1	6

New Procurements/Upgrades

◆ Cyprus has placed an order for Mistral surface-to-air missiles and Exocet anti-ship missiles for a combined worth of €290 million from MBDA for the Cypriot National Guard.

◆ The MoD plans to acquire an additional four new attack helicopters and unmanned aerial vehicles (UAVs).

Naval Service

Personnel: 320s

Equipment

Category	Name	In Service
Patrol Craft		8
	Sa'ar 62 OPV	
ASM	MM40 Exocet	24

New Procurements/Upgrades

No major procurement plans are under consideration at present.

Defence Expenditure

Total defence spending: $414 million (2020), $402 million (2019)

Estimated defence spending in terms of GDP: 1.8%

Defence Production and R&D

Indigenous defence industries have been set up but the levels of research and development have remained nominal. In 2017, the Ministry of Defence in cooperation with the MoD of Greece organised a 'Defence Industry Day,' with an aim to promote cooperation and synergy between the Greek and Cypriot companies active in the defence sector. Cyprus plan to work together with Israel and Greece on defence projects.

Defence Procurement

The Government is reportedly making efforts to equip the National Guard with new weapons systems like drones to be able to deal with asymmetric threats and programmes to boost the army's intelligence gathering capability are also underway. It is moving forward with existing defence contracts and making new agreements for weapons systems like unmanned aerial vehicles, modern air defence and anti-tank systems, and procurement of helicopters.

CONTACT DETAILS
Ministry of Defence
172-174, Strovolos Avenue
2048 Stovolos, Nicosia
Tel.: +357 22807500
Email: defence@mod.gov.cy

CZECH REPUBLIC
(Capital: Prague)

INTRODUCTION
Area: 78,867 sq km
Population: 10,702,596 (July 2021 est.)
Coastline: 0 km (Landlocked)
Maritime claims: None

KEY POLITICAL PERSONS

PRESIDENT & COMMANDER-IN-CHIEF: Milos Zeman

PRIME MINISTER: Petr Fiala

KEY DEFENCE PERSONS

DEFENCE MINISTER: Lubomir Metnar

CHIEF OF GENERAL STAFF: Gen. Ales Opata

LAND FORCES COMMANDER: Maj. Gen. Ladislav Jung

AIR FORCE COMMANDER: Maj. Gen. Petr Mikulenka

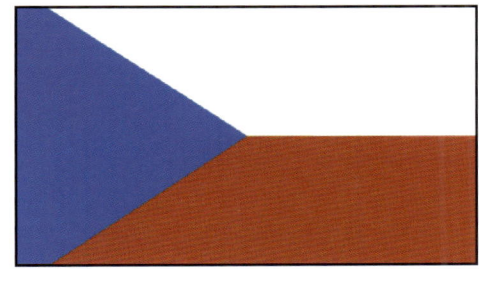

ECONOMY
The Czech Republic is one of the most stable and prosperous economies among the post-Communist states of Central and Eastern Europe. Maintaining an open investment climate has been a key element of Czech Republic's transition from a communist, centrally planned economy to a functioning market economy. As a member of EU, with an advantageous location in the centre of Europe and a well-qualified labour force, the Czech Republic is an attractive destination for foreign investment. The country's service sector is the largest contributor to GDP followed by industry. Prior to its EU accession in 2004, the Czech government harmonised its laws and regulations with those of the EU. The Czech govt. has undertaken reform measures aimed at reducing corruption, attract investment and improve social welfare programmes. The government also plans to remove labour market rigidities to improve business climate, bring procurement procedures in line with EU best practices, and boost wages. The country's low unemployment rate has led to steady increases in salaries, and the government is facing pressure from businesses to allow greater migration of qualified workers, at least from Ukraine and neighbouring Central European countries.

Long-term challenges for the country include dealing with a rapidly aging population, a shortage of skilled workers, a lagging education system, funding an unsustainable pension and health care system, and diversifying away from manufacturing and toward a more high-tech, services-based, knowledge economy. In the wake of Coronavirus pandemic, the Czech economy contracted by 5.6% in 2020, which was lower than a central bank projection of 7.2% fall. The central bank forecasts a growth of 1.7% for the economy in 2021.

GDP (official exchange rate): $250.63 billion (2019 est.)

Real Growth Rate (GDP): 2.27% (2019 est.); 3.18% (2018 est.)

Industries: Motor vehicles, metallurgy, machinery and equipment, glass, armaments

Exports: $229.5 billion (2019 est.); $226.8 billion (2018 est.)

Export Commodities: Cars and vehicle parts, computers, broadcasting equipment, office machinery/parts, seating (2019)

Major Markets: Germany 31%, Slovakia 7%, Poland 6%, France 5% (2019)

Imports: $211.9 billion (2019 est.); $209.2 billion (2018 est.)

Import Commodities: Broadcasting equipment, cars and vehicle parts, office machinery/parts, computers, packaged medicines (2019)

Major Suppliers: Germany 27%, China 12%, Poland 9%, Slovakia 5% (2019)

INTERNATIONAL DISPUTES
Czech Republic has no known international disputes.

DEFENCE
ARMY
Personnel: 5,500+

Equipment

Category	Name	In Service
MBT	T-72M	123 (30 operational)
APC/IFV	Pandur II & BMP-2	127 + 185
	Dingo-2	20
	IVECO	80
Artillery	SPGH-M77 Dana 152mm self-propelled howitzer	33

...continued

Category	Name	In Service
Mortar	M1982 Pram-L 120mm towed	50+
	SPM-85 Pram-S 120mm self-propelled	8
ATGW	Fagot	
	Spike	
	Javelin	
Air Defence Systems	RBS-70 Bofors	
	2K12 Kub-M2	
	9K35 Strela-10M	
	9M32 Strela-2	
	9K33M (OSA-AKM)	

New Procurements/ Upgrades

◆ Upgrade of 30 of the T-72 MBTs is being considered to keep them operational till 2025. New battle tanks would be inducted thereafter as per MoD's plans.

◆ A contract has been awarded to France's Nexter Systems in 2019 for the supply of 62 wheeled TITUS 6x6 armoured vehicles. The vehicles will be licence built in Czech Republic with delivery scheduled between 2022 and 2023.

◆ 80 Iveco multi-role armoured vehicles have been procured.

◆ Additional 20 Pandur II 8x8 armoured vehicles have been acquired between 2019 and 2020.

◆ A contract worth $102 million has been awarded to Tatra Defense Vehicles in 2020 to upkeep the entire fleet of Pandur vehicles for another five years.

◆ Plans are on to replace the BMP-2 tracked infantry fighting vehicles (IFVs).

◆ Acquisition of 50 new self-propelled howitzers is under consideration.

◆ A contract has been signed in 2018 with Sweden's SAAB for the delivery of 16 RBS-70NG short-range air-defence (SHORAD) systems. Deliveries will take place in 2020 and 2021.

◆ A government-to-government deal has been signed with Israel in December 2019 for the procurement of eight Iron Dome multi-mission radars at an estimated cost of US$125 million.

AIR FORCE
Personnel: 6,000+
Equipment

Category	Name	In Service
Fighter Attack/ Reconnaissance	JAS 39 Gripen	14
	L-159/L-159T1	21
	L159T2	3
Transport	CASA C-295M	5 (+1 on order)

...continued

Category	Name	In Service
Transport	L-410, Yak-40, CL-601 Challenger, A-319 CJ	11
Trainer	Aero L-39 Albatros	9
Helicopter	Mi-35/24V (attack)	17
	Mi-8, Mi-17/ Mi-171S (transport)	25
	W-3A Sokol (utility)	10
UAV	Raven RQ-11B	2

New Procurements/ Upgrades

◆ The Defence Ministry has announced to extend the country's lease of SAAB JAS 39 Gripen fighters with Sweden until 2027. The 14 Gripen jets – two JAS 39D two-seat jets and 12 JAS 39C jets – were acquired from Sweden under a 10-year agreement signed in 2004. All the fighters have been upgraded with enhanced combat and communication capability under a contract signed with Sweden's FXM.

◆ Aero Vodochody has been awarded a contract in 2019 to overhaul and modernize the Czech Air Force's entire fleet of 16 single-seat L-159 lightweight fighters. Delivery of the upgraded platforms has started and would continue till 2022-end.

◆ Aero Vodochody has delivered three new two-seat L-159T2 advanced jet trainers to the Czech Air Force. The new platforms are replacing the aging fleet of L-39ZA trainer jets.

◆ A contract has been signed with Airbus in December 2019 for the acquisition of two additional Airbus C295 tactical transport aircraft. Delivery of the first platform has been completed in May 2021 with the sixth and final aircraft set for delivery by 2022.

◆ Acquisition of eight UH-1Y Venom multi-role helicopters and four AH-1Z Viper attack helicopters from the US was announced by the Czech MoD in August 2019 and the contract awarded in 2020. The US-built platforms will phase out the Russian-built Mi-24 'Hind' attack helicopters and most of the fleet of Mil Mi-8/17 'Hip' medium transport helicopters of Czech Air Force in the coming years. Deliveries are scheduled to commence from 2023 onwards.

◆ Acquisition of new light helicopters, up to 30-35, is being considered.

◆ All 10 Polish-made PZL Swidnik W-3A Sokol light helicopters are undergoing mid-life extension upgrades.

◆ Acquisition of Rafael-built SPYDER air defence system has been finalised. The Czech MoD in Sept 2020 announced to start negotiations with the Israeli Government for the acquisition.

Defence Expenditure

Total defence spending (proposed for 2021): CZK 85 billion (US$ 4.01 billion)

Estimated defence spending in terms of GDP: 1.42% (2021)

Major suppliers of military hardware to Czech Republic are Russia, the US and Europe. Czech Republic signed an agreement with Vietnam in August 2014 to collaborate on military technologies, training, maintenance and repair, and wider defence industrial activity. It is one of the biggest suppliers of military hardware to Vietnam.

Defence Production and R&D

The defence industry, which once thrived during the era of Soviet Union, could not survive following the collapse of former Czechoslovakia in 1993. The country's defence industry today is a small fraction of what was. The Czech government intends to privatise the defence sector.

Defence Procurement

The Czech Republic has outlined plans for a major military modernisation programme which aims at phasing out the Armed Force's majority of Soviet-legacy defence hardware and replacing them with modern technological assets from the US and European nations and achieving NATO-standard capability by 2027. The programme is being steadily executed with a phased acquisition of 210 IFVs, 50 self-propelled howitzers (SPHs), 12 multi-role helicopters, two new transport aircraft, short-range air-defence systems), and combat drones, along with other hardware. The country aims to induct all these new weapons and platforms by 2027. The Czech Republic has also steadily increased its annual defence spending with a renewed goal of reaching 1.4% of GDP in 2021 and subsequently, to the NATO goal of 2% by 2024. As part of its modernisation drive, the country also plans to increase recruitment of soldiers so that within five years, by 2025, the Czech Armed Forces could comprise of approximately 25,000 professional soldiers and 5,000 active reservists.

CONTACT DETAILS
Ministry of Defence
Tychonova 221/1
CZ 160 00 Prague 6, Czech Republic
Tel. +420 973 201 111
www.army.cz

DEMOCRATIC REPUBLIC OF THE CONGO
(Capital: Kinshasa)

INTRODUCTION
Area: 2,344,858 sq km
Population: 105,044,646 (July 2021 est.)
Coastline: 37 km
Maritime claims: Territorial sea: 12 nm
Exclusive Economic Zone: Since 2011, the DRC has a Common Interest Zone agreement with Angola for mutual development of offshore resources

KEY POLITICAL PERSONS

PRESIDENT & COMMANDER-IN-CHIEF: Felix Tshisekedi

PRIME MINISTER: Jean-Michel Sama Lukonde Kyenge

KEY DEFENCE PERSONS

MINISTER OF DEFENCE: Kabanda Gilbert

CHIEF OF GENERAL STAFF: Gen. Celestin Mbala Munsense

CHIEF OF ARMY: Gen. Gabriel Amisi Kumba

ECONOMY
The Democratic Republic of the Congo is home to a vast potential of natural resources and mineral wealth. Agriculture is the mainstay of the economy. The economy of the third largest country in Africa relies heavily on mining. However, much economic activity occurs in the informal sector and is not reflected in GDP data. Renewed activity in the mining sector, the source of most export income, boosted Kinshasa's fiscal position and GDP growth until 2015, but low commodity prices led to slower growth, volatile inflation, currency depreciation, and a growing fiscal deficit. Poverty remains widespread in DRC, and the country failed to meet any Millennium Development Goals by 2015. DRC also concluded its programme with the IMF in 2015. The COVID-19 pandemic has dealt a major blow to DRC's economy with the World Bank warning that the outbreak could trigger an economic recession in the country (-2.2% growth) in 2020, stemming from a reduction in exports caused by the global economic downturn.

GDP (official exchange rate): $47.16 billion (2019 est.)
Real Growth Rate (GDP): 3.4% (2017 est.); 2.4% (2016 est.)
Industries: Mining (copper, cobalt, gold, diamonds, coltan, zinc, tin, tungsten), mineral processing, consumer products (textiles, plastics, footwear, cigarettes), metal products, processed foods and beverages, timber, cement, commercial ship repair
Total Exports: $21.16 billion (2019 est.); $20.85 billion (2018 est.)
Export Commodities: Copper, cobalt, crude petroleum, diamonds (2019)
Major Markets: China 53%, United Arab Emirates 11%, Saudi Arabia 6%, South Korea 5% (2019)
Total Imports: $19.5 billion (2019 est.); $21.3 billion (2018 est.)
Import Commodities: Packaged medicines, refined petroleum, sulfuric acid, stone processing machines, delivery trucks (2019)
Major Suppliers: China 29%, South Africa 15%, Zambia 12%, Rwanda 5%, Belgium 5%, India 5% (2019)

INTERNATIONAL DISPUTES
◆ Members of Uganda's Lord's Resistance Army forces continue to seek refuge in Congo's Garamba National Park as peace talks with the Uganda government evolve.
◆ The location of the boundary in the broad Congo River with the Republic of the Congo is undefined except in the Pool Malebo/Stanley Pool area; Uganda and DRC dispute Rukwanzi island in Lake Albert and other areas on the Semliki River with hydrocarbon potential.
◆ A Boundary commission continues discussions over the Congolese-administered triangle of land on the right bank of the Lunkinda River claimed by Zambia near the DRC village of Pweto.

DEFENCE
ARMY
Personnel: 10,000
Equipment

Category	Name	In Service
MBT	T-72	20
	T-55	12
	Type 59	10+
	Type 62	40+
Armoured vehicles	AML-90	40
	AML-30/60	50+
APC	BMP-1	20
	M-113	10
	M-3	70
	YW-531	10
Artillery	M116 75mm	20+
	Type-56 85mm	20
	M1938/D-30 122mm	20
	Type-60 122mm	10+
	Type-59 130mm	8
Mortar	81mm	
	120mm	
	M-30 107mm	
MRL	BM-21 122mm	6
RCL	M18 57mm	
	M20 75mm	
	M40A1 106mm	
AA gun	ZPU-4 14.5mm	
	M1939/Type-63 37mm	
	L/60 40mm	

New Procurements/Upgrades

◆ Ukraine's Ukroboronprom has delivered 25 T-64BV-1 main battle tanks to DRC in 2016. The company had announced a deal in 2014 to deliver at least 50 T-64 MBTs to an unnamed customer, which was then reported to be the DRC.

NAVY
Personnel: 2,000+ (including marines)
Equipment

Category	Name	In Service
Patrol Craft	Ex-Chinese Shanghai II class	2

New Procurements/Upgrades
No major procurement plans are under consideration at present.

AIR FORCE
Personnel: 1,200
Equipment

Category	Name	In Service
Combat	Su-25	8
	MB-326GB	8
	MB-326K	6

...continued

Category	Name	In Service
Transport	DHC-5D Buffalo	3
	C-130H Hercules	5
	C-47	6
	BN-2A Islander	1
Helicopter	SA-330 Puma	4
	SA-332 Super Puma	1
	Alouette III	7
	Mi-2 Hoplite	3
	Mi-8	4
	Mi-24	
	Mi-35	
Trainer	Cessna 150	12
	SF-260 MZ	10
	T-6	10
	Cessna 310	3

New Procurements/Upgrades
No major procurement plans are under consideration at present.

Defence Expenditure
Estimated defence spending in terms of GDP: 1.2%

Defence Production and R&D
No defence production is undertaken in Democratic Republic of the Congo.

Defence Procurement
No confirmed data or information is available on the current acquisition programmes by the DRC military. A number of countries, including Ukraine, China, US, France, Egypt and South Africa have supplied arms and equipment to DRC in the past after the United Nations Security Council, in 2008, decided to lift its arms embargo imposed on the African nation since 2003 due to continued armed conflict in the country. However, in the wake of continuing armed violence, the UNSC has continued to extend the embargo from time to time.

> **CONTACT DETAILS**
> Office of the Prime Minister
> Gombe Avenue
> Hotel du Conseil Executif
> Kinshasa
> Tel: (+243 12) 308 92
> (+243 12) 309 79

DENMARK
(Capital: Copenhagen)

INTRODUCTION
Area: 43,094 sq km
Population: 5,894,687 (July 2021 est.)
Coastline: 7,314 km
Maritime claims: Territorial sea: 12 nm
Contiguous zone: 24 nm
Exclusive Economic Zone: 200 nm
Continental shelf: 200 m depth or to the depth of exploitation

KEY POLITICAL PERSONS

HEAD OF STATE & COMMANDER-IN-CHIEF: Queen Margrethe II

PRIME MINISTER: Mette Frederiksen

KEY DEFENCE PERSONS

MINISTER OF DEFENCE: Trine Bramsen

CHIEF OF DEFENCE FORCES: Gen. Flemming Lentfer

COMMANDER OF ARMY: Maj. Gen. Gunner Arpe Nielsen

COMMANDER OF NAVY: Rear Adm. Torben Mikkelsen

COMMANDER OF AIR FORCE: Maj. Gen. Jan Dam

ECONOMY
A highly modern market economy, Denmark benefits from a high-tech agricultural sector and state-of-the-art industry driven by world-

leading firms in pharmaceuticals, maritime shipping and renewable energy. It also depends on foreign trade to a great extent. Denmark is a net exporter of food and energy and enjoys a comfortable balance of payments surplus. The country is currently experiencing a modest economic expansion. The economy grew by 2.0% in 2016 and 2.1% in 2017. Unemployment stood at 5.5% in 2017, based on national labour survey. The Danish Government offers extensive programmes to train unemployed persons to work in sectors that need qualified workers. Marred by the COVID-19 global health crisis, the Danish economy contracted by 3.7% in 2020, according to the European Commission. The Government has proposed to significantly boost state spending in 2021 to revive the economy.

GDP (official exchange rate): $350.03 billion (2019 est.)

Real Growth Rate (GDP): 2.85% (2019 est.); 2.18% (2018 est.)

Industries: Wind turbines, pharmaceuticals, medical equipment, shipbuilding and refurbishment, iron, steel, nonferrous metals, chemicals, food processing, machinery and transportation equipment, textiles and clothing, electronics, construction, furniture and other wood products

Total Exports: $226.58 billion (2019 est.); $215.72 billion (2018 est.)

Export Commodities: Packaged medicines, electric generators, food items, refined petroleum, medical cultures/vaccines (2019)

Major Markets: Germany 14%, United States 11%, Sweden 10%, United Kingdom 7%, Norway 6%, Netherlands 5%, China 5% (2019)

Total Imports: $197.81 billion (2019 est.); $193.10 billion (2018 est.)

Import Commodities: Cars, refined petroleum, packaged medicines, crude petroleum, broadcasting equipment (2019)

Major Suppliers: Germany 21%, Sweden 11%, Netherlands 8%, China 7% (2019)

INTERNATIONAL DISPUTES

◆ Dispute with Iceland, UK, and Ireland on Denmark's sovereignty claim over the Faroe Islands situated between the Norwegian Sea and the North Atlantic Ocean continues.

◆ Sovereignty dispute with Canada over Hans Island in the Kennedy Channel between Ellesmere Island and Greenland.

DEFENCE

ARMY
Personnel: 8,400

Equipment

Category	Name	In Service
MBT	Leopard 2A5	57
APC/ IFV/ Other Vehicles	M113	200+ (to be retired)
	CV90 35 MkIII	45
	Piranha IIIC	90
	Eagle IV	30
	High mobility vehicle	22
	Heavy tactical recovery vehicle	14
Artillery	M109 155 mm self-propelled howitzer	12
Mortar	60mm	90
	120mm	20
RCL	Carl Gustaf	774

Army Aviation

Category	Name	In Service	On Order
Helicopter	Fennec AS550	8 (4 in reserve)	
	EH-101 Merlin	14	
UAV	RQ11B Raven		12

New Procurements/ Upgrades

◆ Mid-life upgrade of 44 Leopard 2A5 MBTs is going on under a December 2016 contract awarded to Germany's Krauss-Maffei Wegmann. The first batch of upgraded tanks has been delivered in October 2019 with the remaining platforms slated to be handed over by 2022.

◆ First batch of Piranha 5 armoured vehicles has been delivered in March 2019. The Defence Ministry in 2015 had announced to acquire a total of 309 Piranha 5 platforms in six different configurations at a cost of US$600 million to replace the existing fleet of M113 armoured vehicles. Deliveries will continue till 2023.

◆ An order has been placed with General Dynamics European Land Systems (GDELS) for additional 57 Eagle 4 x 4 armoured vehicles (56 patrol variant;1 reconnaissance variant) in December 2020. The first batch

Eagle 4 x 4 armoured vehicle (Photo: GDELS/ www.gdels.com)

of new Eagle vehicles was delivered in March 2019 under a contract awarded to GDELS in 2017 for a total of 36 Eagle platforms. The initial contract had option for other variants of the platform, including electronic warfare, support, and reconnaissance vehicles.

◆ Delivery of CAESAR 155mm wheeled self-propelled howitzers is going on and is slated for completion by 2023. A total of 19 such artillery weapons are on order from French firm Nexter to replace the Danish Army's M109 155 mm tracked SP artillery pieces.

◆ A new 120mm mortar system (Cardom) is being acquired from the Austrian supplier ESL Advanced Information Technology GmbH which would be fitted on 15 of the new Piranha 5 APCs.

NAVY

Personnel: 1,125

Equipment

Category	Name	In Service
Frigate	Iver Huitfeldt-class	3
	Absalon class (support ship)	2
	Thetis-class	4
Patrol vessel	Knud Rasmussen class	2 (+1 on order)
	Agdlek class	1
	Diana class	6
	Flyvefisken class (mine-clearing & combat roles)	2
Auxiliary ship	Icebreakers	3
	ECO-101, Mette & Gunnar Thorson-class environmental control vessels	7
	Svanen-class sail training ships	2
	Torpedo Transport ship Sleipner	1

Naval Aviation

Category	Name	In Service
Helicopter	MH-60 R Seahawk	9

New Procurements/ Upgrades

◆ Three of the Navy's frigates and support ships will be upgraded with anti-submarine warfare (ASW) capability. The Navy's anti-air warfare (AAW) and ASW capabilities will be enhanced under funds allocated in 2018.

◆ Delivery of all nine MH-60R Seahawk helicopters has been completed in August 2018. The ship-based platforms, acquired from the US Navy, have replaced the Danish Navy's Lynx helicopters.

◆ Raytheon-built Standard Missile (SM)-2 Block IIIA anti-air warfare missile variants has been sought from the US under Foreign Military Sales (FMS) programme. Fourty-six (46) such weapons would be procured for the three Iver Huitfeldt class of frigates.

◆ Procurement of longer-range SM-6 missiles from the US is under consideration.

AIR FORCE
Personnel: 2,500
Equipment

Category	Name	In Service
Fighter	F-16A/B	45 (30 operational)
Transport	C-130J Hercules	4
	CL-604 Challenger	3
Trainer	MFI-17 Supporter	27
Helicopter	AS 550 Fennec	8
	EH101 Merlin	14
	Lynx	8

New Procurements/ Upgrades
◆ The first F-35A joint strike fighter platform has officially been handed over to the Danish Air Force in April 2021. In June 2016, Denmark announced to buy 27 F-35A JSF platforms to replace its fleet of aging F-16s. The Lockheed Martin-made F-35 fighters are being acquired at an estimated cost of 20 billion Danish crown. Delivery of all the platforms is slated between 2021 and 2026.

◆ Twenty-eight (28) AIM-120 C-7 Advanced Medium Range Air-to-Air Missiles (AMRAAMs) for an estimated cost of $90 million have been sought from the US under FMS deal. The weapons will arm Denmark's F-16 and F-35 fighters.

◆ Acquisition of Ground Based Air Defence (GBAD) system is under consideration.

Defence Expenditure
Total defence spending: DKK 26.4 billion (proposed for 2021)
Defence spending in terms of GDP: 1.43% (2020)

Being a NATO member, Denmark receives majority of its military equipment from the international block, mostly from the US and also from other Nordic countries. The country has announced to gradually increase its defence budget by 20 percent and reach up to 1.5% of GDP by the year 2023. In 2018, the Government had announced to allocate an additional 12.8 billion crowns to military spending over the next six years.

Defence Production and R&D
The Danish defence industry has been primarily associated with the production of electronics, avionics, communications and radar systems. Terma and Systematic are Denmark's two leading defence manufacturers.

F-35 joint strike fighter of Danish Air Force. (Photo: Royal Danish Air Force website)

Defence Procurement
Denmark has been working on consolidating the military reforms measures started over the past five years. While the Defence Ministry has announced new procurements for the Army, Navy and Air Force, it has focused on training the armed forces to use the new equipment before making them operational. Acquisition of new armoured vehicles, mortars and howitzers for the Army has been announced. Procurement of new ship-borne helicopters for the Navy has been completed with their deployment being planned over the next one or two years. The Air Force is set to receive the new F-35 stealth fighters as a replacement for the aging fleet of F-16 jets.

In January 2018, Denmark adopted a new Defence Agreement for 2018-2023 for the development of Danish armed forces. The Agreement makes provision for an increased defence spending of 20 per cent, as well as a greater balance between "out-of-area operations" and "collective defence". The Agreement provides for a gradual increase in defence spending, which is to rise by 20% (of 2017 levels) by 2023. In 2017, Denmark allocated 1.17% of GDP to defence.

CONTACT DETAILS
Ministry of Defence
Holmens Kanal 9
1060 Copenhagen K
Tel: + 45 7281 0000
E-mail: fmn@fmn.dk
www.fmn.dk

DOMINICAN REPUBLIC
(Capital: Santo Domingo)

INTRODUCTION
Area: 1,138,914 sq km
Population: 10,597,348 (July 2021 est.)
Coastline: 3,208 km (Caribbean Sea 1,760 km, North Pacific Ocean 1,448 km)
Maritime claims: Territorial sea: 6 nm
Contiguous zone: 24 nm
Exclusive Economic Zone: 200 nm
Continental shelf: 200 nm or to the edge of the continental margin

KEY POLITICAL PERSONS

PRESIDENT & COMMANDER-IN-CHIEF: Luis Abinader

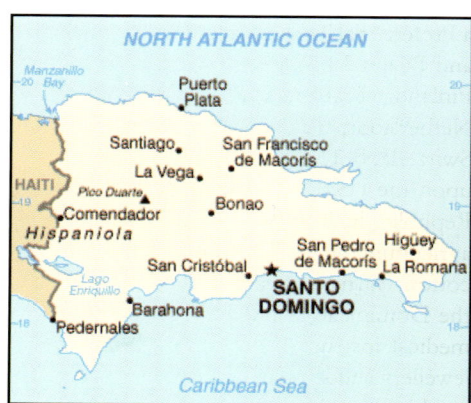

VICE PRESIDENT: Raquel Peña

KEY DEFENCE PERSONS

MINISTER OF DEFENCE: Lt. Gen. Carlos Luciano Diaz Morfa

CHIEF OF STAFF OF ARMY: Maj. Gen. Julio E. Florián Pérez

CHIEF OF STAFF OF NAVY: Vice Adm. Ramón Gustavo Betances Hernández

CHIEF OF STAFF OF AIR FORCE: Maj. Gen. Pilot Leonel Amilcar Muñoz Noboa

ECONOMY

In Dominican Republic, the service sector has overtaken agriculture as the economy's largest employer, due to growth in construction, tourism, and free trade zones. Even the mining sector is performing well. The Dominican Republic has Multilateral Agreements with WTO members; free trade agreements with CARICOM, CARIFORUM - European Community, and Central America; a Preferential Trade Agreement with Panama; and Bilateral Investment Treaties with Chile, Finland, France, Italy, Korea, Morocco, Netherlands, Panama, Taiwan, Spain, and Switzerland. The economy is highly dependent upon the US. US exports to the Dominican Republic include petroleum products, oil, agricultural products, machinery, vehicles, cotton, yarn, and fabric. US imports from the Dominican Republic include optical and medical instruments, electrical components, jewellery and gold, agricultural products, machinery, tobacco, and knit apparel. The Dominican Republic belongs to a number of the international organisations, including the United Nations, Organisation of American States, International Monetary Fund, World Bank, and World Trade Organisation. As per UNDP, Dominican Republic has been affected severely due to the COVID-19 pandemic which has reduced the key activities such as tourism and other economic activities as they were also shutdown. The Govt. is implementing crisis relief measures to uplift the employment and household incomes. According to an October 2020 World Bank report, the Dominican economy was expected to contract by 4.3 percent in 2020. Despite a falling poverty rate, income inequality remains high, and the country faces considerable obstacles to sustaining such robust growth over the long term, as per US Dept. of State.

GDP (official exchange rate): $184.45 billion (2020), $197.74 billion (2019)

Real Growth Rate (GDP): 4.6% (2017 est.), 6.6% (2016 est.)

Industries: Tourism, sugar processing, gold mining, textiles, cement, tobacco, electrical components, medical devices

Total Exports: $14.44 billion (2020), $20.51 billion (2019 est.)

Export Commodities: Gold, medical instruments, cigars, low-voltage protection equipment, bananas (2019)

Major Markets: United States 54%, Switzerland 8%, Canada 5%, India 5%, China 5% (2019)

Total Imports: $20.19 billion (2020), $24.53 billion (2019)

Import commodities: Refined petroleum, cars, jewellery, natural gas, broadcasting equipment (2019)

Major suppliers: United States 50%, China 13% (2019)

INTERNATIONAL DISPUTES

There is no ongoing armed conflict involving the Dominican Republic.

DEFENCE

ARMY

Personnel: 30,000

Equipment

Category	Name	In Service
MBT	AMX13 light	(retired)
	M41A1 light	
APC/MICV/IFV	AMLs	15+
	V150 Commandos	5+
	M3A1 106mm	30
Artillery	M101 105mm Howitzers	5+
	105mm M-45 Bofors	10+
	Reinosa 105mm/26 howitzers	10
Mortar	M-29 81mm	100+
	M-30	
	M-2 60mm	
	ECIA 120 mm	20+

...continued

Category	Name	In Service
RCL	M40A1 106mm	
AA Gun	Hispano-Suiza HS.404	3
	40mm Bofors L/70	

Army Aviation

Category	Name	In Service
Helicopter	Bell OH-58 Kiowa OH-58A	5+
	Robinson R22	4
	Robinson R44	2

New Procurements/ Upgrades

No major procurement plans are under consideration at present.

NAVY

Personnel: 13,000

Equipment

Category	Name	In Service
Patrol boat	USCG 180 Class	1
	USCG 133 White Class	2
Interceptor	32 Defender Class	5+
Auxiliary vessel	Ocean Tug ATR 165 Class	1
Auxiliary vessel	Damen Stan Tug 2608 Class	2
Landing Craft	LCU-1600 Class	1
Rescue craft	Damen Stan Patrol 1500 Class	3

Naval Aviation

Category	Name	In Service
Aircraft	SA316Bs	2
	Cassena T41Ds	5
	CH-146 KIOWA	1

New Procurements/ Upgrades

No major procurement plans are under consideration at present.

AIR FORCE

Personnel: 17,000

Equipment

Category	Name	In Service
Fighter	Super Tucano A-29B	5+
Trainer	ENAER T-35	5+
	Sikorsky S-333	1
	C-172 Skyhawk	2
	R-44, R-22	
Transport	C-212-400	3
Helicopter	Bell 412	
	UH-1H Huey II	5+
	OH-58A	10
	OH-6A	1
	Schweizer 333	3

New Procurements/ Upgrades

No major procurement plans are under consideration at present.

There is a counter-terrorist group formed by members of the three branches. This group is highly trained in counter-terrorism missions.

Defence Expenditure

Total defence spending: $450 million (approx.)

Estimated defence spending in terms of GDP: 0.8% of GDP (2020 est.), 0.7% of GDP (2019)

ECUADOR
(Capital: Quito)

INTRODUCTION

Area: 283,561 sq km
Population: 17,093,159 (July 2021 est.)
Coastline: 2,237 km
Maritime claims: Territorial sea: 200 nm
Continental shelf: 100 nm from 2,500-m isobath

KEY POLITICAL PERSONS

PRESIDENT & COMMANDER-IN-CHIEF: Guillermo Lasso

VICE PRESIDENT: Alfredo Borrero

KEY DEFENCE PERSONS

MINISTER OF DEFENCE: Gen. (Retd.) Luis Hernandez

HEAD OF JOINT COMMAND OF ARMED FORCES: Maj. Gen. Orlando Fabián Fuel Revelo

Domestic suppliers: ELBO, EAB, EBO
Foreign suppliers: United States, Germany, France, Belgium, Brazil, Spain

Defence Production and R&D

The army has expressed an interest in building a small-calibre munitions production facility. Besides this, there has been little significant military procurement in the past 10 years, although the Dominican Army needs to replace its obsolete equipment. To be capable of fulfilling its role, it would require modern armoured fighting vehicles, artillery pieces and both anti-armour and air defence weapons.

CHIEF OF ARMY: Brig. Gen. Luis Enrique Burbano Rivera

CHIEF OF NAVY: Rear Adm. Brumel Vazquez Bermudez

CHIEF OF AIR FORCE: Brig. Gen. Geovanny Espinel Puga

ECONOMY

Ecuador is dependent on its petroleum resources. Ecuador is a member of the Andean Community (CAN), Latin American Integration Association (ALADI), and the WTO. Ecuador also has a bilateral trade agreement with Chile, a partial trade agreement with Guatemala, and a commercial cooperation agreement with Venezuela. China has become Ecuador's largest foreign lender since 2008. In 2017, new administration focussed more on the private sector to improve cash flow in the country. According to report in US Dept. of State, Ecuador has been fully dollarized since 2000.

Defence Procurement

There do not appear to be any plans for either modernisation or procurement in the foreseeable future, and with a military procurement budget of around $15 million there will be little available for anything more than essential spares and ammunition.

CONTACT DETAILS
Ministry of Armed Forces
Avda. 27 de Febrero esq. Luperon
Santo Domingo, Dominician Republic
Tel: +8095305149
Fax: +809-531-1309

The Ecuadorian government is implementing a comprehensive reform program aimed at modernizing the economy and paving the way for strong, sustained, and equitable growth. This new economic policy and an associated IMF program approved in March 2019 are geared towards strengthening the fiscal position and improving competitiveness. Ecuador belongs to a number of the same international organisations, including the United Nations, Organisation of American States (OAS), International Monetary Fund, Inter-American Development Bank, and World Trade Organisation. Ecuador ended its participation in the Bolivarian Alliance for the Americas (ALBA), and the Union of South American Nations (UNASUR) in 2018 and 2019, respectively. Ecuador has been hit badly by the COVID-19 pandemic which has resulted in global oil crisis and is seeing serious dip in GDP in 2020. The sectors which have been hit hardest are tourism, transport and health due to lockdown measures.

GDP (official exchange rate): $182.24 billion (2020), $197.55 billion (2019 est.)

Real Growth Rate (GDP): 0.06% (2019 est.), 1.29% (2018 est.)

Industries: Petroleum, food processing, textiles, wood products, chemicals

Oil - proved reserves: 8.273 billion bbl (1

January 2018 est.)

Natural gas - proved reserves: 10.9 billion cu m (1 January 2018 est.)

Total Exports: $22.23 billion (2020 est.), $26.12 billion (2019 est.)

Export Commodities: Crude petroleum, crustaceans, bananas, fish, refined petroleum (2019)

Major Markets: United States 30%, China 13%, Panama 8%, Chile 7% (2019)

Total Imports: $19.89 billion (2020 est.), $25.89 billion (2019 est.)

Import Commodities: Refined petroleum, coal tar oil, cars, packaged medicines, soybean products (2019)

Major Suppliers: United States 22%, China 18%, Colombia 9%, Panama 5% (2019)

INTERNATIONAL DISPUTES

◆ The Colombian non-state armed group FARC (Fuerzas Armadas Revolucionarias de Colombia) is present near the border with Colombia.

DEFENCE

ARMY

Personnel: 25,000

Equipment

Category	Name	In Service
MBT	Leopard 1	50+
	T-55AM	
	AMX-13 Light Tank	100
APC/ MICV/ IFV	Engesa EE-9	30+
	EE-3 Jararaca	10
	EE-11 Urutu	20+
	AMX-VCI	90+
	Panhard ERC-90	
	BTR-3U	
	BTR-60	
Artillery	M2A1 105mm	20+
	M198 155mm	10
	MkF3 155mm SP	10
Mortar	M29 81mm	400+
	Soltam M-66 160mm	10
	M30 107mm	
MRL	RM-70 122mm	5+
RCL	M67 90mm and M40A1 106 mm	300+
AA Gun	Bofors 40mm	30
	M167 20mm	10
	20 mm M163 Vulcan	50+
	ZSU-23-4	25+
Weapon	Spike, MAPATS, HJ-8, Kornet-E, HOT, MILAN, 9M133 Kornet	
SAM	SA-8, Mistral, Blowpipe, HN-5A, Strela 2, 9K38 Igla, MIM-72	

Army Aviation

Category	Name	In Service
Aircraft	T-41 Mescalero	2
	Cessna 182	3
	Nanchang CJ-6	2
Transport	Pilatus PC-6	1
	Maule M-7	3
	Beechcraft Super King Air	1
	IAI Arava	4
	C-212-400 Aviocar	2
	CASA CN-235	2
	DHC-5D Buffalo	1
Helicopter	Mil Mi-17	5+
	SA342L Gazelle	10
	Eurocopter AS332	5+
	Eurocopter AS350	2

New Procurements/ Upgrades

◆ M28 short takeoff and landing (STOL) aircraft manufactured at PZL Mielec, a facility in Poland owned by Sikorsky, a Lockheed Martin company was delivered to Ecuador Army. Delivered five months after contract award, the twin-engine turboprop will meet the Ecuadorian Army's need for a proven multi-role transport aircraft that can perform in diverse climates and terrain.

NAVY

Personnel: 9,000

Equipment

Category	Name	In Service
Submarine	Type 209/1300	
Frigate	Condell class	2
Corvette	Esmeraldas-class	5+
Patrol Vessel	Damen Stan	3
FAC	TNC 45	2+
Auxiliary Ship	Auxiliaries	5+
Missiles	MBDA Exocet, MBDA Aspide (SAM)	

Naval Aviation

Category	Name	In Service
Aircraft	Super King Air	1
	CASA CN-235	1
Helicopter	206B	3
	TH-57A	3
	230T	1
	430	2
Trainer	T-34C-1	3
	T-35B	5
UAV	Heron I	2
	Searcher III	3

New Procurements/ Upgrades

No major procurement plans are under consideration at present.

AIR FORCE

Personnel: 6,000

Equipment

Category	Name	In Service
Fighters/ attack/ Reconnaissance	IAI Kfir	10+
	Atlas Cheetah	10+
Trainer	EMB 314 Super Tucano	15
	T-35	10+
	Atlas Cheetah	2
	DA20C1	5
	Bell 206	5
Transport	C-130	3
	Boeing 737	1
	Boeing 727	1
	C-295	5
	Hawker Siddeley HS 748	2
	de Havilland Canada DHC-6 Twin Otter	3
Helicopter	AW119 KOALA	2+
AAM	R550 Magic-II, Python MK-IV, Python MK-III, Shafrir MK-II, V-4 R-Darter-BVR	

New Procurements/ Upgrades

◆ Airbus Helicopters has delivered two H145s to the Ecuadorian Air Force, the first military customer in South America for this multi-purpose twin-engine helicopter in 2020. A total of six H145s will be delivered in 2021. The H145 helicopters, known as "Cobra" in the Ecuadorian Air Force, will be assigned to the 22nd Combat Wing in Guayaquil. They will be deployed for national security missions, high-altitude rescue operations, medical evacuations, and disaster relief.

Defence Expenditure

Total defence spending: $2.4 billion (2018 approx.)

Defence spending in terms of GDP: 2.3% of GDP (2020 est.), 2.3% of GDP (2019)

Foreign suppliers: United States, France, Germany, United Kingdom, Israel, Brazil, South Africa, Russia, Chile, China, Venezuela, Spain, Canada, Argentina

Ecuadorian Armed Forces is equipped with western equipment, with some from Russia and China acquired for emergency upgrades. Ecuador receives military assistance from US, Venezuela and Italy. The administration at the Defence Ministry launched a deep restructuring programme under the name of "PATRIA-I". It involves the modernisation of military equipment, improvement of planning and operations within the Ecuadorian territory. "PATRIA-I" was completed by 2011.

Defence Production and R&D
Ecuador has indigenously produced 9mm PAME-90 submachine guns. Its defence industry mainly relies on the external sources.

Defence Procurement
Ecuador's Defence Minister has announced that the plan to strengthen the armed forces would continue despite of the global financial crisis and that the government would invest more into the armed forces. The total defence spending in 2009 was $1,287 million. This hike in defence spending translated into the acquisition of a variety of systems including a fleet of 24 EMB-314 Super Tucano combat aircraft for $270 million, 2 Mi-17 helicopters for $22 million, IAI Heron and Searcher UAV's for $23 million and radars from China for $60 million.

CONTACT DETAILS
Ministry of National Defence
Exposicion No. 28
Quito, Ecuador
Tel: 593-2 295-1951

STRATEGIC INFORMATION
EGYPT
(Capital: Cairo)

INTRODUCTION
Area: 1,001,450 sq km
Population: 106,437,241 (July 2021 est.)
Coastline: 2,450 km
Maritime claims: Territorial sea: 12 nm
Contiguous zone: 24 nm
Exclusive Economic Zone: 200 nm
Continental shelf: 200 m depth or to the depth of exploitation

GEOPOLITICAL IMPORTANCE
Egypt is bordered by the Mediterranean Sea to the North, the Gaza Strip and Israel to the North-east, the Red Sea to the East, and Sudan to the South and Libya to the West. The country is covered with vast swaths of desert in its East and West and the rich Nile River Valley at its heart. Ancient Egypt was considered a cradle of civilisation. It has played a central role in Middle Eastern politics in modern times. The predominantly Sunni Muslim country is the cultural and historic centre of the Arab world. Egypt enjoys military supremacy in the region as well as provides an important place in world trade. The Suez Canal in Egypt connects the Mediterranean Sea to the Red Sea through the Isthmus of Suez. Twelve per cent of all International trade and 22% of the world's total container traffic goes through the Suez Canal. Egypt's geo-strategic location, size and population, its intellectual achievements, its control of the Suez Canal and its position towards Israel have made Egypt a strategically important country. Egypt is a founding member of the United Nations, the Non-Aligned Movement, the Arab League, the African Union, Organisation of Islamic Cooperation and the World Youth Forum.

POLITICAL OVERVIEW
The Arab Republic of Egypt practises a semi-presidential system of government. The president is elected to a six-year term. He is the supreme commander of the armed forces, however, he must consult the National Defence Council and have the approval of the majority of the MPs to declare war or to send armed forces outside state territory. The president appoints the prime minister, ministers, and deputy ministers. In the 2014 presidential election, retired Field Marshal Abdel Fattah al-Sisi was elected president after he ousted the Muslim Brotherhood, Mohammed Morsi, from office in a coup. Mr. Sisi won a second four-year-term in March 2018. A constitutional referendum held in April 2019 proposed changes that allowed President Abdel Fattah el-Sisi to remain in power until 2030. The Parliament may impeach the president. The parliament meets for one eight-month session each year but the president can call an additional session under special circumstances. The House of Representatives known as 'Magles en Nowwáb' is the principal legislative body with a five-year term. The Senate was inaugurated in October 2020 after constitutional amendments passed in 2019 re-established an upper chamber. In the Judiciary, all the judges and justices are selected by the Supreme Judiciary Council and the appointment is done by the president. Judges are appointed for life. The highest court in the country is the Supreme Constitutional Court and the last court of arbitration. The Court of Cessation (CC) is the highest court of appeal for criminal and civil cases and the Supreme Administrative Court (SAC) is the highest court of the state council.

KEY POLITICAL PERSONS

PRESIDENT & SUPREME COMMANDER:
Abdel Fattah El-Sisi

PRIME MINISTER:
Dr. Mostafa Madbouly

ECONOMY
Political uncertainty has caused Egypt's economic growth to slow significantly forcing the government to undertake important measures to restore economic stability. The government announced a wide range of reforms, introducing new taxes, increasing selected taxes, and reducing energy subsidies. These reforms have contributed to stabilise the economy. Showing signs of recovery amid tough reforms and an IMF loan, the country's gross domestic product (GDP) has reportedly increased by 5.3 percent in the 2017-18, the highest rate in ten years. The current account deficit narrowed to 2.4 percent of GDP in fiscal year 2018,

down from 6.0 percent in the previous year, driven primarily by strong remittances and the recovery in tourism, according to the World Bank. Economic activity again slowed down due to the Covid-19 pandemic social distancing measures and the temporary suspension of air traffic. Economic growth declined from 5.6% in fiscal year 2019 to 3.5% in fiscal year 2020. it stated. Most economic activity takes place in the highly fertile Nile Valley. The vital tourism industry has rebounded but Egypt remains dependent on aid from Saudi Arabia and international financial institutions. Egypt's economy depends mainly on petroleum imports, tourism, agriculture, media, and natural gas.

GDP (official exchange rate): $323.763 billion (2019 est.)

Real Growth Rate (GDP): 4.2% (2017 est.), 4.3% (2016 est.)

Industries: Textiles, food processing, tourism, chemicals, pharmaceuticals, hydrocarbons, construction, cement, metals, light manufactures.

Total Exports: $40.1 billion (2020 est.), $53.52 billion (2019 est.)

Export Commodities: Crude petroleum, refined petroleum, gold, natural gas, fertilizers (2019)

Major Markets: United States 9%, United Arab Emirates 6%, Italy 6%, Turkey 6%, Saudi Arabia 6%, India 5% (2019)

Total Imports: $$72.48 billion (2020 est.), $78.95 billion (2019 est.)

Import Commodities: Refined petroleum, wheat, crude petroleum, cars, packaged medicines (2019)

Major Suppliers: China 15%, Russia 7%, United States 6%, Saudi Arabia 6%, Germany 5%, Turkey 5% (2019)

DEFENCE & SECURITY

The Egyptian military, one of the biggest armies in the Middle East, has fought several major wars since its independence. The military with experience in battling militancy has engaged in war on Islamic State of Iraq and the Levant (ISIL) and the Sinai insurgency. Egypt faces serious security challenges including terrorism and Islamic insurgency and its priority is ensuring stability at home. Many terrorist attacks have been linked to Islamic extremism. The breakdown of the Libyan state, crumbling of border outposts, and rise of warring militant factions all threaten Egypt's internal stability. The Sinai Peninsula is the epicentre of an insurgency initiated in early 2011 as fallout of the 2011 Egyptian Revolution. Security officials face resilient jihadist insurgents in the peninsula. In order to improve its own defences and to address mounting challenges, the government has tried to forge a closer security relationship with Libya and its neighbours. President Abdel-Fattah El Sisi has ordered a massive shake-up of the nation's defence establishment to focus on Libya which Egypt now considers the gravest threat to its stability. In view of its security threats, Egypt has purchased hardware across all arms of its military, recently purchasing new fighter jets, submarines and battle tanks. On the international scene Egypt is a long-standing and committed contributor to United Nations peacekeeping operations.

KEY DEFENCE PERSONS

COMMANDER IN CHIEF & DEFENCE MINISTER: Lt. Gen. Mohamed Ahmed Zaki

CHIEF OF STAFF OF ARMED FORCES: Lt. Gen. Osama Askar

COMMANDER IN CHIEF OF NAVY: Lt. Gen. Ahmed Khaled Hassan Said Ahmed

COMMANDER OF AIR FORCE: Lt. Gen. Abbas Helmy Hashem

COMMANDER OF AIR DEFENCE FORCES: Lt. Gen. Mohamed Hegazy Abdul-Mawgoud

Internal Conflict

Egypt continues to face internal conflict with increasing violence and terrorism although the political situation in Egypt reportedly stabilized since Abdel Fattah el-Sisi became the leader and officially took power in 2014. Militant Islamic groups, including the Islamic State and Al-Qaeda, operate in the Sinai Peninsula. An ongoing insurgency in the volatile Sinai Peninsula has become increasingly active with militants involving in suicide bombings, drive-by shootings, assassinations and beheading. The Peninsula has been a hotbed for various armed groups. Since April 2017, the President has maintained a nation-wide state of emergency that gives security forces unchecked powers. The army and pro-government militias have allegedly carried out serious abuses, including demolishing homes and arbitrarily arresting, torturing, and extrajudicially executing residents. ISIS militants also committed horrific violations, including kidnappings, torture, and killings of residents and detained security force members. On October 25, 2021 the President has made an announcement that he is lifting the nationwide state of emergency.

External Conflict

◆ Sudan claims but Egypt de facto administers security and economic development of Halaib region north of the 22nd parallel boundary.

◆ Egypt no longer shows its administration of the Bir Tawil trapezoid in Sudan on its maps.

◆ Gazan breaches in the security wall with Egypt in January 2008 highlight difficulties in monitoring the Sinai border.

◆ Saudi Arabia claims Egyptian-administered islands of Tiran and Sanafir.

THREAT PERSPECTIVE

Libya: Egypt which shares 720-mile long western border with Libya considers its neighbour to be the gravest threat to its stability. Egypt has been affected by instability in Libya and tensions are high with regard to the power of Libya's Islamist groups where they hold 40 percent of the seats in the Libyan parliament. Eastern Libya is home to some of the country's most extreme militant groups.

Israel: Israel is viewed as a threat notwithstanding an Egyptian-Israeli peace treaty and Egypt's role in stabilising West Asia. It has an enormous arsenal of conventional forces that surpasses in efficiency and capability all the Arab states put together. Such an imbalance poses a threat to the weaker side and is thus considered a source of regional instability.

STRATEGIC RELATIONS

United States: The United States and Egypt share a strong partnership based on mutual interest in Middle East peace and stability, economic opportunity, and regional security.

They maintain close military-to-military relations. They have cooperated on counter-terrorism, the Israeli-Palestinian peace process, peacekeeping operations in Africa, deepening regional economic integration and other shared endeavours. Trade in goods between the United States and Egypt was $8.6 billion in 2019.

European Union: Egypt's relation with the EU is based on the 2004 Association Agreement and cooperation is led by a roadmap called the Action Plan. The Euro-Mediterranean Partnership (EMP) is the primary framework guiding Euro-Mediterranean relations and encompassing components and programmes dealing with democracy, while the European Neighbourhood Policy (ENP) addresses reform issues. The EU-Egypt Partnership Priorities 2017 to 2020 aim to address common challenges facing the EU and Egypt, to promote joint interests and to guarantee long-term stability on both sides of the Mediterranean. They also aim to reinforce cooperation in support of Egypt's "Sustainable Development Strategy – Vision-2030". The EU is Egypt's biggest trading partner, covering 24.5% of Egypt's trade volume in 2020.

Russia: Relations between Egypt and Russia have deepened significantly in recent years. The two nations have signed a Strategic Cooperation treaty in 2018. According to a statement from the Russian Foreign Ministry, the document provides continued strengthening of cooperation between Russia and Egypt in political, commercial, economic, cultural fields and more. There have been several exchanges of high-level visits as well. The two countries have signed a 50-year agreement to establish a Russian Industrial Zone (RIZ) in the Suez Canal Economic Zone (SCZone). Military cooperation between Egypt and Russia has grown especially in the fields of armament and training.

China: Egypt was the first country both in the Arab world and Africa to recognise the newly founded People's Republic of China in 1956. They have made great progress in developing their comprehensive strategic partnership over the years. Relations between the two nations have remained sound since then regardless of the changes on both sides and the revolution in Egypt. According to media reports, China has supplied ASN-209 UAVs, Wing Loong-1 drones, and an agreement was signed for the supply of Wing Loong-2 drones. China is the largest exporter for Egypt.

India: India and Egypt have enjoyed good relations from ancient times. Both countries have cooperated in multilateral fora and were the founding members of Non-Aligned Movement. One of the most important aspects of bilateral relations between the two countries is their close defence cooperation. The 8th Joint Defence Committee (JDC) was held in New Delhi in December, 2018 and the 9th JDC was held in Cairo in November, 2019. One of the high points of Indo-Egypt defence cooperation was the training of Egyptian pilots by Indian Air Force pilots. Over the years, the two countries have worked together on a number of mutually beneficial projects in various field of military cooperation especially training.

Saudi Arabia: Egypt and Saudi Arabia continue to be strategic partners in the Middle East. Both are highly influential countries in the Arab world, with Egypt being the most populous Arab country and Saudi Arabia being a member of the G20. They shoulder a big responsibility to realize the Arab solidarity and achieve the aspired goals for Arab nations from Atlantic Ocean to Gulf. The relation between the two countries is growing with increasing number of mutual visits from both sides at high levels.

DEFENCE CAPABILITIES

Egypt has one of the largest military forces and inventories of major weapons in the Middle East and North Africa (MENA). The armed forces enjoy considerable power within the Egyptian State with de facto control over all undeveloped non-agricultural land in Egypt. Having accorded top priority to build the country in view of maritime security threats in the Middle East, the multiple conflicts arising from regional as well as international developments, Egypt has begun the military modernisation programme acquiring new equipment and reconnaissance satellites, enhancing its operational combat capabilities to improve the armed forces' capabilities to meet the critical needs of future missions. As part of the modernisation propgramme, Egypt has inaugurated new military bases – the Bernice Military Base in south of the Red Sea. It consists of a land base, a naval base and an air base. Bernice base is the largest in Africa, with a port that can accommodate huge vessels and aircraft carriers, airports for military and passenger planes and a port for commercial vessels. The Mohammed Naguib Base in El-Hamam city secures the Dabaa nuclear station, the oil fields and the state's western borders. The new "Third of July" naval base, in Gargoub, is the third naval base that had been built during the last five years. In the Space realm, Egypt has launched remote sensing Earth observation satellite EgyptSat 1 in 2007 and EgyptSat2 in 2014 which is now replaced by EgyptSat-A satellite in 2019. The Egyptian Armed Forces newly produced drone called "Nut" can reportedly carry up to 65 kilograms of weight and hide from satellites. The Egyptian Armed Force comprised of the Army, Navy, Air force and the Air Defence force. The supreme commander of the armed forces is the President and the Supreme Council is headed by the Commander-in-Chief and Defence Minister and his deputy, the Chief of Staff of the Armed Forces.

ARMY: The Egyptian Army is one of the oldest armies in history and the largest service branch within the Egyptian Armed Forces. The Army considers itself to be the backbone of the regime and the guarantor of national stability. In recent years the Egyptian army has purchased hundreds of Abrams tanks, anti-tank vehicles, artillery and combat systems, new ground-to-air missiles with a range of hundreds of kilometres. The Army often carries out a number of exercises with the military forces of regional allies Saudi Arabia, the UAE and Sudan as well as international actors including the US, France and Italy.

Personnel: 450,00 (2021)

Equipment

Category	Name	In Service
MBT	M-1A1	1200
	T-62	500
	T-54/55	500
	M-60A3	1,450
AIFV/ APC	BMP-1	4,939 (total)
	YPR-765	
	M-113	
	BMR-600	
	FAHD	
	Commando Scout armoured car	
	M-106A2/M-125A2 mortar carriers	
	M577A2 command posts	
	M-901 ITV tank destroyer	
	YPR-765 Prat tank destroyer	
	M-981 FISTV	
	BRDM 1/-2	
	MRAPs	2000
Artillery	122mm	1,200
	130mm	
	152mm	
	180mm	
	M109A2/A3 155mm SP	680
	122mm SP	124

...continued

Category	Name	In Service
Mortar	120mm	100
	160mm	100
	240mm	200
MRL	BM-11	145
	BM-21	60
	M-88s (all 122mm)	175
	MLRS	26
RCL	82mm	500
	107mm	400
ATK Gun	57mm	300
	76mm	300
	100mm	300
AA Gun	ZSU-23-4	350
	ZSU-57-2 SP	
	M 167A2 Vulcan	
ATGW	TOW	520
	Milan II	220
	Swingfire	200
Weapon	AL SAQR (SA-7) (SAM)	
	Avenger system (SAM)	75
	Patriot-3 missile (SAM)	
	RIM 116B Block (SAM)	
	Scud B/C (SSM)	
	Sakr Eye (SAM)	
	Sakr-36 (SSM)	
	AGM-114 Hellfire (ASM)	
	Frog-7	
	AL-Badr	

New Procurements/Upgrades

◆ The Egyptian Defence Ministry has reportedly signed a major contract with Russia's Uralvagonzavod corporation to acquire 500 T-90MS battle tanks.

◆ The Egyptian military is considering acquiring South Korea's 155 mm K9 Thunder tracked self-propelled howitzers (SPHs) and support vehicles,

◆ Egypt has requested an additional 1000 Mine Resistant Ambush Protected (MRAP) vehicles and associated equipment.

NAVY: The Egyptian Navy established in 1928, is one of the oldest and among the strongest maritime power in the Mediterranean and the Red Sea basins. The Navy's North Fleet operations cover the Mediterranean region with the purpose to secure Egypt's northern and western strategic fronts. The South Fleet is focused at the Suez Canal and the Red Sea region, and is responsible for securing the eastern and southern fronts. The Navy's south fleet plays a crucial role in securing a smooth flow of international trade between Asia, Africa, and Europe via the Red Sea and the Suez Canal. Egypt is one among five countries in the world to own assault aircraft carriers – the mistral-class amphibious assault ships: Gamal Abdel Nasser and Anwar Al-Sadat. The Navy has received new combat missions and units as part of its development plan, including Mistral helicopter carriers, Frame and Gowind-class frigates, Mico-200 stealth frigates, and Type 209 submarines, in addition to a number of near and far traffic vessels. The Navy works closely with the other branches of Egypt's Armed Forces.

Major naval bases: Mersa Matruh, Port Sa'id, Port Tawfiq, Adabiyya, Ras al Tin, Bur Safaga.

Personnel: 16,500

Equipment

Category	Name	In Service
Submarine	Romeo type (ex-Chinese)	4
	Type 209/1400	4
Frigate	FREMM frigate	2
	Tahya Misr	1
	Sharm el-Sheikh class (ex-US Perry class)	4
	Damyat class (ex-US Knox class)	2
	EL Suez class (ex-Spanish Descubierta class (training frigate)	2
	Zaffer class (Chinese Jiang-hu 1 type	2
Corvette	P-32 Molniya-class	1
	Ahmed Fadel	1
	Pohang-class	1
	Gowind 2500	1
Patrol craft	'23 July' class (ex-German type 148 class)	5
	Ambassador MK III	4
	Ramadan class FAC (missile)	6
	Ex-USSR Osa class FAC	4
	Ezzat fast missile craft (Ambassador IV type)	4
	MRTP-20 type fast interceptor craft	6
	Timsah class	12
	Crestitalia type	6
Amphibious force	Mistral Helicopter Carrier	2
	ex-Polish Polnochy class LCT	3
	ex-USSR Vydra class LCU	9
	ex-USSR SMB1 class LCU	4
	LCM	10
Mine-sweeper	ex-US Osprey class (Al Shareen class)	2
	ex-USSR Yurka class	4
	ex-USSR T-43 type (Assiout class) MCMV	3

...continued

Category	Name	In Service
Mine-sweeper	ex-USSR T-301 class	2
	Swiftship type	6
	SRN-6 hovercraft	3
Auxiliaries	Underway replenishment ship (ex-German Glucksburg)	1
	Ammunition transport ship (ex-German Odenwald)	1
Weapon	Harpoon	
	MK-44 Guided Missile Round Pack	
	Exocet	

New Procurements/Upgrades

◆ Germany's Thyssenkrupp Marine Systems has handed over the fourth 209/1400mod class submarine, named "S44", to the Egyptian Navy.

◆ The Navy has taken delivery of the second El Fateh-class corvette ENS Port Said (976). The contract for the acquisition of four Gowind 2500 corvettes was signed in June 2014. The ENS El Fateh (971), the lead ship of the Egyptian Gowind-class corvette, was commissioned on 22 September 2017.

◆ The Navy has received the second Italian FREMM Bergamini-class GP frigate "Bernice" FFG-1003.

◆ The UK Defence Equipment Sales Authority (DESA) has sold the retired Royal Fleet Auxiliary ships Fort Austin and Fort Rosalie to Egypt.

◆ The US State Department has approved McLean, Virginia-based Advanced Technology Systems Co. as prime contractor on a potential $417M foreign military sale of a maritime domain awareness system to the Egyptian government.

Naval Aviation

Category	Name	In Service
Helicopter	Ka-52 Alligator	19
	SA-342L Gazelle	9
	SH-2G Super Seasprite	12

Coastal Defences

Category	Name	In Service
Artillery	100mm	2 brigades
	130mm	
	152 guns	
	Otomat batteries with 2 twin truck-mounted launch units each	3
	P-15 Termit launcher	

AIR FORCE: Egyptian Air Force (EAF) primary role is the air defence of the nation, involving international search-and-rescue operations in the desert, the Mediterranean Sea, and the Red Sea. The Air Force extends support to national security organisations engaged in the war against terrorism – the Sinai Insurgency, the Second Libyan Civil War and the Intervention in Yemen. It is a central body in securing Egypt's borders, in close cooperation with the rest of the armed forces. The EAF has participated in many joint exercises inside and outside the country with friendly countries in an effort to acquire and exchange experiences and skills.

Personnel: 25,000+

Major air bases: Almaza, Cairo West, Bilbeis, Beni Suwayf, Luxor, al-Minya, ras Banas, Hurghada, In Shas, Fayid, Gianaclis, Tanta, Al Mansura, Gabel el Basur, Mersa Matruh.

Equipment

Category	Name	In Service	On Order
Fighter	Rafale DM/EM	24	30
	F4E Phantom II	25 (retired)	
	Mirage 5D/E	48	
	F-16A	34	
	F-16B	12	
	F-16C	154	
	F-16D Block 52	220	
	F-7	54	
	MiG-29M\M2	50	
	Mirage 2000	20	
AWAC	E-2C Hawkeye/Hawkeye 2000	9	
	Beechcraft 1900 Elint	4	
Transport	Il-76	2	
	DH-5D	4 (3 regmnts)	
	C-130H	30	
	C-295	24	
	Falcon 20	2	
	Gulfstream IV-SP	2	
	Gulfstream G400	2	
	An-74T-200A	9	
Trainer/Tanker	Alpha Jet	70 (upgraded to MS)	
	K-8	120	
	EMB-312 Tucano	54	
	L-39	10	
	L-59E	48	
	IL-14	4	
	KC-135 tanker	3	
	Boeing 707 tanker	3	

...continued

Category	Name	In Service	On Order
Helicopter	AW149	5	
	AH-64D Apache	46	
	Ka-52 Alligator	19	27
	UH-60L Blackhawk	24+	
	Commandos	15	
	Mi-4	12	
	Mi-6	10	
	Mi-8 assault	42	
	Mi-8T	15	
	SA.342K Gazelle	65	
	(including 44 with HOT)	18	
	CH-47D	18	
	UH-12	2	
	AS-61	2	
UAV	ASN-209		
	Yabhon United 40		
	CASC Rainbow		
	CAIG Wing Loong		
	RQ-20 Puma		
	324 Scarab		
	Lipan M3		
	Meggitt Banshee		

New Procurements/Upgrades

◆ Egypt has placed an order for additional 30 Rafales to equip its air force. The EAF has earlier acquired 24 Rafales bringing the total number of aircraft to 54.

◆ Egypt has reportedly taken delivery of five of the 24 Russian Sukhoi Su-35 advanced combat aircraft.

◆ Egypt has taken delivery of five of the total 24 of the AW149 helicopters.

◆ The US has approved a possible Foreign Military Sale to Egypt to refurbish 43 AH-64E Apache attack helicopters for an estimated cost of $2.3 billion.

AIR DEFENCE FORCES: The Egyptian Air Defence Forces (EADF) often referred to as the "Fourth Force" is the Anti-aircraft warfare branch of the Egyptian Armed Forces, responsible for protecting the Egyptian airspace against any hostile air attacks. The ADF's capabilities include anti-aircraft guns, rocket and missile units, interceptor planes, and radar and warning installations. Its air-defence system is one of the largest and most complex systems in West Asia.

Personnel: 80,000

Equipment

Category	Name	In Service
SAM	Antey-2500 ABM	
	SA-2	320
	SA-3	180
	SA-6	76
	Tor M1/M2	
	Buk M1/M2	
	Hawk PIP III batteries with 72 systems	1
	Chaparral batteries (Sentinel radars)	12
	Crotale batteries with 36 systems	14
	Skyguard/Amoun	13
AA gun	20mm	250
	23mm	250
	37mm	250
	Twin 35mm (Amoun system)	250
	57mm	350
	85mm	350
	100mm	300

Egypt possesses a limited arsenal of ballistic, cruise, and air defence missiles. The country currently deploys R-300 Elbrus, Project T (Scud-B-100) short range ballistic missiles (SRBM); R-70 Luna-M artillery rockets; and Sakr-80 artillery rockets. It does not possess any intercontinental ballistic missiles (ICBMs) and it is not a member of the Missile Technology Control regime (MTCR). Cairo is a state party to the treaty on the Non-Proliferation of Nuclear Weapons (NPT). It is one of the few states to have used chemical weapons in wartime (North Yemen Civil War (1962-1970), period of Egyptian involvement 1963-1967). Egypt acceded to the Geneva Protocol on December 6, 1928, but has remained outside the Chemical Weapons Convention (CWC). Egypt has one of the largest and best-organised air defence systems in the Middle East, according to NTI. Its arsenals include 12 batteries of MIM-23 Improved Hawk surface-to-air missiles with 78 launchers. Egypt acquired 32 Patriot-3 (MIM-104-F/PAC-3) missile systems from the United States for $1.3 billion. It is the only Arab state with a reconnaissance satellite.

DEFENCE PRODUCTION AND R&D

Egypt boasts one of the most advanced defence industries in the Arab world, supported by a robust industrial complex, particularly in the production of vehicles. Egypt has military-technical cooperation with other countries. In addition to manufacturing small arms and ammunition, Egypt had begun producing advanced weapons systems through licensing and joint venture agreements with companies based in the United States and Western Europe. Egypt and India have decided to co-operate more on defence such as joint production of defence equipment, working together in the maritime domain, holding joint exercises, and increasing training opportunities.

Military industry in Egypt is involved in assembling a variety of trainer aircraft, alongside armoured fighting vehicles (AFVs), artillery pieces, surface-to-air missiles and M1A1 Abrams tanks. Military goods produced in Egypt include: small calibre and heavy ammunition, mortars, mines, grenades and other explosives, antitank rockets, rocket motors, radars and electronic equipment, smoke and pyrotechnic devices, rifles, pistols (Beretta licensee) and machine guns, jet trainer aircraft (Alpha and Tucano), armoured personnel carriers, Alpha jet engines, field and aircraft communications equipment, Gazelle helicopters and engines, gyroscopes, weapon sights, binoculars, periscopes, tanks, MLRs, and artillery pieces.

Egypt's Ministry of State for Military Production has developed an integrated plan to meet the needs of the Armed Forces from 2020 to 2030, and to direct the surplus for export in the period from 2025 to 2030. The plan includes: deepening local manufacturing; increasing the role of technical research; creating cooperation with international companies; and completing the development and rehabilitation of production lines. The Ministry's future vision includes the launch of an integrated medium-range air defence system, the production of an Egyptian tank, and the design and manufacture of a protection system for armoured fighting vehicles.

Major Armament Producers

Arab Organisation for Industrialisation (AOI) supervises nine military factories which produce civilian goods as well as military products. AOI is owned by the Government of Egypt and administered by a Supreme Committee, the chairman of which is the Egyptian president and which includes several cabinet ministers and is considered a division of the Ministry of Military Production.

National Service Products Organisation operates three companies that manufacture military and civilian products.

Arab-American Vehicle Co. (AAVCO): AAV Company is a joint Egyptian and American venture. The company produces military jeeps and other light vehicles.

Arab-British Defence Co. (AB-DCO): AB-DCO is a joint Arab-British project company. The company's product includes ATGM and missiles.

Foreign suppliers: United States, Russia, France, China, Italy, United Kingdom, Germanys

DEFENCE DEALS
Joint Venture Programmes

M1A1 Abrams tank: The Egyptian Ministry of Defence is continuing to produce the M1A1 Abrams Main Battle Tanks locally with the collaboration of US Company General Dynamics. On October 25, 2011, Egypt and the United States resumed the co-production of M1A1 Abrams Tanks. The manufacturing of M1A1s in Egypt is a key part of ongoing U S support for Egypt's crucial role as a factor of security and stability in the region. The Egyptian Defence Company Tank Plant has produced around 1,200 M1A1 Abrams MBT.

Arms Export

Egypt is the only country with a significant arms industry besides Israel in the Middle East. Egypt mainly exports its military-grade jeeps – the Jeep TJL and the Jeep J8. The country is making efforts to export weapons that contained technology of US origin the M1A1 tanks, ammunition to Saudi Arabia, and the provision of technical support for Turkey's arsenal of Hawk Missiles. Egyptian factories are turning out increasing quantities of guns and ammunition. They are also producing military electronics such as radios and telecommunications. France is Egypt's major partner in developing more sophisticated assembly and production facilities. Apart from Iraq, some of Egypt's main clients have been Somalia, Oman, Sudan and North Yemen. The country hosts the Egypt Defence Expo (EDEX) to showcase its military industry on the international stage.

Arms Import

The armed Force of Egypt is one of the biggest in the Middle East. Due to wars and tension, the flow of arms to Middle East has dramatically increased. Egypt faces challenges that require increasing its military capacity, notably in the Suez Canal and the energy-rich eastern Mediterranean. It's arms import tripled from 2010 to 2014 and 2015 to 2019, making it the world's third largest arms importer, according to a report by the Stockholm International Peace Research Institute in March 2020. Egypt received mainly French arms during 2014-18 and secondly Russian weapons. The arms import included Gowind-2500 corvettes, Panthera T6 armoured vehicles, MICA missiles, and radars. Some items on the list with the most hefty price tags include the acquisition of 387 M1 Abrams tanks since 2010 as well as 762 mine-resistant, ambush-protected, armoured trucks; a $1 billion deal for an S-300VM anti-aircraft system; and 50 Mikoyan MiG-29 twin-engine fighter jets in a $2 billion deal. The main suppliers of arms to Egypt were the United States, France, Russia, Spain, Germany, the Netherlands, Canada and Italy.

DEFENCE BUDGET

Total defence spending: $158 billion (2021), US$7.4 to 11.1 billion (2019)

Defence spending in terms of GDP: 1.2% (2020)

Egypt's military budget is largely unknown. The United States State Department in September 2021 decided to release $200 million in military aid to Egypt but will withhold $130 million of $300 million in military financing due to concerns over human rights.

CONCLUSION

Egypt is among the strongest military powers in the Arab world. Modern Egypt is considered to be a regional and middle power, with significant cultural, political, and military influence in North Africa, the Middle East and the Muslim world. The country is central to trade and international relations. Twelve per cent of all international trade goes through the Suez Canal in Egypt and 22% of the world's total container traffic. A destabilised Egypt would disrupt the world's energy security. Egypt remains strategically important to the US and to the EU while Israel's national security rests largely on its treaty with Egypt.

CONTACT DETAILS
Ministry of Defence and Military Production
23 July St., AlKobba bridge, Cairo.s
Ph.: 24032158
Fax: 22916227
E-mail: mmc@afmic.gov.eg
www.mmc.gov.eg

ESTONIA
(Capital: Tallinn)

INTRODUCTION
Area: 45,228 sq km
Population: 1,220,042 (July 2021 est.)
Coastline: 3,794 km
Maritime claims: Territorial sea: 12 nm
Exclusive Economic Zone: Limits fixed in coordination with neighbouring states

KEY POLITICAL PERSONS

PRESIDENT: Alar Karis

PRIME MINISTER: Kaja Kallas

KEY DEFENCE PERSONS

MINISTER OF DEFENCE: Kalle Laanet

COMMANDER OF DEFENCE FORCES: Lt. Gen. Martin Herem

DEPUTY COMMANDER OF DEFENCE FORCES: Maj. Gen. Veiko-Vello Palm

COMMANDER OF NAVAL FLOTILLA: Captain Johan-Elias Seljamaa

CHIEF OF STAFF OF AIR FORCE: Col. Janek Lehiste

ECONOMY

A well-developed modern market economy, Estonia has benefited from its trade ties with other European nations including Finland, Sweden, Germany and Russia. The economy also benefits from strong electronics and telecommunications sectors. Estonia became a member of the European Union in 2004 and adopted the Euro as its national currency in 2011 which boosted foreign investments in the country.

The economy's 4.9% GDP growth in 2017 was the fastest in the past six years, leaving the Estonian economy in its best position since the financial crisis 10 years ago.

Estonia is challenged by a shortage of labour, both skilled and unskilled, although the government has amended its immigration law to allow easier hiring of highly qualified foreign workers, and wage growth that outpaces productivity gains. The government is also pursuing efforts to boost productivity growth with a focus on innovations that emphasize technology start-ups and e-commerce. The outbreak of the Coronavirus pandemic affected the Estonian economy which contracted by 2.9% in 2020. A growth of 3.8% is expected in 2021, according to the Bank of Estonia projections.

GDP (official exchange rate): $31.46 billion (2019 est.)

Real Growth Rate (GDP): 5% (2019 est.); 4.36% (2018 est.)

Industries: Food, engineering, electronics, wood and wood products, textiles; information technology, telecommunications

Total Exports: $23.95 billion (2019 est.); $22.54 billion (2018 est.)

Export Commodities: Broadcasting equipment, refined petroleum, coal tar oil, cars, prefabricated buildings (2019)

Major Markets: Finland 13%, Sweden 9%, Latvia 8%, Russia 8%, United States 7%, Lithuania 6%, Germany 6% (2019)

Total Imports: $23.32 billion (2019 est.); $22.48 billion (2018 est.)

Import Commodities: Cars, refined petroleum, coal tar oil, broadcasting equipment, packaged medicines (2019)

Major Suppliers: Russia 12%, Germany 10%, Finland 9%, Lithuania 7%, Latvia 7%, Sweden 6%, Poland 6%, China 6% (2019)

INTERNATIONAL DISPUTES

Border dispute with Russia over parts of the Narva region has not been resolved even after the two sides signed a border treaty in February 2014.

DEFENCE

ARMY

Personnel: 2,000+

Equipment

Category	Name	In Service
APC/ IFV	Sisu XA-180	56
	Sisu XA-188	60 (+81 on order)
	CV-90	44
Armoured car	Mamba Alvis-4	9
Artillery	D-30 122mm howitzer	42
	FH-70 155mm howitzer	24
	M-40 105mm howitzer	38
Mortar	B455 81mm	40
	NM95 81mm	10
	M252 81mm	80
	2B11 120mm	14
	M-41D 120mm	165
RCL	M40A1 106mm	30
	Pv-1110 90mm	130
ATW	84mm Carl Gustav	
	148mm & 180mm MAPATS	
ATGW	115mm MILAN-2	
ATGM	Javelin FGM-148	128
SAM	90mm Mistral	25

New Procurements/Upgrades

◆ An agreement has been reached with Finland and Latvia in December 2019 to jointly design and develop a new six-wheeled armoured vehicle platform for the three nations' land forces.

◆ Delivery of additional 81 Sisu XA-188 APCs from Netherlands is going on.

◆ Delivery of 44 CV9035 NL infantry fighting vehicles (IFVs) from the Netherlands has been completed with delivery of the final batch in March 2019.

◆ The Army is procuring 37 CV90 IFV

vehicles from Norway which would be rebuilt as armoured support vehicles.

◆ Milrem LCM, a subsidiary of Patria, is providing repair and maintain support for the Patria XA-180 and XA-188 armoured vehicles under a renewed contract signed in 2018.

◆ Delivery of K9 Thunder 155mm self-propelled howitzers ordered from South Korea is going on. The Estonian MoD has placed order for 18 units of the K9 Thunder howitzers. Delivery is slated for completion by 2022.

◆ A tender has been issued in 2018 for buying artillery ammunitions worth €54 million (US$ 66.5 million).

◆ Delivery of Javelin anti-tank launchers and missiles under the US Foreign Military Sales programme has been completed in 2020.

◆ Delivery of Mistral M3 short-range air defence missiles is going on. More such weapons would be acquired under a €50 million contract awarded to MBDA in 2018.

◆ A deal has been signed with Eurospike in 2019 for the procurement of Spike anti-tank guided missiles at a cost of €40 million. The deal includes option for more Spike ATGMs in future. Delivery is scheduled between 2020 and 2021.

◆ Carl-Gustaf M4 weapon systems (anti-tank grenade launchers) are on order from Sweden's SAAB with deliveries slated for 2021-2024.

NAVY

Personnel: 200+

Equipment

Category	Name	In Service
Mine Warfare	Admiral Cowan class	3
Auxiliary ship	Lindormen class (diver and support vessel)	1 (+1 in reserve)
Training ship	Rihtniemi class	1

New Procurements/Upgrades

◆ EML Admiral Cowan, the first of three of Estonian Navy's Admiral Cowan class minehunters, has been upgraded with new sonar, navigation and command & control systems along with other refurbishments by UK-based Babcock in 2019. The other two vessels of the class will also be upgraded under a contract finalised in 2016.

◆ A contract worth €3.9 million has been awarded to Estonian company Baltic Workboats AS to build and deliver two force protection patrol boats to the Navy. The platforms are scheduled to enter service in 2021.

AIR FORCE

Personnel: 300+

Equipment

Category	Name	In Service
Transport / Utility	An-2	2
Transport / Utility	M-28 Skytruck	2
Trainer	L-39	2
Helicopter	Robinson R44	4

New Procurements/Upgrades

◆ The Air Force has acquired M-28 Skytruck twin-turboprop utility transport aircraft from the US to replace the An-2 platforms.

Defence Expenditure

Defence spending: €645.4 million (proposed for 2021); €615 million (2020)

Defence spending in terms of GDP: 2.29% (2021)

As a NATO member, the Estonian Government had targeted to gradually increase its defence spending to 2% of GDP. The defence budget, which had hovered near the 2% mark between 2004 and 2010, reached the 2% target in 2012. Annual defence allocation by the country has exceeded 2% mark since 2017 and continues to rise.

Defence Production and R&D

In recent times, the Estonian defence industry has focused on cyber security, protection against improvised explosive devices (IEDs) and chemical weapons. In the research and development sphere, the country has successfully produced the anti-improvised explosive device IRIS. An Unmanned Ground Vehicle system has been developed while effort is on to develop light armoured panels. Few companies have also developed small UAVs. The allocation of funds for R&D projects has increased significantly since 2001. The country adopted a 10-year National defence development programme spanning from 2013 to 2022 under which it is procuring new weaponry, equipment and ammunitions.

Defence Procurement

The Ministry of Defence in February 2020 unveiled the new development plan for 2021–24 which focuses on improving the Estonian military's intelligence, early warning and communications capabilities. The plan includes NATO-compliant maritime surveillance and development of a tactical communications system inter-operable with Estonia's allies. It lists procurement and deployment of anti-tank weapons, self-propelled howitzers, assault and sniper rifles among other arms/weapons over the next four years.

While all the new K9 Thunder howitzers are expected to be inducted in the Army by 2022, procurement of long-range anti-tank missiles is also advancing. The Estonian Air Force has received the M-28 aircraft in 2019. The Estonian Navy would be obtaining two upgraded vessels and mobile maritime surveillance radars to bolster its maritime warfare capability.

CONTACT DETAILS

Ministry of Defence
Sakala 1, 15094, Tallinn, Estonia
Tel.: +372 717 00 22
www.kaitseministeerium.ee/en

Estonian Defence Forces
Juhkentali 58, 15007, Tallinn, Estonia
Tel: +372 717 1155
Web: www.mil.ee/en/defence-forces

Sisu XA-180 APCs of Estonian Army

ETHIOPIA
(Capital: Addis Ababa)

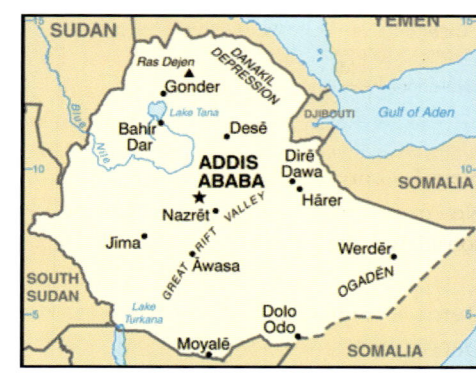

INTRODUCTION
Area: 1,104,300 sq. km
Population: 110,871,031 (July 2021 est.)
Coastline: 0 km (Landlocked)
Maritime claims: None

KEY POLITICAL PERSONS

PRESIDENT: Sahle-Work Zewde

PRIME MINISTER & COMMANDER-IN-CHIEF: Abiy Ahmed

KEY DEFENCE PERSONS

MINISTER OF DEFENCE: Abraham Belay

CHIEF OF GENERAL STAFF: Gen. Birhanu Jula Gelalcha

ECONOMY

Ethiopia is the second most populous country in Africa with a planned economy. For more than a decade before 2016, the country grew at a rate between 8% and 11% annually – one of the fastest growing states among the 188 IMF member countries. This growth was driven by government investment in infrastructure, as well as sustained progress in the agricultural and service sectors. More than 70% of Ethiopia's population is still employed in the agricultural sector, but services have surpassed agriculture as the principal source of GDP. Ethiopia has the lowest level of income-inequality in Africa and one of the lowest in the world. Yet despite progress toward eliminating extreme poverty, Ethiopia remains one of the poorest countries in the world, due both to rapid population growth and a low starting base. The country's foreign exchange earnings are led by the services sector – primarily the state-run Ethiopian Airlines – followed by exports of several commodities. The promising economy of Ethiopia, however, has been affected by the global economic crisis unleashed by the Coronavirus pandemic and is likely to shrink. The IMF had forecast a GDP growth of 3.2% – down from its earlier projection of 6.2% – for the African country in 2020.

GDP (official exchange rate): $92.15 billion (2019 est.)

Real Growth Rate (GDP): 10.9% (2017 est.); 8% (2016 est.)

Industries: Food processing, beverages, textiles, leather, chemicals, metals processing, cement

Total Exports: $3.23 billion (2017 est.); $2.81 billion (2016 est.)

Export Commodities: Coffee, sesame seeds, gold, cut flowers, zinc (2019)

Major Markets: China 17%, United States 16%, United Arab Emirates 8%, Saudi Arabia 6%, South Korea 5%, Germany 5% (2019)

Total imports: $15.59 billion (2017 est.); $14.69 billion (2016 est.)

Import Commodities: Aircraft, gas turbines, packaged medicines, electric filament, cars (2019)

Major Suppliers: China 27%, India 9%, United Arab Emirates 9%, France 9%, United Kingdom 7% (2019)

INTERNATIONAL DISPUTES

◆ Long-standing border dispute with Eritrea has been resolved in June 2018 with Ethiopia announcing to accept the outcome of a 2002 border commission ruling, which awarded disputed territories, including the town of Badme, to Eritrea.

◆ Conflict with Somalia over the un-demarcated former British administrative line having little meaning as a political separation to rival clans within Ethiopia's Ogaden and southern Somalia's Oromo region.

◆ An initial deal has been signed between Ethiopia, Egypt and Sudan in 2015 to end a long-standing dispute over sharing of the Nile waters and the building of Africa's biggest hydroelectric dam, in Ethiopia. Egypt has been opposing the project on the ground that it could diminish its share of Nile River waters, which provides almost all of the desert nation's water needs.

◆ Civil unrest in eastern Sudan has hampered efforts to demarcate the porous boundary with Ethiopia.

DEFENCE

ARMY
Personnel: 180,000

Equipment

Category	Name	In Service
MBT	T-72	200+
	T-62	75
	T-54/55	
APC/IFV	BRDM-1	70
	BMP-1	20
	BTR-40/60/152	90
	WZ551	
Artillery	Howitzer	300
	122 mm	360
MLRS	BM-21 122mm	
SAM, Air Defence	SA-2/3/7	
	Pantsir-S1	
	S-125	

New Procurements/Upgrades

No major procurement plans are under consideration at present.

AIR FORCE
Personnel: 3,500

Equipment

Category	Name	In Service
Fighter	Su-27	15
	Su-25	10
	MiG-21	15
	MiG-23	12
Transport	C-130E	2
	An-26	1
	C-47	8
	Yak-40	1
Helicopter	Mi-6	10
	Mi-8	12
	Mi-24 (attack)	10

...continued

Category	Name	In Service
Helicopter	Mi-14 (anti-submarine)	2
	SA330 Puma	1

New Procurements/Upgrades
No major procurement plans are under consideration at present.

Defence Expenditure
Defence Budget: $520 million (2020)

Estimated defence spending in terms of GDP: 0.6%

Ethiopia receives majority of its military equipment from the US, Israel, Italy and Russia.

Defence Production and R&D
The country does not undertake any defence production activities.

CONTACT DETAILS
Ministry of Defence
Churchill Road, PO Box 1373
Addis Ababa,
Ethiopia

FIJI
(Capital: Suva)

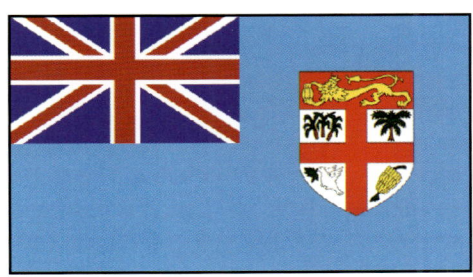

INTRODUCTION
Area: 18,274 sq km
Population: 939,535 (July 2021 est.)
Coastline: 1,129 km
Maritime claims: Territorial sea: 12 nm
Exclusive Economic Zone: 200 nm
Continental shelf: 200 m depth or to the depth of exploitation; rectilinear shelf claim added

KEY POLITICAL PERSONS

PRESIDENT & COMMANDER-IN-CHIEF: Ratu Wiliame Katonivere

PRIME MINISTER: RAdm. (Retd.) Josaia Voreqe (Frank) Bainimarama

KEY DEFENCE PERSONS

MINISTER FOR DEFENCE & NATIONAL SECURITY: Inia B Seruiratu

COMMANDER REPUBLIC OF FIJI MILITARY FORCES (RFMF): Maj. Gen. Jone Logavatu Kalouniwai

ECONOMY
Fiji is endowed with forest, mineral, and fish resources. It is one of the most developed of the Pacific island economies though still with a large subsistence sector. Fiji is a member of the WTO. Fiji's current account deficit peaked at 23% of GDP in 2006, and has been improving since. Fiji's sugar remains a significant industry and a major export. The sugar industry reforms since 2010 have improved productivity and returns. Fiji is a member of the WTO. Fiji is a party to the US-Pacific Islands Multilateral Tuna Fisheries Treaty, which provides access for U.S. fishing vessels in exchange for a license fee from the US industry, as per US Dept. of State reports. Bottled water exports to the US are Fiji's largest domestic export. COVID-19 pandemic and related restrictions and lockdowns have immensely affected the industry especially the tourism sector of Fiji creating a downfall in its GDP for the year 2020 and which may continue to 2021 also. The Govt. of Fiji has provided economic stimulus budget to help the businesses and workers in this situation.

GDP (official exchange rate): $9.86 billion (2020 est.), $12.18 billion (2017 est.)
Real Growth Rate (GDP): 3% (2017 est.), 0.7% (2016 est.)
Industries: Tourism, sugar processing, clothing, copra, gold, silver, lumber
Total Exports: $1.23 billion (2020 est.), $2.64 billion (2019 est.)
Export Commodities: Water, refined petroleum, fish, raw sugar, gold (2019)
Major Markets: United States 29%, Australia 14%, New Zealand 7%, Japan 6%, Tonga 6% (2019)

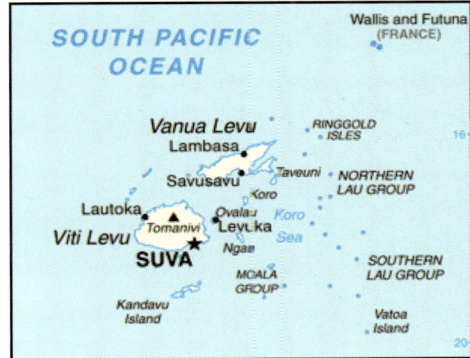

Total Imports: $1.97 billion (2020 est.); $3.21 billion (2019 est.)
Import Commodities: Refined petroleum, aircraft, cars, wheat, broadcasting equipment (2019)
Major Suppliers: Singapore 18%, Australia 13%, China 13.8%, New Zealand 11%, France 11%, South Korea 8% (2017)

INTERNATIONAL DISPUTES
Fiji is not currently engaged in an armed conflict.

DEFENCE
ARMY
Personnel: 3,200

Equipment

Category	Name	In Service
Artillery	25-pdr gun	5+
	105 mm howitzer	2+
Mortar	81 mm	10+
Vehicle	Bushmaster Protected Mobility Vehicle	10

Army Aviation

Category	Name	In Service
Helicopter	Eurocopter AS355F2	
	Eurocopter SA365N	

New Procurements/Upgrades
No major procurement plans are under consideration at present.

NAVY

Personnel: 300

Equipment

Category	Name	In Service
Patrol Vessel	Pacific class	3
	Levuika class	2
	Ex-Israeli Dabur Class	4
Survey Vessel	RFNS Volasiga, RFNS Kacau	2

New Procurements/ Upgrades

No major procurement plans are under consideration at present.

Defence Expenditure

Total defence spending: 13.8 million FJD (2020-21 approx.)

Estimated defence spending in terms of GDP: 1.4% of GDP (2020 est.), 1.6% of GDP (2019)

According to Government of Fiji, the Ministry of Defence, National Security and Policing is allocated a total of $13.8 million in the 2020-2021 Budget. The Republic of Fiji Military Force is to ensure at all times the security, defence and well- being of Fiji and all Fijians. It also makes a significant contribution to United Nations Peacekeeping operations in troubled areas around the world. The RFMF's naval division provides surveillance of Fiji's maritime zone and operates a costal radio station for all vessels within Fijian waters. The US Department of Defence offers defence-related support in two main areas: Foreign Military Financing (FMF), which the government uses to buy military equipment from the US and the International Military Education and Training (IMET) programme, which funds training programmes provided by Washington.

In 2020, the United States of America signed a landmark agreement with Fiji to enhance the bilateral engagements in the areas of Defence and Security. The Defence, International Military Education and Training (IMET) Agreement will deepen the existing partnership between Fiji and the United States. The United States to provide defence and security funding and training opportunities for our Fijian counterparts.

Defence Production and R&D

Fiji does not undertake any defence production activities.

Defence Procurement

The Republic of Fiji Military Forces (RFMF) acquire small amounts of equipment mainly from Australia, South Korea, New Zealand, Singapore, UK and US and some is received in the form of military co-operation/aid. Currently, changes are taking place to meet the military's operational requirements and government demands in areas such as infrastructure development.

CONTACT DETAILS

Republic of Fiji Military Forces
RFMF Headquarters, Berkley Crescent
Suva City, Central, Fiji.
Ph: 679 3313799
Email: info@rfmf.mil.fj
Website: www.rfmf.mil.fj

FINLAND
(Capital: Helsinki)

INTRODUCTION

Area: 338,145 sq km

Population: 5,587,442 (July 2021 est.)

Coastline: 1,250 km

Maritime claims: Territorial sea: 12 nm (in the Gulf of Finland - 3 nm)

Contiguous zone: 24 nm

Continental shelf: 200 m depth or to the depth of exploitation

KEY POLITICAL PERSONS

PRESIDENT: Sauli Niinisto

PRIME MINISTER: Sanna Marin

KEY DEFENCE PERSONS

DEFENCE MINISTER: Antti Kaikkonen

COMMANDER OF DEFENCE FORCES: Gen. Timo Kivinen

COMMANDER OF THE ARMY: Lt. Gen. Petri Hulkko

COMMANDER OF THE NAVY: Rear Adm. Jori Harju

COMMANDER OF THE AIR FORCE: Maj. Gen. Pasi Jokinen

ECONOMY

Finland has a highly industrialized, largely free-market economy with per capita output almost as high as that of Austria, Belgium, the Netherlands, and Sweden. Trade is important with exports accounting for over one-third of GDP in recent years. Finland is strongly competitive in manufacturing – principally the wood, metals, engineering, telecommunications, and electronics industries. Finland excels in hi-tech exports such as mobile phones. Except for timber and some minerals, the country depends on imports of raw materials, energy, and some components for manufactured goods. Finland had been one of the best performing economies within the EU before 2009 and its banks and financial markets avoided the worst of global financial crisis. However, the world slowdown hit exports and domestic demand hard in that year, causing Finland's economy to contract from 2012 to 2014. The recession affected general government finances and the debt ratio. The economy returned to growth in 2016, posting a 1.9% GDP increase before growing an estimated 3.3% in 2017, supported by a strong increase in investment, private consumption, and net exports. Amidst the global economic crisis triggered by the Coronavirus pandemic, Finland's GDP contracted by 2.8% in 2020, as per data from the European Commission. The economy is likely to chart a growth of around 3% in 2021 and 2022, according to projections made by the Bank of Finland.

GDP (official exchange rate): $269.25 billion (2019 est.)

Real Growth Rate (GDP): 1.15% (2019 est.); 1.52% (2018 est.)

Industries: Metals and metal products, electronics, machinery and scientific instruments, shipbuilding, pulp and paper, foodstuff, chemicals, textiles, clothing

Total Exports: $119.88 billion (2019 est.); $111.33 billion (2018 est.)

Export Commodities: Refined petroleum, paper and wood pulp products, cars, stainless steel, lumber (2019)

Major Markets: Germany 14%, Sweden 10%, United States 8%, Netherlands 6%, China 6%, Russia 5% (2019)

Total Imports: $120.43 billion (2019 est.); $116.62 billion (2018 est.)

Import Commodities: Crude petroleum, cars and vehicle parts, refined petroleum, broadcasting equipment, packaged medicines (2019)

Major Suppliers: Germany 16%, Sweden 14%, Russia 13%, China 6%, Netherlands 6% (2019)

INTERNATIONAL DISPUTES

Various groups in Finland advocate restoration of Karelia and other areas ceded to the Soviet Union, but the Finnish Government asserts no territorial demands.

DEFENCE

ARMY

Personnel: 24,000+ (including conscriptions)

Equipment

Category	Name	In Service
MBT	Leopard 2A4	120
	Leopard 2A6	106
APC/IFV	BMP-2	110
	CV90	100
	BTR-50PK	50
	XA-180/102/203	600+
	BTR-60PB	100+
Artillery	Towed pieces (M-46, D-30, 2S5 Giatsint-S, 2S1 Gvozdika)	700+
Mortar	XA 361 - 120 mm	24
	Krh-TeKa - 120 mm	27
MRLS	298 RsRakH 06 (M270)	22
	Rakh 89 122mm	30
ATGW	TOW	
	Spike	
SAM	ITO-90	10
	ITO 2005, ITO 2005 M	16

Army Aviation

Category	Name	In Service
Helicopter	MD 500D/MD 500E (Utility)	7
	NH90 TTH	20
UAV	Ranger	11
	Orbiter	55 systems

New Procurements/Upgrades

◆ Delivery of all Leopard 2A6 main battle tanks from the Netherlands has been completed with the final platform handed over in October 2019. The Finnish Defence Ministry in January 2014 had cleared a contract worth €199.9 million ($271 million) to acquire 106 used Leopard 2A6 MBTs from the Netherlands.

◆ A contract has been signed with BAE Systems in July 2021 for mid-life upgrade of the entire fleet of CV90 infantry fighting vehicles.

◆ State-owned Patria is upgrading the XA-180 Pasi armoured vehicles. The contract involves overhaul of a pre-series vehicle and a series of 70 vehicles alongside an option to modernise 210 vehicles by the end of 2021. The platforms will remain in service till the 2040s after the upgrade.

◆ An agreement has been reached between Finland and Latvia to jointly design and develop a new six-wheeled armoured vehicle for their land forces.

◆ The Defence Ministry in 2017 approved funds to buy the ex-RoK Army K9 Thunder 155 mm self-propelled howitzers from South Korea. 48 of the used howitzers are being acquired from the South Korean Army at a cost of US$155 million.

◆ The Government has requested a possible sale of 40 Guided Multiple Launch Rocket Pods from the US.

◆ Lockheed Martin has received $45.3 million contract to upgrade the Army's entire fleet of M270 Multiple Launch Rocket Systems. The Defence Ministry has also approved the purchase of 90 M31A1 and 150 M30A1 missiles for the 22 M270 MRLS.

◆ The Defence Ministry in October 2020 has approved procurement of 66mm KES 12 single-shot anti-tank weapons.

◆ Acquisition process for mini unmanned air vehicles is going on.

◆ A contract has been awarded to Israel's Elta Systems for the acquisition of ELM-2311 Compact Multi-Mission radars. The counter-battery radars would be procured to enable the Army to locate and track incoming rockets, artillery shells and mortars. Delivery is expected in 2021 – 22.

NAVY

Personnel: 2,000+

Equipment

Category	Name	In Service
FAC	Hamina class	4
	Rauma class	4
Patrol vessel	Kiisla class	2
Amphibious ship	LCUs, LCPs	40+

...continued

Category	Name	In Service
Mine sweeper/ Mine hunter	Kuha class	6
	Kiiski class	7
	Hameenmaa class (minelayer)	2
	Pansio class	3
	Katanpaa class	3
Auxiliary ship	Kemio class	1
	Kampela class	3
	Valas class	5
	Hauki class	8
	Hila class	4
	Jehu class	3

New Procurements/Upgrades

◆ The Government in September 2019 approved contract awards to Rauma Marine Constructions Oy (RMC) and Saab for delivery of the Finnish Navy's €1.32 billion 'Squadron 2020' corvette programme. Under the Laivue 2020 (Squadron 2020) project, four new corvettes would be procured to replace the three minelayers of the Pohjanmaa- and Hameenmaa-classes, as well as four light fast attack craft of the Rauma-class. The new vessels would be built between 2020 and 2024, with initial operational capability expected by 2025.

◆ Delivery of Jehu-class combat/ landing boats is going on. Finland has ordered 12 of these 200-ton fast, manoeuvrable vessels from Marine Alutech Oy Ab.

◆ The Hamina-class fast attack craft are undergoing service-life upgrade by Patria to keep them operational till 2035.

◆ BAE Systems has won a contract in 2018 to produce and deliver the Bofors 40 Mk4 naval guns. The guns will arm the upgraded Hamina-class FACs.

◆ Procurement of Harpoon missiles from the US is advancing.

◆ Gabriel anti-ship missiles would be procured from Israel to equip the Hamina-class missile FACs and the future "Squadron 2020" class of multi-role corvettes. A contract with Israel was signed in 2018 to acquire the new weapons which would replace the Finnish Navy's SAAB-built RBS-15 anti-ship missiles.

AIR FORCE
Personnel: 3,000+
Equipment

Category	Name	In Service
Fighter	F/A-18 C/D	62
Tanker & Transport	Learjet 35	3
	CASA C-295M	3
	Fokker F-27	1

...continued

Category	Name	In Service
Tanker & Transport	C-17 Globemaster	3 (shared with NATO members)
Trainer	Hawk Mk.51/51A (trainer)	49
	Hawk Mk.66 (attack)	16
	L-70 Vinka	28
	L-90 Redigo	7
	Pilatus PC-12	6

New Procurements/Upgrades

◆ New-generation fighter jets will be procured under the HX programme to replace the entire fleet of 62 F/A-18 Hornet fighters. In 2018, the Defence Ministry issued a Request for Quotation (RfQ) to four bidders – UK (Eurofighter Typhoon), France (Dassault Rafale), Sweden (Gripen) and the USA (Boeing F/A-18E/F Super Hornet; Lockheed Martin's F-35 JSF) for the procurement programme. Finland will begin phasing out its Hornet fleet from 2025. The final contract for the new 64 fighter platforms is expected to be awarded in 2021. The deal is likely to cost €7-10 billion (US $9-12 billion).

◆ Procurement of EA-18G Growler airborne electronic attack aircraft (as part of the HX programme) is also under consideration and a request has been made to the US Defence Department in this regard. The US DoD in 2019 has given approval to Boeing and the US Navy to offer the EA-18G Growlers to Finland.

◆ SAAB has offered two GlobalEye Airborne Early Warning and Control (AEW&C) aircraft to the Finnish Air Force (along with the Gripen fighters offered for the HX programme).

◆ Under the US Foreign Military Sales programme, Lockheed Martin has been contracted to support the integration of long-range Joint Air-to-Surface Standoff Missile (JASSM) system onto the Air Force's F-18C/D fighters which have undergone second mid-life upgrade recently to keep them operational till 2025-2030.

◆ 28 used Grob G115E trainer aircraft have been procured from the UK-based Babcock International Corp for about €6.6 million between 2016 and 2018. Finnish firm Patria has been tasked with carrying out avionics modifications and maintenance of the trainer platforms. The upgraded jets are undergoing flight tests.

◆ 12 Ground Master 403 long-range air defence radars are being delivered to enhance the country's air surveillance capability.

▶ The C-295M military transport aircraft are being upgraded with new navigation and identification system.

Defence Expenditure
Defence budget: €4.87 billion (proposed for 2021); €3.17 billion (2020)

Defence spending in terms of GDP: 2.2% (estimated for 2021)

Leading arms suppliers to Finland are the US, Germany and Sweden. The country has exported defence materiel to Turkey, UAE, Sweden, Poland and the US in recent years.

Defence Production and R&D
Finland's domestic defence industry is ruled by Patria Industries, which is majority-owned by the Government. The defence industry is primarily involved in the production of land-based systems, including armoured personnel carriers, self-propelled mortars and air-defence systems among others. However, majority of land and aerospace systems are imported from other countries. The Finnish government is exploring options to cooperate with European nations for the production and maintenance of defence equipment. In 2018, defence exports by Finland increased by 17% over the previous year and totalled €128.3 million.

Defence Procurement
Finland, in the past, has acquired several Soviet-era defence equipment from Russia. However, strained relations with Russia over the ongoing Ukraine crisis has made the Nordic country, which remains "militarily non-aligned", inch closer towards the NATO with Helsinki even considering the option of joining the block in future. Finland has partnered with European countries and has been making defence procurements from both Europe and the USA. Future military procurements, mainly for the Navy and Air Force, have been outlined.

CONTACT DETAILS
Ministry of Defence
Etelainen Makasiinikatu 8
P.O. Box 31
FIN-00131, Helsinki
Finland
Tel.: +358 295 16001
E-mail: kirjaamo@defmin.fi
www.defmin.fi

STRATEGIC INFORMATION
FRANCE
(Capital: Paris)

INTRODUCTION

Area: Total 643,801 sq km; 551,500 sq km (metropolitan France)

Population: : 68,084,217 (July 2021)

Coastline: Total: 4,853 km; 3,427 km, metropolitan France, (has numerous islands under its control in the Pacific Ocean and Indian Ocean).

Maritime Claims: Territorial sea: 12 nm

Contiguous zone: 24 nm

Exclusive Economic Zone: 200 nm (does not apply to the Mediterranean)

Continental shelf: 200 m depth or to the depth of exploitation

GEOPOLITICAL IMPORTANCE

France is the largest western European country with several overseas territories and islands located on other continents. The French overseas territories include French Guiana on the South American continent and several island territories in the Atlantic, Pacific and Indian oceans. Metropolitan France extends from the Mediterranean Sea to the English Channel and the North Sea and from the Rhine to the Atlantic Ocean. It is bordered by Belgium, Luxembourg, Germany, Switzerland, Italy and Monaco, with Spain and Andorra to the Southwest. The country is linked to the United Kingdom by the Channel Tunnel and has land borders with Suriname and Brazil through French Guiana, as well as with the Kingdom of the Netherlands. France is an important player in European geopolitics – it holds the key to the entirety of Europe both in and out of the United Nations. It plays an influential global role as a permanent member of the United Nations Security Council, NATO, the G-7, the G-20, the EU, and other multilateral organisations. France continues to be a major power in the world with its well-developed economy, membership in European organisations, strong military posture and political influence.

POLITICAL OVERVIEW

France's current system of government, known as the Fifth Republic, is based on a constitution that was adopted by popular referendum in 1958. The political system consists of an executive branch, a legislative branch, and a judicial branch. The current constitution has greatly increased the powers of the president making it the most powerful position in the French political system. Since the passing of the 2008 constitutional reform, the maximum number of terms a president can serve has been limited to two. The office of the president under the Third and Fourth Republic was a largely ceremonial one. The presidential term is five years. He is directly elected in a two-stage voting system. A candidate who receives more than 50% of the vote in the first round is elected. However, a second round is held if no candidate receives 50%. The French Parliament consists of two chambers – the National Assembly (lower house) and the Senate (upper house). The prime minister is head of the government. He is nominated by the majority party in the National Assembly and appointed by the president for an indefinite term. The president names the prime minister, presides over the cabinet, commands the armed forces, and concludes treaties. The country's highest appellate court is called the Cour de Cassation and the six chief judges are appointed by the president. The Constitutional Court, a creation of the Fifth Republic, holds the power of judicial review.

KEY POLITICAL PERSONS

PRESIDENT: Emmanuel Macron

PRIME MINISTER: Jean Castex

ECONOMY

France has long been part of the world's wealthiest and most developed national economies. As of September 30, 2020, it was the 3rd largest economy of Europe, after the economy of Germany and the United Kingdom. France economy is dominated by the service sector followed by the industrial sector which accounts for 19.5% of its GDP. The government dominates major sectors of the economy as a large shareholder in many semi-public enterprises. It has substantial agricultural resources, a large industrial base, and a highly skilled work force. The country is a major tourist destinations with 89 million foreign tourists in 2017. France has been successful in developing dynamic telecommunications, aerospace, weapons and features among the top weapons exporter. President Emmanuel Macron has launched a series of economic reforms to improve competitiveness and boost economic growth. He has implemented a range of reforms to increase flexibility in the labour market. In 2018 budget, the government cut public spending, taxes, and social security contributions to spur private investment and increase purchasing power. The government plans to gradually reduce corporate tax rate for businesses from 33.3% to 25% by 2022.

GDP (official exchange rate): $2,715,574,000,000 (2019 est.)

Real Growth Rate (GDP): 1.49% (2019 est.), 1.81% (2018 est.)

Industries: Machinery, chemicals, automobiles, metallurgy, aircraft, electronics; textiles, food processing; tourism

Crude Oil – Proved Reserves: 65.97 million bbl (1 January 2018 est.)

Natural Gas – Proved Reserves: 88.41 billion cu m (1 January 2018 est.)

Total Exports: $746.91 billion (2020 est.), $891.18 billion (2019 est.)

Export Commodities: Aircraft, packaged medicines, cars and vehicle parts, gas turbines, wine (2019)

Major Markets: Germany 14%, United States 8%, Italy 7%, Spain 7%, Belgium 7%, United Kingdom 7% (2019)

Total Imports: $803.66 billion (2020 est.), $919.63 billion (2019 est.)

Import Commodities: Cars, crude petroleum, refined petroleum, packaged medicines, aircraft machinery (2019)

Major Suppliers: Germany 18%, Belgium 9%, Italy 9%, Spain 7%, China 7%, Netherlands 6%, United Kingdom 5% (2019)

DEFENCE & SECURITY

The mission of the French armed forces is protection of the nation's territory and its population. The armed forces have the capacity to set up command structures for the land, sea and air components on the level of an army brigade or equivalent. The Defence White Paper 2013 has accorded priority to develop intelligence capabilities with a greater effort to modernise human resources and upgrade the technical imaging and electromagnetic interception resources, whether space-based, air, naval or land as part of a measure to protect the country. The armed forces model has for the first time included military cyber defence capabilities which will work in close liaison with intelligence and defensive and offensive planning in preparation for or support of military operations. The Special Forces are being reinforced in terms of personnel, command capabilities and their capacity to coordinate with the intelligence services while strengthening the COS (special operations command). The Atlantic Alliance, being an essential component of the defence and national security strategy, France intends to capitalise on its full participation in the military structures of NATO. After being hit by a wave of terrorist attacks, the armed forces are committed to dealing with crises that are simultaneous, complex, and spread out geographically. In addition to ensuring the readiness and safety of the nuclear deterrent, they are deployed in operations in the Sahel region and in the Middle East, in the Counter-Daesh Coalition. They also contribute to the defence and protection of France's homeland and its immediate surroundings. The defence and security plan includes protection of space-based assets.

KEY DEFENCE PERSONS

DEFENCE MINISTER: Florence Parly

CHIEF OF DEFENCE STAFF: Gen. Thierry Burkhard

CHIEF OF STAFF OF THE ARMY: Gen. Pierre Schill

CHIEF OF STAFF OF THE NAVY: Adm. Pierre Vandier

CHIEF OF STAFF OF THE AIR FORCE: Gen. Philippe Lavigne

DIRECTOR GENERAL OF THE GENDARMERIE: Gen. Christian Rodriguez

External Conflict

France is working to ensure long-term stability for the zones freed from Daesh in Iraq and Syria in order to avoid any resurgence from terrorist groups. It is therefore supporting several NGOs as well as multilateral bodies that are active on the ground. France joined the United States led military campaign against the jihadists in Syria and Iraq having pledged to work together on countering the threat from the Islamic State

Peace Operation: France is an active participant in the United Nations peacekeeping missions. The French armed forces are present in a number of conflict zones around the world. France supported the UN peacekeeping operations such as UNTSO, UNIFIL, MINURCAT, MINURSO, MONUSCO, UNMIL, UNOCI, and MINUSTAH.

Territorial disputes: Madagascar claims the French territories of Bassas da India, Europa Island, Glorioso Islands, and Juan de Nova Island. While Comoros claims Mayotte, Mauritius claims Tromelin Island. There is a territorial dispute between Suriname and the French overseas department of French Guiana. France also asserts a territorial claim in Antarctica (Adelie Land) and both France and Vanuatu claim Matthew and Hunter Islands, east of New Caledonia.

THREAT PERSPECTIVE

Terrorism: France has been hit by a series of terrorist attacks consisting of mass shootings, suicide bombings, and hostage-taking. France has suffered several attacks from jihadist individuals from Syria and Iraq. The terrorist threat in France is still very high and today they face a different kind of threats i.e. from individuals already on French soil, individuals who can act in a totally autonomous manner without having any contact with people from Syria or Iraq. In October 2017, the French parliament adopted a controversial anti-terror bill that gives the authorities powers to search homes, shut places of worship and restrict freedom of movement. France determined to combat terrorism in all its forms is taking action at every level with its international partners to combat terrorist networks in the country and abroad. It had joined forces with the Global Coalition against Daesh by launching "Operation Chammal" to support Iraqi authorities engaged in fighting the terrorist group. Faced with heightened terrorist threat, the scope of action of Operation Chammal was extended to include Syria to destroy Daesh's regional hold in the country. In addition to military action, France is actively seeking political solutions to end conflicts and prevent the emergence and strengthening of terrorist actors.

Cyber threat: France plays an active role in promoting a safe, stable and open cyber space. The French Network and Information Security Agency (ANSSI) created in 2009 is responsible for preventing and reacting to IT incidents regarding sensitive institutions. The French Ministry of Defence has a dual mission to ensure the protection of the networks which underpin its action and to integrate digital warfare into military operations. In order to consolidate the Ministry's work in this field, a cyber defence operational chain of command (COMCYBER), placed under the orders of the Armed Forces Chief of Staff, was created in early 2017. The French Ministry of the Interior aims to fight against all forms of cybercrime, aimed at national institutions and interests, economic stakeholders and government authorities, and individuals. The Paris Call for Trust and Security in Cyberspace demonstrates France's active role in promoting a safe, stable and open cyber space. France is actively involved in international forums where cyber security issues are being tackled.

Threats related to power

◆ Rise in military spending particularly in Asia

◆ Power politics between Russia and China

◆ Regional destabilisation in the Middle East

◆ Proliferation of weapons of mass destruction

◆ Cyber-attacks instigated by countries

◆ Risks to maritime security with increase

in piracy
- ◆ Risks to digital infrastructure through cyber attacks
- ◆ Potential threats in outer space

STRATEGIC RELATIONS

India:: France has remained one of India's strongest strategic partners. The two nations have agreed to further strengthen their defence and security partnership by enhancing intelligence and information sharing, bolstering mutual capabilities, expanding military drills and pursuing new initiatives in maritime, space and cyber domains, at a meeting of India-France strategic dialogue in Paris on November 6, 2021. France and its defence industry actively contribute to the "Make in India" programme in the defence sector. The first conventional submarine, Scorpene, was built in India in 2008 with transfer of technology and support from DCNS. The Indian Space Research Organisation (ISRO) and its French counterpart Centre National de Etudes Spatiales (CNES) have a rich history of cooperation and collaboration. They have recently agreed to start a bilateral space security dialogue. They have also committed to expand their military cooperation in the strategically key Indo-Pacific region besides resolving to further ramp up the overall defence and security ties which includes covering of a range of issues – the regional security situation, joint development of defence platforms and expansion of military-to-military ties. Prime Minister Modi has declared India's unwavering commitment to the Paris Accord.

United States: The United States and France have friendly relations and they continue to cooperate closely on many issues, most notably in combating terrorism, efforts to stem the proliferation of weapons of mass destruction, and on regional problems, including in Africa, the Middle East, the Balkans, and Central Asia. The two nations are among the five permanent members of the UN Security Council (P5). In the Israeli-Palestinian conflict, France supports the US engagement in the peace process. France is one of the North Atlantic Treaty Organization's (NATO) top five troop contributors. The US is the top destination for French investment and the US is the largest foreign investor in France. Trade and investment between the two countries are strong. In 2019, the US and France traded more than $138 billion in goods and services. However, in the wake of recent announcement by the US of a new trilateral security partnership between the US, Australia and Great Britain, France has recalled its ambassador to the United States.

United Kingdom: France and the UK have signed a Defence and Security Cooperation Treaty with an aim to develop co-operation between British and French Armed Forces, for sharing and pooling of materials and equipment including through mutual interdependence, the building of joint facilities, mutual access to each other's defence markets, and industrial and technological co-operation. Key planks include the creation of a 10,000-strong joint expeditionary force involving 5,000 troops from each country in all three services, training and exercising together and prepare for high-intensity combat, rescue and peacekeeping missions and the development of an integrated strike force to be deployed on either nation's aircraft carriers. There has been a fallout in the bilateral relations over the new Australia-UK-US defence pact, or AUKUS,

China: France was the first among Western powers to establish diplomatic relations with China. It views China as its very important strategic partner. The two countries are permanent members of the United Nations Security Council and the world's two largest economies. Both the countries have decided to expand nuclear cooperation besides deepening their cooperation in the aerospace industry and participation of French manufacturers in China's C919 aerospace programme. In March 2019, President Emmanuel Macron and President Xi Jinping signed a series of trade agreements further strengthening trade between the two countries.

Israel: France was one of the first countries to establish diplomatic relations with Israel on 11 May 1949, and subsequently played an active role in helping to consolidate the newly formed State by contributing to its defence effort. Efforts have been made to improve their relationship which has become increasingly strained and complex. There has been political dialogue between France and Israel. In recent years' trade between the two countries has remained stable with some major investments or joint ventures. They enjoy good bilateral relations in the cultural, scientific and economic fields and in tourism. Cooperation has been observed in the high-tech fields of defence.

Germany: France and Germany have united after World War II in pursuing political objectives to guarantee that there would never be another war between the two nations. Consequently, the European Union was created with the integration of other European countries. The partnership between Europe's two largest economies has been vital to the functioning of the EU and the 17-nation euro zone. The new currency Euro, a French-German confection, was launched in world money markets on 1 January 1999. The two countries have always been important players in furthering the ideals of European integration. On 22 January 2019, leaders of Chancellor Angela Merkel and President Emmanuel Macron signed the extension to the Elysee Treaty in Aachen, Germany, a historical symbol of European concord.

DEFENCE CAPABILITIES

The French military is one of the most capable forces in Europe. The French Armed Forces encompass the Army, the Navy, the Air Force and the National Gendarmerie. The president of the republic heads the armed forces. He is the supreme authority for military matters and the sole official who can order a nuclear strike. The French military doctrine is based on the concepts of national independence, nuclear deterrence and military self-sufficiency. The force has its own indigenous ballistic missile submarines, maintains its own air and land-based nuclear deterrent. It is equipped with LeClerc MBT, VBCIs, an integrated infantry combat system (FELIN), self-propelled howitzers (CAESER), and attack helicopters (Tiger). It maintains its own nuclear-powered aircraft carrier, combat aircraft including the Rafale and Mirage 2000 fighters and AWACS aircraft. France is carrying out its military modernisation programme – the Scorpion programme – is aimed at transforming the French Army to meet the operational challenges of tomorrow. It brings together all the French Army platform programmes: EBRC – Armoured Reconnaissance and Combat Tank, VBMR – Multirole armoured vehicle, modernised Leclerc heavy tank, Felin, Scorpion Combat and Information System (SIC-S) and communication means. It is integrating different types of unmanned systems, remote weapon stations, tactical cyber capabilities, loitering munitions, energy weapons, electronic warfare (EW) and signature management devices. The Air Force is expected to operate 254 combat aircraft by 2025. These will include 171 Rafales, including 40 Rafale Ms belonging to the navy, and 55 upgraded Mirage 2000Ds. For its Navy, France has ordered six anti-submarine variants, and two self-defence variants of the FREMM European multi-mission frigate. France is equipped with capabilities like the Graves and Satam radars and telescopes operated by CNRS and Ariane group to track satellites. Thales Alenia Space and Airbus Defence and Space are building two Syracuse 4 satellites, and a third is to be added to the constellation. By 2023, nano-satellites between one and 10 kg will be built as a patrol craft for providing eyes in space. France has carried out its first military exercise in space codenamed "AsterX" to test its ability to defend its satellites.

ARMY (Armée de terre): The French army is the largest component of the French Armed Forces comprising of the Troupes de Marine, the Armoured Cavalry Branch, the Artillery, the Military engineers, the Infantry, which includes the Chasseurs Alpins, specialist mountain infantry, Maintenance Matériel, Logistics (Train), Signals (Transmissions), and Commissariat.

Personnel: 115,437

Equipment

Category	Name	In Service	On Order
MBT	Leclerc	254	
Armoured car /AIFV/ APC	Griffon	92	
	ERC-90 (to be replaced)	110	
	AMX-10RC	256	
	VBCI	630	
	VPC	110	
	VAB	3,200	
	Buffalo	5	
	Nexter Aravis	15	
	BVs10 mKII	53	
Artillery	155mm & AUF-1155mm SP howitzer	157	
	155mm TRF-1 towed		
	Ceasar 155mm truck-mounted	577	
Mortar	RTF1 120mm	364	
MRL	MLRS (converted for unitary warhead rockets)	13	
Anti-tank weapon	AT4CS		
	APILAS		
ATGW	Javelin	76	
	Milan	947	
	Hot (on VAB)	135	
	Hot (on helicopters)	110	
	ERYX	700	
AA gun	53T2 20mm	525	
UAV	MQ-9 Reaper	6	
	Crecerelle	12	
	MQ-9 Reaper	6	
	Crecerelle	12	
	Cl-289	54	
	Patroller		14
Weapon	Mistral (SAM)	336	
	Crotale (mobile SAM)		

New Procurements/Upgrades

◆ The government has placed a new order for 271 Griffon vehicles and 42 Jaguar vehicles to be delivered between 2022 and 2023. The order follows an initial contract for 339 vehicles signed in 2017. The Army is set to receive in total 1,872 Griffon and 300 Jaguar vehicles by 2030. About 936 Griffons and 150 Jaguars are set to be delivered by 2025.

◆ The Army has place an order for 14 Patroller tactical UAVs with first deliveries expected this year.

◆ The Army plans to purchase a total of 489 Serval vehicles by the end of 2025, and 978 by 2030. The first 108 Serval vehicles (patrol version) is expected to be delivered in 2022 – 12 in the first half of the year and 96 in the second half of the year. The VBMR Leger nicknamed Serval is part of the Scorpion programme.

◆ The French defence procurement agency DGA has awarded Nexter the mid-life update (MLU) contract for 200 Leclerc main battle tanks on 1 June 2021,

◆ The Missile Moyenne Portee (MMP) programme, a new-generation surface-attack missile system, designed for the French Army will see the delivery of 400 firing posts and 1,750 missiles by 2025.

Army Light Aviation: The French Army Light Aviation was established for observation, reconnaissance, assault and supply duties. It operates numerous helicopters in support of the French Army.

Personnel: 2,200

Equipment

Category	Name	In Service
Combat/ transport helicopter	Tigre HAP	39
	Tigre HAD	3+1
	Gazelle SA.342	147
	EC-725 Caracal	8
	Fennec AS.555	15
	NH-90TTH Caiman	8+
Utility Aircraft	Cougar AS.532	4
	Cessna F406	2
	PC-6	5
	TBM-700	8

New Procurements/Upgrades

◆ NH Industries has signed a contract for the development of an upgraded version of the NH90 Tactical Troop Helicopter (TTH). Under the terms of the contract, the final batch of 10 NH90s already ordered by the French Ministry of Armed Forces through the DGA will be delivered in 2025.

◆ The Ministry of the Armed Forces has launched the Initial Development of the Guépard (Cheetah) military helicopter intended to replace the Gazelle light helicopters. The helicopters will be delivered by 2026.

◆ The Army has placed on order for eight H225M long-range tactical transport military helicopter from Airbus.

NAVY (Marine Nationale): The blue water French Navy has five branches – the Force d'Action Navale, the Forces Sous-marines, the Aviation Navale, the Fusiliers Marins including Commandos de Marine and the Gendarmerie maritime. France aims to continue sailing blue water Navy that is able to project maritime power on the waves, silently below and by striking from the air. The French Navy's area of operation includes the North Atlantic, the Mediterranean Sea, and the Indian Ocean. The French submarine fleet consists of nuclear-propelled attack (SSNs) and ballistic missile submarines (SSBNs). Its SSBN force is the nucleus of the country's strategic deterrent, and maintains a continuous at-sea presence. By 2025, the Navy plans to be equipped with all the capabilities needed to complete a full range of missions, from defence to security. Current important naval programme includes the FREMM multi-mission warship programme and the Barracuda class nuclear attack submarine programme.

Personnel: 36,509

Major naval bases: Brest, Toulon, Ile Longue and Cherbourg in Metropolitan France, Fort de France, Degrad des Cannes, Port des Galets, Nouméa and Papeete.

Equipment

Category	Name	In Service	On order
Aircraft carrier	Charles de Gaulle	1	
Sub-marine	Barracuda class	1	5
	Triomphant class	4	
	Rubis class SSN	6	
Destroyer/ Frigate	Horizon class	2	
	Aquitaine class	7	1
	Georges Leygues class	2	
	Floreal class	6	
	Cassard class	1	
	La Fayette class	5	
Amphibious force	Mistral class LHD	3	
	Batral class assault ship	5	
	LCM (Landing craft mechanised)	20	
	LCT (Tank Landing Craft)	11	
	LST (Landing Ship, Tank)	5	

...continued

Category	Name	In Service	On order
OPV	D'estienne D'orves class	6	
	Loire-class BSAM	4	
Patrol craft	L'Audacieuse class	4	
	Arago	1	
	Leopard PCC	8	
	Flamant class	3	
Mine warfare force	Eridan class mine-hunter	10	
	Antares class sonar towing vessel	4	
Auxiliaries	Durance class tanker	3	
	Hydrographic ship	1	
	Oceanographic ship	2	
	Trial ship	3	
	Command ship	3	
Missile tracking ship	A601 Monge	1	
Electro-magnetic research ship	A759 Dupuy de Lôme	1	
Weapon	Exocet missile (ASM)		
	Aster missile (SAM)		
	Crotale missile (SAM)		

New Procurements/Upgrades

◆ The first of the six Barracuda-class nuclear attack submarine, Suffren, was commissioned on 6 November 2020.

◆ The Naval Group has delivered the FREMM DA Alsace frigate to the French Navy. Alsace is the first of the two air defence frigates with enhanced air defence capability and the seventh FREMM multi mission frigate ordered by OCCAR for the French defence procurement agency (DGA).

◆ The first of the five defence and intervention frigate (FDI) being built by DCNS is expected to be delivered in 2024. The digital multi-mission 4,500 tons-class FDI will be the first French frigate to be protected against cyber threat.

◆ The French Navy has started testing its future landing craft, EDA-S – Arbalète and Arquebuse. The EDA-S will replace the ageing fleet of CTM LCUs.

◆ Orders have been placed for six future POM patrol ships with expected deliveries between 2023 and 2025. The first of them will be christened August Bénébig and will be followed by the Jean Tranape, Teriieroo a teriierooiterai and Philippe Bernardino, Auguste Techer and Félix Éboué.

◆ Construction of the French Navy future aircraft carrier, Porte-avions de nouvelle génération or PANG, is expected to begin around 2025 and enter service in 2038. The nuclear powered next-generation aircraft carrier will replace the in-service Charles Des Gaulle.

◆ The DGA has launched the Future Ocean Patrol Programme (FOPP) to build 10 boats to replace the deep sea patrol boats (PHM). The first deliveries are scheduled for 2025.

◆ France plans to buy Aster 30 missiles; F21 Artemis torpedoes; and four Exocet MM40 Block 3C anti-ship missiles.

Naval Aviation: The Aviation navale is a combination of carrier squadrons and naval patrol air force.

Major naval air bases: Hyeres (main), Landivisiau, Lann-Bihoue and Lanveoc-Poulmic

Equipment

Category	Name	In Service
Interception aircraft	Rafale F3-R	1
	Rafale M F3	39
Attack aircraft	Super Etendard	17
AEW	E-2C Hawkeye (ship-borne)	3
MP/ASW	Atlantique 2	22
Surveillance aircraft	Falcon 50M	4
	Falcon 200	5
	EMB-121AN	6
ASuW	AS565SA Panther	16
Transport/ SAR	EC225 Super Puma (SAR)	2
	AS365N Dauphin SAR	3
	Alouette III	6
	Falcon DA	5
	MER	10
	Alquette II	4
	Rallye	8
	CAP 10	7

New Procurements/Upgrades

◆ The Navy has received the fifth upgraded ATL 2 maritime patrol aircraft. Two aircraft were delivered in 2019, one in 2020, and one last February. Another renovated ATL2 is scheduled for delivery soon.

◆ The French Navy's new Rafale M F3-R has achieved full operational capability. The F3-R upgrade project for all Rafale aircraft in French service was launched in October 2018.

◆ The DGA has signed a $2.3 billion F4-standard development contract for the Rafale fighter jets. France has also approved a proposal to include some F4 functionalities to the last 28 of 180 Rafale aircraft it has on order. The deliveries of these aircraft will begin from 2023. The F4 standard will include upgraded radar sensors and front-sector optronics, as well as improved capabilities in the helmet-mounted display.

◆ The DGA has ordered 27 NH90 NFH from NHIndustries in two different configurations for the Navy.

Air and Space Force (Armée de l'Air et de l'Espace) AAE: On 11 September 2020, the French Air Force was renamed French "Air and Space Force." The name change has been accompanied by a modification of the logo of the Air Force and by the implementation of a new organisation of the Ministry of Defense (MoD). The Air Force was formed in 1909 as the Service Aéronautique, a service arm of the French Army, and then made an independent military arm in 1934, becoming the French Air Force. On 11 September 2020, it assumed its current name. The new Space Command – an organisation of the Air and Space Force – will receives its directives from the Chief of Staff of the Armed Forces. The new military command aims to respond to new threats that could compromise the national freedom of access and action in space: cyber threats, electromagnetic jamming, kinetic (anti-satellites missiles) or more conventional threats. There are currently about 220 personnel spread among four different sites and centres – Paris (management), Toulouse (space operations, command and control), Lyon (a space situational awareness centre called COSMOS) and an observation centre called CMOS in Creil. The Space Command locally known as Commandement de l'Espace (CdE) plans to host 500 military staff by 2025.

Major air bases: Avord, Bordeaux, Cazaux, Cognac, Creil, Dijon, Evreux, Istres, Luxeuil, Monte-de-Marsan, Nancy, Orange, Orleans, Paris, Saint-Dizier, Salon, Solenzara, Toulouse, Tours, Villacoublay, BA104 (UAE). They have airbases on islands in the Pacific and Indian Ocean. Further their friendly relations with African countries, where they had colonized enables them to use their air bases.

Personnel: 42,344

Equipment

Category	Name	In Service	On order
Fighter / tanker	C-130J Hercules	2	
	KC-130J	2	
	KC-135FR, KC-135R	14	
	Rafale B	42+	
	Rafale C	45+	
	Mirage 2000B/C	50	

...continued

Category	Name	In Service	On order
Fighter / tanker	Mirage 2000-5F	34	
	Mirage 2000D	34	
	(being upgraded)	80	
AEW	E-3F AWACS	2	
Transport/ VIP	A330 MRTT	3	3
	A400M Atlas	17	8
	C-130Hs & C-130H-30	14	
	C-135FR	11	
	KC-135R	3	
	C-160 Transall	51	
	A-340	2	
	A-310	3	
	A-319CJ	2	
	Falcon 900	2	
	Falcon 7X	1	
	CN-235	27	
	Falcon 50	4	
	TBM 700	15	
	Twin Otter	5	
	Socata TBM	15	
Trainer aircraft	Alpha jet	85	
	EMB-121 Xingu	23	
	Jodel-D-140	18	
	Walter Extra 300	3	
Helicopter	Puma	24	
	Super Puma	5	
	Cougar	5	
	H225M	11	
	AS555 – Fennec	35+	
UAV	Harfang	4	
	Reaper block1/6	6+6	6
Weapon	Crotale NG	12	
	SAMP-T	8	

New Procurements/Upgrades

◆ The Air and Space Force plans to order 12 additional Rafale fighter jets. Dassault Aviation is already under contract to deliver 28 Rafale to the Air and Space Force between 2022 and 2024.

◆ The AAE has taken delivery of the first of eight VADOR ALSR aircraft. France plans to operate eight by 2030.

◆ The DGA has placed on order for three Airbus A330 planes. These aircraft will eventually be converted into Phenix MRTT (Multi-Role Tanker Transport). They will then complete the 12 MRTTs expected by 2023 bringing the MRTT fleet to 15 aircraft.

◆ The Airbus A400M Atlas transport aircraft of the French Air and Space Force has reached initial tactical capability on June 3, 2021. France is expected to take delivery of another eight A400Ms for a total of 25 aircraft by the end of 2025.

◆ The AAE has taken delivery of the first Mirage 2000D to undergo a major mid-life update (MLU) programme. The upgrade improves the aircraft air-to-air and air-to-ground capabilities through the addition of weapons such as the MBDA Mica IR air-to-air missile and the Sagem AASM precision-guided bomb.

The France Air and Space force upgraded Mirage D no. 639. Image credit: Armée de l'Air et de l'Espace

◆ The AAE has placed on order for eight H225M long-range tactical transport military helicopter from Airbus.. The H225M has the ability to operate both from ships and land in all weather conditions.

◆ France has signed an agreement with the US DoD for 6 additional MQ-9 Reaper Block 5 UAV. The contract will run through to 29 March 2024.

◆ France has announced the signing of a 16 billion-euro (USD 18 billion) armaments mega-contract for the sale of 80 of its upgraded Rafale warplanes to the UAE.

The Gendarmerie National is a branch of the French armed force attached to the Ministry of the Interior. The Gendarmerie National is in charge of public safety, with police duties among the civilian population. It contains a military force and a Special Forces component. It is mandated to fulfil national security duties and duties in support of its parent ministry. It has a personnel of 100,000 personnel, as of 2014.

Major Armament Producers

Airbus designs, manufacture and deliver industry-leading commercial aircraft, helicopters, military transports, satellites and launch vehicles, as well as providing data services, navigation, secure communications, urban mobility and other solutions for customers.

MBDA is a joint venture of European aerospace and defence companies, Airbus, BAE Systems and Leonardo. The group is capable of designing and producing missiles and missile systems to meet the whole range of current and future needs of the three armed forces – air, sea and land.

SAFRAN is a French conglomerate involved in defence, aerospace propulsion and equipment, and security.

The Thales Group products include radars, secure communications, drones, electronic missile systems.

Dassault Aviation is a French aircraft manufacturer of military, regional and business jets, a subsidiary of Dassault Group.

EADS: Co-manufacturer of MBDA missile systems, NH90 helicopters for troop transfer and Tiger combat helicopters, Airbus A400M military transport planes, Harfang drones, Astrium anti missile defence system.

Nexter: Manufacturers Leclerc tanks, VBCI armoured vehicles, Caesar wheeled self-propelled guns, Aravis tanks, munitions. They have recently developed the 155 mm (52 calibre) towed gun.

Naval Group earlier known as DCNS is an international high-tech company which specialises in defence naval systems whose skills cover the whole of the production chain for complex programmes. Naval Group uses its extraordinary know-how and unique industrial resources to meet its customers' requirements.

Foreign suppliers: Austria, Belgium, Germany, Italy, Sweden, United Kingdom, United States

DEFENCE DEALS
Joint Venture Programmes

India

Dassault Reliance Aerospace: India's Reliance Group and France's Dassault have set up a Joint Venture called 'Dassault Reliance Aerospace' for research and development of unspecified defence projects in India. The defence partnership was formed as part of a fighter jet deal agreed between the two nations. Dassault, which is building the aircraft, agreed under the terms of the deal to invest about 50 percent of the value of the contract in India. India has inked an inter-governmental deal with France in September 2016 to procure 36 Rafale jets worth Rs 59,000 crore. So far, Dassault has delivered 29 Rafale jets to India.

Scorpene submarine: France is a major partner for India in developing various key military platforms including the Scorpene submarines. Under a technology transfer agreement with France, India is currently building Scorpene submarines at Mumbai's Mazagon Docks Limited (MDL). The first of six Scorpene diesel-electric attack submarines, INS Kalvari, has been commissioned into the Indian Navy on 14 December 2017, the second, INS Khanderi in September 2019 and the third INS Karanj on 10 March 2021. Trials of two – the Vela and Vagir – are underway while the construction of sixth Vagsheer is under way.

Germany

FCAS: France and Germany have awarded the initial framework contract (called Phase 1A) for the demonstrator phase of the Future Combat Air System (FCAS). The project for the Future Air Combat System (or Système de Combat Aérien Futur, SCAF) was given the formal go-ahead at the ILA Berlin Airshow in April 2018. The New Fighter (NF) or Next-Generation Fighter (NGF), is to be developed to operate in conjunction with a swarm of unmanned 'wingmen' as a next-generation weapon system (NGWS) which will form part of a wider future combat air system that will include the European medium-altitude long-endurance (MALE) remotely piloted aircraft system (RPAS); an ultra-low observable (LO) unmanned combat aerial vehicle (UCAV); future cruise missiles; and other legacy airborne platforms operating in the future battlespace. A test flight of a demonstrator is expected around 2030 and entry into service around 2045.

MGCS: Germany and France have signed another agreements to develop a new Main Ground Combat System (MGCS). The Main Ground Combat System (MGCS) will develop a future land warfare system to replace the German Army's Leopard 2 and the French Army's Leclerc. New European partners are expected to join the MGCS programme. Current plans call for a technology demonstration phase that will last until 2024, followed by a systems demonstrator phase from 2024-2027, followed by the implementation phase, which will commence in 2028.

Italy

FREMM frigate: The FREMM European multi-mission frigate is a joint programme between France and Italy. The project is expected to produce 21 FREMM frigates both for the French and the Italian Navy. FREMM Aquitaine is the first ship of her class. The French Navy has 8 Aquitaine-class FREMM Frigates on order, six have been commissioned and two more will be specialized for air-defence. The Italian Navy has 10 Bergamini-class FREMM Frigates on order – four are configured for ASW missions. The other six are "General Purpose" frigates with two ships still to be commissioned.

Brazil

ProSub: Brazil under the ProSub programme plans to build four diesel-electric attack submarines and a single much larger nuclear-powered submarine with the help of France. The first Scorpène diesel-electric (S-BR) submarines is Riachuelo, the second is Humaitá (S41), third submarine and Tonelero (S42). These submarines being developed with French assistance are based on the French Scorpene class. The Álvaro Alberto, the first Brazilian submarine with nuclear propulsion (SN-BR), is due to be launched in 2031.

Europe

nEUROn: The nEUROn is an experimental unmanned combat aerial vehicle (UCAV) being developed with international cooperation, led by the French company Dassault Aviation. European countries involved in this project include France, Greece, Italy, Spain, Sweden and Switzerland. The nEUROn programme is designed to validate the development of complex technologies representing all mission systems: high-level flight control and stealth, launching real air-to-ground weapons from an internal bay, integration in the C4I environment, innovative industrial collaboration processes, etc.

Arms Export

France ranked third among the world's top arms exporters after the US and Russia, followed by Germany and China as fourth and fifth, according to a Stockholm International Peace Research Institute (SIPRI) think tank. Based on 2016-2020 sales, the US held 37 percent of arms exports, Russia with 20 percent, France 8.2 percent, Germany 5.5 percent, China 5.2 percent, and the UK 3.3 percent, the report from the Swedish think tank said. France reportedly won arms export contracts worth $5.6 billion, down from €8.3 billion in 2019, reflecting lock down and governments freezing military budgets in response to the pandemic crisis.

France military industries have produced the Rafale fighter, the Charles de Gaulle aircraft carrier, the Exocet missile and the Leclerc tank among others. The most exported French defence equipment includes ships, aircraft and missiles. In recent years, France's weapons sales have increased with overseas contracts for Rafale fighter jets. The weapons export in 2018 were worth $10.27 billion, up 30 percent compared to 2017. The French arms industry has benefited from the demand for arms in Egypt, Qatar and India. Other major export client includes the United Arab Emirates. Hungary, Spain, Belgium and the Netherlands.

DEFENCE BUDGET

Total defence spending: $56.1bn (2021), $52.3 billion (2020)

Defence spending in terms of GDP: 2.1% (2020)

France's defence expenditure has generally maintained an upward trend, barring a decrease in spending in 2019, increasing from US$46bn in 2017 to US$56.1bn for 2021, according to GlobalData, a leading data and analytics company. It has stated that France continue to raise defence spending, which will reach EUR40.9 billion (nearly USD48 billion) in 2022, a EUR1.7 billion increase on 2021. The breakdown of the draft budget approved by the Council of Ministers on 22 September will be EUR23.7 billion for equipment, EUR12.6 billion for salaries, and EUR4.6 billion for operating costs. In addition, EUR1.2 billion will be set aside for overseas operations, mainly 'Barkhane' in Africa.

Defence Procurement

The Direction générale de l'armement (DGA) is the French government defence procurement agency responsible for programme management, development and purchase of weapon systems for the French military. The DGA covers three distinct missions within the Ministry of Defence. It is responsible for future weapons systems in terms of conducting targeted research and innovation projects. It equips the armed forces in the context of European industrial and technological policy. The DGA supports and promotes French defence industry exportation.

CONCLUSION

France is among the top countries that can claim to be major powers in the world today. It plays an influential global role as a permanent member of the United Nations Security Council, NATO, the G-8, the G-20, the EU and other multilateral organisations. It ranks as the world's fifth largest national economy, second biggest in Europe behind Germany. France is the only US ally to muster a full-spectrum defence capability across land, air and sea, and with nuclear weapons of its own. France's military is engaged in operations against jihadists in Syria, Iraq and West Africa while also defending against terror attacks on home soil.

CONTACT DETAILS

Ministry of Defence

14, Rue St-Dominique

75700 Paris, France

Postal Address: 00452 ARMEES

Tel: +33-1-44424180, Fax: +33-1-44424171

www.defense.gouv.fr

GEORGIA
(Capital: Tbilisi)

INTRODUCTION
Area: 69,700 sq km
Population: 4,933,674 (July 2021 est.)
Coastline: 310 km
Maritime claims: Territorial sea: 12 nm
Exclusive Economic Zone: 200 nm

KEY POLITICAL PERSONS

PRESIDENT: Salome Zourabichvili

PRIME MINISTER: Irakli Garibashvili

KEY DEFENCE PERSONS

DEFENCE MINISTER: Juansher Burtchuladze

CHIEF OF DEFENCE FORCES: Maj. Gen. Giorgi Matiashvili

COMMANDER OF THE NATIONAL GUARD: Col. Irakli Chumburidze

ECONOMY

The economy of Georgia is an emerging free market. Since the 2003 Rose Revolution, broad and comprehensive reforms were implemented leading to significant inflow of Foreign Direct Investment (FDI) which resulted in the country's high economic growth rates. Construction of the Baku-T'bilisi-Ceyhan oil pipeline, the South Caucasus gas pipeline, and the Kars-Akhalkalaki railroad are part of a strategy to capitalize on Georgia's strategic location between Europe and Asia and develop its role as a transit point for gas, oil, and other goods. Since 2014, Georgia became a part of the European Union's Free Trade Area, with the EU continuing to be the country's largest trading partner, accounting for over a quarter of Georgia's total trade turnover. Georgia's main economic activities include the cultivation of agricultural products such as grapes, citrus fruits, and hazelnuts; mining of manganese and copper; and output of a small industrial sector producing alcoholic and non-alcoholic beverages, metals, machinery, aircraft and chemicals. According to the World Bank, Georgia's economy has grown at an average annual rate of 4.5 percent in the last decade. Since 2014, Georgia is part of the European Union's Free Trade Area, with the EU continuing to be the country's largest trading partner.

GDP (official growth rate): $17.694 billion (2019 est.)

Real Growth Rate (GDP): 5% (2017 est.), 2.8% (2016 est.)

Industries: Steel, machine tools, electrical appliances, mining (manganese, copper, gold), chemicals, wood products, wine.

Total Exports: $5.94 billion (2020 est.), $9.54 billion (2019 est.)

Export Commodities: Copper, cars, iron alloys, wine, packaged medicines (2019)

Major Markets: Russia 12%, Azerbaijan 12%, Armenia 9%, Bulgaria 8%, China 6%, Turkey 6%, Ukraine 6% (2019)

Total Imports: $8.94 billion (2020 est.), $11.11 billion (2019 est.)

Import Commodities: Cars, refined petroleum, copper, packaged medicines, natural gas (2019)

Major Suppliers: Turkey 17%, China 11%, Russia 9%, Azerbaijan 6%, United States 6%, Germany 5% (2019)

INTERNATIONAL DISPUTES

◆ Russia's military support and subsequent recognition of Abkhazia and South Ossetia independence in 2008 continue to sour relations with Georgia.

DEFENCE

The Georgian military is a defence force consisting of the Land Forces, National Guard and the Special Forces. The Georgian Armed Force (GAF) is under the authority of the Ministry of Defence and directly headed by the Chief of Defence Forces. The Armed Force has been extensively reformed with the Georgian Air Force merging into the Army and renamed the Army Air Section. The Navy was abolished and incorporated into the Coast Guard, which is a subunit of the Border Guard of Georgia under the control of Ministry of Internal Affairs. The Coast Guard is responsible for maintenance of the sovereignty of the country and for protection of internal territorial waters and economic zones. The country has carried out the Georgia Defence Readiness Programme (GDRP) launched on 18 May 2018. The programme involves training and equipping nine battalions of the Georgian armed forces.

Land Forces
Personnel: 36,000+ (total active manpower)
Equipment

Category	Name	In Service
MBT	T-72, T54/55	
	Lazika	6
	Didgori	
IFV/APC	BMP-1/2	
	BTR-70/80	
	Otokar cobra	
	Wolf	13 units
Artillery	D30 122mm	25
	D20 152mm	25
	DANA 152mm SP	40
	2S3 152mm SP	30
	2S7 203mm SP	10
	BM-21 122mm	
Mortar	82mm	
	120mm	
ATGW	Metis-M	
	Konkur	
	Fagot	
SAM	OSA-AKM	
	BUK-M1	
	TOR	
	Spyder	

...continued

Category	Name	In Service
SAM	Strela	
	Igla	

Army Air Section
Equipment

Category	Name	In service
Aircraft	Su-25	6
	L-39	
	An-2	10
Helicopter	Mi-24	3
	UH-1H	8
	Mi-8	2
	Mi-17	1
UAV	Elbit Hermes	
	Elbit Skylark	
	Aerostar	
Weapons	Javelin / FIM-92 Stinger/ Strela-2M/9K34 Strela-3/9K38 Igla	

New Procurements/Upgrades

◆ Georgia has reportedly signed an agreement for an air defence system with representatives of Israeli defense company Rafael Advanced Defense Systems. However, specific details of the deal were not released.

◆ The government plans to buy man-portable air defence system- FIM-92 Stingers from the US.

Defence Expenditure

Total defence spending: 900 million GEL (2021), 880 million GEL (2020)

Defence spending in terms of GDP: 1.91%

Defence Production and R&D

Georgia's military industry has their roots in the former Soviet Union providing all types of aircraft and ammunition to the Soviet Army. The industry lost its functionality after the Soviet Union was dissolved. However, the country has retained scientists with considerable expertise from the Soviet military industrial complex and these have targeted foreign technical partnerships to revive Georgia's advanced defence production capabilities. The State Military Scientific-Technical Centre DELTA established in 2005, to co-ordinate military research and development, experimented with unmanned aerial vehicles and modified parts for helicopters and aircraft. With the assistance of designer Zviad Tsikolia, Delta created its first prototype of armoured personnel carrier, the Didgori and the Lazika – a modular infantry fighting vehicle built for multiple tasks. Other main production lines include artillery systems such as MLRS, mortars and anti-tank weapons.

Defence Procurement

The Government of Georgia has purchased its first foreign air-defence component, the Spyder medium-range air-defence system from Israel and in 2017, France's Mistral short-range air-defense system. Ukraine sold its long-range radars to Georgia. It plans to buy man-portable air defence system- FIM-92 Stingers from the US.

CONTACT DETAILS
Ministry of Defence
N20 General Kvinitadze Str
0112 Tbilisi, Georgia
Telephone: (+995 032) 2 543535, (+995 032) 2 723535
Hotline: (+995 032) 2 723535
Email: pr@mod.gov.ge
www.mod.gov.ge/en

STRATEGIC INFORMATION
GERMANY
(Capital: Berlin)

INTRODUCTION

Area: 357,022 sq km
Population: 79,903,481 (July 2021 est.)
Coastline: 2,389 km
Maritime claims: Territorial sea: 12 nm
Exclusive Economic Zone: 200 nm
Continental shelf: 200 m depth or to the depth of exploitation

GEOPOLITICAL IMPORTANCE

Germany, the seventh largest European country in terms of area and the largest in terms of population, is situated partly in Western Europe and partly in Central Europe. It is surrounded by nine countries – Denmark in the north, Poland and Czech Republic in the east, Austria in the southeast, Switzerland in the south, France in southwest, Luxembourg, Belgium and Netherlands in the west. To its northeast lies the Baltic Sea and to its northwest, the North Sea.

After remaining a loosely-controlled territory for several centuries lacking sovereignty and unity, Germany emerged as a strong united empire under the leadership of Otto von Bismarck in the second half of 18th century. Like the other European nations, Germany also followed imperialist policies and acquired overseas colonies in Asia and Africa. Germany's aggressive military posture and its intent to exercise control in entire Europe resulted in World War I in 1914. The country was eventually defeated by the Allied Powers and was forced to pay heavy reparations for causing the devastating war. Later, the rise of Nazi regime led by Adolf Hitler and his audacious territorial expansion designs in the 1930s again saw Germany occupy the centre-stage in the post-World War I period which subsequently led to World War II in 1939. Hitler's attempts to occupy the entire European continent, including the Soviet Russia, failed at the end and Germany was

again defeated in the war. After its defeat, the country was divided into two blocks – East Germany and West Germany, controlled by two Cold War adversaries – the erstwhile Soviet Republic and the US, respectively. It was only after the fall of the Berlin Wall in 1989 that the country was reunited again. Since then, Germany has assumed an important position in the political, economic and military affairs of Europe and to certain extent, in the globe.

POLITICAL OVERVIEW

The Federal Republic of Germany, comprising of 16 states, functions as a

Parliamentary representative democracy with the President as the head of state and the Chancellor as the head of government. While the President is bestowed with nominal powers and responsibilities, the Chancellor carries out executive duties along with the Cabinet. The legislative power is exercised by the country's bi-cameral Parliament constituting of the Bundestag (Federal Diet) and Bundesrat (Federal Council). The federal structure of Germany grants certain degree of autonomy to all its states, with each having its own constitution. The states function as parliamentary republics, parallel to that of the central structure, and are ruled by a cabinet and a unicameral legislative body, called Landtag (State Diet). The independent judiciary of Germany is based on the civil law system with affiliations to the erstwhile Roman law, having its core principles being codified into a referable system and used as the primary source of law.

KEY POLITICAL PERSONS

PRESIDENT: Frank-Walter Steinmeier

CHANCELLOR: Olaf Scholz

ECONOMY

Germany is the largest economy in Europe and thus, regarded as the economic powerhouse of the continent. It is the fourth largest economy in the world in terms of nominal GDP and fifth largest in terms of purchasing power parity (PPP). The country benefits from a highly skilled labour force along with a well-developed infrastructure sector. However, like its Western European neighbours, the country faces significant demographic challenges to sustain long-term growth. Low fertility rates and a large increase in net immigration are increasing pressure on the country's social welfare system and necessitate structural reforms.

The Coronavirus pandemic resulted in an economic contraction of nearly 5% for Germany in 2020. GDP growth is expected to rebound by 3.6% in 2021, according to International Monetary Fund projection.

GDP: $3.86 trillion (2019 est.)

Real Growth Rate (GDP): 0.59% (2019 est.); 1.3% (2018 est.)

Industries: Among the world's largest and most technologically advanced producers of iron, steel, coal, cement, chemicals, machinery, vehicles, machine tools, electronics, automobiles, food and beverages, shipbuilding, textiles

Natural Gas - Proved Reserves: 39.5 billion cu m (1 January 2018 est.)

Crude Oil - Proved Reserves: 129.6 million bbl (1 January 2018 est.)

Total Exports: $2.004 trillion (2019 est.); $1.984 trillion (2018 est.)

Export Commodities: Cars and vehicle parts, packaged medicines, aircraft, medical cultures/vaccines, industrial machinery (2019)

Major Markets: US 9%, France 8%, China 7%, Netherlands 6%, UK 6%, Italy 5%, Poland 5%, Austria 5% (2019)

Total Imports: $1.8 trillion (2019 est.); $1.75 trillion (2018 est.)

Import Commodities: Cars and vehicle parts, packaged medicines, crude petroleum, refined petroleum, medical cultures/vaccines (2019)

Major Suppliers: Netherlands 9%, China 8%, France 7%, Belgium 6%, Poland 6%, Italy 6%, Czech Republic 5%, US 5% (2019)

DEFENCE & SECURITY

The defence and security aspects of present-day Germany have been largely influenced and shaped by its history. While it held centre-stage in the two World Wars of 20th century with its offensive posture and expansionist goals, a unified Germany, after the end of Cold War, has focused more on its internal development, peace and stability and has reoriented its armed forces – the Bundeswehr – and its military doctrine, accordingly. The Bundeswehr operates as a defensive military force. And being firmly tied to the NATO for maintaining its own security and territorial integrity, Germany has adhered to the military doctrine of collective European defence and security cooperation. Safeguarding its interests in the European and transatlantic context forms the basis of Germany's present-day defence policy.

However, the German armed forces, unlike their other leading European counterparts like the British and French military, have lacked a clear-cut strategy and capability of engaging in overseas multinational military missions and thus, assume the role of a static, regional force rather than an expeditionary one. This makes Germany a more continental power, rather than a global power, with limited strategic and security objectives.

The swiftly changing geostrategic realities of 21st century have pushed Berlin to play a more pro-active role in the global order and deploy its military abroad. The European nation, with its strong economic and technological prowess, has charted out plans to steadily increase its defence spending in the coming years, while expanding and securing its strategic interests by engaging more and more with the world.

Germany does not face any direct conventional military threat from any country and has continued to focus on safeguarding its national interests while jointly working with its NATO partners, including the US. There are no border disputes with any of its neighbours. However, the country which until recently was free from any major internal problems except the issues of illicit drug trade and organised crime, is now battling against the increasing threat of Islamic terrorism and extremism that have posed a serious threat to its citizens in present times.

Keeping in view the rapidly changing geostrategic landscape, Berlin in 2016 reversed its earlier policy of troops cut and announced to raise the number of its armed forces for the first time since the Cold War. The major policy shift came at a time when Europe was facing a multitude of security challenges including the growing threat of Islamist terrorism, instability in Africa, civil wars in Syria and Libya, and resurgence of Russia.

In its last Defence Whitepaper released in July 2016, Berlin announced major policy shifts which confirm Germany's increasing willingness to play an important role in the global strategic affairs at large and also lead the European nations to collectively combat the emerging security challenges in the continent. The Government has reversed its earlier decision of troops cut and instead, announced to recruit more troops, thereby bringing the total number of active service personnel to 203,000 by 2025. As of August 2021, a total of 184,127 soldiers (professional & regular soldiers and voluntary military service) are part of the Bundeswehr. A steady rise in annual defence expenses as announced by the Government also promises to bolster Germany's overall military capability in the coming years.

KEY DEFENCE PERSONS

FEDERAL MINISTER FOR DEFENCE & COMMANDER-IN-CHIEF: Christine Lambrecht

CHIEF OF DEFENCE STAFF: Gen. Eberhard Zorn

CHIEF OF ARMY: Lt. Gen. Alfons Mais

CHIEF OF NAVY: (Vacant)

CHIEF OF AIR FORCE: Lt. Gen. Ingo Gerhartz

THREAT PERSPECTIVE

Terrorism: The most serious and significant internal threat Germany faces today is coming from radical Islamic terrorism. The Islamic extremists have targeted the country in recent past with a string of violent attacks occurring at public places. The Angela Merkel Government's open-door migrant policy that allowed an estimated 900,000 asylum seekers from Syria, Iraq, Afghanistan and other such strife-torn regions to enter Germany is being blamed as the root cause for the series of militant attacks by refugees inspired by the Islamic State (ISIS). The German Government has issued high level of security alert after a spate of attacks. The country has joined hands with the US-led NATO forces to fight the ISIS.

STRATEGIC RELATIONS

US: Berlin and Washington strengthened bilateral relations after the end of Cold War when a unified Germany came into existence. Both being primary NATO members, and with Germany positioned at the centre of European affairs, bilateral cooperation in areas of defence and security assumed significance alongside their political, trade and economic ties. Washington played a key role in Germany's integration into the NATO and other leading European institutions. Germany has underlined the importance of the US as its essential security partner and the two sides have conducted joint military wargames and engaged in defence exchanges at regular intervals. As a NATO member, Germany contributed troops in the US-led mission in Afghanistan, although it abstained from the Iraq war. Berlin pulled out all its troops from Afghanistan in August 2021, after staying there for almost 20 years as part of the US-led war.

In the backdrop of swift geostrategic developments, bilateral ties between Berlin and Washington has declined in recent times over several issues, including recent withdrawal of US troops from Afghanistan and the chaotic developments thereafter and also over Germany's inability to meet the NATO's stipulated annual defence spending target of 2% of GDP.

In a setback to Berlin, the then US President Donald Trump in July 2020 announced plans to withdraw about 12,000 US troops out of the German soil and partly deploy them in other NATO member nations. President Joe Biden has put a freeze over this decision.

France: Germany's decades-old relationship with France is based on the Elysee Treaty (Treaty of Friendship) the two sides inked in January 1963 which put an end to centuries-old rivalry, enmity and war between the two neighbours. Both countries have strived for greater European integration for decades. Strategic and military cooperation between the two dates back to the 1950s when they agreed to jointly develop weapons and armament, including missiles, transport aircraft, trainer jets, battle tanks and even nuclear weapons. This relationship further intensified when they agreed to implement the defence clauses of the Élysée Treaty in 1982 and have since then expanded the purview of bilateral military ties. The two countries singed a military agreement in 2012 to renew cooperation in new defence purchases, to undertake joint defence and aerospace projects, and explore possible cooperation on missile defence and related areas. The two countries' Air Forces have also signed a partnership agreement for joint training programme for the Airbus Military-built A400M military transport aircraft aircrew and mechanics. In October 2016, Paris and Berlin signed an agreement to create a joint air transport squadron that will operate the Lockheed Martin-built C-130 Hercules transport aircraft (six platforms of Germany and four of France). The new Franco-German air transport squadron was officially launched in September 2021.

Russia: Even while remaining a major NATO member, Germany has maintained strong bilateral relations with Russia. The multi-faceted German-Russian relationship has often been defined as a strategic partnership between the two sides. The two countries have been especially cooperating in the fields of trade, investment, energy and technology. A major share of Germany's natural gas needs is met by supplies from Russia. And Germany, on its part, has provided technological expertise to Russia. Moreover, Berlin has made efforts over the years for Moscow's inclusion into Europe's economic and security apparatus. The conflict involving Russia and Ukraine, however, has adversely affected Berlin-Moscow ties in recent times. Bilateral ties have further deteriorated over various other political and domestic issues.

Israel: With Israel, Germany shares long-standing military relations and has supplied sophisticated defence technology in the past. Berlin is regarded as one of Israel's closest strategic allies after the US. The two countries have supplied defence technology to each other and also cooperated on jointly developing weapon systems. While Germany has supplied its Dolphin-class submarines to the Israeli Navy, Israel has provided anti-tank missiles to German armed forces.

India: Indo-German relations covering bilateral trade, economic and cultural exchanges exist for several decades. The framework for strengthening their political, scientific and strategic cooperation was laid down towards the end of 20th century. The security and strategic aspects of bilateral ties were further highlighted when the two sides adopted the "Agenda for German-Indian Partnership in the 21st Century" in New Delhi in 2000. Military cooperation between them was strengthened with the singing of a new defence and security agreement in 2006. Germany has supplied weapons and equipment to Indian armed forces and is ranked as the fifth largest arms exporter to India. India has acquired tanks, submarines and aircraft from Germany.

Norway: The two European nations entered into a strategic partnership programme in 2017 by announcing to jointly acquire six Type 212 air-independent propulsion submarines. While Norway will procure four of the subs, Germany will induct two such platforms over the next seven years. Additionally, the two countries will also cooperate on naval missiles. While the submarines would be built by German TKMS, the missiles (Naval Strike Missile variants) would be delivered by Norway's Kongsberg. In February 2020, a revised offer was made by TKMS with regard to the procurement of the platforms with new delivery timeline.

MULTILATERAL ALLIANCES

NATO: West Germany joined NATO on 6 May 1955 when the Western Alliance's second round of enlargement took place. East Germany, which had joined the rival Warsaw Pact, came into NATO fold after the unification of Germany in 1990. Since then, the multinational military block has provided a vital security cover to Berlin that helped Germany grow as a powerful European nation. Berlin has taken part in several NATO-led combat and humanitarian missions since then, including the 1999 Kosovo conflict, 2001 Afghanistan war and in the Libya War as recently as 2011, though it later pulled out of the Libya conflict. From peacekeeping to deterrence, Germany's Bundeswehr has been deployed in several countries across the globe in defence of its allies. According to NATO, Germany is contributing some 4,700 personnel for ongoing operations for whom the security architecture of NATO, the EU, the United Nations and the Organization for Security and Co-operation in Europe (OSCE) form the frame.

Germany also hosts the command centre for the NATO-led European missile defence system located at the Headquarters of Allied Air Command in Germany's Ramstein Air Base controlled by the US military. In July 2016, the Allies declared Initial Operational Capability of the NATO-led ballistic missile defence (BMD) system.

EU: Being at the heart of European affairs, Germany has enjoyed a key position in the European Union. As a founding member of the EU of which it became a part in 1952, Germany has played crucial role in the larger European integration and adoption of Euro as a common currency in the continent. During the global financial crisis and the Euro Zone crisis, the country stood out strongly and maintained a healthy GDP growth as compared to its other European allies. Berlin, which until now had been quite reluctant to take up any leadership role in the European Union's political, financial or security matters, is likely to play a key role in strengthening the Union, particularly after Britain's exit from the EU.

DEFENCE CAPABILITIES

ARMY: The German ground forces, called the Heer, forms the largest part of German armed forces – the Bundeswehr. It is divided into infantry, artillery and armoured forces.

The Government in 2010 announced a reforms plan under which military conscription was abolished from July 2011. The reforms aim to make the ground forces more flexible, well-trained, agile and capable of undertaking overseas military missions with its allied partners in more efficient way. The Government's earlier decision to reduce the number of some existing land platforms has now been reversed and new procurements are lined up to add more platforms, equipment and systems in the Army.

Personnel: 60,000+

Equipment

Category	Name	In Service	On Order
MBT	Leopard 2A5/2A6	225	103
APC/IFV	Fennek	217	
	MTW M113	594	
	Marder 1A5	70 (to be upgraded)	
	Dingo 1 & 2	480	
	Puma	350	
	Boxer	405 (various configurations)	
	Mungo	400+	31
	Fuchs 1 & 2	940	
	BV 206	270	
	Wiesel 1 & Wiesel 2	251	
	Duro	113	100 (Duro III)
	Eagle IV, V	500	
Artillery	PzH 2000 155mm (self-propelled howitzer)	89	
Mortar	120mm	87	
MRL	M270	55	
ATGW	Milan	1500	
	PARS 3 LR		680
ATGM	Spike LR		
SAM	Stinger		
AA gun	Gepard 1 A2	85	

Army Aviation

Category	Name	In Service	On Order
Light transport	C-212-300	2	
	Short 330	2	
	OV-10	75	
	Beech 99	1	
	T-41	23	
	King Air	1	
	Jetstream 41	2	
	ERJ-135	2	

...continued

Category	Name	In Service	On Order
Helicopter	NH90 TTH	74	8
	CH-53	66	
	Bo105	142	
	EC 135	15	
	Tiger	68	
	H145	7	
	Bell UH-1D	65	
UAV	Aladin	115	
	KZO	5	
	Luna X, Luna NG	100+	40+ (Luna NG)
	Mikado (Mini UAV)		

New Procurements/ Upgrades

◆ A total of 328 Leopard 2 MBTs are being inducted.

◆ Some of the existing fleet of Leopard 2 MBTs are being upgraded to 2A7 configuration. A contract worth over €300 million has been awarded to Krauss-Maffei Wegmann in 2019 to upgrade a total of 101 Leopard 2A6 MBTs to the new configuration.

◆ The Defence Ministry is evaluating options to develop a new-generation MBT/Main Ground Combat System (in partnership with other European nations) as a successor to the Leopard 2 MBT which is likely to remain operational until 2030.

◆ A contract has been awarded to Rheinmetall in June 2021 to upgrade 154 of the Puma IFVs to S1 configuration. The contract includes the option for subsequent modernization of a further 143 Puma platforms. Work is scheduled to be completed by 2029.

Puma infantry fighting vehicle (Photo: Rheinmetall)

◆ Plans are advancing to upgrade the Marder 1A5 IFVs.

◆ The Boxer command vehicles (numbering 65) would be upgraded to A2 configuration and delivered from 2024 onward. ARTEC GmbH, under a contract awarded in 2017, is also upgrading the 256 Boxer IFV variants with delivery timeline by 2023.

- ◆ Rheinmetall has upgraded a total of 272 Fuchs wheeled armoured vehicles to the new 1A8 configuration.
- ◆ Diehl Defence has been contracted to deliver 680 PARS 3LR anti-tank missiles for the Army's Tiger attack helicopters. Serial production of the weapon has started.
- ◆ A contract has been signed with Israel's Rafael company to deliver 1,000 Spike LR anti-tank guided missiles.
- ◆ A contract has been awarded to MBDA in 2019 for delivery of Enforcer shoulder-launched anti-tank missiles.
- ◆ Airbus Helicopters is retrofitting 26 of the CH-53 heavy transport helicopters under a 2017 contract. The upgrade will extend the platforms' operational life till 2030.
- ◆ Airbus has completed delivery of all seven H145 search & rescue helicopters. The platforms are replacing the Bell UH-1D helicopters.
- ◆ Additional Luna next-gen UAVs have been ordered from EMT Penzberg.

NAVY: The naval wing of the Bundeswehr, *Deutsche Marine*, functions with the primary mission to defend and protect Germany's maritime territory and secure its sea lanes. Being closely integrated into the NATO system, the Navy also operates with the allied forces and contributes in combat and humanitarian missions overseas. It operates a number of submarines, frigates, corvettes, aircraft and helicopters to carry out its missions. While some of the ageing platforms are being retired from service, acquisition of new maritime platforms and weapons has also started. The naval modernisation programme is aimed at improving the Navy's overall capabilities in order to carry out joint operations internationally.

Major naval bases: Wilhelmshaven, Glucksburg, Kiel

Personnel: 16,400

Equipment

Category	Name	In Service	On Order
Submarine	Type 212A (U212) class	6	2
Frigate	Bremen-class (F-122)	2 (to be retired)	
	Brandenburg-class (F-123)	4	
	Sachsen class (F-124)	3	
	Type F125	3	1
Corvette	Braunschweig class (K130)	5	5
	Korvette K131		6
FAC	Gepard-class (Type 143A)	8	

...continued

Category	Name	In Service	On Order
Mine sweeper	Frankenthal class mine hunter	9	
	Kulmbach class mine hunter	2	
	Ensdorf class mine sweeper	5	
Auxiliary ship	Barbe class (Type 520) utility landing craft	2	
	Elbe class (Type 404) supply boat	6	
	Oste class (Type 423) electronic surveillance ship	3	
	Westerwald (Type 760A) ammunition transport	1	
	Walchensee class (Type 703) fleet oiler	2	
	Rhön class (Type 704) fleet oiler	2	
	Berlin class (Type 702)	2	1
	Fehmarn class	1	
	Wangerooge class	2	
Weapon	ASM AGM84 Harpoon, MM38 Exocet, RBS15 MK3		
	AGM Sea Skua		
	SAM RIM-116 RAM RIM-7-Sea Sparrow RIM-162 Evolved Sea Sparrow SM-2		

Naval Aviation

Category	Name	In Service	On Order
Fighter/ASW/Reconnaissance	P-3C Orion (to be upgraded)	8	
	Dornier DO 228 LM (maritime pollution control)	2	
Helicopter	NH90 Sea Lion	9	9
	NH90 Sea Tiger		31
	Sea King Mk 41	21	
	Sea Lynx Mk 88A	21	
	Camcopter S-100		6

New Procurements/Upgrades

- ◆ Two more Type 212(A) class conventional submarines will be built, taking the total number of such underwater platforms in the Navy to eight. Delivery is scheduled in 2032.
- ◆ Three F125 new-generation frigate platforms have been delivered by ThyssenKrupp Marine Systems as of March 2021. One remaining platform is slated for delivery in 2022.
- ◆ Four F123 (Brandenburg-class) frigates are being upgraded.
- ◆ A contract worth over 2 billion euros has been awarded to a consortium of shipbuilders led by Luerrsen Werft to build additional five (K130 class) corvettes. The warships would be delivered between 2022 and 2025.
- ◆ The Defence Ministry in June 2020 signed a contract worth €4.6 billion with Netherlands-based Damen Shipyards to build four MKS 180 multi-purpose warships for the Navy. The platforms would be built largely in partnership with German shipyards. The first platform would be delivered in 2027.
- ◆ Two new Type 707 replenishment tankers would be procured to replace the two Rhon class (Type 704) tankers.
- ◆ Plans to carry out mid-life upgrade of eight P-3C Orion MPAs has been put off due to cost and technical issues. The MoD is now considering to acquire new maritime patrol platforms for the Navy. The US State Dept. in March 2021 has proposed to sell five P-8A Poseidon aircraft.
- ◆ Delivery of NH-90 (NATO-Helicopter-90) Sea Lion platform is going on (nine out of 18 platforms delivered as of April 2021). The remaining 9 platforms are slated for delivery between 2021 and 2022. These would replace the Westland Mk 41 Sea King maritime platforms.
- ◆ The Navy has selected NHIndustries NH90 (Sea Tiger) NATO Frigate Helicopters (NFH) to replace the Sea Lynx Mk 88A platforms. A €2.3 billion contract was approved by the Parliament in Nov. 2020 to buy the new NH90 ASW (anti-sub warfare) helicopters which would be delivered from 2025 onwards. A total of 31 such platforms would be procured.
- ◆ The Navy has received RBS15 Mk3 anti-ship missiles from Diehl Defence. The missiles are being deployed on the K130-class of corvettes. Diehl Defence, in September 2020, awarded a fresh contract worth $193.4 million to Sweden's Saab to provide the RBS15 anti-ship weapons to the German Navy for arming the Braunschweig class corvettes. Delivery of the weapons is scheduled between 2022 and 2026.
- ◆ Skeldar V-200 UAVs are being procured for the K130 corvettes.
- ◆ Naval Strike Missiles (NSM) would be acquired from Norway's Kongsberg. Deliveries will continue till 2030s.
- ◆ The US has approved sale of 64 MK54 lightweight torpedoes under FMS route.

AIR FORCE: *Luftwaffe* or the German

Air Force operates with the primary mission to protect and defend the national airspace. It also contributes to the military stability of Europe by undertaking joint operations with allied forces of NATO. The Luftwaffe is being restructured with a focus on four priority areas – air-surface integration (ASI), missile defence, military use of outer space and unmanned aircraft systems. While the ASI gives thrust on developing the Air Force's integrated mission capabilities by synergising with the ground and naval wings of the country's military as also with the allied forces, strengthening the Luftwaffe's missile defence apparatus is a key element in the NATO's integrated missile defence programme with an initial thrust on providing short-range defence against missiles. To firm up its network-centric capabilities, the German Air Force is using data and services provided by the SAR-Lupe reconnaissance satellite constellation and the SATCom Bw 2 satellite communication system launched by the country in the last few years. Acquisition of advanced unmanned aerial vehicles is also slated to further bolster the Air Force's reconnaissance and surveillance capabilities.

Major air bases: Wittmundhafen, Neuburg, Büchel, Schleswig, Ramstein, Erding, Holzdorf, Spangdahlem, Frankfurt

Personnel: 27,000+

Equipment

Category	Name	In Service	On Order
Fighter/Attack/AWS	Eurofighter Typhoon	141	38
	PA-200 Tornado	85	
Transport, Tanker, Surveillance	Airbus A319 CJ	2	
	Airbus A310	4	
	Transall C-160D (being retired)	30+	
	Challenger 601	6	
	Airbus A400M	35	18
	Airbus A340-313	2	
Trainer	T-6 Texan II	60+	
	T-38A Talon	35	
Helicopter	Cougar AS 532 U2	3	
	Sikorsky CH-53G	60+	
	H145M	15	
UAV	Heron-1		3
Air Defence System	Patriot SAM	29 (to be cut to 14)	
	Mantis	2 systems	
	Stinger		
	Taurus KEPD 350 ASM	600	
	AGM-88B HARM		
AAM	IRIS-T AIM-120 AMRAAM AIM9-L Sidewinder Meteor		

New Procurements/Upgrades

◆ A contract has been awarded to BAE Systems in November 2020 to help manufacture 38 new Eurofighter Typhoon (tranche 4) aircraft for the German Air Force. The German Parliament has allocated a budget of €5.5 billion to procure the platforms.

◆ The entire fleet of Tornado fighters is slated for retirement by 2030 and would be replaced by new fleet of fighters. No final decision has been taken yet on the new platform. The Govt is weighing between Eurofighter Typhoon and F/A-18 Super Hornet fighters as also the EA-18G Growler electronic warfare aircraft for the replacement.

◆ Delivery of 53 A400Ms transporters is going on.

◆ The Parliament in 2018 approved funds worth €970 million to acquire six Lockheed Martin C-130J military transport aircraft for the Air Force in the wake of delayed delivery of Airbus A400M transport planes. The C-130Js will be operated jointly with French military which has also ordered four of the platforms from US.

◆ Airbus is to deliver five MRTT tanker aircraft which will be funded by Germany and Norway and operated as part of a NATO fleet under a contract signed in 2017.

◆ The military has approved plans to buy up to 60 new heavy-lift helicopters to replace the CH-53G platforms operational in the Air Force. In 2019, US's Boeing and Sikorsky submitted bids for procurement with their CH-47F Chinook and CH-53K helicopter platforms respectively. Final contract for the deal is likely to be awarded in 2021 with deliveries slated to begin in 2023.

◆ Procurement of Bombardier Global 6000 jets for airspace surveillance & reconnaissance purposes is under consideration.

◆ A deal worth $600 million was approved by the Govt. in 2018 for leasing of five Heron TP armed UAVs from Israel for over next nine years. The first UAV undertook its maiden test flight in Israel in July 2020 ahead of delivery expected in 2021.

◆ Development of a European medium altitude long endurance (MALE) UAV in partnership with France, Italy and Spain is under consideration. The new pan-European UAV, MALE 2020, is expected to be operational by 2025.

◆ Two RFPs were issued in 2018 to Europe's MBDA and US's Lockheed Martin-led joint venture entity to develop TLVS – Germany's future Integrated Air and Missile Defense (IAMD) system. The JV entity has submitted proposal in this regard in 2019 to develop, test and deliver the future IAMD system. An updated and final proposal has been submitted by the JV entity in 2020.

◆ The US State Dept. in 2019 has approved possible sale of 50 Patriot Advanced Capability missiles (PAC-3 MSE), along with spare parts and support, to Germany at an estimated cost of $401 million.

◆ Upgrade of existing Patriot missile defence systems is under consideration to keep them operational till 2030.

◆ In 2019, the US State Dept. approved possible sale of 91 Advanced Anti-Radiation Guided Missiles (AARGM AGM-88E) and up to eight Captive Air Training Missiles to German Air Force.

◆ A contract was awarded to MBDA in Dec. 2019 for procurement of additional Meteor BVRAAM weapons for the Luftwaffe. The Air Force has started arming its Eurofighter Typhoons with Meteor missiles for air defence role.

DEFENCE PRODUCTION

Germany has a strong, well-developed defence industry with some 200 companies catering to domestic as well as international defence markets. Avionics and aircraft engine, armoured vehicles, missile systems and naval platforms are some of the leading areas of defence production. The arms production is primarily confined to private sector which accounts for 85% of all military research and development, procurement, and maintenance. Germany has also collaborated with its European allies in defence production. Indeed, nearly 70 percent of Germany's major military equipment is manufactured as part of international projects in collaboration with several NATO member nations.

As regards to defence exports, Germany remains one of the top five arms exporters in the world. Despite its "restrictive and responsible" weapons exports policy, Berlin continues to sell weapons and platforms to several nations. The German Govt. approved arms exports worth €1.16 billion during 2020 period to several nations. German-built submarines, in particular, are steadily gaining strong foothold in the international arms market, according to a 2019 SIPRI report. Overall, the country's cutting-edge defence technology and weapons have found place in the Middle East, Asia, Latin America,

US and Europe. Exports to European nations, however, are categorised as "military transfers" and not military export.

Major Armaments Producers

Rheinmetall Defence is one of Europe's leading manufacturers and suppliers of combat systems, electronic solutions and wheeled vehicles for Army.

Krauss-Maffei Wegmann GmbH is a leading designer, developer and producer of armoured vehicles, tanks and weapon systems for Army.

ThyssenKrupp Marine Systems is a consortium of naval platforms producers. The group is involved in the production of surface ships and submarines. The Kiel-based Howaldtswerke-German Werft (HDW) – a leading shipbuilder – is part of the group.

Diehl BGT Defence GmbH is an arms manufacturer and produces a wide range of missile systems for army, navy and air force. The Diehl Defence Land Systems is involved in repairing and modernisation of various military vehicles.

Joint Ventures Programmes
Europe

Eurofighter **Typhoon:** Germany is one of the four partners in the consortium manufacturing the Eurofighter combat jets along with Spain, Italy and the UK. EADS Germany is the partnering company in the programme.

A400M: Germany is one of the seven NATO member nations in the Airbus A400M military transport plane programme led by European conglomerate EADS.

Eurocopter: Leading European helicopter manufacturer Airbus Helicopter, which was initially created with the merger between the helicopter divisions of Aerospatiale-matra (France) and DaimlerChrysler Aerospace (Germany), today is a subsidiary of larger European defence consortium EADS. The company, which designs, develops and supplies a wide range of rotorcraft, is at present composed of three entities – the parent company Eurocopter, the German subsidiary Eurocopter Deutschland, and the Spanish subsidiary Eurocopter Espana.

France

EuroDrone UAV: Germany and France signed an agreement in September 2012 to jointly develop a medium-altitude, long-endurance (MALE) unmanned aerial vehicle system. Italy and Spain later joined the project which is currently at initial phase of development. It has been named as the EuroDrone unmanned aircraft programme. The partner nations intend to jointly design, build and test fly the new UAV platform by 2025.

Combat Aircraft (FCAS): The two countries in 2017 announced plans to jointly work on the development of a "common European air platform" to replace their current fleets of fighter aircraft in the longer run. As envisioned, the new Franco-German fighter platform – named Future Combat Air System (FCAS) [and likely to use sixth-generation technologies] – would take to the skies by 2040, replacing the fleets of Dassault Rafale and Eurofighter Typhoon fighters in both the air forces. Airbus (Germany) and Dassault (France) are the lead contractors in the programme so far. Spain has subsequently joined the programme. In June 2019, the Defence Ministers of Germany, France and Spain signed a framework agreement at Le Bourget, France, making a true legal commitment for the production of a complete system of combat aircraft and drones, which would enter service with their Armed Forces by 2040.

Poland

APC: *Rheinmetall Defence subsidiary Rheinmetall MAN Military Vehicles (RMMV)* **h**as signed a partnership agreement with Poland's Polska Grupa Zbrojeniowa (PGZ) to develop an amphibious wheeled armoured personnel carrier (APC). The two countries will sell the new APC in the international market.

Japan

The two countries have signed an inter-governmental agreement to collaborate on military technology development and defence equipment production. They have also inked an information sharing accord recently, covering defence technology. Both sides have expressed keenness on jointly undertake military research programmes to develop advanced defence hardware with support from their respective defence industries.

DEFENCE BUDGET

Keeping in view the growing international security challenges, Germany has decided to allocate more funds for defence. Reversing its earlier decision to reduce defence budget which put Berlin at a much lower rank compared to other European countries, including the UK and France, and also way below the NATO stipulated mark of 2% of GDP, the Government has announced plans to steadily increase its annual defence spending. Amidst the Russia-Ukraine crisis, Germany in 2015 pledged to increase its defence spending by 6.2% over the next five years. Accordingly, defence budget was €34.2 billion in 2016; €36.61 billion in 2017; €38.5 billion in 2018; €47.32 billion in 2019 (1.35% of GDP). For 2020, allocation on defence was €51.4 billion. The proposed defence budget for 2021 - 2022 is €53 billion which is an increase of 3.2% over previous year's allocation.

With its decision to reform and expand the Bundeswehr and increase the troops level even while modernising the existing arms inventory as also acquiring new systems/platforms, Germany aims to steadily increase its defence spending in the coming years. The country has also committed to widen its engagement with NATO and meet the NATO-stipulated standard of 2% GDP allocation on defence.

Year	Allocation	% of GDP
2020	€51.4 billion	1.57
2019	€47.32 billion	1.35
2018	€38.5 billion	1.23
2017	€36.61 billion	1.18
2016	€ 34.29 billion	1.2
2015	€ 32.94 billion	1.16
2014	€ 32.44 billion	1.14
2013	€33.3 billion	1.5
2012	€31.87 billion	1.5

COUNTER-TERRORISM & NATIONAL SECURITY

Radical Islamic terrorism and violent extremism has emerged as the primary national security concern for Germany in 21st century. While Islamic terrorism has plagued several parts of Europe, its proliferation in Germany at a faster pace has made the country one of the major terror hubs in the continent. Even as the role of global terror outfits such as the Islamic State (ISIS) and Al-Qaida has been found in some large-scale terror-related plots targetting the country and its citizens, the presence and growth of 'lone-wolf' terrorists in addition to an increasing number of German nationals turning into violent extremism has further exacerbated terror-related problem for Germany. With strict vigilance and a heightened security apparatus, Berlin has managed to avert some major terrorist incidents in the past. Nevertheless, terrorism poses the most serious and significant threat for Germany and its internal security today. The country has joined hands with the US-led NATO forces to fight against the ISIS and other global terror networks

This chapter comprehensively focuses on terrorism and terror-related extremist violence that has afflicted Germany since over the past decade. It also highlights counter-terrorism measures being taken by the country's government to tackle the growing menace.

Types of Terrorism

Germany is primarily fighting against Islamic terrorism/ Salafism and lone-wolf terror threat.

Islamic terrorism: Islamic terrorism reared its ugly head in Germany after Berlin pledged its support to the US-led "war on terror" post the 9/11 World Trade Centre attacks. Even though Germany's military contribution to the fight against global terror outfits such as the Islamic State (ISIS) and Al-Qaida in Iraq, Syria and Afghanistan was defined mostly as "non-combative" in nature, yet, it gave way to rapid rise of radical Islamist ideology within the country. Meanwhile, the German government led by Chancellor Angela Merkel was blamed for having contributed to the Islamist terror threat by opening up the country's borders in 2015 to hundreds of thousands of migrants and asylum seekers, mostly from war-torn Syria, Iraq, Afghanistan and other parts of Middle-east. Among the Islamic radical elements, it is the rise of Salafism or Salafist jihad, having violent political and religious ideology, that has posed a major threat to Germany's internal security in recent times. A large number of people in Germany are believed to be potential supporters of Islamist terrorism, and nearly half of them could be harbouring Salafist/ Jihadist/ extremist ideology, the country's law enforcement authorities have estimated. Moreover, many German citizens (converted to Islam) who travelled to Iraq and Syria to join Islamist terrorist groups, have returned home, and now pose a major security challenge as they could further aggravate the Islamic radicalisation problem within the country.

Lone-wolf terror threat: Germany of late has witnessed more 'lone-wolf' terror attacks on its soil, wherein individual perpetrators harbouring radical ideology, have targeted civilians. In a lone-wolf terror attack, the individual actor may or may not be affiliated with any larger terror group or organisation. Some lone-wolf attacks have been carried out by right-wing extremist elements, thus making it difficult for the security agencies to prevent such acts of violence and terror that have often disturbed social harmony and order in the country. In few other incidents, involvement of global Islamist terror organisations have been found. The terror outfits, by using social media and other cyber networks, have radicalised the individual attacker to perpetrate acts of terror and violence.

Terror Outfits

The terror threat to Germany has primarily emanated from transnational terrorist groups, such as the Islamic State (ISIS), the Al-Qaida and their affiliates. The global terror outfits have been directly or indirectly involved in carrying out some major attacks in different parts of Germany in the past few years.

Major Terror-related Incidents

Germany has faced major terror-related incidents over the past few years even as timely intervention by the country's security and intelligence agencies has prevented few other attacks having possible links to terrorist groups.

Series of terror attacks in 2016: In the year 2016, Germany witnessed a spate of terrorist attacks, including the Ansbach bombing on July 24 in which over a dozen people were injured. The terrorist – a failed asylum seeker from Syria having possible links to the ISIS – blew himself up outside a music festival. Prior to this incident, few other terror-related violent incidents were reported from other parts of the country, some of which were claimed by the Islamic State (IS). On December 19, 2016, Germany witnessed one of the deadliest Islamist terror attacks on its soil when a truck rampaged through a Christmas market in Berlin, killing 12 people and injuring over 60 others. The attacker, a Tunisian national and an asylum seeker, was later neutralised by the German police while he was on the run in Italy. The Islamic State (IS)-Iraq claimed responsibility for the violent attack which was condemned globally.

2017 Hamburg knife attack: The stabbing of civilians at a supermarket in the German city of Hamburg on July 28, 2017 was carried out by a failed Palestinian asylum seeker. One person was killed and seven others were injured in the attack. The perpetrator pledged allegiance to the Islamist State (IS) and was sentenced to life imprisonment. The direct involvement of the ISIS, however, could not be corroborated by investigators.

Right-wing extremism

The rise of right-wing extremist elements of society perpetuating terror and violence has witnessed a sharp increase in the last few years in Germany. While the far-right extremist ideology has plagued other parts of Europe, it has become one of the biggest threats to society, Germany's latest domestic intelligence report states. The number of incidents recorded as being motivated by right-wing extremism has increased to its highest point since the German police began to keep records of such crimes in 2001. As per the official statistics, some 23,064 violent incidents recorded in the year 2020 were counted as right-wing extremist terrorism – an increase of 5.7% over the previous year. Majority of such incidents in Germany are either race-related or anti-Semitic (discrimination against Jews). The far-right attacks – on a synagogue in Halle in October 2019, and a shooting incident in Hanau in February 2020, targeting Jews and people with Turkish roots – have disturbed Germany's delicate social fabric and threatened internal security and peace.

Combating Terrorism & Extremism

Germany has taken up a series of measures to combat terrorism and extremist violence. The overall security, intelligence and surveillance apparatus in the country has been bolstered to maintain strict vigil over the growing menace, resulting in successful prevention of some major terror-related incidents with timely action and intervention. An effective counter-terrorism strategy involves taking up "de-radicalisation and integration" programmes for the radically-motivated individuals of the society, especially those harbouring Islamist ideology. In July 2016, the German government formulated the 'National Strategy on the Prevention of Extremism', pledging to increase funding for integration and prevention (of terror) programmes. Since the Islamist terror threat to Germany is primarily transnational, a robust intelligence sharing mechanism with other European nations and long-term international cooperation has also become necessary to prevent large-scale, coordinated terror attacks inside the country. To effectively counter the ever-evolving threat of terrorism and extremism, Germany has continued to devise new policies and newer counter-terror strategies from time to time.

Agencies & Departments for counter-terrorism operation

Germany, having a federal structure of governance, has a police force (**Federal Police**) and a domestic intelligence service (**Federal Office for the Protection of the Constitution - BfV**) for each of its 16 states. All of them report to the Ministry of the Interior. Besides the domestic intelligence service, it also has the foreign intelligence service (**Federal Intelligence Service - BND**) which reports directly to the German

Chancellor's office. For military intelligence, the Government has set up the **Federal Office for Military Counter-intelligence - MAD,** which operates under the Ministry of Defence.

The highly sophisticated security & intelligence apparatus of Germany involving all the above departments and offices tracks possible terrorist and extremist elements, their illegal activities such as money laundering, terror financing, weapons proliferation etc., collects and evaluates necessary inputs and coordinates with various departments/services to take up effective measures to prevent and deter terrorism and terror-related violence in the country.

CONCLUSION

Germany has so far remained a territorial power rather than an expeditionary power – a position more comfortably accepted by the entire European fraternity. Berlin's allegiance to the NATO has provided it with the necessary security cover for the most part of 20th century. The NATO connection has indeed helped Germany to fully integrate into the European community. However, the changing realities of 21st century has pushed Berlin to prepare its armed forces to take up expeditionary roles in future – an urgent need arising out of the rapidly evolving geostrategic equations wherein the US has steadily shifted its focus away from Europe. The revised military strategy of Germany has taken into consideration the ongoing crisis in Ukraine and resurgence of Russia as a major military power, the prolonged civil wars in Syria and Libya, and the increasing threat of Islamic terrorism to Europe. Berlin has also announced to align its defence expenses to meet NATO standards in the coming years. Ongoing and future military procurements by the country focus less on conventional warfare and more on flexibility, manoeuvrability, deployment and most importantly, force protection capabilities.

Germany, together with its other powerful European allies, is expected to take up an important role in ensuring the European continent's safety and security in the coming years.

CONTACT DETAILS
Ministry of Defence
10785 Berlin
Phone: 030 - 2004-22277
MoD: www.bmvg.de
Army: www.deutschesheer.de/portal/a/heer
Navy: www.marine.de/portal/a/marine
Air Force: www.luftwaffe.de/portal/a/luftwaffe

Tiger attack helicopter of German Armed Forces.

GHANA
(Capital: Accra)

INTRODUCTION

Area: 238,533 sq km
Population: 32,372,889 (July 2021 est.)
Coastline: 539 km
Maritime claims: Territorial sea: 12 nm
Contiguous zone: 24 nm
Exclusive Economic Zone: 200 nm
Continental shelf: 200 nm

KEY POLITICAL PERSONS

PRESIDENT: Nana Akufo-Addo

VICE PRESIDENT: Dr. Mahamudu Bawumia

KEY DEFENCE PERSONS

MINISTER OF DEFENCE: Hon. Dominic Nitiwaul

CHIEF OF DEFENCE STAFF: Vice Adm. Seth Amoama

CHIEF OF ARMY STAFF: Maj. Gen. Oppong Peprah

CHIEF OF NAVY STAFF: Rear Adm. Issah Yakubu

CHIEF OF AIR STAFF: Air Commodore Frank Hanson

ECONOMY

Ghana has a market-based economy. The country is well-endowed with natural resources such as diamonds, manganese ore, and bauxite besides oil. Expanding crude production and rising oil prices have placed Ghana's economy at the top of the GDP growth tables. The country's first gas processing plant at Atubao has started producing natural gas from the Jubilee field. Agriculture accounts for nearly one-quarter of GDP. The country is the second-biggest gold producer and second-largest cocoa producer in Africa. According to the World Bank, Ghana's economy continued to expand in 2019 as the first quarter gross domestic product (GDP) growth was estimated at 6.7%, compared with 5.4% in the same period of last year. Non-oil growth was also strong at 6.0%. The relatively high quarterly growth was driven by a strong recovery in the services sector which grew by 7.2% compared with 1.2% in 2018. Ghana's rapid growth was halted by the COVID-19 pandemic, the March 2020 lock down, and a sharp decline in commodity exports experiencing a sharp contraction in the second and third quarters of 2020. The World Bank stated that economic growth is expected to average 5.1 percent yearly in 2021-23.

GDP (official exchange rate): $65.363 billion (2019 est.)

Real Growth Rate: 8.4% (2017 est.), 3.7% (2016 est.)

Industries: Mining, lumbering, light manufacturing, aluminum smelting, food processing, cement, small commercial ship building, petroleum.

Total Exports: $25.59 billion (2019 est.), $22.51 billion (2018 est.)

Export Commodities: Gold, crude petroleum, cocoa products, manganese, cashews (2019)

Major Markets: Switzerland 23%, India 17%, China 12%, United Arab Emirates 8%, South Africa 8% (2019)

Total Imports: $26.91 billion (2019 est.), $23.22 billion (2018 est.)

Import Commodities: Metal tubing, ships, cars, refined petroleum, rice (2019)

Major Suppliers: China 24%, Nigeria 22%, United States 5% (2019)

INTERNATIONAL DISPUTES

◆ Disputed maritime border between Ghana and Cote d'Ivoire.

DEFENCE

Ghana Armed Forces (GAF) comprised of the Army, Navy and Air Force supervised by the Ghanaian Ministry of Defence and the Chief of Defence Staff. The Army is divided into two brigades - Northern Command (Kumasi) and Southern Command (Accra). There are two operational commands of the Navy - the Western Naval Command at Sekondi and the Eastern Naval Command at Tema. Modernisation programme of the GAF is being carried out. The plan calls for the GAF to be reorganised, re-equipped and restrained with an emphasis on the protection of the country's oil sites.

ARMY

Personnel: 12,000

Equipment

Category	Name	In Service
APC	Piranha	50
	Tactica	20
	Ratel	39
	Sisu XA-185	
	WZ523	50+
	Hunter light strike vehicles	12
Artillery	Type 86 122mm	
MRL	Type 83 122mm	
Mortar	81mm	
	107mm	
	120mm	
ATK weapon	Carl Gustav	50
	RPG-7	

New Procurements/Upgrades

No major procurement plans are under consideration at present.

NAVY

Personnel: 2,000

Equipment

Category	Name	In service
Patrol boat	YAA Asentawaa class	2
	Blika class	4
	Achimota class	2
	(FPB57 type)	2
	Dzata class	7
	(FPB45 type)	2
	Defender class in-shore response boat	7
	Stephen OTU ex-South Korean Cham-suri class	1
	Anzone class transport (ex-USCG Balsam class)	1

New Procurements/Upgrades

No major procurement plans are under consideration at present.

AIR FORCE

Personnel: 1,910

Equipment

Category	Name	In Service
Fighter	MB-339s	2 (stored)
	K-8	4
Transport	C-295M	2
	F-27	2
	Falcon 900	1
Helicopter	Bell 412	1
	A-109	2
	Z-9EH	4
	Mi-17V-5	7

New Procurements/Upgrades

◆ The MoD has signed a contract for the acquisition of five A-29 Super Tucano light attack and advanced training turboprops.

◆ Ghana plans to acquire one Mil Mi-35 attack helicopter from Russia.

◆ Additional Mi-17 helicopters are on order from Russia.

Defence Expenditure

Total defence spending: $237 million (2020), $233 million (2019)

Estimated defence spending in terms of GDP: 0.4 % (2020)

Defence Production and R&D

Ghana does not undertake any major defence production activities; however, in recent years the country has shown interest in developing its local defence industry. The Kantanka Technological Centre of Excellence (KTCE) has unveiled a domestically produced wheeled armoured personnel carrier (APC) - KAI802 APC – at the annual Technology Exhibition of the Kantanka Group in Accra in 2019, representing a development milestone for Ghana's defence industry.

Defence Procurement

The Ghana armed force is acquiring new aircraft and helicopters to enhance its capabilities.

CONTACT DETAILS

Ministry of Defence
Burma Camp, Accra.
Telephone: +233-302-775665
Fax: +233-302-772241
www.gaf.mil.gh/

GREECE
(Capital: Athens)

INTRODUCTION

Area: 131,957 sq km
Population: 10,569,703 (July 2021 est.)
Coastline: 13,676 km
Maritime claims: Territorial sea: 12 Nm
Contiguous Zone: 24 Nm
Exclusive Economic Zone: 200 nm

KEY POLITICAL PERSONS

PRESIDENT & COMMANDER-IN-CHIEF: Katerina Sakellaropoulou

PRIME MINISTER: Kyriakos Mitsotakis

KEY DEFENCE PERSONS

DEFENCE MINISTER: Nikos Panagiotopoulos

CHIEF OF DEFENCE: Gen. Konstantinos Floros

CHIEF OF ARMY STAFF: Lt. Gen. Charalambos Lalousis

CHIEF OF NAVY STAFF: Rear Adm. Stylianos Petrakis PN

CHIEF OF AIR FORCE STAFF: Lt. Gen. Georgios Blioumis

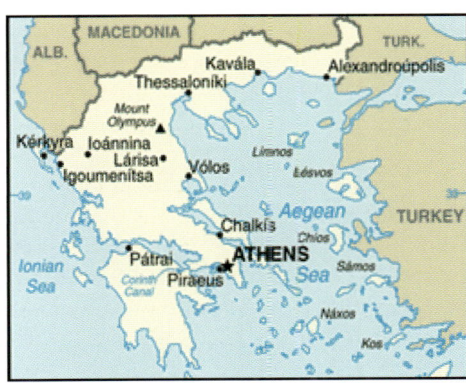

ECONOMY

Greece is a member of the European Union and the Eurozone. The economy of Greece mainly comprises the service sector and industry, while agriculture makes up less of the national economic output. Greece has a capitalist economy with a public-sector accounting for about 40-50% of GDP and with per capita GDP about two-thirds that of the leading euro-zone economies. Greece exited its six-year recession in the second quarter of 2014, but the challenges of securing political stability and debt sustainability remain. Greece achieved a real GDP growth rate of 0.7% in 2014-after 6 years of economic decline-but contracted by 0.3% in 2015 and by 0.2% in 2016. In 2017, Greece saw improvements in GDP and unemployment. Deregulation of Greece's energy sector and the country's central location as a transportation hub for Europe may offer additional opportunities in renewables, gas, refinery, and related sectors, as per US Dept of State report. Greece belongs to a number of the same international organisations, including the United Nations, North Atlantic Treaty Organisation, Euro-Atlantic Partnership Council, Organisation for Security and Cooperation in Europe, Organisation for Economic Cooperation and Development, International Monetary Fund, World Bank, and World Trade Organisation. Greece is also a permanent observer to the Organisation of American States. The COVID-19 lockdown restrictions have inflicted severe damage to the Greece economy and the country now faces steeper recession. Greece has just recently emerged out of last economic meltdown and now with this pandemic the economy may slide down up to 10% in 2020, as per media reports. According to press release by Hellenic Statistical Authority, the available non-seasonally adjusted data indicate that in the 3rd quarter of 2021 the Gross Domestic Product (GDP) in volume increased by 13.7% in comparison with the 3rd quarter of 2020.

GDP (official exchange rate): $292.4 billion (2020 est.), $318.63 billion (2019 est.)

Real Growth Rate (GDP): 1.87% (2019 est.), 1.91% (2018 est.)

Industries: Tourism, food and tobacco processing, textiles, chemicals, metal products; mining, petroleum

Oil - proved reserves: 10 million bbl (1 January 2018 est.)

Natural gas - proved reserves: 991.1 million cu m (1 January 2018 est.)

Total Exports: $59.02 billion (2020), $81.18 billion (2019 est.)

Exports Commodities: Refined petroleum, packaged medicines, aluminium plating, computers, cotton (2019)

Major Markets: Italy 10%, Germany 7%, Turkey 5%, Cyprus 5%, Bulgaria 5% (2019)

Total Imports: $71.76 billion (2020 est.), $83.19 billion (2019 est.)

Imports Commodities: Crude petroleum, refined petroleum, packaged medicines, cars, ships (2019)

Major Suppliers: Germany 11%, China 9%, Italy 8%, Iraq 7%, Russia 6%, Netherlands 5% (2019)

INTERNATIONAL DISPUTES

◆ Greece and Turkey continue discussions to resolve their complex maritime, air, territorial, and boundary disputes in the Aegean Sea.

◆ Greece rejects the use of the name Macedonia or Republic of Macedonia.

◆ The mass migration of unemployed Albanians still remains a problem for developed countries, chiefly Greece and Italy.

◆ The Greek government remained a collaborative CT partner in 2019. The Greek Parliament passed legislation to criminalise terrorist travel and the provision of material support to terrorists.

DEFENCE

ARMY
Personnel: 90,000

Equipment

Category	Name	In Service
MBT	Leopard 2 A6 HEL	150+
	Leopard 2A4	150+
	Leopard 1A5/GR	400+
	M-48A5/MOLF	300+
	M-60A3 TTS	50+
APC/MICV/IFV	VBL	200+
	BMP-1	300+
	G-127 Leonidas	400
	M113A1s/A2	1000+
Artillery	M-56 105mm	15
	M101 155mm	300+
	M114 155mm towed	100+
	PzH-2000	20
	M109A1/A2/A3/A5s 155mm	150+
	M110A2 203mm SP	100+
ATK	Carl Gustaf	900
ATGW	TOW	300
	MILAN	200+
	AT-4 Spigot	200+
	Kornet-E	100+
AA Gun	20mm	200+
	Zu-23-2 23 mm	500+
SAM	I-Hawk PIP IIIs	
	TOR-1Ms	
	OSA-AK (SA-8)	
	Stingers	1000+

Army Aviation

Category	Name	In Service
Helicopter	U-17A/Bs	15+
	C-12C (VIP)	2
	C12/APs	3
	Bell 205s/UH-His	40+
	CH-47D Chinook	10+
	AH-64A/D Apache	10+
	AB-206s	10+
	NH-300C	10+
	B-212	2
UAV	SAGEM Sperwer	

New Procurements/ Upgrades

◆ The US Security Assistance Command has delivered 70 Bell OH-58D Kiowa Warrior armed reconnaissance helicopters and one Boeing CH-47D Chinook heavy-lift helicopter to Greece. The Hellenic army acquired the helicopters through an Excess Defence Articles programme grant.

NAVY
Personnel: 15,000

Equipment

Category	Name	In Service
Submarine	Glavkos class	3
	Poseidon class	4
	Okeanos class	1
	Papanikolis class	4
Frigate	Elli class	8+
	Hydra class	4
OPV/IPV/Missile Boat	Rouseen class	5+
	Laskos missile FAC	4
	Kavaloudis class missile FAC	5
	Votsis class	3
	Niki class	2
	Kasos class	2
	Armatolos class	2
	Machitis class	4
	Tolmi class	2
	Anromeda class	4
	Stamou class	2
Amphibious force	Samos class LSTs	5
	Zubr class	4
	Naxos class	4
Mine Warfare Force	Evniki class	2
	Evropi class	2
Main Auxiliary	Prometheus fleet	
	Axios class	2

Naval Aviation

Category	Name	In Service
Helicopter	S70B6	10+
	AB-212 ASW	5+
	ALOUETTE III	
	P-3B Orion	5

New Procurements/ Upgrades

◆ Greece will buy three frigates from France. France and Greece have announced a multibillion-euro defence deal, including Athens' decision to buy three French warships as part of a strategy to boost its defence capacities in the Eastern Mediterranean. Greece will purchase three French frigates to be built by defence contractor Naval Group. The deal includes an option for the acquisition of a fourth frigate.

◆ The US State Department has approved a possible FMS to the Government of Greece of MEKO Class Frigate Modernization and related equipment for an estimated cost of USD2.5 billion.

◆ The US State Department has approved a possible FMS to the Government of Greece of Multi-Mission Surface Combatant (MMSC) ships and related equipment for an estimated cost of USD6.9 billion.

◆ Lockheed Martin Corp., Owego, New York, is awarded a USD193,980,348 contract. This modification adds a USD180,000,000 not-to-exceed, undefinitised line item for the production and delivery of four MH-60R aircraft, and exercises a USD13,980,348 option to procure three airborne low frequency sonars in support of the government of Greece.

◆ Greece recently signed a Letter of Intent to buy two Belharra frigates similar to those that Naval Group is building for the French Navy.

◆ Hellenic Navy in 2019 received first modernised P-3 Orion maritime patrol aircraft as part of the Hellenic Navy P-3B maritime patrol aircraft mid-life upgrade and modernisation programme implementation. The government-to-government agreement between the United States and Greece was announced in 2015, providing for the re-activation of one Hellenic Navy P-3B Orion maritime patrol aircraft. This agreement also includes the modernisation of four Hellenic Navy P-3B aircraft through the Mid-Life Upgrade (MLU) Programme.

◆ The Expeditionary Sea Base USS Hershel "Woody" Williams (ESB 4), shifted its homeport from Norfolk, Virginia, to Souda Bay, Greece, effective 1, Oct., 2020. Hershel 'Woody' Williams conducts US Africa Command AFRICOM missions in the Mediterranean, and the waters around East, South and West Africa, to include the Gulf of Guinea operating with regional partners.

AIR FORCE
Personnel: 25,000

Equipment

Category	Name	In Service
Fighter/Attack	Lockheed F-16 C/D	100+
	Mirage 2000	40+
	Dassault Rafale	18 (More on Order)
	F-4 Phantom II	20+ (To be replaced by F-35)
	Embraer R-99 AEW	3+
Transport	C-130 Hercules	10+
	C-27J Spartan	8
	Embraer ERJ-135ER	2
	Gulfstream V	
Trainer	T-41 Mescalero	40+
	T-6 Texan II	20+
	T-2 Buckeye	30+

...continued

Category	Name	In Service
Helicopter	AW109	
	AS332 Super Puma	10+
	Agusta-Bell AB205	10+
	Agusta-Bell AB212	4
	Bell 47	5+
SAM	Patriot batteries	6
	Skyguard/Sparrow squadrons	6
	SU-300 PMU1	2
	TOR-M1	4
	Crotale NG/GR	10
AAM	AIM-120, AIM-9M, MICA, IRIS-T	
UAV	HAI Pegasus	10+

New Procurements/ Upgrades

◆ Elbit Systems, Israel was awarded a contract worth $1.65 billion (approx) for the establishment and operation of the International Flight Training Center of the Hellenic Air Force.

Defence Expenditure

Total defence spending: $6.4 billion (2020 approx.)

Estimated defence spending in terms of GDP: : 2.68% of GDP (2020 est.), 2.36% of GDP (2019)

Domestic Suppliers: ELBO, EAS (EBO, Pyrkal), Miltech, KEA, EAB, Barracuda, Elefsis, Hellenic Shipyards, Kioleides, EODH

Foreign Suppliers: Brazil, Canada, France, Germany, Italy, Russia, United Kingdom, United States.

Year	USD (million)
2014	5,234
2015	4,520
2016	4,637
2017	4,752
2018	5,388
2019*	4,843
2020*	5,019
2021*	8,014

(*Figures for 2020 and 2021 are estimates.) Source: Defence Expenditure of NATO Countries (2014-2021), NATO Press Release.

US and Greece recently signed a revised defence cooperation pact. The deal provides for increasing joint US, Greece and NATO activity at Larissa, Stefanovikio, and Alexandroupoli as well as infrastructure and other improvements at the Souda Bay naval base, as per news reports.

Greece occupies a strategic location in the Eastern Mediterranean on the southern flank of the NATO. The enhanced US-Greece Mutual Defense Cooperation Agreement, which was updated in January 2020, provides for the operation by the United States of a naval support facility at the deep-water port and airfield at Souda Bay in Crete, as well as support for US forces present at several other locations in Greece. Greece contributes to NATO operations in Afghanistan and Kosovo, as well as to counterterrorism and law enforcement efforts.

Greece will be bolstering its military with new armament programmes, a boost to military personnel and the development of the country's defence industry, the government spokesman said in Sept 2020. The country is in contact with friendly countries in order to reinforce the equipment of our armed forces. Recently, Greece raised 2.5 billion euros (USD 2.96 billion) in a bond auction as the country seeks to increase military spending and raise funds for businesses affected by the coronavirus pandemic. Greek media have reported the purchases may include French-made Rafale fighter jets and at least one French frigate.

Defence Production and R&D

Greece has a well-developed naval construction industry but it lacks sophisticated production techniques in the battlefield and aerospace sectors. Over the decades, Greece wanted to be as self-sufficient as possible in defence production. Due to the event of hostilities with its neighbour and fellow NATO member such as Turkey, Greece's arms suppliers, mainly the US and Western European states, would impose embargoes on the supply of military equipment. Despite the development of an arms industry, Greece remains largely dependent on imports. Due to the country's poor financial condition, the major arms build-up (covering combat aircraft, MBTs and other equipment) has slowed down. It has also affected on the allocation of the Greek budget, and had generating procurement difficulties for the country.

Defence Procurement

The Armed forces are being steadily modernised and expanded, mainly as a result of national concern over Turkey's larger military forces. The nation has a new EMPAE (Unified Mid-Term Program and Modernization of the Armed Forces), which covers the ten-year timeframe of 2006-2015. It will analyse the overall framework of Greek defence procurement. The Greek defence procurement is used as a main platform to achieve the goals like reducing dependency on foreign sources, expanding the role of the Greek defence forces as a technology developer and cooperating with other European countries towards a more competitive European defence industry.

CONTACT DETAILS

Ministry of Defence
Mesogeion 227-231
Cholargos PC 15561
Greece
Tel.: +30 210 6598100 - 200

National Defence General Staff
General Secretariat of the
National Defence Of
Stratopedos Papagou
Leporos of Mediterranean 227-231
15561 Holargos
Athens
Tel.: 210 657 3035

Army General Staff
Address: Camp PAPAGOU
Mesogion 227-231, Cholargos
PC: 15561 - Greece
Tel: 2106555911

Hellenic Navy General Staff
Public Affairs Directory
229 Mesogion Av.
Zip 15561 Cholargos, Athens
Tel: (+30) 210 6551900
Fax: +30 210-6551440

Air Force General Staff
227-231 Mesogeion Avenue
15561 Chalkaros, Cholargos.
Tel: 210 6593399
Fax: 2106428239

STRATEGIC INFORMATION
INDIA
(Capital: New Delhi)

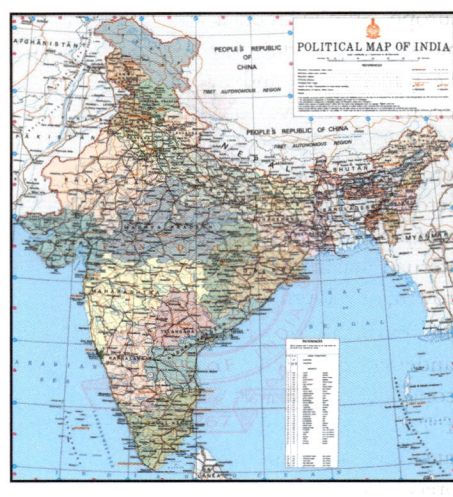

INTRODUCTION

Area: 3,287,263 sq. km
Population: 1,339,330,514 (July 2021 est.)
Coastline: 7,517 km
Maritime claims: Territorial sea: 12 nm
Contiguous zone: 24 nm
Exclusive economic zone: 200 nm
Continental shelf: 200 nm or to the edge of the continental margin

[The Government of India, on August 5, 2019, announced abrogation of Article 370 of the Indian Constitution which had granted special status and autonomy to the state of Jammu & Kashmir since 1949. The Government of India announced to bifurcate Jammu & Kashmir and Ladakh into two separate Union Territories (UTs) which would be directly administered by the Union Government henceforth.]

GEOPOLITICAL IMPORTANCE

The largest country in South Asia in terms of landmass and population, India is bordered by Pakistan in the west, Myanmar and Bangladesh in the east, China, Nepal and Bhutan in the northeast. In its south-east lies the Bay of Bengal and in south-west, the Arabian Sea. To its south lies the Indian Ocean which is a vital sea trading route and connects the Atlantic and Pacific Oceans. India maintains a strategically important position in the Indian Ocean Region (IOR) through its chain of Andaman and Nicobar Islands in the east and through the Lakshadweep islands in the southwest. Sri Lanka, Bangladesh, Maldives and Indonesia are India's major maritime neighbours.

Since centuries, India with its opulent economic, cultural and intellectual strengths has remained an attractive destination for the entire world. Being the largest country in South Asia, it has influenced the regional power play by being actively involved with its immediate and extended neighbourhood in more than one way to maintain peace and prosperity in the entire South Asian region and even beyond. India's predominant geostrategic location in South Asia and proximity to the Indian Ocean has given the country a unique advantage to play a pivotal role in the regional sphere. The rapidly growing market economy and robust workforce coupled with a steady military rise has placed India as a major Asian powerhouse alongside China and Japan. The 21st century India has steadily expanded its strategic outreach at the global arena as well.

POLITICAL OVERVIEW

India is the world's largest democracy. It functions as a multi-party system with a Parliamentary form of government. The Constitution of India defines the country as a "sovereign socialist secular democratic republic." The written Constitution has made provision for a Parliamentary system of governance with a federal structure to dilute power between the Centre and the States. The Union Government comprises of three branches: Executive, Legislature and Judiciary. The Executive includes the President, the Prime Minister and his Council of Ministers. The Legislature constitutes of the two houses of Parliament – Lok Sabha (lower house) and Rajya Sabha (upper house), the President, the Prime Minister and the Council of Ministers. The Judiciary includes the Supreme Court, High Courts and all other subordinate courts in the country. While the President is the nominal head of the state and the Supreme Commander of the Armed Forces, the actual executive power rests with the Prime Minister and his Council of Ministers.

KEY POLITICAL PERSONS

PRESIDENT & SUPREME COMMANDER OF ARMED FORCES:
Ram Nath Kovind

VICE PRESIDENT:
M. Venkaiah Naidu

PRIME MINISTER:
Narendra Modi

ECONOMY

India has transformed itself into a modern, developing economy where agriculture, industry and services sectors are primarily contributing to the national GDP. A major share of the GDP in the past came from agriculture, fisheries, handicrafts and other small enterprises. To expand economic development and catapult domestic growth, India embraced economic reforms in 1991 and opened up its markets for foreign trade and investments. The liberalisation phase, which included industrial deregulation, privatisation of state-owned enterprises, and reduced control over international trade and investment, spearheaded India's economic growth and transformed the economy into one of the leading open-market economies in the world. In 2014, India displaced Japan as the world's third largest economy in terms of purchasing power parity (PPP). In 2019, it became the 5th largest economy in terms of nominal GDP, surpassing the UK and France, as per the World Bank data. In 2018, India was also the fastest growing major economy in the world, overriding China with a GDP growth rate of 6.8% as against China's 6.6%. In 2019, India's GDP growth was 4.2%.

In order to revitalise the economy, the Central Government introduced a series of major economic reforms, including demonetisation in November 2016 followed by the implementation of a uniform Goods and Services Tax (GST) regime in July 2017 with an intent to bring in long-term, widespread economic benefits for the country and its people. The Government has also set forth an ambitious goal of transforming India into a $5 trillion economy by 2024 - 2025. India is also gearing up to host the high-profile annual G-20 global summit in 2023.

To expand its economic outreach beyond its boundaries and immediate neighbourhood, India over the years has also stepped up efforts for major entrepreneurial and financial forays into a number of countries in Asia, Africa,

Europe, South America and other parts of the world. Securing vital natural resources, like minerals, oil and natural gas etc., have become imperative to sustain the country's rapid all-round growth and development. A number of state-owned as well as private-sector enterprises have been actively working to capture a pie of the highly competitive international markets for unhindered national growth, development and prosperity.

The outbreak of the deadly Coronavirus pandemic adversely impacted the Indian economy, resulting in a GDP contraction of 7.3% in 2020, according to Government data. The International Monetary Fund has forecast an economic growth of 9.5% for India for fiscal 2021-22 whereas the World Bank has predicted a growth of 8.3% during the same period.

Meanwhile, to overcome the unprecedented challenges arisen due to the COVID-19 pandemic, Prime Minister Narendra Modi has exhorted the nation to work towards building an "Atma Nirbhar Bharat" (self-reliant India).

GDP (official exchange rate): $2.84 trillion (2019 est.)

Real Growth Rate (GDP): 4.86% (2019 est.); 6.78% (2018 est.)

Industries: Textiles, chemicals, food processing, steel, transportation equipment, cement, mining, petroleum, machinery, software, pharmaceuticals

Natural Gas - Proved Reserves: 1.29 trillion cu m (1 January 2018 est.)

Crude Oil - Proved Reserves: 4.495 billion bbl (1 January 2018 est.)

Total Exports: $572.07 billion (2019 est.); $564.16 billion (2018 est.)

Export Commodities: Refined petroleum, diamonds, packaged medicines, jewellery, cars (2019)

Major Markets: US 17%, United Arab Emirates 9%, China 5% (2019)

Total Imports: $624.31 billion (2019 est.); $656.52 billion (2018 est.)

Import commodities: Crude petroleum, gold, coal, diamonds, natural gas (2019)

Major suppliers: China 15%, US 7%, United Arab Emirates 6%, Saudi Arabia 5% (2019)

DEFENCE & SECURITY

As the largest country in the sub-continent in terms of geographical area and population, India has played a central role in South Asia. It has steadfastly emerged as an economic powerhouse and alongside strengthened its defence forces to counter both conventional and asymmetric military threats of modern times. The country, with its huge population coupled with wide-ranging religious, cultural, ethnic, regional, linguistic and social diversity, has faced varied security challenges, both internal and external, which have posed threat to its sovereignty and territorial integrity from time to time. Even though positioned as the largest country in South Asia having a democratic set up, India has more often faced a very volatile neighbourhood which has directly or indirectly hindered New Delhi's growth and progress in the Asian continent as well as at the global stage. Internal political, social, economic and religious upheavals in almost all of its surrounding countries now and then have spilled into India and directly or indirectly influenced New Delhi's political and larger strategic policies and position vis-à-vis its neighbours. With its strong democratic credentials, India, however, has maintained a peaceful posture towards all of its neighbouring nations even while endeavouring to maintain friendly relations with them so as to create an integrated, vibrant and prosperous South Asia. Yet, New Delhi has often faced mistrust and misconception of being a 'dominant neighbour' and even been perceived as a threat by few of its smaller neighbours.

The decades-old unresolved border dispute with two of its immediate neighbours – China and Pakistan – has resulted in full-scale wars with them in the past. After the 1962 war with China, three wars with Pakistan and the localised Kargil conflict in 1999, India has diligently pursued a massive military modernisation programme to strongly safeguard and defend its sovereignty and territorial integrity. The country's armed forces remain strongly committed and fully prepared to counter any kind of external aggression by any of the neighbours.

Even as the 2017 confrontation with China over the disputed Doklam plateau bordering Bhutan was resolved after a 73-day long bitter stand-off, the unsettled India-China border position once again cropped up in 2020, resulting in violent confrontation between the two countries' armed forces over parts of India's newly carved-out Union Territory Ladakh. High-level military and diplomatic talks have been going on between the two sides to resolve the longstanding boundary dispute, but no visible breakthrough has been achieved yet.

Meanwhile, military preparedness by New Delhi has taken centre-stage with the Indian Army, Navy and Air Force acquiring top-of-the-line modern defence assets including new-generation platforms, weapons and systems as part of a comprehensive modernisation drive. Upgrade of existing fleet of military hardware has also been prioritised. Alongside, India has been mulling to revise its decades-old military doctrine to meet any modern, asymmetric, fourth-generation warfare threats. Steady induction of a large number of modern battle tanks and armoured vehicles, missile frigates, large guided missile destroyers, conventional and nuclear submarines, aircraft carrier, multi-role fighter platforms, helicopters, reconnaissance aircraft, combat drones and sophisticated weapons among other modern military hardware have emboldened the Indian Armed Forces and prepared them well to meet any possible "two-front" conflict scenario with Pakistan and China. To prepare itself for the modern-day network-centric warfare missions, New Delhi has also launched an integrated defence communication network, thus enabling the Indian Army, Navy, Air Force and the Special Forces Command to share situational awareness for a faster decision-making process and greater synergy. The Defence Communication Network (DCN), a strategic, highly secure and scalable system, has a pan-India reach – from Ladakh to the North-east to the forward island territories of the country.

In a major policy decision to further consolidate India's massive defence structure, Prime Minister Narendra Modi on August 15, 2019 announced the creation of the post of Chief of Defence Staff (CDS) with an aim to fully integrate the operations of all three Services – Indian Army, Indian Navy and Indian Air Force. The CDS would act as the principal military adviser to the Defence Minister on all matters relating to the tri-services. The Government also set up the Department of Military Affairs (DMA) under the Defence Ministry, to be headed by the CDS as its Secretary.

Following the creation of the position for CDS, India unveiled major reforms plans involving the entire military structure and functioning, to be steadily implemented over the coming years. v

On December 30, 2019, the Union Government announced the appointment of Late General Bipin Rawat as India's first Chief of Defence Staff (CDS). He assumed charge on January 1, 2020. Late Gen. Rawat served as the Chief of Indian Army from Dec. 2016 to Dec. 2019. Gen. Rawat died in a helicopter crash near Coonor, Tamil Nadu on December 8, 2021. The Government subsequently appointed Army Chief Gen. M M Naravane as the Chairman of the Chiefs of Staff Committee until the appointment of the new CDS.

In order to realise Prime Minister Narendra Modi's ambitious "Atma Nirbhar Bharat" pledge and encourage domestic defence manufacturing, the Defence Ministry in August 2020 announced that India would stop importing a total of 101 weapons and military platforms such as artillery guns, short-range surface-to-air missiles, cruise missiles, transport aircraft, light combat helicopters, conventional submarines, sonar systems etc. under a staggered timeline till 2024. The domestic defence industry would receive contracts worth around Rs 4 lakh crore within the next five to seven years as a result of the decision "to prune the import list of defence platforms and equipment," the Defence Ministry said. The Indian Armed Forces had contracted around Rs 3.5 lakh crore worth of military systems between April 2015 and August 2020 which have now been listed under the restrictions for import. "The embargo on imports is planned to be progressively implemented between 2020 and 2024. The aim behind promulgation of the list is to apprise the Indian defence industry about the anticipated requirements of the armed forces so that they are better prepared to realise the goal of indigenisation," Defence Minister Rajnath Singh said, while announcing the major decision. All necessary steps would be taken to ensure that timelines for domestic production of equipment identified under the negative list for import are met, the Defence Minister said, while adding that the measures would include a co-ordinated mechanism for "hand-holding of the (domestic defence) industry" by the defence services. The Government will also focus on bringing down the percentage of imported components in the indigenously developed systems/ platforms.

In May 2021, Govt. of India notified a second list of 108 military hardware on which import restrictions would be progressively applicable from Dec. 2021 to Dec. 2025. The second list comprises next-gen corvettes, airborne early warning systems, tank engines, radars, sensors, simulators among other items.

In yet another significant development, DRDO successfully tested the indigenously developed Hypersonic Technology Demonstrator Vehicle (HSTDV) in September 2020. The HSTDV is an unmanned scramjet technology demonstrator that uses domestically developed scramjet propulsion system. Besides its utility for developing long-range cruise missiles of the future, the dual-use technology would have other applications, including launching low-cost reusable satellites. The successful test positioned India among select few nations in the world working on similar technology.

Meanwhile, bolstering its capabilities to protect and defend its astess in the outer space, India in March 2019, successfully conducted an ASAT (anti-satellite) weapon test for the first time and became the fourth country in the world after Russia, the US and China, to prove its prowess to shoot down a satellite in low Earth orbit. The direct ascent ASAT weapon, designed and developed by DRDO, successfully targeted and destroyed a live satellite at an altitude of 300-km. The test emphatically demonstrated India's capability to defend its assets in outer space with the anti-satellite missile seen as being a major deterrent in conflict situations.

KEY DEFENCE PERSONS

DEFENCE MINISTER: Rajnath Singh

MINISTER OF STATE FOR DEFENCE: Ajay Bhatt

CHAIRMAN, CHIEFS OF STAFF COMMITTEE & CHIEF OF ARMY STAFF: Gen. Manoj Mukund Naravane

CHIEF OF NAVAL STAFF: Adm. R Hari Kumar

CHIEF OF AIR STAFF: Air Chief Marshal V R Chaudhari

Internal Conflict

Terrorism: India has been fighting cross-border terrorism since its independence. Terrorism-related violence in the country has stemmed mainly from territorial dispute with Pakistan. Armed insurgency and proxy war waged by secessionists and separatists over the Kashmir issue have often taken violent proportions and resulted in large-scale deaths and destruction across India. Deadly terror attacks in many parts of the country from time to time have raised international concern.

Left Wing Extremism: Another major internal security challenge for India spanning over decades has emanated from naxalism or Left-wing extremism (LWE). According to latest Government record, a total of 70 districts in 10 states are currently affected by LWE and related violence. Of these, 25 districts in eight states are categorised as "most affected".

In some of the LWE-affected districts, mostly in central and eastern parts of the country having vast, mineral-rich forests, the Naxalites collect their own taxes and deliver their own system of justice. Security analysts describe the Naxalite-affected areas as a 'Red Corridor' running from eastern to southern India. In 2015, Government launched the 'National Policy and Action Plan' to deal with the vexed issue of Naxalism. Additionally, the Ministry of Home Affairs had drawn up a new 'Red Corridor' to identify the Naxal affected regions.

The decades-old insurgency problem in India's north-eastern states continues to affect internal security and stability. The problem has stemmed from several factors, including the region's geographical distance from the rest of the country and the social, economic and political inequality of its natives, which has been further exacerbated by their ethnic and linguistic diversity. Several armed militant groups in the region, some demanding autonomy while others seeking complete independence, have perpetuated violence in the region for many years from now. Presence of long, porous border with neighbouring countries and a highly inhospitable terrain has also facilitated the movement of militant groups and flow of illegal arms into the region, besides large-scale influx of illegal migrants into the country.

External conflict

Territorial disputes: India has land boundary disputes with two of its immediate neighbours – China and Pakistan. There is also a maritime boundary dispute of Sir Creek with Pakistan and disputes with China over construction of dams on the Brahmaputra River.

Pakistan: The flashpoint between the two neighbours since independence is Kashmir over which they have fought three wars in the past and the localised Kargil military conflict as recently as in 1999. As of 2010, India controls approximately 43% of the region, including most of Jammu, the Kashmir Valley, Ladakh, and the Siachen Glacier. Pakistan occupies approximately 37% or 78,000 sq km of Kashmir, known as Pakistan occupied Kashmir (PoK) and the Northern

Areas of Gilgit-Baltistan. The rest of the territory, around 5,180 sq km, is under the control of China after being illegally ceded to that country by Pakistan under the China-Pakistan Boundary Agreement of 1963. Pakistan has been strongly contesting New Delhi's position that Jammu & Kashmir is an integral part of India.

In a bold and historic move announced on August 5, 2019, the Government of India under Prime Minister Narendra Modi decided to abrogate Article 370 of the Indian Constitution which had granted special status and autonomy to the state of Jammu & Kashmir since 1949. The Government announced to bifurcate Jammu & Kashmir and Ladakh into two separate Union Territories (UTs) which would henceforth be directly administered by the Union Government. This strong and decisive step by the Government of India completely changed the dynamics of India-Pakistan relations involving the decades-old contentious issue of Kashmir.

Another territorial dispute with Pakistan involves the Siachen Glacier located in the eastern Karakoram range in the Himalaya Mountains. The glacier is the highest battlefield on Earth with both India and Pakistan maintaining permanent military presence in the area. The conflict in the region originates from the 1972 Shimla Agreement that did not clearly mention who controlled the glacier. India occupied the entire glacier and its tributary glaciers in 1984 while Pakistan presently controls areas just a few kilometres to the west.

India is also entangled in maritime dispute with Pakistan involving the Sir Creek estuary (spanning an area of 96-km) at the mouth of the Rann of Kutch in the Arabian Sea. The strip of water divides the Kutch region of Indian state of Gujarat with the Sindh Province of Pakistan. Both countries seek a technical resolution of the issue.

China: India and China share a land border of 4,057-km. India's decades-old boundary dispute with its north-eastern neighbour is centred around the Aksai Chin region administered by China. The full-scale Sino-India war in 1962 resulted in China occupying Aksai Chin, covering an area of 37,244 sq km. Pakistan later illegally ceded another 5,180 sq km of the region to China. India is claimant of the area as the eastern most part of Jammu & Kashmir. Even though an uninhabited high-altitude desert, Aksai Chin has remained a strategically vital region, giving China direct access to Pakistan via the Pak-occupied-Kashmir (PoK). China has built a 2,143-km highway running through the disputed land border area (covering some 150-km) that connects Tibet with its Xinjiang prefecture. Beijing has also repaved a road that was built between 1951 and 1957.

The other region of contention between New Delhi and Beijing is the Indian state of Arunachal Pradesh over which China stakes claim. China considers Arunachal Pradesh (formerly North-East Frontier Agency), covering an area of 90,000 sq km, as part of its territory and calls it 'South Tibet', a claim vehemently rejected by India, which says the state is its integral part. In a recent development, Chinese troops have come face-to-face with Indian soldiers along the contested Line of Actual Control (LAC) in Arunachal Pradesh's sensitive Tawang sector. Consequently, India has heightened its operational preparedness and military deployments along forward areas of the region to ward off any misadventure by the Chinese side.

China has also refused to recognise the McMahon Line as the Indo-China border in the North East. While India has regarded the McMahon Line (in Arunachal region) as the effective Sino-Indian boundary which was agreed to by Britain and the then independent state of Tibet as part of the Shimla Accord inked in 1914, the same has been disputed by the Chinese government time and again. The Chinese administration, on the other hand, has recognised the Line of Actual Control (LAC) as the demarcation line that separates the Indian-controlled territory from Chinese-controlled territory. (The term LAC was first used by Chinese Prime Minister Zhou Enlai in 1959.) India rejected the concept of (Chinese propagated) LAC in both 1959 and 1962. India considers the LAC to be 3,488 km long; China considers it to be only around 2,000 km. The LAC has generally been divided into three sectors: the eastern sector spanning Arunachal Pradesh and Sikkim; the middle sector in Uttarakhand and Himachal Pradesh; and the western sector in Ladakh.

India's repeated attempts to clarify the LAC has been rejected by the Chinese government. Mutual agreements reached by the Indian and Chinese sides in the 1990s to the still-unsettled LAC was necessitated to maintain peace and tranquility along the undemarcated border regions, pending a final resolution of the dispute. However, the long-standing unresolved border row has once again cropped up between the two large neighbours, leading to massive deployment of their militaries in the disputed regions.

In June 2020, a major confrontation erupted between the Indian and Chinese soldiers involving the western sector of the LAC, leading to a violent face-off at the Galwan valley in India's eastern Ladakh region. China's increasingly aggressive posture and unilateral attempts to change the status quo in the disputed border region took a violent turn with the Indian Army and People's Liberation Army (PLA) troops clashing over the same. The acrimonious confrontation resulted in both sides' militaries suffering casualties (the first such major military confrontation in decades post the 1962 Sino-India war).

High-level military and diplomatic talks are presently going on to settle the long-pending boundary issue even as both sides have heavily deployed their troops, military platforms and weapons along the LAC for any possible conflict and eventuality. The two sides completed the withdrawal of troops and weapons from the North and South banks of Pangong lake (Ladakh) in February, 2021, following a series of military and diplomatic talks. They are now engaged in talks to extend the disengagement process to the remaining friction points.

While sincerely desiring a peaceful resolution of the differences, India at the same time, has vowed to protect its sovereignty and territorial integrity at all costs to counter the "unilateralism and aggression" by the Chinese side. On 15 June 2021, India marked the first anniversary of the deadly Galwan valley clash in eastern Ladakh in which 20 Indian Army soldiers laid down their lives while defending and protecting the country's territorial integrity and sovereignty against 'unprecedented' Chinese aggression.

Earlier in 2017, the territorial spat between New Delhi and Beijing had taken yet another acrimonious turn when China attempted to unilaterally change the status quo in the disputed Doklam plateau region by trying to build a road there. The Doklam plateau is located on the strategic tri-junction involving Bhutan, the Chumbi Valley in China and the state of Sikkim in India. The plateau is claimed by both Bhutan and China as their territory. India has strongly supported Bhutan's claim as the area is extremely critical to India's own security. Indian soldiers, in mid-June 2017 crossed the Sikkim border to prevent the Chinese side from constructing a road in the Doka La pass located in the middle of the Doklam plateau. The Doka La pass in the Sikkim sector is guarded by Indian Army. The stand-off between the Indian troops and Chinese troops continued for over three months. The escalating tension, which caused international concern, finally subsided after New Delhi and Beijing announced that they were withdrawing their troops from the area. However, later reports of China renewing its efforts once again to build the road there made the Indian Armed Force remain increasingly alert while preparing for a possible conflict in future. (On 14 October 2021, China and Bhutan signed an agreement on a "three-step roadmap" to expedite negotiations to resolve their boundary dispute).

Meanwhile, India has slowly but steadily ramped up efforts to improve its border infrastructure along the 3,488-km long LAC for faster mobility of its troops and weaponry in forward positions in case of any possible conflict. India's border infra revamp has become highly imperative amidst the massive infrastructural built-up (road, rail, air) by the Chinese side over the past decades along the disputed high-altitude stretches of the LAC.

Another source of Sino-India conflict since decades is the Brahmaputra River – one of the major rivers in Asia that flows through India, China and Bangladesh. The river that originates in Tibet and enters India through the state of Arunachal Pradesh is an important source of irrigation, trade and transportation. China has built several hydropower dams on the river to divert water to irrigate its large landmass covering the Gobi Desert during dry seasons, causing concern in India. While Beijing had stopped sharing hydrological data for the river from upstream China for monsoon season in 2017, despite an agreement for the same with India, it resumed the process in 2018 following official-level discussions between the two sides. The data for the years 2020 and 2021 was shared by Beijing.

Since decades, India and China have been intensely engaged at political, diplomatic and military level talks and discussions to find a permanent solution to their long-standing border disputes and build mutual trust, confidence and cooperation, yet they have been unable to reach any consensus or concrete outcome in this direction.

Nepal: The year 2020 marked yet another territorial spat involving India and Nepal. The dispute basically stemmed from India building and inaugurating a new road which connected Dharchula (a Nepalese district) to the Lipulekh pass on the Mansarovar Yatra route (a holy pilgrimage site situated in Tibet, China). The Lipulekh pass is a far western point near Kalapani – a disputed border area between Nepal and India. Both India and Nepal claim Kalapani as an integral part of their territory – India as part of Uttarakhand's Pithoragarh district and Nepal as part of its Dharchula district. Soon after the road's inauguration, Nepal came out with a new official map by adding an area of 370 sq km at the tri-junction of Nepal, India and Tibet (China) to its territory. Despite India maintaining that the recently-inaugurated road section in Pithoragarh district in Uttarakhand lies completely within Indian territory, the Parliament in Kathmandu passed a Constitution amendment bill to legitimize the alteration / addition of Kalapani, Lipulekh and Limpiyadhura regions to Nepal's new political map. This move led to a communication breakdown between New Delhi and Kathmandu. The two countries are currently engaged in military and diplomatic level talks to sort out the dispute.

THREAT PERSPECTIVE

Pakistan: India's relations with Pakistan remain strained over numerous issues. These include border dispute over Jammu & Kashmir as also terrorist activities continuously emanating from the Pakistani soil over which the Pakistan government shows less concern and often denies involvement. Pakistan views India as its main military adversary and has accordingly developed its military capability to match India's strategic outreach. It has also adopted covert tactics against India and engaged in proxy war over the Kashmir issue since decades. Backed by China which has supplied sophisticated nuclear and other weapons and technology to Islamabad, Pakistan is focused on strengthening its military might to take on India. Furthermore, Islamabad has often threatened to use its nuclear arsenal to stall any "provocative offensive" by India.

China: Even as they have steadily emerged as the two top-ranking economic powers of Asia and the world, India and China have at the same time vied to strengthen and expand their military clout to remain influential in the region and beyond. The two immediate neighbours have fought a full-scale war in 1962. China's increasingly aggressive posture and military muscle flexing with regard to its territorial claims, including its reassertion over Arunachal Pradesh, and recently the disputed regions involving the LAC, has escalated regional tensions between the two large neighbours.

Continuing its belligerent posture, China has been robustly engaged in developing massive road and rail infrastructure all along the disputed land border regions, thus enabling swift mobilisation of its troops there in case of a conflict. According to the 2011-2012 annual report released by the Indian Defence Ministry, China had built a network of rail lines and more than 58,000 km of roads in the Tibet Autonomous Region (TAR) along with nuclear missile silos. Beijing has also announced completion of a highway linking the Medog county in Tibet (located near the border of Arunachal) with the rest of China. It has made a number of its airfields in the TAR fully operational which include Gongar, Linzhi, Pangta, Hoping, Gar Gunsa and Kashgar among others. According to latest reports, there are about 14 airbases in the region which are now being upgraded. Regular military manoeuvres involving Chinese fighter jets along with other advanced weapons and platforms in the Himalayan region have increased significantly in recent times. A 2010 Pentagon report stated that China had moved its nuclear-capable advanced CSS-5 (DF-21) ballistic missiles closer to borders with India. Beijing is also engaged in rapid infrastructural development in the disputed Pak-occupied-Kashmir (PoK) region despite India's strong objections. Attempts by Beijing to build a road unilaterally in the disputed Doklam region was thwarted by India in 2017.

To further widen its geopolitical and military outreach and secure vital energy resources across Asia, China, of late, has also expanded its foothold in the Indian Ocean Region (IOR) and beyond. A US Defence Department report published in 2003 stating that China was steadily building up a "String of Pearls" in South Asia – a far-fetched maritime strategy to not only encircle India but also to gain access into the vital energy resources across Asia – has taken concrete shape over the years. The "String of Pearls" refers to Beijing's constant efforts to build strategic sea ports, roadways and airfields along with enhancing its political, diplomatic and military engagements with Asian littoral states that extend from the South China Sea through the Strait of Malacca, across the Indian Ocean, and on to the Arabian Gulf. Beijing's recent efforts to help build the Gwadar port in Pakistan, the Chittagong port in Bangladesh and the Hambantota port in Sri Lanka are all viewed to be a part of that larger "String of Pearls" strategy. The recent docking of Chinese Navy submarines, including one at Sri Lanka's Colombo port and another at Pakistan's Karachi port, are a further confirmation that such a strategy has already been implemented by China, indicating dangerous powerplays at India's backyard to halt its growth trajectory.

Even as India is making a cautious approach to keep any kind of confrontation with China at bay while acknowledging the rapid military rise of that country in its immediate and extended neighbourhood, Indian Armed Forces, nevertheless, are acquiring advanced capabilities and strengthening themselves to remain prepared for any kind of eventuality. The Indian military has identified strategically important infrastructure requirements along the Line of Actual Control (LAC) and they are being developed in a phased manner to counter the overtly growing threat from China. In fact, India's completion of the 255-km Darbuk-Shyok-Daulat Beg Oldie (DBO) all-weather road in 2019 and its fresh move to build additional feeder links and bridges are believed to have triggered the recent clashes between Indian and Chinese soldiers in 2020. The DSDBO road, which has 37 bridges, runs almost parallel to the LAC to provide easier access to the Indian Armed Forces to the Depsang and Galwan Valley regions (the current points of confrontation between India and China) while ending near the strategically-important Karakoram pass. This major development spurred the Chinese military to show aggression towards India.

Meanwhile, the Indian Air Force too has refurbished its helipads and airfields in the north-eastern sector and deployed frontline combat aircraft and advanced weapon systems to defend and protect Indian territory from any external aggression. In a subtle show of strength, the IAF landed its C-130J airlifter at the Daulat Beg Oldie airstrip near the LAC in the Ladakh area of Jammu and Kashmir (now a Union Territory) for the first time in August 2013. Similarly, strategic Advanced Landing Grounds (ALGs) at Fukche and Nyoma airfields located at over 12,000 feet altitude in eastern Ladakh have also been activated by the IAF. It has also re-activated its ALGs at Mechuka in West Siang district of Arunachal Pradesh followed by the Pasighat ALG in that state in 2016. The new ALG is capable of operating all types of aircraft, including the frontline Su-30MKI fighter, as well as helicopters. Work has also progressed on activating other such strategic points in Arunachal Pradesh, including the Walong, Tuting, Along and Ziro ALGs.

The Indian Navy, for its part, has also strengthened its military presence on the frontline islands of Andaman and Lakshadweep chains by setting up new naval bases there so as to secure crucial sea lanes in the IOR. In January 2019, the Navy operationalised a newly enhanced naval air station, INS Kohassa, in the Andaman & Nicobar Islands territory. Another important naval air station, INS Baaz, located at the Campbell Bay on the Great Nicobar island, the southernmost and largest island of the Nicobar islands, is also playing a key role in maintaining strategic vigil in the wider Indian Ocean Region. The Andaman & Nicobar Islands also host India's only operational Tri-Services Command. The strategically important Command, established in 2001, has recently been granted more functional and financial autonomy by the Government.

At the political level, New Delhi is giving more thrust on its "Act East" policy by making renewed efforts to further strengthen and broaden its economic, strategic and military outreach to the East Asian and Southeast Asian nations. India today forms a part of the East Asia Summit and enjoys vibrant relations with the ASEAN. During the 16th East Asia Summit hosted by Brunei in virtual mode in October 2021, Prime Minister Narendra Modi reaffirmed India's focus on a free, open and inclusive Indo-Pacific and the principle of "ASEAN Centrality" in the region. The 18th ASEAN-India Summit was also held subsequently.

STRATEGIC RELATIONS

Russia: India's deep-rooted bilateral relationship with Russia – the erstwhile Soviet Union – dates back to the 1950s when New Delhi was making efforts to become self-reliant after gaining independence from British rule in 1947. From industrial development to advancement of military technology, space science and nuclear energy, the Soviet Union played a pivotal role in shaping up modern India. It also provided strong political and diplomatic support to India in international forums, including in the United Nations. The strategic relationship between the two countries reached its zenith when the Indo-Soviet Friendship Treaty was signed in 1971 which incorporated security clauses in its ambit along with mutual cooperation in other areas. The two countries enjoyed strong strategic ties until the disintegration of USSR in 1991 which gave way to a new world order and the birth of Russian Federation. While both New Delhi and Moscow continued to share deep bilateral bond and bonhomie based on their "common interest" and "strategic convergence", they also began exploring new geostrategic alliances in the emerging world order. Nevertheless, the decades-old and time-tested friendship and trust between the two strategic allies remains crucial even today. In 2017, New Delhi and Moscow celebrated 70 glorious years of their bilateral diplomatic ties. India, whose strategic relationship with Russia has always remained at the forefront of New Delhi's independent foreign policy, continues to be one of the top-most clients of Russian defence industry, receiving majority of weapon systems and technology from Moscow in spite of opening up its arms market to the US and many other Western powers in recent years. According to a report compiled by a think-tank, over 55% of Indian defence imports since 2014 were from Russia. A recent Congressional Research Service (CRS) report has also observed that the Indian military "cannot operate effectively" without Russian-supplied equipment and would continue to rely on its (Russian) weapons systems in the near and middle terms.

In 2018, New Delhi and Moscow signed a mega defence deal under which Russia would supply its advanced S-400 'Triumf' air defence missile systems to India. Other major procurements from the Russian defence industry are also lined up for the Indian military. New Delhi and Moscow are closely cooperating to develop India's nuclear technology for energy security as well. Russia has also been imparting training to Indian astronauts for the ambitious 'Gaganyaan' manned space mission project undertaken by the Indian Space Research Organisation (ISRO). The annual India-Russia summits involving top leadership of the two countries have further enriched bilateral ties between New Delhi and Moscow. During Prime Minister Narendra Modi's Russia visit in September 2019, the two sides signed a proposal to build a full-fledged maritime link connecting the Indian city of Chennai with the Russian city of Vladivostok. New Delhi has also been discussing a reciprocal military logistics support agreement (RELOS) with Moscow. During Russian President Vladimir Putin's New Delhi visit on December 6, 2021, the two countries renewed the military-technical cooperation (MTC) agreement for another 10 years, till 2031.

Israel: India established full diplomatic ties with Israel in 1992. The two countries have become strategic partners thereafter. Israel, with a solid state-of-the-art defence industry, has supplied many sophisticated military technologies and systems to India. India's defence trade with Israel includes a range of military equipment including modernisation of tanks and fighter aircraft, supply of UAVs, missiles, command & control systems and ammunition. The multi-billion-dollar India-Israel defence market has grown quite swiftly in the past few years with Israel emerging as one of the largest defence suppliers to India. The two sides, during a visit by Prime Minister Narendra Modi to Jerusalem in July 2017 – a historic first-ever visit by an Indian Prime Minister to that country – have further bolstered bilateral ties.

Bhutan: The two South Asian neighbours have enjoyed close economic, political and strategic ties since decades. Under the Treaty of Friendship and Cooperation signed between Thimphu and New Delhi in 1949, the two sides agreed for non-interference in each other's internal affairs. Bhutan, under the treaty, also agreed to let India guide its foreign policy and both nations would consult each other closely on foreign and defence affairs. India has provided economic assistance to Bhutan and helped in the Himalayan nation's all-round development. Bhutan's transition to democracy in 2008 has further strengthened Indo-Bhutanese ties. In 2018, the two countries celebrated the Golden Jubilee of the establishment of formal diplomatic relations between them.

Sri Lanka: India's centuries-old relationship with its closest neighbour in the subcontinent Sri Lanka has included historical, cultural, intellectual, linguistic and religious aspects. Their alliance has further expanded to cover economic, political and strategic cooperation in last few decades. India has been actively involved in infrastructure development and modernisation projects in Sri Lanka which is strategically positioned in the Indian Ocean Region (IOR). Bilateral defence ties between the two neighbours have strengthened over the years with India providing military training to the Lankan armed forces. The two sides also conduct joint military exercises on a regular basis as the commonality of concern for both countries include safety and security of their sea lanes of communication in the IOR. India has also delivered two state-of-the-art advanced offshore patrol vessels (AOPVs) to the Lankan Navy in recent past.

Bangladesh: Under New Delhi's "neighbourhood first" policy, India's ties with Bangladesh has gained prominence in recent times. India has extended Lines of Credit to Dhaka for infrastructural and social development. India has also initiated steps to export its defence systems and equipment to Dhaka. The "all-encompassing" bilateral defence cooperation between the two neighbours has gained momentum with high-level military visits in 2021 despite the coronavirus pandemic.

Maldives: The geographic position of Maldives in the Indian Ocean Region makes the island country strategically vital for India. Bilateral relations between the two nations have involved high-level visits, cooperation in defence and security arena, trade and investment and cultural ties. India is backing major infrastructure development projects in the island nation under two lines of credit worth $1.2 billion. At the military front, New Delhi has supplied naval platform, surveillance aircraft and radars to the island nation in the past to secure it from sea piracy and terrorism as also to safeguard its own coastal borders from any sea-borne attack. Maldivian military personnel also receive training in India.

Emphasising New Delhi's "neighbourhood first" policy, Prime Minister Narendra Modi made his first visit to Maldives in June 2019 after securing a decisive win for the second time in India's Parliamentary elections held in April-May 2019. The PM inaugurated there a coastal surveillance radar system built by India. The radar is the primary sensor for Integrated Coastal Surveillance System. The Coastal Surveillance Radar Systems (CSRS) programme contributes in creating a network of information to maritime domain awareness in the strategic Indian Ocean region. In November 2020, the two countries signed four agreements, including a $100 million Indian grant for an ambitious connectivity project, named the Greater Male Connectivity Project (GMCP). A contract was signed in August 2021 for the GMCP infrastructure project (with a Line of Credit of $400 million by India). The project is one of the largest such development plans for Male, involving construction of a 6.74 km long bridge and causeway link connecting the island's capital with adjoining islands of Villingli, Gulhifalhu and Thilafushi.

In February 2021, New Delhi signed an agreement with Male to develop and maintain a naval port at the Uthuru Thila Falhu in the Kaafu atoll of the island. Additionally, India also extended a US$50 million line of credit to Maldives for defence projects during a visit by External Affairs Minister S Jaishankar to that nation. The defence line of credit would facilitate "capability building" in Maldives' maritime domain, the EAM said.

Afghanistan: India and Afghanistan have since long shared close cultural and historic ties. The Treaty of Friendship between the Govt. of India and the Royal Govt. of Afghanistan was inked on 4 January 1950 to strengthen bilateral relations. In the past decade, India generously assisted Afghanistan in its overall development. The two countries signed the Strategic Partnership Agreement in New Delhi on 4 October 2011 to open the doors for training, equipping and capacity-building in defence sector. The accord also sought to impart long-term commitment to their multifaceted bilateral relations and to actively develop them in political, economic, trade, scientific, technological, cultural and other fields. It was the first Strategic Partnership Agreement India had signed within its South Asian neighbourhood. The erstwhile Afghanistan Govt had also expressed its keenness to continue its defence cooperation with India. Reversing its earlier position of refraining from supplying any military and related equipment to the war-torn nation, New Delhi had supplied some defence platforms to Kabul. India also imparted training to Afghan security personnel even as Kabul was seeking more defence supplies and defence-related cooperation from New Delhi. However, the sudden withdrawal of American military personnel from Afghanistan in August 2021 after announcing an "end to the two-decade long war" amidst complete chaos and subsequent capture of power by Taliban has become a major cause of concern for New Delhi even as it is recalibrating its policies and strategies vis-à-vis Afghanistan while maintaining a cautious watch over the evolving situation there.

Singapore: Bilateral relations between India and Singapore have revolved around political, economic, cultural and strategic areas. Singapore has played an important role in reconnecting India with the countries of Southeast Asia since the adoption of New Delhi's "Look East" policy in the early 1990s which was later reframed as "Act East" policy. The two countries signed a Defence Cooperation Agreement in 2003 under which they carry out joint military exercises. The two sides have also decided to further strengthen their naval cooperation while protecting critical sea lanes of trade in the Indo-Pacific region. In June 2018, New Delhi and Singapore signed a Logistics and Services Support agreement.

Seychelles: India and Seychelles share strong trade and economic relations along with cooperation in the fields of science & technology, healthcare and tourism. The most vital aspect of bilateral ties be-tween the two sides is their deep-rooted strategic partnership which has evolved over the years with India providing defence equipment and platform to the island country in the Indian Ocean. India has pro-vided a comprehensive maritime security solution including provisioning of military hardware, training, consultancy as well as hydrographic assistance to the Seychelles Govt. in the past. India has gifted naval vessels to Seychelles to carry out anti-piracy missions and also set up coastal surveillance ra-dars in the island nation. In 2016, the Seychelles Govt. announced that it had provided a piece of land to India in the country's Assumption Island to build a naval base in the Indian Ocean Region. However, continuous opposition in Seychelles over the same made its Govt back out of its earlier stand to lend the island to India. The two sides later on held talks over the issue and decided to work together on the joint project at the Assumption Island, "keeping each other's concerns in mind." In 2018, India gifted a second Dornier aircraft and $100 million defence-related Line of Credit to augment Seychelles' defence capabilities. In April 2021, a fast patrol vessel, 'PS Zoroaster' (fourth platform of the class) funded by the Govt of India, was handed over to Seychelles.

Mauritius: The century-old multi-faceted relationship between India and Mauritius has revolved around historical, cultural, democratic values in addition to intimate ancestral ties. The strategically located island nation had drawn inspiration from India's freedom movement and it gained independence in 1968. In recent times, India has forged extensive defence relations with Mauritius to safeguard vital sea lanes of communication from pirates. New Delhi has provided helicopter, offshore patrol vessel, fast interceptor boats and FACs to the government of Mauritius to bolster its counter-piracy capabilities. Indian naval ships are also conducting regular surveillance and joint patrolling missions in the vast Exclusive Economic Zone of Mauritius.

Vietnam: The decades-old Indo-Vietnam relation has included political, economic and strategic ties between the two Asian countries. Vietnam has played a crucial role in India's "Look East/ Act East" policy. India and Vietnam had signed a protocol on defence cooperation in 1994. The partnership was thereafter elevated to strategic level in 2007 and a pact on boosting bilateral defence cooperation was signed in 2009. The strategic partnership was further elevated to a "comprehensive strategic partnership" in September 2016. The ambit of India's strategic alliance with Vietnam has further expanded in recent times with the two countries agreeing to strengthen their defence cooperation in the backdrop of new evolving geostrategic scenario in Asia. Defence ties between the two sides include high level bilateral visits, training of personnel, upgrading military capabilities, assistance in defence production and joint exercises. India, for the first time, has also provided a $100 million credit line to Vietnam which is being utilised by Hanoi for procurement of Offshore Patrol Boats for its Border Guards. The Southeast Asian country has evinced keen interest in India's defence research programmes and the two sides have identified major areas of cooperation which include upgrade of Soviet legacy systems, upgradation of Thermal Sights and Fire Control Systems for the BMP vehicles, T-54 and T-55 tanks, upgrade of MI-17/ Mi-8 helicopters, shipbuilding programmes, missile systems from India and software defined radios from Vietnam. India has also imparted training to over 500 Vietnam Navy personnel in operating the Russian-origin Kilo-class conventional submarines. The Indian Air Force has agreed to train Vietnam's pilots in flying the Russian-built Sukhoi-30 fighter aircraft. India is presently discussing a logistics support agreement with Vietnam to facilitate military and other logistical inter-operability.

India and Vietnam are also working on an agreement to launch Vietnam's satellites into space. Meanwhile, India is building a Data Reception and Tracking and Telemetry Station at Ho Chi Minh City in southern Vietnam which would essentially help the Indian Space Research Organisation (ISRO) track satellites launched from India and receive data from them. The new space facility would be an important strategic asset for India in the South China Sea region.

Philippines: India-Philippines strategic relations have grown in recent times and touched newer heights under New Delhi's 'Act East' policy. During high level goodwill visits and meeting, the two sides have agreed to further strengthen bilateral defence engagement and maritime cooperation, especially in military training and education, capacity building, and procurement of defence equipment, among others. Amidst the ever-evolving geostrategic developments in Southeast Asia, especially the continuous maritime skirmishes in South China Sea, Manila and New Delhi have identified each other as important strategic partners. India has also reckoned the Philippines as a "vital partner" in the Indo-Pacific region.

Thailand: India and Thailand share maritime boundary in the Andaman Sea. Bilateral relations between the two countries have revolved around trade and economic exchanges, cultural ties and cooperation in the field of defence that includes joint military exercises and training of armed forces. The two countries signed a bilateral Memorandum of Understanding on Defence Cooperation in January 2012. In June 2016, they agreed to forge closer partnership in maritime domain. India plans to take up infrastructure development projects with Thailand and one such project is the construction of India-Myanmar-Thailand Trilateral highway, which will run from Moreh in Manipur, India to Mae Sot in Thailand via Myanmar and connect the three Asian countries by road. India, being instrumental in the grand highway project, has expedited work on it.

Myanmar: India and Myanmar share a land border of 1,650-km and a common maritime boundary in the Bay of Bengal. The geographic position of Myanmar, which connects South Asia with Southeast Asia, has strategic significance for India. The two neighbours have primarily been cooperating in the fields of trade and commerce. Myanmar has received military hardware and software from India in the past and has sought more such assistance from New Delhi. India has also taken up various developmental tasks, including infrastructure build up, in Myanmar. Recently, New Delhi has completed the Sittwe port (Kaladan river) project in Myanmar as part of efforts to promote connectivity with India's North-eastern region. Navies of the two countries have taken part in multilateral exercises; their Armies have conducted bilateral joint exercise in 2017. India has agreed to Myanmar's request for assistance in building OPVs, which are likely to be constructed at an Indian shipyard. India is also considering to train Myanmar pilots to fly the Russian-origin Mi-35 attack helicopters. In 2019, New Delhi delivered the first batch of indigenously-built Shyena lightweight torpedoes to the Myanmar Navy under a deal signed in 2017. In yet another major strategic move, India transferred one of its Navy's Kilo-class attack submarines, INS Sindhuvir, to the Myanmar Navy in 2020. The platform has been inducted in the Myanmarese Navy as 'UMS Minye Theinkhathu'.

Indonesia: As part of India's "Act East" policy, Indonesia has received increasing attention from New Delhi of late. Bilateral cooperation between the two sides covers economic, political, security and military aspects. It was further strengthened with the signing of the 'Joint Declaration on Establishing a Strategic Partnership' in 2005 between the two sides. The two nations have been closely coordinating in defence and security fields and the navies of both sides are regularly conducting coordinated maritime patrols (CORPAT) in the Indian Ocean Region. Their armies also hold joint military training exercises at regular intervals. During the biennial defence dialogue held at Jakarta in Oct 2012, India had agreed to train and support the Indonesian Air Force in operating its fleet of Sukhoi fighter jets acquired from Russia. In 2017, India and Indonesia decided to hold their first-ever joint air combat exercise as well as deepen maritime security cooperation. In 2018, the two countries' leadership decided to elevate bilateral ties to "Comprehensive Strategic Partnership."

Malaysia: The two Asian countries established strategic partnership in 2010. Bilateral ties involve political, regional and international cooperation besides defence and security. While conducting regular military exchanges, the two countries in November 2015 also agreed to set up a "SU-30 Forum" for cooperation in training, maintenance, technical support and safety-related issues, building on the assistance by India for successful completion of the SU-30 MKM (being operated by the Malaysian Air Force) training programme by Indian pilots in Malaysia. The two sides have also announced joint collaboration on projects of mutual interest in the defence sector.

Iran: India and Iran have shared strong cultural and historical relations since several decades. India has always acknowledged the strategic importance of Iran in the Asian continent. Though Indo-Iranian ties have passed through several ups and downs in past few years due to changing regional and global geostrategic developments, nevertheless, the two sides have valued each other as important trading and economic partners. Iran has remained a crucial energy supplier for India and meets major share of New Delhi's crude oil demand. The two countries have especially been making efforts to improve bilateral cooperation in economic, political, energy and security areas. During Prime Minister Narendra Modi's Tehran visit in May 2016, the two countries signed a historic deal to develop the Chahbahar port in Iran. The deal was inked after a meeting between Prime Minister Modi and Iran's President Hassan Rouhani. The port in Southeast Iran having direct road links to Afghanistan border has opened up huge trade opportunities for India as also for Iran in Central Asia and Afghanistan. In October 2017, India sent its first shipment via the Chahbahar port to Afghanistan. Work on the strategic port has reached completion stage and it could become operational in near future.

Oman: The two countries have shared close bilateral ties, including in military domain. Oman is India's oldest defence partner in West Asia. The two sides conduct joint military exercises at regular intervals. New Delhi has further strengthened its strategic ties with Muscat recently. The two countries have signed a pact in 2018 under which India would gain access to Oman's Duqm port. The strategically positioned port, overseeing the coast of Oman in the Arabian sea, would give India access into the wider West Asia and Eastern Africa regions. Indian military vessels would be able to visit the Duqm port as part of the deal. India is also planning to set up defence industrial base in Oman. In 2019, the air forces of India and Oman conducted a 10-day bilateral drill at the Omani air force base in Masirah.

Saudi Arabia: Giving a major boost to bilateral ties, India and Saudi Arabia have signed a "strategic partnership" agreement during Prime Minister Narendra Modi's Riyadh visit in October 2019. India is the fourth country after the UK, France and China with which Saudi Arabia has signed an agreement on strategic partnership. Saudi Arabia has expressed interest to deepen its maritime cooperation with India in the western Indian Ocean, which constitutes busy and sensitive shipping routes such as the Red Sea, the Gulf of Aden, the Arabian Sea, the Gulf of Oman, and the Persian Gulf. India and Saudi Arabia were to hold their first-ever joint naval exercise in March 2020 (as part of the larger MILAN multi-national drill). However, it was cancelled in the wake of the COVID-19 pandemic. The two countries are also exploring new areas of cooperation, including in the defence industry sector.

Japan: While bilateral relationship between the two Asian powers remained confined only to the economic sphere in the past, in recent times, the two countries have made sincere efforts to expand it further so as to include political and strategic tie-ups. Giving a major boost to this strategic partnership, New Delhi and Tokyo in September 2020, inked a landmark agreement on "Reciprocal Provision of Supplies and Services" between the Indian Armed Forces and Japan's Self-Defense Forces (JSDF). The historic pact, inked after years of negotiations, would allow the two militaries to access each other's bases for logistics support besides providing for the creation of an enabling framework for closer cooperation and interoperability. Keeping in mind the changing regional and global geostrategic landscape, India and Japan are also holding joint military exercises involving their defence forces. In the first-ever bilateral maritime engagement, the two countries' navies conducted the 'JIMEX 12' naval exercise in 2012. The two sides are also actively participating in the multi-lateral maritime drill "Malabar" since 2015. In October 2017, the two countries' navies conducted an anti-submarine warfare exercise in the Indian Ocean Region for the first time. India is planning to procure the US-2 amphibious aircraft from Japan.

South Korea: India-South Korea relations have witnessed major transformations in recent years, encompassing bilateral trade, diplomatic and strategic ties. While Seoul views New Delhi as one of its new economic partners in a swiftly changing world-order, India looks at the RoK as an indispensable partner in its 'Act-East' strategy, with the potential to contribute to peace, stability and security in the wider Asia Pacific Region, while aligning with the Indo-Pacific strategic vision. Bilateral defence ties have also gained momentum in recent times between the two Asian nations. Ties between the two countries were raised to the level of 'strategic partnership' during a visit to India by then South Korean President Lee Myung-bak in 2010. The relationship was further elevated to the level of 'special strategic partnership' during the visit of Prime Minister Narendra Modi to Seoul in 2015. Both sides are signatories to a mutual logistics support agreement for naval cooperation. The pact facilitates the two navies to use each other's bases for repair and replenishment of supplies.

Mongolia: Bilateral ties between India and Mongolia date back to 1955 when New Delhi established diplomatic relations with Ulan Bator. The two countries also share deep cultural and historic ties for many centuries. In 2015, India upgraded its bilateral relations with Mongolia to "Strategic Partnership" during Prime Minister Narendra Modi's visit, the first-ever visit by an Indian Premier, to the Central Asian nation. New Delhi has also pledged US$ 1 billion credit line to Mongolia for infrastructure development in that country.

France: India's long-standing partnership with France has widened further to include defence cooperation, maritime security, counter-terrorism, space cooperation, civil nuclear cooperation, economic partnership besides other key areas of mutual convergence. While acknowledging India's political, strategic, diplomatic and economic emergence at the world stage, France has steadfastly supported India's stand on several strategic matters, including a permanent seat for New Delhi at the United Nations Security Council. India-France strategic partnership has become an important pillar of India's foreign policy in 21st century. Even as defence relations between the two sides have become robust after India's signing of the multi-million dollar Rafale combat aircraft deal, New Delhi and Paris have also operationalised the "Logistics Support Agreement", signed between them in March 2018. The agreement makes provision for reciprocal logistics support between India and France, including their armed forces. Under the deal, the two sides' armed forces would receive logistical support, supplies and services from each other during authorised port visits, joint exercises, joint training, humanitarian assistance and disaster relief operations. India is acquiring Scorpene-class attack submarines and Rafale fighter aircraft from France. Indian Armed Forces are also operating other French-built military systems/platforms.

Germany: India and Germany have entered into strategic partnership since 2001 which has been furthered strengthened over the years. Besides sharing close political, economic and cultural ties, Berlin and New Delhi have also cooperated closely on defence and technology spheres. Germany is India's largest trading partner in Europe and second most important partner in terms of technological collaborations. India has invited the German industries to invest in India's mega defence corridors projects in Tamil Nadu and Uttar Pradesh.

Australia: The ambit of bilateral engagements between Australia and India has widened of late keeping in view the increasingly changing regional and global order and newer powerplays. Both nations form an integral part of the now-evolving QUAD coalition which also involves two other countries, the US and Japan. India has expressed its commitment to expand its relations with Australia on a faster and wider pace for regional and global strategic stability. The two Asia-Pacific nations entered into the Mutual Logistics Support Agreement (MLSA) in June 2020, paving the way for their militaries to use each other's bases for repair and replenishment of supplies besides facilitating scaling up of overall defence cooperation.

US: Recalibrating its position vis-à-vis the major world power, India has of late inched closer to establish stronger security and defence relations with the US. Strategic partnership between the two countries has witnessed dramatic transformation wherein the US has acknowledged India as its "security partner of choice" in the broader Indo-Pacific region. The resurgence of China and its increasing military aggressions has also brought New Delhi and Washington further closer to counter Beijing and its increasing belligerence in Asia. High-level joint military exercises are being regularly conducted between the Indian and US armies, navies and air forces in both the countries. India has also been conducting joint maritime exercise with the US in the Indian Ocean region in addition to multilateral drills. The two sides have inked technology exchange agreement and most importantly, India in August 2016, signed the Logistics Exchange Memorandum of Agreement (LEMOA) with the USA. The agreement has paved the way for the two nations to become logistical allies, enabling their militaries to use each other's assets and bases for repair and replenishment of supplies. In 2018, New Delhi and Washington also inked the Communications Compatibility and Security Agreement (COMCASA), paving the way for the transfer of communication security equipment from the US to India to facilitate interoperability between their forces. And in October 2020, India and US signed the Basic Exchange and Cooperation Agreement (BECA) which would help India get "real-time" access to American geospatial intelligence that would enhance the accuracy of automated systems and weapons like missiles and armed drones. Through the sharing of information on maps and satellite images, it would help India access topographical and aeronautical data, and advanced products that will aid in navigation and targeting.

The US has agreed to elevate defence trade and technology sharing with India to a level commensurate with its closest allies and partners. Washington has explored the ever-growing Indian defence market to export its cutting-edge defence equipment and technology. Washington, in fact, has emerged as one of the leading suppliers of defence hardware to India over the past few years. In yet another strategic move, the Pentagon in 2018 renamed its oldest and largest military command – the US Pacific Command (PACOM) as the Indo-Pacific Command, thus reflecting the growing importance of Indian Ocean Region in US strategic thinking and planning. Meanwhile, development and evolution of the quadrilateral (QUAD) coalition involving the US, India, Australia and Japan has taken concrete shape in recent times. India has inked military logistics agreement with all QUAD member countries – the US, Japan and Australia. The QUAD member nations have also conducted mega naval drill "Malabar" in the Indian Ocean Region in November 2020.

EU: India and the European Union have built-up a long-standing relationship since the 1960s and have been coordinating on a broad range of areas, including politics, trade, economy, science & technology, education and strategic sphere. In 2004, India became one of EU's "Strategic Partners". In recent years, some of the leading powers of the EU, including France, Germany and Italy, have evinced interest in the hugely growing Indian defence market.

MULTILATERAL ALLIANCES

Besides maintaining bilateral relations with its neighbouring and other countries, India has also been engaged in several multilateral forums which include SAARC, BIMSTEC, IBSA and BRICS.

SAARC: As one of the founding members of the South Asian Association for Regional Cooperation (SAARC), India has endeavoured to promote political, economic, social and technological cooperation among the member nations in the block which include Afghanistan, Bangladesh, Bhutan, Maldives, Nepal, Pakistan and Sri Lanka. The multilateral forum, founded in 1985 with its headquarters in Kathmandu, Nepal, has accorded observer status to Australia, China, the European Union, Iran, Japan, South Korea, Mauritius, Myanmar and the USA. The forum has been engaged in promoting regional trade and economy, and enhancing mutual cooperation in several fields including agriculture, education, energy, science and technology and social development.

BIMSTEC: The Bay of Bengal Initiative for Multi-Sectoral Technical and Economic Cooperation (BIMSTEC) is a regional block comprising India, Bangladesh, Sri Lanka, Thailand, Myanmar, Nepal and Bhutan. The multilateral forum with the South Asian and Southeast Asian nations has 13 priority areas – trade and investment, technology, energy, transport and communication, tourism, fisheries, agriculture, cultural cooperation, environment and disaster management, public health, people-to-people contact, poverty alleviation, counter-terrorism and transnational crimes. The block, originally named Bangladesh, India, Sri Lanka, and Thailand Economic Cooperation (BISTEC), was formed in 1997 to primarily promote economic and trade cooperation among the member nations. Myanmar, Nepal and Bhutan subsequently joined the forum which was then renamed as Bay of Bengal Initiative for Multi-Sectoral Technical and Economic Cooperation. The block held its fourth summit meeting in 2018 in Kathmandu, Nepal.

IBSA: With a view to promote South-South cooperation, India, Brazil and South Africa joined to form IBSA in 2003, bringing together three developing countries from three continents of the globe – Asia, South America and Africa. The trilateral block has provided a platform to its member nations to engage in cooperation in several areas, including political, trade and economic, social, agricultural, defence and technological relations. The group has also been holding a biennial joint naval drill, called India-Brazil-South Africa Maritime (IBSAMAR) exercise since 2008. The last IBSA summit was held in 2017 at Durban, South Africa. The 9th IBSA Trilateral ministerial meeting was held at Cochin, India in May 2019.

BRICS: The forum was formed in 2006 with Brazil, Russia, India and China (BRIC) as its founding members. South Africa joined the block in 2010 which was then renamed BRICS. The alliance was primarily focused on political, economic and financial cooperation among the member nations. Over the years, the block has expanded its purview of cooperation so as to include evolving issues including international terrorism, climate change, food & energy security, millennium development goals and strategic partnership.

SCO: India joined the strategically important Shanghai Cooperation Organisation (SCO) as a full-time member in 2017. The SCO, with China, Russia, Kazakhstan, Kyrgyzstan, Tajikistan, and Uzbekistan as its founding members, had agreed to include India along with Pakistan as full-time members during its annual summit held at Ufa, Russia in July 2015. Both India and Pakistan formally joined the group as full members at its annual summit in Astana, Kazakhstan in July 2017. Joining the SCO has paved the way for New Delhi to strengthen its connectivity with the resource-rich Central Asian nations. India has renewed efforts in this direction with its "Connect Central Asia" policy. While emphasising on political and economic coordination among its member nations, the SCO is steadily emerging as an influential regional block in the Eurasian space. The organisation is also focused on the rapidly evolving strategic and security issues in the region. The 19th annual summit of the SCO was held in the Kyrgyz capital Bishkek in June 2019 which was attended by the heads of state of all member nations. In the wake of the Coronavirus pandemic, the 20th and 21st annual meetings of the bloc was held virtually in Russia and Kazakhstan, respectively.

Arctic Council: The eight-member Arctic Council is a high-level intergovernmental forum set up to address the issues faced by the Arctic governments and the indigenous people of the Arctic region. Canada, Denmark, Finland, Iceland, Norway, Russia, Sweden, and the US are the Council's permanent members. India, along with 12 other non-Arctic countries including China, have been admitted into the council as permanent observers since 2013. New Delhi has expressed its desire for increased cooperation in the council in view of the geostrategic importance of the Arctic Sea and the region's important role in governing climate change that has global consequences.

DEFENCE CAPABILITIES

ARMY: With a strength of nearly 1.2 million active personnel and around a million reserve force, the Indian Army is presently the largest army in Asia after that of North Korea, and the largest standing volunteer army in the world. The Army is the largest wing of Indian defence forces and it is equipped with conventional and nuclear arsenal to defend and protect national sovereignty and territorial integrity. As India has faced security challenges from both state and non-state actors from time to time, the Indian Army, operating from the remotest and highly difficult, treacherous terrains of the country, has carried out the most complex, delicate and sensitive operations to protect the nation from any internal or external aggressions or threat. It also takes up humanitarian missions across the nation in times of national disasters or adversities.

To add more teeth to its existing warfighting capabilities, the Indian Army is undergoing comprehensive modernisation and acquiring new-generation weapons and platforms, including howitzers, missiles, combat vehicles, helicopters, UAVs, transport, surveillance and fighter aircraft along with other new-age weaponry and hardware. Besides robustly bolstering its overall combat capability to counter enemy threat, Indian Army has also been actively taking part in the United Nations-led peacekeeping missions in several strife-torn countries worldwide.

In 2018, the Government announced plans to carry out major reforms in the Indian Army aimed at enhancing their overall combat capabilities while rebalancing defence expenditure. The reforms would involve redeployment and restructuring of nearly 57,000 officers while ensuring better utilization of resources. The entire process is aimed at making the Indian Army "a leaner and meaner" force. The Defence Ministry, in August 2019, approved the first batch of reforms in the Army including relocation of 206 officers from the Army headquarters. The Defence Ministry has also approved the creation of a new post of deputy chief for military operations and strategic planning in the Army as part of the mega reforms.

In yet another major development, the Army is getting ready to deploy its first Integrated Battle Group (IBG) in near future. The Army plans to form and deploy the IBGs to firmly secure and defend India's volatile western, eastern and northern borders. The IBGs comprising elements of airpower, armour, artillery, mechanised and traditional infantry engineering and ordnance units, would be "self-sustained forces" which could be swiftly mobilised and deployed to carry out strikes against an adversary in a conflict zone at a very short notice and activated without any delay.

Personnel: 1.2 million (+1 million reserve force)

Equipment

Category	Name	In Service	On Order
MBT	Arjun Mk-I	124	124
	Arjun Mk-IA		118
	T-90S/M	700+	1000+
	T-72 M1, M2	2500	
	T-55	900	
IFV, APC, ARV	BMP-1, BMP-2	2000+	500+ (BMP-2)
	Cassipir	250+	
	OT-64 SKOT/ OT-62 TOPAS	200+	
	VT-72B	200	
	WZT-3	550	
Artillery/ Weapon	155mm light field gun	180	
	105mm light field gun	700+	
	FH77B 155mm howitzer	410	
	M46 130mm howitzer (upgraded to 155mm standard)	300	
	M777 howitzer	5	140
	K9 VAJRA-T 155mm	51	753

...continued

Category	Name	In Service	On Order
Artillery/ Weapon	122mm 2S1 howitzer		
	155mm 45-calibre Dhanush howitzer	12	102
	81mm mortar	500	
	106mm RCL		
	Smerch 300mm	62	
	Pinaka Mk-1 MBRL	1 regiment	6 regiments
	BM-21 MRL	100+ (being withdrawn)	
	57mm ATK gun		
	100mm ATK gun		
	AT3 Sagger ATGM	500	
	Milan ATGM		4960
	Snapper ATGM		
	Invar ATGM		
	Nag ATGM		300
	Spike ATGM	200+	200+
	9M113 Konkurs ATGM		
	9K22 Tunguska SPAAG		
	40mm L-70 AAG	1000	
	ZSU-23-2	800	
	SA-6 SAM	180	
	SA-8 SAM		
	SA-13 SAM	50	
	SA-18 SAM		
	SA-9 SAM		
	Akash SAM	2 regiments	More on order
	Prithvi SSM		
	BRAHMOS SSM		

Army Aviation

Category	Name	In Service	On Order
Helicopter	Apache (attack)		6
	Rudra (attack)	21	55
	LCH		114
	Chetak	55	
	Cheetah	120	
	ALH Dhruv/ Mk-III	100+	50+
	Kamov Ka-226T LUH		200
UAV	Searcher I & II		
	Nishant	3	
	Heron		15

New Procurements/Upgrades

◆ Procurement of 118 Arjun Mk-1A advanced main battle tanks has been cleared by the Defence Ministry in Sept. 2021. An order worth Rs. 7,523 crore has been placed with the Heavy Vehicles Factory (HVF), Avadi, Chennai, to deliver the new MBTs to the Army.

◆ Procurement of advanced T-90 tanks is going on. The Army plans to induct over 1500 such tanks, mostly built in India under license from Russia, in its inventory.

◆ The Defence Ministry in 2018 approved plans to upgrade the T-72M1 Ajeya MBTs with new engines. Around 1,000 new engines would be procured under the plan.

◆ In June 2020, the Defence Ministry awarded a contract to Ordnance Factory Board – OFB (now dissolved & organised into seven new defence public sector undertakings) for supply of 156 BMP 2/2k Infantry Combat Vehicles with upgraded features to the Army. The Army is set to receive over 500 new BMP-2 IFVs (to be built by OFB). Additionally, a total of 693 BMP-2 IFVs are undergoing mid-life upgrade under a $375 million contract awarded to OFB and Bharat Electronics Ltd. in 2017.

◆ Indian Army in June 2021 has issued a fresh RFI to procure up to 1,750 Future Infantry Combat Vehicles (FICVs). The new platforms, to be built by an Indian entity in partnership with a foreign company, would replace the BMP-2 IFVs.

◆ The first batch of indigenously-built Armoured Engineer Reconnaissance Vehicles (AERV) has been inducted in December 2021. The vehicles are designed by DRDO and produced by the Ordnance Factory Medak and Bharat Electronics Ltd., Pune.

◆ The Army has signed MoU with DRDO to raise one regiment of the advanced Medium Range Surface to Air Missiles (MRSAM). The Army plans to deploy a total of five regiments of the air defence system. Delivery of the weapon has started in 2021.

◆ A tender has been issued for procurement of a batch of short-range air defence missile systems.

◆ Procurement of advanced Akash-S missile variants has been proposed by the Army.

◆ A total of 12 indigenously-developed 155mm/45-calibre Dhanush howitzers have been inducted as of June 2021. The Defence ministry has approved to induct 114 Dhanush systems in the Army.

◆ The first batch of M-777 howitzers procured from the US was inducted in Sept. 2018. A proposal was cleared to buy 145 of the M-777 ultra-light howitzers. While 25 of the guns are being procured directly through Foreign Military Sales (FMS) programme, the remaining ones are being built locally. BAE Systems, the manufacturer of M-777, has tied up with India's Mahindra Defence for assembling, integrating and testing the howitzers in India. The first batch of the locally-built M-777s was delivered in Dec. 2019.

◆ Procurement of 814 mounted gun systems (MGS) for an estimated $3 billion is being going on. The 155mm/52 calibre guns are being procured under "buy and make" Indian category. India's L&T, which has collaborated with South Korea's Hanwha Tech Win (HTW), bagged a contract in 2017 to supply the initial batch of 100 K9 VAJRA-T self-propelled howitzers over the next three years. Delivery of all 100 Vajra howitzers has been completed in Feb. 2021.

◆ At least six regiments of DRDO-developed Pinaka MBRLs (comprising of 114 launchers, 45 command posts and 330 launch vehicles) are to be inducted in the Army by 2024. The Defence Ministry in Sept. 2020 inked a deal worth Rs 2,580 crore with Tata Power Company Ltd (TPCL), Larsen & Toubro (L&T), and Bharat Earth Movers Ltd (BEML) to procure the indigenous systems for the Army.

◆ An enhanced version of Pinaka MBRL, developed by DRDO and undergoing test firings, features higher range and reduced length among other enhancements. The new system, named Pinaka-ER (extended range), is slated to replace the existing Pinaka (Mk-1) weapons of the Army.

◆ The Defence Ministry in 2018 cleared a proposal to acquire DRDO-built Nag third-gen anti-tank guided missiles. The ATGM successfully completed winter and summer trials in 2019 and would be entering series production soon, the MoD announced. DRDO concluded final phase of user trials for the ATGM in October 2020.

◆ A new Laser-Guided Anti Tank Missile (ATGM) developed by DRDO has undergone successful test firings as part of technical evaluation trials from the Arjun MBT platform in September and October 2020.

◆ DRDO is developing a new man-portable anti-tank guided missile (MPATGM) in partnership with VEM Technologies Ltd. The new weapon is expected to be delivered to the Army by 2021 - 2022.

◆ More Spike anti-tank guided missiles (ATGMs) are being procured from Israel.

◆ Defence Ministry in March 2021 has signed a contract worth Rs 1,188 crore with Bharat Dynamics Ltd (BDL) for supply of 4,960 MILAN-2T anti-tank guided missiles to the Army.

◆ The Army is considering to buy at least eight regiments of the quick reaction air defence missile systems to protect its assets and troops from enemy aircraft and unmanned aerial vehicles. Israel's Spyder QR-SAM has emerged a frontrunner for the likely procurement. DRDO has also developed a similar weapon that has undergone successful test firings.

◆ The US Govt. in 2018 has approved the sale of six AH-64E Apache attack helicopters to Indian Army at a cost of $930 million. The platforms would be armed with Hellfire and Stinger missiles as part of the deal. The Indian MoD had approved the acquisition in 2017.

◆ A proposal has been cleared by the Defence Ministry to acquire Light Combat Helicopters (LCH) for the Army.

◆ HAL has been awarded contract to deliver 25 ALH Mark-III helicopters to Army.

◆ Russia and India are working on the project of joint production of Ka-226T military utility helicopters India plans to produce at least 140 of the Russia-built multi-role rotorcraft locally with "technology transfer" clause which would be inducted in Indian Army and Air Force

◆ 15 Heron UAVs are being procured from Israel at a cost of Rs 1,200 crore. Procurement of more such drones is under consideration as per the Armed Forces' requirement. The Army in 2021 has leased four Heron TP MALE UAVs from Israel for potential deployment along the LAC.

◆ The Defence Ministry in November 2016 cleared procurement of 598 mini UAVs for the Army. An RFI was issued in 2018 for initial batch of 75 such systems.

NAVY: The Indian Navy primarily operates to safeguard India's maritime sovereignty and protect its maritime interests. The vision statement of the Navy reads as follows: "To effectively confront the multifarious challenges it faces in the complex maritime environment of the 21st century, the Indian Navy will strengthen itself continuously as a formidable, multi-dimensional and networked force that maintains high readiness at all times to protect India's maritime interests, safeguard her seaward frontiers and defeat all maritime threats in our areas of interest." Optimum utilisation of every resource, innovation, indigenisation and self-reliance, quality maintenance, timely infrastructure modernisation and effective leadership skills are other priority areas of the Navy.

Besides safeguarding national territorial waters, the Navy also works to strengthen maritime cooperation with other nations and assists in humanitarian missions.

Although smaller than the other two wings of Indian armed forces, the Navy is sizable and well-equipped – a reflection of India's regional power projection capability. Since the 1990s, Indian Navy has made efforts to strengthen its overall capabilities and expand its horizon of operation with an intent to transform itself into a "Blue Water" naval force capable of carrying out both littoral and high sea operations. This transition has become necessary in the wake of swiftly changing geostrategic landscape where Asia has emerged as the new power block amidst a raging China flaunting its military might. Of particular significance for Indian Navy in recent times is the strategically important Indian Ocean Region (IOR) which has witnessed a spurt in maritime activities, mainly by China.

In recent times, Indian Navy has endeavoured to maintain a vigorous presence across the entire Indo-Pacific region. Its naval ships are frequent visitors to ports in the Indian Ocean and Western Pacific. While it is taking part in multi-lateral maritime drills like MILAN and Malabar, the Navy is also undertaking coordinated patrol exercises with some countries like Myanmar, Indonesian and Bangladesh, and bilateral exercises with countries such as Singapore, Oman, Russia, Sri Lanka, UK, and South Africa.

To bolster its overall capabilities, Indian Navy is undergoing full-scale modernisation by acquiring new, top-of-the-line maritime assets including aircraft carriers, submarines, frigates, destroyers, corvettes, naval fighter jets, surveillance aircraft, helicopters and modern combat systems among other equipment. The Navy has, in fact, outlined a plan to acquire around 200 ships, 500 new aircraft and 24 attack submarines in next three to four years. The new maritime assets, equipped with cutting-edge weapons and armaments, promise to transform the Navy into a "world class" maritime force in the 21st century.

The Naval Fleet headquarters is based at New Delhi, while naval commands are located at Mumbai (Western Command), Vishakhapatnam (Eastern Command) and Kochi (Southern Command). The naval aviation HQ is based at Arakonam, while the Marines have a joint command HQ based at Port Blair on the Andaman Islands in the Bay of Bengal.

Major naval & naval air bases: Mumbai, Kolkata, Kochi, Vishakapatnam, Port Blair, Kavaratti, Karwar, Porbandar, Okha, Panaji, Arakkonam, Ramanathapuram

Personnel: 67,228 (Navy); Total 100,000+ (Including Marine Commandos, Naval Air & Coast Guard personnel)

Equipment

Category	Name	In Service	On Order
Aircraft Carrier	INS Vikramaditya	1	
	Indigenous aircraft carrier (IAC) Vikrant		1 (+1 more planned to be built)
Destroyer	Delhi class	3	
	Rajput class	3	
	Kolkata class (Project-15A)	3	
	Project-15B	1	3
Submarine	Shishumar class (German Type 209)	4	
	Sindhughosh class (Russian Kilo-class)	8	
	INS Chakra (Akula II class)	1	1
	Arihant class SSBN	1	5
	Scorpene (Project 75)	4	2
	Project 75-I		6
Frigate	Talwar class	6	4
	Brahmaputra class	3	
	Godavari class	1	
	Shivalik class	3	
	Project 17A		7
Corvette	Khukri class	3	
	Kora	4	
	Veer class	8	
	Abhay class	3	
	ASW Kamorta class	4	
FAC	Bangaram class	4	
	Car Nicobar class	10	
	Car Nicobar class (advanced water-jet)	4	
	Trinkat class	1	
	Super Dovra II class	5	
OPV	Sukanya class	6	
	Saryu class	4	
	P-21 class		5
Amphibious Force	LPD (INS Jalashwa)	1	
	Indigenous LPD		4 (planned)
	Kumbhir class LST	4	
	Magar class LST	2	
	Shardul class LST	3	
	LCU Mk III & Mk IV	3+8	
Fleet tanker	Deepak class	2	
	Jyoti class	1	
	Aditya class	1	
Mine sweeper	Pondicherry class	1	
	MCMV		4 (likely)
Torpedo recovery vessel	Astradharini	1	
Research/ Survey vessel	Sagardhwani	1	
	Sandhayak class	6	
	Makar class	1	
	Large survey ships		4
	INS Dhruv (ocean surveillance ship)	1	
Training/ Sailing ship	Tir	1	
	Tarangini class	2	
Floating dock		1	
Weapon	K-4/ K-15 SLBM		
	Dhanush (ballistic missile)		
	(AShM/ LACM) Brahmos, Klub KH-35, P-20		
	(AAM) R-77		
	(SAM) Barak-1, Barak-8, Shtil, 9K38 Igla (MANPAD)		
	(Torpedo) A244-S, APR-3E, SET-65E/53-65KE, Type 53-65, TEST 71/76 Varunastra		

Naval Aviation Equipment

Category	Name	In Service	On Order
Naval Fighter	MiG-29K/ KUB	42	
Maritime patrol/ Utility	IL-38	5	

...continued

Category	Name	In Service	On Order
Maritime patrol/ Utility	P-8I	11	7
	Dornier Do 28	18	
Trainer	Hawk 132 AJT	11	6
	HJT-16 Kiran	20	
Helicopter	Ka-28	10	
	Ka-31	14	10
	UH-3H Sea King	32	
	Agusta Westland Sea King Mk 42	20	
	Chetak (Aloutte III) utility	56	7
	ALH Dhruv	9	40+
	MH-60R	2	22
UAV	Searcher II		
	Heron		
	MQ-9B SeaGuardian	2 (on lease)	

New Procurements/ Upgrades

◆ The Navy's first indigenous aircraft carrier (IAC) Vikrant has commenced its sea trials in August 2021. The warship is scheduled to be commissioned in 2022.

Indigenous Aircraft Carrier (IAC) Vikrant undergoing sea trials (Photo: Indian Navy)

◆ The first and lead ship of P15-B class stealth destroyer, "Visakhapatnam", has been commissioned on November 21, 2021. The platform is armed with surface-to-surface BRAHMOS supersonic cruise missiles. Work is advancing on three other such platforms – Mormugao, Imphal, Porbandar – which would be launched by 2022. Mazagon Docks Ltd. is building the platforms indigenously.

◆ The second indigenously built nuclear-powered strategic submarine of Arihant-class launched in 2017 is undergoing sea trials and is expected to be commissioned in 2022. INS Arihant, the first platform of the class, joined the Navy in 2016 and has completed its first deterrence patrol. The strategic platform has completed India's nuclear triad by adding maritime strike capability to the country's land- and air-based delivery platforms. The 6,000-tonne submarine is armed with K-4 and K-15 ballistic missiles (SLBMs).

◆ A deal has been signed with Russia in October 2016 to lease a second Akula-II class nuclear submarine. The platform is expected to be delivered in 2025. INS Chakra, the first platform of the class taken on a 10-year lease from Russia in 2012, would be returned to that country in 2022.

◆ INS Karanj, the third Scorpene-class attack submarine, has been commissioned on March 10, 2021. The fourth platform "Vela" has been commissioned on November 25, 2021. The fifth platform, "Vagir", having superior stealth features like advanced acoustic absorption technique, was launched in Nov. 2020.

◆ In July 2021, the Defence Ministry issued an RFP for the acquisition of six (air independent propulsion) AIP-fitted conventional submarines under Project 75(I) for the Navy under "Strategic Partnership" model. The RFP was issued to the Mazagaon Dock Shipbuilders Ltd (MDL) and Larsen & Toubro (L&T), the two Indian companies shortlisted following a long-drawn process. The two companies would collaborate with one of the five already short-listed foreign shipyards – Daewoo Shipbuilding (South Korea), ThyssenKrupp Marine Systems (Germany), Navantia (Spain), Naval Group (France) and JSC ROE (Russia).

◆ Four Kilo-class conventional submarines are being upgraded by Russia in association with an Indian partner under a Rs. 5,000 crore programme. While one of the platforms has re-joined the Navy after undergoing upgrades, a second platform is undergoing fitment there. Two other platforms are being refurbished at an Indian shipyard with Russian assistance.

◆ Germany's Thyssenkrupp Marine Systems has received a contract worth $56.5 million in 2018 from Indian shipyard Mazagon Docks to upgrade the first Shishumar class (Type 209/ 1500) conventional submarine of Indian Navy. The upgraded platform with an extended life of 10 years is expected to be delivered in 2021 - 2022. Plans are on to upgrade three more of the platforms later.

◆ The seventh stealth frigate of P1135.6 class has been launched at Yantar shipyard, Russia in October 2021. Russia had received a contract in 2018 to build two Project 1135.6M (advanced Talwar-class) stealth frigates. The platforms are slated for delivery by 2022. The frigates would be armed with BRAHMOS supersonic cruise missiles. Two more such platforms are also being built at India's Goa Shipyard (GSL) with Russian assistance under a $1.2 billion contract. Keel laying event for the first platform was held in January 2021 followed by the second platform in June 2021. The first ship is slated for delivery in 2026 followed by the second ship after a six-month period

◆ Nilgiri', the lead ship of seven P-17A class of frigates, is undergoing sea trials. The advanced frigates are being built indigenously by MDL and GRSE. GRSE has initiated work on the second and third platforms of the class. The first (GRSE-built) platform, 'Himgiri', was launched in Dec 2020. The seven next-generation frigates are being built as a follow-on project of Project-17 Shivalik-class of frigates. The warships, with advanced stealth features and indigenous weapons and sensors, are being built at MDL, Mumbai (4 frigates) and GRSE, Kolkata (3 frigates) with deliveries scheduled from 2023 onwards.

◆ The MoD in 2019 has issued an RFP to seven shipyards for building six next-generation missile vessels (NGMVs) for the Navy. RFPs have also been issued to shortlisted Indian shipyards for the construction of eight fast-patrol vessels (FPVs) and six air-cushion vehicles (ACVs) for Navy.

◆ The MoD, in August 2019, has cleared a proposal for the procurement of Next Generation Maritime Mobile Coastal Batteries (Long Range) for the Navy. The NGMMCB, armed with BRAHMOS surface-to-surface cruise missiles, would be deployed along India's strategically important coastal regions.

◆ A contract worth Rs 6,311 crore has been awarded each to GRSE and Cochin Shipyard in April 2019 to build and deliver a total of 16 anti-submarine warfare shallow water craft (ASWSWC) to the Navy. The first delivery is slated for 2022 - 2023. Each shipyard will build eight such platforms. The keel laying event for the first GRSE-built ASWSWC platform was held in August 2021.

◆ An RFI has been issued in August 2021 to Indian shipyards (Cochin Shipyard Ltd, GRSE, Mazagon Docks and Larsen & Toubro Shipbuilding) for procurement of four Landing Platform Docks (LPDs).

◆ Eleven (11) indigenously-built next-generation OPVs would be acquired under a tender worth over ₹9,000 crore approved by the MoD in December 2020.

◆ Induction of eight Mk IV LCU platforms built by GRSE has been completed with the commissioning of the final platform in March 2021.

◆ Five new fleet support ships to be built by an Indian shipyard in collaboration with a foreign firm would be acquired by the Navy. India's HSL is finalising an agreement with Turkey's Anadolu Shipyard to build the platforms in India.

◆ An RFI has been issued by the MoD in 2021 for either leasing or procuring three to

- four Mine Countermeasure Vessels (MMCV) from a foreign govt.
- INS Dhruv, an Ocean Surveillance Ship built by HSL, has been commissioned into service in October 2020. The indigenous platform is designed to monitor and track missile/ satellite launches at long distances, as also to support India's classified strategic weapon / ballistic missile defence (BMD) programme.
- INS Anvesh – designed by DRDO and built by Cochin Shipyard as India's first floating missile test range (FTR) vessel – has entered sea trials phase.
- A contract worth around Rs. 2500 crore has been awarded to GRSE in 2018 to design and build four survey vessels for the Navy. Work on initial two platforms has started.
- An RFI has been issued by the Navy in January 2018 for procurement of 57 new Multi-Role Carrier Borne Fighters (MRCBFs) for deployment onboard its aircraft carriers.
- The Defence Ministry has issued a global RFI to procure new amphibious aircraft for the Navy. Discussions are going on with Japanese firm ShinMaywa for its US-2i planes.
- Boeing has delivered three of the four additional P-8I maritime surveillance aircraft in 2021 (as part of a follow-on order placed in 2016). The Navy now has a fleet of 11 P-8Is. The Defence Acquisition Council in Nov 2019 had cleared a proposal to procure six more such platforms at an estimated cost of $1.8 billion. The air platforms would be armed with Harpoon air-launched anti-ship missiles and Mark54 lightweight torpedoes worth US$ 155 million, the procurement of which has been approved by the US Govt in April 2020.
- The Defence Acquisition Council (DAC) in 2018 approved procurement of 111 utility helicopters for the Navy at a cost of around $3.01 billion. The MoD in 2019 had invited proposals from local private-sector companies and foreign original equipment manufacturers (OEMs) to jointly build and deliver the platforms to Indian Navy. The Navy had issued the global RFI in 2017 for procurement of 111 utility helicopters. The RFI also included Navy's requirement for 123 Naval Multi Role Helicopter (NMRH) platforms to enhance its anti-submarine and anti-surface warfare capabilities. The NMRH procurement would be based on "Strategic Partnership" model.
- A government-to-government deal to procure MH-60 multi-role naval helicopters from the US at a cost of US$ 2.6 billion was approved by Indian Govt in February 2020. Under the deal, a total of 24 MH-60Rs would be procured under US's FMS route. The US DoD in May 2020 awarded a contract to Lockheed Martin/ Sikorsky to deliver the rotorcraft to Indian Navy. Delivery of first two platforms took place in July 2021.
- The DAC in 2019 approved a deal worth Rs 3,600 crore for acquisition of 10 Kamov Ka-31 Airborne Early Warning and Control helicopters from Russia. The AEW helicopters would be deployed on aircraft carriers and warships of the Navy including the indigenous aircraft carrier INS Vikrant.
- Six Russian-built Kamov-28 anti-submarine warfare helicopters are undergoing mid-life upgrade in Russia and equipped with new sensors and other systems. Four more of the platforms are getting engine overhaul. A contract worth nearly $300 million has been awarded to Russia's Rosoboronexport to modernize the platforms.
- Two MQ-9B SeaGuardian (non-weaponised) drones have been leased from the US in November 2020 under the Navy's "emergency procurement" provisions. Negotiations are already at an advanced stage with the US to procure up to 30 of the platforms with weapons for maritime surveillance purposes.
- Israel Aerospace Industries (IAI) is delivering Barak-8 LRSAM Air & Missile Defense systems for seven Indian Navy warships under a deal signed in 2018.
- Procurement of new short-range surface-to-air missiles (SR-SAM) is being planned. DRDO has developed and successfully tested the vertical launch short range surface-to-air missile (VL-SRSAM) in 2021 that could equip Indian naval warships.
- The US Govt in November 2019 had proposed foreign military sale of up to 13 MK-45 5-inch/62 caliber (MOD 4) naval guns and related equipment at an estimated cost of US$1.02 billion. Indian Navy is yet to finalise the purchase.
- Bharat Dynamics Ltd has delivered the first indigenously-built Varunastra heavyweight anti-submarine torpedo to the Navy in Nov 2020. BDL has been awarded a contract worth around Rs. 1,188 crore (in June 2019) to deliver over 100 such torpedoes to arm the Navy's frontline warships.
- The MoD has issued an RFP to four foreign firms in July 2019 for procurement of 100 heavyweight torpedoes to arm the six Kalvari (Scorpene)-class conventional attack submarines.
- In October 2020, the DRDO successfully flight tested the Supersonic Missile assisted release of Torpedo (SMART) system. SMART is a missile assisted release of lightweight anti-submarine torpedo system for anti-submarine warfare (ASW) operations for far beyond torpedo range. The technology would help in achieving stand-off capability in ASW environment.
- An advanced anti-torpedo decoy system called 'Maareech' capable of being fired from all frontline ships has been inducted. The decoy, designed and developed indigenously by DRDO, is capable of detecting, locating and neutralizing incoming torpedo.

AIR FORCE: Indian Air Force (IAF), the air arm of Indian defence forces, is primarily tasked to defend and secure national airspace and conduct aerial warfare operations during conflict situations. The IAF coordinates with other wings of Indian armed forces to carry out disaster relief operations and humanitarian assistance as well. It takes part in joint wargames with the Army and Navy and also holds aerial drills with air forces of friendly nations. Over the years, the IAF has grown from a "tactical force" to one with "transoceanic" reach. At a time when air power around the world has assumed increasing significance in deciding the outcome of military conflicts, the IAF too has embarked on an ambitious modernisation drive and reoriented itself to acquire multi-role capability of platforms and equipment, along with multi-skill capability of its personnel. Induction of new generation fighter aircraft, transport planes, refuelling tankers, trainers, helicopters, unmanned aerial platforms, advanced combat systems, radars and network centric warfare systems etc. along with upgradation of existing fleet of platforms and weapons have been taken up expeditiously with an aim to enhance and expand the IAF's operational capability and strategic outreach while preparing it to meet the rapidly evolving modern threats and challenges resulting from swiftly changing security scenario in the continent and beyond.

Major air bases: The IAF is divided into five major air commands – Western Air Command, Eastern Air Command, Central Air Command, Southern Air Command and South Western Air Command. It operates from over 50 air bases spread across the country.

Personnel: 1,50,000+

Equipment

Category	Name	In Service	On Order
Fighter/ Attack	Su 30MKI	250	200+
	Rafale	32	4
	Mirage 2000	47 (being upgraded)	
	MiG-29	59 (being upgraded)	21
	MiG-21	200+ (being phased out)	

Category	Name	In Service	On Order
Fighter/Attack	Jaguar	113	
	LCA Tejas	36 (Mk1 – IOC & FOC configurations)	20 (Mk1) & 83 (Mk1A)
Transport	IL-76	17 (to be upgraded)	
	C-130J	11	
	C-17 Globemaster III	11	
	An-32	55 (being upgraded)	
	Avro	56 (to be phased out)	
	Boeing 737		
	Dornier	40+	
	Embraer (VIP transport)		
Tanker, Trainer	IL-78MKI	6	
	Mid-air refueller		6
	HJT-16 Kiran	190	
	HJT-36 Sitara		70+
	HTT-40		106
	Hawk Mk. 132 AJT	123	
	Pilatus PC-7 Mk II	75	
AWACS, AEW&C	A-50 EI Phalcon	3	
	EMB 145 (Netra) AEW&C	2	1
	AWACS-I (A330)		2
Helicopter	Mi-17 & Mi-17V5	58 + 151	48 (Mi-17V5 proposed)
	Mi-26	3 (to be upgraded)	
	Mi-25/ Mi-35	15	
	LCH	3	62
	HAL LUH		61
	AH-64E Apache	22	
	Cheetah, Chetak	80+	
	ALH Dhruv	40	
	Chinook CH47F (I)	15	
UAV	Searcher II	100+	
	Heron	70	
	Heron (UCAV)		
	Harpy		
	Harop (UCAV)	50+	54
Surveillance Equipment	Aerostat	2	4

Category	Name	In Service	On Order
Weapon	S-13 (rocket)		
	SA-125 Pechora SAM		
	9K38 Igla MANPAD SAM		
	9K33 Osa-Akm SAM		
	SPYDER SAM		
	Akash SAM	2 squadrons	13 squadrons
	MRSAM	1 squadron	17 squadrons
	Land attack BRAHMOS		
	Air-launched BRAHMOS		
	Astra BVRAAM		248
	R-60 AAM		
	R-73, R-77 AAM		
	R-550 AAM		
	Prithvi-II SRBM		
	Mica AAM		500
	Hammer AGM		
	SCALP LACM		
	Meteor AAM		

New Procurements/Upgrades

◆ The Defence Ministry in July 2020 has approved urgent procurement of a total of 33 Russian-origin fighter platforms which includes 21 MiG-29 fighters (from Russia) and 12 Su-30MKI fighters (from Hindustan Aeronautics Ltd). Upgrade of existing fleet of MiG-29 fighters has also been announced. Russia's RAC MiG is comprehensively upgrading the MiG-29s. The procurement of 21 new MiG-29s and upgrade of existing fleet of MiG-29s is estimated to cost Rs 7,418 crore while the purchase of 12 new Su-30MKIs from HAL would be made at a cost of Rs 10,730 crore.

◆ France's Dassault Aviation is continuing the delivery of Rafale fighter platforms. The entire fleet (36) would be delivered by 2022. The first batch of the jets arrived in India on July 29, 2020. India inked a deal worth 7.87 billion Euro with France in Sept 2016 for 36 Rafales (30 fighters; 6 trainers). The contract followed an inter-governmental agreement inked between New Delhi and Paris in January 2016 to acquire the medium multi-role fighters from Dassault Aviation. The fighter platforms are armed with latest missiles and weapons and incorporated multiple India-specific modifications.

◆ Procurement of 114 multi-role fighter platforms is being planned under the 'Make In India' programme to replace the MiG-21 and (now retired) MiG-27 fighters.

◆ The second Squadron of indigenously-built Tejas Mk-1 Light Combat Aircraft (LCA) has been commissioned in May 2020. The squadron comprises of 20 LCA Tejas Mk-1 platforms in final operational clearance (FOC) configuration. More such platforms, built by HAL, would be inducted in service in coming years. The FOC variant features air-to-air refuelling capability, close combat gun, additional drop tanks, BVR missile capability among other upgrades. The first LCA Squadron (totalling 16) with IOC (initial operational capability) standard was operationalised in the IAF in July 2016. The Govt has also cleared procurement of 83 Tejas Mk-1A platforms which would be more capable versions and incorporate AESA radar among other improvements.

◆ Two long-term agreements have been signed in March 2017 between HAL with United Aircraft Corporation and United Engine Corporation of Russia for maintenance and life-cycle support of Russian-origin air platforms, including Su-30MKI fighters and Mi-17 helicopters of the IAF besides other platforms of Indian Army and Navy. The pacts provide for an upgraded schedule for delivery of spares from Russia for the jets, local manufacturing of parts and a proposed logistics hub for the fighter jets in Bengaluru by HAL.

◆ Acquisition of two additional Phalcon airborne warning and control systems (AWACS) from Israel at a cost of around US$ 1 billion is under active consideration. The IAF is currently operating three such platforms.

◆ The Defence Ministry in August 2020 has cleared the purchase of 106 of HAL-built basic trainer aircraft HTT-40.

◆ The Defence Ministry on Sept 24, 2021, awarded a contract at worth over Rs 21,000 crore to Airbus Defence and Space to deliver 56 C-295MW military transport aircraft to the IAF. The platforms would be jointly built Airbus Defence in partnership with Tata Advanced Systems Ltd (TASL). While 16 of the aircraft would be delivered in flyaway condition, 40 would be manufactured in India. The C-295s will replace the IAF's ageing fleet of Avro aircraft

◆ Govt has cleared IAF's proposal to upgrade its entire fleet of Russian-origin IL-76 transport aircraft with new avionics and re-fitting the fleet of IL-78 aerial refuelling aircraft with new engines at a cost of Rs.

4,300 crore. The upgrades could be carried out domestically after getting required permission from Russia.

◆ The IAF in 2018 issued an RFI to procure six flight refueller aircraft and associated equipment. No final decision has been made yet and the IAF is now considering to lease the platforms.

◆ An RFI has been issued by the IAF to procure seven "special mission" aircraft. While two of the aircraft would perform signals intelligence (SIGINT) role, the remaining five aircraft are to be configured for multi-mission role, supporting aerial survey, target towing, communications jamming (COMJAM) and flaring.

◆ A deal worth $5.5 billion has been awarded to Russia in October 2018 for the procurement of five S-400 Triumf air defence missile systems. The delivery has started in 2021.

◆ The highly advanced BRAHMOS air launched cruise missile (ALCM), designed and developed by BrahMos Aerospace, has received "fleet release clearance" (FRC) certification from Bengaluru-based Centre for Military Airworthiness and Certification (CEMILAC), DRDO in June 2020. The FRC certification has paved way for the pilots of Indian Air Force Squadrons to use the missile during live combat missions. The IAF, on January 20, 2020, commissioned the "TigerSharks" Squadron, deploying the deadly combination of Su-30MKI armed with the powerful BRAHMOS ALCM. Prior to its induction, the formidable air-launched cruise missile validated its impeccable precision attack capability against both sea and land-based targets form stand-off, beyond visual ranges in successful test firings conducted between 2017 and 2020.

◆ HAL is upgrading 47 of the Mirage-2000 fighter platforms, of which seven have been delivered in 2018. All upgraded platforms are likely to be delivered by 2023 – 24.

◆ 300 R-27 infrared-guided (IR) or semi-active radar-guided, medium-to-long-range missiles, 300 R-73E IR-guided, short-range missiles, and 400 R-77 active radar-guided, medium-range missiles have been ordered from Russia at a cost of $700 million in 2019 to arm the Su-30MKI and MiG fighter platforms.

◆ Six more Akash missile squadrons would be procured for the IAF, taking the total number of the indigenously-built air defence missile systems in the IAF's arsenal to 15 squadrons. The Govt has cleared the latest procurement worth Rs 5,000 crore in 2019. Meanwhile, Akash NG (new generation) – a new advanced variant of the SAM – has undergone successful test firings in 2021.

◆ Delivery of Medium Range Surface to Air Missile (MRSAM) system has started in September 2021.

◆ Rudram-1, India's first indigenously developed anti-radiation weapon, has been successfully test fired from the Sukhoi-30MKI fighter platform in October 2020. The new weapon, designed and developed by DRDO, is capable of destroying a wide variety of enemy radars, air defence systems and communication networks from large stand-off ranges. The missile would be integrated into a batch of Su-30MKI platforms of the IAF once it is ready for induction.

◆ On December 11, 2021, DRDO and IAF successfully tested the indigenously designed and developed Stand-off Anti-Tank (SANT) missile from a helicopter platform at the Pokhran test range. The weapon can neutralise targets in a range of up to 10 kms.

◆ A deal worth Rs 300 crore has been signed with Israel's Rafael Advanced Defense Systems in 2019 for over 100 of the SPICE 2000 guided bombs to arm the Mirage-2000 and Sukhoi-30 fighter platforms. First batch of the weapon has been delivered in Sept 2019.

◆ A £250 million contact with MBDA-UK has been signed for procurement of advanced short range air-to-air missiles (ASRAAM) for Jaguar fighters. Delivery has started. The IAF is also considering to adopt a new visual range variant of the AAM across its fighters' fleet.

◆ A deal has been signed with Russia in June 2019 for 9M120 Ataka anti-tank missiles to arm the IAF's fleet of Mil Mi-25/35 'Hind' attack helicopters.

◆ A proposal has been cleared in 2018 to procure 10 Heron TP armed drones from Israel. A number of Harop UCAVs have also been ordered from Israel in 2019.

◆ Negotiations are going on with the US to buy the armed Predator C Avenger drones.

STRATEGIC FORCES COMMAND: The Strategic Forces Command of Indian armed forces is responsible for the command and control of the country's tactical and strategic nuclear arsenal. Established in 2003, the SFC forms part of India's Nuclear Command Authority (NCA) which comprises the Political Council chaired by the Prime Minister and an Executive Council headed by the National Security Advisor. The SFC functions under the leadership of a Commander-in-Chief of the rank of Air Marshal (or its service equivalent). The Command works with experts at the Department of Atomic Energy (DAE) and the DRDO. It has the sole responsibility of initiating the process of delivering nuclear weapons and warheads only after securing explicit approval from the NCA as India remains committed to "no first use" of nuclear weapons doctrine.

Potential weapons: India's nuclear doctrine envisages building and maintaining a credible minimum deterrent posture with "second strike capability". The country has successfully built up a "credible and invulnerable" deterrent nuclear triad with retaliatory strike capability through weapon systems from land, air and sea. The potential weapons controlled by the SFC include the Agni and Prithvi family of missiles. Agni is a series of surface-to-surface ballistic missiles developed under India's Integrated Guided Missile Development Programme (IGMDP) in the 1990s. The indigenously-built strategic weapon system is capable of carrying both conventional and nuclear warheads. Prithvi is a short-range surface-to-surface ballistic missile. The single-stage, liquid-fuelled tactical weapon is capable of carrying nuclear warhead. India has also developed and tested submarine-launched ballistic missiles for its indigenously-built nuclear submarine.

Variants

◆ Agni-I is a short to intermediate range road mobile ballistic missile. The single-stage solid-propelled missile has an operational range between 700-km and 1200-km.

◆ Agni-II is a medium range ballistic missile (MRBM). The two-stage solid-propelled missile can hit targets 2,000 km away.

◆ Agni-III is an intermediate-range ballistic missile (IRBM) developed as the successor to Agni-II. The missile has a range of over 3,000 km.

◆ Agni-IV is a modification of Agni II series. It was initially developed as Agni-II Prime. The intermediate range missile has a strike range of about 4,000-km.

◆ Agni-V is an intercontinental ballistic missile (ICBM) having a range of 5,000-km. It is the first canistered road-mobile ballistic missile in India's military arsenal.

◆ Agni-P (prime), a new-generation canister-launched lightweight missile variant having range between 1,000 km and 2,000 km, has been successfully tested by DRDO in 2021.

◆ Prithvi-I is a short-range tactical missile with a range of 150-km.

◆ Prithvi-II is a single stage liquid-fuelled short range ballistic missile. The surface-to-surface missile has a strike range of 250-km to 350-km.

◆ Dhanush has been developed as the naval

variant of Prithvi ballistic missile system.

India has also successfully developed its first submarine-launched ballistic missile (SLBM) for the indigenously-built nuclear submarine (SSBN) INS Arihant. Development of underwater-launched ballistic missile in two variants – the longer-range K-4 (up to 3,500 km) and medium range K-15 (up to 700km) – has enabled India complete its nuclear triad under which it now has the capability to strike from air, land and beneath the sea. With the new DRDO-designed missiles in its arsenal, India has joined an elite club of nations including the US, Russia, UK, France and China who have developed such weapon systems for their armed forces.

In another historic milestone and world-record feat, India has also completed its supersonic cruise missile triad by developing and deploying the world's fastest and deadliest cruise missile BRAHMOS onboard the land, sea and air platforms of its military. The highly versatile BRAHMOS supersonic cruise missile having impeccable anti-ship and land-attack capability has been successfully inducted in the Indian Army, Navy and Air Force, thereby enormously bolstering India's modern warfighting capability against an adversary. The advanced BRAHMOS air-launched cruise missile (ALCM), which was inducted into the Indian Air Force on January 20, 2020 after undergoing successful test firings, has emerged as an unparalleled precision attack weapon in terms of range, lethality, and effectiveness among worldwide conventional airborne weapons. The ALCM has been integrated on the IAF's frontline Sukhoi-30MKI strike fighter.

INTEGRATED SPACE CELL: India officially announced the formation of an Integrated Space Cell (ISC) under the aegis of Integrated Defence Services Headquarters in June 2008. The ISC was created to counter growing threat to national space assets and act as a single window for integration among the Armed Forces, the Department of Space and the Indian Space Research Organisation (ISRO). The establishment of a Tri-Services Aerospace Command is also under consideration since early 2000s and the present Government is deliberating on the issue as part of articulating a national space policy in future. The current Government also finalised broad contours of a new Defence Space Agency (DSA) to develop capabilities to protect India's interests in outer space and deal with threats of space wars. The DSA comprising members of Indian Armed Forces was set up in November 2019. It would primarily be tasked with developing a range of platforms and co-orbital weapons to protect Indian assets in space and to have deterrence. The Govt has also established the Defence Space Research Agency (DSRA) under the DSA to carry out research & development related to military dimensions of use of outer space. All these developments have come after India successfully carried out its first Anti-Satellite (ASAT) weapon test in March 2019.

Major Armaments Developers & Producers

DEFENCE RESEARCH & DEVELOPMENT ORGANISATION (DRDO)

Established in 1958, the state-controlled DRDO is the premier defence research agency of India. It has a network of 50 dedicated defence laboratories all across the country which are engaged in developing critical defence technologies covering a wide array of disciplines ranging from aeronautics, armaments, electronics, combat vehicles, missile systems, engineering systems, electronic warfare systems, radar systems, laser technology, unmanned vehicles, military engineering, life sciences, advanced materials, composites, underwater sensors/weapons and platforms, warship technology to instrumentation, advanced computing, networking and simulation for the Indian armed forces. The defence organisation by its unflinching efforts has designed and produced independently as also with foreign collaboration a whole range of state-of-the-art weapon systems, platforms, sensors and allied equipment for all three wings of the Indian defence forces. Despite of the strict technology denial regime imposed on India by developed nations for several years, DRDO, after starting from the scratch, has made immense contributions to Indian military science and built up the country's defence apparatus in a major way.

In its initial years, DRDO primarily focused on developing basic military equipment and related services like small arms, explosives, machine gun, mountain gun and field gun, military psychology for selection of personnel, physiology for application by troops serving in harsh terrains and electronics systems. Later, it moved to the next stage by successfully developing radars and sonars, flight simulators and electronic warfare systems. In the third phase of its growth, the research agency focused on designing and developing major platforms and weapon systems like battle tanks, combat vehicles, nuclear submarines, supersonic fighter jets, ballistic missiles, radar & sonar systems and other equipment. Today, DRDO has achieved a distinct place in designing, developing and integrating modern military platforms and systems and positioned India as one of the technologically advancing countries not only in Asia but in the world. DRDO has tied up with about 40 academic institutions, 15 national Science and Technology agencies, 50 public sector undertakings and over 250 private sector enterprises to carry out research and development work and fulfilling its foremost objective of making India self-sufficient in defence production.

The defence organisation is presently working on several key projects that include indigenous aircraft carrier, nuclear submarine, guided missile destroyers, frigates, state-of-the-art weapon and systems for the Navy; advanced main battle tanks, combat vehicles and artillery systems for the Army; light combat aircraft, advanced medium combat aircraft and airborne early warning and control (AEW&C) system for the Air Force. It is also working on developing micro UAVs, unmanned combat aerial vehicle (UCAV) and Medium Altitude Long Endurance (MALE) UAV for the armed forces. The premier defence research institution is also designing and developing a wide array of sonar and radar systems alongwith other key system for Indian Defence Forces.

According to the Defence Ministry, DRDO has also been jointly working with a number of other countries, including Russia, Israel, Germany, France, USA, Belarus, Brazil and Singapore, to design and develop new sophisticated military platforms and systems. To further bolster its contribution towards making a self-reliant India in the defence sphere, as exhorted by Prime Minister Narendra Modi under the "Aatma Nirbhar Bharat" mission, DRDO has come up with a list of 108 defence items/technologies identified for local production by the domestic defence industry. Some of the major items on the list include NBC (nuclear, biological and chemical) shelters, missile canisters, navigation radars, satellite navigation receivers, mine-laying equipment, armoured engineering reconnaissance vehicles, mini & micro UAVs, fire detection systems, bullet proof vehicles, tank transporters among other items. The present industry base for DRDO consists of 1800 MSMEs along with defence public sector undertakings, Ordnance Factories (now reorganised into seven new DPSUs) and large scale industries.

Contribution in Aerospace Technology & Systems

LCA: The successful development of Light Combat Aircraft (LCA) Tejas for Indian defence forces is a major feat achieved by DRDO after several years of research work. The indigenous fighter platform has been developed by DRDO's Aeronautical Development Agency (ADA) in partnership with Hindustan Aeronautics Ltd. The project has also involved other DRDO & CSIR laboratories, public and private sector industries and academic institutions of India. The single-seat supersonic all-weather multi-role fourth-generation light fighter is being developed in different configurations for the IAF – Mk-I, Mk-IA and Mk-II. The lightweight jet having a tailless, compound delta wing design, is powered by a single engine. The Mk-I variant is powered by the General Electric F-404 turbofan engine. It is capable of flying at Mach 1.6 (about 2,000 km/h) and can conduct air-to-air, air-to-ground and air-to-sea combat operations. An upgraded variant of the platform would be the Mk-1A configuration having air-to-air refuelling capability and an AESA radar among other improved features. The more powerful Mk-II variant will be equipped with the GE F414 engine. The LCA will carry a wide variety of weapons including Beyond Visual Range (BVR) missiles, air-to-air and air-to-surface missiles, conventional and laser-guided bombs, air defence guns, counter-counter measures and drop tanks to take on surface targets over land or at sea. Two squadrons of LCA Tejas (Mk-1 configuration) have been inducted in the Indian Air Force as of 2020. A naval version of LCA has also been developed and is undergoing test flights for possible deployment onboard India's indigenous aircraft carriers in future.

AEW&C: To provide the IAF with an indigenous "eyes in the sky" capability, India has taken up the project of developing a state-of-the-art Airborne Early Warning and Control (AEW&C) system. Under the programme, DRDO's Bangalore-based Centre for Airborne Systems (CABS) laboratory has developed the internal and external mission systems for integration on-board the Brazilian Embraer-built EMB 145I aircraft. The CABS has developed over 300 mission system items, including the dummy Active Antenna Array Unit having an Active Electronically Scanned Array (AESA) radar for integration on the aircraft. The AEW&C System is mounted on top of the aircraft's fuselage. The indigenous AEW&C system is a multi-sensor system providing for all aspects of airborne early warning & control in present-day defence scenario. It is designed to detect, identify and classify threats present in the surveillance area and act as a command and control centre to support air operations. It can "look" around 270 degrees within a short time and has a range of 350 km.

The first AEW&C platform "Netra" was inducted in the IAF in 2017 while the second platform was delivered by DRDO to the IAF in September 2019. Work on the third system is advancing.

AWACS: DRDO has been entrusted with the task of developing an indigenous Airborne Warning and Control System (AWACS) with the capability to penetrate "longer distances" into the enemy territory by using radars and electronic warfare systems without actually venturing into the region physically. The AWACS, which will be different from the AEW&C system, will have a coverage area of about 360 degrees and it will fly at a higher altitude. It will remain in the sky for longer duration and will have better visibility. In March 2015, the Government approved development of two new AWACS platforms based on the European A330 aircraft. Negotiations with Airbus to acquire two A330 platforms for the programme is on.

UAVs: India has undertaken drone development programme for its military since the past few years. The remotely-controlled pilotless aircraft are being developed in various configurations to meet the needs of the Army, Navy and Air Force. DRDO has played a key role in developing these systems listed below.

Rustom: A Medium Altitude Long Endurance (MALE) UAV, Rustom is being developed by DRDO's Bangalore-based Aeronautical Development Establishment (ADE) in two variants – Rustom I and Rustom-II. The remotely-operated aircraft is capable of undertaking various military missions like reconnaissance and surveillance, target acquisition, target designation, communications, battle damage assessment and gathering signal intelligence. The UAV has been designed for the Indian Army, Navy and Air Force. Both Rustom-I (weighing 700-kg) and its advanced version Rustom-II have been undergoing flight tests. The two-ton Rustom-II has a payload capacity of 350-kg and an endurance of over 24 hours. It has an altitude ceiling of 35,000 feet and an operational range of 250-km.

Nishant: Designed and developed by DRDO's ADE lab, Nishant's role includes battlefield reconnaissance in day and night, surveillance, target tracking and correction of artillery fire. The electro optical, electronic intelligence and communication intelligence payload on-board the UAV make it suitable for a range of operations both during wartime and for counter-insurgency operations. The 380-kg drone can be launched from a hydro pneumatic launcher, without needing a runway and is recovered by parachute. It has an endurance level of five to eight hours and a payload capacity of 45-kg. The tactical UAV has an altitude ceiling of 3,600 km and an operational range of 150 km. The Army has started taking delivery of the new drones from DRDO.

Lakshya: The pilotless target aircraft Lakshya is one of the successful projects undertaken by ADE. The system is manufactured by HAL. The indigenously-built micro-light UAV is a reusable aerial target system which can realistically simulate an enemy aircraft for air-to-air and surface-to-air weapon system operators. Remotely operated from ground, Lakshya is used for the training of gun and missile crew and air defence pilots for all three Services. The subsonic single-engine UAV has a maximum speed of 857km/h and a range of 150 km. It can attain a height of 29,528 ft. It has been developed in two variants – Lakshya I and Lakshya II. DRDO has already delivered the aircraft with ground control and associated systems to the Armed Forces.

UCAV: Keeping pace with the leading global powers' effort to develop unmanned combat aerial vehicles, India too has put forth its endeavour to build one. Three DRDO laboratories – the Aeronautical Development Agency (ADA), the Aeronautical Development Establishments (ADE) and the Defence Avionics and Research Establishment (DARE) – have joined hands to design and develop the stealth UCAV 'Ghatak'. The combat drone, weighing around 15 tonnes, will fly at an altitude of 3,000 feet with combat payloads which would include missiles, bombs and precision guided munitions. It will have short take-off and landing capability on prepared runway.

Rotorcraft: DRDO has played a crucial role in the design and development of rotary-wing aircraft in HAL-led projects like advanced light helicopter (ALH) 'Dhruv', light combat helicopter (LCH) 'Rudra' and armed variant of ALH Dhruv, ALH Weapons System Integrated (ALH-WSI).

Contribution in Naval Technology & Systems

In the naval research domain, DRDO has designed and developed state-of-the-art underwater sensors, weapons and material. Three DRDO laboratories – the Naval Physical Oceanographic Laboratory (NPOL), the Naval Material Research Laboratory (NMRL), and the Naval Science & Technological Laboratory (NSTL) are exclusively dedicated to R&D activities in the field of naval technology. The NPOL is a key contributor in designing and developing a wide array of sonar systems like "HUMVAD" hull-mounted sonar, "Humsa" hull-mounted panoramic sonar, "Panchendriya" and "USHUS" submarine sonars, "Nagan" towed array sonar, "Mihir" airborne sonar for Indian Navy platforms.

Similarly, NSTL has indigenised a wide range of technologies in the field of underwater weapons by developing sophisticated torpedoes like "Varunastra" heavy weight torpedo, "Shyena" light torpedo, "Takshak" thermal torpedo, decoys, targets, counter measures, mines and fire control systems. Research work has also led to the creation of required infrastructure needed for developing and testing such weapons and systems. The NMRL has made key contribution in the field of naval materials technology like high capacity fuel cells, electrochemistry & electrochemical processes, polymer and polymer matrix, composites, elastomers. The Impressed Current Cathodic Protection (ICCP) technology developed by the laboratory to supplement the protection provided by paints to underwater structures against sea water corrosion is widely used by the Navy.

DRDO is also playing a critical role in producing several indigenised components and sub-systems for Navy's warships and submarines as well as equipping them with advanced weapon systems.

Contribution in Land Systems

DRDO has proved its dexterity in the field of combat vehicle and engineering by developing a wide range of multi-disciplinary systems including bridge layer tank, amphibious floating bridge & ferry system, anti-tank ammunition, mine field marking equipment, mortar carrier vehicle, armoured engineering reconnaissance vehicle and armoured amphibious dozer among others. A major achievement in this arena is the development of Arjun MBT for the Army. The MBT has been developed as a world-class combat vehicle and DRDO is presently working on an advanced variant of the MBT, to be called Arjun Mk II which will incorporate a total of 93 improvements, including its fire-power, laser protection suite and improved armoured protection for the vehicle. Besides, it is also developing a Futuristic Main Battle Tank (FMBT) for the Army which will feature stealth technology and more firepower. The Combat Vehicle Research and Development Establishment (CVRDE) is the leading lab dedicated for land systems development projects.

Contribution in Missile Technology

The missile technology programme of India led by DRDO has achieved great heights with the successful development of a number of strategic and tactical missile systems. The foremost among them is the Agni series of ballistic missiles. Developed under the Integrated Guided Missile Development Programme (IGMDP) of India, the Agni family today boasts of several variants – Agni I, Agni II, Agni III, Agni IV and Agni V. Other missile systems designed and developed by the research agency include Akash surface-to-air missile, Prithvi ballistic missile, Astra BVRAAM, BRAHMOS supersonic cruise missile (in partnership with Russia), and the K-4 & K-15 SLBM among others. It has also successfully developed a multi-layered ballistic missile defence (BMD) system.

ORDNANCE FACTORIES: The state-run defence firm was a conglomerate of 41 factories spread across India and engaged in the production of a range of armaments including machine guns, mortar guns, naval guns, ammunition, military vehicles, armoured vehicles like main battle tanks and NBT recce vehicles and related equipment for the Indian armed forces. The Govt in June 2021 approved a plan to dissolve the OFB and restructure it into seven new defence public sector undertakings to increase their efficiency and productivity. On Oct 1, 2021, OFB officially ceased to exist and was replaced by the new entities – Munitions India Ltd, Armoured Vehicles Nigam Ltd, Advanced Weapons and Equipment India Ltd, Troop Comforts Ltd, Yantra India Ltd, India Optel Ltd and Gliders India Ltd.

BHARAT DYNAMICS LTD: BDL manufactures munitions, torpedoes and missile systems for Indian armed forces. The first missile that entered production with BDL was the Prithvi surface-to-surface missile. The state-run firm is now creating infrastructure to enhance manufacturing of other missile systems, especially for the production of Akash air defence systems and Astra air-to-air missiles.

BHARAT ELECTRONICS: This public-sector enterprise produces a whole range of defence equipment, including electronic warfare systems, naval systems, communication systems, radars and weapon systems, for the Indian defence forces.

BEML LTD.: The company, partly owned by the Government, produces a number of defence equipment including TATRA vehicles, missile launchers, missile transporters, armoured recovery vehicles and light recovery vehicles among others. The company has initiated the process of setting up an Aerospace Manufacturing Division at SEZ Park near Bangalore International Airport, Devanahalli, which will pave the way for BEML to enter into aircraft and helicopter manufacturing sector. The company has also set up an Aerospace Manufacturing Division at Mysore and certified to design aircraft, helicopter and engine parts.

HINDUSTAN AERONAUTICS LTD.: India's leading public-sector aerospace company and one of Asia's largest, HAL has built up comprehensive skills in design, manufacture and overhaul of fighters, trainers, helicopters, transport aircraft, engines, avionics and system equipment.

COCHIN SHIPYARD LTD.: The CSL is the largest shipbuilder in the country capable of building and repairing large-sized naval vessels in India. The shipyard is presently building the indigenous aircraft carrier (IAC) for Indian Navy.

GARDEN REACH SHIPBUILDERS & ENGINEERS LTD.: The Government-run GRSE has emerged as a leading shipyard of India, building a wide range of naval vessels, including frigates, corvettes, landing craft, fast interceptor boats and survey ships.

GOA SHIPYARD LTD.: The state-run GSL is involved in designing and building a wide range of sophisticated naval vessels for varied applications in defence and commercial sectors with special expertise in building modern patrol vessels of steel and aluminium hull structure. It also undertakes repairing and modernisation of existing naval platforms. The shipyard's defence repertoire includes OPVs, interceptor craft, missile boat, fast attack craft, sail training ship and landing craft for Navy.

HINDUSTAN SHIPYARD LTD.: The Government-owned HSL is one of the premier shipbuilding organisations in the country catering to the needs of shipbuilding, ship repairs inclusive of sophisticated and state-of-art submarine retrofitting and construction of offshore vessels. The shipyard has built 150 ships and repaired nearly 1800 ships. Previously functioning under the Shipping Ministry, HSL was transferred to the Defence Ministry in 2009 to meet India's security needs and build strategic platforms for the Indian Navy.

MAZAGON DOCK LTD.: One of India's leading shipyards, the state-run MDL is engaged in constructing a wide range of naval platforms, including warships and submarines, as well as offshore platforms. It also undertakes ship repairing work.

LARSEN & TOUBRO LTD.: The leading private sector company in technology, engineering, construction and manufacturing has ventured into the production of defence systems for armed forces. The company has formed alliances with leading global defence firms to develop and market defence products in the fields of electronic warfare, radars and military avionics. It has also recently set up a shipyard at Kattupalli in Tamil Nadu which would enable India to compete globally in building large-sized warships, car carriers and submarines.

RELIANCE NAVAL & ENGINEERING LTD: Formerly known as Pipavav Defence, the private sector entity has been re-christened as Reliance Naval and Engineering Ltd (RNAVAL). The company, with the capability of building a range of naval platforms, has forayed into the defence sector and plans to build warships, submarines and aircraft carriers for Indian Navy in partnership with foreign firms.

ABG SHIPYARDS LTD.: The country's largest private ship-building company, ABL is a manufacturer and service provider for a variety of ships, including bulk carriers, diving support vessels, anchor handling supply ships, anchor handling tugs, and vessels for the defence forces like High speed Interceptor Boats and Pollution Control Vessels. The shipbuilder is currently building two cadet training vessels for Indian Navy.

DEFENCE DEALS

Joint Venture Programmes

Russia

BRAHMOS: World's only supersonic cruise missile system BRAHMOS is a joint venture programme between India and Russia. The two countries partnered to set up the JV company, BrahMos Aerospace, in 1998 to jointly design, develop, produce and market the Universal BRAHMOS weapon system. The tactical BRAHMOS having anti-ship and land-attack capability has been operationalised in the Indian Army, Navy and Air Force. Creating history, the formidable weapon in its highly advanced air-to-surface configuration was successfully test fired for the very first time from the Indian Air Force's Su-30MKI combat aircraft against a sea-surface target on November 22, 2017. On March 22, 2019, the formidable air-launched cruise missile validated its land-attack capability in a second test firing carried out from the Su-30 fighter followed by a third successful test firing on December 17, 2019 to revalidate its ship attack capability. On January 20, 2020, the Indian Air Force commissioned the "TigerSharks" squadron, deploying the BRAHMOS-armed Sukhoi-30MKI fighter aircraft, in Southern India to keep strategic vigil over the Indian Ocean Region.

Since its maiden successful test firing conducted on June 12, 2001, BRAHMOS has undergone a record number of over 80 test firings with an incredible success rate no other weapon of its genre has ever achieved worldwide. As a leading flagbearer of the ambitious "Make In India" (in defence) programme, BrahMos Aerospace over the years has achieved many milestones to incorporate indigenous content and technologies in the BRAHMOS weapon system to enhance national security and also to reduce the weapon's production costs. During a successful test firing of an advanced variant of the land-attack BRAHMOS conducted on 30th Sept, 2020, the weapon featuring indigenous booster and airframe along with other major "Made-In-India" technologies and sub-systems, met all mission objectives. The Indian Navy, on October 18, 2020, also conducted a successful test firing of naval variant of BRAHMOS from its stealth destroyer INS Chennai. The weapon, after performing high-level and extremely complex manoeuvres, successfully hit the target in the Arabian Sea with pin-point accuracy. In yet another successful launch on December 1, 2020, the weapon was tested from the Navy's 'Rajput class' stealth destroyer INS Ranvijay and successfully hit the target in Bay of Bengal. A series of BRAHMOS test firings were conducted successfully by the Indian Army, Navy and Air Force in the year 2020. In 2021, BrahMos Aerospace conducted successful test firings of BRAHMOS, including the air-launched cruise missile (ALCM) from Sukhoi-30MKI fighter platform on December 8. The ALCM featured major indigenous components, including metallic and non-metallic airframe sections comprising its ramjet fuel tank and pneumatic fuel supply system which are an integral part of the ramjet engine. "Structural integrity and functional performance" of the weapon was validated during the successful test firing, the Defence Ministry of India said, adding that the latest successful test firing has paved the way for serial production of the advanced BRAHMOS ALCM in India.

The highly successful BrahMos JV between India's DRDO and Russia's NPOM has opened up newer vistas for more such future joint venture projects between the two strategic allies with greater Indian industry participation. After successfully developing, testing and delivering BRAHMOS in different configurations to the Indian Armed Forces, BrahMos Aerospace would work on designing and developing a smaller, sleeker and lighter variant of BRAHMOS, to be called BRAHMOS-NG (next-generation). The new weapon, with reduced weight, size and dimensions along with higher speed, would be jointly developed by DRDO and NPOM for deployment onto a wider number of modern military platforms on land, sea and air.

Talwar class FFG: Two of the four Project 1135.6M (advanced Talwar-class) stealth frigates are being built for Indian Navy with Russian assistance. The platforms are being built at India's Goa Shipyard (GSL). Deliveries are slated from 2026 onwards. Russia is building two more such platforms.

Israel

LR-SAM: DRDO has jointly developed the Long Range Surface to Air Missile (LR-SAM) system in partnership with Israel Aerospace Industries (IAI) under an offsets contract signed in 2009. The missile has been developed as an advanced naval air defence system to arm Indian Navy warships. The missile has been deployed on the Navy's P-15A Kolkata class guided missile destroyers. The first successful test firing of the weapon, having a range of 70-km, took place on November 10, 2014 in Israel. State-run Bharat Electronics Ltd. (BEL), which had inked an MoU with IAI in December 2012 for cooperation in the programme under the aegis of DRDO, functions as the lead integrator and has produced major sub-systems for the missile while IAI continues to act as the design authority and produces sub-systems as main sub-contractor of BEL. Indian Navy received the first LR-SAM system in August 2017. The final production batch of the weapon was flagged off in February 2021.

MR-SAM: DRDO and IAI have jointly developed the Medium-Range Surface-to-Air Missile (MR-SAM) for the Indian Air Force. The IAF took delivery of the first MR-SAM system in September 2021. The missile is designed as an air defence weapon for the IAF. It is also being developed for Indian Army.

EW System: India and Israel have set up a joint venture to develop advanced electronic warfare (EW) systems for their air forces' fighter aircraft. The proposed joint venture has been signed between India's Defence Avionics Research Establishment (DARE), Bangalore and the Elisra Group, Bene Beraq, Israel.

Next-Gen Technologies: In November 2021, India and Israel inked the Bilateral Innovation Agreement (BIA) to jointly develop next-generation technologies and products such as drones, robotics, artificial intelligence and quantum computing. The agreement was signed between India's DRDO and Israel's Directorate of Defence Research and Development (DDR&D).

France

Scorpene: India's Mazagon Dockyards Limited (MDL) and French shipbuilder DCNS (now renamed 'Naval Group') are building and delivering six Scorpene submarines for Indian Navy. The agreement has incorporated Transfer of Technology to MDL.

Arms Import & Export

While striving to achieve indigenisation and self reliance in defence technology production, India has, nevertheless, relied on arms imports from foreign countries to meet its armed forces' requirements. The country depends on foreign suppliers for nearly 70% of its defence acquisition needs. According to a Stockholm International Peace Research Institute (SIPRI) report, India was the world's second largest arms importer after Saudi Arabia for the period between 2014 and 2018. Russia maintained a strong lead as the top-most defence supplier, accounting for 58% of India's total arms imports during that period, while Israel took the second spot with an import share of 15% followed by the US with 12% share. A large share of defence imports by India has been devoted to acquiring combat vehicles, warships, submarines, new generation fighter aircraft, helicopters, transport planes and other combat weapons from countries including Russia, Israel, US, UK, France and Germany. In 2019, India's defence expenditure stood at US$ 71.1 billion, which was third highest after that of the US and China.

In its latest report published in 2021, SPIRI has noted a decrease in India's arms imports by 33% between 2011 and 2015, and 2016 and 2020. Russia was the most affected supplier, although India's imports of US arms also fell by 46%, the report states.

In this backdrop, attaining self-reliance in defence design, development and production, especially at a critical time when the country's armed forces are undergoing large-scale modernisation and transformation, has become a major focus area for New Delhi. The country is making steady progress in this direction and has been successful to some extent in developing critical defence technologies covering wide areas including weapons and armaments, electronics, combat vehicles, missile systems, engineering systems, electronic warfare systems, radars, military engineering, warship technology, aeronautics, avionics, unmanned aerial systems etc. To further accelerate the pace of indigenisation in the defence sector, the Government has announced several major policy decisions in the past few years, including raising the FDI limit in defence sector from 26% to 100% (on case-to-case basis); streamlining defence industrial licensing processes; creating a level-playing field for both private and public sector entities in payment and tax matters;

a standard operating procedure (SOP) for using MoD-owned trial/ testing facilities by the private sector; and a simplified and streamlined DPP (Defence Procurement Procedure) among many other necessary measures. The MoD has also initiated efforts to boost indigenous defence production by allowing private sector Indian defence firms to form "Strategic Partnership" under the DPP with leading foreign firms to develop and produce cutting-edge military platforms and systems for Indian military. Additionally, it has announced a number of initiatives to support start-ups and innovations in the country, including approving a budgetary support of nearly Rs 499 crore for research and innovation in the defence sector for next five years. The funds would be used to provide financial support to nearly 300 start-ups, micro, small and medium enterprises (MSMEs) and individual innovators with a larger goal of ensuring self-reliance in defence sector.

In key policy initiatives announced in May 2020, the Government permitted foreign direct investment (FDI) of up to 74% (from previous 49%) under 'automatic route' in defence manufacturing sector in order to attract overseas investors. However, foreign investments in defence sector would be subject to scrutiny on the grounds of national security and the Government would have the right to review any foreign investment in the sector that affects or may affect national security. Previously, the Government had permitted 100% overseas investments in the Indian defence industry – 49% under 'automatic route', while for beyond that, Government's approval was required.

In May 2020, the Defence Ministry unveiled the Defence Testing Infrastructure Scheme (DTIS) under which state-of-the-art testing infrastructure would be developed at a cost of Rs 400 crore to help the domestic military firms carry out testing of indigenously developed military hardware in the country. The scheme would run for a duration of five years and envisages to set up six to eight new testing facilities in partnership with the private industry.

Amidst a highly volatile neighbourhood and frequent border escalations, the Defence Ministry has also granted more procurement powers to the Armed Forces to meet their emergency requirements. The special powers granted to the three armed services makes provision for individual capital procurement programme worth Rs 300 crore to meet their "emergent operational requirements."

The MoD in August 2020 unveiled the ambitious 'Defence Production & Export Promotion Policy (DPEPP) 2020' that aims at an indigenous arms production turnover of worth Rs 1,75,000 crore (US$25 billion), including exports of US$5 billion in aerospace and defence goods and services, by 2025. It has subsequently come out with a list of 152 equipment/ sub-systems/ items for export. Some of the top items featured in the list include the BRAHMOS supersonic cruise missile system, Akash air defence system, LCA Tejas, Advanced Towed Artillery Gun System (ATAGS), Pinaka multi-barrel rocket launchers among others.

The Government has also launched two Defence Industrial Corridors – one in Tamil Nadu and the other in Uttar Pradesh – with an initial investment of over Rs 6,800 crore.

The Government's flagship "Make-In-India" programme is aimed at large-scale indigenisation of defence products and systems by the domestic defence industry in the coming years. In a latest report, the Defence Ministry has highlighted some improvements in domestic defence production. It states that the value of defence production recorded by state-owned defence public sector undertakings (DPSUs) including HAL, BEL, OFB etc. increased by 27% between 2014 and 2018. The Department of Defence Production under the MoD set a target of producing equipment worth Rs 90,000 crore in FY 2019-20. In FY 2018-19, the Department had produced equipment worth Rs 80,502 crore.

At the exports front, defence exports by the country, mostly critical components in aerospace sector, witnessed a steady rise. The latest official figures put it at Rs 10,745 crore in FY 2018-19; Rs 9,116 crore in 2019-20; and Rs 8,434 crore in 2020-21. India's overall exports of military hardware and systems in the last seven years stood at worth Rs 35,777 crore, the MoD report mentions.

Indian Defence public sector undertakings have exported products to several countries including the US, UK, Canada, China, Israel, Germany and France. The countries in the Indian subcontinent to which defence products have been exported include Bangladesh, Bhutan, Myanmar, Nepal, Sri Lanka, Afghanistan and Seychelles. With its expanding indigenous military industrial base, India is now eyeing to grab a fair share of the lucrative international defence market and has initiated all-round efforts to sell its cutting-edge military hardware, including missiles, fighter aircraft, helicopters, naval vessels and other equipment to several countries across continents. In 2020, India received a contract worth US$40 million to deliver four indigenously-built Swathi weapon locating radars to Armenia.

DEFENCE BUDGET

Defence spending by India over the past few years has witnessed an upward trajectory, mainly because of all-round modernisation of its armed forces. A large share of the defence budget also goes for the huge manpower as India maintains one of the largest armed forces in the world in terms of personnel strength.

The annual defence allocation has remained around 2 per cent of the country's GDP in the last few years. As the country is rising economically, maintaining a military edge in the Asian region as well as at the world stage has necessitated increased defence spending by New Delhi.

The Government had allocated Rs. 2,95,511.41 crore to defence for FY 2018-19 which was later revised to Rs. 2,98,418 crore. For FY 2019-20, Government earmarked Rs 3,18,931 crore towards defence expenses which was an increase of 6.87% over previous year's (revised) budget of 2.98 lakh crore. The budget was later revised to 3.31 lakh crore (FY 2019 - 20). For 2021 - 22 period, Government has allocated Rs 4.78 lakh crore for defence as against previous year's (2020 – 2021) allocation of Rs 4.71 lakh crore (revised figures). The budget for 2021 – 22 is 1.63% of national GDP and an increase of 1.4% over previous fiscal.

Official Budgetary Allocation

Year	Allocation	% of GDP	% Increase over previous year
2021-22	Rs 4.78 lakh crore	1.63	1.4
2020-21	Rs 4.71 lakh crore (revised)	1.5	1.8
2019-20	Rs. 3.31 lakh crore (revised)	1.6	6.87
2018-19	Rs. 2.98 lakh crore (revised)	1.49	7.8
2017-18	Rs. 2.74 lakh crore ($40.6 billion)	1.56	5.8
2016-17	Rs. 2.58 lakh crore	1.65	13.1
2015-16	Rs. 2.46 lakh crore ($40.4 billion)	1.75	7.74
2014-15	Rs. 2.29 lakh cr ($38.35 billion)	1.81	12.5
2013-14	Rs. 2.03 lakh cr ($37.4 billion)	1.79	5.31
2012-13	Rs 1.93 lakh cr ($41 billion)	1.90	17

COUNTER-TERRORISM & NATIONAL SECURITY

In the past two centuries, terrorism has emerged as one of the deadliest threats to global peace, stability and security. While many nations across the world today are grappling with terrorism and terror-related violence, India has witnessed grisly terror attacks on its soil post independence. The decades-long, deeply entrenched menace of terrorism in India can be traced back to 1947 when India and Pakistan became two separate nations post-partition, and Kashmir became the heart of the problem between them. Despite Kashmir's lawful accession to India, Pakistan refused to accept the same and became the perpetrator of cross-border terrorism as a means of waging a 'proxy war' against India. The scourge of 'state-sponsored' terrorism since then has not only been aimed at destabilising Jammu & Kashmir alone, but disrupted internal peace, harmony and stability in other parts of India as well. Many deadly terror attacks on India have resulted in loss of lives and large-scale devastation, raising international concern and condemnation.

While the term terrorism having "ancient roots" has received different connotations at different times of history in different places worldwide, in the contemporary world, terrorism made its appearance in the 19th century. And terrorism or militancy as a form of starting an asymmetric conflict against a nation has affected India the most. In fact, India has witnessed almost all forms of terrorism in modern times, ranging from suicide bombings to hijacking of civilian aircraft to attacks on political, financial and religious institutions. The increasing use of small drones by terrorist organisations to intrude into Indian airspace and drop small arms and weapons or carry out air-borne attacks in recent times has alerted the authorities against such deadly tactics of waging low-cost, asymmetric war against the nation. Both state-sponsored (by Pakistan) and non-state actors, driven by political, ideological or religious "agenda", have targeted civilians, security and military personnel as well as groups/ institutions and posed a serious threat to national security.

This chapter comprehensively focuses on terrorism, militancy and insurgency-related extremist violence that have afflicted India's peace, security and sovereignty for over the past seven decades. It also highlights counter-terrorism and counter-insurgency efforts undertaken by the Government to deal with the deep-rooted menace.

Types of Terrorism

India has grappled with cross-border terrorism, Islamic terrorism and separatist terrorism. In recent times, cyber terrorism and hybrid terrorism have also afflicted the country's security.

Cross-border terrorism: In the 1980s, Pakistan started pushing its well-trained armed militants into the Indian territory through the Line of Control (LoC) to carry out attacks against military personnel and civilians. The militant outfits used illicit weapons smuggled across the country's porous borders to perpetrate terror and violence. While the erstwhile state of Jammu & Kashmir (presently Union Territory) became worst affected by cross-border terrorism and infiltrations by both state and non-state terror groups acting on behest of Pakistan, the militants carried out deadly attacks on other parts of India too with an intent to disrupt internal peace, harmony and territorial integrity. Many state-sponsored terror groups having their bases in Pakistan and receiving financial help along with training, weapons and equipment, have continued to perpetuate terror and violence in India. Continuing such a proxy war through state-sponsored terrorism has, in fact, formed the very core of Pakistan's ideology and part of its asymmetric warfare strategy against India.

According to a recently released report by the US Congressional Research Service (CRS), an independent think-tank, Pakistan is home to at least 12 groups designated as 'foreign terrorist organisations', including five of them being India- and Kashmir-centric like Lashkar-e-Taiba (LeT), Jaish-e-Mohammed (JeM), Hizb-ul Mujahideen (HM) among others.

The Government of India has listed a total of 42 terrorist organisations (including indigenous armed insurgency groups) in the First Schedule of Unlawful Activities (Prevention) Act, 1967. The Government has banned these outfits for their involvement in various acts of terrorism within the country. Pakistan-sponsored LeT and JeM feature in the list among others.

Islamic terrorism: This form of terrorism has emanated from both within and outside of India. While India's immediate neighbourhood comprising Muslim majority nations (Pakistan, Afghanistan, Bangladesh) has a direct bearing on the spread of Islamic militancy in India, with Pakistan playing most prominent role, radicalisation of Indian Muslims, mainly from Kashmir, has been the root cause of Islamic terrorism inside the country. The radicalised Islamic youth population has often crossed over to Pakistan to receive finances, training, arms & weapons to carry out terror attacks within India. Even as Islamic terrorism has spread to almost all parts of the world today, India remains its biggest victim wherein scores of innocent civilians and military personnel have lost their lives to it. Ironically, it is India's history (repeated Islamic invasions of Indian subcontinent between 12th and 16th century, and eventual 1947 India-Pakistan partition), and its geography (position in South Asia) that have led to the malignant spread of Islamic terrorism in the region and beyond.

Separatist terrorism: Also termed as nationalist / ethno-nationalist terrorism, this form of militancy uses acts of terror and violence with an intent to forcefully create a separate state or nation. Such kind of terrorism essentially seeks 'self-rule' and 'self-determination' for its followers/ propagators. Separatist ideology has spread to many parts of the world in 21st century, and India too is affected by such form of terrorism. Two major terror outfits driven by their "secessionist agenda" which have disrupted peace and harmony within India are the Khalistani group involving the miniscule radicalised Sikh community, and the Kashmir-centric separatist group involving radical Muslims, mostly from Kashmir.

The Khalistani separatist movement found its roots during British colonialism in India and it became all the more evident with the partition of India and Pakistan in 1947 (partly on the basis of religion). The movement gained strength in the early 1980s and continued till the 1990s with the agenda to carve out a separate, sovereign state (Khalistan) for the Sikh community residing in the Indian state of Punjab. The Indian Government has banned few outfits – Babbar Khalsa International, Khalistan Commando Force, Khalistan Zindabad Force, and International Sikh Youth Federation – having purported affiliation to the Khalistani movement. However, many separatist Khalistani groups have continued to receive tacit and often explicit support from Pakistan as also from few other countries internationally to carry out anti-India activities. The movement is largely subdued within India, but the Sikh diaspora residing outside of India has often got political and financial backing to keep the pro-Khalistan secessionist agenda alive.

The Kashmir-centric separatist groups, mostly politically backed by Pakistan, have run vociferous and often vicious campaigns since long to either merge the region with (Muslim-majority) Pakistan or create an independent, self-ruled state out of Jammu & Kashmir. Some leading separatist entities include the All Party Hurriyat Conference (a conglomerate of 26 groups started in 1993 which later split into two factions in 2005), the Jammu and Kashmir Liberation Front (JKLF) and the Jamat-E-Islami. In 2019, the Government of India under the Unlawful Activities [Prevention] Act (UAPA) banned the JKLF and the Jamat-E-Islami. In 2021, the Government was also considering to list both factions of the Hurriyat Conference under the UAPA.

Cyber Terrorism: Such form of terrorism, where terrorist and radical groups worldwide have exploited new-age information and communications technologies in a highly globalised society to build terror networks, incite violence, plan and execute acts of terror, recruit people and do terror funding etc., has spread swiftly in over the past two decades. The terror groups have also rampantly used the internet, especially social media to influence opinions, foment communal tensions and violence, radicalise and recruit youth cadres to carry out cyber espionage, hacking and other forms of cyber attacks against government agencies, organisations and individuals/ groups as also to disrupt critical national and military infrastructure. India has been confronting cyber attacks and disinformation campaigns by both state and non-state actors as a contemporary form of terrorism intended to wage low-cost, asymmetric warfare. The state-sponsored cyber attacks as part of cross-border terrorism have also disturbed internal peace and security. Terrorist groups have used cyberspace to carry out some major attacks within India, including the 26/11 Mumbai attack in 2008.

Hybrid Terrorism: The Indian military establishment has defined "hybrid" terrorists as the ones "who are not listed as ultras but are radicalised enough to carry out a terror strike and then slip back into routine life." The hybrid terrorists are not listed as ultras in the military records, but are radicalised enough to carry out terror attacks and then slip back into their routine self. Such "part-time" terrorists spreading terror and fear by carrying out attacks on 'soft targets', such as civilians and unarmed police/ security personnel etc., have posed a new challenge to the security establishment of late, especially in the Kashmir valley.

Terror Outfits

The major terror outfits working against India are mostly based in Pakistan and Pakistan-occupied-Kashmir (PoK). These include the Lashkar-e-Taiba (LeT), Jaish-e-Mohammed (JeM), Harkat-Ul-Mujahideen (HuM), Hizb-ul Mujahideen (HM) and Al-Umar-Mujahideen (AUM). Global militant outfits such as the Al-Qaida/ Al-Qaida in Indian Sub-continent (AQIS) and the Islamic State (ISIS) have also been included among major terrorist organisations that have been banned by the Indian Government under the UAPA. Some terror groups are also clandestinely operating from within India, mostly from Jammu & Kashmir region, to carry out disruptive activities at the behest of Pakistan and its wide terror network. Few such outfits include the Jamiat-ul-Mujahideen (India), Al Badr, Jammu and Kashmir Islamic Front (JKIF) [operating from both India and PoK], and the Students Islamic Movement of India (SIMI) – an Islamist fundamentalist organisation involving extremist youth population. These terror organisations have been involved in planning and executing major terror attacks against India.

Pakistan has also created Border Action Team (BAT) – an informal unit of Pakistan Army involving army commandos and terrorists to carry out cross-border operations across the Line of Control (LoC). Having expertise in guerrilla warfare tactics and being trained by the Pakistan Army and Air Force, the BAT members operating under the Special Service Group (SSG) of Pakistan Army have perpetuated terror and violence inside Kashmir valley by targetting civilians as well as security personnel.

Major Terror-related Incidents

India has faced terrorism in its most widest, deadliest and ugliest forms with ghastly attacks occurring in many parts of the country at regular intervals, including in national capital Delhi and financial capital Mumbai. According to a Government data released in 2016, a string of terror strikes in India since 2005 had claimed 707 lives and wounded over 3,200 people. The figure has further gone up with grim terror attacks happening as recently as 2016 and 2019 in the Kashmir valley targetting military and security personnel. Terrorists have continued to target civilians in Kashmir despite the Government's efforts for all-round development to restore peace, security and prosperity in the trouble-torn region.

Some major terror incidents in over the past three decades that not only shook the very core of India, but also raised global concern and condemnation include the following:

1985 Air India 'Kanishka' flight bombing: The incident that occurred soon after the 1984 'Operation Blue Star' to flush out militants from the Golden Temple has been blamed on Sikh radical elements spearheading the Khalistan movement. The Montreal-New Delhi Air India 'Kanishka' Flight-182 exploded 45 minutes prior to its landing at London's Heathrow airport on June 23, 1985, killing all 329 people on board, majority of them being Canadians of Indian descent. The flight exploded at around 31,000 feet off the Irish coast as a bomb planted inside the plane by radical Khalistan separatist elements went off. The bombing, one of the world's deadliest acts of terrorism involving a civilian aircraft, was the result of "a conspiracy conceived, planned and executed in Canada," investigations into the incident later revealed. The terror attack is marked as 'National Day of Remembrance for Victims of Terrorism' every year in Canada.

1993 Bombay blasts: The deadly terror attack took place in India's financial capital Mumbai (then Bombay) on March 12, 1993. A series of twelve bombs went off within a span of just over two hours that rocked several parts of the city, killing over 250 people and wounding many others. The explosions were the first large-scale coordinated terror attacks carried out in India where powerful RDX was used as an explosive. One of the time-bombs targeted the Bombay Stock Exchange (BSE) building while the other bombs planted at different locations hit hotels, banks, offices and market complexes at brief intervals.

1998 Coimbatore bombings: The serial bomb blasts took place in the city of Coimbatore, Tamil Nadu on February 14, 1998 in which around 60 people were killed and over 200 others injured. A total of 12 bombs exploded at 11 places, all within a radius of 12 kilometre. The explosives used in the blasts were gelatin sticks, which were activated by timer devices concealed in cars, motorcycles, bicycles, vegetable carts and bags. Several other bombs that failed to detonate were later defused by bomb disposal squads. The Coimbatore terror attacks were in many ways similar to the 1993 Bombay serial blasts.

1999 Air India flight IC-814 hijack: The Indian Airlines flight IC-814 flying from Kathmandu to New Delhi with 179 passengers onboard, including 24 foreigners and 11 crew members, was hijacked by five masked men on December 24, 1999, 45 minutes after its take off. The hijack happened soon after the aircraft had entered Indian airspace. After making the plane land at Amritsar (India), Lahore (Pakistan), and at the Al Minhad Air Base (UAE) for refuelling, the hijackers took the aircraft to Kandahar in Afghanistan. The armed militants were carrying weapons, including rocket launcher. The hijacking incident was orchestrated by Afghanistan-based Taliban terror outfit to secure the release of Islamist terrorists who were imprisoned in India then. After several rounds of negotiations spanning for seven days, the Indian Government finally decided to release three terrorists, including Maulana Masood Azhar – the founder of Jaish-e-Mohammed (JeM), lodged in Indian prison in exchange for the safe return of all the passengers held hostage by the militants. One of the passengers was killed in the hostage crisis while the others were freed safely.

2001 Parliament building attack: In one of the most audacious attacks carried out on India's "temple of democracy", the Parliament, a five-member suicide squad comprising terrorists from Pakistan-based and supported LeT and JeM infiltrated into the high-security zone on December 13, 2001. The terrorists entered the Parliament premises when the Lok Sabha (lower house) was in session with several Parliamentarians and other officials present inside the building. The gunmen, armed with AK-47 rifles and grenades and riding in an Ambassador car, had gained entry into the Parliament complex by showing forged government sticker. Highly alert security personnel of Delhi police and CRPF prevented the terrorists from executing their nefarious plans and all five terrorists were eventually neutralised after a gun battle that lasted for over half an hour. All ministers and MPs inside the Parliament building were unhurt. However, eight people, including security personnel and a photojournalist, lost their life in the terror incident. At least 15 others were injured.

2002 Gujarat Akshardham temple bombing: Two terrorists targeted the Swaminarayan Akshardham temple complex in Gujarat's Gandhinagar district on September 24, 2002. Thirty three people were killed and over 80 others injured in the ghastly incident. Carrying automatic weapons and grenades, the militants went on a rampage and indiscriminately fired at pilgrims and visitors present inside the temple premises. India's National Security Guard (NSG) commandos later took charge of the situation and neutralised both terrorists the following day.

2005 Delhi bombings: The national capital of India witnessed a series of deadly terror blasts on the evening of October 29, 2005 – just a day before Diwali. The multiple bomb-blasts at several places, including in Sarojini Nagar market, at Paharganj railway station and in a DTC bus in Govindpuri – used sophisticated timer devices and RDX. The blasts killed 66 people and wounded over 200 others. Pakistan-based Islamist terrorist organisation, the Islamic Revolutionary Front, claimed responsibility for the attacks. However, Indian investigators believed that Pakistan-based terror outfit, either LeT or JeM, was behind the well-orchestrated, near simultaneous deadly bomb blasts.

2006 Mumbai train bombings: In yet another horrifying attack targeting India's financial capital Mumbai, a series of seven bombs exploded in quick succession within a span of eleven minutes on July 11, 2006. The serial blasts took place on crowded suburban trains plying within the city and killed over 200 people. More than 700 others were injured in the brutal terror attack which was carried out using pressure cooker bombs planted inside first class general compartments of the Mumbai local trains. The explosives used in the blasts were a mixture of RDX and ammonium nitrate. On July 14, 2006, Lashkar-e-Qahhar, a terrorist organisation believed to be linked to LeT, claimed responsibility for the bombings.

2008 Ahmedabad bombings: As many as 21 bombs exploded in Gujarat's Ahmedabad city on July 26, 2008, killing over 50 people and injuring 200 others. The low-intensity blasts took place mostly in crowded area. The bombs were planted in tiffin carriers on bicycles and inside city buses. Two unexploded bombs and other explosive material recovered later from cars were diffused. Terror outfit Indian Mujahideen claimed responsibility for the blasts. Another Islamic militant group (Harkat-ul-Jihad-al-Islami) also claimed responsibility for the bomb attack.

2008 series of attacks in Mumbai: Terror, violence, bloodshed struck Mumbai yet again on November 26, 2008 when a 10-member LeT group launched a scathing, well-coordinated attack at five prominent places in the city. The wave of attacks, also referred to as 26/11 terror attack, took place at the Chhatrapati Shivaji Terminus railway station, Cama Hospital, Nariman House business and residential complex, Leopold Cafe, Taj Hotel & Tower and the Oberoi-Trident Hotel. The terrorists, carrying automatic weapons and grenades, had reached Mumbai on a hijacked fishing trawler from a Pakistani port in Karachi. The vicious attacks lasted for four days in which a total of 166 people lost their lives while over 300 others were injured. While nine of the terrorists were killed in armed operations undertaken by Indian security personnel, including Marine Commandos and NSG commandos, one terrorist (Ajmal Kasab) was captured alive and later executed in November 2012.

2011 Mumbai bombings: Three blasts rocked Mumbai on July 13, 2011 in which 26 people were killed and over 100 injured. The bomb blasts occurred at the Opera House, at Zaveri Bazaar and at Dadar West localities of the city. The bombs, containing IED explosives, were planted on a motorcycle, in a tiffin box and on an electric pole. The role of Indian Mujahideen and LeT was suspected in the blasts, even as no terror outfit claimed responsibility for the blasts.

2016 Uri attack: In one of the worst attacks targeting Indian Army personnel deployed in Jammu & Kashmir, a group of four heavily armed terrorists launched a massive grenade attack in one of the Army's administrative bases at the Uri sector on September 18, 2016. In a pre-dawn ambush, the militants struck the Army camp after breaching tight security cover. 19 soldiers of Indian Army were martyred in the incident while several others were injured. The attack was suspected to be carried out by Pakistan-based LeT terror group. All four terrorists were subsequently neutralised following a six-hour long gun battle with Indian Army personnel. Prior to the 2016 attack, terrorists had attacked Indian Army camp at Mohura, Uri in December 2014, killing nine Army personnel. The 2016 Uri attack was one of the worst attacks on Indian military personnel in J&K in nearly two decades. India avenged the deadly attack eleven days later by carrying out a surgical strike on terror launchpads in the Pakistan-occupied-Kashmir (PoK) region. On September 29, 2016, Indian Army troops including commandos from various units of the Para (Special Forces) units deployed in Jammu and Kashmir carried out raids across the border on multiple targets. The forces crossed the Line of Control (LoC) as part of the highly covert surgical strike operation to annihilate terror camps based deep inside PoK.

2019 Pulwama attack: The deadly fidayeen (suicide bombing) attack was targetted at India's Central Reserve Police Force (CRPF) personnel in Pulwama district of Jammu & Kashmir. A total of 40 security personnel lost their lives in the ghastly terror attack in which an explosives-laden car hit a CRPF convoy travelling on the Jammu-Srinagar National Highway on the afternoon of February 14, 2019. The suicide bomber was a local Kashmiri youth and a member of the JeM terror outfit which later claimed responsibility for the fidayeen attack. On February 26, 2019, India launched an aerial strike in Pakistan's Balakot region, targetting JeM terror camps located in the area. The air raid was carried out based on intelligence inputs provided by Indian agencies that JeM was planning more suicide terror attacks inside India. It was for the first time post the 1971 war that India used its air power wherein the Indian Air Force fighter platforms crossed over the LoC and entered inside Pakistani territory to carry out precision strikes against the JeM terror camps. The aerial raid was termed by India as "intelligence-based, non-military, pre-emptive strike".

Insurgency & Left Wing Extremism

India's internal security apparatus has been affected by insurgency related violence in north-eastern parts of the country. Left-wing extremism (LWE) and naxal-related violent incidents have also hit many other parts of the country, mostly hinterland. The primary causes of insurgency and left-wing extremism are either political, ethnic, linguistic, identity-driven, ideological, or socio-economic backwardness. The Government of India, under the UAPA, has outlawed many outfits involved in carrying out insurgency and Naxal-related violence in the country, including targeting security personnel and civilian population.

Insurgency in north-east India: The majority of India's north-eastern states have been afflicted by insurgency for nearly seven decades, wherein militant outfits have been involved in intermittent acts of armed violence, and at times, resorted to guerilla warfare tactics, in order to achieve their stated objectives. Militant activities of many underground groups and ethnic divisions have created disturbances in north-eastern region having wide diversity based on language, social systems, customs, traditions, economic conditions etc. The insurgency involving the Naga tribe of Nagaland demanding sovereign identity, insurgency over the demand for creation of Bodoland consisting of Bodo tribes by dividing Assam, the separatist rebel groups of Manipur and armed insurgency in Assam primarily led by ULFA for establishing a sovereign state for the indigenous people of Assam has often led to large-scale violence, loss of lives and property in the region. Indian Armed Forces and other security personnel have been deployed in the region to quell any kind of unrest. According to recently released data by the Union Home Ministry, insurgency-related incidents in the north-eastern states have sharply dipped by almost 80 per cent. The overall security situation in Assam, Arunachal Pradesh, Manipur, Meghalaya, Mizoram, Nagaland, and Tripura has improved to satisfactory level, and civilian deaths have reduced by over 90 per cent, while that of the security personnel has gone down by 75 per cent, the data states.

Left Wing Extremism & Naxal-related violence: Left-wing extremism or Maoist ideology has perpetuated India's hinterland primarily because of social injustice, poverty, unemployment, lack of development and exploitation of the poor, uneducated and tribal population. By using violence and force, the armed Maoists / Naxalites have killed scores of security forces and civilians in eastern, central and southern parts of India which forms the "red corridor". Even as the Maoist problem has subsides over the years with latest Government figures indicating relative decline in LWE-related violence, nevertheless, the menace has not been completely eradicated as the Maoists are now exploring the possibility of a transition in their geographical area of operation by making inroads into newer regions/districts. According to latest Government record, a total of 70 districts in 10 states are currently affected by LWE and related violence. Of these, 25 districts in eight states are categorised as "most affected". With all-round development in the LWE-affected areas in addition to strict vigilance and other coordinated measures by both state and central security forces, the LWE problem is being tackled steadily and effectively.

Combating Terrorism & Extremism

Afflicted by both cross-border terrorism and radicalisation within the country in addition to the home-grown insurgency and Maoist problems, India has formulated, revised and reoriented its counter-terrorism and counter-insurgency strategies and policies from time to time to deal with the decades-old menaces. The Pakistan-sponsored terror problem as a proxy war strategy has continued unabated, despite India's all-round efforts to address the same, including raising it at international forums such as the United Nations, time and again. India's strategy to defeat the proxy war had so far been limited to undertaking only defensive actions against the terrorists after they had crossed over to India to carry out attacks. However, there has been a fundamental change in this defensive strategy of late, which has been marked by bold and decisive counter-terror actions such the Uri surgical strike and Balakot air strike undertaken by the Indian Armed Forces to deter and defeat cross-border terrorism. Additionally, the Indian military establishment has significantly increased its troops deployment along the LoC. It is extensively using innovative tools and technology such as cameras, sensors etc. installed along the border to stop infiltration bids by the militants. Selective fencing of the LoC has also been done to prevent infiltration.

To address the problem of radicalisation, the central and state governments along with the Indian Armed Forces have undertaken deradicalisation and rehabilitation programmes in those parts of the country mostly affected by terror-related incidents. By extending their outreach to local communities, especially the youth, the Government through a peaceful and inclusive approach, has been trying to wean away the radical elements of society from the violent path of terrorism and extremism.

The Left-wing extremism and Naxalite issues are being tackled in a holistic manner, by strengthening the security apparatus as well as bringing in development in those backward parts of the country affected by armed insurgency-related violence. The Government has outlined its approach as "to deal with Left Wing Extremism in a holistic manner, in the areas of security, development, ensuring rights and entitlements of local communities, improvement in governance and public perception."

Agencies & Departments for counter-terrorism and counter-insurgency operations

National Investigation Agency (NIA): The agency was set up 2009 as the central counter-terrorism investigation and law enforcement organisation. It was established in the aftermath of the 2008 (26/11) Mumbai terror attacks. The NIA operates under the Ministry of Home Affairs. Its role pertains to investigation of serious national and international offences related to terrorist and extremist activities affecting India's security, sovereignty and integrity. The agency, having its headquarters in New Delhi, has an all-India jurisdiction in addition to nodal officers and branch offices. In July 2019, the Indian Parliament passed the NIA (Amendment) Bill under which the agency was granted more powers to investigate terror attacks targeting Indians and Indian interests abroad.

Anti-Terrorism Squad (ATS): As the tactical unit of the Indian Police Service, the anti-terror squad (ATS) is currently operating from a number of states in India. The first ATS unit was set up in Mumbai, Maharastra in December 1990. The ATS has prevented many terrorist attacks in the country.

Research and Analysis Wing (RAW): RAW was formed in 1968 as India's external intelligence agency for counter-terrorism, counter-insurgency and other such covert and overt operations. Having its headquarters in New Delhi, the agency works closely with India's other intelligence organisations and provides vital intelligence and technical inputs to military and paramilitary forces to prevent and foil potential terror attacks. The agency is also tasked with monitoring terrorist elements and related activities such as smuggling of arms and weapons into India.

Intelligence Bureau (IB): The IB works as India's internal intelligence agency dedicated for internal security, counter-intelligence and counter-terrorism tasks. The agency works in close cooperation with other intelligence services, including the RAW. The IB was founded in 1887 and has its headquarters in Delhi.

Directorate of Military Intelligence: The agency operates under the Indian Army. Counter-terrorism and counter-insurgency intelligence gathering is one of its major tasks, especially in the north and north-east Indian regions affected by cross-border terrorism and insurgency.

Directorate of Naval Intelligence: The agency works under the Indian Navy and provides essential intelligence inputs pertaining to the Navy's operational requirements.

Directorate of Air Intelligence: It is the intelligence wing of Indian Air Force and works to provide vital tactical inputs for the force's operational needs.

Defence Intelligence Agency (DIA): The DIA was created in 2002 under the Ministry of Defence (MoD) to provide military intelligence to Indian Armed Forces. The primary task of the agency is to coordinate among the directorates of military (Army), naval and Air Force intelligence services and provide comprehensive information to Indian Defence Forces for counter-terrorism, counter-insurgency and related operations.

CONCLUSION

The multifarious wars with two of its immediate neighbours in the past, a volatile subcontinent and the swiftly changing geostrategic landscape in Asia and the world has made India strengthen its overall defence capabilities and stand out prominently on global stage in 21st century. With its strong democratic credentials, India has never projected itself as a threatening, expansionist and belligerent power either in its immediate neighbourhood or at the international stage. While sincerely toeing the idea of peaceful co-existence with all its neighbours, New Delhi has, at the same time, staunchly dealt with any kind of transgression against its unity, national sovereignty and territorial integrity. Since independence, India, while maintaining its own strategic autonomy, has pursued a non-aligned policy and propagated a rule-based, multi-polar world order.

With its rising economic clout, New Delhi has been making all-out efforts to maintain regional peace, balance and stability while driving growth, development and prosperity at the home front. The adoption of "Look East" policy in 1991, which subsequently became the prioritised "Act East" policy, has further strengthened India's cause of greater engagement, both economically and strategically, with its East Asian and Southeast Asian neighbours. In a highly globalised world, India too has expanded its horizons to reach out to the world community to secure its national and strategic interests as well as for greater global integration.

In a significant development, India was elected a non-permanent member of the powerful United Nations Security Council (UNSC) with overwhelming support in June 2020, consolidated the country's rising stature at the international stage. New Delhi is holding the position for two years beginning from January 1, 2021. This is the eighth time since 1950-51 that India secured this prestigious seat in the 15-member nation UNSC that consists five permanent members and 10 non-permanent members (elected for two years). India's overall objective during its tenure in the UN Security Council is achievement of N.O.R.M.S – a "New Orientation for a Reformed Multilateral System."

New Delhi has been at the forefront in calling for deep structural reforms within the UN Security Council with Prime Minister Narendra Modi exhorting that "The world needs a reformed multilateralism that reflects today's realities, gives voice to all stakeholders, addresses contemporary challenges and focuses on human welfare." India has been voicing its demand to become a permanent member of the UN Security Council in the backdrop of swiftly changing geopolitical realities of 21st century.

CONTACT DETAILS
Ministry of Defence
South Block
New Delhi-110011, India
Website: www.mod.nic.in
Army: www.indianarmy.nic.in/
Navy: www.indiannavy.nic.in/
IAF: www.indianairforce.nic.in/

INDONESIA
(Capital: Jakarta)

INTRODUCTION
Area: 1,904,569 sq km
Population: 275,122,131 (July 2021 est.)
Coastline: 54,716 km
Maritime claims: Territorial sea: 12 nm
Exclusive Economic Zone: 200 nm

KEY POLITICAL PERSONS

PRESIDENT: Joko Widodo

VICE PRESIDENT: Ma'ruf Amin

KEY DEFENCE PERSONS

MINISTER OF DEFENCE: Lt. Gen. (Retd.) Prabowo Subianto

CHIEF OF ARMED FORCES: Marshal Hadi Tjahjanto

CHIEF OF ARMY: Gen. Dudung Abdurachman

CHIEF OF NAVY: Adm. Yudo Margono

CHIEF OF MARINE CORPS: Maj. Gen. Suhartono

CHIEF OF AIR FORCE: Air Chief Marshal Fadjar Prasetyo

ECONOMY

Indonesia has a mixed economy in which both the private sector and government play significant roles. The country is a member of G-20 major economies. Indonesia, the largest economy in Southeast Asia, has enjoyed steady economic growth over the past decade, averaging between 5-6 percent, with moderate inflation, rising foreign direct investment, and relatively low interest rates. Poverty and unemployment, inadequate infrastructure, corruption, a complex regulatory environment, and unequal resource distribution among its regions are still part of Indonesia's economic landscape. President has pledged to improve infrastructure, diversify the economy, and reduce barriers to doing business in Indonesia as a means of increasing economic growth. The country's GDP per capita has steadily risen, from USD823 in the year 2000 to USD3,932 in 2018. Indonesia's economic planning follows a 20-year development plan, spanning from 2005 to 2025. Indonesia belongs to a number of the same international organizations and forums, including the United Nations, ASEAN Regional Forum, the East Asia Summit, Asia-Pacific Economic Cooperation forum, G-20, International Monetary Fund, World Bank, and World Trade Organisation. The economy of Indonesia has contracted to much lower degree due to the COVID-19 pandemic and restrictions.

GDP (official exchange rate): $1 trillion (2020), $3.25 trillion (2017 est.)

Real Growth Rate (GDP): 5.03% (2019 est.), 5.17% (2018 est.)

Industries: Petroleum and natural gas, textiles, automotive, electrical appliances, apparel, footwear, mining, cement, medical instruments and appliances, handicrafts, chemical fertilizers, plywood, rubber, processed food, jewellery, and tourism

Oil - proved reserves: 3.31 billion bbl (1 January 2018 est.)

Natural gas - proved reserves: 2.866 trillion cu m (1 January 2018 est.)

Total Exports: $178.26 billion (2020), $200.1 billion (2019 est.)

Export Commodities: Coal, palm oil, natural gas, cars, gold (2019)

Major Markets: China 15%, United States 10%, Japan 9%, Singapore 8%, India 7%, Malaysia 5% (2019)

Total Imports: $159.64 billion (2020), $204.23 billion (2019)

Import Commodities: Refined petroleum, crude petroleum, vehicle parts, telephones, natural gas (2019)

Major Suppliers: China 27%, Singapore 12%, Japan 8%, Thailand 5%, United States 5%, South Korea 5%, Malaysia 5% (2019)

INTERNATIONAL DISPUTES

◆ Three stretches of land borders with Timor-Leste have yet to be delimited, two of which are in the Oecussi exclave area, and no maritime

◆ Indonesia challenges Australia's claim to Ashmore Reef. Australia has closed parts of the Ashmore and Cartier Reserve to Indonesian traditional fishing and placed restrictions on certain catches.

◆ Land and maritime negotiations are continuing with Malaysia and disputed areas include the controversial Tanjung Datu and Camar Wulan border area in Borneo and the maritime boundary in the Ambalat oil block in the Celebes Sea.

◆ Indonesia and Singapore continue to work on finalizing their 1973 maritime boundary agreement by defining unresolved areas north of Indonesia's Batam Island.

◆ Indonesia and Vietnam are continuing the Exclusive Economic Zone negotiations. In 2011, the two countries agreed to work together to reduce illegal fishing along their maritime boundary.

◆ Indonesia applied sustained pressure to

detect, disrupt, and degrade terrorist groups operating within its borders and deny them safe haven. ISIS-affiliated Jamaah Ansharut Daulah (JAD) and its offshoots continued to target police and other symbols of state authority.

DEFENCE

ARMY

Personnel: 300,000

Equipment

Category	Name	In Service
MBT	Leopard 2	80+
	AMX-13	100+
	Scorpion	50+
APC/IFV	AMX-VCI MICV	50+
	Ferret	50
	Commando Scout	20+
	AMX-10P	50
	Marder	
	M113	100+
	Stromer	20
	Saracen	50
	Pindad Badak	
	Pindad Anoa	
	BTR-40	100+
	VAB	50
	VBL	10+
	APS-3 ANOA	100+
	P2 protected carrier	
Artillery	FH 2000 155mm	5+
	Astros II 300mm	
	M109 SP	
	105mm	40
	105LG 105mm	20
	122mm	
	76mm gun/howitzer	50
Mortar	81 mm	
	120mm	
MRL	BM14 140mm	20+
RCL	90mm	
	106mm	
SAM	Rapier/Blindfire	20+
	Mistral	
	Starstreak	
	RBS-70	
AA Gun	23mm ZU-23-2	
	35mm Oerlikon	
	57mm	

Army Aviation

Category	Name	In Service
Aircraft	BN-2	1
	Cessna 310P	1
	Aero Commander 680	2

Category	Name	In Service
Aircraft	Cessna 185	2
	Wilga	10+
	Cessna 207	2
	CN-212-200	5+
	DHC-5D Buffalo (VIP)	3
Helicopter	Mi-35	5
	AH-64	5
	AS550	4
	Bell-205	10+
	Mi-17	10+
	Bell 412	30

New Procurements/ Upgrades

No major procurement plans are under consideration at present.

NAVY

Personnel: 65,000

Equipment

Category	Name	In Service
Submarine	Nagapasa class	3
	Cakra class	2
Frigate	Martadinata class	2
	Ahmad Yani class	5+
Corvette	Diponegoro class	4
	Bung Tomo class	3
	Ex-Parchim class	15+
	Fatahillah class	3
Patrol craft/Fast Attack Craft	Mandau class missile FAC	4
	Kakap class SAR	4
	Clurit class	5+
	Singa class FAC	4
	Andau class	4
	Sibarau class	5
	Todak class missile FAC	4
	Siada class	5+
	Waspada class	2
	Pandrong class	2
Mine warfare force	Pulau Rengat class	2
	Ex-Soviet T-43 class	2
	Kondor class	8+
Amphibious vessel	Tanjung Dalpele LSD	1
	Makassar class LPD	4
	Teluk Semangka class LST	6
	Teluk Gelimanuk class	10+
	Teluk Sirebong class	2
	LCU	10+
	Coastal vessel	20+
Support vessel	ARUN fleet oiler	1
	Transport/hospital ship	1
	Driver support ship	1
Anti-ship Missile	RBS-15, Exocet, C-802, Harpoon	

Naval Aviation

Category	Name	In Service
Aircraft	GAF Nomad	10+
	C-212	10+
Transport	Aero Commander 100	3+
	PA-38	5
	CN-235	5
	DHC-5D Buffalo	2
Helicopter	NBO-105C	5
	AS565 Panther	10+
	Bell 412	4
	WASP (ASW)	5+
	NAS.332B/L Super Puma (ASW with AM.39 Exocet missile)	30

New Procurements/ Upgrades

◆ Len Industri and Thales will be modernising Indonesia's naval capabilities. On 10 March 2020, in Jakarta, Len Industri and Thales signed a contract for the complete modernisation of the KRI Usman-Harun multi-role light frigate's mission system. The contract will see Len Industri and Thales install the TACTICOS Combat Management System, the SMART-S Mk2 air and surface surveillance radar, the STIR EO Mk2 radar and EO fire control system and the Vigile Mk2 tactical multi-purpose R-ESM system. These systems are currently also installed on the Indonesian Navy's new Raden Eddy Martadinata class frigates, enabling consistency in operations for the Navy. This upgrade for the KRI Usman-Harun is expected to be completed by the end of 2023, and it will considerably extend the life of the frigate.

Marines

Personnel: 15,000

Equipment

Category	Name	In Service
APC	AMX-10P	10+
	AMX-10PAC 90	30+
	BTR-50, BTR-80	
	PT-76 Tank	50+
	P2 Protected carrier	
	BVP-2 AIFV	30+
	BMP-2, BMP-3	50+
Transport	NC-212-200	3

New Procurements/ Upgrades

◆ Fincantieri and the Ministry of Defence of Indonesia, have signed a contract for the supply of 6 FREMM class frigates, the modernisation and sale of 2 Maestrale class frigates, and the related logistical support.

◆ The MoD has signed a contract

with Russia for an additional 37 BMP-3F amphibious infantry fighting vehicles for the Marine Corps.

◆ The state-owned company PT Dirgantara Indonesia (Persero) will begin shipping nine Bell-412EPI helicopters to the Indonesian Army next year. The total value of the procurement of these assault helicopters reached USD183 million or equivalent to Rp 2.5 trillion. Bell-412EPI is an American aviation production company, Bell Textron Inc. While PTDI will assemble weapons namely gattling gun from Dillon Aerospace and bullets from PT Pindad (Persero).

AIR FORCE
Personnel: 30,000
Equipment

Category	Name	In Service
Fighter	F-16	20+
	EMB 314 Super Tucano	5+
	F-5E/F	(retired)
	KAI T-50	10
	Hawk 209	15
	Hawk 109	5
	Su-27 SKM	4+
	Su-30 Mk2	5+
	Su-30MK	(Upgraded)
Transport	F-28	3
	CN-235	10+
	C-130B/H & KC-130B	30+
	NC-212	10
	C-130-H-30	5+
	L-100-30	2
	AS.332 Super Puma	5+
Maritime Patrol	Boeing 737 surveiller	3
	C-130H-MP	2
	NC-212-200	3
	CN-235-220	1
Helicopter	NAS.332 Super Puma	10+
	MDH-500	10+
	EC-725	1
	NBO-105C	10+
	EC-120B	10
	SA-330J	7
	AS332 Super Puma	5+
Trainer	HAWK Mk.53	5+
	AS-202 BRAVO	40
	SF-260W	10+
	KT-1B	10+
Missile	Aim-9, Aim-120, AMRAAM, MAA-1A, AA-10, AA-2, AGM-65, AS-14/17/13	

New Procurements/ Upgrades

◆ Indonesia plans to buy more than a dozen Russian Sukhoi fighter aircraft and C-130J aircraft.

◆ The US State Department has approved a possible Foreign Military Sale to the Government of Indonesia of 8 MV-22 Block C Osprey aircraft and related equipment for an estimated cost of USD2 billion.

Defence Expenditure

Total defence spending: USD 9 billion (2020 approx.)

Defence spending in terms of GDP: 0.8% of GDP (2020 est.), 0.7% of GDP (2019)

Domestic Suppliers: PT Pindad, PT PAL, LAPAN, IAe, PT Lundin Industry Invest, PT DAHANA, PT SRITEX, PT Sentra Surya Eka Jaya (SSE), CV Maju Mapan, PT Fista Bahari Internusa, PT Sari Bahari Malang, PT Palindo Marine Shipyard, PT Len Industri (Persero), PT CMI Teknologi, PT. Dok dan Perkapalan, (DKB) Kodja Bahari & PT. Tesco Indomaritim.

Foreign Suppliers: France, United Kingdom, Russia, United States, Germany, China, South Korea, Brazil, Spain, Canada, Switzerland, Turkey, Australia, Netherlands, Sweden & Poland

According to the Indonesian Ministry of Finance, Indonesia's financial budget for 2020 provides USD9.26 billion for defence, up more than 19% from 2019.

India and Indonesia in July 2020 agreed to expand strategic cooperation in a range of areas including defence industries and technology sharing, as the two maritime neighbours looked at injecting a new momentum to their security partnership. The possible areas of further expansion of defence and military ties were discussed during talks between Defence Minister Rajnath Singh and his Indonesian counterpart General Prabowo Subianto. Both the ministers agreed to further enhance the bilateral defence cooperation in mutually agreed areas. Potential areas of cooperation in the field of defence industries and defence technology were also identified by the two countries. The two countries inked a new defence cooperation agreement in 2018 during Prime Minister Narendra Modi's visit to Indonesia. The pact was aimed at reflecting the elevation of relationship between the two countries to a comprehensive strategic partnership.

Indonesia and Japan have agreed that the two Asian powers must engage in stronger cooperation, including in the military sector, to contribute to regional security particularly in the Pacific area, which has been tense due to prolonged territorial disputes.

South Korean defence company Daewoo Shipbuilding & Marine Engineering (DSME) has bagged a deal worth USD1.02 billion to build three 1,400-tonne conventional attack submarines for Indonesian Navy in 2019. A contract in this regard was signed on April 12 between DSME and the Indonesian Government in Bandung, West Java, South Korean Defenve Acquisition Programme Administration (DAPA) announced. It is the second such submarine export deal between the two countries, following a 2011 contract worth USD1.08 billion to export three 1,400-tonne submarines to the Southeast Asian country, Yonhap, South Korea's official news agency, said, as quoted by PTI news agency. Under that contract, DSME delivered the first Nagapasa-class submarine to Indonesia in August 2017 while the second platform was delivered last year. Indonesia has announced its plans to acquire at least 12 conventional submarines (SSKs) by 2024 to achieve a minimum essential force (MEF) to secure its maritime regions.

Ulan-Ude Aviation Plant (U-UAP) as part of Russian Helicopters holding company (State Corporation Rostec) launches Mi-8/171 type helicopter test operation program, which is aimed at the assessing of all the advantages of helicopters real operation in conjunction with all available corporate support tools and implemented aftersales services of Russian Helicopters holding company. The pilot project is being implemented in Indonesia, where two Mi-8AMT helicopters are already involved in firefighting operations. In the future, the rotorcraft will be on operational duty on the islands of Sumatra and Kalimantan, as per Russian Helicopters news release.

Defence Production and R&D

Indonesia is committed for the re-establishment of its local defence industry base which was once well-developed and produced a wide range of military equipment. From the recent scenario the country has preferred local assembly of helicopters, ship building and their refurbishment for developing its own defence industrial base but as of now, a majority of defence budget is spent on procuring defence equipment from other countries. The country was planning to introduce a defence offsets policy in 2011 with an objective to strengthen its own defence industry by transfer of technology and local manufacturing of imported weapon systems. Defence and security company Saab underlines its long-term commitment to Indonesia by extending partnerships with the national Agency for Assessment and Application of Technology (BPPT) and the Indonesian Defence University (UNHAN). Saab has signed further agreements with BPPT and UNHAN, to continue working together on technology development and educational advances. Since 2015, Saab has successfully built a programme of defence technology development with BPPT, and academic collaborations with UNHAN. These partnerships have ensured a greater understanding In Indonesia of high-tech defence capabilities such as aeronautics, geo-mapping, missile systems and underwater systems.

Defence Procurement

The major defence procurement drive that Indonesia is planning in the next five years includes its Army and the Air Force in particular. While the air force has recently inducted the new Sukhoi fighters in its fleet, it plans to procure more such fighters in future. Besides, procurement of new transport aircraft, multi-role and ASW helicopters and modernisation of existing aircraft for both the army and air force are also being planned. Indonesia has also announced its plan to join South Korea in the development of the new KF-X fighters.

CONTACT DETAILS
Department of Defence and Security
Jl. Merdeka Barat 13-14 Jakarta Pusat
KOTAK POS 2005 Jakarta 10020
Indonesia
Tel.: ++62-21-366184, -374408
Email: postmaster@dephan.go.id

STRATEGIC INFORMATION
IRAN
(Capital: Tehran)

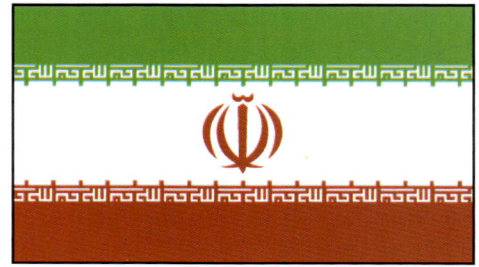

INTRODUCTION

Area: 1,648,195 sq km

Population: 85,888,910 (July 2021 est.)

Coastline: 2,440 km (Iran also borders the Caspian Sea - 740 km)

Maritime claims: Territorial sea: 12 nm

Contiguous zone: 24 nm

Exclusive Economic Zone: Bilateral agreements or median lines in the Persian Gulf

Continental shelf: Natural prolongation

GEOPOLITICAL IMPORTANCE

The largest country in West Asia – Iran – is a country of particular geopolitical significance because of its location. The country is bordered on the North by Armenia, Azerbaijan and Turkmenistan. It is bordered on the East by Afghanistan and Pakistan, on the South by the Persian Gulf and the Gulf of Oman, on the West by Iraq and on the Northwest by Turkey. As Iran is a littoral state on the Caspian Sea; which is an inland sea, Kazakhstan and Russia are Iran's direct neighbours to the North. It is the only country in West Asia which has a direct interface with Europe, Central Asia, West Asia and South Asia. Ethnically, the people are Persian and by religion, most are Shiite Muslims. The Islamic Republic is the main reference point of the Shiite galaxy, the minority branch of the Muslim world whose members live along the coast of the Persian Gulf. This Shiite crescent is perceived as a serious threat by Saudi Arabia, a Sunni country, and by other Gulf States. Iran's clerical leadership believes that the Islamic Republic plays a central role in world affairs as the standard bearer of revolutionary Islam, the defender of the interests of Muslims throughout the world. The country is endowed with oil reserves. Iran's four strategic maritime areas are the Gulf of Oman, the Strait of Hormuz, the Persian Gulf and the Caspian Sea. The Strait of Hormuz is vital to the global supply of both oil and liquefied natural gas. Iran's centrality has lent it geo-strategic importance through the history.

POLITICAL OVERVIEW

The Islamic Republic of Iran was established following the 1979 revolution and a new constitution was introduced that put into place a mixed system of government, in which the executive, parliament, and judiciary are overseen by several bodies dominated by the clergy. The supreme leader is the highest ranking political and religious authority in Iran. He appoints the chiefs of posts such as the commanders of the armed forces, chief judges, prosecutors as well as six of the Islamic jurists who sit on the 12-member Guardian Council. The leader is responsible for declarations of war and is the commander in chief of Iran's armed forces. He also sets the general direction of the nation's policy. The Assembly of Experts, an 86 – member chamber, monitors the highest religious leader's performance.

The president is the second highest-ranking government official elected by popular vote to a four-year term. He selects the Council of Ministers – the cabinet – which must be approved by parliament. He serves as chairman of the Supreme Council for National Security which oversees the country's defence. The president and his ministers are responsible for the day-to-day administration of the government and the implementation of laws. The Parliament known as the Majlis is the national legislative body with 290 publicly elected representatives. Elections for the parliament are held every four years and all potential candidates for the legislature must first be approved by the Guardian Council. The Guardian Council comprised of the speaker of parliament, head of judiciary, chief of the combined general staff of the armed forces, key cabinet ministers and commanders of the regular military and the Revolutionary Guard. The Council has the constitutional authority to veto parliamentary decisions and vet electoral candidates.

The Expediency Council members created in 1988 wields influence through its role as national policy adviser to the supreme leader. Its members include heads of the three government branches, the clerical members of the Guardian Council and various other members appointed by the supreme leader for three-year terms. The Judiciary nominates six lay members of the Guardian Council who are usually lawyers. The Public courts deal with civil and criminal offences. Separate "revolutionary" courts try other categories of offences such as crimes against national security or offences that threaten the Islamic republic. A Special Clerical Court deals with crimes allegedly committed by clerics and occasionally by lay people. Decisions from the revolutionary courts or the clerical court are final and cannot be appealed. The Revolutionary Guard was set up in the wake of the Islamic Revolution to protect the new political leaders and bodies and uphold the spirit of the revolution. The commanders of the Revolutionary Guard are selected by the supreme leader.

KEY POLITICAL PERSONS

SUPREME LEADER OF ISLAMIC REVOLUTION & COMMANDER-IN-CHIEF OF ARMED FORCES: Ayatollah Sayyid Ali Hosseini Khamenei

PRESIDENT: Ebrahim Raisi

ECONOMY

Iran's economy is dominated by oil and gas production. The country ranks second in the world for natural gas reserves and fourth for proven crude oil reserves. Iran also possesses significant agricultural, industrial, and service sectors. The government directly owns and operates hundreds of state-owned enterprises and indirectly controls many companies affiliated with the country's security forces. Private sector activity includes small-scale workshops, farming, some manufacturing, and services, in addition to medium-scale construction, cement production, mining, and metalworking. Most of the country's exports are oil and gas, accounting for a majority of government revenue. In 2012, oil exports reportedly contributed to about 80% of Iranian public revenue and in 2016, oil export revenues enabled Iran to amass well over $135 billion in foreign exchange reserves. However, economic sanctions imposed by the United States that again came into effect in 2018 has greatly affected the economy. The country is also grappling with the impact of COVID-19 crisis. The pandemic has severely affected jobs and income in many labour-intensive activities, including high-contact services and the informal sector. The authorities have adopted a comprehensive strategy of market-based reforms: the development of a resilient economy, progress in science and technology, and the promotion of cultural excellence, the World Bank has stated.

GDP (official exchange rate): $581.252 billion (2019 est.)

Real Growth Rate (GDP): 3.7% (2017 est.), 12.5% (2016 est.)

Industries: Petroleum, petrochemicals, gas, fertilizer, caustic soda, textiles, cement and other construction materials, food processing (particularly sugar refining and vegetable oil production), ferrous and nonferrous metal fabrication, armaments.

Oil-proved reserves: 157.2 billion bbl (1 January 2018 est.)

Natural gas-proved reserves: 33.72 trillion cu m (1 January 2018 est.)

Total Exports: $101.4 billion (2017 est.), $83.98 billion (2016 est.)

Export Commodities: Petroleum 60%, chemical and petrochemical products, fruits and nuts, carpets, cement, ore.

Major Markets: China 48%, India 12%, South Korea 8%, Turkey 6%, United Arab Emirates 5% (2019)

Total Imports: $76.39 billion (2017 est.), $63.14 billion (2016 est.)

Import Commodities: Rice, corn, broadcasting equipment, soybean products, beef (2019)

Major Suppliers: China 28%, United Arab Emirates 20%, India 11%, Turkey 7%, Brazil 6%, Germany 5% (2019)

DEFENCE & SECURITY

Iran's main policy goal has been to be as independent as possible of alliances and foreign arms supplies. Accordingly, the country has avoided military alliances, although it has reached military supply agreements with a number of countries. Iran has two parallel land forces, the regular Artesh (Army), and the Army of the Guardians of the Islamic Revolution, also known as the Pasdaran (IRGC). The regular military defends Iran's borders and maintains internal order. The Pasdaran control Iran's strategic missile and rocket forces. The country has a dedicated force to train and equip non-state actors like Hezbollah, Hamas and Shiite extremists in Iraq. Iran has given the highest priority to the procurement and development of various types of missiles and it reportedly has the largest and most diverse inventory of long-range artillery rockets and ballistic missiles in the Middle East. Its acquisition of long-range missiles and development of its own liquid – and solid – fuelled missiles has given it a strike capability.

Under the Iran nuclear agreement, formally known as the Joint Comprehensive Plan of Action (JCPOA), Iran has agreed to dismantle much of its nuclear programme in exchange for billions of dollars' worth of sanctions relief. The landmark agreement was signed in July 2015 between Iran and several world powers. The United States withdrew from the deal in 2018 claiming it failed to curtail Iran's missile programme and regional influence. Iran is a member of International Atomic Energy Agency, Organisation for the Prohibition of Chemical Weapons, United Nations. The country is a signatory to the Comprehensive Nuclear Test Ban Treaty, Biological Weapons Convention, Chemical Weapons Convention, International Atomic Energy Agency Safeguards Agreement, Partial Test Ban Treaty, and Treaty on the Non-Proliferation of Nuclear Weapons.

KEY DEFENCE PERSONS

MINISTER OF DEFENCE: Brig. Gen. Mohammad-Reza Gharaei Ashtiani

CHIEF OF STAFF OF THE ARMED FORCES: Maj. Gen. Mohammad Hossein Bagheri

COMMANDER-IN-CHIEF OF ARMY: Maj. Gen. Abdolrahim Mousavi

COMMANDER-IN-CHIEF OF ISLAMIC REVOLUTIONARY GUARD CORPS (IRGC): Maj. Gen. Hossein Salami

Internal Conflict

Under the Islamic Republic government which came to power in 1979, the new government forced a mandatory hijab on Iranian women, banned music and forbade all types of independent cultural expression. The cultural war continues to this day. Iranians have been facing decades of unrest with the country placed under sanctions imposed by the US, the EU, and the United Nations over claims Iran breached its nuclear obligations. There have been eruption of political unrest triggering demonstrations.

Protestors have expressed their anger over the country's increasing economic hardship, extending support and funding for foreign conflicts. The punitive economic sanctions and corruption have taken their toll on the people who are struggling to make ends meet. People are suffering due to increased unemployment and decreased access to medicine. In addition to the return of sanctions and the administration's failure to boost the economy, or to extend individual and political freedom and ensure equality for both women and men have shattered their hope of reform. Iranians celebrated the signing of Joint Comprehensive Plan of Action (JCPOA) and the lifting of economic sanctions. However, withdrawal from the JCPOA on May 18, 2018, by the Trump administration and imposition of new sanctions has again inflicted hardships on Iranian people. The overall life in the country remains strictly governed by Islamic rules.

External Conflict
◆ Iran protests Afghanistan's limiting flow of dammed Helmand River tributaries during drought.
◆ Iraq's lack of a maritime boundary with Iran prompts jurisdiction disputes beyond the mouth of the Shatt al Arab in the Persian Gulf.
◆ Iran and UAE dispute Tunb Islands and Abu Musa Island which are occupied by Iran.
◆ Azerbaijan, Kazakhstan, and Russia ratified Caspian seabed delimitation treaties based on equidistance while Iran continues to insist on a one-fifth slice of the sea.
◆ Afghan and Iranian commissioners have discussed boundary monument densification and resurvey.

Cyber Warfare: The Iranian cyberspace system comprises a large number of cyber organisations. One central organisation with a primarily defensive orientation is the Cyber Defence Command, operating under Iran's Passive Defensive Organisation, affiliated with the General Staff of the Armed Forces. According to the Institute for National Security Studies (INSS) Iran has made significant gains in three key areas – creating a defence envelope against cyber-attacks on critical infrastructures, neutralising cyber operations by opposition elements and regime opponents, keeping western ideas and content out of Iranian cyberspace. The Islamic Revolutionary Guard Corps (IRGC) and the Ministry of Intelligence and Security (MOIS) are responsible for carrying out cyber operations. The MOIS reportedly focus on the clandestine acquisition of intelligence. Iran's regime is continuing to improve its cyber capabilities and gaining prominence as member of the cyber superpower club.

THREAT PERSPECTIVE

The greatest threat to Iran has been a foreign power dominating its neighbouring country and using it as a platform to foment ethnic dissent in Iran. Most of Iran's neighbours are unstable and ethnic insurgencies there may impinge upon the internal security of Iran. Iran views NATO's missile defence system, the European Phased Adaptive Approach (EPAA) asset in Turkey, developed to defend Europe against threats originating from outside the Euro-Atlantic area, as a threat to its missile capabilities.

Another threat perspective to Iran is Saudi Arabia. The two counties have been locked in a cold war for decades. The regional confrontation between the two nations separated geographically by the narrow Persian Gulf is deeply rooted in sectarian, political, and economic competition. Iran has a predominantly Shiite Muslim population, while Saudi Arabia is mostly Sunni. The sectarian tension is exacerbated by the fact that hundreds of thousands of Shia Muslims live in Saudi Arabia's Eastern Province – the province in which the bulk of Saudi Arabian petroleum reserves are located. Both countries are major oil and gas exporters and have clashed over energy policy. They fight proxy battles, often violently, in places like Bahrain, Yemen, and Lebanon. Saudi Arabia has no diplomatic relations with Iran since January 2016.

STRATEGIC RELATIONS

Russia: Iran and Russia view each other as integral to its own national security, internal stability, and territorial integrity. They are united by their joint opposition to US foreign policy in the Middle Eastern region and beyond. They are partners in supporting the Assad regime in Syria, and they have common interests in the Caspian Sea and Caucasus region. The Islamic Republic of Iran Navy has made its base at Bandar Abbas available to the Russian Navy as a friendly and secure port where Russian Navy ships can refuel, resupply, and make repairs. Russia is one of the few arms and atomic reactor manufacturer willing and able to sell them to Iran. Russia has assisted Iran with its conventional military, including training and defensive weapons that could serve to protect against air strikes targeting Iran.

China: China and Iran have developed a broad and deep partnership centred on China's energy needs and Iran's abundant resources as well as significant non-energy economic ties, arms sales and defence cooperation. China is Iran's top trading partner and also Iran's top oil export destination. Chinese companies have invested billions in upgrading Iran's gas refinement and oil infrastructure. China was a key player in reviving and developing Iran's nuclear programme in the 1990s. The nuclear facility in Isfahan is the brainchild of Chinese-Iran nuclear cooperation. The country played a crucial role in improving Iran's ballistic missile and naval capabilities. China has been a major arms provider to the Islamic Republic including the HY-2 Silkworm anti-ship missiles. In 2016, Iran and China have signed an agreement to boost defence-military cooperation and fight terrorism.

North Korea: Pyongyang and Tehran have gradually expanded their military, economic and diplomatic cooperation. The two nations have signed an agreement on bilateral support for developing ballistic missiles. Though the two countries appear isolated internationally because of their nuclear programmes, experts said that there are differences in their nuclear perceptions. North Korea has conducted nuclear tests seeking to have strong nuclear deterrence against enemy forces that pose a threat to its regime while Iran has been developing nuclear programmes, arguing that they are purely for peaceful, civilian purposes. Much of the trade relations between Iran and North Korea have included missile sales, mainly from North Korea to Iran.

India: India and Iran have traditionally shared good ties. Relations between the two countries warmed in the 1990s when India collaborated with Iran to support the Afghan Northern Alliance against the Taliban. There are significant trade ties, particularly in crude oil imports into India and diesel exports to Iran. India is one of the largest foreign investors in Iran's oil and gas industry. The trade relations have traditionally been buoyed by Indian import of Iranian crude oil resulting in overall trade balance in favour of Iran. The two countries are involved in the International North-South Transport Corridor (INSTC) which is the ship, rail, and road route based multi modal transportation for moving freight between India, Russia, Iran, Europe and Central Asia.

Pakistan: Iran and Pakistan maintained their bilateral relationship in an atmosphere of Islamic brotherhood and as good neighbours with mutual acceptability. The conflict in Afghanistan in the 1980s brought the two nations closer as each had an interest in the conflict. Pakistan whole-heartedly supported Iranian viewpoint on the issue of its nuclear programme and maintained that Iran has the right to develop its nuclear programme within the ambit of Non-Proliferation Treaty (NPT). Both countries are founding members of the Economic Cooperation Organisation (ECO). Both the countries have conducted joint operations against terrorists and drug traffickers in the border regions.

Germany: Germany and Iran have a special relationship which continue to grow stronger even after the 1979 Islamic revolution and the overthrow of the Shah. From 1979 to this day most Western countries that were considered US allies, including the US, were shut out of the Iranian market except for Germany. The country remains one of Iran's biggest trading partners. In 2019, trade between Germany and Iran fell by 45% compared to 2018 to 1722 million euro. According to a media report, trade between the two countries increased slightly again in 2020 to 1821 million euro. German exports to Iran were worth 1546 million euro, while German imports from Iran amounted to around 275 million euro.

DEFENCE CAPABILITIES

The armed forces of the Islamic Republic of Iran has built up its strike capability by acquiring long-range missiles and by developing its own liquid-and solid-fuelled missiles. The military posses a substantial inventory of missiles capable of reaching targets throughout the region, reportedly including the United States military bases and Israel, and it continues to develop more sophisticated missiles. Iran has acquired the technology to produce fission nuclear weapons and has enriched uranium to levels where it can eventually produce fissile material. Iran's UAV programme capabilities often make the headlines because of their military applications. The country is making efforts to develop its space launch vehicle programme. On April 22, 2020, Iran successfully delivered a military reconnaissance satellite called Nour to orbit. The homegrown defence industry produces light and heavy weapons ranging from mortars and torpedoes to tanks and submarines. In recent years, Iran has built up an impressive list of new weapons systems, including ballistic missiles, and sought to improve its navy and air force. Iran has the largest standing military in the Middle East with a powerful mix of capabilities for both the regular and Islamic Revolutionary Guard Corps (IRGC) forces to defend its territory. The armed forces have been conducting major military drills to enhance its defence capabilities, testing modern military tactics and state-of-the-art equipment. Iran has declared that it is a chemical weapons power, and may have a biological weapons programme.

ARMY: Iran has two parallel land forces with some integration at the command level: the regular Artesh (Army), and the Islamic Revolutionary Guard Corps (IRGC), also known as the Pasdaran. The regular army is responsible for guarding the independence and territorial integrity of the country and maintaining order.

The Islamic Revolutionary Guard Corps (IRGC) was formed by former Supreme Leader Ayatollah Khomeini in the aftermath of the 1979 Islamic Revolution. The IRGC has its own Ground Force, Navy, Air Force, Intelligence, and Special Forces. Over the years, the corps' power has increased militarily, politically, and economically. The Revolutionary Guards controls the country's strategic missile forces, mounts foreign and domestic intelligence operations, and is responsible for protecting the regime; the Guards has sole jurisdiction of patrolling the Iranian capital. The Quds Force, one of the sub groups of the IRGC is mostly tasked with overseas operations predominantly in the Middle East. Another group within the IRCG structure is the Basij militia, a paramilitary force that was first formed as a volunteer force during the Iran-Iraq War. The IRGC's role is enshrined in the constitution and it answers only to Iran's supreme leader.

Personnel: 350,000

Equipment

Category	Name	In Service
MBT	Karrar	400+
	Zulfiqar 1/2/3	150+
	M-60A1	50
	Chieftain	100
	T-62	100
	T-72S	200+
	T-72Z	350
	Scorpions (light)	50
APC/IFV	Boragh	100
	M-113A1	200
	BMP-1	200
	BTR40/50/60/152	320
	EE-9 Cascavel	
	Ferret	
	Greyhound	
	Fox	
Artillery	75mm	2000
	85mm	
	M-101 105mm	
	122mm	200
	130mm towed	22
	GHN45	50+
	G5 155mm towed gun/Howitzer	
	FH77B	18+
	HM41 155MM	

...continued

Category	Name	In service
Artillery	M-107 175mm SP gun	200
	M114 towed	
	M109A1 SP 155mm	
	M115 towed	
	M110 203mm SP	
	RAAD (Thunder) 1 122mm SP	
	RAAD (Thunder) 2 155mm SP	
MRL	BM21	64
	Hadid	
	Fadjr-3 (240mm)	
	Dadjr-5 (333mm)	
Mortar	81mm	
	107mm	
	120mm	
RCL	5mm	
	75mm	
	106mm	
AA gun	23mm	1800
	1800	
	35mm	
	40mm	
	57mm	
	85mm towed	
	ZSU-23-4	
	ZSU-57-2 SP	
ATGW	Entac	130
	SS-11/12	
	Dragon	
	Tow	
	Konkur	
Weapon	1-Hawk (SAM)	
	SA-7 (SAM)	
	Stinger (SAM)	
	Misgah-1 (SAM)	
	Shahab Thaqeb (SAM)	
	Ra'ad	
	Tor M-1 (SAM)	2
	RBS-70 (SAM)	

Army Aviation

Category	Name	In service
Aircraft	F-27	12
	Cessna 185	28
	Cessna 310	6
	Cessna O-2A	10
	Falcon 20	2
	Aero Commander 690	5
	PC-6B	16
Helicopter	AH-1J Twin Cobra	12
	Bell 214	
	Mi-17	50

...continued

Category	Name	In service
Helicopter	Mi-8	
	Boeing CH-47C	40
	AB2/206	84
	NAS.332 Super Puma	7

New Procurements/Upgrades

◆ No major procurement plans are under consideration at present.

NAVY: Iran has two naval forces: The Islamic Republic of Iran Navy or IRIN and the Islamic Revolutionary Guard Corps Navy or IRGN. The IRIN is the naval branch of Iran's Artesh. The Iranian Revolutionary Guard Corps Navy (IRGCN) emerged after the Islamic revolution during the Iran-Iraq war in the 1990s. The regular navy's inventory consists of surface ships, including frigates and corvettes, and submarines. The Revolutionary Guards naval force has a sizeable inventory of small fast attack craft, and specializes in asymmetric, hit-and-run tactics. Both navies maintain large arsenals of coastal defence and anti-ship cruise missiles and mines. After a military reorganisation, the Revolutionary Guard has been given the responsibility for the Persian Gulf, which includes the strategic Strait of Hormuz. The regular navy is tasked with areas including the Gulf of Oman and Iran's Caspian Sea waters. The IRIN is pressing ahead with its modernisation and expansion. Iran has plans for new larger submarines and destroyers, including an ambitious trimaran design.

Personnel: 16,000

Equipment

Category	Name	In Service	On Order
Submarine	Taregh class (Kilo type)	3	
	Nahang class	1	
	Ghadir class midget	23	
	Besat class	1	
	Fateh class	1	2
Destroyer	Dena	1	
	Sahand	1	
Frigate	Alvand class (Vosper Mk5 type)	3	
	Jamaran class	3	
Patrol Craft	ex-North Korean Chaho class	3	
	ex-Chinese	3	
	Hudong class FAC	10	
	Kaman class FAC	1	
	(Combattante II type)	8	

...continued

Category	Name	In Service	On Order
Patrol Craft	ex-Iraqi Osa II	10	
	type missile FAC	1	
	ex-Iraqi Bogomol	3	
	type missile FAC	1	
	ex-Chinese	2	
Mine warfare force	Shahin	1	
	ex-US Bluebird class minesweeper (Schahrokh)		
	ex-US Cape class	1	
	Harishi class	1	
Amphibious force	Hengham class LSL	4	
	Iran AJR class LST	2	
	Iran Hormuz class LST	3	
	Rotork craft type	6	

Naval Aviation

Category	Name	In service
Aircraft	F-27	4
	Strike Commander	6
	Falcon 20E	4
	P-3F Orion	2
Helicopter	AB205	15
	AB206	10
	RH53D	4
	SH3D Sea King	10
	AB.212	6
	M-17	5

New Procurements/Upgrades

◆ The IRGC has unveiled a new warship, Abdollah Roudaki, capable of carrying helicopters, drones and missile launchers. The warship is reportedly equipped with surface-to-surface missile and surface-to-air missiles.

◆ The Iranian Navy has inducted two new domestically manufactured naval platforms, Dena destroyer and Shahin minesweeper, into its fleet.

◆ The Besat class submarine is an Iranian designed class of submarines currently under construction.

◆ The IRGCN has received 188 new naval drones and helicopters including Sepehr vertical take-off and landing (VTOL) drone, Shahab-2, and Hodhod-4 VTOL drone, capable of taking aerial images of fixed and mobile naval targets in combat operations.

AIR FORCE: The Islamic Republic of Iranian Air Force (IRIAF) was established in the early 1980s when the former Imperial Iranian Air Force was renamed. The Air Force is organised on geographical lines has three regional commands, namely the Western Area Command (WAC), the Southern Area Command (SAC) and the Eastern Area Command (EAC).

Major air bases: Ahwaz, Bushire, Chahbahar, Dezful, Doshen-Tappeh, Galeh-Marghi, Hamadan, Isfahan, Mashad, Mehrabad, Shiraz, Tabriz, Zahidan, Abu Musa.

Personnel: 35,000

Equipment

Category	Name	In Service
Fighter	MiG-29	15
	Su-24	25
	F-14A Tomcat	20+
	F-5E/F Tiger II	50
	Saegheh	12
	F-4D/E	40
	RF-4E	6
	F-6	20
	Chengdu F-7	15+
	SU-25	6
Transport	Boeing 747	9
	Boeing 707	14
	C-130H Hercules	15
	F-27	13
	Falcon 20	2
	Aero Commander	2
	DHC-2	7
	Y-7	4
AEW	IL-76 Mainstay	2
Maritime patrol	P-3F Orion	
Trainer	Yasin	
	MF1-17 Mushshak	45
	F-33A	49
	U-22	25
	EMB.312 Tucano	35
	PC-7	6
	TB21	6
	TB200	45
	MF1-17 Mushshak	45
Helicopter	AB-205	6
	AB-206	72
	HH-34F	10
	AB-212	5
	CH-47C	24
	Bell 214C	22
	S-61	2
SAM	AB-205	6
	AB-206	72
	HH-34F	10
	AB-212	5
	CH-47C	24

...continued

Category	Name	In Service
SAM	Bell 214C	22
	S-61	2
UAV/UCAV	Ababil	
	Mohajer I/II/III/IV	
	Ra'ad	
	Nazir	
	Hod Hod	
	Saeghe	
	MQM-107	
	Yasir	
	Karrar	
	Shahed 129	
	Hamaseh	
	H-110 Sarir	
	Fotros	

New Procurements/Upgrades

◆ Iran and Russia are reportedly working on a possible contract for the co-production of an undisclosed number of Russian-made Sukhoi Su-30 multirole fighter aircraft.

AIR DEFENCE FORCE:

The Air Defence Force is the anti-aircraft warfare service branch of Iran's regular military, the Islamic Republic of Iran Army (Artesh). It controls all of Iran's military land-based air defence systems. Iran has imported surface-to-air missiles from China and Russia. It also possess obsolete and modern indigenous designed SAMs which feature significant improvements including increased range, digital fire control systems and electro-optical fire control systems. The country has designed and manufactured a variety of indigenous missiles, including Sayyad-2, Khalij-e-Fars (Persian Gulf), Mehrab (Altar), Ra'd (Thunder), Qader (Mighty), Nour (Light) and Zafar (Triumph), Mersad-16, Tabas, Khordad-3, Khordad-15, Majeed, and Dezfoul.

New Procurements/Upgrades

◆ The IRGC Aerospace Force has unveiled a SAR imaging radar mounted on the Shahed 129 drone.

SAR imaging radar and Shahed 129 drone.

◆ On September 1, 2021, the Army Air Defence Forces unveiled a new 450 km Alborz 3D phased-array radar capable of intercepting and revealing long-range stealth targets or small aerial threats.

DEFENCE PRODUCTION AND R&D

After the 1979 Islamic revolution and the start of the Iran–Iraq War, economic sanctions and an international arms embargo coupled with a high demand for military hardware forced Iran to rely on its domestic arms industry for repair and spare parts. The Islamic Revolutionary Guards Corps was put in charge of re-organising the domestic military industry. Under its command, Iran's military industry was dramatically expanded. Over the years, considerable investment has been made in new equipment and facilities for research, development and production. Iran has a sophisticated coterie of engineers and technicians with the capability to work on sophisticated, high-tech projects. It has specialised in the "reverse-engineering" of western equipment. Iran continues to conduct research on military electronics, battlefield command and communications equipment, and integrated control systems. Key product lines include missiles, ammunition, armaments, vehicles, communications, marine, chemical and aviation. The most significant growth area has been in the missile industries. Other equipment being produced includes Anti-Tank Guided Weapons (ATGW) and long-range artillery rockets. Iran is one of the leading countries in the development of drones. Its extensive unmanned aerial vehicle programme dates back to the Iraqi war of the 1980s against the Islamic Republic. Iran's UAV programme has expanded in recent years with more than a dozen models operating for a variety of functions ranging from surveillance, to intelligence gathering, carrying bombs and Kamikaze operations. Iran is reportedly expanding and modernising its submarine fleet. Iran's military industries are run by the Ministry of Defence's Defence Industrial Organisation (DIO) and the Revolutionary Guard's military production authority.

Major Armament Producers

Defence Industries Organisation is a conglomerate of companies run by the Islamic Republic of Iran whose function is to provide the military of Iran with the necessary manufacturing capacity and technical abilities. It produces tanks, rockets, bombs, guns, armoured vehicles, etc.

Iran Electronics Industries is a state-owned subsidiary of Iran's Defence Industries Organisation. IEI was established as a government company in 1972 in order to develop military materials for the Iranian Military. Its products include missile electronics, radar, and electronic warfare.

Aviation Industries Organisation acts as a policy maker and coordinator to promote an indigenous Iranian aeronautical industry by providing and assisting the Iranian aircraft industries with needed technologies, knowledge and parts.

Aerospace Industries Organisation is a subsidiary of Defence Industries Organisation responsible for managing Iran's missile programme.

Marine Industries Organisation produces Ships, hovercraft and submarines.

DEFENCE DEALS

Arms Import

The UN arms embargo against Iran ended On October 18, 2020. The lifting of the embargo had been agreed in the 2015 Joint Comprehensive Plan of Action (JCPOA). Iran can now import and export weapon systems. Iran imported most of its weapons from the United States and Europe before the Islamic revolution. However, due to economic sanctions and a weapons embargo put on Iran by the United States it was forced to rely on its domestic arms industry for weapons and spare parts. China began to sell weapons directly to Iran, strategic weapons such as coast-to-sea missiles. Gradually, Russia also began to start selling weapons to Iran. All weapons used by the IRGC today are either produced by countries such as Russia, China, Ukraine, North Korea and Belarus, or are the result of reverse engineering those products or produced under license from one of these countries. The IRGC has procured hundreds of tanks and armoured personnel carriers from Russia. The Russian arms included the Sukhoi Su-25 Frogfoot ground support aircraft and S-300 SAM, other items such as speed boats, cruise and ballistic missiles from China and North Korea increasingly steering its defence organisation toward that of Eastern countries. The purchase of four Russian S-300 air defence systems in 2016 was Iran's first significant import of major arms since 2007. According to reports, Ninety six per cent of Iran's imports in 2014 to 18 came from Russia and the rest from China.

Arms Export

With the lifting of the UN arms embargo, Iran reportedly plans to export arms. The potential export products include communication systems, short-range multiple rocket launchers, recoilless rifles, and sniper rifles, some anti-tank systems, both guided missiles (ATGMs) and RPGs, and unmanned aerial vehicles (UAVs). Iran's defence industries claim to offer a wide variety of armaments, spanning from watercraft to armoured vehicles, from rockets to small arms ammunition, and from artillery to missiles. Due to Iran's nuclear programme, the United Nations Security Council placed sanctions on Iran forbidding it from exporting any form of weapons. Military equipment exported by Iran includes small arms and ammunition, communications equipment, night-vision goggles, thermal scopes, high-power sniper rifles, long-range mortars, man-portable air-defence systems (MANPADS), and artillery rockets. Iran has reportedly started sending the T-72S main battle tank to Iraq.

DEFENCE BUDGET

Total defence spending: $20.5 billion(2020), $17.4 billion (2019)

Defence spending in terms of GDP: 3.8% (2019)

According to media reports, Iran's military spending peaked in 2006 during the period 1994–2018 and fell by 30 per cent between 2006 and 2014 being affected by the European Union imposed economic and financial sanctions on Iran. Iran's military spending increased by 25 per cent between 2015 and 2017 when sanctions were lifted in 2015 by the United States. However, in 2018 military spending decreased again after sanctions were reimposed by the Trump administration.

CONCLUSION

Iran has managed to become self-sufficient in the production of a vast range of weapons and military equipment despite sanctions. A large portion of Iran's military equipment is presently met by domestic production. In recent years, Iran has designed and manufactured different weapons and military systems in aerospace, naval, aerial, ground, electronic and optic fields. It has large arsenal of anti-ship cruise missiles and a wide-range of unmanned aerial vehicles while the Navy has been increasing its presence in international waters. Iran is likely to continue to focus on the domestic development of increasingly capable missiles, naval platforms and weapons, and air defences while it attempts to upgrade some of its deteriorating air and ground capabilities primarily through foreign purchases. With the lifting of a 13-year UN arms embargo on their military, Iran now appears ready to establish a serious and effective presence in the international armament market. The country holds a position of immense strategic importance in the world today as well as a regional importance among the nations of the Persian Gulf.

CONTACT DETAILS
Ministry of Defence and Logistics
Tehran, Iran
E-mail: vds@isiran.com
Website: http://www.mod.ir/

Aerospace Research Institute
15th Street, PO Box 834-14665
Tehran, Iran
Tel: (+98 21) 88 36 60 30 39
Fax: (+98 21) 88 36 20 11
e-mail: info@ari.ac.ir

IRAQ
(Capital: Baghdad)

INTRODUCTION

Area: 438,317 sq km
Population: 39,650,145 (July 2021 est.)
Coastline: 58 km
Maritime claims: Territorial sea: 12 nm
Continental shelf: not specified

KEY POLITICAL PERSONS

PRESIDENT: Barham Salih

PRIME MINISTER & COMMANDER-IN-CHIEF : Mustafa Al-Kadhimi

KEY DEFENCE PERSONS

DEFENCE MINISTER: Juma Inad

CHIEF OF STAFF: Lt. Gen. Abdul Amir Rashid Yarallah

COMMANDER -IN-CHIEF OF THE ARMY: Maj. Gen. Qassem Al-Mohammadi

COMMANDER-IN-CHIEF OF THE NAVY: Rear Adm. Ahmed Jasim

COMMANDER-IN-CHIEF OF THE AIR FORCE: Gen. Shihab Jahid Ali

ECONOMY

Iraq has a mixed economic system with oil as the major economic driver. The Oil sector provides roughly 85% of government revenue and 80% of foreign exchange earnings. Iraq is the second-largest producer in the Organisation of the Petroleum Exporting Countries (OPEC). The government has signed several trade agreements with its neighbours while the country's reconstruction efforts have been proceeding at a moderate pace. The government is enacting laws and developing the institutions needed to implement its economic policy. After the country's devastations by war, the economy was gradually picking up, however, the drop in oil prices and COVID-19 pandemic are placing unprecedented strains on its economy. According to the World Bank, the recovery outpaced the slowdown in the oil sector as Iraq adjusted to its OPEC+ quota. The economy is forecast to gradually recover on the back of rising oil prices and OPEC+ production quotas, which are planned to be phased out in 2022.

GDP (official exchange rate): $231.994 billion (2019 est.)

Real Growth Rate (GDP): -2.1% (2017 est.), 13.1% (2016 est.)

Industries: Petroleum, chemicals, textiles, leather, construction materials, food processing, fertilizer, metal fabrication/processing.

Total Exports: $50.61 billion (2020 est.), $88.9 billion (2019 est.)

Export Commodities: Crude petroleum, refined petroleum, gold, dates, petroleum coke (2019)

Major Markets: China 26%, India 24%, South Korea 9%, United States 8%, Italy 6%, Greece 6% (2019)

Total Imports: $54.72 billion (2020 est.), $72.28 billion (2019 est.)

Import Commodities: Refined petroleum, broadcasting equipment, cars, jewellery, cigarettes (2019)

Major Suppliers: United Arab Emirates 28%, Turkey 21%, China 19% (2019)

INTERNATIONAL DISPUTES

◆ Iraq's lack of a maritime boundary with Iran prompts jurisdiction disputes beyond the mouth of the Shatt al Arab in the Persian Gulf.

◆ Turkey has expressed concern over the autonomous status of Kurds in Iraq.

DEFENCE

The Iraqi Armed Forces have been rebuilt with substantial assistance from the United States Armed Forces after the 2003 invasion which toppled the Saddam Hussein regime. Iraqi security forces are composed of forces serving under the Ministry of Interior (MOI) and the Ministry of Defence (MOD), as well as the Iraqi Counter Terrorism Bureau which reports directly to the Prime Minister of Iraq. MOD forces include the Iraqi Army, the Iraqi Air Force and the Iraqi Navy. In 2015, a large-scale programme for the complete reconstruction of the Army was announced as the Army effectively collapsed during the Islamic State (IS) offensive in mid-2014. The US and other militaries came to support as the Islamic State took over and routed the Iraqi military.

The Air Force is designed to support the Ground Forces with surveillance, reconnaissance and troop lift capabilities and the Navy to protect Iraq's shoreline, inland waterways and offshore oil platforms. The Iraqi Special Forces – the Counter Terrorism Service – created by coalition forces after the 2003 invasion is funded by the Iraq Ministry of Defence. The Popular Mobilisation Forces (PMF) - an Iraqi state-sponsored umbrella organisation composed of some 40 militias – has been called the new Iraqi Republican Guard after it was fully reorganised in early 2018.

ARMY

Personnel: 54,000

Equipment (figures as of 2014)

Category	Name	In Service
MBT	T90	
	T-72	77
	T-55	50
	M1A1 Abrams	146
AFV/APC	BMP-1	150
	M113	1026
	MTLB	1200+
	BTR-80	115
	FUCH	20
	BTR-4	150
Mortar	120mm	(55 batteries)
	81mm	(108 platoons)
Artillery	M109A4/A5 155mm SP howitzer	50
	M198 155mm towed howitzer	128
	152 mm D-20 towed howitzer	18
Weapon	Stinger	
	Avenger	40
	Pantsir S1	40
	Igla - Manpad	

New Procurements/Upgrades

No major procurement plans are under consideration at present.

Army Aviation

Category	Name	In Service
Helicopter	UH-1HP Huey II	2
	Bell 206-B3	10
	Mi-8T	20
	Mi-17	20
	Bell IA-407	24
	EC635	20
	Gazelle 20mm canon	6
	Mi-35M	28
	Mi-28NE	15

NAVY

Personnel: 2,300 (including 800 marines)

Equipment

Category	Name	In service
Patrol craft	Al Basrah class 60m OSV	2
	Fatah-class OPV (Fincantieri Saettia Mk type)	4
	140t 'Predator' type patrol boat	5
	AL FAW-class patrol	6
	PB-301	12
	'Defender'-type RIHB fast small boat	26

New Procurements/Upgrades

No major procurement plans are under consideration at present

Marines

Two battalions of Marines Regiment have been established. The first battalion consists of 12 platoons, six of which execute point of defence of the oil platforms, while the other six are trained to conduct vessel board, search and seizure (VBSS) operations). The second battalion also consists of 12 platoons tasked with port security and other ground security duties.

AIR FORCE

Personnel: 3,000

Equipment

Category	Name	In Service
Attack Aircraft	T-50 IC	6
	Su-25	12
	L-159A	
	F-16	36
Reconnaissance	Sama CH2000	8
	SB7L-360 Seeker	6
	King Air 350	6
Trainer	Lasta 95	20
	Cessna AC-208B Caravan	12
	T-6A Texan II	15
Transport	C-130E	3
	An-32	6
	C-130J	6
Helicopter	Mi-17	
UAV	CH-4B	

New Procurements/Upgrades

No major procurement plans are under consideration at present.

Defence Expenditure

Total defence expenditure: $7.6 Billion

(2019), $6200 million (2018)

Estimated defence spending in terms of GDP: 3.5% (2019)

Defence Production and R&D

The military industry in Iraq has been destroyed due to war. The importance of reviving the military industry has been felt but Iraq is looking for partners from the private sector to proceed with the work. Earlier, Iraq has made considerable efforts in armoured fighting vehicle development, combat aircraft conversion and repair, aerial weapon production, artillery system and rocket development and small arms production.

Defence Procurement

Iraq seeks to achieve 'strategic independence'. The aim of the military is to be able to defend its international borders without external support. It is keen to diversify the purchase of defence equipment away from excessive reliance on the United States. Baghdad has expressed interest in acquiring Russian-made S-300 and S-400 long-range surface-to-air missile systems.

CONTACT DETAILS
Ministry of Defence
Bab Al-Muadam
Baghdad, Iraq
Tel: (+964 1) 888 90 71

STRATEGIC INFORMATION
ISRAEL
(Capital: Jerusalem)

INTRODUCTION

Area: 20,770 sq km
Population: 8,787,045 (July 2021 est.)
Coastline: 273 km
Maritime claims: Territorial sea: 12 nm
Continental shelf: to depth of exploitation

GEOPOLITICAL IMPORTANCE

Israel – the only Jewish majority state – became a nation on 16 May 1948. Israel is positioned between three continents or sub-continents, Africa, the Arab Peninsula (sub-continent) and Europe. The country is bordered by Egypt on the West, Syria and Jordan on the East, and Lebanon on the North. Its maritime plain is extremely fertile. The southern Negev region, which comprises almost half the total area, is largely a desert. The Jordan River flows from the North through Lake Hule (Waters of Merom) and Lake Kinneret (also called Sea of Galilee or Sea of Tiberias), finally entering the Dead Sea 1,349 ft (411 m) below sea level. Israel contains the occupied areas of Jerusalem from which it has not withdrawn after 1967 war. The nation of Israel is endowed with archaeological and religious sites considered sacred by Jews, Muslims and Christians alike. With the growth in high-tech sector, and massive defence industry, Israel has emerged as a regional economic and military powerhouse.

POLITICAL OVERVIEW

Israel is a parliamentary democracy, consisting of Legislative, Executive and Judicial branches. Its institutions are the Presidency, the Knesset (parliament), the Government (cabinet), the Judiciary and the State Comptroller. The president is elected by the Knesset to a seven-year term. He has no veto powers and exercises mainly ceremonial functions. The 120 members of the Knesset are elected in nation-wide elections from party lists. The Knesset is the parliament of the State of Israel; its main function is to legislate. The Government (cabinet of ministers) is the executive authority of the state, charged with administering internal and foreign affairs, including security matters. The government usually serves for four years. The head of the government is the Prime Minister.

The Judicial branch is an independent branch of the government. The judicial structure consists of three main types of courts – civil, religious, and military. There are special courts for labour, insurance, traffic, municipal, juvenile, and other disputes. Judges for all courts are appointed by the Judicial Selection Committee. The committee is composed of nine members – two cabinet members (one being the Minister of Justice), two Knesset members, two members of the Israel Bar Association, and three Supreme Court justices (one being the President of the Supreme Court). The committee is chaired by the Minister of Justice.

Israel does not have a constitution, but it does have a number of basic laws that govern how the government is structured, rights of individuals and similar matters. Scheduled general elections are held regularly four years after the last elections. In addition, a government may fall either by a motion of the government dissolving the Knesset, or on a no confidence motion of parties in the Knesset. To limit the number of such motions and stabilise the government, a no confidence motion requires 61 votes to be carried out, and the initiators must name a candidate whom they will back to form a government.

KEY POLITICAL PERSONS

PRESIDENT: Isaac Herzog

PRIME MINISTER: Naftali Bennett

KEY DEFENCE PERSONS

DEFENCE MINISTER: Benny Gantz

CHIEF OF GENERAL STAFF: Lt. Gen. Aviv Kochavi

COMMANDER OF ARMY: Maj. Gen. Yoel Strick

COMMANDER OF NAVY: Vice Adm. Aluf David Salama

COMMANDER OF AIR FORCE: Brig. Gen. Alif Tomer Bar

ECONOMY

Israel is among the world's most resilient and technologically-advanced market economies. The world demand for Israeli advanced technologies, software, electronics, and other sophisticated equipment has stimulated industrial growth attracting significant foreign investment. The number of new start-ups is very high due to the extraordinary innovative talent in Israel, coupled with the availability of highly skilled manpower. Israel's diamond-cutting and polishing industry, centred in Tel Aviv, is the largest in the world and is a significant source of foreign exchange. Cut diamonds, high-technology equipment, and pharmaceuticals are among its leading exports.

The Israeli Defence industry is a strategically important sector and a large employer within the country. It is a major player in the global arms market and it is among the largest exporter of weapons in the world. There are over 150 active defence companies based in the country and Israel is considered to be the world's leading UAV exporter. Natural gas fields discovered off Israel's coast have also brightened Israel's energy security outlook. The Tamar and Leviathan fields were some of the world's largest offshore natural gas finds in the last decade. In 2020, Israel began exporting gas to Egypt and Jordan. Israel is a major tourist destination. Visitors are drawn to Israel's numerous religious, archaeological, and historic sites such as the Western Wall and the Dome of the Rock and biblical cities such as Nazareth, and Bethlehem in the West Bank.

GDP (official exchange rate): $394.93 billion (2019 est.)

Real Growth Rate (GDP): -2.6% (2020 est.), 3.28% (2019 est.)

Industries: High-technology products (including aviation, communications, computer-aided design and manufactures, medical electronics, fiber optics), wood and paper products, potash and phosphates, food, beverages, and tobacco, caustic soda, cement, pharmaceuticals, construction, metal products, chemical products, plastics, cut diamonds, textiles, footwear.

Oil – proved reserves: 12.73 million bbl (1 January 2018 est.)

Natural gas – proved reserves: 176 billion cu m (1 January 2018 est.)

Total Exports: $104.992 billion (2019 est.), $101.389 billion (2018 est.)

Export Commodities: Diamonds, packaged medicines, medical instruments, integrated circuits, refined petroleum (2019)

Major Markets: United States 26%, China 9%, United Kingdom 7% (2020)

Total Imports: $116.23 billion (2019 est.), $111.652 billion (2018 est.)

Import Commodities: Diamonds, cars, crude petroleum, refined petroleum, broadcasting equipment (2019)

Major Suppliers: United States 12%, China 11%, Germany 7.5%, Switzerland 7%, Turkey 6% (2020)

DEFENCE & SECURITY

Israel's military priority is to defend the integrity of the State and uphold its values – its character as a Jewish and democratic state and as the homeland of the Jewish people. As the armed forces of the country, the military has been entrusted to defend its territorial integrity and the security of its citizens and inhabitants, strengthen the state of Israel's international and regional status while striving toward peace with its neighbours.

The state's security doctrine was laid down by the first Prime Minister, David Ben-Gurion, in the 1950s. The doctrine was founded based on three principles – Deterrence, Early Warning and Military Superiority. Later, it was proposed to add four new components to the security doctrine – Prevention and Pre-emption, Alliance with the United States, Regional alliances and Adaptation. Prevention and pre-emption refer to a policy that Israel has already adopted, using all the means at its disposal in order to pre-empt threats of non-conventional weapon use against it. In recent years, Israel has adopted a new military doctrine relying on high tech defence, quick reaction to counter terrorism and special operations forces with focus on countering threats from guerrilla armies such as Hezbollah and Hamas. Instability in Egypt and Syria has also prompted Israel to build up forces against cross-border terrorist attacks from small militias.

Israel's external threats has compelled the country to invest heavily in cyber security. The military's Unit 8200, an elite group of the Israeli Defence Forces, focuses on intelligence and collects information and code decryption. Israel's National Cyber Directorate – the national security and technological agency – is responsible for defending Israel's national cyberspace and for establishing and advancing Israel's cyber power. The Directorate operates at the national level to constantly strengthen the level of defence of organisations and citizens, to prevent and handle cyberattacks and to strengthen emergency response capabilities. As part of its roles, the Directorate advances innovative cyber solutions and forward-looking technological solutions, formulates strategies and policies in the national and international arenas and develops its cyber manpower.

External Conflict

Palestinian-Israeli conflict: The main sticking points preventing peace between Israelis and Palestinians is that Palestinians want Israel to withdraw to pre-1967 borders. The West Bank and the Gaza Strip are Israeli-occupied with current status subject to the Israeli-Palestinian Interim Agreement. The Palestinians in the West Bank and Eastern Jerusalem have lived under Israeli occupation since 1967. The settlements that Israel has built in the West Bank are home to nearly 500,000 people and are deemed to be illegal under international law, although Israel disputes this. The West Bank has enormous strategic importance to any country wishing to invade Israel. Israel, therefore, insists on guarantees that the Palestinian state would not allow a foreign army to enter its borders. Israel evacuated its settlers from the Gaza Strip in 2005 and withdrew its forces, ending almost four decades of military occupation. However, after the militant Islamic group Hamas seized control of Gaza in June 2007, Israel intensified its economic blockade of the Strip. Peace process began with the Palestinians after years of an uprising known as the Intifada. Despite the handover of Gaza and parts of the West Bank to Palestinian control, a final agreement is yet to be reached. The latest round of peace negotiations began in July 2013 and was suspended in 2014. For nearly a century, world leaders have debated the issues and attempted to resolve this conflict. On 28 January 2020, US President Donald Trump unveiled the Trump peace plan but the plan was rejected by the Palestinians. Peace agreements were signed between Israel and Egypt in 1979, and Israel and Jordan in 1994. Israel seized the Golan Heights from Syria during the Six-Day War. Israel also annexed Shebaa Farms as part of the Golan Heights, a move not recognised by the international community. Syria tried to retake the Golan Heights during the 1973 Middle East war. Both countries signed an armistice in 1974 and a UN observer force has been in place on the ceasefire line since then. Syria wants to secure the return of the Golan Heights as part of any peace deal. However, public opinion in Israel does not favour withdrawal.

THREAT PERSPECTIVE

The geographically tiny state of Israel has been plagued by the threat of both low-intensity conflict and full-scale war throughout its entire history. Major threats facing the country include the growing number of foreign fighters joining jihadist groups in the Middle East, cyber warfare, the Iranian nuclear and missile threat, the transforming of the Mediterranean Basin into a launch pad for terrorism in Europe, and threats to maritime and energy security. Israel is rattled by Iran's arsenal of missiles capable of striking the Jewish state, its frequent talk of Israel's annihilation, and its alliances with anti-Israel militants like the Palestinian Hamas in the Gaza Strip and Hezbollah based in Lebanon, who control tens of thousands of rockets. Hezbollah's enormous rocket stores pose an unprecedented threat to Israel. Syria reportedly funds and arms terrorist organisations like the Hamas and Hezbollah, as proxies to attack Israel. Another threat about Iran's alleged nuclear weapons programme is constant in Israel.

STRATEGIC RELATIONS

United States: Israel and the US maintain a strategic alliance which represents a clear interest for both sides. Israel is one of the United States' two original major non-NATO allies in the Middle East. In both military and non-military spheres, Israeli technological achievements – often developed with US support – are shared with America. Israel is the largest annual recipient of US foreign assistance. Almost all US aid to Israel is now in the form of military assistance. The US-Israel bilateral relationship is strong, anchored by over $3 billion in Foreign Military Financing annually. In addition to financial support, the US participates in a high level of exchanges with Israel, to include joint military exercises, military research, and weapons development. Through the Joint Counterterrorism Group and a semi-annual Strategic Dialogue, the US and Israel have enhanced their cooperation in fighting terrorism. The United States is Israel's largest single trading partner.

India: Israel has consolidated defence ties with India into a strategic relationship. India is among the world's largest customer of Israeli arms. The first major military deal between the two countries was the sale of Israeli EL/W-2090 AEW radars. The two nations have signed many important defence deals and also embarked on extensive space cooperation. They have held numerous joint anti-terror training exercises. There are regular exchanges between the armed forces and defence personnel. Cyber has emerged as one of the areas in which both countries have started to collaborate. Israel currently has plans for fresh joint ventures and technology transfer in developing weapons systems and ensuring implementation of Make in India initiative in the key sectors. Cooperation in other spheres, like agriculture and education, has witnessed a significant rise.

Azerbaijan: Relations between Israel and Azerbaijan have strengthened in the political, military, and technology spheres. Israel's strategic partner Azerbaijan became an oil producer and the volume of Azerbaijani oil delivered to Israel did not stop to increase more than 45 % of Israeli supplies. Azerbaijan is the biggest supplier of oil to Israel while Israel sells sophisticated arms including missile systems and drones. Azerbaijani-Israeli trade cooperation flourishes and amounts to nearly $4 billion. Israel's drone planes are as much in demand in Azerbaijan. Israel also sells its Azeri partner armoured troop carriers, multiple rocket launchers, Tavor rifles, and ammunition.

Germany: Germany and Israel maintain a special relationship based on shared beliefs, Western values and a combination of historical perspectives. The relationship has developed impressively since 1965, the year full diplomatic relations were established between the two countries. The two nations have significant and long-standing military cooperation. Germany has supplied Israel with Dolphin class submarines while Germany utilizes the Israeli-designed Spike Anti-Tank Missile. Both the countries have jointly developed a nuclear warning system, dubbed Operation Bluebird. Germany is Israel's largest trading partner in Europe and Israel's second most important trading partner after the United States.

Myanmar: Myanmar has become one of Israel's strongest allies. The two nations achieved independence in the same year, 1948 and diplomatic relations between the two countries were established at the beginning of the 50's. In the years since the establishment of diplomatic relations, the two countries have nurtured a strong bond of friendship, which have included visits of high level officials from both countries. Israel and Myanmar have undertaken many international cooperation ventures in the fields of agriculture, health and education. Israel over the last several decades have sold military hardware and provided technology and training.

DEFENCE CAPABILITIES

The Israel Defence Forces (IDF) is one of the world's best battle-trained armed force. The IDF consists of the Ground Forces, Air Force and Navy, headed by the Chief of General Staff, the Ramatkal, is subordinate to Israel's Defence Minister. Israel follows a conscript model for its armed forces. It is unique in that military service is compulsory for both men and women. The 'Nachshol' IDF's first company consisting entirely of female combat soldiers was established in 2006 whose mission is to patrol and gather field intelligence in real time. The IDF maintains a qualitative advantage by deploying advanced weapons systems, many of which are developed and manufactured in Israel for its specific needs.

The IDF has reportedly begun the roll out of its five-year 'multi-year Momentum Plan' in an effort to make the military better equipped to fight in future warfare. The plan envisages to take full advantage of the areas in which the IDF has expertise – air power, intelligence and technology- in order to ensure the military maintains a constant and significant edge over its foes. The momentum plan includes the purchasing of new equipment for ground troops, including better rifle scopes, shoulder-launched missiles, and small drones, as well as training soldiers in new methods, creating new divisions and improving communication between units. The military is working to improve its ability to attack the enemy and at the same time giving considerable focus on the growing problem of finding the enemy.

The IDF is equipped with top-of-the-line weapons and computer systems and uses several technologies developed in Israel such as the Merkava main battle tank, Achzarit armoured personnel carrier, high tech weapons systems, the Iron Dome missile defence system, Trophy active protection system for vehicles, and the Galil and Tavor assault rifles. The armed forces have deployed a variant of the Samson RCWS, a remote-controlled weapons platform, which can include machine guns, grenade launchers, and anti-tank missiles on a remotely operated turret, in pillboxes. It has developed observation balloons with sophisticated cameras and surveillance systems used to thwart terror attacks and possess advanced combat engineering equipment which includes the IDF Caterpillar D9 armoured bulldozer, IDF Puma CEV, Tzefa Shiryon and CARPET minefield breaching rockets, and a variety of robots and explosive devices. It also possesses a sizeable arsenal of short and medium-range ballistic missiles, land, sea, and air-launched cruise missiles, and is working towards a layered and comprehensive missile defence capability. Israel's missile defence system includes the Arrow system, the Iron Dome system, David's Sling. It is believed that Jericho intercontinental ballistic missile is capable of delivering nuclear warheads.

Israel's major military operations include the 1948 War of Independence, 1951-1956 Retribution operations, 1956 Sinai War, 1964-1967 War over Water, 1967 Six-Day War, 1967-1970 War of Attrition, 1968 Battle of Karameh, 1973 Operation Spring of Youth, 1973 Yom Kippur War, 1976 Operation Entebbe, 1978 Operation Litani, 1982 Lebanon War, 1982-2000 South Lebanon conflict, 1987-1993 First Intifada, 2000-2005 Second Intifada, 2002 Operation Defensive Shield, 2006 Lebanon War, 2008-2009 Gaza War, 2012 Operation Pillar of Defence.

ARMY: The IDF Ground Forces is responsible for the general organisation and structure of field forces, infantry, paratroopers, artillery, armour, engineering and field intelligence. The primary duty of the branch is the development, acquisition and maintenance of combat facilities besides taking responsibility for planning and the administration of manpower, training and military exercises. The service branches are the Infantry Corps, Armoured Corps, Artillery Corps, Engineering Corps and the Intelligence Corps.

Personnel: 133,000

Equipment

Category	Name	In Service
MBT	Merkava Mk4	700 (target figure)
	M113 (all versions)	5,500
	Namer	100+
APC	Achzarit	150
	Nagmachon & Nakpadon	150
	ZE'EV	150
	David (urban warfare roles)	
	Wolf Armoured Vehicle	
Artillery	D30s (122mm)	100
	Soltam M68/71	
	(155mm) towed	300+
	M107 175mm (SP)	175
	L33 M-50 155mm (SP)	120
	M-109 155mm (SP)	500
	M-110 203mm (SP)	72
Mortar	160mm	
	122mm	
MRL	135mm	
	240mm	
	290mm	
	MRLS	
ATGW	TOW	48
	MAPATS	
	SPIKE	
	TAMUZ	
AA gun	20mm missile/gun	
	30mm & 40mm	
	FIM-92 Stinger (SAM)	500
Weapon	Machbet	400
	Pereh Guided Missile Carrier	

New Procurements/Upgrades

◆ Israel will begin serial production of a new Eitan (APC) developed to give troops greater speed and mobility. Eitan will replace the M113 APCs.

The IDF's new 'Eitan' APC. (Image credit: Defence Ministry)

◆ Israeli Ministry of Defence has awarded Elbit Systems of America, LLC, a $200 million contract as part of the automatic self-propelled howitzer gun systems programme to replace its tank-like M109 howitzers with Elbit's wheeled ATMOS mobile howitzer.

◆ The MOD has placed an order for Rafael's Spike FireFly loitering munition jointly developed by Rafael and the IMOD. FireFly provides behind-cover precision attack capabilities for the dismounted soldier.

NAVY: The Israeli Navy is officially known as the Sea Corps (Hel Yam). Although the Navy is relatively small compared to other IDF corps, it plays a significant role in the IDF's warfare capabilities. The Navy's primary objectives are to defend and protect the country from threats emanating from the sea, to warn of impending warfare and to achieve the goals set by the IDF during warfare. The Navy is responsible for protecting strategic infrastructure along Israel's coast, including natural resources and ports including Israel's natural gas platforms in the Mediterranean Sea, which provide about 75 percent of the country's electricity. The Navy's defence capability has been strengthened with the delivery of the Sa'ar 6 class missile corvettes. The vessels are part of the IDF's new multidimensional warfare strategy that is a key part of the IDF's Momentum multiyear plan. Other ships include corvettes of the Sa'ar 5 class equipped with Harpoon and Gabriel sea-to-sea missiles, Barak-8 sea-to-air missiles. Smaller and more agile ships comprised of the Sa'ar 4.5 and Sa'ar 4 classes besides two dozen Dvora and Daburclass patrol boats. The Navy also operates the AS-565 helicopter for a variety of missions, including reconnaissance and rescue.

The principal units of the Navy: Routine Security Company (Palgot Habatash), Missile boats (Shayetet 3), Submarines (Shayetet 7), Special Forces of the Navy (Shayetet 13), Naval control unit.

Main naval bases: Ashdod, Eilat, Haifa, Atlit

Personnel: 9,500

Equipment

Category	Name	In Service
Submarine	Dolphin class	5+1
Corvette	Sa'ar 6 class	4
	Sa'ar 5 class	3
Missile Boat	Sa'ar 4.5 class	8
Patrol Boat	Super Dvora Mk I I/II	9
	Shaldag Mk I/II	7
	Dabur	
Unmanned Vehicle	Protector USV	
	Orbiter Mini	

...continued

Category	Name	In Service
Weapon	Harpoon (ASM)	
	Popeye	
	Gabriel	
	Barak 1 & Barak 8	
	Typhoon	
	Rafael overhead weapon station	
	Samson remote controlled weapon station	

New Procurements/Upgrades

◆ With the delivery of the third and fourth next-generation SA'AR-6 class missile corvettes – the INS Atzmaut and INS Nitzachon – to the Israeli Navy, Germany has now successfully handed over all the four SA'AR-6 class missile corvettes under contract to the Navy.

The Israeli Navy SA'AR-6 corvettes. (Image credit: © thyssenkrupp AG.)

◆ The Defence Ministry has approved the purchase of four Shaldag 5-class fast petrol boats (FPBs) for the Israeli Navy from a domestic shipyard in a $30.6 million deal. The ships will be delivered in stages over the next four years.

◆ The Navy's sixth Dolphin-class submarine, Dragon, is being built for Israel by Germany. The first three submarines were commissioned between 1999 and 2000 and delivery of the second batch submarines began from 2014.

Naval Aviation
Equipment

Category	Name	In Service
Helicopter	SA-366G (shipborne)	2
	AB-206B	6
	AS565MA (shipborne on the Eilaths)	5
	C-130 Hercules	2
	UH-1N Twin Huey	15+

New Procurements/Upgrades

◆ The Israeli MoD plans to purchase a total of 12 AW119KX training helicopters. Israel had earlier ordered seven helicopters and later placed an order for the remaining five units. The aircraft will replace the Sayfan helicopters.

AIR FORCE: The Israeli Air Force officially known as the "Kheil HaAvir" in Hebrew meaning "Air Corps" is among the world's most powerful aerial fighting forces. The Air Force, a central pillar of the IDF, has played a major role in securing the country's numerous military victories since the creation of the state of Israel in 1948. Its combat policy, strategy, and ability were put to a test in a long series of air clashes with Egypt, Syria and Jordan. One third of the IDF's manpower is in the IAF taking on a variety of roles in defending Israel's home front. The IAF is also known for its distinguished staff of pilots, which ranks among the most elite in the world. As part of the expansion of the IDF's defensive capabilities under the military's Momentum multi-year plan, the Israel's Air Force will be making changes over the next five years to streamline the force, including closing an air squadron and opening a third F-35i Adir squadron. In 2020, the Air Force opened a new unit '7th Aerial Special Forces Wing' aimed at bringing all of its special forces units under one roof o streamline their operations and make them more effective. The Unit will include the air force's elite search-and-rescue Unit 669, the Shaldag commando unit, the Frontal Landing Unit, which builds ad hoc landing strips behind enemy lines; a dedicated intelligence unit for the wing; and a special forces school.

Major air bases: Ramat David, Sdot Micha, Hatzerim, Ovda, Hatzor, Tel Nof, Ramon, Nevatim, etc

Personnel: 30,000

Equipment

Category	Name	In Service
Fighter	F-35I 'Adir'	16
	F-15A/B/C/D	52
	F-15I	25
	F-16A/B	25
	F-16C/D	137
	F-16I	102
Tanker	KC-130H	5
	KC-707	3
AWE&C/EW	Gulfstream G550	
	Oron	
Transport	C-130J Super Hercules	1+
	C-130E/H	16
	Do28	10
	King Air B200	3

...continued

Category	Name	In Service
Trainer	AW119KX	7
	F-16A	30 (lavi)
	M-346 LAVI	
	G-120	
	Beechcraft T-6A Texan II	
	M-D500 (helicopters)	
Helicopter	AH-64A	29
	AH-64D-1	18
	AH-1 G	30
	Bell 206	38
	S-70A-50 Peace Hawk	25
	CH-53A/D	40
	UH-60A Blackhawk	34
	CH-53 Sea Stallion	
Liaison	Cessna U-206C	20
	Beech Queen Air	18
UAV	Heron	
	Eitan	
	Harpy	
	Harop	
	Hermes 450	
	Skylark	
Weapon	MIM-23 Hawk (SAM)	
	MIM-104 Patriot (SAM)	
	Arrow (ABM)	
	Shafrir missile	
	Python (AAM)	
	Popeye (ASM)	
	AGM-65 Maverick (ASM)	
	AGM-45 Shrike (ASM)	
	AGM-114 Hellfire (ASM)	
	AIM-120 AMRAAM (AAM)	
	AGM-65 Maverick (AGM)	
	AIM-9 Sidewinder (AAM)	
	MIM-72 Chaparral (SAM)	
	Delilah cruise missile	
	Iron Dome	
	David's Sling (SAM)	
	Jericho II ICBM	
	Jericho III ICBM	

New Procurements/Upgrades

◆ The Israeli Air Force has received a new intelligence aircraft called "Oron" equipped with an advanced radar system. The airplane is developed to provide the military with unprecedented reconnaissance capabilities.

◆ The IAF has placed an order for 50 F-35i Adir aircraft. The first nineteen will be standard F-35A models and the following 31 will adhere to the F-35I standard.

- The Israeli Ministry of Defence (IMOD) has issued a price and availability request to the US Navy's international programmes office for the acquisition of Boeing V-22 aircraft. Earlier the IDF had planned to purchase 12 to 14 V-22 Osprey aircraft.
- The IMOD has signed a Letter of Acceptance covering the purchase of two Boeing KC-46 tanker/transports following recent parliamentary approval for the acquisition of a number of new aircraft for the Air Force.
- Israel will acquire 15 CH-53k heavy-lift helicopters worth $2.4 billion from the United States, to replace its aging fleet of Sikorsky CH-53 Yasur helicopters.

AIR DEFENCE

- MIM-104 Patriot "Yahalom" a high to medium air defence (HIMAD)
- Iron Dome short-range air defence system
- Spyder short and medium range mobile air defence system
- David's Sling medium-to long-range rocket SAM
- Arrow anti-ballistic missile system

DEFENCE PRODUCTION AND R&D

Israel invests heavily in research and development and with the participation of the research institutes, the defence industry it has produced a high-tech weapons factory. Israel's defence industry is reportedly dominated by companies such as Israel Aerospace Industries (IAI), Rafael Advanced Defence Systems and the publicly-owned Elbit Systems which has acquired the Israel Military Industries (IMI). The companies have a diverse portfolio of products and services, including space and airborne reconnaissance systems, radar systems, UAVs, avionics and electro-optical systems, munitions, tanks and armoured personnel carriers. They produce structural components and parts and operate maintenance, repair and upgrade facilities. In addition, there are several hundred Small and Medium Sized Enterprises (SMEs) active in the sector.

The industry has a high concentration of well-qualified scientists, engineers, and technicians. The arms industry is also acknowledged as the world leader in the area of unmanned aerial vehicles (UAVs), manufacturing variants for both intelligence-gathering examples – Heron, Hermes and Searcher Mk III and unmanned combat air vehicles (UCAVS) like Harop and Jaguar. Other defence industry products are weapons and vehicles such as the Merkava battle tank series, the Kfir fighter aircraft, and various small arms such as the Galil and Tavor assault rifles, and the Uzi submachine gun. Much of the IDF's electronic systems (intelligence, communication, command and control, navigation etc.) are developed indigenously. Israel has a space research programme with scientific and commercial goals and has developed indigenous launch capabilities. It's first mission to the moon in February 2019 made Israel the 4th nation to attempt to soft land on the moon.

Major Armament Producers

IAI: Israel Aerospace Industries is Israel's prime aerospace and aviation manufacturer, producing aerial systems for both military and civilian usage. It also designs, develops and manufactures naval and ground systems, electronic warfare and radar equipment and missiles.

IMI: Israel Military Industries (IMI) manufactures assault weapons – from the classic Uzi sub-machine gun to the Tavor assault rifle – heavy ammunition, aircraft and rocket systems, armoured vehicles like the Merkava tank, and integrated security systems.

The Rafael Arms Development Authority: Rafael designs and develops a wide range of high technology-based defence systems for air, land, sea and space applications.

Elbit Systems: The Company is involved in manufacturing electronic equipment, artillery guns, radio communications systems, unmanned aerial vehicles, remote weapon systems, radar and naval systems.

Aeronautics Defence Systems Ltd. specializes in providing comprehensive defence solutions.

Israel Weapons Industries is an Israeli firearms manufacturer.

Astronautics C.A Ltd is a leading provider of airborne, naval and ground forces defence systems and solutions.

Israel Shipyards is one of the largest shipbuilding and repair facilities in the eastern Mediterranean.

Automotive Industries is an Israeli auto maker and major supplier of the Israeli security forces.

Plasan develops, manufactures and assembles custom-built vehicle armour systems and chassis up-armour designs as well as add-on armour protection kits for lightweight military tactical trucks and APCs, commercial vehicles, and a major supplier of personnel protection armour.

Defence firms in the private sector: Cyclone Aviation, Urdan Industries makers of the Merkava tank; Magal Security Systems, BVR Technologies, the Elul Group and RSL Electronics.

Foreign Suppliers – United States and Germany

DEFENCE DEALS

Joint Venture Programmes

India: Israel has exteded support and is actively participating in the 'Make in India' initiative forming a number of joint ventures with Indian partners besides taking a number of steps to encourage and facilitate collaboration between Israeli and Indian start-ups. Israel's Elbit group has formed a joint ventures with Adani-Elbit Advanced Systems India Ltd., to manufacture UAVs in India. Elbit Security Systems and Alpha Design Technologies are engaged in another joint venture-Alpha-Elsec Defence and Aerospace Systems. Israel Aerospace Industries (IAI) has inked an MoU with Kalyani Strategic Systems to develop, build and market selected air defence systems and lightweight special purpose munitions while IAI's Golan Industries Division has signed an MoU with Taneja Aerospace & Aviation Ltd. (TAAL) to cooperate in the development, production, marketing and sale of civil and military aircraft seats. IAI and Wipro Infrastructure Engineering (WIN) have announced a strategic alliance to manufacture composite aero structure parts and assemblies. Rafael Advanced Defence Systems, which is government owned, has entered into a JV with Kalyani Strategic Systems, a defence arm of Kalyani group. Rafael has also signed an agreement with Hyderabad-based Astra Microwave Products Ltd. to build tactical radio communication systems, electronic warfare systems and signal intelligence systems. Mahindra group's Mahindra Telephonics has an agreement with Israel's Shachaf Engineering to jointly develop strategic electronics sub-assemblies and systems for aerospace, marine and automotive applications. The Barak 8 (LR-SAM or MR-SAM) is a product of the joint efforts of IAI and India's Defence Research & Development Organisation (DRDO), MAFAT (a joint administrative body of the Israeli Defence Ministry and IDF), Rafael, and Bharat Dynamics Ltd.

United States: The United States and Israel cooperate closely in a number of technology development programmes. Israel is a participant in the F-35 Lightning II fighter development programme. The two nations also cooperate jointly on the Arrow missile system and the Tactical High Energy Laser also known as Nautilus. They have jointly developed the David's Sling designed to intercept medium-to long-range rockets and cruise missiles and other missile defence systems such as the Patriot and the Iron Dome. Under a 2019 agreement, Israel sold two Iron Dome batteries to the US, the first being delivered in late 2020 and the second in January 2021. The Iron Dome originally designed to intercept rockets has been upgraded and improved to allow it to also shoot down mortar shells, unmanned aerial vehicles and cruise missiles.

Singapore: The land systems arm of Singapore Technologies Engineering (ST Engineering) has signed an agreement with state-owned Israel Aerospace Industries (IAI) to set up a joint-venture (JV) company in Singapore named Proteus Advanced Systems. The new venture will develop and market advanced naval missile systems including a next-generation anti-ship missile system.

Greece: Israel and Greece have reportedly signed a defence deal which includes a $1.65 billion contract for the establishment and operation of a training centre for the Hellenic Air Force by Israeli defence contractor Elbit Systems over a 22-year period. The training centre will be modelled on Israel's own flight academy and will be equipped with 10 M-346 training aircraft produced by Italian company Leonardo. Elbit will supply kits to upgrade and operate Greece's T-6 aircraft and also provide training, simulators and logistical support.

Arms Export

Israel is among the top exporters of military equipment. The Israeli defence industries have won great prestige around the world with its advanced quality technology. The major Israeli defence companies are: Elbit Systems, Israel Aerospace Industries and Rafael. In 2020, Israeli military exports reached $8.3 billion buoyed by a 15 percent spike in the number of agreements signed compared with the previous year, according to the government. It is the second highest sales figure ever, behind 2017, when the total hit $9.2 billion. As in previous years, the bulk of the military exports went to countries in Asia and the Pacific region. The government figures said radar and early warning systems, and ammunition and armament, each contributed 16 percent of sales, while manned aircraft and avionics accounted for 13 percent, as did observation and optronics. Missiles, rockets and air defence systems sales contributed 10 percent. Other areas included communication, drone and intelligence systems. Sales to the Asia and the Pacific region comprised 44 percent, with 30 percent going to Europe, 20 percent to North America, four percent to Africa and two percent to Latin America. In addition, IAI has signed a $200 million deal to supply drone technology and services to an unspecified Asian country. The deal is for the sale of the IAI's Heron drone, including the more advanced MK II version. According to a new report by the Stockholm International Peace Research Institute (SIPRI), from 2015-2019, Israeli arms exports accounted for 3% of the global total. The top three buyers of Israeli arms were India (45% of the total amount), Azerbaijan (17%) and Vietnam (8.5%). The top three arms suppliers to Israel were the US (78%), Germany (16%) and Italy (6.2%).

Arms Import

Most of the arms used by the IDF are manufactured locally. However, for its arms Israel rely mainly on the United States. The US is by far the biggest supplier of arms to Israel. In 2016, the US agreed to provide Israel a record $38 billion in new military aid over the next decade. The agreement which equates to $3.8 billion a year, is the largest bilateral military aid package ever and includes $5 billion for missile defence, additional F-35 joint strike fighters and increased mobility for its ground forces. In 2014, Israel reportedly imported 600 air-to-air AIM-9 Sidewinder missiles, together with about 50 training missiles, replacement parts and technical support. Other Israeli arms supplier include the UK. Israel has imported Dolphin-class submarine and Sa'ar corvettes from Germany. Italy also sold 30 M-346 training aircraft to Israel.

DEFENCE BUDGET

Total defence spending: $21.3 billion (2019), $18.5 billion (2018)

Defence spending in terms of GDP: 5.3% (2019)

The Israel government has reportedly announced a new annual defence budget for 2022, worth USD17.95 billion net. The last time that Israel approved a new defence budget was in 2019, totalling ILS55.5 billion. In a statement released on 28 July, Defence Minister Benny Gantz said that the new budget "will enable a safeguarding of our defence superiority in the face of growing threats, safeguarding the State of Israel's interests and those of other government ministries, and it will allow the IDF to implement its Momentum multi-year programme". In addition to that funding from the government, Israel also received an additional 3.8 billion from the United States each year as military aid. The MoD and IDF have been operating without a proper budget for the past two years as the government failed to pass a national budget for 2020 and 2021.

Defence Procurement

The Israel Ministry of Defence is responsible for procurement, contractual, legal, financial and economic aspects of IDF activities. The Procurement and Production Directorate (PPD) handles procurement and oversees the manufacture of systems and products, maintenance services for the military and civilian defence systems, and ministry agencies' overseas procurement activities. The PPD oversees the development of the country's military-industrial infrastructure and administers the maritime and air transport of equipment and goods acquired abroad for the MoD and other government ministries, as well as equipment and goods exported from Israel. The PPD is composed of five executive and several staff units.

COUNTER-TERRORISM & NATIONAL SECURITY

Israeli society perceives terrorism as an ever present threat. The state of Israel has been accused of being a state-sponsor of terrorism, and also committing acts of state terrorism. The Jewish state has experienced numerous terrorist attacks for several decades and its counter-terrorism experience has developed in the context of complex territorial, ethnic and religious conflict with the Palestinians. Conventional threats to Israel emanated from Egypt, Syria, Iraq, and Jordan. In the last few years, the primary source of threat to Israel has come from non-state actors. The Balfour Declaration of 1917 provided for the creation of a Jewish state in Palestine. The Jews claimed Palestine – the land inhabited by a Jewish minority and Arab majority – as their ancestral land. The Palestinian Arabs also claimed the land and opposed the move to carve out a separate state, However, in 1948, Jewish leaders declared the creation of the state of Israel. War ensued and the fighting ended in a ceasefire. Israel occupied East Jerusalem and the West Bank, as well as most of the Syrian Golan Heights, and the Egyptian Sinai peninsula. It has pulled out of Gaza, ruled by the Hamas. Most Palestinian refugees and their descendants live in Gaza and the West Bank, as well as in neighbouring Jordan, Syria and Lebanon. Israel claims the whole of Jerusalem as its capital, while the Palestinians claim East Jerusalem as the capital of a future Palestinian state. Terrorists attacks in Israel have included hijackings, hostage takings, kidnappings, mass shootings, car bombings, stabbings and suicide bombings. Following the Iranian Revolution in 1979, Iran which had good relations with Israel earlier adopted a strong anti-Israel stance accusing Israel as an imperialist power in the Middle East. It has been accused of funding, weapons and training to groups, including Hezbollah, Hamas and Palestinian Islamic Jihad (PIJ) which have vowed and carried out attacks on Israel.

Terrorist groups

Different militant groups have launched attacks against Israel including the Lebanese Hizballah, Hamas, the Palestinian Islamic Jihad (PIJ), the Popular Front for the Liberation of Palestine (PFLP), the Democratic Front for the Liberation of Palestine (DFLP), and more recently the Popular Resistance Committees (PRC) and other groups.

Hizballah aka the Party of God, Hezbollah, Islamic Jihad, Islamic Jihad Organisation, Islamic Jihad for the Liberation of Palestine. The Shia militant group Hizballah ideologically inspired by the Iranian revolution is closely allied with Iran. It also shares a close relationship with the Syrian Asad regime and has provided assistance including thousands of fighters to regime fighters in the Syrian civil war. The group targets included Israeli security forces, civilians, Jews and other symbols of Western influence in the Middle East.

HAMAS (Harakat al-Muq wamah al-Isl miyyah) aka the Islamic Resistance Movement, Harakat al-Muqawama al-Islamiya, Izz al-Din al Qassam Battalions. The Hamas, the de facto ruler of Gaza, has continued to engage in sporadic clashes with Israeli security forces. They have claimed responsibility for numerous rocket attacks from Gaza into Israel and organised protests at the border between Gaza and Israel resulting in clashes that killed its members, Palestinian protesters, and Israeli soldiers.

Palestine Islamic Jihad (PIJ) aka PIJ-Shaqaqi faction, Islamic Jihad of Palestine, Abu Ghunaym Squad of the Hizballah Bayt al-Maqdis. The PIJ committed to the creation of an Islamic state in Palestine has conducted attacks on Israel including a barrage of mortar and rocket strikes in February 2020.

Popular Front for the Liberation of Palestine (PFLP) aka Halhul Gang, Halhul Squad, Palestinian Popular Resistance Forces, PPRF. The group has earned a reputation for large-scale international attacks including high-profile hijackings of Israeli and Western aircraft. Now the group has been in decline.

Democratic Front for the Liberation of Palestine (DFLP) aka Democratic Front, or al-Jabha al-Dimuqratiyah. The DFLP has been responsible for attacks against Israeli targets in Israel and the occupied territories. Its armed wing, the National Resistance Brigades, has taken part in fighting against Israeli forces in Gaza.

Popular Resistance Committees (PRC) (Lijān al-Muqāwama al-Shahbiyya). The Popular Resistance Committees (PRC), a loose grouping of armed factions, is reportedly responsible for a large number of attacks against Israelis in the Gaza Strip, both civilians and soldiers.

Islamic State of Iraq and ash-Sham – Sinai Province (ISIS-SP) aka Islamic State-Sinai Province (IS-SP), ISIS-Sinai, ISI. Initially known as Ansar Bayt al-Maqdis (ABM), the group has conducted a bloody insurgency under the ISIS banner and become one of the most deadly of the ISIS affiliates continuing to conduct attacks through 2020 and into 2021.

Army of Islam (AOI) aka Jaysh al-Islam, Jaish al-Islam. The AOI has allegedly pledged allegiance to the Islamic State and declared itself part of the Islamic State's Sinai Province (IS-SP). The group targets the Israeli governments and its citizens, conducts rocket attacks against Israel, kidnapping civilians, and attacking Christians.

Major Incidents

Israel has experienced a wave of terror perpetrated by various militant groups. Some incidents have been listed that occurred in the last ten years:

2021: Fighting broke out between Israel and Palestinian militants in Gaza on 10 May 2021 after weeks of rising Israeli-Palestinian tension in East Jerusalem that culminated in clashes at al-Aqsa, a holy site revered by both Muslims and Jews. Hamas allegedly began firing rockets after warning Israel to withdraw from the site, triggering retaliatory air strikes. At least 243 people, including more than 100 women and children, were killed in Gaza, according to its health ministry. Israel said it has killed at least 225 militants during the fighting. Hamas has not given casualty figures for fighters. In Israel 12 people, including two children, were killed, according to its medical service. Israel and Hamas have announced a ceasefire mediated by Egypt after ending an 11-day war that caused widespread destruction in the Gaza Strip and brought life a standstill.

2020: On February 23, 2020, rockets were fired toward southern Israel after Israel said it had killed a Palestinian militant who allegedly tried to place a bomb along the Israel-Gaza barrier fence. Palestine Islamic Jihad (PIJ) launched several rockets at Israel by the time the ceasefire was announced, according to a media report.

2019: On February 7, 2019, a teenager, 19-year-old Ori Ansbacher, was violently assaulted and stabbed to death in the EinYael forest near Jerusalem. According to a report, police arrested Arafat Irfiya, a 29-year-old Palestinian man from Hebron who allegedly admitted the attack was "nationalistically motivated." In the same year, several militant groups, including Hamas and Palestine Islamic Jihad (PIJ) launched rocket attacks against Israel from Gaza. According to Israel's Eshkol regional council, the total damage in the year was estimated at $3.46 million.

2012: On July 18, 2012, a Hezbollah operative blew himself up on an Israeli tourist bus in Burgas, Bulgaria, in which six people were killed and 36 wounded. The bus was meant to take a group of Israeli tourists who were spending their vacation in the area, according to a media report.

Combating Terrorism

Israel passed the Counterterrorism Law of 2016 to replace and update older laws. The law authorises the Minister of Defence to declare that an association is a terrorist organisation upon being convinced that the association, in a systematic and continuous plan is perpetrating or intentionally promoting the perpetration of terrorist acts. The Law further authorised the Prime Minister, in special circumstances, to determine that the declaration decision will be made by a ministerial committee or the government. The Law also authorised the Ministerial Committee for National Security to declare that a foreign association is a terrorist organisation if that association has been subject to a similar declaration by a foreign authority in accordance with powers granted to that authority under the relevant foreign law. The Law provides procedures for periodic reviews of declarations as well as for appeals of declaration decisions. The Law empowered the regional police commanders to issue decrees to prevent activities by or in support of terrorist organisations, including organising meetings, marches, or training. The changes include provisions addressing use of the internet and social media for terrorist purposes.

The Israeli law enforcement agencies, military and intelligence community have accumulated a unique experience fighting non-state violence for several years. They are no strangers to the counter-terrorist world of special operations. They have developed several Special Operations units each with a specific function.

Agencies & Departments

Mista'arvim: The Mista'arvim are the elite undercover counter-terrorism units who operate in the West Bank and Gaza while disguised as local Arabs. They are specifically identified, selected, trained, and operate among the Arab population. Their primary missions are performing intelligence gathering, law enforcement, hostage rescue, and counter-terrorism. Stealth and disguise are their primary means of accomplishing their mission.

Duvdevan: 'Unit 217' commonly known as the 'Duvdevan' is the military's elite counter-terrorism unit established in June 1986. The Duvdevan a part of the IDF Commando Brigade, operate undercover in high-risk urban areas and complicated operations, including targeted killing of terrorists. They are are trained in human and mechanical counter-surveillance. Unlike other special forces units, they can operate independently in more than one place at a time. In the wave of terrorism that began in 2015, the unit played a significant role in the daily struggle against terrorists in Judea and Samaria. The unit is a recipient of the Israeli Chief of Staff Citation.

YAMAM: Yamam, an elite Israeli counter-terrorism unit, is capable of both hostage-rescue operations and offensive take-over raids against targets in civilian areas. Yamam is basically a SWAT unit. They have won the 'Urban Shield', the world's most prestigious international SWAT teams contest. The unit is subordinate to the Ministry of Internal Security central command. It is part of the civilian Israel Police force, specifically the Israel Border Police. Most of Yamam's activity is classified.

The Israeli National Police (INP): The INP, established as a brigade in the Israeli army, primary responsibility is to maintain public safety by preventing crimes, investigating and clearing crimes, identifying offenders and bringing them to justice, supervising and controlling traffic, preserving public order and safety, providing prison security, and maintaining homeland security. The government has officially assigned the police with "internal security" responsibilities within the Gaza Strip and West Bank. Their main task is to allow Israeli citizens to continue their normal routines despite terrorist threats.

Israel also closely coordinate with the United States on a range of counterterrorism initiatives. They held numerous inter-agency counterterrorism dialogues to discuss the broad range of threats in the Middle East and to determine areas of collaboration to address these challenges. This included the annual meeting of the US-Israel Joint Counterterrorism Group, launched in the early 1990s.

Military Intervention

Ranked among the world's most battle-tested militaries, the Israeli Defense Forces (IDF) objectives are "to defend the sovereignty and territorial integrity of the State of Israel, deter all enemies, and curb all forms of terrorism that threaten daily life." Its main tasks include protecting the peace agreements; ensuring overall security in the West Bank; fighting terrorism inside and outside Israel, and maintaining a deterrent capability to prevent the outbreak of hostilities. The IDF is actively involved in fighting terror.

January 13, 2019 – Operation Northern Shield: In December 2018, the IDF launched Operation Northern Shield to expose and neutralise the underground attack tunnels allegedly dug by the terror organisation Hizballah from Lebanon into Israel. For years, Hizballah, the Iran-backed terror group, dug cross-border attack tunnels as part of a "top secret" offensive plan to launch a wide-scale attack on Israel. These attack tunnels, some dug from under civilian areas inside Lebanon, were dug toward civilian communities in northern Israel in violation of UN Security Council Resolution 1701. On January 13, 2019, the IDF exposed the final attack tunnel of Operation Northern Shield. According to an IDF report, the latest tunnel is one of the most strategically important due to not only its location, but also in light of its size. "The tunnel was 800 metres long on its Lebanese side and infiltrated dozens of metres into Israel. The tunnel is two metres high, one metre in diametre, and approximately 55 metres deep,. It is equipped with railway tracks, steps carved into the rock, as well as electric power and lighting system."

Military Intelligence & Operations

Israel has three main intelligence agencies: Shin Bet (domestic), Mossad (international), and Aman (military). The Israeli Military Intelligence Directorate is one of the oldest Directorates in the IDF. The main mission of the Directorate is to supply the government and IDF with intelligence warnings and alerts daily and during wartime to protect Israel from threats. The directorate is made up of three 3 main units – the 8200 Unit, the 9900 Unit and the 504 Unit.

Unit 8200 is subordinate to Aman, the military intelligence directorate. The Unit also referred to as Israeli SIGINT National Unit (ISNU) is responsible for collecting signal intelligence (SIGINT) and code decryption. The unit established in 1952 is composed primarily of 18 to 21 year olds. Soldiers in the unit are in charge of developing and utilizing information gathering tools, analysing, processing and sharing of the gathered info to relevant officials. The unit operates in all zones and in wartime, they join combat field headquarters in order to enable a faster flow of information.

Unit 9900: The IDF's secretive Unit 9900, is responsible for gathering visual intelligence including geographical data from satellites and aircraft, as well as mapping and interpreting such intelligence for troops on the battlefield as well as for decision-makers. The information allow for troops on the ground as well as fighter pilots to get the full picture of enemy territory even before they head into the battlefield. A new drone unit has been introduced in the unit for gathering high-precision intelligence at high resolutions using multi-rotor drones and other advanced technologies.

Unit 504: The Israeli Military Intelligence's Unit 504 employs agents in foreign countries and within the West Bank and Gaza Strip. They provide intelligence that is analysed within the Military Intelligence Directorate. The specific activities of the highly secretive unit is not known.

Sayeret Matkal: The General Staff Reconnaissance Unit, commonly known as Sayeret Matkal is an elite special forces unit of the IDF. The primary task of the unit unit is field intelligence-gathering, conducting deep reconnaissance behind enemy lines. It is also tasked with counter-terrorism and hostage rescue beyond Israel's borders.

Aman: Israel's Military Intelligence Organisation, Aman, controls most signals intelligence and aerial reconnaissance assets. It collects human intelligence and commands Sayeret Maktal, Israel's primary counter-terrorism and intelligence-gathering entity. Aman represents Israel in a very exclusive club of states that design, launch and operate espionage satellites and produces comprehensive national intelligence estimates for the Prime Minister and the Cabinet, as well as daily intelligence reports, risk of war estimates, target studies on neighbouring Arab countries, and communications intercepts.

Shin Bet: Shin Bet also known as Shabak, is Israel's internal security service with its headquarters in Ramat Aviv, a northern neighbourhood in Tel Aviv. The agency is responsible for safeguarding state security, exposing terrorist rings, interrogating terror suspects, providing intelligence for counter-terrorism operations in the West Bank and the Gaza Strip, counter-espionage, personal protection of senior public officials, securing important infrastructure and government buildings, and safeguarding Israeli airlines and overseas embassies. It reports directly to the prime minister of Israel. It is believed to have three operational wings: the Arab Department, the Israel and Foreigners Department, the Protective Security Department.

Mossad: The Mossad, meaning Central Institute for the Intelligence and Special Missions, was established in 1951 as Israel's foreign intelligence agency with headquarters in Tel Aviv. The Mossad is in charge of collection of human intelligence, covert action, and counter-terrorism. Its main tasks include collection of intelligence against enemy states and preventing terror against Israeli and Jewish targets. The Mossad has a Collections Department, a Political Action and Liaison Department, a Special Operations Division, a Psychological Warfare Department, a Research Department, and a Technology Department.

CONCLUSION

Israel has made remarkable advancements despite its war-torn history particularly in the area of innovative defence technologies and emerging as a major player in the global arms market. The development of a sophisticated defence industry inevitably led to exports which today account for a majority of its revenues and allows the country's defence industry to compete against some of the largest companies in the world for foreign contracts, in addition to producing many of the arms needed for Israel's own defence. Israel military is the most powerful in the Middle East. The country has a qualitative edge over the region – this edge includes space assets, advanced fighter jets, drones, and nuclear weapons.

CONTACT DETAILS
Ministry of Defence
The Kirya, Tel Aviv 64734, Israel
Phone: 972-3-6084548
Fax: 972-3-6084529
Email: anordan@mailto.mod.gov.il
www.mod.gov.il

STRATEGIC INFORMATION
ITALY
(Capital: Rome)

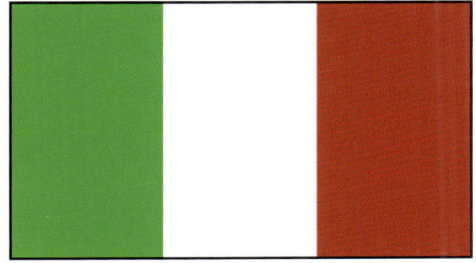

INTRODUCTION
Area: 301,340 sq km
Population: 62,390,364 (July 2021 est.)
Coastline: 7,600 km
Maritime claims: Territorial sea: 12 nm
Continental shelf: 200 m depth or to the depth of exploitation

GEOPOLITICAL IMPORTANCE
Situated in Southern Europe, Italy with a large coastline, is bordered by Switzerland and Austria in the north, France and Monaco in the northwest, Slovenia and San Marino in the northeast. The country takes the shape of a peninsula and extends to the central Mediterranean Sea. It is surrounded by the Tyrrhenian Sea in the west, the Ionian Sea in the south, and the Adriatic Sea in the east. Italy enjoys a unique geostrategic position in Europe. Its proximity to the Balkan states of Albania, Bosnia and Herzegovina, Bulgaria, Croatia, Greece, Macedonia, Montenegro, Romania, Serbia and Slovenia in the south-eastern Europe, and to the littoral states of North Africa – Morocco, Algeria, Libya and Egypt – makes the country strategically important. Sicily, Sardinia and the surrounding minor islands administered by Italy help the country occupy a vital position in the Mediterranean Sea. The country also has a number of gulfs, bays and ports that are suitable for being used as strategic military bases.

POLITICAL OVERVIEW
An erstwhile monarchy, Italy today functions as a parliamentary democratic republic with the President as the ceremonial head of the state. The three branches of the government include the executive, the legislature and the judiciary. While the executive powers are exercised by the Council of Ministers led by the Prime Minister, the legislative power is vested with the two houses of Parliament – the Chamber of Deputies and the Senate of the Republic. The judiciary, constituting of all courts of law, functions independently.

KEY POLITICAL PERSONS

PRESIDENT & COMMANDER-IN-CHIEF: Sergio Mattarella

PRIME MINISTER: Mario Draghi

ECONOMY

With a diversified economy, which primarily includes industry, agriculture and services sector, Italy remains the third-largest economy in the Euro zone. The country's economy is largely dependent on manufacturing and services sector which contribute a major share of the GDP. Italy is a member of the European Union, the World Trade Organisation and Organisation for Economic Co-operation and Development (OECD). The country's exceptionally high public debt and structural impediments to growth rendered it vulnerable to scrutiny by financial markets. Public debt increased steadily since 2007 and reached around 135% in 2019 – the highest in the entire European Union.

In 2020, Italy became the worst-hit European nation to be affected by the deadly Coronavirus pandemic. Even while the Government took various measures to contain the large-scale economic devastation unleashed by the global health crisis, Italy's GDP contracted by record 8.6% in 2020. The Government hopes that the economy will rebound by 4.5% in 2021. Meanwhile, Rome has sought funds worth 200 billion euro from the European Union's proposed 800 billion euro (US$948 billion) "Recovery Fund" designed to help the European nations hardest hit by the Coronavirus crisis.

GDP (official exchange rate): $2.002 trillion (2019 est.)

Real Growth Rate (GDP): 0.34% (2019 est.); 0.83% (2018 est.)

Industries: Tourism, machinery, iron and steel, chemicals, food processing, textiles, motor vehicles, clothing, footwear, ceramics

Natural Gas - Proved Reserves: 38.11 billion cu m (1 January 2018 est.)

Crude Oil - Proved Reserves: 487.8 million bbl (1 January 2018 est.)

Total Exports: $687.34 billion (2019 est.); $678.788 billion (2018 est.)

Export Commodities: Packaged medicines, cars and vehicle parts, refined petroleum, valves, trunks/cases, wine (2019)

Major Markets: Germany 12%, France 11%, United States 10%, United Kingdom 5%, Spain 5%, Switzerland 5% (2019)

Total Imports: $647.05 billion (2019 est.); $649.96 billion (2018 est.)

Import Commodities: Crude petroleum, cars, packaged medicines, natural gas, refined petroleum (2019)

Major Suppliers: Germany 16%, France 9%, China 7%, Spain 5%, Netherlands 5%, Belgium 5% (2019)

DEFENCE & SECURITY

After remaining a colonial power for over half a century and influencing the two World Wars in the 19th century, Italy joined the international military alliance North Atlantic Treaty Organisation (NATO) as one of the founding members in 1949. The country spent heavily in building up a strong military force. Today, Italy commands a prominent position in the entire European continent as well as in global military affairs. Though it does not face any direct military threat from any foreign country, Italy's geostrategic position makes it particularly vulnerable to sea piracy, proliferation of weapons, illegal immigration, drug trade, human trafficking and other forms of organised crime. The country has grappled with illegal immigration from neighbouring regions, especially from the strife-torn Libya. Islamic terrorism has become a major security concern for the country in recent times. To counter these asymmetric threats, Italy has maintained a strong and well-organised military force. The two primary roles assigned to the Italian armed forces include territorial control/protection operations and peacekeeping operations. Italy's allegiance to NATO has strengthened its national security while helping it to standardise and upgrade its own military capabilities. Italy's military strategy and policies are primarily influenced by those of the NATO. The country is engaged in several multilateral operations and peacekeeping missions led by the international military alliance. It also regularly takes part in joint military exercises conducted by NATO. With the rise of Islamic State (IS) and its terror acts which have emerged as the most serious security threat to the entire European continent in present times, Italy has pitched for a stronger European defence mechanism to fight the menace collectively.

Under a large-scale defence reforms plan announced by the Defence Ministry in 2016, Italy plans to cut down the strength of its armed forces by 40,000 personnel over the next 20 years (from 1,90,000 to 1,50,000 by January 2025); shut many of its military bases and reduce its defence equipment and platforms by selling them off to other countries. Such a widespread reduction is aimed at making the Italian armed forces a leaner force in consonance with NATO and European standards of building up a flexible, expeditionary military capable of undertaking operations outside the country more efficiently. In its Defence Whitepaper which was released in April 2015 after a gap of 13 years, Italy announced to take up a key role in the Mediterranean military affairs to ensure regional stability.

KEY DEFENCE PERSONS

MINISTER OF DEFENCE: Lorenzo Guerini

CHIEF OF DEFENCE STAFF: Adm. Giuseppe Cavo Dragone

CHIEF OF STAFF OF ARMY: Lt. Gen. Pietro Serino

CHIEF OF NAVY: Adm. Enrico Credendino

CHIEF OF AIR FORCE: Gen. Luca Goretti

Internal Conflict

Italy's major security challenges are regional in nature and originate in the country's vicinity. Its geostrategic position with a large coastline makes it vulnerable to illegal immigration, illicit drug trade, human trafficking, weapons proliferation, organised crime and terrorism-related activities. To counter these internal and transnational threats, Italy maintains a large police force.

External Conflict

Italy does not face direct external military threat from any country. In the past two decade, it has taken part in the US-led and NATO-backed military interventions in a number of countries including Afghanistan, Iraq and Libya. While its role in the Afghanistan conflict was confined to peacekeeping and nation building (Rome pulled out all its troops from the strife-torn Afghanistan in June 2021), Italy has carried out combat operations against Libya in 2011. In Iraq, the Italian military's role began after the war ended and remained confined mainly to stabilization of the Coalition forces. The country also provided transit routes – land and maritime – to the participating nations for deploying troops in Iraq, although it did not permit use of its territory for carrying out direct attacks against the West Asian country.

THREAT PERSPECTIVE

Terrorism: Like other parts of Europe, Italy too is facing the threat of Islamic terrorism in recent times. Terrorism has posed a serious security challenge to the country, especially to its capital city Rome. The country remains vigilant over any purported terror attacks and has tightened its overall security apparatus to counter any kind of violent act by Islamic extremists.

STRATEGIC RELATIONS

US: Bilateral strategic ties between Italy and the US root in their allegiance to NATO. Under longstanding bilateral agreements flowing from NATO membership, Italy hosts US military forces at some of its major bases including at Vicenza and Livorno (Army); Aviano (Air Force); and Sigonella, Gaeta, and Naples – home port for the US Navy's Sixth Fleet. The US has over 10,000 military personnel – army, navy, marine and air force – stationed in Italy (across more than 40 bases). The US Govt. led by the previous President Donald Trump had announced plans to shift some 12,000 US troops from Germany and relocate nearly half of them in Italy and Belgium. The proposed strategic plan also included to move a squadron of fighter jets to Italy. All the above plans have been put on hold by President Joe Biden who has, in fact, ordered the US Defence Department to conduct a review of how American forces are deployed around the world.

EU: As an important member of the European Union (EU), Italy has traditionally supported the idea of greater European integration. Its affiliation to the EU also makes it less vulnerable to the peripheral threats it faces from its surrounding regions. While economic cooperation is the main driving force for the multinational block, it has also been working on several military projects to cater to the European defence market as well as for importing to foreign countries. Italy plays a key role in several such projects, including the Eurofighter Typhoon fighter aircraft, nEUROn unmanned combat aerial vehicle (UCAV) programme and MBDA-led missile systems programme. It has also recently tied up with France and Germany-led EuroDrone medium-altitude long endurance (MALE) UAV programme.

Russia: Since decades, Italy has made efforts to build strong relations with Russia, despite being a NATO member. The two sides share deep economic and energy ties. They have explored ways to develop multi-dimensional and strategic relations in recent times. Italy also entered the Russian defence market in 2010 when Moscow acquired the design, technology, and local assembly rights over the Iveco M65 LMVs. Moscow too had expressed interest in involving Italian shipbuilder Fincantieri in developing Russian shipyards. The two countries had initiated work on a joint project to design and develop a next-generation diesel submarine, called S-1000, for exporting to international customers. It was, however, stalled following the Russia-Ukraine development.

Turkey: Italy and Turkey have shared long-standing economic, political and strategic relations. Italy has supported the idea of Turkey's inclusion as a European Union member.

DEFENCE CAPABILITIES

ARMY: The Italian Army, which was traditionally been assigned the task of defending national sovereignty, has focused more on enhancing internal stability in recent times in the wake of peripheral dangers emanating from its porous borders. It has also been taking part in several peacekeeping missions led by the United Nations. Being a NATO member, Italy's Army personnel have been part of multinational combat operations from time to time. The Army aims at becoming a lighter-weight, digital fighting force in the 21st century.

Personnel: 99,000+

Equipment

Category	Name	In Service
MBT	Ariete	200
	Leopard 1A5	120 (in reserve)
Armoured Car	B1 Centauro	240
APC/ IFV	M113	250+
	VCC-1/ VCC-2	2,000+
	Bv 206	105
	Puma	540
	Cougar	6
	VAB NBC	15
	Dardo	200
	VBM Freccia	249 (+381 on order)
	VTLM Lince	1260
	LMV 2	16 (+18 on order)

...continued

Category	Name	In Service
Artillery	M109L SP howitzer	130+
	PzH 2000 SP howitzer	70
	FH-70 towed howitzer	160
Mortar	120mm F1	200
	60mm M6-111	300
MLRS		22
ATGW	TOW (to be withdrawn)	244
	Milan	2000+
ATGW	Spike MR/LR	990 (with 90 launchers)
AA Gun	Sidam 25	275
SAM	MIM-23 Hawk	60+
	SPADA 2000	50
	SAMP/T	6

Army Aviation

Category	Name	In Service	On Order
Transport	Dornier Do 228	3	
	P180 Avanti	3	
Helicopter	A129 Mangusta (attack)	60	
	Agusta A109	12	
	Bell 205	42 (to retire)	
	Bell 206	30 (to be replaced)	
	Bell 412	23	
	CH-47C Chinook	17 (being phased out)	
	ICH-47F Chinook	2	14 (+4 option)
	NH90 TTH	31	29
UAV	Raven RQ-11A/11B	58	

New Procurements/ Upgrades

◆ Additional funds have been allocated in 2019 for the procurement of more Centauro II armoured vehicles. An order was placed with Iveco-Oto Melara consortium in 2018 for an initial batch of 10 Centauro II platforms. Production of a second batch of 40 Centauro IIs (tank destroyer vehicles) was approved by the MoD in May 2020. The Army is expected to procure up to 150 of the new platforms.

◆ Additional 381 Freccia armoured vehicles are being procured.

◆ 34 LMV-2 (light multi-role vehicle-2) platforms are on order with deliveries going on.

◆ The first of two AW169 basic training twin engine helicopter (designated UH-169B) has been delivered by Leonardo in July 2020.

Delivery of the second platform is awaited.

◆ Acquisition of 15 new Leonardo AW169MA advanced multi-role helicopters for the Army has been approved by the MoD in April 2020. The platforms would be delivered by Leonardo at a cost of €337 million.

◆ The AW129C Mangusta attack helicopters are to be upgraded to new 'G19' configuration featuring new observation, targeting and weapon system. Initial contract is to upgrade 32 helicopters with option for 16 more.

◆ AgustaWestland is delivering 16 ICH-47F Chinook transport helicopters.

◆ The SAMP/T missile defence systems, deployed in the Army base in Mantova, have reached Full Operational Capability.

NAVY: The Italian Navy, which was the fourth largest navy in the world during World War II, has transformed itself into a modern naval power. The geostrategic position of Italy near the Mediterranean Sea has rendered it necessary to build and project a strong naval force. The Italian Navy, called the Marina Militare, maintains a fleet of advanced battleships, including aircraft carriers, submarines, frigates and destroyers. The Navy operates with a mission "to support and to contribute to the safety of navigation and to the National Defence, to promote the study of all sea related matters and the protection of the marine environment." It has also taken part in several NATO-led peacekeeping operations.

Major naval bases: Taranto, La Spezia, Naples

Personnel: 30,000+

Equipment

Category	Name	In Service	On Order
Aircraft Carrier (STOL)	Cavour	1	
	Giuseppe Garibaldi	1	
Destroyer	Orizzonte class	2	
	Durand de la Penne class	2	
Submarine	Todaro class (U212A Type)	4	2 (+2 more)
	Sauro III/ IV	4 (To be retired)	
Frigate	Maestrale class (being phased out)	8	
	Bergamini class FREMM	8	2
Patrol vessel	Cassiopea class	4	
	Esploratore class	4	
	Comandanti class	4	
	Multipurpose Offshore Patrol Ship		7

...continued

Category	Name	In Service	On Order
Amphibious assault dock	San Giorgio class	3	
Mine sweeper	Lerici class 1 series	4	
	Lerici class 2 series	8	
Auxiliary ship	Etna class	3	
	Stromboli class	2	
Weapon	Aspide (SAM)		
	Aster 15 & Aster 30 (SAM)		
	Otomat (ASM)		
	(Torpedo) MU-90 Mk 32 A-184 Black Shark		

Coast Guard

Category	Name	In Service
OPV	Diciotti-class	2
APC, IFV	AAV-7	18
	VCC 1/VCC 2s	70
Mortar	120mm	4
	81mm	8
ATGW	Milan	12
	TOW	3
	Panzerfaust	25
SAM	Stinger	4

Naval Aviation

Category	Name	In Service	On Order
Fighter/ Attack/ AWS	AV-8B Harrier II	16	
	F-35A/ B Lightening II		90 (navy and air force)
Transport, Surveillance/ MPA	P-180 Avanti	3	
	ATR-72 ASW	4	
Helicopter	AW101 (ASW/ ASuW)	24	
	EH101	20	
	AB-212	20	
	NH-90 TTH & NFH	10 + 38	8

New Procurements/Upgrades

◆ Fincantieri has been awarded a contract worth €1.35 billion ($1.63 billion) in February 2021 to build the first two of four planned U212 NFS submarines for the Italian Navy. The Navy has announced plans to buy four new submarines in order to maintain a fleet of eight underwater platforms. An initial funding was made in this regard in 2018 for the two new submarines of the 212A class. The new platforms would replace the Sauro-class conventional subs, four of which are currently in service.

◆ The eighth FREMM multi-role frigate, "Antonio Marceglia", was delivered to the Navy in April 2019. A total of 10 FREMM frigates are being acquired to replace the Maestrale class and Lupo class platforms of the Navy. The final two platforms would be delivered by 2024.

◆ Fincantieri, in May 2019, launched the Italian Navy's future LHD (landing helicopter dock), "Trieste". Displacing 33,000 tonnes, the new platform is the largest warship built in Italy since 1945. It is slated for delivery in 2022. Fincantieri and Finmeccanica had received a contract worth over €1.1 billion in 2015 for the construction of the multi-purpose amphibious platform for the Navy.

◆ Seven Multi-Purpose Offshore Patrol Ships (PPAs) will be acquired with the first delivery expected by 2021 - 2022. "Paolo Thaon di Revel", the first unit of the new platforms, was launched in Sept. 2019. Fincantieri Shipyard is building the vessels.

Multi-role vessel "Paolo Thaon di Revel" (Image credit: Fincantieri Shipyard)

◆ The first two F-35B STOVL variants built for the Navy are undergoing sea trials from the Cavour aircraft carrier.

◆ Delivery of NH90 helicopters (TTH and NFH variants) is going on. Italy has ordered a total of 56 NH90 naval helicopters (46 NFH and 10 TTH).

AIR FORCE: Primarily tasked with defending the country's airspace and preventing and neutralising any aerial threat, the Italian Air Force has also supported peacekeeping and humanitarian missions outside its territory. The Air Force, in coordination with the other two wings of the Italian military, ensures homeland security. It also acts as an advanced and technological organisation which drives the scientific and industrial progress of the country.

Major air bases: Amendola, Aviano, Ghedi, Sigonella, Trapani, Vicenza

Personnel: 45,000

Equipment

Category	Name	In Service	On Order
Fighter/ Attack	AMX/ AMX-T Ghibli	60+	
	F-16	28	
	Eurofighter Typhoon	95	
	Tornado	60+	
	F-35A/ B Lightening II	12 + 3	90 (total order for Air Force & Navy)
Transport, Tanker, Surveillance	C 27J Spartan	12	
	C-130J/C-130J-30 Hercules II	21	
	P180 Avanti	15	
	Airbus A319 (VIP transport)	3	
	Falcon (VIP transport)	7	
	Boeing KC-767A (aerial refuelling)	4	
	ATR 72MP	4	3
Trainer	MB-339A/ MB-339CD	137 (to be replaced)	
	SF.260EA	30	
	M-346 Master	18	
	M-345		45
Helicopter	HH-139A	10	
	HH 101A (AW101)	8	4 (+3 in option)
	AB-212	32	
	NH-500E	49	
AEW	G-550 Conformal	2	
UAV	RQ-1 Predators	10+	
	MQ-9 Reaper	6	
Weapon	(AAM) AIM-9 Sidewinder, AIM-132 ASRAAM, AIM-120 AMRAAM, IRIS-T		
	Storm Shadow (AGM)	200+	
	JDAM		
	Paveway (laser guided bomb)		

New Procurements/Upgrades

◆ Six C-27J Spartan cargo aircraft are being converted into multi-mission gunship configuration called the MC-27J Pretorian under a contract awarded in 2013. The modifications involve new sensors, communications and cannon. Italy's Alenia Aermacchi has partnered with US' defence and aerospace company ATK to carry out the conversion.

◆ Delivery of three more ATR 72MP fixed-wing maritime patrol aircraft platforms are slated for delivery in 2022. Leonardo-Finmeccanica was awarded the contract in this regard in 2019.

◆ Delivery of HH-101A (AgustaWestland AW101) medium twin-engine helicopters is going on. The new choppers are replacing the HH-3F Pelicans.

◆ Delivery of F-35 stealth fighters is going on. Italy is buying a total of 90 F-35 platforms – 60 F-35A variants for the Air Force and 15 F-35B variants each for the Air Force and Navy.

◆ The final Eurofighter Typhoon platform has been delivered by Eurofighter GmbH in October 2020 to complete the order for 96 such platforms in total (1 platform crashed).

◆ Mid-life upgrade of Tornado fighters is going on.

◆ A new contract has been awarded to Leonardo in June 2019 for 13 more M-345 jet trainers, taking the total number of such platforms on order to 18. Italy had previously awarded a contract to Leonardo for an initial procurement of five Alenia Aermacchi M-345 High Efficiency Trainer aircraft (HET) out of a total requirement of 45.

◆ General Atomics Aeronautical Systems has been contracted to provide weapons (HELLFIRE missiles, bombs, M36-E8 Captive Air Training Missiles, laser guided bombs) and other logistical support for the MQ-9 Reaper UAVs.

DEFENCE PRODUCTION AND R&D

Major Armaments Producers

Finmeccanica: The second largest industrial group and the largest among hi-tech industrial groups based in Italy, Finmeccanica works in the strategic fields of defence, aerospace and security. The defence conglomerate in March 2016 decided to rename itself as "Leonardo". It is one of Europe's leading defence systems company and its subsidiaries include Alenia Aermacchi, AgustaWestland, SELEX Sistemi Integrati and Oto Melara among others. The conglomeration is partially owned by the Italian government and produces aerospace systems, helicopters, trainer and fighter aircraft, UAVs, missile, naval artillery and armoured vehicles in cooperation with other leading European defence firms.

Fincantieri: The leading shipbuilder in Italy and one of the largest in Europe, Fincantieri constructs both commercial ships and military naval vessels. It also undertakes repair and modernisation work of naval vessels.

DEFENCE DEALS

Joint Venture Programmes

Europe

EADS: The largest conglomerate of defence and aerospace companies in Europe, the EADS group includes Airbus, Airbus Military, Cassidian and Eurocopter which produce civilian and military aircraft, defence equipment including land, naval and aerial systems, and a range of helicopters respectively. Italy is a part of the mega conglomerate.

Eurofighter Typhoon: Italy has partnered with Germany, Spain and UK to produce Eurofighter Typhoon – Europe's largest military collaborative programme. Finmeccanica subsidiary Alenia Aermacchi joined hands with other European firms in manufacturing the fourth-generation multi-role fighter aircraft.

nEUROn UCAV: Six European countries – France, Sweden, Italy, Spain, Greece and Switzerland – are jointly developing an unmanned combat aerial vehicle (UCAV) called nEUROn. The programme was launched by the French defence ministry in 2003 with the aim to design and develop an advanced combat unmanned aerial vehicle capable of fighting futuristic warfare and perform stealth missions. Sweden's Saab, Italy's Alenia Aermacchi, Spain's EADS-CASA, Greece's HAI and Switzerland's RUAG later joined the programme led by French major Dassault Aviation.

Missile Systems: MBDA – the leading European missile manufacturer – is a partnership company between BAE Systems, EADS (Europe's largest defence and aerospace organisation) and Italy's Finmeccanica. The company produces a wide range and family of missile systems for European nations as well as for foreign supply.

France

FREMM Frigate: The FREMM programme is a joint Italian-French defence industrial co-operation project to build new generation multi-mission frigates. Italy's Fincantieri and France's DCNS have been partnering in the project which has been pegged as Europe's largest naval programme

Germany

Type 212A class submarine: In joint partnership with Germany, Italy has built two additional Type-212A Todaro-class submarines for its Navy. The platforms have been delivered in 2017.

Naval Defence Cooperation: The French and Italian governments have reached an agreement to launch a joint process, paving the way for future creation of a progressive alliance in the naval defence sector.

US

F-35 Joint Strike Fighter: The Joint Strike Fighter, pegged as the most expensive weapons programme in the US defence history, has been developed as a joint programme between nine partnering nations. Italy is one of the allies in the project led by US defence major Lockheed Martin. The Italian Govt. in 2018, however, has announced that it would not buy more of the JSF platforms for its military in future. The country has committed to buy total of 90 F-35 platforms with deliveries going on.

Russia

S-1000 Submarine: Under a deal inked in 2004, Italy's Fincantieri and Russia's Rubin Central Design Bureau are developing the S-1000 new-generation conventional submarine. The two sides had renewed efforts to upgrade the submarine's previous design and make it smaller so as to market it in Middle East and Southeast Asia. However, the ongoing Ukraine crisis has stalled the project.

UK

Tempest Fighter Jet: Italy, in September 2019, has signed a statement of intent with the UK to work on the proposed next-generation Tempest fighter jet programme, being led by Britain.

Arms Export

Led by a well-developed defence industry, Italy is one of the major suppliers of military equipment in the international market. It has also partnered with leading European countries to manufacture and supply military hardware. In past few years, Italian defence exports have witnessed an upward trajectory.

The country's leading defence firms have collectively clinched deals, both civilian and military, with countries like Saudi Arabia, UAE, Qatar, Egypt, Turkey, Germany, US, UK, India, Israel, Singapore and Australia worth several million Euros. According to latest SIPRI figures, Italy ranks 10th in the world in military exports.

Arms Import

Majority of military imports by Italy have been sourced from its European partner countries and also from the US. Israel too has supplied some defence hardware to Rome. While maintaining self-sufficiency in defence production, Italy has acquired sonar and radar systems, missiles, combat vehicles and unmanned aerial vehicles from other countries.

DEFENCE BUDGET

Military spending by Italy remains obscured as the annual defence budget announced by the Defence Ministry does not include spending on procurement, defence R&D and global peacekeeping operations which are sourced from the Ministry of Economic Development. Annual defence expenditure by the country has maintained an uneven graph over the years.

Even while the country's defence spending continues to focus on military modernisation programmes and UN peacekeeping missions, plans to reduce its overall military strength reflects its reduced defence spending as part of austerity measures. The defence budget for FY 2015-16 stood at €13.19 billion, a decline over previous year's budget. The funding, however, increased slightly in 2016-17 with the country allocating €13.36 billion. In 2017, total defence expense was €13.21 billion which was a drop from previous year's allocation.

Defence allocation for 2018 was €13.8 billion (1.15% of GDP). For 2019, total defence outlay earmarked by the Defence Ministry was €13.98 billion. In 2020, the Govt. allocated €15.3 billion towards defence which was an increase of 9.6% over previous year. For 2021, the country has announced a defence budget of €16.8 billion – an increase of 5% over last year.

CONCLUSION

The 21st century Italy, even though subdued than what it was during the two World Wars, has nevertheless maintained a military prominence not only in Europe but also in the global stage largely due to its allegiance to NATO. Its involvement in some NATO-led combat operations, including the intervention in Libya in recent past, has provided a scope for its military to actively exercise and showcase its prowess outside its territory while at the same time, gauge its operational readiness to defend and protect the homeland. The country, led by a strong domestic defence industry, has focused on modernising its armed forces by acquiring new-age military hardware and equipment despite the ongoing financial crunch in Europe. As per the 2015 national Defence Whitepaper, Italy is now willing to take leadership role in the military affairs of the Mediterranean region.

CONTACT DETAILS
Ministry of Defence
Baracchini Palace
Via XX Settembre 8-00187, Rome
www.difesa.it
Tel: (+39) 06-4882126

STRATEGIC INFORMATION
JAPAN
(Capital: Tokyo)

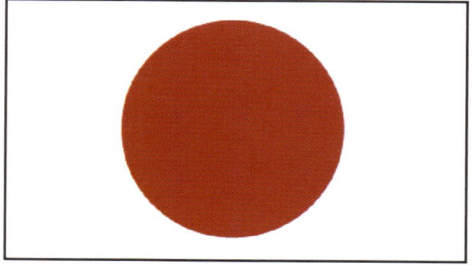

INTRODUCTION

Area: 377,915 sq km
Population: 124,687,293 (July 2021 est.)
Coastline: 29,751 km
Maritime claims: Territorial sea: 12nm
Contiguous zone: 24 nm
Exclusive Economic Zone: 200nm (Including the Senkaku group of islands by purchasing it from the owners in September 2012).

GEOPOLITICAL IMPORTANCE

Japan, a country of islands, is situated in East Asia. Located in the Pacific Ocean, it lies to the East of the Sea of Japan, China, North Korea, South Korea and Russia, stretching from the Sea of Okhotsk in the North to the East China Sea and Taiwan in the South. Philippines also share maritime boundary with the country. The four largest

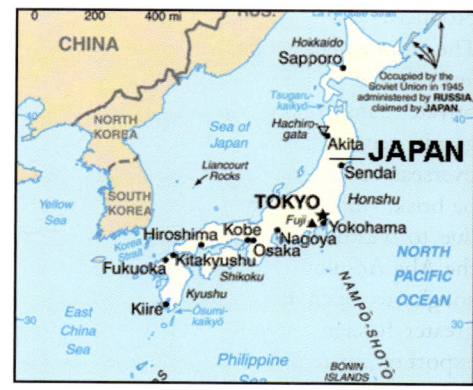

islands (from North to South) are Hokkaido, Honshu, Shikoku, and Kyushu. The Ryukyu Islands, including Okinawa, are a chain to the south of Kyushu. Together they are often known as the Japanese Archipelago.

POLITICAL OVERVIEW

Japan is one of the world's most successful democracies and largest economies. Japan is a constitutional monarchy with a parliamentary government. The Emperor has limited powers and is defined as "the symbol of the state and the unity of the people". Power is held primarily by the Prime Minister of Japan and other elected members of the Diet, while sovereignty is vested in the Japanese people. The judiciary is independent.

KEY POLITICAL PERSONS

HEAD OF STATE:
Emperor Naruhito

PRIME MINISTER:
Fumio Kishida

ECONOMY

Japan is one of the world's most successful democracies and largest economies. In 2018, Japan was the world's fourth-largest importer and the fourth-largest exporter. According to the Website of the Ministry of Economy, Trade and Industry of Japan, the national economic situation is improving moderately. Production shows steady performance as seen in the brisk performance of semiconductor-related products in the general-purpose, production, and business-oriented machinery industries as well as products in the electronic parts and devices industry for automobiles. Business investment shows proactive movement in investments in productivity and labour-saving equipment. The employment situation remains at a high level in the jobs-to-applicants ratio. As for private consumption, sales of high-priced goods remain brisk and consumption by overseas tourists to Japan also continues to be brisk, while sales of clothing are sluggish due to weather and other conditions. Under the Abe Administration, Japan's government sought to open the country's economy to greater foreign competition and create new export opportunities for Japanese businesses, including by joining 11 trading partners in the Trans-Pacific Partnership (TPP). Japan is an indispensable partner in the United Nations and the second-largest contributor to the UN budget. In 2019, the Japanese economy faced considerable challenges posed by a declining population. Manufacturing in Japan focuses primarily on high-tech and precision goods, such as optical instruments, hybrid vehicles, and robotics due to significant competition from China and South Korea. Japan economy has been hit badly since World War II with record 27% drop due to the ongoing COVID-19 pandemic. Consumption and trade has been affected badly. Due to social distancing restriction and stay at home advisory, the economy has weakened. Japan's economy contracted at a 3.6% annual rate in July-September 2021, according to a revised govt. estimate. The world's third-largest economy has been mired in recession and struggling to recover from the impact of waves of coronavirus infections.

GDP (official exchange rate): $5.224 trillion (2019 est.), $5.210 trillion (2018 est.)

Real Growth Rate (GDP): 0.7% (2019 est.), 0.29% (2018 est.)

Industries: Among world's largest and most technologically advanced producers of motor vehicles, electronic equipment, machine tools, steel and nonferrous metals, ships, chemicals, textiles, processed foods

Crude oil - proved reserves: 44.12 million bbl (1 January 2018 est.)

Natural gas - proved reserves: 20.9 billion cu m (1 January 2018 est.)

Total Exports: $793.32 billion (2020 est.), $904.63 billion (2019 est.)

Export Commodities: Cars and vehicle parts, integrated circuits, personal appliances, ships (2019)

Major Markets: United States 19%, China 18%, South Korea 6%, Taiwan 6% (2019)

Total Imports: $799.52 billion (2020 est.), $913.25 billion (2019 est.)

Import Commodities: Crude petroleum, natural gas, coal, integrated circuits, broadcasting equipment (2019)

Major Suppliers: China 23%, United States 11%, Australia 6% (2019)

DEFENCE & SECURITY

The Japan Self-Defence Forces or JSDF, occasionally referred to as JSF or SDF, are the unified military forces of Japan. The Self Defence Force is divided into three branches: Ground Self Defence Force (Army); Maritime Self Defence Force (Navy); Air Self Defence Force (Air Force). The purpose of Self Defence Forces is to preserve peace, public order and Japan's independence and safety. The Prime Minister is the commander-in-chief of the Self Defence Forces and is advised by the Chief of Staff of the Joint Staff Council consisting of all the three services. Military authority runs from the Prime Minister to the cabinet-level Minister of Defence of the Japanese Ministry of Defence. The defence policy of Japan is pursued under the Constitution and is based on the "Basic Policy on National Defence" adopted by the National Defence Council and the Cabinet in May 1957. The "Basic Policy on National Defence" first states the promotion of efforts for peace such as international collaboration and the establishment of a basis for national security through the stabilisation of livelihood of the people, etc., and then the build-up of efficient defence capability and Japan-US security arrangements as the basis of Japan's defence. The objective of national defence is to prevent direct and indirect aggression, but if invaded, to repel such aggression, and thereby, to safeguard the independence and peace of Japan based on democracy. For most of the post-war period the JSDF was confined to the islands of Japan and not permitted to be deployed abroad. In recent years they have been engaged in international peacekeeping operations. Recently, Japan has stressed the need to step up its military presence in its annual defence white paper. The document says Japan is coping with "increasingly severe security environment," and has named the DPRK, China, and Russia as major security threats. The country made an overhaul to its defence status, including a decision on exercising the right to collective self-defence, a shift away from post-war Pacifism. Japan's Prime Minister in the year 2015 won a crucial vote in Parliament for legislation that would give Japan's military limited powers to fight in foreign conflicts for the first time since World War II. A total of 11 security-related bills were approved. Japan is strengthening bilateral cooperative relationships, including the Japan-U.S. alliance, as well as regional cooperation in the Asia-Pacific region and cooperation with the United Nations (UN), in order to prevent and resolve conflicts and confrontations and to promote economic development, arms control and disarmament, maritime security, and mutual understanding and trust.

KEY DEFENCE PERSONS

MINISTER OF DEFENCE:
Kishi Nobuo

CHIEF OF JOINT STAFF OFFICE:
Gen. Koji Yamazaki

CHIEF OF GROUND SELF-DEFENCE FORCE: Gen. Yoshihide Yoshida

CHIEF OF MARITIME SELF-DEFENCE FORCE: Adm. Hiroshi Yamamura

CHIEF OF AIR SELF-DEFENCE FORCE: Gen. Izutsu Shunji

Internal Conflict

There are no internal security problems in Japan.

External Conflict

◆ The sovereignty dispute over the islands of Etorofu, Kunashiri, and Shikotan, and the Habomai group, known in Japan as the "Northern Territories" and in Russia as the "Southern Kuril Islands," occupied by the Soviet Union in 1945, now administered by Russia and claimed by Japan, remains the primary sticking point to signing a peace treaty formally ending World War II hostilities.

◆ Japan and South Korea claim their control over islands known as Dokdo in Korean and Takeshima in Japanese. On August 2012, Japan delivered a diplomatic document to South Korea proposing that the two countries should take their territorial dispute over a group of small islets to the primary judicial entity of the United Nations. South Korea responded by saying that Japan's suggestion to take the issue to the International Court of Justice has no value because no territorial dispute exists and thus there is no need for negotiations. According to reports, South Korea has maintained a presence on the islets since 1952 when its coast guard was dispatched to the rocks nearly equidistant from the Korean peninsula and the main Japanese island of Honshu.

◆ Japan is in dispute with both China and Taiwan for their claims to the uninhabited islands of the Senkaku-shoto (Diaoyu Tai) and Japan's unilaterally declared exclusive economic zone in the East China Sea, the site of intensive hydrocarbon prospecting.

THREAT PERSPECTIVE

China: Japan and China are both strategically important neighbours. Actions over the Senkaku Islands dispute have brought relations between these East Asian neighbours to a standstill. The islands, known as Senkaku to the Japanese and Diaoyu to the Chinese, are also claimed by Taiwan. The islands, which are also claimed by Taiwan, sit near an important shipping lane and nearby waters are believed to harbour valuable mineral resources. Recently, Prime Minister Shinzo Abe of Japan said that he believed his country and China had taken a major step forward in repairing relations, and that from now on, for the sake of the Asia-Pacific region, there should be frequent dialogue between them. Prime Minister Shinzo Abe and Chinese President Xi Jinping, in Nov 2016, agreed to improve bilateral ties ahead of the 45th anniversary of their normalisation of relations. In 2018, the two countries pledged to further deepen tie, also working on One Belt One Road Initiative, etc. In 2019, Japan and China hold first joint maritime drills in eight years. The ties between both the nations also started warming up keeping the recent US trade policy and North Korea's nuclear programme in the scenario. Both recently agreed to work together to promote free and fair trade as both are Asia's largest economies.

North Korea: Relations between the two countries are severely strained and marked by tension and hostility. The ties between Japan and North Korea are not established formally but diplomatic discussions are on between both the governments on issues such as North Korea's nuclear programme. North Korean missile tests are also a concern for Japan because the missiles sometimes travel over Japanese territory and through its airspace. According to the annual white paper of Defence of Japan, North Korean military behaviour has increased tension over the Korean Peninsula, and constitutes a serious destabilising factor for the entire East Asian region. There have also been several confrontations between the two nations over North Korean clandestine activity in Japan besides the abductions including drug smuggling, marine poaching, and spying. Relations between the two countries are severely strained and marked by tension and hostility. In 2017, North Korea in a six-party talks agreed to shut down one of its nuclear facility in exchange for fuel. This is a positive step in the normalisation of ties between USA, Japan and North Korea. In 2020, during Pyongyang's military parade, various weapons and ICBMs were displayed which led Japan to vow to strengthen its military deterrence capabilities.

Russia: Both the governments of Japan and Russia have taken positive efforts to improve relations which include Japanese investments in Russia, military cooperation, etc. Relations between the two nations are hampered by the long-running Northern Territories (Kuril) dispute. The dispute also over the Southern Kuril Islands deteriorated Russia-Japan relations. Recently in 2019, in a move to build trust, Japanese tourists began a visit to two disputed Russian-held islands off Hokkaido, as part of joint economic activities by the Japanese and Russian governments. Relation between Russia and Japan is thus improving and getting closer. Prime Minister Shinzo Abe of Japan and President Vladimir V. Putin of Russia discussed concluding a Japanese-Russian peace treaty in time for the 70th anniversary of the end of World War II in 2015. Russia and Japan are again holding consultations between their foreign and defence ministries, which will improve their bilateral ties and intensify trade & economic cooperation. In June 2018, Russia and Japan inked a Memorandum of Understanding (MoU) in Russia's Far Eastern Republic of Sakha (Yakutia) to expand cooperation between the two countries. Japan & Russia's relations are developing steadily and the Far East is one of the important areas of bilateral cooperation. In Sept 2020, Prime Minister Yoshihide Suga and Russian President Vladimir Putin agreed to promote territorial negotiations between both the nations based on a 1956 joint declaration, as per media reports.

STRATEGIC RELATIONS

USA: The US-Japan alliance is the cornerstone of US security interests in Asia and is fundamental to regional stability and prosperity. Japan relies on the United States for its national security to a high degree as the latter is former's closest ally. Japan and US being world's top economic powers, both also rely on close economic ties for their wealth. The Treaty of Mutual Cooperation and Security between US and Japan declares that both nations will maintain and develop their capacities to resist armed attack in common and that each recognises that an armed attack on either in territories administered by Japan will be considered dangerous to the safety of the other. US has positioned close to 50,000 troops in Japan, the headquarters of the US 7th Fleet and more than 10,000 Marines to undertake military operations. Japan's limited intelligence gathering capability and personnel are focused on China and North Korea, as the nation primarily relies on the US NSA. US and Japan in 2015 enhanced their military relationship by strengthening ties between the two nations on cyber, space and industrial programmes. Japan and the United States collaborate closely on international diplomatic initiatives. USA consults with Japan and South Korea on policy regarding North Korea. USA coordinates with Japan and Australia under the the Trilateral Strategic Dialogue and the Security and Defence Cooperation Forum. USA and Japan coordinate with India trilaterally and in the US-Australia-India-Japan Consultations. In Southeast Asia, US-Japan cooperation advances maritime security and economic development. Also, Japanese political and financial support has significantly assisted US efforts on a variety of global issues arising, including countering ISIL, terrorism, etc. 2020 marks the 60th anniversary of the signing of the US-Japan Security Treaty. The U.S.-Japan Alliance was strengthened in 2015 through the release of the revised US-Japan Defence Guidelines, which provide for new and expanded forms of security-oriented cooperation. Japan provides bases as well as financial and material support to US forward-deployed forces, which are essential for maintaining stability in the region.

India: The friendship between India and Japan has a long history rooted in spiritual affinity and strong cultural and civilisational ties. Both the countries have close military relations. Both the nations have shared interests in maintaining the security of sea-lanes in the Asia-Pacific and Indian Ocean, and in cooperation for fighting international crime, terrorism, piracy and proliferation of weapons of mass destruction. The United States and Japan coordinate with India trilaterally and in the US-Australia-India-Japan Consultations. The two nations have frequently held joint military exercises and cooperate on technology. India and Japan concluded a security pact on 22 October 2008. Both the countries have also decided to enhance cooperation in anti-piracy operations off the coast of Somalia in the Gulf of Aden and launched a maritime dialogue mechanism. In Dec 2015, the two countries signed a pact regarding the transfer of defence equipment and technology after the annual summit between Prime Minister Narendra Modi and his Japanese counterpart Shinzo Abe. Prime Minister Narendra Modi, in November 2016, during the meeting, India and Japan signed the Agreement for Cooperation in Peaceful Uses of Nuclear Energy. In FY 2017-2018 India-Japan bilateral trade reached USD 15.71 billion. Exports from Japan to India during this period were USD 10.97 billion and imports were USD 4.74 billion. Year 2019 was significant in the commencement of negotiations for the Japan-India Acquisition and Cross-Servicing Agreement (ASCA). In June 2020, the Indian Navy carried out a maritime exercise with the Japanese navy as part of efforts to bolster military cooperation. In Nov 2020, India and Japan will participate in the Malabar naval exercise along with USA and Australia that will bring the four key defence partners and democracies in the region together, demonstrating their collective resolve to support an open and prosperous Indo-Pacific. It will be the first military-level engagement between the four-member nation grouping - the Quad.

Australia: Japan and Australia have established good bilateral relationships based on mutually harmonising the economic relations. Japan is one of Australia's major economic partners. In recent years, the two countries have also strengthened political, defence and scientific cooperation, which has made them a strategic partner in the Asia-Pacific region. The Australia-Japan-United States Trilateral Strategic Dialogue is a key security policy mechanism for Japan in the Asia-Pacific region. Australia and Japan also have a strong history of cooperation in United Nations peacekeeping missions. Australia and Japan have been maintaining dialogue on humanitarian assistance and disaster relief, maritime security, cyber security, and peacekeeping activities, in order to not only deepen practical cooperation, but also prepare for future challenges. The Japan Australia Economic Partnership Agreement (JAEPA) was signed in Canberra on 8 July 2014. In 2017, Japan was Australia's second-largest trading partner, second-largest export market, and second-largest source of foreign direct investment. Australia and Japan regularly participate in joint defence exercises and frequently consult on regional security issues, such as the nuclear tests and ballistic missile launches undertaken by North Korea. Australia and Japan are close partners in regional forums such as Asia Pacific Economic Cooperation (APEC) and the East Asia Summit (EAS).

South Korea: Japan and South Korea are close neighbours. The General Security of Military Information Agreement is aimed at better coping with North Korea's missile threats. Japan and South Korea planned to have military talks on accords aimed at strengthening defence cooperation by sharing important intelligence, mostly on North Korea, and assisting each other's military with fuel and medical supplies during peacekeeping operations abroad. Seoul and Tokyo are important trading and diplomatic partners, but the possibility of such a military treaty is a sensitive topic in South Korea, where many people still harbour strong resentment against Japan's 35-year occupation until the end of World War II. Therefore, as a result of a political firestorm in South Korea's cabinet on the issue, the country was forced to postpone signing of the military agreement with Japan. And now the fate of the accord is uncertain. At present, sharing and protecting of sensitive military data about North Korea and China and missile defences between Japan and South Korea take place through Washington. The Liancourt Rocks dispute is a territorial dispute between South Korea and Japan. Both countries claim sovereignty over the Liancourt Rocks, a group of small islets in the Sea of Japan. General Security of Military Information Agreement (GSOMIA) pact signed between both the countries in 2016.

Multilateral Alliances: Japan, a member of G7, G-20, Organization for Economic Cooperation and Development, Asia-Pacific Economic Cooperation forum, ASEAN Regional Forum, International Monetary Fund, World Bank, and World Trade Organisation., participant in the East Asia Summit, continues to hold many international cooperations within the United Nations since 1956. Japan, has participated in many areas such as UN peacekeeping / peacebuilding, international humanitarian relief, nuclear-non-proliferation/ disarmament, and also earned a unique status as a non-nuclear weapon state and one of the world's largest economies. The country is the second-largest contributor to the UN budgets among the Member States, bearing 12.5% of the total budget. It is one of the G4 nations seeking permanent membership in the Security Council. Japan is also a strong advocate of a Reform of the United Nations Security Council (UNSC), in a joint campaign with Germany, India, and Brazil. Japan is striving to gain the permanent seat in the chamber.

DEFENCE CAPABILITIES

ARMY: The Japan Ground Self-Defence Force, or JGSDF, is the armed force of Japan. The largest of the three services of the Japan Self-Defence Forces, the Ground Self-Defence Force operates under the command of the chief of the ground staff. Regionally the JGSDF is organised into five armies, the Northern Army, North Eastern Army, Eastern Army, Central Army, and Western Army. JGSDF divisions and brigades are combined arms units with infantry, armoured, and artillery units, combat support units and logistical support units.

Personnel: 145,000

Equipment

Category	Name	In Service
MBT	Type 10	63
	Type 90	200+
	Type 74	200+

...continued

Category	Name	In Service
APC/ MICV/ IFV	Type 89	50+
	Type 16	3
	Type 60	25
	Type 73	300
	Type 87 Recon. & Warning Vehicle	70+
	Type 82 (Command & Comm.)	200
	Type 96	250+
	Komatsu LAV	1,000+
Artillery	Towed FH70 155mm	400+
	Type 75 155 mm self-propelled	100
	Type 99 155 mm self-propelled	15
	M110 203mm howitzers	80
Mortar	Type 96 120mm self-propelled	350
	120mm rifled towed	350
	M2 107mm	80
	M6C-210 60 mm	
	L16 81mm	
MRL	Type 75 130mm	200+
	M270	100
RCL Gun	Type 60 106mm	90
Anti-Tank GW	Type 01	1,000+
	Type 64	100+
	Type 79	200
	Type 87 Chu-MAT	40
	Chu-MPM	40
	Carl Gustaf	
	Panzerfaust-3	
SSM	Type 88	
	Type 12	
SAM	I-HAWK system	500
	Type 81	50
	Type 91	100+
	Type 93	60+
	Type 03 Chu-SAM	
	FIM-92A Stingers	50
AA gun	35mm twin	20
	Type 87 self-propelled	50+ (200 planned)
SSM (Coastal Defence)	Type 88 (SSM-1)	40+ systems (each with six cell)

Army Aviation

Category	Name	In Service
Aircraft	Beechcraft Super King Air LR-2	5
	MU-2 LR-1	3
Combat Helicopter	AH-1S Cobra	80
	Tilt-rotor aircraft (V22)	3
	CH - 47JA	On Order

...continued

Category	Name	In Service
Combat Helicopter	AH-64D Apache Longbow	11
	OH-1	30
Liaison & light transport Helicopter	EC225 Super Puma (VVIP)	4
	UH-1H/J	100+
	CH-47J/JA	50+
	OH-6D	To be replaced
	UH-60 Blackhawk	30
	TH-480B	10
	V-22B	15+
UAV	ScanEagle, R-MAX, RQ-16 T-Hawk	

New Procurements/ Upgrades

◆ Patria's armoured modular vehicle AMVXP has been chosen to a one-year field testing in Japan after a competitive bidding. The Japanese Ministry of Defence will buy two vehicles from Patria for the tests. The final selection is to be expected after the trials.

NAVY: The Japan Maritime Self-Defence Force, or JMSDF, is the naval branch of the Japan Self-Defence Forces, tasked with the naval defence of Japan. The JMSDF has a large fleet and its main tasks are to maintain control of the nation's sea lanes and to patrol territorial waters.

Naval Bases: Maritime Staff Office (Tokyo), Self Defence Fleet Headquarters (Yokosuka), main bases (Yokosuka, Kure, Sasebo, Maizuru and Ominato), other bases (Yoichi, Hakodate, Kobe, Shimonoseki, and Katsuren) and air bases (Hachinohe, Ominato, Simofusa, Tateyama, Atsugi, Komatsujima, Tokushima, Iwakuni, Ozuki, Oomura, Kanoya, Naha, Matzuru).

Personnel: 45,000

Equipment

Category	Name	In Service
Helicopter Destroyer (DDH)	Hyuga class	2
	Izumo-class	2
Guided Missile Destroyer (DDG)	Kongo class	4
	Hatakaze class	1
	Atago class	2
	Maya-class	1 (1 on order)
Destroyer (DD)	Takanami class	5
	Asagiri class	8
	Hatsuyuki class	2
	Murasame class	9
	Akizuki class	4
	Asahi-class	2
Frigate/ Destroyer Escorts (DE)	Abukuma class	6

...continued

Category	Name	In Service
Submarine	Soryu class	12
	Oyashio class	10
	Taigei-class	On order
Patrol vessel	Hayabusa class	6
Landing ship	Osumi class	3
	1-Go class	2
	Yura class	2
Landing craft	YF 2121 class	11
	YF 2150 class	2
	Landing Craft Air Cushion	6
Mine warfare ship	Uraga class	2
	Yaeyama class	1
	Uwajima class	2
	Sugashima Class	12
	Enoshima class	3
	Ieshima-class	2
	Hirashima class	3

Naval Aviation

Category	Name	In Service
Aircraft	P-3C Orion	60+
	U 36-A Learjet 35	3
	KC-130R	5
	US-2	4
	EP-3C	3
	UP-3D	
	Fuji T-5 (trainer)	30
	Beechcraft King Air	20
	Kawasaki P-1	10+
Helicopter	UH-60J	15
	SH-60J	30
	SH-60K	40+
	MCH-101	
	MD 500	3+
	CH-101	2
	Eurocopter EC 135 (TH-135)	10+

New Procurements/ Upgrades

◆ The US State Department has approved a possible Foreign Military Sale to the Government of Japan of AEGIS Class Destroyer Support and related equipment for an estimated cost of USD134 million.

◆ The US State Department has approved a possible Foreign Military Sale to the Government of Japan of RAM Block 2 Tactical Missiles and related equipment for an estimated cost of USD61.5 million.

◆ The US State Department has approved a possible Foreign Military Sale to Japan of 8 Standard Missile-3 (SM-3) Block 1B Missiles and 13 Standard Missile-3 (SM-3) Block 2A Missiles for an estimated cost of USD 561 million.

- The US State Department has approved a possible Foreign Military Sale to Japan of MK 15 Phalanx Close-in Weapon System (CIWS) Block IB Baseline 1 to MK 15 Phalanx Block IB Baseline 2 conversion kits for an estimated cost of USD 45 million.
- The US State Department has approved a possible Foreign Military Sale to Japan of Standard Missile-3 (SM-3) Block IIA missiles for an estimated cost of USD 133.3 million.

US Navy and Japan Maritime Self-Defence Force ships steam in formation while participating in a photo exercise with the aircraft carrier USS George Washington (CVN 73) at the culmination of ANNUALEX 2008.

AIR FORCE: : The Japan Air Self-Defence Force, or JASDF, is the aviation branch of the Japan Self-Defence Forces responsible for the defence of Japanese airspace and other aerospace operations. The JASDF carries out combat air patrols around Japan, while also maintaining an extensive network of ground and air early warning radar systems. The JASDF also provides air support for ground and sea operations of the JGSDF and the JMSDF and air defence for bases of all the forces. The JASDF is not allowed to have strategic bombers for that would go against the self-defence—only policy.

Air Bases: Kasuga, Hamamatsu, Komaki, Niigata, Shizuhama, Chitose, Naha, Hofu, Komatsu, Iruma, Misawa, Ashiya, Tsuiki, Gifu, Miho, Kasuga, Miho

Personnel: 45,000

Equipment

Category	Name	In Service
Combat	F-35A	10+ (more on order)
	Mitsubishi F-2 A/B (fighter/fighter trainer)	60
	F-4 Phantom II (fighter/reconnaissance)	70
	F-15 Eagle (fighter/fighter trainer)	150+
Transport/ Aerial refueling/ Aerial Surveillance	C-130H	10+
	Kawasaki C-1 (EW)	1
	Boeing 747-400	2
	Boeing KC-767	4
	KC-130H	1
	Gulfstream IV	5
	Boeing KC-767 (refueling)	4

...continued

Category	Name	In Service
Transport/ Aerial refueling/ Aerial Surveillance	Hawker 800	20+
	Kawasaki C-1/C-2	20+
	NAMC YS-11 (EW)	7
	U-125A BAe	30
AWACS	E-2 Hawk Eye	10+
	Boeing E-767	4
Helicopter	UH-60 Mitsubishi	30+
	CH-47J	16
Trainer	Kawasaki T-4	100+
	Mitsubishi F-2B	15+
	Hawker T-1 Jayhawk	12
	NAMC YS-11	2
	Fuji T-3	40+
Weapon	AIM-9 Sidewinder	
	Mitsubishi AAM-3	
	Mitsubishi AAM-4	
	AIM-7 Sparrow	
	ASM-1 and ASM-2 anti-ship missiles	
	J/AAQ-2 FLIR	

Air Defence

- PAC-2, PAC-3 (MIM-104 Patriot) systems 6 group with 24 batteries.
- Type 81 SAM systems about 36 of such units are still in service.
- Type 91 SAM more than 350 systems.
- M167 Vulcan Air Defence System (VADS).

New Procurements/ Upgrades

- The US State Department has approved a possible Foreign Military Sale to Japan for the upgrade of up to 98 F-15J aircraft to a Japanese Super Interceptor (JSI) configuration for an estimated cost of USD4.5 billion.
- The US State Department has approved a possible Foreign Military Sale to Japan of 32 AIM-120C-7 Advanced Medium Range Air-to-Air Missiles (AMRAAM) for an estimated cost of USD 63 million.
- The US State Department has approved a possible Foreign Military Sale to Japan of up to nine E-2D Advanced Hawkeye (AHE) Airborne Early Warning and Control (AEW&C) aircraft for an estimated cost of USD 3.135 billion.
- The US State Department has approved a possible Foreign Military Sale to Japan for AIM-120C-7 Advanced Medium-Range Air-to-Air Missiles (AMRAAMs). The estimated cost is USD 113 million.
- The US State Department has approved a possible Foreign Military Sale to the Government of Japan of 105 F-35 Joint Strike Fighter aircraft and related equipment for an estimated cost of USD23.11 billion.

The Government of Japan has requested to buy 63 F-35A Conventional TakeOff and Landing (CTOL) aircraft, 42 F-35B Short Take-Off and Vertical Landing (STOVL) aircraft, and 110 Pratt and Whitney F135 engines (includes 5 spares). Also included are Electronic Warfare Systems; Command, Control, Communications, Computers and Intelligence/Communications, Navigation and Identification; Autonomic Logistics Global Support System, Autonomic Logistics Information System; Flight Mission Trainer; Weapons Employment Capability, and other Subsystems, Features, and Capabilities; F-35 unique infrared flares; reprogramming center access and F-35 Performance Based Logistics; software development/integration; flight test instrumentation; aircraft ferry and tanker support; spare and repair parts; support equipment, tools and test equipment; technical data and publications; personnel training and training equipment; US Government and contractor engineering, technical, and logistics support services; and other related elements of logistics support.

Anti-Ballistic Missile Programme

Japan decided to join in the American anti-ballistic missile (ABM) defence programme in 1998, soon after North Korea's Taepodong-1 missile launch over northern Japan. In August 1999, Japan, Denmark and the US governments signed a Memorandum of Understanding (MoU) of joint research and development on the Aegis Ballistic Missile Defence System. In 2003, the Japanese government decided to deploy two types of ABM system, sea-based Aegis and land-based Patriot Advanced Capability 3 (PAC-3) ABM. On April 2012, Japan deployed Patriot missilesat three military facilities in the greater Tokyo region and the defence ministry dispatched three Aegis destroyers carrying sea-based interceptor missiles, reportedly to the East China Sea, as a precautionary measure to boost its defences against a planned North Korean rocket launch.

The Aegis Ballistic Missile Defence System (Aegis BMD) is a United States Department of Defence's Missile Defence Agency programme developed to provide defence against ballistic missiles. In 2010, Japan, in partnership with the US, has successfully conducted an Aegis Ballistic Missile Defence (BMD) intercept flight test off the coast of Hawaii. The JMSDF has equipped three vessels for Long Range Surveillance and Tracking (LRST) and engagement: JS Kongo, JS Chokai, JS Myoko, and in 2010 the JS Kirishima. In 2018, Japan selected Lockheed Martin Corp. to build a USD 1.2 billion radar for two ground-based Aegis ballistic missile defence stations, which will be used to guard against missile strikes. In Sept 2018, the Japan's JS ATAGO (DDG-177), supported by the US Navy, Missile Defence Agency and Lockheed Martin, used an upgraded Aegis Combat System, testing their Ballistic Missile Defence (BMD) capability for the first time. The JS ATAGO Aegis Weapon System merges BMD into an Integrated Air and Missile Defence capability using commercial-off-the-shelf and open architecture technologies including the Aegis Common Source Library (CSL). In Aug 2019, United States has approved a 3.3 billion dollar sale of anti-ballistic missiles to Japan following close behind a series of new ballistic missile tests by North Korea. According to Pentagon as per news reports, Japan will buy up to 73 of the Raytheon-made SM-3 Block IIA missiles, which are designed to be fired by the ship-board Aegis system to intercept incoming ballistic missiles. The sale came as North Korea is expanding its offensive missile capabilities, having proven over the past two years the ability to launch medium- and long-range ballistic missiles, potentially nuclear-tipped, that could hit both Japan and the United States.

Major Armaments Producers

The Japanese defence industry is the major supplier of the nation's own Self-Defence Forces. The country has a strong base of defence R&D and production the major contribution in the defence development & production are from Mitsubishi Heavy Industries (MHI) and Kawasaki, apart from these industries there is consortium of the industries which also work for defence equipment development & production.

Domestic suppliers: Mitsubishi Heavy Industries, Mitsubishi Electric, Fuso, Toyota, Kawasaki Heavy Industries, IHI Corporation, Japan Marine, United Mitsui Engineering & Shipbuilding, NEC, Japan Radio Company, Toshiba, Fujitsu, Oki Electric Industry, ShinMaywa, Japan Steel Works, Subaru Corporation, MinebeaMitsumi, Komatsu Limited, Yamaha Motor Company, Kayaba Industry, Toray Industries, Showa Shell Sekiyu, Daicel.

Foreign suppliers: United States, United Kingdom, Germany, Italy, Switzerland, France, Australia, Sweden, Canada.

DEFENCE DEALS

The country is going to expand its defence capabilities in the entire horizon, as per the policy change the procurement of the arms is going to be raise in the coming decade.

Joint Venture Programmes

Lockheed Martin, Mitsubishi Electric Corporation, SAMPA Kogyo K.K. and Mitsubishi Corporation have formed a joint venture company that will serve the emerging combat system engineering and lifetime support requirements of the Japan Maritime Self-Defence Forces (JMSDF). The joint venture company, MLS Corporation, represents a full service partnership arrangement between industry and government, and leverages Japanese and US industry expertise in life cycle support and integration services to benefit the JMSDF. Through the MLS partnership, Lockheed Martin will transfer its proven models to Japan for application across JMSDF surface ship programmes.

Arms Export

Japan has recently relaxed ban on military exports to make its defence manufacturers more competitive. According to media reports, the country has cancelled its self-imposed decades-old ban on export of military equipment. The move will open new corridors for defence contractors. The ban was issued in 1967 when Japan decided not to sell defence products to communist nations and those involved in international conflicts. Later, the country extended the ban on exports with defence industries barred from engaging in any development or production of weapons with any country other than United States. With the relaxation, Japan can now indulge in joint development and production of weapons with other countries and also provide military weapons and support for humanitarian missions. Though the ban has been lifted, Japan will limit its exports to strategic allies like the USA. The move is intended to bolster the domestic arms industry and reduce national defence spending. Under the new standards, Japan will be able to transport military equipment for missions of peace-building and international cooperation. The new rules will allow Japan to develop and produce arms jointly with the US and European countries and to export military equipment for peaceful and humanitarian purposes such as UN peace-keeping operations. Tokyo will also be allowed to provide defensive equipment, such as helmets and bullet-proof vests, to the limited number of countries in which its Self-Defence Forces are deployed.

Arms Import

The Japan Ministry of Defence (MoD) has released the five-year mid-term defence programme which lists major equipment purchases and envisions a total budget of approximately 23, 490 billion yen (USD 267.6 billion) to be spent over the next five years. The US-Japan security alliance is the cornerstone of relation between US contractors and Japan defence market. Major US defence contractors, as well as other US defence makers of defence-related technologies and equipment, play important role in the Japanese defence market, participating through product licensing and direct sales. The Equipment Procurement and Construction Office (EPCO), under Japan Ministry of Defence (MoD) conducts all procurement of necessary equipment for executions of self-defence force missions (firearms, guided weapons, telecommunications, ships, aircraft, vehicles, machinery, ammunitions, foods, fuel, textile, other necessary materials) and designated primary materials by Minister of Defence for the services. EPCO is a procurement agency that executes the big budget of about 1.3 trillion yen which is equivalent of almost 1/4 of whole defence related costs.

After years of negotiations, India and Japan have inked a landmark agreement that will allow their militaries to access each other's bases for logistics support, a key development that comes in the backdrop of growing concerns over China's military muscle flexing in the region. The acquisition and cross-servicing pact was signed by Defence Secretary Ajay Kumar and Japanese Ambassador Suzuki Satoshi, a defence ministry spokesperson said in Sept 2020. The agreement provides for creation of an enabling framework for closer cooperation and interoperability, besides allowing militaries of the two countries to use each other's bases and facilities for repair and replenishment of supplies. The agreement will promote closer cooperation between the militaries of the two countries, and enable them to actively contribute to international peace and security. The defence ministry said the pact will enhance the interoperability between the armed forces, resulting in further expansion of bilateral defence engagement under the Indo-Japan special strategic and global partnership.

Japan's National Security Council has endorsed plans to cancel the deployment of two costly land-based US missile defence systems aimed at bolstering the country's capability against threats from North Korea, the country's defence minister said in Sept 2020. The reason found to be that the safety of one of the two planned host communities could not be ensured without a hardware redesign that would be too time consuming and costly. The council made its decision recently, and now the government will need to enter negotiations with the US about what to do with payments and the purchase contract already made for the Aegis Ashore systems.

DEFENCE BUDGET

Total defence spending: $50 billion (2020-21 est.)

Estimated defence spending in terms of GDP: 1% of GDP (2020), 1% of GDP (2019)

According to the Ministry of Defence, Japan website, the Japan's Self-Defence Forces (SDF) will acquire and strengthen capabilities in new domains, which are space, cyberspace and electromagnetic spectrum by focusing resources and leveraging Japan's superb science and technology. In addition, SDF will enhance capabilities in maritime and air domains, stand-off defence capability, comprehensive air and missile defence capability and manoeuvre and deployment capability to effectively respond to various situations during cross-domain operations in close combination with capabilities in new domains.

Japan's Cabinet in Nov 2021 approved a 770 billion yen (6.8 billion) request for an extra defence budget through March to expedite the purchase of missiles, anti-submarine rockets and other weapons amid rising concern over the escalation of military activities by China, Russia and North Korea. The request brings Japan's military spending for the current year to a new high of more than 6.1 trillion yen (53.2 billion), up 15% from 5.31 trillion yen in 2020. As per official sources, the goal is to beef up Japan's defences against North Korea's missile threat and China's increasingly assertive maritime activity around remote Japanese south-western islands.

As per the PTI news release, the budget request includes nearly 100 billion yen (870 million) for the advanced version of PAC-3 mobile surface-to-air missile interceptors and related equipment, as well as cruise missiles.

Separately, more than 800 billion yen (7 billion) will go to speed up the purchase of reconnaissance planes and equipment, including three P-1s, equipment for P-3Cs and vertical launch systems to be placed on two destroyers, to step up surveillance around Japan's territorial waters and airspace. Japan has been stepping up defences in its south-western regions and islands, including Ishigaki Island, where a new military base with a land-to-sea missile defence system will be operational. Ishigaki is north of the uninhabited Japanese-controlled Senkaku Islands, which are also claimed by China, which calls them Diaoyu. The defence budget is part of a nearly 36 trillion yen (316 billion) draft extra budget approved by the Cabinet Friday to fund an economic stimulus package focusing on COVID-19 preparedness and support for the pandemic-hit households and businesses. The combined budget for 2021 will be just over 1% of Japan's GDP.

Overview of JFY2021 Budget Request:

Overall Defence-Related Expense (Overview of JFY2021 Budget – (Unit: JPY 100 million)
Source: MOD/Budget, Japan

Categories	FY2021 Budget	FY2022 Budget
Defence related expenditures	50,688	51,235
Personnel & Provisions expenses	21,426	21,919
Material Expenses	29,262	29,316
Obligatory outlay expenses	19,336	19,377
General material expenses	9,926	9,939
Future Obligations concerning new contracts	24,050	24,090

Major Programmes in JFY2021 Defence Budget
Source: MOD/Budget, Japan

Capabilities in Space, Cyber, Electromagnetic Domain:
- Procurement of SSA satellite (space-based optical telescope) (¥17.5 billion)
- Development of SSA systems (¥11.3 billion)
- Study on utilisation of satellite constellations for missile defence
- Enhance resiliency of satellite communication system (¥0.9 billion)
- Enhance resiliency of satellite positioning capability by utilizing "QZSS" (¥0.4 billion)
- Strengthening Information-Gathering Capability Using Outer Space
- Enhancing Posture of Cyber Defence Group, etc.
- Improving Security of System Networks
- Development of stand-off electronic warfare aircraft (¥10 billion)
- Procurement of network electronic warfare system (1 set: ¥8.7 billion)
- Study of naval vessels' radio detection and jamming capabilities (¥20 million)

Enhancing capabilities in Ground, Maritime and Air Domains:
- Improvement of capability of the Japan Aerospace Defense Ground Environment (JADGE) (¥22.1 billion)
- Procurement of fixed-wing patrol aircraft (P-1) (3 aircraft: ¥66.5 billion)
- Life extension of fixed-wing patrol aircraft (P-3C) (4 aircraft: ¥1.5 billion)
- Refurbishment of a patrol helicopter (SH-60K) to rescue specification (1 helicopter: ¥1 billion)
- Procurement of a search and rescue amphibian (US-2) (1 amphibian: ¥7.1 billion)
- Construction of destroyers (2 ships: ¥94.4 billion)
- life extension for 4 ships and parts procurement for 4 ships: ¥12.3 billion
- Construction of a submarine (1 ship: ¥68.4 billion)
- Life extension of submarines (life extension for 9 ships and parts procurement for 4 ships: ¥6.4 billion)
- Procurement of fighters (F-35A) (4 fighters: ¥39.1 billion)
- Procurement of fighters (F-35B) (2 fighters: ¥25.9 billion)
- Improvement of capability of fighters (F-2) (¥3 billion)
- Procurement of rescue helicopters (UH-60J) (5 helicopters: ¥26.1 billion)
- Refurbishment of Izumo-class destroyers (¥20.3 billion)
- Procurement of Type-03 Medium-Range Surface-to-Air Missile (modified) (1 set: ¥12 billion)
- F-X (approx. ¥73.1 billion [including related expenses])
- Research on advanced radar technology (¥4.1 billion)
- Development of sonar system for future submarines (¥3.5 billion)
- Research on a noise-reducing torpedo-launcher (¥1.8 billion)
- Procurement of Type-12 surface-to-ship guided missiles (1 set: ¥5.5 billion)
- Procurement of stand-off missile (¥14.9 billion)
- Procurement of fighters (F-35A) (4 fighters: ¥39.1 billion)
- Development of upgraded Type-12 surface-to-ship guided missile ¥33.5 billion
- Research on Hyper Velocity Gliding Projectile (HVGP) for defense of remote islands (¥15 billion)
- Improvement of capability of electronic warfare information of the Japan Aerospace Defense Ground Environment (JADGE) (¥22.1 billion)
- Research on the feasibility of linking FC networks to CEC (¥200 million)
- Procurement of enhanced capability type PAC-3 missiles (PAC-3MSEs) (¥35.6 billion)
- Procurement of Type-03 Middle-Range

- Surface-to-Air Missile (modified) (1 set: ¥12 billion)
- ◆ Procurement of Type-16 mobile combat vehicles (22 vehicles: ¥15.8 billion)
- ◆ Procurement of new utility helicopter (UH-2) (7 helicopters: ¥12.5 billion)

Breakdown by Organisation
(Source: MoD, Japan) (Unit: JPY100 million)

Classification	JFY2021 Budget
Defence-related expenses	51,235
Ministry of Defence	51,235
(Ministry of Defence Head Office)	49,593
GSDF	18,264
MSDF	13,088
ASDF	11,237
Subtotal	42,590

CONCLUSION

Japan, keeping in view the regional security environment, the country plans to substantially bolster its defence capability, thereby establishing a defence posture that squarely addresses the reality. There is also a need to develop cross-domain defence capability that leverages capabilities in new domains such as space, cyber and electromagnetic spectrum on top of the existing domains of land, sea, and air. Moreover, the Japan-US alliance as well as defence cooperation with India, Australia, ASEAN countries and other partners can work very effectively in maintaining peace and stability of Japan and the region. According to the MoD, Japan report in Budget 2019, Japan should develop a defence capability that can further deepen and expand these endeavours. Furthermore, Japan's capability development should take into account Japan's demographic trends, other countries' military developments and future technological, given that defence capability development requires time. The security environment surrounding Japan has become increasingly severe, with various challenges and destabilising factors becoming more tangible and acute. Japan is striving to develop appropriate defence capabilities to protect the life and properties of its nationals and to defend the territorial land, sea, and airspace of Japan. At the same time, it is strengthening the Japan–US Alliance with the United States, which shares basic values and interests with Japan. The peace and security of Japan is ensured through developing seamless defence measures by coupling Japan's own defence capabilities with the Japan-US security arrangements. Japan and the United States are revising their mutual defence guidelines for the first time in nearly two decades to respond to China's military expansion and increase Japan's role in regional defence. US and Japan are pursuing a wider partnership that requires enhanced capabilities and greater shared responsibilities. Japan is gradually building up its forces in the region. This strategic shift of raising the prowess of its armed forces and equipment are seen as a significant step to defend and respond strongly to China's and North Korea's military growth in East Asia. Japan and India have been increasing cooperation in the field of maritime security. The country, in an effort to protect its territories and waters, is strengthening the naval and air force by acquiring submarines, ships, next generation fighter aircraft and adding new amphibious infantry vehicles. Japan relies to a large degree for its defence on its alliance with the United States, which has a significant number of fighters and other aircraft, along with some 50,000 troops, stationed around the Japanese archipelago. Japan is already started focusing on making its military presence more visible in the region, in a move to discourage China from extending its reach into the waters controlled by Japan. In July 2014, in a historic shift in Japan's post World War II defence policy, Abe's Cabinet approved a new interpretation of Japan's pacifist constitution. The reinterpretation allows the military to defend the US and other allies under what is known as collective self-defence. In order to realise cross-domain operations, the Japan's Self-Defence Forces (SDF) will acquire and strengthen capabilities in new domains, which are space, cyberspace and electromagnetic spectrum by focusing resources and leveraging Japan's superb science and technology.

CONTACT DETAILS

Japan Ministry of Defense
5-1 Honmura-cho, Ichigaya,
Shinjuku-ku, Tokyo 162-8801
Phone: 03-5366-3111
Website: http://www.mod.go.jp
E-mail: infomod@mod.go.jp

Equipment Procurement and Construction Office (EPCO)
http://www.epco.mod.go.jp/en/

JORDAN
(Capital: Amman)

INTRODUCTION
Area: 89,342 sq km
Population: 10,909,567 (July 2021 est.)
Coastline: 26 km
Maritime claims: Territorial sea: 3 nm

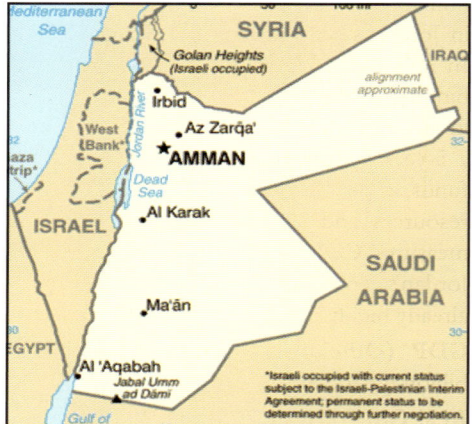

KEY POLITICAL PERSONS

HEAD OF STATE & COMMANDER-IN-CHIEF: King Abdullah II

PRIME MINISTER & DEFENCE MINISTER: Dr. Bishr Al-Khasawneh

KEY DEFENCE PERSONS

CHAIRMAN OF JOINT CHIEF OF STAFF: Maj. Gen. Yousef Huneiti

COMMANDER OF THE AIR FORCE: Brig. Gen. Zaid Ali Ngresh

ECONOMY

Jordan's economy is among the smallest in the Middle East, with insufficient supplies of water, oil, and other natural resources. Significant economic reforms, such as expanding foreign trade and privatising state-owned companies were implemented to attract foreign investment. It contributed to the annual economic growth. Jordan is nearly completely dependent on imported energy - mostly natural gas - and energy consistently makes up 25-30% of Jordan's imports. In 2016, Jordan and the IMF agreed to a USD723 million 'Extended Fund Facility' that aims to build on the three-year. Jordan belongs to a number of the same international organisations, including the United Nations, International Monetary Fund, World Bank, and World Trade Organisation. Jordan also is a Partner for Cooperation with the Organisation for Security and Cooperation in Europe. Jordan is also a major non-NATO ally, and a key partner in the US and Arab Coalition to defeat ISIS. The United States is Jordan's single largest provider of bilateral assistance, providing more than USD1.5 billion in 2019, including USD1.082 billion appropriated by the US Congress to Jordan through USAID in the 2019 fiscal year budget, and USD425 million in Foreign Military Financing. The United States has also provided nearly USD1.5 billion in humanitarian assistance to support refugees in Jordan since the start of the Syria crisis. In 2018, the U.S. and Jordan signed a non-binding MoU to provide USD6.375 billion in bilateral foreign assistance to Jordan over a 5-year period, pending the availability of funds, as per US Dept. of State. With limited resources and strict lockdown and curfew measures, COVID-19 pandemic has affected Jordan's economy badly. The country is already highly dependent on foreign aid.

GDP (Official exchange rate): $100.16 billion (2020), $101.74 billion (2019)

Real Growth Rate (GDP): 2% (2019 est.), 1.94% (2018 est.)

Industries: Tourism, information technology, clothing, fertilizer, potash, phosphate mining, pharmaceuticals, petroleum refining, cement, inorganic chemicals, light manufacturing

Oil – proved reserves: 1 million bbl (1 January 2018 est.)

Natural gas - proved reserves: 6.031 billion cu m (1 January 2018 est.)

Total Exports: $16.29 billion (2019), $15.09 billion (2018)

Export Commodities: Fertilizers, calcium phosphates, packaged medicines, clothing and apparel, phosphoric acid (2019)

Major Markets: United States 21%, Saudi Arabia 13%, India 8%, Iraq 7%, United Arab Emirates 5%, China 5% (2019)

Total Imports: $22.04 billion (2019), $22.92 billion (2018)

Import Commodities: Cars, refined petroleum, natural gas, crude petroleum, clothing and apparel (2019)

Major Suppliers: China 17%, Saudi Arabia 15%, United States 6%, United Arab Emirates 6%, Egypt 5%, India 5% (2019)

INTERNATIONAL DISPUTES

◆ A 2004 agreement settled border dispute with Syria pending demarcation.

◆ Jordan continued to face a persistent threat of terrorist activity both domestically and along its borders, owing in part to its proximity to regional conflicts in Iraq and Syria.

◆ As a regional leader in the Global Coalition to Defeat ISIS, Jordan played an important role in Coalition successes in degrading the terrorist group.

DEFENCE

ARMY

Personnel: 75,000

Equipment

Category	Name	In Service
MBT	Al Hussein Challenger 1	250+
	Khalid	300+
	M60A1/A3	300+
	Scorpion	50+
APC/IFV	M113 A2	1000+
	Ratel	300
	Spartans	100
	Saracen	100+
	Saladin	100+
	Ferret	100
Artillery	105 mm. M102	50
	155 mm. M59	10+
	155 mm. M114	30+
	203 mm. M114A2	100+
	105 mm. M52	30
	155 mm. M44	20+
	155 mm. M109	200+
	203 mm. M110A2	100
	Norinco 120mm. Howitzer	15+

...continued

Category	Name	In Service
Mortar	120 mm.	
	107 mm.	
	81 mm.	
Anti-Tank GW	TOW launchers	300+
	DRAGON	300+
	Javelin	30
AA Gun	40 mm. M42	150+
	Vulcan	100
	ZSU234 Shilka	10+
SAM	Redeye	200+
	Hawk	500+
	SA6, SA8, SA9, SA13, SA14, Starburst	10+

New Procurements/Upgrades

◆ The US State Department has approved a possible Foreign Military Sale to Jordan of up to 700 Advanced Field Artillery Tactical Data System (AFATDS) software license copies and related equipment for an estimated cost of USD300 million.

NAVY

Personnel: 500

Equipment

Category	Name	In Service
Patrol Craft	Al Hussein Class	3
	Faysal Class	4
	Abdullah Class	5+
	Al Hashim	3
	Bremse Class	2
	Coastal craft	5

New Procurements/Upgrades

No major procurement plans are under consideration at present.

AIR FORCE

Personnel: 12,500

Equipment

Category	Name	In Service
Fighter	F-16A	10+
	AT-802	4
	AC-235	1
	AC-295	1
Transport	CASA C-212 Aviocar	2
	An-28	1
	C-208	2+
	C-130H	4
Helicopter	AS332	10
	EC-635	10+
	UH-60L	5+
	Challenger 604	2

...continued

Category	Name	In Service
Helicopter	L-1011 Tristar	1
	S-70A	5
	SA-316C	1
	AH-1SW Cobra	20+
Trainer	C-101 Aviojet	10+
	Slingsby T-67 Firefly	10+
	TB 20 Trinidad	2
	MD 500D	5+
Weapons	MANPADS, MIM-23B/E, MIM-104 Patriot, 9K33 Osa, 9K35 Strela-10, SA-22 Pantsir-S1E	

New Procurements/ Upgrades

◆ The US State Department has approved a possible Foreign Military Sale to the Government of Jordan of an F-16 Air Combat Training Center and related equipment for an estimated cost of USD60 million.

◆ The US State Department has approved a possible Foreign Military Sale to the Government of Jordan of one UH-60M Black Hawk helicopter and related equipment for an estimated cost of USD23 million. The Government of Jordan has requested to buy one UH-60M Black Hawk helicopter in standard US Army configuration with standard Government Furnished Equipment (GFE), including two T700-GE-701D engines and one Common Missile Warning System. Also included is one AN/APR-39 Radar Signal Detecting Set; one AN/AVR-2B Laser Detecting Set; two AN-ARC-231 Radios; two AN-ARC-201D Radios; one AN/APX-123A Identification Friend or Foe (IFF) Transponder; two Embedded Global Positioning System with Inertial Navigation (EGIs); one Common Missile Warning System User Data Module; Aviation Mission Planning System (AMPS); AMPS software development and support services; and other related elements of logistical, engineering, and programme support.

Defence Expenditure

Total defence spending: $2.5 billion (approx.)
Estimated defence spending in terms of GDP: 4.7% of GDP (2020 est.)

Domestic Suppliers: King Abdullah Design and Development Bureau.
Foreign Suppliers: US, UK, France, Russia, China, Germany, Pakistan, Poland, Japan, Egypt, South Korea, Serbia, Taiwan, Turkey, Ukraine, Croatia, Mexico, Brazil, Italy, Greece, India,, Australia, Bulgaria, Netherlands.

Defence Production and R&D

The Jordanian Armed Forces own much of the country's defence industry and are closely involved in research, development, production and marketing of its products. The King Abdullah II Design and Development Bureau, KADDB was established to provide an indigenous capability for the supply of scientific and technical services to the Jordanian Armed Forces (JAF). KADDB was also created to provide a one-stop solution for the supply of defence and commercial equipment optimised for Middle East requirements.

Jordan Light Vehicle Manufacturing LLC (JLVM) is a joint venture between KADDB and the Jankel Group Ltd. of the UK to design, develop, produce, and market military vehicles.

Jordan Ammunition Manufacturing and Services Co (JORAMMO) caters for the ammunition needs of the Jordanian Armed Forces as well as other armed forces in the region and worldwide. The Laboratory has a full capability to test and evaluate different type of Small Arms, Light Weapons Ammunition, Armour Materials and Ballistic Resistance Systems for Military and Law Enforcement applications according to various international testing standards. KADDB's numerous products in the field of defence industries includes Al-Washaq ATV Model, the Stallion 4x4 LAV Model, in addition to the 8x8 wheeled Armoured Vehicle Model.

Defence Procurement

The Directorate of Procurement is part of General Headquarter of Jordan Armed Forces. It was established with the mission of executing the whole purchases of Jordan Armed Forces requirements and needs. The Directorate of Procurement carries out sales surplus and unserviceable equipment, Vehicles, Weapons, spare parts and other types of goods. The main duties of the Directorate of Procurement are:

◆ Executing the policy of General Headquarters of the Jordan Armed Forces.

◆ Producing and developing the rules and regulations related to procurement in cooperation with concerned government department.

◆ Specifying the best and optimal sources of purchase whether locally or abroad.

◆ Signing, implementing and pursuing of contracts regarding buying, items, Services Etc. with the concerned parties.

◆ Implementing the laws, regulations and customs instructions regarding purchasing process.

◆ Authenticating the latest references, contract, catalogues, specifications and standardization.

◆ Classifying and arranging local and foreign purchasing resources.

CONTACT DETAILS
Ministry of Defence
PO Box 79, Amman, Jordan

King Abdullah II Design and Development Bureau
928125 Amman, 11190, Jordan
Tel: +962 6 4603230
Fax: +962 6 5627203 - +962 6 4626804, (962) 6 5001186
E-Mail: info@kaddb.mil.jo

Directorate of Defence Procurement
P. O. Box: 926680
Tel: (+962) 6 5000108
Fax: (+962) 6 5001186
Vehicles, Weapons & Ammunitions
vehicle@jafdop.mil.jo
Communications & Electronic Systems.
commsys@jafdop.mil.jo
Quartermaster, Food, and Medical Supplies.
qmaster@jafdop.mil.jo
Shipping & Insurance.
shipin@jafdop.mil.jo
Military Customs & Clearance.
customs@jafdop.mil.jo
Loans & Eastern Supply.
loans@jafdop.mil.jo
Central Tenders Committee
ctc@jafdop.mil.jo

General Command of the Jordanian Armed Forces
Amman – Tabarbour
Abu Alia - in front of Military Sports Union
Tel: 06/5000800

Royal Jordanian Air Force
Amman - Marka - Versus the State Security Court
Postal Code: 11134 | P.O.Box: 340766
Tel: +962 6 4896351

KAZAKHSTAN
(Capital: Nur-Sultan)

INTRODUCTION

Area: 2,724,900 sq. km

Population: 19,245,793 (July 2021 est.)

Coastline: 0 km (Landlocked) Note: Kazakhstan borders the Aral Sea, now split into two bodies of water (1,070 km), and the Caspian Sea (1,894 km)

Maritime claims: None

Note: Astana, the capital of Kazakhstan since 1997, was renamed Nur-Sultan after former president Nursultan Nazarbayev on 23 March 2019 following a unanimous vote in Kazakhstan's parliament.

KEY POLITICAL PERSONS

PRESIDENT & SUPREME COMMANDER OF THE ARMED FORCES: Kassym-Jomart Tokayev

PRIME MINISTER: Askar Mamin

KEY DEFENCE PERSONS

DEFENCE MINISTER: Lt. Gen. Bektanov Murat Karibaevch

CHIEF OF THE GENERAL STAFF: Maj. Gen. Marat Khusainov

COMMANDER OF GROUND FORCE: Maj. Gen. Talgat Koibakov

COMMANDER OF THE NAVAL FORCE: Captain 1st rank Saken Bekzhanov

COMMANDER OF AIR DEFENCE FORCE: Lt. Gen. Nurlan Ormanbetov

ECONOMY

Kazakhstan has transitioned from lower-middle-income to upper-middle-income status. It's economy is the largest in Central Asia and is supported by enormous oil reserves, minerals, and metals such as uranium, copper and zinc. The vast hydrocarbon and mineral reserves form the backbone of its economy. The oil sector is the main driver of economic growth. Oil output reportedly increased by 12.5% in the first nine months of 2017 due to the launch of production at the long-awaited off-shore oil field Kashagan in October 2016. Kazakhstan also has a large agricultural sector featuring livestock and grain. To boost its economy the government has embarked on an ambitious diversification programme aimed at developing targeted sectors like transport, pharmaceuticals, telecommunications, petrochemicals and food processing. The main export commodities included oil and oil products, ferrous metals, chemicals, and machinery. Other export products include coal, wool, grain, and coal. According to the World Bank, the course of the COVID-19 pandemic is likely to affect the balance and pace of the economic recovery. The recovery has been uneven, with manufacturing activities recovering faster than the services sector, which had employed a larger share of workers and was hit hardest by the pandemic.

GDP (official exchange rate): $181.194 billion (2019 est.)

Real Growth Rate (GDP): 6.13% (2019 est.), 4.41% (2018 est.)

Industries: Oil, coal, iron ore, manganese, chromite, lead, zinc, copper, titanium, bauxite, gold, silver, phosphates, sulphur, uranium, iron and steel; tractors and other agricultural machinery, electric motors, construction materials.

Total Exports: $51.75 billion (2020 est.), $65.91 billion (2019 est.)

Export Commodities: Crude petroleum, natural gas, copper, iron alloys, radioactive chemicals (2019)

Major Markets: China 13%, Italy 12%, Russia 10%, Netherlands 7%, France 6%, South Korea 5% (2019)

Total Imports: $44.3 billion dollars (2020 est.), $51.5 billion (2019 est.)

Import Commodities: Packaged medicines, natural gas, cars, broadcasting equipment, aircraft (2019)

Major Suppliers: Russia 34%, China 24% (2019)

INTERNATIONAL DISPUTES

◆ In January 2019, the Kyrgyz Republic ratified the demarcation agreement of the Kazakh-Kyrgyz border

◆ The demarcation of the Kazakh-Uzbek borders is ongoing

◆ The ongoing demarcation with Russia began in 2007

◆ Demarcation with China completed in 2002

DEFENCE

Kazakhstan military had some difficult periods after the fall of the Soviet Union but due to good national military governance the country has emerged as the armed forces with the highest professional standards. Kazakhstan military comprised of the Ground Forces, Air and Air Defence Forces and the Naval Forces. As member of the Collective Security Treaty Organization (CSTO), Kazakhstan takes part in military operations with the other organisation's participants. Kazakhstan has adopted a new military doctrine giving priority to armed conflict along the border introducing the concept of "hybrid" warfare. According to the 2017 Military Doctrine, "hybrid" warfare is defined as the "ways of achieving military-political and military-strategic objectives of an integrated military force including special operations forces, private military security companies on the territory of the opposing side, via non-military means, as well as by using the potential of other states, terrorist and extremist organisations, and separatist movements to destabilise the situation in the territory of the opposing state." Meanwhile, Kazakhstan and Russia have signed the strategic partnership programme in the defence sector for 2022-2024.

Ground Force
Personnel: 30,000
Equipment

Category	Name	In Service
MBT	T-72	650
	T-62	280
AIFV/APC	Otokar Cobra	
	MRAP Arlan	60
	BMP1/2	508
	BTR-60/70/80 (many stored)	
	BTR-82	12
	BTR-4	
	BMPT	30+
Artillery	D-30 122mm	200
	M-46 130mm	200
	D-20 152mm (towed)	100
	2S1 12mm	150
	2S3 152mm SP	
MRL	BM21 122mm	
	TOS-1 Buratino 220mm	
	Uragan 220mm	

New Procurements/Upgrades
◆ Kazakhstan Paramount Engineering (KPE) has started production of the Barys 6×6 Infantry Fighting Vehicle (IFV) for the Kazakh military. The Armed Forces Special Units have placed an initial order for three vehicles.

◆ Kazakh vehicle manufacturer KPE has signed an agreement with the Kazakh Ministry of Defence (MoD) for a further batch of 4×4 Arlan MRAP vehicles.

NAVAL FORCES
Landlocked Kazakhstan operates a small Navy on the Caspian Sea – the world's largest inland body of water – base at Aktau. The former Soviet Union's Caspian Sea Flotilla was divided between Russia, Azerbaijan, Turkmenistan, and Kazakhstan in 1993. Kazakhstan is developing its Navy by creating the coastal navies infrastructure, further improvement of training programmes and increasing the number of the military vessels within the Naval Forces.

Personnel: 3,000
Equipment:

Category	Name	In Service
Vessels	Almaty class	4
	Dauntless class	1
	Guardian class	5
	Turk	2

...continued

Category	Name	In Service
Minesweeper	Alatau	
Patrol Craft	Project1400M Grif class	2
Aircraft	Su-27	
Missile Boat	-	3+

New Procurements/Upgrades
No major procurement plans are under consideration at present.

AIR and AIR DEFENCE FORCE
Personnel: 10,000
Equipment

Category	Name	In service	On Order
Fighter	Su-30SM	20	4
	MiG-31		
	MiG-29	40	
	MiG-27		
	Su-27	12	
	Su-24	20+	
	Su-25	14	
	MiG-23	20	
	MiG 25		
Transport	Y-8		
	Airbus C295	4	
	An-26	12	
	An-72	10	
	An-12		
	L-39	4 (upgraded)	
Helicopter	Mi-35M	4	
	EC145	6	8
	UH-1H	6	
	Mi-8	40	
	Mi-17	20	
	Mi-24	30	
	Mi-26	10	
	Ka-32A11BC	2	
SAM	S-300	1 battery	

New Procurements/Upgrades
◆ The Air Force has taken delivery of the four modernised L-39s. The overhaul included an extensive modernisation of the avionics.

◆ The Kazakhstan Air Defence Forces (KADF) will receive four more Russian Sukhoi Su-30SM 'Flanker-H' multirole fighter aircraft by the end of 2022. So far, 20 Su-30SMs have been delivered to the KADF.

◆ An agreement has been signed for local assembly of 20 BC725 Caracals.

◆ A MoU has been signed to develop fully digital 3D air surveillance radars, Ground Master 400 (GM400).

Defence Expenditure
Total defence spending: $1752 million (2020), $1929 million (2019)
Estimated defence spending in terms of GDP: 1.1% (2018)

Defence Production and R&D
Kazakhstan has announced ambitious plans to become the leading regional exporter of arms in Central Asia by transforming its defence industry capabilities in order to export mainly artillery systems. Its military is armed primarily with Russian and Soviet equipment but Astana is trying to diversify its sources for armaments from other countries so as not to be too dependent on one. A joint venture has been set up with the European helicopter manufacturer to produce EC145 helicopters for the Kazakh military and other government agencies. South Africa's Paramount Group and Kazakhstan have entered a deal to jointly produce armoured vehicles and has signed a military technical cooperation with Israel. Kazakhstan has also signed an agreement with Russia to boost bilateral military cooperation between the two countries.

Defence Procurement
The government has signed a decree approving a state programme to modernise the Kazakh military. The defence ministry is actively introducing modern and advanced military systems and platforms. Both the Navy and the Air Force are acquiring new platforms, weapons and systems as part of the modernisation drive. The government has outlined the priority areas for military procurement as: manufacture and repair of aircraft, motor vehicles, missile and artillery systems, automated C2 as well as communications and other specialist military equipment.

CONTACT DETAILS
Ministry of Defence
Dostyk ave., Bld 14
Nur-Sultan-010000, Republic of Kazakhstan
Office: +7(7172) 72-13-84
E-mail: mork@mod.gov.kz

KENYA
(Capital: Nairobi)

INTRODUCTION
Area: 580,367 sq km
Population: 54,685,051 (July 2021 est.)
Coastline: 536 km
Maritime claims: Territorial sea: 12 nm
Exclusive Economic Zone: 200 nm
Continental shelf: 200 m depth or to the depth of exploitation

KEY POLITICAL PERSONS

PRESIDENT & COMMANDER-IN-CHIEF: Uhuru Muigai Kenyatta

DEPUTY PRESIDENT: William Ruto

KEY DEFENCE PERSONS

DEFENCE SECRETARY: Monica Juma

CHIEF OF DEFENCE FORCES: Gen. Robert Kibochi

ARMY COMMANDER: Lt. Gen. Walter Raria Koipaton

NAVY COMMANDER: Maj. Gen. Jimson Longiro Mutai

AIR FORCE COMMANDER: Maj. Gen. J M Omenda

ECONOMY

Kenya is the economic, financial, and transport hub of East Africa. The country's real GDP growth has averaged over 5% for the last decade. Since 2014, Kenya has been ranked as a lower middle income country because its per capita GDP crossed a World Bank threshold. The market-based mixed economy of Kenya has registered positive growth in the last few years despite being marred by corruption. It is the most industrially developed country in East Africa and an attractive destination for foreign trade in the continent. While the services sector is the major contributor to the GDP, agriculture and industry too have a visible share in it. Tourism also holds a significant place in Kenya's economy.

A prolonged election cycle in 2017 hurt the economy, drained government resources, and slowed GDP growth. Drought-like conditions in parts of the country pushed 2017 inflation above 8%, but the rate had fallen to 4.5% in February 2018. The COVID-19 pandemic has affected the Kenyan economy which has shrunk for the first time in almost three decades due to the deadly virus. According to the Kenyan Government, GDP growth was 0.6% in 2020, and it could rebound in 2021 with a growth forecast of 6.6%.

GDP (official exchange rate): $95.52 billion (2019 est.)

Real Growth Rate (GDP): 5.39% (2019 est.); 6.32% (2018 est.)

Industries: Small-scale consumer goods (plastic, furniture, batteries, textiles, clothing, soap, cigarettes, flour), agricultural products, horticulture, oil refining; aluminum, steel, lead; cement, commercial ship repair, tourism, information technology

Total Exports: $10.07 billion (2019 est.); $10.1 billion (2018 est.)

Export Commodities: Tea, cut flowers, refined petroleum, coffee, titanium (2019)

Major Markets: Uganda 10%, United States 9%, Netherlands 8%, Pakistan 7%, United Kingdom 6%, United Arab Emirates 6%, Tanzania 5% (2019)

Total Imports: $18.72 billion (2019 est.); $19.11 billion (2018 est.)

Import Commodities: Refined petroleum, cars, packaged medicines, wheat, iron products (2019)

Major Suppliers: China 24%, United Arab Emirates 10%, India 10%, Saudi Arabia 7%, Japan 5% (2019)

INTERNATIONAL DISPUTES

The boundary that separates Kenya's and Sudan's sovereignty is unclear in the "Ilemi Triangle," which Kenya has administered since colonial times.

DEFENCE

ARMY
Personnel: 19,000

Equipment

Category	Name	In Service
MBT	T-72	70
	Vickers Mk3	80
Armoured Car	Saladin	3
	Ferret	16
	AML90	30
	AML60	20
	Shorland	8
	Saracen	5
APC	UR-416	38
	Panhard M3	8
	BRM SP	85
Artillery	2S7 203mm SP	25
	NORA 152mm SP	18
	122mm towed	48
	105mm light gun	40
	L5 105mm pack	
Mortar	L16 81mm	20
	120mm	8

...continued

Category	Name	In Service
ATGW	Swingfire	14
	Milan	40
SAM	Mistral/ASPIC	
	BUK	
AA gun	TCM20 20mm	50
	ZPU-4	70
ATK weapon	Carl Gustav 84mm	56
Helicopter	Harbin Z9WA	4

New Procurements/Upgrades
◆ The Army has received 12 French-made Arquus Bastion armoured personnel carriers (APCs) donated by the United States in 2018.

NAVY
Personnel: 1,400

Equipment

Category	Name	In Service
Fleet	Nyayo class large missile FAC	2
	Ex-Spanish P101 type patrol boat	5
	Shupavu class OPV	2
	LSM	1

New Procurements/Upgrades
No major procurement plans are under consideration at present.

AIR FORCE
Personnel: 2,500

Equipment

Category	Name	In Service
Fighter	F-5E/F Tiger II	20

KOSOVO
(Capital: Pristina)

INTRODUCTION
Area: 10,887 sq km
Population: 1,935,259 (July 2021 est.)
Coastline: 0 km (Landlocked)
Maritime claims: None

KEY POLITICAL PERSONS

PRESIDENT: Vjosa Osmani

...continued

Category	Name	In Service
Transport	Fokker 70 (VIP)	1
	Piper NAVAJO	1
	Piper Chieftain	1
	Harbin Y-12	11
	DASH 8	3
Trainer	Tucano	11
Helicopter (attack & utility)	MD 500M	10
	MD 530F	6
	SA.330 Puma	3
	IAR330	6
	Bell UH-1 Huey II	8
	Bell AH-1F Cobra (attack)	
	Mi-17	
	AW139	3
UAV	ScanEagle	

New Procurements/Upgrades
◆ Italy's Leonardo has completed delivery of all three Alenia C-27J Spartan transport aircraft in 2020.
◆ Three AW139 helicopters delivered by Leonardo have been inducted in service.
◆ Six MD 530F Cayuse Warrior light attack helicopters have been delivered by US's MD Helicopters in 2019.
◆ The US Government has proposed to sell 12 armed L3 Technologies-Air Tractor AT-802L Longsword intelligence, surveillance, and reconnaissance (ISR) and light attack turboprop aircraft to the Kenyan Air Force.

KEY DEFENCE PERSONS

PRIME MINISTER: Albin Kurti

MINISTER OF DEFENCE: Armend Mehaj

Defence Expenditure
Defence spending: Sh121 billion (2020)
Estimated defence spending in terms of GDP: 1.4%

Major defence suppliers to Kenya are the US, Russia and Europe.

Defence Production and R&D
Kenya has very limited defence production and research facilities. Majority of its military equipment are procured from outside Africa. The state-owned Kenya Ordnance Factories Corporation (KOFC) is primarily involved in manufacturing small arms and ammunition.

Defence Procurement
The Kenyan Army, Navy and Air Force have inducted several new equipment and platforms in the past decade as part of their modernisation drive. The country, however, maintains secrecy over its defence procurement programmes. In the past over two years, Kenya has acquired armoured vehicles, main battle tanks, multiple rocket launchers, armed helicopters and transport aircraft among other platforms and equipment for its military.

CONTACT DETAILS
Ministry of Defence
The Principal Secretary
Ministry of Defence
Ulinzi House, Lenana Road
P O Box 40668 - 00100, Nairobi
Tel: +254 20 2721100
www.mod.go.ke

COMMANDER OF KOSOVO SECURITY FORCE: Maj. Gen. Bashkim Jashari

ECONOMY

After gaining independence in 2008, Kosovo's relatively new economy has grown significantly by transitioning into a modern free market system from a centralist and controlled economy. Foreign investments into the country are mostly from Europe, including Germany, Austria and Switzerland, among others. It also receives remittances from citizens working in neighbouring Nordic and other countries. Imports are higher than exports and the country has been making efforts to bridge the huge trade deficit. Kosovo's citizens are the second poorest in Europe, after Moldova, with a per capita GDP (PPP) of $10,400 in 2017. While Kosovo's economy continues to make progress, unemployment has not been reduced, nor living standards raised, due to lack of economic reforms and investment.

To accelerate economic growth, the Government has taken initiatives to privatise state-owned enterprises. In June 2009, Kosovo joined the World Bank and International Monetary Fund. In order to help integrate Kosovo into regional economic structures, the United Nations Interim Administration Mission in Kosovo (UNMIK) signed the country's accession to the Central Europe Free Trade Area (CEFTA) in 2006. Serbia and Bosnia previously had refused to recognise Kosovo's customs stamp or extend reduced tariff privileges for Kosovo products under CEFTA, but both countries resumed trade with Kosovo in 2011. The official currency of Kosovo is the euro, but the Serbian dinar is also used illegally in Serb enclaves. Kosovo's tie to the euro has helped keep core inflation low.

Due to the COVID-19 outbreak, Kosovo's economy was predicted to contract by over 4% in 2020, according to World Bank.

GDP (official exchange rate): $7.92 billion (2019 est.)

Real Growth Rate (GDP): 3.7% (2017 est.); 4.1% (2016 est.)

Industries: Mineral mining, construction materials, base metals, leather, machinery, appliances, foodstuff and beverages, textiles

Total Exports: $428 million (2017 est.); $340 million (2016 est.)

Export Commodities: Mining and processed metal products, scrap metals, leather products, machinery, appliances, prepared foodstuffs, beverages and tobacco, vegetable products, textiles and apparel

Major Markets: Albania 16%, India 14%, North Macedonia 12.1%, Serbia 10.6%, Switzerland 5.6%, Germany 5.4% (2017)

Total Imports: $3.223 billion (2017 est.); $2.876 billion (2016 est.)

Import Commodities: Foodstuff, livestock, wood, petroleum, chemicals, machinery, minerals, textiles, stone, ceramic and glass products, electrical equipment

Major Suppliers: Germany 12.4%, Serbia 12.3%, Turkey 9.6%, China 9.1%, Italy 6.4%, Macedonia, The Former Yugo Rep of 5.1%, Albania 5%, Greece 4.4% (2017)

INTERNATIONAL DISPUTES

◆ Boundary dispute with Serbia continues as Serbia and a number of other countries do not recognise Kosovo as an independent sovereign state.

◆ Kosovo and North Macedonia completed demarcation of their boundary in September 2008.

◆ Kosovo ratified the border demarcation agreement with Montenegro in March 2018, but the actual demarcation has not been completed.

DEFENCE

The Kosovo Security Force (KSF), formed in March 2008 with the initiatives of NATO-led Kosovo Force (KFOR) and the Kosovo Protection Corps (KPC), assumed full operational capability in July 2013. Constituted as a lightly armed and uniformed security force primarily responsible for civil protection operations and assisting civil authorities in responding to natural disasters and other emergencies the KSF has been trained to NATO standards. The security force has been assigned the task of conducting non-military security functions such as search and rescue operations, explosive ordnance disposal, control and clearance of hazardous materials, fire-fighting and other humanitarian assistance tasks.

The Kosovo Government, in March 2014, had proposed to create a 5,000-strong regular army to "protect sovereignty" of the ethnic Albanian territory. According to the proposal, the future army would have about 3,000 reservists in a decade's time and a yearly budget of around €65 million. The new military structure was expected to be fully operational after 2019; however, it has been staunchly opposed by Serbia and the Serbian minority community living in Kosovo.

The Kosovo Parliament in December 2018 gave its approval for the creation of the National Army despite opposition from several quarters, including from NATO and the US, who advocated a final settlement with Serbia first before moving forward to form the national (regular) Army Kosovo's defence budget for the year 2019 was increased to help begin the process of transforming the Kosovo Security Force (KSF) into a regular army. The 2021 defence budget, however, has not much provision to increase military personnel or equipment in the KSF which still retains its old name.

Existing Personnel: 4,500 (+2,000 reserve force)

Defence Expenditure

Defence Budget: €63.6 million ($78 million) proposed for 2021; €58.7 million (2019)

Estimated defence spending in terms of GDP: 1%

Defence Production and R&D

Kosovo has not undertaken any defence production activities and no defence production facilities exist in the country.

Defence Procurement

No major procurement plans are under consideration at present.

Kosovo Security Forces Personnel

CONTACT DETAILS
Ministry of the Kosovo Security Force
Kazerma "Adem Jashari"
10 000 Pristina, Republic of Kosovo
mod.rks-gov.net/

KUWAIT
(Capital: Kuwait City)

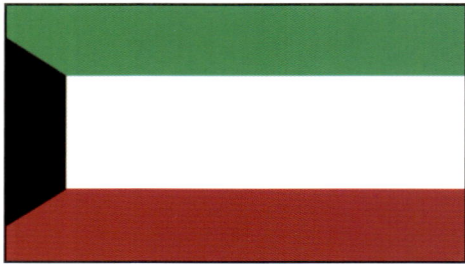

INTRODUCTION
Area: 17,818 sq km
Population: 3,032,065 (July 2021 est.)
Coastline: 499 km
Maritime claims: Territorial Sea: 12 nm

KEY POLITICAL PERSONS

CHIEF OF STATE & SUPREME COMMANDER OF ARMED FORCES: Sheikh Nawaf Al Ahmad Al Sabah

PRIME MINISTER: Sheikh Sabah-al-Khalid-al-Sabah

KEY DEFENCE PERSONS

DEPUTY PRIME MINISTER & MINISTER OF DEFENCE: Sheikh Hamad Jaber Al-Ali Al-Sabah

CHIEF OF GENERAL STAFF: Lt. Gen. Khaled Saleh Al-Sabah

ECONOMY

Kuwait has a geographically small, but wealthy, relatively open economy with self-reported crude oil reserves of about over 6% of world reserves. Kuwaiti officials plan to increase production to 4 million barrels of oil equivalent per day by 2020. Petroleum accounts for over half of GDP, 92% of export revenues, and 90% of government income. Kuwait, however, has done little to diversify its economy or bolster the private sector, because of a poor business climate and a large public sector that employs about 74% of citizens. The Kuwaiti Government has made little progress on its long-term economic development plan first passed in 2010. While the government planned to spend up to $104 billion over four years to diversify the economy, attract more investment, and boost private sector participation in the economy, many of the projects did not materialize because of an uncertain political situation or delays in awarding contracts. To increase non-oil revenues, the Kuwaiti Government in August 2017 approved draft bills supporting a Gulf Cooperation Council-wide value added tax scheduled to take effect in 2018.

Severely affected by the Coronavirus pandemic coupled with a sharp drop in oil prices, the Kuwaiti economy contracted 8% in 2020, according to the IMF. The economy was expected to recover by about 1% in 2021.

GDP (official exchange rate): $134.63 billion (2019 est.)

Real Growth Rate (GDP): -3.3% (2017 est.); 2.2% (2016 est.)

Industries: Petroleum, petrochemicals, cement, shipbuilding and repair, water desalination, food processing, construction materials

Natural gas - proved reserves: 1.784 trillion cu m (1 January 2018 est.)

Crude oil - proved reserves: 101.5 billion bbl (1 January 2018 est.)

Total Exports: $84.82 billion (2018 est.); $89.09 billion (2017 est.)

Export Commodities: Crude petroleum, refined petroleum, aircraft, natural gas, industrial hydrocarbon products (2019)

Major Markets: China 20%, South Korea 16%, India 15%, Japan 10%, Taiwan 6%, Vietnam 5% (2019)

Total Imports: $54.55 billion (2018 est.); $55.02 billion (2017 est.)

Import Commodities: Cars, broadcasting equipment, natural gas, packaged medicines, jewellery (2019)

Major Suppliers: China 14%, United Arab Emirates 12%, United States 10%, Saudi Arabia 6%, Japan 6%, Germany 5%, India 5% (2019)

INTERNATIONAL DISPUTES

Kuwait and Saudi Arabia continue to negotiate a joint maritime boundary with Iran.

DEFENCE

ARMY
Personnel: 10,000+

Equipment

Category	Name	In Service
MBT	M1A2 Abram	236
	M84	150
	Chieftain	45 (storage)
APC, AFV	Desert Warrior	254
	BMP-2	40
	BMP-3	55
	M113	60
	Ferret	80
Artillery	Norinco PLZ45 155mm SP	51
	M-109 155mm SP	23
	GCT 155mm SP	15
	F3 155mm SP	18
MLRS	Smerch 300mm	25
ATGW	TOW	118

New Procurements/Upgrades

◆ A total of 218 new M1A2 Abrams tanks are being procured from the US. General Dynamics Land Systems has received an initial contract of US$24.3 million to design, build and deliver the new improved M1A2-K Abrams variants. The first platform has officially been handed over to the Kuwaiti Army in July 2021.

◆ Up to 300 Sherpa Light armoured 4 x 4 vehicles built by France's Renault Trucks Defence are on order with deliveries going on.

NAVY
Personnel: 1,500

Equipment

Category	Name	In Service
Corvette	Baynunah-class	6
FAC (missile & gun)	Al Sanbouk class (Type TN C45)	1
	Istiqlal class (Type FPB 57)	1
	Um Al Maradim class (CMN PB-37BRL)	8

...continued

Category	Name	In Service
Landing Craft & High Speed Vessels		8
Patrol Craft	ASI 315 Type	2
	NAJA 12 Type	12
	Seagull	4
	In-shore patrol craft	57
	Al Tahaddy class LMC	2
	Haditah Class LC	2

New Procurements/Upgrades

◆ 15 fast patrol boats from the US at a cost of US$100 million under foreign military sales (FMS) programme has been sought. The US State Dept. has approved the sale in 2018.

◆ Plans are on for mid-life upgrade of eight P37 (Um Al Maradim class) fast patrol boats. The Navy is also planning to order a range of ship-launched missiles to equip the boats.

◆ Delivery of 15 MkV-C fast Interceptor boats on order from the US is going on. The vessels are being procured to conduct coastal patrol, surveillance and interdiction missions.

AIR FORCE
Personnel: 2,500
Equipment

Category	Name	In Service
Fighter	F/A-18C/D	39
Transport	L100-30 Hercules	2
	C-17 Globemaster	1
	KC-130J	3
Trainer	Tucano	8
	Hawk Mk. 64	10
Helicopter	AS.332 Super Puma	5
	SA 330 Puma	5
	SA342K Gazelle	13
	AH-64D Apache Longbow	16
SAM	I-Hawk battery	1
	Skyguard	10
	Patriot (PAC-3)	
	Starburst	50

New Procurements/Upgrades

◆ A deal has been signed with Eurofighter GmbH in April 2016 for 28 Eurofighter Typhoon jets at a cost of €7.957 billion. The Eurofighter consortium will deliver 22 single-seat and six twin-seat (all third tranche configuration) Eurofighters. Delivery is expected between 2020 and 2023.

◆ Boeing has received a US$1.5 billion contract in 2018 for the production and delivery of 28 F/A-18E/F Super Hornet combat aircraft to Kuwait. Delivery is expected by 2021. The US Govt in 2016 had cleared the proposal to sell the fighters to Kuwait. Kuwait had made a request for acquiring 28 of the jets with an option for 12 more such platforms. The cost of the deal is estimated to be US$10.1 billion.

◆ Four King Air 350ER Intelligence, Surveillance, and Reconnaissance (ISR) aircraft for an estimated cost of $259 million have been sought from the US under FMS route.

◆ The US Govt in 2020 has proposed to sell 24 of the Boeing AH-64E Apache Guardian attack helicopters to Kuwait at an estimated cost of $4 billion.

◆ Under a deal worth US$ 1.1 billion finalised with France, 30 Airbus-built H225M Caracal helicopters and associated weapons are being procured for the Kuwait Air Force and National Guard. Delivery is going on. The rotorcraft would be used for conducting combat search & rescue, and naval operations.

◆ The US State Department in May 2020 has approved a possible Foreign Military Sale (FMS) of over 80 Patriot Advanced Capability (PAC-3) missile systems to Kuwait.

◆ Potential sale of AIM-9X-2 Sidewinder Block II missiles and associated equipment has been notified by the US's DCSA.

◆ Sale of 300 AGM-114R Hellfire air-to-surface missiles has been approved by the US Government.

◆ Possible foreign military sale of 60 units of AIM-120C-7 advanced medium range air-to-air missiles (AMRAAM) and upgrade of AH-64D Apache helicopters worth over $500 million by the US is under consideration.

◆ The UK's Marshall Aerospace and Defence Group has received a contract from the US Govt to provide in-service support for three of the Lockheed Martin KC-130J tanker-transport aircraft of the Kuwait air force.

◆ Procurement of a second C-17 Globemaster III strategic airlifter platform from the US is under consideration.

◆ Procurement of UAVs is under consideration.

Defence Expenditure
Defence budget: US$7.8 billion (proposed for 2021); US$6.9 billion (2020)
Estimated defence spending in terms of GDP: 3.7%

The Kuwait Parliament in January 2016 announced to allocate an additional US$ 10 billion for defence over the next 10 years to finance the ongoing military procurement programmes, including the purchase of new fighter jets, tanks and air defence systems among other defence hardware. The US is a major military supplier to the country.

Defence Production and R&D
Kuwait does not undertake any defence production activities.

Defence Procurement
Kuwait opted for completely restructured armed forces after the Iraqi invasion and the subsequent war in 1990-91. The Government signed a 10-year defence cooperation agreement with the US that allowed US military equipment to be stored in its territory and joint military operations. Of late, Kuwait has undertaken comprehensive, all-round military modernisation by acquiring new weapons and platforms for all three wings of its defence forces.

CONTACT DETAILS
Ministry of Defence
P.O Box 1170
Safat 3012, Kuwait

KYRGYZSTAN
(Capital: Bishkek)

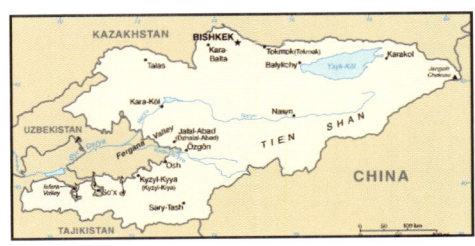

INTRODUCTION
Area: 199,951 sq. km
Population: 6,018,789 (July 2021 est.)
Coastline: 0 km (landlocked)
Maritime claims: None

KEY POLITICAL PERSONS

PRESIDENT: Sadyr Japarov

CHAIRMAN OF THE CABINET OF MINISTERS OF KYRGYZSTAN: Akylbek Japarov

KEY DEFENCE PERSONS

MINISTER OF DEFENCE: Maj. Gen. Baktybek Bekbolotov

CHIEF OF GENERAL STAFF: Maj. Gen. Erlis Terdikbayev

COMMANDER OF ARMY: Col. Almazbek Karasartov

COMMANDER OF AIR FORCE: Kylychbek Aidaraliev

COMMANDER OF NATIONAL GUARD: Col. Talantbek Ergeshov

ECONOMY

The mountainous landlocked country with a dominant agricultural sector produces cotton, tobacco, wool, and meat but only tobacco and cotton are exported. Other exports include gold, mercury, uranium, natural gas. The economy depends heavily on remittances from Kyrgyzstani migrant workers. Kyrgyzstan has carried out market reforms, such as improving the regulatory system and instituting land reform. It was the first Commonwealth of Independent States (CIS) country to be accepted into the World Trade Organisation. The Kyrgyz government remains dependent on foreign donor support to finance its annual budget deficit of approximately 3 to 5% of GDP. Despite some reforms, the overall economic improvement has been slow and continues to be hampered by corruption, lack of administrative transparency, lack of diversity in domestic industries, and difficulty attracting foreign aid and investment. The country went through major turmoil following the parliamentary elections on October 4, 2020.

GDP (official exchange rate): $8.442 billion (2019 est.)

Real Growth Rate (GDP): 4.6% (2017 est.), 4.3% (2016 est.)

Industries: Small machinery, textiles, food processing, cement, shoes, lumber, refrigerators, furniture, electric motors, gold, rare earth metals

Total Exports: $3.11 billion (2019 est.), $2.73 billion (2018 est.)

Export Commodities: Gold, precious metals, various beans, refined petroleum, scrap copper (2019)

Major Markets: United Kingdom 56%, Kazakhstan 13%, Russia 13%, Uzbekistan 5% (2019)

Total Imports: $5.67 billion (2019 est.), $5.86 billion (2018 est.)

Import Commodities: Refined petroleum, footwear, clothing and apparel, broadcasting equipment, walnuts (2019)

Major Suppliers: China 53%, Russia 17%, Kazakhstan 7%, Uzbekistan 7%, Turkey 5% (2019)

INTERNATIONAL DISPUTES

◆ Disputes in Isfara Valley delay completion of delimitation with Tajikistan.

◆ Delimitation of approximately 15% or 200 km of border with Uzbekistan is hampered by serious disputes over enclaves and other areas.

DEFENCE

Kyrgyzstan is a Central Asian republic that became independent with the collapse of the Soviet Union in 1991. The Armed Forces of the Republic of Kyrgyzstan, originally formed from former Soviet forces of the Turkestan Military District, includes the Army, Air Force and the National Guard. Russia help patrol Kyrgyz airspace as part of the Joint CIS Air Defence System.

ARMY
Personnel: 12,000

Equipment

Category	Name	In Service
MBT	T-72	150
AIFV/APC	BTR-60	53
	BTR-70	25
	BTR-80	10
	BMP-1	230
	MBP-2	90

...continued

Category	Name	In Service
AIFV/APC	BRDM-2	30
	BRDM-2M 4×4	9 (upgraded)
Artillery	100mm BS-3 towed	18
	122mm howitzer D-30	72
	122mm howitzer M-30	35
	152mm D-1	16
	2S9 Anona SP	12
	2S1	18
	M120	48
	2S12 120mm Sani mortar	6
AA gun	100mm T-12	18
MRL	BM-21 GRAD	15

New Procurements/Upgrades

No major procurement plans are under consideration at present.

AIR FORCE
Personnel: 1,000

Equipment

Category	Name	In Service
Aircraft	L-39 Albatross	30
Helicopter	Mi-8	3
	Mi-8T	2
	Mi-24	12
VIP transport/ liaison	An-26	2
	Tu-154	2
	Boeing 737	2

New Procurements/Upgrades

◆ Kyrgyzstan to acquire Bayraktar TB2 UAVs from Turkey.

◆ Kyrgyzstan has procured Orlan-10 UAVs from Russia,

Defence Expenditure

Total defence spending: $130 million (2020), $129 million (2019)

Estimated defence spending in terms of GDP: 3.74%

Defence Production and R&D

Kyrgyzstan does not have any defence production capability.

Defence procurement

Kyrgyzstan relies on foreign aid and military assistance from Russia. Arms transferred by Russia include small arms, mountain guns and mortars, several attack and transport helicopters and individual combat kits. Other Commonwealth of Independent States

(CIS) also supply Kyrgyzstan with military equipment. Bishkek has received military supplies from China, Turkey, the US and Germany. India and Kyrgyzstan have signed an agreement to bolster defence cooperation and hold annual joint military exercises.

CONTACT DETAILS
Ministry of Defence
Bishkek, Kyrgyzstan
Tel., Fax: (312) 66-18-04
E-mail: ud@mil.gov.kg
www.mod.gov.kz

LAOS
(Capital: Vientiane)

INTRODUCTION
Area: 236,800 sq. km
Population: 7,574,356 (July 2021 est.)
Coastline: 0 km (Landlocked)
Maritime claims: None

KEY POLITICAL PERSONS

PRESIDENT & COMMANDER-IN-CHIEF: Thongloun Sisoulith

PRIME MINISTER: Dr. Phankham Viphavanh

KEY DEFENCE PERSONS

DEFENCE MINISTER: Gen. Chansamone Chanyalath

CHIEF OF GENERAL STAFF OF ARMY: Lt. Gen. Suvon Luongbunmi

ECONOMY
The economy of landlocked Laos is growing rapidly averaging 8% a year in GDP growth with the government having decentralise control and encouraging private enterprise while pursuing poverty reduction and education for all children as key goals. The economy is heavily dependent on capital-intensive natural resource exports. It has benefited from high-profile foreign direct investment in hydropower dams along the Mekong River, copper and gold mining, logging, and construction. The government has begun an initiative to become a "land-linked" country by undertaking projects like the ongoing construction of the nearly $6 billion high-speed rail from Kunming, China to Vientiane, Laos. The government has committed to raising the country's profile among foreign investors and has developed special economic zones replete with generous tax incentives. Tourism is the fastest growing industry in the economy and plays a vital role in the Lao economy. However, according to the World Bank, Economic growth declined to an estimated 0.4% in 2020, the lowest level in three decades, and a second wave of the pandemic in 2021 has dented hopes of a rebound, with a growth rate of just 2.2% forecast for 2021.

GDP (official exchange rate): $16.97 billion (2017 est.)
Real Growth Rate (GDP): 6.9% (2017 est.), 7% (2016 est.)
Industries: Mining (copper, tin, gold, gypsum); timber, electric power, agricultural processing, rubber, construction, garments, cement, tourism.
Total Exports: $6.99 billion (2019 est.), $6.39 billion (2018 est.)
Export Commodities: Electricity, copper, rubber, gold, flavoured water (2019)
Major Markets: Thailand 36%, China 28%, Vietnam 16% (2019)
Total Imports: $7.52 billion (2019 est.), $7.56 billion (2018 est.)
Import Commodities: Refined petroleum, cars, cattle, iron structures, steel products (2019)
Major Suppliers: Thailand 53%, China 26%, Vietnam 10% (2019)

INTERNATIONAL DISPUTES
◆ Southeast Asian states have enhanced border surveillance to check the spread of avian flu.
◆ Talks continue on completion of demarcation with Thailand but disputes remain over islands in the Mekong River.

◆ Cambodia and Laos have a longstanding border demarcation dispute.
◆ Concern among Mekong River Commission members that China's construction of eight dams on the Upper Mekong River and construction of more dams on its tributaries will affect water levels, sediment flows, and fisheries.
◆ Cambodia and Vietnam are concerned about Laos' extensive plans for upstream dam construction for the same reasons.

DEFENCE
ARMY
Personnel: 35,000

Equipment

Category	Name	In Service
MBT	T-54/54 (3)/T-55	30
	PT-76	25
	T-72 E1	
APC	BTR-40/60	30 (upgraded)
	BTR-152	40
	M-113	
	BRDM	
Artillery	75mm	
	105mm	
	M1938 & D30 122 mm	40
	M46 130mm	10
Mortar	81 mm	20
	155 mm	20
	107 mm	
RCL	75mm, 106mm	

...continued

Category	Name	In Service
MRL	9K51 Grad 122 mm	
AA gun	37mm	
	23mm twin	
	D-74 122 mm	
	D-20 152 mm	
	D-30 122 mm	

Army Aviation: 4 Cessna U-17A

New Procurements/Upgrades

No major procurement plans are under consideration at present.

NAVY (Riverine section of the Army): The Lao People's Navy operates vessels on the Mekong River. Personnel - 500. Patrol craft – 40 and 8 LCM.

AIR FORCE

Personnel: 3,500

Equipment

Category	Name	In Service
Fighter	MiG-21	21 (most grounded)

...continued

Category	Name	In Service
Transport	Yak-130 'Mitten'	
	AN-24	7
	AN-2	6
	An-74	1
	YAK-40	2
	Y7-100C	
Helicopter	Mi-8	10
	Mi-6	1
	Mi-17	10
	Ka-32T	6
	Z-9A	6
Trainer	MiG-21U	4
	Yak-130 Mitten	
SAM	9K35 Strela-10	
	SA -3, SA - 7	
Air Defence	9K38 Igla MANPADS	

New Procurements/Upgrades

No major procurement plans are under consideration at present.

Defence Expenditure

Total defence spending: $18.5 million (2019)

Estimated defence spending in terms of GDP: 0.5% (2006)

Defence Production and R&D

Laos does not undertake any defence production activities.

Defence Procurement

Laos has developed a close defence relationship with Russia. The two nations have reportedly signed a contract on military and technical cooperation, deals on assistance on helicopter repair and procurement. Russia has reportedly delivered a second batch of T-72 main battle tanks (MBTs) and BRDM-2M 4×4 armored reconnaissance vehicles (ARVs) to the Lao People's Armed Forces (LPAF) in the recent past.

CONTACT DETAILS
Ministry of National Defence
Phon Kang Road
Vientiane, Laos
www.mod.gov.la/

LEBANON
(Capital: Beirut)

INTRODUCTION

Area: 10,400 sq km
Population: 5,261,372 (July 2021 est.)
Coastline: 225 km
Maritime claims: Territorial sea: 12 nm

KEY POLITICAL PERSONS

PRESIDENT: Gen. Michel Aoun

PRIME MINISTER: Najib Mikati

KEY DEFENCE PERSONS

MINISTER OF DEFENCE: Maurice Slim

CHIEF OF STAFF OF THE ARMED FORCES: Maj. Gen. Amin Al-Aram

COMMANDER OF ARMY: Gen. Joseph Aoun

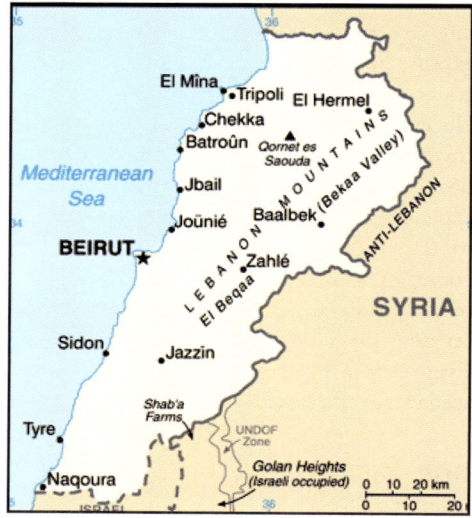

COMMANDER OF NAVY: Capt. Haissam Dannaoui

COMMANDER OF AIR FORCE: Maj. Gen. Ziad Haykal

ECONOMY

Lebanon has a free-market economy and a strong laissez-faire commercial tradition. The Lebanese economy is service-oriented; main growth sectors include banking and tourism. Lebanon's economy and markets are based on private and liberal economic activity and openness to abroad with perfect capital and labour mobility. The private sector covers the totality of economic sectors and is a major pillar for growth and recovery. Services and banking sectors predominate, representing 70% of the country's gross national product. Agriculture constitutes 10% and the industrial sector constitutes the remaining 20%, as per Embassy of Lebanon Washington, DC. The Port of Beirut plays an important role in Lebanon's commercial activities. The Lebanese economy is based primarily on the service sector, which accounts for approximately 60% of GDP. Currently, the main financial services offered are commercial banking, investment banking and insurance. Lebanon and the European Free Trade Association (EFTA) signed a Free Trade Agreement (FTA) in 2004. Lebanon also signed the Greater Arab Free Trade Agreement. Lebanon belongs to a number of the same international organisations, including the United Nations, International Monetary Fund, and World Bank. Lebanon is an observer to the Organisation of American States and is working toward accession to the World Trade Organisation. In early 2018, the Lebanese government signed long-awaited contract agreements with an international consortium for petroleum exploration and production as part of the country's first offshore licensing round. The US and Lebanon have signed a Trade and Investment Framework Agreement to help promote an attractive investment climate, expand trade relations, and remove obstacles to trade and investment between the two countries. The COVID-19 outbreak and related containment measures have affected severely the economic situation of Lebanon. Even before the coronavirus the economic scenario in the country was dismal.

GDP (official exchange rate): $79.51 billion (2020 est.), $99.76 billion (2019 est.)

Real Growth Rate (GDP): 1.5% (2017 est.), 1.7% (2016 est.)

Industries: Banking, tourism, real estate and construction, food processing, wine, jewellery, cement, textiles, mineral and chemical products, wood and furniture products, oil refining, metal fabricating

Total Exports: $18.17 billion (2019), $19.16 billion (2018)

Export Commodities: Gold, jewellery, shotguns, diamonds, scrap copper (2019)

Major Markets: Switzerland 27%, United Arab Emirates 15%, South Korea 11%, Saudi Arabia 7%, Kuwait 6% (2019)

Total Imports: $31.34 billion (2019 est.), $32.78 billion (2018 est.)

Import Commodities: Refined petroleum, cars, packaged medicines, jewellery, gold (2019)

Major Suppliers: United Arab Emirates 11%, China 10%, Italy 8%, Greece 8%, Turkey 7%, United States 6% (2019)

INTERNATIONAL DISPUTES

◆ Lacking a treaty or other documentation describing the boundary, portions of the Lebanon-Syria boundary are unclear with several sections in dispute.

◆ Since 2000, Lebanon has claimed Shab'a Farms area in the Israeli-occupied Golan Heights.

◆ The roughly 2,000-strong UN Interim Force in Lebanon has been in place since 1978.

◆ Terrorist groups operating in Lebanon included Hizballah, ISIS, Hamas, and the Abdullah Azzam Brigades.

DEFENCE

ARMY
Personnel: 75,000
Equipment

Category	Name	In Service
MBT	T-54/T-55	200+
	M48A5	50+
	M60A3	10
APC/IFV	M113	1000+
	Panhard AML-90	50
	VAB	50+
Artillery	105 mm M101-A1	100+
	122 mm D-30	
	130 mm	
	155 mm M114-A1	
	155 mm M109-A3	10+
Mortar	120 mm	40+
Recoilless rifle	106 mm	
Anti-Tank GW	Milan, TOW	
AA Gun	20 mm	120+
	23mm	
	30mm	

New Procurements/ Upgrades

◆ The US Embassy in Lebanon reports that the United States has delivered laser-guided rockets worth more than USD16 million to the Lebanese army.

NAVY
Personnel: 1,500

Equipment

Category	Name	In Service
Patrol Vessel	Tabarja Class	1
	Amchit Class	1
	Tracker Class	7
	MK2 combat support	20+
	Fast patrol boats	10+
Landing Craft	EDIC-III Class	2

New Procurements/ Upgrades

No major procurement plans are under consideration at present.

AIR FORCE
Personnel: 1,500
Equipment

Category	Name	In Service
Aircraft	AC-208B Combat Caravan	3
	Hawker Hunter	3
	Scottish Aviation Bulldog T1	3
	Embraer A-29A	On order
Helicopter (attack & utility)	AB-205/UH-1H	20+
	Aérospatiale SA-342L Gazelle	5+
	IAR 330SM / Aérospatiale SA-330 Puma	10+
	AgustaWestland AW139	1
	Mil Mi-24	5
	Robinson R44	4
	Sikorsky S-61N Mk II	3
UAV	RQ-11B Raven	10+

New Procurements/ Upgrades

◆ The United States has delivered six MD-530F+ Light Attack Helicopters, valued at over $40 million dollars, to the Lebanese Armed Forces (LAF) Air Force. This helicopter is the first light attack helicopter of its kind to integrate APKWS missiles and live downlink of targeting data.

Defence Expenditure

Total defence spending: USD 2 billion (2018 est.)

Estimated defence spending in terms of GDP: 3% of GDP (2020 est.), 4.2% of GDP (2019)

Lebanon's military spending remains far behind most countries in the region, allocating only 2.8 percent of its GDP to military expenditures. Recently, the Lebanese government approved a five-year plan to arm the Lebanese military.

Foreign suppliers: United States, France, United Kingdom, Russia, Saudi Arabia.

The United States is Lebanon's primary security partner and has provided more than $2 billion in bilateral security assistance to the Lebanese Armed Forces (LAF) since 2006. US assistance supports the LAF's ability to secure Lebanon's borders, counter internal threats, and demonstrate it is the sole legitimate defender of Lebanon's sovereignty. Through the provision of fixed- and rotary-wing aircraft, munitions, vehicles, and associated training, the LAF has become a committed partner and greatly increased its capability as a fighting force against violent extremists, as per US Dept. of State.

According to US Embassy in Lebanon, the United States recently announced an additional $67 million in annual Foreign Military Financing support for this year 2021. This is in addition to the $120 million that we had already set aside for Lebanon bringing the total to $187 million for this year.

Defence Production and R&D

There are no defence production capabilities in Lebanon.

Defence Procurement

Lebanese Army/Navy/Air Force has not done any major defence procurements in recent years.

CONTACT DETAILS
Ministry of Defence, Yarzé
Beyrouth Lebanon
Tel: (+961 5) 45 24 00
Fax: (+961 5) 95 87 57
(+961 1) 44 47 62
E-mail: ministry@leb-army.gov.lb
Lebanese Armed Forces
Yarzeh, Lebanon
www.lebarmy.gov.lb

LIBYA
(Capital: Tripoli)

INTRODUCTION
Area: 1,759,540 sq km
Population: 7,017,224 (July 2021 est.)
Coastline: 1,770 km
Maritime claims: Territorial sea: 12 nm
Exclusive Fishing Zone: 62 nm

KEY POLITICAL PERSONS

PRESIDENT (Libyan Presidential Council): Mohamed Yunus al-Menfi

PRIME MINISTER & DEFENCE MINISTER (Interim Govt.): Abdul Hamid Dbeibeh

(Libya plunged into deep political crisis and military chaos soon after its long-time powerful leader Moamer Kadhafi was captured and killed by NATO-led forces in October 2011. The Commander of Libyan Armed Forces, Field Marshal Khalifa Haftar, with his self-styled 'Libyan National Army', launched a major offensive in April 2019 to conquer the capital, Tripoli and overthrow the then United Nations-recognised Government of National Accord led by Fayed al-Sarraj. The uninterrupted military lock-down has continued to push the North African country into the brink of a full-scale civil war. The United Nations has called for international efforts to immediately end the conflict.

In March 2021, a new interim Government led by Prime Minister Abdul Hamid Dbeibah assumed charge. The Government of National Unity (GNU), selected through a United Nations-supported process, replaced the Government of National Accord (GNA) which was being led by Fayed al-Sarraj.

Meanwhile, the two warring sides during a UN-backed meeting held in November 2020, had agreed to hold general elections [both parliamentary and presidential] in the country on December 24, 2021. It has been deferred.)

ECONOMY

Libya's economy, almost entirely dependent on oil and gas exports, has struggled since 2014 given security and political instability, disruptions in oil production, and decline in global oil prices. The Libyan dinar has lost much of its value since 2014 and the resulting gap between official and black market exchange rates has spurred the growth of a shadow economy and contributed to inflation. The country suffers from widespread power outages, caused by shortages of fuel for power generation. Living conditions, including access to clean drinking water, medical services, and safe housing have all declined since 2011. Oil production in 2017 reached a five-year high, driving GDP growth, with daily average production rising to 879,000 barrels per day. However, oil production levels remain below the average pre-Revolution highs of 1.6 million barrels per day.

The Central Bank of Libya continued to pay government salaries to a majority of the Libyan workforce and to fund subsidies for fuel and food, resulting in an estimated budget deficit of about 17% of GDP in 2017. Low consumer confidence in the banking sector and the economy as a whole has driven a severe liquidity shortage. Libya's economy was adversely affected by COVID-19 pandemic in 2020.

GDP (official exchange rate): $52.25 billion (2019 est.)

Real Growth Rate (GDP): 64% (2017 est.); -7.4% (2016 est.)

Industries: Petroleum, petrochemicals, aluminium, iron and steel, food processing, textiles, handicrafts, cement

Natural gas - Proved Reserves: 1.505 trillion cu m (1 January 2018 est.)

Crude oil - Proved Reserves: 48.36 billion bbl (1 January 2018 est.)

Total Exports: $18.38 billion (2017 est.); $11.99 billion (2016 est.)

Export Commodities: Crude petroleum, natural gas, gold, refined petroleum, scrap iron (2019)

Major Markets: Italy 18%, China 16%, Germany 15%, Spain 15%, United Arab

Emirates 6%, France 6%, United States 5% (2019)

Total Imports: $11.36 billion (2017 est.); $8.66 billion (2016 est.)

Import Commodities: Refined petroleum, cars, broadcasting equipment, cigarettes, jewellery (2019)

Major Suppliers: China 16%, Turkey 14%, Italy 9%, United Arab Emirates 9%, Egypt 5% (2019)

INTERNATIONAL DISPUTES

Libya claims more than 32,000 sq km in south-eastern Algeria and about 25,000 sq km in the Tommo region of Niger in a currently dormant dispute.

DEFENCE

ARMY

Personnel: No exact data available

Equipment: While the Libyan Army maintained a large inventory of mostly Soviet-supplied equipment, including main battle tanks, armoured fighting vehicles, small arms and artillery, it lost majority of them during the NATO-led war in 2011. No definitive data is available on the Army's present equipment level other than the recent new procurements. Meanwhile, some countries have reportedly supplied military weapons secretively to the Libyan National Army (led by Commander Khalifa Haftar) to fight the war against the UN-recongnised Government of National Accord (GNA) under Fayed al-Sarraj.

New Procurements/ Upgrades

◆ 10 Khrizantema-S tank destroyers ordered from Russia have been inducted in the Army, taking its total number to 14.

◆ 20 PUMA armoured vehicles were delivered by Italy in 2013.

◆ Jordan has delivered 49 NIMR wheeled armoured military vehicles.

◆ Delivery of 287 Humvee multi-role vehicles from the US is in progress.

NAVY

Personnel: 2,000+

Equipment

Category	Name	In Service
Frigate	Koni class	1
Corvette	Nanuchka class	1
Minesweeper	Ex-USSR Natya class	1

New Procurements/Upgrades

◆ Procurement of new warships for the Navy is under consideration.

◆ An offshore patrol vessel has joined the Navy in 2018.

AIR FORCE

Personnel: 2,000+

Equipment

Category	Name	In Service
Fighter	Su-27	4
	MiG-23	2
	MiG-21	2 or more
	Mirage F1 AD/ED	2
Transport	C-130H	1
	An-26	2
	An-32	2
Helicopter	Mi-8	
	Mi-24/ Mi-35	3
Trainer	L39 Albatros	2

New Procurements/ Upgrades

◆ Four new Russian-made Su-27 Flanker fighter aircraft have been delivered in 2015.

◆ Libyan Air Force plans major overhaul of its fleet by acquiring new fighter jets, transport aircraft and helicopters.

Defence Expenditure

Defence budget allocated for 2019-20: 40 million Libyan dinars (US$28.5 million)

Estimated defence spending in terms of GDP: Over 1%

Libya has procured arms and equipment mostly from the erstwhile Soviet Union and France in the past. In recent times, the US is eying a share of the country's defence market. Libya has also requested the US to impart personnel training for 6,000 to 8,000 of its troops.

Defence Production and R&D

Libya does not undertake any defence production activities.

Defence Procurement

After most of its defence equipment was destroyed in the 2011 NATO-led war, the present regime in Libya intends to restructure and modernise the armed forces by acquiring new platforms and weapons for the Army, Navy and Air Force. Many of the previously signed deals during Muammar Gaddafi's regime have been scrapped by the present Government. Acquisition of new armoured vehicles for the Army is going on while for the air force, purchase of new airlifters, helicopters and fighter jets have been planned. The country plans to spend some $4.7 billion for new military acquisitions. Continuous political instability, however, has marred the Government's military procurement plans in the longer run.

CONTACT DETAILS
Ministry of Defence
Shatt Road,
Abu Sitta Naval Base, Tripoli

LUXEMBOURG
(Capital: Luxembourg)

INTRODUCTION

Area: 2,586 sq km
Population: 639,589 (July 2021 est.)
Coastline: 0 km (Landlocked)
Maritime claims: None

KEY POLITICAL PERSONS

HEAD OF STATE & COMMANDER-IN-CHIEF: Grand Duke Henri

PRIME MINISTER: Xavier Bettel

KEY DEFENCE PERSONS

DEPUTY PRIME MINISTER & MINISTER OF DEFENCE: Francois Bausch

CHIEF OF DEFENCE STAFF: Gen. Steve Thull

ECONOMY

The small, stable, high-income economy of Luxembourg has historically recorded solid growth, low inflation, and low unemployment. The landlocked country is surrounded by Belgium, France, and Germany. Despite its small landmass and small population, Luxembourg is the fifth-wealthiest country in the world when measured on a gross domestic product (PPP) per capita basis. It has one of the highest current account surpluses as a share of GDP in the euro zone, and it maintains a healthy budgetary position, with a 2017 surplus of 0.5% of GDP, and the lowest public debt level in the region. The economy has evolved and flourished, posting strong GDP growth of 3.4% in 2017, far outpacing the European average of 1.8%. In the wake of the Coronavirus pandemic, Luxembourg's GDP could decline by as much as 6% in 2020, according to the country's national statistics institute STATEC. American credit rating agency Fitch Ratings has forecast Luxembourg's GDP contraction by 5.8% in 2020 before recovering with a 6% growth in 2021.

GDP (official exchange rate): $71.08 billion (2019 est.)

Real Growth Rate (GDP): 2.31% (2019 est.); 3.14% (2018 est.)

Industries: Banking and financial services, iron and steel, information technology, chemicals, glass, telecommunications, cargo transportation, food processing, metal products, engineering, aluminium, tires, tourism, biotechnology

Total Export: $133.61 billion (2019 est.); $132.48 billion (2018 est.)

Export Commodities: Iron and iron products, tires, cars, broadcasting equipment, clothing and apparel (2019)

Major Markets: Germany 23%, France 13%, Belgium 12%, Netherlands 6%, Italy 5% (2019)

Total Import: $111.28 billion (2019 est.); $110.27 billion (2018 est.)

Import Commodities: Cars, refined petroleum, broadcasting equipment, scrap iron, aircraft (2019)

Major Suppliers: Belgium 27%, Germany 24%, France 11%, Netherlands 5% (2019)

INTERNATIONAL DISPUTES

Luxembourg has no known international disputes.

DEFENCE

ARMY
Personnel: 400

Equipment

Category	Name	In Service
Vehicle	Dingo 2	48
	HMMWV Hummer (armoured)	30
	HUMMER (TOW Carrier)	6
	MLST	
	MAN 4T truck	
Artillery	105mm howitzer	
ATGW	BGM-71 TOW	6

Army Aviation

Category	Name	In Service
Aircraft	E-3A Sentry (NATO)	17
	Boeing 707	2
	A400M	
Helicopter	H145M	2

New Procurements/Upgrades

◆ Funds worth €367 million has been cleared by the Government in 2021 to procure up to 80 lightly armoured vehicles for the Army to replace some of the obsolete platforms.

AIR FORCE

Luxembourg does not have an air force, though the 17 NATO AWACS (E-3A Sentry) aircraft are for convenience registered as aircraft of Luxembourg. The country has received the sole A400M heavy transport aircraft from Airbus in October 2020 which would be jointly operated by a bi-national unit of Luxembourg Armed Forces and Belgium. Airbus has delivered two A330 MRTT tanker/transport aircraft to be jointly operated by six NATO member nations – Netherlands, Luxembourg, Norway, Germany, Belgium and the Czech Republic. The aircraft platforms would form a part of the NATO Multinational MRTT Fleet (MMF). A total of eight A330 MRTTs would be delivered by 2024 as part of the multi-national programme.

Defence Expenditure
Estimated defence spending in terms of GDP: 0.6%

Defence Production and R&D
Luxembourg does not undertake any defence production or related activities.

Defence Procurement
Being one of the smallest military forces in the NATO group of countries with a very limited defence budget, Luxembourg has not done any major military procurements in the past. The country, without a Navy and Air Force, has procured equipment for its Army, mainly bought from the US. Belgium and Luxembourg have jointly formed the Office of Defence Cooperation, Belgium-Luxembourg (ODC BELLUX), with an objective to support the US and other NATO militaries through the acquisition of defence goods and services and by participating in international armaments cooperation activities. Luxembourg plans to increase its annual defence spending to up to 0.72% of its GDP by 2024.

CONTACT DETAILS
Directorate of Defence
6, Rue l'anvien Athenee
L-1144, Luxembourg
Phone: (+352) 247-82800
www.defense.gouvernement/.lu/

STRATEGIC INFORMATION
MALAYSIA
(Capital: Kuala Lumpur)

INTRODUCTION
Area: 329,847 sq km
Population: 33,519,406 (July 2021 est.)
Malay 50.4%, Chinese 23.7%, indigenous 11%, Indian (Tamils) 7.1%, others 7.8%
Coastline: 4,675 km
Maritime claims: Territorial sea: 12 nm
Exclusive Economic Zone: 200 nm
Continental shelf: 200 m depth or to the depth of exploitation; specified boundary in the South China Sea

GEOPOLITICAL IMPORTANCE
Malaysia is a Southeast Asian country located partly on a peninsula of the Asian mainland and partly on the northern third of the island of Borneo. Land borders are shared with Thailand, Indonesia, and Brunei, and maritime borders exist with Singapore, Vietnam, Brunei and the Philippines. It has coastlines on the South China Sea and the Straits of Malacca. Kuala Lumpur, Malaysia's capital, and Putrajaya, the administrative and government centre are located in the western part of peninsular Malaysia. The states of Sabah and Sarawak occupy roughly the northern fourth of the island of Borneo and share land boundaries with Indonesia and Brunei.

POLITICAL OVERVIEW
Malaysia is a federal constitutional monarchy. It consists of thirteen states and three federal territories. The head of state is the 'Yang di-Pertuan Agong', commonly referred to as the king and the Prime Minister of Malaysia is the head of government. Malaysia has a diverse democracy.

KEY POLITICAL PERSONS

HEAD OF STATE & COMMANDER-IN-CHIEF: Sultan Abdullah Sultan Ahmad Shah of Pahang

PRIME MINISTER: Ismail Sabri Yaakob

ECONOMY
Malaysia is rich in natural resources and its traditional economic strength lay in commodities. It is still an important source of tin and rubber, produces more than half the world's palm oil and is a net exporter of oil and gas. Malaysia is an upper middle-income country and has transformed itself from a producer of raw materials into a multi-sector economy. Malaysia signed the 12-nation Trans-Pacific Partnership (TPP) free trade agreement in February 2016. Services and manufacturing accounts for 73 percent of GDP in 2017. Malaysia's GDP projection for 2018 is 5.3 percent while the 2017 GDP was 5.9 percent. Malaysia recognises the importance of international trade and relations to the nation's growth and development and has therefore adopted liberal trade policies. Malaysia through the ASEAN has established the ASEAN Free Trade Area. According to Surviving the Storm, the latest edition of the World Bank's Malaysia Economic Monitor, released in June 2020, Malaysia's economy is projected to contract by 3.1 percent in 2020 due to a sharp slowdown in economic activity caused by COVID-19 and measures to contain its spread. The World Bank expects growth to resume in 2021-22 as the outbreak eases.

GDP (official exchange rate): $855.6 billion (2020 est.), $906.24 billion (2019 est.)
Real Growth Rate (GDP): 4.31% (2019 est.), 4.77% (2018 est.)
Industries: Peninsular Malaysia - rubber and oil palm processing and manufacturing, petroleum and natural gas, light manufacturing, pharmaceuticals, medical technology, electronics and semiconductors, timber processing; Sabah - logging, petroleum and natural gas production; Sarawak - agriculture processing, petroleum and natural gas production, logging
Oil Proved Reserves: 3.6 billion bbl (1 January 2016 est)
Natural Gas Proved Reserves: 1.183 trillion cu m (1 January 2016 est)
Total Exports: $207.37 billion (2020 est.), $237.83 billion (2019 est.)
Export Commodities: Integrated circuits, refined petroleum, natural gas, semiconductors, palm oil (2019)
Major Markets: Singapore 13%, China 13%, United States 11%, Hong Kong 6%, Japan 6%, Thailand 5% (2019)
Total Imports: $185.59 billion (2020 est.), $210.68 billion (2019 est.)
Import Commodities: Integrated circuits, refined petroleum, crude petroleum, broadcasting equipment, coal (2019)
Major Suppliers: China 24%, Singapore 14%, Japan 6%, United States 6%, Taiwan 5%, Thailand 5% (2019)

DEFENCE & SECURITY
The Malaysian Armed Forces (Angkatan Tentera Malaysia, ATM) have three branches, the Royal Malaysian Navy, the Royal Malaysian Army, and the Royal Malaysian Air Force. The military of Malaysia is responsible for assisting civilian authorities to overcome all international threats, preserve public order, assist in natural disasters and participate in national development programmes. Malaysia's Armed Forces are responsible for the protection of the country against internal and external threats. They serve in a wide variety of situations such as assisting civil authorities in addressing domestics threats, maintaining public security, providing aid following the onset of natural disasters, and assisting in national development programmes.

KEY DEFENCE PERSONS

DEFENCE MINISTER: Hishammuddin Bin Tun Hussein

CHIEF OF DEFENCE FORCES: Gen. HJ Affendi Bin Buang

CHIEF OF ARMY: Gen. Zamrose bin Mohd Zain

CHIEF OF NAVY: Adm. Mohd Reza Bin Mohd Sany

CHIEF OF AIR FORCE: Gen. Ackbal Bin Haji Abdul Samad

Internal Conflict

Terrorism: Malaysia has experienced terrorism since 1948 during the battle against communists. Malaysian Special Operations Force is a multi service force tasked with a counter-terror mission. Malaysia maintains a high level of security and has not suffered incidents of terrorism for several years, but was vulnerable to terrorist activity and continued to be used as a transit and planning site for terrorists. Malaysia has implemented series of measures in the name of counter-terrorism to detect and prevent terrorism, and to minimise damage from such terrorist acts should they occur. These measures involve all levels of society, including military, police, border and infrastructure security, civil defence, medical readiness, and psychological preparedness. Malaysia also participates actively in international counter-terrorism schemes. It is working closely with intelligence agencies of the United States, Britain, China, Pakistan and India to combat international terrorism. Malaysia is a member of the Asia/ Pacific Group on Money Laundering, a Financial Action Task Force-style regional body. The country has an established Financial Intelligence Unit and capacity to report suspicious transactions. In January 2016, the Malaysian police said the country was on the highest security alert. Malaysian authorities in June 2016 faced a terrorist attack by individuals with links to Daesh (formerly referred to as ISIL). In 2017, Malaysian Police foiled a terrorist plot on the closing ceremony of the SEA Games in Bukit Jalil and the 60th National Day parade in Merdeka Square. While no ISIS-affiliated attacks were carried out in 2019, Malaysia remained a transit point and hub for kidnap-for-ransom activities perpetrated by other terrorist networks.

External Conflict

Since independence, Malaysia, bordered by Thailand, Indonesia, Singapore and Brunei, has been involved in territorial disputes and overlapping maritime claims with almost all its neighbours. Malaysia's territorial and maritime disputes are located in the Gulf of Thailand, the Andaman Sea, the Straits of Malacca, the Straits of Singapore, the South China Sea, the Sulu Sea and the Celebes Sea. Some of these disputes were resolved through bilateral and multilateral treaties.

◆ Disputes continue over deliveries of fresh water to Singapore, Singapore's land reclamation, bridge construction, and maritime boundaries in the Johor and Singapore Straits.

◆ Land and maritime negotiations with Indonesia are ongoing, and disputed areas include the controversial Tanjung Datu and Camar Wulan border area in Borneo and the maritime boundary in the Ambalat oil block in the Celebes Sea.

◆ While the 2002 "Declaration on the Conduct of Parties in the South China Sea" has eased tensions over the Spratly Islands, it is not the legally binding "code of conduct" sought by some parties.

◆ Malaysia was not party to the March 2005 joint accord among the national oil companies of China, the Philippines, and Vietnam on conducting marine seismic activities in the Spratly Islands.

◆ In 2008, ICJ awarded sovereignty of Pedra Branca (Pulau Batu Puteh/ Horsburgh Island) to Singapore, and Middle Rocks to Malaysia, but did not rule on maritime regimes, boundaries, or disposition of South Ledge.

◆ Separatist violence in Thailand's predominantly Muslim southern provinces prompts measures to close and monitor border with Malaysia to stem terrorist activities.

◆ Philippines retain a dormant claim to Malaysia's Sabah State in northern Borneo.

◆ As per Letters of Exchange signed in 2009, Malaysia in 2010 ceded two hydrocarbon concession blocks to Brunei in exchange for Brunei's sultan dropping claims to the Limbang corridor, which divides Brunei.

◆ Another serious non-military security challenges confronting Malaysia is piracy. The Straits of Malacca, situated between Indonesia and Malaysia, was long considered to be the world's most dangerous waters for pirate attacks. Malaysia, Singapore and Indonesia have increased their patrols in the Straits of Malacca and Singapore Straits to combat piracy. Malaysia has established the Maritime-Enforcement Co-ordination Centre (MECC) to co-ordinate anti-piracy activities and surveillance. Pirate activity in the region, has thereby declined significantly since 2005 due to increased military patrols and vessel security, according to the International Maritime Bureau (IMB).

THREAT PERSPECTIVE

Philippines: Both Malaysia and Philippines have a long history of close economic and political ties; the relationship is often overshadowed by a series of territorial disputes such as claim over the Sabah state in northern Borneo and ongoing disputes over ownership of the Spratly Islands. The Philippines has a claim over the Sabah state in northern Borneo though this is currently not being actively pursued. Malaysia and the Philippines both claim a portion of the disputed Spratly Islands. The archipelago lies off the coasts of the Philippines and Malaysia, about one third of the way from there to southern Vietnam. Malaysia's claims are based upon the continental shelf principle, and have clearly defined coordinates. The Philippines base their claims of sovereignty over the Spratly Islands on the issues of Res nullius and geography. Both are founding members of the Association of Southeast Asian Nations, both countries are of Malayo-Polynesian language group, and also are important trading partners.

Thailand: Relationship between Malaysia and Thailand has been soured by territorial issues. The Malaysia–Thailand border consists of both a land boundary across the Malay Peninsula and maritime boundaries in the Straits of Malacca and the Gulf of Thailand/South China Sea. Malaysia lies to the south of the border while Thailand lies to the north. There are two stretches of the Malaysia–Thailand border which are subject to dispute. The first involves the land border in the Bukit Jeli (Jeli Hill) at the headwaters of the Golok River and the second involves the continental shelf boundary in the Gulf of Thailand. Both disputes have not resulted in any aggression between the two countries. Both Malaysia and Thailand participate in the Cooperation Afloat Readiness and Training (CARAT) annually together with other ASEAN countries.

Indonesia: The border between Indonesia and Malaysia consists of both a land border separating the two countries' territories on the island of Borneo as well as maritime boundaries along the length of the Straits of Malacca, in the South China Sea and in the Celebes Sea. The border in the Celebes Sea is subject to dispute between the two countries. Part of the dispute was settled by the judgement of the International Court of Justice in the Sipadan and Ligitan Case in 2002 and is now awaiting delimitation between the two countries. The two countries however still have overlapping claims over the continental shelf which Indonesia refers to as Ambalat, a sea block in the Celebes Sea which is currently under Indonesia sovereignty. Both Malaysia and Indonesia are the founding members of ASEAN and APEC, and also members of the Non-aligned Movement, Developing 8 Countries and Organisation of Islamic Cooperation. Both Malaysia and Thailand also announced a plan to replace their border fence into a wall border.

STRATEGIC RELATIONS

United States: United States and Malaysia enjoy strong security cooperation. Both the countries share a strong military-to-military relationship with numerous exchanges, training, joint exercises, and visits. The United States and Malaysia cooperate closely on security matters, including counter terrorism, maritime domain awareness, and regional stability. Security cooperation and training builds capabilities among Malaysia's armed forces and coast guard, allowing it to take on an expanded international role, including peacekeeping operations. The United States supports Malaysia's counterterrorism efforts through information sharing, capacity building programmes for law enforcement and judicial authorities, and assistance to improve immigration security and border controls. Bilateral trade in goods with the United States was USD50.2 billion in 2017. The United States is Malaysia's fourth-largest trading partner. Malaysia is the United States' 18th largest trading partner and the third-largest trading partner among the 10 ASEAN members in Southeast Asia. US assistance to Malaysia focuses on education, exchanges, counterterrorism, non-proliferation, security cooperation, and enhancing transparency, accountability and responsiveness of government.

China: Malaysia and China share close bilateral ties and cordial regional cooperation. Friendship and cooperation between China and Malaysia have achieved significant progress in recent years. Leaders of both countries exchanged visits frequently and cooperation in all areas deepened continuously. The two countries have also agreed to further strengthen military cooperation between the two countries in a bid to maintain peace and stability in the region. During a recent defence and security consultation in September 2012, the two sides reached consensus in a broad range of issues to strengthen exchange and cooperation between the PLA and Malaysian Armed Forces. Both sides agreed to maintain high level military exchanges between the armed forces, make good use of the defence and security consultation mechanism, strengthen exchange and communication in training cooperation and training systems, while deepening cooperation in non-conventional security issues. Malaysia and China signed a series of agreements in Nov 2016 which cover among other things energy and defence coordination. Malaysia has been China's one of the top trading partner. China's investment in Malaysia had shown significant increase and it expected to be an important new source of investment for Malaysia.

Russia: Russia and Malaysia share strong ties since 1967 when diplomatic relationships were established between Malaysia and former USSR. Both countries maintain political dialogue and regular meetings on current bilateral issues and international concerns. Malaysia is also one of the largest MTC (military-technical cooperation) partners of Russia in Southeast Asia. The Russian-Malaysian Intergovernmental Joint Commission on cooperation in defence, defence technologies, and defence industry is a working body through which both nations maintain their relationships. Malaysia is one of the main Russia's trading partners in South East Asia. Palm oil is supplied to Russia in accordance with an agreement on extending Malaysian credit facility signed in Moscow in July 2002 as well as through private channels. In 2016, a Russian-Malaysian business council was established with the intent to strengthen cooperation on economic, scientific, technological issues and culture. Russia's initiatives to develop its eastern provinces will open up new market opportunities for Malaysia.

India: India and Malaysia have traditionally been close and friendly. India-Malaysia defence relations have also steadily grown over the years. A MoU on Defence Cooperation was signed in 1993. Malaysia-India Defence Cooperation meetings at the level of Defence Secretary are held regularly. The IAF Training Team deployed in Malaysia trained Malaysian pilots on the SU-30SKM aircraft for two-and-a-half years from February 2008. Indian naval ships regularly make port calls in Malaysia. Malaysia participates in the biennial MILAN event regularly. Malaysia is one of the significant investors in India. It is estimated that, if the Mauritius route is also included, the investment of Malaysia in India could be as high as USD 7 billion. Malaysia is India's third largest trading partner in ASEAN besides Indonesia and Singapore. India is the largest trading partner for Malaysia from among the countries of the South Asia, excluding Singapore and China. New Delhi and Kuala Lumpur have been working closely through the Wuhan virus pandemic.

Brunei: The close relationship between Malaysia and Brunei has seen some changes in the past few years. Both countries have recently agreed to step up bilateral cooperation in the oil and natural gas sector. The two countries share a land border on the island of Borneo. Significant progress has also been made on joint demarcation and survey of the land boundary with survey going on for the complicated process of border demarcation. Regarding South China Sea developments, both countries have proposed the idea of a cooperation package which includes cooperation in trade, investment, defence, finance, and transportation. Such joint cooperation will further develop Malaysia-Brunei relations. The two countries share a land border on the island of Borneo. Both are full members of ASEAN and the Commonwealth of Nations.

Australia: Australia's economic and trade relationship with Malaysia is strong. Malaysia and Australia's defence relationship is based on practical cooperation including the Malaysia-Australia Joint Defence Programme, an ongoing Australian presence at the Royal Malaysian Air Force (RMAF) Base at Butterworth, and common membership of the Five Power Defence Arrangements (FPDA). Australia and Malaysia cooperate closely on a range of security issues, and have signed a MoU on co-operation to combat international terrorism. MAJDP is the cornerstone of the bilateral defence relationship under which both countries have defence officers posted in each other's country, involved in training and professional exchanges.

Pakistan: Both Pakistan and Malaysia enjoy close and cordial relations. Pakistan and Malaysia have a convergence of views on world affairs that translates into cooperation and support for each other, at various international stage. Both are members of Organization of Islamic Conference (OIC) and the Commonwealth of Nations. Both countries have signed a number of agreements and Memoranda of Understanding to enhance bilateral cooperation. The two countries have also signed agreements and MoUs for cooperation in defence, education, science & technology, and a number of economic and commercial agreements on palm oil, etc. In 2019, Royal Malaysian Navy Ships KD KASTURI and KD MAHAWANGSA arrived in Karachi to participate in the bilateral MALPAK-II exercise.

Singapore: Singapore and Malaysia have a broad and multi-faceted relationship. Bilateral trade, investment, and tourism ties are robust.

Singapore got separated from the Federation of Malaysia in 1965. Certain factors such as geography, history, politics, ideology, economy, culture and ethnicity of both the nations are inextricably linked. On May 2010, Malaysia and Singapore announced that they have resolved their long-standing disputes over land and water. Malaysia decided to relocate its railway station, close to one of the two bridges linking the two countries, freeing up land in the city-state for redevelopment. Singapore decided it would not seek to extend a water agreement dating back to 1961. Singapore will also hand over the waterworks it operates in Johor to the Malaysian state government when the current agreement lapses. Singapore and Malaysia are full members of the Commonwealth of Nations. Both countries are part of the Five Power Defence Arrangements (FPDA) along with New Zealand, Australia and the United Kingdom. Both sides along with Indonesia help each other when threatened with threats posed by Jeemah Islamiyah (JI). Both countries are full members of the Commonwealth of Nations and ASEAN. Ties between the two countries remain intact despite several diplomatic issues that have arisen.

MULTILATERAL ALLIANCES

Malaysia is an active member of various international organisations, including the Commonwealth of Nations, the United Nations, the Organisation of Islamic Cooperation (OIC), Asia-Pacific Economic Cooperation (APEC) forum and the Non-Aligned Movement (NAM). It was a founding member of the Association of Southeast Asian Nations (ASEAN). Malaysia is a frequent contributor to UN and other peacekeeping and stabilisation missions, including recent deployments to Lebanon, Timor-Leste, Philippines, Indonesia, Pakistan, Sierra Leone, Sudan, Western Sahara, Nepal, and Kosovo. Malaysia has also deployed a medical unit to Afghanistan. Malaysia is also an active member of Five Power Defence Arrangements (FPDA) along with United Kingdom, Australia, New Zealand and Singapore.

DEFENCE CAPABILITIES

ARMY: The Royal Malaysian Army (Tentera Darat Malaysia) is the land component of the Malaysian Armed Forces. The Malaysian Army (RMA) is responsible for the safeguarding the nation against land-based threats.

Personnel: 80,000

Equipment

Category	Name	In Service
MBT	PT91M	40+
	FV101 Scorpion	20+
APC/MICV/IFV	ACV-300 Adnan	200+
	K-200 KIFVs	100+
	AV8	200+
	Condor 4x4	250+
	Sibmas	100+
	AV4	10+
	Stormer	20+
Artillery	G5 Mk3 155mm towed	20+
	FH70 155mm towed	10+
	OTO Melara Mod 56 105mm	100+
	Astros II MLRS	50
	M109 howitzer	20
Mortar	82 mm 2B14 Podnos	
	81 mm L16	
RCL	106mm	100+
Anti-Tank GW	ERYX	
	9K115 Metis-M	
	AT-4, M-40, M72 LAW	
	INGWE	200+
SAM	Rapier 2000	10
	FN-6	
	9K38 Igla	75
	Anza 72 mm	100
	Starstreak	
	Starbrust	
AA gun	12.7mm	50+
	Bofors 40mm	20+
	Oerlikon 35mm	20+

Army Aviation

Category	Name	In Service
Helicopter	A-109 LOH	10
	MD 500 Defender	
	S-61A-4 Nuri	10+

New Procurements/ Upgrades

▶ Denel delivered the 100th modular turret for armoured vehicles used by the Malaysian armed forces in terms of a multi-million-rand export contract. The Euro 342-million contract is the largest export contract in Denel's history. In terms of the contract, Denel Land Systems supplied 177 modular turrets in four variants that are fitted onto the Malaysian AV8 vehicles as well as 216 laser-guided Ingwe anti-tank missiles. The contract deliverables consist of 69 armoured fighting vehicle turrets fitted with GI30 30mm cannons; 54 missile turrets with combined GI30 cannons and Ingwe missiles and 54 remotely-operated weapon systems.

NAVY: The Royal Malaysian Navy (Tentera Laut Diraja Malaysia) is the naval arm of the Malaysian Armed Forces. The Royal Malaysian Navy (RMN) protects Malaysia's coastlines, territorial waters, and economic zones from potential trespass or illegal activity. The Navy Future Fleet programme is component of the second batch of Lekiu class frigates, Scorpene class submarines, New Generation Patrol Vessels (NGPV), Multi-Purpose Support Ship (MPSS) and maritime patrol aircraft. The ultimate goal is to build a six vessels squadron of each class by year 2020. The Special Forces arm of the Royal Malaysian Navy is known as PASKAL (Pasukan Khas Laut or Naval Special Forces). In peacetime, the unit is tasked with responding to maritime hijacking incidents as well as protecting Malaysia's numerous offshore oil and gas platforms. On 15 April 2009, PASKAL was renamed KD Panglima Hitam.

Naval Bases: TLDM Lumut, Perak, TLDM Tanjung Gelang, Pahang, TLDM Sepanggar, Sabah, TLDM Tanjung Gerak, Langkawi, Kedah, TLDM Tanjung Pengelih, Johor, TLDM Sandakan, Sabah, TLDM Semporna, Sabah, TLDM Sejingkat, Sarawak, TLDM Bintulu, Sarawak.

Personnel: 18,000

Equipment

Category	Name	In Service
Submarine	Scorpene class	2
Frigate	2nd generation PV	On order
	Lekiu class	2
Corvette	Kasturi class	2
	Laksamana class	4
OPV	Kedah class (Meko A100)	6
	Littoral Mission Ship	On order
Missile Boat	Perdana	4
	Handalan	4
	Jerung	6
	CB-90	17
	Kris	2
	Sri Tiga	2
Mine Hunter	Mahamiru class	4
Amphibious Force	Sri Indera Sakti	1
	Mahawangsa	1
Auxiliaries	Bunga Mas Lima, Bunga Mas Enam, Mega Bakti	
Missile	Exocet, Sea Skua, Aspide, Otomat, MICA, Sea Wolf, Naval Strike Missile	

Naval Aviation

Category	Name	In Service
Aircraft (Maritime Patrol)	Beech King A 200	4

...continued

Category	Name	In Service
Helicopter	Super Lynx 300 (with sea SUKA anti-ship missile)	6
	AS 555SN Fennec	6

New Procurements/ Upgrades

◆ Kongsberg Defence & Aerospace AS has entered into contract worth Euro 124 million with the Royal Malaysian Navy for delivery of the Naval Strike Missile (NSM) to their six new Littoral Combat Ships. Boustead Naval Shipyard Sdn Bhd is building the ships based on Naval Group's Gowind Class design. This contract is a follow-on to the agreement announced 9 April 2015 for NSM shipboard equipment. The NSM will be deck mounted and integrated to the SETIS combat management system provided by Naval Group.

◆ Boustead Naval Shipyard Sdn Bhd (BNS), associate of Boustead Heavy Industries Corporation Bhd (BHIC), has been awarded a contract valued at RM95.99 million for the refit works for KD Terengganu for the Royal Malaysian Navy (RMN).

AIR FORCE: The Royal Malaysian Air Force (Tentera Udara Diraja Malaysia) maintains and operates a capability that is ready and able to project aerospace power to secure Malaysia's airspace and protect her national interests.

Air Bases: Kuala Lumpur Air Base, Subang Air Base, Butterworth Air Base, Kuantan Air Base, Gong Air Base Kedak, Labuan Air Base, Kuching Air Base, College of the Air Force Air Base, Jugra Air Base, Hill Air Force Base Lunchu, Hill Air Force Base Ibam.

Personnel: 17,000

Equipment

Category	Name	In Service
Fighter	Su-30MKM	18
	F/A-18D	8
	BAE Hawk	20
	MB-339	18
Transport	C-130H	10
	KC-130 Tanker	4
	A400M	
	CN-235	8
	Falcon 900	1
Helicopter	SA316B/ SA319B Alouette III	30
	S-70 Black Hawk	6
	EC120 Colibri	1
	SH-3 Sea King	17
	A109C	1

...continued

Category	Name	In Service
Helicopter	AS-61N1	2
	EC725 Cougar	12
Trainer	PC-7 MkI	30
	PC-7 MkII	17
	MD3-160	20
UAV	CTRM Aludra, ScanEagle, CTRM Eagle ARV	
Missile	AIM-7 Sparrow, AIM-120 AMRAAM, AIM-9 Sidewinder AA-12 Adder, AGM-65 Maverick, AS-14 Kedge, AS-13 Kingbolt	

New Procurements/ Upgrades

◆ Malaysia is planning to buy 18 combat aircraft to replace its ageing fleet of Russian-made MiG-29s and have shortlisted Eurofighter, Gripen, Rafale, Super Hornet, Sukhoi SU-30MKM. The Air Force will fly its MiG-29N/NUB fighter aircraft until 2020 or longer and will receive upgrades to keep them up to date.

◆ EPI and the Royal Malaysian Air Force (RMAF) extended the TP400 service contract for technical and logistic support, parts availability and MRO services for their TP400 engines fleet. The Royal Malaysian Air Force began operating the Airbus A400M in March 2015 and currently operates four aircraft.

The Malaysian Air Defence Ground Environment Sector Operations Centre III (MADGE SOC III) programme provides the Royal Malaysian Air Force with significant upgrades to their legacy capabilities. The contract, originally for the addition of a single command and control operations centre and long-range air defence radar, was expanded to include multiple operations centres with either Sector Operations Centre or Air Defence Operations Centre functionality derived from the Sentry command and control software. Sentry is the basis for the Battle Control System, which is used operationally by the US Air Force and Canadian Air Force. The MADGE SOC III programme continues a long history of cooperation between ThalesRaytheonSystems and the Royal Malaysian Air Force, which dates back to the installation of their first automated command and control air defence system.

Major Armaments Producers

The government of Malaysia recognises that there is a significant need to upgrade the nation's military assets. Malaysia decided to undertake defence industrialisation for both economic and military reasons. Since the 1970s, Malaysia had defence programmes aimed at improving military capabilities with procurement of weapon systems and in general, military modernisation. In the sector of defence R&D, Malaysia mostly relies on partnerships with international contractors. The Malaysian Defence Industry Council (MDIC) was formed in August 1999 to ensure coordinated and orderly development of the defence industry sector in Malaysia. It was later renamed as Malaysian Defence, Security and Enhancement Industry Council (MIDES). MIDES also discusses common issues and challenges encountered by defence, enforcement and security related companies. Domestic companies are now engaged in joint venture projects such as shipbuilding, manufacturing small arms & explosives, aerospace sector and assembling of military vehicles for the armed forces. The government has given more focus on indigenisation of defence industry in order to attain the goal of self-reliance. The government has been actively engaging & marketing the Malaysian Defence Industry through exhibitions. International exhibitions such as LIMA and DSA hosted by Malaysia periodically have geared up the defence industry to new heights. The Langkawi International Maritime and Aerospace (LIMA) Exhibition is one of the largest defence and civil showcases in the Asia Pacific, regularly attracting the global maritime and aerospace industry to Langkawi. DSA is Asia's largest defence and security exhibition. Thus, the Government of Malaysia is fully committed to developing the nation's competitiveness by enhancing its economic and technological capabilities. According to the US Department of Commerce's International Trade Administration report, the industry currently lacks critical mass to encourage diversification of markets and users to support the export initiatives of the defence industry. High capital investments both at the initial and continuing operational stages inhibits ease of entry into the sector. Malaysia has enforced a robust defence offset policy to enhance the participation of its local industries.

Domestic suppliers: Astronautic Technology, Boustead Heavy Industries, Composites Technology Research Malaysia, DefTech, Malaysian International Shipping Corporation, SME Ordnance, Weststar Defence.

Foreign suppliers: Australia, Austria, Belgium, Brazil, Brunei, Canada, China, European Union, Finland, France, Germany, Italy, Japan Netherlands, Norway, Pakistan, Poland, Russia, South Africa, South Korea, Spain, Sweden, Switzerland, Thailand, United Kingdom, United States.

DEFENCE DEALS

European defence firm Thales has teamed European defence firm Thales has teamed up with Malaysia's Global Komited Sdn Bhd, a wholly owned subsidiary of the Weststar Group of Companies, to develop, promote, market, and distribute a wide range of ground-based air defence systems for the Malaysian Armed Forces. The partnership agreement was inked on the inaugural day of the Defence Services Asia (DSA) exhibition on April 14 in Kuala Lumpur. The event marked the appointment of Global Komited Sdn Bhd as a key industrial partner agent for Thales in the region. The GK-M1 is capable of mounting a lightweight multiple missile launcher that can fire the Thales-built STARStreak high velocity missiles. The STARStreak is the latest addition to Thales-developed Ground-based Air Defence systems. The new missile will enable the Malaysian Armed Forces, particularly the Royal Malaysian Air Force, to replace the previously commissioned Starburst missile system, according to Thales.

BAE Systems is planning to expand its existing Malaysian joint venture with Boustead Heavy Industry Corporation, BHIC Bofors Asia Sdn Bhd (BHIC Bofors), which already has an industrial facility in Kota Kinabalu. This expansion will include manufacture and supply of gun systems for the Royal Malaysian Navy (RMN) and the wider Southeast Asian region. Through the joint venture, BHIC Bofors will produce new guns locally, using an increased number of parts from local suppliers. The Malaysian supplier base will be expanded through a 'vendor development programme' which includes technology transfer from BAE Systems Bofors' factory in Karlskoga, Sweden. BAE Systems has supplied Malaysia with Bofors naval guns for decades and today there are about 140 in service. BAE Systems' Malaysian joint venture, with BHIC Bofors Asia currently supports the RMN with spares, maintenance, through-life support, training, lifetime extension, test, installation and setting to work on ships. Eurofighter Typhoon is a leading contender in the Malaysian Multi-Role Combat Aircraft competition.

Based on agreements concluded from 1989 onwards (and in particular the Defence Agreement signed in 1993 by Defence Ministers), the French-Malaysian cooperation has been focusing on three key points: strategic issues, defence and armament co-operation. France is one of the main military partners of Malaysia as far as the supply of military equipment and defence services—such as training, assessments and technical assistance—is concerned. Since 2002, Malaysia has chosen to develop a closer co-operation with France to create a submarine force. Malaysia ordered two Scorpene units along with an ex-French Navy Agosta boat for training purposes. The second submarine entered service with the Royal Malaysian Navy in 2010. Malaysia govt. has also chosen French military helicopters and missiles, military electronics and some important equipment in new heavy tanks, new fighting aircraft and the tactical radios of the armed forces.

Malaysia is a key Rolls-Royce customer, with over 100 Rolls-Royce military engines in service across a number of platforms. The Royal Malaysian Navy (RMN) was the first defence force to take delivery of the Super Lynx 300 helicopter in 2003, powered by the T800 engine from LHTEC, a joint venture between Rolls-Royce and Honeywell. The RMN now operates six of the highly sophisticated Super Lynx helicopters at sea from its two frigates, the KD Jebat and KD Lekiu. The Royal Malaysian Air Force (RMAF) is one of the most experienced operators of the Adour Mk871-powered Hawk trainer aircraft and also operates the Aermacchi MB339 trainer, powered by the Viper engine and the VVIP Global Express powered by the BR710.

Raytheon awarded an initial contract to Malaysian-based Contraves Advanced Devices Sdn. Bhd. for the production and supply of components for the Evolved Sea Sparrow Missile (ESSM). This is the first contract of its type awarded to a Malaysian company and is aligned with US and Malaysian strategic initiatives as well as the Malaysian Economic Transformation Programme. Raytheon has proposed ESSM to Malaysia for its upcoming Second Generation Patrol Vessel programme for the Royal Malaysian Navy. Selection of ESSM for the SGPV programme would significantly enhance the capabilities of the Royal Malaysian Navy and provide for interoperability with the US Navy and with the Australian, Japanese and Canadian navies in the Pacific theatre. Raytheon has also issued requests for quotation to Malaysian industry for additional components for the ESSM, the MK56 ESSM vertical launching system, MK73 illuminator, and test equipment in support of the Malaysian SGPV programme as well as other international production programmes. ESSM is the world's most advanced ship self-defence and local area defence surface-to-air missile system.

Arms Imports

The Malaysian defence arm requirements are supplied by the Russians and the US. The current trend indicates the domination of the Russian weapons systems in the Malaysian defence market.

On November 2016, Malaysia and China signed a major defence deal and promised significant cooperation in the South China Sea, which is seen worldwide as a potential strategic shift by Malaysian Prime Minister Najib Razak. Both the countries signed nine agreements covering defence, business and other areas of mutual interests with special focus on naval cooperation.

Global Komited, a member of the Weststar Group and Thales in 2018 announced that the ForceSHIELD Ground-Based Air Defence system project has reached its final milestone with Full System Acceptance (FSA). ForceSHIELD Ground Based Air Defence (GBAD) system project for the Malaysian Armed Forces (MAF) reaches final milestone with Full System Acceptance (FSA). The next generation of Short-Range Air Defence (SHORAD) capability to the Malaysian Army, Air Force and Navy will now enter service with MAF, according to Thales.

Arms Exports

Malaysia External Trade Development Corporation (Matrade) has secured RM761 million (USD 248 million) from export of defence equipment to neighbouring countries- Cambodia and Vietnam, according to Matrade. Cambodia recorded potential sales of RM629.5 million while Vietnam concluded potential sales of RM131.5 million. Items for sale included unmanned aerial vehicles; fast interceptor crafts; fire, rescue and specialised vehicles; simulation training equipment and software; communications and command systems; maintenance, repair and operations as well as design services. Eight companies participated in its first ever specialised marketing mission on the defence industry to Phnom Penh, Cambodia and Hanoi, Vietnam in 2012. The mission's objective was to expand on trade and economic collaboration between Malaysia, Cambodia and Vietnam specifically in the area of defence related products and services, at the same time further strengthening existing business networks with the two nations.

DEFENCE BUDGET

Total defence spending: $3.60 billion (2017)

Defence budget in terms of GDP: 1.1% of GDP (2020 est.), 1% of GDP (2019)

Malaysia's defence budget may be affected due to the ongoing COVID-19 pandemic. The Defence Ministry's allocation of RM15.6

billion was the fifth largest in the 2020 Budget. Of the total amount, RM5.7 billion would go to the Army, RM2.5 billion to the Royal Malaysian Air Force, RM2 billion to the Navy and RM1.4 billion for the Joint Forces. Also, as part of efforts to safeguard the Sabah waters, the government had opened bids to provide 20 fast interceptor crafts at a cost of RM220 million. The overall budget deficit for 2018 was 3.7 percent of GDP and the government aim to reduce this to 3.4 percent in 2019 and 3.0 percent by 2020. The country is projected to cumulatively spend USD 20.3 billion during 2018-2022. Malaysia's defence policy outlines the three main bases, the country's strategic interests, the principles of defence and defence concepts. It emphasises the need to maintain the strategic importance of a stable and secure environment. Malaysia's budgeting system for defence is based on a formal five-year planning structure and process which establishes force-manpower-ringgit planning levels to guide the formulation of annual budget. The five-year plans projects spending trends into the future and is used as the primary planning instrument for development or acquisition of new capabilities. The Ministry of Defence will include strategies to make the Malaysian Armed Forces a premium organisation in its first Defence White Paper (DWP). The White Paper will bring a significant contribution to the country's defence and security landscape as it will provide a clearer description of every agency and its purpose.

CONCLUSION

Malaysia's present and future interests are tied to an uncertain and ever-changing security environment. As a result of the uncertainties at the regional and global levels, the international strategic landscape is becoming more complex and unpredictable in the coming years. Although Malaysia is not beset by military threats or conflicts at the present moment, the nation still faces three main security challenges. Malaysia which shares common land boundaries with Thailand, Brunei and Indonesia, as well as maritime boundaries with Thailand, Brunei, Indonesia, Singapore, the Philippines, Vietnam, China and Taiwan is entwined in complex interdependence with its neighbours with strategic interests in economic, political, cultural and defence arenas. The complexity is further heightened with the constant presence and influence of extra regional powers such as US, Russia, Japan and China The main security challenge which Malaysia currently faces is safeguarding and defending the country's national interests which include political stability and peace and harmony of the citizens. From the defence point of view, Malaysia, as an independent sovereign nation, is growing its defence capabilities by building up armed forces and tying strong relations with strategic neighbours in order to defend itself from any external interference and armed attack. Malaysia's security perspective is influenced by the geographical, political, military and economic realities of the region and its strategic location in Southeast Asia. The defence of these national interests is crucial to Malaysia's sovereignty, territorial integrity and economic well-being. Other than this, the country also faces security challenges from terrorism, illegal immigrants and piracy. Malaysia's defence policy is an extension of its foreign policy. It is a capability-driven policy as opposed to a threat-dependent. It simply means that while it does not foresee immediate threats to sovereignty and territorial integrity, the possibility of threats arising in the future cannot be totally ignored. In order to safeguard the security of the country and strengthening the socio-economic and politics, Malaysia must promote and contribute for a stable regional security environment and have closer regional co-operation by resolving territorial disputes and focus more on shared economic interests in the region. The Malaysian Ministry of Defence will soon be introducing the Defence White Paper, the first of such being introduced in the country, which will be a 10-year plan for the national policy on defence and security.

CONTACT DETAILS

Ministry of Defence
Tingkat 5, Wisma Pertahanan,
Jalan Padang Tembak,
50634 KUALA LUMPUR
www.mod.gov.my

Malaysian Armed Forces Headquarters,
Secretariat, Ministry of Defence
Jalan Padang Tembak, 50634
Kuala Lumpur, Malaysia
Phone: +603 - 20712004 | 2014
Email: sek[dot]matm[at]mod[dot]gov[dot]my

MEXICO
(Capital: Mexico City)

INTRODUCTION

Area: 1,964,375 sq km
Coastline: 9,330 km
Population: 130,207,371 (July 2021 est.)
Maritime claims: Territorial sea: 12 nm
Contiguous zone: 24 nm
Exclusive Economic Zone: 200 nm
Continental shelf: 200 nm or to the edge of the continental margin

KEY POLITICAL PERSONS

PRESIDENT & COMMANDER-IN-CHIEF: Andrés Manuel López Obrador

KEY DEFENCE PERSONS

SECRETARY OF NATIONAL DEFENCE: Gen. Luis Cresencio Sandoval Gonzalez

CHIEF OF NATIONAL DEFENCE STAFF: Gen. Staff Ricardo Trevilla Trejo

COMMANDER OF ARMY: Gen. Eufemio Alberto Ibarra Flores

SECRETARY OF NAVY: Adm. José Rafael Ojeda Duran

COMMANDER OF AIR FORCE: Gen. José Gerardo Vega Rivera

ECONOMY

Trade currently accounts for 63% of Mexico's GDP, making it the 5th most open economy in the G-20. According to the President of Mexico as quoted in the official website, an FTA has been signed with Panama, a trade agreement has been completed with the Pacific Alliance and the Trans-Pacific Partnership (TPP) negotiations have been finalised. When the TPP comes into force, Mexico will have 13 FTAs and access to 1.309 potential consumers in 52 countries. He added that, Mexico's economy is moving along the correct path, and that the country is growing and reaching higher levels of development, despite the adverse scenario in the world. The United States, Mexico, and Canada are parties to the North American Free Trade Agreement (NAFTA). Mexico is a member of the World Trade Organisation (WTO), the Asia-Pacific Economic Cooperation (APEC), the G-20, and the Organisation for Economic Cooperation and Development (OECD). Mexico's exports rely heavily on supplying the US market, but the country has also sought to diversify its export destinations. Mexico is a strong promoter of free trade, maintaining free trade agreements with the most countries of any nation in the world, including pacts with Japan, the EU, and many Latin American partners. Mexico is a strong supporter of the United Nations (UN) and Organization of American States (OAS). Mexico belongs to a number of the same international organisations, including the Asia-Pacific Economic Cooperation (APEC) forum; Organisation for Economic Cooperation and Development (OECD); International Energy Agency (IEA); International Monetary Fund (IMF); World Bank (WB); World Trade Organisation (WTO); International Maritime Organisation (IMO); and the Wassenaar Arrangement on conventional arms. COVID-19 pandemic has affected the economy hard by putting tremendous pressure on jobs and output. Recently US demand has helped greatly in bringing back the economy as Mexico is largely dependent on US economy. The United States is working closely with the Mexican government and partners to combat the pandemic and reduce secondary economic impacts in both countries. Mexico is the United States' second largest trading partner and second-largest export market after Canada. In 2020, all three countries began implementation of the United States-Mexico-Canada Agreement (USMCA). The recovery in 2021 is going strong which relies on vaccination programmes and recovery in labor markets.

GDP (official exchange rate): $2 trillion (2020 est.), $2.463 trillion (2019 est.)

Real Growth Rate (GDP): -0.3% (2019 est.), 2.19% (2018 est.)

Industries: Food and beverages, tobacco, chemicals, iron and steel, petroleum, mining, textiles, clothing, motor vehicles, consumer durables, tourism

Oil - proved reserves: 6.63 billion bbl (1 January 2018 est.)

Natural gas - proved reserves: 279.8 billion cu m (1 January 2018 est.)

Total Exports: $434.93 billion (2020 est.), $492.73 billion (2019 est.)

Export Commodities: Cars and vehicle parts, computers, delivery trucks, crude petroleum, insulated wiring (2019)

Major Markets: United States 75% (2019)

Total Imports: $410.66 billion (2020 est.), $495.79 billion (2019 est.)

Import Commodities: Integrated circuits, refined petroleum, cars and vehicle parts, office machinery/parts, telephones (2019)

Major Suppliers: United States 54%, China 14% (2019)

INTERNATIONAL DISPUTES

◆ The US has intensified security measures to monitor and control legal and illegal personnel, transport, and commodities across its border with Mexico. Through the Merida Initiative, the United States and Mexico have forged a partnership to combat transnational organised crime and drug trafficking, while strengthening human rights and the rule of law. From 2008-2018, the United States has appropriated USD2.8 billion in equipment, training and capacity building support under the Merida Initiative.

◆ Belize and Mexico are working to solve minor border demarcation discrepancies arising from inaccuracies in the 1898 border treaty.

◆ Counterterrorism cooperation between Mexico and the United States is strong.

DEFENCE

ARMY

Personnel: 1,80,000

Equipment

Category	Name	In Service
APC/ IFV/ Light Tank	AMX-VCI	300+
	M2A1	30+
	Buffalo	20+
	BDX	80+
	ERC 90	
	VBL M11	40
	HWK11	40
	VCR/TT	40
	Mowag Roland	20+
Artillery	105 mm M2A1	40+
	105 mm M101	
	155mm M-114	
	105 mm. M90	20+
Mortar	120 mm.	30
	81 mm.	300
	60 mm.	1,000+
Anti-Tank GW	Milan	

New Procurements/ Upgrades

No major procurement plans are under consideration at present.

NAVY

Personnel: 56,000

Equipment

Category	Name	In Service
Destroyer	Quetzalcoatl class	1
	Manuel Azueta class	1
Frigate	Allende Class	4
	Nicolas Bravo Class	2
Patrol Vessel/ Patrol Craft	Huracan Class	2
	Oxaca Class	6
	Durango Class	4
	Uribe Class	5+
	Valle Class	10+
	Azteca Class	20

...continued

Category	Name	In Service
Patrol Vessel/ Patrol Craft	Democrata Class	2
	Yaqui Class	2+
	Point Class	5
	Olmeca Class	10+
	Polimar Class	5+
	Acurio A	5+
	Acurio B	2
	Inshore patrol	2+
	River Patrol	5
Amphibious Force	Transport Ship	2
	LST	3
	Auxiliary vessel	10+
	Rio Tuxpan hydrographic vessel	1

Naval Aviation

Personnel: 1,200

Equipment

Category	Name	In Service
Aircraft	C212-200 MPA Aviojet	5+
	An-32	5+
	E-2C Hawkeye	2+
	Dash-8 Q200	1
	Cessna 180	2
	Cessna 310	3
	Cessna 150	2
	Cessna 337	3
	Cessna 402	3+
	DHC-5	1
	L-90 TP RediGo	10+
	King Air 90	1
	CN-235	2
Helicopter	MD Explorer	5+
	MBB BO-105	10
	SA.319B Alouette III	4
	MD500E	5
	AS-555 Fennec	4
	AS 565 Panther	2
	Mi-8	20
	Mi-17V1	10+
	R-44 Clipper	1
	R22 Mariner	2
	Schweizer 300	4

Marines

Personnel: 10,000

Equipment

Category	Name	In Service
APC/IFV	Pegaso VAP 3550	20+
	BTR-70	
	VAP 3560/1	
Artillery	105 mm. M56	5+

...continued

Category	Name	In Service
MRL	Firos-6	
Mortar	60 mm.	100
	81 mm.	
Recoilless rifle	106 mm.	
Patrol Vessel	Pollaris/ Pollaris II Class FAC	30+

New Procurements/ Upgrades

No major procurement plans are under consideration at present.

AIR FORCE

Personnel: 8,000

Equipment

Category	Name	In Service
Fighters/ attack/ Reconnaissance/ bomber	F-5E	5+
	F-5F	2
	Cessna C-182 Skylane	50+
	EMB-145 AEW&C	1
	EMB-145MP	2
Transport/ Tanker	C-130S/C-130K/C-130E/L-100-20	10+
	Boeing 727	3
	An-32	2
Attack/ Transport Helicopter	Mi-8	10
	Mi-17	15+
	Mi-26	2
	MD-530F	20+
	Bell 212	20+
	S-70	10+
	CH-53	2
	Bell 412EP	5
Trainer	PC-7	30+
	T-6C+	5+

New Procurements/ Upgrades

No major procurement plans are under consideration at present.

Mexico is one of the few countries which has capabilities to manufacture nuclear weapons but has renounced them and pledged to only use its nuclear technology for peaceful purposes following the Treaty of Tlatelolco in 1968. In the 1970s Mexico's national institute for nuclear research successfully enriched weapons-grade uranium which is used in the construction of nuclear weapons. However, in April 2010, Mexico agreed to turn over its weapons-grade uranium to the United States. This agreement hasn't been approved by the Mexican Congress and the uranium remains in Mexico.

Defence Expenditure

Total defence spending: 10 billion (2019 approx.)

Estimated defence spending in terms of GDP: 0.6% of GDP (2020 est.), 0.5% of GDP (2019)

Mexico has the second largest defence budget in Latin America, spending about 0.5% GDP on its military.

Major foreign suppliers: United States, Russia, Spain, Israel, Germany, France, Switzerland, UK, Italy, Sweden, Brazil, Denmark, Norway, South Africa and Colombia.

Defence Production and R&D

Mexico has a small but long-established defence industry. The Mexican defence industry is fairly active producing "soft" items: manuals, uniforms, etc. The "Industria Militar" (owned by the government) produces uniforms and other supplies, and small arms, including G3 machine guns. No equipment such as tanks, aircraft, etc., is manufactured and there are no known plans to produce this type of equipment. Mexico's major shipyards at Tampico on the Gulf of Mexico and Salina Cruz on the Pacific Ocean have been involved in the construction of patrol craft and auxiliary vessels. The largest programme, involving the manufacture of Azteca-class patrol craft, was carried out under a licensed production agreement with a British firm. Mexico has improved its aerospace manufacturing capabilities, moving from production of components, small parts, and harnesses, to manufacturing of airframes, flight surfaces, small drones, and flight control and avionic assemblies. Successful engineering and design activities have extended to production of small unmanned aerial vehicles (UAVs) and light aircraft projects.

Defence Procurement

The Mexican Armed Forces are currently under-equipped as much of their inventories are ageing. To meet the present requirements of the forces, Mexico needs a significant procurement programme.

A Mexican Navy MI-8 helicopter standby on the flight deck aboard USS Bataan (LHD 5)

CONTACT DETAILS

Secretariat of National Defence
Boulevard Manuel Avila Camacho
Avenida Industria Militar
Col. Lomas de Sotelo
11640 Delegacion Miguel Hidalgo
Distrito Federal
Tel: (+52 21) 22 88 00
Website: https://www.gob.mx/sedena

Secretary of the Navy
Heroic Naval Military School
Avenue. No. 861,
Cypresses, Coyoacan, Mexico City. CP 04830
Telephone: 56 24 65 00
www.gob.mx/semar

MONGOLIA
(Capital: Ulaanbaatar)

INTRODUCTION

Area: 1,564,116 sq. km
Population: 3,198,913 (July 2021 est.)
Coastline: 0 km (Landlocked)
Maritime claims: None

KEY POLITICAL PERSONS

PRESIDENT & COMMANDER-IN-CHIEF: Ukhnaagiin Khurelsukh

PRIME MINISTER: Luvsannamsrain Oyun-Erdene

KEY DEFENCE PERSONS

MINISTER OF DEFENCE: Brig. Gen. Gürsediin Saikhanbayar

CHIEF OF GENERAL STAFF: Maj. Gen. Dovchinsurengiin Ganzorig

COMMANDER OF ARMY: Brig. Gen. B. Amgalanbaatar

COMMANDER OF AIR FORCE: Brig. Gen. Ochir Enkhbayar

ECONOMY

Foreign direct investment has transformed Mongolia's landlocked economy from its traditional dependence on herding and agriculture. The country is endowed with extensive mineral deposits such as copper, coal, molybdenum, tin, tungsten, and gold. The main export commodities are copper, gold and coal. Exports now account for more than 40% of GDP. The economy expanded rapidly with GDP growth increasing from 1.2% in 2016 to 5.1% in 2017 and 6.1% in the first quarter of 2018. The main driver of this rapid economic expansion has been the mining industry making up 30% of all Mongolian industry, and the government's macro-fiscal adjustment programme. Another important industry is the production of cashmere. Mongolia is the world's second largest producer of cashmere. Mongolia's economic growth rebounded in the first half of 2021 on the back of robust exports and a surge in private investment, mainly in the mining sector, according to the World Bank. Mongolia joined the WTO in 1997 and seeks to expand its participation in regional economic and trade regimes.

GDP (official exchange rate): $11.14 billion (2017 est.)

Real Growth Rate (GDP): 5.1% (2017 est.), 1.2% (2016 est.)

Industries: Construction and construction materials; mining (coal, copper, molybdenum, fluorspar, tin, tungsten, gold); oil; food and beverages; processing of animal products, cashmere and natural fiber manufacturing.

Total Exports: $7.65 billion (2020 est.), $8.42 billion (2019 est.)

Export Commodities: coal, copper, gold, iron, crude petroleum (2019)

Major Markets: China 81%, Switzerland 9% (2019)

Total Imports: $7.34 billion (2020 est.), $9.25 billion (2019 est.)

Import Commodities: Refined petroleum, cars, delivery trucks, construction vehicles, aircraft (2019)

Major Suppliers: China 31%, Russia 29%, Japan 10%, South Korea 5% (2019)

INTERNATIONAL DISPUTES

Mongolia has no known international disputes.

DEFENCE

The Mongolian Armed Forces has no Navy being a landlocked country. The Armed Forces consists of the Ground Forces and the Air Force. The General Staff of the Mongolian Armed Forces is the main managing body and operates independently from the Ministry of Defence, the government - controlled parent body. The Mongolian armed forces have been performing peacekeeping missions around the world. This peace-time structure could be changed and reorganised in case of war or a war-like situation. Mongolian armed forces have been performing peacekeeping missions in South Sudan, Chad, Georgia, Ethiopia, Eritrea, Congo, Western Sahara, Sudan (Darfur), Iraq, Afghanistan, and in Sierra Leone under the mandate of the United Nations Mission in Liberia.

ARMY

Personnel: 20,500

Equipment

Category	Name	In Service
MBT	T-54/55	350
	T-72	50
MICV/APC	BMP-1	400
	BRDM-2	130
	BTR-60/70/80	250
Artillery	D-30	300
	M-30 122mm	
	M-46 130mm	
	M-20 152mm Howitzer	
MRL	BM-21 122mm	
ATGW	Snapper	
	Sagger AT-3	
AA gun	37mm, 57mm	

New Procurements/Upgrades

No major procurement plans are under consideration at present.

AIR FORCE (Army Air Wing)

Personnel: 3,000

Equipment

Category	Name	In Service
Transport	MiG-29	2
	An-24	6
	An-2	15
	An-26	1
	An-32	1
Helicopter	Mi-8	11
	Mi-24	11
	Mi-171	
SAM	SA-2	1 battalion

New Procurements/Upgrades

No major procurement plans are under consideration at present.

Defence Expenditure

Total defence spending: $210 million (2019), $150 million (2018)

Estimated defence spending in terms of GDP: 1.5%

Defence Production and R&D

Mongolia does not undertake any defence production activities.

Defence Procurement

The main suppliers of arms to Mongolia are Russia and China. Mongolia and the United States have signed a joint statement to strengthen military cooperation and increase joint training programmes. A defence co-operation agreement has been signed with Russia. Turkey and India have extended military assistance to Mongolia. India has been imparting training to Mongolian military officers in Indian training establishments.

CONTACT DETAILS

Ministry of Defence
Government Building 7
Dandar Street 51
Bayanzurkh District
Ulaanbaaatar, Mongolia

Tel: +97-51-261718
Fax: +976-51-322904
http://www.mod.gov.mn/

MOROCCO
(Capital: Rabat)

INTRODUCTION

Area: 446,550 sq km
Population: 36,561,813 (July 2021 est.)
Coastline: 1,835 km
Maritime claims: Territorial sea: 12 nm
Contiguous zone: 24 nm
Exclusive Economic Zone: 200 nm
Continental shelf: 200 m depth or to the depth of exploitation

KEY POLITICAL PERSONS

HEAD OF STATE, COMMANDER-IN-CHIEF & CHIEF OF GENERAL STAFF: King Mohammed VI

PRIME MINISTER: Aziz Akhannouch

KEY DEFENCE PERSONS

MINISTER DELEGATE FOR NATIONAL DEFENCE: Abdellatif Loudiyi

INSPECTOR GENERAL OF ROYAL ARMED FORCES (FAR): Gen. Belkhir El Farouk

ECONOMY

Morocco has become a major player in African economic affairs, and is the 5th largest African economy by GDP (PPP). Morocco's economy is considered a relatively liberal economy governed by the law of supply and demand. Additionally, High food and fuel prices strained the government's budget and widened the country's current account deficit. Key economic challenges for Morocco include fighting corruption, reducing government spending, reforming the education system and judiciary, addressing socioeconomic disparities, and building more diverse, higher value-added industries. Key sectors of the economy include agriculture, tourism, aerospace, automotive, phosphates, textiles, apparel, and subcomponents. The U.S. - Moroccan FTA is comprehensive and includes chapters detailing commitment on intellectual property rights, labour, and environmental protection. Morocco also

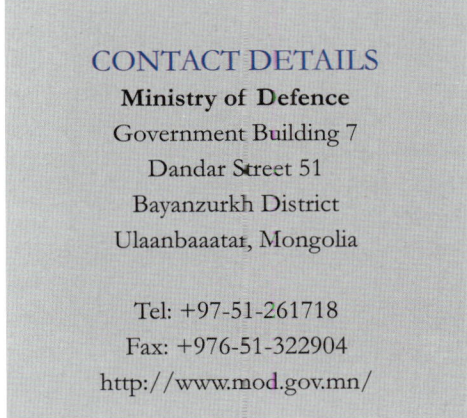

has FTAs with United Arab Emirates, Jordan, Tunisia, Egypt, and Turkey and has an advanced status with the EU. Morocco seeks to establish itself as a hub for shipping, logistics, finance, assembly, and sales. More than 100 US companies operate in Morocco, particularly in the renewable energy, infrastructure, aviation, and environmental technology sectors, as per US Dept of State report. Morocco maintains close relations with Europe and the United States. Morocco belongs to the United Nations, Arab League, Arab Maghreb Union, Organisation of Islamic Cooperation (OIC), the Non-Aligned Movement, and the Community of Sahel-Saharan States. King Mohammed VI chairs the OIC's Al-Quds (Jerusalem) Committee. Morocco re-joined the African Union in January 2017. Morocco seeks to expand its renewable energy capacity with a goal of making renewable more than 50% of installed electricity generation capacity by 2030. As per US Dept. of State, Morocco plans to become a hub for shipping, logistics, finance, assembly, and sales. 100-plus US companies operate in Morocco, mainly in the renewable energy, infrastructure, aviation, and environmental technology sectors. To safeguard the economy from COVID-19 pandemic, Morocco has taken strict and rapid health and security measures along with financial steps.

GDP (official exchange rate): $259.42 billion (2020 est.), $279.3 billion (2019 est.)

Real Growth Rate (GDP): 2.5% (2019 est.), 2.96% (2018 est.)

Industries: Automotive parts, phosphate mining and processing, aerospace, food processing, leather goods, textiles, construction, energy, tourism

Oil - proved reserves: 684,000 bbl (1 January 2018 est.)

Natural gas - proved reserves: 1.444 billion cu m (1 January 2018 est.)

Total Exports: $37.52 billion (2020 est.), $44.05 billion (2019 est.)

Export Commodities: Cars, insulated wiring, fertilizers, phosphoric acid, clothing and apparel (2019)

Major Markets: Spain 23%, France 19% (2019)

Total Imports: $46.26 billion (2020 est.), $54.1 billion (2019 est.)

Import Commodities: Refined petroleum, cars and vehicle parts, natural gas, coal, low-voltage protection equipment (2019)

Major Suppliers: Spain 19%, France 11%, China 9%, United States 7%, Germany 5%, Turkey 5%, Italy 5% (2019)

INTERNATIONAL DISPUTES

◆ Claims and administers Western Sahara whose sovereignty remains unresolved.

◆ Morocco protests Spain's control over the coastal enclaves of Ceuta, Melilla, and Penon de Velez de la Gomera, the islands of Penon de Alhucemas and Islas Chafarinas, and surrounding waters. Both countries claim Isla Perejil (Leila Island).

◆ Discussions have not progressed on a comprehensive maritime delimitation, setting limits on resource exploration and refugee interdiction, since Morocco's 2002 rejection of Spain's unilateral designation of a median line from the Canary Islands.

◆ Algeria's border with Morocco remains an irritant to bilateral relations, each nation accusing the other of harbouring militants and arms smuggling.

The National Liberation Front's assertion of claim to Chirac Pastures in south-eastern Morocco is a dormant dispute.

DEFENCE

ARMY

Personnel: 175,000

Equipment

Category	Name	In Service
MBT	T-72B/BK	150+
	M60/ M60A3TTS	400+
	M48A5	200+
	Kurassier	100
	M1A1SA	200+
	VT-1A	100+
APC/ MICV/IFV	AMX13	50
	M113	1000+
	UR416	50
	VAB VCI/VTT	300+
	Ratel IFV	50+
	EBR75	10+
	AMX10RC	100+
	AMX10P	10
	AML90	100+
	AML60	30+
	ERC90 Lynx	20
Artillery	L118	30+
	M101	10+
	105 mm. M101A1	40
	130 mm. M46	10+
	M114	20
	155 mm. FH70	30
	155 mm. M109	250
	155 mm. Mk F3	50+
	203 mm. M-110 A2 SP	50+
	M198 155 mm.	30+
	M1950 155 mm.	30+
Mortar	81 mm.	20
	120 mm.	50+
Recoilless rifle	75 mm.	
	106 mm.	
	M72 Law	
	Strim89	
Anti-Tank GW	Milan	
	Tow	
	Dragon	
	HOT	
	Sagger	
AA Gun	20 mm.	100
	Twin 200 mm. mounts	30+
	ZPU232	100+
	M163 Vulcan	40
SAM	SA-7	150+
	Chaparral	50
	Tunguska M-1	10
	Crotale	30

Army Aviation

Category	Name	In Service
Helicopter	Alouette II	4
	Gazelle	3
	A-109	5+

New Procurements/ Upgrades

◆ The US State Department has approved a possible Foreign Military Sale to Morocco of 25 M88A2 Heavy Equipment Recovery Combat Utility Lift and Evacuation System (HERCULES) vehicles and/or M88A1 long supply HERCULES refurbished vehicles and related equipment for an estimated cost of USD239.35 million.

◆ The US State Department has approved a possible Foreign Military Sale to Morocco of 36 AH-64E Apache attack helicopters and related equipment for an estimated cost of USD4.25 billion. The Defence Security Cooperation Agency delivered the required certification notifying Congress of this possible sale on November 19, 2019. The proposed sale will improve Morocco's capability to meet current and future threats, and will enhance interoperability with US forces and other allied forces. Morocco will use the enhanced capability to strengthen its homeland defence and provide close air support to its forces. Morocco will have no difficulty absorbing the Apache aircraft into its armed forces.

◆ GE Aviation's T700 turboshaft engine has been chosen by the Kingdom of Morocco to power its new Defence fleet of Boeing AH-64E Apache attack helicopters. Morocco will acquire 48 T700-701D engines and two spares as part of a recent contract announcement for 24 Apache helicopters.

◆ The US State Department has approved a possible Foreign Military Sale to Morocco of various TOW-2A missiles for an estimated cost of USD776 million.

◆ The US State Department has approved a possible Foreign Military Sale to Morocco of enhancements to 162 Abrams tanks for an estimated cost of USD1.259 billion. The Government of Morocco has requested to purchase enhancements to 162 Abrams tanks procured through the Excess Defence Article (EDA) programme to one of the following variants: M1A1 Situational Awareness (baseline version), M1A2M (includes Commander's Independent Thermal Viewer) or M1A1 US Marine Corps version (includes Slew to Cue).

NAVY

Personnel: 10,000

Equipment

Category	Name	In Service
Frigate	SIGMA class	3
	Mohammed V Class	1
	Hassan II	1
	Mohammed VI FREMM Class	1

...continued

Category	Name	In Service
Corvette	Lieutenant-Colonel Errahmani	1
Patrol Vessel	Rais bargach Class OPV	5
	El Khattabi Class ex-FAC	4
	Okba Class FAC	2
	El Lahiq	4
	LV Rabhi	5+
	El Wacil Class/ Erraid Class	
Auxiliary ship/ Amphibious Force	Sidi Mohammed Ben Abdallah	1
	Batral Type	3
	Dakhla logistics support	1

Naval Aviation

Category	Name	In Service
Aircraft	Britten-Norman Defender	10+
Helicopter	Eurocopter AS565 MA	3

New Procurements/ Upgrades

◆ The US State Department has approved a possible Foreign Military Sale to the Government of Morocco of 10 AGM-84L Harpoon Block II Air Launched missiles and related equipment for an estimated cost of USD62 million. Also included are containers, spare and repair parts, support and test equipment, publications and technical documentation, personnel training and training equipment, US Government and contractor representatives' technical assistance, engineering and logistics support services, and other related elements of logistics support.

AIR FORCE
Personnel: 15,000

Equipment

Category	Name	In Service
Fighters/ attack/ Reconnaissance/ bomber	Mirage F-1 MF2000	20+
	F-5E	20+
	Dassault Falcon 20 ELINT / ESM	2
	F-16C/D Block 52+	20+
Transport/ Tanker	KC-130H	2
	C-130H	10+
	CN-235	6
	Gulfstream II/III	2
	King Air 200/300/350	8
	Alenia C-27J	3
	Boeing 707	1
	Citation V	2

...continued

Category	Name	In Service
Attack/ Transport Helicopter	SA341	20+
	SA 330 Puma	25+
	Bell 205	40+
	Bell 206	5
	Bell 212	4
	CH47C Chinook	3
Trainer	Super King Air 100	4
	Bell 206	17
	T-6C Texan II	20+
	Alpha Jet	20+
	F-5F	4

New Procurements/ Upgrades

◆ Thales delivered its 100th radar from the Ground Master family - a Ground Master 400 (GM400) to Morocco end July 2021, under a contract signed in 2019 with the Royal Moroccan Air Force (in addition to a previous order placed in 2013).

◆ The US State Department has approved a possible Foreign Military Sale to Morocco of additional F-16 ammunition for an estimated cost of USD209 million. The Defence Security Cooperation Agency delivered the required certification notifying Congress of this possible sale on September 11, 2019.

◆ The US State Department has approved a possible Foreign Military Sale to Morocco of continuation of sustainment support to its current F-16 fleet for an estimated cost of USD250.4 million.

◆ The US State Department has approved a possible Foreign Military Sale to Morocco to upgrade its existing twenty-three F-16 aircraft to the F-16V configuration and related equipment for an estimated cost of USD985.2 million.

◆ The US State Department has approved a possible Foreign Military Sale to Morocco of F-16C/D Block 72 aircraft and related equipment for an estimated cost of USD3.787 billion.

ROYAL MOROCCAN GENDARMERIE
Personnel: 25,000

The Moroccan Royal Gendarmerie is the Gendarmerie body of Morocco, and comes under the authority of the Ministry of Defence. The service aim of the gendarmerie is to ensure especially administrative, judicial and military policing activities directly and to help to the competent authorisations with the envisaged laws. It is a public force designed to guarantee public security and public order and the implementation of laws.

Category	Name	In Service
Helicopter	SA315	5+
	SA342 Gazelle	5
	Eurocopter AS355	3
	Sikorsky S-70 S-70A-26	2
	SA 330 Puma C/F/H	5+
	Eurocopter EC145	2
	Eurocopter AS332 AS332/ EC225	2
	Eurocopter EC135	3

Defence Expenditure

Total defence spending: USD 3 billion (approx.)

Estimated defence spending in terms of GDP: 4.5% of GDP (2020 est.), 3.1% of GDP (2019)

Moroccan defence spending has raised from USD 3.8 billion in 2014 to USD 4.5 billion in 2018 because of the procurement of military aircraft, armoured vehicles, radar systems, diesel-electric submarines and patrol ships. The Moroccan army ordered from the United States 222 main battle tanks, including Abrams tanks, delivery was completed in 2018. Morocco also signed a contract in 2019 to be provided with technical support for their Abrams tanks. The Royal Moroccan Air Force flies F-16 fighters, C-130 transport aircraft, and CH-47D helicopters, among other US-origin equipment, while the Royal Moroccan Navy operates modern frigates equipped with US-origin digital communications. The Moroccan defence budget is expected to grow to USD3.9 billion by 2022, as per the US Department of Commerce's International Trade Administration news reports.

Major foreign suppliers: USA, France, Russia, China, Spain, Netherlands, UK, South Africa, Italy, Germany, Turkey.

India and Morocco signed cooperation on defence industry, including collaboration in Ship Building and manufacturing support. Both Defence Ministers agreed to enhance bilateral cooperation in the field of defence and security. The Minister identified fields of Hydrography, Peacekeeping, Telemedicine, Information Technology and Communications as well as Counter Terrorism and Counter Insurgency as potential areas for bilateral engagement.

Morocco and the United States renewed the alliance between the two nations as a foundation stone for peace in Africa in Oct 2020. Both countries signed the defence cooperation road map in Rabat, Morocco. The road map charts cooperation between the two nations through 2030. The road map will allow the United States and Morocco to improve defence cooperation, partnerships and interoperability.

Defence Production and R&D
Morocco's small aerospace sector is entirely based at Casablanca's Muhammad V Airport and has civil and military applications. There are no defence production facilities in Morocco.

Defence Procurement
Moroccan procurement has been limited by financial constraints and the European Code of Conduct on arms sales, which some member states interpret as prohibiting weapons sales to Morocco due to the Western Sahara dispute. Morocco allocates around USD 180 million per year for military capital spending, including procurement and defence construction.

CONTACT DETAILS
National Defence Administration
6Bis, Rue Patrice Lumumba
Rabat, Morocco

MYANMAR
(Capital: Naypyidaw)

INTRODUCTION
Area: 676,578 sq. km
Population: 57,069,099 (July 2021 est.)
Coastline: 1930 km
Maritime claims: Territorial sea: 12 nm
Contiguous zone: 24 nm
Exclusive Economic Zone: 200 nm
Continental shelf: 200 nm or to the edge of the continental margin

Note: NAYPYIDAW was unveiled as Myanmar's new administrative capital in November 2005 by the then military regime.

KEY POLITICAL PERSONS

PRESIDENT (Acting): Myint Swe

KEY DEFENCE PERSONS

DEFENCE MINISTER: Gen. Mya Tun Oo

COMMANDER-IN-CHIEF OF THE ARMED FORCES: Sr. Gen. Min Aung Hlaing

COMMANDER OF THE NAVY: Adm. Moe Aung

COMMANDER OF AIR FORCE: Gen. Maung Maung Kyaw

ECONOMY
Myanmar is an emerging economy. The major agricultural produce is rice which covers about 60% of the country's total cultivated land area. However, the most productive sectors are oil and gas, mining, and timbre. Since its transition to a civilian-led government in 2011, the government has taken steps toward reforming and opening up the economy by lowering export taxes, easing restrictions on its financial sector, and reaching out to international organisations for assistance. Following the US sanctions lift in 2016, State Counsellor Aung San Suu Kyi and the ruling National League for Democracy have sought to improve Myanmar's investment climate. The economic growth rate recovered from a low growth under 6% in 2011 but has been volatile between 6% and 8% between 2014 and 2018. According to the World Bank, prior to the COVID-19 pandemic, the economic was projected to pick up to 6.3 percent in FY2019/20 and 6.4 percent in FY2020/21. The economy is estimated to have grown by 1.7 percent in FY19/20, down from 6.8 percent in FY/19. The national economy reportedly has been paralysed since a military power-grab which pushed civilian leader Aung San Suu Kyi out of office in February 2021. Livelihoods have been lost after strikes and factory closures, indiscriminate and brutal crackdown on dissent. Myanmar remains one of the poorest countries in Asia with approximately 26% of the people living in poverty.

GDP: $75.50 billion (2020 est), $76.606 billion (2019 est.)
Real Growth Rate (GDP): 6.8% (2017 est.), 5.9% (2016 est.)
Industries: Agricultural processing; wood and wood products; copper, tin, tungsten, iron; cement, construction materials;

pharmaceuticals; fertilizer; oil and natural gas; garments; jade and gems.

Total Exports: $16.267 billion (2018 est.), $14.611 billion (2017 est.)
Export Commodities: Natural gas, clothing products, rice, copper, dried legumes (2019)
Major Markets: China 24%, Thailand 24%, Japan 7%, Germany 5% (2019)
Total Imports: $14.958 billion (2018 est.), $16.21 billion (2017 est.)
Import Commodities: Refined petroleum, broadcasting equipment, fabrics, motorcycles, packaged medicines (2019)
Major Suppliers: China 43%, Thailand 15%, Singapore 12%, Indonesia 5% (2019)

INTERNATIONAL DISPUTES
◆ Over half of Myanmar's population consists of diverse ethnic groups who have substantial numbers of kin in neighbouring

countries.

◆ Bangladesh struggles to accommodate 912,000 Rohingya, Myanmar Muslim minority from Rakhine State, living as refugees in Cox's Bazar.

◆ Myanmar border authorities are constructing a 200 km (124 mi) wire fence designed to deter illegal cross-border transit and tensions from the military build-up along border with Bangladesh in 2010.

◆ Bangladesh referred its maritime boundary claims with Myanmar and India to the International Tribunal on the Law of the Sea.

◆ Myanmarese forces attempting to dig in to the largely autonomous Shan State to rout local militias tied to the drug trade, prompts local residents to periodically flee into neighbouring Yunnan Province in China.

◆ Fencing along the India-Myanmar international border at Manipur's Moreh town is in progress to check illegal drug trafficking and movement of militants.

◆ Over 100,000 mostly Karen refugees and asylum seekers fleeing civil strife, political upheaval, and economic stagnation in Myanmar were living in remote camps in Thailand near the border as of May 2017.

DEFENCE

In 1948, Myanmar also know as Burma, became independent from Britain. The military ruled the country from 1962 until 2011 when a new government began ushering in a return to civilian rule. On 1 February 2021, Min Aung Hlaing – commander-in-chief of the country's armed forces – staged a coup d'état and took over the reigns of the country. The democratically elected members of Myanmar's ruling party, the National League for Democracy (NLD) were deposed by the Tatmadaw. President Win Myint and State Counsellor Aung San Suu Kyi were detained along with ministers and their deputies and members of Parliament. The coup led to a civil disobedient movement which included political parties that have rejected the military's offer to participate in the State Administration Council.

The Myanmar Armed Forces officially known as Tatmadaw is composed of the Army, the Navy and the Air Force. The Army has the largest service and has always received the lion's share of the country's defence budget. The Air Force was formed on 16 January 1947, while Myanmar was still under British rule. The Navy has expanded in recent years to provide blue water capability and external threat defence role in Myanmar's territorial waters.

ARMY (Tatmadaw Kyee)

Personnel: 300,000

Equipment

Category	Name	In Service
MBT	Type 59D	160
	Type 69/69II	130
	Type 63	100
	T-72	50
	PTL-02 6×6 tank destroyers	
APC/AIFV	Type 85	100
	Type 90	55
	BTR-3U	500
	MTLB IFV	26
Artillery	Type WP52 155mm	
	Soltam 155mm	36
	140mm	
	M1948 76mm	100
	M101 105mm	80
	NORA B-52 155mm	30
	Norinco SH1 155mm	
Mortar	81mm	
	120mm	
MRL	Type 81	20 units
	Type 90B 122mm	20 units
	Type 63 107mm	30
	M-1985 240mm	30
ATK weapon	Carl Gustaf	
SAM	HN-5A	
	SA-18 Manpads	
AA gun	Type 80 57mm	
	M1 40mm	10
	Tunguska gun SP systems	
	Type 74 37mm twin	

New Procurements/Upgrades

◆ Myanmar and Ukraine have reportedly signed a joint venture agreement to build a plant capable of manufacturing BTR-4U wheeled APCs and 2S1U Gvozdika self-propelled howitzers.

NAVY (Tatmadaw Yay)

Personnel: 18,000+

Equipment

Category	Name	In Service
Frigate	Kyansittha class	2
	Mahar Bandoola class	2
	Haung Zeya	1
Submarine	UMS Minye Theinkhathu	1
Corvette	Anawratha class	3

...continued

Category	Name	In Service
Patrol craft	Super-Dvora Mk III	2
	FAC	10
	55m missile FAC	5
	Houxin class (missile) FPB	6
	ex-Chinese Hainan	1
	coastal patrol boat	10
	INDAW class OPV	1
	PGM-type	12
	PB-90	3
	river patrol craft	40
	river gun boat	16
Landing craft	LCU	4
	ex-US LCM	10

New Procurements/Upgrades

◆ The Navy has commissioned India's submarine INS Sindhuvir called UMS Minye Theinkhathu.

◆ The Navy has also inducted a stealth fast attack craft and Yan Nyein Aung-class submarine chaser ship designed to perform anti-submarine warfare missions.

◆ The Navy plans to purchase an additional 4 Kyansittha class light frigates.

◆ A new series of 21m coastal patrol boats are under construction to replace the Hainans.

◆ Israel has reportedly agreed to provide the Myanmar Navy with four or more Super-Dvora Mk III gunboats.

The Myanmar Navy commissions UMS Minye Theinkhathu and some other vessels on 24 December 2020. Image credit: Tatmadaw Information Team

AIR FORCE (Tatmadaw Lay)

Personnel: 23,000

Equipment

Category	Name	In Service	On Order
Fighter	Su-30SM		6
	JF-17B2/17A/17B	7++5+2	
	NAMC A-5C	21	
	MiG-29B/SE/LB	31	
	F-7M	25	

...continued

Category	Name	In Service	On Order
Fighter	K-8	12+	
Transport/Trainer	Yak-130	12	
	Beechcraft 1900D	8	
	FH-227E	1	
	ATR 42	3	
	Y-8D	2	
	PC-6B turboporter	5+	
	CASA C295		2
	BN-2 Islander	2	
	PC-9	4	
	Super Galeb	4	
	Grob 120TP	20	
Helicopter	Mi-35	12	
	AS365 Dauphin 2	3	
	Bell UH-1	12	
	Mi-2	10	
	W-3 Sokol	12	
	Mi-17V	13	
SAM	SA-3		
	SA-6		
	TOR M1		
	KS-1A		

New Procurements/Upgrades

◆ Russia is reportedly assembling six Sukhoi SU-30SM fighter jets for Myanmar under a contract worth about US$204 million signed between the two nations in 2018.

◆ The Air Force has placed an order for two Airbus CASA C295 transport aircraft worth $38.6 million from the Royal Jordanian Air Force to replace the military's ageing fleet of Chinese-made Y-8s.

◆ The defence ministries of Russia and Myanmar have reached an agreement for the supply of Pantsir-S1 air defence systems. As part of the agreement, Myanmar will also receive Orlan-10E UAVs and radar stations.

Defence Expenditure

Total Defence Spending: $2.4 billion (2020), $2.2 billion (2019)

Defence spending in terms of GDP: 2.7% (2019)

Defence Production R&D

The defence industry in Myanmar is relatively underdeveloped and defence manufacturing is reliant on foreign technology transfers. Myanmar does not export any arms to foreign countries. The Tatmadaw's, Myanmar Defence Industries (DI), products include automatic rifles, machine guns, sub-machine guns, anti-aircraft guns, complete range of mortar and artillery ammunition, aircraft and anti aircraft ammunition, tank and anti-tank ammunition, bombs, grenades, anti-tank mines, anti-personnel mines such as the M14 pyrotechnics, commercial explosives and commercial products, and rockets. DI has produced new assault rifles and light machine-guns for the infantry. In recent times, Myanmar has developed the Chinese Sky 02A UAV's in-country as Yellow Cat A2 to perform basic surveillance missions. Heavy Industries were established with Ukrainian assistance mainly to assemble the BTR-3U fleet of the Myanmar Army. This industry has produced APC/IFV such as MAV 1, MAV 2, BAAC APCs and military trucks and jeeps for the defence forces.

Defence Procurement

Myanmar mainly import weapons from China, North Korea, India, Israel, the Philippines, Russia and Ukraine such as fighter jets, armoured fighting vehicles, warships, missiles and missile launchers. According to a report, China and Russia are the largest suppliers of arms to Myanmar over the last decade. China emerged as the largest supplier of defence equipment, accounting for 70% of the country's total defence imports, followed by Russia with 19% during 2012–2016.

CONTACT DETAILS
Ministry of Defence
Building 24, Nay Pyi Taw, Myanmar.
Tel: 067 - 404300, Fax: 067 - 404299
Email: admm.myanmar@mptmail.net.mm
adsom.myanmar@mptmail.net.mm
admmewg.myanmar@mptmail.net.mm

NEPAL
(Capital: Kathmandu)

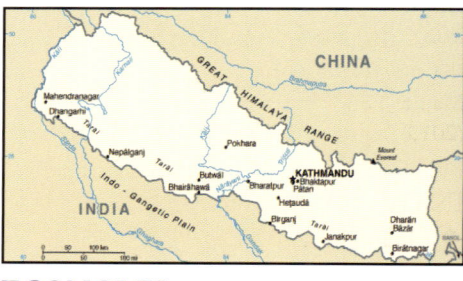

INTRODUCTION

Area: 147,181 sq km
Population: 30,424,878 (July 2021 est.)
Coastline: Landlocked
Maritime claims: None

KEY POLITICAL PERSONS

PRESIDENT & COMMANDER-IN-CHIEF: Bidya Devi Bhandari

PRIME MINISTER: Sher Bahadur Deuba

KEY DEFENCE PERSONS

DEFENCE MINISTER: Dr. Minendra Rijal

CHIEF OF ARMY STAFF: Gen. Prabhu Ram Sharma

ECONOMY

Nepal is a landlocked country located in South Asia. Nepal is among the poorest and least developed countries in the world, with almost one-quarter of its population living below the poverty line. Major contribution in the state GDP is from agriculture products. Additional challenges to Nepal's growth include its landlocked geographic location, inconsistent electricity supply, and underdeveloped transportation infrastructure. Agriculture employs 76% of the workforce, services 18% and manufacturing and craft-based industry 6%. Nepal has considerable scope for exploiting its potential in hydropower. Nepal and India signed trade and investment agreements in 2014 that will increase Nepal's hydropower potential. Massive earthquakes hit Nepal in the year 2015, which destroyed infrastructure and homes and set back economic development of the country. Nepal has ratified the South Asian Association for Regional Cooperation (SAARC) Agreement on a South Asian Free Trade Area (SAFTA). Nepal became the 147th member of the World Trade Organisation (WTO) in April 2004. Nepal also became a member of the BIMSTEC. In 2016, Nepal became one of few countries in the world with a single-country trade preference programme with the United States. The outbreak of the COVID-19 virus has created an abrupt and widespread economic shutdown in Nepal affecting almost all the sectors including tourism, trade and production linkages, supply, aviation, hospitality and health.

GDP (official exchange rate): $110.72 billion (2020), $113.08 billion (2019 est.)

Real Growth Rate (GDP): 1% (2020), 7.9% (2017 est.)

Industries: Tourism, carpets, textiles; small rice, jute, sugar, and oilseed mills; cigarettes, cement and brick production

Total Exports: $1.79 billion (2020 est.), $2.73 billion (2019 est.)

Export Commodities: Palm oil, clothing and apparel, carpets, soybean oil, flavored water (2019)

Major Markets: India 68%, United States 10% (2019)

Total Imports: $10.68 billion (2020 est.), $13.83 billion (2019 est.)

Import Commodities: Refined petroleum, iron, broadcasting equipment, natural gas, rice (2019)

Major Suppliers: India 70%, China 15% (2019)

INTERNATIONAL DISPUTES

◆ Joint Border Commission continues to work on contested sections of boundary with India, including the 400 square kilometre dispute over the source of the Kalapani river.

◆ India has instituted a stricter border regime to restrict transit of Maoist insurgents and illegal cross-border activities.

NETHERLANDS
(Capital: Amsterdam)

INTRODUCTION

Area: 41,543 sq km
Population: 17,337,403 (July 2021 est.)
Coastline: 451 km
Maritime claims: Territorial sea: 12 nm
Contiguous zone: 24 nm

DEFENCE

ARMY
Personnel: 95,000
Equipment

Category	Name	In Service
APC/ MICV/IFV	BTR-70	100+
	Indian Mine Protected Vehicle/APC	50+
	Ferret Armoured Car	30+
Artillery	105 mm artillery pack	10
	3.7 inch Mountain Howitzer	100
	105 mm (Indian Field Gun)	100
	81 mm & 120mm mortar	1000+
AA Gun	94 mm QF 3.7 inch AA gun	10
	14.5 mm Type 56 AD Guns	20+
	40 mm L60 AD Guns	10

New Procurements/ Upgrades
No major procurement plans are under consideration at present.

Nepal became a member of the United Nations in 1955 and since then, has been an active participant of most UN peace operations. The participation of the Nepali Army in UN peace support operations spans a period of over a half century covering some 43 UN missions, in which over 1,28,588 personnel have participated.

Nepalese Army Air Service
Personnel: 500

Category	Name	In Service
Aircraft (Trainer/ Transport)	M28 Sky truck	2
	BN-2T islander	2
	HS-748	1
Helicopter	Mi-17	5
	HAL Lancer	2
	HAL Dhruv	2+
	HAL Chetak	3
	HAL Cheetah	2
Helicopter (VIP Transport)	Super Puma (VIP)	1

New Procurements/ Upgrades
No major procurement plans are under consideration at present.

Defence Expenditure
Total defence spending: $400 million (approx.)
Estimated defence spending in terms of GDP: 1.40% (2020 est.)
Major foreign suppliers: India, Russia, China, United States, North Korea, Bangladesh, Sri Lanka, Thailand, Pakistan, Israel.

Defence Production and R&D
Nepal does not possess any defence R&D base. There are certain facility for repair and maintenance of the combat vehicles.

Defence Procurement
According to news report in Press Trust of India, China has pledged to provide assistance of RMB 150 million to the Nepalese Army over a period of five years for humanitarian and disaster relief equipment. The Chinese assistance - equivalent to Nepalese Rs 2.5 billion - was announced during Nepal Deputy Prime Minister and Defence Minister Ishwor Pokhrel's visit to China. With the latest aid, China's financial support to the Nepalese Army has increased by 50 per cent. Last year, China had extended RMB 100 million for humanitarian and disaster relief equipment to Nepal's Army. China has hiked defence assistance to the Nepalese Army in recent years.

CONTACT DETAILS
Ministry of Defence
Singha Durbar, Kathmandu, Nepal.
Phone: +977-1-4211289
Fax: 977-1- 4211294,
E-mail: info@mod.gov.np
www.mod.gov.np

KEY POLITICAL PERSONS

HEAD OF STATE:
King Willem-Alexander

PRIME MINISTER:
Mark Rutte

KEY DEFENCE PERSONS

DEFENCE MINISTER:
Henk Kamp

CHIEF OF DEFENCE: Gen. Onno Eichelsheim

COMMANDER OF ARMY: Lt. Gen. Martin Wijnen

COMMANDER OF NAVY: Vice Adm. René Tas

COMMANDER OF AIR FORCE: Lt. Gen. Dennis Luyt

ECONOMY

The Netherlands has the 6th largest economy in the European Union and 17th largest economy in the world, and ranks 10th in GDP (nominal) per capita. The Netherlands is part of the euro zone. The Netherlands is the fifth-most competitive economy in the world, according to the World Economic Forum's Global Competitiveness Report. The country is a founding member of the European Union, the OECD and the World Trade Organisation. Netherlands has a prosperous and open economy, which depends heavily on foreign trade. The Netherlands is part of the Eurozone, and as such, its monetary policy is controlled by the European Central Bank. The Netherlands continues to be one of the leading European nations for attracting foreign direct investment and is one of the five largest investors in the United States. The government's policy plans to increase demand for workers in the public and private sector, forecasting a further decline in the unemployment rate, which hit 4.8% in 2017. The fiscal policy by the new government in the 2018-2021 plans for increases in government consumption and public investment. The United States is the largest foreign investor in the Netherlands and has its largest bilateral trade surplus in the world with this country (USD24 billion in 2015). The Netherlands belongs to a number of the same international organisations, including the United Nations, North Atlantic Treaty Organisation, Euro-Atlantic Partnership Council, Organisation for Security and Cooperation in Europe, Organisation for Economic Cooperation and Development, International Monetary Fund, World Bank, and World Trade Organisation. The Netherlands is an observer to the Organisation of American States. Due to the COVID-19 pandemic restrictions, the Dutch economy has suffered an unprecedented 8-8.5% downfall in the second quarter in 2020 affecting spending, exports and investments. Corona has caused unprecedented economic damage to the country. According to De Nederlandsche Bank, the Dutch economy is expected to recover strongly and rapidly, starting in the second quarter of 2021. GDP is expected to have grown by 3.0% in 2021, 3.7% in 2022 and 1.9% in 2023.

GDP (official exchange rate): $945.48 billion (2020), $982.22 billion (2019 est.)

Real Growth Rate (GDP): 1.63% (2019 est.), 2.32% (2018 est.)

Industries: Agro-industries, metal and engineering products, electrical machinery and equipment, chemicals, petroleum, construction, microelectronics, fishing

Oil - proved reserves: 81.13 million bbl (1 January 2018 est.)

Natural gas - proved reserves: 801.4 billion cu m (1 January 2018 est.)

Total Exports: $719.78 billion (2020 est.), $755.77 billion (2019 est.)

Export Commodities: Refined petroleum, packaged medicines, broadcasting equipment, photography equipment, computers (2019)

Major Markets: Germany 20%, Belgium 12%, United Kingdom 9%, France 7%, United States 5% (2019)

Total Imports: $622.66 billion (2020 est.), $661.18 billion (2019 est.)

Import Commodities: Crude petroleum, refined petroleum, broadcasting equipment, computers, cars (2019)

Major Suppliers: Germany 15%, China 11%, Belgium 9%, United States 8%, Russia 7%, United Kingdom 5% (2019)

INTERNATIONAL DISPUTES

Netherlands has no known international disputes.

DEFENCE

ARMY

Personnel: 15,000

Equipment

Category	Name	In Service
MBT	Leopard 2A6	15+
APC/MICV/IFV	CV9035 MkIII	150
	PzH 2000	50
	XA-188	50+
	Luchtmobiel Speciaal Voertuig MWV	100+
	Bushmaster	50+
	Fennek	300+
	Boxer AFV	200
Artillery	155 mm. SP PzH-2000	50+
Mortar	81 mm.	40
	120 mm.	100+
Anti-Tank GW	SPIKE launchers	300
ATK Weapon	SRAT	250+
	VSRAT	700+
	AT4	
SAM	FIM-92 Stinger	300+
	NASAMS II	
	MIM-104 Patriot	
UAV	ScanEagle, RQ-11 Raven	

New Procurements/ Upgrades

◆ The US State Department has approved a possible Foreign Military Sale to the Government of the Netherlands of 199 Excalibur Increment IB M982Al tactical projectiles and related equipment for an estimated cost of USD40.55 million.

NAVY

Personnel: 7,500

Equipment

Category	Name	In Service
Submarine	Walrus Class	4
Frigate	De Zeven Provincien Class	4
	Karel Doorman Class	2
Patrol Vessel	Holland class	4
Mine Warfare Force	Alkmaar Class Mine-hunters	10
Amphibious Force	Rotterdam Class LPDs	2
	LCVP	10+
	LCU	5
Support Vessel	Amsterdam Class	1
	Karel Doorman	1
	Zuiderkruis Class	2
Helicopter	NH-90	

New Procurements/ Upgrades

◆ Thyssen Krupp Marine Systems is ready to exclusively share and transfer our Submarine Key Technology in accordance with the Dutch requirements with regard to the full scope of Industrial Participation. Including knowledge institutes like TNO, Marin and NLR, aim to explore all possible synergies with the Dutch Triple Helix and its submarine knowledge base. HDW Class Submarines can be built entirely in the Netherlands with the support of Thyssen Krupp Marine Systems. Building the submarines in Den Helder is a perfect preparation for sustaining them during their whole life-cycle. It resembles a good public-private partnership and creates opportunities for transfer of technology.

◆ The US State Department has approved a possible Foreign Military Sale to the Netherlands of 16 MK-48 Mod 7 Advanced Technology (AT) torpedo conversion kits and related equipment for an estimated cost of USD85 million.

◆ The Royal Netherlands Navy has ordered 8 Thales radars. The Royal Netherlands Navy already operates the latest generation of Thales 4D AESA radars on the majority of its vessels. The NS100 on the Royal Netherlands Navy's other LPD, HNLMS Rotterdam, will be updated, so that the radars on both LPDs will be identical. The same contract specifies the delivery of Scout Mk3 surveillance radars to be installed on HNLMS Johan de Witt and on the Combat Support Ship along with a Thales IFF system.

◆ GE to provide electric propulsion systems to Royal Netherlands Navy new Combat Support Ship. Damen Schelde Naval Shipbuilding, in partnership with GE, will deliver a new Combat Support Ship to the Royal Netherlands Navy. GE's Power Conversion business have signed a contract with Damen Schelde Naval Shipbuilding (DSNS) to deliver an energy management and electric propulsion package intended for the new Combat Support Ship (CSS) in use at Royal Netherlands Navy.

AIR FORCE

Personnel: 6,500

Equipment

Category	Name	In Service
Fighters/ attack/ Reconnaissance	F-35A Lightning II	8+ (more on order)
	F-16AM/BM Fighting Falcon	50+
Transport/ Tanker	KDC-10	2
	A330 MRTT	2+
	Gulfstream IV	1
	C-130/C-130H-30 Hercules	4
	C-17 Globemaster III	3 (shared with NATO)
Trainer	PC-7 Turbo Trainer	10+
	F-16 MLU	10+
Helicopter	CH-47D, CH-47F Chinook	15+
	AS 352U2 Cougar	15+
	SA316B Alouette III	4
	AH-64D Apache	20+
	Agusta-Bell 412	3
	Westland Lynx	20+
	NH-90	20
UAV	MQ-9 Reaper	4
	ScanEagle	10+
	RQ-11 Raven	70+

New Procurements/ Upgrades

◆ The US State Department has approved a possible Foreign Military Sale to the Government of the Netherlands of AH-64 Pilot Training and Logistics Support and related equipment for an estimated cost of USD190 million.

◆ The US State Department has approved a possible Foreign Military Sale to the Government of the Netherlands of 16 AIM-120C-8 Advanced Medium Range Air-to-Air Missiles (AMRAAM) and related equipment for an estimated cost of USD39 million.

◆ The Netherlands will buy the remaining 3 F-35 fighter aircraft as per the Defence Ministry, thus confirming the Dutch purchase of at least 37 aircraft. The full operational capability of the Dutch F-35 fleet is planned for 2024.

◆ The US State Department approved a possible Foreign Military Sale to the Netherlands of defence articles and services in support of continuation of a Continental United States (CONUS) based Royal Netherlands Air Force F-16 Formal Training Unit for an estimated cost of USD 110 million.

◆ The US State Department approved a possible Foreign Military Sale to the Netherlands of items and services to support the upgrade/remanufacture of AH-64D Block II Apache Attack Helicopters to the AH-64E configuration for an estimated cost of USD 1.191 billion.

◆ The Netherlands Ministry of Defence has signed an agreement with the United States of America for the procurement of 4 MQ-9 Reapers. The unmanned aircraft are expected to arrive in the Netherlands from mid-2020.

The Netherlands participates in the NATO "smart defence" initiative, including missile defence. The Netherlands is a military contributor to the Counter-ISIL Coalition, and co-chair of the Coalition's Foreign Terrorist Fighters Working Group. The Netherlands supports counterterrorism efforts with leadership, personnel, and materiel.

Defence Expenditure

Total defence spending: $14 billion (2020 approx.)

Estimated defence spending in terms of GDP: 1.49% of GDP (2020 est.), 1.35% of GDP (2019)

Year	USD (Millions)
2014	10,349
2015	8,673
2016	9,112
2017	9,643
2018	11,172
2019*	12,092
2020*	13,125
2021*	14,378

(*Figures for 2020 and 2021 are estimates.) Source: Defence Expenditure of NATO Countries (2014-2021), NATO Press Release.

The Dutch defence and security industry sells military goods, such as ships and radar equipment, to the Ministry of Defence. It also exports goods worth approximately € 1.5 billion every year. The Commissariat for Military Production (CMP) helps the companies concerned by putting them in touch with potential buyers. The CMP is part of the Ministry of Economic Affairs and Climate Policy. The government also promotes the participation of Dutch companies in international cooperation programmes to develop or purchase military materiel.

Defence Production and R&D

Despite its relatively small size, the Dutch defence industry supplied the majority of defence items to the Netherlands. The Netherlands' defence industrial base is best described as one that supports major projects. The Industrial Marketing Association of The Netherlands (NIID) is an independent group financed by Dutch industry and aims at promoting optimal participation of Dutch industry in the field of defence production for both national and foreign forces. NIID operates in close liaison with the Ministeries van Defensie en Economische Zaken (Ministries of Defence-MOD, and Economic Affairs-MEA). They also assist foreign companies with offset obligations in finding potential partners in The Netherlands. NIID also assists small and medium sized Dutch firms in obtaining defence orders, especially as subcontractors. OGMA and the Netherlands Aerospace Centre signed a Memorandum of Understanding (MoU), as part of the State Visit of King Willem-Alexander and Queen Maxima of the Netherlands. The main purpose of this MoU is to provide for a cooperative relationship between the two parties regarding research and development projects, and to bring those parties to work together in technical cooperation for the development and improvement of aeronautical maintenance, repair and overhaul technologies.

Defence Procurement

The Defence Materiel Organisation (DMO) is responsible for all materiel within the Defence organisation: from procurement and major maintenance to disposal. The DMO also establishes internal materiel policy. The DMO works closely with the Netherlands Organisation for Applied Scientific Research (TNO), educational institutions and national and international industry on new technological developments. In addition, the DMO is in contact with similar materiel organisations of foreign ministries of defence, in order to enable international coordination. The Directorate of Materiel Policy is the only DMO unit that is part of the Central Staff of the Ministry of Defence. Its tasks include developing materiel logistics policy and policy in respect of scientific research and development (R&D) and supporting the National Armaments Director (NAD). Contributing to the administrative and political decision-making process concerning major materiel projects, managing the materiel logistics process and R&D and supporting the administrative and political leadership in those areas are also among the directorate's tasks. The Directorate of Projects & Procurement (DP&V) is responsible for the process of providing materiel, which consists of procurement and project management. The Directorate manages all procurement activities for the armed forces at a functional level and issues strict guidelines to all procurers. It obtains new materiel and/or services on a project basis and ensures that materiel is maintained by carrying out large-scale and/or complex modification programmes, also on a project basis. The directorate also negotiates contracts for the disposal of surplus Defence goods. The Directorate of Weapon Systems is responsible for ensuring high-quality materiel for the entire armed forces during all stages of its life cycle in a cost-effective way. This is achieved by setting standards in weapon systems management and by working on a project basis. The services of the required in-house, high-quality expertise base are also rendered to the Directorate of Projects & Procurement, the Directorate of Logistic Agencies and the external clients of the Directorate of Weapon Systems.

CONTACT DETAILS

Ministry of Defence
PO Box 20701
NL-2500 ES's-Gravenhage
Netherlands

Ministry of Defence, Press and Information Service
Kalvermarkt 38, PO Box 20701
NL-2500 ES's-Gravenhage
Tel: (+31 70) 318 88 88
Fax: (+31 70) 318 78 88
E-mail: persvoorlichting@mindef.nl
www.mindef.nl

National Agency for Aerospace Programmes - NIVR
PO Box 35, NL-2600 AA Delft
Netherlands

Defence Materiel Organisation
Van der Burchlaan 31,
Frederik Barracks, building 35,
A-L towers, P.O. Box 90822
2509 LV The Hague, Netherlands

Directorate of Materiel Policy
Tel: +31 (0) 70-3161551
Fax: +31 (0)70-3161553

Directorate of Projects & Procurement
Tel: +31 (0)70-3168079
Fax: +31 (0)70-3162577

Directorate of Weapon Systems
Tel: +31 (0)70-3162610
Fax: +31 (0)70-3166810

Directorate of Logistic Agencies
Tel: +31 (0) 70-3164474
Fax: +31 (0) 70-3164275

The ships of Standing NATO Maritime Group (SNMG) 1 transit in formation for a photo exercise. From left, Portuguese frigate NRP Alvares Cabral (F331), Canadian frigate HMCS Toronto (FFH 333), American guided-missile cruiser USS Normandy (CG 60), German replenishment tanker FGS Spessart (A1442), Dutch frigate HNLMS Evertsen (F805), and Danish corvette HDMS Olfert Fischer (F355). Image Credit: US Navy

NEW ZEALAND
(Capital: Wellington)

INTRODUCTION
Area: 267,710 sq km
Population: 4,991,442 (July 2021 est.)
Coastline: 15,134 km
Maritime claims: Territorial sea: 12 nm
Contiguous zone: 24 nm
Exclusive Economic Zone: 200 nm
Continental shelf: 200 nm or to the edge of the continental margin

KEY POLITICAL PERSONS

HEAD OF STATE: Queen Elizabeth II

GOVERNOR GENERAL & COMMANDER-IN-CHIEF: Dame Cindy Kiro

PRIME MINISTER: Jacinda Ardern

KEY DEFENCE PERSONS

DEFENCE MINISTER: Peeni Henare

CHIEF OF THE DEFENCE FORCE: Air Marshal Kevin R. Short

CHIEF OF ARMY: Maj. Gen. John Boswell

CHIEF OF NAVY: Rear Adm. David Proctor

CHIEF OF AIR FORCE: Air Vice-Marshal Andrew Clark

COMMANDER JOINT FORCES NZ: Rear Adm. James Gilmour

ECONOMY

According to the New Zealand's Treasury, the Treasury forecasts economic growth of about 3.0 per cent per year on average over the period to June 2022. The New Zealand economy is forecast to grow at a rate faster than that expected for our major trading partners. Unemployment is expected to remain steady over 2018 before falling to 4.1 per cent in late 2019, in line with the Government's target of reducing the unemployment rate to 4.0 per cent by the end of this parliamentary term. The most recent month-end financial results show strong tax revenue which is expected to persist for the remainder of the current year and into the future. As a percentage of GDP, core Crown expenses are forecast to gradually fall to 28.0 per cent in 2022, below the historical average of around 30.0 per cent of GDP. Improving the Government's fiscal position makes New Zealand more resilient to future economic shocks and natural disasters. It helps to deal with the costs associated with future

challenges such as an ageing population. The United States is New Zealand's second most important investment partner, after Australia. The United States was the second largest source of foreign investment into New Zealand, accounting for almost USD5.5 billion in investment in 2017. New Zealand belongs to a number of the international organisations, including the United Nations, Organization for Economic Cooperation and Development, Asia-Pacific Economic Cooperation forum, ASEAN Regional Forum, International Monetary Fund, World Bank, and World Trade Organisation. New Zealand also belongs to the Pacific Islands Forum, of which the United States is a Dialogue Partner. China is also one of New Zealand's most important trading partners. The Treasury, which is the Government's lead economic and financial adviser, is supporting the Govt.'s COVID-19 economic response by helping workers, businesses and communities from the impacts of pandemic restrictions and lockdown.

GDP (official exchange rate): $215.6 billion (2020), $213.5 billion (2019 est.)

Real Growth Rate (GDP): 2.22% (2019 est.), 3.22% (2018 est.)

Industries: Agriculture, forestry, fishing, logs and wood articles, manufacturing, mining, construction, financial services, real estate services, tourism

Oil - proved reserves: 51.8 million bbl (1 January 2018 est.)

Natural gas - proved reserves: 33.7 billion cu m (1 January 2018 est.)

Total Exports: $50.43 billion (2020 est.), $57.16 billion (2019 est.)

Export Commodities: Dairy products, sheep/goat meats, lumber, beef products, fresh fruits (2019)

Major Markets: China 28%, Australia 14%, United States 9%, Japan 6% (2019)

Total Imports: $47.86 billion (2020 est.), $57.75 billion (2019 est.)

Import Commodities: Cars, crude petroleum, refined petroleum, delivery trucks, gas turbines (2019)

Major Suppliers: China 18%, Australia 15%, United States 9%, Japan 6%, Germany 5% (2019)

INTERNATIONAL DISPUTES

◆ Asserts a territorial claim in Antarctica (Ross Dependency).

DEFENCE
ARMY

Personnel: 4,170 (1,841 reserve)

Equipment

Category	Name	In Service
APC/MICV/IFV	NZ Light Armoured Vehicle (NZLAV)	80+
	Infantry Mobility Vehicle (IMV)	50+
	Light Obstacle Blade Vehicle (LOB)	7
	Pinzgauer High Mobility ATV	250+
	Recovery Vehicle (LAV-R)	3
Artillery	105 mm. L-118	20+
Mortar	81 mm.	50
Anti-Tank GW	Javelin	20+
Recoilless Rifle	84 mm. Carl Gustav	50+
SAM	Mistral	10

New Procurements/ Upgrades

◆ The Coalition Government has approved the purchase of a fleet of Bushmaster vehicles to replace the New Zealand Army's armoured Pinzgauers, Defence Minister Ron Mark has announced. The new fleet of 43 Australian-designed and built Bushmaster NZ5.5 will provide better protection for personnel and improved carrying capacity. Funding of $102.9 million will deliver the vehicles, along with training, a desk top simulator, support equipment and infrastructure upgrades at Linton Camp.

NAVY

Personnel: 2,343 (535 reserve)

Equipment

Category	Name	In Service
Frigate	Anzac class	2
Patrol Vessel	Protector class OPV	2
	Protector class Inshore	2+
Logistics and Support	HMNZS Canterbury	1
	HMNZS Endeavour	1
Survey Vessel	HMNZS Resolution	1

Naval Aviation

Category	Name	In Service
Helicopter	SH-2G Super Seasprite	5

New Procurements/ Upgrades

No major procurement plans are under consideration at present.

AIR FORCE

Personnel: 2,586 (317 reserve)

Equipment

Category	Name	In Service
Patrol aircraft	Lockheed P-3K Orion	5+
Transport/Tanker	Boeing 757-200	2
	Lockheed C-130H Hercules	5
Helicopter	Kaman SH-2G	5+
	AW109	5
Trainer	Super King Air	4
	T-6 Texan II	5+

New Procurements/ Upgrades

◆ The US State Department has approved a possible Foreign Military Sale to New Zealand of five C-130J aircraft and related equipment for an estimated cost of USD1.4 billion. This purchase also includes sensors and performance improvements that will assist New Zealand during extensive maritime surveillance and reconnaissance as well as improve its search and rescue capability.

◆ he US State Department has approved a possible Foreign Military Sale to New Zealand for P-8A aircraft and associated support. The estimated cost is USD1.46 billion. New Zealand plans to purchase four Boeing P-8A Poseidon maritime patrol aircraft to replace the aging six P-3K2 Orion maritime patrol aircraft that have been in operation since the 1960s. The current Orion fleet will reach the end of their expected operational life in 2025. The new P-8As, training systems, infrastructure and introduction into service costs will total USD2.346 billion. They will be delivered and begin operations from 2023, Defence Minister Hon Ron Mark said in a statement. No. 5 Squadron, which currently operates the Orions, will shift from Whenuapai to Ohakea air force base to operate the P-8As.

◆ CAE announced that it officially handed over a CAE 700MR Series NH90 flight training device to the New Zealand Defence Force (NZDF) and Royal New Zealand Air Force (RNZAF). This advanced NH90 simulator means Royal New Zealand NH90 aircrews can train safely and cost-effectively in New Zealand.

There are currently around 250 NZDF personnel serving on 11 operations overseas

Defence Expenditure

Total defence spending: $4 billion (2020 approx.)

Estimated defence spending in terms of GDP: 1.5% of GDP (2020), 1.5% of GDP (2019)

Foreign suppliers: United States and European Union.

Summary Tables for the Estimates of Appropriations 2021/22:

Appropriations for Output Expenses

Vote	2020/2021		2021/2022		
	Final Budgeted ($000)	EstimatedActual ($000)	Departmental Transactions Budget ($000)	Non-Departmental Transactions Budget ($000)	Total Budget ($000)
Defence	14,185	13,839	24,832	-	24,832
Defence Force	2,352,288	2,317,074	2,371,612	746	2,372,358

(Source: Budget 2021. The Treasury, Govt. of New Zealand. Updated 20 May 2021.)

Appropriations for Other Expenses

Vote	2020/2021		2021/2022		
	Final Budgeted ($000)	Estimated Actual ($000)	Departmental Transactions Budget ($000)	Non-Departmental Transactions Budget ($000)	Total Budget ($000)
Defence Force	150,722	143,462	-	62,028	62,028

(Source: Budget 2021. The Treasury, Govt. of New Zealand. Updated 20 May 2021.)

Appropriations for Capital Expenditure

Vote	2020/2021		2021/2022		
	Final Budgeted ($000)	Estimated Actual ($000)	Departmental Transactions Budget ($000)	Non-Departmental Transactions Budget ($000)	Total Budget ($000)
Defence	696,545	696,225	350	-	350
Defence Force	856,395	856,395	1,164,711	-	1,164,711

(Source: Budget 2021. The Treasury, Govt. of New Zealand. Updated 20 May 2021.)

Total Appropriations for Each Vote

Vote	2020/2021		2021/2022		
	Final Budgeted ($000)	Estimated Actual ($000)	Departmental Transactions Budget ($000)	Non-Departmental Transactions Budget ($000)	Total Budget ($000)
Defence	726,522	720,492	25,182	875,354	900,536
Defence Force	4,023,041	3,967,081	4,223,864	62,774	4,286,638

(Source: Budget 2020. The Treasury, Govt. of New Zealand. Updated 14 May 2020.)

Defence Production and R&D

The New Zealand defence and homeland security industry comprises over 250 companies with the capability and capacity to participate in international defence and security markets. New Zealand companies have major defence acquisition and maintenance contracts with Australia, Singapore, the United Kingdom and the United States, and also export to China, Southeast Asia, South America and Europe. Australia is the most significant market destination, accounting for almost half of all exports. The ANZAC frigates project – a joint venture between the governments of New Zealand and Australia signed in 1989 – saw New Zealand companies provide more than USD800 million of work to construct 10 frigates. New Zealand Trade and Enterprise estimates that the value of New Zealand exports of defence and security and services is USD 200 to USD 250 million per annum. Defence products and services range from VT-Fitzroy servicing of the French Navy's Light Transport Ship Jacques Cartier, to Rakon's quart crystal components. New Zealand's defence and security industry was confirmed by the United States Defence Director Ted Glum in 2009 to be a secure supply chain partner.

Industry contacts

The New Zealand Defence Industry Association has a broad mandate to support New Zealand companies operating in the defence and homeland security sector (www.nzdia.co.nz).

Defence Procurement

NZ DEFENCE Procurement has three aspects:

◆ Capital Equipment: This is procured by the Ministry of Defence.

◆ Minor Capital Equipment: Capital equipment procured by the NZDF. It is generally items or projects below $NZ 7 million.

◆ Operating Requirements: These are day to day needs to keep the NZDF, its equipment and its people functioning. It includes basic necessities such as fuel, food, clothing etc, and a wide range of other specialist items to meet particular needs.

According to the Ministry of Defence, New Zealand, the Defence White Paper 2016 signalled investment of around $20 billion over the next 15 years in new capability and infrastructure for the Defence Force. This includes replacing our aged C-130 Hercules, P-3 Orions and Boeing 757 aircraft, ANZAC frigates, and investment in associated infrastructure for the Defence Force.

The New Zealand Defence Force (NZDF) purchases:

◆ Assets with a life cost of under $15 million

◆ Every day goods and services, such as clothing, food, medical gear and supplies

◆ Products and services to help run the Defence Force's camps and bases.

> **CONTACT DETAILS**
> **Ministry of Defence**
> Defence House
> 34 Bowen Street, Pipitea,
> Wellington 6011, New Zealand
> www.defence.govt.nz
>
> PHONE: +64 4 496 0999
> FAX: +64 4 496 0859
>
> ENQUIRIES: info@defence.govt.nz
> Postal: Ministry of Defence, PO Box 12703
> Molesworth Street,
> Wellington 6144 New Zealand
>
> New Zealand Defence Force
> Defence House, 2-12 Aitken St, Wellington
> +64 4 496 0999
> www.nzdf.mil.nz

HMNZS Te Kaha (front) forms part of the Navy fleet concentration in the Cook Strait. Image Credit: HMNZS Te Kaha, New Zealand Defence Force from Wellington, New Zealand

NIGER
(Capital: Niamey)

INTRODUCTION
Area: 1.267 million sq km
Population: 23,605,767 (July 2021 est.)
Coastline: 0 km (Landlocked)
Maritime claims: None

KEY POLITICAL PERSONS

PRESIDENT & COMMANDER-IN-CHIEF:
Mohamed Bazoum

PRIME MINISTER:
Ouhoumoudou Mahamadou

KEY DEFENCE PERSONS

DEFENCE MINISTER:
Alkassoum Indatou

ARMED FORCES CHIEF OF STAFF:
Gen. Salifou Modi

CHIEF OF ARMY: Brig. Gen. Seidou Bague

ECONOMY

Niger is a landlocked, sub-Saharan nation, whose economy centres on subsistence crops, livestock, and some of the world's largest uranium deposits. Agriculture contributes nearly 40% of GDP and provides livelihood for most of the population. The UN ranked Niger as the second least developed country in the world in 2016 due to multiple factors such as food insecurity, lack of industry, high population growth, a weak educational sector, and few prospects for work outside of subsistence farming and herding. Since 2011, public debt has increased in part from a large loan financing a new uranium mine. The government relies on foreign donor resources for a large portion of its fiscal budget. The economy in recent years has been hurt by terrorist activity and kidnappings near its uranium mines and instability in Mali, and concerns about security have boosted fiscal spending on defence. Future growth may be sustained by exploitation of oil, gold, coal, and other mineral resources. Niger has sizable reserves of oil and oil production. Food insecurity and drought remain perennial problems for Niger, and the government plans to invest more in the agriculture sector, most notably irrigation. Formal private sector investment needed for economic diversification and growth remains a challenge, given the country's limited domestic markets, access to credit, and competitiveness. To mitigate the deep crisis arisen due to the deadly Coronavirus pandemic, the World Bank and IMF have provided financial aid to Niger to improve its healthcare system and bolster economic recovery.

GDP (official exchange rate): $12.92 billion (2019 est.)

Real Growth Rate (GDP): 4.9% (2017 est.); 4.9% (2016 est.)

Industries: Uranium mining, cement, brick, soap, textiles, food processing, chemicals, slaughterhouses

Total Exports: $1.52 billion (2018 est.); $1.46 billion (2017 est.)

Export Commodities: Gold, sesame seeds, uranium, natural gas, refined petroleum (2019)

Major Markets: United Arab Emirates 54%, China 25%, France 7%, Pakistan 5% (2019)

Total Imports: $2.99 billion (2018 est.); $2.88 billion (2017 est.)

Import Commodities: Rice, packaged medicines, palm oil, cars, cement (2019)

Major Suppliers: China 19%, France 9%, United Arab Emirates 7%, Cote d'Ivoire 6%, India 6%, Nigeria 5%, Togo 5%, Turkey 5% (2019)

INTERNATIONAL DISPUTES

◆ Libya claims about 25,000 sq km in a currently dormant dispute in the Tommo region.

◆ The location of the Benin-Niger-Nigeria tri-point is unresolved.

◆ Only Nigeria and Cameroon have heeded the Lake Chad Commission's admonition to ratify the delimitation treaty that also includes the Chad-Niger and Niger-Nigeria boundaries.

DEFENCE

ARMY
Personnel: 5,000+

Equipment

Category	Name	In Service
Armoured Car/ APC	AML-60	12
	AML-90	88
	M-3	14
Mortar	60mm	
	81mm	
	120mm	
RCL	M20 75mm	6
	106mm	6
AA gun	20mm	30+

New Procurements/ Upgrades
No major procurement plans are under consideration at present.

AIR FORCE
Personnel: 300

Equipment

Category	Name	In Service
Fighter	Su-25	2
Transport/ Liaison/ Utility	C130H	1
	Do-28D	1
	Do-228	1
	Boeing 737-200 (VIP)	1
	ULM TETRA	3
	Cessna	2

...continued

Category	Name	In Service
Helicopter	SA341F Gazelle (armed)	3

New Procurements/ Upgrades
No major procurement plans are under consideration at present.

Defence Expenditure
Estimated defence spending in terms of GDP: 10%

(Annual defence spending by Niger has increased significantly in recent times as the Government has tried to build up defences against several militant and terror groups emanating from neighbouring countries, including Mali and Nigeria.)

Defence Production and R&D
Niger does not undertake any defence production activities.

Defence Procurement
Recent military procurements by Niger remain obscure as no official information is available on the same.

CONTACT DETAILS
Ministry of Defence
P.O. Box 626 , Niamey, Niger

NIGERIA
(Capital: Abuja)

INTRODUCTION
Area: 923,768 sq km
Population: 219,463,862 (July 2021 est.)
Coastline: 853 km
Maritime claims: Territorial sea: 12 nm
Exclusive Economic Zone: 200 nm
Continental shelf: 200 m depth or to the depth of exploitation

KEY POLITICAL PERSONS

PRESIDENT & COMMANDER-IN-CHIEF: Muhammadu Buhari

VICE PRESIDENT: Yemi Osinbajo

KEY DEFENCE PERSONS

DEFENCE MINISTER: Maj. Gen.(retd) Bashir Salihi Magashi

CHIEF OF DEFENCE STAFF: Gen. Leo Irabor

CHIEF OF ARMY STAFF: Lt. Gen. Farouk Yahaya

CHIEF OF NAVAL STAFF: Vice Adm. A Z Gambo

CHIEF OF AIR STAFF: Air Marshal Isiaka Oladayo Amao

ECONOMY
Oil-rich Nigeria, long hobbled by political instability, corruption, inadequate infrastructure, and poor macroeconomic management, has undertaken several reform measures over the past decade. As a result, the country has witnessed strong economic growth. While it still remains overtly dependent on the capital-intensive oil sector, which provides 95% of foreign exchange earnings and about 80% of budgetary revenues, the present Government has taken initiatives to diversify the economy. It is taking steps towards developing stronger public-private partnerships for building up national infrastructure. Economic diversification and strong growth, however, have not translated

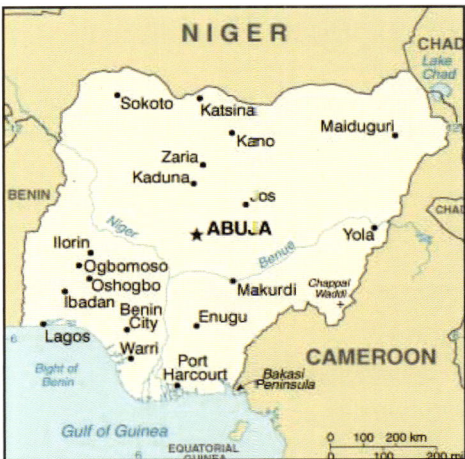

into a significant decline in poverty levels; over 62% of Nigeria's over 180 million people still live in extreme poverty. Following an April 2014 statistical "rebasing" exercise, Nigeria emerged as Africa's largest economy, with 2015 GDP crossing $1 trillion figure. However, it entered a recession in 2016 partly because of lower oil prices in international market. GDP growth turned positive in 2017 as oil prices recovered and output stabilized.

In the wake of the Covid-19 pandemic, the economic outlook for Nigeria remains fragile. The International Monetary Fund (IMF) projected a GDP contraction of 5.4% in 2020 – the country's biggest in nearly 40 years. Economic recovery would remain slow in 2021.

GDP (official exchange rate): $475.06 billion (2019 est.)
Real Growth Rate (GDP): 0.8% (2017 est.); -1.6% (2016 est.)
Industries: Crude oil, coal, tin, columbite; rubber products, wood; hides and skins, textiles, cement and other construction materials, food products, footwear, chemicals, fertilizer, printing, ceramics, steel
Crude Oil - Proved Reserves: 37.45 billion bbl (1 January 2018 est.)
Natural Gas - Proved Reserves: 5.475 trillion cu m (1 January 2018 est.)
Total Exports: $34.54 billion (2020 est.); $62.53 billion (2019 est.)
Export Commodities: Crude petroleum,

natural gas, scrap vessels, flexible metal tubing, cocoa beans (2019)

Major Markets: India 16%, Spain 10%, United States 7%, France 7%, Netherlands 6% (2019)

Total Imports: $32.67 billion (2017 est.); $35.24 billion (2016 est.)

Import Commodities: Refined petroleum, cars, wheat, laboratory glassware, packaged medicines (2019)

Major Suppliers: China 30%, Netherlands 11%, United States 6%, Belgium 5% (2019)

INTERNATIONAL DISPUTES

◆ Land and maritime boundary dispute with Cameroon continues over the potentially oil rich Bakassi peninsula and around Lake Chad.

◆ Location of Benin-Niger-Nigeria tri-point remains unresolved.

DEFENCE

ARMY

Personnel: 100,000+

Equipment

Category	Name	In Service
MBT	VT-4	
	Vickers Mks3	100+
	T-55	20+
APC	AML-60/90	100+
	SALADIN	15
	FOX	50
	EE-9 Cascavel	50+
	BTR-3U	42
	Piranha	70
	K7AFA	250+
	MT-LB	60
	Otokar Cobra	100+
	Ara	20+
Artillery	M-56 105mm	200
	D30/D74 122mm	200
	FH77 155mm	25
	PALMARIA 155mm	25
Mortar	81mm towed	200+
MRLS	BM21 122mm	
RCL	Carl Gustav 84mm	
	M40A1 106mm	
AA Gun	20mm	
	40mm	
	ZSU-23-4 SP	
SAM	Roland	
	Blowpipe	40

New Procurements/ Upgrades

◆ China's NORINCO has delivered the VT-4 MBTs along with the ST-1 wheeled tank destroyer and two types of self-propelled howitzers to the Nigerian Army in April 2020.

◆ Delivery of Streit 4x4 APCs by Canada's STREIT Group is going on. Nigerian Army has ordered a total of 177 such platforms in different configurations.

◆ Delivery of new indigenously-built 'Ara' armoured vehicles developed by Nigerian company Proforce is going on since 2018. The vehicle can be developed in different configurations.

◆ 28 of the locally built 'Ezugwu' mine-resistant ambush-protected vehicles (MRAPs) have been ordered in 2019. The platforms, designed and produced by DICON/NAVMC (Defence Industries Corporation of Nigeria), are fitted with Chinese turbo-diesel engines.

NAVY

Personnel: 5,000

Equipment

Category	Name	In Service
Frigate	Aradu class	1
Corvette	Erin'mi class	2
	Thunder class (cutter) ex-US	2
OPV	PN18 (Chinese Type 056 variant)	2
Light Forces	NNS Andoni FAC	1
	Siri class missile FAC	2
	Ekpe class missile FAC	1
	Manta class 17mm inshore patrol boats	6
	Shaldag type patrol craft	5
	Swiftship type patrol craft	4
	Kyanwa class patrol craft	4
	Seaward Defence Boat	2
	Ocea fast patrol boat	6
Mine sweeper	Ohue class mine hunter	2
Auxiliary ship	Ambe class LST	2
	Oton class LCU	2

Naval Aviation

Category	Name	In Service
Fighter/ Surveillance / AWS role	AW139	1
	Lynx Mk89	2
	A-109	3

New Procurements/ Upgrades

◆ Procurement of four 'whaler boats' and two tug boats has been proposed in the 2018-19 defence budget.

◆ Work on a landing ship (LST 100) on order from Damen Shipyards has started with delivery scheduled for 2022.

AIR FORCE

Personnel: 9,000

Equipment

Category	Name	In Service
Fighter/ Light attack aircraft	JF-17	3
	F-7NI	8
	L39 Albatross	21
	A-29 Super Tucano	6
	Dornier Alpha	10
Transport/ Surveillance	C130H/H-30	8
	Dornier Sky-Servant	16
	Gulfstream	1
	Do-228	5
	ATR-42 (maritime patrol)	2
	Falcon 90	1
	BBJ 737	1
Helicopter	SA 330 Puma	2
	AS 332 Super Puma	6
	Mi-171	4
	Mi-24	2
	Mi-35	6 (+8 on order)
	AW101	2
	AW109(LUH)	
	AW109 (gunship)	4+(2 on order)
	AW139	2
	Bell 412	2
	AS365 Dauphin	
	H135	
Trainer	F-7NI, FT-7NI	12 + 3
	Air Beetle	20
	Super Mushshak	10
UAV	Wing Loong II	2
	Tsaigumi	1

New Procurements/ Upgrades

◆ Three JF-17 fighter aircraft, jointly developed by China and Pakistan, have been delivered and inducted in NAF in May 2021.

◆ The first batch of six A-29 Super Tucano light attack aircraft has been delivered July 2021. An order was placed with Brazilian firm Embraer and its US partner Sierra Nevada Corporation in February 2019 for the procurement of 12 A-29 platforms for the Nigerian Air Force under the US Foreign Military Sales programme.

◆ Russia has delivered two more Mi-35M attack helicopters in April 2018. The first two platforms of the class were commissioned in April 2017. A contract has been signed with Russia's Rosoboronexport for the acquisition of a total of 12 Mi-35 combat helicopters and over 20 Mi-171Sh transport helicopters.

◆ Five C-130 transport aircraft and Do-

228 aircraft are being upgraded.
- 17 new F-7NI fighters and 3 FT-7NI trainers have been ordered from China.
- An order has been placed for six AW109 utility/attack helicopters from Italy's Leonardo Company in 2018 with deliveries going on.
- China has delivered at least two Wing Loong II armed UAVs to the NAF in 2020.
- First indigenously-built UAV, Tsaigumi, has been inducted in service in 2018. The platform, built in partnership with Portugal, is used for ISR operations.
- US's Textron Systems has been awarded a contract in May 2020 to deliver three Aerosonde Mk 4.7 UAVs.
- An undisclosed number of Marauder mine-resistant ambush-protected (MRAP) vehicles have been received from South Africa's Paramount Group in 2019.

Defence Expenditure
Defence budget: NGN 840.56 billion (proposed for 2021); NGN 878.4 billion (2020)
Estimated defence spending in terms of GDP: 1%

Nigeria has imported arms and equipment from several European countries including Germany, Italy and Bulgaria in the past. Present military suppliers include China, Pakistan, and Israel.

Defence Production and R&D
Previously engaged in the production of only small arms, the Nigerian defence industry has steadily entered into major defence production activities in recent times. The state-owned Defence Industry Corporation (DIC) was set up in 1964 with the objective to make the country self-reliant in defence production and provide all necessary equipment to the Nigerian armed forces. Of late, Nigeria has explored cooperation with a number of countries in military hardware manufacturing and production. While the Army has started inducting the indigenously-built 'Ara' armoured vehicles, the country has also entered naval shipbuilding domain and inducted few indigenously-built naval vessels, including a warship in 2012. The Nigerian air force too has commissioned indigenous unmanned aircraft (UAV) built in cooperation with a foreign partner nation.

Defence Procurement
Nigeria has mostly relied on foreign countries in acquiring weapons and equipment for its defence forces. Most of its weapons were bought from European countries in the 1980s. In the 1990s, the country, in an effort to give boost to domestic defence industry, sought military partnership with a number of countries including Romania, Yugoslavia, France and China. Abuja has also discussed naval cooperation with India in the past. The African country has announced plans to acquire new weapons and equipment for its military and train them for internal stability while also strengthening their role in international peace keeping efforts.

CONTACT DETAILS
Ministry of Defence
By Ship House, Area 10- Abuja, Nigeria
E-mail: contact@defence.gov.ng
www.defence.gov.ng

STRATEGIC INFORMATION
NORTH KOREA
(Capital: Pyongyang)

INTRODUCTION
Area: 120,538 sq km
Population: 25,831,360 (July 2021 est.)
Coastline: 2,495 km
Maritime Claims: Territorial sea: 12 nm
Exclusive economic zone: 200 nm

(Note: Military boundary line 50 nm in the Sea of Japan and the exclusive economic zone limit in the Yellow Sea where all foreign vessels and aircraft without permission are banned.)

GEOPOLITICAL IMPORTANCE
North Korea or the Democratic People's Republic of Korea (DPRK) is an East Asian country and occupies the northern half of Korean Peninsula. The country is bordered by China and Russia in the north and South Korea in the south. It is surrounded by the Sea of Japan in the East and Yellow Sea and Korean Bay in the West. The Korean peninsula, constituting North Korea (DPRK) and South Korea or Republic of Korea (ROK), has strategically remained an important region for four major global powers – China, Japan, Russia and the US. The peninsula is part of the Northeast Asian

region which is gradually gaining prominence among the leading continental and sea powers intending to wield greater economic and military clout in the Asia-Pacific region. Hence, a unified Korea is being viewed as a strategically important region as it could emerge as a new maritime zone in East Asia. Uniting the two Koreas is regarded to be the key for establishing regional security and stability alongside economic prosperity in the region. The two Koreas, which remained undivided till 1948, continue their spat over sovereignty claims of the entire peninsular region.

POLITICAL OVERVIEW
North Korea functions as a single-party republic country. It is run by the Workers' Party of Korea (WPK) which has been in power since the establishment of DPRK in 1948. The political system of North Korea is widely viewed as totalitarian dictatorship having Communist credentials. The head of the state is also the Chairman of the National

Defence Commission which is the highest military leadership body in the country.

KEY POLITICAL PERSONS

HEAD OF STATE, CHAIRMAN OF NATIONAL DEFENCE COMMISSION & SUPREME COMMANDER OF KOREA PEOPLES REPUBLIC ARMY: Kim Jong-un

ECONOMY
The state-controlled economy of North Korea witnessed a sharp decline following

the collapse of Soviet Union in the 1990s. The country, once boasting a modern, industrialised and productive economy, has been marred by chronic financial problems. It has mostly relied on international aid to feed the population. The mid 1990s through mid-2000s were marked by severe famine and widespread starvation. Significant food aid was provided by the international community through 2009. Since that time, food assistance has declined significantly. In the last few years, domestic corn and rice production has improved, although domestic production does not fully satisfy demand.

Over the last decade, China has been North Korea's primary trading partner. The Government in Pyongyang often highlights its goal of becoming a "strong and prosperous" nation, attracting foreign investment to improve the overall standard of living. The Government, however, has taken few steps to make that goal a reality for its populace. The primary reasons for the economic dishevel is DPRK's isolation from international trade and its large-scale military spending by diverting funds needed for investment and production. The country's economic woes have been further compounded by a plethora of sanctions imposed by the US, South Korea and Japan.

Since 2017, North Korea's intermittent nuclear and missile tests have led to a tightening of UN sanctions, resulting in full sectoral bans on DPRK exports and drastically limited key imports. As a result, the economy shrank by 3.5% in 2017; and by 4.1% in 2018. It charted a positive growth of 0.4% in 2019.

However, the Coronavirus outbreak in 2020 exacerbated Pyongyang's economic problems with the country imposing strict restrictions, including halting import of non-essential items from its major trading partner and neighbour China and closing its borders with Beijing, to contain the deadly health crisis. As a result, North Korea's economy suffered its biggest contraction of 4.5% in 23 years in 2020, as estimated by South Korea's central bank that keeps track of reclusive Pyongyang's economy-related activities.

GDP (official exchange rate): $28 billion (2013 est.)

Real Growth Rate (GDP): -1.1% (2015 est.); 1% (2014 est.)

Industries: Military products; machine building, electric power, chemicals; mining (coal, iron ore, limestone, magnesite, graphite, copper, zinc, lead, and precious metals), metallurgy; textiles, food processing; tourism

Total Exports: $222 million (2018); $4.582 billion (2017 est.)

Export Commodities: Watch components, fake hair, iron alloys, instructional models, tungsten (2019)

Major Markets: China 67%, Suriname 6% (2019)

Total Imports: $2.32 billion (2018 est.); $3.86 billion (2016 est.)

Import Commodities: Clothing and apparel, soybean oil, rice, wheat products, clocks/watches (2019)

Major Suppliers: China 96% (2019)

DEFENCE & SECURITY

A unified Korean Peninsula, which was ruled by Japan till the end of World War II, split into two parts with North Korea coming under the Soviet command and South under the US. While both the sovereign states intended to rule over the entire region, the Cold War prevailing between the then two superpowers – Soviet Union and the US – further heightened military tensions between the two Koreas. But it was North Korea which launched a surprise attack against the South in 1950 with a motive to bring that region under its control. Though the two countries signed the Armistice Agreement in 1953 to end the fight, they have not shunned military conflict altogether since then.

North Korea's decades-long military build-up and acquisition of large number of weapons and equipment has intensified tensions between the two neighbours. The Communist state's unabated attempts to possess nuclear weapons and develop asymmetric warfare capabilities continue to remain a major cause of concern for international community, especially for the US which strongly supports South Korea militarily.

North Korea maintains one of the largest militaries in the world. It has over one million armed personnel – the fifth largest in the world. Along with the massive conventional armed forces, the country also appears to have acquired asymmetric warfare capabilities in the form of nuclear, biological and chemical weapons in addition to possessing long-range ballistic missiles and related technology. Pyongyang follows the Songun or "Military First" doctrine meaning that the country's armed forces have first priority over national resources. This policy also guides the political and economic life in the Communist country.

DPRK's military doctrine aims at invading South Korea (RoK) and bringing the entire peninsula under one regime. Though this offensive doctrine still prevails, a strong US backing to South Korea has deterred the North from waging a full-scale war against its neighbour.

In recent times, Pyongyang has been relentlessly working to develop a wide range of weapons at an unprecedented pace. In 2017, the world witnessed a flurry of belligerent activities by the North. The isolated country conducted over two dozen missile tests, including an inter-continental ballistic missile test, thus hinting at its growing command over missile technology development. On November 29, 2017, Pyongyang conducted a powerful missile test (Hwasong-15) which many military analysts presumed to be an ICBM having a range of over 12,000 km. According to US media reports, North Korea has successfully developed nuclear warheads for its missiles which are capable of reaching the US mainland. Some of the missiles test launched by DPRK have flown over Japan, further intensifying the conflict in the entire Korean Peninsula region as well as in the East Asian region.

In an attempt to denuclearise North Korea, the US Government led by the then President Donald Trump had reached an agreement with Pyongyang during a summit held in Singapore in June 2018. Under a comprehensive deal signed between the two sides during that summit, the North Korean Government, led by President Kim Jong-un, had agreed to work towards "complete denuclearisation of the Korean peninsula" while promising "new relations" between Washington and Pyongyang.

Consequently, North Korea also imposed a voluntary moratorium on its nuclear and long-range missile tests and shut down its underground nuclear test site. It had also agreed to dismantle some of its missile-test facilities. However, the country refused to allow any outside inspectors to review the actual progress it had made towards denuclearisation.

In February 2019, Washington and Pyongyang held a second summit at Vietnamese capital Hanoi, but failed to reach any agreement on North Korea's denuclearisation efforts. The summit was abruptly cut short. Amidst the deadlocked dialogue process initiated by the US, North Korea resumed its ballistic missiles tests after an interval of nearly 17 months (from November 2017 to May 2019). The missile tests were restarted as a defiant protest against the joint military drills conducted by South Korea and the US in the Korean Peninsula, amidst warnings from Pyongyang that the "hostile" drills could further derail the nuclear talks.

In June 2019, former US President Trump stepped foot onto the North Korea soil after crossing the demarcation line to meet Kim Jong-un in the Demilitarized Zone (DMZ) – the area that divides the two Koreas. While official talks between Pyongyang and Washington have continued thereafter, no meeting has taken place between the two nations' leaders since their last meeting over the denuclearisation issue.

Meanwhile, N Korea has continued its missile development programme and conducted test launches of long-range cruise and ballistic missiles. In September 2021, the country claimed to have conducted test firing of a new hypersonic missile, named Hwasong-8. The missile was termed a "strategic weapon" by the state media, indicating it could have nuclear capabilities. A submarine-launched ballistic missile (SLBM) was tested in October 2021 in an attempt to bolster the military's underwater operational capability, the country announced.

KEY DEFENCE PERSONS

MINISTER OF PEOPLE'S ARMED FORCES: Ri Yong-gil

CHIEF OF GENERAL STAFF: Gen. Pak Jong Chon

External Conflict

The inter-Korean conflict is the only major external military conflict North Korea is engaged in. The decades-old conflict has often resulted in open confrontation between the two Koreas with each threatening to launch war against the other. The ROK's closer military tie-up with the US and their regular joint military exercises off the Korean coast has intensified DPRK-RoK conflict in recent times. The test firing of lethal missiles conducted by DPRK at regular intervals continue to exacerbate the conflict in the Korean Peninsula, raising international concern.

Territorial disputes: DPRK's territorial disputes revolve mainly around some islands in the region. The disputes include the following:

S Korea: The South-controlled Yeonpyeong Island in the Yellow Sea, which is nearly 12-kms from the North Korean border, has often witnessed confrontations between the two Korean navies since the past decade. The two countries are engaged in a maritime border dispute as the North wants the western maritime line or the Northern Limit Line, which separates the two countries, to be drawn farther south.

China: North Korea and China dispute the sovereignty of certain islands in Yalu and Tumen rivers though it has not hampered their bilateral ties. The Baekdu mountain lying in the border between the two countries has become another region of contention in recent times. Though both countries jointly administer the mountain and its surrounding lake, Chinese attempts to bring the area under its command and control has resulted in friction with DPRK.

THREAT PERSPECTIVE

South Korea: The RoK is preparing itself to counter the DPRK in the eventuality of a full-scale war by acquiring a range of weapons and equipment. Though it maintains a military smaller than that of the North, South Korea has steadily strengthened its conventional warfare power with support from the US. Its strategy is to use its fleet of advanced fighter jets, warships, missiles along with other weapons to deter the North. The country has acquired the new KDX-class warships equipped with US-made Aegis air defence systems along with new submarines. Procurement of new-generation stealth planes, spy drones and missile systems is also going on. However, RoK lacks the capability to counter the ever-increasing asymmetric threat posed by DPRK, especially from its ballistic missiles and nuclear weapons. Accordingly, it is believed that South Korea is also developing nuclear weapons. According to recent reports, Seoul is developing a surface-to-surface ballistic missile as powerful as a tactical nuclear warhead. The country, however, has dismissed the possibility of deploying any nuclear weapons in its territory amidst growing threat from DPRK. The South Korean President has ruled out the deployment of US tactical nuclear weapons on the Korean peninsula to deter threats from the North.

US: The United States views North Korea as a rouge state and believes that it can launch a sudden, surprise attack not only on Seoul, but even on Washington. DPRK's opaque military intentions have thus strengthened US-RoK military tie up. Being an RoK ally, the US has stationed around 28,500 troops – air, naval and ground forces – in South Korea since the end of the Korean War. It has also pledged to help defend Seoul in the wake of another war. Both countries' navies conduct joint military exercises off the Korean coast by deploying advanced warships and weapons. In yet another recent development, the US has gone ahead with its plan to deploy the THAAD (Terminal High Altitude Area Defence) anti-missile system in South Korea despite strong resistance from Russia, China and North Korea. The THAAD missile defence system has been positioned to defend South Korea against North Korea's nuclear and ballistic missile attacks. The system became operational in 2017.

Japan: North Korea's secretive nuclear programme has worried Japan. Rockets launched by the North have flown over Japan, prompting the latter to deploy missile interceptors to shoot down any such weapon flying over its airspace. Japan's military alliance with South Korea in recent times has also infuriated DPRK. South Korea has also joined the Japan-US military exercises as an observer.

STRATEGIC RELATIONS

China: North Korea is regarded as China's strategic buffer zone in Northeast Asia. The two countries share a 1,400 km-long border. Since China perceives the US as its biggest military threat over the issue of Taiwan, the DPRK acts as a guard post for Beijing against the US troops deployed in South Korea. This allows China to deploy its military away from the north-eastern region and focus more on the Taiwan Strait. North Korea's development of nuclear weapons is viewed to be acting as a shield in the wake of possible US military intervention in the Asia Pacific region. China's economic support to DPRK has helped the latter in its nuclear armaments development programme. China was also a major supplier of military weapons and equipment to North Korea in the 1970s.

Russia: The military tie-up between the then Soviet Union and North Korea was at its peak in the 1990s when the former world power was supplying a large number of defence equipment to DPRK that included tanks, submarines, warplanes and missiles among other hardware. The two countries were also engaged in bilateral military wargames involving their navies and air forces. Following the disintegration of Soviet Union in 1991, the military relationship froze. Recently, there has been a thaw in their bilateral defence ties. Moscow and Pyongyang are also discussing economic and energy cooperation with each other.

Iran: North Korea for over three decades has helped Iran in building nuclear and ballistic missiles. The clandestine Iran-DPRK military affair of sharing sophisticated weapons technology, mostly provided by China, has continued despite the United Nations' sanctions against both North Korea and Iran.

Pakistan: North Korea has close relations with Pakistan. It is reported that North Korean missile technologies have been supplied to Pakistan in the past.

DEFENCE CAPABILITIES

ARMY: North Korea maintains one of the

largest militaries in the world. The ground force is called the Korean People's Army (KPA). With nearly a million-strong active ground personnel, the KPA forms the largest and most formidable branch of North Korean armed forces. The KPA is equipped with a large number of arms and weapons to carry out DPRK's offensive military doctrine of bringing the entire Korean Peninsula under one regime and also the defensive policy of protecting its territory from any threat posed by South Korea. The Army also assists in maintaining internal security of the country.

Personnel: 9,50,000 (Including reserves, total strength is estimated to be around 4 million)

Equipment

Category	Name	In Service
MBT	Type-59	700
	T-62	800
	T-54	1600
	PT-85	50+
	Pokpung-ho	250+
APC	BMP-1	2500
	BA-64	
	VTT-323	
	YW-531	
	BTR-60	
	BTR-50	
	BTR-40	
	BTR-152	
Artillery	M-1989 170mm SP	8000
	M-1978 170mm SP	
	M-1977 152mm SP	
	M-1974 152mm SP	
	M-1992 130mm SP	
	M-1991 130mm SP	
	M-1981 130mm SP	
	M-1991 122mm SP	
	M-1985 122mm SP	
	M-1981 122mm SP	
	M-1977 122mm SP	
	M-1992 120mm SP	
	M-1985 towed 152 mm	
	M-1943 towed 152 mm	
	M-1937 ML-20	
	Type 66 towed 152 mm	
	M-46 / Type-59 130 mm	
	D-74 122 mm	
	D-30 122 mm	
	A-19 122 mm	
	M-30 / Type-54 122 mm	
	M-1931 122 mm	
Mortar	82 mm	5000

...continued

Category	Name	In Service
MLRS/ Vehicle mount rocket launcher	M-1991 240 mm	2500+
	M-1989 240 mm	
	BM-24	
	M-1985	
	BMD-20 200 mm	
	BM-14, 140 mm	
	RPU-14	
	Type-63, 130 mm	
	M-1993	
	M-1992	
	M-1985	
	M-1977	
	BM-21	
	BM-11	
	Type-63	
ATGW	Susong-Po (Sagger)	
SSM	Scud B (SRBM) Hwasong-5	100
	Scud C (SRBM) Hwasong-6	36
	9K52 & 2K6 Luna	24
	Scud-ER	~350
	Nodong-A	~200
	Nodong-B	20+
	Taepodong-1	
	Taepodong-2	~2
SAM	Hwasung-Chong (SA-7)	
	SA-2	800
	SA-3	30
	SA-5	24
AA gun	KS-19, 100 mm	500
	KS-12, 85 mm	400
	M-1985 SP, 57 mm	
	ZSU-57-2, 57 mm	250
	S-60, 57 mm	
	M-1992,SP,37 mm	
	M-1939, 37 mm	500+
	M-1992,SP,30 mm	
	M-1992,SP,23 mm	
	ZSU-23-(Quad),23 mm	100
	ZU-23,23 mm	1500
	ZPU-4, ZPU-2, ZPU-1	

New Procurements/Upgrades

No official information is available on recent military procurements made by DPRK.

NAVY: The North Korean Navy has often been designated as a "brown water" navy that operates mostly in the country's surrounding waters. The Navy, called the Korean People's Army Naval Force, acts as a coastal defence force. It deploys small patrol-sized craft capable of defending the country's territorial waters. The Navy possesses some 50 to 60 submarines acquired from Russia and China. The exact number of naval platforms is not known due to extreme secretiveness of the country's military programme and acquisitions. The large number of submarines along with other amphibious vessels can covertly insert troops into the S Korean territory. The country also claims to have conducted submarine-launched ballistic missile (SLBM) tests in recent times, thus confirming its aggressive weapons development programme for self defence.

Personnel: 60,000

Major naval bases: Pipagot, Sagon Ni, Najin, Wonsan

Equipment

Category	Name	In Service
Submarine	SSG Soviet Golf class	
	Golf II class	1
	SS PRC Type-031 (Soviet Romeo Class)	22
	SS Whiskey (Soviet)	4
	Sang-O class (Midget)	15
	SSI (Midget)	30
Frigate	FF Soho	1
	FFL Najin	2
Corvette	PG Sariwon	4
	Tral	2
Patrol vessel (Missile)	PTG Soju (OSA)	15 + 8
	PRC Huangfeng	4
	PTG Sohung	6
	PTG Komar	10
Patrol Boat (Tarpedo)	PT Shershen	3
	PT Sinnam	
	PT Sin Hung	40
	PT P-4 19.3	
	Ku Song	60
Patrol Craft	PG T Class	5
	PG Mayang	10
	PC Taechong I/II	13
	PC Hainan	6
	PC Chodo	3
	PC/PT/PTG/WPC Chong-Ju	6
	PC SO-142	18
	PC Shanghai II	12
	PB Chongjin	16
	PB Chaho	50+
	PB/PT P-6 PB Shantou	10
LCU	Hantae class	10
LCM	Hungnam class	15
LCVP	Nampo class	100+
ACV	Kongbang class	140+
Amphibious		10

...continued

Category	Name	In Service
Mine sweeper	MSI Yukto I/II	20+
Auxiliary ship		10+
ASM	Silkworm	
	P-15 Termit	
	KN-01	
	KN-02	
	Kh-35	

Coastal Defence

Category	Name	In Service
Artillery	M-1931/-37	
	SM-4-1	
	M-1992	
	M-1937	
ASM (Coastal Defence)	Silkworm	1 Regiment

New Procurements/Upgrades

◆ Images of a new submarine platform built at a local shipyard was released by the official news agency of North Korea in July 2019. The submarine would operate in waters of the East Sea of Korea (also Sea of Japan) and implement "military strategic intentions" of the North Korean regime, the agency said in a news report.

◆ An old Soviet-era Golf-II class ballistic missile submarine (SSBN) has been launched after being refurbished. The DPRK plans to use the vessel either for active service or for constructing a similar submarine of its own.

◆ Modernisation of conventional submarine fleet continues.

AIR FORCE: The Korean People's Army Air Force operates with the primary mission of defending the country's airspace. It maintains a large but mostly obsolete inventory of Soviet-era fighter planes, bombers, attack helicopters, transport aircraft and other fixed wing planes along with a range of air defence weapons. Some military hardware have also been acquired from China. The air force also provides tactical support to the Army and Navy.

Personnel: 110,000

Major air bases: Chongjin, Haeju, Hwangsuwon, Hyesan, Hyon-ni, Kanch'on, Taetan, Sunchon

Equipment

Category	Name	In Service
Fighter/ Ground Attack	Su-25	10
	MiG 19/Q5	30
	MiG-21	140
	MiG-23	50
	MiG-29	40

...continued

Category	Name	In Service
Fighter/ Ground Attack	F7B	40
	F6/F5	180+
	A5 Fantan	40
Bomber	H-5	~50
Transport	Y-2	300+
	An-24	6
	Il-18	2
	Il-62M	2-3
	Tu-134	2
	Tu-154	4
Attack/ Transport/ Surveillance Helicopter	Mi-8	20+
	MDH 300/500	27
	MDH300/500(AT)	~60
	Mi-24	50+
	Mi-26	4
	Mi-18	
	Z-5	40+
Trainer	MiG 23	4
	Yak 18	120
	L-39 Albatross	5
AEW	An-24	2
Air Defence System	KN-06, SA-2/3 SA-5, SA-6 SA-7, SA-17	

New Procurements/ Upgrades
No official information is available on recent military procurements made by DPRK.

STRATEGIC FORCE COMMAND:
Though it is not officially known whether North Korea has built-up a strategic force command, the country certainly possesses a large number of ballistic missiles (according to some estimates over 1,000) and appears to be advancing in its nuclear weapons programme. The country's missile programme has been developed from the Soviet-made Scud tactical ballistic missiles.

North Korea officially declared its nuclear weapons programme in 2003 and detonated its first nuclear device in 2006 followed by more such tests in 2009 and 2013. In 2016, the North conducted two nuclear tests in January and September. In confirming its nuclear weapons programme in 2003, the Asian country nullified the Agreed Framework signed between it and the United States on 21 October 1994 in Geneva.

Pyongyang is believed to be possessing ICBM capability. Latest attempts by the country are focused on building long-range missiles having the potential of reaching up to the mainland United States. According to some US media reports, North Korea has succeeded in making a nuclear warhead small enough to fit inside its missiles. The country is developing nuclear weapons capable of hitting the US at a much faster rate than expected.

In July 2017, Pyongyang claimed that it had carried out its first successful test of an inter-continental ballistic missile (ICBM). The Hwasong-14 could hit "any part of the world", the country claimed. On 28 July 2017, it carried out its second ICBM test, with the missile reaching an altitude of about 3,000km and landing in the sea off Japan. The North Korean regime conducted over 20 missile tests in the year 2017.

The country has displayed two types of ICBMs, known as the KN-08 and KN-14, at military parades since 2012. The KN-08 is believed to have a range of about 11,500km while the KN-14 appears to have a range of around 10,000km. Neither of the weapon has been tested yet.

In May 2015, N Korea released images indicating the launch of a missile from one of its Navy's submarines. Previously, it was reported that DPRK was on the verge of developing a submarine-launched ballistic missile (SLBM) capable of being launched from the Navy's Golf-class SSBN. A second test of the missile in November 2015 ended in failure. The country has also reportedly acquired the sea-based copy of a Russian cruise missile, believed to be the Kh-35.

In 2016, DPRK for the first-time test fired an inter-mediate range ballistic missile (IRBM) named Musudan or BM-35. The IRBM is believed to have been deployed with the N Korean military since 2007. In 2016, the missile, having a reported range of 3,500-km, underwent a series of test firings.

DEFENCE PRODUCTION

The secretive military regime of N Korea does not disclose any details about its defence industry. While in the past it has acquired majority of weapons from Soviet Union and China, DPRK appears to have become steadily self-reliant in indigenous defence production. The domestic defence manufacturing includes a whole range of military equipment for the Army, Navy and Air Force including artillery, armoured vehicles, tanks, submarines, warships, helicopters, trainer aircraft, missiles and air defence systems. The country possesses indigenous R&D facilities for development of almost all types of missiles including long range SSM, ICBM, IRBM, SRBM and other variants. Some defence analysts suggest that the missiles can be armed with nuclear warheads.

DEFENCE BUDGET

North Korea appears to be allocating a major share of its GDP to defence. The annual defence budget is estimated to be between 15% and 20% of GDP in the last few years. According to a recent report, annual defence expenditure of North Korea could be as high as 22% of its GDP which amounts to around US$10 billion a year.

According to the US State Department's World Military Expenditures and Arms Transfers 2019 report, the North's military expenditure averaged about US$ 3.6 billion a year between 2007 and 2017. That accounts for 13.4% to 23.3% of the country's average GDP of US$17 billion during that period.

DPRK has constantly put up an aggressive and offensive military stance despite the stiff economic sanctions against it by international powers. The huge defence budgetary allocations have been aimed at developing nuclear and missile programmes as well as for strengthening the domestic defence industry. The following table provides a rough overview of the defence expenditure made by Pyongyang over the past few years.

Year	Allocation	% of GDP
2017	$10 billion	22
2016		16
2011	$5.5 billion	15
2010	No Data available	
2009	76.250 billion won ($8.77 billion)	15.8
2008	71.330 billion won	15.8

CONCLUSION

The extremely secretive and isolated North Korea has since long been viewed as a steadily rising military threat, particularly by South Korea and the US. The country has maintained a belligerent and offensive posture to unify the Korean Peninsula and bring it under its control. With a massive military force and ever-growing asymmetric warfare capabilities, DPRK poses the greatest threat to the RoK. Recent developments related to its nuclear weapons and missiles development programme have become one of the major causes of global concern in the 21st century. The historic US-North Korea summit held in Singapore in June 2018 was being viewed as a major step towards denuclearization of the Korean Peninsula. The 2019 Hanoi summit also failed to bring in any tangible outcome in this regard. Bilateral talks between Pyongyang and Washington has since been stalled over many contentious issues.

CONTACT DETAILS
Ministry of Defence – DPRK
Pyongyang, North Korea

NORWAY
(Capital: Oslo)

INTRODUCTION
Area: 323,802 sq km
Population: 5,509,591 (July 2021 est.)
Coastline: 25,148 km
Maritime claims: Territorial Sea: 12 nm
Contiguous Zone: 10 Nm
Exclusive Economic Zone: 200 Nm
Continental Shelf: 200 nm

KEY POLITICAL PERSONS

CHIEF OF STATE & COMMANDER-IN-CHIEF: King Harald V

PRIME MINISTER: Jonas Gahr Støre

KEY DEFENCE PERSONS

DEFENCE MINISTER: Odd Roger Enoksen

CHIEF OF DEFENCE: Maj. Gen. Eirik Johan Kristoffersen

CHIEF OF ARMY: Maj. Gen. Lars Lervik

CHIEF OF NAVY: Commodore Rune Andersen

CHIEF OF AIR FORCE: Maj. Gen. Tonje Skinnarland

ECONOMY

As the world's second-largest exporter of natural gas and eleventh-largest exporter of oil, Norway plays an important stabilizing role in energy markets and energy security. The Norwegian economy is doing well. Businesses are investing more and employment is rising throughout the country. We are using the good times to secure a sustainable welfare state and a safer Norway. The restructuring of the economy must

continue in order for us to reach the climate goals and further diversify the economy to promote growth. As per the official press release, a tighter fiscal stance now allows the majority of new jobs to be created within the private sector. The 2019 fiscal budget has a neutral impact on the Norwegian economy. Spending of oil revenue amounts to 2.7 per cent of the Government Pension Fund Global. This is well in line with the fiscal rule, which says that transfers from the GPFG to the central government budget shall, over time, follow the expected real return on the fund, estimated at 3 per cent. The government maintains its growth-supporting policies by cutting taxes and duties also in the 2019 budget. Prioritized areas continue to be knowledge, transport and communication, health, and an efficient provision of services at the local level. Norway belongs to a number of international organisations and fora, including the African Development Bank, Arctic Council, Asian Development Bank, Euro-Atlantic Partnership Council, Inter-American Development Bank, International Monetary Fund, Organisation for Economic Cooperation and Development, Organisation for Security and Cooperation in Europe, the North Atlantic Treaty Organisation (NATO), United Nations, World Bank, and World Trade Organisation. Norway also is an observer to the Organisation of American States. Economic growth is expected to remain constant or improve slightly in the next few years. The COVID-19 pandemic restrictions and lockdown has affected gravely the economic situation of Norway causing a financial crisis. The country is facing milder recession than rest of the Europe.

GDP (official exchange rate): $342.06 billion (2020 est.), $344.69 billion (2019 est.)

Real Growth Rate (GDP): 0.86% (2019 est.), 1.36% (2018 est.)

Industries: Petroleum and gas, shipping, fishing, aquaculture, food processing, shipbuilding, pulp and paper products, metals, chemicals, timber, mining, textiles

Oil - proved reserves: 6.376 billion bbl (1 January 2018)

Natural gas - proved reserves: 1.782 trillion cu m (1 January 2018 est.)

Total Exports: $117.06 billion (2020 est.), $146.71 billion (2019 est.)

Export Commodities: Crude petroleum, natural gas, fish, refined petroleum, aluminum (2019)

Major Markets: United Kingdom 18%, Germany 14%, Netherlands 10%, Sweden 9%, France 6%, United States 5% (2019)

Total Imports: $119.08 billion (2020 est.), $140.14 billion (2019 est.)

Import Commodities: Cars, refined petroleum, broadcasting equipment, natural gas, crude petroleum (2019)

Major Suppliers: Sweden 17%, Germany 12%, China 8%, Denmark 7%, United States 6%, United Kingdom 5%, Netherlands 5% (2019)

INTERNATIONAL DISPUTES

◆ Norway asserts a territorial claim in Antarctica (Queen Maud Land and its continental shelf)

◆ Russia and Norway reached an agreement on aligning the Barents Sea and Arctic Ocean boundaries over EEZ and continental shelf on 15 September 2010; this agreement is pending ratification by the respective national assemblies.

◆ As a founding member of the North Atlantic Treaty Organisation, Norway has been an active participant in NATO since the signing of the treaty in Washington. The Norwegian Delegation to NATO is staffed by personnel from the Norwegian Ministry of Foreign Affairs and the Ministry of Defence.

◆ Norway is a member of the Global Coalition to Defeat ISIS.

DEFENCE

ARMY

Personnel: 8,500

Equipment

Category	Name	In Service
MBT	Leopard 2A4NO	30+
AIFV & APC	CV-9030N	90+
	Supacat HMT Extenda	20+
	M113	300+
	Patria XA series	50+
Artillery	M109A3GN 155mm	20+
	M125A2	10
MLRS	MLRS	10
ATK Weapon	M72 LAW	
SAM	RBS70 MKII	300
UAV	RQ-11 Raven, PD-100 Wasp III, RQ-20 PUMA	

New Procurements/ Upgrades

◆ The US State Department has approved a possible Foreign Military Sale to the Government of Norway of Javelin FGM-148 Missiles and related equipment for an estimated cost of USD36 million. The Government of Norway has requested to buy 120 Javelin FGM-148 Missiles; and 2 Javelin FGM-148 Missiles Fly to Buy. Also included are 24 Javelin Block 1 Command Launch Units (CLUs) retrofit kits; spare parts; publications and technical documentation; personnel training; US Government and contractor engineering, technical and logistics support services; and other related elements of logistical and programme support.

NAVY

Personnel: 3,500

Equipment

Category	Name	In Service
Submarine	Ula Class	6
Frigate	Fridtjof Nansen class	4
Corvette	Skjold class	6
Mine warfare force	Oksoy class	4
	Alta Class	3
Auxiliary	Reine class	1

Naval Aviation

Category	Name	In Service
Aircraft	Mk86P3E Orion	2
Helicopter	LYNX	6

New Procurements/ Upgrades

◆ Kongsberg Defence & Aerospace AS (KONGSBERG) signed two contracts, valued at MNOK 1,426, with the Norwegian Defence Materiel Agency (FMA). KONGSBERG will deliver a new batch of Naval Strike Missile (NSM) to the Norwegian Navy's frigates and corvettes. The existing inventory of missiles will go through a series of maintenance actions to extend their operational timeline and continue providing state of the art defence capabilities for the Navy. Kongsberg Defence & Aerospace AS (KONGSBERG) signed two contracts, valued at MNOK 1,426, with the Norwegian Defence Materiel Agency (FMA). KONGSBERG will deliver a new batch of Naval Strike Missile (NSM) to the Norwegian Navy's frigates and corvettes. The existing inventory of missiles will go through a series of maintenance actions to extend their operational timeline and continue providing state of the art defence capabilities for the Navy.

AIR FORCE

Personnel: 3,500

Equipment

Category	Name	In Service
Fighter	F16	40+
	F-35	12+ (50+ on order)
ASW Maritime Patrol	P3C Orion	5+
	P3Ns	2
EW/ AEWCS	Falcon 200	2
Transport	C-130J-30s	5+
Helicopter	Bell 412SPs	15+
	NH-90	5+

...continued

Category	Name	In Service
Helicopter	Sea King Mk4	10
	LYNX Mk86s	5
Trainer	SAAB Supporter	10+
SAM	NASAMS	2

New Procurements/ Upgrades

◆ The Norwegian Defence Materiel Agency (NDMA) in Nov 2021 accepted the first of five Boeing P-8A Poseidon maritime patrol aircraft (MPA) that will be operated by the Royal Norwegian Air Force (RNoAF). Norway's first P-8A aircraft named Vingtor, was delivered to the NDMA during a ceremony at the Museum of Flight in Seattle, Washington. Norway's four remaining aircraft are all in advanced stages of production and will be delivered to the NDMA in 2022.

◆ SAS has won a contract with the Armed Forces in Norway, in direct competition with Norwegian. The contract is worth a total value of ca. NOK 1 billion over four years. The Norwegian Armed Forces have chosen SAS as their carrier of choice for the proud men and women in the military service. The contract has a four-year duration, which will also lead to additional SAS flights to routes such as Oslo to Bergen, Trondheim, Bodø and Evenes, which will help boost passenger volumes.

◆ Norway will replace its P-3C Orion and DA-20 Jet Falcon maritime patrol aircraft with five new P-8A Poseidon MPAs. The first aircraft delivery is expected in 2022.

◆ First of 16 AW101 helicopters delivered to the Norwegian Ministry of Justice & Public Security for its All-Weather Search and Rescue Helicopter programme by Leonardo Company. The AW101s will be operated by the Royal Norwegian Air Force and replace the Sea King helicopters currently in service.

The Norwegian Special Operations Command (NORSOCOM) is a joint staff that runs the Armed Forces' two special forces: the Norwegian Special Operations Commando and the Norwegian Naval Special Operations Commando.

The Cyber Defence is responsible for establishing and maintaining the Armed Forces freedom of action in the digital domain. It also protects the Armed Forces' ICT systems against any digital threat from military and civilian actors. The Cyber Defence provides other military departments with sensor and radar data. The department also runs and maintains the Armed Forces' jointly integrated management system (FIF).

Defence Expenditure

Total defence spending: 37.1 billion Norwegian krone (2020)

Estimated defence spending in terms of GDP: 2% of GDP (2020 est.), 1.86% of GDP (2019)

Year	USD (Millions)
2014	7,772
2015	6,142
2016	6,431
2017	6,850
2018*	7,544
2019*	7,536
2020*	7,272
2021*	8,292

(*Figures for 2020 and 2021 are estimates.) Source: Defence Expenditure of NATO Countries (2014-2021), NATO Press Release.

Norwegian Defence Spending

The Norwegian Ministry of Defence submitted a White Paper on a new National Defence Industry Strategy in March 2021.

Defence Production and R&D

Norwegian Defence Research Establishment (FFI) is the prime institution responsible for defence-related research in Norway. It conducts research and development on behalf of the Norwegian Armed Forces and provides expert advice to political and military defence leaders. In particular, its task is to keep track of advances in the fields of science and military technology which might affect the assumptions on which Norwegian security policy and/or defence planning is based. The Norwegian Defence and Security Industries Association (FSI) is the largest and most important association in Norway advocating the interests of the Norwegian Defence and Security Industry and the primary interlocutor for the government in matters of importance to the industry. The association comprises more than 100 companies from all parts of Norway. It is a diversified group ranging from the major national defence contractors to one-man businesses with unique niche capabilities built on innovation and advanced technology serving both the military and civilian markets. Norway plays a significant role in global security and the production of defence products. The high growth, which occurred in this sector over the last years, is due to the fact that the Norwegian defence industry is highly competitive and to the constructive relationship that exists between the armed forces and industry. Kongsberg Gruppen is a Norwegian defence contractor and maritime automation supplier. It is an international technology corporation that delivers advanced and reliable solutions that improve safety, security and performance in complex operations and during extreme conditions. KONGSBERG works with demanding customers in the global defence, maritime, oil and gas and aerospace industries. Kongsberg Defence & Aerospace AS (KDA), one of two operating companies of Kongsberg Gruppen (KOG) of Norway, is a supplier of defence and space related systems and products, mainly anti-ship missiles, military communications, and command and weapons control systems for naval vessels and air-defence applications. In 2016, Norway exported arms and military equipment for around NOK 3.6 billion. This is an increase of 10 % from 2015. Exports of arms and munitions accounted for around NOK 2.9 billion of this amount, and other defence-related products for NOK 650 million. In addition, there were exports of dual-use items, in other words civilian products with military uses, with a total value of around NOK 300 million. A total of 34 applications for licences to export defence-related products were refused in 2016, according to the white paper on exports of defence-related products. Other NATO and Nordic countries are still the main importers of these products.

Most Norwegian defence companies are relatively small compared to international defence companies. According to the EU definition of sizable companies, only three Norwegian defence companies can be considered large, and these are Kongsberg Defence and Aerospace, Nammo and AIM Norway (recently acquired by the Kongsberg Group).

Defence Procurement

The Norwegian Defence Materiel Agency (NDMA) is an important partner for Norwegian industry. The Defence White Paper 38 stipulates that the Norwegian Armed Forces and Norwegian defence industry are strategic partners. Norway has set up a defence equipment agency called Forsvarsmateriell in 2015, responsible for acquisition and production in the sector. Forsvarsmateriell's foremost mission and raison d'être is to support the Armed Forces and the country's defence capability. The agency is directly under the Ministry of Defence. The main tasks of the agency include material investments and material management in the defence sector. The Norwegian Armed Forces are tasked with contributing to increased national economic growth and a competitive industry. The Defence industry strives to ensure the Armed Forces has sufficient access to competence, material (armaments) and services.

CONTACT DETAILS
Ministry of Defence
Myntgt. 1, P.O. Box 8126 Dep
0032 Oslo 1, Norway
Tel: +4723098000
Fax: +4723092323
E-mail: postmottak@fd.dep.no

Norwegian Armed Forces
P.O. box 800, Postmottak
2617 Lillehammer, Norway
Tel: (+47) 915 03 003
Email: forsvaret@mil.no

OMAN
(Capital: Muscat)

INTRODUCTION

Area: 309,500 sq km
Population: 3,694,755 (July 2021 est.)
Coastline: 2,092 km
Maritime claims: Territorial sea: 12 nm
Contiguous zone: 24 nm
Exclusive Economic Zone: 200 nm

KEY POLITICAL PERSONS

HEAD OF STATE, PRIME MINISTER & MINISTER OF DEFENCE: Sultan Haitham bin Tariq Al Said

DEPUTY PRIME MINISTER FOR COUNCIL OF MINISTERS: Sayyid Fahd Bin Mahmoud Al Said

KEY DEFENCE PERSONS

DEPUTY PRIME MINISTER FOR DEFENCE AFFAIRS: Sayyid Shihab bin Tarik bin Taimur Al Said

CHIEF OF STAFF OF ARMED FORCES: Vice Admiral Abdullah Khamis Abdullah Al Raisi

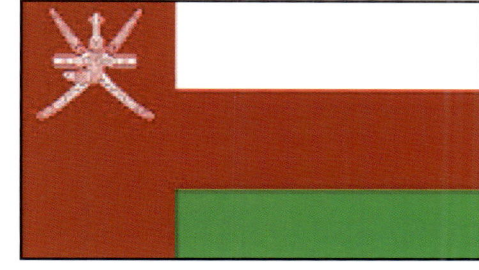

COMMANDER OF ARMY: Maj Gen Matar Bin Salim Bin Rashid Al Balushi

COMMANDER OF NAVY: Rear Admiral Saif bin Nasser bin Mohsen Al-Rahbi

COMMANDER OF AIR FORCE: Air Vice Marshal Khamis Bin Hammad Bin Sultan Al Ghafri

ECONOMY

Oman is heavily dependent on oil and gas resources, which can generate between and 68% and 85% of government revenue, depending on fluctuations in commodity prices. In 2018, Oman has sufficient foreign assets to support its currency's fixed exchange rates. It is issuing debt to cover its deficit. Growth is projected to slow to 1.2% in 2019 as Oman's commitment to the December 2018 OPEC+ output cut constrains oil production. The 2019 budget assumes a 3% increase in total expenditure compared to 2018. Omani officials imposed austerity measures on its gasoline and diesel subsidies in 2016. These spending cuts have had only a moderate effect on the government's budget. Oman is a member of United Nations, International Monetary Fund, World Bank, and World Trade Organisation. Oman is also a member of the Organisation of Islamic Cooperation, the Arab League, and the Gulf Cooperation Council. The country is not a member of the Organisation of the Petroleum Exporting Countries. Oman's economy contracted in 2020 due to the oil price slide and the COVID-19 public health response.

GDP (official exchange rate): $135.79 billion (2020), $136.92 billion (2019 est.)

Real Growth Rate (GDP): -0.9% (2017 est.), 5% (2016 est.)

Industries: Crude oil production and refining, natural and liquefied natural gas production; construction, cement, copper, steel, chemicals, optic fiber

Oil - proved reserves: 5.373 billion bbl (1 January 2018 est.)

Natural gas - proved reserves: 651.3 billion cu m (1 January 2018 est.)

Total Exports: $43.69 billion (2020 est.), $46.32 billion (2019 est.)

Export Commodities: Crude petroleum, natural gas, refined petroleum, iron products, fertilizers (2019)

Major Markets: China 46%, India 8%, Japan 6%, South Korea 6%, United Arab Emirates 6%, Saudi Arabia 5% (2019)

Total Imports: $32.55 billion (2019 est.), $35.37 billion (2018 est.)

Import Commodities: Cars, refined petroleum, broadcasting equipment, gold, iron (2019)

Major Suppliers: United Arab Emirates 36%, China 10%, Japan 7%, India 7%, United States 5% (2019)

INTERNATIONAL DISPUTES

◆ Boundary agreement reportedly has been signed and approved with UAE in 2003 for entire border, including Oman's Musandam Peninsula and Al Madhah exclave.

◆ The Omani government remains concerned about the conflict in Yemen and the potential for al-Qa'ida in the Arabian Peninsula and ISIS-Yemen to threaten Oman's land and maritime borders. Omani officials regularly engages with US officials on the need to counter terrorism.

◆ The Omani security establishment has deployed assets to address increased insecurity along Oman's land and sea border with Yemen.

DEFENCE

ARMY
Personnel: 50,000

Equipment

Category	Name	In Service
MBT	Challenger 2	30+
	M60A3/ A1	50+
	Scorpion	30+
APC/MICV/ IFV	AT105 Saxon	10+
	Stormer	10
	Piranha 8X8	100+
	WZ5516X6	50
	Saladin	30+
	V150 Commando	150+
	VBC90	15
	Fahd	50
Artillery	155 mm G6	20+
	155 mm FH70	10+
	155 mm M109	10+
	130 mm	10+
	105 mm towed	30
Mortar	81 mm	
	107 mm	
	120 mm	
MRL	122 mm Type 90	5+
Anti-Tank GW	Milan	50
	TOW	10+
	Javelin	30
AA Gun	ZU232	
	35 mm twin GDF-005	10
SAM	SA7	30+
	Javelin	30
	Albi/Mistral	
	THAAD anti-missile system	

New Procurements/ Upgrades
No major procurement plans are under consideration at present.

NAVY
Personnel: 4,500

Equipment

Category	Name	In Service
Corvette	Qahir class	2
	Khareef Class	3
Patrol Vessel	Province Class	2+
	Al Bushra Class	3
	Al Ofouq	4
HSSV	Al Mubshir	1
Amphibious Force	Nasir Al Bahr	1
	Fulk al Salamah	1
	Al Sultana	1
Missile	Crotale	30+
	Exocet MM-40	100+
	Harpoon	
	Mica	

New Procurements/ Upgrades
No major procurement plans are under consideration at present.

AIR FORCE
Personnel: 5,000

Equipment

Category	Name	In Service
Aircraft	Eurofighter Typhoon	10+
	F-16C Fighting Falcon	20+
	Hawk 203/103	10
	CASA C-295	2+
	Skyvan	2+
Transport/ Tanker	Airbus A320 Prestige	2
	C130H	2+
	C-130J	2+
Attack/ Transport Helicopter	Bell 205	5
	Bell 206	2+
	SA330	2
	Puma	3
	AS332	2
	Super Lynx300	10+
	NH90	10+
Trainer	Pilatus PC-9	10+
	Hawk 128	5
	F-16D Block Fighting Falcon	4

New Procurements/ Upgrades
No major procurement plans are under consideration at present.

Defence Expenditure
Total defence spending: $9 billion (approx.)
Estimated defence spending in terms of GDP: 11% of GDP (2020 est.), 8.8% of GDP (2019)

Domestic Suppliers: Engine Engineering Company, Sultanate of Oman

Foreign Suppliers: US, UK, India, Turkey, Arab League, Russia, Malaysia, Singapore, Pakistan, China.

India and Oman in Sept 2021 inked an agreement for exchange of white shipping information and to boost maritime security cooperation in reflection of growing cooperation between the two sides. Information would be exchanged between the Indian Navy's Information Fusion Centre and the MSC (Maritime Security Centre), Oman, and contribute to enhanced maritime safety and security in the region.

Defence Production and R&D
The Head of State is very much interested in promoting the development of defence and technology in the country and encourages the involvement of the Omani companies or state organisations. In 2000, Alenia Marconi Systems (AMS) signed an agreement with the Royal Air Force of Oman (RAFO) to jointly set up and manage an air controller training school in the Sultanate.

Defence Procurement
The Gulf Cooperation Council (GCC) was established in an agreement concluded on 25 May 1981 in Riyadh, Saudi Arabia between: Bahrain, Kuwait, Oman, Qatar, Saudi Arabia and UAE. These countries declared that the GCC is established in view of the special relations between them, their similar political systems based on Islamic beliefs, joint destiny and common objectives. The GCC is a regional common market with a defence planning council as well. The geographic proximity of these countries and their general adoption of free trade economic policies are factors that encouraged them to establish the GCC. The GCC States seek to build up their defence forces according to a common conception. In this context, they have unified operational procedures, training, and military curricula. They also endeavour to accomplish compatibility of their military systems. The Office of the Secretary General of Ministry of Defence Oman main roles and responsibilities include managing and implementing the financial and procurement policy, as well as paying invoices to MOD suppliers. The office provides e-Services to

facilitate improved communications with external organisations that deal with the Ministry of Defence.

CONTACT DETAILS
Ministry of Defence
PO Box 113, Muscat 113
http://www.mod.gov.om/

Office of Deputy Prime Minister for Security and Defence
P.O. Box 113, Muscat, Oman
Tel: +968704096
www.omanet.om

STRATEGIC INFORMATION
PAKISTAN
(Capital: Islamabad)

INTRODUCTION
Area: 796,095 sq km
Population: 238,181,034 (July 2021 est.)
Coastline: 1,046 km
Maritime claims: Territorial sea: 12 nm
Contiguous Zone: 24 nm
Exclusive Economic Zone: 200 nm
Continental Shelf: 200 nm or to the edge of the continental margin

GEOPOLITICAL IMPORTANCE
The Islamic Republic of Pakistan is a South Asian country and was once part of the larger Indian subcontinent. It is bordered by India in the east, Iran and Afghanistan in the west, and China in the far northeast. In its south lies the Arabian Sea. The geographic location of Pakistan makes it a vital access point between South Asia and Southwest Asia. The four neighbours of Pakistan – India, China, Afghanistan and Iran – all play important roles in the Asian continent as well as in the international sphere. Pakistan, being positioned in the midst of all these countries, plays a key role in some or other ways. The Islamic Republic's relative proximity to the resource-rich Central Asian region also gives it a strategic edge. The Arabian Sea in the south connects Pakistan with the Gulf countries. In the present-day world order, Pakistan has attained an important stature and is influencing the international geostrategic sphere for numerous reasons.

POLITICAL OVERVIEW
The Constitution of Pakistan defines the country as a federal republic with the President as head of the state and Commander-in-Chief of armed forces, and the Prime Minister as head of the Government. However, intermittent political instability in the country has given way to authoritarian military regimes several times in its history. Hence, the political system of Pakistan has remained volatile in nature with the country ruled either by democratically elected governments or by the military. The last Parliamentary/ General election in the country was held in July 2018 following the completion of five-year term by the outgoing Government.

KEY POLITICAL PERSONS

PRESIDENT: Arif ur Rehman Alvi

PRIME MINISTER: Imran Khan

ECONOMY
The developing economy of Pakistan has suffered setbacks due to national and international political turmoil. According to the World Bank's 2018 data, the country ranked 40th largest in terms of GDP. In the last decade, Islamabad witnessed economic inconsistency with the GDP rising from 5% to 8% between 2004 and 2007 and sliding down thereafter largely due to global recession. GDP growth gradually increased from 2012 onward, and was 5.5% in 2018. Foreign investments in the country also significantly declined due to continuous internal unrest and terrorism-related incidents. Foreign aid, mostly from the US, and financial assistance from global institutions including the World Bank, IMF and Asian Development Bank, helped Pakistan to revive its economy to an extent.

The deadly Coronavirus pandemic battered

Pakistan's economy which shrank by 0.47% in 2020. The economy is expected to chart a positive growth of 1.3% in 2021, according to estimates made by the World Bank.

In an effort to boost growth and development, Pakistan and its "all-weather" ally China have initiated work on implementing the "China-Pakistan Economic Corridor" (CPEC) project – a $62 billion (revised estimate of $87 billion by some analysts) investment programme targeted towards energy sector and other infrastructure projects that Islamabad and Beijing had agreed on in 2013. Pakistan believes the CPEC investments would enable its growth rates to touch over 6% of GDP by laying the groundwork for increased exports. CPEC-related obligations, however, have raised IMF concern about Pakistan's capital outflows and external financing needs over the medium term.

GDP (official exchange rate): $253.18 billion (2019 est.)

Real Growth Rate (GDP): 5.4% (2017 est.); 4.6% (2016 est.)

Industries: Textiles and apparel, food processing, pharmaceuticals, construction materials, paper products, fertiliser, shrimp

Natural Gas - Proved Reserves: 588.8 billion cu m (1 January 2018 est.)

Crude Oil - Proved Reserves: 332.2 million bbl (1 January 2018 est.)

Total Exports: $31.5 billion (2019 est.); $27.60 billion (2018 est.)

Export Commodities: Textiles, clothing and apparel, rice, leather goods, surgical

instruments (2019)

Major Markets: US 14%, China 8%, Germany 7%, UK 6% (2019)

Total Imports: $42.27 billion (2019 est.); $51.60 billion (2018 est.)

Import Commodities: Refined petroleum, crude petroleum, natural gas, palm oil, scrap iron (2019)

Major Suppliers: China 28%, United Arab Emirates 11%, US 5% (2019)

DEFENCE & SECURITY

Pakistan, which was once a part of Indian subcontinent, has throughout its existence maintained an aggressive posture towards India. This has resulted in three wars – in 1948, 1965 and 1971. The 1971 War led to the creation of a new nation, Bangladesh, which was carved out from East Pakistan. Further, there was a localised military conflict over Kargil in 1999. A militarily "imbalanced" Pakistan has also adopted covert war tactics against India since decades and is engaged in a prolonged proxy war over the Kashmir issue.

Pakistan has maintained a sizable military force since its creation in 1947 after separation from India. It ranks sixth in the world in terms of active armed personnel. The armed forces of Pakistan constitute the Army, Navy and Air Force. The country has built up a large conventional armed force, though its size and strength pales in comparison to India's massive military power. By possessing nuclear arsenal, Islamabad has tried to add teeth to its overall military capability against New Delhi which still adheres to a "no first use" policy of nuclear weapons.

Drawing lessons from the past Indo-Pak wars, Pakistan, while maintaining that it follows a defensive military doctrine, however, has felt the need for an "offensive defence" strategy to counter the superior conventional military might of India. The Islamic nation has always regarded India as its foremost military rival in the entire Asian continent. To overcome the conventional military asymmetry against India, Pakistan has acquired nuclear weapons capability over the years. Its increased inclination towards the other rising Asian power, China, has also enabled Islamabad procure advanced arms, weapons and related technology to further strengthen its military posture. The two "all-weather allies" have been regularly conducting joint defence drills. In the last few years, Pakistan and China have worked on joint development and production of sophisticated weapon systems and military platforms. The two partner nations, in fact, have made aggressive efforts to "strategically contain" India and hinder New Delhi's peaceful rise as an influential regional and global economic and military powerblock. The contentious China-Pakistan Economic Corridor (CPEC) project being collectively executed by Beijing and Islamabad is believed to be directly aimed at the strategic containment of India in the South Asian region.

A part of the broader One Belt One Road (OBOR) initiative of China, the CPEC project is a massive infrastructural undertaking involving large-scale Chinese investments into Pakistan, including in the contested Pak-occupied Kashmir (PoK) region. The CPEC aims to connect China's largest province Xinjiang with Pakistan's Gwadar port in Balochistan. New Delhi has vehemently opposed the project having strategic implications for India's own security, sovereignty and territorial integrity.

KEY DEFENCE PERSONS

DEFENCE MINISTER: Pervez Khattak

CHAIRMAN JOINT CHIEFS OF STAFF COMMITTEE: Gen. Nadeem Raza

CHIEF OF ARMY: Gen. Qamar Javed Bajwa

CHIEF OF NAVY: Adm. Amjad Khan Niazi

CHIEF OF AIR FORCE: Air Chief Marshal Zaheer Ahmad Babar Sidhu

Internal Conflict

Pakistan is grappling with several internal problems, including terrorism, religious, ethnic and sectarian violence, and organised crime.

Terrorism: The foremost internal threat Pakistan faces today is terrorism. Recurrent political instability and volatility, alternating military regimes and the country's support to US-led war on terror post 9/11 have aggravated the Islamic extremism problem which has become a major cause of concern for the country's internal security apparatus in present times. The armed conflict in North West Pakistan has also intensified over the years with militant elements in the region, which were once nurtured by the country, posing a serious internal security threat. The Pakistan Army in its 2013 military doctrine described home-grown militant groups and non-state actors as the "biggest threat" to the country's internal security. In fact, in the aftermath of American troops' withdrawal from the strife-torn Afghanistan in August 2021 and the subsequent take over of Kabul by Taliban, Pakistan has witnessed a sharp rise in terror-related attacks within its territory.

Ethnic and religious unrest: Pakistan has been dealing with religious and ethnic unrest since its creation in 1947. The religious violence in Pakistan has largely been rooted in the country's birth as a theocratic state. The sectarian strife between Shia and Sunni Muslims in the country has often taken violent form. Political, economic and social factors have also played a role in the ethnic, religious and sectarian conflicts in the country.

Organised crime: Pakistan deals with the issues of drug trafficking, money laundering, extortion, fraud and other forms of organised crime which have often been linked to terrorist groups operating in the country.

External Conflict

The external conflict area for Pakistan has solely revolved around India ever since both the nations got separated over seven decades ago. While Kashmir remains the flashpoint in bilateral ties between the two neighbours, several other factors have further accentuated Indo-Pak dispute, including Islamabad sponsored cross border terrorism and proxy war against India since decades.

Territorial disputes: Pakistan is engaged in land border disputes with two of its immediate neighbours, India and Afghanistan.

India: The central point of territorial dispute between Pakistan and India is Kashmir. While India controls approximately 43% of the region, including most of Jammu, the Kashmir Valley, Ladakh, and the Siachen Glacier, Pakistan has occupied approximately 37% of Kashmir, namely 'Azad Kashmir' (PoK) and the northern areas of Gilgit and Baltistan. The rest of the territory is under the control of China after being illegally ceded to that country by Pakistan under the China-Pakistan Boundary Agreement of 1963. Islamabad has contested New Delhi's position that Jammu and Kashmir is an integral part of India. The troubled history of Partition and Jammu and Kashmir's accession to India has resulted in bitter conflicts between the two countries from time to time.

(Indian Government on August 5, 2019 decided to abrogate Article 370 of the Indian Constitution which had granted special status and autonomy to the state of Jammu & Kashmir since 1949. The Government of India announced to bifurcate Jammu & Kashmir and Ladakh into two separate Union Territories which would be directly administered by the Union Government henceforth. The decisive move has radically changed the dynamics of India-Pakistan relations involving the contentious issue of Kashmir.)

Another territorial dispute between Pakistan and India involves the Siachen Glacier located in the eastern Karakoram range of the Himalaya Mountains. The glacier is the highest battlefield on Earth with both India and Pakistan maintaining permanent military presence in the area. The conflict in the region originates from the 1972 Simla Agreement that did not clearly mention who controlled the glacier. India occupied the entire glacier and its tributary glaciers in 1984 while Pakistan presently controls areas just a few kilometres to the west. A ceasefire agreement is effective in the area since 2003.

A maritime dispute between Pakistan and India involves the Sir Creek estuary at the mouth of the Rann of Kutch in the Arabian Sea. The strip of water divides the Kutch region of Indian state Gujarat with the Sindh province of Pakistan. Both countries seek a technical resolution of the issue.

Afghanistan: Pakistan and Afghanistan, which share a land boundary spanning for over 2,400 km and mostly covering mountainous terrain, spar over the Durand Line that separates the two countries. The Durand Line was drawn in 1893 between British government and then Afghan king Abdur Rahman Khan. It brought some tribal regions under the British administration which was reigning over the undivided India at that time. The line became the border between Pakistan and Afghanistan in 1947 after India's partition. Afghanistan, however, does not recognise it as the Af-Pak border and stakes claim over some of the areas the Durand Line runs through that are inhabited by Pashtun tribes and fall in Pakistan's territory. Pakistan's repeated attempts to convert the Durand Line into international border have been opposed by Afghanistan. Pakistan-based militant groups have been blamed for most of the deadly attacks inside Afghanistan in recent times. The (erstwhile) Government in Kabul had accused Islamabad of causing instability and unrest in Afghanistan.

THREAT PERSPECTIVE

India: Pakistan has historically perceived India as its foremost military threat. India's conventional military prowess has outclassed that of Pakistan's in all aspects. The Indo-Pak wars in the past have clearly determined the military imbalance between the two neighbouring nations. India's obvious dominance in this lopsided equation stems from the very fact that while New Delhi has always aspired to rise as a major regional and global powerhouse with military strength being an important part of it, Pakistan, on the other hand, has single-mindedly focused on building up its defence arsenal only to counter India and its steady rise. The Islamic country lives in the "perpetually pseudo" fear of an Indian invasion of its territory and hence bears an aggressive posture towards New Delhi.

Though India does not pose an "existential threat" to Pakistan and has, in fact, adopted a "Cold Start" military strategy which is meant to deter its powerful military from eliminating the neighbour, nevertheless New Delhi has prepared itself well to face any asymmetric and fourth-generation warfare tactics raised by both state and non-state actors of Pakistan. The Indian Army, Navy and Air Force with all necessary modern military assets are fully equipped and well-trained to counter any misdemeanour by Pakistan.

India has pursued a comprehensive military modernisation programme over the years and added the requisite strength to its armed forces. Acquisition of new-generation weapons and platforms for the Army, Navy and Air Force along with modernisation of existing military hardware has been carried out even as New Delhi is evaluating options to revise its decades-old military doctrine to meet asymmetric and fourth-generation warfare tactics. Steady induction of a large number of advanced battle tanks, naval frigates and destroyers, submarines, aircraft carriers, multi-role fighters, combat drones and new missile systems have immensely bolstered the military might of India to counter any "two-front" simultaneous war scenario with Pakistan and China.

Marred by the decades-long proxy war strategy of Pakistan which sends scores of terrorists into the Indian soil to carry out deadly attacks, the Indian military has adopted a tougher posture against any kind of provocations by Islamabad. New Delhi had conducted a "surgical strike" on the terror launch pads along the LoC following a terror attack at an Indian Army camp at Uri, Kashmir in September 2016.

Conflict between India and Pakistan has intensified in recent times with both sides continuously exchanging fire at their border regions for many months from now. The border dispute has further escalated and touched new low after India's strategic move to abrogate Article 370 of the Indian Constitution. Relentless cross-border firings and related skirmishes by the Pakistani Army has made the Indian Army give a befitting reply to the adversary. In recent months too, Pakistan has once again revived its proxy war strategy against India by infiltrating terrorists and even flying drones carrying ammunitions across the LoC to disturb peace and prosperity in the region.

Afghanistan: Afghanistan, which provides direct access to Pakistan to enter the resource-rich Central Asian region, has been engaged in military skirmishes with Islamabad, mostly over the border issue. Alleged attempts by Pakistan to establish a "proxy regime" in Afghanistan to gain strategic benefits has caused tension between the two nations in the past. While the recent withdrawal of American troops from Afghanistan in August 2021 followed by the seizure of Kabul by Taliban might have been welcomed at some Pakistani quarters, it may exacerbate Islamabad's troubles in the longer run.

For decades, the cross-border insurgency issue has caused acrimony between the two neighbours, with each accusing the other of harbouring militants in its territory. The border situation between Pakistan and Afghanistan also remains tense with both sides engaged in heavy gunfire exchanges and clashes at frequent intervals, resulting in civilian and military casualties.

STRATEGIC RELATIONS

China: China has remained Pakistan's most important strategic and military ally for the last sixty years or so. Beijing has supplied several key defence equipment, jointly developed sophisticated weapon systems & platforms, and conducted joint military drills with Pakistani forces from time to time. The Chinese assistance to Pakistan is mostly aimed at building up and strengthening the latter's indigenous conventional military power with a special thrust on air combat and naval capabilities. Most of Pakistan's nuclear arsenal and missile technology have also been provided by China. The ever-growing defence ties between the two countries is widely being viewed as a strategy to counter India and its rising regional and global power status. The conventional military equipment supply contracts China has clinched with Pakistan include those for main battle tanks, naval frigates, combat jets and fighter bombers, some of which also include transfer of technology. Pakistan has also signed deals to acquire larger warships, submarines and unmanned aerial vehicles from China. From the economic perspective, the ambitious but controversial CPEC (China Pakistan Economic Corridor) project under the Chinese leadership claims to bring in huge economic dividends for Islamabad in the coming years. The multi-billion dollar trade and investment project, with major strategic implications for the entire South Asian region, has brought the two "all-weather" allies further closer in recent times.

US: The US military assistance to Pakistan dates back to 1950s when the two countries signed the Mutual Defence Assistance Agreement in 1954 and the US later supplied a large number of F-86 Sabre fighters to the Pak Air Force. Military cooperation between the two sides deepened following the 9/11 terror attacks on the US. As a major non-NATO ally of the US in the war against terror since 2001, Pakistan has received a number of sophisticated platforms and weapons including fighter jets, surveillance aircraft, attack helicopters, naval craft and anti-missile defence systems from Washington. The US Government has also provided Pakistan financial aid worth billions of dollars since 2002. The annual funding, however, has declined in recent years owing to deteriorating relations between the two sides. Pakistan's continuous and clandestine support to Islamic militant groups hiding inside its territory which are hostile to the US has resulted in the dwindling Pak-US relationship of late. Washington sharply cut both military and economic aid to Pakistan, showing its resentment over the nuclear-armed Islamabad's tacit support to the terror outfit Taliban in the neighbouring Afghanistan. The recent withdrawal of US troops from Afghanistan in August 2021 may appear to be a welcome development for the supporters of Taliban regime in Pakistan. However, it could have wider and deeper security implications for Pakistan in the longer run, such as an influx of refugees from Afghanistan and the resurgence of local militant groups emboldened by Taliban victories. In fact, terrorism and related violence may engulf the peripheral region due to the strategic vacuum caused by the sudden US withdrawal from war-torn Afghanistan, military analysts have warned.

Russia: Pakistan's growing closeness to Russia, especially in the military domain, has come at a time of rapid geopolitical developments in the Asian continent. While being increasingly alienated by its once-strong strategic ally – the US, Islamabad is now steadily inching closer to Moscow from which it has received some military hardware, including attack helicopters, in recent times. The Armies of the two countries have been holding annual joint military drill, "Druzhba", since 2016, indicating revival of bilateral military ties between them after decades of hiatus. In 2017, a military-technical cooperation agreement between Islamabad and Moscow was signed involving arms supply, weapon development and upgrade of military products. Additionally, Islamabad signed an agreement with Moscow in 2018 under which Pakistani military personnel would receive training in Russia.

Iran: The two South Asian countries have maintained close strategic relationship over the last six decades. Defence cooperation between Iran and Pakistan has involved joint development of defence equipment including armoured vehicles, battle tanks, helicopters and unmanned systems. The two countries have also conducted joint military exercises in the past. The Iran-Pakistan strategic relationship has often been termed a 'clandestine affair' with the latter supplying nuclear technology to the former, thus raising international concern. The Pak-Iran bilateral ties, however, has witnessed some strains in recent past with some points of contention, including apparent growing proximity of Iran with India.

Saudi Arabia: The decades-old close strategic and military ties between Pakistan and Saudi Arabia has largely remained an interdependent affair. While Saudi Arabia has provided extensive financial and other aid to Pakistan, in return it has received military aid and expertise from the latter. Pakistan-Saudi Arabia relation extends to close military cooperation including provision of Pakistan Army Contingents for Saudi security in crisis situations. Pakistan has also provided training teams for Saudi Armed Forces. The most significant aspect of this relationship in recent times, however, has been Pakistan's secret attempts to provide nuclear technology to Saudi Arabia. Recently, the two sides have pledged to enhance strategic relations between their armies and increase joint exercises. Saudi Arabia is also reportedly planning to buy the JF-17 fighter jets jointly produced by China and Pakistan.

Turkey: The two countries, which were once part of the Central Treaty Organisation during the Cold War era, have remained strong partners in the area of military cooperation. Defence ties between the two sides has reached unprecedented level in recent times. Turkey has supplied defence equipment to Pakistan. Presently, both countries are exploring options of collaboration in defence production with Ankara offering its military hardware, including combat vehicles, naval vessels and Unmanned Aerial Vehicles to Islamabad along with assistance in manufacturing the systems. A Turkish firm has assisted a Pakistani shipbuilder in manufacturing a fleet tanker for the Pak Navy. Turkey has also won a contract to build four new corvettes for the Pakistani Navy. Pakistan has delivered indigenously-built parts for the Turkish UAV "ANKA" to Turkish Aerospace Industry (TAI). TAI, which manufactures the UAVs, has signed a contract with Pakistan's National Engineering and Science Commission (NESCOM) in August 2021 to jointly produce the ANKA military drones.

The TAI has also carried out avionics and structural modernisation of 41 F-16 fighter jets operated by the Pakistani Air Force. Pakistan has evinced interest in buying Turkish-built "Altay" main battle tanks. Islamabad won a major defence contract in 2017 to supply 52 Super Mushshak jet trainers to Turkey. In 2018, the two sides inked their largest-ever defence deal worth US$1.5 billion under which Turkey was to deliver 30 of its indigenously-built T129 attack helicopters to Pakistan. The deal, however, was later blocked by the US after Turkey's failure to replace the US-made engines onboard the rotorcraft.

Malaysia: Bilateral strategic and defence cooperation between Pakistan and Malaysia has gained momentum in recent times with the two countries holding regular dialogue to boost relations. Military ties between the two sides date back to the 1950s and involve joint exercises, training programmes and defence exchanges. The two countries are also exploring joint production of military equipment and systems.

DEFENCE CAPABILITIES

ARMY: The Pakistan Army is the largest wing of Pakistan's armed forces and is a voluntary force. It is primarily tasked with defending the homeland from external aggression. The powerful Army, however, has attempted to control the entire Pakistan from time to time with an intention to usher in effective administration and make the country corruption-free while instilling a sense of unity among the citizens. All military regimes in Pakistan's history have been headed by an Army official.

The modernisation plans of Pakistan Army include upgradation/ rebuilding of existing main battle tanks (MBTs) and armoured vehicles, acquisition of new artillery, attack and transport helicopters along with other hardware while phasing out obsolete ground platforms and systems. According to recent reports, the country is also planning to procure around 600 new MBTs under a mega plan to significantly revamp its armoured fleet by 2025.

Personnel: 5,50,000 (+ 5,20,000 reserves)

Equipment

Category	Name	In Service
MBT	Al Khalid I	300+
	Al Khalid II	20+ (more on order)
	VT-4	
	T85-IIAP	250 (up-graded)
	Type 69	250
	T-80 UD	330
	Type 59 (Al Zarrar)	500+ (being upgraded)
Light tank	T60	100+
APC	M113	800+
	Al Fahd	140
	Talha	500+
	BTR-70	120
Artillery	155mm Panter	12
	M198 155mm	120+
	M114 155mm	65
	Type-59 130mm	200
	Type-60 122mm	600
	M101 105mm	300+
	Type-56 85mm	180
	M7 105mm	12
	M109A2	300
	M109A5 155mm	115
	M110 203mm	12
	Norinco SH1 155mm wheeled	85+
Mortar	120mm	
MLRS	BM2 122mm	30+
	A-100	
RCL	75mm	
	106mm	
ATGW	TOW (I & II)	5000
	M901 TUA	24
	Cobra	
	Baktar Shikan	
SSM	Ghauri-1	10+
SAM	HQ-7B (FM-90)	
	HQ-9	
	HQ-16 (LY-80)	
	RBS 70	410
	CSA1	6+

...continued

Category	Name	In Service
SAM	Stringer	100
	Anza (MK I /II)	
AA Gun	ZU23 30mm	
	ZU23 35mm	
	37mm	
	40mm	60
	57mm	
	90mm	15

Army Aviation

Category	Name	In Service
Combat/ Utility helicopter	Mi-35	4 (more on order)
	Z-10	3
	Cobra AH-1S/1F	40
	SA.330 Puma	33
	Bell 206	10
	Mi-8	7
	Mi-17	28+
	Alouette III	24
	UH-1	15
	Bell 412EP	26
	AW-139	2
Liaison & Light Transport	Cessna O-1E	35
	Mushshak	130+
VIP Transport	Cessna 421	2
	Queen Air	
	Y-12	2
	Turbo commander	

New Procurements/Upgrades

◆ The first batch of advanced Al Khalid-II main battle tank (MBT) has been inducted in service in July 2020. The new platform, featuring enhanced power pack, fire-control/gun-control system among other upgrades, has been developed indigenously in partnership with China and Ukraine.

◆ The first batch of China's NORINCO-built VT-4 MBTs has been deployed in service. Delivery of the platforms started in April 2020.

◆ Induction of upgraded T-59 'Al Zarrar' (Chinese built) MBTs is going on.

◆ Around 150 of the Type-85IIAP MBTs have been upgraded and inducted in service.

◆ Delivery of 155mm M109L self-propelled artillery guns by Italy is going on. A total of 245 guns are being delivered from Italian Army's surplus inventory.

◆ Russian-built 9K129 Kornet-E anti-tank guided missiles are on order.

◆ Nearly 300 of the Chinese-made FN-16 MANPADs are on order.

◆ A domestically developed 300-mm multiple rocket launch system, designated A-100, has been inducted in service. The weapon is derivate of a Chinese MRLS.

◆ A deal has been signed with Turkey in 2018 for 30 T129 attack helicopters built by Turkish Aerospace Industries (TAI). All the platforms were to be delivered by 2023. The deal, however, was blocked by the US in 2019 after Turkey's failure to replace the US-made engines onboard the helicopter platforms. Pakistan, meanwhile, has extended the deadline to get delivery of the platforms.

◆ Four Mi-35 'Hind E' attack helicopters have been delivered by Russia in 2017. More such platforms are reportedly on order.

◆ A deal to acquire 12 AH-1Z Viper attack helicopters from the US under a 2015 agreement has been stalled over political issues.

◆ US's Bell Helicopter has been awarded a contract to develop weapon system for the Army's AH-1S/1F Cobra attack helicopters.

◆ CH-4 UAVs have reportedly been acquired from China.

NAVY: The Pakistan Navy is the maritime wing of Pakistan Armed Forces and also includes marine forces and coast guard. The Navy operates a few submarines, destroyers, frigates, corvettes and missile boats along with fixed-wing aircraft and helicopters. The primary task of the Navy is to protect and defend the country's territorial waters and guard Pakistan's sea frontiers, sea trade and maritime interests. The Navy also operates with the mission to be a technologically driven and sustainable force; maintain qualitative superiority in conventional forces and asymmetric fighting capability to offset the advantage of numerically superior adversaries; and to operate in synergy with other services, especially the PAF and be ready to participate in Joint Operations whenever required. To strengthen its maritime strike capability, Pakistan Navy is undergoing modernisation as part of the Armed Forces Development Programme 2019 and inducted new maritime platforms in recent past. Additionally, acquisition of new attack submarines along with surface combat ships including frigates, corvettes and OPVs has been lined up as part of the comprehensive naval modernisation drive.

Major naval bases: Ormara, Pasni, Gwadar, Karachi, Jiwani

Personnel: 20,000+

Equipment

Category	Name	In Service	On Order
Submarine	Yuan class (Chinese Type 041)		8

...continued

Category	Name	In Service	On Order
Submarine	Khalid class (French-Agosta 90B)	3 (being upgraded)	
	Hashmat class (French - Agosta)	2	
	Sx404 class (Midget)	3	
Frigate	Zulfiquar class (F-22P)	4	
	Tariq class (ex-UK Type 21)	5	
	Alamgir (ex-USS McInerney)	1	
	Type 054A/P	1	3
Corvette	MILGEM-class		4
Missile boat/ FAC	Larkana class	2	
	Quwwat class	2	
	Jalalat class	4	
	Azmat class	3	1
	MRTP-33	2	
OPV/MPV	Yarmook-class (Damen multi-role OPV)	2	
	600-ton MPV	4	2
Mine Sweeper & Mine Hunter	Munsif class (French Tripartite Type)	3	
Auxiliary ship	Fleet tanker	1	
	Fleet oiler	2	
	Coastal tanker	2	
	Inshore tanker	1	
	Small tanker/ utility ship	2	
	Survey ship	1	
Weapon	(ASM) C-602, Zarb (new C-602 variant for coastal defence), C-802A, Harpoon, SM 39 Exocet		
	Babur LACM		
	(Torpedo) Tp 45, (lightweight) Mk-46, Black Shark		

New Procurements/Upgrades

◆ A deal has been announced in 2015 to buy eight diesel-electric attack submarines from China at an estimated cost of US$5 billion. The platforms would be based on Chinese Yuan-class (Type 039B/ 041) of conventional attack submarines. Delivery is expected to commence from 2022. While four of the submarines will be built by China, four others would be manufactured locally at a Pakistani shipyard.

◆ A contract has been awarded to Turkish company STM in 2016 to carry out mid-life upgrade of all three of the Khalid-class (French Agosta 90B) submarines of Pak Navy. The upgrades would be carried out in collaboration with a Pakistani shipyard (KSEW). All upgraded platforms are slated for delivery by 2022.

◆ PNS Tughril – the first of four advanced Type 054A/P class of frigates on order from China, has been commissioned in January 2022. Work on three other such multi-role platforms is advancing.

◆ Three Azmat-class missile FACs have been inducted in service. Fourth platform of the class was launched in November 2019.

◆ First MILGEM-class corvette ordered from Turkey has been launched at a Turkish shipyard in August 2021 followed by the second platform in November 2021. Delivery is slated for 2023. Turkish defence engineering firm STM won a contract in 2018 to build and deliver four MILGEM (Ada-class) corvettes to Pak Navy. While two platforms would be built in Turkey, Pakistan's Karachi Shipyard & Engineering Works Ltd (KSEW) will locally manufacture other two platforms with assistance from STM. KSEW laid the keel for the first platform in June 2020 and that of the second platform in June 2021. The new warships would be deployed to guard the Gwadar and Karachi ports.

◆ The second Yarmook-class multi-role OPV, locally built by Pakistan's KSEW in assistance with Netherlands' Damen Shipyards, has been commissioned in November 2020. The first platform was inducted in February 2020.

◆ Four new maritime patrol vessels constructed with Chinese assistance have been delivered to the Navy. Two more similar platforms are under construction.

Naval Aviation

Category	Name	In Service
ASW/ Surveillance	P-3 Orion	7
	Atlantic	2
	F-27	6
	ATR-72	3
ASW/Utility Helicopter	Sea King	20
	Alouette III	15
	Z-9C	12
	AW139	
UAV	Scaneagle	1
	Uqab-II	1 squadron

New Procurements/Upgrades

◆ Two ATR-72 turboprop aircraft have been refurbished to maritime patrol configuration.

AIR FORCE: The Pakistan Air Force (PAF) operates with the mission to provide aerial defence to Pakistan in synergy with the Army and Navy. The PAF operates over 500 fighter aircraft along with some reconnaissance, transport and trainer aircraft. Under the Armed Forces Development Programme 2019 initiated by the Government, the PAF is undergoing modernisation by acquiring new platforms and weapons, including fighter aircraft, airborne early warning aircraft, mid-air refuellers, UAVs and long-range missiles among others.

Major air bases: Karachi, Peshawar, Quetta, Kamra, Mianwali, Shorkot, Jacobabad, Chaklala (Rawalpindi) and Sargodha

Personnel: 70,000

Equipment

Category	Name	In Service
Fighter	JF-17 Block I, II	90+ (more on order)
	JF-17 Block III	50 (to be inducted)
	JF-17B	12 (+14 more on order)
	F-16 A/ B	54
	F-16 C/ D	18
	Mirage IIIEP	16
	F-7P	270+
	F-7PG	
	Mirage IIIRP	3
	Mirage 5PA/ DPA	56
	Mirage 5EF	34
	Mirage IIIEA	33
	Mirage IIIDA	5
	Mirage 5DF	5
	A5III	120+
Transport/ Surveillance/ Tanker	C130B/ E	16
	CN-235-200	3 + 1 (VIP)
	F-27	1
	Falcon 20	1
	Boeing 707	2
	A310	1
	Cessna 172	4
	Y-12	2
	Il-78	4
AWACS / AEW	Falcon 20F	2
	Mi-171	3
	Saab 2000 Erieye	6
	ZDK-03	4
Trainer	MFI-178	78
	FT5	25
	T-37	50+
	K-8	55
Helicopter	Alouette-III	12
	AW-139	2
	Bell 412EP	24

...continued

Category	Name	In Service
UAV	ScanEagle	
	Wing Loong II	
Weapon	(AAM) AIM-9B Sidewinder, PL-5E, PL-9 PL-12 (SD-10), Hatf-8 (Raad)	
	(SAM) Crotale AD systems Aspide 2000 HQ-2B	
	(AGM) AM 39 Exocet, AGM-65 Maverick, C-802	

New Procurements/ Upgrades

◆ Possible acquisition of Su-35 Flanker-E multi-role fighters from Russia is under consideration.

◆ Acquisition of additional six second-hand F-16 fighters from Jordan is under consideration.

◆ The US State Department in 2019 approved an FMS (foreign military sales) worth $125 million to provide technical support services to the PAF's fleet of F-16 fighters.

◆ A decision is yet to be taken on the PAF's plans to acquire two squadrons (36) of the advanced J-10B multi-role, all-weather fighter aircraft from China, negotiations for which were initiated in 2009.

◆ Progressive induction of JF-17 fighters, jointly built with China, is going on. PAF plans to induct over 200 JF-17s in Block I, II and III configurations in coming years. The new multi-role fighters are replacing the Mirage and F-7 aircraft of the PAF. Serial production of the advanced Block III variant has started with the PAF looking forward to deploy all the 50 Block III fighters by 2024. The Block III variant is upgraded with China-built AESA radar to improve its combat capability.

◆ 12 of the JF-17B 'Thunder' fighters (advanced variant of JF-17) have been inducted. 14 more such platforms are to be commissioned. Pakistan has built some of these fighters while the remaining have been manufactured by China.

◆ A total of 60 CM-400AKG air-launched cruise missiles (export variant of Chinese-made YJ-12) have likely been acquired to arm the JF-17 fighters. Plans are also afoot to equip the platforms with indigenously-built Ra'ad II (Hatf 8) air-launched cruise missiles.

◆ Three more SAAB 2000 AEW&C aircraft with EriEye radar have been delivered.

◆ All four Karakorum Eagle 03 (KE-03/ ZDK-03) airborne early warning and control (AEW&C) aircraft have been received from China, forming the KE-03 AEW&C squadron of the PAF.

◆ Rockwell Collins is upgrading the entire fleet of C-130 Hercules transport aircraft.

◆ China has announced to sell at least 50 Wing Loong II high-end reconnaissance, strike and multi-role endurance unmanned aircraft systems to Pakistan.

◆ The US Govt has cleared a $15.2 million FMS deal to supply ScanEagle UAVs to PAF.

STRATEGIC FORCES COMMAND:

Pakistan formed the National Command Authority (NCA) on February 2, 2000, to oversee the country's strategic nuclear arsenal and related organisations. The NCA operates with a unified central command structure and comprises of the Strategic Plans Division (SPD) and Strategic Forces Commands of the three military branches – Army, Navy and Air Force. The SPD has an elaborate Security Division which includes a counter-intelligence network to safeguard the activities of strategic organisations. It also has in place a dedicated multi-layered security apparatus to safeguard strategic assets. The Strategic Forces Command comprises of Army Strategic Forces Command, Naval Strategic Forces Command and Air Force Strategic Command. Pakistan raised the strength of its SPD Security Force to 25,000 in 2013 to provide fool-proof security to the country's nuclear weapons and strategic assets. In May 2012, the Navy also inaugurated a new Naval Strategic Force Command (NSFC). The new command was set up to perform a pivotal role in the development and employment of the Naval Strategic Force and would be the custodian of the nation's 2nd strike capability. The future submarine-based nuclear capability is also being managed by the NSFC.

Potential weapons

Hatf is a series of ballistic and cruise missiles of Pakistan with different ranges. The missile has been developed as an offensive weapon. The indigenously-built missiles can carry both conventional and nuclear warheads.

Variants

◆ Hatf-1 is a two-stage solid propelled short range ballistic missile (SRBM) having a range between 70 km and 100 km.

◆ Hatf-2 (Abdali-1) is a short-range surface-to-surface ballistic missile. The weapon has a range of 180 km and can carry nuclear and conventional warheads.

◆ Hatf-3 (Ghaznavi) is a road mobile, solid propellant, single warhead ballistic missile with a range of 290 km.

◆ Hatf-4 (Shaheen-1) is a single stage SRBM having a range between 750 km to 900 km. A new improved variant of the missile, known as Shaheen-1A, was tested in April 2012. The range of the missile has not been revealed.

◆ Hatf-5 and Hatf-5B (Ghauri-1, Ghauri-2) are MRBMs having operational range of 1300 km and 2,300 km respectively.

◆ Hatf-6 (Shaheen-2) is a medium range ballistic missile (MRBM) having a range between 2,000 km and 2,500 km. Another advanced variant, Shaheen-3, has been developed as a multi-stage surface-to-surface MRBM having an estimated range of 2,750 km. It can carry both nuclear and conventional warheads.

◆ Hatf-7 (Babur) is a nuclear-capable cruise missile having a range of 700 km. The multi-tube cruise missile can carry both conventional as well as nuke warhead. Pakistan has also developed and tested the improved Babur 2 and the submarine-launched Babur 3 missile variants in 2016-17. In 2018, yet another enhanced version – Babur Weapon System-1 (B) was tested. The weapon has been described as "a low-flying, terrain-hugging missile having certain stealth features."

◆ Hatf-8 (Raad) is an air-launched cruise missile having a range of 350 km. The weapon can carry both conventional and nuclear warhead and has been developed exclusively for launch from combat aircraft. An extended range Raad-2 having a stated range of 600 km was unveiled in 2017. The air-launched missile was test fired in February 2020.

◆ Hatf-9 (Nasr) is a short-range surface-to-surface ballistic missile capable of carrying nuclear warhead. The missile has a range of 60 km.

◆ Ababeel, a surface-to-surface medium range ballistic missile, was tested for the first time in January 2017. The weapon is reportedly capable of carrying multiple nuclear warheads (MIRVs) and has a maximum range of 2,200 km. (Operational deployment of the weapon is not confirmed)

Major Armaments Producers

Heavy Industries Taxila (HIT) is a state-controlled defence firm that produces main battle tanks, combat vehicles, artillery and related equipment for the Pakistan Army. Government has initiated steps to turn it into a corporate entity.

Pakistan Ordnance Factories (POF)

is the leading producer of small arms and ammunitions.

Karachi Shipyard and Engineering Works (KSEW) is the leading producer of naval vessels, including warships and submarines.

Pakistan Aeronautical Complex (PAC) is the state-owned aerospace firm engaged in assembly, overhaul and production of aircraft and related components for the PAF.

Air Weapons Complex produces air-borne weapons systems.

National Development Complex has been established as an aerospace and defence agency to undertake research and development of various missile programmes.

Surveillance and Target Unmanned Aircraft (SATUMA) is a private-run firm that produces unmanned aerial vehicles and related equipment.

DEFENCE DEALS

Joint Venture / Collaboration Programmes

China

Al-Khalid MBT: Pakistan developed the Al-Khalid main battle tank with Chinese assistance in the 1990s. The MBTs are operational with the Pakistan Army.

Hongdu JL-8 jet trainer: The Pakistan Aeronautical Complex (PAC) joined hands with China's Hongdu Aviation Industry Corporation (HAIC) to manufacture the Hongdu JL-8 (export variant Karakorum-8 or K-8) single engine two-seat advanced jet trainer aircraft with light attack capabilities. Pakistan's share in the joint venture is 25%. PAF uses the K-8P variant of the jet trainer.

JF-17 Thunder (FC-1) combat aircraft: The multi-role JF-17 Thunder combat aircraft was jointly developed by China and Pakistan in the 1990s. Pakistan announced serial production of the new fighter jet in February 2011. Pakistan Air Force plans to acquire as many as 250 such fighters and also intends to sell the platform in the international market. The two countries have announced to jointly export an upgraded variant of the multi-role fighter to foreign customers.

F-22 naval frigate: Pakistan, with China's assistance, has built four F-22 guided missile frigates. The Pakistan Navy has inducted the warships along with the Chinese Harbin Z-9EC helicopters.

Turkey

Ada-class corvette: The two countries have finalised a deal to build Ada-class (Milgem) corvettes for the Pakistan Navy. While two platforms are being built in Turkey, Pakistan's Karachi Shipyard & Engineering Works Ltd. (KSEW) is locally manufacturing two more such warships with assistance from Turkish defence engineering firm STM.

LST: Turkey has assisted Pakistan in locally building a new fleet tanker, PNS Moawin. It is the largest-ever warship built in Pakistan by the Karachi Shipyard (KSEW).

Saudi Arabia

Pakistan has expressed interest to form joint ventures with Saudi Arabia to produce defence systems, including tanks, armoured vehicles and missiles. Saudi Arabia has also evinced interest in the JF-17 Thunder fighter. Pakistan has reportedly offered to sell the fighters to Saudi Arabia along with technology transfer and co-production.

Arms Export

Pakistan, while attempting to attain self-sufficiency in defence production, mainly with Chinese assistance, has been exporting some military parts and weapons to other countries. Defence exports worth $300 million have been made mostly to countries in South Asia, Middle East and Africa in the last few years. Islamabad targeted to earn over $100 million in military exports to some 30 countries in 2015, and in 2016-17, it achieved the target. The country registered defence exports worth around US$213 million in 2018-19, according to official data released by the Ministry of Defence Production. Presently, the country is making persistent efforts to export the JF-17 Thunder fighters it has built in partnership with China. In May 2021, Pakistan delivered three JF-17 platforms to Nigeria.

Arms Import

Pakistan has mostly relied on the US and China to acquire military hardware. Other countries, including France, Germany, Switzerland, Italy and Brazil have also supplied defence equipment to Pakistan. According to a Pentagon report, Pakistan is the top-most buyer of a whole range of Chinese defence equipment that includes fighter aircraft, frigates, helicopters, jet trainers, early warning and control aircraft, tanks, air-to-air missiles and anti-ship cruise missiles. In recent years, Pakistan has inclined more towards China in acquiring new military hardware, leaving behind the US. It has also inched closer to Russia and received attack helicopters even while negotiating to acquire more military platforms from Moscow.

DEFENCE BUDGET

The Pakistan Govt. has traditionally made defence allocations with an objective to maintain conventional parity with India. To keep pace with India's rising defence expenditure, Pakistan too has increased its defence allocation over the years. However, its annual defence expenditure is much less when compared to that of India's. Pakistan's association with the US-led war on terror had also pushed up Islamabad's annual defence expenses as the country's defence budget was supplemented by military aid provided by the US. In 2018, Pakistan was the 20th biggest military spender in the world.

Defence budget for 2017-18 was PKR 999 billion. For 2018-19, Govt. allocated PKR 1,100 billion which was later revised to PKR 1,137 billion. For 2019-20 period, defence budgetary allocation was PKR 1,152 billion (US $7.6 billion) – a nominal increase of 4.5% over previous year.

For FY 2020-21, defence budgetary allocation was PKR 1,289 billion (US $7.8 billion) – an increase of 11.9% over previous year's allocation. For FY 2021 - 22, Pakistan has announced a defence budget of PKR 1.37 trillion (US $8.8 billion) – a hike of 6.28% over past year's allocation.

Official Budgetary Allocation

Year	Allocation	% Increase over previous year
2021-22	Pkr 1.37 trillion (US $8.8 billion)	6.28
2020-21	Pkr 1,289 billion (US $7.8 billion)	11.9
2019-20	Pkr 1,152 billion (US $7.6 billion)	4.5
2018-19	Pkr 1,137 billion (US $9.5 billion)	20
2017-18	Pkr 920.16 billion (US $8.7 billion)	9.3
2016-17	Pkr 860.2 billion (US $8.2 billion)	11
2015-16	Pkr 781 billion (US $7.8 billion)	11
2014-15	Pkr 700. 2 billion (US $7 billion)	11.64
2013-14	Pkr 627 billion (US $6.36 billion)	10
2012-13	Pkr 570 billion (revised) (US $5.82 bn)	10
2011-12	Pkr 495 billion (US $5.75bn)	12

CONCLUSION

Pakistan has maintained a large military force since its inception to counter the conventional military power of India. The small country has built-up and prepared its armed forces to maintain a minimum credible deterrence against India which it regards as its most potent adversary. Toeing the doctrine of "offensive defence" strategy against militarily superior India, Pakistan has focused on acquiring latest weapons and equipment for which it has increased its defence expenditure over the years. Though in terms of size, strength, strategic, military and technological perspective, India overpowers Pakistan, in terms of nuclear prowess though, the latter has perhaps surpassed India by possessing more nuke warheads, according to defence analysts. Pakistan continues to expand its nuclear arsenal with more warheads, more delivery systems, and a growing fissile materials production industry. In a recent report published by a US-based think-tank, Pakistan's current stockpile of nuclear warheads is estimated to be around 165 (as of 2021). If the country continues in the same manner, it would have 200 nuclear warheads by 2025, the report predicts. The country has deployed or is developing a number of delivery systems/ platforms for its nuclear warheads, including aircraft, ballistic and cruise missiles etc. Moreover, the absence of a "no first use" nuclear policy by Pakistan (unlike that of India) has somehow helped Islamabad maintain a credible military deterrence against India which, being a very responsible nation, fully acknowledges the cost and consequences of a full-scale nuclear fallout in the entire Asian continent.

CONTACT DETAILS
Ministry of Defence
www.mod.gov.pk/

Ministry of Defence Production
www.dgmp.gov.pk/

PERU
(Capital: Lima)

INTRODUCTION
Area: 1,285,216 sq km
Population: 32,201,224 (July 2021 est.)
Coastline: 2,414 km
Maritime claims:
Territorial sea: 200 nm
Continental shelf: 200 nm

KEY POLITICAL PERSONS

PRESIDENT: Jose Pedro Castillo Terrones

PRIME MINISTER: Mirtha Esther Vásquez Chuquilin

KEY DEFENCE PERSONS

MINISTER OF DEFENCE: Juan Manuel Carrasco Millions

CHIEF OF JOINT COMMAND OF THE ARMED FORCES: Maj. Gen. Manuel Gómez de la Torre

COMMANDER OF ARMY: Maj. Gen. Walter Horacio Córdova German

COMMANDER OF NAVY: Adm. Alberto Alcalá Luna

COMMANDER OF AIR FORCE: Gen. Alfonso Artadi Saletti

ECONOMY
The Peruvian economy grew by an average of 5.6% per year from 2009-13 with a stable exchange rate and low inflation. Since the US-Peru Trade Promotion Agreement entered into force in February 2009, total trade between Peru and the US has doubled. The country is focusing on economic reforms and free market policies aimed at boosting investment in Peru. Peru is the world's second largest producer of silver and copper. As per Peru's UK Embassy, Peru, as a participant country in the Investment Committee of the OECD, it promotes the implementation of the Guidelines for Multinational Enterprises,

aimed at promoting a healthy business climate and enhancing relations between Peruvian authorities and the international investment community. The country is focusing on economic reforms and free market policies aimed at boosting investment in Peru. Mining output increased significantly in 2016-17, which helped Peru attain one of the highest GDP growth rates in Latin America, and Peru should maintain strong growth in 2018. Peru belongs to many international organisations, including the United Nations, Organisation of American States, Asia-Pacific Economic Cooperation forum, International Monetary Fund, World Bank, and World Trade Organisation. Two-way trade in goods between the United States and Peru has increased from USD9.1 billion in 2009 to USD15.8 billion in 2019, driving growth and employment in both countries, as per US Dept. of State. COVID-19 pandemic restrictions have heavily impacted the mining-driven economy of Peru as mining dropped sharply. Peru has now gradually pushed the reopening of the Peruvian economy.

GDP (official exchange rate): $371.29 billion (2020), $417.88 billion (2019 est.)

Real Growth Rate (GDP): 2.18% (2019 est.), 3.97% (2018 est.)

Industries: Mining and refining of minerals; steel, metal fabrication; petroleum extraction and refining, natural gas and natural gas liquefaction; fishing and fish processing, cement, glass, textiles, clothing, food processing, beer, soft drinks, rubber, machinery, electrical machinery, chemicals, furniture

Oil - proved reserves: 434.9 million bbl (1 January 2018 est.)

Natural gas - proved reserves: 455.9 billion cu m (1 January 2018 est.)

Total Exports: $54.88 billion (2019 est.), $55.84 billion (2018 est.)

Export Commodities: copper, gold, refined petroleum, zinc, fishmeal, tropical fruits, lead, iron, molybdenum (2019)

Major Markets: China 29%, United States 12%, Canada 5%, South Korea 5%, Switzerland 5% (2019)

Total Imports: $51.38 billion (2019 est.), $51.41 billion (2018 est.)

Import Commodities: refined petroleum, crude petroleum, cars, broadcasting equipment, delivery trucks (2019)

Major Suppliers: China 24%, United States 22%, Brazil 6% (2019)

INTERNATIONAL DISPUTES

◆ Peru's November 2005 unilateral legislation to shift the axis of their joint treaty-defined maritime boundaries along the parallels of latitude to equidistance lines was rejected by Chile and Ecuador.

◆ Peru rejects Bolivia's claim to restore maritime access through a sovereign corridor through Chile along the Peruvian border.

DEFENCE

ARMY

Personnel: 55,000

Equipment

Category	Name	In Service
MBT	T-55	40+
	Al-Khalid	30+
	AMX13	30+
APC/IFV	M8 armoured cars	50+
	M113A1	200
	UR416	200
	M325	200+
	Fiat/OTO 6616	20
	BRDM2	30
	BTR-60	10+
	Casspir	20
	V-100 Commando	20+

...continued

Category	Name	In Service
Artillery	105 mm M101	100+
	105 mm M2	50+
	105 mm M56	50
	155 mm M114	30+
	130 mm M46	30
	122 mm towed D30	30+
	155 mm M109A2	10
	155 mm MkF3	10
	122 mm 2S1	
Mortar	81 mm, 120 mm, 160 mm	
	Fiat/OTO 6614 mortar carriers	
	122 mm. BM21	
MRL	Spike	
Anti-Tank GW	Kornet	
AA Gun	4X23 mm. Shilka	20+
	Zu-23-2	20+
	Bofors	20
SAM	SA7	250+
	SPYDER	
	SA-14	100
	SA-16	100+
	TOR M1	
	TOR M1	

Army Aviation

Category	Name	In Service
Aircraft	An-32	3
	An-28	3
	L410	1
	Beechcraft Queen Air	1
	Il-103	5+
Helicopter	SA 315B Lama	5+
	Alouette II/III	8
	Mi8/17	30+
	Mi-171	10+
	Mi26	3
	Agusta A-109	10+
Trainer	Cessna 150	3
	Cessna 172	2
	Cessna 182	1
	Enstrom F-28	3

New Procurements/ Upgrades

No major procurement plans are under consideration at present.

NAVY

Personnel: 25,000

Equipment

Category	Name	In Service
Submarine	Type 209/1200	5+

...continued

Category	Name	In Service
Cruiser	De Zeven Provincien-class	1
Frigate	Carvajal class	3
	Lupo class	4
Corvette	PR-72P-class	5+
Patrol Vessel/ Gun Boat	Loreto class	2
	Clavero class	2
	Maranon class	2
Amphibious Force	Terrebonne Parish class	2
Missile	Exocet, Otomat, Aspide, FN-6, Igla	

Naval Aviation

Category	Name	In Service
Aircraft	An-32	2
	Fokker 60	1
	Beechcraft B200T Super King Air	5
	T-34 C.1 "Turbo Mentor"	5
	Cessna 206	1
	F27-200	3
	De Havilland Canada DHC-6 Twin Otter	1
Helicopter	AB 212 ASW	5
	Bell 206 Jet Ranger	3
	ASH3D Sea King	3
	Mi8T	3
	Enstrom F28F	5

New Procurements/ Upgrades

No major procurement plans are under consideration at present.

AIR FORCE

Personnel: 15,000

Equipment

Category	Name	In Service
Fighters/ attack/Reconnaissance	MiG-29	10+
	A-37B	10+
	Su-25	10+
	Mirage-2000	10
	C-26 Metroliner III	3
Transport/ Tanker	L-100-20	3
	C-27J	1 (More on order)
	DHC-6 Twin Otter	10+
	C-130A	1
	C-130D	
	DC-862CF	1
	C-26A Metro III	
	737-200	3
	An-32B	5+
Helicopter	Bell 212	10+
	Bell 412	2

...continued

Category	Name	In Service
Helicopter	Bell 206	
	MBB Bo 105	10
	SA.316B Alouette III	10
	Mi-8 / Mi 17 Hip	20+
	AB 214ST	
	Mi-25 Hind	
Trainer	Il-103	5+
	Z242L	10+
	EMB 312 Tucano	20
	MB-339	10+
	Cessna 150	2
	Bell 206	2

New Procurements/ Upgrades

◆ The State Concern Ukroboronprom and the Ministry of Interior of the Republic of Peru have signed a number of cooperation agreements in the field of life extension of the Antonov aircraft fleet. Under these agreements, the Ukrainian party will develop the plan to overhaul, retrofit and service the Antonov aircraft previously operated by different agencies of the Ministry of Interior of Peru. After considering the solutions offered by Ukroboronprom enterprises, the customer will determine the terms and conditions of the work. In 2019, SFTE Spetstechnoexport, the enterprise-member of Ukroboronprom, has signed a contract with the Ministry of Interior of the Republic of Peru for supply of An-178 medium transport aircraft.

◆ Viking Air Limited of Victoria, British Columbia, Canada has renewed Twin Otter series 400 "maintenance plus" support contract with Peru Air Force.

◆ Antonov Company has started the general assembly of the fuselage of the AN-178 transport intended for delivery to the Ministry of Internal Affairs of the Republic of Peru. Ukraine's Antonov has begun production of a single An-178 twin-jet military transport ordered by Peru.

Defence Expenditure

Total defence spending: $1,900 million (approx.)

Estimated defence spending in terms of GDP: 1.2% of GDP (2020 est.), 1.2% of GDP (2019)

Major defence suppliers: Russia, United States, France, Italy, Belarus, Spain, China, Ukraine, South Korea, Serbia, Israel, Argentina, Mongolia, Malaysia, Brazil, India & Cuba.

Peru's budget proposal places top priority on national security and defence. The budget provides financing for a new remuneration scale for the Peruvian armed forces and police as well as improved logistics. Giving a boost to its ties with the fastest growing Latin American country, India has signed four agreements with Peru including one on defence cooperation and another on establishment of a Joint Commission. Peru is the largest importer of Russian helicopters in Latin America, with more than 100 Russian-made helicopters operating in the country.

Defence Production and R&D

The Peruvian Army's weapon and ammunition factory (FAME) was re-organised and established in 2009 as an independent entity in the defence industry sector of the Ministry of Defence. Currently, Peru is concentrating on maintenance and upgrade capabilities. Shipbuilding is also developing there.

Defence Procurement

The Peruvian Armed Forces' existing arsenal is impressive but is extraordinarily heterogeneous in origin and much of it is ageing, in storage, or out of service. Plans to retire most unnecessary equipment will improve overall readiness. Major acquisitions might take place in areas such as armoured weapons and air defence systems and also improvements in command and control assets.

CONTACT DETAILS

Ministry of National Defence
Av. De la Peruanidad s / n
Jesús María, Lima, Lima, Peru
Tel: (+511) 209 8530
www.mindef.gob.pe

Joint Command of the Armed Forces of Peru
Nicolás Corpancho street 289, Santa Beatriz
Lima, Peru
Tel: (511) 3151030
Email: informaciones@ccffaa.mil.pe

FAME
Ex. Hacienda Nievería Km. 3.5
Carretera Cajamarquilla
LURIGANCHO
CHOSICA
PERU
E-mail: ventas@famesac.com
Tel: (+511) 717 8791
Fax: (+511) 356 4119
http://www.famesac.com

A Peruvian Agusta AB 212 helicopter approaches the flight deck of the guided missile cruiser USS Thomas S. Gates (CG 51) during a helicopter cross deck training exercise in the Caribbean Sea in 2005.

STRATEGIC INFORMATION
PHILIPPINES
(Capital: Manila)

INTRODUCTION

Area: 300,000 sq km
Population: 1110,818,325 (July 2021 est.)
Coastline: 36,289 km
Maritime claims: Irregular polygon extending up to 100 nm from coastline as defined by 1898 treaty; Since late 1970s has also claimed polygonal-shaped area in South China Sea as wide as 285 nm
Exclusive Economic Zone: 200 nm
Continental shelf: to depth of exploitation

GEOPOLITICAL IMPORTANCE

The Philippines, an archipelago with one of the world's longest coastlines, an important and strategic gateway to Asia from the Pacific. The country is located in South-Eastern Asia, between the Philippine Sea and the resource-rich South China Sea. Forming part of the Malay archipelago, it consists of 7,107 islands and islets of which only 2,773 have names and about 500 are larger than a square kilometre. The three major island groups are Luzon, Visayas and Mindanao. More than half of the world's shipping tonnage and 80 percent of crude oil shipments headed to Japan and South Korea pass through the Philippines which lies at a vital maritime crossroad. The archipelago, situated at the confluence of major trade routes and its proximity to other Asian countries makes it an ideal hub for industry and commerce. Its strategic location makes it crucial to the rest of the world. The country is a founding member of the United Nations, World Trade Organisation, Association of Southeast Asian Nations, and East Asia Summit.

POLITICAL OVERVIEW

The Philippines is a republic with a presidential form of government wherein power is equally divided among its three branches: Executive, Legislative, and Judiciary. One basic corollary in a presidential system of government is the principle of separation of powers wherein legislation belongs to Congress, execution to the Executive, and settlement of legal controversies to the Judiciary.

The Executive branch is composed of the president and the vice president who are elected separately by direct popular vote. While the president cannot contest for a second term in office, the vice president is eligible to do so. The Constitution grants the president authority to appoint his cabinet. These departments form a large portion of the country's bureaucracy. The president functions as both the head of the state, the head of the government and the commander-in-chief of the country's armed forces. The vice president is second in line to succession should the president resign, been impeached or die in office. The Legislative branch is authorised to make laws, alter, and repeal them through the power vested in the Philippine Congress. This institution is divided into the Senate and the House of Representatives. The Senate or Senado or upper chamber consists of 24 seats. They can be re-elected for a maximum second term. The House of Representatives or Kapulungan ng mga Kinatawan or lower chamber consists of 212 members representing districts plus 24 sectoral party-list members. The constitution prohibits the House of Representatives from having more than 250 members. The president, vice-president, and the senators are elected for a six-year term, while the members of the House of Representatives and others are elected to serve for a three-year term.

The Judicial branch holds the power to settle controversies involving rights that are legally demand-able and enforceable. This branch determines whether or not there has been a grave abuse of discretion amounting to lack or excess of jurisdiction on the part and instrumentality of the government. The Judiciary is made up of a supreme court and lower courts. The constitution expressly grants the supreme court the power of Judicial Review as the power to declare a treaty, international or executive agreement, law, presidential decree, proclamation, order, instruction, ordinance or regulation unconstitutional.

KEY POLITICAL PERSONS

PRESIDENT & COMMANDER-IN-CHIEF OF THE ARMED FORCES: Rodrigo Roa Duterte

VICE PRESIDENT: Leni Robredo

KEY DEFENCE PERSONS

SECRETARY OF NATIONAL DEFENCE: Delfin Negrillo Lorenzana

CHAIRMAN OF THE JOINT CHIEFS: Gen. Jose Faustino Jr

COMMANDER OF THE ARMY: Maj. Gen. Andres Centino

COMMANDER OF THE NAVY: Rear Adm. Adeluis Bordado

COMMANDER OF THE AIR FORCE: Lt. Gen. Allen T. Paredes

ECONOMY

The Philippines is among the fastest growing economies in the Asia-Pacific region and is named as one of the Tiger Cub economies together with Indonesia, Malaysia and Thailand. Primarily considered a newly industrialised country, its economy has transitioned from one based on agriculture to one based more on services and manufacturing. Business activities are buoyant with notable performance in the services sector including the business process outsourcing, real estate, and finance and insurance industries. The Philippines is one of the richest countries in terms of minerals with an unexploited mineral wealth reportedly estimated at more than USD 840 billion. The Philippines reserves of copper, gold and zinc are also among the largest in the world. The main exports include semiconductors and electronic products, transport equipment, garments, copper products, petroleum products, coconut oil, and fruits.

According to the World Bank, the Philippines economic growth contracted significantly in 2020 due to the Covid-19 pandemic driven by heavy declines in consumption and investment growth, and exacerbated by the sharp slowdown in exports, tourism, and remittances. Nevertheless, according to the IMF's April 2021 forecast, GDP growth is expected to pick up to 6.9% in 2021 and 6.5% in 2022, subject to the post-pandemic global economic recovery. The Philippines is a participant in the Asia-Pacific Economic Cooperation, Asian Development Bank, the Colombo Plan, Group of 24, G-20, G-77, the World Bank, Next Eleven and the World Trade Organisation.

GDP (official exchange rate): $377.205 billion (2019 est.)

Real Growth Rate (GDP): 6.04% (2019 est.), 6.34% (2018 est.)

Industries: Semiconductors and electronics assembly, business process outsourcing, food and beverage manufacturing, construction, electric/gas/water supply, chemical products, radio/television/communications equipment and apparatus, petroleum and fuel, textile and garments, non-metallic minerals, basic metal industries, transport equipment

Total Exports: $78.82 billion (2020 est.), $94.74 billion (2019 est.)

Export Commodities: Integrated circuits, office machinery/parts, insulated wiring, semiconductors, transformers (2019)

Major Markets: China 16%, United States 15%, Japan 13%, Hong Kong 12%, Singapore 7%, Germany 5% (2019)

Total Imports: $97.58 billion (2020 est.), $131.01 billion (2019 est.)

Import Commodities: Integrated circuits, refined petroleum, cars, crude petroleum, broadcasting equipment (2019)

Major Suppliers: China 29%, Japan 8%, South Korea 7%, United States 6%, Singapore 6%, Indonesia 6%, Thailand 5%, Taiwan 5% (2019)

DEFENCE & SECURITY

As security risks persist in the Philippines, the Government is engaged in a concerted effort to modernise its military into a service capable of projecting a posture of credible external deterrence. The Armed Forces of the Philippines (AFP) Modernisation Act, passed in 2012 aims to equip the AFP with necessary capabilities to protect the territorial integrity of the state, offset evolving foreign defence challenges, combatting militias and terrorist groups and ensure the attainment of the country's strategic maritime interests, particularly in the contested South China Sea region. The most contentious region in the SCS covers the Spratlys Island. The Philippine Department of National Defence (DND) framework for bringing reforms is based on an environment of increasing economic prowess to address AFP capability gaps, implement capability for seamless interoperability by developing proficiency in the conduct of joint operations, eliminating crisis handling by individual major services, improve effectiveness of internal security operations, enhance capability to counter terrorism and other transnational threats, provide sustainment or long-term viability of acquired capabilities, improve cost-effectiveness of operations, improve accountability and transparency in the DND, increase professionalism in the AFP through reforms in areas such as promotions, assignments, and training.

The Enhanced Defence Cooperation Agreement signed with the United States in 2014 saw the return of the US forces to the country's bases after a 20-year absence. While primary security threats against the country are internal such as separatism, communist insurgency and terrorism, recent national policies under the present government have shifted the strategic direction of the AFP towards external threat and territorial defence. The Mutual Defence Treaty signed between the two nations on August 30, 1951, states that the Philippines and the US will come to each other's aid in case of armed attacks. The Philippines conducts bilateral and multilateral naval exercises with countries such as Indonesia, Malaysia, South Korea, Japan, India, Australia, and Russia. These exercises are significant in light of the tensions resulting from conflicting territorial claims in the South China Sea.

Internal Conflict

The Philippines has been confronted with multiple and simultaneous insurgencies. The country has a long history of conflict in the southern regions, mostly in the remote islands of central Mindanao, especially on Basilan and Jolo. The myriad of rebel groups including Muslim separatists, communists, clan militias and criminal groups are active in the area. Three groups comprise the Muslim separatists – the Moro National Liberation Front (MNLF), the Moro Islamic Liberation Front (MILF) and the Abu Sayyaf. The MILF and the Abu Sayyaf are breakaway factions of the MNLF. The communist insurgency, on the other hand, is allegedly propagated by the Communist Party of the Philippines' (CPP) military wing, the New People's Army (NPA).

In March 2014, the government and the MILF signed a peace deal granting the Muslim areas of Mindanao greater political autonomy in exchange for an end to armed rebellion while other rebel groups vowed to keep fighting for full independence of the region. The conflict involving the Moros has killed tens of thousands of people and displaced millions of people, according to the Internal Displacement Monitoring Centre (IDMC).

In May 2017, the city of Marawi, parts of which had been overrun by insurgents sympathetic to Daesh, was declared free of militants by the Philippines Army after a fierce five-months long battle. At least 1,131 people were reportedly killed in the fighting, including 919 militants and 165 soldiers and police. At least 1,780 of the hostages seized by the militants, including a Roman Catholic priest, were rescued. In 2019 the Senate passed the Bangsamoro Organic Law, to form the Bangsamoro Autonomous Region in Muslim Mindanao (BARMM), replacing the Autonomous Region in Muslim Mindanao.

The interim Bangsamoro Transitional Authority (BTA) is governing the region until 2022. The BTA comprises 80 representatives headed by the chief minister, who is also chairman of the MILF.

External Conflict

The Philippines is one of the contenders in the South China Sea (SCS) dispute. Both the Philippines and China lay claim to the Scarborough Shoal (known as Huangyan Island in China) – a little more than 160 km from the Philippines and 800 km from China. The dispute involves the Paracels and the Spratly Islands also claimed by Malaysia, Taiwan, and Vietnam. The Philippines invokes its geographical proximity to the Spratly Islands as the main basis of its claim. Malaysia and Brunei are the other claimants of the territory in the South China Sea. Brunei does not claim any of the disputed islands, but Malaysia claims a small number of islands in the Spratly. The interests of different nations include acquiring fishing areas around the two archipelagos; potential exploitation of suspected crude oil and natural gas under the waters of various parts of the South China Sea; and the strategic control of important shipping lanes. The sea is a major shipping route and home to fishing grounds that supply the livelihoods of people across the region. In July 2016, Philippines won an arbitration case against China over the South China Sea in the International Tribunal for the Law of the Sea (ITLOS). The tribunal ruled that Philippines has exclusive sovereign rights over the West Philippine Sea (in South China Sea) and that China's "nine-dash line" is invalid. Philippines had filed its case in January 2013 following a tense stand-off between Chinese and Philippines ships at Scarborough shoal in April 2012. After Manila's initiation of the arbitration case, China had conducted several massive reclamation projects to turn submerged reefs into artificial islands capable of hosting military structures and equipment. It continues to construct military and industrial outposts on artificial islands it has built in disputed waters.

THREAT PERSPECTIVE

China's island-building and military activities in the South China Sea has threatened Philippine sovereignty and security. None of the other claimant countries in the SCS pose a threat to Philippine interests the way China does. China reportedly occupies seven features in the Philippine claim, while Malaysia and Vietnam occupy three and 19, respectively. The issue of far greater concern for the Philippines is that five of the nine dotted lines in China's map are clearly on the Philippines' continental shelf and well within 200 nautical miles of its main islands, recognised by China as the sovereign territory of the Republic of the Philippines. China has consistently refused to recognise the jurisdiction of any international body over territorial delimitation and sovereignty-related issues while accusing the Philippines of unnecessarily provoking a crisis by internationalizing what it sees as an essentially bilateral territorial dispute, which should be resolved primarily through diplomatic channels. Bilateral consultations continue between the two parties to resolve the maritime dispute.

Maritime threats: According to the International Maritime Bureau, the territorial waters of littoral states and offshore waters in the South China Sea are high risk for piracy and armed robbery against ships; an emerging threat area lies in the Celebes and Sulu Seas between the Philippines and Malaysia where three ships were attacked in 2020; numerous commercial vessels have been attacked and hijacked both at anchor and while underway; hijacked vessels are often disguised and cargoes stolen.

STRATEGIC RELATIONS

United States: The Philippines and the US have a long history of close bilateral relations and common strategic purposes that date back to joint anti-Japanese operations during World War II. On 26 March 2021, the two nations celebrated 75 years of diplomatic relations. The US has for decades been the Philippines' defence treaty ally and its biggest source of military hardware and training, providing about US$1 billion in equipment since 2000. Bilateral ties, however, witnessed some changes under President Rodrigo Duterte. While Manila had postponed or cancelled some of the military drills it regularly conducts with the US, most now focus on counter-terror operations and internal security operations. In the past decade alone, the Joint United States Military Assistance Group (JUSMAG) has reportedly delivered $147 million of military equipment to the AFP to enhance counter-terrorism capabilities. In June 2021, the State Department approved plans to sell the Philippines $2.6 billion worth of fighter jets, missiles and related equipment.

Australia: The Philippines and Australia have signed the Joint Declaration on Philippines-Australia Comprehensive Partnership on 18 November 2015 marking a new era in their bilateral relations. Defence cooperation between the two nations dates back to the early decades of the Cold War. Australia is the Philippines' primary partner along with the US in the implementation of the Coast Watch System programme which seeks to improve the Philippines' maritime domain awareness and border security. The Status of Visiting Forces Agreement (SOFVA) in force since 2012 provides a comprehensive legal and operational framework for defence cooperation and presence of Australian forces in the Philippines and the latter's forces in the former. Both the armed forces of the Philippines (AFP) and Australia Defence Force (ADF) regularly conduct exercises under the PH-AUS Defense Cooperation.

Japan: The Philippines-Japan Strategic Partnership formalised in 2011 originally began as an enhanced economic relationship. A common strategic interest in protecting the sea lines of communication of the two maritime countries was identified as a foundation of the enhanced relationship. Tokyo has decided to extend a stand-by credit loan for the Philippines' disaster preparedness and offer continuous assistance to the Mindanao peace process where the Philippine government has been negotiating for a comprehensive peace pact with the Moro Islamic Liberation Front (MILF). Manila has expressed willingness to provide Japanese maritime vessels access to some of its naval bases, alongside the US.

South Korea: South Korea is one of the Philippines' most important bilateral partners and military allies. South Korea is the fourth largest trading partners and trade between the two countries remains active. The gross trade scale of both countries in 2018 was $15.7 billion. South Korea is an active arms donor and supplier for the Armed Forces of the Philippines (AFP). The country has donated numerous military hardware to the Philippines such as a number of F-5A/B fighter jets for the Philippine Air Force, two guided-missile frigates over the past year. The two nations have signed an agreement on Logistics and Defence Industry Cooperation.

DEFENCE CAPABILITIES

The Armed Forces of Philippines (AFP) is a voluntary force. The three major services – Army, Navy, and Air Force – are unified under the Chief of Staff who is assisted by the Vice Chief of Staff. Each of the three major branches is headed by an officer. The AFP is currently carrying out its military modernisation programme. The Revised Armed Forces of the Philippines Modernisation Programme (RAFPMP) is divided into three Horizons, with the first lasting from 2013 to 2017, the second from 2018 to 2022 and third 2023 to 2028. The modernisation programme was initially aimed at strengthening the AFP's capability to address external threats, particularly to protect its territorial waters, and advance its maritime domain awareness, however, due to the continued presence of terrorist activity in some parts of the Mindanao region, the Government's defence spending, apart from the modernisation effort, is expected to focus on the AFP's counterterrorism efforts. The military modernisation programme will renew old and obsolete naval vessels, military aircraft and army equipment, some of which dates back to the II World War era. Under the Horizon 2, the Philippine military planned to purchase multi-role fighters, offshore patrol vessels, corvettes, light tanks, and other assets that would boost its effective force presence.

ARMY: The Philippine Army (PA) is the largest branch of the AFP responsible for ground warfare. The PA is headed by the Chief of the Army with the rank of Lieutenant General. The Army has several regular units: Infantry, Armour and Cavalry, Artillery, Special Forces, Intelligence, Signalling and Engineering units and five regular support units dedicated to counter-insurgency and conventional army operations. A reorganisation programme is underway to reduce the number of infantry units.

Personnel: 67,500 (+30,000 reserves)

Equipment

Category	Name	In Service
Tank	Scorpion (light)	11
APC/AIFV	FNSS	6+
	M113	250+
	V150 Commando	70
	AIFV	33
	GKN Simba	135
Artillery	Soltam M71	2
	M114A1 155 Howitzer	4
	M101A1 105 mm	229
Mortar	M81 81 mm	358
RCL	M67 90 mm	189

New Procurements/Upgrades

◆ In the second phase of the military modernisation programme, Horizon 2, the Army is likely to be equipped with both towed and self-propelled howitzers, multiple launch rocket systems, armoured recovery vehicles, and general support vehicles.

◆ UK Military Bridge manufacturer, WFEL, is to supply a number of its Dry Support Bridges (DSB) to the Philippine Army under the Horizon 2 phase of the revised AFP modernisation programme.

NAVY: The Philippine Navy (PN) is the naval warfare service branch of the AFP. The senior naval officer is the Chief of the Navy who usually holds the rank of vice admiral. Currently, the Navy is composed of two type commands, the Philippine Fleet and Philippine Marine Corps (PMC). It is further organised into seven naval operational commands, five naval support commands, and seven naval support units. In the recent past, the Navy has procured landing docks, corvettes, multi-purpose attack crafts, and offshore patrol vessels, two South Korean-made multi-role frigates designed for green-water missions, an Israeli-made Mark III MPACs with Spiker-ER missiles designed for surface-to-surface combat. The PN plans to acquire two submarines and powerful land-based anti-ship missiles for its coastal defence. It possesses two aircraft carriers and few frigates, destroyers, corvettes, destroyers, and submarines, many of which are employed in the South China Sea.

Major naval bases: Sangley Point (Cavite), Naval Operating Base San Vicente (Aparri, Cagayan), Naval Operating Base Mactan (Cebu), Naval Operating base Ulugan (Palavan), Naval Operating base Batu-Batu (Tawi-Tawi), Naval training Base San Miguel (Zambales)

Personnel: 21,000 (includes 8,500 Marines)

Equipment

Category	Name	In Service
Frigate	BRP Antonio Luna	1
	BRP Jose Rizal	1
	Rajah Humabon class (ex-US Cannon class)	1
	Gregorio Del Pilar (ex-USCG Hamilton cutter)	2
Corvette	BRP Conrado Yap	1
	Rizal class	2
	Cebu class	7
Patrol craft	General Mariano Alvarez (ex-US Cyclone class)	1
	Emilio Jacinto class (ex-RN Peacock class)	3
	PCF 370 class (Halter marine type)	22
	PC 394 class (ex-UCG Cutter type)	2
	PG118 (ex-ROK navy)	1
	Tomas Batilo	6
Amphibious Force	MPAC	12
	AAV	8
	LCH	2
	LCU	2
	LSV	2
	LST	5
	LPD	2
Auxiliary ship		10

Naval Aviation

Category	Name	In Service
Aircraft	Beechcraft TC-90	5
	BN-2 Islander	6
	Cessna 172	2
	C-23 Sherpa	2
	Fokker F27 Friendship	1
Helicopter	AW-109 Wildcat	4

Marines

Category	Name	In Service
IFV	V150 Commando	19
APC	V300 with 90 mm gun	12
	LVT	12
	GKN Aqua tracks	2
Gun	40 mm	4
	Twin 12.7 truck mount	4
	20mm AA gun	
	M101 105 mm	23
	L10A1 Otomelara 105mm	5
RCL	M40 A1 106 mm	

New Procurements/Upgrades

◆ The Philippines' second-guided missile frigate, BRP Antonio Luna (FF-151) was delivered in February 2021 and officially commissioned in March.

The Philippines Navy BRP Antonio Luna. (Image credit: Naval Public Affairs Office)

◆ The Navy plans to procure additional AW-159 "Wildcat" anti-submarine helicopters for deterrence and undersea warfare missions.

◆ The Navy will purchase eight Shaldag-class patrol boats. Four of the eight ships reportedly will be armed with non-light-of-sight (NLOS) missiles that have a range of 25 km while the other four will have machine guns and light automatic cannons.

◆ Procurement of a Shore-Based Anti-ship Missile System (SBMS) has been finalised under Phase 2 of the military modernisation programme.

◆ Israel Shipyards is set to supply three fast-attack interdictor craft missile (FAIC-M) boats to the Philippine Navy.

◆ The Navy plans to acquire its first-ever submarines by 2027. The planned acquisition of submarines was already approved by the President.

◆ The AFP has taken delivery of the country's first Mistral 3 surface-to-air missiles (SAM) to be installed on the Navy's two missile-capable Jose Rizal-class frigates, BRP Jose Rizal (FF150) and BRP Antonio Luna (FF151).

AIR FORCE: TThe Philippine Air Force (PAF) is commanded by the Chief of the Air Force holding the rank of Lieutenant General. The PAF consists of three tactical commands, three support commands, seven air wings including one separate search and rescue wing, one engineering brigade, one air control and warning wing, one air weather group and one special operations unit. The Air Force has embarked on a transformation process to enhance its capabilities. The Flight Plan 2028 is aimed at building the PAF capability to detect, identify, intercept and neutralise intrusions in the Philippine Air Defense Identification Zone (PADIZ) and the South China Sea. The plan calls for reorienting the PAF from a primarily internal security role to a territorial defence force. Major air assets acquired in the current modernisation programme includes the FA-50 light fighters, while those programmed for future procurements are multi-role fighters and maritime patrol aircraft, among other equipment.

Major air bases: Basa, Fernando, Mactan Ebuen, Edwin Andrews, Antonio Bautista, Kalayaan Island, Sangley Point, Vilamor

Personnel: 14,389

Equipment

Category	Name	In Service
Fighter, Light Attack	A-29B Super Tucano	6
	S-211	5 (13 in inventory)
	FA-50 Fighting Eagle	12
	OV-10 Bronco	24
	SF-206TP	7
	MG-520	24
Transport	Airbus C295	4
	NC212i aircraft	2
	C-130/H	4
	F-27/F-28	1 each
	Nomad	3
VIP Transport	F-28, F-27, S-70	1 each
	Black Hawk	16
	PZL-Swidnik W-3 Sokol	7
Helicopter	Bell 412s	8
	UH-1H Iroquois	25
	AW-109E	8
	UH-1D	7

...continued

Category	Name	In Service
SAR	S-76	7
	Bell 205	6
UAV	Scan Eagle	6
	Hermes 450	4
	Hermes 900	9
Trainer	FA-50PH	12
	SF-260F	18
	SF-260M	21
	T4-1D	30
	LC-210	1

New Procurements/Upgrades

◆ The Department of National Defence (DND) plans to acquire UH-1H and MD500 helicopters from the Republic of Korea.

◆ The Philippines plans to buy six AH-64E Apache attack helicopters to modernise its attack helicopter capabilities.

◆ A contract has been signed for the purchase of Horizon 2 Air Surveillance Radar System (ASRS) from Japan with expected delivery this year.

◆ The US military has handed over four ScanEagle UAS worth $4 million to the PAF.

◆ The Air Force has taken delivery of the last five of the 16 Black Hawks it ordered to replace the UH-1D helicopters.

◆ The Philippine House of Representatives has approved additional funding for the Air Force to acquire five new C-130J Super Hercules military transport aircraft.

DEFENCE PRODUCTION AND R&D

The Philippines indigenous arms manufacturing engages mainly in small arms and ammunition manufacturing. The Self-Reliant Defence Posture (SRDP) programme, initiated in 1974, took the development of a domestic defence industry as its objective. Defence officials contracted SRDP projects with the government arsenal and local manufacturers, encouraging the use of indigenous raw materials and production capacity. Projects included domestic production of small arms, radios, and assorted ammunition. One of the most significant SRDP operations was the manufacturing of the M-16A1 rifle under license from Colt Industries, an American company. The government has proposed Philippine Defence Industry Development Act of 2019 to enhance the self-reliance of the country's defence industry and promote domestic suppliers.

The Philippine and Japan have signed a defence agreement to allow the transfer of defence equipment and technology from Japan to the Philippines. The agreement allows the two nations to conduct joint research and development, and even joint production, of defence equipment and technology. The Philippines has signed a MoU with Jordan on Defence Cooperation while the Thailand government has ratified an agreement with the Philippines to expand defence industrial collaboration. The MOU which runs for an initial five years provides a formal framework for the two countries to engage in defence trade with each other and to undertake joint research, development, and production projects. The Philippines has also signed a similar defence agreement with India. This accord – known as the 'implementing arrangement concerning the procurement of defence material and equipment' – was signed between the Philippines Department of National Defense (DND) and Indian Ministry of Defence (MoD).

Domestic suppliers: Government Arsenal, Armscor, FERFRANS, Floro International Corporation, United Defence Manufacturing Corporation, Steelcraft Industrial & Development Corporation

Foreign suppliers: United States, South Korea, Israel, Italy, Germany, United Kingdom, France.

DEFENCE PROCUREMENT

As part of a comprehensive military modernisation programme, the Philippines Government has steadily moved ahead in several major acquisition projects. The AFP is now transitioning from Horizon 1 to Horizon 2 of its modernisation programme. Around PHP600 billion has been allocated for Horizon 2 projects, according to AFP public affairs office chief Navy Capt. Jonathan Zata. He said some 107 projects were completed under Horizon 1. The equipment delivered for Horizon 1 included six A-29B "Super Tucano" close-air support aircraft, S-70i "Black Hawk" helicopters and two new missile frigates BRP Jose Rizal and BRP Antonio Luna. The AFP Modernisation Programme has three horizons – Horizon 1 which started in 2013 and ended in 2017, Horizon 2 from 2018 to 2022, and Horizon 3 from 2023 to 2028

DEFENCE BUDGET

Proposed defence budget: $4.3 billion (2021), $3.6 billion (2020)

Defence spending in terms of GDP: 1.17% (2021)

The Philippines' Department of National Defense (DND) will receive 222 billion pesos (roughly 4.39 billion US dollars) in the largest ever proposed national budget for 2022, according to a media report. The proposed defence budget saw a 7.87 percent increase compared with the amount of 205.8 billion pesos in 2021.

Apart from its modernisation program, the Philippine Security Forces (which includes the AFP and all Service Commands, and the Philippine Coast Guard) receive an average of $120-125 million annually in US grant funds inclusive of both Department of State (DoS) Foreign Military Fund (FMF) and International Military Education and Training (IMET) and Defence Security Cooperation Agency (DSCA) Building Partnership Capacity (BPC) programmes 333 and 1263 which is separate from defence-related construction projects, as well as Defence Threat Reduction Agency (DTRA) projects in the Philippines.

CONCLUSION

The Philippines, an island country in Southeast Asia in the western Pacific Ocean, is considered to be an emerging market and a newly industrialised country. The Philippines Armed Forces through its military modernisation programme has taken initial steps to build a more credible military defence against its neighbouring countries not only for the bounty that the Spratly offers but for its own territorial integrity. Manila's recent major shift in political stance towards the US has fuelled speculations with regard to its future policies and priorities. Other than its old-time ally the US, the Philippines is now exploring new trading partners, including China and Russia, with whom it is steadily renewing its ties, including strategic and defence relations.

CONTACT DETAILS
Department of National Defence
DND Building, Segundo Ave.
Camp General Emilio
Aguinaldo Quezon City,
Philippines 1110
Tel: (+632) 982 – 5600
email: info@dnd.gov.ph
www.dnd.gov.ph/

POLAND
(Capital: Warsaw)

INTRODUCTION

Area: 312,685 sq km
Population: 38,185,913 (July 2021 est.)
Coastline: 440 km
Maritime claims: Territorial sea: 12 nm
Exclusive Economic Zone: defined by international treaties

KEY POLITICAL PERSONS

PRESIDENT: Andrzej Duda

PRIME MINISTER: Mateusz Morawiecki

KEY DEFENCE PERSONS

MINISTER OF NATIONAL DEFENCE: Mariusz Błaszczak

CHIEF OF GENERAL STAFF OF THE ARMED FORCES: Lt. Gen. Rajmund Andrzejczak

INSPECTOR OF LAND FORCES: Brig. Gen. Wojciech Grabowski

INSPECTOR OF NAVY: Vice Adm. Jarosław Ziemiański

INSPECTOR OF AIR FORCE: Brig. Pilot Jacek Pszczoła

ECONOMY

Poland has the sixth-largest economy in the European Union and has long had a reputation as a business-friendly country with largely sound macroeconomic policies. The Polish economy performed well during the 2014-17 period. Poland is the largest recipient of EU development funds and their cyclical allocation can significantly impact the rate of economic growth. As an EU member, Poland applies the EU's common external tariff to goods from other countries, including the United States. Poland belongs to number of international organisations, including

the United Nations, North Atlantic Treaty Organisation, Euro-Atlantic Partnership Council, Organisation for Security and Cooperation in Europe, Organisation for Economic Cooperation and Development, International Monetary Fund, World Bank, and World Trade Organisation. Poland is an observer to the Organisation of American States. As of 2019 the Polish economy has been growing steadily, as per media reports. COVID-19 pandemic restriction economically affected the growth of Poland, but now with ease of pandemic-related restrictions and normalisation of economic activity in many sectors. According to the World Bank, growth in Poland is expected to reach 3.5% in 2021. In 2020, US goods imports from Poland totalled USD8.3 billion, as per US Dept. of State.

GDP (official exchange rate): $1 trillion (2020), $1.126 trillion (2017 est.)

Real Growth Rate (GDP): 4.55% (2019 est.), 5.36% (2018 est.)

Industries: Machine building, iron and steel, coal mining, chemicals, shipbuilding, food processing, glass, beverages, textiles

Oil - proved reserves: 126 million bbl (1 January 2018)

Natural gas - proved reserves: 79.79 billion

cu m (1 January 2018 est.)

Total Exports: $333.54 billion (2020 est.), $330.68 billion (2019 est.)

Export Commodities: cars and vehicle parts, seats, furniture, computers, video displays (2019)

Major Markets: Germany 27%, Czechia 6%, United Kingdom 6%, France 6%, Italy 5% (2019)

Total Imports: $292.44 billion (2020 est.), $302.87 billion (2019 est.)

Import Commodities: Cars and vehicle parts, crude petroleum, packaged medicines, broadcasting equipment, office machinery/parts (2019)

Major Suppliers: Germany 25%, China 10%, Italy 5%, Netherlands 5% (2019)

INTERNATIONAL DISPUTES

◆ As a member state that forms part of the EU's external border, Poland has implemented the strict Schengen border rules to restrict illegal immigration and trade along its eastern borders with Belarus and Ukraine.

◆ Poland has contributed to operations in Afghanistan, Iraq, Kosovo, as well as to operations against ISIS.

DEFENCE

ARMY
Personnel: 60,000

Equipment

Category	Name	In Service
MBT	Leopard 2A4/2A5	200+
	PT-91	200+
	T-72M	500+
APC/IFV	BWP-1	1,000
	Rosomak	300+
	Cougar	40
	BRMD-2	250+
Artillery	122 mm SP 2S1 Gvozdika	100+
	152 mm SP Dana	80+
Mortar	120 mm M120	70+
	98 mm M98	50+
Anti-Tank GW	Spike	50+
	9K11	100
	9K111 Fagot	
	9K113	
	9K115	
MRL	122 mm. BM21	
	RM70	30
	WR-40 Langusta	1
AA Gun	ZSU-23-4 SPAAG	30+
	ZSU-23-2 Towed	300+
SAM	SA-6 KUB	80
	SA-8 OSA	50+

...continued

Category	Name	In Service
SAM	Poprad	
	SA-7 STRZALA	200+
	GROM	300+
UAV	Orbiter, FlyEye	

Army Aviation

Category	Name	In Service
Helicopter	W-3A	30+
	Mi-2	45
	Mi-8	10+
	Mi-17	10+
	Mi-24	25+

New Procurements/ Upgrades

◆ The US State Department has approved a possible Foreign Military Sale to Poland of 20 High Mobility Artillery Rocket System (HIMARS) M142 Launchers, and other related equipment for an estimated cost of USD655 million.

◆ The first part of the 53 000 modular assault rifles (GROT) will be soon available for the military. This contract amounts to almost half a billion of PLN and the procurement is to be executed by 2020.

◆ Contract for the delivery of 28 buses for the military was signed in Sanok. The value of the contract amounts to 18 million PLN.

◆ The US State Department has approved a possible Foreign Military Sale to Poland of 180 Javelin missiles and 79 Javelin Command Launch Units (CLUs) and related equipment for an estimated cost of USD100 million.

◆ Polska Grupa Zbrojeniowa will be providing equipment and ammunition for the Polish Army.

NAVY
Personnel: 7,000

Equipment

Category	Name	In Service
Submarine	Kilo class	1
	Kobben class	3+
Frigate	Oliver Hazard Perry class	2
Mine Warfare Force	Krogulec Class	3
	Gardno Class	5+
	Mamry Class	4
Amphibious Force	Lubin Class	5
	Deba Class	2+
Corvette	Kaszub class	1
FAC	Orkan class	2+
Support Vessel	Czernicki Class	1
	Heweliusz Class	2
	Nawigator Class	2

...continued

Category	Name	In Service
Support Vessel	Baltyk Class	1
	Piast Class	2
	Zbyszko Class	2
	Wodnik Class	1
	Iskra Class	1

Naval Aviation
Personnel: 1,300

Equipment

Category	Name	In Service
Aircraft	M-28	3+
	Mi-17	2
	Mi-2	1
	SH-2G	2+
Helicopter	W-3RM	5
	W-3T	2
	Mi-14PL	5+
	Mi-14PS	2
	Mi-2	1

New Procurements/ Upgrades

◆ The Navy received five modernised W-3 WARM ANAKONDA rescue helicopters and the following three will be delivered in 2018. The modernised helicopters are equipped with the Full Authority Digital Engines Control system (FADEC), which replaced the analogue system, as well as new rescue equipment, new thermal imagining cameras compatible with searchlights. All new helicopters are equipped with the Automatic Identification System (AIS), which significantly improves all evacuation operations of victims from vessels.

◆ Contract signed for the delivery of additional two, modern minehunters with three logistic support packages and one rescue vessel, with a possibility to order a second one.

◆ OSI Maritime Systems (OSI) has entered in to a strategic partnership with PGZ Stocznia Wojenna Shipyard (PGZ SW), located in Gdynia, Poland to provide Integrated Navigation and Tactical Systems (INTS) to the Polish Navy.

AIR FORCE
Personnel: 17,000

Equipment

Category	Name	In Service
Fighters/ attack/ Reconnaissance	MiG-29A	20+
	F-16 C/D Block 52+	40+
	Su-22M4/Su-22UM3K	40+
	F-35 Lightning II	On order

...continued

Category	Name	In Service
Transport/Tanker	C-295M	10
	PZL M-28 Bryza	20
	C-130E	5
	Tu-154M	2
	Yak-40	2+
	M-28	2
	Bell 412HP	1
Trainer	TS-11 Iskra	35+
	PZL SW-4	10
	PZL-130	30+
	SA-3 Goa	50+
	SA-3	50
	SA-4	15+
	SA-45	10+

New Procurements/ Upgrades

◆ The US State Department has approved a possible Foreign Military Sale to Poland of 32 F-35 Joint Strike Fighter aircraft with support for an estimated cost of USD6.5 billion. Poland has requested to buy 32 F-35 Joint Strike Fighter Conventional Take Off and Landing (CTOL) Aircraft and 33 Pratt & Whitney F-135 Engines.

◆ The signing of the contract for deliveries of the JASSM-ER air-to-ground missiles, which are of strategic importance, as well as DAGLEZJA bridges.

◆ Contract was signed with PZL Warszawa- Okęcie S.A. for the modernisation of 12 PZL-130 TC-I ORLIK aircrafts to PZL-130 TC-II ORLIK version in the years 2017-2020. This contract amounts to 186 million PLN. The modernised PZL-130 TC-II ORLIK aircrafts will be used for basic and advanced military pilot training in the field of piloting and navigation technique under different weather conditions.

Defence Expenditure

Total defence spending: $14 billion (2020 approx.)

Estimated defence spending in terms of GDP: 2.2% of GDP (2021 est.), 2.31% of GDP (2020 est.)

Domestic suppliers: Polish Defence Holding, WZM S.A., PZL-Świdnik, HSW S.A., OBRUM

Foreign suppliers: European Union, Israel, Norway, Switzerland, South Korea & United States

Annual Exports: European Union, Nigeria, Libya, Iraq, Malaysia & Vietnam

Year	USD (Millions)
2014	10,107
2015	10,588
2016	9,397
2017	9,940
2018	11,857
2019*	13,590
2020*	13,369
2021*	13,369

(*Figures for 2020 and 2021 are estimates.)
Source: Defence Expenditure of NATO Countries (2014-2021), NATO Press Release.

Spending on Defence in Poland
(Source: International Trade Administration, US Department of Commerce)

Year	2019	2020	2021
Approximate Defence Spending $ billion	12.5	12.5	13.3

The 2021 defence budget of Poland raised defence spending to $13.1 billion (PLN 51.83 billion), a 3.7 percent increase over 2020 expenditures and an increase from 2.1 percent of 2020 GDP to 2.2 percent of estimated 2021 GDP. Polish legislation mandates a gradual increase of annual defence spending to at least 2.5 percent of GDP by 2030, as per the International Trade Administration, US Department of Commerce and Poland Ministry of Defence. Major recent Foreign Military Sales include F-35 fighter aircraft, the PATRIOT air and missile defence system, High Mobility Artillery Rocket System (HIMARS), Joint Air-to-Surface Standoff Missiles-Extended Range (JASSM-ER), and Javelin Anti-Tank Missiles.

In 2019, Polish Ministry of National Defence announced its new, 15-year Technical Modernisation Plan 2020-2035, which outlined a number of procurement programmes such as acquisition of 32 new F-35 aircraft, requirement of additional F-16 aircraft, acquisition of stealthy UAVs, modernisation of Poland's short range air-and-missile defence capability, modern attack helicopters for Polish Land Forces, acquisition of satellites, microsatellites, and reconnaissance aircraft, acquisition of cyber defence tools and software, modernisation of Poland's medium air and missile defence capability, acquisition of tactical medium-range UAVs, acquisition of reconnaissance aircraft, acquisition of two coastal defence vessels, acquisition of 155 mm fire division modules, acquisition of light anti-tank guided missile launchers, new generation main battle tanks, indigenously produced advanced engineering robots for bomb disposal units, acquisition of tank destroyers for the anti-tank regiment, pods for combat aircraft, unmanned search-strike systems, high-mobility trucks and passenger vehicles, etc.

Defence Production and R&D

The Polish defence industry comprises 38 manufacturing companies, 12 renovation and manufacturing military enterprises, 10 research-and-development establishments, and three companies specialising in trading arms. Revenue from this sector of the economy amounted to $1.27 billion in 1999, while the sector's corporate assets are estimated at over $1.71 billion. Up to now, out of the 38 companies recognised as strategically important for the country, only two have been successfully privatised.

Defence Procurement

Poland's Ministry of National Defence (MND) created a new 'Armaments Inspectorate' '(Inspektorat Uzbrojenia - IU) in January 2011. The Armament Inspectorate performs analytical-conceptual tasks in the process of the acquisition of the armament for the Polish Armed Forces needs.

CONTACT DETAILS

Ministry of National Defence
Al. Niepodległości 218
00-909 Warszawa
Tel. + 48 261 874 124
Fax + 48 261 874 490
E-mail: bsiw@mon.gov.pl

General Staff of Polish Armed Forces
ul. Rakowiecka 4a
00-904 Warszawa
Tel. +48 261 870-335
Fax +48 261 870 568

Armament Inspectorate
Aleje Niepodległości 218
Warsaw
Tel: (+48 22) 68 461 77
E-mail: rzecznik.iu@mon.gov.pl

PORTUGAL
(Capital: Lisbon)

INTRODUCTION
Area: 92,090 sq. km
Population: 10,263,850 (July 2021 est.)
Coastline: 1,793 km
Maritime claims: Territorial sea: 12 nm
Contiguous Zone: 24 nm
Exclusive Economic Zone: 200 nm
Continental Shelf: 200 m depth or to the depth of exploitation

KEY POLITICAL PERSONS

PRESIDENT & SUPREME COMMANDER OF THE ARMED FORCES: Marcelo Rebelo de Sousa

PRIME MINISTER: Antonio Luis Santos da Costa

KEY DEFENCE PERSONS

DEFENCE MINISTER: Jao Gomes Cravinho

CHIEF OF THE GENERAL STAFF: Adm. António Silva Ribeiro

CHIEF OF STAFF OF THE ARMY: Lt.Gen. José Nunes da Fonseca

CHIEF OF THE NAVY: Admiral Antonio Mendes Calado

CHIEF OF STAFF OF THE AIR FORCE: Gen. Joaquin Manuel Nunes Borrego

ECONOMY
Portugal's economy is based primarily on services and industrial production. The country has been a part of the Eurozone since its inception. The country joined the Economic and Monetary Union in 1999 and began circulating the euro on 1 January 2002 along with 11 other EU members. The largest industries are clothing, textiles, and footwear; food processing; wood pulp, paper, and cork; metal working; oil refining; chemicals; fish canning; wine; and tourism. After the global financial crisis in 2008, Portugal's economy contracted in 2009 and fell into recession from 2011 to 2013. Portugal exited the EU-IMF programme in May 2014, and its economic recovery gained traction in 2015 because of strong exports and a rebound in private consumption. Portugal is home to a number of notable leading companies with worldwide reputations, such as The Navigator Company, a major world player in the international paper market; Sonae Indústria, the largest producer of wood-based panels in the world; Amorim.

GDP (official exchange rate): $237.698 billion (2019 est.)

Real Growth Rate (GDP): 2.24% (2019 est.), 2.85% (2018 est.)

Industries: Textiles, clothing, footwear, wood and cork, paper and pulp, chemicals, fuels and lubricants, automobiles and auto parts, base metals, minerals, porcelain and ceramics, glassware, technology, telecommunications; dairy products, wine, other foodstuffs; ship construction and refurbishment; tourism, plastics, financial services, optics.

Total Exports: $85.28 billion (2020 est.), $104.77 billion (2019 est.)

Export Commodities: Cars and vehicle parts, refined petroleum, leather footwear, paper products, tires (2019)

Major Markets: Spain 23%, France 13%, Germany 12%, United Kingdom 6%, United States 5% (2019)

Total Import: $89.31 billion (2020 est.), $103.05 billion (2019 est.)

Import Commodities: Cars and vehicle parts, crude petroleum, aircraft, packaged medicines, refined petroleum, natural gas (2019)

Major Suppliers: Spain 29%, Germany 13%, France 9%, Italy 5%, Netherlands 5% (2019)

INTERNATIONAL DISPUTES
◆ Portugal does not recognise Spanish sovereignty over the territory of Olivenza based on a difference of interpretation of the 1815 Congress of Vienna and the 1801 Treaty of Badajoz.

DEFENCE
The Portuguese Armed Forces (Forças Armadas) is responsible for protecting the country as well as supporting international peacekeeping efforts when mandated by the North Atlantic Treaty Organisation (NATO), the United Nations and/or the European Union. The three service branches – Army, Navy and Air Force – are independent but co-ordinated by a Defence General Staff, with the Chief of General Staff acting as operational commander of all the three branches. In 2013, the Government approved structural reform of the national defence,

"Defence 2020" with an aim to establish the guidance parametres for strategic planning, reinforcing the leading responsibility of the Chief of the General Staff in the execution of the approved military strategy, reducing human resources while at the same time improving their management and enhancing the coordination between the General Staff of the Armed Forces, the branches of the Armed Forces and the Ministry of National Defence.

ARMY (Exercito Portuguesa)
Personnel: 16,565
Equipment

Category	Name	In service
MBT	Leopard 2A6	37
	M-60A3 TTS	21
Armoured car/APC/AIFV	URO VAMTAC ST5	139
	V-150 Chaimite	14
	M-113A1	170
	M-113A2	32
	M-577A2	50
	M-106A1	3
	M-106A1	15
	M-125A1	3
	M-125A2	12
	Pandur II	233
	V-200 Chaimite	20
	Panhard M11	32
	HMMWV	42
	Pandur II 30mm	22
Artillery	M-119 light gun	18
	M-101A1 105mm	8
	M-114A1 155mm	24
	Oto Melara 105mm pack	5
	M-109A2	6
	M-109A5	17
AAA	Rh 202 20mm twin	26
Mortar	81mm	164
	107mm M30	31
	120 mm Tampella	54
SAM	Stinger Manpads	20
	M-48A2 Chaparral	5
	M-48A3 Chaparral	24
ATGW	Tow	43
	Milan	69
ATK	Carl Gustav 84mm	162
	90mm	29
	M-40A1 106mm	45

New Procurements/Upgrades

◆ The NATO Support and Procurement Agency (NSPA) has delivered the last batch of 139 armoured vehicles to the Portuguese Army, consisting of eight Emergency Response Vehicles, under the Light Armoured Tactical Vehicle programme or Viaturas Taticas Ligeiras Blindadas (VTLC). Portugal to buy tactical mini-unmanned aerial vehicles (UAVS).

NAVY (Marinha Portugues)
Personnel: 8,038
Equipment

Category	Name	In Service
Submarine	Tridente class (Type 209PN)	2
Frigate	Bartolomeu Dias class	2
	Vasco Da Gama class	3
	Baptista De Abdrade class (patrol)	3
	Joao Coutinho class (patrol)	2
Patrol craft	Viana Do Castelo class OPV	4
	Tejo class	4
	Cacine class large patrol craft	3
	Centauro class (coastal)	4
	Argos class (coastal)	5
	Rio Minho class (inshore)	1
	Albatroz class (coastal)	2
Amphibious force	Bacamarte LCT	1
Miscellaneous	Replenishment ship	1
	Hydrographic ships	4
	Training ships	6

New Procurements/Upgrades

◆ NRP Bartolomeu Dias (F 333), the first of two Portuguese Navy M frigates, has undergone a mid-life upgrade. The second ship, NRP D Francisco de Almeida (F 334) remains in the Netherlands for the same upgrade. The upgrade included weapons, sensor and communication systems, while work is also undertaken on propulsion and power distribution.

◆ Portugal plans to procure new replenishment ships.

AIR FORCE (Forca Aerea Portuguesa, FAP)
Personnel: 6,147
Equipment

Category	Name	In service
Fighter	F-16 AM 15MLU	26
	F-16 BM 15MLU	4
Trainer	Alpha JET	6
	TB30 Epsilon	16
	Chipmunk	6
	ASK-21 gliders	3
Maritime patrol	P-3C Orion	5
Transport/Support	C-130H	3
	C-130H-30	3
	Falcon-50	3
	C-295M	12
Helicopter	EH.101	12
	SA.316 Alouette III	6

New Procurements/Upgrades

◆ Portugal has placed an order for five multi-mission air-lifters Embraer KC-390 with delivery scheduled to start in 2023.

Defence Expenditure

Total defence expenditure: $3.358 billion (2019), $3969 million (2013)

Defence spending in terms of GDP: 1.59% of GDP (2020 est.)

Defence Production and R&D

Portugal imports the majority of its defence equipment as its domestic defence industry is relatively under-developed. The Portuguese industry landscape is mainly based on small and medium enterprises (SMEs). The country produces licensed equipment such as assault rifles. Portugal's membership of the consortiums involved with the production of the NH90 helicopter and KC-390 transport aircraft is expected to increase the country's defence exports.

Defence Procurement

The military is currently undertaking several major acquisitions supported by national industries. These include two new submarines with air-independent propulsion that feature communications, information systems and integration. The Ministry of Defence is acquiring armoured vehicles for the Army and Navy with communications systems provided by home companies. The Government has announced a firm order of five multi-mission air lifters Embraer KC-390 as part of the process to modernise Portuguese Air Force capability.

CONTACT DETAILS
Ministry of Defence
Madeira, 1 - 1400-204 Lisbon.
Phone: 21 303 85 20
Fax: 21 301 95 55
E-mail: dscrp@defesa.pt
Public Relations of CEMGFA
Madeira, 1 - 1449-004 Lisbon.
Phone: 21 304 37 89
Fax: 21 304 32 62
E-mail: emgfa_rp@emgfa.pt

STRATEGIC INFORMATION
QATAR
(Capital: Doha)

INTRODUCTION

Area: 11,586 sq km

Population: 2,479,995 (July 2021 est.)

Coastline: 563 km

Maritime claims: Territorial sea: 12 nm

Contiguous zone: 24 nm

Exclusive Economic Zone: as determined by bilateral agreements or the median line

GEOPOLITICAL IMPORTANCE

Qatar, also known as the State of Qatar, is an Arab emirate, in the Middle East, occupying the small Qatar Peninsula on the north-easterly coast of the much larger Arabian Peninsula. Its sole land border is with Saudi Arabia to the south, with the rest of its territory surrounded by the Persian Gulf. A strait of the Persian Gulf separates Qatar from the nearby island state of Bahrain. The country is in a strategic location near major petroleum deposits. Qatar is therefore, one of the richest countries in the region due to the exploitation of large oil and gas fields since the 1940s. Qatar is a peninsula located halfway down the west coast of the Arabian Gulf. Its territory comprises a number of islands including Halul, Sheraouh, Al-Ashat and others.

POLITICAL OVERVIEW

Qatar has an unelected, monarchic, emirate-type government. There are no democratic institutions or elections, and power is assumed on a hereditary basis. The head of state is the Emir, and the right to rule Qatar is passed on within the Al Thani family. The Emir's role is influenced by continuing traditions of consultation, rule by consensus, and the citizen's right to appeal personally to the Emir. The Emir, while directly accountable to no one, cannot violate the Sharia (Islamic law) and, in practice, must consider the opinions of leading notables and the religious establishment. Their position was institutionalised in the Advisory Council, an appointed body that assists the Emir in formulating policy. There is no electoral system. Political parties are banned. But Qatar on the other hand, claims that it is developing into a constitutional monarchy. Suffrage is currently limited to municipal elections, with the voting age set at 18. Elections in 1999 for a 29-member municipal council were the first in which Qatari women were allowed to vote and stand for office. A constitution, providing for democratic reforms, came into force in 2005. Qatar has a discretionary system of law controlled by the Emir, although civil codes are being implemented; Islamic law (Sharia) is significant in personal matters.

KEY POLITICAL PERSONS

HEAD OF STATE, COMMANDER-IN-CHIEF & MINISTER OF DEFENCE: Sheikh Tamim Bin Hamad Al Thani

PRIME MINISTER & MINISTER OF INTERIOR: Sheikh Khalid bin Khalifa bin Abdulaziz Al Thani

ECONOMY

Qatar is one of the richest country in the world. Qatar has prospered in the last several years with continued high real GDP growth. The country has one of the highest incomes per capita in the world. GDP was driven largely by the oil and natural gas sector and are the main economic and government's revenue source. Following trade restriction imposed by Saudi Arabia, the UAE, Bahrain, and Egypt in 2017, Qatar has established new trade routes with other countries to maintain access to imports, notably Turkey, Oman, Kuwait, and India. Qatar has also strengthened its manufacturing, construction and financial services. Qatar's National Vision aims that, by 2030, Qatar becomes an advanced society capable of sustaining its development and providing a high standard of living for its people. Qatar's National Vision defines the long-term goals for the country and provides a framework in which national strategies and implementation plans can be developed. Qatar's economy has largely overcome the constraints posed by the continuing diplomatic rift with Gulf Cooperation Council (GCC) neighbours. Growth is estimated to have recovered to 2.1% in 2018, as activity has gradually recovered from the effects of diplomatic issues between Qatar and some GCC neighbours. Hamad Port is Qatar's main seaport, located south of Doha also helped in the wake of blockade, which started in 2017. In August 2019, Qatar Central Bank stated that the country's economic growth will see a boost over the next two years amid expectations of stable oil prices and continued strong exports. Qatar ranked 14 in The World Competitiveness Yearbook 2020 - which it is annually published by the International Institute for Management Development (IMD) located in Lausanne of Switzerland - out of 63 countries, mostly high-income countries. Qatar's rank has been positively influenced by many factors including strong economic performance as represented by, Qatar's low unemployment rate, high percentage of gross fixed capital formation, capital investments, and saving to GDP, percentage of trade balance to GDP, the high overall productivity and low inflation rate whereby other factors had negatively influenced the rank as real GDP growth per capita, Office rents, Business expenditure on R&D. Due to lockdown measures with regard to COVID-19, Qatar's economy performed its worst since at least 2012 during the second quarter, as per news reports in Oct 2020. The Minister of Finance, stated that total revenue in the 2022 State Budget is estimated at QR196.0 billion, representing an increase of 22.4% over the 2021 Budget. The 2022 Budget is based on an oil price assumption of $55 per barrel given the robust recovery in international energy prices. The Minister of Finance added that total expenditure, compared to the 2021 fiscal year, is set to increase by 4.9% and reach QR204.3 billion in 2022.

GDP (official exchange rate): $245.66 billion (2020 est.), $255.01 billion (2019 est.)

Real Growth Rate (GDP): 1.6% (2017 est.), 2.1% (2016 est.)

Industries: Liquefied natural gas, crude oil production and refining, ammonia, fertilizer, petrochemicals, steel reinforcing bars, cement, commercial ship repair

Crude Oil - proved reserves: 25.24 billion bbl (1 January 2018 est.)

Natural gas - proved reserves: 24.07 trillion cu m (1 January 2018 est.)

Total Exports: $70.93 billion (2020 est.), $92.05 billion (2019 est.)

Export Commodities: Natural gas, crude petroleum, refined petroleum, ethylene polymers, fertilizers (2019)

Major Markets: Japan 17%, South Korea 16%, India 14%, China 13%, Singapore 7% (2019)

Total Imports: $59.06 billion (2020 est.), $66.77 billion (2019 est.)

Import Commodities: Aircraft, gas turbines, cars, jewellery, iron piping (2019)

Major Suppliers: United States 15%, France 13%, United Kingdom 9%, China 9%, Germany 5%, Italy 5% (2019)

DEFENCE & SECURITY

The Qatar Armed Forces are the military forces of Qatar. The country plays an active role in the collective defence efforts of the Gulf Cooperation Council; the other five members are Saudi Arabia, Kuwait, Bahrain, the UAE, and Oman. Qatar maintains a modest defence establishment which includes army, navy, and air force. The country lacks strategic depth, have small populations, and small, untrained armies. Qatar's significant oil and natural gas reserves have made the country the potential target for aggression and dependent on outside forces for defence and security. The country has a public security force of about 8,000-plus men, including a coast guard, national fire fighting force, air wing, marine police, and an internal security force. Qatar also has signed defence pacts with the US, UK, and France. Qatari forces played an important role in the first Gulf War.

KEY DEFENCE PERSONS

MINISTER OF STATE FOR DEFENCE AFFAIRS: Dr. Khalid bin Mohammed Al Attiyah

CHIEF OF STAFF OF QATAR ARMED FORCES: Staff Lt. Gen. (Pilot) Salem bin Hamad bin Mohammed bin Aqeel Al Nabit

COMMANDER OF LAND FORCE: Maj. Gen. Saeed Hassen Mohammad Al-Khayareen

COMMANDER OF NAVY: Staff Major General Abdullah Bin Hassan Al Sulaiti

COMMANDER OF AIR FORCE: Brig. Gen. (Pilot) Jassem Mohamed Al Mannai

Internal Conflict
Qatar is not currently engaged in any armed conflict.

External Conflict
Bahrain: The territorial dispute with Bahrain over the Hawar Islands and the maritime boundary dispute with Bahrain were solved by the International Court of Justice (ICJ) in The Hague. In the June 2001 decision, Bahrain kept the Hawar Islands and Qit'at Jaradah but dropped claims to Janan Island and Zubarah on mainland Qatar, while Qatar retained significant maritime areas and their resources. On 5 June 2017, Bahrain cut diplomatic ties with Qatar. On 6th Jan, 2021, Qatar and Bahrain have agreed to fully restore diplomatic ties.

Other Issues: Qatar has played an important role in mediating regional conflicts including in Lebanon, where it deployed peacekeepers as part of the UN Mission in Lebanon (UNIFIL) and, more recently, in Darfur, Somalia and Yemen. Qatar also mediated the Eritrea-Djibouti border dispute. The country also chairs the Follow-Up Committee of the Arab Peace Initiative and has in recent months hosted a series of ministerial meetings of the Committee in Doha.

Libyan crisis: Qatar pledged 4-6 fighter aircraft and a cargo plane as part of its contribution to the March 2011 military intervention in Libya following UN Security Council Resolution 1973 of 2011.

ISIS: Qatar, in response to ISIS (or ISIL) militants, has joined many states along with USA and Russia on a coalition against them in Syria and Iraq. The country has done airstrikes against ISIL targets in Syria

THREAT PERSPECTIVE

Qatar in order to prevent militants traveling to and from Syria and nearby conflict zones has joined hands with international organisations and also taken number of new counterterrorism measures in recent years to secure its critical infrastructure. In March 2005, a car bomb blast occurred at the Doha Players theatre outside the capital, Doha, near a British school. It was the first attack of its kind in the Gulf Arab state, which hosts the US military's Central Command. Since then, the country fears that it would become a regular target for militant attacks. Currently, the threat status remains low in Qatar but still military, security agencies maintain a high alert scenario and readiness to face any impending threat. The country is active on the regional and world arena, having mediated in disputes in the Middle East and Africa. It is pursuing an Afghan peace deal.

Qatar-Gulf Crisis: The 2017 Qatar diplomatic crisis began when several countries abruptly cut off diplomatic relations with Qatar in June 2017. These countries included Saudi Arabia, United Arab Emirates, Bahrain, and Egypt. Yemen, the Maldives and Libya's eastern-based government later followed suit. The severing of relations included withdrawing ambassadors, and imposing trade and travel bans. The Saudi-led coalition cited Qatar's alleged support for terrorism as the main reason for their actions, insisting Qatar has violated a 2014 agreement with members of the Gulf Cooperation Council (GCC). Saudi Arabia and other countries have criticised Al Jazeera and Qatar's relations with Iran. Qatar claims that it has assisted the United States in the War on Terror and the ongoing military intervention against ISIL. On August 2017, Qatar announced that they would restore full diplomatic relations with Iran. Two states in the six-member Gulf Co-operation Council (GCC) did not cut ties with Qatar - Kuwait and Oman. Kuwait has offered to mediate in the dispute. Qatar refused to comply with an initial list of 13 demands, saying it would not agree to any measures that threatened its sovereignty or violated international law. The emirate has now been told by its neighbours that they want it to accept six broad principles on combating extremism and terrorism. Initial supply issues were mitigated by additional imports from Iran and Turkey, and Qatar did not agree to any of the Saudi-led coalition's demands. In Jan 2021, Saudi Arabia and allies restored diplomatic ties with Qatar following a deal to resolve the crisis. Gulf leaders signed a "solidarity and stability" agreement towards ending the diplomatic rift with Qatar at a summit in Saudi Arabia in Jan 2021.

STRATEGIC RELATIONS

Gulf Cooperation Council (GCC): Qatar plays an active role in the collective defence efforts of the Gulf Cooperation Council (GCC--the regional organisation of the Arab states in the Gulf; the other five members are Saudi Arabia, Kuwait, Bahrain, the UAE, and Oman). In 2017, Saudi Arabia, UAE, Bahrain and Egypt had officially cut diplomatic ties with Qatar, and also put a ban on Qataris and their businesses. Diplomatic relations have been restored since Jan 2021 between Qatar and four Arab states including Saudi Arabia. Kuwait and US played the key role as mediators to end the stand-off. Qatar's Emir arrived in Al-Ula in Jan 2021 for an annual summit of Gulf Arab leaders that is expected to produce a détente between Qatar and four Arab states.

US: Bilateral relations are strong and expanding. Qatar and the United States coordinate closely on regional diplomatic initiatives, cooperate to increase security in the Gulf, and enjoy extensive economic links, especially in the hydrocarbons sector. Qatar has supported US military operations critical to the success of Operation Enduring Freedom and Operation Iraqi Freedom. The two countries have a Defence Cooperation Agreement that provided for US access to Qatari bases, pre-positioning of United States material, and combined military exercises. The United States and Qatar also cooperate on security in the Persian Gulf region, notably via hosting the Al-Udeid Air Force Base and CENTCOM Forward Headquarters, and Qatar's support of North Atlantic Treaty Organization and US military operations in the region. Both the countries have extensive economic ties. Qatar announced a plan to invest USD45 billion in the United States, in addition to billions of dollars' worth of military and aviation contracts. Qatar is an active participant in the Global Coalition to Defeat ISIS, is active in all Defeat-ISIS Coalition working groups, and facilitated U.S. military operations in the region. Qatar hosts roughly 10,000 US service members on two military installations critical to Coalition efforts. The United States and Qatar signed an accord in 2021 for Qatar to represent US diplomatic interests in Afghanistan. Qatar will establish a US interest section within its embassy in Afghanistan to provide certain consular services and monitor the condition and security of US diplomatic facilities in Afghanistan.

UK: Bilateral relations are strong and there is good co-operation in a number of areas. Qatar and the UK enjoy a special defence relationship underpinned by the Defence Cooperation Arrangement (DCA) signed in May 2006. The spirit of the DCA is to recognise UK support to the Qatari Armed Forces through training and exercises both in Qatar, providing Loan Service Officers and Training Teams to the Emiri Guard, Qatar Military Academy and the Infantry School; and in the UK with many Qatari officers graduating each year from Sandhurst, Dartmouth, the Joint Command and Staff College Shrivenham, and the Royal College of Defence Studies. Britain and Qatar signed a Defence Cooperation Agreement in November 2014.

India: The India-Qatari strategic engagement is based on the Qatari interests to engage India as a big market for its natural gas. Recently, India and Qatar have signed a landmark defence cooperation pact based on defence and security, dealing with key areas like maritime security, intelligence sharing on terrorism, money laundering and transnational crime. India-Qatar Defence Cooperation Agreement, signed during the visit of former PM to Qatar in November 2008 and extended till 2018, is implemented through the Joint Defence Cooperation Committee (JDCC). India is considered to be the fourth largest export destination for the Qatar followed by Japan, South Korea and Singapore.

Iran: Qatar is investing in missile defence systems to counter the threat across the Gulf from Iran, which has built up its missile arsenal. Stronger relations between Tehran and Doha contribute to peace and stability in the Middle East region. Qatar and Iran share close ties and membership in the Organisation of Petroleum Exporting Countries (OPEC), the Non-Aligned Movement (NAM) and the Organisation of the Islamic Conference (OIC). Qatar and Iran have made several bilateral agreements for to further develop their economic relationship. Iran and Qatar have a close economic relationship, particularly in the oil and gas industries. Iran and Qatar also cooperate in the shipping sector.

Iraq: Following the 1990-91 Gulf War, in which Qatar and Iraq were on opposing sides, Qatar closed their embassy in Baghdad. They reopened the embassy for the first time twenty-five years in mid-2015. A shipping line between Qatar and Iraq was launched recently.

Multilateral Alliances: Qatar, which is a member of NATO's Istanbul Cooperation Initiative (ICI) launched in 2004, has also contributed actively to the NATO-led Operation Unified Protector in Libya. The country was also an early member of OPEC. It is a member of the Arab League and Organisation of Islamic Cooperation (OIC). The country is a member of United Nations, International Monetary Fund, World Bank, and World Trade Organisation. Qatar is an observer to the Organisation of American States and a member of the Organisation for Islamic Cooperation, the Gulf Cooperation Council, and the Arab League. The new shipping line will transport goods from Jordan, Kuwait, Turkey and Iran through Iraqi territory to Qatar.

DEFENCE CAPABILITIES

ARMY: Qatari Emiri Land Force (QELF) is the largest branch of the Qatar Armed Forces and maintains a modest military force.

Personnel: 10,000 (including Emiri Guard)

Equipment

Category	Name	In Service
MBT	Leopard 2A7	20+ (more on order)
APC/ MICV/IFV	EE-9 Cascavel	25+
	AMX 10RC	10
	Piranha II 8x8	30+
	AMX 10P	20+
	AMX-VTT	10
	VAB	100+
	Commando vehicle	10
Artillery	155 mm G5	10
	PzH 2000 self-propelled	
	155 mm F3	20
Mortar	81 mm	22
	120 mm	14
MLRS	Astros II	5
	HIMARS	
	122mm BM-21 Grad	
Anti-Tank GW	Milan	500+
	Hot	900+
	Swingfire	
Missile	SA-7	
	Patriot PAC-3	15
	Stinger	50
	Starburst	
	Roland MK-II	100+
	Blowpipe	50+
	Mistral	300+
	MIM-23 Hawk	
	Rapier	200+
	THAAD	10+

New Procurements/ Upgrades

◆ The US State Department has approved

a possible Foreign Military Sale to Qatar of defence articles and services in support of a Direct Commercial Sale of the National Advanced Surface to Air Missile System (NASAMS) for an estimated cost of USD 215 million. The Government of Qatar has requested to buy defence articles and services from the US Government in support of a Direct Commercial Sale of the National Advanced Surface to Air Missile System (NASAMS). The items Qatar requests include the following: 40 AIM 120C-7 AMRAAM missiles, 1 spare AIM 120C-7 AMRAAM guidance section, 1 spare AIM-120C-7 control section, 8 AMRAAM Captive Air Training Missile (CATM-120C), missile containers, classified software for the AN/MPQ-64F1 Sentinel Radar, spare and repair parts, cryptographic and communication security devices, precision navigation equipment, other software, site surveys, weapons system equipment and computer software support, publications and technical documentation, common munitions and test equipment, repair and return services and equipment, personnel training and training equipment, integration support and test equipment, and US Government and contractor, engineering, technical and logistics support services, and other related elements of logistical and programme support.

◆ In January 2018, Russian state media TASS reported that Qatar was in an advanced state of talks to procure the S-400 air defence system from Russia.

NAVY: Qatari Emiri Navy (QAN) has a small number of 1,500-man navy, including its marine police force and coastal defence artillery. The navy headquarters is at Doha there is also a base at Halul island.

Personnel: 2,000 (including Marine Police)

Equipment

Category	Name	In Service
Fast Attack Craft	Barzan Class (Vita Class)	4
	Damsah Class	3
Patrol Vessel	Vosper class	6
	Damen Polycat	6
	MV-45	3
	P-1500 class	5
	DV-15 class	3
	Fast Interceptor	5+
Missile	Exocet MM40 Block-III, MM-38, Mistral, Goalkeeper	

New Procurements/ Upgrades

◆ Fincantieri, one of the world's top shipbuilding groups, and Barzan Holdings, a company wholly owned by the Qatari Ministry of Defence and responsible for empowering the military capabilities of the national armed force in the state, signed a letter of intent aimed at studying possible forms of cooperation in the coastal defence surveillance sector, through the implementation of new technologies and cutting-edge program management and maintenance services within the Qatari naval programmes.

AIR FORCE: The Qatar Emiri Air Force (QEAF) is the aerial branch of the Qatar Armed Forces. It was formed in 1974, three years after achieving independence from Great Britain in 1971.

Personnel: 2,000

Equipment

Category	Name	In Service
Fighters/ attack/Recon-naissance/ bomber	Dassault Mirage 2000-5	12
	Boeing F-15E	On order
	Boeing 737 AEW&C	On order
	Dassault Rafale	4+ (More on order)
Transport/ Tanker	C-17A Globemaster III	1 (More on order)
	C-130J Super Hercules	4
	Boeing 747-SP	2
	Airbus A330 MRTT	On order
	Airbus 300/310/320	
Helicopter	Gazelle SA 342	10+
	AH-64 Apache	On order
	AW139	20
	NH-90	On order
	UH-60R Sea Hawk	On order
	Westland Commando	10+
	UH-60R Sea Hawk	On order
Trainer	Alpha Jet-A	5+
	Pilatus PC-21	On order
SAM	I-Hawk Battery	1
	Roland II	5+
	Rapier Battery	1
AAM	AIM-9M Sidewinder, Mica-RF, Magic-II R.55O, Matra R.530	
AGM	AS-30L	
ASM	AM-39 Exocet	

New Procurements/ Upgrades

◆ The joint Royal Air Force & Qatar Emiri Air Force (QEAF) Typhoon squadron was officially opened at RAF Coningsby. The UK has offered to base Qatar's recently acquired nine Hawk aircraft at a British RAF station, which could also be home to a joint RAF & QEAF Hawk training squadron.

◆ Qatar bought 36 F-15QAs with staged delivery by summer 2021 and committed to developing Al Udeid AB to accommodate F-15's and other fighter jets.

◆ In June 2019, Qatar received its first five of the 36 purchased Rafale fighter jets from France.

◆ The US State Department has approved a possible Foreign Military Sale to Qatar of Advanced Precision Kill Weapon Systems (APKWS) II Guidance Sections for an estimated cost of USD300 million.

◆ The US State Department has approved a possible Foreign Military Sale to Qatar of equipment and support to upgrade the Qatari Emiri Air Force's (QEAF) Air Operation Center (AOC) for an estimated cost of USD197 million.

◆ BAE Systems and the Government of the State of Qatar have entered into a contract, valued at approximately £5 billion, for the supply of Typhoon aircraft to the Qatar Emiri Air Force along with a bespoke support and training package. The contract provides for 24 Typhoon aircraft with delivery expected to commence in late 2022. In addition, the agreement signed by the Qatar and British Governments, it also includes a clear intention to proceed with the purchase of Hawk aircraft. The deal also includes an agreement with MBDA for Brimstone and Meteor missiles and Raytheon's Paveway IV UK-manufactured weapon for the jets. Substantial progress has been made on the contract between BAE Systems and the Government of Qatar for the provision of 24 Typhoon aircraft, 9 Hawk Advanced Jet Trainers and a six-year availability support service.

◆ The US State Department has approved a possible Foreign Military Sale to Qatar for support of its F-15QA multi-role fighter aircraft program for an estimated cost of USD1.1 billion.

◆ CAE wins contract to provide Qatar Emiri Air Force (QEAF) with comprehensive NH90 training solution. The contract is valued at more than C$150 million. The QEAF signed a contract with Leonardo Helicopters to acquire a fleet of both NH90 tactical transport helicopters (TTH) and NH90 NATO frigate helicopters (NFH).

◆ USAF has awarded Boeing USD500 million for Qatar Emiri Air Force F-15QA aircrew and maintenance training. This is a sole-source requirement as the Boeing Co. has been country-designated as the sole-source provider for the F-15QA program, including F-15QA specific training, under the QEAF Foreign Military Sales (FMS) case QA-D-TAH.

◆ The US State Department has approved a possible Foreign Military Sale to Qatar of two AN/AAQ-24(V)N Large Aircraft Infrared Countermeasures (LAIRCM) systems and related equipment for an estimated cost of USD86 million.

◆ The US State Department has approved a possible Foreign Military Sale to Qatar of 24 AH-64E Apache Attack helicopters and related equipment for an estimated cost of USD3.0 billion.

A Qatar Emiri Air Force Dassault Mirage 2000-5 fighter jet takes off as part of a Joint Task Force Odyssey Dawn mission in 2011. Image Credit: US Navy photo by Paul Farley

Major Armaments Producers

There is no domestic production facility in Qatar for defence related products and equipments. Qatar also has no military research and development programmes in progress. The Gulf Cooperation Council (GCC) was established in an agreement concluded on 25 May 1981 in Riyadh, Saudi Arabia between: Bahrain, Kuwait, Oman, Qatar, Saudi Arabia and UAE. These countries declared that the GCC is established in view of the special relations between them, their similar political systems based on Islamic beliefs, joint destiny and common objectives. The GCC is a regional common market with a defence planning council as well. The geographic proximity of these countries and their general adoption of free trade economic policies are factors that encouraged them to establish the GCC. The GCC States seek to build up their defence forces according to a common conception. In this context, they have unified operational procedures, training, and military curricula. They also endeavour to accomplish compatibility of their military systems.

Barzan Holdings is responsible for empowering the military capabilities of the Qatari Armed Forces. The defence and security company has made its official public launch on the first day of DIMDEX 2018. Barzan Holdings' mission is to strengthen Qatar's sovereignty and support the long-term development of R&D, knowledge transfer, human capital, industry and innovative technology in Qatar's defence and security sector. Barzan Holdings has also signed a Memorandum of Understanding (MoU) with Qatar Navigation (Milaha) for enhancing Qatar's defence and security capabilities. Barzan has signed multiple MoU and partnership agreements with many defence and aerospace companies in order to empower the military capabilities of Qatar Armed Forces.

DEFENCE DEALS
Arms Import

Qatar has a less significant military and therefore the procurement percentage is mere compare to other Gulf States. Qatar is enhancing its military capability to strengthen its homeland defence. Major purchases since 2014 include Apache helicopters, Javelin missiles, Early Warning Radar, PAC 3 Patriot systems, and F-15 aircraft. The Qatari military is also sponsoring an initiative to create a vast network of military training facilities and programs focused on supporting their recent defence acquisitions.

At DIMDEX international exhibition held in March 2018, both Turkey and Qatar signed an agreement that would allow Turkey to construct a naval base in the north of Qatar which would include a training facility. Qatar's Ministry of Defence recently signed a three-year, USD 43.92 million contract with UK-based Serco to run courses for mid-level officers, such as majors and lieutenant-colonels, from the Qatari Emiri Navy, Army and Air Force. The Qatari Armed Forces recently during the DIMDEX exhibition announced deals with US weapons manufactures worth USD 7.6 billion, including Apache helicopters, Javelin missiles and PAC 3 Patriot systems and also included 17 Turkish fast patrol vessels and German tankers.

According to Kongsberg news release in 2018, KONGSBERG has signed a cooperation agreement in Qatar for long-term technology development programs within defence, maritime industry and digitalisation. The first programme in relation to the cooperation will be delivery of communication, digitalization and tower solutions for military vehicles, a programme with a potential of approximately NOK 15 billion over the next eight years. KONGSBERG plans to deliver tower solutions, and digitalization and communication solutions to 490 armoured vehicles delivered by the French company Nexter. The next steps in the process will be detailing and final negotiations prior to signing the final contract for the programme. KONGSBERG plans to deliver the solutions "PROTECTOR Remote Weapon Station" and "Medium Caliber Turret" to the programme, both tower solutions developed for increased protection of personnel.

Qatar also ordered and has in service 62 tanks and 24 self-propelled guns from Germany including 24 combat helicopters and 3 AEW aircraft from the US, and 2 tanker aircraft from Spain. Qatar maintains advanced anti air and anti ship capabilities with deliveries of Patriot PAC-3 MSE Batteries, Exocet MM40 Block 3 and Marte ER anti-ship missiles. Defence imports also include ballistic anti-missile systems and a new generation of warplanes. Military electronics and cyber systems, helicopters for special forces, light tactical armoured vehicles with weapons systems, GBU-35 bunker-buster ammunition to be used against concrete-protected nuclear facilities, guided air-to-air and air-to-ground missiles, Apache attack helicopters, and Patriot and Javelin air defense systems are also common purchases.

DEFENCE BUDGET

Total defence spending: $12.6 billion (approx.)

Estimated defence spending in terms of GDP: 4% of GDP (2020 est.), 3.6% of GDP (2019 est.)

The State of Qatar has witnessed rapid economic growth in recent years with a predicted GDP growth forecast to hit 7.8 % in 2015, its fastest rate since 2011. Oil and gas have given Qatar one of the highest per capita incomes in the world and made it one of the fastest-growing economies. Qatar's military spending follows the Middle Eastern trend by investing increasing amounts of GDP to modernise and strengthen its military forces, with $23 billion of deals announced at DIMDEX 2014 with the Qatar Armed Forces. Qatar, during DIMDEX 2016, Qatar penned eight new MoUs totalling QAR 1.29 billion. DIMDEX 2018 saw record number of contracts being signed with special focus on the Barzan Holdings. Qatar, along with other Middle East GCC nations like Saudi Arabia and UAE are continuing with their massive military spending despite falling oil prices. Qatar is planning to modernise its armed forces and secure its maritime borders by signing agreements for approx. USD 8.95 billion. Qatar is one of the wealthiest countries in the world and has strong bonds with the European Union especially USA and France. Qatar has defence pacts with the US, UK, Russia and France and other countries. There is a little transparency in the military spending. The country does not report their military spending separately from their broader spending on security (including internal security). Qatar's procurement and military spending is growing rapidly. There is therefore a greater need for the development of efficient, effective and interoperable logistics systems and strategies. Recent military operations have highlighted both the importance of coalitions as well as the logistics capabilities of Qatar.

CONCLUSION

Qatar is classified by the UN as a country of very high human development and is widely regarded as the most advanced Arab state for human development, as per news reports. Qatar has a very high per capita income and is strongly involved in nearby regional conflicts. The Middle East nation plays an active role in the collective defence efforts of the Gulf Cooperation Council. The presence of a large American military base in the country provides the country with a guaranteed source of defence and national security. The country has one of the most creative foreign policies in this unstable region. Qatar is planning to emerge as a world player and also as a strong nation among the rest of the Gulf States. Qatar, one of the wealthiest nations in the middle-east is rich in oil and natural gas has the world's largest per capita production and proven reserves of both oil and natural gas. The country thus shares a mutual interest with western countries. The US military has a substantial military presence in Qatar, including the operational headquarters for the US Central Command (CENTCOM) and the Central Air Operational Component at Al-Udeid Air Base. The country, having less population, minimal military power, is fully economy driven with major investments in banking, financial services, wealth and education, as well as in development of industrial plants. From military point of view, she is friendly to Iran and also serves as a base for the US armed forces. Qatar has been historically sensitive to outside military intervention in the Gulf and was eager to bolster regional security measures. Also, it is focusing all its energies on improving cooperation and coordination on mutual defence issues while also continuing to work together in social, cultural, political, and economic spheres with other GCC members. The Qatar Armed Forces is aiming to develop a technically advanced military force which will ensure its readiness to meet the challenges of the maritime domain in the 21st Century. Qatar has played a constructive financial, political, and military role in addressing regional turmoil, and in partnership with the United States, has contributed to progress, stability, and prosperity in the region. In 2017, the governments of Saudi Arabia, the United Arab Emirates, Bahrain, and Egypt severed diplomatic relations with the State of Qatar and imposed a series of economic restrictions, including shuttering the Saudi-Qatar land border, closing airspace to Qatari-registered aircraft, and limiting certain maritime traffic.

CONTACT DETAILS

Ministry of Defence and Armed Forces HQ
P.O. Box 37, Doha, Qatar
Tel: +974-4614111
Procurement Directorate – Logistics Department
Tel: 44612959
Tender and Auction Committee
Tel: 44612734
www.gov.qa

REPUBLIC OF THE CONGO
(Capital: Brazzaville)

INTRODUCTION

Total Area: 342,000 sq km
Population: 5,417,414 (July 2021 est.)
Coastline: 169 km
Maritime claims: Territorial sea: 12 nm
Contiguous zone: 24 nm
Exclusive economic zone: 200 nm

KEY POLITICAL PERSONS

PRESIDENT & COMMANDER-IN-CHIEF: Denis Sassou-Nguesso

PRIME MINISTER: Anatole Collinet Makosso

KEY DEFENCE PERSONS

DEFENCE MINISTER: Gen. Charles Richard Mondjo

ECONOMY

The Republic of the Congo's economy is a mixture of subsistence farming, an industrial sector based largely on oil and support services, and government spending. Oil has supplanted forestry as the mainstay of economy, providing a major share of government revenues and exports. Natural gas is increasingly being converted to electricity rather than being flared, greatly improving energy prospects. New mining projects, particularly iron ore, which entered production in late 2013, may add as much as $1 billion to annual government

revenue. The Republic of the Congo is a member of the Central African Economic and Monetary Community and shares a common currency – the Central African Franc – with five other member states in the region. The current administration faces difficult economic challenges of stimulating recovery and reducing poverty. The drop in oil prices that began in 2014 has constrained government spending; lower oil prices forced the government to cut more than $1 billion in planned spending. The fiscal deficit amounted to 11% of GDP in 2017. In the wake of a multi-year recession, the country reached out to the IMF in 2017 for a new programme; the IMF noted that the country's continued dependence on oil, unsustainable debt, and significant governance weakness are key impediments to economy. The IMF urged the government to renegotiate debts levels to sustainable levels before it agreed to a new macroeconomic adjustment package.

Amidst the deadly COVID-19 outbreak and declining global oil prices, the Congo-Brazzaville economy contracted by 6.8% in 2020, according to data by the African Development Bank. The Bank projects a GDP growth of 1.2% in 2021 for the country if the world economy rebounds.

GDP (official exchange rate): $8.71 billion (2017 est.)

Real Growth Rate (GDP): -3.1% (2017 est.); -2.8% (2016 est.)

Industries: Petroleum extraction, cement, lumber, brewing, sugar, palm oil, soap, flour, cigarettes

Natural Gas - proved reserves: 90.61 billion cu m (1 January 2018 est.)

Crude Oil - proved reserves: 1.6 billion bbl (1 January 2018 est.)

Total Exports: $4.139 billion (2017 est.); $4.116 billion (2016 est.)

Export Commodities: Crude petroleum, copper, lumber, ships, refined petroleum (2019)

Major Markets: China 49%, United Arab Emirates 15%, India 6%, Italy 5% (2019)

Total Imports: $2.501 billion (2017 est.); $5.639 billion (2016 est.)

Import Commodities: Ships, chicken products, refined petroleum, processed fish, packaged medicines (2019)

Major Suppliers: China 15%, France 12%, Belgium 6%, Angola 5% (2019)

INTERNATIONAL DISPUTES

Most of the Congo River boundary with the Republic of the Congo is undefined as no agreement has been reached on the division of the river or its islands, except in the Pool Malebo/Stanley Pool area.

DEFENCE

ARMY
Personnel: 10,000

Equipment

Category	Name	In Service
Battle Tank	T-54/55	26
	T-59	14
	PT-76 light	3
	Type 62	8
Armoured Vehicle	BRDM1/2	24
	Panhard M3	
	BTR-152	20
	BTR-50	18
	BTR-60	28
Artillery	75mm	6
	100mm guns	10
	122mm D-30 howitzers	8
Mortar	81mm	
	120mm	
MRL	122mm	
ATGW	AT-3 SAGGER	
AA gun	14.5mm	16
	37mm	40
	57mm	8
ATK gun	100mm	

New Procurements/ Upgrades

No major procurement plans are under consideration at present by the Army.

NAVY
Personnel: 300

Equipment

Category	Name	In Service
Patrol Vessel	Arco class river patrol	4
Tug	Hinda class	1

New Procurements/ Upgrades

No major procurement plans are under consideration at present by the Navy.

Note: Angola, Cameroon, the Democratic Republic of Congo, the Republic of the Congo, Gabon, Equatorial Guinea and Nigeria have reached an agreement for the establishment of a joint force (Gulf of Guinea Guard Force, GGGF) to monitor their shared interests in the Gulf of Guinea, in particular the valuable offshore oil facilities in the region.

AIR FORCE
Personnel: 500

Equipment

Category	Name	In Service
Fighter	MiG-21	12
	L-39 Albatross	4
Transport	An-26	1
	F-28	1
	An-24	5
	Nord 2501	1
Helicopter	Mi-26	1
	Alouette II/III	4
	SA-365 Dauphin	1

New Procurements/ Upgrades

No major procurement plans are under consideration at present by the Air Force.

Defence Expenditure

Estimated defence spending in terms of GDP: 1.7%

Most of the defence equipment and hardware of the Congo military are of Soviet, Chinese and Czech origin.

Defence Production and R&D

No defence production facility exists in the Republic of Congo.

Defence Procurement

No military procurement plans are under consideration by the Government at present.

CONTACT DETAILS
Ministry of National Defence
Quartier General
Brazzaville, Congo
Armed Forces HQ
P.O. Box 138, Brazzaville, Congo

ROMANIA
(Capital: Bucharest)

INTRODUCTION

Area: 238,391 sq km
Population: 21,230,362 (July 2021 est.)
Coastline: 225 km
Maritime claims: Territorial sea: 12 nm
Contiguous zone: 24 nm
Exclusive Economic Zone: 200 nm
Continental shelf: 200 m depth or to the depth of exploitation

KEY POLITICAL PERSONS

PRESIDENT & SUPREME COMMANDER OF THE ARMED FORCES: Klaus Iohannis

PRIME MINISTER: Gen. Nicolae Ionel Ciuca

KEY DEFENCE PERSONS

DEFENCE MINISTER: Vasile Dîncu

CHIEF OF THE GENERAL STAFF: Lt. Gen. Daniel Petrescu

CHIEF OF ARMY STAFF: Lt. Gen. Dunitru Scarlat

CHIEF OF NAVY STAFF: Contraamiral Mihai Panait

CHIEF OF AIR STAFF: Maj. Gen. Viorel Pană

ECONOMY

Romania is an upper-middle income mixed economy. The country is a regional leader in multiple fields, such as IT and motor vehicle production. Exports remained the engine of economic growth. The top exports of Romania are vehicles, machinery, chemical goods, electronic products, electrical equipment, pharmaceuticals, transport equipment, basic metals, food products, and rubber and plastics. Romania's economic growth rate was 4.8% in 2016, 7.1% in 2017, 4.4% in 2018, and 4.1% in 2019, the highest in the EU. The World Bank has classified Romania as a high-income country for the first time, based on the 2019 data (per capita income of $12,630). However, the pandemic-triggered crisis pulled the country back into the upper-middle-income group. Romania's economy contracted by 3.9 percent in 2020, one of the lowest contractions in the European Union (EU), and recovered strongly at 6.5 percent in the first half of 2021, the World Bank has stated.

GDP (official exchange rate): $249.543 billion (2019 est.)

Real Growth Rate (GDP): 4.2% (2019 est.), 4.54% (2018 est.)

Industries: Electric machinery and equipment, auto assembly, textiles and footwear, light machinery, metallurgy, chemicals, food processing, petroleum refining, mining, timber, construction materials.

Oil – Proved Reserves: 600 million bbl. (1 January 2018 est.)

Natural Gas – Proved Reserves: 105.5 billion cu m (1 January 2018 est.)

Total Exports: $93.01 billion (2020 est.), $100.9 billion (2019 est.)

Export Commodities: Cars and vehicle parts, insulated wiring, refined petroleum, electrical control boards, seats (2019)

Major Markets: Germany 22%, Italy 10%, France 7% (2019)

Total Imports: $104.16 billion dollars (2020 est.), $111.18 billion (2019 est.)

Import Commodities: Cars and vehicle parts, crude petroleum, packaged medicines, insulated wiring, broadcasting equipment (2019)

Major Suppliers: Germany 19%, Italy 9%, Hungary 7%, Poland 6%, China 5%, France 5% (2019)

INTERNATIONAL DISPUTES

◆ The ICJ ruled largely in favour of Romania in its dispute submitted in 2004 over Ukrainian-administered Zmiyinyy/Serpilor (Snake) Island and Black Sea maritime boundary delimitation; Romania opposes Ukraine's reopening of a navigation canal from the Danube border through Ukraine to the Black Sea.

DEFENCE

The Romanian Military is modernising its armed forces carrying out structural changes including command, doctrine, training and personnel levels besides defence procurement. Having completed two short-term stages, the long-term stage is expected to be finished in 2026. The modernisation programme which started in 2017 aims to improve the structure of the armed forces, reducing personnel as well as acquiring newer and more improved technology that is compatible with NATO standards. Romania plans to acquire the Patriot air defence system and equip its navy with new submarines under the modernisation programme.

ARMY

Personnel: 42,000

Equipment

Category	Name	In Service
MBT	Piranha V	36
	T-55	190
	TR-85	103
	TR-85MI	54
IFV/APC	MLI-84 JDER	101
	MLI-84	15
	B33 TAB Zimbru	69
	TAB-71	247
	TAB-77	153
	TAB-79	372
	Panhard PVP	12
	Piranha IIIC	24
Artillery	M30 122mm howitzer	84
	M81 152mm	217
	M85 152mm	
	M85 152mm	104
Mortar	82mm	299
	120mm	281
MLRS	APR-40	134
	Larom 160mm	54
ATK gun	M77 100mm	199
ATGW	9P122	12
	9P133	51
	9P148	48
AA Gun	35 mm twin	24
	Gepard SPAAG	42

New Procurements/Upgrades

◆ Romanian will produce locally about 191 Piranha V armoured fighting vehicles.

NAVY

Personnel: 7,000+

Equipment

Category	Name	In Service
Submarine	Kilo class	1

...continued

Category	Name	In Service
Frigate	Regela Ferdinand class	2
	Marasesti class	1
Corvette	Tetal class	4
Patrol craft	ex-USSR Tarantul class missile corvettes	3
	Epitrop class torpedo boats	3
Mine warfare Force	Corsar class minelayers	1
	Musca class minesweepers	4
River squadron	Mihail Kogalniceanu class river monitors	3
	Brutar class river monitors	5
	VD 141 class river patrol minesweepers	12
Marine	TABC-79	
	TAB-1M	
Helicopter	PUMA	3

New Procurements/Upgrades

◆ Romania plans to purchase four vessels for its Navy under a procurement estimated to be worth about $1.96 billion. Deliveries are scheduled for 2018 to 2024, according to the Ministry of National Defence.

◆ The government plans to overhaul and modernise two Type 22 frigates acquired second hand from the United Kingdom in 2003.

◆ The US State Department has approved a possible Foreign Military Sale (FMS) of naval strike missile (NSM) coastal defence systems (CDS) worth $300m to Romania.

AIR FORCE

Personnel: 11,000
Equipment

Category	Name	In Service	On Order
Fighter	F-16	16	1
	MiG-21 Lancer	36	
Transport	C-130B	4	
	C-130H	1	
	C-27J	7	
	An-30	2	
Helicopter	IAR-330 L/M/Medevac	33	
	IAR-330 Socat (attack)	23	
	IAR-316B	6	
Air defence artillery	S-60 57mm gun	96	
SAM	SA-2	7	
	Hawk XXI system	4	

New Procurements/Upgrades

◆ The United States Air Force has donated C-130H Hercules to the Romanian Air Force.

◆ The Romanian Ministry of Interior has ordered six new-generation S-70M Black Hawk utility helicopters. This first order follows the recent signing of a four-year framework agreement that will see up to 12 Polish-built S-70M Black Hawks supplied to Romania over the next four years. The first six aircraft, three configured to support maritime and three to support land operations, will be delivered in 2023.

◆ Romania plans to purchase 32 additional F-16 fighters from Norway to modernise the country's air force.

◆ The Romanian military will receive three Phased Array Tracking Radar to Intercept on Target (PATRIOT) batteries from 2022.

◆ Five new Shorad/VShorad integrated systems to be procured to replace the S-60 guns.

◆ Israel Aerospace Industries has signed Agreement of Cooperation with Romanian IAR-Brasov to manufacture tactical Heron UAV.

◆ Romania expects to receive a mobile coastal defence system based on the Naval Strike Missile.by the end of 2024. Romania in May 2021 became the first country to officially order the Raytheon Naval Strike Missile (NSM) Coastal Defence System (CDS) via the FMS programme.

Defence Expenditure

Total defence spending: $5.785 billion (2021), $5.050 billion (2019)

Defence spending in terms of GDP: 2.02% (2021)

Starting from 2017, Romania has committed to spend at least 2.0% of GDP on defence through 2027. Romania is carrying out its military modernisation programme and it is also looking to develop its own defence industry through international partnerships.

Defence Production and R&D

Romania is in the process of recapitalising its defence industry, especially in terms of producing modern weapon systems even as it carries out the military modernisation programme for the armed forces. New steps have been taken for finding a fundamental solution for the defence industry, such as, reorganising and resizing the sector according to the real needs of the Romanian Defence Forces and Romania's potential in the external market. Towards this effort, Romania has decided to collaborate with Pakistan on defence production. Romania and Poland are currently negotiating an agreement for broadening of defence cooperation between the two countries for production of advanced military equipment and joint participation in research and development (R&D) projects. Meanwhile, Romania and the United States have signed a ten-year road map for defence cooperation that captures the nations' common strategic goals and shared interests, such as defence modernisation and Black Sea-area security.

Defence Procurement

The Ministry of National Defence – Armaments Department is responsible for armament systems acquisition management, Romanian defence policy for enhancing the country's defence capability and the interoperability of the armed forces with NATO and EU countries. Being the authority in the acquisition domain for the Ministry of National Defence, the Armaments Department acts towards the harmonisation of the national with international laws by concerning the product and services procurement organisation, establishing the goals of modern technology integration, and optimum resource utilisation and keeping balance between domestic and foreign acquisitions. The country's defence modernisation acquisition programme includes purchase of four multifunctional corvettes, rocket launcher mobile systems, modernisation of MLI 84 M combat machines, 8×8 and 4×4 armoured carriers, C4I systems, ASAM large-scale rocket systems, short and very short range air defence (SHORAD/VSHORAD) systems and a multiple missile launcher, expansion of the fighter plane fleet, acquisition of combat and utility helicopters, upgrade of the training plane fleet (IAR 99 Soim), the modernisation of the two frigates Regele Ferdinand and Regina Maria, acquisition of military trucks and the beginning of a small submarine fleet programme. The government has signed several important military contracts in 2017.

CONTACT DETAILS
Ministry of Defence
Izvor Street, nr. 110
Sector 5, cod 050561
050561, Bucharest.
Information and Public Relations Directorate
E-mail: presamapn@mapn.ro
Contact: 021-319.60.22

STRATEGIC INFORMATION
RUSSIAN FEDERATION
(Capital: Moscow)

The map of Russia is according to the Federal Constitutional Law dated 21.03.2014 No. 6-FCL/FKZ (Version 31.12.2014)

"On accession of Crimean Republic to Russian Federation and on formation of new constituent entities of Crimean Republic and Sevastopol – the city of Federal status." (Valid with amendments and addenda from 01.01.2015)

INTRODUCTION

Area: 17,098,242 sq km
Population: 142,320,790 (July 2021 est.)
Coastline: 37,653 km
Maritime claims: Territorial sea: 12 nm
Contiguous zone: 24 nm
Exclusive Economic Zone: 200 nm
Continental shelf: 200m depth or to the depth of exploitation

GEOPOLITICAL IMPORTANCE

The Russian Federation is a large country which is carved out of the erstwhile Soviet Union. Following the dissolution of the Soviet Union in 1991, the Russian Soviet Federative Socialist Republic (SFSR) reconstituted itself as the Russian Federation and is recognised as the successor of the Union of Soviet Socialist Republics (USSR). Russia, a major great power, occupies most of Eastern Europe and North Asia, stretching from the Baltic Sea in the West to the Pacific Ocean in the East, and from the Arctic Ocean in the North to the Black Sea and the Caucasus in the South. It is bordered by Norway and Finland in the Northwest; Estonia, Latvia, Belarus, Ukraine, Poland, and Lithuania in the West; Georgia and Azerbaijan in the Southwest; and Kazakhstan, Mongolia, China, and North Korea along the Southern border. The country is endowed with the largest reserves of mineral and energy resources and is among the largest producer of oil and natural gas. It is one of the five recognised nuclear weapons states and possesses the largest stockpile of nuclear warheads. The Russian Armed Forces have been ranked as the world's second most powerful. Russia remains an important international actor both in the Eurasian region and in the world at large even after the disintegration of the Soviet Union, an era which witness significant technological achievements including launching of the first human in space.

POLITICAL OVERVIEW

After the dissolution of the USSR, Boris Yeltsin became the first directly elected president of the Russian Soviet Federative Socialist Republic in June 1991, which later became the independent Russian Federation. A new constitution was adopted in 1993 and since then Russia has been governed as a federal semi-presidential republic.

The head of the Russian Federation is the president who is elected after every six years. The president, who is also the supreme commander in chief of the Russian military has the right to lead international politics of the country. He is eligible for a second term but constitutionally the president is barred from a third consecutive term. The Government consists of the Prime Minister, Deputy Chairman of the Government and Federal ministries. The prime minister is appointed by the president with the approval of the Duma. The upper chamber of the Russian parliament – the Federation Council – consists of two members from each of the 83 federal subjects: 21 republics, 46 oblasts, nine krais, two federal cities, four autonomous okrugs and an autonomous oblast. The Council has special powers to declare a presidential election, impeachment of the president and to decide on the use of the armed forces outside Russian territory. The federal bodies include federal ministries, federal services and federal agencies. The lower chamber in the Russian Federal Assembly is the State Duma. The chamber has 450 members who are known as deputies. All the bills, even those proposed by the Federation Council must first be considered by the Duma. The Constitutional Court consists of 19 judges, one being the Chairman and another one being Deputy Chairman. Judges are appointed by the president with the consent of the Federation Council. The Constitutional Court and general courts are headed by the Supreme Court and arbitration courts by the Supreme Arbitration Court.

On 18 March 2014, Russian President Vladimir Putin added the Crimean Peninsula to the map of Russia, a day after Crimea's regional assembly declared independence from Ukraine and applied to join the Russian Federation. Crimea is home to Russia's Black Sea fleet. The Crimean Peninsula is a multi-ethnic region which until February 2014 was administered by Ukraine. Russia now administers the territory consisting of the Autonomous Republic of Crimea and the city of Sevastopol as two federal subjects within the Crimean Federal District – the Republic of Crimea and the federal city of Sevastopol.

KEY POLITICAL PERSONS

PRESIDENT & SUPREME COMMANDER-IN-CHIEF OF THE ARMED FORCES: Vladimir Putin

PRIME MINISTER: Mikhail Mishustin

ECONOMY

Following the collapse of the Soviet Union, Russia changed from a centrally planned economy to a globally integrated market economy. Market reforms in the 1990s privatised much of Russian industry and agriculture, with notable exceptions in the energy and defence-related sectors. The country has an abundance of natural resources, including oil, natural gas and precious metals which make up a major share of Russia's exports. In 2019, Russia's Natural Resources and Environment Ministry estimated the value of natural resources to $844 billion or 60% of the country's GDP. Russia, also known for its large and sophisticated arms industry, is capable of designing and manufacturing a wide range of high-tech military equipment including launch vehicles, satellites. Top military exports from Russia include combat aircraft, air defence systems, ships and submarines. Falling oil prices and sanctions imposed by western countries with the annexation of Crimea pushed the Russian economy into a deep recession in

2015, with GDP falling by close to 2.8%. The downturn continued through 2016, with GDP contracting another 0.2%, but was reversed in 2017 as world demand picked up. Russia's economic recovery continued amidst relatively high oil prices, enhanced macroeconomic stability, gradual monetary loosening, and ongoing momentum in global economic growth and real GDP growth surpassed expectations in 2018, reaching 2.3 percent, the World Bank has stated. The Russian economy expanded by 10.5% year on year in the second quarter of 2021 as it recovered after a sharp contraction caused by the Covid-19 pandemic. After shrinking by 3.0% in 2020, the economy has reached pre-pandemic levels buoyed by a rebound in global commodity prices, according to Rosstat, the federal statistics service.

GDP (official exchange rate): $1,702,361,000,000 (2019 est.)

Real Growth Rate (GDP): 1.34% (2019 est.), 2.54% (2018 est.)

Industries: Complete range of mining and extractive industries producing coal, oil, gas, chemicals, and metals; all forms of machine building from rolling mills to high-performance aircraft and space vehicles; defence industries (including radar, missile production, advanced electronic components), shipbuilding; road and rail transportation equipment; communications equipment; agricultural machinery, tractors, and construction equipment; electric power generating and transmitting equipment; medical and scientific instruments; consumer durables, textiles, foodstuff, handicraft.

Natural Gas – Proved Reserves: 47.8 trillion cu m (1 January 2018 est.)

Crude Oil – Proved Reserves: 80 billion bbl (1 January 2018 est.)

Total Exports: $551.128 billion (2019 est.), $564.314 billion (2018 est.)

Export Commodities: Crude petroleum, refined petroleum, natural gas, coal, wheat, iron (2019)

Major Markets: China 14%, Netherlands 10%, Belarus 5%, Germany 5% (2019)

Total Imports: $366.919 billion (2019 est.), $355.022 billion (2018 est.)

Import Commodities: Cars and vehicle parts, packaged medicines, broadcasting equipment, aircraft, computers (2019)

Major Suppliers: China 20%, Germany 13%, Belarus 6% (2019)

DEFENCE & SECURITY

The Russian armed forces main tasks is protection of the individual, society and state from terrorism, including international terrorism, from extraordinary situations both natural and man-made, and their consequences, and in times of war from the dangers arising from the conduct and consequences of military action. As part of its new national security priorities, Moscow has reoriented its armed forces to meet four major objectives – deterring the military and political threats to the security or interests of the Russian Federation; supporting economic and political interests; mounting other-than-war enforcement operations; and using military force.

The country's strategic goal seeks to prevent global and regional wars and conflicts. It is increasing its security cooperation with other Soviet successor states that belong to the Commonwealth of Independent States (CIS). The updated military doctrine released in 2014 calls for a more aggressive stance toward NATO, boosting Moscow's presence in the Arctic and strengthening its cooperation with India and China. It exhorts for joint setting up of missile defence systems by Russia and allied countries, to extend its air and anti-missile defence coverage over Europe. The doctrine has highlighted the deterrent capacity of Russia's conventional weapons in addition to its nuclear arsenal which can be used only in the event of an existential threat, referring to the country's growing conventional might. As a major nuclear power, Russia has inherited the arsenal of all the former Soviet states which consists of silo-based as well as rail and road mobile ICBMs, sea-based SLBMs, strategic bombers, strategic aerial refuelling aircraft, and long-range tactical aircraft capable of carrying gravity bombs, stand-off missiles, and cruise missiles. The Kremlin has approved a new "information security doctrine" aimed at bolstering the country's defences against cyber attacks. A separate Arctic command has been formed and the military has restored long-abandoned Soviet-era airfields and built radar stations in the region. Russia is a member of the Missile Technology Control Regime (MTCR) and the Hague Code of Conduct Against Ballistic Missile Proliferation (HCOC).

KEY DEFENCE PERSONS

MINISTER OF DEFENCE: Gen. Sergei Shoigu

CHIEF OF THE GENERAL STAFF: Gen. Valery Gerasimov

COMMANDER IN CHIEF OF THE LAND FORCES: Col. Gen. Oleg Salyukov

COMMANDER IN CHIEF OF THE NAVY: Adm. Nikolai Yevmenov

COMMANDER IN CHIEF OF THE AEROSPACE FORCES: Col. Gen. Sergei Surovikin

COMMANDER IN CHIEF OF THE AIR FORCE: Lt. Gen. Sergey Dronov

COMMANDER OF THE AIRBORNE FORCES: Col. Gen. Andrey Serdyukov

COMMANDER OF THE STRATEGIC MISSILE FORCES: Col. Gen. Sergei Karakaev

Internal Conflict

Russia's internal problems stem mainly from separatist uprisings and attempts to secede. The disintegration of the Soviet Union on 26 December 1991 resulted in political instability leading to ethnic conflict in Russia. The minority groups have been fighting for autonomy to control their own people, language, culture, and religion. The Russia-Chechen conflict was a major internal area of concern for Moscow. The Southern Caucasus region is a strategic pathway from Russia to oil reserves in Central Asia and the Caspian Sea. In 1991, secessionist movements developed in Chechnya were strongly resisted by Moscow. Russia's implacable opposition to Chechen independence was based on the region's importance as a centre of the oil industry and home to several chemical factories. Even though Russia has established its firm control over the autonomous region after decades of fighting for independence, separatist groups continue low-level guerrilla attacks even today. Besides, jihadist groups, including those aligned with Islamic State terrorist organisation, also exist in the region.

External Conflict

Ukraine: Russia is involved in a conflict with Ukraine over the control of Crimea, a Black Sea peninsula. Prior to the crisis, Crimea was a part of Ukraine as the Autonomous Republic of Crimea and the administratively separate municipality of Sevastopol. On 17 March 2014, the Crimean Parliament declared independence from Ukraine and asked to join the Russian Federation. The next day Russia and the separatist government of Crimea signed a treaty of accession of the Republic of Crimea and Sevastopol into the Russian Federation. However, on 27 March 2014, the UN General Assembly passed a non-binding resolution that declared the Crimean referendum invalid and the incorporation of Crimea into Russia as illegal. On 15 April 2014, the Ukrainian parliament declared Crimea a territory temporarily occupied by Russia. Several hundreds of people have been killed since the start of the conflict. Ukraine had been the second-most important contributor supplying heavy industrial equipment and raw materials to the former Soviet Union's economy.

Georgia: Georgia and Russia had a military conflict over the autonomous region of South Ossetia, which had been de-facto independent from Georgia. On 26 August 2008, Russia unilaterally recognised the independence of South Ossetia and Abkhazia. This recognition was strongly condemned by the European Union, the United Sates, North Atlantic Treaty Organisation (NATO) and the Organisation for Security and Co-operation in Europe (OSCE). Russia's military support and subsequent recognition of Abkhazia and South Ossetia independence continue to sour Moscow's relations with Georgia.

Territorial Disputes

Japan: Russia's territorial dispute with Japan over a group of islands in the Pacific Ocean continues. The islands administered by Russia and called the Southern Kurils are being claimed by Japan. These islands of Etorofu, Kunashiri, Shikotan, and the Habomai island, known in Japan as Northern Territories, were annexed by the then Soviet Union in 1945 following Japan's defeat in World War II. The long-standing dispute has prevented the two countries from signing a formal peace treaty following WWII. In September 2019, the leader of the two countries, Russian President Vladimir Putin and Japanese Prime Minister Shinzo Abe agreed to accelerate negotiations based on the 1956 document, which stated that the Habomai islets and Shikotan would be handed back to Japan, and the question of Kunashiri and Etorofu was to be settled during negotiations for a peace treaty.

Estonia: Russia and Estonia signed a technical border agreement in May 2005, but Russia recalled its signature in June 2005 after the Estonian parliament added to its domestic ratification act a historical preamble referencing the Soviet occupation and Estonia's pre-war borders under the 1920 Treaty of Tartu. Russia contends that the preamble allows Estonia to make territorial claims on Russia in the future, while Estonian officials deny that the preamble has any legal impact on the treaty text.

Lithuania: Lithuania and Russia committed to demarcating their boundary in 2006 in accordance with the land and maritime treaty ratified by Russia in May 2003 and by Lithuania in 1999; Lithuania operates a simplified transit regime for Russian nationals travelling from the Kaliningrad coastal exclave into Russia, while still conforming, as an EU member state with an EU external border.

Ukraine: Preparations for the demarcation delimitation of land boundary with Ukraine have commenced; the dispute over the boundary between Russia and Ukraine through the Kerch Strait and Sea of Azov is suspended due to the occupation of Crimea by Russia.

Russian Duma has not yet ratified the 1990 Bering Sea Maritime Boundary Agreement with the US; Denmark (Greenland) and Norway have made submissions to the Commission on the Limits of the Continental Shelf (CLCS) and Russia is collecting additional data to augment its 2001 CLCS submission

THREAT PERSPECTIVE

NATO: The North Atlantic Treaty Organisation (NATO) is regarded by Moscow as its main military threat. The bloc is seen as one of the instruments of America's anti-Russian policies. NATO's building up of a missile defence shield over Europe with the US deploying interceptor missiles in Eastern European countries, including in Poland and Romania, has been viewed by Russia as a direct threat to its territory. The US has advanced in its plans to deploy air defence missiles, including the Patriot, THAAD and Standard Missile systems in several parts of Europe and on ships in the Black Sea and Mediterranean. The missile shield deployed in Romania has been activated in May 2016, further escalating the tensions with Moscow. According to Russia's military doctrine of 2014, NATO's military build-up and the bloc's expansion toward the Russian borders are among the main external threats to Russia's security and territorial integrity. Other external threats include the development and deployment of strategic missile defence systems, the implementation of the "global strike" doctrine, plans to place weapons in space, as well as the deployment of high-precision conventional weapon systems.

United States: Tension between the United States and Russia have increased due to Russia's annexation of Crimea in 2014 and subsequent launch of war in South-Eastern Ukraine, Russian military intervention in the Syrian Civil War, Moscow's alleged interference in the 2016 US presidential election and extending support to Venezuela's Nicolas Maduro. The United States responded to these events with the imposition of sanctions against Russia. The EU has strongly condemned Russia's annexation of Crimea and its military intervention in Eastern Ukraine following Ukraine's intention to sign an Association Agreement (AA) with the European Union.

Separatism/Terrorism: Russia is surrounded by a fairly unfriendly environment. Its neighbours, mostly the former Soviet Republics, are not keen to see Russia re-emerge as a great world power in the 21st century and become an influential centre of a multi-polar world order as it was once upon a time. Many of its neighbours could hinder Moscow in pursuing its national interests, while trying to weaken its position in Europe, West Asia Trans-Caucasus, Central Asia and in the Asia-pacific Region. Islamic terrorism poses another major threat to the security of Russia.

STRATEGIC RELATIONS

India: Russia has shared a very deep strategic partnership with India for decades. Over the years, defence ties between the two countries have transformed from a buyer-seller relationship to one involving joint research, design, development, and production of advanced military hardware. India and

Russia's close cooperation in military and military-technical fields is a pillar of their bilateral special and privileged strategic partnership. They have welcomed the successful implementation of the 2011-2020 Long-Term Programme for Military and Technical Cooperation. The two sides have expressed their commitment to upgrading their defence cooperation, including by fostering joint development and production of military equipment, components and spare parts, improve the after-sales service system and continue holding regular joint exercises of the armed forces of the two countries. Russia has shared defence technology of a strategic nature with India, including that of the aircraft carriers and nuclear submarines. The two nations are also working together on indigenous production of tanks and fighter jets.

China: The rapidly changing global geostrategic equations have firmed up strategic ties between Russia and China in recent times. The two nations have upgraded their relationship to a comprehensive strategic partnership in June 2019. Both are permanent members of the UN Security Council and have called for a multi-polar world order. They have often presented a united front against the West and its allies and stood together on the 2011 Libyan conflict and the civil war in Syria. Moscow has allied with Beijing in the South China Sea dispute which has flared up in recent times, especially after an international tribunal's decision favouring Philippines over territorial claims in the region. Both Russia and China have conducted a joint naval drill in the region in September 2016 following the ruling. Their militaries have carried out joint drills in Central Asia and East Asia regularly. In response to a call to form an alliance against China, Russia has said that it will not join any alliance against China as Moscow and Beijing share special relations.

Iran: Irand and Russia have generally enjoyed very friendly relations and they have been increasing their military cooperation. The Russian Defence Ministry and the General Staff of the Iranian Armed Forces have signed a MOU that seeks to expand military ties between the two countries who were military allies in the conflicts in Syria and Iraq. Russia has assisted Iran with its conventional military, including training and defensive weapons that could serve to protect against air strikes targeting Iran while Iran has helped Russia with its drone technology. Moscow has supplied the S-300 long-range air defence systems to Tehran. Although Russia has voted in favour of United Nations Security Council (UNSC) sanctions against Iran's nuclear programme, it has helped Iran develop the Bushehr facilities and has supported Iran's right for peaceful use of nuclear technology in the International Atomic Energy Agency (IAEA). Due to Western economic sanctions on Iran, Russia has become a key trading partner.

Armenia: After the disintegration of Soviet Union, Armenia has been considered as the only ally of Russia in all of Transcaucasia. The two countries are members of an inter-governmental military alliance called the Collective Security Treaty Organisation (CSTO) along with four other ex-Soviet countries – a relationship that Armenia finds essential to its security. Both countries are engaged in vigorous political dialogue. Bilateral relations have been successfully developing on the basis of good traditions and reached the level of strategic partnership, with Russia supplying critical military equipment to Armenia. Armenia hosts a Russian military base in the East of the country across Turkey's Kars province. They have signed an agreement in 2016 on joint force grouping of the two countries in the Caucasus region. Russia is Armenia's largest trade partner.

North Korea: The fall of the Soviet Union have shaken the historical relations between the two nations, however, Russia has maintained a diplomatic presence in Pyongyang. Moscow has gained unique and exclusive communications capabilities with Pyongyang based on the development of trust between the two states' leaderships at the highest political levels. Using its special relations in the political sphere, Moscow indirectly stimulated the beginning of economic reforms in North Korea and its gradual involvement in the processes of international cooperation in Northeast Asia. There is an exchange of Defence Ministry delegations on the basis of an agreement signed back in 1992.

Kazakhstan: Russia and Kazakhstan have good bilateral relationship. The two nations work together within the Collective Security Treaty Organization (CSTO). Agreements and conventions are periodically renewed which outline the general framework and other aspects of their close cooperation. The trade turnover between Russia and Kazakhstan over eight months of 2018 reportedly amounted to $11.3 billion. In June 2021, a media report quoted President Putin as saying "Although the pandemic stole 4-5% of our trade volume, during the first half of this year, we observe a growth of almost 20% - I think, 18% plus," regarding Russia's trade relations with Kazakhstan.

Belarus: Russia and Belarus have made great strides in regional military alignment, coordinated air defence and joint military manoeuvres in the past decade. They have decided to take their bilateral relationship further by signing a draft treaty on the exchange of geostrategic information between their militaries. The two nations military are engaged in various joint military-scientific activities. Russia operates several military bases and radars in Belarus which includes the Hantsavichy Radar Station an early warning radar run by the Russian Aerospace Defence Forces.

MULTILATERAL ALLIANCES

Russia is a major world power as well as a regional power. The country is a member of several important international organisations and multilateral alliances:

UNSC: Russia – a permanent member of the United Nations Security Council (UNSC) - is actively involved in shaping UN Security Council policy regarding the international crises that required the intervention of the international community and investing its effort in regional peace operations. The UNSC permanent members can veto any substantive resolution, including those on the admission of new member states or nominees for the office of Secretary-General. The remaining ten members are elected on a regional basis to serve a term of two years. The body's presidency rotates monthly among its members. Its powers include establishing peacekeeping operations, enacting international sanctions, and authorizing military action. The UNSC is the only UN body with the authority to issue binding resolutions on member states.

SCO: The Shanghai Cooperation Organisation (SCO) is an inter-governmental group of Central Asian countries founded by Russia, China, Kazakhstan, Uzbekistan, Kyrgyzstan and Tajikistan. India and Pakistan officially joined SCO as full members in June 2017. The organisation aims to promote economic, political and strategic cooperation between its member states. The SCO's main goal is to serve as a forum to ease tensions in the region and fight against "terrorism, extremism and separatism." In the recent past, the organisation's activities have expanded to include increased military cooperation, intelligence sharing, and counterterrorism.

BRICS: Russia is an important member in BRICS, an association of five major emerging national economies – Brazil, Russia, India, China and South Africa – formed with an aim to encourage cooperate between the member nations for development, provide financial assistance, support various projects and infrastructure.

RIC: RIC a trilateral group of Russia, India and China is conceived by the then Russian foreign minister Yevgeny Primakov in 1998. All three are nuclear powers and two, Russia and China, are permanent members of the UN Security Council, while India is a non permanent member. The RIC trilateral academic conference engages in deliberation on deepening of cooperation in diverse areas. The group is known for its creative innovation and thinking in the field of international relations.

DEFENCE CAPABILITIES

The Supreme Commander of the Russian Armed Forces is the President of the Russian Federation. Direct leadership of the armed forces is vested with the Ministry of Defence and the General Staff exercises operational control. As a result of its military reforms, the Ground Forces now consist of armies subordinate to the four new military districts – Western, Southern, Central, and Eastern Military Districts. The Russian armed force is divided into the Ground Forces, Russian Aerospace Forces, Russian Navy, Strategic Missile Forces and the Russian Airborne Troops.

A substantial share of the conventional weapon systems which Russia inherited from the Soviet Union remains in operational use with the Russian armed forces, while another part is in storage. Russia has been striving to rebuild its military power. In an effort to accelerate the modernisation of its armed forces, it is speeding up its weapons upgrading and equipment – heavy artillery, missile artillery, and electronic warfare units. The Ground Forces have received improved main battle tanks as part of State Armament Programme (SAP) 2020, taking delivery of the T-72B3, T-80BVM and T-90M. The Aerospace Forces similarly were the beneficiary of new combat aircraft – Su-35S Flanker M and Su-30SM Flanker H – which were upgrades of existing designs. Development of digital technology equipment, artificial intelligence, drones and robot systems are on its agenda besides development of nuclear and aerospace defence forces and strengthening its "triad" strategic nuclear power comprising the land-based, sea-based and space-based forces. Russia plans to continue improvement of its national defence procurement system, boost the scientific and technological levels and support capabilities of its national defence industry and develop further the command, communication, reconnaissance and electronic warfare systems. Russia is known for its robust and advanced missile programmes and maintains the capability to produce highly sophisticated liquid- and solid-propelled missiles of all ranges. Russia possesses some of the world's most advanced air and missile defence systems such as the long-range systems S-200, S-300, and S-400, Iskander ground-to-ground ballistic missiles. The introduction on naval platforms of the 3M14 Kalibr (SS-N-30A Sagaris) 2,500 km-range land-attack cruise missile has greatly improved the Navy's land-attack capability. Russia's military deployments in the Syrian frontier has helped the Russian Armed Forces develop combat-proven capabilities. The experiences gained in the Syrian theatre and, more recently, in the Libyan conflict have allowed the Russian military to train its personnel and test a range of new capabilities.

ARMY: The Land Forces are primarily tasked with repelling the aggression of the enemy in continental theatres of military operations, protect territorial integrity and national interests of the Russian Federation. It is equipped with a wide range of weapons and trained in various methods of warfare, including in joint operations alongside the other wings of the Armed Forces. The Land Forces consists of the following units: Motorised Rifle Troops, Tank Troops, Missile Troops and Artillery, Air Defence Troops, Reconnaissance formations and military units, Engineer Troops, Troops of Radiological, Chemical and Biological Defence, Signal Communications Troops.

Personnel: 280,000 active duty (2021)

Equipment

Category	Name	In Service
MBT	T-14 Armata	100+
	T-90	400
	T-72B4	20+
	T-80	3,500
	T-72	9000
	T-72B3 (being upgraded)	250+
	T-72B3M	20
Armoured car/IFV/APC	Kurganets-25	
	T-15 Armata	
	BMD4	105 +
	BMD-4M	12
	BMD	2000
	BMP-1/ 2	25,000
	BMP-3	700
	BRDM-2	2000+
	ATOM	
	Boomerang	
	Kurganets-25	
	BTR-50/-60/-70/-80	25,000
	BTR-90	

...continued

Category	Name	In Service
Armoured car/IFV/APC	BTR-82A/AM	300
	BTR-MDM Rakushka	12
	BPM-97	200+
	MT-LB	3000+
	2S25 Sprut-SD	24
	IVECO LMV	358
Artillery	2S35 Koalitsiya-SV	8
	122mm	40,000
	130mm	
	152mm (towed)	
	122mm & 152mm (SP guns & howitzers)	
Mortar	82mm	14,000
	120mm	
	160mm	
	240mm	
	Gun/mortars	1,100
MLR	122mm	7,500
	140mm	
	220mm	
	240mm	
	300mm Smerch (Tornado)	
	TOS-1 Buratino	
RL	RPG 30	
	40mm RPG-7	
	64mm RPG-15	
	73mm RPG-16	
ATK gun	57mm	8,000
	76mm	
	85mm	
	100mm (towed)	
	ASU-57/85 SP gun	
ATGW	3M11 Fleyta	
	3M6 Shmel	
	9M14 Malyutka	
	9K111 Fagot	
	9M113 Konkurs	
	9K114 Shturm	
	9K115 Metis	
	9K112 Kobra	
	9M117 Bastion	
	9M119 Svir	
	9M133 Kornet	
	9M13 Metis-M	
	9M112 Kobra	
	9M120 Atakas	
	9M123 Khrizantema	
Weapon	SS-21 Tochka (SSM)	100+
	Iskander-M (SSM)	57
	2K11 Krug/SA-4 (SAM)	500
	2K12 Kub/SA-6 (SAM)	400
	9K33 Osa/SA-3 (SAM)	400

...continued

Category	Name	In Service
Weapon	9K31 Strela-1/SA-9 (SAM)	200
	Buk/SA-11 (SAM)	250
	S-300V/SA-12 (SAM)	100
	9K35Strela-10/SA-13 (SAM)	350
	Tor missile/SA-15 (SAM)	100
	Igla/SA-16/-18/-19 (SAM)	
	Pantsir-S1/SA-22 (SAM)	
	S-400 Trium (SAM)	24
	Tor-M2DT	
	Tor-M2	6 battalions

New Procurements/Upgrades

◆ The Defence Ministry has signed an order for a pilot batch of over 100 state-of-the-art T-14 "Armata" main battle tanks. Delivery of the new MBT is expected to start from 2022 onwards.

◆ A new IFV Boomerang is being developed by the Military Industrial Company (MIC) to replace the BTR-82A and BTR-80 APCs currently in service with the Russian army. Russia plans to export the two variants of the Bumerang vehicle – the K-16 APC and K-17 IFV.

◆ The MoD has signed another contract with Kupol for the delivery of additional Tor-M2 and Tor-M2DT systems worth approximately $1.57 billion.

◆ The Russian military will receive three regiments of the S-400 Triumf anti-aircraft missile systems along with four sets of the S-350 Vityaz battlefield air defence launchers by 2023 under new contracts signed with Almaz-Antey.

◆ About 2,500 BTR-MD Rakushka tracked APCs are to be delivered to the Russian military by 2025.

◆ The MoD has signed another 10-year contract with Instrument Design Bureau (KBP) for the upgrade of 540 BMP-2 IFVs and BMD-2 airborne IFVs.

◆ A new armoured recovery vehicle (ARV) based on the Kurganets-25 IFV is under development. The ARV will be deployed to support infantry and marine battalions.

◆ About 300,000 Ratnik combat outfits to the troops over eight years. The Ratnik combat outfit integrates over 60 elements.

Army Aviation

Category	Name	In Service
Helicopter	Ka-52 Alligator	
	Mi-28N(E) Night Hunter	10
	Mi-24/V/PN (attack)	700
	Mi-8 (transport)	700

...continued

Category	Name	In Service
Helicopter	Mi-26 (transport)	12
	Mi-17V-5	10

Russia plans to add six more Army Aviation airbases to the eight existing ones in the near future.

NAVY: The Russian Navy consist of the Northern Fleet, the Pacific Fleet, the Black Sea Fleet, the Baltic Fleet, the Caspian Flotilla, Naval Aviation, and the coastal troops including the Naval Infantry and the Coastal Missile and Artillery Troops. The Navy can support the Ground Forces during operations in the continental theatre of war, insert maritime forces into the area, repel enemy's assaults and accomplish a number of other missions. It is capable of attacking enemy land-based facilities with nuclear weapons, destroying enemy naval forces at sea and on bases, disrupting its maritime lines of communication and protecting friendly maritime shipping operations. Major naval platforms can perform multi-mission tasks and they are armed with the latest capabilities in weapons, sensors, and command and control, communications, computer, intelligence, surveillance, and reconnaissance (C4ISR) systems. As its primary surface combatants frigates of the Russian Navy are equipped with Vertical Launch Systems to house an array of hypersonic anti-ship missiles, cruise missiles, and antisubmarine missiles. The submarine forces comprised of new nuclear-powered ballistic submarines, nuclear-powered cruise missile submarines, and diesel-electric attack submarines. Over the last decade, Russia has expanded its military footprint in the Mediterranean deploying several warships including the Admiral Grigorovich, Admiral Essen and Pytlivy frigates, along with landing ship Nikolai Filchenkov and the Vishny Volochek missile corvette.

Major naval bases: Northern Fleet – Severonmorsk HQ, Motovskij Gulf, Polyarny, Severodvinsk, Archangelsk

Baltic Fleet – Baltiysk, Kaliningrad HQ, Kronstad

Black Sea Fleet – Sevastopol HQ, Poti, Novrissisk

Pacific Fleet – Vladivostok HQ, Petrapavlovsk, Sovyetskaya Gavan, Korsakov, Providenie, Magadan, Najin

Personnel: 150,000-160,000 active duty (2020)

Equipment

Category	Name	In Service	On Order
Aircraft Carrier	Admiral Kuznetsov class	1	

...continued

Category	Name	In Service	On Order
Cruiser	Pyotr Velikiy (nuclear powered)	1	
	RFS Admiral Nakhimov	1	
	Moskva Slava class	1	
	Marshal Ustinov Slava class	1	
	Kerch class	1	
Destroyer	Admiral Chebanenko (Udaloy II type)	1	
	Udaloy class (+1 reserve)	7	
	Sovremenny class (+5 reserve)	5	
Submarine/ Research submarine	Borei class SSBN	4	4
	Typhoon class (test boat)	1	
	Delta IV class	6	
	Oscar II class	4	
	Yasen-class	1+1	7
	Sierra I/II class	2	
	Akula I/Akula II class	11	
	Lada class	1	2
	Kilo class (+8 reserve)	9	
	Varshavyanka-class (Project 636.3)	6	
	Kalitka	1	
	Orenberg	1	
Frigate	Admiral Gorshkov class	2	8
	Neustrashimy class	2	
	Krivak I/II/III class (+4 reserve)	3	
	Tatarstan class	2	
Corvette	Buyan-M class	12	
	Steregushchiy class	5	
	Grisha I/II/III/IV/V class	8	
	(+ some 20 reserve)	8	
	Parchim class (+4 reserve)	8	
	Tarantul I/II/III class	10	
	Nanuchka I/III class	6	
Patrol craft	Vasily Bykov		
	Grad Sviyazhsk	7	
	Murayev class attack hydrofoils	9	
	Matka class FAC missile hydrofoils	8	

...continued

Category	Name	In Service	On Order
Patrol craft	Babochka class FAC hydrofoils	3	
	Pauk I/II (patrol)	24	
	Svetlyak class	30	
	Stenka class	20	
	Astrakan class river gunboats	3	
Mine-sweeper	Alexandrit-class	3	
	Evgenya class	12	
	Natya class	30	
	Sonya class	51	
	Gorya class	2	
	Lida class	11	
Amphibious Force	Ivan Rogov class	1	
	Dyugon-class	5	
	Ropucha class	19	
	Aligator class IST	7	
	Polnocny class LCT	5	
Hovercraft	Pomornik class	10	
	Aist class	9	
	Lebed class	2	
	Utka class (WIG)	1	
	Drakon class (WIG)	2	
Auxiliaries & Support ship	Boris Chilkin class AOs	4	
	Ugra class submarine tender	2	
	Don class submarine tender	1	
	Don class	2	
	Susanin ice-breaker	13	
	Lama class (missile support ship)	5	
	Amga class (missile support ship)	3	
Air Defence	Igla – 1M		
Weapon	3M-54 Klub		
	K-300P Bastion-P		
	Kh-35 (ASM)		

New Procurements/Upgrades

◆ Ten vessels of Admiral Gorshkov class project 22350 have been contracted for delivery by 2027. The lead ship of the class Admiral Gorshkov was commissioned on 28 July 2018. The Navy has commissioned the second frigate Admiral Kasatonov which will enter service with Russia's Northern Fleet.

◆ The Navy has commissioned the third Project 22160 patrol ship, Pavel Derzhavin. The first ship, the Vassily Bykov and the second ship, Dmitry Rogachov is in active service. In all, six ships of the class have been ordered for the Navy's Black Sea Fleet.

◆ Ivan Papanin, the first Project 23550 multi-purpose Arctic-class patrol vessel is likely to be commissioned in November, 2023. The ice-breaker will be equipped with a portable anti-aircraft missile system, a shipborne helicopter, a radar station and a hydrometeorological station.

◆ Russia has started construction of two more nuclear-powered Yasen-M class submarines, Voronezh and the Vladivostok. The subs are likely to be delivered in 2027 and 2028. The Severodvinsk is already in operation. The first modernised Yasen-M class vessel – the Kazan is undergoing sea trials, while the Novosibirsk, Krasnoyarsk, Arkhangelsk, Perm and Ulyanovsk are in various phases of construction.

◆ One of Russia's largest submarine, the K-329 Belgorod, has officially started its sea trials. The six hundred foot long submarine which can dive to a depth of 1,700 feet is designed to support a variety of military missions.

◆ The fourth-generation nuclear-powered missile submarine, Borei Class, are being built to replace the Delta III and Typhoon Class submarines. The Yury Dolgoruky, Alexander Nevsky, Vladimir Monomakh, and Knyaz Vladimir submarines have been commissioned. Four other submarines of the Borei-A project, Knyaz Oleg, Generalissimus Suvorov, Emperor Alexander III, and Knyaz Pozharskiy, are at various stages of construction.

◆ Russian design bureau Malakhit is working on a new nuclear attack submarine identified as the Laika (Husky) class. The lead boat in the Husky class is planned to be built by the end of 2030. The submarine will reportedly have a displacement of just over 11,000-13,000 tons and speed of 35 knots.

◆ A new class of fifth-generation conventional submarines under Project Kalina are being developed by TsKB Rubin with air-independent propulsion (AIP) system.

◆ The Project 636.3 diesel-electric submarine (SSK) Volkhov, the second of a six-boat series, has entered service. Admiralty Shipyards is now building the third and fourth submarines of the series – Magadan and Ufa.

◆ St. Petersburg, the lead submarine of the diesel-electric attack submarine Project 677 Lada, entered the Northern Fleet in September 2021. Kronshtadt, the second of this project was laid down in 2005. The Admiralty Shipyard is building one more Lada-class submarine named Velikiye Luki.

◆ The MoD has decided to overhaul the Project 971 (Akula class) of nuclear-powered attack submarines. The refurbished platforms will feature better stealth capabilities and improved electronics among other upgrades.

◆ The Kirov-class nuclear-powered battlecruiser Admiral Nakhimov is currently being overhauled and modernised. Current upgrades include the fitting of Kalibr and Oniks cruise missiles.

◆ The Navy's sole aircraft carrier, Admiral Kuznetsov, commissioned in 1985, is undergoing overhaul and is due to return to service in this year.

◆ The Navy plans to order 12 advanced Leader-class (Project 23560) destroyers expected to enter service from 2023-2025. The new platforms will be built in two variants – one with nuclear power plant and another with gas turbine power generating units.

◆ The Amur Shipyard has begun construction of Steregushchiy-Class Project 20380 corvette Bravy which will join the Pacific Fleet. The fleet now operates three Project 20380 corvettes, namely, the 'Sovershenniy', the 'Gromkiy', and the 'Aldar Tsydenzhapov'. The fourth surface combatant of the class, 'Rezkiy', is set to join the Pacific Fleet soon. The 'Grozniy' is expected to be commissioned in the same

Russian Navy's diesel-electric submarine Volkhov. (Image credit: Admiralty Shipyards)

fleet in 2024. By 2028, the Pacific Fleet will operate six Project 20380.

◆ The Navy has commissioned the Gremyashchy, lead corvette in a series of two Project 20385 ships. The corvettes are due to enter service with the Pacific Fleet in 2024-2028.

Russian Navy Project 20385 Corvette 'Gremyashchy.' (Image credit: Russian MoD)

◆ The Navy has begun building its new corvette of Project 20386. The corvette 'Mercury' will be the first of the Russian Navy to be fully stealth.

◆ The Kerch Shipyard in Crimea has floated the second Karakurt-class corvette project 22800 "Askold". The first warship, the Tsiklon, is undergoing trials while the third corvette, the Amur, is at the stage of construction. The Karakurt-class corvettes are set to be commissioned with the Russian Navy by 2026.

◆ Construction of project 11711 landing ship, Vladimir Andreyev and Vasily Trushin have started with an expected commissioning by the Navy in 2023 and 2024 respectively. They are an improved version of the first two ships of the class, Ivan Gen and Pyotr Morgunov, which were commissioned in June 2018 and December 2020.

Naval Aviation
Equipment

Category	Name	In Service
Fighter	MiG-29K	20
	MiG-29KUB	4
	Su-30SM	22+
	Su-33 (shipborne)	12
Bomber	Tu-22M Backfire	58
	Su-24 Fencher	51
ASW	Tu-142 Bear F	30
	Be-12 Mail	30
	IL-38/38N May	33 (upgraded)
	Mi-14 Haze	20
	Ka-25 Hormone-A	20

...continued

Category	Name	In Service
ASW	Ka-27 Helix	100
	Ka-31	
Transport	Tu-134	4
	An-12 Cub	31
	An-24 Coke	12
	An-26 Curl	39
	An-72	2
	An-140	1
Recce/EW/Targeting	Tu-142D	15
	An-12	7
	Su-24	6
	Kamov Ka-27	1
	Kamov Ka-52K	
	Ka-29	8
Helicopter	Ka-29	
	Ka-27M	
	Mi-8	63
	Mi-14	9

New Procurements/Upgrades

◆ The future ship-borne helicopter being developed under the Minoga programme to replace the Ka-27 helicopter will enter production in 10 years. The advanced rotorcraft would be capable of cruising at 500 km/h.

◆ An order has been placed for 21 Su-30SM2s.

Naval Infantry
Personnel: 8,000
Equipment

Category	Name	In Service
MBT	T-80	150
	T-72	150
	BRDM	60
	BTR-82A	30
APC	BTR-60/-70/-80	300
	MT-LB	300
Artillery	2SI 122mm	120
	2S3 152 SP	60
AA Gun	ZSU-23-4 SPAAG	50
SAM	SA-7/-8/-9/-13	

Coastal Artillery & Rocket Troops: 7,000+ personnel

AEROSPACE FORCES: The Russian Government has merged the country's Air Force along with the Aerospace Defence Forces and the Air Defence Troops into a new branch of the Armed Forces known as the Russian Aerospace Forces. According to a December 2020 Centre for Naval Analyses report, Russia's modern air force is smaller yet far more capable. The Air Force had stepped up efforts to significantly modernise its aerial fleet. Russian military aircraft feature numerous types of capable fighters, fighter interceptors, and tactical bombers. The development of new military transport aircraft, refuelling aircraft, AWACS aircraft and other platforms and weapons systems are advancing. The aerospace force has successfully replaced its older-generation combat aircraft with newer variants such as the Su-35S multi-role jets and Su-34 fighters/bombers. Russian military intervention in Syria has given the Aerospace Forces significant operational experience and has been used as a testing ground for new capabilities, including precision-strike and air-launched cruise missiles by both tactical and long-range assets.

Personnel: 490,000 (2019)
Equipment

Category	Name	In Service	On Order
Fighter/Interceptor	MiG-35	2	4
	MiG-31BM	24	
	MiG-31	122	
	MiG-29	120	
	MiG-29UB/UBT	36	
	MiG-29SMT	44	
	Su-57	1	22
	Su-27/27SM	340	
	Su-27SM	12	
	Su-30M2	19	
	Su-30SM	92	
Bomber/Strike/Ground Attack	Tu-95MS	63	
	Tu-160/160M Blackjacks	16	
	Tu-22M Backfire	145	
	Tu-95SM Bear H6	25+	
	Tu-95SM Bear H16	30	
	Su-34	129	20
	Su-24M/M2 Fencer	400	
	Su-25B/SM	180	
Reconnaissance/EW	MiG-25R	40	
	Su-24M2	32	
	Su-24M	70	
AWACS/AEW&C	A-50 Mainstay	15	
	A-50U	3	
Tanker	IL-78 Midas	20	
Helicopter	Mi-24/-6/-8/-26/-14		
	Mi-28N	126	
	Kazan Ansat		

...continued

Category	Name	In Service	On Order
Transport aircraft	Il-76MD-90A	4	32
	An-12	700	
	An-124	11	
	IL-76MD/TD	120	
	An-24	100	
	An-32	50	
	An-72	30	
	Tu-134s/154	20	
	L410	150	
Trainer	Yak-52	350	
	L-29/L-39	1500	
	Yak-130	100+	
Weapon	SA-10/12 (SAM)		
	S-500 (SAM)		
	SA-21 Growler (SAM)		
	Pantsir M (SAM)		
	S400 (SAM)		
	S-300V4 (ABM)		
	S-300 PMU-2		
	Antey 2500		

New Procurements/Upgrades

◆ The Aerospace Forces will receive 22 Su-57 fighters by late 2024 and their number will increase to 76 by 2028. The first Su-57 fighter was delivered to the Russian military in 2020.

◆ Russia's latest MiG-35 generation-4++ multi role fighter jet has received a preliminary certificate for the limited series production even as it is undergoing state joint trials. Meanwhile, the Aerospace Forces has inducted 2 of the six MiG-35 jets in June 2019 first ordered in August 2018.

◆ The Aerospace Defence Force is scheduled to receive 8 of the 20 Su-34 multi-role supersonic fighter-bomber aircraft. The deliveries will stretch over 3 years. The Su-34 will replace the Su-24 fighter and the Tu-22M3 long-distance bomber.

◆ The modernised Tu-160M2 Blackjack strategic bomber made its maiden flight in February 2020. The MoD plans to begin serial production of the aircraft by 2023 and buy around 50 such platforms.

◆ The Beriev A-100 airborne early warning and control (AWACS) aircraft based on the Il-76MD-90A (Il-476) transport aircraft is currently under development and it is expected to be delivered by 2024.

◆ The Ilyushin Il-112V military turboprop is being developed by Ilyushin Aviation Complex to replace the An-26 and An-24 turboprop planes. By 2023, Russia is expected to be able to serially produce up to 12 Ilyushin IL-112V. The first test prototype of the IL-112V made its maiden flight in late March 2019.

◆ Work on the development of a new interceptor aircraft has started to replace the existing 122 MiG-31 Foxhound planes which are set for retirement by 2028. The new sixth-generation stealth interceptor, the Mikoyan MiG-41 or PAK DP, will take to the skies by 2025.

◆ A contract has been signed for the delivery of 100 Mi-28NM combat helicopters, a version of Mi-28Ns already in service with the Russian Aerospace Forces by 2028.

◆ A new variant of Mi-26, the Mil Mi-26T2V heavy-lift helicopter is being developed for the Aerospace Forces. Preliminary flight tests of helicopter has been completed.

◆ The Russian military plans to acquire over 114 newly upgraded Ka-52 attack helicopters in the coming years. Development of the Ka-52M is expected to be completed this year.

◆ Russia has completed tests of its new S-500 surface-to-air missile system and has started supplying it to the armed forces. The S-500 missile system will replace the S-400 currently in use.

STRATEGIC MISSILE FORCES

The Strategic Missile Forces (SMF) represents the main component of the country's strategic nuclear force. They are designed for nuclear deterrence of a possible aggression. They control Russia's land-based Inter Continental Ballistic Missiles (ICBMs). The SMF operates missile systems such as the silo-based R-36M2 which carries ten warheads, the UR-100NUTTH, the single warhead mobile RT-2PM Topol, and the upgraded Topol-M called RS-24 Yars. Russia has been modernising its ICBMs by replacing legacy Soviet ICBMs with new post-Cold War systems. The RS-28 Sarmat is a liquid-fueled intercontinental ballistic missile currently under development at the Makeye Rocket Design Bureau. The MIRV-equipped (multiple independently targetable re-entry vehicle) Sarmat is among the six new weapons of mass destruction unveiled by President Putin in 2018. The other five missiles are: Avangard, Tsirkon, Poseidon, Kinzhal, and a nuclear-propelled cruise missile. More trials of the missile are being conducted and the first operational missile regiments is expected to be activated by the end of 2022. The re-armed formations of the SMF have reportedly received about 100 units of the latest equipment of the nuclear, biological and chemical (NBC) protection troops – modern machines, including the ARS-14KM, RHM-6 and the first samples of the UTM-80M.

Personnel: 50,000 (2020)

Equipment

Category	Name	In Service
ICBM/SLBM	R-36M2 Voyevoda	40+
	RT-2PM2 Topol-M	18
	RS-24 Yars	150+
	RS-12M Topol	70+
	UR-100 NUTTH	55+
	R-29 Sineva	
	Iskander-M (BM)	

New Procurements/Upgrades

◆ More trials of the RS-28 Sarmat ICBM are being conducted and the first operational missile regiments is expected to be activated by the end of 2022. The Sarmat will replace the R-36M2 Voevoda and RS-18A Stilet missiles.

AIRBORNE FORCES

Russia's elite Airborne Force (AbF), established in the 1930s, is one of the world's largest and most highly-mechanised best trained forces. The AbF fought during World War II, in Afghanistan, in the Five-Day War with Georgia. They are deployed in Crimea and eastern Ukraine. Recent changes in manning levels, coupled with equipment modernisation and operational experience, has made the (AbF) an ever more formidable force. The AbF is primarily tasked "to flank enemy around by air and performing tasks in its rear to disrupt control of troops, seize and destruct ground elements of precision weapons, frustrate advance and deployment of reserves, violation of logistical support and communications, as well as to defend some directions, areas, open flanks, block and destroy air assaults, along with other tasks." The main armaments of the airborne formations and units were predominantly light and heavy machine guns, 50mm and 82mm mortars, 45mm anti-tank and 76mm mountain guns, light tanks (T-40 and T-38), flame-throwers. The artillery of the AbF includes such systems as the 2S9 Nona, the D-30 howitzer or the 2S25 self-propelled tank destroyer. The AbF formations are receiving new, modern armament and military hardware, including up to 150 BMD-4M airborne IFVs and BTR-MDM APCs, BREM-D armoured maintenance-recovery vehicle, 2S9-1 Nona self-propelled artillery systems, Verba MLRS, modern EW stations, about 40 BTR-82A APCs as well as around 6,000 parachute systems and about 100 pieces of different airborne hardware. Current personnel is 60,000 paratroopers.

Major Armaments Producers

Domestic suppliers

- Rostec (military industrial complex)
- United Aircraft Corporation (fixed-wing air planes)
- Russian Helicopters (helicopters)
- Uralvagonzavod (MBT)
- Almaz-Antey (air defence systems)
- Tactical Missiles Corporation (air and naval-based missiles)
- Moscow Institute of Thermal Technology (engineering and scientific research institute)
- NPO Mashinostroyenia (NPOM)
- High Precision Systems (weapons)
- Kalashnikov Concern (small arms etc)
- Military Industrial Company
- Kurganmashzavod (infantry fighting vehicles)
- KAMAZ (truck company)
- United Shipbuilding Corporation (submarines, corvettes, frigates, aircraft carriers)

Foreign suppliers: France, Finland, Austria and Italy

DEFENCE DEALS

Joint Venture Programmes

India and Russia have inked an agreement for joint production of over six lakhs AK-203 assault rifles at a manufacturing facility in Amethi, Uttar Pradesh, India besides firming up another pact on military cooperation for 10 years. The rifles will be manufactured for the Indian armed forces at a cost of around Rs 5000 crore. The agreements were signed at the 20th meeting of the India-Russia Inter-Governmental Commission on Military and Military-Technical Cooperation (IRIGC-M&MTC) on 07 December 2021.

The world-class BRAHMOS supersonic cruise missile system is one of the product of India-Russia Joint Venture programmes. The missile has been inducted in the Indian Army, Navy and Air Force. Meanwhile, the governments of the two nations have decided to take forward inter-governmental arrangements for facilitating joint manufacturing of spares for Russian origin equipment in India, under the 'Make in India' initiative. The joint ventures aims to cover a range of equipment from modern T-90 tanks to legacy Pechora air defence systems. The MoUs were signed during the 5th India Russia military industry conference held during the Defexpo 2020 in Lucknow.

An Indo-Russian Helicopter Pvt Ltd (IRHL), a joint venture between Hindustan Aeronautics Ltd (HAL) and Russian Helicopters has been formed to produce 200 Kamov Ka-226T multi-role military helicopters under a $1 billion deal signed in 2015. Sixty would be supplied to India in fly-away condition.

China and Russia is jointly developing a 40-ton class heavy helicopter expected to be delivered by 2032. Under the contract, at least 200 heavy helicopters will be built in China. China will be responsible for the design of the helicopter and production and Russia would act as a technical partner. The heavy helicopter, dubbed Advanced Heavy Lift, would reportedly have a weight-lift capability of 15 tons, a range of 630 km and a top speed of 300 km an hour. Russia is also reportedly designing a non-nuclear submarine with China. A media report quoted an official, Viktor Kladov, Director for International Cooperation and Regional Policy of the state arms export corporation Rostec as saying, "We are currently cooperating with the Chinese side on a joint project of a new generation non-nuclear submarine..."

The United Arab Emirates' defence and security industry development arm Tawazun and VR Technologies, a unit of Russian Helicopters have announced a joint venture for establishing an assembly line in the UAE for the VRT-500 helicopter, a light helicopter which is currently under development. Serial production of the helicopter is expected to begin in 2023. The company is targeting sales of 1,000 VRT-500s by 2035.

Russia has signed agreements with Saudi Arabia and Egypt to develop joint military cooperation. Iraq and Russia have also discussed prospects for deepening military coordination.

Arms Export

Russia remains the world's second-largest arms exporter after the United States, between 2016 and 2020, as per the latest data on international arms transfers compiled by the Stockholm International Peace Research Institute (SIPRI), an independent research institute that tracks global military expenditures, according to the report published in March 2021. Russia's main customers included India, China and Algeria during that period. In the last two decades, Moscow has managed to deepen its connection with Africa and became the biggest arms supplier on the continent besides building up its weapons sales to Asia-Pacific region. The region reportedly absorbs over 60% of Russia's arms shipments, with most of them going to Southeast Asia. Russian Sukhoi Su-30 fighters, diesel submarines and medium and long-range air defence systems are particularly popular in the region. Meanwhile, Russia is moving ahead with the sale of the S-400 anti-aircraft system to Turkey. India has also signed signed a USD 5.43-billion deal with Russia in 2018 for the air defence missile system. State-owned Rostec, Russia's largest weapons exporter, is the sole entity responsible for the supply and export of Russian arms and military equipment abroad. Russia exports a variety of weaponry, including legacy and advanced aircraft, air defence systems, naval vessels and submarines, radars, missiles, tanks, armoured vehicles, small arms, and artillery.

DEFENCE BUDGET

Total defence spending: $61.7 billion (2020), $65.1 billion (2019)

Estimated defence spending: 4.3% (2019)

According to SIPRI data, Russian military expenditure has grown significantly over the past two decades. It increased by 30 per cent in real terms between 2010 and 2019 and by 175 per cent between 2000 and 2019. Although Russian military spending decreased in 2017 and 2018, it rose again in 2019 to reach $65.1 billion. It was the fifth largest spender in 2018 and rose to fourth place in 2019, after the United States, China and India. Military expenditure increased by 2.5 per cent in 2020 to reach $61.7 billion which was the second consecutive year of growth. However, Russia's actual military spending in 2020 was 6.6 per cent lower than its initial military budget, a larger shortfall than in previous years, it stated. Exact figures for military funding are considered a state secret in Russia.

COUNTER-TERRORISM & NATIONAL SECURITY

Terrorism is a persistent global threat that knows no border, nationality or religion. Russia faces a largely subdued rebel movement in Chechnya and some other surrounding regions, although violence still occurs throughout the North Caucasus. In the early 20th century, Marxist revolutionaries used terrorism as a tool to disrupt the social, political, and economic system and enable rebels to bring down the Tzarist government. More recently terror threats against the Russian Federation are primarily presented by the Islamist insurgents in the North Caucasus, who are organised into several groups that are loosely allied with al-Qaeda's global

Jihad. In the North Caucasus's republics of Chenchnya, Dagestan, Ingushetia, and Kabardno-Balkariya, the extremist ethno-nationalist and Islamist militants have been waging an insurgency for the past decades against Russian rule which they seek to replace with their own Islamist regime. As the nature and scope of the Caucasus Emirate underwent a transformation with a large segment of its recruits and fighters joining the Islamic State's insurgency in Syria and Iraq, the frequency and number of its terrorists attacks in the Russian federation has declined in recent years. However, there continues to be frequent attacks and skirmishes between rebel groups and Russian forces. The threat from terrorism could rise quickly in relation to any escalation of violence in the North Caucasus.

Terrorist groups

The list of organisations designated as terrorist according to the Law of the Russian Federation:

Islamic State of Iraq and ash-Sham – Caucasus Province aka Wilayat Qawqaz. The ISIS-Caucasus Province (ISIS-CP) claimed responsibility for the attack against a Russian Army barrack in September 2015 and also claimed at least two attacks on local security forces in 2020 including a suicide bomber who blew himself up in the North Caucasus region of Karachay-Cherkessia, injuring six police officers. It targets local security and military forces, as well as non-Muslim civilians, with small arms, improvised explosives, and knives.

Aum Shimrikyo (AUM/Aleph) aka Aum Shinrikyo Shiryu Ha, A.I.C. Sogo Kenkyusho. The group has allegedly sought to overthrow the Japanese Government and to spark a nuclear war between Japan and the US to create a global armageddon 'cleansing' the world so its members could achieve salvation. In 2004, Asahara was found guilty on charges of masterminding the 1995 sarin gas attack in Tokyo. Asahara along with 12 other AUM members were executed in July 2018 for the crime, while 85 others were sentenced to prison terms up to life.

Islamic State of Iraq and ash-Sham (ISIS) aka Islamic State in the Levant (ISIL), Islamic State. The group adopted the moniker ISIS to express regional ambitions and expanded operations to Syria. After losing to the US and allied military forces, the group has transitioned to an insurgency, reverting to guerrilla warfare and more traditional terrorist tactics. The group claims to have 14 wilayats or networks in more than 20 countries including the Caucasus (Russia). It continues to maintain a considerable presence particularly in Iraq and Syria and conduct operations into 2021.

Al-Qaeda: aka al-Qa'eda, the Islamic Army, Islamic Salvation Foundation. The al-Qaeda formed under Usama Bin Ladin (UBL) is one of the world's longest operating jihadist organisations. The group extended support for the Afghan resistance against the former Soviet Union in the 1980s. The group based in Afghanistan is known for use of suicide bombers, car bombs, conducted the September 11, 2001 attacks on the US.

Hizb ut-Tahrir al-Islami aka 'Party of Liberation'. The Hizb ut-Tahrir, an international pan-Islamist and fundamentalist political organisation, was put on the list of terrorist organisations in February 2003 by the Russian Supreme Court due to their "militant Islamic propaganda combined with intolerance to other religions" and "subversive activities to fracture the society" aimed at the removal of the non-Islamic regimes and establishing the global Caliphate, primarily within the regions where Muslim populations are present. The HT have appeared in the cities of Nizhnevartovsk, a city in the oil-rich region of Yugra, and Dagestan, North Caucasus, and in Tatarstan, Volga region. In October 2018, the head of Russian wing of HT was reported to have been arrested in Tatarstan.

Major Incidents

Significant terrorist activity have taken place in Russia, most notably the Budyonnovsk hospital hostage crisis, the 1999 apartment bombings, the Moscow theatre hostage crisis and the Beslan school siege. Following are some of the major terror incidents that occurred in the recent past:

2019: On 11 January 2019, officers of Russia's road patrol service were attacked near the village of Agachaul, Karabudakhentsky district in Dagestan. The suspects opened fire on law enforcement officers with automatic rifles before being killed by the authorities. The authorities reportedly found additional weapons and ammunition in the suspects' car.

2017: On 3 April 2017, at least 15 people were reported dead including the attacker and 45 others injured in a terrorist attack on the Saint Petersburg Metro. The explosive device used in the attack was contained in a briefcase. A second explosive device was found and defused at Ploshchad Vosstaniya metro station.

2013: On 29 and 30 December 2013, two suicide bombings occurred targeting the public transport system – train station and a trolley bus – in the city of Volgograd. The bombings were carried out weeks before the start of the 2014 Winter Olympics, being held about 400 miles away in the Russian Black Sea resort of Sochi. A total of 34 people were reportedly killed including the attackers.

2011: On 24 January 2011, about 37 people were reportedly killed and 172 wounded in a suicide bombing at Moscow's Domodedovo airport. The attack was claimed by Doku Umarov, a powerful Chechen warlord who runs an Islamist extremist group called the Caucasus Emirate movement.

2004: On 1 September 2004, militants seized a school in Beslan, in the province of North Ossetia, and took children, teachers and parents hostage. In the attack which lasted for thee days more than 300 people were reportedly killed, many of them children.

2002: On 23 October 2002, militants seized Moscow's crowded Dubrovka theatre holding them hostage. Russian forces pumped a chemical agent into the building's ventilation system to incapacitate the militants. In the incident, at least 170 people reportedly died, including 130 of the nearly 1,000 hostages.

1999: About 300 people reportedly lost their lives in bombings carried out between 4 and 16 September 1999 of apartment buildings in Moscow, Buynaksk and Volgodonsk. The attacks were blamed on Chechen separatists and eventually led to the second Chechen war.

1995: In June 1995, more than 100 people were allegedly killed when Chechen fighters stormed a hospital in Budyonnovsk near the border with Russia, taking many civilians hostage and threatening to kill them. Attempts by Russian forces to raid the hospital failed. The deaths occurred before an agreement could be reached.

Combating Terrorism

The Russian Federation is taking a comprehensive approach to combating international terrorism. It has been steadily improving its legislative framework and law enforcement practices and strengthening its counter-terrorism cooperation with interested states and international and regional organisations. According to an official report, inter-agency cooperation has played a role in the successful detection and suppression of criminal activity by law enforcement authorities. It is actively cooperating with foreign law enforcement agencies in the investigation of terrorism-related crimes and the prosecution of persons complicit in such activity. The government has established the National Antiterrorism Committee, a collegiate body tasked with coordination and organisation of counter terrorism activities of government bodies at the federal level, at the level of the subjects of the Russian Federation and local governments. Russia has deliberated with other countries including India, regarding measures to further strengthen and deepen counter-terrorism cooperation. The two nations have stressed the need for elimination of all safe havens of terrorist and emphasized the need for strengthening international cooperation to combat terrorism in a comprehensive and sustained manner without any double standards.

Agencies & Departments responsible for counter terrorism:

Federal Security Service (FSB): The FSB, successor to the KGB, is responsible for the internal security of the Russian state, counter-intelligence, and the fight against organised crime, terrorism, and drug smuggling, The director of the FSB is directly answerable to the president of Russia. The elite Alpha Group and the Vympel are FSB's dedicated counter terrorism special forces. FSB Alpha and Vympel aka Vega Groups took part in rescue efforts along with the Russian Ministry of Internal Affairs (MVD) SOBR unit in the Moscow theatre hostage crisis.

Spetsnaz: The Spetsnaz was officially formed in 1950 in the erstwhile Soviet Union. The Spetsnaz unit is the Special Operations Forces' or 'Special Purpose Military Units'. The term mainly refers to special operations units controlled by the military intelligence service GRU (Glavnoye Razvedyvatelnoye Upravlenie). Spetsnaz GRU plays an important role in Russia's foreign and national security policies. As an arm of the military, the GRU is responsible for all levels of military intelligence, from tactical to strategic. It maintains its own special forces units.

Unit 29155 is tasked with foreign assassinations and other covert activities.

Unit 54777 is responsible for psychological warfare capabilities.

Unit 26165 is a cyber operations/hacking group.

Unit 74455 is the Main Center for Technologies.

SATCOM is GRU satellite communications interception.

Navy Spetsnaz: Russian Naval Spetsnaz also known as "frogmen" is a special forces unit of the Russian Naval Infantry comprising of highly trained and elite marines within the Naval Infantry.

Airborne Forces Vozdushno-Desantnye Voyska (VDV)/Spetsnaz (VDV)s: It has been reported that approximately 300 commandos, intelligence officers and other GRU personnel died during the fighting in Chechnya. The highly skilled Spetsnaz have been instrumental in the takeover of the 2014 Crimea and in the war in Donbas.

KSSO: The elite Special Operations Forces Command or Komandovaniye Sil Spetsialnykh Operatsiy (KSSO), established in March 2013, is responsible for special operations and counter-terrorism. The KSSO was reportedly deployed in Russia's military operations in Ukraine and Syria. It is distinctive in the way it is trained to support and conduct operations abroad.

Centre for Countering Extremism: The Centre for Combating Extremism, a unit within the Ministry of Internal Affairs, also known as Centre E functions as a secret police force. Their main task is suppression of extremism, e.g. suppression of the Jehovah Witnesses in Russia. The unit operates in the North Caucasus and Crimea following its annexation in 2014.

Military Intervention/Military Intelligence

Beslan school siege: In the Beslan school siege by terrorist on September 1, 2004, Russian troops took part in the hostage rescue efforts. The forces comprised of the Russian police, Internal Troops, Russian Army forces, Spetsnaz including the Alpha and Vympel units of the FSB, and the OMON special units of the Russian Ministry of Internal Affairs (MVD). The siege lasted for three days in which more than 1,100 people were taken hostages including 777 children and ended with the deaths of 333 people, 186 of them children, as well as 31 of the attackers.

Apart from the military, the Spetsnaz have actively participated in the Hungary Revolution, invasion of Czechoslovakia, war in Afghanistan (1979 – 1989), kidnappings and various hostage rescue operations, conflict in Chechnya, Georgia and Ukraine,

CONCLUSION

Russia is rising in its influence once again at the global stage even as it is preparing to project power in the military, economic, and political spheres across Eastern Europe, Central Asia, and the North Pacific. Simultaneously, it has strengthened its relations in the Middle East, especially with Iran and Syria, and also with Egypt. Russia is beginning to bolster its geopolitical presence and military might by expanding the Collective Security Treaty Organization (CSTO). Moscow is carrying out sweeping military reforms. The rearmament programme focuses on equipping the military with new ships, submarines, air planes, nuclear missiles and battlefield equipment for soldiers and completely overhaul the strategic nuclear arsenal of the country. The Crimean Peninsula continues to give Moscow access to the naval base at Sevastopol, which is home to Russia's Black Sea Fleet. Operating from Sevastopol, the Black Sea Fleet provides Russia with the ability to project power in and around the Black Sea while serving as a potent symbol of Russian military power. Russia has also launched a military push in the Arctic region to restore its Soviet-era stake in a hotly contested area that contains the world's largest untapped energy resources. The larger Russian goal appears to be building up a strong military force in the 21st century to recover the economic, political, and geostrategic assets lost by the Soviet state in the previous century. By virtue of its great economic, scientific, technological and military potential and its unique strategic location on the Eurasian continent Russia continues to play an important role on the world's stage.

CONTACT DETAILS
Ministry of Defence
19 Znamenka Str., Moscow
Russia-119169
Tel.: 8 (495) 696-71-71
Website: http://eng.mil.ru/

Information Desk of the
Ministry of Defence
Phone: 8 (495) 696-88-00

STRATEGIC INFORMATION
SAUDI ARABIA
(Capital: Riyadh)

INTRODUCTION

Area: 2,149,690 sq km
Population: 34,783,757 (July 2021 est.)
Coastline: 2,640 km
Maritime claims: Territorial sea: 12 nm
Contiguous zone: 18 nm
Continental shelf: not specified

GEOPOLITICAL IMPORTANCE

The Kingdom of Saudi Arabia, commonly known as Saudi Arabia is the largest state in the Middle East by land area, constituting about 80 percent of the Arabian Peninsula, and the second-largest in the Arab World. It is bordered by Jordan and Iraq on the north and northeast, Kuwait, Qatar and the United Arab Emirates on the east, Oman on the southeast, and Yemen on the south. It is also connected to Bahrain by the King Fahd Causeway. The largest and most influential nation on the Arabian Peninsula, Saudi Arabia is strategically located between the Red Sea and the Arabian Gulf. Saudi Arabia's geography is dominated by the Arabian Desert and associated semi-desert and shrub land. Its extensive coastlines on the Persian Gulf and Red Sea provide great leverage on shipping (especially crude oil) through the Persian Gulf and Suez Canal. Saudi Arabia's maritime claims include a twelve-nautical-mile territorial limit along its coasts. The Saudis also claim many small islands as well as some sea-beds and sub-soils beyond the twelve-nautical-mile limit. Saudi Arabia sees itself as the leader of the Arab countries. Being a rich state it champions the Middle-east cause in all forums.

POLITICAL OVERVIEW

Saudi Arabia is an absolute monarchy with a Council of Ministers and Consultative Council. Although, according to the Basic Law of Saudi Arabia adopted by royal decree in 1992, the king must comply with Sharia (i.e., Islamic law) and the Quran. The Basic Law specifies that the king must be chosen from among the sons of the first king, Abdul Aziz Al Saud, and their male descendants subject to the subsequent approval of religious leaders (the ulema). The country has given the ulema (the body of Islamic religious leaders and jurists) a direct role in government. The king combines legislative, executive, and judicial functions and royal decrees form the basis of the country's legislation. The king is also the prime minister, and presides over the Council of Ministers, which comprises the first and second deputy prime ministers (usually the first and second in line to the throne respectively) and 23 ministers with portfolio and five ministers of state. The Quran and the Sunna (the traditions of Muhammad) are declared to be the country's constitution, but no modern constitution has ever been written for Saudi Arabia, and it remains the only Arab nation where no elections have ever taken place, since its creation. No political parties or national elections are permitted. The royal family dominates the political system. On September 2011, King Abdullah announced that women will have the right to stand and vote in future local elections and join the advisory Shura council as full members.

KEY POLITICAL PERSONS

HEAD OF STATE & PRIME MINISTER:
King Salman bin Abdulaziz Al Saud

CROWN PRINCE & DEP. PRIME MINISTER:
Mohammad Bin Salman Abdulaziz Al Saud

ECONOMY

Saudi Arabia has the largest economy in the Arab world and the Middle East. Saudi Arabia has an oil-based economy with strong government controls over major economic activities. The country has the largest economy in the Arab World with a GDP of USD 683 billion (approx.). It is the only G-20 member country in the region. It plays a leading role in OPEC, is one of the world's largest producers and exporters of crude oil, possesses large percentage of proven petroleum reserves and is also a large-scale oil refiner and producer of natural gas. Saudi Vision 2030 is a plan to reduce Saudi Arabia's dependence on oil, to diversify its economy, and develop public service sectors such as health, education, infrastructure, recreation and tourism. This could be possible by more dedicated focus on economic and investment activities, increasing trade using goods and consumer products and increasing government spending on the military, manufacturing equipment and ammunition. Saudi Arabia's oil reserves and production are largely managed by the state-owned corporation Saudi Aramco. Saudi Arabia's economy shrank to record low due to the ongoing COVID-19 pandemic affecting the oil and non-oil sectors badly due to curbed global crude demand. Saudi Arabia's economy was affected badly in 2020 due to COVID-19 pandemic and record-low oil prices, but it rebounded in 2021 because of easing coronavirus restrictions, higher oil prices and production hikes, as per media reports.

GDP (Official exchange rate): $1.5 trillion (2020), $1.6 trillion (2019 est.)

Real Growth Rate (GDP): -0.9% (2017 est.), 1.7% (2016 est.)

Industries: Crude oil production, petroleum refining, basic petrochemicals, ammonia, industrial gases, sodium hydroxide (caustic soda), cement, fertilizer, plastics, metals, commercial ship repair, commercial aircraft repair, construction

Crude Oil - proved reserves: 266.2 billion bbl (1 January 2018 est.)

Natural gas - proved reserves: 8.619 trillion cu m (1 January 2018 est.)

Total Exports: $184.11 billion (2020 est.), $285.86 billion (2019 est.)

Export Commodities: Crude petroleum, refined petroleum, polymers, industrial alcohols, natural gas (2019)

Major Markets: China 20%, India 11%, Japan 11%, South Korea 9%, United States 5% (2019)

Total Imports: $179.8 billion (2020 est.), $218.94 billion (2019 est.)

Import Commodities: Cars, broadcasting equipment, refined petroleum, packaged medicines, telephones (2019)

Major Suppliers: China 18%, United Arab

Emirates 12%, United States 9%, Germany 5% (2019)

DEFENCE & SECURITY

The Saudi military consists of the Saudi Army, the Royal Saudi Air Force, the Royal Saudi Navy, the Royal Saudi Air Defence, the Saudi Arabian National Guard – the 'SANG' (an independent military force), and paramilitary forces. In addition, there is a military intelligence service. The armed forces are mainly the responsibility of the Ministry of Defence and Aviation. However, the Saudi Arabian National Guard is independent of the Ministry, and is commanded by King Abdullah's son, Prince Mutaib bin Abdullah. Khalid bin Sultan, son of Crown Prince Sultan bin Abdulaziz, is the Assistant Minister of Defence and Aviation of Saudi Arabia.

KEY DEFENCE PERSONS

MINISTER OF DEFENCE: Prince Mohammed bin Salman

CHAIRMAN OF THE GENERAL STAFF: Gen. Fayyad bin Hamed Al Ruwaili

COMMANDER OF THE JOINT FORCES: Lt. Gen. Mutlaq bin Salem Al-Azima (Acting)

COMMANDER OF THE LAND FORCES: Lt. Gen. Fahad bin Abdullah Al Mutair

COMMANDER OF THE NAVY: Adm. Fahd bin Abdullah Al-Ghafily

COMMANDER OF THE AIR FORCE: Maj. Gen. Turki bin Bandar bin Abdulaziz al-Saud

COMMANDER OF THE AIR DEFENCE FORCES: Lt. Gen. Mazyad Bin Sulaiman Al-Amro

COMMANDER OF THE STRATEGIC MISSILE FORCES: Lt. Gen. Jarallah Mohammed Alaluwayt

Internal Conflict

Political opposition: The Al Saud dynasty holds a monopoly of power in Saudi Arabia and any form of political parties are banned. This has encouraged the growth of dissident groups and militant Islamists. They face opposition from four sources: Sunni political activism (which itself takes on many forms, from moderate voices to militant Jihadi ideologies), liberal criticism, Shiite minority agitation, and tribal and regional politics.

Terrorism: Saudi Arabia has a growing terrorism problem unleashed by radical Islamic fighters. Their targets include foreign civilians - mainly Westerners affiliated with its oil-based economy - as well as Saudi civilians and security forces. After the terrorist attacks on New York and Washington of 11 September 2001 - carried out mainly by Saudi nationals - the Saudi authorities were further torn between their natural instincts to step up internal security and pressure to allow a greater degree of democracy. Al-Qaeda in the Arabian Peninsula (AQAP) is a militant Islamist organisation, primarily active in Yemen and Saudi Arabia. The group has carried a number of attacks in Saudi Arabia. Saudi security services have waged an active counterterrorism campaign that has largely neutralised terrorist organisations, though sporadic instances of terrorism still occur.

◆ In May 2006, terrorists attempted to attack the major ARAMCO oil-processing facility at Abqaiq.

◆ In February 2007, four French nationals were killed in western Saudi Arabia in a suspected terrorist attack.

◆ In August 2009, an al-Qaeda in the Arabian Peninsula (AQAP) suicide bomber attempted to assassinate a Saudi royal and senior Ministry of Interior official.

◆ The Specialised Criminal Court in 2011 started hearing charges including possessing explosives, missiles, military weapons, and chemical materials and smuggling items.

◆ In 2012 special security police arrested two Saudis and six Yemenis from cells operating in Riyadh and Jeddah.

◆ In 2014, the Saudi interior ministry issued a royal decree branding all 'deviants' as terrorists.

◆ In 2015, a suicide bomber attacked the Imam Ali mosque for which ISIS claimed responsibility.

◆ In 2016, four suicide bombs exploded in three locations in Saudi Arabia. No group has claimed responsibility for the attacks but the ISIS is under the suspicion radar.

◆ On 7 January 2017, two ISIL terrorists were killed by police in the Al Yasmin suburb of Riyadh.

◆ In 2018, gunmen belonging to Islamic State killed Saudi security officer and foreign national in Buraidah attack.

◆ In 2019, Saudi Arabia has been granted a full membership of the Financial Action Task Force (FATF) becoming the first Arab country awarded this full membership.

◆ In 2019, Saudi Arabian government officials continued to work closely with their US counterparts to deploy a comprehensive and well-resourced CT strategy that included vigilant security measures, regional and international cooperation, and measures to counter terrorist radicalization and recruitment.

Saudi Arabia has undertaken several initiatives to counter extremism and to promote moderation and tolerance among its citizenry. It has built a special counterterrorism force and increased the size, training and professionalism of its security forces. These forces are equipped with cutting-edge technology, and have been deployed aggressively against terrorists that threaten targets inside the Kingdom and around the world. The Kingdom has implemented the use of aerial reconnaissance aircraft to help patrol remote areas to protect against smuggling and infiltration. New barriers, motion detectors and thermal imaging systems have been installed which provide additional coverage, helping to seal the Kingdom's borders. Saudi Arabia has also shared its counterterrorism expertise with its allies. It has put in place one of the world's strictest financial control systems to prevent funds going to support terrorism.

External Conflict

Yemen: Saudi Arabia began a military intervention alongside eight other Arab states and with the intelligence and logistical support of the United States against the Yemini Houthi rebels, at the request of

Hadi's government, in 2015. The intervention included a bombing campaign, naval blockade and deployment of ground forces in Yemen. Later, Saudi Arabia and its coalition partners said they would launch political and peace efforts after Operation Decisive Storm and will be called Operation Restoring Hope. However, the coalition did not rule out using force in order to eliminate enemy forces. The coalition has yet to dislodge the Houthi group from the capital Sanaa. King Salman meanwhile has doubled his country's Yemen aid pledge to USD 540 million, as per news reports. The border between Saudi Arabia and Yemen has long been a source of political dispute, particularly from 1990 - when North Yemen and South Yemen unified - to 2000, when the two countries signed an agreement. As per media reports in Oct 2019, Saudi Arabia is considering a proposal by Yemen's Iran-aligned Houthi movement for some form of ceasefire. The Houthis also offered ceasefire from their end if the coalition does the same.

ISIS: The Government of Saudi Arabia is working closely with United States since 2014 to fight against ISIS militants. The country is supporting by providing training and equipping Syrian fighters in this coalition battle against ISIS and its propaganda. The Saudi government's counter-terrorism actions have considerably helped, such as by cutting off money flows to terrorist groups, according to a statement by the then US Secretary of State John Kerry. Saudi Arabia has also put USD 500 million into the coffers of the UN humanitarian aid agencies in Iraq.

Kuwait and Saudi Arabia continue discussions on a maritime boundary with Iran.

Saudi Arabia claims Egyptian-administered islands of Tiran and Sanafir.

THREAT PERSPECTIVE

Saudi Arabia is one of the key powers in the region given both its position as the world's most important oil producer and also the two holiest sites of Islam, Mecca and Medina, are located in the kingdom. Saudi Arabia, in the initial times, was primarily concerned about the safety and security of royal blood(s) of the kingdom mainly king and the royal family. Their defence systems were concerned chiefly about the safety of the holy places and the security of the borders. Since the discovery of oil in the country, and its overwhelming export to nations around the world, gave rise to new security concerns engulfing Saudi Arabia and added precautionary measures were taken in maritime security, since majority of its oil exports are through waterways in the Persian Gulf.

A series of drone and missile attacks on the oil facilities of Saudi Aramco, the country's largest petroleum company, on Sept 14 knocked out half its daily oil production, severely impacting the global oil market and triggering fresh tension between Saudi Arabia and Iran. Yemen's Houthi terror group has taken responsibility for the biggest-ever attacks on Saudi oil facilities. Saudi Arabia and its ally, the US, have blamed Iran for the attacks but Tehran has strongly denied the allegations. After worst ever drone and missile attacks on its oil facilities, Saudi Arabia has said it will ramp up cooperation with India in combating terrorism, including by choking flow of funds to terror groups and boosting intelligence sharing.

Iran: Saudi Arabia broke off diplomatic relations with Iran on January 4, 2016. The Iranian government barred its citizens from making the hajj. Iran's relations with Saudi Arabia have been a function of the two countries' geopolitical situation in the Middle East and political rivalries between Tehran and Riyadh. Both Saudi Arabia and Iran have aspiration for Islamic leadership and both countries possess different visions of regional order. Iran, which after the Islamic Revolution strictly followed an anti-US policy, always deemed Saudi Arabia as an agent of the US in the Persian Gulf region that speaks for the US interests. Saudi Arabia's concerns about Iran are mainly associated to its plans of expanding influence to other parts of the Persian Gulf region, especially in post-Saddam Iraq and the quest to build its own nuclear arsenal. Both the countries share a hate-hate relationship. Saudi Arabia announced in January 2016 it was severing its ties to Iran after its embassy in Tehran was attacked in protest at the kingdom's execution of Shiite cleric Sheikh Nimr al-Nimr. The oil-rich rivals have also been divided over the nearly five-year war in Syria, where Iran is backing the regime, and the conflict in Yemen where a Saudi-led coalition is battling Shiite rebels. Both countries are major oil and gas exporters and have clashed over energy policy. There are international efforts going on to normalise the relations between two countries.

Iraq: In 2019, Saudi Arabia opened its consulate in Baghdad after many years of stale relations. Post-war Saudi policy focused on ways to contain potential Iraqi threats to the kingdom and the region. The Saudi leadership opposed the US plan to invade Iraq, and did not join the Coalition. The Kingdom stands behind Iraq, and desires to see a stable, peaceful, united and independent Iraq that is representative of all Iraqis. Saudi Arabia's efforts in diplomacy have been coupled with support for humanitarian relief and assistance to the Iraqi people. The Saudi Arabia-Iraq border is one of the most patrolled borders in the world, and the Kingdom has dramatically increased its presence to stop illegal border crossings. In August 2016, Iraq has called on Saudi Arabia to replace its ambassador to Baghdad over comments he made about Iran's involvement in Iraq. The Saudi embassy in Baghdad only reopened in December 2015 after being closed since the Iraqi invasion of Kuwait. Currently, relations are improving between the Saudi Arabian government and the Iraqi government. To improve trade ties, Saudi Arabia and Iraq decided to open the borders in October 2019. In 2021, Saudi Arabia's King Salman held talks with Iraqi Prime Minister Mustafa Al-Kadhimi to discuss relations and developments in the region and stressed on strengthening cooperation in political, security, trade, investment and tourism.

STRATEGIC RELATIONS

US: Saudi Arabia's unique role in the Arab and Islamic worlds, its possession of the world's largest reserves of oil, and its strategic location make its friendship important to the United States. The United States and Saudi Arabia share common concerns about regional security, oil exports and imports, and sustainable development. Although Saudi Arabia's relations with the United States were strained after 11 September 2001, Saudi Arabia is now one of the United States' strongest partners against terrorism. Saudi Arabia is a strong partner in the campaign against terrorism, providing military, diplomatic, and financial cooperation. Counterterrorism cooperation between Saudi Arabia and the United States increased significantly since 2013. Saudi Arabia and the US have established two Joint Task Forces - one to combat terrorists, another to combat terror financing. Experts from both governments work side-by-side, share real-time information about terror networks. The United States has provided logistical and intelligence support to Saudi Arabia in their military intervention in Yemen, establishing a Joint Planning Cell with Saudi Arabia. The United States has sold Saudi Arabia military aircraft, air defence weaponry, armoured vehicles, and other equipment. Saudi Arabia is the United States' largest foreign military sales customer. The US would deploy the one Patriot Battery, four Sentinel RADARs and approximately 200 support personnel in the Kingdom. This deployment will augment the kingdom's air and missile defence of critical military and civilian infrastructure. The United States and Saudi Arabia have a longstanding security relationship. Saudi Arabia is the United States' largest foreign military sales (FMS) customer, with nearly USD100 billion in active FMS cases. The United States has supported three key security assistance organisations in the Kingdom - the Saudi Ministry of Defence, the Saudi Arabian National Guard, and the Ministry of Interior. The United States is Saudi Arabia's second largest trading partner, and Saudi Arabia is one of the United States' largest trading partners in the Middle East. Saudi Arabia is the second leading source of imported oil for the United States, providing just under one million barrels per day of oil to the US market.

UK: The United Kingdom and Saudi Arabia have long been close strategic allies. Saudi Arabia is the United Kingdom's primary trading partner in the Middle East. There are more than 150 joint ventures between British and Saudi Companies. Both the countries share strong military cooperation with each other. Both the countries are strong strategic partners with shared regional and wider interests. Saudi Arabia is one of UK's most vital partners in global counter-terrorism. The Ministry of Defence Saudi Armed Forces Projects (MODSAP) is responsible for fulfilling the UK Government's obligations under arrangements signed between the UK and Saudi Arabian Governments covering the supply of defence equipment and services to the Saudi Armed Forces under the Saudi British Defence Cooperation Programme and the SALAM Project.

Pakistan: Bilateral relations between the Islamic Republic of Pakistan and the Kingdom of Saudi Arabia are exemplary. Pakistan is the closest non-Arab ally of Saudi Arabia. Saudi Arabia and Pakistan are leading members of the Organisation of Islamic Cooperation (OIC). Pakistan maintains close military ties with Saudi Arabia, providing extensive support, arms and training for the Military of Saudi Arabia. They have had a deep strategic military relationship for decades and today have an unacknowledged nuclear partnership to provide the kingdom with a nuclear deterrent on short notice if ever needed. Pakistan, on the other hand, has received more aid from Saudi Arabia than any country outside the Arab world since the 1960s. In 2015, Pakistan has declined a Saudi Arabian request to join the coalition against Yemen intervention and maintained a neutral diplomatic stance. However, Pakistan said it will come to Saudi Arabia's defence if the country's sovereignty or territorial integrity is threatened. In 2018, Saudi Arabia has agreed to give Pakistan USD3 billion in foreign currency support for a year and a further loan worth up to USD3 billion in deferred payments for oil imports, totalling to USD 6 billion. In 2019, Saudi Arabia paid USD20 billion to finance developmental projects in Pakistan. In Dec 2021, Pakistan received $3 billion loan from Saudi Arabia, as part of economic support package, as per media reports.

India: Saudi Arabia values India as a close friend and a strategic partner and continuously enhances the defence and security cooperation. Saudi Arabia is the one of largest suppliers of oil to India. Saudi Arabia has supported granting observer status to India in the OIC and has expanded its cooperation with India to fight terrorism. In Sept 2012, India and Saudi Arabia have decided to enhance their military exchanges during the first meeting of their joint committee on defence cooperation held in New Delhi. The Joint Committee was mandated to formulate a programme to develop areas of cooperation between the defence establishments of both countries. Both nations also agreed on joint ventures and the development of oil and natural gas in public and private sectors. Reflecting growing congruence in bilateral ties, India and Saudi Arabia have inked a defence cooperation pact to take their strategic partnership further in areas of security. The defence cooperation pact will allow exchange of defence-related information, military training and education as well as cooperation in areas varying from hydrography and security to logistics. The visit by Prime Minister Narendra Modi to Riyadh in 2016 is seen as a turning point in growing engagement with the Kingdom of Saudi Arabia, which has taken an upward strategic direction. India and Saudi Arabia are also closely cooperating with each other in fighting terrorism and enhancing their level of engagement to deal with the menace. Saudi Arabia, known to be a key ally of Pakistan, has been siding with India in its campaign to rid the region of terrorism and pledged to extend all cooperation to effectively deal with the challenge. Both countries already signed several agreements in the field of security, including an extradition treaty. In 2021, both India and Saudi Arabia conducted their first-ever naval exercise, in reflection of their growing defence and military cooperation.

MULTILATERAL ALLIANCES

Saudi Arabia, a member of UN, is also a founder member of the Arab League, Persian Gulf Cooperation Council, Muslim World League, and the Organisation of Islamic Cooperation (OIC). The country plays a prominent role in the International Monetary Fund and the World Bank, and in 2005 joined the World Trade Organisation. According to the Saudi Ministry of Foreign Affairs, Saudi foreign policy is focused on co-operation with the Gulf States, the unity of the Arab world, solidarity with Muslim countries, and support for the UN. Saudi Arabia also is an observer to the Organisation of American States.

DEFENCE CAPABILITIES

ARMY: Royal Saudi Land Forces (RSLF) is a branch of the Saudi Armed Forces. The combat strength of the Saudi Army consists of 4 armoured brigades, 17 mechanised infantry brigades, three light motorised rifle brigades, and one airborne brigade. It also has five independent artillery brigades and an aviation command. The primary task of the army is to protect the kingdom's borders against attack by a conventional force.

Personnel: 75,000

Equipment

Category	Name	In Service
MBT	M1A2S Abrams	400+ (more on order)
	M60A3	400+
	AMX30	120+
APC/MICV/IFV	Al-Fahd	75+
	AMX-10P	400+
	M2A2 Bradley	350
	BMP-3	
	M113	1000+
	Panhard M3	50+
	TPz Fuchs	100+
	HMMWV	10000+
	Nyoka Mk2	1500+
Artillery	105 mm M101	75
	105 mm M102	75
	155 mm M198	80
	155 mm FH70	30
	M109A2/A5	275
	155 mm. AMX GCT	40+
	M198	42+
	155 mm. M114	55+
	PLZ-45	60+
Mortar	M224	
	107 mm	
	60 mm	100+
	120 mm	100+
MLRS	Astros II MLRS	50+
Anti-Tank GW	Dragon	3500+
	BGM-71 TOW	
	ITOW	1750+
	HOT/HOT-2	3000+
	Javelin	
	Swingfire	
	MILAN	

...continued

Category	Name	In Service
IRBM	DF3A	
SAM	Stinger	
	Mistral	500

Army Aviation

Category	Name	In Service
Helicopter	UH-60A	10+
	S-70	5+
	Bell 406 Combat Scout	12+
	CH-47	
	AH64/64D Apache	100 (More on order)
UAV	Aeryon Scout, Saqr	

New Procurements/ Upgrades

◆ Raytheon Missiles & Defence, a Raytheon Technologies business, received a USD2.3 billion US Missile Defence Agency production contract for seven gallium nitride (GaN)-based AN/TPY-2 radars as part of the Terminal High Altitude Area Defense (THAAD) system, which is designed to protect against incoming ballistic missile threats. The contract is part of a foreign military sale to the Kingdom of Saudi Arabia.

◆ The US State Department has approved a possible Foreign Military Sale to Saudi Arabia of a Royal Saudi Land Forces Ordnance Corps Foreign Military Sales Order (FMSO) II Case for an estimated cost of USD300 million. The Government of the Kingdom of Saudi Arabia has requested a possible purchase of a new Foreign Military Sales Order (FMSO) II to provide funds for blanket order requisitions under a Cooperative Logistics Supply Support Agreement (CLSSA) for common spares/ repair parts to support Saudi Arabia's fleet of M1A2 Abrams tanks, M2 Bradley Fighting Vehicles, High Mobility Multipurpose Wheeled Vehicles (HMMWVs), Light Armoured Vehicles (LAVs), M198 Towed Howitzers, additional support, and other related elements of logistics and program support.

◆ The US State Department has approved a possible Foreign Military Sale to Saudi Arabia of TOW 2B (BGM-71F-Series) missiles for an estimated cost of USD 670 million. The Government of the Kingdom of Saudi Arabia has requested to buy up to 6,600 TOW 2B missiles (BGM-71F-Series) and 96 TOW 2B (BGM-71F-Series) fly-to-buy lot validation missiles. Also included is government furnished equipment; technical manuals and publications; essential spares and repair parts; consumables; live fire exercise and ammunition; tools and test equipment; training; transportation; US Government technical support and logistic support; contractor technical support; repair and return support; quality assurance teams; in-country Field Service Representative (FSR); other associated equipment and services in support of TOW 2B missiles; and other related elements of logistics and program support.

◆ The US State Department has approved a possible Foreign Military Sale to Saudi Arabia of equipment and services for the continuation of the Maintenance Support Services (MSS) contract that supports the Royal Saudi Land Forces Aviation Command for an estimated cost of USD 106.8 million.

NAVY: Royal Saudi Naval Forces (RSNF) is the naval force of the Kingdom of Saudi Arabia. It also includes Marine Forces and Special Forces. The Naval headquarters is in Riyadh. The Western Fleet is based in the Red Sea with the main base at Jeddah. The Eastern Fleet is based in the Persian Gulf with the headquarters at Jubail. Other naval facilities were located at Yanbu, Dammam, and Ras al Mishab.

Naval Bases: Jeddah, Jubail, Dammam, Ras Tanura, Ras-al-Mishab

Personnel: 14,000

Equipment

Category	Name	In Service
Frigate	Al Riyadh class	3
	Al Medinah	4
Corvette	Badr Class	4
Patrol Boat	Al Siddiq	9
	Naja 12	30+
	Halter Type	15+
Mine Warfare Force	Sandown-class	3
Auxiliary ship	Boraida Class (Fleet Tanker)	2
Amphibious Force	Afif Class Landing Craft Utility	4
	LCM	4
SSM	Exocet MM40 Block II	
	Otomat	
SAM	Aster 15	
	Crotale	20+

Naval Aviation

Category	Name	In Service
Helicopter	MH-60R	15+
	AS332	15+
	AS565	22+

New Procurements/ Upgrades

◆ Navantia successfully carried out the launching of AL-JUBAIL, the first of five corvettes built for the Royal Saudi Naval Forces (RSNF). The Commander of RSNF highlighted the importance of ALSARAWAT Project, contracted to Navantia, as one of the largest capability-acquisition programmes for the RSNF.

◆ The US government awarded Lockheed Martin an Undefinitised Contract Action (UCA) award for the production of the Multi-Mission Surface Combatant for the Kingdom of Saudi Arabia. Lockheed Martin is being awarded a contract totalling USD 450 million to begin the detailed design and planning for construction of four Multi-Mission Surface Combatants (MMSC) that will be built at Fincantieri Marinette Marine shipyard in Marinette, Wisconsin. The Kingdom of Saudi Arabia (KSA) will acquire four Multi-Mission Surface Combatants as part of a larger agreement between the United States and KSA to enhance global security and stimulate economic progress in the two regions. MMSC utilises the COMBATSS-21 Combat Management System, built from the Aegis Combat System Common Source Library, enabling anti-air and anti-surface capabilities in a small surface combatant platform.

◆ Navantia has carried out, in its San Fernando shipyard facilities in Oct. 2019, the official keel-laying act of the first of the five corvettes it is building for the Royal Saudi Arabian Navy (RSNF). The contract, which calls for the last vessel to be delivered in 2022, includes, in addition to construction, the Life Cycle Support for five years, from the delivery of the first vessel, with an option for an additional five years.

AIR FORCE: The Royal Saudi Air Force is the aviation branch of the Saudi Arabian armed forces. The RSAF maintains the third largest fleet of F-15s after the JASDF and the USAF.

Personnel: 36,000

Equipment

Category	Name	In Service
Fighters/ attack/ Reconnaissance/ bomber	F-15E	80+ (More on order)
	F-15C/D Eagle	65+
	F-15S Strike Eagle	60+ (to be upgraded to SA standard)
	Eurofighter Typhoon	50+ (More on order)
	Panavia Tornado IDS	75
	An-178	On order
Transport/ Tanker	E-3 Sentry (AWACS)	
	A330 MRTT	5
	C-130 Hercules	20+

...continued

Category	Name	In Service
Transport/ Tanker	C-130H Super Hercules	20+
	Gulfstream III/IV	4
	Saab 2000 AEW&C	3
	L-100 Hercules	5+
	CN-235	5+
	An-132	
	KC-130J	3
Attack/ Transport Helicopter	Bell 212	20+
	Bell 205	20+
	AS-532 Cougar	10
	AS365 Dauphin	20+
	SA-332 Super Puma	10+
	AS-61	
	Alouette III	5
	S-70 Blackhawk	10+
	Cougar MkII	10+
Trainer	BAe Hawk	30
	BAe Jetstream	
	Super Mushshak	15+
	F-5B	10+
	F-15D	14
	Pilatus PC-9	40+
	Pilatus PC-21	30+
	SR22	15+
	King Air 350	10+
	T-41A	10+

New Procurements/ Upgrades

◆ The US State Department has approved a possible Foreign Military Sale to the Kingdom of Saudi Arabia of AIM-120C Advanced Medium Range Air-to-Air Missiles (AMRAAM) and related equipment for an estimated cost of USD650 million.

◆ The US State Department has approved a possible Foreign Military Sale to the Kingdom of Saudi Arabia of Continuation of Maintenance Support Services (MSS) and related equipment for an estimated cost of USD500 million.

◆ The Boeing Co., Defence, Space & Security, St. Louis, Missouri, has been awarded a USD9,800,000,000 indefinite-delivery/indefinite-quantity contract for F-15 support for Saudi Arabia.

◆ The US State Department has approved a possible Foreign Military Sale to the Kingdom of Saudi Arabia of aircraft follow-on support and services for an estimated cost of USD1.8 billion. Saudi Arabia has requested to buy follow-on logistics support and services for the Royal Saudi Air Force aircraft, engines, and weapons; publications and technical documentation; support equipment; spare and repair parts; repair and return; calibration support and test equipment; personnel equipment; US Government and contractor technical and logistics support, and other related elements of programme support. Equipment and spares will be procured for support of, but not limited to, F-5, F-15, KA-350, C-130, KC-130, E-3, RE-3, and KE-3 aircraft.

◆ The US State Department has approved a possible Foreign Military Sale to Saudi Arabia of continuation of missile system support services for an estimated cost of USD 500 million. The Government of the Kingdom of Saudi Arabia has requested a possible purchase for continued participation, technical assistance, and support in the Patriot Legacy Field Surveillance Programme (FSP); the Patriot Advanced Capability 3 (PAC-3) FSP; and the Patriot Engineering Services Programme (ESP). Also included are Patriot and HAWK Missile System spare parts and repair and return management services and component repairs, and other related elements of logistics and programme support.

◆ The US State Department has approved a possible Foreign Military Sale to the Government of Saudi Arabia for Terminal High Altitude Area Defence (THAAD) and related support, equipment and services for an estimated cost of USD 15 billion. The Government of Saudi Arabia has requested a possible sale of 44 Terminal High Altitude Area Defence (THAAD) launchers, 360 THAAD Interceptor Missiles, 16 THAAD Fire Control and Communications Mobile Tactical Station Group, 7 AN/TPY-2 THAAD radars. Also included are THAAD Battery maintenance equipment, 43 prime movers (trucks), generators, electrical power units, trailers, communications equipment, tools, test and maintenance equipment, repair and return, system integration and checkout, spare/repair parts, publications and technical documentation, personnel training and training equipment, US Government and contractor technical and logistics personnel support services, facilities construction, studies, and other related elements of logistics and program support.

◆ The US State Department has approved a possible Foreign Military Sale to the Kingdom of Saudi Arabia of aircraft follow-on support and services for an estimated cost of USD800 million. Saudi Arabia has requested to purchase follow-on support and services for Royal Saudi Air Force aircraft, engines, and weapons; publications and technical documentation; support equipment; spare and repair parts; repair and return; calibration support and test equipment; personnel equipment; US Government and contractor technical and logistics support, and other related elements of programme support. Equipment and spares will be procured for support of, but not limited to, F-5, RG-5, F-15, C-130, KC-130, E-3, RE-3, and KE-3 aircraft.

◆ The US State Department has approved a possible Foreign Military Sale to the Kingdom of Saudi Arabia of continued Tactical Air Surveillance System Aircraft support for an estimated cost of USD136 million. Saudi Arabia has requested to purchase spare and repair parts, US Government and contractor engineering, technical, and logistics support services, and other related elements of programme support for their TASS (Tactical Air Surveillance System) aircraft programme.

◆ The US State Department has approved a possible Foreign Military Sale to the Kingdom of Saudi Arabia of GBU-39 Small Diameter Bomb I (SDB I) Munitions and related equipment for an estimated cost of USD290 million.

ROYAL SAUDI AIR DEFENCE: Royal Saudi Air Defence is the fourth branch of Saudi Armed Forces. It was a part of the Army until 1981, when it was made independent by Field Marshal Khalid bin Sultan. The RSADF has its headquarters in Riyadh.

Personnel: 36,000

Equipment

Category	Name	In Service
AA Gun	35 mm. twin towed	150+
	Vulcan towed	75+
	30 mm. AMX30	10+
Missile	Improved HAWK	15 batteries
	Shahine I/ Shahine II	150
	MIM-104 Patriot	10 system (to receive PAC-3 missiles)
Radar	AN/FPS-117	10+
	AN/TPS-43	5+

SAUDI ARABIAN NATIONAL GUARD (SANG): The Saudi Arabian National Guard (SANG) is a separate military force of the Kingdom of Saudi Arabia. It is not part of the Saudi Arabian Defence Forces. It is a tribal force forged out of those tribal elements loyal to the Saud Family. It serves both as defence force against external threats and as a security force against internal threats. Its duties include protecting the royal family, guarding against coups, protecting strategic facilities and resources, and protecting the Holy Places of Mecca and Medina. It is always commanded by a high ranking member of the royal family.

Prince Mutaib bin Abdullah bin Abdul-Aziz Al-Saud is the Commander of the Saudi National Guard since 2010. He is also a state minister. He is a son of King Abdullah of

Saudi Arabia. He conducted a major USD 3 billion reorganisation of SANG to develop its firepower and artillery.

Personnel: 100,000

Equipment

Category	Name	In Service
APC/ IFV	LAV-25	
	LAV-III	10+ (LAV 6.0 on order)
	Al-Fahd	70+
	EE-11 Urutu	15+
	Piranha II	900+
Mortar/ Assault	120 mm. AMS	70+
	90 mm. LAV Assault Gun	100+
Artillery	155 mm. M198	20+
AA Gun	M167 Vulcan	
Helicopter	AS532U Super Puma (Jointly with Navy & Coast Guard)	10+
	AH-6	

New Procurements/ Upgrades

No major procurement plans are under consideration at present.

The Royal Saudi Strategic Missile Force or RSSMF is the fifth branch of the Saudi Arabian Armed Forces, responsible for commissioning long-range strategic missiles.

Major Armaments Producers

Domestic suppliers: Advanced Electronics Company, Military Industries Corporation, Abdallah Al Faris Company for Heavy Industries, Alsalam Aircraft Company, BAE Systems Saudi Arabia, SELEX Galileo, King Abdulaziz City for Science and Technology, Prince Sultan Advanced Technology Research Institute

Foreign suppliers: France, China, Germany, United Kingdom, Russia, Brazil, United States, Spain, Turkey, Austria, Pakistan, Japan, Switzerland, Italy, Brazil, Australia, Canada

Saudi Arabian Military Industries company (SAMI) is a new national defence industry, launched in May 2017 to provide a sustainable vehicle to deliver world class defence products and services to Saudi Arabia and the region. SAMI is a key part of Vision 2030 and aims to act as a catalyst to drive localisation of military spending in the Kingdom of Saudi Arabia. Its main goals are: to increase the local content of military, products and services; to invest in strategic, profitable areas; to ensure that the military industries contribute to the wider economy. SAMI will manufacture products and provide services across four business units: Air Systems, which includes maintenance and repair of fixed-wing aircraft as well as manufacturing and repair of unmanned air vehicles; Land Systems, which includes manufacturing and repair of military vehicles; Weapons and Missiles, including ammunition; and Defence Electronics, which includes radars and sensors as well as communication systems and electronic warfare. It will directly contribute around SR14 billion to the Kingdom's GDP in 2030, invest over SR6 billion in research and development by 2030.

The Abdallah Al Faris Company for Heavy Industries, based in Dammam manufactured Al-Fahd Infantry fighting vehicle and the Al-Faris 8-400 armoured personnel carrier. After the collapse of Arab Organisation for Industrialisation (AOI), Saudi Arabia established its own small arms industry at 'Al Kharj', producing rifles, machine guns, and ammunition under license. In 1985 a royal decree by King Fahd led to the creation of the 'General Establishment of Military Industries' to oversee and coordinate the kingdom's existing and proposed domestic defence projects. The Al-Fahd Infantry fighting vehicle and the Al-Faris 8-400 armoured personnel carrier, used by Saudi land forces, were manufactured by the Abdallah Al Faris Company for Heavy Industries, based in Dammam. Saudi Arabia, despite budget hurdles, remains a major buyer of defence arms and equipment. The country, like other Gulf States, devotes a larger share of their gross domestic product (GDP) to military spending than the global average.

Saudi Arabia is a member of the Gulf Cooperation Council (GCC) which consists of Kuwait, Qatar, Bahrain, the UAE, Oman, and Saudi Arabia. These countries declared that the GCC is established in view of the special relations between them, their similar political systems based on Islamic beliefs, joint destiny and common objectives. The GCC is a regional common market with a defence planning council as well. The geographic proximity of these countries and their general adoption of free trade economic policies are factors that encouraged them to establish the GCC. The GCC States seek to build up their defence forces according to a common conception. In this context, they have unified operational procedures, training, and military curricula. They also endeavour to accomplish compatibility of their military systems.

Prince Sultan Advanced Tech. Research Institute (PSATRI) was established to conduct applied scientific and technical research and development to support the Royal Saudi Air Force and other Saudi military and security users in becoming more effective and efficient regional leaders. PSATRI benefits from its close collaboration with MOD, Private organizations and strong interaction with KSU, local and global universities and research centres.

The King Abdulaziz City for Science and Technology (KACST) is Saudi Arabia's national science agency and home to its advanced laboratories. KACST is promoting the development and investment in the national system of science, technology and innovation, by orienting research outputs towards industrial diversification. KACST has created the Joint Centres of Excellence Program (JCEP) to conduct cutting-edge research ideas via partnerships with leading academic and industrial establishments from around the world. In May 2017, Saudi Arabia's KACST unveiled its Saqr 1 unmanned aerial vehicle, which has a range of 2,500km and features a satellite communication system.

DEFENCE DEALS

Arms Import

Saudi Arabia is expected to remain one of the biggest buyers defence equipment globally over the coming decade. According to a report by the US Department of Commerce's International Trade Administration, in August 2016, the US State Department announced that the sale of 153 Abrams battle tanks and 20 M88 Hercules armoured recovery vehicles had been approved, in a contract worth around USD1.15 billion. In 2017, Boeing was awarded a multi-year contract (running until 2022) to supply 24 newly-built AH-64E Apache Guardians to the Saudi Army. Also, in 2017, the US DSCA announced that the sale of 10 Lockheed Martin 74K Persistent Threat Detection Systems (PTDS) to Saudi Arabia. In May 2017, arms contracts worth USD109 billion were signed during President Donald Trump's visit to Riyadh. Saudi Arabia is planning to buy THAAD ballistic missile interception system and other equipments from Lockheed Martin. They are also planning to acquire in BAE Systems' 155 mm M109 self-propelled howitzers and Bradley IFVs. Saudi Arabia is interested in Raytheon's Paveway guided bombs. As per various reports, USD109 billion arms deal signed during President's Trump's visit to Saudi Arabia has yet to be finalised. Saudi Arabia is also close to a USD 7 billion deal for 48 Eurofighter Typhoons. The country also negotiated a contract with Spain for five warships for the Royal Saudi Navy worth

USD1.8 billion, but none is finalised yet. Saudi Arabia is also equipped with C4ISR (Command, Control, Communications, Computer, Intelligence, Surveillance, and Reconnaissance) platforms. The Kingdom has Boeing E-3A, RC-135, Erieye on Saab 340, Bombardier Q300 MPA, and others in its service.

The Saudi Arabian Military Industries (SAMI) announced in Oct 2017 the signing of a Memorandum of Understanding (MoU) and a General Terms and Conditions Contract with Rosoboronexport, Russia's state company for exporting military products. According to SAMI, the MOU focuses on localising the manufacturing and sustainment of advance armament systems in the Kingdom of Saudi Arabia in line with the objectives of Vision 2030. The MOU includes the transfer of technology for the local production of the Kornet-EM anti-tank guided missile (ATGM) system, the TOS-1A advanced multiple rocket launcher and AGS-30 automatic grenade launchers with grenades. The parties will also cooperate in setting a plan to localize the manufacturing and sustainment of parts of the S-400 air defence system. The contract covers the local production of the Kalashnikov AK-103 and its ammunition which will contribute to raising the local content and enhancing self-sufficiency in line with Vision 2030.

Despite falling oil prices, Saudi Arabia is seeing surge in military spending. The vast majority of Saudi Arabia's military equipment is imported from European and North American suppliers. Canada's General Dynamics has received USD 10 billion contract to sell armoured vehicles to Saudi Arabia. General Dynamics Land Systems is the manufacturer of the LAV III armoured vehicle Canada used in Afghanistan. It also makes similar Stryker armoured vehicles for the United States. The United Kingdom has sold USD8.2billion of arms to Saudi Arabia in five years.

Saudi Arabia's modern high-technology arsenal makes Saudi Arabia among the world's most densely armed nations, with its military equipment being supplied primarily by the US, France and Britain.

DEFENCE BUDGET

Total defence spending: $82.9 billion (2018)

Estimated defence spending in terms of GDP: 7.9% of GDP (2020 est.), 8% of GDP (2019)

According to the US Department of Commerce's International Trade Administration, Saudi Arabia's defence and security expenditures reached USD63.2 billion in 2019 and are expected to reach USD83 billion in 2020. Saudi Arabia is expected to maintain its defence spending over the coming years, driven by both internal and external security threats. Vision 2030 encompasses two key goals that are central to the defense sector. First, to establish a holding company for the military industry that is 100 percent owned by the Saudi government. The Saudi Arabian Military Industries (SAMI) was created in 2017 for the fulfillment of this goal and will be instrumental in advancing the Kingdom's defense industry capabilities and leading to new defense investments. The Government established the General Authority of Military Industries (GAMI) in late 2017, which will oversee regulation of the military industry and will support the Kingdom in achieving its sector-related objectives of Vision 2030.

According to Ahmed bin Abdulaziz al-Ohali, Governor of the General Authority for Military Industries (GAMI) in the year 2021, Saudi Arabia plans to spend more than USD10 billion in arms industry and research and development in the country for the next 10 years.

CONCLUSION

Saudi Arabia plays a unique role in the Arab and Islamic worlds, also holds the world's second largest reserves of oil, and is positioned in a strategic location. Saudi Arabia maintains a complex diplomatic position between the Middle East and the West. It has consistently sought to promote Arab unity, defend Arab and Islamic interests, and support a peaceful resolution of the Israeli-Palestinian conflict. Saudi Arabia plays an important leadership role in working toward a peaceful and prosperous future for the region and is a strong partner in security and counterterrorism efforts, providing military, diplomatic, and financial cooperation. The kingdom spends 25% of its budget, or about nearly USD 88 billion on military and safeguarding its borders. On the other hand, Saudi Arabia has been a partner with the West in economic endeavours and the war against terrorism. Saudi Arabia's military, the best-equipped in the Gulf region, is a force to be reckoned with. It ranks among the world's most densely armed nations, and it has ambitious plans to further upgrade its arsenal. It has always devoted significant resources to improving its military. Since the Cold War era, it has been militarily aligned with the US. Saudi Arabia imports most of its military arms and equipment. The strategic position of Saudi Arabia is directly related to its impact on the stability of the Gulf, which encompasses the military forces, defence expenditures, arms imports, military modernisation, readiness, and war fighting capability. In general, Saudi foreign policy objectives are to maintain its security and its paramount position on the Arabian Peninsula, defend general Arab and Islamic interests, promote solidarity among Islamic governments, and maintain cooperative relations with other oil-producing and major oil-consuming countries. The country, because of its possession of the world's largest reserves of oil and its strategic location, is having good diplomatic relations with western countries, especially United States. The US is Saudi Arabia's largest trading partner, and Saudi Arabia is the largest US export market in the Middle East. Saudi Arabia's local defence industry remains underdeveloped, leaving the country's armed forces heavily reliant on imports of military equipment. Meanwhile, the Saudi government is one of the largest defence spenders globally. Saudi Arabia has one of the highest percentages of military expenditure in the world, spending more than 10% of its GDP in its military. Saudi Arabia ranks among the top 10 in the world in government spending for its military.

CONTACT DETAILS

Ministry of Defence and Aviation
Airport Road
11165 Riyadh
Saudi Arabia
Tel: +96614785900/477313
Fax: +96614011336
Website: https://www.mod.gov.sa/

Armed Forces HQ
C/o Ministry of Defence
Tel: +96614023106

National Guard HQ
Riyadh, Saudi Arabia
Tel: +96614024600, 4024277

SERBIA
(Capital: Belgrade)

INTRODUCTION
Area: 77,474 sq km
Population: 6,974,289 (July 2021 est.)
Coastline: 0 km (Landlocked)
Maritime claims: None

KEY POLITICAL PERSONS

PRESIDENT & SUPREME COMMANDER OF ARMED FORCES: Aleksandar Vucic

PRIME MINISTER: Ana Brnabic

KEY DEFENCE PERSONS

DEPUTY PRIME MINISTER & MINISTER OF DEFENCE: Nebojsa Stefanovic

CHIEF OF GENERAL STAFF: Gen. Milan Mojsilovic

COMMANDER OF ARMY: Lt. Gen. Milosav Simovic

COMMANDER OF AIR FORCE & AIR DEFENCE: Lt. Gen. Dusko Zarkovic

ECONOMY

Serbia has a transitional economy mostly dominated by market forces, but the state sector remains large and many institutional reforms are needed. The economy relies on manufacturing and exports, driven largely by foreign investment. Serbia has made progress in trade liberalisation and enterprise restructuring and privatisation, but many large enterprises – including power utilities, telecommunications, natural gas company, national air carrier, and others – remain in state hands. Serbia has made some progress towards EU membership, signing a Stabilization and Association Agreement with Brussels in May 2008, and with full implementation of the Interim Trade Agreement with the EU in February 2010, gained candidate status in March 2012. In January 2014, Serbia's EU accession talks officially opened, and as of December 2017, Serbia had opened 12 negotiating chapters including one on foreign trade. Serbia's negotiations with the WTO are also advancing, with the country's complete ban on the trade and cultivation of agricultural biotechnology products representing the primary remaining obstacle to accession. The government has shown progress implementing economic reforms, such as fiscal consolidation, privatisation, and reducing public spending. Unemployment in Serbia, while relatively low (16% in 2017) compared with its Balkan neighbours, remains significantly above the European average. Serbia is slowly implementing structural economic reforms needed to ensure the country's long-term prosperity.

Due to the Coronavirus pandemic, the Serbian economy shrunk by 1% in 2020 – one of the smallest GDP declines in Europe. Growth is expected to accelerate in 2021, according to projections made by the country's Government.

GDP (official exchange rate): $51.44 billion (2019 est.)

Real Growth Rate (GDP): 4.18% (2019 est.); 4.4% (2018 est.)

Industries: Automobiles, base metals, furniture, food processing, machinery, chemicals, sugar, tires, clothes, pharmaceuticals

Total Exports: $15.92 billion (2017 est.); $13.99 billion (2016 est.)

Export Commodities: Insulated wiring, tires, corn, cars, iron products, copper (2019)

Major Markets: Germany 12%, Italy 10%, Bosnia and Herzegovina 7%, Romania 6%, Russia 5% (2019)

Total Imports: $20.44 billion (2017 est.); $17.63 billion (2016 est.)

Import Commodities: Crude petroleum, cars, packaged medicines, natural gas, refined petroleum (2019)

Major Suppliers: Germany 13%, Russia 9%, Italy 8%, Hungary 6%, China 5%, Turkey 5% (2019)

INTERNATIONAL DISPUTES

◆ Serbia with several other states protested the US and other states' recognition of Kosovo declaring itself as a sovereign and independent state in February 2008; Ethnic Serbian municipalities along Kosovo's northern border challenge the final status of the Kosovo-Serbia boundary.

◆ Serbia has delimited about half of the boundary with Bosnia and Herzegovina, but sections along the Drina River remain in dispute.

DEFENCE

ARMY

Personnel: 12,000+

Equipment

Category	Name	In Service
MBT	M-84/84A	200
MBT	T-72M	11 (+19 to be delivered)
APC, IFV	M-80/80A	320
APC, IFV	M-86	49
APC, IFV	BTR-50	
APC, IFV	Lazar-I, II, III	
Armoured car	BRDM-2	80 (+20 to be delivered)
Armoured car	BOV	12

...continued

Category	Name	In Service
Artillery	M84 152mm	36
	M46 130mm	36
	122 mm D30	
	MI5 155mmSP	6
	2SI 122mm Sp	72
Mortar	M74, M75	6
MRLS	M-63/94 128mm	18
	M77 128mm	60
	M87 ORKAN 262mm	4
	Morava 128mm	
AA Gun, SAM	L-70 Bofors	
	9K35M Strela-10M	
	9K31M Strela-1M	
	9K32M Strela 2M	

New Procurements/ Upgrades

◆ The M-84A MBTs and M-80A IFVs are being progressively upgraded. The upgraded platforms have been unveiled in 2020.

◆ 30 T-72S main battle tanks and 30 BRDM-2 armoured reconnaissance vehicles are being donated by Russia with deliveries going on since 2019.

◆ Indigenously-built Lazar III 8X8 multi-role armoured personnel carrier (APC) has entered service.

◆ An upgraded variant of the BVP M-80A infantry fighting vehicle (IFV), designated as BVP M-80AB1, has been unveiled in 2017.

◆ The indigenously developed Morava 128mm multiple rocket launchers (MRL) are being progressively inducted.

◆ Upgrade of existing short-range and medium-range air defence systems is being planned.

◆ A contract has been signed with MBDA in 2019 for the acquisition of Mistral 3 short-range air defence missile systems.

AIR FORCE

Personnel: 4,000+

Equipment

Category	Name	In Service
Fighter, Trainer	MiG-21/21-U (being phased out)	10+
	MiG-29/MiG-29UB	10 (+4 more to be delivered)
	Galeb G-2	1
	Galeb G-4 (to be upgraded)	15
	Soko J-22 Orao (to retire)	
Transport, Laison	AN-26	14
	AN-2TD	1
	Seneca V	1

...continued

Category	Name	In Service
Helicopter	SA-341H/SA-342L Gazelle	50
	Mi-24, Mi-8, Mi-17	2+8+1
	Mi-17, Mi-17V-5	3 + 2
	Mi-35 (attack)	4
	H145M (utility)	9
UCAV	CH-92A Wing Loong	6
SAM	S-125M NEVA	6
	2K12 KUB	20+
	S-10/S-2M	100+
	Pantasir-S1	6

New Procurements/ Upgrades

◆ Eight MiG-29 Fulcrum fighters donated by Russia have entered service.

◆ Belarus donated four of its MiG-29 fighters in 2018 and is set to deliver four more such platforms in 2021.

◆ A total of 15 Utva Lasta (designated V-54 by Serbia) basic trainers being delivered by YugoImport.

◆ Funds have been allocated to upgrade the Supergaleb G-4 jet trainers to keep them operational till 2030.

◆ Nine H145M light utility helicopters have been acquired from Airbus Helicopters.

◆ Seven Mi-35 combat helicopters are being acquired from Russia with deliveries going on.

◆ The 2K12 Kub-M1 mobile surface-to-air missile (SAM) systems are being upgraded.

◆ Negotiations are going on with Russia for Buk-M1 and Buk-M2 air defence missile systems and Tunguska anti-aircraft missile/gun weapons.

◆ Six CH-92A (Wing Loong) medium altitude long endurance (MALE) unmanned combat aerial vehicles (UCAVs) have been received from China and inducted in service in 2020. More such platforms are likely to be procured. Serbia plans to produce the drones domestically by acquiring necessary technology from the Chinese source company Chengdu Aerospace Corporation.

◆ The FK-3 medium range radar guided surface-to-air missile defence systems have been acquired from China in 2020.

Defence Expenditure

Defence Budget: US$1.45 billion (2021)
Estimated defence spending in terms of GDP: 1.4%

Defence Production and R&D

Serbia has a well-developed defence industry. Once part of erstwhile Yugoslavia – a leading arms exporter – Serbia, until the 1990s, was a hub of weapons manufacturing units. Several of these arms factories were destroyed by NATO during the Kosovo War in 1999. Serbia again revived defence production and presently is one of the leading producers and exporters of military equipment in the region. Serbia has eight state-owned military plants. The country has exported weapons and military hardware to a number of countries in the Middle East, Africa, Asia, Europe and the US. Military exports by the country was over US$500 million in 2017. In 2018, it recorded an increase in defence exports which reached up to US$900 million.

Serbia has also jointly produced weapon systems with its neighbours Bosnia, Macedonia and Croatia. Russia too has expressed interest in establishing military-technical cooperation with the Balkan nation to jointly work on the production and modernisation of some types of weapons and equipment. The Serbian Government is now considering to allow the Russian Defence Ministry to open its office in Belgrade.

Defence Procurement

Serbia has revived its defence procurement plans in recent times following a decade of inactivity due to lack of funds. While the Army is procuring modern armoured vehicles and upgrading some of the existing land platforms to strengthen its fleet, acquisition of MiG-29 fighter aircraft donated by Russia and Belarus has bolstered the Serbian Air Force's air combat capabilities. Acquisition of transport, attack and utility helicopters and Chinese-built unmanned aerial vehicles in addition to new air defence systems has also strengthened the Armed Forces of the country.

CONTACT DETAILS
Ministry of Defence
Republic of Serbia
5th Bircaninova Street, Belgrade
Website (MoD): www.mod.gov.rs/
Armed Forces website: www.vs.rs/

SINGAPORE
(Capital: Singapore)

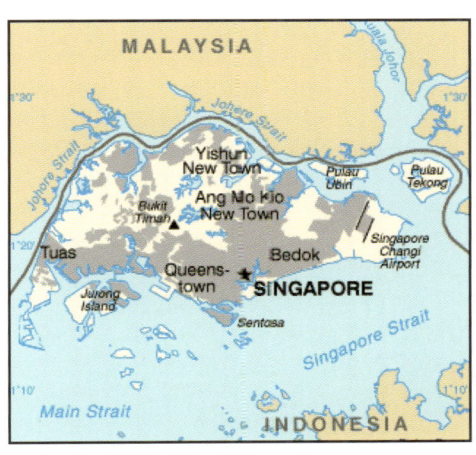

INTRODUCTION
Area: 697 sq km
Population: 5,866,139 (July 2021 est.)
Coastline: 193 km
Maritime claims: Territorial sea: 3 nm

KEY POLITICAL PERSONS

PRESIDENT & COMMANDER-IN-CHIEF: Halimah Yacob

PRIME MINISTER: Lee Hsien Loong

KEY DEFENCE PERSONS

DEFENCE MINISTER: Dr. Ng Eng Hen

CHIEF OF DEFENCE FORCE: Lt. Gen. Melvyn Ong

CHIEF OF ARMY: Brig. Gen Goh Si Hou

CHIEF OF NAVY: Rear Adm. Aaron Beng

CHIEF OF THE AIR FORCE: Maj. Gen. Kelvin Khaong

ECONOMY

Singapore has a highly developed and successful free-market economy. Manufacturing is the leading sector in the country's economic growth besides pharmaceuticals, and medical technology production. It places great emphasis on high-end manufacturing – semi-conductors and consumer electronics, as well as machinery, transport equipment, and ships. According to advance estimates from the Ministry of Trade & Industry, the manufacturing sector continued its strong performance in 2017. Singapore has attracted investments from more than 3,000 multinational corporations (MNCs) from the United States, Japan, and Europe due to its largely corruption-free government, skilled workforce, and advanced and efficient infrastructure. Foreign firms are found in almost all sectors of the economy. The country is a member of the Regional Comprehensive Economic Partnership. In 2015, Singapore formed the ASEAN Economic Community. The overall growth of the Singapore economy was 3.2% in 2018. Value-added manufacturing, particularly in the electronics and precision engineering sectors, remain key drivers of growth, as are the services sector, according to the World Bank. Singapore has taken measures to promote innovation, to encourage entrepreneurship and to re-train its workforce.

GDP (official exchange rate): $372.088 billion (2019 est.)

Real Growth Rate (GDP): 30.73% (2019 est.), 3.48% (2018 est.)

Industries: Electronics, chemicals, financial services, oil drilling equipment, petroleum refining, biomedical products, scientific instruments, telecommunication equipment, processed food and beverages, ship repair, offshore platform construction, entrepot trade.

Total Exports: $599.2 billion (2020 est.), $658.54 (2019 est.)

Export Commodities: Integrated circuits, refined petroleum, gold, gas turbines, packaged medicines (2019)

Major Markets: China 15%, Hong Kong 13%, Malaysia 9%, United States 8%, Indonesia 7%, India 5% (2019)

Total Imports: $490.68 billion (2020 est.), $552.71 billion (2019 est.)

Import Commodities: Integrated circuits, refined petroleum, crude petroleum, gold, gas turbines (2019)

Major Suppliers: China 15%, Malaysia 11%, United States 9%, Taiwan 7%, Japan 5%, Indonesia 5% (2019)

INTERNATIONAL DISPUTES

◆ Disputes with Malaysia over territorial waters, airspace, the price of fresh water delivered to Singapore from Malaysia, Singapore's extensive land reclamation works, bridge construction, and maritime boundaries in the Johor and Singapore Straits.

◆ In 2008, ICJ awarded sovereignty of Pedra Branca (Pulau Batu Puteh/Horsburgh Island) to Singapore, and Middle Rocks to Malaysia, but did not rule on maritime regimes, boundaries, or disposition of South Ledge.

◆ Indonesia and Singapore continue to work on finalisation of their 1973 maritime boundary agreement by defining unresolved areas north of Indonesia's Batam Island.

◆ Piracy remains a problem in the Malacca Strait.

DEFENCE

The Singapore Armed Forces (SAF) is the bedrock of Singapore's defence and security. Its mission is to enhance Singapore's peace and security through deterrence and diplomacy, to secure a swift and decisive victory over the aggressor in times of war. The SAF enjoys interactions with other militaries which range from exchanges of visits and joint exercises to attendance on each other's courses. A Special Operations Command Centre (SOCC) has been set up as part of a wide-ranging effort to enhance the SAF's ability to conduct counter-terrorism operations. The SOCC provides the SAF's Special Operations Task Force (SOTF) with the capability to centrally plan, monitor and manage multiple Counter-Terrorism (CT) and contingency operations. The SOTF comprises elite soldiers from the Army's Commandos and the Navy's Naval Diving Unit. Singapore works closely with its ASEAN neighbours and hosts the annual Shangri-La Dialogue (SLD) organised by the International Institute of Strategic Studies since 2002. Singapore is a part of the Five Power Defence Arrangement. The country has contributed to international operations like Afghanistan and also took part in disaster relief missions to affected nations.

ARMY

Personnel: 40,000+

Equipment

Category	Name	In Service
MBT	Leopard 2A4SGP	102
	AMX-13SM1	(Stored)
AIFV/APC	Hunter	
	Terrex AV-81	135
	Spider Light Strike vehicles	
	Bionix I/II	500+
	M113A2 Ultra IFV	250
Artillery	M-71 155mm	35
	FH-88 155mm	50
	FH2000 155mm	50+
	Pegasus 155mm light-weight	54
	SPH-1 Primus 155mm SP	54
Mortar	160mm	
	120mm	
	81mm	
	60mm	
MLR	Himars	18
ATGW	Milan-2	30
	Spike	
ATK weapon	Matador	
	Carl Gustaf 84mm	

New Procurements/Upgrades

◆ SAF plans to acquire more military systems and platforms such as the next-generation armoured fighting vehicles and Terrex infantry carrier vehicles.

NAVY

Personnel: 4,000

Equipment

Category	Name	In Service
Submarine	Challenger class (ex-Sjoormen class)	6
	Archer class (ex-Vastergotland class)	2
Frigate	Formidable class (modified La Fayette design)	6
Littoral Mission Vessel	RSS Independence	
	RSS Sovereignty	
	RSS Unity	
	RSS Justice	
	RSS Indomitable	
	RSS Fortitude	
	RSS Dauntless	
	RSS Fearless	
Patrol craft	Victory class missile corvette	6
	Fearless class ASW/patrol vessel	11
	Littoral Mission Vessel (LMV)	8
Mine warfare force	Bedok class (Landsort design)	4
	FB 31-42 class inshore patrol vessel	12
Amphibious Force	Endurance class LPD	4
	Perservance LSL	1
	LCM	6
	LCU	30

New Procurements/Upgrades

◆ Republic of Singapore Navy (RSN) first Invincible-class submarine 'Invincible' has started sea trials. The other three under construction submarines -Impeccable, Illustrious, and Inimitable are expected to be delivered by 2025.

◆ The RSN will acquire Multi-Role Combat Vessels (MRCVs) to replace the ageing Victory-class missile corvettes. Delivery is expected to begin from 2025 to 2030.

◆ The Navy plans to replace its Landing Ships Tank (LSTs) with bigger Joint Multi Mission Ships (JMMS) that has double the lifting capability of the LSTs.

◆ The Navy's Archer-and Challenger-class submarines will be replaced with four new Type 281SG submarines.

AIR FORCE

Personnel: 8,000

Equipment

Category	Name	In Service
Fighter	F-16C/D	62
	F-5S Tiger II	30
	F-15SG	12
	RF-5S Tigereye	6

...continued

Category	Name	In Service
Transport/ Tanker	A330 MRTT	6
	C-130 H	5
	KC-130B	4
	KC-130H	1
	KC-135	4
Trainer	Northrop F-5	9
	Alenia M-346	12
	EC-120B Colibri	5
	Pilatus PC-21	19
Helicopter	H225M	1
	AH-64D Apache Longbow	27
	AS.332 Super Puma	23
	CH-47D/SD	14
	S-70B Sea Hawk	6
Maritime patrol	F-50 Enforcer	5
UAV	Searcher	
	Heron 1	
	Hermes 450	
SAM	Aster	
	I-Hawk	6
	Mistral	36
	IGLA	75
	Spyder launchers	12
	RBS-70	330
AA Gun	35mm AA gun	24
Air Defence	Python-5	
	Spyder	

New Procurements/Upgrades

◆ Republic of Singapore Air Force (RSAF) has taken delivery of its first H225M helicopter. The Air Force has placed an order for 16 H-225M medium-lift utility helicopters from Airbus.

◆ The RSAF has taken delivery of new CH-47F Chinook heavy-lift helicopters from Boeing to replace the older Chinooks that have been in operation since 1994. Singapore has placed on order for 16 of the helicopters.

◆ The US has approved the sale of 12 Lockheed F-35Bs worth $2.7 billion to Singapore.

Defence Expenditure

Total defence spending: : $15.36 billion (2021), $10.77 billion (2020)

Defence spending in terms of GDP: 3.2% (2020)

Defence Production and R&D

Economic reforms over the past decades have enabled Singapore to invest heavily in defence and developing its military. As a result of this investment, Singapore Technologies

Engineering (ST Engineering) has become one of the world's most important defence firms, with over 100 subsidiaries. ST Engineering has a very close working relationship with the country's armed forces. Singapore has sold defence products to Indonesia, Chad, Nigeria, the Philippines, the United Arab Emirates and Brazil since 2000. Besides manufacturing small arms and munitions, the Bionix, the Terrex AV81 armoured fighting vehicles and the Bronco all-terrain tracked carrier are some vehicles designed and developed by ST Kinetics, a subsidiary of ST Engineering. The Defence Science and Technology Agency (DSTA) is responsible for performing acquisitions management, systems management, systems development for the Singapore Ministry of Defence (MINDEF) and the Singapore Armed Forces.

Defence Procurement

The Defence Science and Technology Agency (DSTA) is responsible for all aspects of defence procurement process such as contract preparations, pricing and risks, identification of contractors, as well as the evaluation of tenders received, and the subsequent contract award.

With an aim to make the Royal Singapore Army (RSA) a faster, heavier and deadly force, the government plans to acquire better platforms doubling the number of tracked and wheeled vehicles. This will include the next generation Howitzer, a fully automated 155mm weapon system. The Royal Singapore Navy (RSN) will receive more advanced vessels to replace the missile corvettes with Multi-Role Combat Vessels (MRCVs) by 2025. The Mechanised Combat Repair Vehicle (MCRV) will act as a manned "mothership" and be equipped with unmanned systems, such as drones, to boost its capabilities.

CONTACT DETAILS
Ministry of Defence
MINDEF Building
303 Gombak Drive
Tel: +656760-8828
Fax: +656764-6119
www.mindef.gov.sg

SLOVAKIA
(Capital: Bratislava)

INTRODUCTION
Area: 49,035 sq km
Population: : 5,436,066 (July 2021 est.)
Coastline: 0 km (Landlocked)
Maritime claims: None

KEY POLITICAL PERSONS

PRESIDENT & COMMANDER-IN-CHIEF: Zuzana Caputova

PRIME MINISTER: Eduard Heger

KEY DEFENCE PERSONS

DEFENCE MINISTER: Jaroslav Nad

CHIEF OF DEFENCE STAFF: Gen. Daniel Zmeko

COMMANDER OF LAND FORCES: Brig. Gen. Ivan Pach

COMMANDER OF AIR FORCE: Brig. Gen. Robert Toth

ECONOMY

Slovakia has made significant economic reforms since its separation from the Czech Republic in 1993. With a population of 5.4 million, the Slovak Republic has a small, open economy driven mainly by automobile and electronics exports, which account for more than 80% of GDP. Slovakia joined the EU in 2004 and the euro zone in 2009. The country's banking sector is sound and

predominantly foreign owned. Slovakia has been a regional FDI champion for several years, attractive due to a relatively low-cost yet skilled labour force, and a favourable geographic location in the heart of Central Europe. Exports and investment have been key drivers of Slovakia's robust growth in recent years. The unemployment rate fell to historic lows in 2017, and rising wages fueled increased consumption, which played a more prominent role in 2017 GDP growth. A favourable outlook for the Eurozone suggests continued strong growth prospects for Slovakia during the next few years, although inflation is also expected to pick up. Among the most pressing domestic issues potentially threatening the attractiveness of the Slovak market are shortages in the qualified labour force, persistent corruption issues, and an inadequate judiciary, as well as a slow transition to an innovation-based economy. The energy sector in particular is characterized by unpredictable regulatory oversight and high costs, in part driven by government interference in regulated tariffs.

The COVID-19 pandemic has adversely affected economic activities and the GDP is estimated to have shrunk by 7% in 2020, according to IMF data. The Slovak economy is projected to grow by 4.2% in 2021.

GDP (official exchange rate): $105.38 billion (2019 est.)

Real Growth Rate (GDP): 2.4% (2019 est.); 3.9% (2018 est.)

Industries: Automobiles; metal and metal products; electricity, gas, coke, oil, nuclear fuel; chemicals, synthetic fibers, wood and paper products; machinery; earthenware and ceramics; textiles; electrical and optical apparatus; rubber products; food and beverages; pharmaceutical

Total Exports: $113.96 billion (2019 est.); $113.09 billion (2018 est.)

Export Commodities: Cars and vehicle parts, video displays, broadcasting equipment, tires, refined petroleum (2019)

Major Markets: Germany 22%, Czechia 11%, Poland 7%, France 7%, Hungary 6%, Austria 5%, United Kingdom 5% (2019)

Total Imports: $107.88 billion (2019 est.); $105.67 billion (2018 est.)

Import Commodities: Cars and vehicle parts, broadcasting equipment, crude petroleum, natural gas, insulated wiring (2019)

Major Suppliers: Germany 18%, Czech Republic 18%, Poland 8%, Hungary 7%, Russia 5% (2019)

INTERNATIONAL DISPUTES

◆ Bilateral government, legal, technical and economic working group negotiations continue between Slovakia and Hungary over Hungary's completion of its portion of the Gabcikovo-Nagymaros hydroelectric dam project along the Danube.

◆ As a member state that forms part of the EU's external border, Slovakia has implemented the strict Schengen border rules.

DEFENCE

ARMY

Personnel: 6,000+

Equipment

Category	Name	In Service
MBT	T-72	17
APC, IFV	BMP-1/2	200
	Tatrapan T1	
	OT-90	50+
Armoured Car	Aligator	40
Artillery	D-30	8
	155mm ZUZANA	16
Mortar	81mm, 82mm, 98mm	
MRLS	RM 70/85 Modular	20+
ATGW/ATW	9P135	90
	9P148	6
	9S428	100
	Carl Gustaf 84mm	

New Procurements/ Upgrades

◆ A new 8×8 wheeled infantry fighting vehicle (IFV) would be developed in a joint programme with Finland's Patria. Slovakia plans to acquire up to 81 of the new IFVs in the coming years.

◆ The Government has approved funds to buy multi-purpose four-wheeled armoured vehicles.

◆ Delivery of eight ZUZANA-2 155mm self-propelled howitzers from Konstrukta-Defence has been completed in July 2021. A total of 25 such systems are being acquired as part of a deal finalised in 2018.

AIR FORCE

Personnel: 4,000

Equipment

Category	Name	In Service
Fighter, Trainer	MiG-29	5
	L-39	8
Transport	C-27J	2
	L-410	5
Helicopter	Mi-17	9
	UH-60M	6 (+3 on order)
SAM	2K12KUB	4
	S-300 PMU	1 Battery
	9K38 Igla	

New Procurements/ Upgrades

◆ The Defence Ministry has announced in 2018 to buy 14 new F-16V fighter platforms from the US under Foreign Military Sales (FMS) programme at the cost of €1.6 billion to replace its aging fleet of MiG-29 fighters. The new fighters are scheduled to be delivered from 2022 onwards.

◆ Acquisition of Bell 429 light utility helicopters has been approved by the US Government under foreign military sales. Slovakia has sought nine such platforms.

◆ A deal has been finalised in March 2021 to acquire seventeen 3D radars (six medium-range; five short-range; and six very short-range systems) from Israel Aerospace Industries (IAI). Delivery is expected to start from 2022 onward.

Defence Expenditure

Defence budget: €1.6 billion (proposed for 2021)

Defence spending in terms of GDP: 1.73% (2021)

Defence Production and R&D

The Slovakian defence industry is expanding ties with a number of countries in an attempt to find markets for its products while meeting its own procurement needs. A 2010 European Defence Agency assessment stated that Slovakia has a good research & development base for future high-tech military production.

Defence Procurement

The Government has moved ahead in its plans to acquire modern platforms for the Army and Air Force, which include new armoured vehicles, transport aircraft and helicopters to replace the ageing inventory of Soviet-era weaponry and systems. Acquisition of new fighter jets for the Air Force has also been finalised in 2018. The country intends to be self-reliant in defence production and planning. The Government has also announced to progressively boost defence spending to 2% of GDP by 2022, thereby achieving the NATO stipulated standard two years faster than planned.

CONTACT DETAILS
Ministry of Defence
Kutuzovova 8
832 47, Bratislava, Slovakia
Tel: 0960 11 22 33
E-mail: minister@mod.gov.sk
Website: www.mosr.sk/

ZUZANA-2 155mm self-propelled howitzers being delivered to the Slovak Army (Image credit: Slovak MoD website)

STRATEGIC INFORMATION
SOUTH AFRICA
(Capital: Pretoria)

INTRODUCTION
Area: 1,219,090 sq km
Population: 56,978,635 (July 2021 est.)
Coastline: 2,798 km
Maritime claims: Territorial sea: 12 nm
Contiguous zone: 24 nm
Exclusive Economic Zone: 200 nm
Continental shelf: 200 nm or to edge of the continental margin

GEOPOLITICAL IMPORTANCE

South Africa (Republic of South Africa) is located at the southern tip of Africa. It is divided into nine provinces. To the north of the country lie the neighbouring territories of Namibia, Botswana and Zimbabwe; to the east are Mozambique and Swaziland; while Lesotho is an enclave surrounded by South African territory. South Africa is the 25th largest country in the world. Mafadi in the Drakensberg at 3,450 m (11,320 ft) is the highest peak in South Africa. South Africa is a maritime nation, endowed with a double geo-political identity, both land and the sea. It is strategically situated along vital sea routes of the world, the South Atlantic, the Indian Ocean and the Southern Oceans. South Africa's maritime border extends from the Orange River in the West to Punta do Ouro in the East - a coastline of about 3,000 km and along which its marine resources are spread. The geo-strategic position of the country is also defined by its maritime zones, marine resources, marine ecology and conservation - as well as its maritime trade.

POLITICAL OVERVIEW

South Africa is a parliamentary republic and the President is both head of state and head of government. The President, Deputy President and the Ministers make up the executive branch of the national government. Executive power is exercised by the government. Legislative power is vested in both the government and the two chambers of Parliament, the Council of Provinces and the National Assembly. The judiciary is independent of the executive and the legislature. Government is three-tiered, with representatives elected at the national, provincial and local levels. Since the end of apartheid in the 1990s the African National Congress (ANC) has dominated South Africa's politics. The ANC is the ruling party in the national legislature, as well as in eight of the nine provinces. Nelson Mandela served as president of South Africa from 1994 to 1999, the first ever to be elected in a fully representative democratic election. He joined the African National Congress in 1944 and was engaged in resistance against the ruling National Party's apartheid policies after 1948. His negotiations in the early 1990s with South African President F.W. de Klerk helped end the country's apartheid system of racial segregation and ushered in a peaceful transition to majority rule. Mandela and de Klerk were jointly awarded the Nobel Prize for Peace in 1993 for their role in the ending of apartheid.

KEY POLITICAL PERSONS

PRESIDENT & COMMANDER-IN-CHIEF: Matamela Cyril Ramaphosa

DEPUTY PRESIDENT: David Mabuza

ECONOMY

South Africa is a middle-income emerging market with an abundant supply of natural resources. The economy of South Africa is the second largest in Africa, after Nigeria. South Africa enjoys relative macroeconomic stability and a largely pro-business environment. The country is the world's largest producer of platinum, vanadium, chromium, and manganese. South Africa is the most advanced, diversified, and productive economy in Africa. South Africa is well integrated into regional economic infrastructure as formalized by membership in the Southern African Development Community (SADC). In 2017, its GDP grew by 0.5% to an estimated USD 736.3 billion. As per the Statistics Department, South Africa, after shrinking sharply in the first quarter of 2019, the economy rebounded from a low base to record positive growth of 3,1% in the second quarter (April–June). Mining, finance, trade and government services were the main drivers of growth. Three industries (construction, agriculture and transport) registered a slump in production. Finance, real estate and business services - the largest industry in the South African economy - grew by 4.1%. This was on the back of stronger performances by the banking and insurance sectors. Government saw its biggest increase since the second quarter of 2014. A rise in contract employment in the public sector, particularly during May's general elections, underpinned the growth in government activity. South African exports of goods and services edged lower (-0.7%), largely influenced by a fall in the trade of pearls, precious and semi-precious stones. Imports jumped by 18.8% in the second quarter, driven mostly by a rise in trade of machinery and electrical equipment, mineral products and chemical products. Due to COVID-19 pandemic worldwide and lockdown restrictions, the economy of South Africa shrank by more than half in the second quarter, as per news reports. GDP growth is expected to rebound to 3% in 2021.

GDP (official exchange rate): $680.04 billion (2020), $730.91 billion (2019 est.)

Real Growth Rate (GDP): 0.06% (2019 est.), 0.7% (2018 est.)

Industries: Mining (world's largest producer of platinum, gold, chromium), automobile assembly, metalworking, machinery, textiles, iron and steel, chemicals, fertilizer, foodstuffs, commercial ship repair

Crude Oil - proved reserves: 15 million bbl (1 January 2018 est.)

Natural gas - proved reserves: 0 cu m (1 January 2012 est.)

Total Exports: $93.01 billion (2020 est.), $104.85 billion (2019 est.)

Export Commodities: Gold, platinum, cars, iron products, coal, manganese, diamonds (2019)

Major Markets: China 15%, United Kingdom 8%, Germany 7%, United States

6%, India 6% (2019)

Total imports: $77.86 billion (2020 est.), $103.12 billion (2019 est.)

Import Commodities: Crude petroleum, refined petroleum, cars and vehicle parts, gold, broadcasting equipment (2019)

Major Suppliers: China 18%, Germany 11%, United States 6%, India 5% (2019)

DEFENCE & SECURITY

The South African National Defence Force (SANDF) is the name of the present-day armed forces of South Africa. SANDF was created in 1994, following South Africa's first post-apartheid national elections and the adoption of a new constitution. The SANDF is subdivided into- the South African Army, the South African Air Force, the South African Navy, Joint Operations Command, Military Intelligence and the South African Medical Service. The commander of the SANDF is appointed by the President from one of the armed services and is accountable to the Minister of Defence. The SANDF continues to be part of the United Nations Peace support and enforcement missions in the DRC. The SANDF plays a key role in peace keeping operations on the African continent as well as providing election observers from time to time. Recent peacekeeping actions by the South African military include the South African intervention in Lesotho in order to restore the democratically-elected government after a coup, as well as extensive contributions to United Nations and African Union peacekeeping operations in the Democratic Republic of the Congo (MONUSCO) and Burundi.

KEY DEFENCE PERSONS

MINISTER OF DEFENCE & MILITARY VETERANS: Thandi Modise

CHIEF OF NATIONAL DEFENCE FORCE: Gen. Rudzani Maphwanya

CHIEF OF ARMY: Lt. Gen. Lawrence Khulekani Mbatha

CHIEF OF NAVY: Vice Adm. Mosuwa Samuel Hlongwane

CHIEF OF AIR FORCE: Lt. Gen. Wiseman Mbambo

Internal Conflict

South Africa is not currently engaged in an armed conflict.

External Conflict

◆ South Africa has placed military units to assist police operations along the border of Lesotho, Zimbabwe, and Mozambique to control smuggling, poaching, and illegal migration.

◆ As of January 2007, South Africa also supports large numbers of refugees and asylum seekers from the Democratic Republic of the Congo (33,000), Somalia (20,000), Burundi (6,500), and other states in Africa (26,000).

◆ The governments of South Africa and Namibia have not signed or ratified the text of the 1994 Surveyor's General agreement placing the boundary in the middle of the Orange River.

◆ In 2006, Swazi king advocated resort to the ICJ to claim parts of Mpumalanga and KwaZulu-Natal from South Africa.

THREAT PERSPECTIVE

South Africa at present is not faced with any military threats. Most identified threats are transnational in nature, related to the illegal flow of immigrants, terrorism, organised crime, climate change (connected to food and water security), regional instability and other socio-economic threats. In 1948, South Africa introduced apartheid as a systematic extension of pre-existing racial discrimination in the country. As a result, the country became increasingly isolated internationally until apartheid was ended and racial equality introduced in 1993. After South Africa held its first non-racial election in April 1994, most sanctions imposed by the international community in opposition to the system of apartheid were lifted. On 1 June 1994, South Africa rejoined the Commonwealth, and on 23 June 1994, the UN General Assembly accepted its credentials. South Africa served as the African Union's (AU) first president from July 2003 to July 2004. South Africa after emerging from the international isolation of the apartheid era has become a leading international actor.

Its principal foreign policy objective is to promote the economic, political, and cultural regeneration of Africa, through the New Partnership for African Development (NEPAD); to promote the peaceful resolution of conflict in Africa; and to use multilateral bodies to ensure that developing countries' voices are heard on international issues.

South Africa has played a key role in seeking an end to various conflicts and political crises on the African continent, including in Burundi, the Democratic Republic of the Congo, Madagascar, Sudan, Comoros, and Zimbabwe.

South African democracy is not under terminal threat. The country currently has no major defence and security related issues with other nations around the world and is more focused and determined in developing excellent and long-lasting relations with all countries, especially its neighbours in the Southern African Development Community (SADC) and the other members of the African Union.

In 2016, the United States embassy in Pretoria issued a statement warning US citizens about the threat of near-term attacks against places where US citizens assemble in South Africa. The embassy issued the warning after threats of terrorist attacks from ISIS. Later, South Africa disagreed with the assessment of the US and a statement in this regard was also issued the Department of International Relations and Cooperation (DIRCO) and the State Security Agency (SSA). South Africa Govt. noted that the information provided as a basis for the latest terror alerts on South Africa has been found to be unsubstantiated.

South Africa saw a decrease in suspected terrorism-related incidents in 2019, following an unusually high number of incidents in 2018. ISIS facilitation networks and cells remained a threat, after being first publicly acknowledged by the South African government in 2016. South Africa is a member of FATF and of ESAAMLG. South Africa's FIU, the Financial Intelligence Centre, is a member of the Egmont Group.

STRATEGIC RELATIONS

Africa: Africa is at the centre of South Africa's foreign policy. South Africa's development is inextricably linked to the development of Africa and the southern African region. Africa faces the challenge of positioning itself to address the marginalisation of the continent by engaging global role-players on socio-economic development and facilitating a fair and just global order. Angola-South Africa relations are quite strong as both fought together during Angolan Civil War and South African Border War. Botswana and South Africa issued a communiqué which said the two heads of state reviewed bilateral, regional and international issues of mutual interest such as the Agreement on the Establishment of a Joint Permanent Commission for Cooperation between Botswana and South Africa. Bilateral political and economic relations between Egypt and South Africa have improved greatly since 1993. The relationship is in good terms with Malawi also where the two countries in 2008 has signed a Memorandum of Understanding designed to enhance the relationship between the two countries through enhanced security cooperation. South Africa–Zimbabwe relations have been generally cordial since the end of apartheid in South Africa, although there have been tensions due to political troubles in Zimbabwe in recent years. Both the nations have recently agreed maintain border control simple and also discussed on progress made on a MoU on migration. Finally, in order to ensure peace, stability and security in the African continent, South Africa should continue to play leading role with initiatives from African Union (AU) and UN in conflict prevention, peacekeeping, peace-building, post-conflict reconstruction and in providing lasting solutions to other outstanding issues in the continent by keeping the commitment to African unity and integration within the framework of the Constitutive Act of the AU. As a strong democracy and sub-Saharan Africa's most developed economy, South Africa plays a key economic and political role on the African continent.

India: The bilateral relations between the Republic of India and the Republic of South Africa have grown strong since the end of apartheid in South Africa in 1994. Both nations have since developed close strategic, cultural and economic ties. The strategic significance of South Africa for India is undeniable. Both the countries have also developed defence cooperation, trading military equipments and joint exercises and programmes to train their armed forces. A number of bilateral agreements have been concluded between the two countries in diverse areas ranging from economic and commercial cooperation, defence, culture, heath, human settlements, public administration, science and technology and education. The year 2017 marked the 20 years of signing of the Red Fort Declaration for Strategic Partnership between India and South Africa. Indian Naval Ships and Sailing Vessels also regularly make port calls to South Africa. IN Ships Tarkash and Kolkata visited Cape Town from 1 to 13 October 2018 and participated in the 6th IBSA Maritime Exercise (IBSAMAR). INSV Tarini visited Cape Town from 2-14 March 2018 as part of Navika Sagar Parikrama. The South African Army participated in the Multinational Field Training Exercise for African Nations conducted by Indian Army at Pune in March 2019. There is substantial potential for trade growth between the two countries. Major Indian exports to South Africa include vehicles and components, transport equipment, drugs and pharmaceuticals, engineering goods, footwear, dyes and intermediates, chemicals, textiles, rice, and gems and jewellery, etc. Major Indian imports from South Africa include gold, steam coal, copper ores & concentrates, phosphoric acid, manganese ore, aluminium ingots & other minerals.

United States: The bilateral relations between South Africa and United States have been more significant and beneficial since the abolition of apartheid and 1994 democratic elections. The two countries share development objectives throughout Africa, and South Africa plays a key economic and political role in the African continent. South Africa is a strategic partner of the United States, particularly in the areas of health, security, and trade. South Africa and US belong to a number of the same international organizations, including the United Nations, International Monetary Fund, World Bank, G-20, and World Trade Organisation. South Africa qualifies for preferential trade benefits under the African Growth and Opportunity Act. South Africa is the largest U.S. trade partner in Africa, with a total two-way goods trade of USD14 billion in 2018, and more than 600 US firms operating in South Africa.

China: The relationship between China and South Africa was officially established in January 1998. The two countries currently enjoy an increasingly close relationship. Increasingly numerous official visits to each other's countries by their respective officials and rapidly increasing trade between the two countries has drawn them ever increasingly together. Relationship scaled new heights in 2010, with the comprehensive strategic partnership established between the two countries. In the 2010 Beijing Declaration, South Africa was upgraded to the diplomatic status of Strategic Comprehensive Partner by the Chinese government. There are over 140 medium-sized or large Chinese companies in South Africa. In July 2018, China announced to invest USD15 billion in South Africa's economy. South Africa also supports China's multilateral trade system.

Russia: The historical links between South Africa and the Russian Federation are strong. Full diplomatic relations were established between South Africa and the Russian Federation on 28 February 1992. Russia and South Africa distinguishes close positions on key international issues such as the strengthening of multilateralism, the role of the UN and international law, the fight against terrorism, non-proliferation, regional conflicts (North Africa, Middle East, Iraq, Afghanistan, the Iranian "nuclear dossier"), and in sub-Saharan Africa. Both the countries cooperate in various international platforms such as the UN, BRICS, the Group of Twenty, the format of Group of Eight plus five, IAEA, and others. Both of them are coordinating efforts on foreign policy issues. Relations and trade between the two countries are rapidly improving, citing an increase of 92% in trade turnover between them. Russia had also added South Africa to a list of developing countries, thus laying the groundwork for even larger increases in the future. In Oct 2019, Russian President Vladimir Putin opened the first-ever Russia Africa Summit in Sochi on the Black Sea as Kremlin has been working to expand its influence across the continent. The two leaders also confirmed mutual commitment to further develop strategic partnership and enhance collaboration of Moscow and Pretoria in the international arena on the sidelines of G20 Summit in Osaka on 28 June, 2019.

MULTILATERAL ALLIANCES

South Africa is active in the United Nations (UN), the African Union (AU), the Commonwealth of Nations, and International Atomic Energy Agency (IAEA), Inter-State Defence and Security Committee (South Africa), and others. Considered a possible permanent addition to the United Nations Security Council, South Africa was elected by the UN General Assembly to serve on the Security Council in 2007 for the first time ever. South Africa was a non-permanent member of the United Nations Security Council from October 2006 until 2008. The relationship between European Union (EU) and South Africa increased significantly since 1994 when both the countries entered into a broad framework agreement that would cover all spheres of cooperation. South Africa and the EU now cooperate with each other at various levels and in many forums. Other than trade and development cooperation, various dialogue meetings address issues pertinent to South Africa, the EU, Africa and the rest of the world. South Africa is a member of BRICS.

DEFENCE CAPABILITIES

ARMY: The South African Army is an integral part of the new South African National Defence Force. It is now becoming increasingly involved in peacekeeping efforts in southern Africa, often as part of wider African Union operations. The South African Army released its ARMY VISION 2020 guidelines document during 2006. This strategic guide is an attempt to transform the South African military into a professional, effective, well-equipped and well-trained force that is able to deploy quickly. As per the vision, the objective of the army is to defend and protect South Africa and its territorial integrity and vital interests by providing prepared and supported landward combat forces, also to contribute to peacekeeping operations in the continent at large.

Personnel: 38,000

Equipment

Category	Name	In Service
MBT	Olifant 1A/1B	130+
APC/ MICV/IFV	Rooikat 76	150+
	Ratel ZT3 tank destroyer	50
	Ratel IFV	900+
	Casspir	300+
	Mamba	480
Artillery	GV5 155mm towed	50
	GV6 155mm SP	40+
Mortar	M1/M4 60mm	
	M3 81mm	1100
	M5 120mm	20+
RCL Gun	M40 105mm	150+
MRL	Bateleur 127mm	20+
	Valkiri Mk 1 127mm	20+
SAM	Cactus (Crotale)	50+
	Starstreak	50+
Anti-Tank GW	Ingwe	
	MILAN ER	250+
AA gun	Oerlikon 35mm	35
	23mm	35
UAV	Vulture	

New Procurements/ Upgrades

◆ South African developer and supplier of defence and security products, Milkor, was recently awarded a contract to supply 40mm, handheld grenade launchers to the South African Army. Part of the Armscor contract was the supply of a full logistic support package for the Y4 grenade launchers, encompassing a Logistic Support Analysis Plan (LSAP), operator support publications and training, and technical support publications and training.

◆ South Africa Army is upgrading their mine-detection and electronic warfare systems along with unmanned aerial vehicles and other components.

NAVY: The South African Navy is the navy of the South African National Defence Force. The role of the navy is to prepare for and to conduct naval operations in defence of the Republic of South Africa, its citizens and interests and to carry out peacetime operations in support of other national objectives. Other responsibilities include the maintenance, preservation and the provision of naval services in support of other state departments and authorities, including search and rescue, protection of maritime resources, and diplomatic sea transport support.

Naval Bases: Simons Town (main naval base and dockyard), Naval Station Port Elizabeth, Naval Station Durban.

Personnel: 65,00

Equipment

Category	Name	In Service
Submarine	Heroine Class	3
Frigate	Valour class	4
Light Force	Warrior class FAC	4
	T Craft Class IPV	3
	Namacurra Class HPB	
Mine warfare force	River Class	4
	CITY Class type 351	4
Auxiliary	SAS Drakensberg	1
	SAS Protea	1
SAM	Umkhonto	
ASM	Exocet MM40 Block 2	8

Naval Aviation

Category	Name	In Service
Helicopter	Atlas Oryx M2	1
	Westland Super Lynx 300 Mk64	4
Aircraft	Douglas Jet Prop DC-3 AMI	5

The South African Navy does not operate any aircraft itself. The aircraft used on ships or supporting the Navy are operated by 22 Squadron of the South African Air Force.

New Procurements/ Upgrades

◆ Cybicom Atlas Defence has been awarded a support and maintenance contract in partnership with ThyssenKrupp Marine systems by South African Navy.

◆ Damen Shipyards Cape Town (DSCT) has been awarded a second major contract from the South African Department of Defence. After a public tender, DSCT received the order for three 62 metre, multi-mission Inshore Patrol Vessels (IPV) in December 2017. Armscor, the acquisition agency for the South African Department of Defence, ordered the three IPVs – known as the Damen Stan Patrol (SPa) 6211 – as part of the government's efforts to boost maritime security.

◆ South Africa Navy awards defence contract to Kongsberg Maritime for integrated hydro acoustic and bridge system technology package.

◆ On 28th August 2020, Damen Shipyards Cape Town (DSCT) held a keel-laying. The keel-laying was for the second of three Multi-Mission Inshore Patrol Vessels (MMIPV) that DSCT is building for the South African Navy's Project BIRO.

AIR FORCE: The South African Air Force (SAAF) is the air force of South Africa, with headquarters in Pretoria. SAAF is involved in regional peace-keeping, disaster relief and maritime patrol operations. Current air combat capabilities are limited to the Gripen multi-role fighter and the Rooivalk combat support helicopter to allow regional deployments while maintaining national air space protection and training obligations.

Air Bases: Bloemspruit, Durban, Waterkloof, Langebaanweg, Overberg, Swartkop, Thaba Tshwane, Ysterplaat, Hoedspruit, Makhado, Port Elizabeth, TEK Base, Valhalla, & Air Force Mobile Deployment Wing.

Personnel: 9,500

Equipment

Category	Name	In Service
Fighter	Gripen C & D	25+
Helicopter	Oryx - MKI and MKII	40+
	Rooivalk MKI	10
	MBB/ Kawasaki BK 117	5
	A109LUH	20+
	Westland Super Lynx Mk300	4
Trainer	BAE Hawk Mk120	20+
	Pilatus PC-7 MkII	50+
Transport	C-130BZ Hercules	7
	Cessna 208B	10
	Super King Air 200/ 300	
	Pilatus PC-12	
	CASA C-212-200 / 212-300	4
	Cessna Citation 550	
Maritime Patrol	C-47TP	10+
Weapon	IRIS-T (AAM)	
	A-Darter (AAM)	
	Mokopa (ASM)	
	Lightning III targeting pod	
	Type 159 Rocket Launcher	

...continued

Category	Name	In Service
Weapon	FZ90 70mm FFAR	
	GBU-12 Paveway II	
	Umbani PGM	
Ground defence	RADAR sector control centres	2
	Mobile long range radar	2
	Static radar	2
	Tactical mobile radar	4
	Protection squadrons	10+

New Procurements/ Upgrades

◆ GKN Aerospace has signed a three year contract extension with ARMSCOR for technical product support, maintenance and parts supply agreement for the South African Air Force's Gripen RM12 engines. The contract extension is worth over USD 8 million (Initial order value R89 million).

◆ Defence and security company Saab has received a support contract for the South African Gripen weapon system. The order has a total value of SEK 206 million (ZAR 314 million) over the period November 2017 to February 2020. The South African Air Force has been operating the Gripen fighter system since 2008 when the first Gripen was delivered. The support contract, signed between Saab and Armscor, enables Saab to deliver efficient support in a sustainable manner with a long-term horizon. Through the contract, Saab will deliver support related services like airworthiness management, engineering support, maintenance, repair and overhaul, spares replenishment and updates of technical publications.

South African soldiers board a C-130 Hercules aircraft for a practice jump at Air Force Base Bloemspruit in Bloemfontein, South Africa, July 23, 2013, in preparation for exercise Shared Accord 2013. Image Credit: defenseimagery.mil, US

Nuclear Weapons Programme

South Africa was the first and only country to build nuclear weapons and then possibly voluntarily dismantle them in 1989. The country was involved in research and development of strategic weapon systems including nuclear, biological, and chemical weapons from 1960s to 1980s. South Africa also acquired the technology to build nuclear weapons. South Africa developed at least six nuclear warheads, which it later acknowledged, along with a variety of missiles and other conventional weapons. Later, after intensive diplomatic efforts by other nations, the South African government dismantled all of its nuclear weapons. The country has been a signatory of the Biological Weapons Convention since 1975, the Nuclear Non-Proliferation Treaty since 1991, and the Chemical Weapons Convention since 1995. The country also banned any further development, manufacture, marketing, import, or export of nuclear weapons or explosives, as required by the NPT. The country joined the Nuclear Suppliers Group (NSG) in 1995 and also played a leading role in the establishment of the African Nuclear Weapons Free Zone Treaty, also known as the Treaty of Pelindaba in 1996. South Africa also signed the Comprehensive Test Ban Treaty (CTBT) in 1996 and ratified it in 1999. The Treaty of Pelindaba came into effect on 15 July 2009 and the African Commission on Nuclear Energy, in order to verify compliance with the treaty, has been established and headquartered in South Africa.

Major Armament Producers

Domestic suppliers: Denel, Paramount Group, Reutech Radar Systems, BAE Systems Land Systems South Africa, Land Systems OMC.

Foreign suppliers: AgustaWestland, BAE Systems, Heckler & Koch, IVECO, MAN, Saab AB, Thales, ThyssenKrupp.

Foreign supplier countries: US, France, Switzerland, Israel, UK, Belgium.

South Africa's Defence Industry is recognised as being among the most technologically advanced in the world. There are in excess of 180 businesses registered with the National Conventional Armaments Control Committee (NCACC) with a primary focus on the manufacturing of weapons of war. The Defence Industry is recognised by Government as a fully fledged economic sector and should it be adequately funded, has the potential to significantly contribute to the economy of South Africa. In the past, South Africa has attempted to attain a level of self-sufficiency in the design and manufacture of complete armament systems commensurate with the high threat perception prevalent at the time. Since the fall of the Berlin Wall and the negotiated settlement in South Africa which followed shortly thereafter, the strategic environment within the region has undergone a dramatic change. The central strategic challenge is no longer that of deterrence, but of building common regional security.

Armscor (also ARMSCOR), the Armaments Corporation of South Africa, was a government-supported weapons producing conglomerate officially established in 1968, primarily as a response to the international sanctions by the United Nations against South Africa that began in 1963 and were formalised in 1967. The corporation later assumed the role of a procurement agency for the South African National Defence Force (SANDF). ARMSCOR's primary function is to provide a cost-effective service to the SANDF for the execution of its capital acquisition programmes and the logistical and maintenance support that it requires. Armscor maintains strategic capabilities and technologies and promotes the local defence industry. Following the split off of Armscor and its manufacturing subsidiaries, the South African government established Denel, a leading state-owned manufacturer of defence and aerospace systems, in 1991. Denel inherited most of Armscor's production and research facilities. According to a recent budget speech by South African Minister of DoD, Armscor has developed a new strategy which strongly focuses on the SANDF as its primary client. This strategy deals with the rapid acquisition of equipment in support of urgent operational requirements for the SANDF. Armscor is assisting the DOD with developing the Funding Model to support the implementation of the Defence Review 2015. The mission of the Armaments Corporation of South Africa SOC Ltd (ARMSCOR) is to become the premier defence technology and acquisition service provider for the South African Government and its allies on the African continent and in the world. The corporation maintains strategic capabilities and technologies, and promotes the local defence related industry, ensuring that the South African National Defence Force receives quality equipment to carry out its mandate.

Denel along with its associated companies has been manufacturing a number of weapons, including artillery, air defence missiles, anti-tank missiles, UAVs and aircraft components for the South African armed forces as well as for the global market. Reutech Radar Systems (RRS) is a subsidiary of Reunert Limited, a South African defence and aerospace technology company. The company manufactures radar and radar-related systems. Paramount Group, a South African group of companies, offers a range of armoured vehicles, military aircraft, equipment and training to governments. Land

Systems OMC is a South African company that produces a range of armoured vehicles. BAE Systems Land Systems South Africa is a South African defence company and a subsidiary of BAE Systems Land Systems. Denel currently has nearly USD 744 million in export contracts on its books. Denel's output is primarily directed to meet the requirements of the South African military, which recently purchased state-of-the art Rooivalk helicopters manufactured by Denel.

DEFENCE DEALS

While acquisition of new naval vessels for the navy is over, delivery of new fighter aircraft for the Air Force is going on as part of the modernisation and transformation programme. Procurement of a large number of BADGER Armoured Fighting Vehicles for the Army is also going on. Development of a new Main Battle Tank under project 'Aorta' and a new generation armoured personnel carrier under project 'Sepula' for the Army are in planning stage. Under project Protector, the government is planning the development and partial acquisition of a mobile ground-based air defence system. For the Navy, acquisition of nine indigenous multi-purpose hull vessels is being planned under project Biro. Under project Millennium, one to three multi-mission strategic support ships are being planned. The South African Aerospace Maritime and Defence Export Council (Saamdec) is developing a collaboration with Indian defence industry in the field of ammunition (small and medium calibre), artificial intelligence, cybersecurity, electronic warfare, landward weapons (especially artillery), robotics and unmanned aerial vehicles. India and South Africa are also focusing on maritime security and joint defence ventures.

Joint Venture Programmes

◆ Russia's Rosoboronexport and South Africa are discussing the possibility of joint development of defence-related products primarily in the area of radar equipment and rocket engines.

◆ Russia and South Africa are also planning to work together to develop and manufacture weapons and military equipment, as per Director of the Russian Federal Service for Military-Technical Cooperation Dmitry Shugayev.

◆ South Africa's Denel has confirmed the establishment of a joint venture (JV) with United Arab Emirates (UAE) company Tawazun Holdings. The JV is called Tawazun Dynamics. The joint venture will develop, manufacture and integrate guided systems for conventional air munitions. The UAE's Air Force will be the first customer of Tawazun Dynamics.

◆ Saudi Arabian Military Industries (SAMI) and South Africa's Paramount Group have signed a collaboration agreement as part of Saudi Arabia's efforts to develop its own domestic defence industry.

◆ The Advanced High-Performance Reconnaissance Light Aircraft (Ahrlac), is a light reconnaissance and counter-insurgency aircraft developed in South Africa by AHRLAC Holdings, a joint venture between the Paramount Group and Aerosud. A joint venture between Paramount Group and Aerosud has given South Africa's aviation sector an important boost, creating a world-class Mirage F1 supply, support and upgrade capability for worldwide customers.

DEFENCE BUDGET

Total defence spending: $4.092 billion (est.)

Estimated defence spending in terms of GDP: 0.9% of GDP (2021 est.), 1.1% of GDP (2020 est.)

Defence Budget Summary (Source: National Treasury Department, South Africa)

Vote expenditure trends and estimates by programme and economic classification:

Budget Programme	Medium-term Expenditure Estimates		
	R Million 2021/2022	R Million 2022/2023	R Million 2023/2024
Administration	5 514.1	5 623.4	5 640.2
Force Employment	3 596.5	3 586.4	3 606.2
Landward Defence	14 523.4	14 532.2	14 833.6
Air Defence	5 969.2	5 914.7	5 902.5
Maritime Defence	4 278.1	4 471.0	4 511.5
Military Health Support	5 306.1	5 241.1	5 246.8
Defence Intelligence	758.0	1 116.0	1 140.7
General Support	6 323.1	6 292.1	6 278.3
Total	46 268.7	46 777.0	47 159.8

According to treasury.gov.za, Govt. of South Africa, Cabinet has approved an overall reduction of 4.5 per cent (R15.4 billion) on the department's budget over the medium term. Accordingly, expenditure decreases at an average annual rate of 4.5 per cent, from R54.2 billion in 2020/21 to R47.2 billion in 2023/24. This includes reductions of R119.9 million in 2021/22, R145.2 million in 2022/23 and R140 million in 2023/24 on transfers to the Armaments Corporation of South Africa.

CONCLUSION

South Africa's national security focuses on human security, sovereignty and the related priorities of territorial integrity, constitutional order, the well-being, prosperity and upliftment of its people, economic growth and good governance. Regionally, South Africa's national security hinges on the stability, unity and prosperity of the Southern African Region in particular, and the African continent in general. The growth and success of the South African economy depend on peace, stability, economic development and deepened democracy on the African continent, thereby placing Africa at the centre of South Africa's foreign policy and Defence's diplomacy efforts. The primary object of the SANDF is to defend and protect the country, its territorial integrity and its people, in accordance with the Constitution and the principles of international law regulating the use of force. South Africa and SANDF continues to support regional and continental processes to respond to and resolve crises, promote peace and security, strengthen regional integration, significantly increase intra-African trade and champion sustainable development in Africa. South Africa is a major player in the African continent which aspires to shape the peace and security of the region. South Africa's vision for 2025 is to be a successful and influential member of the international community, supported by a globally competitive economy on a continued growth path that has made significant inroads in addressing unemployment, inequality and poverty in South Africa and contributing to the development of the region and continent. South Africa's longer-term stability is linked to the success of the South African government and its partners in fighting poverty and reducing the toll of the AIDS pandemic. The country is the only African nation with strength and industrial capability to develop a wide variety of military products. South Africa's influence in the African continent by playing a leading role both on specific issues and within their regions such as taking policy initiatives, building institutions and originating solutions has created unprecedented opportunities for the country in the international arena. The next strategic challenge is for South Africa to utilise this opportunity to take the initiative in shaping a new global order. Hence, South Africa should continue keep strong bilateral relations in order to enhance the strength of South Africa's international positions and influence in multilateral organizations. SANDF, as a national asset, is defending the country's borders and supporting the national security imperatives, foreign policy objectives and its' economic interests. In terms of domestic security, the SANDF is currently employed in co-operation with the SAPS in the maintenance of law and order and in border protection against non-military threats. Securing South Africa's borders remains a matter of national security for South African DoD, requiring adequate resources supported by an appropriate sensor capability and infrastructures.

CONTACT DETAILS

Ministry of Defence
Defence Headquarters
Armscor Building
cnr Delmas Avenue and Nossob Streets
Erasmusrand, PRETORIA
Tel: 012 355 6200
Web: http://www.dod.mil.za/
Email: info@dod.mil.za

Information Centre
Department of Defence (Defence Corporate Communication)
Private Bag X161
Pretoria 0001
Tel: (012) 355 6321; Fax: (012) 355 6398
E-mail: info@mil.za

STRATEGIC INFORMATION
SOUTH KOREA
(Capital: Seoul)

INTRODUCTION
Area: 99,720 sq km
Population: 51,715,162 (July 2021 est.)
Coastline: 2,413 km
Maritime claims: 12 nm; between 3 nm and 12 nm in the Korea Strait
Contaguous Zone: 24nm
Exclusive Economic Zone: 200 nm

GEOPOLITICAL IMPORTANCE

South Korea occupies the southern portion of the Korean Peninsula. It shares a land border with North Korea. The mountainous and strategically located peninsula is flanked by the Yellow Sea to the West, and Sea of Japan (East Sea) to the East. Its southern tip lies on the Korea Strait and the East China Sea. South Korea is a regional power and a world leader in IT, shipbuilding and vehicle manufacturing. The country has demonstrated incredible economic growth to become a high-tech industrialised economy. South Korea participates in various United Nations Peace Keeping Operations and peace activities in Multi-National Forces (MNF). The country has multiple organisational memberships, including the ASEAN Plus mechanism, Uniting for Consensus, G20 and OECD. It is a founding member of APEC and the East Asia Summit.

POLITICAL OVERVIEW

The Republic of Korea (ROK) is a republic with powers nominally shared among the Presidency, the Legislature, and the Judiciary, but traditionally dominated by the President. The president is the chief of state and is directly elected by the people for a single term of five years with no additional terms being allowed. The president who is head of the Executive Branch cannot dissolve the National Assembly, but the Assembly can hold the President ultimately accountable to the Constitution by means of an impeachment process. The prime minister is appointed by the president and approved by the National Assembly. As the principal executive assistant to the president, the prime minister supervises the administrative ministries and manages the Office for Government Policy Coordination under the direction of the president. The 299 members of the unicameral National Assembly are elected for a 4-years term.

The State Council is the highest body for policy deliberation and resolution in the executive branch. The Cabinet is made up of between 15 and 30 members, and includes the president, the prime minister, the vice prime minister, and cabinet-level ministers of 17 ministries. The president is constitutionally the chairperson of the Cabinet, with the Prime Minister as the vice chairperson. South Korea's Judicial system comprises of the Supreme Court, Regional Appellate Courts, and the Constitutional court. The Judiciary is independent under the constitution. The Supreme Court is the head of the judicial branch and is the final court of appeal. Appellate courts are below the Supreme Court, which are stationed in five of the country's major cities.

KEY POLITICAL PERSONS

PRESIDENT & COMMANDER IN CHIEF: Moon Jae-in

PRIME MINISTER: Chung Sye-kyun

ECONOMY

South Korea is known for its spectacular rise from one of the world's poorest country to a developed, high-income country. It achieved an incredible record of growth and global integration from the 1960s to become a high-tech industrialised economy today. The growth of the industrial sector was the principal stimulus to its economic development. The country's mixed economy is dominated by family-owned conglomerates called 'chaebols.' South Korea adopted an export-oriented economic strategy to fuel its economy, and in 2014, it was the world's seventh largest exporter and seventh largest importer. It has expanded its network of free trade agreements to help bolster exports, and has since implemented 16 free trade agreements covering 58 countries including the United State and China. It is an important contributor to the International Development Association (IDA), the fund established to support the world's poorest countries. The World Bank has described Korea as one of the fastest-growing major economies of the next generation along with BRIC and Indonesia. South Korea ranks 10th among the world's largest economic powers and 4th in Asia in 2021.

GDP (official exchange rate): $1,646,604,000,000 (2019 est.)

Real Growth Rate (GDP): 2.04% (2019 est.), 2.91% (2018 est.)

Industries: Electronics, telecommunications, automobile production, chemicals, shipbuilding, steel.

Total Exports: $683.996 billion (2019 est.), $672.442 billion (2018 est.)

Export Commodities: Integrated circuits, cars and vehicle parts, refined petroleum, ships, office machinery (2019)

Major Markets: China 25%, United States 14%, Vietnam 9%, Hong Kong 6%, Japan 5% (2019)

Total Imports: $599.705 billion (2019 est.), $603.535 billion (2018 est.)

Import Commodities: Crude petroleum, integrated circuits, natural gas, refined petroleum, coal (2019)

Major Suppliers: China 22%, United States 12%, Japan 9% (2019)

DEFENCE & SECURITY

The country has laid out a major defence reforms plan under which it intends to transform its military from a manpower-intensive force to a technology-intensive force, from a military-dominated one to a civilian-dominated one, and from a service-oriented force structure to having one with joint operational capability with a long-term vision. It has adopted the 'Advanced Elite Military' as its vision to achieve the objectives of national security and national defence. To this end, it has identified eight policy tenets which it is actively pursuing, i.e. establishing a defence posture for comprehensive security; strengthening the ROK-US military alliance and expansion of defence diplomacy and cooperation; providing military support for the advancement in inter-Korea relations; bolstering advanced military capabilities; nurturing highly qualified military personnel and improving the training and education system; enhancing management efficiency; nurturing an attractive and rewarding military; striving to become a defence force that serves the people.

KEY DEFENCE PERSONS

MINISTER OF DEFENCE: Gen. Suh Wook

CHAIRMAN OF THE JOINT CHIEFS OF STAFF: Gen. Won In-choul

CHIEF OF STAFF OF THE ARMY: Gen. Nam Yeong-shin

CHIEF OF STAFF OF THE NAVY: Adm. Boo Suk-jong

CHIEF OF STAFF OF THE AIR FORCE: Lt. Gen. Park In-ho

External Conflict

South and North Korea have remained technically in a state of war ever since the 1950-53 Korean War which ended in a truce and not a peace treaty. Over the past decades, small-scale skirmishes have flared up repeatedly along their land and sea borders. Tensions were particularly high in the Korean peninsula after the sinking of the South Korean warship Cheonan in 2010. Tension between the two neighbours have escalated after repeated nuclear weapons tests carried out by the North. The Northern Limit Line or North Limit Line (NLL) is a disputed inter-Korea maritime demarcation line in the Yellow (West) Sea between the Democratic People's Republic of Korea (DPRK) in the North, and the Republic of Korea (ROK) in the South. This line of military control acts as the de facto maritime boundary between North Korea and South Korea. Tensions escalated in 2017 when North Korea conducted its sixth nuclear test in September and a new, successful test of an intercontinental ballistic missile in November. In June 2018, at the Singapore Summit, the United States and North Korea committed to build "new US-DPRK relations" and work for peace on the Korean Peninsula. The leaders, President Donald J. Trump and Kim Jong-un met again in Vietnam in late February 2019. However, the two countries have been mired in a diplomatic stalemate since then.

Territorial disputes

◆ The Liancourt Rocks, called Dokdo in Korean and Takeshima in Japanese, are a group of islets in the Sea of Japan (East Sea) whose ownership is disputed between Japan and South Korea. Although Liancourt Rocks are claimed by both Korea and Japan, the islets are currently administered by South Korea, which has its Korean Coast Guard stationed there.

◆ Military Demarcation Line within the 4-km-wide Demilitarized Zone has separated North from South Korea since 1953. Periodic incidents with North Korea in the Yellow Sea over the Northern Limit Line, which South Korea claims as a maritime boundary.

THREAT PERSPECTIVE

North Korea, a nuclear power, in particular poses a major security threat to South Korea by developing and increasing its large stockpile of conventional military hardware while advancing in its nuclear weapons programme, and other weapons of mass destruction. The attack and sinking of a ROK Navy ship and the shelling of Yeonpyeongdo Island in 2010 have further escalated the military conflict between Seoul and Pyongyang. The collapse of the de-nuclearisation negotiations between the United States and North Korea and renewed long-range missile testing by DPRK continue to pose a threat. Ballistic missiles tests in the recent past by both South and North Korea have revealed an escalating arms race. The dual launches have raised fresh regional security fears. North Korea announced it had test-fired cruise missiles that can carry a nuclear warhead and evade detection which the North Korean media described as the "railway mobile missiles system." South Korea also announced it had successfully tested its first submarine-launched ballistic missile. The escalations are fomenting tensions not seen since 2017, when Kim Jong-un of North Korea and President Donald Trump held peace talks.

STRATEGIC RELATIONS

United States: South Korea and the United States have strong economic, diplomatic, and military ties, although they have at times disagreed with regard to policies towards North Korea. The United States helped establish the modern state of South Korea and fought on its UN-sponsored side in the Korean War and South Korea has extended support to the US in every war since the Vietnam War, and most recently during the Iraq War. The two countries work together to combat regional and global threats and to strengthen their economies. Under the US-ROK Mutual Defence Treaty, the United States has maintained Army, Air Force, Navy, and Marine personnel in South Korea to extend support and help the ROK defend itself against external aggression. In 2020, the two countries commemorated the 67th anniversary of the U.S-ROK alliance and the 70th anniversary of the outbreak of the Korean War.

India: ROK and India, the two largest democracies in Asia, have declared their relationship as a strategic one. In the recent past the two sides have agreed to boost defence ties through more military exercises and training as part of efforts to expand their relationship beyond economic partnership. In 2021, South Korean Defence Minister Suh Wook visited India giving a boost to their growing defence and security ties. The two sides reviewed the state of relations and appreciated the depth and breadth of their bilateral defence ties across the three services of the two militaries as well as between the agencies handling defence technology and industry.

European Union: The EU-Korea relationship has evolved over the past few years, based on shared values, common issues of global concern and the increasing role of both partners on the world stage. This is demonstrated by the signing of two agreements during 2010 – the new Framework Agreement and Free Trade Agreement (FTA). The agreements address a wide range of international concerns, including non-proliferation of weapons of mass destruction, human rights, cooperation in the fight against terrorism, climate change, energy security and development assistance. On the basis of these two agreements, the EU and South Korea decided at their October 2010 summit to upgrade their relationship to a strategic partnership.

Japan: Tokyo has recognised South Korea as the only legitimate government in the whole Korean peninsula based on the Treaty on Basic Relations between Japan and the Republic of Korea. And despite not having any defence relationship with Seoul, Tokyo has nonetheless backed the US's contingency plans to dispatch the United States' armed forces based in Japan to South Korea in the event of a North Korean attack on the South. Japan is South Korea's second-biggest trading partner.

China: The ROK-China relationship has been elevated to a 'strategic cooperative partnership' level, leading to active defence cooperation and exchange. Visits by naval vessels, military sports teams, and military history and training institutions have been very active. Despite a robust economic relationship, China and South Korea diverge over a number of issues, notably the nuclear issue on the Korean peninsula, fishing in disputed territories as well as a lack of mutual trust in strategic terms.

Russia: South Korea's relations with Russia has been elevated to strategic cooperative partnership. The two sides are strengthening their cooperation to resolve the North Korean nuclear issue and to develop energy resource opportunities. They are stepping up the level of cooperation and exchange in the area of defence and security through senior level exchange visits and cooperation in the defence industry and technology sectors. They have decided to hold defence strategic dialogues on a regular basis.

DEFENCE CAPABILITIES

In South Korea, military service is a constitutional duty, and the Law on Conscription applies to all males. The Ministry of National Defence (MND) is gradually reducing the service period to relieve citizens' burden and allow more people to fulfil their obligations by assigning service duties fairly.

The president is the commander-in-chief of the South Korean armed forces. The chairman of the joint chiefs of staff, a 4-star general or admiral is the senior officer of the armed forces and has the operational authority over the armed forces, with directions from the president through the defence minister. The joint chiefs of staff (JCS) enables close mutual support between the country's Army, Navy, and Air Force and the integration of the three services. The JCS carry out joint and combined operations by executing operational command over joint units and operations commands. Under the "Defence Reform 2.0", announced in July 2018 by MND, the number of generals and soldiers will be reduced and the length of compulsory military service will be reduced to 18 – 22 months by 2022.

South Korea is undertaking an ambitious slate of defence reforms to keep its conventional military edge. A prototype K-21 fighter jet was unveiled on April 21, 2021. The borders of the country is planned to be protected by an AI-based surveillance systems known as the Mobile Rail Robot Surveillance System. South Korea is already exporting indigenous tanks, missiles, and other weapons. Reportedly, it has decided to mass produce by 2025 a new type of tactical ground-based missiles designed to destroy underground artillery bases. The South Korean navy has commissioned its first indigenously developed submarine capable of launching ballistic missiles to enhance South Korea's underwater defence capabilities. Reportedly there are plans to develop an indigenous version of Israel's Iron Dome missile defence system. South Korea has its own arsenal of missiles. The country has successfully developed a ballistic missile called the "Frankenmissile." South Korea does not possess nuclear weapons. South Korea also has anti-missile defence systems – Patriot missiles and THAAD. Seoul's military plans to embrace weaponised drones, unmanned aircraft and other technologies.

With restrictions now lifted, South Korea has launched a task force to further develop space capabilities for its military. In May 2021, the United States and South Korea agreed to end a 42-yea-old bilateral missile guideline that restricted Seoul's ballistic missile range to 800 kilometers. Towards this effort, the Defence Acquisition Programme Administration (DAPA) has endorsed a plan to invest nearly $13 billion over the next decade to help local industries develop technologies for military satellites.

ARMY: The Republic of Korea Army is one of the largest standing armies in the world. The Army boasts of weapons such as K2 main battle tanks and K9 howitzers Apache attack helicopters. It has unveiled an ambitious plan to equip all of its army squads nationwide with advanced armoured vehicles and other transportation by 2030. Under the Mount Paektu Tiger project, worth $1.1 billion, all ground troops will move by wheeled-armoured carriers, such as the K200 armed vehicle and other small tactical vehicles, rather than on foot. The Army's command and control system has been upgraded to improve the commanders' ability to make decisions in real time in combat situations. The upgraded Army's C4I – command, control, communication, computer and intelligence – has been deployed to some front-line corps. The new systems has analytical functions, such as the automatic calculation of combat capabilities and recommendation of optimal attack methods, to help commanders make decisions faster.

The ROK Army consists of the Army Headquarters, two Field Army Commands, Operations Command, Capital Defence Command, Special Warfare Command, Army Aviation Operations Command, Army Missile Command, and other supporting units.

Personnel: 420,000

Equipment

Category	Name	In Service	On Order
MBT	K-2 Black Panther	100	100+
	Type 88 K1/K-1 A1E/K2	1500+	
	M-48A2C		
	M-48A3	950	
	M-48A5K		
	T-80U	35	
MICV/APC	K-21 IFV	65+	
	KIFV	1400 (to be replaced)	
	M-577	500	
	M-113		
	BMP-3	110	
	KM-900	400	
	LVTP-7	61	
	BV-206	93	
	M-8	45	
Artillery	M101/KH178 105mm	500	
	M114/KH179 155mm towed howitzer	500	
	M115 203mm towed howitzer	1000	
	K55 155mm	1000	
	K9 thunder 155mm SP	1,178	
	M110 203mm SP howitzer		
	M107 175mm	100	
Mortar	81mm towed	5000	
	107mm		
SSM	Hyunmoo 2B (ballistic)/ Hyunmoo 3C (cruise)		

...continued

Category	Name	In Service	On Order
MLRS	MLR 227mm ATACMS Block1A missile	58	
	130mm Kooryong	156	
RCL	57mm, 75mm, 106mm LAW		
ATGW	TOW, Metis		
AT weapon	Panzerfaust	3	
SAM	Hyyyunmoo 1/2/3		
	K-SAM Pegasus	113	
	Javelin	100	
	Mistral	35	
	IGLA		
	Sin Gung		
AA gun	40mm	40	
	Vulcan 20mm	500	
	35mm twin		

New Procurements/Upgrades

◆ ROKA has received its final units of the K9 Thunder 155mm self-propelled howitzer. No production figure has been disclosed.

◆ Hyundai Rotem has been awarded USD481.4 million contract by DAPA for production of a third batch of 54 K2 Black Panther MBTs. Delivery is scheduled to be completed by 2023. The first batch of 100 K2s was delivered in 2015. The second batch of 106 K2s is expected to completed soon.

◆ The K1A2 MBT fleet is slated to undergo upgrade work to enhance its overall operational performance.

◆ South Korea has decided to mass-produce a newly developed 120 millimetre self-propelled mortar system. The new weapon to be developed with indigenous technologies will replace the aging 107-mm mortars on K200A1 armoured tracked vehicles.

◆ The government has decided to produce more than 200 units of the Korean Tactical Surface to Surface Missile (KTSSM) by 2025.

◆ The South Korea government has approved plans to develop an artillery interception system, similar to Israel's Iron Dome. It will spend approximately $2.5 billion on research and development of this new system, with a target to deploy it by 2035.

Army Aviation
Equipment

Category	Name	In Service
Helicopter	Surion	65

...continued

Category	Name	In Service
Helicopter	MDH – 500 Defender	150 (to be replaced)
	Bo - 105	12
	OH-6S	100
	KH-4	5
	AH-1F Cobra (attack)	60
	CH-47 Chinook	15
	UH-60P Black Hawk	120
	DHC-2 Beaver	10
	O-1A	10
	Mi-172	2

New Procurements/Upgrades

◆ Korea Aerospace Industries (KAI) is scheduled to supply the Army and Marine Corps with about 220 Surion units by 2023 under contracts with the DAPA.

◆ KAI building about 200 light heavy helicopter (LAH) to replace Bell AH-1 Cobras and older MD 500 helicopters flown by the Army.

NAVY: In order to bolster its blue-water capabilities, the ROK Navy is carrying out modernisation programmes which include building aircraft carriers, a task fleet comprising of three task squadrons to carry its high-tech assets such as the Aegis-equipped destroyers. Under the FFX programme new Daegu-class frigates are being built. Stepping up its security, the Navy has deployed more submarines and anti-torpedo weapons as well as an increased number of artillery shells on front-line islands. It plans to create a "first operational command" to counter North Korean threats.

The ROK Navy consists of the Navy HQs, Naval Operations Command, Marine Corps HQs/Northwest Islands Defence Command (NWIDC), and other supporting units. The Marine Corps functions as a branch of the Navy.

Major naval bases: Chinhae, Tonghae, Pyontaek, Pusan, Pohang

Personnel: 70,000 (to be reduced to 64,000 under Defence Reforms Plan)

Equipment

Category	Name	In Service	On Order
Destroyer	Sejong Daewang (KDX-3) (DDG)	3	3
	Chungmugong Yi Sun Shin (KDX 2)	6	
	King Kwang-Gae-to class (KDX-1)	3	
Submarine	Son Won IL class (Type 214)	8	1

...continued

Category	Name	In Service	On Order
Submarine	Chang Bogo class (Type 209)	10	
	Tolgorae class (midget)	2	
	Cosmos type (midget)	7	
Frigate	Daegu class	3	4
Corvette	Po Hang class (being withdrawn)	12	
Patrol craft	Yoon Young Ha-Ham class missile FAC	12+	
	Chamsuri (being phased out)	50+	
Mine warfare forces	Yangyang-AM	3+4	
	MLS-II class	2	
	Kang Keong class MCMV	6	
	Dokdo class (LHD)	1	2
Amphibious ship	Alligator	4	
	LST-II	4	
	LSMR	1	
	ex-US LSM	2	
	ex-US LCU	3	
	ex-US LCM	10	
	Chung Jee class logistic support vessel	3	
Auxiliary ship	Soyang class combat support ship	1	
	Submarine rescue vessel	1	
	T-Agor type ship	2	
	T-Agor type ship	10	

New Procurements/Upgrades

◆ The Navy has commissioned the country's first 3,000-ton diesel air-independent propulsion (AIP) submarine – Dosan Ahn Chang-ho – the first developed under the Navy's Changbogo-III (KSS-III) Batch-I construction project.

AIP submarine – the Dosan Ahn Chang-ho. (Image credit: Republic of Korea Navy).

◆ Hyundai Heavy Industries (HHI) has started construction of the country's first aircraft carrier, the LPX-II-class ship expected to enter service in 2030.

◆ South Korea's DSME has launched ROKS Pohang (FFG-825), the sixth Daegu-class FFX Batch II frigate. The first ship, ROKS Daegu, was commissioned in 2018 and the second, ROKS Gyeongnam in January 2021. The third and fourth frigates of the class ROKS Seoul and ROKS Donghae were launched in November 2019 and April 2020 respectively. The fifth vessel in the class, ROKS Daejeon (FFG-823 was launched in May 2021.

◆ The HHI has started construction of the first KDX-III Batch-II AEGIS destroyer Commissioning by the ROK Navy is expected to take place in 2024. The HHI has also signed a US$565 million contract with DAPA for the first of three Gwanggaeto-III Batch II (KDX-III Batch II) destroyers.

◆ South Korea has commissioned the new 14,500-ton amphibious assault ship known as Landing Platform Helicopter-II or LPH-II. The LPH ship Marado is the second large-scale transport ship after the Dokdo.

◆ DAPA has signed a $11 million contract to develop a robot capable of autonomously searching for mines underwater.

Naval Aviation

Category	Name	In Service
ASW/ Surveillance/ Utility Helicopter	P-3CK/P-3C Orion	16
	F406 Caravan II	5
	500 MD	25
	Super Lynx	22
	AW159 Wildcat	8

New Procurements/Upgrades

◆ South Korea plans to buy 12 Sikorsky MH-60R Seahawk anti-submarine warfare helicopters. A total of 12 Seahawks is expected to be delivered by 2025 in phases.

◆ The Ministry of National Defence has decided to procure 20 F-35B short take off and vertical landing (STOVL) variant for its light aircraft carrier project known as LPX-II.

MARINE FORCES: The Marine Corps founded as a reconnaissance force just prior to the start of the Korean War, operates as a distinct arm of the South Korean armed forces. South Korea plans to develop the Marine Corps into a force that can readily adapt to carry out a variety of tasks based on situations and missions such as multi-dimensional high-speed landing, rapid response, and ground operations among others.

Personnel: 27,000+

Equipment

Category	Name	In Service
MBT	M47	40
APC	LVTP7	100
Helicopter	SA-316B/SA-319B	11
Weapon	Mistral	
	Spike NLOS	

AIR FORCE: The ROK Air Force consists of the Air Force HQs, Air Force Operations Command, and other supporting units. The Air Force Operations Command (AFOC) controls air operations in a centralised manner. The Northern and Southern Air Combat Commands, under the AFOC's centralised command, execute decentralised missions in order to defend the airspace of their respective areas of operation. The Air Defence Artillery Command (ADAC) carries out all-directional air defence missions in preparation against air attacks by enemy aircraft and missiles. The Air Defence and Control Wing executes missions such as air control within the ROK theatre, air surveillance and aircraft identification, and air support operations.

In a move to enhance the country's military capabilities, South Korea has launched a new Air Force unit in-charge of operating the country's key reconnaissance assets, such as the RQ-4 Global Hawk aircraft, RF-16 and RC-800 Geumgang reconnaissance aircraft, and a medium-altitude unmanned aircraft system. South Korea's four RQ-4 Block 30 Global Hawk Remotely Piloted Aircraft (RPA) will be equipped with advanced radar and sensors capable of detecting any unusual signs regardless of weather conditions.

Major air bases: Ch'ongju, Kangnong, Kunsan, Kwangju, Osan, Sunch'on, Suwon, and Taegu

Personnel: 65,000

Equipment

Category	Name	In Service	On Order
Fighter/ AWS	F-35A	24	
	RF-16 C/D Block 52	140	
	F-16 C/D Block 32	40	
	F-15K Slam Eagle	60	
	F-5E/F (to be withdrawn)	60	
	F-4E	50	
Transport	KC-330 Cygnus (A330 MRTT)	2	2
	C-130J	4	
	C-130H-30	4	
	C-130H	8	

...continued

Category	Name	In Service	On Order
Transport	CN-235 (including 2 VIP)	20	
	Boeing 737 AEW&C	4	
ELINT/ SIGINT/ EW	Falcon 2000	2	
	Hawker 800SIG	4	
	800RA	4	
Helicopter	CH-47D Chinook	5	
	AS.332 Super Puma	3	
	Bell UH-1D/N (VIP)	5	
	Bell 212/412 (SAR)	10	
	UH-1H (SAR)	5	
	Ka-32 (SAR)	7	
	S-92 (VVIP)	3	
Trainer	KT-1	85	
	T-35 (on lease)	30	
	Hawk (T-59)	16	
	T-50 Golden Eagle	50	
	TA-50	22	
	T-50B	10	
UAV	RQ-4 Global Hawk	4	
SAM	Patriot PAC-3	18	
	Cheongung		
	Hawk (to be withdrawn)		
	Mistral		

New Procurements/Upgrades

◆ KAI has unveiled South Korea's first homegrown fighter jet prototype, named the KF-21 Boramae, five years after the KF-X program began. ROKAF will receive 40 KF-21s by 2028 and 80 more jets by 2032.

◆ ROK Air Force has received a total of 24 F-35A next-generation fighter jets from the United States.

◆ South Korea has taken delivery of the second of four A330-200 Multi Role Tanker Transport (MRTT) aircraft ordered in 2015. The other two aircraft are expected to be delivered in the near future.

◆ Korea Aerospace Industries (KAI) has signed a USD15.6 million contract to support the US company Boeing in upgrading RoKAF's four Boeing E-737 airborne early warning and control (AEW&C) aircraft with new mission systems.

◆ South Korea plans to buy from the US, 205 AIM-9X Block II Tactical Sidewinder, Captive Air Training Missile, Tactical Missile Guidance and CATM Guidance systems under foreign military sales FMS agreement.

◆ KAI has signed a deal with the DAPA to manufacture additional 20 TA-50 lead-in fighter aircraft for radar tactical and combat mission training.

◆ South Korea plans to invest US$2.3 billion in the next 10 years to develop drones for military use.

◆ South Korea to invest USD13.6 billion over the next 10 years to accelerate the development of defence-related space technologies following the termination of range restrictions for the country's ballistic missiles under the US-South Korea missile guidelines agreement.

◆ South Korea's first locally developed anti-aircraft guided missile system, Cheongung, has been delivered to the military.

Nuclear capability: Seoul has signed the Non-Proliferation of Nuclear Weapons (NPT) treaty in April 1975. It is a state party to the Comprehensive Nuclear Test Ban Treaty (CTBT), and a member of the Nuclear Suppliers Group and the Zangger Committee.

Biological Weapons: South Korea has ratified the Biological and Toxin Weapons Convention (BTWC) in June 1987 and joined the Australia Group in October 1995.

Chemical weapons: South Korea has ratified the Chemical Weapons Convention (CWC) in April 1997. According to Nuclear Threat Initiative (NTI) report, South Korea completed the destruction of its entire chemical weapons stockpile in July 2008, becoming only the second CWC member to do so..

DEFENCE PRODUCTION

South Korea has progressively built up a formidable defence industry. The country has developed faster than the regional average possibly due to security threat from neighbouring countries. The existence of a modern industrial base, consistent financial backing and encouragement from the government, generous technological assistance from the US and Japan, and a well-educated, skilled work force has contributed to the success of the South Korean defence industry. The defence sector has developed competence in a number of areas such as manufacturing of armoured vehicles, naval vessels and aircraft. Domestic manufacturers provide approximately 77 per cent of the weapon systems to the country's armed forces. In the reform acquisitions mandated under the Defence Reform 2020 plan, emphasis has been placed on improvement of individual and joint C4ISR capabilities of the armed services. The defence industry develops, designs and manufactures a full range of military systems, including imaging satellites, armoured vehicles, artillery, missiles and rockets, C4I systems, fixed- and rotary-wing aircraft, surface combatants and submarines. South Korea's Defence Acquisition Program Administration or (DAPA), is responsible for improving the defence capabilities of the nation, and fostering the defence industry. South Korea recently celebrated its entry into the elite group of fighter jet producers by unveiling its domestically-developed KF-21 Boramae fighter jet. Development of the fourth generation aircraft began more than 20 years ago under former president Kim Dae-jung. The fighter will be a replacement for the country's ageing fleet of F-4s and F-5s.

Major Armaments Producers

Korea Aerospace Industries Ltd.: KAI is a South Korean aerospace company involved in the development and production of military aircraft. Major products are T-50 Golden Eagle supersonic jet trainer, KT-1 turboprop trainer, and Korea Utility Helicopter.

Samsung Thales: The Company is a leading high-tech company, with its main operations focused on defence. Its core business areas are command, control and tactical communication systems, radar systems, naval combat management systems, electro-optics and fire control systems, aviation/electronics warfare systems, Land C2 systems.

Samsung Techwin: Samsung Techwin Defence Company produces huge artillery system for the South Korean military which includes: K9 Thunder, K10 Ammunition Resupply Vehicle, K77 Fire Direction Centre Vehicle, K55A1 Self-propelled Howitzer, K-56 Ammunition Resupply Vehicle. It also constructs Hybrid-Unmanned Vehicle, Hybrid Tactical Vehicle and Unmanned Ground Combat Vehicle.

Hanwha: Hanwha's Defence Products Division is involved in developing and manufacturing various state-of-the-art weapons ranging from precision munitions to precision guided weapon systems, underwater equipment and satellite launch vehicles.

Poongsan: The company has made significant contribution towards defence indigenisation through mass production and localisation of ammunitions. The military products include ammunition for small arms, anti-aircraft guns, mid-to large-size arms.

Hanjin Heavy Industries: The company has built a variety of special ships for the Korean Navy such as Dokdo-ham, a mega transporter, corvettes, landing ships, air cushion vehicles and patrol boats.

LIG Nex1: The company has produced a wide range of advanced precision electronic systems including missile, underwater weapon systems, radars, electronic warfare, avionics, tactical communication systems, fire control systems, naval combat systems, and electro-optics.

Major foreign suppliers: European Union, Israel, Russia, United States

DEFENCE DEALS
Joint Venture Programmes

Europe: Korea Aerospace Industries (KAI) and Airbus Helicopters are jointly developing two 5-ton class rotorcraft to meet South Korea's requirements for its next-generation Light Civil Helicopter (LCH) and Light Armed Helicopter (LAH). Both the LCH and LAH are based on Airbus Helicopters' H155. As part of the agreement, Airbus Helicopters will transfer the company's technical know-how.

Indonesia: Indonesia and South Korea have signed an agreement to continue joint development of the Korean Fighter Experimental, Indonesian Fighter Experimental – Ed (KFX/IFX) aircraft. The KF-X/IF-X development cooperation programme is being undertaken in three phases, including the technology development (TD), engineering and manufacturing development (EMD), as well as the production development (PD) phase.

United States: South Korea has secured technologies from the US to support its programme to develop the KFX fighter aircraft through defence offset of F-35 deal between both the countries. Technologies include active electronically scanned array (AESA) radars, electro-optical targeting pods, infrared search and track systems, and radio frequency jammers. KAI's T-50 supersonic jet trainer was jointly developed and produced in partnership with US' Lockheed Martin.

India: India and South Korea have agreed to go for joint production and export of military hardware, enhance intelligence sharing and boost cooperation in cyber and space domains as part overall expansion of defence and security ties. In 2019, the two countries finalised a roadmap for cooperation in joint production of various land and naval systems.

Israel: Sharp Elbit Systems Aerospace (SESA), a joint venture entity between Israel's Elbit Systems and ROK's Sharp Aviation K, has been established to provide capabilities in the domains of maintenance, repair and production of advanced avionics for military applications. The company will manage research & development of systems and avionics for ROK military's existing and future projects, including the Korean Light Attack Helicopter (LAH) and the Korean Future Fighter (KFX) development programmes.

Arms Import

South Korea is progressively bolstering its military strength by purchasing warplanes, anti-missile systems and other weapon systems. The country inked its biggest-ever arms deal worth US$7.04 billion for the procurement of 40 Lockheed Martin-built F-35 fifth-generation fighter jets. Defence Acquisition and procurement Agency (DAPA) has announced the purchase of four aerial tankers to enhance its air defence system in addition to upgrading its missile system with PAC-3 interceptors. The ROK Government is making efforts to boost other military capabilities, such as the development of advanced army tanks, navy frigates, new-generation submarines, surveillance systems including UAVs as well as launching military satellites. A recent report has stated that the US State Department has agreed to a sale of precision-guided weapons worth about $258 million to South Korea.

Arms Export

Faced with constant threats South Korea has been developing its own arms production to reduce dependency on foreign suppliers. In the last few decades South Korea has been making efforts emerging as a significant arms producer and supplier rising from the 31st ranked arms exporting country in 2000, to number six in 2020, according to SIPRI arms transfer database. The Global Defence Market Yearbook 2020 has stated that Britain, Iraq and Indonesia were the main buyers of South Korea's defence products during the 2015-2019 period. Its trade involves armoured vehicles, tanks and fighter jet trainers which are sold such as cluster bombs and rocket launchers, to a wide variety of countries. Its missiles, howitzers, submarines and warplanes are particularly popular in Southeast Asia, Eastern Europe and South America. South Korean companies – Samsung, Korea Aerospace Industries, and LIG Nex1 are among the world's leading arms-producing and military services companies.

DEFENCE BUDGET
Total defence spending: $48 billion (2021), $41 billion (2020)

Defence spending in terms of GDP: 2.8% (2020)

According to the budget plan approved by the National Assembly, military spending for 2021 was set at 52.8 trillion won ($48 billion). The national defence budget has been on a constant rise, from 20.8 trillion won in 2005 to 31.4 trillion won in 2011 and 40.3 trillion won in 2017. It surpassed the 50 trillion-won mark for the first time in 2020. a media report stated. South Korea's Ministry of National Defense (MND) has reportedly decided to seek a 4.5% increase to the national defence budget for 2022

CONCLUSION
South Korea is seen as an emerging maker of high-end military systems and advanced military technologies with the country making advancements in defence technology due to perceived threat from North Korea, Seoul has strengthened its conventional deterrence capabilities by boosting defence spending and developing new weapons systems as evidenced by the submarine-launched ballistic missile (SLBM) test. Its military has become a great regional naval power in the span of a decade and its shipbuilding industry and general munitions industries have seen successes abroad. In 2020, South Korea introduced its new Hyunmoo-4 short-range ballistic missile (SRBM) that could carry a 2-ton warhead. South Korea has also unveiled its domestically-developed KF-21 Boramae fighter jet joining the elite group of fighter jet producers.

CONTACT DETAILS
Ministry of National Defence
22, Itaewon-ro, Yongsan-gu,
Seoul-04383
Tel: 02748-1111
mail: cyber@mnd.go.kr
Web: www.mnd.go.kr

SOUTH SUDAN
(Capital: Juba)

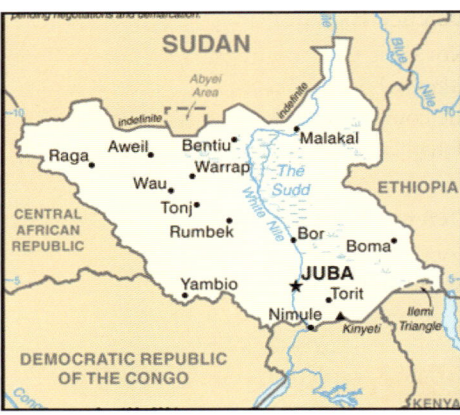

INTRODUCTION
Area: 644,329 sq km
Population: 10,984,074 (July 2021 est.)
Coastline: 0 km (Landlocked)
Maritime claims: None

(On 9 July 2011, South Sudan became an independent country called Republic of South Sudan and on 14 July 2011, the country became the 193rd member state of the United Nations. The government has formed various organs which constitute the state.)

KEY POLITICAL PERSONS

PRESIDENT & COMMANDER-IN-CHIEF: Salva Kiir Mayardit

FIRST VICE PRESIDENT: Riek Machar

KEY DEFENCE PERSONS

DEFENCE MINISTER: Angelina Teny

CHIEF OF GENERAL STAFF: Gen. Santino Deng Wol

ECONOMY

Industry and infrastructure in landlocked South Sudan are severely underdeveloped and poverty is widespread following several decades of civil war with Sudan. Subsistence agriculture provides a living for the vast majority of population. Property rights are tentative and price signals are missing because markets are not well organized. South Sudan has little infrastructure. The government spends large sums of money to maintain a large army; delays in paying salaries have periodically resulted in riots by unruly soldiers. South Sudan depends largely on imports of goods, services, and capital from the North. Despite these disadvantages, the country has abundant natural resources. It produces nearly three-fourths of the former Sudan's total oil output of nearly a half million barrels per day. The government of South Sudan derives nearly 98% of its budget revenues from oil.

South Sudan is burdened by considerable debt because of increased military spending and high levels of government corruption. Economic mismanagement is prevalent. The African country has received more than $11 billion in foreign aid since 2005, largely from the US, the UK, and the EU. Inflation peaked at over 800% per year in October 2016 but dropped to 118% in 2017. The government has funded its expenditures by borrowing from the central bank and foreign sources, using forward sales of oil as collateral. Long-term challenges include rooting out public sector corruption, improving agricultural productivity, alleviating poverty and unemployment, improving fiscal transparency – particularly in regard to oil revenues, taming inflation, improving government revenues, and creating a rules-based business environment.

The outbreak of Coronavirus pandemic has created disruptions in the country's economy and also reduced oil production.

GDP (official exchange rate): $3.06 billion (2017 est.)

Real Growth Rate (GDP): -5.2% (2017 est.); -13.9% (2016 est.)

Agricultural Products: Sorghum, maize, rice, millet, wheat, gum arabic, sugarcane, mangoes, papayas, bananas, sweet potatoes, sunflower seeds, cotton, sesame seeds, cassava (manioc, tapioca), beans, peanuts; cattle, sheep

Natural Gas - Proved Reserves: 63.71 billion cu m (1 January 2016 est.)

Crude Oil - Proved Reserves: 3.75 billion bbl (1 January 2017 est.)

Total Exports: $1.13 billion (2016 est.)

Export Commodities: Crude petroleum, gold, forage crops, lumber, insect resins (2019)

Major Markets: China 88%, United Arab Emirates 5% (2019)

Total Imports: $3.795 billion (2016 est.)

Import Commodities: Cars, delivery trucks, packaged medicines, foodstuffs, clothing and apparel (2019)

Major Suppliers: United Arab Emirates 37%, Kenya 18%, China 18% (2019)

INTERNATIONAL DISPUTES

◆ The South Sudan-Sudan boundary represents the 1 January 1956 alignment. A final alignment pending negotiations and demarcation; and the final sovereignty status of Abyei Area are pending negotiations between South Sudan and Sudan.

◆ Periodic violent skirmishes with South Sudanese residents over water and grazing rights persist among related pastoral populations along the border with the Central African Republic.

◆ The boundary that separates Kenya and South Sudan's sovereignty is unclear in the "Ilemi Triangle," which Kenya has administered since colonial times.

DEFENCE

Following the independence of South Sudan in 2011, the Sudan People's Liberation Army (SPLA) became the regular army of the new republic. The SPLA was founded as a guerrilla movement in 1983 and was a key protagonist of the Second Sudanese Civil War. The US Security Council established the United Nations Mission in South Sudan (UNMISS) for an initial period of one year starting from 9 July 2011 in view of the security situation in South Sudan where a series of deadly ethnic clashes had occurred.

The SPLA maintains some military platforms such as the T-72 MBTs, T-55 MBTs, APCs and Mi-17 helicopters along with few small arms and weapons to carry out its operations

Defence Expenditure
No exact data is available on the country's defence budget. According to some estimates, the country spends over 10% of its GDP on defence.

Defence Production and R&D
South Sudan does not undertake any defence production activities.

Defence Procurement
SPLA has not officially announced any major defence procurements, but it has reportedly procured amphibious vehicles, ATGWs and other small arms and ammunition from China in recent past. The country has also acquired MANPADs, also believed to be from China, which have been delivered to it through its neighbouring countries Kenya and Uganda. With these new acquisitions, South Sudan hopes to modernize and professionalize its armed forces.

CONTACT DETAILS
SPLA Headquarters,
Juba, South Sudan

SPAIN
(Capital: Madrid)

INTRODUCTION
Area: 505,370 sq km
Population: 47,260,584 (July 2021 est.)
Coastline: 4,964 km
Maritime claims: Territorial sea: 12 nm
Contiguous zone: 24 nm
Exclusive Economic Zone: 200 nm (applies only to the Atlantic Ocean)

KEY POLITICAL PERSONS

SUPREME COMMANDER & CHIEF OF STATE: King Felipe VI

PRESIDENT: Pedro Sanchez Perez Castejon

KEY DEFENCE PERSONS

MINISTER OF DEFENCE: Margarita Robles Fernandez

CHIEF OF DEFENCE STAFF: Gen. Adm. Teodoro Esteban Lopez Calderon

CHIEF OF STAFF OF THE ARMY: Lt. Gen. Amador Fernando Enseñat y Berea

CHIEF OF STAFF OF THE NAVY: Adm. Antonio Martorell Lacave

CHIEF OF STAFF OF THE AIR FORCE: Gen. Javier Salto Martinez Avial

ECONOMY
Spain's economy is the world's 14th largest by nominal GDP and also among the largest by purchasing power parity. The Spanish economy plunged into recession during the financial crisis of 2007–2008. The economic situation started improving by 2013–2014. In 2015, the Spanish GDP grew by 3.2%, the highest among larger EU economies that year. Strong GDP growth was registered in 2016 with the country reportedly growing twice as fast as the eurozone average. One of the main drivers of economic recovery is international trade. The country's diversified economy includes manufacturing, financial services, pharmaceuticals, textiles and apparel, footwear, chemicals, and a booming tourism industry. Spain is a member of the European Union, the Organisation for Economic Co-

operation and Development, the World Trade Organisation, the International Development Association (IDA), the Multilateral Investment Guarantee Agency (MIGA), the International Finance Corporation (IFC), and the International Centre for Settlement of Investment Disputes (ICSID).

GDP (official exchange rate): $1,393,351,000,000 (2019 est.)

Real Growth Rate (GDP): 1.95% (2019 est.), 2.43% (2018 est.)

Industries: Textiles and apparel (including footwear), food and beverages, metals and metal manufactures, chemicals, shipbuilding, auto mobiles, machine tools, tourism, clay and refractory products, footwear, pharmaceuticals, medical equipment.

Crude Oil – Proved Reserves: 150 million bbl (1 January 2018 est.)

Natural Gas – Proved Reserves: 2.548 billion cu m (1 January 2018 est.)

Total Exports: $392.85 billion (2020 est.), $486.15 billion (2019 est.)

Export Commodities: Cars and vehicle parts, refined petroleum, packaged medicines, delivery trucks, clothing and apparel (2019)

Major Markets: France 15%, Germany 11%, Portugal 8%, Italy 8%, United Kingdom 7%, United States 5% (2019)

Total Imports: $373.67 billion (2020 est.), $444.31 billion (2019 est.)

Import Commodities: Crude petroleum, cars and vehicle parts, packaged medicines, natural gas, refined petroleum (2019)

Major Suppliers: Germany 13%, France 11%, China 8%, Italy 7% (2019)

INTERNATIONAL DISPUTES

◆ In 2002, Gibraltar residents voted overwhelmingly by referendum to reject any "shared sovereignty" arrangement.

◆ The Government of Gibraltar insists on equal participation in talks between the UK and Spain.

◆ Spain disapproves of UK plans to grant Gibraltar greater autonomy.

◆ After voters in the UK chose to leave the EU in a June 2016 referendum, Spain again proposed shared sovereignty of Gibraltar. UK officials rejected Spain's joint sovereignty proposal

◆ Morocco protests Spain's control over the coastal enclaves of Ceuta, Melilla, and the islands of Penon de Velez de la Gomera, Penon de Alhucemas, and Islas Chafarinas, and surrounding waters; both countries claim Isla Perejil (Leila Island).

◆ Morocco serves as the primary launching site of illegal migration into Spain from North Africa.

◆ Portugal does not recognise Spanish sovereignty over the territory of Olivenza based on a difference of interpretation of the 1815 Congress of Vienna and the 1801 Treaty of Badajoz.

DEFENCE

The Spanish Armed Forces (Fuerzas Armadas Españolas) is one of the oldest active armies dating back to the late 15th century. The commander in chief of the Armed Forces is the King of Spain with the ex officio rank of Capitán General in the Army, Navy and Air Force. Spain is one of the most militarily powerful nations of the European Union (EUFOR) and Eurocorps. It occupies a prominent position in the structure of the North Atlantic Treaty Organization (NATO) which it joined in 1982.

ARMY (Ejército de Tierra)

Personnel: 80,000

Equipment

Category	Name	In Service
MBT	Leopard 2/E	216
	Leopard 2/A4	100+
Armoured Car	VEC-M1 Pegaso	95
	Centauro B1	84
APC/AFV/IFV	Pizarro	260
	BMR-600	682
	LINCE	395
	RG-31	180
Artillery	155mm/62mm APU SBT	84
	L-118 105 Light Guns	53
	Mountain howitzer 105/14mm	18

...continued

Category	Name	In Service
Artillery	M-109A5 155mm SP howitzer	96
Mortar	120mm on M-106	192
	81 mm (medium mortar)	1200
	120mm on BMR	8
	120 mm towed	265
MRL	Teruel 140 mm	14
ATGW	Tow	200
	Milan	442
	Spike	260
	Hot	28
ATK weapon	C-90CR M3	
	C-100 Alcotan	
SAM	I-Hawk PIP III	36
	Patriot	8 batteries
	Roland	16
	Aspide	6
	Mistral	105
	Nasams	8
AA gun	35mm twin	48
UAV	Raven System	27
	Searcher	4

New Procurements/Upgrades

◆ The programme to deliver up to 1,000 wheeled combat vehicles (VCR) to the Spanish Army under the Dragón project has entered the construction phase Dragón VCR will replace the Pegaso 3560 BMR armoured personnel carriers and Pegaso VEC-M1 reconnaissance vehicles.

A file photo of an 8×8 VCR demonstrator. (Image credit: Spanish Defence Ministry)

Army Aviation

Category	Name	In Service
Helicopter	CH-47D Chinook	17
	NH90	23
	Tiger HAP-E/HAD-E	6+2
	AS.332B Super Puma	15
	AS-532AL Cougar	22
	EC-135 (UME)	14+8
	Bo-105	10

New Procurements/Upgrades

◆ The MoD has taken delivery of 13 NH90 Spain has reportedly ordered a second batch of NH90 Helicopters worth $1.57 billion.

NAVY (Armada Española)

Personnel: 22,000

Equipment

Category	Name	In Service
Submarine	Galerna class	3
Mine warfare	M-30 Segura class	6
Frigate	Alvaro De Bazan class	5
	Santa Maria class (to be withdrawn)	6
Amphibious force	LCM-1 E landing craft	14
	Galicia class LPD	2
	Juan Carlos-I (LHD)	1
Patrol ship	Cabo Fradera class	1
	Descubierta class	4
	Serviola class	4
	Anaga class	3
	Toralla class	2
	Meteoro class	6
	P-114 (coastal surveillance)	2
	Chilreu class	3
Auxiliary ship	Patino AOR	1
	Cantabria	1

New Procurements/Upgrades

◆ Spain's state-owned shipbuilder Navantia has won US $4.9 billion contract to build five F-110 frigates for the country's Navy. The new frigates will replace the Santa Maria class between 2023 to 2028.

◆ Four Spanish designed new generation submarines with AIP propulsion are under construction to replace the Galernas with the first vessel expected to be delivered in 2022.

Naval Aviation

Category	Name	In Service
Fighter/Attack/AWS role	AV-8B	12
Trainer	TAV-8B	1
Transport/Surveillance	Cessna Citation II/VII	3
Helicopter	AB-212	10
	Hughes 500	9
	SH-3W AEW	3
	SH-60B (Sea Hawk)	12
	SH-3D	7

Marines

Personnel: 5,836

Equipment

Category	Name	In Service
Vehicle	M-60A3 TTS	15
	AAV-7A1	19
	Piranha IIIC	39
	BLR	35
Artillery	M-109A2 (155 mm howitzer)	6
	M-56 105 mm pack howitzer	12
	C-90/CR	
ATGW	Tow 2A	24
	Spike	24
SAM	Mistral	12

AIR FORCE (Ejercito del Aire Espanola)
Personnel: 24,000
Equipment

Category	Name	In Service	On Order
Fighter/Attack	Tranche 1 Eurofighter (upgraded)	1	
	Eurofighter Typhoon	61	
	EF-18	87	
	Eurocopter EC120 Colibri	15	
Transport/Surveillance	A400M	2	25
	PA-3A/B Orion	7	
	Casa C-212	24	
	Casa CN-235	20	
	Casa C-295	13	
	C-130-Hercules	7	
	Falcon 900	5	
	Falcon 20	2	
	Airbus A-300	2	
Trainer	Northrop F-5	19	
	Casa C-101-Aviojet	70	
	Sikorsky S-76 Spirit	8	
	Enaer T-35C	36	
	Beechcraft Bonanza F-33C	35	
	Northrop F-5M	20	

...continued

Category	Name	In Service	On Order
Helicopter	NH90	1	11
	AS.330-Puma	7	
	AS.332 Super Puma	16	
	AS.532 Cougar		
	Eurocopter EC-120 Colibri	17	
	Sikorsky S-76	8	
	Beechcraft C-90 King Air	4	
UAV	Reaper MQ-9Block 5		

New Procurements/Upgrades

◆ The Spanish government has approved the procurement of 20 new Eurofighter Typhoon combat aircraft under Project Halcon (Falcon), as well as a mid-life upgrade (MLU) for a portion of the country's existing fleet.

◆ The Spanish MoD has signed the formal order for the acquisition of three Airbus A330 Multi-Role Tanker Transport aircraft (MRTT).

◆ The Air Force first 14 A400Ms turboprop military transport aircraft are expected to be delivered by 2022 and the remaining 13 aircraft will be delivered from 2025.

◆ The US has approved the sale to Spain for 100 AIM-120C-7/8 Advanced Medium Range Air-to-Air Missiles (AMRAAM).

Defence Expenditure
Total defence spending: $17160 million (2020), $17189 million (2019)
Defence spending in terms of GDP: 1.4% (2020)

Defence Production and R&D

The Spanish defence industry has been producing varieties of military equipment for its armed forces that included light arms, vehicles, ships, and light transport aircraft. Several firms in the country are engaged principally in defence production that primarily involves aerospace, shipbuilding and land armaments. As a member of NATO, Spain has collaboration with other European countries in a number of defence projects like Eurofighter Typhoon and Airbus A400M programmes. Navantia, Bazan and CASA are some of the leading defence manufacturing companies in the country. The participation in the (FCAS)/Système de Combat Aérien Futur (SCAF) programme, the new F-110 frigates and the 8×8 armoured fighting vehicle projects is expected to give a boost to the defence industry.

Defence Procurement

Spain has continued acquisition of weapon systems for all three branches of the military. While the Army is in the process of acquiring a number of infantry vehicles and other ammunitions, a new class of submarines, frigates and patrol vessels along with new aircraft and helicopters for the Navy are scheduled to be inducted in the coming years. The Air Force has completed deploying the Eurofighter combat jets while delivery of the A400M strategic transport aircraft is continuing.

CONTACT DETAILS
Ministry of Defence
Paseo de la Castellana,
109 28071, Madrid, Spain

Tel: + 34 91 395 50 00
E-mail: infodefensa@mde.es
Website: www.mde.es

SRI LANKA
(Capital: Colombo)

INTRODUCTION
Area: 65,610 sq km
Population: 23,044,123 (July 2021 est.)
Coastline: 1,340 km
Maritime claims: Territorial sea: 12 nm
Contiguous zone: 24 nm

Exclusive Economic Zone: 200 nm
Continental shelf: 200 nm or to the edge of the continental margin

KEY POLITICAL PERSONS

PRESIDENT, MINISTER OF DEFENCE & COMMANDER-IN-CHIEF: Gotabaya Rajapaksa

PRIME MINISTER: Mahinda Rajapaksa

KEY DEFENCE PERSONS

CHIEF OF DEFENCE STAFF AND COMMANDER OF THE ARMY: Gen. Shavendra Silva

COMMANDER OF THE NAVY: Vice Adm. Nishantha Ulugetenne

COMMANDER OF THE AIR FORCE: Air Marshal Sudarshana Pathirana

ECONOMY

Sri Lanka is a middle-income country with a GDP per capita of USD 3,852 in 2019. The economy is transitioning from a predominantly rural-based economy towards a more urbanised economy oriented around manufacturing and services. The main economic sectors of the country are tourism, tea export, apparel, textile, rice production and other agricultural products. In 2017, the government promulgated plans to transform the country into a knowledge-based, export-oriented Indian Ocean hub by 2025. Sri Lanka is known for producing a variety of gemstones, including chrysoberyl, corundum, garnet, ruby, spinel, and tourmaline. The country is a leading producer of the Ceylon Blue sapphire. The economy contracted by 1.6 percent y-o-y in the first quarter of 2020 after growing by 2.3 percent in 2019. Growth is expected to recover to 3.3 percent in 2021, but the medium-term outlook is clouded by pre-existing macroeconomic weaknesses and the economic scarring from the COVID-19 pandemic. according to the World Bank.

GDP (official exchange rate): $84.016 billion (2019 est.)

Real Growth Rate (GDP): 2.29% (2019 est.), 3.32% (2018 est.)

Industries: Processing of rubber, tea, coconuts, tobacco and other agricultural commodities; telecommunications, insurance, banking; tourism, shipping; clothing, textiles; cement, petroleum refining, information technology services, construction.

Total Exports: $19.41 billion (2019 est.), $20.26 billion (2018 est.)

Export Commodities: Clothing and apparel, tea, used tires, rubber products, precious stones, cinnamon (2019)

Major Markets: United States 24%, India 8%, United Kingdom 7%, Germany 7% (2019)

Total Imports: $24.56 billion (2019 est.), $26.84 billion (2018 est.)

Import Commodities: Refined petroleum, textiles, gold, cars, broadcasting equipment (2019)

Major Suppliers: India 24%, China 23%, Singapore 7%, United Arab Emirates 6%, Malaysia 5% (2019)

INTERNATIONAL DISPUTES

Sri Lanka has no known international disputes.

DEFENCE

As head of state, the President of Sri Lanka, is nominally the Commander-in-Chief of the Armed Forces. The Ministry of Defence is responsible for the management of the armed forces – The Army, Navy and Air Force. The three services have their own respective professional chiefs: the Commander of the Army, the Commander of the Navy and the Commander of the Air Force. The Joint Operations Command (JOC) is headed by the Chief of the Defence Staff who is the most senior officer in the Armed Forces. The Sri Lankan military is set to be modernised Army by 2025.

ARMY

Personnel: 180,000+

Equipment

Category	Name	In Service
MBT	T-55/AM2/AM2 MP	68
AIFV	BMP-1/II	40
	Type 85 (Saladin turrets)	8

...continued

Category	Name	In Service
APC	BTR 80	426
	Type 63	
	WMZ 551 A/B	
	Type 89 VP	
	Type 86	
	South African Buffel	
Artillery	Type 66 152mm	100
	Type 59 130mm	50
	122mm	74
	120mm	50
	85mm	50
Mortar	107 mm	
	81mm	
MRL	122mm	20
AA gun	528 12.7mm	

New Procurements/Upgrades

No major procurement plans are under consideration at present.

NAVY

Personnel: 54,000

Equipment

Category	Name	In Service
Frigate	P625	1
Patrol vessel	SLNS Sindurala	1
	SLNS Samudura	1
	SLNS Sayura	1
	Jayesegra class large patrol Boat	1
	Oshadi	2
	Rana class patrol craft	3
	Sooraya (Shanghai II) class FAC	8
	Parakramabahu class gun patrol Boat	1
	South Korean Killer type P430	3
	P463 class Israeli Dvora type	6
	Colombo class FAC	10
	Patrol craft-coastal	25
	Harbour patrol craft	40+
	Speed boat-Arrow type	100+
Amphibious Force	Wuhu class LSM	2
	LCM	2
	Yunnan class LCU	1
	M10 Hovercraft	1

New Procurements/Upgrades

No major procurement plans are under consideration at present.

Marine Infantry: Personnel 5,300 and seven battalions to protect harbour facilities.

Coast Guard: Personnel 1000. The Coast Guard is under the Ministry of Defence and Urban Development.

AIR FORCE
Personnel: 38,000
Equipment

Category	Name	In Service
Fighter/attack/AWS role	MiG-23/ 27	8
	F-7/ FT-7	5
	KFIR C-2	5
	KFIR TC-2	2
Transport/Surveillance	An-32	4
	C-130B	2
	Y-12	5
	Beech 200	3
Helicopter	Mi-24/Mi-35 Hind	5-6
	Bell 212	8
	Bell 206	7
	Bell 412	6
	Mi-17	11
Trainer	K-8	5+
	PT-6	
	Cessna 150	
UAV	Searcher	

New Procurements/Upgrades
No major procurement plans are under consideration at present.

Defence Expenditure
Total defence spending: $1560 million (2020), $1700 million (2019)
Defence spending in terms of GDP: 2 % (2020)

Defence Production and R&D
Sri Lanka does not undertake any defence production activities. Meanwhile, India and Sri Lanka have agreed to enhance bilateral cooperation in the defence sector, including training Sri Lankan military personnel.

Defence Procurement
The Sri Lankan government has procured two advanced offshore patrol vessel in the recent past and it has made the announcement that it was seeking to procure between eight and 12 combat aircraft to replace its ageing air force assets.

CONTACT DETAILS
Ministry of Defence
15/5 Baladaksha Mawatha
Colombo 03, Sri Lanka
Tel: (+94 1) 2430860
Fax: (+94 1) 254 15 29
E-mail: modsec@sltnet.lk
webinfo@defence.lk
www.defence.lk

Sri Lanka Army (SLA) indigenously developed Mine-Resistant Ambush-Protected Vehicle (MRAPV), 'Unicob.' (Image credit: Sri Lanka MoD)

SUDAN
(Capital: Khartoum)

INTRODUCTION
Area: 861,484 sq km
Population: 46,751,152 (July 2021 est.)
Coastline: 853 km
Maritime claims: Territorial sea: 12 nm
Contiguous zone: 18 nm
Continental shelf: 200 m depth or to the depth of exploitation

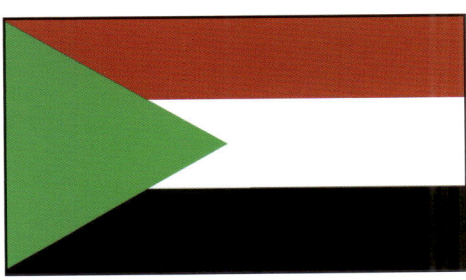

KEY POLITICAL PERSONS

HEAD OF STATE & COMMANDER-IN-CHIEF: Gen. Abdel Fattah Abdelrahman al-Burhan

PRIME MINISTER: Abdalla Hamdok

KEY DEFENCE PERSONS

DEFENCE MINISTER: Maj. Gen. (Retd.) Yassin Ibrahim Yassin

CHIEF OF GENERAL STAFF: Gen. Mohammed Othman al-Hussein

COMMANDER OF ARMY: Maj. Gen. Essam Mohamed-Hassan Karar

COMMANDER OF NAVY: Rear Adm. Mahjoub Bushra Ahmed Rahma

COMMANDER OF AIR FORCE: Lt. Gen. Essam al-Din Said Koko

ECONOMY
The oil sector had driven much of Sudan's GDP growth since 1999. Economy boomed because of rising oil production, high oil prices, and significant inflows of FDI. South Sudan's secession created economic instability in Sudan. Sudan was subject to comprehensive US sanctions, which were lifted in October 2017. Agriculture continues to employ 80% of the work force. Since late 2017, Sudan has suffered a currency and fiscal crisis that has led to hyperinflation, a collapse of the banking system, and shortages of basic goods, such as fuel. Inflation has declined to 57 percent. Sudan is a member of the Common Market for Eastern and Southern Africa, which has a Trade and Investment Framework Agreement with the United States. The COVID-19 pandemic has hurt the Sudanese economy badly including rice in basic amenities, rising unemployment and downgrade in export. The government is

addressing these challenges with help from the World Bank in the strengthening its preparedness and response time.

GDP (official exchange rate): $176.4 billion (2020), $179.2 billion (2019 est.)

Real Growth Rate (GDP): 1.4% (2017 est.), 3% (2016 est.)

Industries: Oil, cotton ginning, textiles, cement, edible oils, sugar, soap distilling, shoes, petroleum refining, pharmaceuticals, armaments, automobile/light truck assembly, milling

Oil - proved reserves: 5 billion bbl (1 January 2018 est.)

Natural gas - proved reserves: 84.95 billion cu m (1 January 2018 est.)

Total Exports: $5.11 billion (2019 est.), $5 billion (2018 est.)

Export commodities: Gold, crude petroleum, sesame seeds, sheep, goats, cotton, ground nuts (2019)

Major Markets: United Arab Emirates 31%, China 19%, Saudi Arabia 14%, India 12%, Egypt 5% (2019)

Total Imports: $9.79 billion (2019 est.), $8.24 billion (2018 est.)

Import commodities: Raw sugar, wheat, packaged medicines, jewelry, tires, cars and vehicle parts (2019)

Major Suppliers: China 31%, India 14%, United Arab Emirates 11%, Egypt 6% (2019)

INTERNATIONAL DISPUTES

◆ The effects of Sudan's almost constant ethnic and rebel militia fighting since the mid-20th century have penetrated all neighbouring states - Chad, Ethiopia, Kenya, Central African Republic, Democratic Republic of the Congo, and Uganda.

◆ In February 2006, Sudan and DROC signed an agreement to repatriate 13,300 Sudanese and 6,800 Congolese.

◆ Sudan accuses Eritrea of supporting Sudanese rebel groups.

◆ Efforts to demarcate the porous boundary with Ethiopia proceed slowly due to civil and ethnic fighting in eastern Sudan.

◆ The boundary that separates Kenya and Sudan's sovereignty is unclear in the "Ilemi Triangle," which Kenya has administered since colonial times.

◆ Sudan claims but Egypt de facto administers security and economic development of Halaib region north of the 22nd parallel boundary.

◆ Periodic violent skirmishes with Sudanese residents over water and grazing rights persist among related pastoral populations along the border with the Central African Republic.

Bilateral relations between South Sudan and Sudan were officially started on 9 July 2011 following the former's independence from the latter.

DEFENCE

ARMY

Personnel: 60,000

Equipment

Category	Name	In Service
MBT	T-62	20
	Type 88	
	M-60	30+
	T-54/55	30+
	T-59	30+
Light Tank	Type 62 light	50
Armoured car	SALADIN	10+
	V-150 COMMANDOS	20+
	FERRET	20+
	AML-90	5
	BRDM-2	20+
AIFV/APC	BMP-2	5
	BTR-50/-152	30
	OT-64	30+
	M113	50
	WALID	100
	BTR-80	20+
Artillery	M101	20
	M56 (105mm)	
	D-74	
	M-1938	
	Type 54/D-30 (122mm)	50+
	Type 59-1/M-46 (130mm)	20+
	D-20 (155mm)	40+
	M114A1 (155mm) towed	10
	AMX F3 155mm SP	
Mortar	81mm	
	M-43	10
	AM-49 (120mm)	
ATGW	SWINGFIRE	
	SAGGER	
AA Gun	M-3 20mm SPAAG	10
	Bofors 40mm	50+
	37mm	80
	VULCAN	20
SAM	SA-2	20
	SA-7	
	REDEYE	

New Procurements/ Upgrades

No major procurement plans are under consideration at present.

NAVY

Personnel: 1,500

Equipment

Category	Name	In Service
Light Force	Swiftship type patrol boat	1
	Ex-Yugoslav patrol boat (GIHAD class)	2+
	SEWART type patrol craft	3
	Ex-Iranian coastal patrol craft (KADIR class)	2

New Procurements/ Upgrades

No major procurement plans are under consideration at present.

AIR FORCE

Major air bases: Atbara, Dongola, El Fashir, El Obeid, Geneima, Juba, Khartoum, Malakal, Merowe, Port Sudan, Wad Medani, Waw.

Personnel: 3,000

Equipment

Category	Name	In Service
Fighter	MiG-29	10+
	MiG-23	2
	MiG-21	5+
	F-6	10+
	F-7	10+
	Su-24	
	Su-25	10
	COIN	1
	K-8	10+
Maritime reconnaissance	C-212 AVIOCAR	5
Transport	F-27 FRIENDSHIP	1
	C-130H	2+
	DHC-5D	3
	An-32	5
	An-24	3
	C-212 AVIOCAR	
	EMB-110P	5+
	FALCON 20/50	2
Utility/Liaison	TURBO PORTER	5+
	TWIN OTTER	1
	KING AIR 90	1
Helicopter	Mi-4	4
	Mi-8	5
	SA.330 PUMA	10+
	BO-105	10+
	AB-412	8
	Mi-24	5+
	Mi-35P	3
Trainer	F-5F	1
	MiG-29UB	2

New Procurements/ Upgrades

No major procurement plans are under consideration at present.

Defence Expenditure

Total defence spending: $4 billion (approx.)
Defence spending in terms of GDP: 1.1% of GDP (2020 est.), 1.7% of GDP (2019 est.)
Domestic suppliers: Military Industry Corporation
Foreign suppliers: China, Russia, Ukraine, UAE, Jordan, Saudi Arabia, Iran, UK, Turkey

Military spending stood at USD3.308 billion in 2010 and increased to USD3.923 billion in 2011, amounting to 22.2% of GDP. More than three quarter of South Sudan's 2014/2015 budget was spent on government employees and the military. The minister apportions 28% (i.e.; 4.4 billion SSP) to the national army and approximately 13% (i.e.; 1.573 billion SSP) to police, prison and fire services for 2014-2015 fiscal year.

Defence Production and R&D

The Sudanese military research is believed to be limited to conventional and unsophisticated weapons programmes. It is looking to expand its indigenous defence industry with Russian and Chinese assistance. Sudan has signed an agreement with Pakistan on joint military co-operation at all levels. In January 2002, the International Atomic Energy Agency (IAEA) confirmed that the country was not pursuing nuclear weapons technology.

Defence Procurement

Sudan Army/Navy and Air Force have not made any major defence procurements in recent years.

CONTACT DETAILS

Ministry of Defence
P.O. Box 291, Khartoum, Sudan
Tel: +249-11-74910, -72771

Ministry of Foreign Affairs
Intersection of University Avenue
Street Pain Tiger, PO Box 873
Khartoum, Sudan
Tel: (+249 183) 77 31 01
Fax: (+249 183) 77 29 41
E-mail: ministry@mfa.gov.sd
Website: www.mfa.gov.sd

STRATEGIC INFORMATION
SWEDEN
(Capital: Stockholm)

INTRODUCTION

Area: 450,295 sq km
Population: 10,261,767 (July 2021 est.)
Coastline: 3,218 km
Maritime claims: Territorial sea: 12 nm (adjustments made to return a portion of straits to high seas)
Exclusive Economic Zone: agreed boundaries or midlines
Continental shelf: 200 m depth or to the depth of exploitation

GEOPOLITICAL IMPORTANCE

Sweden is a Scandinavian country in Northern Europe. At 450,295 square kilometres, it is the third-largest country in the European Union by area. Sweden lies west of the Baltic Sea and Gulf of Bothnia, providing a long coastline, and forms the eastern part of the Scandinavian Peninsula. To the west is the Scandinavian mountain chain (Skanderna), which separates Sweden from Norway. Finland is located to its north-east. It has maritime borders with Denmark, Germany, Poland, Russia, Lithuania, Latvia and Estonia, and it is also linked to Denmark (south-west) by the Öresund Bridge. Its border with Norway (1,619 km long) is the longest uninterrupted border within Europe. About 15% of Sweden lies north of the Arctic Circle. Southern Sweden is predominantly agricultural, with increasing forest coverage northward. Around 65% of Sweden's total land area is covered with forests.

POLITICAL OVERVIEW

Politics of Sweden takes place in a framework of a parliamentary representative democratic constitutional monarchy. The Swedish institutions are represented by the King Carl XVI Gustav whose functions stay honorary and led by a government called Regering and by a parliament "Riskdag". The Swedish government is formed by ministers and a Prime Minister called Statminister. The Prime Minister is named by the head of Parliament and chooses the ministers of his government. The Judiciary is independent, appointed by the government and employed until retirement.

KEY POLITICAL PERSONS

HEAD OF STATE:
King Carl XVI Gustaf

PRIME MINISTER:
Magdalena Andersson

ECONOMY

The economy of Sweden is a developed export-oriented economy. Sweden, with a

GDP of USD 511 billion and a population of 10 million, is the largest Nordic economy and boasts a transparent, highly developed, sophisticated and diversified market. Sweden also consistently ranks among the top 10 worldwide for its connectivity, governance, investment in R&D, etc. Sweden is a member of the European Union (EU). Sweden is highly dependent on exports, is strongly pro-free trade, and has one of the most internationally integrated economies in the world. Exports, including engines and other machines, motor vehicles, and telecommunications equipment, account for more than 44% of GDP. Sweden's gross domestic product (GDP) per capita is among the highest in the EU, it has low inflation and a healthy banking system. The World Economic Forum ranks Sweden among the top ten most competitive countries in the world. Sweden is also one of the easiest countries in the world to do business with, according to the World Bank. Stable economic policies combine with competitiveness, innovation and an open approach to trade to make Sweden a model for economic success. Sweden is highly dependent on exports, is strongly pro-free trade, and has one of the most internationally integrated economies in the world. The government has been expanding its export base away from the traditionally European market, seeking to grow in Asia, South America, and the United States, but the bulk of Sweden's exports still remains within the EU. During the peak period, Sweden avoided a lockdown to suppress the spread of COVID-19 and saw the shrink in economy to 8% in the months of April to June 2020. Swedish economy is expected to recover in the second half of 2020, just like the global economy in general. The Government has proposed extensive fiscal policy stimulus measures and reforms worth more than SEK 105 billion for 2021 and more than SEK 85 billion for 2022.

GDP (official exchange rate): $524.75 billion (2020 est.), $539.96 billion (2019 est.)

Real Growth Rate (GDP): 1.29% (2019 est.), 2.06% (2018 est.)

Industries: Iron and steel, precision equipment (bearings, radio and telephone parts, armaments), wood pulp and paper products, processed foods, motor vehicles

Total Exports: $240.08 billion (2020 est.), $254.53 billion (2019 est.)

Export Commodities: Cars and vehicle parts, packaged medicines, refined petroleum, broadcasting equipment, lumber (2019)

Major Markets: Germany 10%, Norway 9%, United States 8%, Denmark 7%, Finland 6%, United Kingdom 5%, Netherlands 5%, China 5% (2019)

Total Imports: $217.68 billion (2020 est.), $232.81 billion (2019 est.)

Import Commodities: Cars and vehicle parts, crude petroleum, refined petroleum, broadcasting equipment, computers (2019)

Major Suppliers: Germany 18%, Netherlands 9%, Denmark 7%, Norway 7%, China 6%, Finland 5%, Belgium 5%, Poland 5% (2019)

DEFENCE & SECURITY

The primary task of the Swedish Armed Forces is to train, organise and deploy military forces, domestically and abroad, while maintaining the long-term ability to defend the country in the event of war. The Ministry of Defence is responsible for Sweden's military defence and civil emergency preparedness. The head of the armed forces is the Supreme Commander, the most senior officer in the country. Swedish units have taken part in peacekeeping operations in the Democratic Republic of Congo, Cyprus, Bosnia and Herzegovina, Kosovo, Liberia, Lebanon, Afghanistan and Chad. The total defence comprises military and civil defence. The task of the civil defence is to plan support to the Armed Forces in a state of emergency. From 2016, the objectives for the military defence is to, independently and jointly with others, within and outside the country, defend Sweden and promote security in the country. The military units are designed firstly to be able to face an armed attack. These units are also fundamentally equipped to resolve tasks in peacetime, for example, protection of the territorial integrity and participation in international crisis managing operations.

KEY DEFENCE PERSONS

MINISTER FOR DEFENCE: Peter Hultqvist

SUPREME COMMANDER OF ARMED FORCES: Gen. Micael Byden

CHIEF OF ARMY: Maj. Gen. Karl Engelbrektson

CHIEF OF NAVY: Rear Adm. Ewa Skoog Haslum

CHIEF OF AIR FORCE: Maj. Gen. Carl-Johan Edström

Internal Conflict

Sweden is not engaged in any internal conflict in the region.

External Conflict

The Swedish Armed Forces are increasingly active on the international stage. The Swedish Armed Forces are active in over twenty countries. Sweden is a member of the Defeat-ISIS Coalition. In addition to being a leader in humanitarian support to ISIS-affected communities, Sweden deployed 70 military trainers to Iraq in support of Defeat-ISIS efforts.

Swedish Neutrality: Swedish neutrality refers to its policy of neutrality in armed conflicts, which has been in effect since the early 19th century. After the end of the Cold War and the fall of the Soviet Union, Sweden has officially dropped the principle of neutrality. The present policy of Swedish neutrality is not laid down in the Constitution or required by any international agreement. In 2016 Sweden became a NATO Affiliate, and signed a treaty allowing NATO operations to take place within the country's borders. Sweden is engaged in armed conflict in Afghanistan as part of an UN-authorised, NATO-led mission, the International Security Assistance Force – ISAF. Sweden does contribute to various NATO and EU battlegroups and is involved in international organisations. Today, Sweden is one of the Allies' most visible supporters among NATO's many partnering countries.

THREAT PERSPECTIVE

The National Centre for Terrorist Threat Assessment (NCT) is a permanent working group within the Swedish Counter-Terrorism Cooperation Council. The NCT is staffed by personnel from the National Defence Radio Establishment (FRA), the Military Intelligence and Security Directorate

(MUST) and the Swedish Security Service. The NCT produces long and short-term strategic assessments of the terrorist threat against Sweden and Swedish interests. The NCT is also tasked with producing strategic analyses of incidents, trends and international developments with a bearing on terrorism that may affect Sweden and Swedish interests, both today and in the future. According to the Swedish Security Service website, as reported in the one-year assessment by the National Centre for Terrorist Threat Assessment (NCT), the main terrorist threat to Sweden in 2018 is posed by Islamist-motivated terrorism. There are individuals both in Sweden and abroad who consider attacks against targets in Sweden legitimate.

As per 2019 assessment of NCT, the main terrorist threat to Sweden is likely from Islamist-motivated terrorism. There are individuals both in Sweden and abroad who consider terrorist attacks against targets in Sweden as legitimate. These circles are inspired by propaganda spread by groups such as al-Qaeda and ISIS. There is also report on threat to Sweden from violence-promoting right-wing and left-wing extremism. Sweden is a member of the EU and supports CT efforts in regional and multilateral organizations, including the European Commission's Radicalization Awareness Network, the EU-9 (focusing on FTFs), the Counter-Terrorism Group, the Police Working Group on Terrorism, and Europol.

STRATEGIC RELATIONS

United States: Sweden was one of the first countries to recognise US independence in 1783 and the two countries have maintained a strong bilateral friendship since then, based on shared values and mutual interests. The United States provides no development assistance to Sweden. Although Sweden has a longstanding policy of political neutrality in international affairs, it is a participant in the Euro-Atlantic Partnership Council. Sweden currently participates with around 500 troops in the International Security Assistance Force (ISAF), under the command of NATO, in Afghanistan. During the Libyan Civil War of 2011, the Swedish Air Force worked close with NATO and USA. Sweden is also a member of the Global Coalition to Defeat ISIS and participates in the United Nations Multidimensional Integrated Stabilisation Mission in Mali (MINUSMA). USA has collaborated with Sweden to strengthen Internet freedom in countries emerging from oppressive and autocratic regimes to more effectively promote and protect freedom of expression. Finland, Sweden and the US have signed a new letter pledging to increase the national security relationship between the two nations. The United States and Sweden's two way trade for 2019 is USD25.5 billon (including trade in goods and services). Sweden and the US invest over USD94 billion in each other's economies.

Nordic defence cooperation: NORDEFCO (Nordic Defence Cooperation) is a collaboration amongst the Nordic countries in the area of defence. Its five members are Denmark, Finland, Iceland, Norway, and Sweden. The purpose of NORDEFCO is to strengthen the participants' national defence, explore common synergies and facilitate efficient common solutions. NORDEFCO is the organisation responsible for implementing this in areas such as logistics and maintenance, training and exercises, operational activities, such as air and maritime surveillance and international operations. Defence partnerships with other countries are becoming an increasingly important way of enabling Sweden to develop and maintain its military capabilities in Sweden, and on international missions. The cooperation includes troop contributions to international peace missions, development, procurement, maintenance and further development of materiel, officer training and exercises. In 2016, the Nordic Ministers of Defence made a Joint Statement, after having signed a Memorandum of Understanding on enhanced and easier access to each other's territories in peacetime. The agreement will improve the operational effect and quality of air, land and maritime operations. Also, the Northern Group consisting of Denmark, Estonia, Finland, Germany, Iceland, Latvia, Lithuania, the Netherlands, Norway, Poland, the United Kingdom and Sweden, came together informally for discussions on defence and security issues. In 2019 Sweden holds the chairmanship of the Nordic Defence Cooperation (NORDEFCO). Sweden's priorities during its chairmanship were enhanced military cooperation as well as facilitation of armaments cooperation. The Nordic cooperation is central for Swedish defence and security policy. In 2013, Sweden and Finland announced their intent to strengthen their defence cooperation. In the joint final report, submitted by the Swedish Armed Forces and the Finnish Defence Forces, a number of cooperation areas were presented such as the development of a bilateral standing Naval Task Group, the Swedish-Finnish Naval Task Group (SFNTG), with full operational capability by 2023, an increased level of interoperability between the Swedish and Finnish Air Forces with the capacity for joint operation, common base operations and common command and control (C2) capability and the development of a combined Finnish - Swedish Brigade Framework.

India: The ties between India and Sweden were established in 1949 and are founded on shared democratic values. India and Sweden in 2015 signed several agreements to boost ties and decided to restart the bilateral strategic dialogue besides finding ways for investment by the Nordic country in India's defence sector under the ambitious 'Make in India' initiative. A MoU on defence between Sweden and India was signed in November, 2009. The MoU set out several areas for cooperation between the defence authorities of the two countries for the purpose of mutual benefit. Sweden is the third-largest contributor of Foreign Direct Investment (FDI) to India besides being the country's third-largest trade partner after China and Japan. In 2018, both the Govt. announced that India and Sweden have agreed on an innovation partnership and a joint action plan. Sweden and India would also work towards a security agreement, including cyber security, which would allow the countries to exchange intelligence information. Sweden has declared his support for India's candidature as a permanent member of the UNSC. The main Swedish exports to India are communication equipment, motor vehicles, paper & pulp products, pharmaceuticals, chemicals and engineering products. The main items of Indian exports are garments, textiles, chemical products, food products, and semi manufactured and manufactured goods.

Multilateral Alliances: Sweden belongs to a number of international organisations, including the United Nations, European Union (EU), Euro-Atlantic Partnership Council, the Arctic Council, Organisation for Security and Cooperation in Europe, Organisation for Economic Cooperation and Development, International Monetary Fund, World Bank, and World Trade Organisation. Sweden also is an observer to the Organisation of American States and a participant in the North Atlantic Treaty Organisation's (NATO) Partnership for Peace programme. Sweden is also a member of Partnership for Peace (PfP) a practical partnership programme between NATO and various OSCE states (Organisation for Security and Co-operation in Europe). Sweden is an Enhanced Opportunities Partner (EOP) of the NATO and plays an active leadership role on the international stage, from its long-term investment in Afghanistan to its role as a global peacemaker.

DEFENCE CAPABILITIES

ARMY: The Swedish Army has the task of organising and training ground forces and air defence units. Army units operate both on the ground and in the air. They are trained and equipped for combat with all types of enemy in different types of terrain and urban environments. The Army units are categorised into Mechanised Units, Cavalry Units, Artillery Units, Air Defence Units, Command and Control Units, Engineer Units, Support Units and CBRN Units.

Personnel: 19,200

Equipment

Category	Name	In Service
MBT	Stridsvagn 122	110+
APC/ MICV/IFV	CV-90	400+
	Pbv-302	40+
	Patria XA-200 6x6	155+
	Patria AMV	120
	Bv-206S	90
	RG-32M SCOUT	200+
	Stridsfordon 90	400+
	Pansarterrängbil 360/203	300+
Artillery	155 mm. towed FH-77B	40
Mortar	120 mm.	55
Anti-Tank GW	TOW	
	BILL	
	Robot-57	
Recoilless rifle	Carl Gustav	
	AT-4	
AA Gun	CV90 AA	20+
SAM	HAWK	
	I-HAWK	
	RBS-70	
	RBS-23 BAMSE	

New Procurements/ Upgrades

◆ Rheinmetall has been awarded a contract from the Swedish armed forces to supply vehicles for transporting Patriot air defence systems made by Rheinmetall's partner Raytheon. Starting in the first quarter of 2021, Rheinmetall MAN Military Vehicles (RMMV) will supply Sweden with a total of forty high-mobility trucks from its HX series, including 16 tractor trucks and 24 transport vehicles. The order is in the double-digit million-euro range. FMV, the Swedish procurement authority, has already ordered other HX vehicles for its logistics corps.

◆ The US State Department has approved a possible Foreign Military Sale to Sweden of Patriot Configuration-3+ Modernised Fire Units for an estimated cost of USD 3.2 billion. The Defence Security Cooperation Agency delivered the required certification notifying Congress of this possible sale. The Government of Sweden has requested to buy 4 Patriot Configuration-3+ Modernised Fire Units consisting of: 4 AN/MPQ-65 radar sets, 4 AN/MSQ-132 engagement control stations, 9 antenna mast groups, 12 M903 launching stations, 100 Patriot MIM-104E Guidance Enhanced Missile-TBM (GEM-T) missiles, 200 Patriot Advanced Capabilty-3 (PAC-3) Missile Segment Enhancement (MSE) missiles, and 4 Electrical Power Plants (EPP) III. Also included with this request are communications equipment, tools and test equipment, range and test programmes, support equipment to include associated vehicles, prime movers, generators, publications and technical documentation, training equipment, spare and repair parts, personnel training, Technical Assistance Field Team (TAFT), US Government and contractor technical, engineering, and logistics support services, Systems Integration and Checkout (SICO), field office support, and other related elements of logistics and programme support.

◆ Swedish Defence Materiel Administration (FMV) has received the Mjölner vehicle mounted mortar system from BAE Systems for the Swedish Army's CV90 combat vehicles.

◆ The Swedish Defence and Material Administration has awarded BAE Systems a contract to deliver additional rounds of Bofors 155mm BONUS ammunition to the Swedish Army.

◆ The Swedish Patriot system is in production with delivery of the first fire unit to FMV during the second quarter of 2021.

NAVY: The Swedish Navy has the task of organising and training naval and amphibious units and operates in navigable coastal waters, in the archipelago and on the open sea. Naval units are categorised into Naval flotillas, Submarine flotilla, Amphibious battalion and Naval base. Karlskrona naval base (MarinB) is located at Karlskrona with detachments at Berga, Goteborg and Skredsvik.

Personnel: 9,500

Equipment

Category	Name	In Service
Submarine	Gotland Class	3
	Sodermanland Class	2
Corvette	Visby Class	3
	Goteborg Class	2
	Stockholm Class	2
Mine Warfare Force	Landsort Class	2
	Styrso Class	4
	Koster class	5

...continued

Category	Name	In Service
Patrol Vessel	Tapper class	10
	CB90 HSM (Combat)	20
Auxiliary Force	Submarine rescue ship	1
	Supply ship	1
	Survey Vessel	1
Amphibious Force	Landing Craft Mechanised (LCM)	17
	Landing Craft Utility (LCU)	20+
	LCPFM	140+
	Light Combat Aircraft (LCA)	50+
	Griffon 8100TD Hovercraft	3

New Procurements/ Upgrades

◆ The first out of 18 of the all-new CB90 HSM has been delivered to the Swedish defence material administration (FMV). A brand-new boat, equipped with a lot more than its predecessors: improved speed and manoeuvrability – as well as attack power and surveillance capabilities.

◆ CAE has been awarded a contract from the Swedish Defence Materiel Administration (FMV) to upgrade and expand the capabilities of the Naval Warfare Training System (NWTS) located at the Swedish Naval Warfare Centre (NWC) in Karlskrona, Sweden.

◆ Saab has received an order from the Swedish Defence Material Administration (FMV) for delivery of advanced anti-submarine warfare training, including the autonomous underwater vehicle AUV62 in training configuration. Deliveries will take place during the period 2016-2019.

◆ Kockums AB signed a contract with the Swedish Defence Materiel Administration (FMV) concerning overall of the design phase of the next-generation submarine. Sweden is planning to purchase two new submarines that will be commissioned by 2018-19 replacing the two submarines of the Södermanland class. The plans also included upgrades to two submarines of the Gotland class. Additional submarines could later be orderd to replace the Gotland class, however this will not be decided before 2020.

◆ Saab in 2019 launched the special-purpose signal intelligence (SIGINT) ship for the Royal Swedish Navy.

AIR FORCE: The Swedish Air Force is tasked with organising and training aircraft units, and base and command units and completes its tasks by means of fixed-wing aircraft and helicopters. These tasks include protecting Swedish airspace, conducting rescue operations, performing air transport duties and gathering intelligence. Air Force units are categorised into Fighter Aircraft Units, Transport Aircraft Units, Signal Reconnaissance Units, Radar Surveillance Units, Helicopter Units, Base and Command Units.

Personnel: 6,600

Equipment

Category	Name	In Service
Fighters/attack/Reconnaissance	JAS 39C/D	70
	JAS 39 E/F	On order
	Dassault nEUROn	Under development
Transport/Tanker	C130H	6
	C-17 Globemaster III	5+
	Saab 340	6
Trainer	Saab-105	30
SIGINT	Gulfstream IV	2
UAV	Shadow 200, Elbit Skylark, Wasp III, RQ-20 PUMA	3+

Swedish Helicopter Flotilla

Personnel: 700

Equipment

Category	Name	In Service
Helicopter	NH90	15+
	A109	15
	UH-60M Black Hawk	10+
Missile	Sidewinder, Maverick, Hawk, Robot 05, RB 04	

New Procurements/ Upgrades

◆ Saab is in the fray for a contract to supply around 110 Gripen E fighter planes to India under the Multi Role Fighter Aircraft (MRFA) programme. The Indian Air Force in April 2018 issued an initial tender or Request for Information (RFI) for the billion dollar procurement deal.

◆ Saab signed an agreement with the Swedish Defence Materiel Administration (FMV) regarding development and modification of 60 Gripen E for Sweden during the period 2013-2026 as well as a possible order for new production of Gripen E for Switzerland. The Swedish Air Force wants to upgrade 60–80 Gripens to this standard by 2020. The Swedish Riksdag has also approved the purchase of 40 to 60 E/F aircraft, but with an option to cancel if at least 20 aircraft are not ordered by other customers. The Government of Sweden approved the deal for 60 Gripen Es on 17 January 2013. Deliveries will begin in 2018 and be completed in 2027.

◆ Saab has received a serial production order from the Swedish Defence Materiel Administration (FMV) amounting to SEK16,4 billion for operations during 2013-2026. The order includes modification of 60 Gripen C to Gripen E for Sweden with initial deliveries in 2018.

◆ FMV, the Swedish Defence Materiel Administration, signed a production order contract with United Kingdom MOD regarding the Meteor missile. With the Meteor missile the JAS39 Gripen system will get a significantly increased capability to operate against air targets at long distances with very high performance.

◆ Sweden and Switzerland have signed a framework agreement for procurement of the next generation Gripen. The Swedish government plans to buy 40-60 new Gripens over the next decade at a cost of 242 million euros.

◆ According to a white paper by Sweden's defence committee, Gripen C/D will be an important part of the Swedish Air Force even beyond 2030.

Swedish air force JAS 39 Gripen fighters arrive at Nellis AFB, Nev., on July 14 for Red Flag 08-3. Image Credit: US Air Force

Major Armaments Producers

Sweden has a well-developed defence industry. The Swedish Security and Defence Association is open to companies whose production of security and defence equipment and services constitutes an essential part of their output, i.e. companies engaged in research, development, production, trade and marketing of military and security equipment, material and services. The Association currently has 65 member companies including 50 SMEs.

3M Svenska AB, 4C Group AB (4C Strategies), Actea Consulting AB, Aimpoint AB, Aqeri AB, BAE Systems Bofors AB, BAE Systems Hägglunds AB, Carmenta AB, CGI Sverige AB, Cobham, Combitech AB, Comex Electronics AB, Condesign AB, CRD Protection AB, CybAero AB, Datapath (f.d Rockwell Collins Sweden AB), Dockstavarvet AB, Eltel Networks Infranet AB, Eurenco Bofors AB, FLIR Systems AB, GSS, GKN Aerospace AB, Habia Cable CS Technology, Hewlett-Packard Sweden AB, IBM Svenska AB, Imdar Systems AB, Kaller, Kitron AB, Life Time Engineering AB, Marinediesel Sweden AB, Micro Systemation AB, Mildef AB, MSE Engineering AB, Nammo Sweden AB, PartnerTech Karlskoga AB, Patria Helicopters AB, Polyamp AB, PrimeKey Solutions AB, Qinetiq Sweden AB, Rolls-Royce AB, Rote Consulting AB, RSG connexion AB, Saab AB, Saab Bofors Test Center AB, SCAMA AB, Scania CV AB, Secana AB, Sepson AB, Sjöland & Thyselius AB, Skyddsprodukter i Sverige AB, SRS Group AB, Swede Ship Marine AB, Svensk Konstruktionstjänst AB, Syntell AB, Systecon AB, Teleanalys AB, T-kartor, Sweden AB, Venatio AB, Volvo Defense AB, Woolpower AB, ÅAC Microtec AB, ÅF Technology AB, Åkers Krutbruk Protection AB, etc. are the member companies.

DEFENCE DEALS

Arms Export

Swedish defence major Saab has unveiled its next generation fighter aircraft, Gripen E, which the company in 2016 said is being offered to India under the 'Make In India' initiative with transfer of technology. Gripen E has significantly improved avionics system when compared to previous versions of the Gripen. The Gripen E is a specific configuration of Gripen NG that has been chosen by the Swedish customer. The exact configuration for another customer such as India will depend on discussions with that customer. Saab is offering the next generation Gripen to India, under 'Make In India' with transfer of technology. The company has not only offered to set up a base here but also help in the development of aerospace capability for the next 100 years. It has also offered to partner in developing the next version of indigenous Light Combat Aircraft Tejas and the Advanced Medium Combat Aircraft (AMCA), being developed and designed by Aeronautical Development Agency. Gripen E is equipped with a highly integrated and sophisticated sensor suite including an Active Electronically Scanned Array (AESA) radar, Infra-Red Search and Track (IRST), Electronic Warfare (EW) suite and datalink technology, which, when combined gives the pilot, and co-operating forces exactly the information needed at all times.

The Swedish Defence and Security Export Agency (FXM) promotes defence export which benefits Swedish defence and security policies. The agency represents the Swedish Government in contracts between governments (G2G contracts). The Government intends to close FXM during 2015. The planned closure of the FXM is expected to trigger a major redevelopment of the country's arms export rules and infrastructure.

DEFENCE BUDGET

Total defence spending: $6.8 billion (2019 approx.)
Estimated defence spending in terms of GDP: 1.1% of GDP (2020 est.), 1.1% of GDP (2019)

Government bill 'Totalförsvaret 2021–2025':

According to Government of Sweden report in Dec 2020, Sweden's military defence is being designed and dimensioned to be able to respond to an armed attack against Sweden. Annual spending on military defence will increase with approximately EUR 2.7 billion totalling EUR 8.9 billion by 2025. This is an increase of around 45 percent compared with 2020 and 95 percent compared with 2015.

◆ Two new Blekinge-class submarines will be commissioned. Preparations for the procurement of new surface combat vessels will begin with the aim of two new vessels being delivered during the period 2026–2030. Increase in the number of submarines from the four at present to five in 2021-25 period.

◆ An additional amphibious battalion will be organised and based in Gothenburg.

◆ The new combat aircraft system JAS 39 E will be commissioned during the period 2021–2025 and will along with the existing JAS 39 C/D be organised in six fighter squadrons. Additional missiles and electronic warfare capabilities will be procured.

◆ Home Guard units should receive additional equipment.

◆ Ability to conduct defensive and offensive operations in the cyber domain.

◆ Sweden's civil defence and military defence need to be developed in a coordinated fashion and there should be coherent planning for total defence. The Government's focus is a gradual strengthening that includes EUR 0.1 billion in 2021, EUR 0.15 billion in 2022, EUR 0.25 billion in 2023, EUR 0.3 billion in 2024 and EUR 0.38 billion in 2025. Together with the funds allocated in the Budget Bill for 2018, total civil defence funds will amount to EUR 0.42 billion in 2025.

Material Planning
The task of material planning is carried out jointly by the Armed Forces, the Swedish Defence Materiel Administration (FMV) and the Swedish Defence Research Agency (Totalförsvarets forskningsinstitut). These agencies decide how to direct resources, guided by the guidelines set by parliament and the government.

The Armed Forces are engaged in both developing new material and decommissioning that which is outdated. New equipment is often developed in cooperation with other countries in order to spread the costs. The country also decommissions old material, which is often too costly to store when it is no longer in use. Also, materials are donated to certain kinds of organisations that might need it. Otherwise it is sold or destroyed.

Swedish defence and aerospace company Saab has started the assembly of the next generation Gripen, the Gripen E. Following a short and intense period of design using the latest tools and methods, through so called 'Model Based Design', the construction of the Gripen E begins with the manufacturing and assembly of all parts of the fuselage; the largest and most time-consuming part of the airframe. These parts will then be joined together and assembled into a complete airframe. This is followed by an intensive construction period to install cables, mount systems, the outer shell and other equipment. Based on the design of previous versions of the Gripen system, the Gripen E offers a next generation sensor suite, new communication links, revolutionary avionics architecture, more thrust, increased flight time, more weapon stations and load capability, a fully digital cockpit including HUD (Head-Up Display) and a brand new electronic warfare system. The test aircraft 39-8 will be the first complete pre-production version of the Gripen E and will be used to demonstrate new features and capabilities. The technological leaps in the Gripen E have been proven in the Gripen demonstrator programme with the Gripen E/F demo aircraft that has flown over 250 hours in countries such as Sweden, the UK, India and Switzerland (in Emmen in October 2012, January and April 2013) since 2008.

Swedish Defence Commission
The Defence Commission is a forum for consultation between the Government and representatives of the political parties in Riksdag (national legislature and the supreme decision-making body of Sweden). The objective is to achieve the broadest possible unity with respect to how Sweden's defence and security policy is to be designed. The Government forms its proposals for Riksdag based on reports from the Defence Commission. On 9 January 2017, the Defence Commission were given instructions for its continued work. Not later than 14 May 2019, the Commission is to submit a defence and security policy report to the Government. The report will constitute an important basis for the next defence bill.

Defence Procurement
The Armed Forces are engaged in developing new systems, and decommissioning older systems that have reached the end of their service life. New equipment tends to be developed in co-operation with other countries with a view to minimising costs. Sweden has a well-developed defence industry, so a considerable proportion of Armed Forces' equipment is manufactured domestically. The Swedish Defence Materiel Administration (Försvarets materielverk, FMV) is a Swedish government agency that reports to the Ministry of Defence. The agency is responsible for the supply of materiel to the Swedish defence organisation. Requests for new materials are drafted within the Swedish Armed Forces and then submitted to the FMV for action. FMV is charged with technical preparation work, inspection of materials and equipment, and modifications or upgrades deemed necessary for a given system or piece of equipment. Most military procurement contracts are awarded to Swedish defence companies. However, companies often partner with foreign suppliers. FMV is located in Stockholm. In 2014, Sweden's new coalition government announced plans to shut down the Swedish Defence and Security Export Agency ('FXM'), a division of the Defence Ministry, whose primary role is to promote arms exports.

CONCLUSION

International defence and security cooperation, in particular Nordic and Baltic cooperation, strengthens the security of Sweden as a nation. A strong transatlantic link is crucial for Europe's security. It is in Swedish interests to maintain and further deepen the bilateral relationship with the United States. The deepening of bilateral cooperation with Finland is critical. The task of the Swedish Armed Forces is to defend Sweden and safeguard its sovereignty and securing its borders. Sweden gives support to the United Nations (UN) in order to contribute to global peace, security and development. Units from the Swedish Armed Forces are currently on deployment in several international operations either actively or as military observers, including Afghanistan as part of the Resolute Support Mission and in Kosovo. Through its membership in the European Union (EU) Sweden assumes joint responsibility for the security of Europe and the ability of the EU to promote peaceful and democratic development.

Sweden's cooperation with NATO allows the Swedish Armed Forces to develop military capabilities and, by contributing to qualified international crisis management operations, Sweden contributes to building security together with partners. The Swedish Armed Forces receive approximately SEK 40 billion to perform important military tasks. Around half of the money goes to the activities conducted by the units. The other half goes to research, development and materiel systems. Sweden takes part in EU rationalisation and cooperation on equipment, and has contributed to every EU crisis management operation. Over a twenty-year period, Sweden has developed close cooperation with the NATO defence alliance within the Partnership for Peace. By taking part in all major NATO operations under a UN mandate and in major exercises with NATO member countries in Europe, Sweden has developed cooperation capabilities with the Alliance and its member countries on a par with that of many NATO members.

This cooperation is crucial to the operational capabilities of the Swedish Armed Forces. Sweden has long enjoyed well-developed defence cooperation, including cooperation on equipment, with the Nordic countries, certain large European countries and the US. Swedish Armed Forces contribute as the lead nation for an EU Battle Group once every three years through the Nordic Battlegroup. Sweden has close relations with NATO and NATO members.

CONTACT DETAILS
Ministry of Defence
Jakobsgatan 9
SE-103 33 Stockholm
SwedenTel: (+46 8) 405 10 00
Fax: (+46 8) 723 11 89
E-mail: registrator@defence.ministry.se
Website: www.sweden.gov.se

Swedish Armed Forces
Försvarsmakten
107 85, Stockholm
Phone: (+46) 08-788 75 00
Fax: (+46) 08-788 77 78
E-mail: exp-hkv@mil.se
Web: www.forsvarsmakten.se/en/

Swedish Defence Materiel Administration
Försvarets materielverk (FMV)
Banérgatan 62
S-115 88 STOCKHOLM
Visiting address: Banérgatan 62
Sweden
Telephone: +46 (0)8 - 782 4000
Fax: +46 (0)8 - 661 8220
E-mail: annons@fmv.se
registrator@fmv.se
Website: www.fmv.se

SWITZERLAND
(Capital: Bern)

INTRODUCTION
Area: 41,277 sq km
Population: 8,453,550 (July 2021 est.)
Coastline: 0 km (Landlocked)
Maritime claims: None

KEY POLITICAL PERSONS

PRESIDENT: Guy Parmelin

KEY DEFENCE PERSONS

HEAD OF THE FEDERAL DEPARTMENT OF DEFENCE: Viola Amherd

CHIEF OF ARMED FORCES: Maj. Gen. Jean-Paul Theler

ECONOMY

Switzerland is a peaceful, prosperous, and modern market economy with low unemployment, a highly skilled labour force, and a per capita GDP among the highest in the world. Switzerland's economy benefits from a highly-developed service sector, led by financial services, and a manufacturing industry that specializes in high-technology, knowledge-based production. Its economic and political stability, transparent legal system, exceptional infrastructure, efficient capital markets, and low corporate tax rates also make Switzerland one of the world's most competitive economies. The Swiss have brought their economic practices largely into conformity with the EU's to enhance their international competitiveness, but some trade protectionism remains, particularly for its small agricultural sector. The fate of the Swiss economy is tightly linked to that of its neighbours in the euro zone, which purchases half of all Swiss exports. The sovereign debt crises unfolding in neighbouring euro-zone countries, coupled with ongoing economic instability in Russia and other eastern European economies continue to pose a significant risk to the Swiss economy, driving up demand for the Swiss franc by investors seeking a safe-haven currency.

In recent years, Switzerland has responded to increasing pressure from neighbouring countries and trading partners to reform its banking secrecy laws, by agreeing to conform to OECD regulations on administrative assistance in tax matters, including tax evasion. The Swiss government has also renegotiated its double taxation agreements with numerous countries, including the US, to incorporate OECD standards, and is openly considering the possibility of imposing taxes on bank deposits held by foreigners.

Hit by the COVID-19 pandemic, the Swiss economy contracted by 2.9% in 2020, Government data showed. GDP is expected to recover moderately in 2021.

GDP (official exchange rate): $731.502 billion (2019 est.)

Real Growth Rate (GDP): 1.11% (2019 est.); 3.04% (2018 est.)

Industries: Machinery, chemicals, watches, textiles, precision instruments, tourism, banking, insurance, pharmaceuticals

Total Exports: $443.99 billion (2019 est.); $444.60 billion (2018 est.)

Exports Commodities: Gold, packaged medicines, medical cultures/vaccines, watches, jewellery (2019)

Major Markets: Germany 16%, United States 14%, United Kingdom 8%, China 7%, France 6%, India 6%, Italy 5% (2019)

Total Imports: $344.47 billion (2019 est.); $344.55 billion (2018 est.)

Import Commodities: Chemicals, vehicles, machinery, metals; textiles

Major Suppliers: Germany 21%, Italy 8%, United States 6%, France 6%, United Kingdom 5%, United Arab Emirates 5% (2019)

INTERNATIONAL DISPUTES

Switzerland has no known international disputes.

DEFENCE

ARMY

Personnel: 100,000+

Equipment

Category	Name	In Service
MBT	Leopard 2 (Pz 87 Leo)	134
APC, IFV	Duro IIIP	290
	M113	371
	CV90 (Spz 2000)	186
	APC 93 (Piranha)	521
	Duro	290 (+130 on order)
Reconnaissance vehicle	93, 93/97, 97/06	326
Howitzer	M109 calibre	150+
Anti-tank vehicle	Piranha TOW	110
SAM	Stinger	96

New Procurements/ Upgrades

◆ 130 Duro IIIP APCs are on order from General Dynamics Land Systems with deliveries going on.

◆ Modernized Duro-I WE troops transport vehicles are being delivered since 2018. The Army has placed an order for a total of 2,220 Duro-Is which would be delivered by 2022.

◆ An order has been placed with General Dynamics European Land Systems-Mowag in 2019 for procurement of 100 protected Eagle 6x6 reconnaissance vehicles.

◆ Norway's Kongsberg has received an order to supply the Protector Weapon Control System to the Swiss Army.

◆ Spanish company EXPAL has been awarded a contract to deliver 81mm mortars to Swiss Army.

◆ Procurement of mini UAVs for reconnaissance role is under consideration.

AIR FORCE

Equipment

Category	Name	In Service
Fighter	F/A-18 Hornet C/D	31
	F-5 E/F Tiger II	36 (26 operational)
Transport	Beechcraft 1900	1
	Pilatus PC-6 Turbo-Porter	15
	Dassault Falcon 50	1
	Pilatus PC-12	1
	Cessna Citation Excel	1
Trainer	Pilatus PC-7	28
	Pilatus PC-9	8
	Pilatus PC-21	8
UAV	ADS-95 Ranger	15
Helicopter	Super Puma	15
	Cougar	11
	EC 635	20
Air Defence System	Stinger	96
	Rapier	40
	Skyguard	

New Procurements/ Upgrades

◆ The Government in June 2021 has announced to buy 36 of the Lockheed Martin's F-35A Joint Strike Fighter aircraft at an estimated cost of $5.5 billion under the "Air2030" programme. The new platforms will replace the Swiss Air Force's ageing fleet of F-5 planes and subsequently the F/A-18 Hornets. Deliveries are slated to begin from 2025 onwards.

◆ The Government has announced procurement of five PAC-3 Patriot missile defence systems from US's Raytheon Technologies under the "Air2030" programme. The new long-range ground-to-air missile defence systems would be acquired at a cost of $2.1 billion. The US State Department in September 2020 had approved the potential sale of Patriot systems and related equipment to Switzerland under the FMS route.

◆ The entire fleet of Boeing F/A-18 Hornet fighters is being modernised under a $535 million programme to keep them operational beyond 2025. The US Defense Security Cooperation Agency in 2017 had notified the Congress of a potential $115m foreign military sale of F/A-18 Super Hornet upgrades to Switzerland.

◆ Six Hermes 900 unmanned aerial vehicles built by Israel's Elbit Systems are being procured for the Air Force's ADS-15 project. Delivery is expected to start from 2022.

Defence Expenditure

Total defence spending: CHF6 billion (2019)

Estimated defence spending in terms of GDP: 0.6%

Defence Production and R&D

The well-developed and self-sufficient defence and aerospace industry of Switzerland has been catering to domestic needs and also exports military products to international customers. Some of the leading defence and aerospace companies include RUAG Holding, Pilatus Flugzeugwerke AG and Oerlikon-Contraves AG which has been renamed as Rheinmetall Air Defence AG.

A decline in the annual defence budget over the years has adversely affected Switzerland's domestic defence production.

Reduced military spending has resulted in cutback in armaments production. Besides, a strict export regime has led to the Swiss defence industry facing strong competition from international arms majors.

Defence Procurement

Switzerland has announced the acquisition of new F-35 Joint Strike Fighter platforms as replacement for the Air Force's ageing fleet of frontline fighters. The Government has earmarked CHF6 billion Swiss Francs for the major acquisition programme. In total, around CHF15 bn is estimated to be required to fund Switzerland's equipment procurement plans between 2023 and 2032. To accommodate this, the defence budget's real growth would need to increase by about 1.4% annually from 2021 onwards.

Meanwhile, the Government has announced plans to gradually reduce the size of its armed forces from the present strength of over 140,000 to 100,000 starting from 2018 onwards.

CONTACT DETAILS

Federal Department of Defence
Federal Palace East
CH-3003, Bern
Tel: +41 58 462 21 11
www.vbs.admin.ch

SYRIA
(Capital: Damascus)

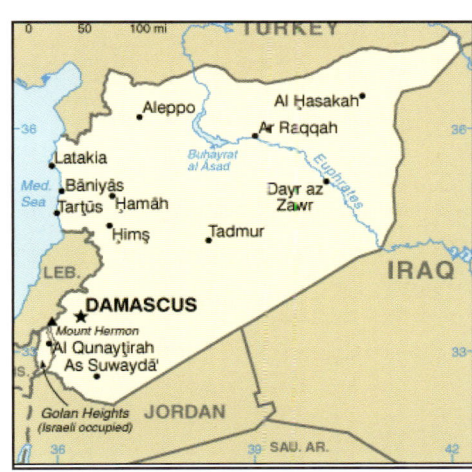

INTRODUCTION
Area: 187,437 sq km
Population: 20,384,316 (July 2021 est.)
Coastline: 193 km
Maritime claims: Territorial Sea: 12nm
Contiguous Zone: 24 nm

KEY POLITICAL PERSONS

PRESIDENT & COMMANDER-IN-CHIEF OF ARMED FORCES: Bashar al-Assad

PRIME MINISTER: Hussein Arnous

KEY DEFENCE PERSONS

DEFENCE MINISTER: Gen. Ali Abdullah Ayyoub

ECONOMY

Syria's economy has deeply deteriorated amid the ongoing conflict that began in 2011, declining by more than 70% from 2010 to 2017. The government has struggled to fully address the effects of international sanctions, widespread infrastructure damage, diminished domestic consumption and production, reduced subsidies, and high inflation, which have caused dwindling foreign exchange reserves, rising budget and trade deficits, a decreasing value of the Syrian pound, and falling household purchasing power. In 2017, some economic indicators began to stabilize, including the exchange rate and inflation, but economic activity remains depressed and GDP almost certainly fell.

During 2017, the ongoing conflict and continued unrest and economic decline worsened the humanitarian crisis, necessitating high levels of international assistance, as more than 13 million people remain in need inside Syria, and the number of registered Syrian refugees increased from 4.8 million in 2016 to more than 5.4 million. Long-run economic constraints for the country include foreign trade barriers, declining oil production, high unemployment, rising budget deficits, increasing pressure on water supplies caused by heavy use in agriculture, industrial contraction, water pollution, and widespread infrastructure damage.

Syria's economic woes have further deepened in the wake of the Coronavirus pandemic.

GDP (official exchange rate): $24.6 billion (2014 est.)

Real Growth Rate (GDP): -36.5% (2014 est.); -30.9% (2013 est.)

Industries: Petroleum, textiles, food processing, beverages, tobacco, phosphate rock mining, cement, oil seeds crushing, automobile assembly

Natural Gas - Proved Reserves: 240.7 billion cu m (1 January 2018 est.)

Crude Oil - Proved Reserves: 2.5 billion bbl (1 January 2018 est.)

Total Exports: $1.85 billion (2017 est.); $1.705 billion (2016 est.)

Export Commodities: Olive oil, cumin seeds, pistachios, tomatoes, apples, pears, spices, pitted fruits (2019)

Major Markets: Saudi Arabia 23%, Turkey 18%, Egypt 14%, United Arab Emirates 8%, Jordan 7%, Kuwait 5% (2019)

Total Imports: $6.279 billion (2017 est.); $5.496 billion (2016 est.)

Import Commodities: Wheat flours, refined petroleum, Cigarettes, broadcasting equipment, sunflower oil (2019)

Major Suppliers: Turkey 27%, China 22%, United Arab Emirates 14%, Egypt 5% (2019)

INTERNATIONAL DISPUTES

The province of Hatay in Turkey (containing Antakya) and the Golan Heights were all originally part of French Mandate Syria, but are now outside the boundaries of the modern Syrian state. Golan Heights is Israeli-occupied with the almost 1,000-strong UN Disengagement Observer Force patrolling a buffer zone since 1964. Since 2000, Lebanon has claimed Shab'a Farms in the Golan Heights. Lacking a treaty or other documentation describing the boundary, portions of the Lebanon-Syria boundary are unclear with several sectors in dispute.

DEFENCE

The Syrian military consists of the Air, Ground, Navy and the Air Defence Forces. The President of Syria is the Commander-in-Chief of the Armed Forces. The military is a conscripted force. The current enlisted members of the Syrian military have dropped by over half from a pre-civil war figure. As the uprising in the country progressed into civil war in 2011, several soldiers began to defect from the Syrian Armed Forces and came together under the banner of Free Syrian Army (FSA). Various rebel forces such as the Islamic State (ISIS/ISIL), the Al-Nousra Front, the Army of Conquest and the FSA fought against Government troops. Air strikes against ISIS positions have been carried out by foreign countries like the United States, Australia, Bahrain, Canada, France, Jordan, Saudi Arabia, Turkey and United Arab Emirates.

On the other side, the Government of Russia has been involved directly in the Syrian conflict by supporting and strongly backing the internationally-recognised Syrian regime led by President Bashar al-Assad. Moscow has not only supported the Syrian Government politically, but also made direct military intervention by deploying troops and fighter jets to Syria starting from 2015 onward and carrying out combat missions to fight the terror groups as well as the rebels/anti-Government forces. The Russian Defence Minister in 2017 announced that Moscow had started establishing a permanent military presence at naval and air bases in Syria. Iran too has strongly supported the Syrian regime led by President Bashar al-Assad.

ARMY
Personnel: 150,000

Equipment

Category	Name	In Service
MBT	T-90/T-72	1000+
	T-62	500+
	T-55MV	
Armoured Car	BRDM-2	700
AIFV & APC	BMP-1/2	2000+
	BTR 40/50/60/152	1500
	OT-64	
Artillery	82mm, 120mm, 160mm, 240mm	1500
	2-S1 122mm SP	200+
	2-S3 152mm SP	50+
Mortar	81mm	
	120mm	
	160mm	
MRL	122mm, 140mm, 240mm	
ATGW	Snapper	2000+
	Sagger	
	Swatter	
	Spigot	
	Spandrel	
	Hot	
	Milan	
	Kornet	
AA gun	23mm, 37mm	900
	57mm, 85mm	900
	100mm towed	100+
	ZSU-23-4	300
	ZSU-57-2 SP	10
SAM	SA6/-7/-8/-9/-11/-13/-18	
SSM	Frog-7	24
	Scud B launchers	18
	SS-12	
	SS-21	18

New Procurements/Upgrades

No major procurement plans are under consideration at present.

NAVY

Personnel: 4,000 (+2,500 Reserves)

Equipment

Category	Name	In Service
Corvette	ex-USSR Petya II class	2
Patrol craft	ex-USSR Osa I/II class missile FAC	8
	ex-USSR Zhuk class	8
Amphibious force	ex-USSR Polnochny class	3
Mine warfare force	ex-USSR Ocean minesweeper (Natya class)	1
	ex-USSR coastal minesweeper (I Sonya class, 2 Vanya class)	3

Naval Aviation: 12 Mi-4, 4 Ka-25, 11 Mi-14, 5 Ka-28

New Procurements/Upgrades

No major procurement plans are under consideration at present.

AIR FORCE

Personnel: 20,000

Equipment: (Figures represent pre-civil war inventory)

Category	Name	In Service
Fighter	Su-24	20
	MiG-21F	150
	MiG-23	70
	MiG-29	40 (+12 on order with deliveries going on)
	MiG-25	30
	MiG-23BN	40
	Su-20/22	40
	MiG-25R	6
Transport	Il-76	4
	An-26	6
	An-12	6
	An-24	2
	Il-14	8
	TU-134	4
Trainer	MiG-21U	20
	L-39 Albatross	83
	L-29 Delphin	60
	MBB-223 Flamingo	30
	MiG-17	30
	PAC Shahbaz	6
Helicopter	Mi-24	36
	Gazelle/Hot	55
	Mi-8	100
	Mi17	100
	Mi-2	10
	Mi-25	50
	Mi-14 Haze	16
	Ka-25 Hormone	5

New Procurements/Upgrades

- Delivery of 12 MiG-29M/M2 fighters is going on. Russia has delivered a second batch of the advanced fighters in May 2020.
- Delivery of 36 Yak-130 advanced trainers is awaited under an older contract.

AIR DEFENCE FORCE

Equipment

Category	Name	In Service
Air Defence Systems	9K37 Buk-M2E	
	SA-2/3	400
	SA-9	200
	SA-5	48
	SA-8	60
	Pantsyr-SIE	36

New Procurements/Upgrades

No major procurement plans are under consideration at present.

Defence Expenditure

Total defence spending: No reliable data available

Defence spending in terms of GDP: 5% (est.)

Defence Production and R&D

Limited resources allocated for research & development has impeded Syria's defence industry, making the country dependent on foreign arms suppliers. Its relative backwardness in technological and industrial development, compounded by limited funds, has meant that most of its capability has been developed using outside help.

Defence Procurement

Syria has imported most of its arms and weapons primarily from Russia, Iran and North Korea. Arms supplies from other countries is limited, given the extensive embargoes placed on the country. Russia in the past has offered assistance to Syria with the supply and modernization of helicopters, heavy armoured vehicles, tactical missiles, various types of surface warships and other weapons. A contract was awarded to Russia for the delivery of Yak-130 jet trainers along with other fighter platforms before the Syrian crisis began in 2011. Russia has also announced the transfer of S-300 air defence missile systems to Syria.

CONTACT DETAILS

Ministry of Defence
Ommayad Sq.
Damascus, Syria
Tel: +936-11-112101 through -05
112100 through -04

STRATEGIC INFORMATION
TAIWAN
(Capital: Taipei)

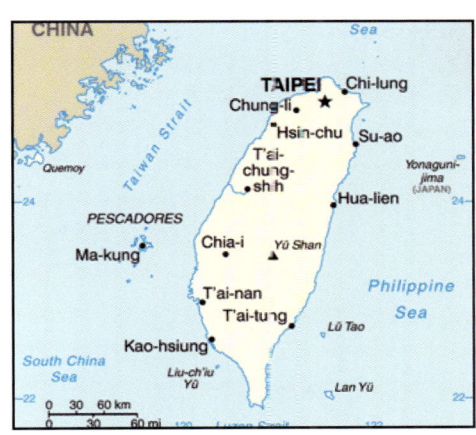

INTRODUCTION

Area: 35,980 sq km
Population: 23,572,052 (July 2021 est.)
Coastline: 1,566.3 km
Maritime claims: Territorial Sea: 12 nm
Exclusive Economic Zone: 200 nm

GEOPOLITICAL IMPORTANCE

The island state of Taiwan, also called the Republic of China (ROC), is a sovereign state in East Asia. The ROC constitutes a chain of islands among which Taiwan occupies 99 per cent of its territory. The other islands administered by ROC include Penghu, Kinmen, Matzu and few other small islands. Taiwan is neighboured by the People's Republic of China (PRC) in the west, the Philippines in the south and Japan in the northeast. It is bordered by the Pacific Ocean, East China Sea, South China Sea, Luzon Strait and the Taiwan Strait. The Taiwan Strait separates ROC from mainland China. It is one of the busiest transportation routes in the world with hundreds of commercial ships plying its waters everyday. The Strait is also believed to be rich in gas and oil reserves.

The independently positioned Taiwan has direct access to the Pacific Ocean, thereby making it a strategically important region to build up and project naval power in the Pacific waters. The island has often been associated with the term "unsinkable aircraft carrier" since it can be used as an airbase to launch air strikes as done from on-board an aircraft carrier without physically destroying the landmass. Hence, the archipelago holds the possibility of being used to extend power projection by a military force.

POLITICAL OVERVIEW

The political status of Taiwan remains a contentious issue even today as the autonomously-ruled island has not been recognised as an independent country by the United Nations. Taiwan was part of mainland China or erstwhile Republic of China until 1949. The Chinese Civil War split the entire territory into two parts i.e., Republic of China or Taiwan and People's Republic of China or mainland China. Taiwan claimed independence from mainland China following the end of Chinese Civil War between the ruling party of Republic of China and the Communist Party of China. While the mainland China became People's Republic of China (PRC) and came to be recognised as an independent country after receiving United Nations Permanent Member status in 1971, Taiwan or ROC has struggled to find an independent identity for itself since then.

Taiwan identifies itself as an independent sovereign state. It functions as a multi-party democracy having its own Constitution. The President of Taiwan, who is also the commander-in-chief of the armed forces, is elected by universal suffrage. The island state maintains its own military.

KEY POLITICAL PERSONS

PRESIDENT & SUPREME COMMANDER OF ARMED FORCES:
Tsai Ing-wen

VICE PRESIDENT:
Lai Ching-te

ECONOMY

Following its transition to democracy from the previous authoritarian regime in the 1980s and 1990s, Taiwan has transformed itself into a modern dynamic market economy. The industrially-advanced country has established itself as one of the leading economic powerhouses in Asia and is counted as one of the "Four Asian Tigers" along with South Korea, Singapore and Hong Kong. The country's economy mostly relies on exports carried through marine lanes. The island runs a trade surplus with many economies, including China and the US, and its foreign reserves are the world's fifth largest. Despite confrontations with China over reunification issue, Taiwan has maintained healthy economic and trade relations with Beijing. China is also the island's number one destination for foreign direct investment.

Taiwan has joined several international organisations, including the World Trade Organisation, under a politically neutral name. However, an ambiguous political and diplomatic status has prevented Taiwan's wider economic participation and integration with the world market. The country had registered an annual GDP growth of 3.8% in 2014-15. However, following a global economic slump and falling domestic exports, the economy contracted even as the Government announced measures to boost infrastructure investment and corporate credit to bolster the economy. The new President of the country since taking office in May 2016 has promoted greater economic integration with South and Southeast Asia through the New Southbound Policy initiative and has also expressed interest in Taiwan joining the Trans-Pacific Partnership (TPP) as well as bilateral trade deals with partners such as the US.

While the Coronavirus pandemic battered the global economy in 2020, Taiwan was only the second Asian nation apart from China to register a positive GDP growth of over 3%. The island nation effectively controlled the deadly pandemic and its economic activities remained uninterrupted. GDP growth rate is projected to cross 5% in 2021.

GDP (official exchange rate): $611.39 billion (2019 est.)

Real Growth Rate (GDP): 2.71% (2019 est.); 2.75% (2018 est.)

Industries: Electronics, communications and information technology products, petroleum refining, chemicals, textiles, iron and steel, machinery, cement, food processing, vehicles, consumer products, pharmaceuticals

Natural Gas - Proved Reserves: 6.229 billion cu m (1 January 2018 est.)

Crude Oil - Proved Reserves: 2.38 million bbl (1 January 2018 est.)

Total Exports: $383.4 billion (2019 est.); $383.4 billion (2018 est.)

Export Commodities: Integrated circuits, office machinery/parts, computers, refined petroleum, liquid crystal displays (2019)

Major Markets: China 26%, United States 14%, Hong Kong 12%, Japan 7%, Singapore 7%, South Korea 5% (2019)

Total Imports: $308.7 billion (2019 est.); $305.4 billion (2018 est.)

Import Commodities: Integrated circuits, crude petroleum, photography equipment, natural gas, refined petroleum (2019)

Major Suppliers: China 21%, Japan 16%, United States 11%, South Korea 6% (2019)

DEFENCE & SECURITY

Taiwan, until 1945, was ruled by Japan that transferred its administration to mainland China or erstwhile Republic of China (ROC) after facing defeat in World War II. Following the Chinese Civil War of 1949, the mainland China came to be known as People's Republic of China (PRC) but Taiwan retained the original name Republic of China (ROC) which was established in 1912. Both regions claimed to represent the state China and wanted to govern each other's territory. But after the People's Republic of China (PRC) secured 'permanent member' status in the United Nations and came to be recognised as an independent country, Taiwan or ROC's political status became vague. From time to time, the official status of Taiwan as part of Chinese territory has remained unclear with some countries, including the United States, maintaining silence over the issue.

The self-proclaimed sovereign state of Taiwan faces the biggest security threat from China which considers the archipelago as part of its territory and intends to unify it with mainland China even by military force. Taiwan's growing military relations with the US has also resulted in friction between China and the US. China, with its rapidly growing economy and expanding military might, has maintained a belligerent stand over the issue of Taiwan which it regards as its "core area of interest."

The ROC's independent military, constituting the Army, Navy and Air Force, has been groomed with the primary objective of defending the homeland from an invasion by China. Guided by the military strategy of "resolute defence and credible deterrence", the ROC armed forces have focused on enhancing joint operational capabilities with the aim to prevent war and maintain effective deterrence. Keeping pace with the evolving military technology and new warfare methodology in the information era, the ROC armed forces have strived to develop information and electronic warfare tactics, missile defence systems, joint counter-air, joint sea control and joint ground defence, and acquiring asymmetric military capabilities even with the country's limited defence personnel and resources. The technologically advanced Taiwanese armed forces have gone on to acquire modern military hardware and weapons, mostly from the US, to counter and prevent any attack by the People's Republic of China.

As part of a comprehensive military restructuring programme, the Taiwanese Defence Ministry announced to implement the "Jingtsui Programme" from 2011 to 2014. The programme gave emphasis on future warfare, enemy situation and threats and the nation's overall resource distribution, as well as "military strategy," "national financial resources and policy guidance" and "voluntarism," finding a balance between "combat requirements" and "financial capabilities." The programme aimed at gathering defence resources together and utilise them to "prevent the enemy from landing and establishing lodgement"; streamlining of high level command organisations to establish a "small but superb, strong and smart" defence force. Enhancement of early warning capabilities and integrating them with the existing intelligence, surveillance and reconnaissance capacity have also become a thrust area for the ROC military so as to counter any sudden and highly intense attack from the PRC.

In its last biannual report released in December 2017, Taiwan explicitly designated China as the island's biggest security threat. The report made specific reference to increased frequency of Chinese military activities in and around the Taiwanese territory. The report highlighted Taiwan's current security situation, combat readiness and defense strategies, including bolstering the island's asymmetric warfare capabilities.

In September 2019, Taiwan released its latest defence report which detailed its military's plans to repel invading Chinese forces along the coast of Taiwan as part of the country's new defence strategy adopted since President Tsai Ing-wen took office in 2016. The National Defence Report, issued by the Ministry of National Defence, also included a graphic showing exactly how the ROC Armed Forces would repel a potential Chinese invasion along the coastline, such as by dispatching larger military vessels along the country's outer perimeter in coastal areas as the first line of defence against possible invaders. Naval mines would be used as the second line of defence behind those vessels together with other smaller naval vessels. Armoured vehicles and other weapon systems would be positioned to eliminate enemy forces on beach areas. Military aircraft and missiles would be used next as further deterrence, the graphic showed.

China, on the other hand, has continued its provocative actions over the contentious Taiwan Strait region by scrambling warplanes and bombers. As a counter-measure, Taiwan too has sent its warplanes to warn off the Chinese fighters. The frequent skirmishes have escalated regional tensions.

KEY DEFENCE PERSONS

MINISTER OF NATIONAL DEFENCE: Chiu Kuo-cheng

CHIEF OF GENERAL STAFF: Gen. Chen Pao-yu

COMMANDER-IN-CHIEF OF ARMY: Gen. Hsu Yen-pu

COMMANDER-IN-CHIEF OF NAVY: Adm. Liu Chih-pin

COMMANDER-IN-CHIEF OF AIR FORCE: Gen. Hsiung Hou-chi

Internal Conflict

Terrorism: Though not a potential threat to the state, terrorism has often reared its head in Taiwan. Terrorist incidents like bombing and aircraft hijacking have struck Taiwan in the past. The military often conducts anti-terrorist military drills to counter any terror-related eventualities.

Organised crime: The island state faces the problem of illegal smuggling of firearms and drugs across the Taiwan Strait. Human trafficking, gang wars, extortion and money laundering have also affected its internal security apparatus.

External Conflict

The self-governed Taiwan has not been involved in military conflict with any of its neighbours barring China which has, from time to time, threatened the sovereignty of the former. The cross-Strait relations between Taiwan and China have remained tense, especially after vociferous and rapid Chinese military expansion in the last few years. To counter the militarily rising and aggressive China, Taiwan has intensified its efforts to acquire modern military platforms and weapons, mostly from the US. It is also developing asymmetric warfare capabilities and strengthened its conventional forces to meet internal and external security challenges.

Territorial disputes: Taiwan is engaged in territorial water disputes with Brunei, China, Malaysia, the Philippines, and Vietnam over the Spratly Islands in the South China Sea. The archipelago is also claiming authority over the Paracel Islands occupied by China.

Taiwan has been opposing Japan's claims over the uninhabited islands of the Senkaku-shoto (also called Diaoyu Tai) in the East China Sea. The islands, which are around 160 kilometres from Japan's Okinawa chain and about 200 kilometres from Taiwan, lie on vital shipping lanes, and are believed to be near potentially rich gas fields. China too claims sovereignty over the islands.

THREAT PERSPECTIVE

China: The sole and foremost military threat that Taiwan faces comes from China. Taiwan's National Defence Report 2013 had predicted that by 2020, China would acquire "full capability" to launch an attack on the island nation to forcibly reunite it with the mainland. "China has been upgrading its major weapons systems and building up the People's Liberation Army (PLA) as part of its goal to have a strong enough fighting force to attack Taiwan by 2020," the 2015 National Defence Report of ROC had stated.

With its massive all-round military modernisation programme continuing unabated, China has shifted the balance of power in the Taiwan Strait in Beijing's favour. According to the Taiwanese Defence Ministry, China has renewed its earlier military strategy of "using military force to oppose Taiwan independence" to "opposing Taiwan independence and advancing the unity of China". The PRC has rapidly built up its capabilities to launch large-scale operations against Taiwan while deterring, delaying or denying any kind of intervention by a foreign military power in the wake of a conflict in the Taiwan Strait. Even while continuing its military intimidation tactics against Taiwan, Beijing has also put forth in place an elaborate strategy of "air and sea blockade" to encircle the island state if necessary.

China has deployed large number of missiles along its south-eastern coast targeting Taiwan. The Chinese arsenal deployed along its east coast includes some 1,400 tactical ballistic missiles, short-range missiles, cruise missiles, and laser or electronically guided missiles capable of delivering warheads over long distances. The PLA has also deployed amphibious assault vehicles, long-range MLRS, warships, long-range anti-ship missiles, ballistic missiles and advanced fighter jets in its southern provinces of Guangdong and Fujian, according to the Taiwanese Defence Ministry. The Defence Ministry's Five-Year Military Reform and Policy Plan Report states that China's Second Artillery Corps (now renamed as PLA Rocket Force) has increased its deployment of Dong Feng 16 (DF-16), DF-21D and DF-31 series of ballistic missiles, thus enabling the People's Liberation Army to carry out multiple-wave precision strikes against Taiwan.

China is also intensely building up its air defence and anti-ship bases along the south-eastern coast. Ships and missile boats armed with long-range anti-ship missiles have also been deployed in the coast. Chinese unmanned aerial vehicles and high-speed anti-radiation missiles are capable of attacking Taiwan's command-and-control bases, according to Taiwan's National Defence Report. Moreover, Taiwan's military strength consisting of around 190,000 active soldiers (+ some 260,000 estimated reserve forces), coupled with its meagre defence budget of around US$15 billion, has been dwarfed by China's massive military force and huge annual defence spendings.

STRATEGIC RELATIONS

US: The tiny island state has solely relied on weapons and technology supplied by the US to face any possible attack from China. The US has continued its efforts to supply arms to Taiwan, irking Beijing. According to a US report, the United States has announced over $12 billion in arms sales to Taiwan since 2010. In 2008, Pentagon announced an arms package worth $6.6 billion for Taiwan which included the Patriot Advanced Capability-3 guided missile systems, Apache attack helicopters, Harpoon missiles and Javelin anti-tank missiles among other weapons and hardware. The announcement resulted in China suspending bilateral military exchanges with the US. In January 2010, the US Govt. further announced an arms deal worth $6.4 billion for the island state. The arms sales included Patriot missiles, Black Hawk helicopters, and communications equipment for Taiwan's F-16 fighters' fleet. The Obama administration in December 2015 had announced a $1.83 billion arms sale to Taipei. China's continuous opposition to the proposed military sales held back Washington from supplying some of the weapons and platforms to Taiwan. The US Govt. under then President Donald Trump in June 2017 approved military sales worth $1.42 billion to the island state. The arms package included advanced missiles, torpedoes and early warning systems among other hardware. Further infuriating Beijing, the US Govt in September 2018 approved a military contract worth $330 million which involved an inventory of spare parts and repairs to be bought from the US for Taiwanese military aircraft. In July 2019, the American Govt. gave approval to potential arms sale worth a whopping $2.2 billion to Taiwan, which included M1A2T Abrams battle tanks, Stinger portable anti-aircraft missiles along with related equipment and support. China lodged a strong protest over the possible deal, demanding that the US should "immediately cancel" the potential sale. In August 2020, the US administration approved defence sales worth over US$ 7 billion to Taiwan that included the new, more advanced F-16V fighter platforms.

DEFENCE CAPABILITIES

ARMY: The primary task of the Taiwanese Army or ROC Army is to defend the integrity of the national territory and sovereignty; guarding the outer islands region; building up its combat strength through military training and acquiring technological specialization; carrying out joint operations with the Navy and Air Force in the event of war.

With China steadily expanding its naval and air power capabilities in recent times, the Taiwanese Army has faced cutbacks in personnel and overall strength as the island state has shifted its focus more on strengthening its Navy and Air Force. Nevertheless, equipping the ground forces with new tanks, combat vehicles, attack helicopters, UAVs, advanced air defence systems and C4I2SR (command, control, communications, computer, information, intelligence, surveillance and reconnaissance) capabilities have been undertaken to bolster the Army's capability while preparing it to jointly fight modern-day hi-tech war in consonance with the Navy and Air Force.

Personnel: 115,000+

Equipment

Category	Name	In Service	On Order
MBT	M60 A3	250	
	Modified M-48 (CM11/12)	300	
Light Tank	Type 64 (M41)	400	
APC/IFV	M113	1090	
	V-150 Commando	300	
	CM-32 Cloud Leopard	200	300+ (advanced variant CM-34)
Artillery	M109A5 155mm	50	
	M109A2	100	Being upgraded to M109 A5 155mm variant
	M108	150	
	155mm field artillery	6	
	105mm field artillery	500	
	M110A2 203mm SP	25	
	M107 175mm SP	50	
Mortar	81mm towed		
	120mm towed		
	107mm		
	60mm		
MLRS	RT-2000	50+	100
ATGW	TOW	1000+	
	Javelin	60 launchers, 360 missiles	40 launchers, 400 missiles
	Kun Wu	5 launchers	
SAM	Patriot air defence system (PAC-2)	1 battalion with 3 batteries	4 batteries on order. Missile systems upgraded to Configuration-3
	PAC-3		
	Tien Kung air defence system	1 battalion with 6 batteries	
	Hawk air defence system	6 battalion each with 6 batteries i.e. (each battery armed with 54 missiles	
	Stringer	1000+	

...continued

Category	Name	In Service	On Order
AA gun	40mm	300	
	20mm SP	20	
SSM	Hsiung Feng IIE (600km SSCM)		
	Ching Feng		

Army Aviation
Equipment

Category	Name	In Service
Combat helicopter	AH-1W Super Cobra	64
	OH-58D Kiowa	13
	AH-64E Apache Longbow	29
Transport/ Utility helicopter	CH-34	7
	UH-1H	100
	Kh-4	8
	Boeing 234 Chinook	3
	CH-47SD	3
	OV-1 Bird Dog	20
	OH-6A	5
	UH-60M Black Hawk	59 (deliveries going on)

New Procurements/Upgrades

◆ The US State Dept. in July 2019 has approved arms sale worth US$2.2 billion which include 108 of the M1A2T Abrams main battle tanks (and 250 Stinger anti-aircraft missiles) along with other support equipment. The Taiwan Army plans to induct the M1A2 Abrams to replace its aging fleet of M60A3 and CM-11 battle tanks.

◆ Upgrade of M60A3 MBTs is being considered under a US$ 6.6 million programme. The upgrades will be carried out domestically.

◆ Mass production of domestically-built CM-34 infantry fighting vehicle (IFV) – an advanced variant of CM-32 Cloud Leopard IFV – has started and deliveries going on since 2019. Plans are on to produce over 300 such IFVs in different configurations by 2023.

◆ BAE Systems has been awarded a $84 million contract in 2018 to produce 36 assault amphibious vehicles (AAVP7A1) for the Taiwanese Army under a US DoD deal.

◆ PAC-2 air defence missiles have been upgraded to PAC-3 configuration. Additional units of PAC-3 systems have also been delivered.

◆ Additional Javelin anti-tank guided missile systems along with launchers are on order from the US.

NAVY: The Taiwanese Navy or the Republic of China (ROC) Navy outlines its primary role as safeguarding maritime security in the Taiwan Strait and actively engage in disaster relief operations. It operates with the mission to maintain and defend the safety of the country's maritime regions and secure its international shipping lanes in the Pacific Ocean. The Navy, also consisting of ROC Marine Corps, is deployed in the Taiwan Strait and its surrounding waters. With a stated vision to build "a modernised force" that will be able to control the sea, the Taiwanese Navy, however, has lagged way behind the ferociously growing China. The "Force Build-up Plans and Objectives" outlined in the 2011 National Defence Report of the Taiwanese Defence Ministry had emphasised on the procurement of diesel-electric submarines, long-range anti-submarine aircraft, new-generation missile motorboats and mine-hunters to enhance the armed forces' 3-dimensional joint sea control capabilities, and strengthen counter blockade and joint interdiction capabilities. In addition, fuel and ammunition supply ships would be constructed to maintain the capabilities of surface operation groups, thus building a sea control force equipped with anti-submarine, air defence and regional ocean surveillance capabilities. In a recent move, the RoC Navy, under a 20-year force modernisation programme, has expressed its intent to acquire new destroyers, frigates, corvettes and submarines to replace all the older-generation US and French-built warships in its fleet. All the new platforms and systems are planned to be built indigenously by the domestic defence industries with Western assistance, if necessary.

Major naval bases: Suao, Keelung, Kenting, Makung

Personnel: 45,000 appx. (Including Marine Corps)

Equipment

Category	Name	In Service
Destroyer	Keelung-class DDG (ex-US Kidd class)	4
Submarine	Hai Lung (Dragon) class	2
	Hai Shih (Guppy II class for training)	1
Frigate	Cheng Kung class (modified Perry design)	10
	Chi Yang class (ex-US Knox class)	6
	Kang Ding class (French La Fayette type)	6
Corvette	Tuo Jiang class	2 (+9 on order)
Patrol vessel	Jin Jiang class OPV	11
	Lung Chiang class missile FAC	2

...continued

Category	Name	In Service
Patrol vessel	Sui Kiang class missile FAC	2
	PLC coastal patrol boat	22
	Kuang-Hwa class (New Hai Ou class) FAC	31
LST	Ex-US	22
	Chung He class (ex-US Newport class)	2
LCU		26
LSM	Ex-US	4
LSD	Xu Hai-Class (ex-US Anchorage class)	1
LCVP		150
Mine sweepers & Mine hunters	Ex-US Osprey class	2
	Yeong Feng-class	4
	Yeongyang class	4
	Adjutant type	4
Auxiliary ship	Wu Yi class supply ship	1
	Combat support ship "Panshih"	1
Weapon	(Naval guns) Mk42 127mm Mk45 127mm Oto Melara 76mm Bofors 40mm	
	Phalanx close-in weapon system	
	(ASM) Hsiung Feng II Hsiung Feng III Syongfong II Harpoon RIM-66 Standard Missile	
	(Torpedo) Mk46 Wire-guided surface and underwater target torpedo	

New Procurements/Upgrades

◆ With an intent to build its own submarines and maritime platforms after failing to acquire the same from the US over the years, the island state under the new Govt. has announced plans to spend around $15 billion from 2018 through 2040 for indigenous construction of new battleships. The new platforms would include an amphibious transport dock (LPD), high-speed mine-laying vessels and Tuo Jiang-class of corvettes in addition to submarines.

◆ In May 2019, the country unveiled a miniature model of the first domestically-designed diesel-electric attack submarine, construction on which was expected to start by 2021 followed by possible delivery by 2024. The US Govt. has approved the transfer of some key technologies to build the underwater platform. Taiwan plans to build at least eight conventional submarines indigenously.

◆ Two Hai Lung-class submarines are to be upgraded by Netherlands' RH Marine and delivered by 2024.

◆ Indigenous development of a new class of guided missile destroyers having AESA radar capability is under consideration.

◆ Plans are advancing to upgrade all six of the French-built La Fayette (Kang Ding class) of frigates. The upgrade work would start in 2022.

◆ The first amphibious landing helicopter dock ship (LHD), Yu Shan, has been launched in April 2021. It is likely to be inducted in the Navy by 2022. A contract was awarded to local shipbuilder CSBC Corporation in 2018 to build the multi-role platform for the RoC Navy.

◆ The first Tuo Jiang-class corvette having a displacement of 500-ton was commissioned in 2014. An upgraded variant of the platform having higher displacement, length and width to accommodate more personnel and equipment has also been built and commissioned into service in August 2021. A total of 11 such corvettes are planned to be built and inducted over the years.

◆ A contract has been awarded to an international team, led by Taiwan's Ching Fu Shipbuilding, to deliver six mine countermeasures vessels (MCMVs) by 2024. International partners in the programme include US's Lockheed Martin and Italian shipbuilder Intermarine. Construction work is advancing.

◆ The Defence Ministry has stepped up production of the indigenous Hsiung Feng IIE subsonic and Hsiung Feng III supersonic anti-ship cruise missiles. A next-generation version of the Hsiung Feng III is also reportedly under development.

◆ Acquisition of Harpoon anti-ship missiles from the US to serve as a coastal defence cruise missile system is under consideration. If approved by the US Govt., the weapons would be delivered by 2024.

◆ The US State Dept. in May 2020 has approved possible sale of 18 MK-48 Mod6 heavy weight torpedoes and related equipment for an estimated cost of $180 million.

Naval Aviation
Equipment

Category	Name	In Service
ASW Aircraft	P-3C Orion	12
	S-2T Turbo Tracker	11
ASW/ Minesweeper helicopter	S-70B Sea Hawk	6
	MH-53E	(12 on order)
	S-70 CM1/CM2	18
	MD500 Defender	8

New Procurements/Upgrades

◆ The Navy is evaluating options of acquiring new anti-submarine warfare (ASW) helicopters to replace its aging fleet of MD500 Defender choppers. Eight MH-60R Seahawk ASW helicopters could be purchased via the US Foreign Military Sales programme.

◆ Plans are on to upgrade the entire fleet of Sikorsky S-70 CM1/CM2 helicopters.

◆ The US State Dept. has approved the sale of four MQ-9B SeaGuardian armed drones to Taiwan in November 2020.

AIR FORCE: The Republic of China Air Force (ROCAF) operates with the primary missions of keeping vigil over the Taiwan Strait, maintaining airspace security over the region with effective combat readiness, defending the island's territory against any "surprise enemy attack" and ensuring homeland security. The Taiwanese Air Force has focused on enhancing its long-range reconnaissance capabilities, integration of C4I2SR systems and battlefield management capabilities effectively. It also aims to procure next-gen fighter aircraft and counter-strike weapons to strengthen its overall combat capability for offensive manoeuvre against the People's Liberation Army of China. Procuring advanced variants of US-made F-16 fighters and upgrading the Chingkuo indigenous defence fighters by deploying advanced electronic warfare systems along with air-to-ground, air-to-sea and air-to-air missiles are being planned to strengthen joint counter-air operations by the RoC Air Force.

Major air bases: Sungshan, Makung, Tainan, Ching Chuan Kang, Chiayi

Personnel: 35,000+ (including Air Defence Missile Command)

Equipment

Category	Name	In Service
Fighter/ Attack/ AWS role	F16A/B (being upgraded)	141
	F-16V	(66 on order)
	F-5E/F / RF-E	65 + 5
	Chingkou IDF	127
	Mirage 2000-5E/5D	54
Trainer	AIDC AT-3	50+
	Beechcraft T-34C	30+
Transport/ Surveillance	C130H/HE	19
	E-2K/E-2T Hawkeye	4+2
	Beech B-1900C	10
Helicopter (SAR)	EC225 Super Puma Mk2	3
	S-70C Blue Hawk	12

...continued

Category	Name	In Service
Weapon	(AAM) R.550 Magic, MICA AIM-7 Sparrow AIM-120 AMRAAM Tien-Chien I Tien-Chien II	
	Wan Chien stand-off AGM	

New Procurements/Upgrades

◆ Acquisition of 66 new F-16V fighters from the US at an estimated cost of $7.96 billion has been approved by the US State Dept. in August 2020. Delivery would be completed by 2026.

◆ The Air Force has started taking delivery of upgraded F-16V fighter platforms (42 platforms delivered as of 2021). The entire fleet of F-16A/B fighters is being upgraded to F-16V configuration under a 2012 contract. It includes fitment of AESA radars, embedded global positioning, as well as upgrades to electronic warfare and other avionics systems of the fighters. Work would continue till 2023, with Lockheed Martin refitting some of the fighters in the US and Taiwan's Aerospace Industrial Development Corporation (AIDC) upgrading the rest of them locally.

◆ The Defence Ministry in 2017 announced plans to indigenously develop a new advanced stealth fighter jet. The new fighter will be a double-engine stealth plane developed with Taiwanese technology.

◆ Comprehensive upgrade of Chingkou indigenous fighters has been completed.

◆ The first prototype of AT-5 'Brave Eagle' jet trainer being built by domestic aerospace firm AIDC has undergone maiden successful test flight in June 2020 and is likely to be handed over to the Air Force in 2021-2022. The Defence Ministry had announced plans to purchase new advanced jet trainers to replace the Air Force's aging fleet of F-5E/F jet fighters and AT-3 jet trainers. The Govt in 2017 launched a $2.1 billion investment programme to indigenously build the new platforms. The Air Force plans to acquire up to 66 of the new AT-5 jet trainers.

◆ The Govt is negotiating to buy six Alenia Aermacchi C-27J Spartan tactical transport planes.

◆ Acquisition of PAC-3 Missile Segment Enhancement (MSE) missiles – an advanced version of PAC-3 air defence system – is being planned with delivery expected by 2025.

Nuclear Weapons Programme

To achieve asymmetric warfare capabilities, Taiwan pursued coveted nuclear weapons programme twice in the past. The programme, however, was eventually abandoned following intense US pressure. After China conducted its first nuclear weapons test on 16 October 1964, Taiwan raised concern over its powerful neighbour's military intension, fearing that use of such weapons could completely annihilate the tiny island state off the map. To counter the threat, the Taiwanese Defence Ministry in the following years decided to take up nuclear weapons development programme which was code-named "Hsin Chu". The Institute of Nuclear Energy Research (INER), established in 1965, was authorised to carry out nuclear research programme, which the Taiwanese government tagged with civilian energy purposes. The INER, however, was set up near the Chung-Shan Institute of Science and Technology (CSIST) – the country's leading military research and development centre and received support from it. Taiwan bought heavy water reactors and other nuclear technology from a number of countries, including the US, Canada, Norway, Germany and France. In 1968, Taiwan signed the Nuclear Non-Proliferation Treaty (NPT) even while it was secretly pursuing nuclear weapons programme. The programme was subsequently scrapped following strong US opposition. The island state again restarted the stalled nuclear weapons programme for a brief period in the late 1980s, but eventually abandoned it. Some defence experts believe that Taiwan is still capable of successfully developing nuclear weapons as it has already acquired the basic technologies needed to make such weapons. The island state currently has six nuclear reactors and three active nuclear power plants producing around 5,000 MW of nuclear energy.

Major Armaments Producers

Chung-Shan Institute of Science and Technology (CSIST) is Taiwan's leading institution for defence R&D and is engaged in the development, management and integration of advanced weapon systems.

CSBC Corporation, formerly known as China Shipbuilding Corporation is a leading state-owned naval conglomerate that designs and builds warships and other vessels for the ROC Navy.

Aerospace Industrial Development Corporation (AIDC) is a state-owned aviation firm and manufactures fighter jets, trainers and transport aircraft. Taiwan decided to privatise the aircraft manufacturer in 2014.

Indigenous Weapon Systems: Some indigenous weapons produced by Taiwan's defence industry include the Tien Kung I and Tien Kung II multi-level advanced air-defence missile systems. An advanced variant of the weapon, Tien Kung III, has also been developed by the Chungshan Institute of Science and Technology (CSIST). Taiwan plans to spend US$2.5 billion over the years to acquire the new anti-missile system to boost its aerial defences against China. The Tien Kung III SAMs are being acquired to replace the ageing Hawk missiles of the ROC military.

In 2019, the Taiwanese Navy successfully tested a modified variant of the Tien-Kung III, dubbed as Hai-Kung III system from a naval platform. The Ray Ting-2000 or Thunder 2000 multiple launch rocket system (MLRS) has been developed with long range and wide impact area for anti-landing operation.

The Syongfong II anti-ship missiles have been deployed on Cheng Kung-class and Kang Ding-class frigates and Keelung-series DDGs.

The Hsiung Feng II subsonic and Hsiung Feng III supersonic anti-ship cruise missiles have been developed to counter Chinese attack.

The Tien-Chien I and Tien-Chien II air-to-air missiles are deployed on the IDF fighters.

The Wan Chien (Ten Thousand Swords) is the new air-to-ground cruise missile developed by the CSIST for the ROCAF's Chingkou combat aircraft. The stand-off weapon has an estimated range of over 200 km and it has been declared fully operational in 2018.

DEFENCE DEALS
Joint Venture/ Collaboration Programmes

USA: Taiwan has achieved self-reliance to some extent in military equipment production by tying up with leading US defence firms. The Aerospace Industrial Development Corporation (AIDC) has produced aircraft, helicopters and other aerospace components in partnership with US companies Lockheed Martin, Northrop Grumman, Sikorsky and Bell Helicopters among others.

F-5A/E/F Fighter: The AIDC, under license from the US Government, has co-produced over 300 F-5A/E/F Tiger fighters with Northrop Grumman since the 1970s. A few of the fighters are presently operational in the ROCAF.

Indigenous Defence Fighter: Taiwan began development of the Chingkou indigenous defence fighters in 1980 following US's refusal to sell its F-20 and F-16 fighters to the ROCAF. The AIDC designed, developed and manufactured the new fighters with assistance from US defence firms, including General Dynamics, Honeywell and others.

AT-3 Trainer Jet: The advanced trainer jets, currently operated by the Taiwanese Air Force, were developed by the AIDC in partnership with US' Northrop Grumman between 1984 and 1990.

UH-1 H Helicopter: The multi-utility transport helicopters were assembled by AIDC under license from Bell Helicopter in the 1970s.

Arms Import

Due to the heightened threat posed by its neighbour, Taiwan remains one of the major arms buyers in the Asia-Pacific region. In the 1990s, Taipei was a leading arms importer in the world. The island state has received majority of its military weapons, equipment and systems from the US. Few European countries, including Germany, Italy and France, have also supplied defence equipment to Taiwan. However, many import deals under which Taipei has sought to acquire advanced weapons and platforms for its military, have been stalled in the wake of stiff Chinese opposition.

Meanwhile, defence indigenisation efforts by Taiwan has gathered momentum in recent times with the country planning to set up a military technology department under the MoD. The new department would work on developing "ground-breaking" and "innovative" defence technologies as well as supporting the advancement of the local defence industrial base, according to the Defence Ministry.

DEFENCE BUDGET

The defence budget of Taiwan which witnessed a declining trend few years ago has recorded a rise in recent times. The escalating tensions with Beijing has forced Taipei to massively bolster its military build-up and increase annual defence allocation.

While defence budget earmarked for 2017 was TWD 321.7 billion (US$10.4 billion), the Govt increased it to TWD 327.8 billion (US$10.79 billion) in 2018. For 2019, defence budgetary allocation was TWD 346 billion (US$11.3 billion) – a rise of 5.6% over previous year. For 2020, the Govt approved TWD 358 billion (US$11.4 billion) for defence, which was later revised to TWD 411.3 billion ($13.1 billion).

The proposed military spending for 2021-22 is TWD 453.4 billion (US$15.42 billion) – an increase of 10.2% over last year, and 2.4% of national GDP.

Budgetary allocation

Year	Allocation	% of GDP
2021-22	TWD 453.4 billion ($15.42 bln)	2.4
2020-21	TWD 411.3 bln ($13.1 bln)	2.26
2019-20	TWD 346 billion ($11.3 bln)	2.16
2018-19	TWD 327.8 billion ($10.8 bln)	
2017-18	TWD 321.7 billion ($10.4 bln)	
2016-17	TWD 323 billion ($ 10.2 bln)	2.9
2015-16	TWD 321.7 billion ($ 9.7 bln)	2.8
2014-15	TWD 319.3 billion ($10.7 bln)	2.6
2013-14	TWD 313 billion ($10.52 billion)	2.1

CONCLUSION

At a time when China has clearly asserted its military strategies and coercive policies, Taiwan's perennial concern to protect itself from its mighty neighbour's possible attack has heightened. The large-scale military build-up by China has shifted the balance of power in the Taiwan Strait in Beijing's favour. Even though increasing territorial tensions in the Asia-Pacific region in recent times have involved several littoral states, with China being at the centre, yet Beijing has not entirely shifted its focus away from Taiwan – the region it considers its "core area of interest" and an "inalienable part" of 'One-China'. Acknowledging the all-round rapid military rise of mainland China, Taiwan has intensified its efforts to acquire advanced military systems, weapons and platforms to counter the imminent threat. The ROC military has focused on building up asymmetric warfare capabilities as well as strengthening its conventional forces to counter the ever-rising PLA power. With a strong military and political backing from the US, Taiwan has so far maintained a tough and defiant posture against any possible attack which could be launched to reunite the archipelago into the mainland China by force.

CONTACT DETAILS
Ministry of National Defence
No. 409, Bei An Road,
Zhongshan District
Taipei-10462,
Taiwan
Contact: (+886) 2-2311-6117
www.mnd.gov.tw/

TAJIKISTAN
(Capital: Dushanbe)

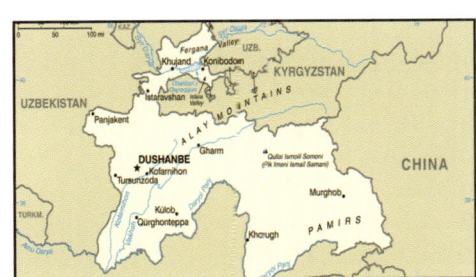

INTRODUCTION

Area: 144,100 sq km
Population: 8,990,874 (July 2021 est.)
Coastline: 0 km (landlocked)
Maritime claims: None

KEY POLITICAL PERSONS

PRESIDENT & COMMANDER-IN-CHIEF:
Emomali Rahmon

PRIME MINISTER:
Qohir Rasulzoda

KEY DEFENCE PERSONS

DEFENCE MINISTER: Col. Gen. Sherali Mirzo

CHIEF OF THE GENERAL STAFF: Lt. Gen. Emomali Sobirzoda

ECONOMY

Tajikistan's economy is dominated by minerals extraction, metals processing, agriculture, and reliance on remittances from citizens working abroad. The country imports approximately 70% of its food. Cotton is the most important crop. Mineral resources include silver, gold, uranium, antimony, and tungsten. Tajik citizens mainly work abroad, around 90% in Russia, supporting families back home through remittances. Tajikistan has a high poverty rate. As of August 2009, an estimated 60% of Tajikistani citizens reportedly live below the poverty line. Between 2000 and 2018, the poverty rate fell from 83 percent of the population to 27.4 percent, while the economy grew at an average rate of 7 percent per year, according to the World Bank. The social and economic well-being of the population severely deteriorated following the outbreak of COVID-19. The economy has been experiencing a fast recovery in 2021, however, the labour market remained weak and food insecurity more prevalent compared to pre-pandemic levels, it stated. The National Development Strategy (NDS) has set a target of increasing domestic income by up to 3.5 times by 2030 and reducing poverty by half.

GDP (official exchange rate): $2.522 billion (2019 est.)

Real Growth Rate (GDP): 7.1% (2017 est.), 6.9% (2016 est.)

Industries: Aluminium, cement, coal, gold, silver, antimony, textile, vegetable oil.

Oil – Proved Reserves: 12 million bbl (1 January 2018 est.)

Natural gas – Proved Reserves: 5.663 billion cu m (1 January 2018 est.)

Total Exports: $1.41 billion (2020 est.), $1.24 billion (2019 est.)

Export Commodities: Gold, aluminium, cotton, zinc, antimony, lead (2019)

Major Markets: Turkey 24%, Switzerland 22%, Uzbekistan 16%, Kazakhstan 12%, China 10% (2019)

Total Imports: $3.13 billion (2020 est.), $3.41 billion (2019 est.)

Import Commodities: Refined petroleum, wheat, natural gas, bauxite, aircraft (2019)

Major Suppliers: China 40%, Russia 38%, Kazakhstan 19%, Uzbekistan 5% (2019)

INTERNATIONAL DISPUTES

◆ In 2006, China and Tajikistan pledged to commence demarcation of the revised boundary agreed to in the delimitation of 2002.

◆ Talks continue with Uzbekistan to delimit border and remove minefields.

◆ Disputes in Isfara Valley delay delimitation with Kyrgyzstan.

DEFENCE

Tajikistan armed forces consist of the National Army, Mobile Forces, Air Force, National Guard, Internal Troops and Border Troops. The Mobile Forces similar to the Russian Airborne Troops are the paratroopers of the armed forces of Tajikistan. The Air Force is mostly used for search and rescue missions, transportation, and the occasional attack on militant groups. The Tajik National Guard is a special task force under direct command of the President. The Border Troops are responsible for border security and the Internal Troops are tasked with state security, operating under the Interior Ministry.

A long-term military cooperation agreement with Russia establishes the legal framework for the presence of Russian troops in Tajikistan. The soldiers and officers are being trained by Russians and its forces are fully integrated into exercises organised by Moscow. A five-nation agreement to improve military capability in border areas has been signed between China, Kazakhstan, Kyrgyzstan, Russia and Tajikistan. The Commonwealth of Independent States (CIS) Collective Security Treaty includes Armenia, Belarus, Kazakhstan, Kyrgyzstan, Russia and Tajikistan. Tajikistan has formed a 'Defence Union' with Uzbekistan, Kyrgyzstan and Kazakhstan aimed at coordinating their activities against Islamic Fundamentalist terrorism and pledging mutual support and joint military intervention if any one of the signatories comes under attack. Tajikistan and Iran have signed a Memorandum of Understanding on defence cooperation and an agreement with the United States allows for US troops to be deployed in and operate from base at Dushanbe and Kulyab. Tajikistan's armed forces total active manpower is reportedly around 25,000+.

ARMY

Equipment

Category	Name	In Service
MBT	T-62/T-72	35+
IFV	BMP-1/2	100
	BRDM-2M	6
APC	BTR-60/70/80	
Helicopter	Mi-8/Mi-24	19
MRL/Mortar	BM21/PM-38	
SAM	SA-2/SA-3	

New Procurements/Upgrades

No major procurement plans are under consideration at present.

AIR FORCE

Equipment

Category	Name	In Service
Aircraft	L-39 Albatros	4
	Tupolev Tu-134 Crusty	1
Helicopter	Mi-8 Hip	11
	Mi-24 Hind	4

New Procurements/Upgrades

No major procurement plans are under consideration at present.

Defence Expenditure

Total defence spending: $80 million (2020), $84 million (2019)

Defence spending: 10% of GDP (2020)

Defence Production and R&D

Tajikistan does not undertake any defence production activities.

Defence Procurement

Marking the founding of the 27th anniversary of the Tajik Armed Forces on 21 February 2020, Tajikistan has reportedly showcased its newly acquired equipment which included the VP11 mine-resistant, ambush-protected (MRAP) vehicles Dongfeng EQ2050F Mengshi 4×4 unprotected light tactical vehicle, the Norinco CS/VN3 light tactical armoured vehicle, and the China Tiger patrol vehicle. Other Chinese-made infantry weapon included the Type 56-3 7.62 mm assault rifle and the LR2 12.7 mm anti-matériel rifle. In the past, the Russian government has transferred military hardware to support the country's security forces. The hardware included a radar station that provides detection, tracking and control of the use of national airspace and at least six BRDM-2M modern armoured reconnaissance and patrol vehicle.

CONTACT DETAILS
Ministry of Defence
Ulitsa Bokhtar 59
734002 Dushanbe, Tajikistan

TANZANIA
(Capital: Dar es Salaam)

INTRODUCTION
Area: 947,300 sq km
Population: 62,092,761 (July 2021 est.)
Coastline: 1,424 km
Maritime claims: Territorial sea: 12 nm
Exclusive Economic Zone: 200 nm

KEY POLITICAL PERSONS

PRESIDENT & COMMANDER-IN-CHIEF: Samia Suluhu Hassan

PRIME MINISTER: Kassim Majaliwa

KEY DEFENCE PERSONS

MINISTER OF DEFENCE: Stergomena Lawrence Tax

CHIEF OF DEFENCE FORCES: Gen. Venance Mabeyo

COMMANDER OF NAVY: Rear Adm. Richard Mutayoba Makanzo

COMMANDER OF AIR FORCE: Maj. Gen. William Ingram

ECONOMY
Tanzania has achieved high growth rates based on its vast natural resources and tourism with GDP growth in 2009-17 averaging 6%-7% per year. Dar es Salaam used fiscal stimulus measures and easier monetary policies to lessen the impact of global recession and in general, benefited from low oil prices. Tanzania has largely completed its transition to a market economy, though the government retains a presence in sectors such as telecommunications, banking, energy, and mining. The economy depends on agriculture, which accounts for slightly less than one-quarter of GDP and employs about 65% of the work force, although gold production in recent years has increased to about 35% of exports. All land in Tanzania is owned by the government, which can lease land for up to 99 years. The financial sector in Tanzania has expanded in recent years and foreign-owned banks account for about 48% of the banking industry's total assets. Banking reforms have helped increase private-sector growth and investment. The World Bank, the IMF, and bilateral donors have provided funds to rehabilitate Tanzania's aging infrastructure, including rail and port, which provide important trade links for inland countries. The new government elected in 2015 has developed an ambitious development agenda focused on creating a better business environment through improved infrastructure, access to financing, and education progress, but implementing budgets remains challenging for the government.

The World Bank data showed a GDP growth rate of 2% for Tanzania in 2020 due to the raging Coronavirus pandemic. For 2021, economic outlook for the country appears positive, with real GDP projected to grow 4.1%, according to the African Development Bank.

GDP (official exchange rate): $60.63 billion (2019 est.)

Real Growth Rate (GDP): 6.98% (2019 est.); 6.95% (2018 est.)

Industries: Agricultural processing (sugar, beer, cigarettes, sisal twine); mining (diamonds, gold, and iron), salt, soda ash; cement, oil refining, shoes, apparel, wood products, fertilizer

Total Exports: $7.82 billion (2017 est.); $5.69 billion (2016 est.)

Export Commodities: Gold, tobacco, cashews, sesame seeds, refined petroleum (2019)

Major Markets: India 20%, United Arab Emirates 13%, China 8%, Switzerland 7%, Rwanda 6%, Kenya 5%, Vietnam 5% (2019)

Total Imports: $9.97 billion (2017 est.); $8.46 billion (2016 est.)

Import Commodities: Refined petroleum, palm oil, packaged medicines, cars, wheat (2019)

Major Suppliers: China 34%, India 15%, United Arab Emirates 12% (2019)

INTERNATIONAL DISPUTES
Dispute with Tanzania over the boundary in Lake Nyasa (Lake Malawi) and the meandering Songwe River; Malawi contends that the entire lake up to the Tanzanian shoreline is its territory, while Tanzania claims the border is in the centre of the lake. The conflict was reignited in 2012 when Malawi awarded a license to a British company for oil exploration in the lake.

DEFENCE
ARMY
Personnel: 40,000+

Equipment

Category	Name	In Service
MBT	Type-59	26
	T-62/ Type-63	30+
	Scorpion	36
APC	BTR-40/-152	50
	Type 56	20+

...continued

Category	Name	In Service
Mortar	M43 82mm	300
	M43 120mm	50
Artillery	ZIS-3 76mm gun	24
	Type 56 85mm	80
	D-30	20
	M-30 122mm	85
	M46 130mm	30+
AA gun	ZPU-2 & ZPU-4 14.5mm	250+
	ZU-23 23mm	40
	Type 55 37mm	100+
SAM	SA-3/6/7	

New Procurements/ Upgrades

No major procurement plans are under consideration at present.

NAVY

Personnel: 1000+

Equipment

Category	Name	In Service
Patrol boat	Haiqing-class	2
	Ex-Chinese Shanghai II class	2
	Ex-Chinese Huchuan class	4
LCM		1

New Procurements/ Upgrades

◆ Two new landing craft have reportedly been acquired from China.

AIR FORCE

Personnel: 900+

Equipment

Category	Name	In Service
Fighter	J-7G	14
	J-6	8
	J-4	4
Helicopter	Bell 412	2
	AB206A/B	4
	AB-205	4
	SA.316B ALOUETTE III	4
	BO-105	1
Trainer	PA-28	4
Transport	DHC-5D	5
	Cessna 404	2
	Cessna 310	7
	HS-748	3
	Y-5	1
	F-28 (VIP)	2

New Procurements/ Upgrades

No major procurement plans are under consideration at present.

Defence Expenditure

Defence spending: Sh1.84 trillion (2019-20)

Estimated defence spending in terms of GDP: 1.5%

Defence Production and R&D

Tanzania does not have the financial or technical resources to pursue any significant defence-related production or research & development. Defence spending remains very low and hence, little funding is available for the defence industry. The country is not subjected to any international arms embargo but there has been international concern at its intentions to develop small-arms manufacturing capabilities.

Defence Procurement

Procurement plans for the Armed Forces have not been officially announced, but the country has acquired some naval platforms from China of late. It has also expressed interest in Russian military hardware, including fighter jets and armoured vehicles. No deals have been signed so far.

CONTACT DETAILS

Ministry of National Defence
PO Box 9544, Ismani Road,
Dar es Salaam

STRATEGIC INFORMATION
THAILAND
(Capital: Bangkok)

INTRODUCTION

Area: 513,120 sq km
Population: 69,480,520 (July 2021 est.)
Coastline: 3,219 km
Maritime claims: Territorial Sea: 12 nm
Exclusive Economic Zone: 200 nm
Continental Shelf: 200 m depth or to the depth of exploitation

GEOPOLITICAL IMPORTANCE

Situated at the centre of Southeast Asian peninsula, Thailand or the Kingdom of Thailand, shares its land border with Cambodia in the southeast, with Laos in the north and northeast, with Myanmar in the north and west, and with Malaysia in the south. The country shares maritime boundary with Vietnam in the Gulf of Thailand to the southeast, and with India and Indonesia in the Andaman Sea to the southwest. With a varied geographical terrain, Thailand is broadly divided into four different regions: the central region (plains), northern region (mountainous), north-eastern region (plateau) and southern region (peninsula). The central region comprising of the Bangkok metropolitan region and the central plains is often called the "rice bowl" of Thailand and is the most fertile part of the country with high population density.

Sitting at the heart of mainland Southeast Asia which has traditionally remained a key trading and transition point for the world, Thailand has historically yielded great influence in and around its neighbourhood. Situated almost at equidistance from India and China – the two rapidly growing countries of Asia in the 21st century – Thailand has gained greater strategic importance in present times. Pursuing a goal to rise economically and politically, and transform itself from a developing to a developed nation, Thailand,

over the past few years, has steadily expanded its reach across Asia, especially in South Asia, by taking various diplomatic initiatives like forming regional and sub-regional forums and participating in leading multilateral blocks in the region. The country has aimed at a balanced development of the Southeast Asian region where it could emerge as an important geostrategic and economic hub.

POLITICAL OVERVIEW

Thailand functions as a constitutional monarchy where the King (Bhumibol Adulyadej, who ruled the country since 1946, died in October 2016 and was succeeded by his son King Maha Vajiralongkorn), is the head of state and the Prime Minister is the head of government, as per a new written Constitution adopted in 2007. The King, however, does not hold much real power and is more of a symbol of national unity and identity. The Prime Minister and his council of ministers carry out the executive tasks. The country's legislature and judiciary function independently. The bicameral legislature, called the National Assembly, consists of the Senate of Thailand (upper house), and the House of Representatives of Thailand (lower house). The judiciary consists of all the courts in the country.

Despite its democratic credentials, political volatility has continued to affect Thailand since long. After being ruled as an absolute monarchy for several centuries, the country transitioned into democratic monarchy in 1932 wherein the king became the titular head of state and the prime minister became the head of government. However, the influence of military over the political dispensation did not cease and the country has witnessed military coups several times in its history.

The Southeast Asian country yet again witnessed political turmoil in the latter half of 2013 wherein violent anti-Government protests against the elected Yingluck Shinawatra-led dispensation resulted in the Thai Army taking control of the situation and imposing martial law all over the nation in May 2014. This resulted in the ouster of the Shinawatra government and appointment of a military junta led by Army Chief General Prayuth Chan-ocha. The Army scrapped the 2007 charter and rolled out an interim Constitution, giving the military sweeping powers. The military dispensation had promised to hold democratic elections in the country in early 2016 but deferred it several times. In August 2016, Thailand approved a new Constitution in a referendum which gave the military extensive powers.

The military junta in October 2017 had announced plans to hold general elections in November 2018 which was ultimately held in March 2019 in which Prime Minister Prayuth Chan-ocha secured his position for another 5-year term and further consolidated the military's grip on power. While he formally resigned as the head of the military Government on July 15, 2019, saying that the country would function as a "normal democracy" after five years of military rule, Prayuth Chan-ocha stays on as the Thai PM with the backing of pro-military parties in Parliament and a military-appointed upper house under the new Constitution. He has also kept the Defence Ministry with him.

KEY POLITICAL PERSONS

HEAD OF STATE: King Maha Vajiralongkorn

PRIME MINISTER & DEFENCE MINISTER: Prayuth Chan-ocha

ECONOMY

As one of the economic powerhouses in Southeast Asia, Thailand has witnessed rapid economic growth in the past two decades. The free-market economy, with a well-developed infrastructure, has relied heavily on exports which contribute a major share to its GDP. Exports by the country include electronics, agricultural commodities, automobiles and parts, and processed food. The industry and services sector produce about 90% of GDP. The agricultural sector, comprised mostly of small-scale farms, contributes only 10% of GDP but employs about one-third of the labour force. The World Bank, in July 2011, upgraded Thailand's income categorisation from a lower-middle income economy to an upper-middle income economy. This was due to Thailand's progress in social and economic development, despite facing a number of financial/ economic and political challenges. With an investment-friendly economy, Thailand has also attracted foreign direct investments. Over the last few decades, the country has sustained strong growth and reduced poverty substantially.

The country's economy had been recovering from slow growth during the years since the 2014 military coup. Thailand's economic fundamentals are sound, with low inflation, low unemployment, and reasonable public and external debt levels. Tourism and government spending – mostly on infrastructure and short-term stimulus measures – have helped to boost the economy.

While largely successful in containing the deadly Coronavirus pandemic, the Thai economy suffered collateral damages arisen out of the global health crisis. The national trade and tourism sectors were particularly hit. The country's GDP contracted by 6.1% in 2020. The Thai Government has forecast a GDP growth between 1.5% and 2.5% in 2021 amidst resurgence of Covid-19 cases.

GDP (official exchange rate): $543.79 billion (2019 est.)

Real Growth Rate (GDP): 2.62% (2019 est.); 4.31% (2018 est.)

Industries: Tourism, textiles and garments, agricultural processing, beverages, tobacco, cement, light manufacturing such as jewellery and electric appliances, computers and parts, integrated circuits, furniture, plastics, automobiles and automotive parts; world's second-largest tungsten producer and third-largest tin producer

Natural Gas - Proved Reserves: 193.4 billion cu m (1 January 2018 est.)

Crude Oil - Proved Reserves: 349.4 million bbl (1 January 2018 est.)

Total Exports: $291.16 billion (2019 est.); $298.96 billion (2018 est.)

Export Commodities: Office machinery/ parts, cars and vehicle parts, integrated circuits, delivery trucks, gold (2019)

Major Markets: US 13%, China 12%, Japan 10%, Vietnam 5% (2019)

Total Imports: $257.87 billion (2019 est.); $269.45 billion (2018 est.)

Import Commodities: Crude petroleum, integrated circuits, natural gas, vehicle parts, gold (2019)

Major Suppliers: China 22%, Japan 14%, United States 7%, Malaysia 6% (2019)

DEFENCE & SECURITY

Having deep-rooted affiliation with monarchy since centuries, Thailand professes a policy of avowed allegiance to the Nation, Religion, People and the King. The Kingdom is the only country in mainland Southeast Asia which has never been colonized by any Western power. Being at the heart of mainland Southeast Asia, Thailand, nevertheless has remained strategically critical for leading global powers since centuries. In the absence of any specific conventional military threat to Southeast Asia barring the border/maritime disputes involving some littoral countries and China (which does not include the Kingdom of Thailand), the country has largely focused on building up its armed forces in consonance with evolving global as well as regional geostrategic changes. The national defence policy has emphasised on enhancing military capabilities with a "right-sized Armed Forces" and enhancing security cooperation with neighbouring states, and with the regional and international community.

Thailand has remained a traditional strategic ally of the US in Southeast Asia for over six decades since the two sides inked the Manila Pact in 1954 to form the Southeast Asia Treaty Organization (now dissolved) and the Rusk-Thanat agreement in 1962 that pledged US support for Thailand's defence and security. The country's military still relies on US military doctrine and structure and receives military training from the latter. In 2003, the Kingdom became the first country in the region to be designated as the US's major non-NATO ally. However, in the wake of evolving geostrategic equations and shifting balance of power in the Asian continent, Thailand has realigned its strategic perspective and tilted towards its north Asian neighbour, China. The two countries have become important strategic allies in recent times. Thailand, indeed, is the only Southeast Asian country sharing a "comfort zone" with the economically and militarily growing China which, on its part, has been entangled in maritime territorial disputes with several other regional littoral states, including Vietnam, the Philippines, Brunei and Malaysia. While toeing a flexible "rebalancing" policy with both the US and China, Thailand has also beefed up bilateral engagements with its South Asian neighbour, India, in recent times.

Focused on becoming an economically developed country and play a leading role in the regional and international arena, Thailand, despite having few border disputes with its neighbouring countries, does not pursue any exclusive and extensive military goal. It has rather strived to maintain a balanced, cordial relation within its surrounding regions and beyond.

KEY DEFENCE PERSONS

DEPUTY DEFENCE MINISTER: Gen. Chaichan Changmongkol

CHIEF OF STAFF OF DEFENCE FORCES & SUPREME COMMANDER: Gen. Chalermpol Srisawasdi

COMMANDER-IN-CHIEF OF ARMY: Gen. Narongpan Jittkaewtae

COMMANDER-IN-CHIEF OF NAVY: Adm. Somprasong Nilsamai

COMMANDER-IN-CHIEF OF AIR FORCE: Air Chief Marshal Naphadej Thupatemi

Internal Conflict

Ethnic insurgency: For several decades, Thailand has been fighting insurgency in its predominantly Muslim-populated southern provinces. The insurgency problem in the south, remotely located from the country's capital, is rooted over the demand for an independent Pattani state and inclusion of Malay as an official language. Five provinces in the remote south – Pattani, Yala, Narathiwat, Satun and Songkhla – have been seeking the restoration of Pattani which was an independent Sultanate before being annexed by Thailand (then Kingdom of Siam) in 1909. The conflict has mainly stemmed from ethnic identity, economic inequality, religious issues and political exclusion. Insurgency-related violence where armed Islamic militants have targeted civilians has resulted in loss of life and property over the years. After remaining relatively peaceful in 2017 and 2018, violence once again erupted in the region in 2019 with religious killings. More violence was reported in the region in 2020 as well.

Proximity of the southern region with the Thai-Malaysian border, which has become a haven for drug-trafficking and illegal arms trading, has further deepened the problem in the area. The Thai government has often linked the violence with terrorism and deployed armed forces in the region to deal with the issue.

Organised crime: Thailand has been fighting human trafficking, illegal drug trade, money laundering, smuggling, financial fraud and other forms of organised crime.

External Conflict

Territorial disputes: Thailand is engaged in land border dispute with two of its neighbours – Cambodia and Myanmar. With Malaysia, it has land as well as maritime dispute, though neither country has taken an aggressive stand over it. Thailand is also locked in maritime disputes with Laos and Cambodia.

Cambodia: The two neighbours spar over the 11th century Hindu temple of Preah Vihear in the Thai-Cambodian border. Historically recognized as a Cambodian temple, Preah Vihear (called Phra Viharn by the Thais) was occupied by Thai forces in 1954 soon after Cambodia gained independence. However, the ownership of the temple was eventually given to Cambodia under a 1962 ruling of the International Court of Justice. The dispute over the temple remained subdued for some decades as an internal conflict-ridden Cambodia was busy sorting out its domestic issues. The Preah Vihear dispute resurfaced again in 2008 when Cambodia sought to list the temple as a UNESCO World Heritage site which mounted tensions between the two neighbours. While Thailand does not claim any official ownership over the temple, the main area of contention is its surrounding region roughly covering some 4.6 square kilometres, having direct transport links to Thai cities and giving a free access to its citizens and tourists. Hence, the area remains a subject of overlapping territorial claims. Efforts are going on by the two sides to resolve the centuries-old conflict.

The maritime dispute between the two countries involves some 26,000 sq kms of area in the Gulf of Thailand. Both sides have overlapping claims in the region, believed to be rich in oil and natural gas.

Myanmar: Thailand shares a land boundary of 2,401-km with its north-western neighbour Myanmar of which only 60-km is officially demarcated. The border conflict between the two countries dates back to the British colonization of Myanmar (erstwhile Burma) in 1824 and the inking of the Burney Treaty between Thailand and Britain in 1826, which redefined the Thai-Burmese border. Myanmar, since its independence in 1948, has opposed the current border, most of which has not been officially demarcated. The area of dispute, in particular, is the region along the Moei River which forms a natural border between Thailand and Myanmar. The border issue has also given rise to illegal arms and drugs trade, human trafficking, illegal immigration and ethnic insurgency originating in Myanmar and spilling into Thailand.

Laos: Thailand and Laos share a 1,810-km long common border – 702-km of land and 1,108-km of the Mekong River. Dispute over the land border resulted in a brief war between the two sides in 1987-88. The two neighbours set up the Thai-Lao Joint Boundary Commission (JBC) in August 1996 to demarcate the 1,810-km common border. Talks are going on to resolve the issue, even as disputes remain over several islands in the Mekong River.

Malaysia: While the maritime boundary dispute involving delimitation of continental shelf in the Gulf of Thailand has been resolved between the two countries, a dispute still remains over an area adjacent to the continental shelves with overlapping claims by Thailand, Malaysia and Vietnam. The land border dispute involving the Bukit Jeli (Jeli Hill) is yet to be resolved between the two countries.

THREAT PERSPECTIVE

Barring the border disputes in its immediate neighbourhood, Thailand has over the years successfully maintained a friendly posture and endeavoured to elevate its regional as well as international profile by promoting peace, stability and security. There is no direct military threat to Thailand's national security and sovereignty from any country at present. The only primary threat the country faces today is non-traditional in nature and stems from internal unrest and related violence. At the regional level, Thailand has been making efforts to resolve all boundary disputes with its neighbours. At the global stage, while retaining strong ties with its traditional allies, Thailand is also extending its hand of friendship to newer countries with the larger goal of securing its national interests and rise as an economic power.

STRATEGIC RELATIONS

US: As the US's only "treaty ally" in the entire Southeast Asia, Thailand has immensely benefited from its ties with the world's superpower. While traditional relations between the two countries dates back to 1833 when they inked the bilateral Treaty of Amity and Commerce, strategic alliance between them was established in the post Word War-II phase, when both sides became signatories to the 1954 Manila Pact. The pact led to the formation of Southeast Asia Treaty Organization (SEATO) in 1955 as an "Asian equivalent of Western military alliance NATO". The organisation, with its headquarters at the Thai capital Bangkok, was established as an international forum for collective defence of Southeast Asia, though, barring from Thailand and Philippines, the rest of the member countries in the block were from outside the region. SEATO was eventually dissolved in 1977 after many member nations withdrew from it. In 1962, Thailand and the US signed the landmark Rusk-Thanat agreement, under which the latter pledged support to Thailand's defence and security that subsequently paved the way for the US military gaining access into the Southeast Asian country. During the US-Vietnam war in the 1950s, Thailand became an indispensable ally of Washington and provided its crucial airfields, ports and other infrastructure for military use against Vietnam. The Thai armed forces, in return, received a wide range of military equipment and training from the US. In subsequent years, the Thai-US military relations were subdued, particularly after the end of the Vietnam War. The relationship revived again in the late 1970s when Vietnam occupied Cambodia in 1978. The US undertook the task of modernising and professionalising the Thai armed forces and in 1982, the two countries staged the first "Cobra Gold" annual military exercise, which today is pegged as one of the largest multi-national field exercises in the Asia Pacific region with nearly 30 countries taking part in it. The two countries also conduct the annual Cooperation Afloat Readiness and Training (CARAT) exercise involving their militaries.

Over the past few years, US-Thai relations have witnessed changes in the backdrop of evolving regional and global strategic environment. Nevertheless, bilateral ties between the two sides remain firmly in place, with the US providing military as well as economic assistance to Thailand. In 2003, Washington designated Thailand as its major non-NATO ally (MNNA), after the Kingdom contributed troops and support for US military operations in Afghanistan and Iraq. The MNNA tag allowed Bangkok to buy advanced medium-range air-to-air missiles for its US-built F-16 fighter aircraft – a first for any Southeast Asian nation.

Even as Washington announced plans to shift its strategic focus towards the Asia-Pacific by bolstering its military presence in the region, it started exploring ways to further reinvigorate its strategic alliance with Thailand by reviving some of its old defence bases there and also by increasing joint naval cooperation with the Southeast Asian nation. However, the developments in Thailand's political landscape which jeopardized the democratic set up in the country following the military-led coup in 2014 adversely affected Thai-US relations. It subsequently led to Washington suspending military aid worth US$ 4.7 million to Bangkok. Bilateral ties between the two nations improved during the tenure of former US President Donald Trump when he came to power in 2016. The current US administration led by President Joe Biden has re-focused on making the Thai-US alliance stronger and secure as before.

China: Relations between Beijing and Bangkok has grown unprecedentedly in recent times with the former supplying major military platforms and systems to the Thai defence forces. A deal signed in 2017 to acquire three conventional submarine from China for the Royal Thai Navy has further bolstered the bustling strategic ties between the two Asian nations.

Though it initially harboured a policy of suspicion and hostility towards the Communist China, the Thai Kingdom later established diplomatic ties with Beijing in 1975 and since then, the two Asian neighbours have cooperated on several areas of mutual interest. The two sides started the Sino-Thai Defence and Security Consultation in 2001 which later gave way to defence cooperation, including joint development and technological transfers. China began supplying a range of military equipment, including tanks, APCs, small arms, missiles and frigates to the Thai armed forces in the late 1980s. In the past few decades, Beijing has sought to further strengthen military ties with Thailand, given the strategic importance of the Kingdom in the Asian neighbourhood. China has come to be reckoned as a major strategic partner of Thailand. The two countries are holding joint military training exercises, and also partnered in developing equipment for the Thai armed forces. Bilateral ties also include cooperation in areas of trade, infrastructure and energy. The two nations have declared their "comprehensive strategic partnership" in 2012. Thailand has also become a signatory to the China-led Regional Comprehensive Economic Partnership (RCEP) Agreement.

India: Toeing the policy of balancing its regional and foreign relations, Thailand has made efforts to deepen its ties with India in recent times. The two countries share maritime boundary in the Andaman Sea and hence, reckon each other's strategic importance in the region. While bilateral trade, economic and cultural ties between the two neighbours have flourished in the past, cooperation in the field of defence and security has also assumed significance. India has held regular bilateral naval drills with Thailand since 1995. The navies are also regularly conducting coordinated maritime patrols in the Indian Ocean Region since 2005. The two countries signed a bilateral Memorandum of Understanding on Defence Cooperation in January 2012. India has evinced interest in taking up infrastructure development projects with Thailand. High-level political and diplomatic visits and exchanges between the two sides in recent years have paved way for future activities and cooperation at a broader level.

Vietnam: The two neighbours upgraded their partnership into a strategic one in June 2013. Vietnam thus became Thailand's first strategic partner among the ASEAN member nations. The two sides have also agreed to effectively carry out bilateral defence cooperation agreement while establishing a defence policy dialogue mechanism.

Australia: Thailand has good defence relations with Australia since World War II. The two countries continue to cooperate in the field by regularly holding bilateral military exchanges and high level defence visits. Thai armed forces also receive training in Australia.

Ukraine: Thailand and Ukraine share defence relations, with the latter extending military and technical cooperation to the Kingdom. The Thai Army has inducted the Ukrainian BTR-3E1 armoured vehicles. Thailand has also started assembling the vehicles locally. The two sides are planning joint production of other Ukraine-designed military vehicles and exploring ways to set up joint industrial facilities for the same.

MULTILATERAL ALLIANCES

ASEAN: The Association of Southeast Asian Nations (ASEAN) has emerged as one of the most prominent regional multilateral blocks in Asia. The 10-member ASEAN, established on 8 August 1967 with the primary objective to promote regional trade, peace and stability along with social and cultural development of the region, has successfully pursued its goals and made great strides in achieving regional integration. The absence of any conventional military threat to Southeast Asia aided by the member countries' pledge to resolve all their bilateral issues through political and diplomatic means has further strengthened the ASEAN. The foreign policy of Thailand, which is one of the founding members of ASEAN, has been largely guided by the regional forum. Bangkok has made foremost efforts to transform the association into a regional economic stronghold and a vibrant marketplace. Moreover, having maintained an equation of bonhomie with its immediate and extended neighbourhood, in particular with China which is entangled in maritime dispute with several Southeast Asian littoral states, Thailand's importance in the regional forum as an arbitrator to resolve conflicts has amplified in recent times.

APEC: Thailand is one of the 12 founding members of the Asia-Pacific Economic Cooperation (APEC). The 21-member organisation, established in 1989 as a regional economic forum among the Pacific Rim nations, has solely focused on free and open trade and investment, promoting and accelerating regional economic integration and encouraging economic and technical cooperation among the member countries to build a dynamic and harmonious Asia-Pacific region.

East Asia Summit: Initially proposed as part of the ASEAN forum, the East Asia Summit, over the years, has evolved as a platform for strategic dialogue and cooperation on key issues in the East Asian region. The first meeting of the forum was held at Kuala Lumpur, Malaysia in 2005. Besides the 10 ASEAN member nations, the EAS also comprises of Australia, China, India, Japan, New Zealand, South Korea, the US and Russia.

BIMSTEC: The Bay of Bengal Initiative for Multi-Sectoral Technical and Economic Cooperation (BIMSTEC) is a regional block comprising of India, Bangladesh, Sri Lanka, Thailand, Myanmar, Nepal and Bhutan. The multilateral forum with the South Asian and Southeast Asian nations has 13 priority areas, including trade and investment, technology, energy, transport and communication among others. The block, originally named Bangladesh, India, Sri Lanka, and Thailand Economic Cooperation (BISTEC), was formed in 1997 to primarily promote economic and trade cooperation among the member nations. Myanmar, Nepal and Bhutan subsequently joined the forum which was then renamed as BIMSTEC.

DEFENCE CAPABILITIES

ARMY: The Royal Thai Army (RTA) in terms of personnel strength is the largest of all three wings of Thai armed forces, constituting over 60 percent of the total active force. The Army operates with the primary mission to protect the Kingdom's sovereignty and integrity from any internal and external threat. The land forces have played a crucial role in dealing with insurgency-related problems in the country's south. Thailand is also a regular contributor to the UN peacekeeping missions by sending troops for overseas operations. While focusing on its modernisation, the Thai Defence Ministry has emphasised on transforming the Army into "a compact and integrated force." Having an armoured inventory consisting of Cold War-era battle tanks, combat vehicles and other weapons, most of which are now obsolete, Thailand has inked deals with a number of countries including China, Ukraine and South Africa in last few years to acquire new tanks and armoured vehicles for its land forces. Alongside, it is also acquiring new artillery systems, multiple rocket launchers, missiles and helicopters as part of the renewed 10-year "Modernisation Plan: Vision 2026" cleared by the Government in 2017 which aims at military modernisation along with an eventual increase in annual defence budget at 2% of GDP.

Personnel: 190,000+

Equipment

Category	Name	In Service
MBT	VT4	48
	M60 A1	53
	M48A5	70
	M60 A3	125
	T-69	110
	T-59	24
	BM Oplot	20
Light Tank	M41(light)	150 (reserve)
	Stingray	100
	Scorpion	144
APC	VN-1	75
	V150 Commando	150
	Type 85	600+
	M113	340
	WMZ-55B1	96
	Reva protected Carrier	97
	BTR-3EI 8X8	251
	First Win 4x4 (light armoured)	200+
Artillery	M109A5 155mm SP	20+
	Caesar 155mm wheeled SP	6
	M101 105mm	286
	LG1Mk2 105mm	24
	L119 105mm	22
	M114	60
	M198	50
	Type 59 130mm	30+
	75mm	300+
Mortar	81mm towed	217
	120mm towed	86
	M106A3 120mm mortar carrier	12
	M125A3 81mm	21
MLRS	130mm	60
	DTI-1 300mm	10
RCL	57mm, 75mm & 106mm	
ATGW	Tow	
	Dragon	
	M901A3 ITOW	18
AA gun	Vulcan SP	48
	40mm	48
	57mm	24
SAM	I-Hawk	
	Redeye	

...continued

Category	Name	In Service
SAM	Spada	1 battery
	SA-18 Igla	
	Short Blowpipe	

Army Aviation

Category	Name	In Service
Light Transport Aircraft	C295	2 (+1 on order)
	C-212-300	1 (to retire)
	Short 330	2
	OV-10	75
	Beech 99	1
	T-41	23
	King Air	1
	JETSTREAM 41	2
	ERJ-135	2
Helicopter	Bell 206	12
	UH-1H	50+
	UH-60L	9
	UH-60M	3 (+4 on order)
	UH-72A Lakota	6 (+9 in option for future order)
	AS550 C3 Fennec	8
	Bell 212/412	20
	OH13	18
	Bell 214 B	6
	Bell AH-1F	3
	Boeing 234 Chinook	3
	TH300	45
	Bell 206B	5
	Mi-17V5	7
	AW139	12
UAV	Hermes	4
	Searcher Mk II	4

New Procurements/Upgrades

◆ The US State Department in July 2019 approved the sale of 60 M1126 Stryker infantry carrier vehicles (ICVs) with equipment and support for an estimated cost of $175 million. The Thai Govt. had made a request in this regard. Delivery of the initial batch started in August 2019 with Thailand now planning to acquire 50 more such platforms.

◆ A total of 48 MBT-3000 (export designation "VT-4") MBTs have been acquired from China between 2017 and 2019.

◆ China's NORINCO has completed delivery of all VN-1 armoured vehicle variants in 2021.

◆ Indigenously developed First Win (4x4) light armoured vehicles (LAVs) have been delivered. More orders have been placed.

◆ The indigenously developed Black Widow Spider 8×8 APC has been handed over to the Army in 2020 for conducting field trials. The armoured platform has been developed by the Defence Technology Institute (DTI) of Thailand.

◆ An order has been placed with Airbus to deliver an additional C295 transport aircraft with delivery slated for 2023. Two such platforms are already operational in the Thai Army.

◆ Ten Mi-17V5 helicopters procured from Russia have been inducted as of 2021. Acquisition of more such platforms is being planned to replace the Boeing-made Chinook transport helicopters.

◆ Delivery of six UH-72A Lakota multi-role helicopters from the US under FMS has been completed. Thailand has made a further request for nine more Lakotas to replace its ageing fleet of Bell UH-1H helicopters.

◆ Acquisition of new combat helicopters to replace the ageing fleet of Bell AH-1F Cobras is under consideration. The US State Department, in September 2019, has cleared a potential sale of eight AH-6i light attack reconnaissance helicopters and associated equipment as a replacement for the older platforms in the Thai Army.

◆ The US State Dept. has approved sale of Javelin anti-tank missiles under FMS route.

NAVY: To defend and protect over 3,000-km long national coastline, Thailand has built up a modern naval force capable of conducting combat missions. The Royal Thai Navy (RTN), indeed, is the only naval power in entire Southeast Asia having an aircraft carrier. Besides, it possesses a number of frigates, corvettes and other naval craft to carry out its missions. The Govt. in 2017 also cleared the purchase of the Navy's first submarine from China, with delivery expected in 2024. In 2019, the Thai Navy inked a deal with China to acquire an amphibious transport dock as well.

The RTN mainly operates in the Gulf of Thailand, Malacca Strait and the Indian Ocean Region. Though Thailand does not face any conventional external maritime threat and its only areas of focus are fighting piracy, illegal drug trade and related incidents, nevertheless, a naval modernisation programme is going on to maintain the Kingdom's strategic parity with neighbouring countries and enhance its regional force projection capabilities.

Major naval bases: Sattahip, Bangkok, Nakhon Phanom, Phang Nga, U-Tapao (naval air base)

Personnel: 56,000+

Equipment

Category	Name	In Service
Submarine	S26T (Chinese Yuan-class)	1 (On Order)
LHD	Chakri Nareubet	1
LPD	HTMS Ang Thong (Endurance class)	1
	Type 071E	(On Order)
Frigate	HTMS Bhumibol Adulyadej	1
	Phutthayotfa class (ex US Knox class) to be phased out	2
	Naresuan class (Type F52T)	2
	Chao Praya class (Chinese 053HT & 053HTH design)	4
Corvette	Rantanamkosin class	2
	Tap class	2
Training vessel	Makut Rajakumarn	1
Patrol vessel	Pattani class	2
	Hua Hin class	3
	Khamrosin class	3
	Chonburi class gun FAC	3
	Ratcharit class missile FAC	2
	Prabparapak class missile FAC	3
	Sattahip class	6
	T991 class	3
	T81 class	9
	T81 class	3
	PC30 class	10
	T213	18
	Marsun M36 & M21	3 + 4 (2+5 on order)
	Kravi class	2
LST	Sichang class & ex US	6
LCU	Tongkaew + ex US	12
LSM	Ex-US	2
LCM+LCI	Ex-US	24+1
LCVP	Ex-US	12
Hovercraft	Griffon 100TD	3
Mine hunter	M48 class	2
Auxiliary ship		29
Weapon	RIM-7 Sea Sparrow SAM	
	RIM-162 Evolved Sea Sparrow SAM	
	Harpoon ASM	
	Exocet ASM	
	C-802A ASM	
	(Torpedo) Mk.32, Mk.46	

Marines

Personnel: 14,000

Equipment

Category	Name	In Service
MBT	M60 A3	5
APC	AAV71A	30+
	BTR-3EI 8X8	12 (on order)
	V-150 Commando	50+
Artillery	GC 45 howitzer	20+
	M101 105mm	30
	LG1Mk2 105mm	6

Naval Aviation

Equipment

Category	Name	In Service
Fighter/ Attack/ AWS role	A-7E Corsair II	14
	TA-7C	4
	AV-8S	7
	TAV-8V	2
	P-3T Orion	2
	UP 3T	1
	F27 Mk200/Mk400	4+2
Transport/ Surveil-lance	ERJ-135Lr	1
	CL215	2
	Nomad Searchmaster	5
	Do228	6
	Cessna 337	6
Helicopter	S-70B Sea Hawk	6
	MH-60S Sea Hawk	2
	UH-1H	3
	S-76B	4
	Super Lynx 300	2
	H145M	5

New Procurements/ Upgrades

◆ Work is progressing on the first S26T diesel-electric submarine (derivative of Yuan-class / Type-041) ordered from China. Delivery is awaited by 2024. Procurement of two additional platforms of the class, however, has been put off over funding issues and budgetary constraints following the Covid-19 pandemic.

◆ A contract has been awarded to a UK company in 2018 to support Royal Thai Navy's new midget submarine programme. Under the programme approved by the Govt in July 2018, Thailand plans to build the small underwater platform having displacement of 150-300 tons over the next seven years.

◆ Acquisition of a second medium-sized frigate to replace the two ex-US Knox-class ships is under consideration. Britain's BAE Systems has offered its Type 31 multipurpose frigate. The first platform of the class, renamed as HTMS Bhumibol Adulyadej, built by South Korean shipbuilder Daewoo Shipbuilding, was commissioned in Jan. 2019.

◆ A deal has been signed with China Shipbuilding Industry Cooperation in September 2019 to acquire one Type 071E amphibious transport dock (export variant of Chinese Navy's Type 071 LPD) for the Thai Navy.

◆ The US Govt has approved sale of Harpoon Block II anti-ship missiles worth $24.9 million under foreign military sales. The weapon would be fitted on the HTMS Bhumibol Adulyadej frigate.

◆ The US Govt has approved sale of 16 RIM-162 Evolved SeaSparrow Missile (ESSM) units and associated equipment under Foreign Military Sales. The missiles would be deployed on Chinese-built Naresuan class frigates.

◆ First batch of three VN-16 amphibious assault tanks has been delivered in May 2021. A contract was awarded to China's NORINCO in June 2020 to supply the VN-16 platforms to Thai Marine Forces.

AIR FORCE: The Royal Thai Air Force (RTAF) is structured and equipped to carry out conventional air warfare as well as internal security missions. It is the smallest wing of Thai armed forces in terms of personnel strength and yet the most modern among them. The air force inventory, which mostly consisted of the US and European fighter jets and other aircraft acquired in the 1980s and 1990s, has been revamped to accommodate new platforms, weapon systems and equipment. Deployment of European Gripen fighters, reconnaissance aircraft, command and control system and new military radar have been completed recently. Refurbishing of existing platforms and systems has also been going on to enhance the combat capabilities of RTAF which is regarded as the third largest air force in Southeast Asia after that of Malaysia and Singapore.

Major air bases: Khorat, Takhli, Udorn, Surat Thani

Personnel: 45,000+

Equipment

Category	Name	In Service
Fighter/ Attack/ AWS role	F16A/ B	66
	F-5E/ F	23 (10 in store)
	Gripen C/ D	11
	Alpha Jet	25
Trainer/ Light Attack	T-50 Golden Eagle	8 (+6 on order)
	Pilatus PC-9	23
	L-39ZA/ MP Albatros	24

...continued

Category	Name	In Service
Transport/ Surveil-lance	C130H-30/ C13J/30	12 + 6
	A-310-300	1
	Boeing 737-300ER	1
	ATR72-500 (VIP)	4
	N-22B Nomad	16
	BT-67 Basler	6
	CN-235	3
	Merlin IV	3
	Learjet	4
	Saab 340	2
	Sukhoi 100	3 (on order)
Helicopter	S-92 Hawk	3
	Bell 412	15
	H225M	8 (+4 on order)
	Bell UH-1H	15
Weapon	IRIS-T AAM	
	AIM-9 Sidewinder AAM	
	AIM-120 AM-RAAM	
	Python 3 AAM	
	RBS 15-F ASM	

New Procurements/ Upgrades

◆ Phased acquisition of at least 24 new F-16A/B platforms over the next few years is under consideration as a replacement for equal number of existing F-16 fighters.

◆ Acquisition of a Gripen fighter to supplement the one that crashed in Jan. 2017 is under consideration. Upgrade of the existing fleet of Gripen platforms' software suite to MS20 configuration is also being planned.

◆ Delivery of T-50 advanced jet trainers ordered from South Korea's Korean Aerospace Industries is going on. The platforms are replacing the ageing fleet of L-39ZA jet trainers. A total of 14 T-50 aircraft are on order with deliveries slated for completion by 2023.

◆ In 2019, KAI received another contract from the RTAF to upgrade the entire fleet of T-50 platforms with radar systems, radar warning receivers, and countermeasures dispenser systems. Work is scheduled to be completed by 2021 – 2022.

◆ An order has been placed with US-based Textron Aviation in Sept. 2020 to acquire 12 Beechcraft T-6C Texan II trainer aircraft. The military trainer platforms would be delivered by 2023.

◆ Israel's Elbit Systems is upgrading 14 of the Northrop Grumman F-5E/F light fighters under contracts signed in 2014 and 2017. Delivery of the upgraded platforms has started. The upgrades would keep the platforms operational until 2030.

◆ Rolls-Royce in June 2019 has received a contract to upgrade the RTAF's entire fleet of C-130H tactical transport aircraft (totalling 12) with new engines to keep them operational till 2040. Thailand was earlier planning to replace the ageing fleet of C-130H configurations with new planes.

◆ Two new H225M (previously called EC725) multi-role utility helicopters were delivered in 2018 under a 2016 contract. Four more such platforms were ordered in 2018 from Airbus with delivery scheduled for 2022. The helicopters are being used for search-and-rescue/combat search-and-rescue (SAR/CSAR) missions as well as for troops transport and other roles.

◆ More number of IRIS-T short-range air-to-air missiles have been ordered from Germany's Diehl Defence in 2018 for arming the F-5E/F Tiger II fighter platforms.

DEFENCE DEALS
Joint Venture Programmes

China: Thailand and China have agreed to jointly develop multiple rocket launchers with a guidance system. Under the agreement, the Thai Defence Technology Institute (DTI) has worked with China to develop the multiple rocket launcher called "DTI-1G (Guided)" having a higher range than existing systems. Thailand successfully tested the new rocket launcher in 2015. In an earlier joint deal, the two countries developed the DTI-1 system. The two sides are also exploring ways to jointly set up defence industrial facility in Thailand to support and maintain Chinese land platforms operated by the Thai Army. The Thai Army has procured the VT4 MBTs and VN-1 APCs from China. Plans are also advancing to develop a tactical UAV (based on Chinese design) for the Thai Army.

UK: The Bangkok Dock has designed and developed the offshore patrol vessel HTMS Krabi for the Royal Thai Navy under a transfer of technology agreement with UK's BAE Systems inked in 2009. The state-run DTI has also worked with UK's Ricardo for the development of the indigenous Black Widow Spider 8×8 infantry fighting vehicle programme.

Defence Industry: The Thai armed forces has mostly relied on foreign military exports as the country lacks a robust defence industry. According to official figures, there are 48 defence-related industries operating under the Ministry of Defence. The defence firms are capable of producing small arms, artillery, rockets and other weapons primarily for the Royal Thai Army and small coastal patrol craft for the Navy. Dearth of defence related research and development programmes, which receive less than 0.1% of the overall defence budget, has led to an underdeveloped domestic defence sector. To augment national defence production, the Government has incorporated technology transfer clause in some of the recent military acquisition deals with foreign firms, including with Sweden's Saab and UK's BAE Systems. The present military dispensation has particularly focused on defence industrial collaboration with major arms importing nations to galvanize the indigenous defence production capability of Thailand. The Government-owned Defence Technology Institute (DTI), set up in January 2009, is also working on few areas of defence research & development programmes including rockets and missile systems, unmanned aerial vehicle (for Army), and vertical take-off and landing unmanned aerial vehicle (for Navy).

DEFENCE BUDGET

Thailand, since the past few years, has allocated a visible amount of its GDP for military expenditure. The annual defence budget of the Kingdom witnessed a northward trend between 2006 and 2011. While in 2010, it allocated 1.5% of GDP on defence, the 2011 defence budget was 1.6% of GDP, at US$5.52 billion. In 2013, the government announced defence spending worth 178.4 billion baht.

Following the taking over of power by the country's military in 2014, defence spending received major boost with an average annual increase of around 5%. Defence budget for 2015 was 193.07 billion baht, while in 2016, it rose to 206.4 billion baht, an increase of nearly 7% over previous year's spending. For 2017, a budget of 210.7 billion baht (US$6.1 billion) was approved. The budget amounted to around 1.5% of GDP. While budgetary figure for 2018-19 period was 222.4 billion baht (US$6.5 billion), for 2019-20, the Government earmarked 227.67 billion baht (US$7.4 billion) which was an increase of 4.2% over previous year's budget and 1.4% of the country's GDP.

For 2020-21, the Government allocated around 215 billion baht (revised amount) which was a reduction of 7% over previous year's allocation. Proposed defence allocation for 2022 is 203 billion baht – a further cut of 5% over last fiscal as a result of economic constraints arisen due to the Covid-19 pandemic.

The ongoing comprehensive military modernisation drive had resulted in a steady rise in Thailand's defence budget in past few years. The country is swiftly acquiring new platforms and systems for its Army, Navy and Air Force, including armoured vehicles, main battle tanks, submarines, frigates, OPVs, jet trainers, helicopters in addition to upgrading the existing military inventory.

CONCLUSION

In the absence of any conventional military threat, Thailand has primarily focused on its socio-economic development, though maintaining military edge in the region has also been prioritised by the Government. Driven by the larger goal of achieving self-reliance and securing its national interests, the Kingdom has adopted a flexible and balancing policy towards its larger Asian neighbours, China and India, even while continuing the deep-rooted relations with its traditional strategic ally, the US. In recent times, bilateral ties between Thailand and China, especially their military relations, have scaled newer heights. Military acquisitions by Bangkok have been diversified in the past few years and do not exclusively rely on US-supplied weapons and systems. The fast evolving geostrategic developments have reshaped Thailand as a major strategic player, especially in the Southeast Asian region, in the present century.

CONTACT DETAILS
Ministry of Defence
The Department of Defence
Defence Town Hall Road,
Phra Nakhon, Bangkok 10200
Sanamchai Road
www.mod.go.th/

LPD HTMS Ang Thong of Royal Thai Navy (Internet photo)

TUNISIA
(Capital: Tunis)

INTRODUCTION
Area: 163,610 sq km
Population: 11,811,335 (July 2021 est.)
Coastline: 1,148 km
Maritime claims: Territorial sea: 12 nm
Contiguous zone: 24 nm
Exclusive Economic Zone: 12 nm

KEY POLITICAL PERSONS

PRESIDENT & COMMANDER-IN-CHIEF: Kais Saied

PRIME MINISTER: Najla Bouden Romdhane

KEY DEFENCE PERSONS

MINISTER OF DEFENCE: Imed Memiche

INSPECTOR GENERAL OF ARMED FORCES: Gen. Abdelmoneim Belati

CHIEF OF STAFF OF ARMY: Maj. Gen. Mohamed al Ghoul

CHIEF OF STAFF OF NAVY: Rear Adm. Adel Jhen

CHIEF OF STAFF OF AIR FORCE: Maj. Gen. Mohammad Al Hajjem

ECONOMY

Tunisia's diverse, market-oriented economy has long been cited as a success story in Africa and the Middle East, but it faces an array of challenges following the 2011 revolution. Following an ill-fated experiment with socialist economic policies in the 1960s, Tunisia embarked on a successful strategy focused on bolstering exports, foreign investment, and tourism, all of which have become central to the country's economy. Key exports now include textiles and apparel, food products, petroleum products, chemicals, and phosphates, with about 80% of exports bound for Tunisia's main economic partner, the European Union. Tunisia's liberal strategy, coupled with investments in education and infrastructure, fuelled decades of 4-5% annual GDP growth and improving living standards. Since its establishment in late 2014, Tunisia's new government led by then President Mohamed Beji Caid Essebsi (passed away in July 2019), faced challenges reassuring businesses and investors, bringing budget and current account deficits under control, shoring up the country's financial system, lowering high unemployment, and reducing economic disparities between the more developed coastal region and the impoverished interior. The government remained under pressure to boost economic growth quickly to mitigate chronic socio-economic challenges, especially high levels of youth unemployment, which had persisted since the 2011 revolution. Successive terrorist attacks against the tourism sector and worker strikes in the phosphate sector, which combined account for nearly 15% of GDP, slowed growth from 2015 to 2017. Tunis is seeking increased foreign investment and working with the IMF through an Extended Fund Facility agreement to fix fiscal deficiencies.

Hit by the global Coronavirus health crisis, Tunisia's economy contracted by 8.8% in 2020, according to the World Bank. GDP growth is expected to accelerate to 4% in 2021.

GDP (official exchange rate): $38.88 billion (2019 est.)

Real Growth Rate (GDP): 2% (2017 est.); 1.1% (2016 est.)

Industries: Petroleum, mining (particularly phosphate and iron ore), tourism, textiles, footwear, agribusiness, beverages

Total Exports: $13.82 billion (2017 est.); $13.57 billion (2016 est.)

Export Commodities: Insulated wiring, clothing and apparel, crude petroleum, olive oil, vehicle parts (2019)

Major Markets: France 29%, Italy 17%, Germany 13% (2019)

Total Imports: $19.09 billion (2017 est.); $18.37 billion (2016 est.)

Import Commodities: Refined petroleum, natural gas, low-voltage protection equipment, cars, insulated wiring (2019)

Major Suppliers: France 17%, Italy 16%, Germany 8%, China 8%, Algeria 7% (2019)

INTERNATIONAL DISPUTES

Tunisia has no known international disputes.

DEFENCE

ARMY

Personnel: 25,000+

Equipment

Category	Name	In Service
MBT	M60A1	24
	M60A3	50
	Kurassier (tank destroyer)	54
Armoured car	Saladin	22
	AML-90	20
	AML-60	10
	EE-9 Cascavel	15
APC	M113A2	100+
	EE11 URUTU	18
Artillery	M-101A1/A2 (105mm)	45
	M-114 (155mm) towed	12
	M-198 (155mm) towed	50
	M108 105mm SP	10
	M109 155mm SP	18
Mortar	81mm	100
	107mm	50+
	120mm	
SAM	Chaparral	
	RBS-70	
ATGW	SS-11	
	MILAN	
	TOW	
ATK weapon	STRIM-89	
AA gun	M55 20mm	100
	M-1939/Type 55 37mm	

New Procurements/ Upgrades

◆ Delivery of Kirpi (4x4) mine-resistant ambush-protected (MRAP) vehicles from Turkey is going on. A total of 100 such platforms are on order.

◆ Turkey has reportedly been awarded a contract in 2020 to deliver more armoured platforms to the Tunisian Army. The platforms are nine Medium Class Multi-Purpose Armored Vehicles (MPAVs) built by Turkey's BMC defense company.

NAVY

Personnel: 4,500

Equipment

Category	Name	In Service
Fleet	Ex-German ALBATROS class FAC (Type 143B)	6
	La Galite class missile FAC (Combattante III type)	3
	BIZERTE class large patrol craft (P48 Type)	3
	UTIQUE class large patrol craft (Chinese HAIZHUI Type)	3

...continued

Category	Name	In Service
Fleet	ISTIQLAL class patrol craft	4
	US-built 65-ft SAFE patrol boat	2
	TAZARKA class attack craft	2
	Damen class multi-role OPV	4
UAV	ScanEagle	

Coast Guard

Category	Name	In Service
Fleet	RAS EL BLAIS class patrol craft	5
	SBEITLA class inshore patrol craft (ex-GDR BREMSE class)	5
	Light patrol boats	10

New Procurements/ Upgrades

◆ The Tunisian Government and local private shipbuilding company Societe de Construction Industrielle et Navale (SCIN) have partnered to build patrol boats for the Navy indigenously.

◆ ScanEagle UAVs are being procured from the US.

AIR FORCE

Personnel: 3,000

Equipment

Category	Name	In Service
Fighter	F-5E/F	16
	MB326K/L	10
	L-59T	9
	SF-260WT	12
	SF-260C	6
Transport/ Surveillance	C130 B/H Hercules	2
	C-130J Super Hercules	2
	King Air	1
	L410	3
Helicopter	Alouette II, III	11
	UH-1H/ 1N	8
	Puma	1
	Ecureuil	6
	AB-205	15
	Gazelle	6
	UH-60M Black Hawk	12
	Bell OH-58D Kiowa Warrior	10 (+more with deliveries going on)

New Procurements/ Upgrades

◆ The US will deliver eight T-6C Texan II trainer aircraft to Tunisia under FMS route. A $12.5 million contract has been awarded by the US DoD to Textron in June 2021 to supply the air platforms to the Tunisian Air Force.

◆ Delivery of 24 Bell OH-58D Kiowa Warrior helicopters from the US is going on since 2017. The US Government in 2016 had approved the sale of US Army's surplus Bell OH-58D Kiowa Warrior scout and light attack helicopters along with weapon systems and other equipment for worth US$100.8 million.

◆ Under a US FMS deal, Northrop Grumman has been awarded a contract to carry out avionics upgrade for the Tunisian Air Force's 12 F-5 supersonic fighter aircraft fleet.

◆ Turkish Aerospace Industries (TAI) has received a contract in 2020 to deliver six ANKA-S unmanned aerial vehicles (UAVs) and associated equipment to Tunisia.

Defence Expenditure

Defence budget (2018): 2,233 million dinars ($824 million)

Estimated defence spending in terms of GDP: 1.4%

Leading arms suppliers are the US and Europe. Turkey has emerged as a new military supplier to the North African nation of late.

Defence Production and R&D

The domestic defence industry of Tunisia has very few manufacturing facilities. The country does not undertake any major defence research and development activities.

Defence Procurement

Tunisia has initiated steps to modernise its armed forces as majority of its military equipment is now obsolete. The Army, Navy and Air Force are presently acquiring new platforms to bolster their overall capability. Following its transition to democracy in 2014, the country's military has also received military aid and weapons, mostly from the US.

CONTACT DETAILS

Ministry of National Defence
The Kasbah Bab al-Manara
Tunis 1008, Tunisia
Phone: 71 560 244 (00216)
www.defense.tn

STRATEGIC INFORMATION
TURKEY
(Capital: Ankara)

INTRODUCTION

Area: 783,562 sq km

Population: 82,482,383 (July 2021 est.)

Coastline: 7,200 km

Maritime claims: Territorial sea: 6 nm in the Aegean Sea; 12 nm in Black Sea and in Mediterranean Sea

Exclusive Economic Zone: in Black Sea only: to the maritime boundary agreed upon with the former USSR

GEOPOLITICAL IMPORTANCE

Turkey, known officially as the Republic of Turkey, is a Eurasian country located in Western Asia and in East Thrace in Southeastern Europe. Turkey is bordered by eight countries: Bulgaria to the northwest; Greece to the west; Georgia to the northeast; Armenia, Azerbaijan and Iran to the east; and Iraq and Syria to the southeast. The Mediterranean Sea and Cyprus are to the south; the Aegean Sea to the west; and the Black Sea is to the north. The Sea of Marmara, the Bosphorus and the Dardanelles (which together form the Turkish Straits) demarcate the boundary between East Thrace and Anatolia; they also separate Europe and Asia.

POLITICAL OVERVIEW

Turkey is a democratic, secular, unitary, constitutional republic with an ancient cultural heritage. The President of the Republic is the head of state and has a largely ceremonial role. Executive power is exercised by the Prime Minister and the Council of Ministers which make up the government, while the legislative power is vested in the unicameral parliament, the Grand National Assembly of Turkey. The judiciary is independent of the executive and the legislature, and the Constitutional Court is charged with ruling on the conformity of laws and decrees with the constitution. The Council of State is the tribunal of last resort for administrative cases, and the High Court of Appeals for all others. A constitutional referendum was held throughout Turkey in April 2017 on whether to approve 18 proposed amendments to the Turkish constitution that were brought forward by the governing Justice and Development Party (AKP) and the Nationalist Movement Party (MHP). With approval by voting, it abolished the office of the Prime Minister, and the existing parliamentary system of government was replaced with an executive presidency and a presidential system.

KEY POLITICAL PERSONS

PRESIDENT: Recep Tayyip Erdogan

ECONOMY

Turkey's performance in the economic and social development sector since the year 2000 has been impressive, leading to increased employment and incomes and making Turkey an upper middle-income country in the region. Turkey, Currently the 17th largest economy, has grand ambitions to become a top ten economy by 2023. In 2017, Turkey's economy reported 7.4% growth, with GDP per capita at approximately $11,000. This rapid economic growth is being driven in part by massive public investment in infrastructure projects, including in bridges, airports, highways, and railways. Turkey's geographic position makes it an important energy and logistics corridor. Turkey remains highly dependent on imported oil and gas but is pursuing energy relationships with a broader set of international partners and taking steps to increase use of domestic energy sources including renewables, nuclear, and coal. Since August 2018, Turkey has been going through a currency and debt crisis. The growth of Turkish GDP since 2016 has revealed the persistent underlying imbalances in the Turkish economy. In particular, Turkey's large current account deficit means it must rely on external investment inflows to finance growth. Turkey's economy contracted by 9.9 per cent in the second quarter of the year 2020 from the previous three-month period in the wake of lockdown measures put in place to deal with the COVID-19 pandemic.

GDP (Official exchange rate): $2.393 trillion (2020 est.), $2.352 trillion (2019 est.)

Real Growth Rate (GDP): 0.98% (2019 est.), 3.04% (2018 est.)

Industries: Textiles, food processing, automobiles, electronics, mining (coal, chromate, copper, boron), steel, petroleum, construction, lumber, paper

Natural gas - proved reserves: 5.097 billion cu m (1 January 2018 est.)

Crude oil - proved reserves: 341.6 million bbl (1 January 2018 est.)

Total Exports: $203.29 billion (2020 est.), $245.84 billion (2019 est.)

Export Commodities: Cars and vehicle parts, refined petroleum, delivery trucks, jewellery, clothing and apparel (2019)

Major Markets: Germany 9%, United Kingdom 6%, Iraq 5%, Italy 5%, United States 5% (2019)

Total Imports: $232.01 billion (2020 est.), $227.06 billion (2019 est.)

Import Commodities: Gold, refined petroleum, crude petroleum, vehicle parts, scrap iron (2019)

Major Suppliers: Germany 11%, China 9%, Russia 9%, United States 5%, Italy 5% (2019)

DEFENCE & SECURITY

The Turkish Armed Forces is the second largest standing armed force in NATO, after the US Armed Forces, with a combined strength of just over a million uniformed personnel serving in its five branches. Turkey is considered to be the strongest military power of the Middle East region besides Israel. The Turkish Armed Forces consists of the Army, the Navy and the Air Force. The Gendarmerie and the Coast Guard operate as parts of the Ministry of Internal Affairs in peacetime, although they are subordinated to the Army and Navy Commands respectively in wartime, during which they have both internal law enforcement and military functions. The Chief of the General Staff is the Commander of the Armed Forces. In wartime, he acts as the Commander in Chief on behalf of the President, who represents the Supreme Military Command of the TAF on behalf of the Grand National Assembly of Turkey.

Forces deployed abroad: Turkey still contributes to several peace keeping operations executed in Bosnia Herzegovina, Kosovo, Afghanistan, Lebanon and offshore and territorial waters of Somalia. Lists also includes EU Operation Althea, Kosovo Force (NATO KFOR), United Nation

Interim Administration Mission in Kosovo (UNMIK), Contributions of Turkey to the International Security Assistance Force (ISAF) and Resolute Support Mission (RSM), UN Interim Force in Lebanon (UNIFIL), United Nations Assistance Mission in Somalia (UNSOM), Combined Task Force 150/151 (CTF 150/151), Operation Sea Guardian (OSG), Defence and Related Security Capacity Building (DCB) Initiative, Konya Forward Operating Base Support to NATO Airborne Early Warning & Control (NAEW&C) Force, and NATO Mission Iraq (NMI).

KEY DEFENCE PERSONS

MINISTER OF DEFENCE:
Hulusi Akar

COMMANDER OF ARMED FORCES:
Gen. Yasar Guler

COMMANDER OF LAND FORCES:
Gen. Musa Avsever

COMMANDER OF NAVY: Adm. Adnan Ozbal

COMMANDER OF AIR FORCE: Gen. Hasan Kucukakyuz

COMMANDER OF GENDARMERIE:
Gen. Arif Cetin

Internal Conflict

Turkey continues its efforts to defeat terrorist organisations both inside and outside its borders, including the PKK and ISIS. Turkey remained an active contributor in international CT fora, including the GCTF. Turkey is an active member of the Global Coalition to Defeat ISIS, co-chairs the Defeat-ISIS Coalition FTF Working Group, and continued to provide access to its airspace and facilities for Coalition CT operations in Iraq and Syria. Turkey is a member of the UN, NATO, the CT Committee for the CoE, and the Global Coalition to Defeat ISIS, and it co-chairs, with Kuwait and the Netherlands, the Defeat-ISIS FTF Working Group.

2016 failed coup attempt in Turkey: In July 2016, a coup was attempted in Turkey with military tanks in the city of Ankara, and Istanbul. Fethullah Gulen Terrorist Organisation (FETO) was blamed for last months failed coup to topple President Tayyip Erdogan in Turkey. Later, members of Turkey's armed forces took control of the country as explosions, gunfire and a reported air battle between loyalist forces and coup supporters erupted in the capital. Turks also took to the streets, marching and waving Turkish flags to show support to Turkey's President and his government. Erdogan, after the situation became completely under control, dismissed the military action as an attempt at an uprising by a minority within the armed forces, and a probe has been initiated in this regard. Turkey's relations with the US also deteriorated because of this incident, as US refused to extradite US-based cleric Fethullah Gulen, whom the Turkish government blames for the failed coup attempt. Gulen has denied the claims and has condemned the coup.

Turkish – Kurdish conflict: It is an armed conflict between the Republic of Turkey and various Kurdish insurgent groups, which have demanded separation from Turkey to create an independent Kurdistan, or to have autonomy and greater political and cultural rights for Kurds inside the Republic of Turkey. The main rebel group is the Kurdistan Workers' Party or PKK, which is considered a terrorist organisation by Turkey and the United States and was on the European Union terrorist list, but was removed due to court order. Year 2011 showed a sharp increase in violence in recent history of the Kurdish–Turkish conflict. In 2012, the conflict with the PKK took a violent curve. The PKK's recent campaign against ISIS has caused many politicians to reconsider the PKK's position as a terrorist organisation. The conflict between Turkey and PKK escalated following the 2015 Suruc bombing attack. Later, the PKK allegedly carried out a revenge attack. During the Operation Martyr Yalçın, Turkey bombed alleged PKK bases in Iraq and PYD bases in Syria. The conflict then escalated, with pro-PKK Kurdish organisations staging attacks across the country, and Turkish forces attacks in the form of aerial bombardments and military operations. Following mainly negotiations, a largely successful ceasefire was put in place by AKP and PKK. The ceasefire broke in summer 2015 due to political tensions.

External Conflict

◆ Complex maritime, air, and territorial disputes with Greece in the Aegean Sea. The Aegean dispute is a set of interrelated controversial issues between Greece and Turkey over sovereignty and related rights in the area of the Aegean Sea.

◆ The Cyprus dispute is the result of the ongoing conflict between the Republic of Cyprus and Turkey, over the Turkish occupied northern part of Cyprus. Also, the status of Northern Cyprus has become a recurrent issue especially during the recent talks for Turkey's membership of the EU where the division of the island is seen as a major stumbling block in Turkey's long road to membership.

◆ Syria and Iraq protest Turkish hydrological projects to control upper Euphrates waters.

◆ Turkey has expressed concern over the status of Kurds in Iraq. Recently, in response to a series of attacks by Kurdish rebels, Turkey has deployed active military operations against them. Kurdistan Workers Party (PKK) has threatened Ankara with an open war in case of continuation of previous policies aimed at infringement of the national interests of the Kurds.

◆ Border with Armenia remains closed over Nagorno-Karabakh.

◆ On 2 September 2011, Turkey downgraded diplomatic ties with Israel to second secretary level and suspended military co-operation between the countries as the UN released its report into Israel's controversial raid of a Gaza-bound ship. As of 2 September 2011, all military agreements between Turkey and Israel have been suspended. Turkey is currently planning to appeal the International Court of Justice in The Hague as soon as next week in order to probe the legality of Israel's naval blockade on the Gaza Strip.

◆ Turkey's government has recently requested the deployment of NATO's Patriot surface-to-air missiles on to bolster its defences along its border with Syria and prevent a spill over of the civil war in that nation. NATO allies installed the long-range Patriot batteries on Turkish territory twice before, during the 1991 and 2003 Iraq wars. They were never used and were quietly withdrawn a few months later. Around 600 foreign troops are expected to accompany six Patriot missile systems to be deployed in Turkey to reinforce the NATO member country's air defence.

♦ Diplomatic relations between Turkey and Syria were severed in March 2012, due to the Syrian civil war and Turkish involvement in the Syrian Civil War.

♦ Ankara is currently facing off against Greece and Cyprus over oil and gas exploration rights in the eastern Mediterranean. Greece and Turkey have deployed naval and air forces to assert their competing claim in the region.

THREAT PERSPECTIVE

Turkey is engaged in intensive efforts to defeat terrorist organisations both inside and outside its borders, including the Kurdistan Workers' Party (PKK), the Revolutionary People's Liberation Party/Front (DHKP-C), and ISIS.

The Kurdistan Workers' Party, commonly known as PKK, is a major threat looming in the heart of Turkey. Turkey labelled the organisation as an ethnic secessionist organisation that uses terrorism and the threat of force against both civilian and military targets for the purpose of achieving its political goal. The main aim of the Kurdish terrorist groups in Turkey has been to establish an independent Kurdish state on the south-eastern part of Turkey which is heavily populated by people with Kurdish ethnicity. 2015-2016 saw eruption in Kurdish–Turkish conflict between various Kurdish insurgent groups and the Turkish government. The 2015 conflict between Turkey and the PKK broke out following two year-long peace negotiations, which began in late 2012. According to the Turkish government, between July 2015 and May 2016, huge number of Kurdish rebels were killed in Turkey and in northern Iraq, while many were killed among Turkish security forces, as reported in local media. Turkey's President Recep Tayyip Erdogan in Oct 2017 offered his country's support to Iraq in the wake of Kurdistan Region's independence referendum, including helping to bring back online a damaged oil export pipeline that runs to Turkey's Ceyhan port. The PKK has its headquarters in Kurdistan Region's Qandil mountains. It also has a presence in the Yezidi region of Shingal, also known as Sinjar, where it has remained after helping defeat ISIS.

Turkey has been fighting against terrorism since its establishment. During its establishment, it faced three threats. Each of the three threats, (1) religious fundamentalism, (2) ethnic (Kurdish) separatism and (3) Soviet (communist) domination somewhat manifested itself in terms of terrorist attacks after the establishment of the Republic. The terrorist organisations in Turkey were strengthened in the 1960s and 1970s especially during the student movements. Radical Islamist terrorist groups in Turkey are also a dominating threat to the country. The most important Islamist terrorist group in Turkey is the Turkish Hizbullah which has no apparent connection with the Lebanese Hizbullah. After the 2003 Istanbul Bombings were linked to Al-Qaeda, Turkey deployed troops to Afghanistan to fight Taliban forces and Al-Qaeda operatives, with the hope of dismantling both groups. Turkey's responsibilities include providing security in Kabul, as well as in Wardak Province, where it leads PRT Maidan Shahr.

2019 Turkey's conflict in Northern Syria: The 2019 Turkish offensive into north-eastern Syria is an military operation conducted by the Turkish Armed Forces (TAF) and the Syrian National Army (SNA) against the Syrian Democratic Forces (SDF) and the Syrian Army in north-eastern Syria. President Erdoğan called United States President Trump and informed him that Turkey is preparing an imminent invasion of Syria to create a buffer zone between Turkey and Syria. Soon, US troops withdrew from North-eastern Syria where they have been providing support to Kurdish allies. Turkey's military operation is intended to defeat SDF as they are having close ties with Kurdistan Workers Party (PKK). In Oct 2019, Kurdish fighters belonging to the SDF withdrawn from the besieged Syrian border towns under a ceasefire deal with Turkey brokered by the United States.

STRATEGIC RELATIONS

Turkey has strengthened its relations both with the US and the European countries; while further developing its relations with the countries in the Balkans, Middle East and North Africa, Southern Caucasus, South Asia and Central Asia by making use of its close ties. Turkey is also deepening its policies of reaching out to Sub-Saharan Africa, Latin America and Asia-Pacific regions that is home to many emerging powers.

US: US-Turkish relations focus on areas such as strategic energy cooperation, trade and investment, security ties, regional stability, counterterrorism, and human rights progress. Relations were strained when Turkey refused in March 2003 to allow US troops to deploy through its territory to Iraq in Operation Iraqi Freedom, but regained momentum steadily thereafter and mutual interests remain strong across a wide spectrum of issues. Turkey also seek advanced military equipment from US sources, particularly with respect to fighter and drone aircraft, helicopters, and missile defence systems. US also continue to provide cooperation on counterterrorism, law enforcement, and military training and education. US exports to Turkey include aircraft, iron and steel, agricultural products, oil, cotton yarn and fabric, and machinery. US imports from Turkey include vehicles, machinery, iron and steel and their products, agricultural products, travertine, and marble. Syrian Civil War has deteriorated to some extent the relationship shared between Turkey and US especially in regard to Kurdish fighters. Ankara aims to push both IS and Kurdish fighters away from its border. US termed the clashes in places where so-called Islamic State (IS) was not present were a source of deep concern. Recently, Turkey and USA saw further strain in their relations attributing to many disagreements and restrictions from both sides. Relations between the US and Turkey have been particularly tense since the failed coup. Turkey contributes to international security alongside US forces in Afghanistan, the seas bordering Somalia, and in the Mediterranean. Turkey borders Greece, Bulgaria, Georgia, Armenia, Azerbaijan, Iran, Iraq, and Syria, and is a key partner for US policy in the surrounding region. Following Turkeys' continued acquiring of Russian S-400 missile system, the United States decided to end the F-35 before July 31, 2019. President Trump and President Erdogan in 2019 agreed to work toward increasing annual bilateral trade to USD100 billion annually. Turkey is also the 10th largest purchaser of US LNG exports worldwide and an emerging regional energy hub.

Russia: After the failed coup attempt in Turkey, the country's foreign policy has gradually re-orientated towards seeking partnerships with other powers such as Russia. The warm bilateral relations of the past two decades was earlier strained after the November 2015 jet shoot down incident, when a Turkish F-16 combat aircraft shot down a Russian Su-24 fighter aircraft during an airspace dispute close to the Turkish-Syrian border. In response, Russia imposed a number of economic sanctions on Turkey. After the dissolution of Soviet Union, relations between Turkey and Russia dramatically and strongly improved. Russia is Turkey's second largest trade partner with the 2012 bilateral trade figure expected to reach USD 35 billion. The countries aim to bring this figure to USD 100 billion. Russia is the biggest and the most reliable supplier of natural gas to Turkey. The leaders of Russia and Turkey have signed a series of major trade and energy deals in the Turkish capital on December 2014 amid differences over the crises in Syria and Ukraine. In 2016, the normalisation of relations between both the countries began with Erdogan expressing regret to Putin for the downing of the Russian aircraft. The trade ties has since been normalised between both the countries. In February & July 2017, the two countries further normalised their ties through Syria peace talks in Astana, Kazakhstan on the creation of de-escalation zones in the conflict region. In September 2017, Turkey announced that it had signed a deal to purchase the Russian S-400, surface-to-air missile system. Both the Turkish and Russian presidents confirmed that they agreed to closely cooperate on ending Syria's civil war. In Oct 2019, Turkey reached a deal with Russia for Kurdish fighters to withdraw from a Turkish-ruled safe zone in northeast Syria.

Egypt: Egypt and Turkey are bound by strong religious and historical ties, and diplomatic ties between the two have remained extremely friendly. Turkey is planning to sign strategic cooperation agreements with Egypt in the military, diplomatic and commercial fields, after the relationship between Turkey and Israel strained due the 'Palmer Report' on Gaza Strip. Both countries are full members of the Union for the Mediterranean. Turkey and Egypt are among the leading countries of both the Middle East and Mediterranean regions, and are often said to be key in Middle East peace. Turkey and Egypt have been in strained relationship since 2013 due to diplomatic crisis.

Pakistan: Turkey is a close ally of Pakistan. Both enjoy close relations during both democratic and military regimes, reflecting the depth of the relations between the two nations. Both Turkey and Pakistan are Muslim-majority states and share extensive cultural and geopolitical links. Turkey has been supplying a variety of arms, military equipment to Pakistan. In 2016, Pakistan and Turkey have reaffirmed commitment to transform their special relationship into a strong strategic partnership by signing a joint communique. The two nations are in the process of strengthening economic relations with a Pakistan-Turkey Free Trade Agreement aiming to raise bilateral trade volume to USD10 billion by 2020. Turkey and Pakistan have a strong defence relationship consisting of joint exercises and a substantial portion of the Pakistan Navy's fleet consisting of joint Pakistan-Turkish naval ships such as fleet tankers and fast attack craft. Turkey supports Pakistan's membership of the Nuclear Suppliers Group. Turkey and Pakistan are founding members of the Economic Cooperation Organisation and part of the Developing 8 Countries (D-8) organisation.

India: India and Turkey are friendly countries. Turkey and India have undergone an immense social, political and economic transformation since the end of the Cold War. Bilateral relations between both the countries are characterised by warmth and cordiality. They share common values including commitment to secularism and democratic principles. Bilateral relations have been strengthened by the exchange of visits of leaders of both countries in recent times. A Protocol on setting up a Joint Working Group on Counter Terrorism was signed in September, 2003. As far as the military exercises between India and Turkey is concerned, there has been a regular but a low-profile passage exercises (PASSEX) between the Navies of the two countries. The major Indian exports to Turkey include: petroleum products, auto components/parts, man-made yarn, fabrics, made ups, aircraft & spacecraft parts, plastic raw materials, organic chemicals, dyes, industrial machinery, etc. Imports from Turkey include: industrial machinery, broken/unbroken poppy seeds; machinery and mechanical appliances, iron and steel articles thereof, inorganic chemicals, pearls and precious/semi precious stones and metals (including imitation jewellery), granite and marble, etc.

MULTILATERAL ALLIANCES

Turkey has become increasingly integrated with the West through membership in organisations such as the Council of Europe, NATO, OECD, OSCE and the G-20 major economies. Turkey began full membership negotiations with the European Union in 2005. The country is also Turkic Council, Joint Administration of Turkic Arts and Culture, Organisation of Islamic Cooperation, the Black Sea Economic Cooperation (BSEC) Council, the Euro-Atlantic Partnership Council and the Economic Cooperation Organisation. Turkey, a member of NATO, was granted dialogue partner status in the Shanghai Cooperation Organisation (SCO) at the group's 2012 summit in Beijing. Turkey is also granted chairman of the energy club of SCO for 2017.

NATO: Turkey has maintained forces in international missions under the United Nations and NATO since 1950, including peacekeeping missions in Somalia and former Yugoslavia, and support to coalition forces in the First Gulf War. Turkey also pledged five ships and a submarine as part of its contribution to the March 2011 military intervention in Libya following UN Security Council Resolution 1973 of 2011. Turkey is a non-permanent member of the United Nations Security Council since 1 January 2009. Turkey has attached the utmost importance to NATO's role in maintaining security and stability in the Euro-Atlantic area and in providing a forum for political-military consultations on topics of interest to its members. Turkey also strongly supports NATO's partnerships. Turkey believes that a constructive relationship based on mutual understanding, transparency and cooperation between NATO and Russia is important for Euro-Atlantic peace and stability and that the NATO-Russia Council provides the necessary forum for such a relationship. Turkey also believes that the integration of all Western Balkan countries in Euro-Atlantic structures is the key to lasting peace and stability in the region.

DEFENCE CAPABILITIES

ARMY: The Turkish Army or Turkish Land Forces is the main branch of the Turkish Armed Forces responsible for land-based military operations. The land force has a total active manpower of 402,000, including 325,000 conscripts with approximately 258,700 troops in reserve. The army is by far the largest of the three service components. The structure of the Turkish Army has historically had two facets: operational and administrative. The operational chain consists of the field fighting formations, and the administrative the arms and service branches - infantry, armour, artillery etc.

Personnel: 325,000

Equipment

Category	Name	In Service
MBT	Leopard 1	350+
	M60 Patton	900
	Leopard 2	300+
	Altay	10+ (200+ on order)
	M-48 Patton	700+
APC/ MICV/IFV	ACV-15	1500+
	Mortar carrier	150
	TOW carrier	45
	M113	3000+
	BTR-80	500+
	Cobra MRAP	800+
	ZPT	1000
	Kirpi MRAP	400
Artillery	105 mm towed M52	200+
	105 mm towed M101A1	75
	J-600T Yildirim	20+
	203 mm towed M115	150
	155 mm towed Panter	210+

...continued

Category	Name	In Service
Artillery	155 mm M44T	130+
	175 mm M107 SP	30
	155 mm M114	500
	155 mm Firtina	210+
	M110 A2	210+
Mortar	60 mm	5,000+
	81 mm	
	107 mm	
	120 mm	
MLRS	T-300 Kasirga	60
	122 mm T-122 Sakarya	50+
	T-107	90
	ATACMS rockets	70
Anti-Tank GW	MILAN	400+
	BGM-71 TOW	300+
	ERYX	500
	Mizrak-U	
	Roketsan Cirit	
Recoilless rifle	57 mm	3,000+
	75 mm	
	105 mm	
	Carl Gustaf 84 mm	
SAM	FIM-92 Stinger	2000+
	9K38 Igla	30
AA Gun	40 mm Bofors	720+
	Atilgan	70
	Zipkin	70+
	35 mm towed	100
	40 mm M42A1 Duster	200

Army Aviation

Category	Name	In Service
Helicopter	CH-47 Chinook	5 (More on order)
	T/S-70 Black Hawk	45
	AS532 Cougar	20
	AH-1 P/S/W Cobra	40+
	T-129 ATAK	10 (More on order)
	UH-1H	50
	205 JetRanger	50+
Aircraft	T-41	20+
	U-17A	70
	T-42	3
	Super King Air 200	5
UAV	Heron, Anka, Firebee, Harpy, CL-89, Bayraktar Mini	

New Procurements/ Upgrades

◆ Russia signed contract with Turkey on 2nd batch of S-400 air defence systems. The sides are discussing the contract's financial terms, as per Head of Russia's state arms seller Rosoboronexport Alexander Mikheyev. Russia announced in September 2017 that it had signed a USD2.5 billion deal with Turkey on the delivery of S-400 anti-aircraft missile systems to Ankara.

◆ The works on the Hisar national air defence system are continuing at full speed. The Hisar project, expected to be finished by 2020. Aselsan and Roketsan are the prime contractor and subcontractor of the Hisar project.

◆ BMC Otomotiv Sanayi ve Ticaret A.Ş., Turkey's largest manufacturer of commercial and military vehicles, officially signed altay tank mass production contract. Under contract, first of 250 Altay next-generation battle tanks will roll off assembly line by 2020-2021 and will be delivered to the Turkish Land Forces.

◆ BMC signed a contract with the Turkish government to produce and sell a total of 529 tactical wheeled armoured vehicles.

NAVY: The Turkish Navy is one of the three branches of the Turkish Armed Forces. The mission of the Turkish Navy is national defence, although it also participates in coordinated security and humanitarian efforts as part of Black Sea Naval Cooperation Task Group (BLACKSEAFOR). The Turkish Navy maintains several Marines and Special Operations units. These include the Amphibious Marines Brigade (Amfibi Deniz Piyade Tugayi), several commando detachments and two special operations forces. The Turkish Navy is the eighth largest navy in the world. It currently has approximately 55,000 active personnel. The Turkish Navy is also the third largest navy in Europe, in terms of the total displacement of its fleet, which is 258,948 tonnes.

Personnel: 50,000

Equipment

Category	Name	In Service
Submarine	Gur Class Type 209T2/1400	4
	Preveze Class Type 209T1/1400	4
	Atilay class Type 209/1200	5
Frigate	Barbaros Class	4
	Gabya Class	8
	Yavuz Class	4
Corvette	Ada Class	3
	Burak Class	6
Fast Attack Craft	Ruzgar Class	3
	Kilic Class	9
	Yildiz Class	2
	Kartal Class	2
	Dogan Class	4

...continued

Category	Name	In Service
Patrol Boat	Tuzla-class	8
Mine Warfare Force	Seydi Class	4
	Aydin Class	5
	Engin Class	3
Auxiliary ship	Training	2
	Submarine support ships	2
	Fleet replenishment tankers	2
	Tankers (fleet oil tanker)	3
	Transports	10
	Hydrographic ships	2
Amphibious Force	Osman Gazi Class LST	1
	Ertugrul Class LST	1
	Yeni Class	1
	Landing craft tank (LCT)	20+
	Landing Craft Mechanized (LCM)	15+

Naval Aviation

Category	Name	In Service
Fixed wing aircraft	CN-235 (Maritime/ Transport)	5
	TB-20	7
	ATR 72–600	3+
Helicopter	S-70B SeaHawks	20+
	AB-204	3
	AB-212 ASW	10

New Procurements/ Upgrades

◆ Turkish Navy is planning for the acquisition of Multi-Functional Helicopter Platform Dock (LHD). LHD Project includes LCMs, AAVs, LCVPs, guidance purposed Commander Boat and RHIBs. LHD shall be capable of carrying helicopters, amphibious vehicles including tanks and AAV, and an Amphibious Marine Battalion. The LHD contract has been signed on 1st of June 2015 and the project work has been started in September 2015. It is planned that LHD will be taken into service by April 2020.

◆ Presidency of Defence Industries (SSB) has inked defence contract for mass production and procurement of ATMACA cruise missiles with Roketsan. Aselsan will produce production control systems and other equipment. The ATMACA Project was launched for the Navy's cruise ship missile deployment on MILGEM platforms.

◆ MiLDEN (Milli Denizalti - National Submarine) is an ambitious project by Turkey to design and develop a new class of indigenous submarines along with electronics, telecommunications, sensors, propulsion and weapon systems.

AIR FORCE: The Turkish Air Force is

one of the oldest air forces in the world and operates one of the largest combat aircraft fleets of NATO. The Turkish Air Force was one of the first air forces in the world to be established. Supported by the TuAF's in-flight refuelling capability, the fighter aircraft of the Turkish Air Force can participate in international operations and exercises on every major continent and return back to their home bases. The Turkish Air Force currently has over 930 different aircraft and it is the third largest air force in NATO, in terms of its fleet size.

Personnel: 50,000

Equipment

Category	Name	In Service
Fighters/ attack/ Recon- naissance/ bomber	F-4E/ 2020	40+
	F-16C	150+
	F-16D	40+
	NF5/2000	15
	NF-5B	15
	Boeing 737-700 AEW&C	4
Transport/ Tanker	C-160D	10
	C130 Hercules	8
	C130B	15
	CN-235	50
	A400M	2 (More on order)
	C.550 Citation II (VIP)	2
	Gulfstream IV	1
	CN-235	30+
	KC-135R	5+
Helicopter	UH-1H Iroquois	15
	Cougar	20
Trainer	T-38M	30+
	T-41 Mescalero	20+
	T37	50+
	SF-260D	30+
SAM	Rapier 2000	80+
	Hawk XXI	15
	FIM-92 Stinger	100+
	Atilgan PMADS	30+
AAM	AIM-120 (A/B/C-7) AMRAAM, AIM-7(E/F) Sparrow, AIM-9 Sidewinder	
AGM	SOM, AGM-84, AGM-88 HARM, AGM-65 Maverick, AGM-154 JSOW, SLAM	
UAV	RQ/MQ-1, GNAT, TAI Anka	

At present, the Turkish Air Force operates MALE UAVs such as the TAI Anka, the IAI Heron and the I-GNAT ER. The Turkish Air Force is procuring 10 MQ-1 Predator and 4 MQ-9 Reaper MALE UAV/UCAVs in the short term.

On 17 July 2019, following the delivery of Russian S-400 air defence systems, the United States announced that Turkey would be removed from the F-35 programme. Besides the ban on training of pilots and delivery of the aircraft, the move would also include removing Turkey from the supply chain.

New Procurements/ Upgrades

No major procurement plans are under consideration at present.

TURKISH GENDARMERIE: The Gendarmerie of the Republic of Turkey, which is responsible for the maintenance of safety and public order as well as carrying out other duties assigned by laws and regulations, is an armed security and law enforcement force, having military nature. As a part of Turkish Armed Forces, the General Command of the Gendarmerie is subordinated to the General Staff in matters related to training and education in connection with the Armed Forces and to the Ministry of Interior in matters related to the performance of the safety and public order duties.

Personnel: 150,000

Equipment

Category	Name	In Service
APC	Kirpi	100+
	Cobra	100+
	V-150S	70+
	BTR-60	
	Condor	
Helicopter	UH-60	20
	UH-1	10
	Mil Mi-17	10+

Major Armaments Producers

Domestic suppliers: MKEK, ASELSAN, BMC, FNSS, GIRSAN, TISAS, Havelsan, Transvaro, TAI, Otokar, Roketsan, ASFAT, TÜBİTAK.

Foreign suppliers: United States, South Korea, Germany, United Kingdom, Russia, France, Ukraine, Israel, China, Pakistan, Australia, India, Canada.

Other defence and aerospace companies: Howaldtswerke-Deutsche Werft (HDW), Lockheed Martin, BAE Systems, Makina ve Kimya Endüstrisi Kurumu (MKEK), Tusas Engine Industries, Inc (TEI), FNSS Defence Systems Co, Istanbul Shipyard.

Otokar, a Koc Group Company, is leading supplier of the Turkish Military and Security Forces for wheeled tactical vehicles.

The Undersecretariat for Defence Industries (SSM) has made significant achievements in building the blocks for a modern national defence industry in Turkey, with notable results in certain vital areas. Turkey's Defence Industry Executive Committee is the main decision-making body of the system. It is chaired by the Prime Minister and consists of the Chief of General Staff and the Minister of National Defence. SSM was affiliated to the Presidency of Republic in December 2017 and renamed as Presidency of Defence Industries (SSB) in July 2018.

Turkish Aerospace Industries, Inc. (TAI) is the center of technology in design, development, manufacturing, integration of aerospace systems, modernisation and after sales support in Turkey. ASELSAN is a Turkish corporation which produces tactical military radios and defence electronic systems for the Turkish Army. The Mechanical and Chemical Industry Corporation (MKEK) established in 1950, is a reorganisation of government-controlled group of factories in Turkey that supplied the Turkish Army with supplies, munitions and equipment. The corporation mainly produces equipment for the Turkish Armed Forces, such as the ammunition for small arms and heavy weapons, heavy weapons and artillery systems, aerial bombs, mines, explosives, and rockets.

Defence Industry Manufacturers Association, SASAD was established by 12 companies in 1990 with the support of Ministry of National Defence, Turkey. SASAD is the association for producers of defence systems and equipment for domestic and international markets. As of 2010, SASAD encompasses more than 120 members and associate members. SASAD's members include government-owned companies, such as the Machinery and Chemicals Industry, or MKEK, and the military's naval shipyards; firms owned by the Turkish Armed Forces Foundation, including Aselsan, Turkish Aerospace Industries (TAI), Havelsan and Roketsan; and private companies.

DEFENCE DEALS

Arms Export

Turkey now produces over 70% of its own military equipment and is also a significant exporter of arms. Between 2014 and 2018, Turkish arms exports increased by 170%. Also, according to SASAD (Defence and Aerospace Industry Manufacturers' Association), Turkey's defence exports reached USD 1.8 billion in 2017. The total value of orders received in 2017, including civilian aviation products, was close to USD 8 billion. The Turkish government is about to finalise its efforts to ink two major naval export deals totalling between USD 1.5 billion and USD 2 billion. Turkish defence industry exports rose 35 percent in the first two months of 2016. By 2018 it was the 14th largest arms exporter in the world, with Saudi Arabia, the UAE and Turkmenistan the major buyers. The country had made significant progress in developing weaponised drones. The country's defence industry is making rapid strides with the mass production of locally-developed infantry rifles and joint production of the aircraft being started in 2016.

The country mainly exports armoured vehicles of many sorts, rockets and other ammunition, as well as military electronics like radios, to more than 10 Islamic countries. It also sells aviation equipment as part of offset deals. The Turkish government is making determined efforts to promote its indigenously produced armaments. The Turkish defence industry plans to promote its military products at various international defence and security exhibitions in future.

Turkish firm under the Ministry of Defence Production collaborated with Pakistan Navy and Karachi Shipyard and Engineering Works (KS&EW) in the design and construction of the 17,000 tonne naval fleet tanker. Pakistan will also receive 34 trainer-cum- fighter aircraft from Turkey free of cost under a major defence deal inked between the two countries. The agreement was reached during the meeting of Pakistan-Turkey High Level Military Dialogue Group which concluded in Ankara. Turkey will also be selling 30 T129 ATAK helicopters to Pakistan worth USD 1.5 billion.

AIS, founded by the owners of the top five leading shipyards of Turkey to offer expert and innovative solutions in naval shipbuilding, has received a $2.3-billion tender to build five ships for the Indian Navy. No official contract as been signed yet due to some serious security concerns raised over the firm, as per media reports.

Arms Import

The US has been the largest exporter of arms to Turkey, providing approximately 60% of its total imports between 2014 and 2018. According to SASAD, Turkey's total defence imports reached USD1.54 billion in 2017. Turkey's military procurement consists almost exclusively of imports. At USD 19 billion (approx.), it is the 15th largest military spender globally. The majority of weapons, including advanced systems, are imported from the major arms producers. Turkey had the second largest defence budget (after Saudi Arabia) in the Middle East. Turkey is rapidly expanding its military forces by domestically producing many weapons and importing many more. Turkey is using its imports to build up indigenous arms industries by requiring as part of tenders that foreign companies transfer technology, capital and production capabilities to Turkey. Turkey is still reliant on foreign imports for about 35 per cent of critical military technologies.

Turkey has awarded Eurosam, Aselsan and Roketsan a contract for the definition study of the future Turkish Long Range Air and Missile Defence System. According to a press release by MBDA, this definition study aims at preparing the development and production contract for the future system meeting the operational requirements of the Turkish Air Force. The contract was awarded by the SSM (the Undersecretariat for Defence Industries), jointly to Turkish companies Aselsan and Roketsan, and to the Franco-Italian consortium Eurosam; backed by its two shareholders MBDA and Thales. This study paves the way for the launch of a three-country joint Long Range Air and Missile Defence Programme. The future system will be ready by the middle of the next decade with a state-of-the-art military capability designed to counter the most challenging threats (stealth aircraft, UAVs, cruise missiles, and ballistic missiles). The system is expected to meet three countries' basic operational needs and it will guarantee Turkey has full employment autonomy and will allow a sovereign choice of integration level within NATO. The joint development activity is expected to support Turkey's indigenous air and missile development programme in addition to opening up prospects for exports and longer-term co-operation of Turkey, Italy and France.

In 2017, Turkey and Russia jointly signed an agreement worth of USD2.5 billion for delivery of the S-400 air defence system to Turkey. Turkey received its first installment of Russian S-400 missile defence system on 12 July 2019. By Septt 2019, Russia completed the deliveries of S-400 missile defence systems to Turkey. As per media reports, Turkish personnel are currently ongoing training by Russian specialists to operate the delivered equipment. The air defence systems will be activated when the training period completes.

In terms of Turkey domestic defence industry, the 10th Development Plan (2014-2018) calls for a competitive structure of the defence industry, defence system and logistics needs to be met in an integrated and sustainable way by the country's industry based on indigenous design, civilian use of appropriate technologies, increase in the domestic ratio and the share allocated for R&D as well as supporting networks and clustering structures in specific areas of the defence industry.

DEFENCE BUDGET

Total defence spending: USD20 billion (2019 approx.)

Estimated defence spending in terms of GDP: 1.86% of GDP (2020 est.), 1.85% of GDP (2019)

Defence Expenditure

Year	USD (Millions)
2014	13,577
2015	11,953
2016	12,644
2017	12,971
2018	14,168
2019*	14,089
2020*	13,396
2021*	13,057

(*Figures for 2020 and 2021 are estimates.) Source: Defence Expenditure of NATO Countries (2014-2021), NATO Press Release.

Turkey's Defence Industry Executive Committee is planning to increase Ankara's own military production capabilities. USD 4.5 billion of the total budget will consist of domestic production. The Turkish government has approved nearly USD 6 billion in defence programme. The SSM Undersecretariat for Turkish Defence Industries has undergone major modernisation projects to achieve their 2023 defence export target of USD 25bn by 2023. After 2020, Turkey is planning to design, develop and produce another fighter plane to close the JSF' s deficiencies either by itself, or through its other, most likely with South Korea. Few years back, Turkish defence companies spent USD 228 million on research and development from their own assets which is a major increase from USD 64 million in 2004 and USD 120 million in 2007. Turkey's official defence policy is based on Ataturk's principle of 'peace at home, peace in the world'. Turkey's newly published defence industrial strategic plan 2012-2016 will modernise the country's critical technologies, ensure the indigenous development of defence capabilities and progressively reduce dependency on foreign imports. The 2010 budget was 26 billion liras. The total value of the contracts signed in 2011 was some USD 27.3 billion. According to the new plan the total turnover target for the defence industry exports for 2016 is USD 2 billion. The Law on the Court of Accounts provides for external ex-post audits of armed forces' expenditure. It also paves the way for audits of extra budgetary resources earmarked for the defence sector, including the Defence Industry Support Fund.

CONCLUSION

Turkey's Armed Forces, whose geopolitical and geo-strategic importance is ever increasing, is composed of the Land Forces, Air Forces and Navy that are directly affiliated to the Turkish General Staff. The General Command of the Gendarmerie and the Coast Guard Command serving as elements of inland security during peacetime take their due positions under Land Forces and Navy in wartime. Turkey, as a founding member of the UN, member of NATO and all European leading institutions, and a negotiating country with the EU for full membership, has pursued a proactive foreign policy to develop strategic cooperation in its region and beyond. Turkey's economy and diplomatic initiatives led to its recognition as a regional power while its location has given it geopolitical and strategic importance throughout history. The main elements of Turkish Defence Politics are the commitment towards national defence, NATO solidarity and the Turkish Armed Forces. The Turkish Armed Forces collectively rank as the second largest standing military force in NATO, after the US Armed Forces, with large number of military, civilian and paramilitary personnel. In recent years Turkey is standing out as one of the growing defence markets in Asia. The Turkish military perceived itself as the guardian of Kemalist ideology, the official state ideology, especially of the secular aspects of Kemalism. The TAF still maintains an important degree of influence over the decision-making process regarding issues related to Turkish national security, albeit decreased in the past decades, via the National Security Council. The country's defence expenditure is expected to continue growing, largely be driven by a strained relationship with neighbouring countries and Ankara's aspirations in becoming a leading power in the region, along with the need to meet the threat of persistent terror threats and instability within the region. Peacekeeping initiatives will also continue to put pressure on the government to increase defence expenditure. Turkish Armed Forces, till date, has undertaken and is still undertaking peacekeeping and other operations under the aegis of the UN and NATO in order to settle the crises in the Balkans, Caucasus, Middle East, Africa and Asia. Turkey's Defence Industry Under secretariat (SSM) is responsible for the modernisation of Turkish Armed Forces and development of defence industry.

CONTACT DETAILS

Ministry of Defence
Devlet Mahallesi,
Yahya Galip Caddesi,
Bakanlıklar
ANKARA 06100
Tel: +90 312 402 61 00
Website: www.msb.gov.tr

Undersecretariat of Defence Industries (SSM)
Nasuh Akar Mah.
Ziyabey Caddesi 1407.
Sokak No:4 (06520) Balgat
Ankara, Turkey
Tel: +90 (312) 411 90 00 - 400
Fax: +90 (312) 411 93 86

E-Mail: posta@ssm.gov.tr
Website: www.ssm.gov.tr

Defence Industry Manufacturers Association (SASAD)
Paris Caddesi Yazanlar Sok. No: 4/106
06680 Kavaklidere, ANKARA
TURKIYE
Tel: +90 312 426 22 55
Fax: +90 312 426 22 56
Email: sasad@tr.net
Website: www.sasad.org.tr

Turkish Aerospace Industries, Inc.
Fethiye Mahallesi,
Havacılık Bulvarı No:17 06980
Kazan-ANKARA / TÜRKİYE
Tel : +90 312 811 1800
Fax: +90 312 811 1425
Marketing
E-mail: marketing@tai.com.tr
Procurement
E-mail: procurement@tai.com.tr
Website: www.tai.com.tr

ASELSAN
PK 1, 06172, Yenimahalle / Ankara, Turkey
E-mail: marketing@aselsan.com.tr
Website: www.aselsan.com.tr

MKEK
Tandogan 06330 ANKARA
TURKEY
Tel: +90 (312) 296 10 00-09
Website: www.mkek.gov.tr

TURKMENISTAN
(Capital: Ashgabat)

INTRODUCTION

Area: 488,100 sq km
Population: 5,579,889 (July 2021 est.)
Coastline: landlocked
Maritime claims: None

KEY POLITICAL PERSONS

PRESIDENT:
Gurbanguly Berdymukhammedov

KEY DEFENCE PERSONS

DEFENCE MINISTER: Maj. Gen. Begenc Gundogdyyew

CHIEF OF THE GENERAL STAFF: Lt. Col. Akmurad Anamedov

ECONOMY

Turkmenistan, a largely desert country, has been classified as an upper-middle-income country. The country is among the world's largest reserves of natural gas and substantial oil resources. Cotton and wheat are the two main agricultural crops. Turkmenistan is also among the world's top ten producers of cotton. In addition to cotton and natural gas, the country is rich in petroleum, sulphur, iodine, salt, bentonite clays, limestone, gypsum, and cement. The Government's National Socio-Economic Development Programme for 2011–2030 and the National Rural Development Programme focus on inclusive economic growth while preserving economic independence, modernising the country's infrastructure, and promoting foreign direct investment. The country is in the process of constructing the Turkmenistan-Afghanistan-Pakistan-India (TAPI) pipeline. China is the country's largest export market, especially for gas, but natural gas deliveries to Russia were resumed in 2019. The economy is still recovering from a deep recession that followed the late 2014 collapse in global energy prices.

GDP (official exchange rate): $40.819 billion (2018 est.)

Real Growth Rate (GDP): 6.5% (2017 est.), 6.2% (2016 est.)

Industries: Natural gas, oil, petroleum products, textiles, food processing.

Crude Oil – Proved Reserves: 600 million bbl (1 January 2018 est.)

Natural Gas – Proved Reserves: 7.504 trillion cu m (1 January 2018 est.)

Total Exports: $7.458 billion (2017 est.), $6.987 billion (2016 est.)

Export Commodities: Natural gas, refined petroleum, crude petroleum, cotton fibres, fertilizers (2019)

Major Markets: China 82% (2019)

Total Imports: $4.571 billion (2017 est.), $5.215 billion (2016 est.)

Import Commodities: Iron products, harvesting machinery, packaged medicines, broadcasting equipment, tractors (2019)

Major Suppliers: Turkey 25%, Russia 18%, China 14%, Germany 6% (2019)

INTERNATIONAL DISPUTES

◆ Cotton monoculture in Uzbekistan and Turkmenistan creates water-sharing difficulties for Amu Darya river states.
◆ Field demarcation of the boundaries with Kazakhstan commenced in 2005.
◆ Bilateral talks continue with Azerbaijan on dividing the seabed and contested oilfields in the middle of the Caspian.

DEFENCE

The Armed Forces of Turkmenistan consists of the Army, Navy, Air and Air Defence Forces, Border Troops, and Internal Troops, and a National Guard. An agreement with Russia formalizes the presence of Russian troops in Turkmenistan.

ARMY

Personnel: 17,000

Equipment

Category	Name	In Service
MBT	T-72	700 (most in storage)
	T-90	10+
AIFV/APC	Al Shibl 2	8
	BMP-1/2	600
	BTR-60/70/80	700 (many is storage)
Artillery	D-20 152mm	125
	D-30 122mm towed	125
	2S3 152mm SP	12
MRL	BM-21 122mm	
	SMERCH 300mm	8

New Procurements/Upgrades

No major procurement plans are under consideration at present.

NAVY

Turkmenistan has created its own Naval forces necessary to protect the huge water area of the Caspian Sea and the coastline over 800 kilometres long. A naval force established for patrol duties includes two Russian built Type 21418 missile boats (Eldermen class) and Two Sobol class patrol boats. Other vessels in the inventory include: Kalkan-type patrol boats, ten GRIF-T multi-purpose launches and four Dearsan YTKB-type patrol boats (Arkadag class), two missile boats of project 12418 Molniya class. The naval personnel is 2000

New Procurements/Upgrades

◆ The Turkmenistan Navy has commissioned a new corvette named Deñiz Han, reportedly constructed at a new shipyard near Dzhanga, in Turkmenistan's Balkan Region.

AIR FORCE

Personnel: 3,000

Equipment

Category	Name	In service
Aircraft	MiG-29A/UB	24
	MiG-23	60+
	MiG-25	12
	Su-25	
	An-26	
Helicopter	Mi-24	10
	AW101	2
	Mi-17-1B	2
	Mi-8	10
	S-92	2

New Procurements/Upgrades

◆ Turkmenistan reportedly plans to acquire the Turkish-built Bayraktar TB2 unmanned aircraft system.

Defence Expenditure

Exact defence expenditure figures are unavailable

Defence spending in terms of GDP: 1.6% (est.)

Defence Production and R&D

Turkmenistan does not undertake any defence production activities due to the absence of its base for the development of the military-industrial complex (MIC). However, in order to supply the Army with weapons and military equipment, the country receives support from other states in the framework of military-technical cooperation. It has developed military-technical cooperation with Georgia and the United States.

Defence Procurement

Arms procurement by Turkmenistan has included delivery of modern 36D6 radar and Kolchuga-M radio technical intelligence stations by Ukraine. The Russian company JSC Rosoboronexport has delivered T-90C tanks. Other purchase from Russia included at least eight BMP-3 infantry fighting vehicles, more than 1,000 KamAZ trucks, Smerch with a calibre of 300 mm, two Mi-17-1B helicopters and two missile boats of project 12418 Molniya for the Navy. From Turkey, two patrol vessels of Tuzla class.

CONTACT DETAILS
Ministry of Defence
Galkynysh str. 4, 744000 Ashgabat, Turkmenistan
Tel: +99-312-3516666, -357948
Fax: +99-312-511430, -397745

UGANDA
(Capital: Kampala)

INTRODUCTION

Area: 241,038 sq km
Population: 44,712,143 (July 2021 est.)
Coastline: 0 km (landlocked)
Maritime claims: none (landlocked)

KEY POLITICAL PERSONS

PRESIDENT: Yoweri Kaguta

PRIME MINISTER: Rabinah Nabbanja

KEY DEFENCE PERSONS

DEFENCE MINISTER: Vincent Bamulangaki Ssempijja

CHIEF OF DEFENCE FORCES: Gen. Wilson Mbaddi

COMMANDER OF LAND FORCE: Lt. Gen. Muhoozi Kainerugaba

COMMANDER OF AIR FORCE: Lt. Gen. Charles Lwanga Lutaaya

ECONOMY

Uganda has significant natural resources which include fertile soils, regular rainfall, substantial reserves of recoverable oil, and small deposits of copper, gold, and other minerals. Agriculture with 72% people working in it, is one of the most important sectors of the economy. Uganda has a small industrial sector that is dependent on imported inputs such as refined oil and heavy equipment. Uganda is eligible for preferential trade benefits under the African Growth and Opportunity Act. Uganda belongs to a number of the same international organisations, including the United Nations, International Monetary Fund, World Bank, and World Trade Organisation. Uganda is also a member of East African Community and with the Common Market for Eastern and Southern Africa COVID-19 pandemic and lockdown restrictions had real and potential economic impact on the economy of Uganda. Uganda, in order to secure the economy and financing has taken significant policy measures that will benefit many low-income households and many businesses.

GDP (official exchange rate): $99.61 billion (2020 est.), $96.84 billion (2019 est.)

Real Growth Rate (GDP): 4.8% (2017 est.), 2.3% (2016 est.)

Industries: Sugar processing, brewing, tobacco, cotton textiles; cement, steel production

Oil - proved reserves: 2.5 billion bbl (1 January 2018 est.)

Natural gas - proved reserves: 14.16 billion cu m (1 January 2018 est.)

Total Exports: $6.12 billion (2019 est.), $5.63 billion (2018 est.)

Export Commodities: gold, coffee, milk, fish and fish products, tobacco (2019)

Major Markets: United Arab Emirates 58%, Kenya 9% (2019)

Total Imports: $9.54 billion (2019 est.), $8.65 billion (2018 est.)

Import Commodities: Packaged medicines, aircraft, delivery trucks, cars, wheat (2019)

Major Suppliers: China 19%, India 17%, Kenya 16%, United Arab Emirates 7%, Japan 5% (2019)

INTERNATIONAL DISPUTES

◆ Uganda is subject to armed fighting among hostile ethnic groups, rebels, armed gangs, militias, and various government forces that extend across its borders.

◆ Uganda hosts 209,860 Sudanese, 27,560 Congolese, and 19,710 Rwandan refugees, while Ugandan refugees as well as members of the Lord's Resistance Army (LRA) seek shelter in southern Sudan and the Democratic Republic of the Congo's Garamba National Park.

◆ The Government of Uganda continues to make important contributions toward Counter Terrorism efforts in East Africa and the Horn of Africa. As the largest troop contributing country to AMISOM, Uganda remained a key partner in regional efforts to neutralize al-Shabaab, as per US Dept. of State.

DEFENCE

ARMY

Personnel: 38,000

Equipment

Category	Name	In Service
MBT	T-55	50+
	T-90	40+
	T-34	7
	T-85	
Light Tank	PT76s	10
APC	BMP-2s	20
	BTR 40/-52	20
Artillery	M1942 76mm	50+
	M1938 122mm	15+
Mortar	82mm	
	Soltam 120 mm	
ATGW	SAGGER	
AA Gun	ZSU23 23 mm	
	M1939 37 mm	
SAM	SA7	

New Procurements/ Upgrades

No major procurement plans are under consideration at present.

NAVY

Personnel: 200

Equipment

Category	Name	In Service
Patrol vessel	Yugoslav AL8K Type	3

New Procurements/ Upgrades

No major procurement plans are under consideration at present.

AIR FORCE

Personnel: 1300

Equipment

Category	Name	In Service
Fighter	MiG-21 MF	5
	Su-30MK2	6
	L-39 ALBATROS	3
	AS-202 BRAVO	1
Transport	Y121V	2
	L-100 HERCULES	1
	GULSTREAM II	1
Helicopter	AB306	2
	AB205	3
	AB212	2
	Mi24PN	6

New Procurements/ Upgrades

◆ Uganda received another two Su-30MK fighters from Russia, after taking delivery of the first aircraft in July, 2011. The country has six on order. Uganda's ministry of defence paid USD 446m as a first part payment to an 'unidentified supplier' from Russia for fighters as well as tanks. In total, Uganda bought between six and eight fighters and other military equipment from Russia, worth USD 744 million.

Defence Expenditure

Total defence spending: $600 million (approx.)

Estimated defence spending in terms of GDP: 2.5% of GDP (2020 est.), 2.1% of GDP (2019)

Foreign suppliers: Russia, China, United States, Italy and Poland, South Africa

The United States provides significant development and security assistance to Uganda, with a total assistance budget exceeding USD970 million per year, as per US Dept. of State.

Defence Production and R&D

Uganda runs Luwero Industries Limited, a subsidiary of the National Enterprise Corporation (NEC) established in 1989 by an Act of Parliament, which acts as a commercial arm for the defence forces under the Ministry of Defence. NEC redeploys soldiers who were involved in the war to produce goods and services for the army and use the profit for soldier's welfare. Uganda produces its arms at the country's only production centre located at Nakasongola. The government is rethinking to modernise and professionalise its armed forces, including the procurement of modern equipment.

Defence Procurement

Future procurement possibilities were hindered by the government's obligation to its donors to not spend more than 2 per cent of GDP on defence. Uganda manufactures some ammunition and mainly depends on Eastern Europe for heavy weaponry. Second-hand equipment from the former Warsaw Pact states is likely to continue to dominate procurement through unorthodox channels. Indonesia has invited Uganda to purchase weapon systems such as bulletproof vests, helmets, boots and uniforms. Uganda has shown interest in procuring Indonesian-made weapons.

> **CONTACT DETAILS**
> Ministry of Defence and Veteran Affairs
> P.O. Box 3798, Kampala, Uganda.
> Tel: 0414-565100
> Website: www.defence.go.ug

UKRAINE
(Capital: Kyiv)

INTRODUCTION

Area: 603,550 sq km
Population: 43,745,640 (July 2021 est.)
Coastline: 2,782 km
Maritime claims: Territorial sea: 12 nm
Exclusive Economic Zone: 200 nm
Continental shelf: 200 m or to the depth of exploitation

Crimea Republic is now a part of Russian Federation according to the Federal Constitutional Law dated 21.03.2014 No. 6-FCI/FKZ (Version 31.12.2014) "On accession of Crimea Republic to Russian Federation and on formation of new constituent entities of Crimean Republic and Sevastopol-the city of Federal status." (valid with amendments and addenda from 01.01.2015).

KEY POLITICAL PERSONS

PRESIDENT: Volodymyr Oleksandrovych Zelenskyy

PRIME MINISTER: Shmyhal Denys

KEY DEFENCE PERSONS

DEFENCE MINISTER: Reznikov Oleksii

COMMANDER-IN-CHIEF OF THE ARMED FORCES: Lt. Gen. Valerii Zaluzhnyi

COMMANDER OF THE ARMY: Lt. Gen. Oleksandr Syrskyi

COMMANDER OF THE NAVY: Rear Adm. Oleksii Neizhpapa

COMMANDER OF THE AIR FORCE: Col. Gen. Serhii Drozdov

COMMANDER OF JOINT FORCES: Lt. Gen. Serhii Naiev

ECONOMY

According to the Government portal of Ukraine, in the third quarter of 2018 Ukraine's economy increased by 0.4% as compared with the previous quarter. This figure strengthened the positive tendency of sustainable economic growth for the 11th consecutive quarter. According to data released by the State Statistics Service, the growth reached 2.8% as compared with the third quarter of last year. The situation is in line with the forecasts of the Government and international partners. Exports of goods and services from Ukraine in 9 months of 2018 grew by 9.3% and amounted to USD 41.7 billion, according to the data of the State Statistics Service of Ukraine. The EU's share in total exports made up USD 14.6 billion (42.3%). Commodity exports grew by 10.3%. In the sectoral terms, growth was demonstrated by the chemical industry, wood products, textiles, metals, building materials. Ukrainian roads, ports and railways are the pillars of economic growth. The development of creative industries adds 4% to the country's GDP. Ukraine returned to international debt markets in September 2017, issuing a USD 3 billion sovereign bond. Ukraine belongs to a number of the international organisations, including the United Nations, Euro-Atlantic Partnership Council, Organisation for Security and Cooperation in Europe, International Monetary Fund, World Bank, and World Trade Organisation. Ukraine also is an observer to the Organisation of American States. The country has many of the components of a major European economy - rich farmlands, a well-developed industrial base, highly trained labour, and a good education-system. In April 2017 the World Bank stated that Ukraine's economic growth rate was 2.3% in 2016, thus ending the recession. Ukraine's economy has been hit badly because of the COVID-19 outbreak and lockdown restrictions. But the country is currently getting back on track in the economic front through adaptive quarantine measures and boosting the economy growth by implementing various business support programmes and privatising state-owned enterprises.

GDP (official exchange rate): $516.68 billion (2020), $538.33 billion (2019 est.)

Real Growth Rate (GDP): 3.24% (2019 est.), 3.41% (2018 est.)

Industries: Coal, electric power, ferrous and nonferrous metals, machinery and transport equipment, chemicals, food processing

Oil-Proved Reserves: 395 million bbl (1 January 2018 est.)

Natural Gas Proved Reserves: 1.104 trillion cu m (1 January 2018 est.)

Total Exports: $60.67 billion (2020 est.), $63.56 billion (2019 est.)

Export Commodities: Corn, sunflower seed oils, iron and iron products, wheat, insulated wiring, rapeseed (2019)

Major Markets: Russia 9%, China 8%, Germany 6%, Poland 6%, Italy 5%, Turkey 5% (2019)

Total Imports: $62.46 billion (2020 est.), $76.07 billion (2019 est.)

Import Commodities: refined petroleum, cars, packaged medicines, coal, natural gas (2019)

Major Suppliers: China 13%, Russia 12%, Germany 10%, Poland 9%, Belarus 7% (2019)

INTERNATIONAL DISPUTES

◆ Crimean Peninsula: Former President Viktor Yanukovych's backtracking on a trade and cooperation agreement with the EU in November 2013 in favour of closer economic ties with Russia led to a three-month protest occupation of Kyiv's central square. Later Russia control in the Ukrainian autonomous region of Crimea resulted in the annexation of Crimea by Russia on 18 March 2014. Russian forces now control Crimea and Russian authorities claim it as Russian territory while the Ukrainian Government asserts that Crimea remains part of Ukraine.

◆ Dispute over the boundary between Russia and Ukraine through the Kerch Strait and Sea of Azov remains unresolved despite a December 2003 framework agreement. The boundary delimitation treaty (1997) with Belarus is yet to be ratified due to unresolved financial claims.

DEFENCE

The overall strategic situation around Ukraine and the events that took place in 2014 have required the government to revise its approaches towards protecting the sovereignty, territorial integrity and independence of the state. A new military doctrine has been developed. Ukraine has scrapped compulsory military service for young men and brought back military conscription by Presidential decree.

ARMY

Personnel: 1,50,000 (including Airborne/Air Assault Forces)

Equipment

Category	Name	In Service
MBT	T-80	1,000+
	T-64	
	T-72	
	T-84	
AIFV/APC	BMP-1, BMP-2, BMP-3	3,000+
	BMD-1/2	
	BTR-60/70/80	
	BRDM-2	
	Dozor-B	10
	Saxon	50+
Artillery	D-30 122mm	1,500+
	D-20 152mm	
	2A36 152mm towed	
	2C1 122mm	
	2C3 152mm SP	
	2C19 152mm	
MRL	300mm	300+
	BM-21 122mm	
	220mm	
Mortar	120mm	150+
SSM	SS-21 Tochka/Tochka-U	
ATGW	9P148, 9P149	
SAM	SA-4, 6, 8, 11, 12, 15	

New Procurements/Upgrades

◆ The US State Department has approved a possible Foreign Military Sale to Ukraine for 150 Javelin missiles and related equipment and support for an estimated cost not to exceed USD39.2 million The Government of Ukraine has requested to buy 150 Javelin missiles and 10 Javelin Command

Launch Units (CLUs). Also included are training devices, transportation, support equipment, technical data and publications, personnel training and training equipment, US government, engineering, technical, and logistics support services, and other related elements of logistics support tools and test equipment; support equipment; publications and technical documentation; spare and repair parts; equipment training and training devices; US Government and contractor technical, engineering and logistics support services; and other related elements of logistical, sustainment, and programme support.

◆ According to Ukroboronprom, NVK Iskra company started mass production of Ukrainian 1L220UK counter-battery radar, also known as Zoopark-3. The first operational unit is scheduled for delivery to Ukrainian Army by the end of 2020.

NAVY
Personnel: 12,000
Equipment

Category	Name	In Service
Frigate	Hetman Sahaydachniy (Krivak III)	1
Patrol craft	Matka Class	1
	Gurza-M Class	3+
	Zhuk Class	1
	Island Class	1
Mine Sweeper	Yevgenya Class	1
Amphibious force	Polnocny Class	1
	Centaur Class	1
Auxiliaries	Ondatra Class	1
		10+

New Procurements/Upgrades

◆ The US State Department has approved a possible Foreign Military Sale to the Government of Ukraine of up to 16 Mark VI Patrol Boats and related equipment for an estimated cost of USD600 million. The Government of Ukraine has requested to buy up to 16 Mark VI Patrol Boats; 32 MSI Seahawk A2 gun systems; 20 Electro-Optics-Infrared Radar (FLIR) (16 installed and 4 spares); 16 Long Range Acoustic Device (LRAD) 5km loudspeaker systems; 16 Identification Friend or Foe (IFF) systems; 40 MK44 cannons (32 installed and 8 spares); communication equipment; support equipment; spare and repair parts; tools and test equipment; technical data and publications; personnel training and training equipment; US government and contractor engineering, technical, and logistics support services; and other related elements of logistics support.

◆ Minister of Defence of Ukraine signed an order on the adoption of the coastal missile system 360MC "Neptune".

Ukrainian Naval Infantry: They are used by the Ukrainian Navy as a component part of amphibious, airborne and amphibious-airborne operations.

AIR FORCE
Personnel: 40,000
Equipment

Category	Name	In Service
Fighter	Su-24M	10
	Su-27	20+
	MiG-29	20+
	Su-25	10
Transport	IL-76MD	25+
	An-30	
	An-70	
	An-26	
Helicopter	Mi-8	10+
	Ka-226	
SAM	SA-11	
	SA-5	
	SA-10	
UAV	RQ-11	

New Procurements/Upgrades
No major procurement plans are under consideration at present.

Defence Expenditure
Total defence spending: $5 billion (2020 approx.)
Estimated defence spending in terms of GDP: 3.2% of GDP (2020 est.), 3.9% of GDP (2019)

Domestic Suppliers: Ukroboronprom
Foreign Suppliers: US, UK, European Union, Canada, France, Australia, Canada, Israel, Japan

Key suppliers of defence equipment to Ukraine have been the US and the UK, as per US Department of Commerce's International Trade Administration. The primary suppliers of defense and military equipment to Ukraine's armed forces are the state-owned company UkrOboronProm (UOP).

In 2021, National Security and Defence Council (NSDC) recommended to the government, when preparing the draft state budget for next year, to increase funding for the security and defence sector to 5.95% of GDP, or UAH 319.4 billion (from 5.93% of GDP in 2021). In total, UAH 319.4 billion (USD11,949,514,172) will be spent on national security and defence, which corresponds to 5.95% of GDP.

A memorandum of intent between the Ministry of Defence of Ukraine and the Ministry of Defence of the United Kingdom of Great Britain and Northern Ireland on cooperation in developing and enhancing the capabilities of the Navy of the Armed Forces of Ukraine was signed during the official visit of President Volodymyr Zelenskyi to Great Britain in October 2020, as per Ukrainian Ministry of Defence.

The US Department of Defence announced in June 2020 its plans for USD250 million in Fiscal Year 2020 Ukraine Security Assistance Initiative (USAI) funds for additional training, equipment, and advisory efforts to strengthen Ukraine's capacity. The USAI funds – USD125 million of which was conditional on Ukraine's progress on defense reforms – will provide equipment to support ongoing training programs and operational needs, as per US DoD news.

Ukraine has stepped up its efforts to join services and partnership of NATO Support and Procurement Agency (NSPA). In this way, Ukraine will have full access to the Alliance's procurement system. Moreover, Ukrainian manufacturers will be able to participate in NATO tenders and sell their products to foreign customers, as well as approaching Alliance standards, as per Ministry of Defence, Ukraine news release.

Defence Production and R&D
Ukrainian national military exports have been suspended while it focuses on the production of materiel for domestic armed forces during the unrest in the country. One of the products that the Ukrainian industry has been successful within Asia is the Oplot main battle tank (MBT) produced by the Malyshev Plant (ZIM) in Kharkiv. The country's intercontinental ballistic missiles, tactical ballistic missiles, and radar and avionics systems are mostly designed in Donetsk and Dnipropetrovsk, while the cities of Kharkiv and Luhansk are production hubs for main battle tanks such as the T-34, T-64, T-80UD, and other types of armoured vehicles. Military aircraft engines are mostly designed and produced in the south-eastern city of Zaporizhia. Ukraine remains a leader in missile-related technology, navigation electronics for combat vessels and submarines, guidance systems, and radar for military jets.

Defence Procurement

The Ukrainian government has approved a change to the procurement law in which the country's State-owned military industries are to be exempted from the need to competitively tender for government work while the Ministry of Defence has announced the priorities of the state defence order for 2018, focusing on anti-tank weapons, armoured infantry vehicles, means of combating unmanned aerial vehicles, as well as upgraded aircraft and helicopters.

CONTACT DETAILS
Ministry of Defence
6, Povitroflots'ky Avenue,
Kyiv, Ukraine 03168
Ph: (044) 253-04-71
E-mail: priymalna_mou@mil.gov.ua
Website: http://www.mil.gov.ua

UNITED ARAB EMIRATES
(Capital: Abu Dhabi)

INTRODUCTION

Area: 83,600 sq km
Population: 9,856,612 (July 2021 est.)
Coastline: 1,318 km
Maritime claims: Territorial sea: 12 nm
Contiguous zone: 24 nm
Exclusive Economic Zone: 200 nm
Continental shelf: 200 nm or to the edge of the continental margin

KEY POLITICAL PERSONS

PRESIDENT & COMMANDER OF UNION DEFENCE FORCE: Sheikh Khalifa bin Zayed Al Nahyan

VICE PRESIDENT, PRIME MINISTER & DEFENCE MINISTER: Sheikh Mohammed bin Rashid Al Maktoum

KEY DEFENCE PERSONS

DEPUTY SUPREME COMMANDER OF THE ARMED FORCES: Crown Prince Mohamed bin Zayed Al Nahyan

CHIEF OF STAFF: Lt. Gen. Hamad Mohammed Thani Al Rumaithy

COMMANDER OF THE ARMY: Lt. Gen. Saleh Mohamed Saleh Al Ameri

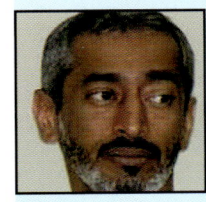

COMMANDER OF THE NAVY: Rear Adm. (Pilot) Saeed Bin Hamdan Al Nahyan

COMMANDER OF THE AIR FORCE & AIR DEFENCE: Vice Marshal Ibrahim Nasser Mohammed Al Alawi

ECONOMY

The UAE has an open economy with a high per capita income and a sizeable annual trade surplus. Petroleum and natural gas exports play an important role in the economy. Oil continues to be the mainstay of the economy. Non-oil sectors account for 69 per cent of GDP. Tourism is one of non-oil sources of revenue. A massive construction boom, an expanding manufacturing base, and a thriving services sector are helping the UAE diversify its economy. The UAE has reportedly spent billions of dirhams in economic stimulus measures to support businesses since the Covid-19 outbreak began. Business activity in the non-oil private sectors continued to improve boosted by the easing of Covid-19 restrictions, a rise in tourism and increased spending amid the economic recovery. The economy is expected to grow 4.2 per cent in 2022, higher than the previous forecast of 3.8 per cent.

GDP (official exchange rate): $421.077 billion (2019 est.)

Real Growth Rate: (GDP) 0.8% (2017 est.), 3% (2016 est.)

Industries: Petroleum and petrochemicals; fishing, aluminium, cement, fertilizer, commercial ship repair, construction materials, handicrafts, textiles.

Crude Oil – Proved Reserves: 97.8 billion bbl (1 January 2018 est.)

Natural Gas – Proved Reserves: 6.091 trillion cu m (1 January 2018 est.)

Total Exports: $308.5 billion (2017 est.), $298.6 billion (2016 est.)

Export Commodities: Crude petroleum, refined petroleum, gold, jewelry, broadcasting equipment (2019)

Major Markets: India 11%, Japan 10%, Saudi Arabia 7%, Switzerland 6%, China 6%, Iraq 6% (2019)

Total Imports: $229.2 billion (2017 est.), $226.5 billion (2016 est.)

Import Commodities: Gold, broadcasting equipment, jewellery, refined petroleum, diamonds (2019)

Major Suppliers: China 15%, India 12%, United States 7% (2019)

INTERNATIONAL DISPUTES

◆ Boundary agreement was signed and ratified with Oman in 2003 for entire border, including Oman's Musandam Peninsula and Al Madhah enclaves, but contents of the agreement and detailed maps showing the alignment have not been published.

◆ Iran and UAE dispute Tunb Islands and Abu Musa Island, which Iran occupies.

DEFENCE

The President of the United Arab Emirates is the supreme commander of the Armed Forces. The military forces consist of the Army, Navy, Air force, and the Presidential Guard (PG) Special forces. The UAE armed forces are considered highly capable among other militaries in the Arabian Gulf. The number of the armed forces have grown significantly over the years and are presently equipped with some of the most modern weapon systems. The military has actively involved itself in supporting other nations. The member states of the Gulf Cooperation Council – Bahrain, Kuwait, Oman, Qatar, Saudi Arabia and the UAE – have signed a defence pact to consider an attack on one of them as an attack on all.

ARMY

Personnel: 59,000

Equipment

Category	Name	In Service
MBT	Leclerc	390
	Scorpion light	80
Amoured car	NIMR N35	3000
	AML-90	60
AIFV/APC	BMP-3	450 (upgraded)
	ACV (all versions)	133
	AMX-13P	11
	RG-31	28
	M-ATV	794
	Patria AMV	40
	Fuchs NBC	32
	BAE Caiman	222
Artillery	155 mm/39 Howitzer	6
	Norinco AH4 Howitzer	
	M198 155mm towed	12
	105mm towed	6
	AMX MkF3 155mm SP	20
	G6 155mm SP	76
	M-109L47 155mm SP	85
MRL	Astros II	
	Firos-25	
	HMARS	20
	Smerch	6
Mortar	81mm	
ATGW	Vigilant	
	Tow	
	Milan	50
	Javelin	
SAM	1-Hawk	(5 batteries)
	Rapier	
	Crotale	
	RBS-70	

...continued

Category	Name	In Service
SAM	SA-14	
	Javelin	
	9K69 Pantsir S1 gun/missile	50
	Avenger fire units with Stinger RMP Block 1 missile	780
	THAAD	2
	Patriot/PAC-3	9

New Procurements/Upgrades

◆ The US State Department has given its approval to sell 4,569 Mine Resistant Ambush Protected (MRAP) vehicles not used by the US Army, to the UAE for $556 million.

NAVY

Personnel: 2,000

Equipment

Category	Name	In Service
Corvette	Baynunah class	6
	Muray Jib class	2
	Abu Dhabi class	2
Patrol Craft	OPV Arialah	
	Mubarraz class FAC	2
	Mubarraz class missile FAC	2
	Ban Yas class FAC	6
	Ghannatha class	24
	Ardhana class	6
Mine warfare Force	ex-German Type 332 minehunters	2
Amphibious Force	Landing craft tank	7
	Landing craft utility	5
	LCP	4
	LCM	1

New Procurements/Upgrades

◆ French shipbuilder Naval Group announced that it has launched the first Gowind corvette, Bani Yas (P110), for the UAE Navy. The UAE ordered two Gowind corvettes in 2019 to be built in France. The second vessel is set to be launched in 2022.

AIR FORCE

Personnel: 4,500

Equipment

Category	Name	In Service
Fighter	Mirage 2000-9/9D	58
	F-16E/F Block 60 Desert Falcon	79
AEW&C	GlobalEye	3
Transport	Airbus A330 MRTT	3
	C-17ERC-130J	8
	CN-235	11
	Cessna 208B	8

...continued

Category	Name	In Service
Trainer	Hawk Mk102	15
	Hawk Mk63	30
	MB339A	10
	PC-21	25
Helicopter	CH-47C/D	12+
	AW139	60+
	CH-47F	4+
	AH-64A/ 64D	50+
	IAR-99 Puma	6
	AS.550 Fennec	12
	AB-412	4
	UH-60L/60M Black Hawk	25+
Missile	AGM-65, AGM-84, AGM-88, AIM-9M, AIM-120B, Black Shahine	
UAV	Predator XP, Seeker II, Falcon Eye 1	

New Procurements/Upgrades

◆ Swedish firm Saab has handed over the UAE's third GlobalEye airborne early warning and control (AEW&C) aircraft. In September 2021, the UAE took delivery of the second GlobalEye and the first was handed over in April.

◆ Production underway for eight Piaggio P.1HH Hammerhead UAV ordered by the UAE.

◆ The UAE to purchase 80 French Rafale jets in $19bn arms deal.

◆ The UAE has placed an order for 12 Airbus H225M Caracal helicopters.

Defence Expenditure

Total Defence Expenditure: $2.3 billion (2019), $1.66 billion (2018)

Defence spending in terms of GDP: 4.86% (2017)

Defence Production and R&D

Through joint ventures with international leading industrial partners, the UAE has now begun to design, manufacture and sell a wide array of armaments and services for the UAE armed forces and global clients. In a bid to reduce foreign dependence and help with national industrialisation, the UAE indigenous defence industry is aggressively pushing to enter the global market showcasing its defence technology capabilities overseas in markets such as the US, Brazil, France and the Far East. Stringent offset policy has contributed to significant growth in the domestic defence sector in the fields of shipbuilding, systems integration and naval logistics. The country has secured deals to supply weapons and hardware to Algeria, Turkey, Russia and Italy. Tawazun, the country's strategic defence investment company has inked agreements with the Algerian and Turkish governments to set up joint ventures for its Nimr Automotive subsidiary and partnered with Swedish company, Saab, for radar development.

Defence Procurement

The UAE's Tawazun will take control of the management of procurements for the UAE's armed forces in a resolution signed by Sheikh Mohamed bin Zayed Al Nahyan on 24, 2021 February at the IDEX trade show in Abu Dhabi. The organisation will manage procurement for the armed forces and Abu Dhabi police, as well as other bodies that include the Presidential Guard and critical national infrastructure protection force.

The organisation has now been given end-to-end control of procurement, ranging from developing and articulating concept development for the armed forces through to contract management, quality assurance and control, as well as vendor registration and management, and the approval and supervision of offset projects.

Over the past few years, the UAE has made major investments in its air, land and sea and critical infrastructure defence capabilities, including significant purchases of F-16 aircraft, Patriot and Terminal High Altitude Air Defence (THAAD) systems. The UAE has awarded contracts to firms from Russia, Turkey, Pakistan and South Africa. The Saudi Arabian Military Industries (SAMI), the kingdom's state defence company, has signed partnerships with France's Naval Group, Spain's Navantia, and Abu Dhabi state fund Mubadala.

CONTACT DETAILS

Ministry of Defence
P O Box 2838
Abu Dhabi, UAE
Tel: +9712532330
Fax: +971253 406

Armed Forces HQ
P O Box 309
Abu Dhabi, UAE
Tel: +971234392

STRATEGIC INFORMATION
UNITED KINGDOM
(Capital: London)

INTRODUCTION

Area: 243,610 sq km
Population: 68.2 million (2021 est.)
Coastline: 12,429 km
Maritime claims: Territorial sea: 12 nm
Continental shelf: As defined in continental shelf orders or in accordance with agreed upon boundaries
Exclusive fishing zone: 200 nm

GEOPOLITICAL IMPORTANCE

Located off the north-western coast of European continent, the United Kingdom comprises a chain of islands including Great Britain and the north-eastern part of the island of Ireland. The Kingdom mainly consists of four countries – England, Scotland, Wales and Northern Ireland, with greater devolution of power among the last three. Scotland went for a referendum on 18th Sept 2014 for independence, with voters rejecting a proposal to separate from the 307-year-old political union with Great Britain. The Scottish Government proposed to go for a second referendum in 2021, seeking independence from the UK; the exercise was put off due to the Coronavirus pandemic. Scotland is now considering to hold the referendum before the end of 2023.

The UK is surrounded by the Atlantic Ocean in North West, by the North Sea in North East and by the English Channel in the South. In its West lies the Irish Sea. The Kingdom occupies a unique geostrategic position in the entire Europe. Though separated from mainland Europe, the UK since centuries has wielded more power over the entire continent than any other country in the region. Dubbed as the modern world's first superpower that went on to build imperial colonies all around the globe and established an extensive empire on which the "sun never set", the UK even today projects a strong military posture globally. Especially its formidable naval fleet is deployed in several strategic parts of the world.

POLITICAL OVERVIEW

A unitary state, the UK functions as a Constitutional monarchy and a Parliamentary democracy. While the monarch (currently Queen Elizabeth II) is a ceremonial head of the state, the real political power is exercised by the Executive and Legislature constituting the Prime Minister and Cabinet Ministers (functioning as government) and the two houses of Parliament – House of Lords and House of Commons, respectively. The country does not have a written Constitution. As one of five permanent members of the United Nations Security Council, a founding member of NATO, and of the Commonwealth, the UK has pursued global approach in its strategic and foreign policies.

KEY POLITICAL PERSONS

HEAD OF STATE & COMMANDER-IN-CHIEF: Queen Elizabeth II

PRIME MINISTER: Boris Johnson

ECONOMY

The United Kingdom is a leading trading power and financial centre in the world with London being one of the "command centres" of global economy. Based on its GDP, the UK was the 5th largest economy in the world as of 2019. It is the third largest economy in Europe after France and Germany.

UK's service sector, primarily constituting of banking, insurance, and business, contributes the largest share of national GDP. Once a leading industrial nation in the world, Britain's industrial sector, however, has declined over the years. Manufacturing, meanwhile, has declined in importance but still accounts for about 10% of economic output. The highly modernised agricultural sector is capable of meeting more than half of the country's food need. The country is a member of leading international financial institutions, including the World Trade Organisation (WTO), International Monetary Fund (IMF) and Organisation for Economic Co-operation and Development (OECD) along with the financially powerful G-7 and G-20 group of nations and the Commonwealth states.

UK officially exited the European Union (EU) on January 31, 2020 and was on an 11-month long "transition phase" to renegotiate its future relationship with the EU covering trade & economy, security and other aspects of cooperation. On December 24, 2020, the UK and the EU finally struck the historic "Brexit deal", covering trade and other areas of cooperation just ahead of Britain's official exit from the European Union on December 31, 2020. UK's exit after 47 years of membership in the EU has reduced the number in the bloc to 27.

The Coronavirus pandemic further deepened UK's economic woes with its GDP contracting by a whopping 9.9% in 2020 – the worst in almost 300 years. The GDP recorded the sharpest fall of 22.1% in the first half of 2020 during the nationwide lockdown phase to contain the spread of the deadly virus, pushing the country into deep recession. GDP growth is projected to be over 7% in 2021 with steady acceleration in economic activities; however, appearance of new Covid strains still poses risk for possible downturn.

GDP (official exchange rate): $2.82 trillion (2019 est.)

Real Growth Rate (GDP): 1.26% (2019 est.); 1.25% (2018 est.)

Industries: Machine tools, electric power equipment, automation equipment, railroad equipment, shipbuilding, aircraft, motor vehicles and parts, electronics and communications equipment, metals, chemicals, coal, petroleum, paper and paper products, food processing, textiles, clothing, other consumer goods

Natural Gas - Proved Reserves: 176 billion cu m (1 January 2018 est.)

Crude Oil - Proved Reserves: 2.069 billion bbl (1 January 2018 est.)

Total Exports: $901.88 billion (2019 est.); $877.50 billion (2018 est.)

Export Commodities: Cars, gas turbines, gold, crude petroleum, packaged medicines (2019)

Major Markets: US 15%, Germany 10%, China 7%, Netherlands 7%, France 7%, Ireland 6% (2019)

Total Imports: $987.01 billion (2019 est.); $955.65 billion (2018 est.)

Import Commodities: Gold, cars, crude petroleum, refined petroleum, broadcasting equipment (2019)

Major Suppliers: Germany 13%, China 10%, US 8%, Netherlands 7%, France 6%, Belgium 5% (2019)

DEFENCE & SECURITY

Driven by commercial and trade interests, the United Kingdom, which was the world's first industrialised nation in the 18th century, had expanded its imperial rule worldwide, mainly through the projection of a powerful and formidable military force. Even during the two World Wars and the Cold War era in the 19th century, Britain remained a mighty military power. An active member of NATO, and by allying with the United States as its "indispensable partner" in international military affairs, the UK continued to maintain its global military edge well into the early part of 20th century. UK's defence and security perspective has not merely been confined to defending the homeland from internal and external threat, but pursuing wider global interests, ranging from protecting its overseas territories (It still retains some of the colonial territories under its control) to maintaining energy security and conducting international trade. Being a NATO member, its armed forces take part in international coalition operations, including humanitarian missions. With a robust domestic defence industry, the country has equipped its armed forces with cutting-edge military systems. Its naval fleet maintains a worldwide presence to secure the country's interests overseas. UK is also one of the leading exporters of military hardware to other countries, thereby becoming a key player in international arms trade.

Hit by economic constraints in the past few years and stringent austerity measures, the British military is facing an erosion in its overall capability. The armed forces have braced up for major cuts in terms of weapons and personnel strength due to overall budgetary curtailment. The British Government's decision in 2016 to break away from the Europe Union is likely to further diminish the country's defence prowess in future. Continuous decrease in military expenditure coupled with troops reduction and curtailment of new military acquisition programmes could result in the UK withdrawing completely from world affairs in the next few years or so. The total strength of the UK service personnel was around 159,000 (as of April 2021).

The present Government, under PM Boris Johnson in November 2020 unveiled the biggest programme of investment in British defence since the end of Cold War, announcing to pump in an extra £4 billion a year over the next four years. The mega investment plan would fund space and cyber defence projects and is expected to create thousands of new jobs in the country. A new agency dedicated to Artificial Intelligence (AI), the creation of a National Cyber Force and a new Space Command, capable of launching UK's first rocket in 2022, are among the areas for the investment focus. There would be a record investment of at least £1.5 billion extra and £5.8 billion total on military R&D and a commitment to invest further in the Future Combat Air System.

KEY DEFENCE PERSONS

SECRETARY OF STATE FOR DEFENCE: Robert Ben Wallace

MINISTER FOR THE ARMED FORCES: James Heappey

CHIEF OF DEFENCE STAFF: Adm. Tony Radakin

CHIEF OF NAVAL STAFF: Adm. Ben Key

CHIEF OF THE GENERAL STAFF, ARMY: Gen. Mark Carleton-Smith

CHIEF OF THE AIR STAFF: Air Chief Marshal Mike Wigston

COMMANDER OF STRATEGIC COMMAND: Gen. Patrick Sanders

Internal Conflict

Terrorism: Terrorism poses the gravest threat to UK's internal security at present. A spate of deadly attacks at public places across the country, including one in capital London in September 2017, had increased the official terror threat level to "critical" from "severe". In the last few years, there have been many attempts to carry out terrorist strikes at different locations across the UK. Terrorism is not associated with any single area of the UK, and individuals convicted of terror-related offences have lived in different parts of the country. Attacks related to terrorism have occurred in London, Glasgow, Manchester and other sub-urban areas of the country. Thwarted terrorist plots have been aimed at targets outside the capital in recent past. The rise of extremist terror organisation Islamic State (ISIS) has further accentuated the terror threat level for Great Britain.

Racism: Racism in one form or other has been widespread in Britain since ages and race-related crimes have taken ugly form at times. Violence against ethnic groups living in the country has increased over the years. Though race relations have improved significantly in the last thirty years or so, racial segregation, however, remains an important but largely unaddressed problem in the UK.

Organised crime: The country deals with the issues of drug trafficking, gang wars, human trafficking, financial fraud and other forms of organised crime.

External Conflict

The United Kingdom had previously been engaged in external conflict with few countries including Iraq and Afghanistan. Although it did not face any direct military threat from any country, especially after the disintegration of Soviet Union in 1991, the British armed forces, nevertheless, have been involved in major international military operations led by the US and NATO. At present, the country is involved in air strikes over Syria and Iraq to fight the terror outfit Islamic State (ISIS).

Britain's territorial disputes are with Northern Ireland, Argentina, Spain, Denmark and Mauritius.

Overseas Conflict

Iraq: The UK was a major contributor to the US-led invasion of Iraq in 2003. Despite a public mandate going against the country's involvement in the war, UK sent a 46,000-strong army personnel to the region. The British Army controlled the southern regions of Iraq and maintained a peace-keeping presence in the city of Basra until their withdrawal from the war-torn nation on 30 April 2009. Later on, British troops were fully withdrawn from Iraq after the Iraqi government refused to extend their mandate. UK military operations in Iraq were conducted under the name 'Operation TELIC'. The UK operated as part of a coalition called the Multi-National Force – Iraq (MNF-I) alongside troops from 25 other nations. In February 2007, the-then British Prime Minister, Tony Blair, announced the first large-scale withdrawal of British troops from Iraq. Presently there are no British soldiers in Iraq.

Afghanistan: UK has played a key role in the Afghanistan conflict which began as a war in October 2001. Led by the US and NATO coalition members, the war against Afghanistan was waged to eliminate Taliban rule in that country as well as to annihilate Al-Qaida and its global terror network. The UK was the second country after the US to deploy a large number of troops in the war-ravaged country. NATO announced withdrawal of its combat troops from Afghanistan by 2014-end, even as it continued sending non-combat forces for training and other missions in the country. After the US Govt in 2021 announced an "end to the two-decade long war" and complete withdrawal of its troops from the Afghan soil, Britain too followed suit and pulled out all its forces from the strife-torn nation in August 2021.

Libya: British armed forces took part in the March 2011 military intervention in Libya led by NATO coalition forces to stop civil war in the North African country. The Royal Navy and Royal Air Force were actively involved in carrying out combat operations along with the French military during the conflict. The war came to an end with the capture and death of Libyan leader Muammar Gaddafi in October 2011.

Territorial Conflict

Northern Ireland: The centuries-old conflict between Great Britain and Northern Ireland has both political and religious roots. It has revolved around whether the latter should remain a part of the former. While the Catholics in Northern Ireland have opposed partition of the territory from UK, the Protestants have supported the idea of its inclusion in the Republic of Ireland which gained independence from British administration in 1922. In the south, 26 counties formed the separate state of Republic of Ireland while six counties in the north stayed within the UK. Despite several efforts to resolve the dispute, problems still persist between UK and Northern Ireland over devolution of power.

Argentina: The British-Argentina conflict over a chain of islands in the South Atlantic Ocean has flared up nearly three decades after the Falklands War in 1982. Argentina claims sovereignty over the Falkland Islands, which it calls Las Malvinas. The archipelago, located near Argentina, is a self-governing British Overseas Territory with the UK looking after the region's defence and foreign affairs. The two countries are also engaged in territorial dispute over the South Georgia and the South Sandwich Islands in South Atlantic Ocean. The uninhabited region is a British Overseas Territory over which Argentina claims sovereignty.

Spain: UK and Spain spat over Gibraltar – a British Overseas Territory near the Mediterranean. Spain does not acknowledge British sovereignty over the region and the two sides have fought a war over it in 1704. The self-governed region, spread over an area of 6.8 square kilometres, has rejected proposals of Spanish sovereignty twice in 1967 and 2002. UK looks over the region's defence and foreign affairs.

Mauritius & Seychelles: The region of contention between UK, Mauritius and Seychelles is the Chagos archipelago – a chain of over 60 islands in the Indian Ocean. The area was part of Mauritius till the 18th century, but later came under British rule and presently falls under the British Indian Ocean Territory (BIOT). Mauritius has contended UK's claims over the region and has taken the issue to the United Nations.

Denmark: UK along with Iceland and Ireland dispute Denmark's claim that the Faroe Islands' continental shelf extends beyond 200 nm. The island, situated between the Norwegian Sea and the North Atlantic Ocean, is administered by Denmark.

THREAT PERSPECTIVE

After the collapse of Soviet Union in 1991 and the end of Cold War, UK did not face any direct military threat from any country. Due to the absence of any conventional military threat to its territory, the British armed forces were structured as Expeditionary forces. While maintaining a forward military presence globally, Britain's military alliance with the US and NATO had fortified its security position at the global stage. However, the military resurgence of Russia after the Ukraine crisis followed by the ongoing Syria conflict, and the increasing threat of terrorism from the Islamic State have significantly altered power equations for the entire European continent, as well as for Britain which is now reeling under defence budgetary cuts along with an ever-shrinking military power. Furthermore, the country's decision to exit the European Union could jeopardise its overall security position vis-à-vis its potential adversaries, including non-state actors, according to military analysts.

The Strategic Defence and Security Review, launched in 2015, had highlighted extremist terrorism, state-based threats, technology advancement and gradual loss of rules-based international order as four major threat areas for Great Britain. The latest review report, released in 2021, has listed Russia as a potential adversary. Increasing cyber warfare has become the other major area of concern.

STRATEGIC RELATIONS

US: The UK and the US have enjoyed deep-rooted historic, cultural, linguistic, and political ties for several centuries. Alongside, the two countries' governments have shared an intense politico-military and intelligence cooperation since World War II. Bilateral relations is based on a long history of "shared interests and common values" between the two nations. As permanent members of the UN Security Council and also of the NATO, the US and UK have taken more or less similar stand over key international issues that have influenced or affected their own national / security interests. Though in terms of projecting power, the US has surpassed the UK, the latter has nevertheless supported the former, both militarily and diplomatically, in some of its major decisions, including the last decade's wars against Iraq and Afghanistan, despite domestic public opposition. While the UK sent its troops to take part in the wars, it also provided its territory to the US to carry out combat strikes against Iraq in 2003. The two countries' multi-dimensional relationship has enormously benefited both in the past. Even while the US has steadily shifted its focus away from Europe, the UK has, nevertheless, acknowledged that its strategic allegiance to the world's leading power America is vital for its own security and strategic stability. The swiftly shifting geostrategic dimensions of 21st century, however, has resulted in Britain appearing to be steadily drifting away from the US for whom it was once an indispensable and most credible political, strategic and military partner. The US Air Force maintains few military bases in the UK.

France: The UK and France are active members of the NATO, EU and UN Security Council. Both are nuclear weapon states, and have similar national security interests. Though historic rivals since centuries, the two European powers have made efforts in recent years to deepen bilateral cooperation with a thrust on defence and strategy. The two signed a landmark treaty in November 2010 to strengthen bilateral defence cooperation by agreeing to create a Combined Joint Expeditionary Force (CJEF) and share nuclear test facilities. The deal also made provision for shared use of aircraft carriers by the two countries' navies as also jointly working on nuclear capabilities. Britain and France have also joined hands to design and develop new-generation aerospace systems including an unmanned air combat system while identifying other areas of cooperation to jointly invest and develop futuristic defence technologies and weapon systems in the coming decade.

Turkey: Acknowledging the importance of Turkey as a major regional power, Britain has made efforts to build a strong relationship with Ankara. Britain and Turkey signed the "Strategic Partnership" agreement in 2010 which among other areas includes defence relations, regional stability and international security issues. Bilateral ties between the two sides have strengthened since then with high-level political and diplomatic visits. In 2011, the two sides inked a "Military Co-operation Treaty". The Treaty is aimed at facilitating greater bilateral co-operation across a range of military activities. Trade ties between the two sides also remain robust.

India: Reckoning India as a growing economic and strategic power, the UK has laid stress on strengthening its ties with New Delhi. The countries share strong economic and social relations besides historic and cultural affinity. Their bilateral relationship got the "strategic partnership" stamp in 2004 when they signed an agreement in this regard. Defence cooperation has also received a boost in recent times with high-level official visits, joint military training and military exercises and technological collaboration in science and technology. India has procured some defence equipment from Britain.

Japan: Bilateral relations between Britain and Japan have primarily involved economic and social ties as well as cooperation in nuclear energy sector. The two sides have also been discussing cooperation in the field of defence, including joint research, development and production of defence equipment, and joint military training and exercises. They have taken up a joint programme to develop new air-to-air missile.

MULTILATERAL ALLIANCES

NATO: As a founder member of the North Atlantic Treaty Organisation (NATO), Britain has given highest priority to its allegiance to the multinational military block to reinforce its own defence and security while protecting its interests overseas. The country regards NATO as the "bedrock" of its defence and has been a major financial contributor to the alliance. British armed forces have actively taken part in most of the NATO-led combat operations overseas. The country's nuclear forces also make substantial contribution in ensuring NATO's nuclear deterrence as part of the block's overall military strategy. The multilateral block, formed primarily as a military alliance to counter the then potential threat of former Soviet Union to Western Europe, has evolved over the years to meet present-day changing security challenges. While acknowledging the importance of collective defence through the military alliance to ensure its own territorial sovereignty as well as the security of European neighbourhood, Britain has laid emphasis on closer cooperation with all its NATO allies. Despite having exited the EU, the UK has, nevertheless, reiterated its military commitment to the NATO alliance for collective defence of their territories.

AUKUS: The new trilateral pact involving the Governments of US, UK and Australia was announced in September 2021 amidst the rapidly evolving geostrategic landscape. Under the new military-strategic pact, Australia will build nuke-powered submarines for the first time, using technology provided by the US and UK. The pact would cover AI and other emerging technologies as well. The 'historic' pact has been formed to counter China's increasing presence and aggression in the strategically vital Indo-Pacific region and establish an international "rules-based order".

DEFENCE CAPABILITIES

ARMY: Bestowed with the primary task of safeguarding and protecting the country's interests, the British Army is organised to undertake operations in two broad scenarios – standing tasks (maintaining its presence in the territories controlled by it), and contingent operations in response to international crisis. The country maintains a Territorial Army to carry out exercises and operations overseas. The British Army personnel are actively deployed at present in 16 major countries across the globe. Britain sent the second highest number of troops to Afghanistan after the US and ended its combat operations in that country in 2014, even though few soldiers remained stationed there as part of support mission. It completely withdrew all its troops from Afghanistan in August 2021.

The British Army is being steadily transformed into a "smaller, more flexible and agile force" in order to meet divergent security scenarios of future warfare. Both the regular and reserve forces are being integrated into a single force structure. In March 2021, the Secretary of State for Defence, Robert Ben Wallace, announced that the Royal Army would be reduced from just over 82,000 fully trained soldiers at present to 72,500 by 2025. Many of the new procurement/ upgrade programmes for the Army is also under review amidst deliberations over reallocation of funds to other important defence projects.

Personnel: 117,560 (Regular + Reserve Force + Other personnel as of April 2020)

Equipment

Category	Name	In Service	On Order
MBT	Challenger 2	227 (to be reduced to 148)	
Light Tank	Scimitar	318	
APC/IFV	Warrior	786	
	FV432	541	
	Stormer	151	
	Jackal	400	
	Coyote (TSV light)	70	
	Mastiff	400	
	Spartan & other CVR(T) vehicles	138	
Armoured Car	Land Rover Snatch 2	(To be replaced by Foxhound LPPV)	
	Vector	166	
	Viking BVS10	158	
	Panther	350	
	Husky	325	
	Wolfhound	125	
	Foxhound	400	

...continued

Category	Name	In Service	On Order
Artillery	L115A3	600	
	L118 light gun (105 mm towed howitzer)	126	
	AS90 self-propelled gun	89	
Mortar	M6-895 60 mm	640	
	L16A2 81mm	371	
MRLS	M-270	35	
RCL	M72 LAW		
ATGW	Javelin	144	
SAM	Rapier	24	
	Starstreak	147	200
	Javelin	335	
	Stinger	120	

Army Aviation Equipment

Category	Name	In Service
Light transport aircraft	Defender	9
	Islander AL1, CC2	6
Helicopter	Lynx AH-9A (utility)	
	Wildcat Mk1	34 (being delivered)
	Gazelle (reconnaissance)	20+
	Merlin	28
	Chinook	48
	Puma	38
	Bell 212	8
	Apache Mk 1 (attack)	50
	Sea King	28
UAV	Hermes 450	
	Watchkeeper	40+
	Desert Hawk	200+

New Procurements/Upgrades

◆ A contract worth £800 million (US$1 billion) has been awarded to Rheinmetall BAE Systems Land in May 2021 to upgrade 148 of the Challenger-2 MBTs to Challenger-3 configuration under life-extension project to keep the platforms operational till 2040.

The Challenger MBT (Image Credit: Royal Army)

◆ Lockheed Martin in 2019 has delivered the first batch of upgraded Warrior 2 infantry combat vehicles for qualification and verification trials. A final production contract award is yet to signed by the UK MoD which would allow Lockheed Martin-UK to upgrade the entire fleet of Warrior vehicles, numbering around 280, to be upgraded and delivered by 2028.

◆ A £3.5 billion contract has been awarded to General Dynamics-UK for delivery of new Ajax armoured fighting vehicles (AFVs). Under the contract, GD will supply a total of 589 new vehicles in six variants to provide essential capability to the Armoured Cavalry. The new AFVs will replace the Scimitar light tanks. Initial batch of 14 platforms has been delivered and undergoing acceptance trials. However, the trials have been halted over noise and vibration issues in the platforms.

◆ Acquisition of new 8 x 8 mechanised infantry vehicle (MIV) is advancing. Over 300 such platforms are planned to be inducted by 2023. The UK MoD in 2018 announced plans to re-join the Boxer wheeled armoured vehicle development programme which could be acquired under the MIV project. Germany's Rheinmetall MAN Military Vehicles (RMMV) manufactures the Boxer in cooperation with fellow German defence contractor Krauss-Maffei Wegmann (KMW) under a bi-national programme. Serial production of the platforms for British Army has started.

◆ Procurement of a total of 2,747 Joint Light Tactical Vehicles and accessories from the US's Oshkosh company is under consideration.

◆ NP Aerospace is upgrading the entire fleet of around 2,200 protected mobility vehicles based in the UK and on operations. The vehicles include Foxhound, Mastiff, Wolfhound, Jackal, Coyote, Husky and other platforms. Work will continue till 2024.

◆ An RFI has been issued by the MoD in 2019 for planned procurement of a new 155mm self-propelled howitzer to replace the AS90 SP guns. Final contract is yet to be awarded.

◆ The Defence Ministry is buying 34 Army Wildcat Mk1 helicopters which will replace the Lynx fleet of choppers operated by the Army Air Corps. The new choppers will primarily be used in reconnaissance role and provide protection to soldiers on the ground. Delivery is going on.

◆ The existing fleet of Apache Mk1 attack helicopters would be re-manufactured into AH-64E configuration.

◆ A £93 million contract has been awarded to Thales UK to upgrade the Army's Starstreak short-range air defence missiles.

♦ Six Drone Dome anti-drone systems have been acquired from Israel's Rafael Advanced Defense Systems.

NAVY: Britain has maintained its force projections across the globe through its formidable Royal Navy which, for over three centuries, exerted great power and played a key role in establishing the British Empire. As an island nation, the UK had reckoned the importance of naval power in securing sea lanes for trade and transport to gain economic prosperity. Hence, the Royal Navy has been operating as a "blue water" navy, carrying out operations far beyond the British territory. Driven by the primary goal of protecting and promoting the country's interests worldwide, the Royal Navy not only undertakes combat operations wherever and whenever necessary, but it has also been used strategically to prevent any conflict in the international stage. The British Naval fleet is deployed in several parts of the globe, including in the South Atlantic, Gulf region, Northern Europe (North Atlantic and Mediterranean) and Far East. It is also building up maritime relations in the Asia-Pacific and Indian Ocean regions. The Royal Navy operates and regularly exercises with allies, coalition partners and other countries to build trust and understanding that contributes to stability in regions of interest to the UK. The Navy also undertakes humanitarian missions overseas.

To meet the future challenges, the Royal Navy aims to be an increasingly versatile, network-enabled expeditionary force, continuing to operate on, under and over the sea, on land (along with Royal Marines) and ever more frequently in the littoral, fully interoperable and integrated with the UK and allied forces. To support this transformation, the Navy is acquiring a range of new warships, including aircraft carriers, submarines, destroyers and frigates, naval fighter jets along with advanced weapon systems and equipment. The recently commissioned two large aircraft carriers, capable of operating the F-35 Joint Strike Fighter, promise to significantly transform the carrier strike capabilities of the Royal Navy and enhance its ability to project power onto the land environment.

Major naval bases: Gateshead, Tyne & Wear, England, Ceres Division (Leeds), Greenock, Scotland, Govan Division (Glasgow), Liverpool, Whale Island, Portsmouth, Hampshire, Medway Division, Chatham, HMNB Devonport, Plymouth

Personnel: 39,050 (Navy + Marines + Other personnel as of April 2020)

Equipment

Category	Name	In Service	On Order
Aircraft carrier	Elizabeth class	2	
Destroyer	Type 45 Daring class	6	
Submarine	Vanguard class (SSBN)	4	
Submarine	Dreadnought class (SSBN)		4
Submarine	Astute class (SSN)	4	3
Submarine	Trafalgar class (SSK)	3	
Frigate	Type 23 Duke class	12	
Frigate	Type 26 (To replace Type 23)		8
Frigate	Type 31		5
Amphibious ship	LPH, LPD, LSD, LCU, LCVP, LCAC etc.	60+	
Patrol vessel	Antarctic patrol ship	1	
Patrol vessel	River class	5	4
Fast Patrol boat	Archer class	14	
Fast Patrol boat	Scimitar class	2	
Mine sweeper	Hunt class MCMV	3	
Mine sweeper	Sandown class SRMH	4	
Auxiliary Ship	Oilers, Tankers, Repair Ships, Ice Patrol Ships etc.	15+	
Weapon	(Naval Gun) Mk8, Phalanx 20mm, Goalkeeper 30mm		
Weapon	(ASM)/ (LACM) Harpoon, Tomahawk		
Weapon	Sea Viper system with Aster 15 & Aster 30 SAM		
Weapon	Seawolf SAM		
Weapon	Trident D5 SLBM		
Weapon	(Torpedo) Spearfish, Sting Ray		

Royal Marines

The Marine forces, also called the Royal Marines, constitute of the Marine Corps and amphibious infantry that work alongside the Royal Navy. With specialisation in amphibious warfare capabilities, including the operation of landing craft, mountain warfare, and Arctic warfare, the Royal Marines operate a number of key military equipment, including landing craft, combat vehicles and other weapons.

Equipment

Category	Name
APC	Viking BvS 10
APC	Land Rover Wolf
APC	Jackal
APC	Pinzgauer
Mortar	L9A1 51 mm
Mortar	L16A2 81 mm
ATGW	Javelin
ATGW	LAW 80 (Light Anti-tank Weapon)
SAM	Starstreak

Naval Aviation

Category	Name	In Service	On Order
Fighter	F-35B		
Maritime Patrol Aircraft	P-8A Poseidon	6	3
Helicopter	Merlin HM2 (ASW/ASuW)	30	
Helicopter	AW101 Merlin (troops transport)	25	
Helicopter	Wildcat	28	

New Procurements/Upgrades

♦ HMS Queen Elizabeth, the lead ship of the two Elizabeth-class aircraft carriers commissioned into service in 2017, is slated for its first operational deployment in 2021. The second platform, HMS Prince of Wales, was commissioned into service in December 2019. BAE Systems has built the two large aircraft carriers designed to deploy and operate the F-35 Joint Strike Fighter platforms.

♦ The Govt in 2016 announced an initial £1.3 billion funding for the Successor-class (renamed "Dreadnought" class) of nuclear submarines programme. Led by BAE Systems, the project will deliver four new submarines to the Navy and replace the current Vanguard class of platforms, with the first submarine, named 'Dreadnought', likely to enter service in the early 2030s. The new submarines, to be armed with Trident nuclear weapons, would provide the UK nuclear deterrence into the 2060s.

♦ Fourth Astute class nuke-powered attack submarine has been commissioned into service in September 2021. BAE Systems is building the platforms.

♦ BAE Systems, under a £3.7 billion contract awarded to it in 2017, has started work on the first batch of three Type 26 next-generation frigates. The Royal Navy would acquire the new platforms, designated as "Global Combat Ships". While eight of these warships will be designed and built by BAE as "Type 26", the remaining five would be the cheaper "Type 31" general purpose frigates to be built at different shipyards across the UK. A competition for the Type 31 class of frigates, first launched in 2017, was cancelled and relaunched again in 2018.

In 2019, an industry team led by Babcock was selected to deliver the Type 31 frigates. The first platform is slated for delivery in 2025.

◆ Delivery of all four Tide-class tankers built by South Korea's Daewoo Shipbuilding and Marine Engineering (DSME) under a £452 million contract has been completed in 2018. The new vessels have been acquired to maintain the Royal Navy's ability to refuel at sea and provide fuel to warships and task groups, including the Elizabeth class aircraft carriers.

◆ BAE Systems has built and delivered the second batch of five new River-class offshore patrol vessels. The final platform was commissioned in June 2021.

◆ 18 of the F-35B ski-jump jet (STOVL) variants of Joint Strike Fighter have been delivered as of 2019. 24 of the new stealth fighters are scheduled to be deployed on two Elizabeth class aircraft carriers by 2024 as part of a total order of 138 platforms (which could be reduced to only 48 platforms due to over-pricing and other issues, but no final decision made yet) for the Royal Navy and Royal Air Force.

◆ Six of the Boeing-built P-8A Poseidon submarine-hunting aircraft have been delivered as of 2021; delivery of three more platforms is scheduled.

◆ Babcock has won a contract in 2019 to provide in-service support to the Navy's Tomahawk land-attack cruise missiles. The company would work in partnership with Lockheed Martin UK for the programme.

◆ Thales UK has been contracted to produce and deliver 1,000 lightweight multi-role missiles (LMM) for the UK forces. The LMM will enter service with the UK Armed Forces aboard the new Lynx Wildcat helicopter. The low-cost, lightweight missile, the development of which began in 2008, is designed to be launched from a variety of air, sea and land platforms against wide range of threats.

AIR FORCE: The Royal Air Force (RAF) is the aerial wing of British armed forces. The RAF operates with the stated objectives of defending the UK and its interests; strengthening international peace and stability; and 'be a force for good' in the world. The RAF has been structured to carry out a broad range of activities across full spectrum of operations ranging from warfighting to humanitarian missions and expeditionary roles. It is one of the powerful and technologically advanced air forces in the world. It is the largest air force in the European Union and second largest in NATO after the US Air Force. The RAF has played an important role in World War II and in most modern overseas conflicts. In order to meet the divergent security threats and challenges of the present century, the RAF has focused on developing itself as a more agile, adaptable and capable expeditionary air power and contribute to the UK's overall defence capability by working alongside the Army and the Royal Navy as also by harmonizing its capability, concepts and doctrine with those of the US Forces. In pursuance of this goal, the RAF has emphasised on developing and strengthening its command and control, and intelligence, surveillance, target acquisition and reconnaissance (ISTAR) capabilities; integrated air-land operation capabilities, and introduction of unmanned air vehicle systems along with the induction of state-of-the-art weapons and platforms. Integrating its various platforms and sensors with an effective network is also a key aspect of the modernisation drive.

Major air bases: Alconbury, Barkston Heath, Barkway, Boulmer, Brampton, Brize Norton, Coningsby, Cosford, Cranwell, Digby, Donna Nook, Fylingdales, Halton, Henlow, High Wycombe, Holbeach, Honington, Kirton in Lindsey, Leeming, Linton-on-Ouse, Lossiemouth, Marham, Northolt, Odiham, Pembrey Sands, Scampton, Shawbury, Spadeadam, St. Mawgan, Syerston, Tain, Topcliffe, Trimingham, Valley, Waddington, Weston-on-the-Green, Wittering, Woodvale, Wyton

Personnel: 37,370 (Regular + Reserve + Other personnel as of April 2020)

Equipment

Category	Name	In Service	On Order
Fighter, Attack	Eurofighter Typhoon	160	
	F-35 Joint Strike Fighter		
Reconnaissance/ Maritime Patrol	RC-135/Rivet Joint	3	
Tanker, Transport	C-17A Globemaster	8	
	C-130J Hercules	25	
	Voyager	14	
	A400M Atlas	20	2
Helicopter	Chinook CH-47	60	
	Griffin	3	
	Puma	20+	
	Sea King	18	
AEW	E3-D Sentry	4	
	E-7 Wedgetail		5
Trainer	Hawk	157	
	King Air	5	
	Tucano	55	

...continued

Category	Name	In Service	On Order
Trainer	Tutor T Mark 1	100	
	Vigilant T1	50+	
	Viking T1	60+	
UAV	MQ-9A Reaper	10	
	MQ-9B Sky-Guardian		3 (option for more)
Weapon	AAM AIM-120B AMRAAM, AIM-132 ASRAAM		
	ASM Brimstone, Storm Shadow		
	Paveway II, III, IV & Enhanced Paveway laser-guided bomb		

New Procurements/Upgrades

◆ The last of the Eurofighter Typhoon combat jet has entered service after being delivered by BAE Systems in September 2019. The delivery of the final Tranche 3 aircraft marks the conclusion of the programme which started in 2003 to deliver a total of 160 Eurofighter Typhoons to the RAF. Some of the Tranche 1 aircraft (numbering 30) would be retired by 2025.

◆ Development of a new sixth-gen fighter aircraft, named Tempest is under active consideration. The new platform could be ready for operations by 2035. The UK Govt. in 2018 announced plans to invest around £2 billion by 2025 to develop necessary technology to build the new aircraft, to be developed by a joint team of BAE Systems, Leonardo, MBDA and Rolls-Royce. Italy and Sweden have joined the programme as international partners. The UK is expected to lay out a roadmap for the new fighter platform that could be fielded to replace the Eurofighter Typhoons in future.

◆ A new project to develop a novel unmanned combat aircraft (UCAV) has been announced by the RAF Rapid Capabilities Office (RCO) and the Defence Science and Technology Laboratory (Dstl). The Lightweight Affordable Novel Combat Aircraft (LANCA) concept looks to offer additional capability when deployed alongside fighter jets like the F-35 and Typhoon of the RAF. First flight of the new unmanned platform is expected by 2023.

◆ The Defence Ministry has announced to buy a total of 138 F-35B (short takeoff/vertical landing -STOVL variant) Lightning II Joint Strike Fighter aircraft for the RAF and Navy. The RAF has made the first overseas deployment of its F-35B platform at its air base in Akrotiri, Cyprus in May 2019.

- Twenty A400M heavy-lift transport aircraft have been delivered by Airbus as of 2018. A total of 22 A400Ms are on order to replace the C-130J planes. Delivery of the remaining two platforms is awaited.
- The first RC-135W Rivet Joint surveillance/ signals intelligence aircraft has joined service after undergoing avionics upgrade in the US. The two other platforms would rejoin later after due upgrades. Full operational capability for the Rivet Joint platforms was achieved in 2018.
- A contract has been awarded to US's Boeing in 2019 to deliver five E-7 Airborne Early Warning and Control (AEW&C) aircraft for US$ 1.98 billion. The new platforms would replace the RAF's existing six Boeing E-3D Sentry AEW aircraft. Deliveries would be completed by 2023.
- Engine maker Rolls-Royce has been awarded £865 million contract to upkeep RAF's fleet of Eurofighter Typhoon aircraft which are powered by EJ200 engines. In 2019, the company received an additional amount worth £350 million to provide maintenance support to the EJ200 engines up to 2024.
- A deal worth £110 million has been awarded to British company Marshall Aerospace and Defence Group to extend the lifespan of the RAF's Hercules C-130J aircraft (totalling 14) until 2035.
- A £260m foreign military sale (FMS) agreement has been signed with the US in 2018 to support the RAF's fleet of C-17 Globemaster III transport aircraft.
- 14 of the H-47 Chinook extended range (ER) helicopters would be bought from the US under FMS route at a price of £1.4 billion. Deliveries would be completed by 2030.
- Up to 16 MQ-9B SkyGuardian medium-altitude long-endurance (MALE) aerial drones would be procured from the US under the "Protector" programme. A contract worth £65 million (US$80 million) for the first three platforms has been placed in July 2020. The UAVs are expected to be operational by 2024 and subsequently replace the MQ-9A Reaper drones.
- General Atomics has been awarded a contract worth $91 million in 2019 to support the RAF's fleet of MQ-9A UAVs. The contract provides for depot repair, life cycle sustainment, software maintenance services for the MQ-9A fleet.
- The RAF has outlined plans to develop hypersonic weapons for its existing and future fighter platforms. UK's leading defence industry players, including BAE Systems, Rolls Royce and other entities, would jointly work on the future project.
- The LANZA 3D long-range air-defence radar system is being procured from Spanish firm Indra.
- The US State Dept in August 2020 has approved a possible Foreign Military Sale of 395 AGM-114R2 Hellfire missiles for an estimated cost of $46 million.

Major Armaments Producers

BAE Systems: The largest defence manufacturer in the UK and one of the leading defence and aerospace contractors worldwide, BAE Systems designs, develops and produces a whole range of military platforms and equipment for the Army, Navy and Air Force. The company is presently involved in several multi-national, mega-budget defence projects including the F-35 Joint Strike Fighter, Eurofighter Typhoon and the A400M heavy-lift transport plane. It has also built and delivered the Elizabeth-class aircraft carriers and Type-45 destroyers to the Royal Navy besides delivering the Astute class of attack submarines. In September 2012, BAE Systems and European defence major EADS revealed that they were in merger talks to create a global aerospace and defence leader. The negotiations, however, broke off due to a lack of consensus among the leading partnering nations and stiff opposition from Germany.

Thales UK: The second largest defence and aerospace company in the UK, Thales's defence portfolio includes missile systems, electronic warfare and radar systems, avionics, C4ISR systems and naval equipment among others.

Rolls Royce: A leading aircraft engine manufacturer, Rolls Royce provides defence aero-engine products and services to 160 customers in over 100 countries around the world. The company produces engines for transport planes, combat jets, reconnaissance aircraft, trainer jets, helicopters, and unmanned aerial vehicles. It also produces equipment and systems for naval vessels.

Babcock: Babcock is UK's leading engineering support services organisation. The company is a major industrial support partner to the Royal Navy and also supplies equipment and services to a number of other navies in the world, including the US, Canada, Spain and New Zealand. It also provides flight training, aircraft provision and through-life support to the UK's armed forces and manages armoured and support vehicle training fleets of the UK Army. The company has also bagged a multi-million contract from the UK Defence Ministry to design the next generation of nuclear deterrent submarines for the Royal Navy.

Government Organisations in Defence Sector

UKTI Defence & Security Organisation: UKTI Defence & Security Organisation (UKTI DSO) is part of the UK Trade & Investment (UKTI) - a UK Government department working with businesses based in the country to ensure their success in international markets. The UKTI DSO works with the domestic defence industry and the Ministry of Defence to promote UK equipment, products and services all across the world.

ADS Group Limited: The Aerospace Defence Security (ADS) is the premier trade organisation advancing the UK Aerospace, Defence, Security and Space industries. The organisation explores opportunities and priorities in the fields of defence, aerospace, security and space.

DEFENCE DEALS
Joint Ventures/ Collaboration Programmes

US

F-35 Joint Strike Fighter: Britain's BAE Systems is one of the main industrial partners of US's Lockheed Martin in the F-35 Lightening II Joint Strike Fighter programme. Britain is one of the leading financial contributors to the programme and over 100 British firms are involved in the project, including Rolls-Royce. The US has built the fifth-generation stealth fighter in partnership with eight countries, including the UK.

Europe/NATO

Eurofighter Typhoon: Four NATO member countries – Germany, UK, Italy and Spain – have collaborated in the design and development of the multi-role combat aircraft Eurofighter Typhoon. The Eurofighter Typhoon is Europe's largest military collaborative programme.

A400M: Seven NATO nations – Belgium, Britain, France, Germany, Luxembourg, Spain and Turkey – have partnered in the Airbus A400M military transport plane programme led by European conglomerate EADS. It is pegged as Europe's biggest defence project under which the new airlifter has been developed to replace the ageing military cargo carriers of several European air forces.

Sixth Generation Fighter: Britain has initiated talks with few European nations to develop a new sixth-generation fighter platform under the name "Tempest". The new advanced combat jet could be fielded to replace the Eurofighter Typhoons in future.

France

UAV & UCAV: Following the signing of a landmark defence cooperation treaty between UK and France in 2010, Britain's BAE Systems has joined hands with French giant Dassault Aviation to develop a medium altitude long endurance (MALE) unmanned aerial vehicle (UAV) system. The two firms have also agreed to collaborate on designing and building an unmanned combat air system (UCAS) for Europe.

Combat Aircraft Engine: Rolls-Royce and French aircraft engine maker Snecma – a subsidiary of Safran Group – have signed a contract with the UK Ministry of Defence to undertake studies into the next generation of UK and French combat aircraft engines, through their 50:50 Rolls-Royce Snecma Ltd joint venture, established in 2001.

India

BAeHAL: A joint venture between BAE Systems and India's Hindustan Aeronautics Ltd (HAL), BAeHAL provides Information Technology solutions and services to aerospace, defence and engineering industries.

DLSI: The Defence Land Systems India (DLSI) is a partnership between BAE Systems and private sector Indian firm Mahindra & Mahindra. The company manufactures military vehicles and select artillery systems.

Arms Export

Home to a vibrant domestic defence industry, UK is one of the leading exporters of military equipment worldwide. According to official data, total defence exports by the country in 2013 was worth £9.8 billion and in 2014, it sold £8.5 billion worth of defence equipment abroad. For 2015, military exports totalled £7.7 billion. The official export figure for 2016 was £5.9 billion. Largest military export markets for the UK were the Middle East, North America and Europe in 2016. In 2017, British defence firms secured export orders worth £9 billion, according to official figures. Saudi Arabia, India and Qatar remained three largest importers of defence equipment from Great Britain. In 2018, UK won defence orders worth £14 billion (US$17 billion) which was around 19% of global defence exports share for the year. The largest defence export markets were the Middle East, North America and Europe. In 2019, defence export order totalled £11 billion (US$14.2 billion) which was a decline of 21% from 2018. Major export markets were Middle East, Europe and North America.

Arms Import

UK significantly relies on its large and diverse domestic defence industry to meet the needs of its armed forces. It imports some defence equipment like missiles, armoured vehicles and aircraft, mostly from the US and often from Europe. With gradual reduction in its defence expenditure, the country has aimed at reducing its military imports while focusing on increasing exports.

DEFENCE BUDGET

UK is one of the world's largest defence spenders, positioning itself among the top ten in the global military expenditure index. It is the seventh largest military spender in the world. As a NATO member, Britain has so far met the alliance's commitment to spend at least 2% of its GDP on defence. However, marred by global economic slowdown and European financial crisis, the country has announced defence budgetary cuts. The Defence Ministry, however, remains committed to acquire new state-of-the-art military equipment and hardware including new armoured vehicles, ballistic missile submarines, destroyers, and a range of other advanced weapons and systems. For FY 2014-15, the official budgetary allocation was £36.43bn – adhering to the NATO stipulated standard of 2% of GDP. For 2015-16, the Govt. announced defence spending of £34.3 billion. For FY 2016-17, £35.1 billion was allocated for defence; for 2017-2018, it was £36.6 billion. For 2018-19 period, defence budget was £38.8 billion. Proposed defence budget for financial year 2020 - 21 was set at £41.5 billion (US $53 billion).

COUNTER-TERRORISM & NATIONAL SECURITY

International terrorism refers to terrorism that goes beyond national boundaries in terms of the methods used, the people that are targeted or the places from which the terrorists operate. According to UK Security Service MI5, the majority of terrorist attack plots in this country have been planned by British residents. There are several thousand individuals in the UK who support violent extremism or are engaged in Islamist extremist activity. Some British nationals travel overseas to train with extremist groups and return to the UK with the view to plan attacks, but increasingly the terrorist threat from within the UK emanates from individuals radicalised by individuals and material online. Once radicalised, an individual might decide to conduct an attack in the name of Islam without any prior signs of radicalisation. Simple, self-organised attacks by UK-based Islamist extremists have increased and are inherently harder to detect than more complex and ambitious plots.

The United Kingdom Terror Threat Levels, often referred to as UK Threat Levels, are the alert states that have been in use since 1 August 2006 by the British government to warn of forms of terrorist activity. Threat levels were originally produced by MI5's Counter-Terrorism Analysis Centre. The MI5 also added that, terrorist groups in Syria and Iraq, including Al Qaeda and the Islamic State of Iraq and the Levant (ISIL), possess both the intention and the capability to direct attacks against the West. Daesh, Al Qa'ida and affiliates remain committed to attacking UK and Western targets. The UK is a high-priority target for Islamist extremists and they pose a significant threat to our country and to our interests and citizens abroad. Despite the current main focus on terrorism originating from Syria and Iraq, the threat of terrorism also emanates from other parts of the Middle East and regions such as North, East and West Africa, South and South East Asia. Northern Ireland-related terrorism continues to pose a serious threat to British interests. Although the Provisional Irish Republican Army (PIRA) has ceased its terrorist campaign and is now committed to the political process, some dissident republican groups continue to mount terrorist attacks, primarily against the security forces. MI5 took on responsibility for national security intelligence work in Northern Ireland in 2007 and are working along with Police Service of Northern Ireland (PSNI).

MI5 has countered terrorist threats to UK interests, both at home and overseas, since the 1960s and the threat has developed significantly since then. Insurgency is organised armed resistance to authority. Counter-insurgency is a comprehensive civilian and military effort made to defeat an insurgency and address any core grievances. According to an address by MI5 Director General Ken McCallum in 2020, MI5's largest mission remains countering terrorism, Firstly Northern Ireland, where 22 years on from the Good Friday Agreement, great things have been achieved; Northern Ireland today does not suffer in the way that it did. Nearly everyone has moved on - but a few rejectionist terrorist groups, without meaningful community backing, persist. Secondly, Islamist extremist terrorism, which by volume remains UK's largest threat. Thirdly, Right Wing Terrorism. This threat is not, today, on the same scale as Islamist extremist terrorism. But it is growing. In order to deal with this, MI5 operate entirely the same system as on Islamist extremist terrorism.

Cyberterrorism is a new level of threat where a wide range of hostile actors use cyber to target the UK. Hostile actors conducting cyber espionage can target the government, military, business and individuals. They use computer networks, for example, to steal large volumes of sensitive data undetected. This might include intellectual property, research and development projects, strategic data on a company's merger and acquisition plans, or any other information that the owner might want to protect. According to MI5, the Centre for the Protection of National Infrastructure (CPNI) produces a range of advice and guidance to help protect the country's essential services against threats to national security. This includes protective measures for cyber security. CPNI also works in partnership with the National Cyber Security Centre (NCSC) on cyber security.

Proscribed terrorist groups or organisations

According to the gov.uk, 78 terrorist organisations are proscribed under the Terrorism Act 2000 and 14 organisations in Northern Ireland that were proscribed under previous legislation. List of proscribed international terrorist groups, as per UK.Gov website: 17 November Revolutionary Organisation (N17), Abdallah Azzam Brigades, including the Ziyad al-Jarrah Battalions (AAB), Abu Nidal Organisation (ANO), Abu Sayyaf Group (ASG), Ajnad Misr (Soldiers of Egypt), Al-Ashtar Brigades including Saraya al-Ashtar, Wa'ad Allah Brigades, Islamic Allah Brigades, Imam al-Mahdi Brigades and al-Haydariyah Brigades, Al-Gama'at al-Islamiya (GI), Al Ittihad Al Islamia (AIAI), Al Murabitun, Al-Mukhtar Brigades including Saraya al-Mukhtar, Al Qa'ida (AQ), Al Shabaab, Ansar Al Islam (AI), Ansar al-Sharia-Benghazi (AAS-B), Ansar Al Sharia-Tunisia (AAS-T), Ansar Al Sunna (AS), Ansar Bayt al-Maqdis (ABM), Ansaroul Islam, Ansarul Muslimina Fi Biladis Sudan, Armed Islamic Group (Groupe Islamique Armée) (GIA), Asbat Al-Ansar, Atomwaffen Division (AWD), Babbar Khalsa (BK), Basque Homeland and Liberty, Baluchistan Liberation Army (BLA), Boko Haram (Jama'atu Ahli Sunna Lidda Awati Wal Jihad) (BH), Egyptian Islamic Jihad (EIJ), Feuerkrieg Division (FKD), Global Islamic Media Front (GIMF), Groupe Islamique Combattant Marocain (GICM), Harakat al-Muqawamah al-Islamiyyah (Hamas), Harakat-Ul-Jihad-Ul-Islami (HUJI), Harakat-Ul-Jihad-Ul-Islami (Bangladesh) (HUJI-B), Harakat Mujahideen (HM), Haqqani Network (HQN), Hasam including Harakat Sawa'd Misr, Harakat Hasm and Hasm, Hizballah, Imarat Kavkaz (IK), Indian Mujahideen (IM), Islamic Army of Aden (IAA), Islamic Jihad Union (IJU), Islamic Movement of Uzbekistan (IMU), Islamic State of Iraq and the Levant (ISIL) also known as Dawlat al-'Iraq al-Islamiyya, Islamic State of Iraq (ISI), Islamic State of Iraq and Syria (ISIS) and Dawlat al Islamiya fi Iraq wa al Sham (DAISh) and the Islamic State in Iraq and Sham, Jaish e Mohammed (JeM) and splinter group Khuddam Ul-Islam (KuI) – JeM, Jamaah Anshorut Daulah, Jamaat Nusrat al-Islam Wal-Muslimin (JNIM) also known as Jamaat Nusrat al-Islam Wal-Muslimin (JNIM), Nusrat al-Islam, Nusrat al-Islam wal Muslimeen (NIM), including Ansar al-Dine (AAD), Macina Liberation Front (MLF), al-Murabitun, al-Qa'ida in the Maghreb and az-Zallaqa, Jamaat ul-Ahrar (JuA), Jammat-ul Mujahideen Bangladesh (JMB), Jamaat Ul-Furquan (JuF), Jaysh al Khalifatu Islamiya (JKI), Jeemah Islamiyah (JI), Jund al Khalifa-Algeria (JaK-A), Kateeba al-Kawthar (KaK), Lashkar e Tayyaba (LT), LTTE, Liwa al-Thawra, Minbar Ansar Deen, National Action, Mujahidin Indonesia Timur, Palestinian Islamic Jihad - Shaqaqi (PIJ), Partiya Karkeren Kurdistani (PKK), Popular Front for the Liberation of Palestine-General Command (PFLP-GC), Revolutionary Peoples' Liberation Party - Front (Devrimci Halk Kurtulus Partisi - Cephesi) (DHKP-C), Salafist Group for Call and Combat (Groupe Salafiste pour la Predication et le Combat) (GSPC), Saved Sect or Saviour Sect, Sipah-e Sahaba Pakistan (SSP) (Aka Millat-e Islami Pakistan (MIP), Sonnenkrieg Division (SKD), Tehrik Nefaz-e Shari'at Muhammadi (TNSM), Tehrik-e Taliban Pakistan (TTP), The Base, Turkestan Islamic Party (TIP), Turkiye Halk Kurtulus Partisi-Cephesi (THKP-C).

List of proscribed groups linked to Northern Ireland related terrorism, as per UK.Gov website: Continuity Army Council, Cumann na mBan, Fianna na hEireann, Irish National Liberation Army, Irish People's Liberation Organisation, Irish Republican Army, Loyalist Volunteer Force, Orange Volunteers, Red Hand Commando, Red Hand Defenders, Saor Eire, Ulster Defence Association, Ulster Freedom Fighters, Ulster Volunteer Force.

Major Incidents

Since 1970 the worst terrorist attack in the United Kingdom was the downing of Pan Am Flight 103. 270 people had lost their lives in the **bombing of Pan Am Flight 103** on December 21, 1988. The jet had exploded over Lockerbie, Scotland. Until 9/11, it was one of the world's most lethal acts of air terrorism and one of the largest and most complex acts of international terrorism ever investigated by the FBI.

The **Birmingham pub bombings** were carried out on 21 November 1974, when bombs exploded in two public houses in Birmingham, England. Police have said they believe the Provisional IRA planted the devices in the Mulberry Bush and the nearby Tavern in the Town. The Provisional Irish Republican Army never officially admitted responsibility for the Birmingham pub bombings.

The Warrenpoint ambush, also known as the Narrow Water ambush, the Warrenpoint massacre or the Narrow Water massacre, was a guerrilla attack by the Provisional Irish Republican Army on 27 August 1979.

The **Droppin Well bombing** or Ballykelly bombing occurred on 6 December 1982, when the Irish National Liberation Army (INLA) exploded a time bomb at a disco in Ballykelly, Northern Ireland.

On 4 December 1971, the Ulster Volunteer Force, an Ulster loyalist paramilitary group, detonated a bomb at **McGurk's Bar in Belfast, Northern Ireland.**

The **La Mon restaurant bombing** was an incendiary bomb attack by the Provisional Irish Republican Army on 17 February 1978.

The **M62 coach bombing** happened on 4 February 1974 on the M62 motorway in northern England, when a Provisional Irish Republican Army (IRA) bomb exploded in a coach carrying off-duty British Armed Forces personnel and their family members.

The **Omagh bombing** was a car bombing on 15 August 1998 in the town of Omagh in County Tyrone, Northern Ireland, United Kingdom. It was carried out by a group calling themselves the Real Irish Republican Army (Real IRA), a Provisional Irish Republican Army (IRA) splinter group who opposed the IRA's ceasefire and the Good Friday Agreement, signed earlier in the year.

The 7 July 2005 **London bombings,** often referred to as 7/7, were a series of four coordinated suicide attacks carried out by Islamist terrorists in London that targeted commuters travelling on the city's public transport system during the morning rush hour.

On 22 May 2017, an Islamist extremist suicide bomber detonated a shrapnel-laden homemade bomb as people were leaving the **Manchester Arena** following a concert by American singer Ariana Grande.

The **Parsons Green terror attack** was an explosion on a Tube train at a London station on September 15, 2017. 30 people were treated in hospital or an urgent care centre.

In 2020, on June 20 a Libyan refugee fatally stabbed three men and injured at least three others in **Reading.** Same year on January 9, two Islamic violent extremist inmates at a **maximum-security prison in Cambridgeshire,** stabbed one prison officer. On February 2, 2020 a recently released convicted terrorist under active counterterrorism surveillance stabbed two persons in Streatham, London.

On 14 November 2021, a taxi carrying a passenger arrived at the main entrance of **Liverpool Women's Hospital in Liverpool, England.** An improvised explosive device carried by the passenger ignited, killing him and injuring the driver.

The British people have endured many such multiple politically motivated attacks, attacks by right-wing extremists and attacks by Islamic extremists over the last few decades.

Combating Terrorism

The UK has a counter-terrorism strategy to prevent and disrupt plots against this country. According to the Counter Terrorism Policing, the **Counter Terrorism Policing network** stretches across the UK. They work alongside MI5 and other partners to find information and evidence to thwart terrorist planning and help bring perpetrators to justice. The Security Service, **MI5**, is responsible for protecting the UK against threats to national security. The Joint Terrorism Analysis Centre (JTAC) analyses and assesses all intelligence relating to international terrorism, at home and overseas. JTAC works especially closely with MI5's International Counter-Terrorism branch, which manages investigations into terrorist activity in the UK.

Around the UK there are eleven regional counter terrorism units (CTUs) and intelligence units (CTIUs). These units collaborate daily to confront the threat from terrorism. At the centre of the network sits the **Counter Terrorism Policing Headquarters** (CTPHQ), which devises policy and strategy, coordinates national projects and programmes, and provides a single national Counter Terrorism Policing voice for key stakeholders including government, intelligence agencies and other partners. Alongside the headquarters is the **National Operations Centre**, a central command made up of units that provide operational support to the national network. The **National CBRN Centre** brings together the emergency services to protect and prepare the UK against the chemical, biological, radiological and nuclear (CBRN) threat. Counter Terrorism Policing, therefore, is a collaboration of UK police forces working with the UK intelligence community to help protect the public and our national security by preventing, deterring and investigating terrorist activity. The **National Counter Terrorism Security Office** (NaCTSO) is a police hosted unit that supports the 'protect and prepare' strands of the government's counter terrorism strategy. It is a part of the National Police Chiefs' Council (NPCC).

United Kingdom passed the **Terrorism Act 2000**, which is the first of a number of general Terrorism Acts passed by the Parliament of the United Kingdom. It superseded and repealed the Prevention of Terrorism (Temporary Provisions) Act 1989 and the Northern Ireland (Emergency Provisions) Act 1996. Under the act, UK Home Secretary may proscribe an organisation if they believe it is concerned in terrorism. The **Terrorism Act 2006** is an Act of the Parliament of the United Kingdom that received royal assent on 30 March 2006, after being introduced on 12 October 2005. The Act creates new offences related to terrorism, and amends existing one. According to The Crown Prosecution Service (CPS), the **Counter-Terrorism and Border Security Act 2019** updates existing counter-terrorism legislation to ensure that it is fit for the digital age and reflect contemporary patterns of radicalisation. The **Counter-Terrorism and Sentencing Act (2021)** ends the prospect of early release for anyone convicted of a serious terror offence and forces them to spend their whole term in jail. The most dangerous offenders - such as those found guilty of preparing or carrying out acts of terrorism where lives were lost or at risk - now face a minimum of 14 years in prison and up to 25 years on licence, with stricter supervision. The **Independent Reviewer of Terrorism Legislation** is an independent person, appointed by the Home Secretary and by the Treasury for a renewable three-year term and tasked with reporting to the Home Secretary and to Parliament on the operation of counter-terrorism law in the UK.

According to US State Department, Country Reports on Terrorism 2020, the UK launched the 2025 Border Strategy consultation in June to seek views on strengthening UK border security by 2025, using new digital systems. The UK is a member of FATF and has observer or cooperating status in the following FATF-style regional bodies: observer of the Asia/Pacific Group on Money Laundering, observer of the Eastern and Southern Africa Anti-Money Laundering Group, observer of MENAFATF, and a cooperating and supporting nation of CFATF. Its FIU, the UK Financial Intelligence Unit, is a member of the Egmont Group. The UK is a member of the Defeat-ISIS CIFG.

Military Intervention

Operation Banner was the operational name for the British Armed Forces' operation in Northern Ireland from 1969 to 2007, as part of the Troubles. It was the longest continuous deployment in British military history. This involved counter-insurgency and supporting the police in carrying out internal security duties such as guarding key points, mounting checkpoints and patrols, carrying out raids and searches, riot control and bomb disposal.

Operation Shader is the operational code name given to the contribution of the United Kingdom in the ongoing military intervention against the Islamic State of Iraq and the Levant. British Army troops are not in a combat role in Iraq but are on the ground with coalition partners providing training and equipment to Iraqi Security Forces (ISF) and Kurdish Security Forces (KSF). The Royal Air Force began the first airstrikes against Daesh (also known as ISIL, Islamic State, or ISIS) in 2014. Between then and 2017, RAF Typhoon, Tornado and Reaper aircraft have struck Daesh more than 1,300 times in Iraq and over 260 times in Syria. The UK's Carrier Strike Group joined in June 2021 the fight against Daesh with F-35 jets carrying out their very first combat missions from HMS Queen Elizabeth.

Daesh poses a threat to UK national security as it seeks to expand its terror network, using propaganda to radicalise and recruit citizens from the UK and across the world. The United Kingdom deployed sea, air and land assets for the invasion against the Taliban/al-Qaeda in 2001, designated *Operation Veritas.*

Operation Herrick was the codename under which all British operations in the War in Afghanistan were conducted from 2002 to the end of combat operations in 2014. It consisted of the British contribution to the NATO-led International Security Assistance Force (ISAF), and support to the American-led Operation Enduring Freedom (OEF).

Operation Temperer is a British government plan to deploy troops to support and free up police officers in key locations following a major terrorist attack or major public disorder. The plan was activated for the first time on 23 May 2017 following the Manchester Arena bombing. Military personnel again replaced police officers on armed guarding duties when the operation was activated again on 15 September 2017 during the Parsons Green bombing when the threat level was raised to critical.

CONCLUSION

Being a key strategic ally of the US, Britain

(Image Credit: NATO)

has over the years maintained its military force projection capability in the world. It has been engaged in a significant number of combat as well as peacekeeping operations around the globe. The nation has followed a cardinal principle of defence and security operations to seek and maintain an edge over potential adversaries, both to increase its chances of success in hostile situations, and also to protect its national assets and interests. However, in the wake of rapid geostrategic alterations at global stage where Europe no longer remains the cynosure of world affairs and Asia Pacific steadily taking up that position, the United Kingdom's military prowess appears to be steadily eroding. After the country decided to exit from the European Union following a referendum in 2016, future military policies to be adopted by Britain also appear uncertain. In recent past, plans to create a European Union (EU) Army with its headquarters at Brussels, Belgium, has been aborted following strong opposition from London. The country is already facing defence budgetary constraints and funding issues involving mega military projects which could get complicated further in the wake of Covid-19 health crisis as well as Brexit (UK's exit from the EU). Consequently, Britain may lose key military capabilities that could deal a major blow to its global power projection capabilities as well as in countering home-grown security threats, including terrorism, in the foreseeable future.

CONTACT DETAILS
Ministry of Defence
Main Building
Whitehall, London
SW1A 2HB
United Kingdom
Tel: 020 7218 9000

Websites
Ministry of Defence: www.mod.uk
British Army: www.army.mod.uk/
Royal Navy: www.royalnavy.mod.uk/
Royal Air Force: www.raf.mod.uk/

STRATEGIC INFORMATION
UNITED STATES OF AMERICA
(Capital: Washington, DC)

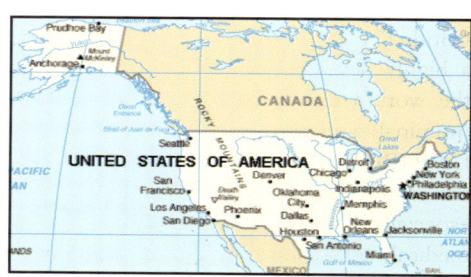

INTRODUCTION
Area: 9,833,517 sq km
Population: 334,998,398 (July 2021 est.)
Coastline: 19,924 km
Maritime claims: Territorial sea: 12 nm
Contiguous zone: 24 nm
Exclusive Economic Zone: 200 nm
Continental shelf: not specified

GEOPOLITICAL IMPORTANCE
The United States of America (USA) is situated in North America, and consists of 48 contiguous states and the non-contiguous states of Alaska and Hawaii. Alaska, separated from the contiguous USA by Canada, is the largest state. Hawaii, occupying an archipelago is in the central Pacific, southwest of North America. The 48 states are between the Atlantic and Pacific oceans, south of Canada and north of Mexico. The state of Alaska is in the northwest of the continent, with Canada to the east and Russia to the west across the Bering Strait. The country also possesses several territories in the Caribbean and Pacific. The country shares land borders with Canada and Mexico and maritime (water) borders with Russia, Cuba, and The Bahamas. The United States also has overseas territories with varying levels of independence and organisation.

POLITICAL OVERVIEW
The United States is a Federal Union of fifty states. It is a constitutional republic and representative democracy. Citizens are usually subject to three levels of government: federal, state, and local. The federal government is composed of three branches; Legislative, Executive & Judicial. The House of Representatives has 435 voting members.

The Senate has 100 members with each state having two senators. The President of the United States, Congress, and judiciary share powers reserved to the national government, and the federal government shares sovereignty with the state governments. The executive branch consists of the President and those to whom the President's powers are delegated. The President is both the head of state and government, as well as the military commander-in-chief and chief diplomat.

KEY POLITICAL PERSONS

PRESIDENT: Joe Biden

VICE-PRESIDENT: Kamala Harris

SECRETARY OF STATE: Antony Blinken

ECONOMY

The US economy is the second largest in the world. The economy of the United States is a highly developed mixed economy. It has the world's eighth-highest per capita GDP (nominal) and the tenth-highest per capita GDP (PPP) in 2019. US firms are at or near the forefront in technological advances, especially in computers, pharmaceuticals, and medical, aerospace, and military equipment. Imported oil accounts for more than 50% of US consumption and oil has a major impact on the overall health of the economy. In the US, private individuals and business firms make most of the decisions, and the federal and state governments buy needed goods and services predominantly in the private marketplace.

The US is the world's largest importer and the second-largest exporter. It has free trade agreements with several nations, including NAFTA, Australia, South Korea, Israel, and few others. Real gross domestic product (GDP) increased at an annual rate of 2.0 percent in the third quarter of 2021, following an increase of 6.7 percent in the second quarter. The increase in third quarter GDP reflected the continued economic impact of the COVID-19 pandemic.

GDP (official exchange rate): USD 22,600.270 billion (2021 est.), USD 20,900.700 billion (2020 est.)

Real Growth Rate (GDP): -3.5 % (2021), -5.907 % (2020)

Industries: Highly diversified, world leading, high-technology innovator, second-largest industrial output in the world; petroleum, steel, motor vehicles, aerospace, telecommunications, chemicals, electronics, food processing, consumer goods, lumber, mining

Crude oil – proved reserves: 44.191 million barrels (2019 est.)

Natural gas - proved reserves: 494.91 Tcf (209 est.)

Shale gas – proved reserves: 353 trillion cubic feet (2019 est.)

Total Exports: USD2,127,250,000,000 (2020), USD2,528,270,000,000 (2019 est.)

Export Commodities: Refined petroleum, crude petroleum, cars and vehicle parts, integrated circuits, aircraft (2019)

Major Markets: Canada 17%, Mexico 16%, China 7%, Japan 5% (2019)

Total Imports: USD2,808,960,000,000 (2020), USD3,105,130,000,000 (2019 est.)

Import Commodities: Cars, crude petroleum, computers, broadcasting equipment, packaged medicines (2019)

Major Suppliers: China 18%, Mexico 15%, Canada 13%, Japan 6%, Germany 5% (2019)

DEFENCE & SECURITY

The US military is one of the largest militaries in terms of number of personnel. They consist of the Army, Navy, Marine Corps, Air Force, and Coast Guard. The Dept. of Defence (DoD) is America's oldest and largest government agency. Five of the branches, the United States Army, United States Marine Corps, United States Navy, United States Air Force, and United States Space Force are organised under the Department of Defence's military departments. The United States Coast Guard is nominally under the Department of Homeland Security, The DoD is charged with coordinating and supervising all agencies and functions of the government relating directly to national security and the United States armed forces. Among the many DoD agencies are the Missile Defence Agency, the Defence Advanced Research Projects Agency (DARPA), the Pentagon Force Protection Agency (PFPA), the Defence Intelligence Agency (DIA), the National Geospatial-Intelligence Agency (NGA), and the National Security Agency (NSA). The United States has a strong tradition of civilian control of the military. The President is the overall head of the military, and helps form military policy but the United States Dept. of Defence (DoD), a federal executive Dept., is the principal organ by which military policy is carried out. The US military is one of the largest armed forces in terms of number of personnel. The US Air Force is the world's largest air force, the US Navy is the world's largest navy by tonnage, and the US Navy and the US Marine Corps combined are the world's second largest air arm. There are eleven unified combatant commands that come in two types. Geographic commands, such as Africa, Central, European, Indo-Pacific, Northern, Southern and Space commands are responsible for planning and operations in a certain geographic area. Functional commands, such as Cyber, Special Operations, Strategic, and Transportation commands are responsible for a functional activity that crosses geographic boundaries.

The US armed forces as a whole possess large quantities of advanced and powerful equipment, along with widespread placement of forces around the world, gives them significant capabilities in both defence and power projection. Personnel are deployed in many countries around the world, with more than 369,000 of its 1,580,255 active-duty personnel serving outside the United States and its territories.

The US is currently moving towards strategic re-balance in the Asia-Pacific region, which is also known as Washington's 'pivot-to-Asia' policy. The rebalancing to this region is a very important part of the new US Defence strategy. US have also appointed a new military commander in Asia-Pacific. The United States continues to face a rapidly changing security environment, as warfare evolves across all domains. US continue to rebalance the Dept.'s posture and presence to the Asia-Pacific while maintaining a focus on the Middle East. It also means working closely with European partners to strengthen their capabilities, maximising the impact of a relatively small US presence in Africa.

KEY DEFENCE PERSONS

DEFENCE SECRETARY: Lloyd J. Austin III

CHAIRMAN, JOINT CHIEFS OF STAFF: Gen. Mark Alexander Milley

CHIEF OF STAFF OF ARMY: Gen. James C. McConville

CHIEF OF NAVAL PERSONNEL: Adm. Michael Gilday

CHIEF OF STAFF OF AIR FORCE: Gen. Charles Q. Brown, Jr.

COMMANDANT OF MARINE CORPS: Gen. David H. Berger

COMMANDER OF STRATEGIC COMMAND: Gen. Charles A. Richard

CHIEF OF SPACE OPERATIONS: Gen John W. "Jay" Raymond

Internal Conflict

Terrorism: The Bureau of Counterterrorism and Countering Violent Extremism's mission is to promote US national security by taking a leading role in developing coordinated strategies and approaches to defeat terrorism abroad and securing the counterterrorism cooperation of international partners. The National Counterterrorism Centre (NCTC) is a United States government organisation responsible for national and international counterterrorism efforts. NCTC advises the United States on terrorism. The Counterterrorism Division (CTD) is a division of the National Security Branch of the Federal Bureau of Investigation. CTD investigates terrorist threats inside the United States, provides information on terrorists outside the country, and tracks known terrorists worldwide. The USA PATRIOT Act is an Act of Congress that was signed into law by President George W. Bush on October 26, 2001. The act arms law enforcement with new tools to detect and prevent terrorism, also improves counter-terrorism efforts in several ways. USA PATRIOT Act stands for "Uniting and Strengthening America by Providing Appropriate Tools Required to Intercept and Obstruct Terrorism Act of 2001". On May 26, 2011, President Barack Obama signed the PATRIOT Sunsets Extension Act of 2011. Parts of the Patriot Act expired on June 1, 2015. In 2020, efforts to extend the provisions were not passed by the House of Representatives, and as such, the law has expired. The USA Freedom Act is a US law enacted on June 2, 2015 that restored in modified form several provisions of the Patriot Act. USA FREEDOM stands for "Uniting and Strengthening America by Fulfilling Rights and Ending Eavesdropping, Dragnet-collection and Online Monitoring Act". According to a 2017 report by the US Government Accountability Office, of the 85 violent extremist incidents that resulted in death since September 12, 2001, right-wing violent extremist groups were responsible for 62 (73%) while radical Islamist violent extremists were responsible for 23 (27%). Terrorist threats have evolved from large-group conspiracies toward lone-offender attacks. These individuals often radicalize online and mobilize to violence quickly. International and domestic violent extremists have developed an extensive presence on the Internet through messaging platforms and online images, videos, and publications. Social media has also allowed both international and domestic terrorists to gain unprecedented, virtual access to people living in the United States in an effort to enable homeland attacks. The ISIS, in particular, encourages sympathizers to carry out simple attacks wherever they are located—or to travel to ISIS-held territory in Iraq and Syria and join its ranks as foreign fighters. This message has resonated with supporters in the United States and abroad, as per FBI.

External Conflict

Afghanistan War (Present): On 28 December 2014, NATO formally ended combat operations in Afghanistan and transferred full security responsibility to the Afghan government, via a ceremony in Kabul. In May 2014, the United States announced that its combat operations would end in 2014, leaving just a small residual force in the country until the end of 2016. Obama also announced that all US forces, with the exception of a normal embassy presence, would be removed from Afghanistan by the end of 2016. These plans were confirmed with the signing of the Bilateral Security Agreement between the United States and Afghanistan on 30 September 2014. The relatively small American presence there has been active in executing airstrikes as well as providing close air support for the Afghan forces. As of December 2016, there are 9,800 US service members in Afghanistan. The US and its 39 coalition partners in Afghanistan are committed to providing support to Afghanistan for through 2020. On 21 August 2017, US President Donald Trump stated that he would be expanding the American presence in Afghanistan, without giving details on how or when. On 19 September 2017, the Trump Administration deployed another 3,000 US troops to Afghanistan. They will add to the approximately 11,000 US troops already serving in Afghanistan, bringing the total to at least 14,000 US troops stationed in Afghanistan. As of May 2017, over 13,000 foreign troops remain in Afghanistan without any formal plans to withdraw, and continue their fight against the Taliban, which remains by far the largest single group fighting against the Afghan government and foreign troops. In 2020, the US and Taliban have signed a peace deal in Doha, Qatar bringing closure to 18 years of conflict and if the Taliban upholds their side of the deal then US and troops from NATO allies will withdraw from Afghanistan in 14 months. The Afghan government was not a party to the deal and rejected its terms regarding release of prisoners. The US, under the presidency of Joe Biden, completed the withdrawal of its forces from Kabul, ending 20 years of war that culminated in the Taliban's return to power on August 15. The Taliban insurgents stormed across the country, capturing all major cities in a matter of days, two weeks before the US was set to complete its troop withdrawal after a costly two-decade war, which followed by the dramatic fall of the Afghan national government to the Taliban. US Secretary of State Antony Blinken said the US engaged with the Taliban during the past few weeks for evacuation operations. The Taliban on August 15 declared victory after President Ghani fled the country and his government collapsed. According to the US Department of Defence, the total military expenditure in Afghanistan (from October 2001 until December 2020) was USD825 billion, with about another USD130 billion spent on reconstruction projects.

Iraq (2014-Present): The US-led intervention in Iraq took place in 2014, to eliminate threat by ISIL in the region. By December 2017, ISIL had no remaining territory in Iraq, following the 2017 Western Iraq campaign. Currently, the US estimates to have around 4,500 troops in Iraq. In 2014, an increase of 350 servicemen was announced to be sent to Baghdad, increasing US forces in Baghdad to 820, and increasing US forces in Iraq to 1,213. With the arrival of a new administration, a change in policy was instituted regarding the disclosure of current troop levels as well as the timing of any additional deployments to the area. As of July 2, 2018, the US still maintains a military presence of 5,000 troops stationed in Iraq with the task of helping train and assist Iraqi forces. In addition to direct military intervention, the American-led coalition provided extensive support to the Iraqi Security Forces via training, intelligence, and personnel. The total cost of coalition support to the ISF, excluding direct military operations, was officially announced at USD3.5-plus billion by March 2019.

Southeast Asia: Southeast Asia has a long history of important security and economic ties to the United States and is also of strategic interest. The Special Operations Command Pacific, known as SOCPAC provides unconventional warfare task force support for operations in Southeast Asia. SOCPAC annually conducts small unit exchanges, joint and combined training events, and operational deployments throughout the Pacific. Units are used for counterdrug and humanitarian demining operations, training forces in countries such as Thailand, Laos, Cambodia, Vietnam, and the Philippines. As a subordinate unified command of the United States Pacific Command, SOCPAC units deploy throughout the Pacific. Political and security discussions have focused on the role of the United States in maintaining peace and stability in the region, the South China Sea disputes and the threat of terrorism.

Africa: US AFRICOM is responsible for all US Dept. of Defence operations, exercises, and security cooperation on the African continent, its island nations, and surrounding waters. Operation Enduring Freedom-Horn of Africa (OEF-HOA) is the name of the military operations for combating terrorism and piracy in the Horn of Africa and is run by the Africa Command. In North-eastern Africa, allies of the OEFHOA effort include Sudan, Somalia, Djibouti, Ethiopia, Eritrea, Seychelles and Kenya. US Africa Command (AFRICOM) Operation Enduring Freedom Trans Sahara (OEF-TS) provides military support to the Trans Sahara Counter Terrorism Partnership (TSCTP) programme. OEF-TS partnership comprises the United States and ten African countries: Algeria, Burkina Faso, Morocco, Tunisia, Chad, Mali, Mauritania, Niger, Nigeria, and Senegal. United States has also committed to work with African partners to rid the continent and the world of terrorism by addressing drivers of conflict that lead to radicalisation and recruitment in the first place, and building the institutional law enforcement capacity of African nations. In the Horn of Africa, CJTF-HOA is the US Africa Command organisation that conducts operations in the region to enhance partner nation capacity, promote regional security and stability, dissuade conflict, and protect US and coalition interests. US Army Africa (USARAF) conducts sustained security engagement with African land forces to promote security, stability, and peace. As the air component of USAFRICOM, US Air Forces Africa (AFAFRICA) conducts sustained security engagement and operations to promote air safety, security, and development in Africa. US Marine Forces Africa (MARFORAF) conducts operations, exercises, training, and security cooperation activities throughout the African continent. NAVAF's primary mission is to improve the maritime security capability and capacity of African partners. SOCAFRICA conducts persistent, networked and distributed special operations in direct support of the United States Africa Command to promote regional stability and prosperity in Africa.

Syria: In Oct 2019, President Donald Trump ordered the remaining US forces out of northern Syria, as a Turkish invasion targeting US-allied Syrian Kurdish fighters against the Islamic State expanded deep into Syrian territory. Since September 2014, the US had been conducting air strikes on IS and other jihadist groups in Syria as part of an international coalition against the jihadist group. Operation Inherent Resolve officially refers to the US's military actions against ISIL, specifically the campaign in Iraq and the campaign in Syria. US and partner nation military forces continued to attack ISIL terrorists in Syria in Nov 2014 using bomber, fighter and remotely piloted aircraft to conduct twenty-three airstrikes. US Special Operations Forces are playing an important role on the ground in the fight against ISIS in Syria. The missile strike on the Shayrat Airbase conducted by the US on April 2017, marked the start of deliberate direct military action by the US military against the Syrian Ba'athist government's and pro-government forces. The US government has worked closely with the Global Coalition remains committed to ISIS's enduring defeat through stabilisation support to liberated areas, facilitating the return of displaced individuals, finding long-term solutions for detained foreign ISIS fighters, and promoting justice and accountability efforts in Syria and Iraq.

THREAT PERSPECTIVE

United States face a spectrum of challenges, including violent transnational extremist networks, hostile states armed with weapons of mass destruction, rising regional powers, emerging space and cyber threats, natural and pandemic disasters, and a growing competition for resources. The range of security challenges the country faces right now are beyond Iraq and Afghanistan. There are issues which pertain to Iran, North Korea and modernisation.

Iran: US fears about Iran's nuclear intentions, mainly after the country said it plans to triple its output of higher-grade uranium. Iran, on the other hand, says the aim of its enrichment programme is energy security. Iran currently has short- and medium- range missiles with improved lethality and more accurate guidance systems. Iran's launch of a medium range, solid fuel ballistic missile demonstrates its ability to hit targets in Israel and southern Europe. Iranian citizens were temporary banned from entering the United States by the executive order "Protecting the Nation From Foreign Terrorist Entry Into the United States by the Trump administration." On October 13, 2017, US President Donald Trump announced that the US would not make the certification provided for under US domestic law, but stopped short of terminating the Iran nuclear deal. In May 2018, Donald Trump decided to pull out of the JCPA, announcing he would reimpose economic sanctions on Iran effective from 4 November that year. In response, the Iranian president Hassan Rouhani said that if needed he would start industrial enrichment without any limitations. In July 2018, Iran threatened to close off the Strait of Hormuz if US decided to reimpose oil sanctions on Iran following US withdrawal from the JCPOA. As of 2018, Supreme Leader of Iran Ali Khamenei banned direct talks with the United States. In March 2019, US urged UN to impose new sanctions on Iran over launches. In Sept 2019, Iran ruled out the accusations of the United States of it conducting drone attacks on Saudi Arabia's oil fields. Iran also warned that it is ready for a "full-fledged" war. Military tensions escalated between USA and Iran in 2019-2020 in the Persian Gulf region. With the rise in confrontation, USA withdrew from Joint Comprehensive Plan of Action (JCPOA), designated Islamic Revolutionary Guard

Corps (IRGC) as terrorist organisation and imposed fresh sanctions against Iran. By the end of 2021, Iran, Russia, China and the European countries resumed negotiations in Vienna to revive the 2015 nuclear agreement, known as the Joint Comprehensive Plan of Action (JCPOA), as Iran has refused to hold direct talks with the US.

North Korea: US President met with North Korean Supreme Leader Kim Jong-un on June 12, 2018, in Singapore, in the first summit meeting between the leaders of USA and North Korea. They signed a joint statement, agreeing to security guarantees for North Korea, new peaceful relations, reaffirmation of the denuclearisation of the Korean Peninsula, recovery of soldiers' remains, and follow-up negotiations between high-level officials. As per media reports, interactions between the Washington and Pyongyang continue where President Trump commended Kim Jong-Un for ceasing nuclear testing, dismantling several military facilities, releasing American hostages, and returning POW/MIA remains. Trump reaffirmed that sanctions will continue to be held on North Korea until total denuclearisation is achieved. In June 2019, US President Donald Trump and South Korean President Moon Jae-in visited North Korean leader Kim Jong-un at the Joint Security Area. At present the diplomatic relations between US and North Korea is ceased due to differences in denuclearisation. In 2021, US President attempted a new outreach to North Korea to discuss a possible declaration to end conflict between both North and South Korea.

China: The partnership between US & China is such that both nations regards each other as a potential adversary as well as a strategic partner. China and the US have mutual political, economic, and security interests. China is one ascendant country with the potential for competing with the United States. China and USA have been described as engaging in a race of military technology. China's arsenal poses serious threat to the United States. Cyber-threats coming from China are also on the rise. China is also developing capacity for attacking satellites and for cyberwarfare. The two countries remain in dispute over territorial issues in the South China Sea. China and the US maintain effective communication and coordination on major regional and international as well as global issues such as Korean Peninsula, Iranian nuclear issue, South Asia and other security issues. In recent years, China and the US have conducted constructive dialogues and productive cooperation on Asia-Pacific affairs. Both the countries are engaged in a race of advancing military technology. The then US administration has concentrated on two issues in its relationship with China- North Korea and trade. The US has emphasised the need to enhance bilateral trust through increased high-level exchanges, formal dialogues, and expanded people-to-people ties. China and USA are locked in an ongoing trade war as each country has introduced tariffs on goods traded with the other. The trade war has caused a significant deterioration in China–United States relations as the countries exchanged tit-for-tat tariffs for over a year. Since May 2020, the relationship between both the countries deteriorated with the blame-game for worldwide COVID-19 pandemic. Tension remained between both the countries under Joe Biden administration. President Biden in his foreign policy address had described China as the most serious competitor to the US and vowed to confront Beijing on various fronts, including human rights, intellectual property and economic policy. Secretary of State Antony Blinken in his first major foreign policy speech described the US' relationship with China as the "biggest geopolitical test" of the 21st century and say that Washington will engage Beijing from a position of strength.

Russia: The relationship between the United States and Russia is among the most critical bilateral relationships in the world. Both the countries have diverse interests in nuclear security and non-proliferation, regional security in Europe and Eurasia, countering terrorism and violent extremism, and conflict situations in the regions of Middle East. Ukraine crisis, Syrian civil war and mutual sanctions imposed has casts shadow on US relationship with Russia. On Sept 2015, US and Russia resume military relations to increase fighting against the Islamic State. Representatives from both the countries also met in UN Headquarters to discuss the situation in Syria and Ukraine. On April 2010, US President Barack Obama and Russian President Dmitry Medvedev signed a new START treaty to reduce the number of active nuclear weapons from 2,200 to 1,550. The grant of temporary asylum to US whistle-blower Mr. Edward Snowden by Russia has created a diplomatic turmoil between US and Russia. Both the countries have conducted joint military manoeuvres, training and counter-terrorist exercises in recent past. Currently, as per reports, US-Russian relations have deteriorated sharply, amid a salvo of accusations and disagreements, to their lowest point since the end of the Cold War. During the start of Trump administration, both governments initially were positive about improvement of relations between the US and Russia. In March 2017, the US military for the first time publicly accused Russia of having deployed a land-based cruise missile. On 25 March 2017, the US imposed new sanctions against eight Russian companies in connection with the Iran, North Korea, and Syria Non-proliferation Act. Both Donald Trump in April and the Russian government in May characterised the relationship between the countries as frozen and lacking any progress. In July 2018, Russia and US summit between both the Presidents took place in Helsinki, Finland. Topics of discussion included the situation in Syria, the Ukrainian crisis and nuclear arms control. US under Trump administration is withdrawing from the landmark Intermediate-Range Nuclear Forces (INF) Treaty with Russia. As per media reports, the reason for exit from INF are that US need to counter a Chinese arms build-up in the Pacific. The US formally suspended the treaty in February 2019 and Russia too did so in response. The US formally withdrew from the treaty in August 2019. In 2021, Presidents Biden and Putin, at the summit in Geneva, discussed ambassadors, nuclear weapons and more. Putin also said the Russian foreign ministry and the US State Department would begin consultations on other vexing diplomatic issues. Biden and Putin also instructed their diplomats to begin laying the groundwork for a new phase of arms control.

STRATEGIC RELATIONS

India: India and the US share an extensive and expanding cultural, strategic, military, and economic relationship. India and US relations has recently achieved significant milestones with increase in bilateral trade & investment, cooperation on global security matters, upgraded representation in trade & investment forums and admission into multilateral control regimes like MTCR and joint-manufacturing through technology sharing arrangements. India and US work closely at United Nations, G-20, Association of Southeast Asian Nations (ASEAN) Regional Forum, International Monetary Fund, World Bank, and World Trade Organisation. US support for India's bid for permanent membership to UN Security Council as well as India's entry to Nuclear Suppliers Group, Wassenaar Arrangement and Australia Group. In 2016, India and United States signed Logistics Exchange Memorandum of Agreement, a bilateral deal on military logistics exchange including defence technology collaboration, expanding military-to-military exchanges. India-US bilateral cooperation is broad-based and multi-sectoral, covering trade and investment, defence and security, education, science and technology, cyber security, high-technology, civil nuclear energy, space technology and applications, clean energy, environment, agriculture and health. India and the US share an extensive cultural, strategic, military, and economic relationship. Over the years, the defence relationship between India and the United States has steadily improved. US recognise India as a key to its strategic interests as India plays a more active role in the broader Asia-Pacific region. India and USA are making efforts to transform defence ties to pursue opportunities for technological collaboration in the field of joint research and co-production of major defence equipment. India and the US have established a Defence Trade and Technology Initiative (DTTI) aimed at simplifying technology transfer policies and exploring possibilities of co-development and co-production to invest the defence relationship with strategic value. Both countries continue to engage under several bilateral institutional mechanisms. In Sept 2018, India and the US signed the foundational agreement COMCASA on the sidelines of the inaugural 2+2 dialogue. COMCASA stands for Communications Compatibility and Security Agreement and is one of the four foundational agreements that the US signs with allies and close partners to facilitate interoperability between militaries and sale of high end technology. COMCASA allows India to procure transfer specialised equipment for encrypted communications for US origin military platforms like the C-17, C-130 and P-8Is. India had signed the General Security Of Military Information Agreement (GSOMIA) in 2002 and the Logistics Exchange Memorandum of Agreement (LEMOA) in 2016. In December 2019, the United States hosted the second 2+2 Ministerial Dialogue in Washington led by the US Secretaries of State and Defence and their Indian counterparts, at which both sides reaffirmed India's status as a Major Defence Partner and deepened cooperation on maritime security, interoperability, and information sharing. India is also a member of the Indian Ocean Rim Association (IORA), at which the US is a dialogue partner. Recently, in a reflection of their fast expanding strategic ties, India and US ink the landmark defence pact, Basic Exchange and Cooperation Agreement (BECA), that will provide for sharing of high-end military technology, geospatial maps and classified satellite data between their militaries.

Japan: The relationship between the United States and Japan is very strong which includes political, economic and military alliances. Japan provides bases as well as financial and material support to US forward-deployed forces, which are essential for maintaining stability in the region. Because of the two countries' combined economic and technological impact on the world, the US-Japan relationship has become global in scope. Japan and the United States have closely cooperated on a vast array of global issues. In 2012, both the countries have agreed to discuss updating 15-year-old guidelines on their security alliance in view of China's growing military presence in the region. The two sides would be involved in strategic discussions reviewing their defence roles in the face of China's military build-up and its naval expansion, formulating joint plans and promoting joint use of defence bases. At present, around 50,000 US troops and more than 10,000 marines are stationed in Japan, many of them on the far southern island chain of Okinawa. Japan contributes irreplaceable political, financial, and moral support to US-Japan diplomatic efforts. The US consults with Japan and the South Korea on policy regarding North Korea. The United States coordinates with Japan and Australia under the auspices of the Trilateral Strategic Dialogue and the Security and Defence Cooperation Forum. In Southeast Asia, US-Japan cooperation advances maritime security and economic development. Outside Asia, Japanese political and financial support has significantly assisted US efforts on a variety of global issues arising, including countering ISIL and terrorism, etc. Japan and US together participates in the United Nations, G7, G-20, Organisation for Economic Cooperation and Development, Asia-Pacific Economic Cooperation forum, ASEAN Regional Forum, International Monetary Fund, World Bank, and World Trade Organisation. Japan and the United States are also making progress toward our shared vision of a free and open Indo-Pacific region through partnerships such as the Japan-U.S. Strategic Energy Partnership (JUSEP), Japan-U.S. Strategic Digital Economy Partnership (JUSDEP), and the Japan-U.S. Mekong Power Partnership (JUMPP).

Pakistan: Pakistan is a major non-NATO ally of the United States, which is the second-largest supplier of military equipment to Pakistan after China and largest economic aid contributor. US security assistance to Pakistan is focused on strengthening the counterterrorism (CT) and counterinsurgency (COIN) capabilities of the Pakistan security forces, and promoting closer security ties and interoperability with the US. After the September 11 attacks, Pakistan became a key ally in the war on terrorism with the United States. The country provides key intelligence and logistical support for the United States. Though both the countries are allies and share strong strategic relationship, there were various setbacks and constantly remains a significant mistrust, which continues to deter successful cooperation in defeating terrorist organisations. Though the relationship between both countries became increasingly strained in recent years, US continue to supply military equipment & assistance to Pakistan and is one of Pakistan's largest donors of foreign aids and counterinsurgency funds. In Jan 2018, US suspended about USD 2 billion in security aid to Pakistan, freezing all security assistance, for failing to clamp down on the Afghan Taliban and the Haqqani Network terror groups and dismantle their safe havens, a White House official noted. In Sept 2018, the US DoD announced that they would postpone the transfer of approximately USD 300 million in military aid to Pakistan. The reason is due to a lack of effort by the Pakistan Government in combating terrorist organisations in their country. In August 2019, the United States slashed the aid to the cash-strapped nation by nearly USD440 million, bringing down its commitment to just USD4.1 billion.

Israel: The United States and Israel maintain a strategic and supportive alliance which is an important part of US Govt's overall Middle East policy. While Israel receives massive security support and a diplomatic umbrella from the United States, the US knows it can view Israel as a military extension of their policies. The US-Israel bilateral relationship is strong, anchored by over USD3 billion in Foreign Military Financing annually. Israel is one of the United States' two original major non-NATO allies in the Middle East. The US and Israel are engaged in extensive strategic, political and military cooperation. This cooperation is broad and includes American aid, intelligence sharing, and joint military exercises. The US also participates in a high level of exchanges with Israel, to include joint military exercises, military research, and weapons development. In addition to financial and military aid, the United States also provides political support to Israel. USA was the first country to recognise Israel as a state in 1948, and the first to recognise Jerusalem as the capital of Israel in 2017. In 2019, President Trump signed the United States recognition of the Golan Heights as part of Israel.

South Korea: South Korea is one of America's closest allies. The relationship have been most extensive since 1948, when the US helped establish capitalism in South Korea and fought on its UN-sponsored side in the Korean War (1950–1953). The United States has maintained Army, Air Force, Navy, and Marine personnel in South Korea in support of its commitment under the US-ROK Mutual Defence Treaty to help South Korea defend itself against external aggression. A Combined Forces Command coordinates operations between US units and South Korea armed forces. South Korea has also been designated as a major non-NATO ally of USA. USA provides significant military and economic assistance to South Korea.

Vietnam: US relations with Vietnam have become deeper and more diverse in the years since political normalisation. The two countries have broadened their political exchanges through regular and regional security. Cooperation in other areas, such as defence, non-proliferation, counterterrorism, and law enforcement, is also expanding steadily. In 2013, Presidents Obama and Sang launched the US-Vietnam Comprehensive Partnership, an overarching framework for advancing the bilateral relationship. In May 2016, President Obama announced the full lifting of the embargo on Vietnam. Vietnam is a partner in non-proliferation regimes, including the Global Initiative to Combat Nuclear Terrorism. South Korea is United States' sixth-largest goods trading partner with a trillion-dollar economy.

MULTILATERAL ALLIANCES

United States is a permanent member of the United Nations Security Council. It is also a member of the G8, G20, East Asia Summit (EAS) and Organisation for Economic Co-operation and Development and works closely with fellow NATO members on military and security issues. US have contributed support to various UN peacekeeping missions worldwide. The country has strong relationship with UK and close ties with Canada, Australia, New Zealand, the Philippines, Japan, South Korea, Saudi Arabia and Israel and several European countries such as France and Germany. The US military is building up its presence in Australia's Northern Territory in phases and plans to send a 2,500-strong Marine Air Ground Task Force to Darwin on six-month rotations each year starting in 2016.

North Atlantic Treaty Organisation (NATO): The United States is one of the founding members of NATO, a military alliance that was formed in 1949. NATO is a security alliance of 28 countries from North America and Europe. NATO's fundamental goal is to safeguard the Allies' freedom and security by political and military means. US supports in many of NATO operations. As of May 2012, the US participation in NATO operation are- 824 troops in Kosovo (KFOR, Kosovo Force) and 90,000 troops in Afghanistan (ISAF, International Security Assistance Force). US Missions' operation and issues in NATO includes Ballistic Missile Defence, Assurance Measure & European Security, Afghanistan, NATO Russia Relations, Kosovo, Monitoring the Mediterranean Sea and Counter-piracy off the Horn of Africa. USA's NATO allies have increased defence spending by more than 9% from 2016 to 2018 - the largest increase is 25 years. By 2020, NATO allies are projected to increase their defence spending by approximately USD100 billion. In addition to contributing to the war effort in Afghanistan, NATO member nations helped the US military with airspace defence and security over the United States and with maritime patrols in the Mediterranean Sea to guard against movement of weapons and terrorists.

DEFENCE CAPABILITIES

ARMY: The United States Army is the main branch of the United States Armed Forces responsible for land-based military operations. It is the largest and oldest established branch of the US military. The United States Army is made up of three components: the active component, the Regular Army; and two reserve components, the Army National Guard and the Army Reserve. The Army is headed by the Secretary of the Army (SECARMY), and by a chief military officer, the Chief of Staff of the Army (CSA) who is also a member of the Joint Chiefs of Staff.

Personnel: 482,000

Equipment

Category	Name	In Service
MBT	M1 Abrams	2,384 (3,500 in storage)
APC/IFV	M2/M3 Bradley	3500+ (both included)
	M1120 Series	4,300
	M113	3600+
	M1117	2,777
	M88 Hercules	1000+
	M9	500
	M1200	300+
MRAPs	M-ATV	5,000
	Couger H/HE	4,000
	International MaxxPro	2,700
	RG-33 & RG-33L	2,300
	RG-31	1500+
	Buffalo	750
MWV	HMMWV	1,00,000
	L-ATV	53,000
	RSOV	50
Artillery	M109 155 mm self-propelled howitzer	850+
	M777 155 mm gun-howitzer	456
	M119 105 mm howitzer	400

...continued

Category	Name	In Service
Mortar	60 mm M224	2,000
	81 mm M252	450
	120 mm M120/M120A1	1060
MLRS	M270 MRL	130
	M142 HIMARS	215
Recoil-less rifle	84 mm M-136 (AT-4)	2,70,000
Air Defence	THAAD	2
	PATRIOT	10
	AN/TWQ-1 Avenger	800+
	Stinger MANPADS	
	C-RAM	
	MIM-104	1,000
Portable Weapons/ Anti-Tank	AT4, FGM-148 Javelin, FIM-92 Stinger, M72 LAW, M141	

Army Aviation

Category	Name	In Service
Fixed wing aircraft	C-12 (C,D,F,MC-12W)	60
	C-26	11
	C-31	2
	C-37	3
Recon-naissance	EO-5	5
	RC-12	50
Trainer	TH-55	200
	TH-67 Creek	137
	OH-58A	
Helicopter	AH-6	60
	AH-64	700
	CH-47	400
	EH-60	60
	MH-47	25
	UH-60	1,500
	UH-72	200+
UAV	RQ-11B, RQ-20A, RQ-7B, MQ-1C, AeroViron-ment Switchblade	

New Procurements/ Upgrades

◆ Microsoft has won a US Army contract to build more than custom HoloLens augmented reality headsets worth USD21.9 billion for 10 years.

◆ Oshkosh Defence has been awarded USD591.61 million US Army contract for JLTV trucks.

◆ Elbit Systems Ltd.'s US subsidiary, Elbit Systems of America, LLC, was awarded an Indefinite Delivery/Indefinite-Quantity (ID/IQ) contract with a maximum value of approximately USD50 million to produce spare parts in support of the Aviators' Night Vision Imaging System Head-Up Display system (ANVIS HUD) of the US Army.

◆ General Dynamics Land Systems

(GDLS), a business unit of General Dynamics, was awarded a USD1.219 billion contract to produce, test and deliver Interim Maneuver Short-Range Air Defence (IM-SHORAD) systems to the US Army. The Army's initial order on the contract calls for 28 Stryker IM-SHORAD vehicles for USD230 million.

◆ Lockheed Martin Missile Fire Controls, Grand Prairie, Texas, was awarded an USD183,182,541 for M142 High Mobility Artillery Rocket System launchers.

◆ SAIC, Reston, Virginia, was awarded a USD36,290,371 hybrid (cost-no-fee, time-and-materials) contract for the procurement of information technology services.

◆ BAE Systems Technology Solutions & Services Inc., Rockville, Maryland, was awarded an USD11,723,000 firm-fixed-price contract to provide US Army Cyber Command with command, control, communications, computers and information management augmentation services.

◆ GM Defence awarded an USD214.3M contract to produce the US Army's Infantry Squad Vehicle. Designed to provide rapid ground mobility, the expeditionary ISV is a light and agile all-terrain troop carrier intended to transport a nine-Soldier infantry squad moving throughout the battlefield.

◆ NV5 Global, Inc.'s subsidiary, Quantum Spatial, Inc. ("Quantum Spatial"), North America's largest geospatial services firm, has been awarded contracts totaling USD28 million to support the US Army Corps of Engineers (USACE) and the US Geological Survey's (USGS) Earth Mapping Resources Initiative.

◆ Ibis Tek Inc., Butler, Pennsylvania, was awarded a USD229,062,184 firm-fixed-price contract for the Family of Heavy Tactical Vehicles protection kit.

◆ General Atomics Aeronautical Systems Inc., Poway, California, was awarded a USD131,596,627 for Gray Eagle aircraft, satellite communications air data terminals, programme management and government-furnished equipment maintenance and repair.

◆ Palantir, Washington, D.C., was awarded a USD91,176,844 firm-fixed-price contract for general research and development support of the Army Research Laboratory.

◆ Raytheon Co., Tucson, Arizona, was awarded a USD398,329,554 for tube-launched, optically tracked, wire-guided missiles (TOW), TOW obsolescence and safety missiles and practice missiles.

◆ L3Harris Technologies has received a third low-rate initial production (LRIP) order valued at USD95 million by the US Army under the HMS (Handheld, Manpack & Small Form-Fit) IDIQ contract to bring AN/PRC-158 multi-channel radios to the battlefield.

◆ Sierra Nevada Corporation was recently awarded a US Army contract for USD318.9 million for continued Simple Key Loader (SKL) production, engineering and sustainment support services.

◆ Boeing recently signed a USD265 million contract for nine more MH-47G Block II Chinook helicopters that employees in its Philadelphia plant will assemble for the US Army Special Operations Aviation Command (USASOAC).

NAVY: The United States Navy (USN) is the naval warfare service branch of the United States Armed Forces and one of the seven uniformed services of the United States. There are nine components in the operating forces of the US Navy: the United States Fleet Forces Command, United States Pacific Fleet, United States Naval Forces Central Command, United States Naval Forces Europe, Naval Network Warfare Command, Navy Reserve, United States Naval Special Warfare Command, Operational Test and Evaluation Force, and Military Sealift Command. The Navy is administratively managed by the Dept. of the Navy, which is headed by the civilian Secretary of the Navy. The Dept. of the Navy is itself a division of the Dept. of Defence, which is headed by the Secretary of Defence. The highest ranking naval officer is the Chairman of the Joint Chiefs of Staff.

Major naval bases: China Lake, CA; Lemoore, CA; Monterey, CA; Point Mugu, CA; San Diego, CA; Seal Beach, CA; Groton, CT; Washington, DC; Jacksonville, FL; Key West, FL; Pensacola, FL; Atlanta, GA; Kings Bay, GA; Pearl Harbor, HI; Great Lakes, IL; Crane, IN; New Orleans, LA; Annapolis, MD; Patuxent River, MD; Brunswick, ME; Gulfport, MS; Meridian, MS; Fallon, NV; Earle, NJ; Willow Grove, PA; Newport, RI; Charleston, SC; Millington, TN; Corpus Christi, TX; Fort Worth, TX; Ingleside, TX; Kingsville, TX; Norfolk, VA; Silverdale, WA; Bremerton, WA; Everett, WA; Whidbey Island, WA

Personnel: 3,47,000

Equipment

Category	Name	In Service
Aircraft Carrier	CVN Nimitz Class	10
	Gerald R. Ford class	10 Planned
Destroyer	DDG Arleigh Burke Class	68 (80+ planned)
Cruisers	Zumwalt class	2 (3 planned)
	Ticonderoga	20+
Submarine	SSBN/SSGN Ohio Class (Ballistic missile sub)	14

...continued

Category	Name	In Service
Submarine	SSBN/SSGN Ohio Class (Cruise missile sub)	4
	Columbia class	12 planned
	SSN Virginia Class	14 (50+ planned)
	SSN Seawolf Class	3
	SSN Los Angeles Class	30+
Frigate	USS Constitution	1
Mine Warfare Force	MCM Avenger Class	8
Command ship	Freedom Class	10 (10+ planned)
	Independence Class	10 (10+ planned)
Amphibious Force	Wasp Class (LHD)	8
	San Antonio Class (LPD)	11 (more on order)
	Harpers Ferry Class (LSD)	4
	Whidbey Island Class (LSD)	8
	Harpers Ferry (LSD)	4
	America Class (LHA)	2 (8+ planned)
Coastal	Cyclone Class	10+
Missiles	AIM-7 Sparrow, AIM-9 Sidewinder, AIM-120 AMRAAM, AGM-65 Maverick, AGM-84 Harpoon, AGM-88 HARM, AGM-154 JSW, AGM-114, BGM-109 Tomahawk (ASM)*, SLAM-ER, SM-3, RIM-116 RIM-162, RIM-67, etc	

(The United States Navy has a stockpile of approx. 3,500 Tomahawk cruise missiles of all variants, with a combined worth of approximately USD 2.6 billion. In 2016, the US DoD purchased 149 Tomahawk Block IV missiles for USD 202.3 million.)

Naval Aviation

Category	Name	In Service
Fighter/ attack/Re- connaissance aircraft	C-2A	34
	CMV-22B Osprey	30+ On Order
	F/A-18E/F	500+
	E-2C Electronic warfare / E-2D Advanced Hawkeye	40 / 50
	E-6B Electronic warfare	12+
	EP-3 ARIES II	10
	EA-18 Growler	100
	F-35 Lightning II	100+ (300+ planned)
	P-3C (Maritime)	70 (to be replaced)
Helicopter	HH-60H	7
	MH-53E	25+

...continued

Category	Name	In Service
Helicopter	MH-60R	200+
	MH-60S	250+
	SH-60B	120+
	SH-60F	40+
Trainer	T-6A, T-6B	40, 100+
	T-44A	50+
	T-45C	100+
	TH-57B	44
	TH-57C	80+

New Acquisition/Procurements

◆ General Dynamics Electric Boat, Groton, Connecticut, is awarded a USD50,598,114 cost-plus-fixed-fee modification to previously awarded contract to exercise options for the New England Maintenance Manpower Initiative for non-nuclear maintenance on submarines based at Naval Submarine Support Facility New London, Connecticut.

◆ Lockheed Martin Rotary and Mission Systems, Baltimore, Maryland, is awarded a USD78,530,376 cost-plus-fixed-fee modification to previously awarded contract to exercise options for the accomplishment of class design services for the Littoral Combat Ship programme.

◆ Rolls-Royce has secured recent agreements with the US Navy for ship engines, propulsion components and services valued at up to USD115.6 million. The engine contract, for USD34.4 million, is a follow-on production agreement for 16 new MT7 gas-turbine engines for Navy Ship-to-Shore Connector Landing Craft.

◆ Peraton, a national security company, received a contract award from the Naval Air Warfare Center Weapons Division (NAWCWD) to expand its Test and Evaluation (T&E) support on the Mission, Maintenance, Future Requirements (MMFR) programme for range instrumentation systems. The contract is valued at USD33 million over a five-year period.

◆ The Department of Defence and the US Navy awarded to Fincantieri's subsidiary, Marinette Marine (FMM), a USD7 million contract for design and engineering work of the Large Unmanned Surface Vessel (LUSV), the future large-size unmanned surface vessels, able to operate without crew on board. The award process will follow the scheme of the tender for the 10 first-in-class guided-missile FFG(X) frigates of the US Navy, awarded to Fincantieri Marinette Marine four months ago, collectively worth USD5.5 billion. In addition to the recent milestone of the FFG(X) frigates, the Group is currently developing the Littoral Combat Ships programme for the US Navy, envisaging the construction of 16 vessels (10 of which already delivered).

◆ The US Navy has awarded Boeing a combined USD3.1 billion in contracts for Harpoon and Standoff Land Attack Missile Expanded Response (SLAM ER) weapon systems in support of FMSs (FMS). About USD2.6 billion of that was contracted in May 2020 while the remainder had been previously awarded.

◆ BAE Systems has been awarded a contract worth up to USD11,35,25,865.00 (approx.) by the US Department of Defence (DoD) to manufacture and deliver Archerfish mine neutralisers for the US Navy. Archerfish is a remote-controlled underwater mine neutraliser that can be launched and operated from a surface ship, helicopter or an unmanned underwater vehicle (UUV).

◆ Oceaneering International, Inc. announced that its Aerospace and Defence Technologies (ADTech) segment has secured a contract with Naval Sea Systems Command (NAVSEA) to operate and maintain the US Navy's submarine rescue systems. The contract duration is one year, with four one-year extension options, with a potential value of USD119 million.

◆ The US Navy has awarded a USD25-million contract to Saab Inc. on Sept. 25, 2020, for two AN/SPN-50(V)1 Shipboard Air Traffic Radars and one Installation and Checkout kit. The new fixed-price incentive fee contract is a sole-source procurement with the first AN/SPN-50(V)1 scheduled for delivery in September 2021. It will replace the Navy's current radar system, AN/SPN-43C, on Nimitz-class aircraft carriers and amphibious assault ships in fiscal 2021 timeframe.

◆ The US Navy awarded Boeing a USD1.5 billion production contract for the next 18 P-8A Poseidon aircraft. The contract includes eight aircraft for the US Navy, six aircraft for the Republic of Korea Navy and four aircraft for the Royal New Zealand Air Force.

◆ The US Navy has awarded L3Harris Technologies a USD104 million follow-on contract to supply the next production lot of the electronic warfare (EW) system that protects F/A-18 Hornet and Super Hornet aircraft against electronic threats.

◆ Northrop Grumman Systems Corp., Mission Systems Sector, Linthicum Heights, Maryland, was awarded a USD100,798,804 fixed-price-incentive-fee and firm-fixed-price contract for follow-on production of Surface Electronic Warfare Improvement Programme Block 3 electronic attack systems and hardware design modifications required for aircraft carrier and amphibious assault ship installation.

◆ Raytheon Missiles & Defence, Marlborough, Massachusetts, was awarded a USD273,353,649 firm-fixed-price, cost-plus-fixed fee, and cost only modification to previously awarded contract to exercise options and add advanced radars detection laboratory generator support for Air and Missile Defence Radar; and Enterprise Air Surveillance Radar, integration and production support efforts.

F/A-18 Super Hornets assigned to the "Black Aces" of Strike Fighter Squadron Forty One (VFA-41) fly over the Western Pacific Ocean in a stack formation. (Image Credit: US Navy)

MARINE CORPS: The United States Marine Corps (USMC) is a branch of the United States Armed Forces responsible for providing power projection from the sea, using the mobility of the United States Navy to deliver combined-arms task forces rapidly. The Dept. of the Navy, led by the Secretary of the Navy, oversees both the Marine Corps and the Navy. The most senior Marine officer is the Commandant of the Marine Corps, responsible for organising, recruiting, training, and equipping the Marine Corps so that it is ready for operation under the command of the Unified Combatant Commanders. The Marine Corps is organised into four principal subdivisions: Headquarters Marine Corps (HQMC), the Operating Forces, the Supporting Establishment, and the Marine Forces Reserve (MARFORRES or USMCR).

Personnel: 181,000

Equipment

Category	Name	In Service
MBT	M-1A1 Abrams	483
APC/IFV	LAV	735
	LVTP-7A1	400
	MRAP	2,200
Artillery	155 mm M777A1 Ultra-Light Howitzer	380
	155 mm M-109	140
Mortar	81 mm M252	500
MLRS	MLRS	42
Anti-Tank GW	TOW	
	Javelin	
SAM	Stinger	30000
	Avengers	79
	LAV-AD	16

Marine Aviation

Category	Name	In Service
Fighter/attack/Reconnaissance aircraft	F/A-18A/C/D	250+
	AV-8B+	100+
	F-35B	60
	C-12	10+
	EA-6B Prowler	20
	C-130J	50+
Helicopter	UH-1Y	170
	AH-1Z	70
	AH-1	100
	MV-22B	250
	CH-53K/CH-53E	140
Trainer	T-34	3
	F-5	10+
	F/A-18	15+
	TAV-8	16
UAV	Wasp, AeroVironment Switchblade, RQ-7 Shadow, RQ-11 Raven, RQ-14 Dragon Eye, RQ-20 Puma, T-20, ScanEagle, RQ-21A Blackjack	

New Acquisition/Procurements

◆ The US Marine Corps (USMC) has awarded BAE Systems a contract worth approximately USD19 million to develop a prototype design for a new state-of-the-art Wargaming Center to be built at Marine Corps Base Quantico in Virginia. BAE Systems will integrate advanced technologies into the prototype, including artificial intelligence, machine learning, game theory, multi-domain modeling and simulation, and predictive data analytics, which will provide greater metrics and training on many wargaming processes.

◆ Kongsberg Defence & Aerospace AS (KONGSBERG) has been selected by BAE Systems, Inc. to design and manufacture the remote Medium Caliber Turret (MCT) for the United States Marine Corps' Amphibious Combat Vehicle (ACV) -30 programme.

◆ Marshall Aerospace and Defence Group (MADG) has won a ten-year multi-million dollar contract with the US Marine Corps to provide depot-level maintenance to its 66-strong fleet of KC-130J tanker aircraft deployed worldwide. The contract, one of the biggest in the company's history, enables MADG to perform scheduled and unscheduled maintenance, repair and overhaul (MRO) services in support of Naval Air Systems Command's Tactical Airlift Program Office (PMA-207).

◆ Northrop Grumman Corporation has received an order from the US Marine Corps for two additional AN/TPS-80 Ground/Air Task-Oriented Radar (G/ATOR) systems as part of the full-rate production Lot 2 award received in December 2019. This order completes the planned Lot 2 procurement for a total of eight systems for the Marine Corps.

◆ Lockheed Martin recently delivered the first KC-130J Super Hercules tanker assigned to Marine Aerial Refueler Transport Squadron 452 (VMGR-452), the Marine Forces Reserve squadron at Stewart Air National Guard Base, New York.

AIR FORCE: The United States Air Force (USAF) is the aerial warfare service branch of the United States Armed Forces. The US Air Force provides air support for surface forces and aids in the recovery of troops in the field. The Dept. of the Air Force is headed by the civilian Secretary of the Air Force. The Dept. of the Air Force is a Military Dept. within the Dept. of Defence. The highest ranking military officer in the Dept. of the Air Force is the Chief of Staff of the Air Force who exercises supervision over Air Force units, and serves as a member of the Joint Chiefs of Staff.

Personnel: 3,36,000

Equipment

Category	Name	In Service
Fighter/attack/Reconnaissance/bomber	A-10 Thunderbolt II	280+
	AC-130/ AC-130J	30 (AC-130 being replaced by AC-130J)
	F-15C	250+
	F-15E	150
	F-16	700+ (To be replaced by F-35A)
	F-22A	184
	F-35A Lightning II	170+
	B-1B Lancer	52
	B-2A Spirit	15
	B-52H Stratofortress	70
	E-3 Sentry AWACS	30
	E-4B	4
	E-8C Joint STARS	14+
	EC-130H Electronic Warfare	14
	EC-130J Electronic Warfare	7
Transport/Tanker	C-130H Hercules	261
	KC-10A Extender	59
	KC-135 Stratotanker	397
	KC-46 Pegasus	15+
	C-144	2
	VC-25	2
	C-20	7
	C-130J Super Hercules	120
Cargo	C-5-B/C/M Galaxy	55
	C-12 Huron	67
	C-17A Globemaster III	222
	C-21A Learjet	31
Helicopter	UH-1N Twin Huey	59
	TH-1H Iroquois	37
	HH-60 Pave Hawk a	100
	CV-22B Osprey	42 (50 on order)
	HH-60G Pave Hawk	50+
Trainer	T-1 Jayhawk	157
	T-6A Texan II	449
	T-38 Talon	480
UAV	RQ-4 Global Hawk	37
	RQ-11 Raven	Classified
	RQ-170 Sentinel	
	Wasp III	Classified
	MC-1B Predator	150
	MQ-9B Reaper	93
Missiles	AGM-65, AGM-86, AGM-88, AGM-129, AGM-130, AGM-154, AGM-158 AIM-7, AIM-9, AIM-120, LGM-30G Minuteman III ICBM	

Spacecraft

Category	Name	In Service
Launch vehicle	Atlas V	
	Delta II	
	Delta IV	
Satellite	Defence Satellite Communications System	9
	Global Positioning System	30
	Milstar Satellite Communications System	5
	Defence Support Programme	
	Ground-Based Electro-Optical Deep Space Surveillance	

...continued

Category	Name	In Service
Satellite	Defence Meteorological Satellite Programme	
	Wideband Global SATCOM Satellite	
	Boeing X-37B	2

New Acquisition/Procurements

◆ The US Air Force Life Cycle Management Center's MQ-9 Programme Office has awarded a USD7.4 billion ceiling Agile Reaper Enterprise Solution (ARES) contract to General Atomics Sept. 17.

◆ The US Air Force awarded Boeing a nearly USD1.2 billion contract to build the first lot of eight F-15EX advanced fighter jets to help the service meet its capacity requirements and add capability to its fighter fleet. The award also covers support and one-time, upfront engineering costs. Already under construction at the Boeing F-15 production facility in St. Louis, the first two jets will be delivered next year. The F-15EX will replace the oldest F-15C/Ds in the service's inventory. Eight F-15EX aircraft were approved in the fiscal year 2020 budget and 12 were requested in the FY21 budget. The Air Force plans to purchase a total of 76 F-15EX aircraft over the five-year Future Years Defence Programme.

◆ AirMap, the leading digital airspace and automation company serving the drone economy, was awarded a contract to provide unmanned aircraft system (UAS) traffic management (UTM) services to the United States Air Force (USAF)'s Agility Prime programme. The USAF will use AirMap's UTM platform to support testing of electric vertical takeoff and landing (eVTOL) aircraft in preparation for scaling of advanced air mobility operations.

◆ Northrop Grumman Corporation was selected by the US Air Force to modernise the nation's aging intercontinental ballistic missile (ICBM) system under a USD13.3 billion contract awarded for the engineering and manufacturing development (EMD) phase of the Ground Based Strategic Deterrent (GBSD) programme. The Air Force Nuclear Weapons Center announced that the effort will span 8.5 years and include weapon system design, qualification, test and evaluation and nuclear certification.

◆ Northrop Grumman Corporation has delivered a pair of sensors to enhance the capability of its Global Hawk high-altitude long-endurance autonomous aircraft system. Enhancements include the deployment of the MS-177 multi-spectral camera system to provide additional high resolution imaging capability for operational users. The second new capability is the first fielding of the increment 1 upgraded AN/ASQ-230 system on Global Hawk to meet expanded electronic threats.

◆ KBR has been awarded an eight-year contract to perform day-to-day base operations for the US Air Forces in Europe and Air Forces Africa (USAFE-AFAFRICA) - a major command of the Air Force. This new indefinite-delivery/indefinite-quantity contract has a USD974 million maximum ceiling value.

◆ Sarcos Defence, a wholly-owned subsidiary of Sarcos Robotics, recently announced that the company has been awarded a contract by the US Air Force Technology Acceleratory Programme (AFWERX) to develop an artificial intelligence (AI) platform, on behalf of Sarcos' customer, the Center for Rapid Innovation (CRI) at Air Force Research Labs (AFRL), that will enable human-scale dexterous robotic systems.

◆ The Boeing Co., Seattle, Washington, has been awarded a USD2,122,841,088 for KC-46 Lot 3 production. Contractor will provide 15 KC-46 aircraft, data, two spare engines, and five wing refueling pod kits.

◆ Kratos Defence & Security Solutions, Inc. has been awarded a USD950,000,000 ceiling indefinite-delivery/indefinite-quantity contract for the maturation, demonstration and proliferation of capability across platforms and domains, leveraging open systems design, modern software and algorithm development in order to enable Joint All Domain Command and Control (JADC2). This contract is part of a multiple award multi-level security effort to provide development and operation of systems as a unified force across all domains (air, land, sea, space, cyber, and electromagnetic spectrum) in an open architecture family of systems that enables capabilities via multiple integrated platforms.

◆ L-3 Communications Integrated Systems, Greenville, Texas, has been awarded a USD44,651,345 cost-plus-fixed-fee delivery order for engineering, procurement and fabrication that will result in modification, installation and test of the aircraft mission system.

◆ Raytheon Co., El Segundo, California, has been awarded a USD7,107,820 for miniaturised airborne Global Positioning System (GPS) Receiver 2K-M development.

◆ The Boeing Co., El Segundo, California, has been awarded a USD298,369,312 firm-fixed-price contract for the Evolved Strategic Satellite Communications programme. This contract provides a prototype payload to develop hardware and software.

◆ Lockheed Martin Missiles and Fire Control Global Logistics Support Services, Lexington, Kentucky, has been awarded a USD19,316,175 cost-plus-fixed-fee contract for a Situational Awareness Communications Upgrade (SACU). This contract provides for design, integration and validation of hardware and software to improve on-board situational awareness of the operational environment between disparate tactical network systems.

The United States also have 41,000 Coast Guard; 16,000 Space Force; 336,000 Army National Guard; 106,000 Air National Guard.

SPACE FORCE: The US Space Force (USSF) is a new branch of the Armed Forces. It was established on December 20, 2019 with enactment of the Fiscal Year 2020 National Defence Authorisation Act and will be stood-up over the next 18 months. The USSF was established within the Department of the Air Force, meaning the Secretary of the Air Force has overall responsibility for the USSF, under the guidance and direction of the Secretary of Defence. Additionally, a four-star general known as the Chief of Space Operations (CSO) serves as the senior military member of the USSF. The Chief of Space Operations, US Space Force, serves as the principal uniformed adviser to the Secretary of the Air Force on Space Force activities. Barbara M. Barrett is the 25th Secretary of the Air Force and leads the affairs of the Department of the Air Force, which is comprised of the US Air Force and US Space Force. Gen. John W. "Jay" Raymond is the Chief of Space Operations, United States Space Force.

US STRATEGIC COMMAND

The United States Strategic Command, or USSTRATCOM, is headquartered at Offutt Air Force Base in Nebraska. The command is one of nine US unified commands under the Dept. of Defence. Strategic Command was established in 1992 as a successor to Strategic Air Command (SAC).

USSTRATCOM is the command and control centre for US strategic forces and controls military space operations, computer network operations, information operations, strategic warning and intelligence assessments as well as global strategic planning. The command is responsible for both early warning of and defence against missile attack and long-range conventional attacks. The command is charged with deterring and defending against the proliferation of weapons of mass destruction. The command has worldwide functional responsibilities not bound by any single area of operations. The command's scope of responsibilities includes the interrelated areas of space operations, information operations, computer network operations, and strategic defence and attack. Tying these areas together is a globally focused command and control, communications and intelligence, surveillance and reconnaissance network (C3ISR).

The US Cyber Command (USCYBERCOM) was activated as a subordinate unified command under USSTRATCOM in September 2009, with a mission to coordinate computer-network defence and direct US cyber-attack operation. US Cyber Command (USCYBERCOM), located at Fort Meade, Maryland, is the nation's 10th Unified Combatant Command. USCYBERCOM directs, synchronises, and coordinates cyberspace planning and operations in defence of the US and its interests. The components under this command are Army Cyber Command, Fleet Cyber Command/Tenth Fleet, Air Forces Cyber/Twenty-Fourth Air Force and Marine Corps Forces Cyberspace Command.

Service Commands
- US Army Space and Missile Defence Command (USASMDC)
- US Fleet Forces Command
- Air Force Global Strike Command (AFGSC)
- Marine Corps Forces US Strategic Command (MARFORSTRAT)

Functional Components are JFACC (Joint Force Air Component Commander) Barksdale AFB, LA, JFCC-IMD (Joint Functional Component Command for Integrated Missile Defence) Schriever AFB, CO and JFMCC (Joint Force Maritime Component Command) Naval Station Norfolk, VA.

Current Unified Commands

United States Africa Command (USAFRICOM): United States Africa Command (USAFRICOM) is responsible for military relations with African nations, the African Union and African regional security organisations.

United States Central Command (USCENTCOM): United States Central Command (USCENTCOM) is responsible for operations in twenty countries that fall in the "central" area of the globe: Afghanistan, Bahrain, Egypt, Iran, Iraq, Jordan, Kazakhstan, Kuwait, Kyrgyzstan, Lebanon, Oman, Pakistan, Qatar, Saudi Arabia, Syria, Tajikistan, Turkmenistan, United Arab Emirates, Uzbekistan and Yemen.

United States Cyber Command (USCYBERCOM): US Cyber Command's mission is to direct, synchronise, and coordinate cyberspace planning and operations to defend and advance national interests in collaboration with domestic and international partners.

United States European Command (USEUCOM): United States European Command (USEUCOM) works with NATO and other partner nations to address the security and Defence needs of nations in Europe and parts of the Middle East and Eurasia.

United States Northern Command (USNORTHCOM): United States Northern Command (USNORTHCOM) operates in the area of responsibility encompassing the continental United States, Alaska, Mexico, Canada, portions of the Caribbean and surrounding waters.

United States Indo-Pacific Command (USINDOPACOM): United States Indo-Pacific Command (USINDOPACOM) oversees an area of responsibility encompassing about half the earth's surface, stretching from the waters off the west coast of the US to the western border of India, and from Antarctica to the North Pole.

United States Southern Command (USSOUTHCOM): United States Southern Command (USSOUTHCOM) oversees an area of responsibility encompassing 31 nations in Latin America south of Mexico, Central and South America, and the Caribbean Sea.

United States Strategic Command (USSTRATCOM): The United States Strategic Command (USSTRATCOM) is headquartered at Offutt Air Force Base in Omaha, Nebraska. It conducts global operations in partnership with other Combatant Commands, services and US government agencies to deter and detect strategic attacks against the United States.

United States Transportation Command (USTRANSCOM): The United States Transportation Command (USTRANSCOM) provides the Dept. of Defence with an aggregate of transportation capabilities and assets.

United States Space Command (USSPACECOM): The USSPACECOM mission is to deter aggression and conflict, defend US and allied freedom of action, deliver space combat power for the Joint/Combined force, and develop joint warfighters to advance US and allied interests in, from, and through the space domain.

United States Special Operations Command (USSOCOM): USSOCOM develops and employs fully capable Special Operations Forces to conduct global special operations and activities as part of the Joint Force to support persistent, networked and distributed Combatant Command operations and campaigns against state and non-state actors to protect and advance US policies and objectives.

US President 2019 formally launched the Space Command, which he said will defend America's vital interests in "the next war-fighting domain". Gen. John W Raymond is the commander of the US Space Command, which has been established as the 11th Unified Combatant Command of the American armed forces. Notably, it is re-establishment of the US Space Command, which existed between 1985 and 2002.

Currently, the United States nuclear arsenal is deployed in three areas:
- Land-based intercontinental ballistic missiles, or ICBMs;
- Sea-based, nuclear submarine-launched ballistic missiles, or SLBMs; and
- Air-based nuclear weapons of the US Air Force's heavy bomber group

The Pentagon is aiming to invest about 10 percent more over the next five years to upgrade the nation's nuclear deterrent. THE US has begun a USD10 billion upgrade of its nuclear weapons arsenal after two hard-hitting reviews found decades of neglect have left its most significant line of defence in disrepair. The US had already put itself on the path to modernise ageing weapons at a cost of up to USD 1 trillion over the next three decades, including a dozen ballistic missile submarines, up to 100 new bombers and 400 land-based missiles.

New START Treaty Aggregate Numbers of Strategic Offensive Arms

(Data in this Fact Sheet comes from the biannual exchange of data required by the Treaty. It contains data declared current as of September 1, 2021. Data will be updated each six-month period after entry into force of the Treaty.).) Source: BUREAU OF ARMS CONTROL, VERIFICATION AND COMPLIANCE, State.Gov)

Category of Data	USA	Russia
Deployed ICBMs, Deployed SLBMs, and Deployed Heavy Bombers	665	527
Warheads on Deployed ICBMs, on Deployed SLBMs, and Nuclear Warheads Counted for Deployed Heavy Bombers	1389	1458

Deployed and Non-deployed Launchers of ICBMs, Deployed and Non-deployed Launchers of SLBMs, and Deployed and Non-deployed Heavy Bombers	800	742

Major Armaments Producers

Top 20 US government defence contractors:

Lockheed Martin Corp., Northrop Grumman Corp., Boeing Co., Raytheon Co., General Dynamics Corp., KBR Inc., Science Applications International Corp., L-3 Communications Corp., Computer Sciences Corp., ITT Corp., CACI International Inc., BAE Systems Inc., Hewlett-Packard Co., Harris Corp., United Technologies Corp., URS Corp., Jacobs Engineering Group Inc., DRS Technologies Inc., Dell Computer Corp., and Rockwell Collins Inc.

The Defence Advanced Research Projects Agency (DARPA) is the research and development office for the US Dept. of Defence. DARPA funds unique and innovative research through the private sector, academic and other non-profit organizations as well as government labs. DARPA research runs the gamut from conducting scientific investigations in a laboratory, to building full-scale prototypes of military systems. They fund research in biology, medicine, computer science, chemistry, physics, engineering, mathematics, material sciences, social sciences, neuroscience, and more. DARPA is independent from other more conventional military R&D and reports directly to senior Dept. of Defence management.

The Missile Defence Agency (MDA) is a research, development, and acquisition agency within the Dept. of Defence. The MDA's mission is to develop, test, and field an integrated, layered, ballistic missile defence system (BMDS) to defend the United States, its deployed forces, allies, and friends against all ranges of enemy ballistic missiles in all phases of flight. There are several other agencies and military commands which play a role, such as the United States Army Space and Missile Defence Command. Missile defence elements are operated by United States military personnel from US Strategic Command, US Northern Command, US Indo-Pacific Command, US Forces Japan, US European Command and others. The United States has missile defence cooperative programmes with a number of allies, including United Kingdom, Japan, Australia, Israel, Denmark, Germany, Netherlands, Czech Republic, Poland, Italy, France, Poland, Romania, Spain, Turkey, Kuwait, Qatar, Saudi Arabia, UAE, and South Korea. The Missile Defence Agency also actively participates in NATO activities to maximise opportunities to develop an integrated NATO ballistic missile defence capability.

DEFENCE DEALS

Arms Export

The USA alone accounts for one-third of arms exports worldwide. 94 countries imported US made weaponry, with the Middle East accounting for 32 percent of the purchases. USA has been continually restocking supplies in the Middle Eastern crisis region. US has taken a firm lead as the major arms exporter globally. The main customers include Saudi Arabia, UAE & Turkey in the Middle East. US has done overseas arms sales agreements with countries like Afghanistan, Algeria, Africa, Bahrain, Bangladesh, Bhutan, British Indian Ocean Territories, Egypt, India, Iran, Iraq, Israel, Jordan, Kuwait, Lebanon, Libya, Maldives, Morocco, Nepal, Oman, Pakistan, Qatar, Saudi Arabia, Sri Lanka, Syria, South Korea, Tunisia, United Arab Emirates, Yemen and many more. Over the past decade, US arms sales have grown manifold, and they are likely to continue growing in coming years. Sales to Afghanistan alone totalled nearly USD 20 billion for fiscal years 2009 through 2011. Among the biggest potential arms deals on the table now are armaments sale in India and Brazil, various modernisation programmes for Saudi Arabia, and continuing support for arms sales to Iraq, Afghanistan, Pakistan and Lebanon. The USA delivered weapons to 75 recipients in 2006–10, more than any other supplier. Asia and Oceania was the biggest recipient region of US weapons—accounting for 44 per cent of US deliveries, including 22 per cent in total for South Korea, Japan and Taiwan. The Middle East accounted for 28 per cent and Europe for 19 per cent. The US defence market is the largest and most advanced in the world with ample opportunities given the vast size of the defence market.

As per the US Defence Security Cooperation Agency, following arms sales were approved in 2021:

◆ The US State Department has approved a possible FMS to the Government of Finland of Extended Range Guided Multiple Launch Rocket Systems and related equipment for an estimated cost of USD91.2 million.

◆ The US State Department has approved a possible FMS to the Government of Egypt of Rolling Airframe Missiles (RAM) Block 2 Tactical Missiles and related equipment for an estimated cost of USD197 million.

◆ The US State Department has approved a possible FMS to the Government of Jordan of an F-16 Air Combat Training Center and related equipment for an estimated cost of USD60 million.

◆ The US State Department has approved a possible FMS to the NATO Communications and Information Agency (NCIA) of UHF SATCOM Radio Systems and related equipment for an estimated cost of USD65 million.

◆ The US State Department has approved a possible FMS to the Government of Chile of Standard Missile-2 (SM-2) Block IIIA Missiles and related equipment for an estimated cost of USD85.0 million.

◆ The US State Department has approved a possible FMS to the Republic of Korea of AGM-114R Hellfire Missiles and related equipment for an estimated cost of USD36 million.

◆ The US State Department has approved a possible FMS to the Government of Norway of Javelin FGM-148 Missiles and related equipment for an estimated cost of USD36 million.

◆ The US State Department has approved a possible FMS to the Government of the Netherlands of AH-64 Pilot Training and Logistics Support and related equipment for an estimated cost of USD190 million.

◆ The US State Department has approved a possible FMS to the Government of the Netherlands of CH-47 Pilot Training and Logistics Support and related equipment for an estimated cost of USD125 million.

◆ The US State Department has approved a possible FMS to the Government of North Macedonia of Stryker Vehicles and related equipment for an estimated cost of USD210 million.

◆ The US State Department has approved a possible FMS to the Government of Germany of P-8A Aircraft and Associated Support, and related equipment, for an estimated cost of USD1.77 billion.

◆ The US State Department has approved a possible FMS to the Government of India of six (6) P-8I Patrol aircraft and related equipment for an estimated cost of USD 2.42 billion.

◆ The US State Department has approved a possible FMS to the Government of Australia of CH-47F Chinook Helicopters and related equipment for an estimated cost of USD 259 million.

◆ The US State Department has approved a possible FMS to the Government The US State Department has approved a possible FMS to the Government of Australia of Heavy Armored Combat Systems and related equipment for an estimated cost of USD1.685 billion.

◆ The US State Department has approved a possible FMS to the Government of Australia of MQ-9B Remotely Piloted Aircraft and related equipment for an estimated cost of USD1.651 billion.

◆ The US State Department has approved a possible FMS to the Government of Spain of Follow-on Contractor Logistics Support (CLS) for MQ-9A Blk 5 Aircraft and related equipment for an estimated cost of USD110 million.

◆ The US State Department has approved a possible FMS to the Government of Greece of FMSO II, CLSSA Services, and related equipment for an estimated cost of USD165 million.

◆ The US State Department has approved a possible FMS to the Government of Canada of AEGIS Combat System and related equipment for an estimated cost of USD1.7 billion.

◆ The US State Department has approved a possible FMS to the Government of the Philippines of F-16 Block 70/72 Aircraft and related equipment for an estimated cost of USD2.43 billion.

◆ The US State Department has approved a possible FMS to the Government of the Philippines of AIM-9X Sidewinder Block II Tactical Missiles and related equipment for an estimated cost of USD42.4 million.

◆ The US State Department has approved a possible FMS to the Government of the Philippines of AGM-84L-1 Harpoon Air Launched Block II Missiles and related equipment for an estimated cost of USD120 million.

◆ The US State Department has approved a possible FMS to the Government of Australia of AH-64E Apache Helicopters and related equipment for an estimated cost of USD3.5 billion.

◆ The US State Department has approved a possible FMS to the Government of Thailand of Javelin Missiles and related equipment for an estimated cost of USD83.5 million.

◆ The US State Department has approved a possible FMS to the Government of Israel of CH-53K Heavy Lift Helicopters with Support and related equipment for an estimated cost of USD3.4 billion.

◆ The US State Department has approved a possible FMS to the Government of the Philippines of F-16 Block 70/72 Aircraft and related equipment for an estimated cost of USD2.43 billion.

◆ The US State Department has approved a possible FMS to the Government of the Philippines of AIM-9X Sidewinder Block II Tactical Missiles and related equipment for an estimated cost of $42.4 million.

◆ The US State Department has approved a possible FMS to the Government of the Philippines of AGM-84L-1 Harpoon Air Launched Block II Missiles and related equipment for an estimated cost of $120 million.

◆ The State Department has made a determination approving a possible Foreign Military Sale to the Government of Australia of AH-64E Apache Helicopters and related equipment for an estimated cost of $3.5 billion.

◆ The US State Department has approved a possible FMS to the Government of Thailand of Javelin Missiles and related equipment for an estimated cost of $83.5 million.

◆ The US State Department has approved a possible FMS to the Government of Israel of CH-53K Heavy Lift Helicopters with Support and related equipment for an estimated cost of USD3.4 billion.

◆ The US State Department has approved a possible FMS to the Government of Kuwait of Heavy Tactical Vehicles with support and related equipment for an estimated cost of USD445 million.

◆ The US State Department has approved a possible FMS to the Government of Australia of Defense Services Related to Future Standard Missile Production and related equipment for an estimated cost of USD350 million.

◆ The US State Department has approved a possible FMS to South Korea of Precision Guided Munitions and related equipment for an estimated cost of USD258 million.

◆ The US State Department has approved a possible FMS to the Taipei Economic and Cultural Representative Office in the United States (TECRO) of 155mm M109A6 Paladin Medium Self-Propelled Howitzer System and related equipment for an estimated cost of USD750 million.

◆ The US State Department has approved a possible FMS to the Government of Japan of AEGIS Class Destroyer Support and related equipment for an estimated cost of USD134 million.

◆ The US State Department has approved a possible FMS to the Government of Japan of RAM Block 2 Tactical Missiles and related equipment for an estimated cost of USD61.5 million.

◆ The US State Department has approved a possible FMS to the Government of Georgia of Javelin Missiles and related equipment for an estimated cost of USD30 million.

◆ The US State Department has approved a possible FMS to the Government of Greece of F-16 Sustainment Materiel and Services and related equipment for an estimated cost of USD270 million.

◆ The US State Department has approved a possible FMS to the Government of India of Harpoon Joint Common Test Set (JCTS) and related equipment for an estimated cost of USD82 million.

◆ The US State Department has approved a possible FMS to the Government of Australia of EA-18G Growler Aircraft, Related Defense Services, and related equipment for an estimated cost of USD125 million.

◆ The US State Department has approved a possible FMS to the Kingdom of Saudi Arabia of Continuation of Maintenance Support Services (MSS) and related equipment for an estimated cost of USD500 million.

◆ The US State Department has approved a possible FMS to the Government of Australia of MH-60R Multi-Mission Helicopters, Related Defense Services, and related equipment for an estimated cost of USD985 million.

◆ The US State Department has approved a possible FMS to the Kingdom of Saudi Arabia of AIM-120C Advanced Medium Range Air-to-Air Missiles (AMRAAM) and related equipment for an estimated cost of USD650 million.

◆ The US State Department has approved a Foreign Military Sale to the Government of Greece of MEKO Class Frigate Modernization and related equipment for an estimated cost of USD2.5 billion.

◆ The US State Department has approved a possible Foreign Military Sale to the Government of Greece of Multi-Mission Surface Combatant (MMSC) ships and related equipment for an estimated cost of USD6.9 billion.

Defence Procurement

Defence Procurement and Acquisition Policy (DPAP) is responsible for all acquisition and procurement policy matters in the Dept. of Defence (DoD). The DPAP office serves as the principal advisor to the Under Secretary of Defence for Acquisition, Technology and Logistics (AT&L) and the Defence Acquisition Board on acquisition/procurement strategies for all major weapon systems programs, major automated information systems programmes, and services acquisitions.

DEFENCE BUDGET

Total defence spending: USD715 billion (2021); USD703 billion (2020)

Defence spending in terms of GDP: 3.73% of GDP (2020 est.), 3.51% of GDP (2019)

Defence Expenditure

Year	USD (Miions)
2014	653,942
2015	641,253
2016	656,059
2017	642,933
2018	672,255
2019	730,149
2020*	784,952
2021*	811,140

(*Figures for 2020 and 2021 are estimates.) Source: Defence Expenditure of NATO Countries (2014-2021), NATO Press Release.

According to the press release by the US Department of Defence, The Biden-Harris Administration recently submitted to Congress the President's Fiscal Year (FY) 2022 Budget request of USD752.9 billion for national defence, USD715 billion of which is for the Department of Defence (DOD). The FY 2022 Defence Budget submission reflects President Biden's priorities to end the "forever wars," invest in cutting-edge capabilities for our military and national security advantage in the future, and revitalise America's unmatched network of alliances and partnerships. The FY 2022 President's Budget request of USD715 billion when compared to the FY 2021 enacted amount of USD703.7 billion, reflects a 1.6% increase. For the Navy and Air Force, there are additional investments to address strategic competition with China. For the Army, the request reflects the President's decision to withdraw all US troops from Afghanistan prior to the beginning of FY 2022, the release added.

US Defence Department's FY 2022 Budget contains: COVID-19 and pandemic preparedness - over USD500 million; Pacific Deterrence Initiative - USD5.1 billion; Preparing for, adapting to and mitigating climate change - USD617 million.

Nuclear Modernisation (USD27.7 billion): B-21 Long Range Strike Bomber - USD3 billion; COLUMBIA Class Ballistic Missile Submarine - USD5 billion; Long-Range Stand-Off (LRSO) Missile - USD609 million; Ground Based Strategic Deterrent (GBSD) - USD2.6 billion.

Missile Defeat and Defense (USD20.4 billion): Sea-Based Interceptors (SM-3 IIA and SM-3 IB) - USD647 million; Sea-Based Ballistic Missile Defense System (AEGIS BMD) - USD1 billion; Ground-Based Midcourse (GMD) and Improved Homeland Defense/Next Generation Interceptors (NGI) - USD1.7 billion; Terminal High Altitude Area Defense (THAAD) Ballistic Missile Defense - USD562 million; Patriot Advanced Capability Missile Segment Enhancement - USD777 million.

Long Range Fires (USD6.6 billion): Includes funds to develop and field multi-Service, multi-domain offensive Long Range Fires.

Science and Technology and Advanced Capability Enablers: Largest ever RDT&E request - USD112 billion; Science and Technology - USD14.7 billion; Microelectronics - USD2.3 billion; Artificial Intelligence - USD874 million; 5G - USD398 million.

Air Force (USD52.4 billion): 85 F-35 Joint Strike Fighters - USD12 billion; 14 KC-46 Tanker Replacements - USD2.5 billion; 9 CH-53K King Stallion - USD1.7 billion; 12 F-15EX - USD1.5 billion; 30 AH-64E Apache Attack Helicopters - USD825 million

Navy (USD34.6 billion): COLUMBIA Class Ballistic Missile Submarine - USD5 billion; CVN-78 FORD Class Aircraft Carrier - USD2.9 billion; 2 Virginia Class Submarines - USD6.9 billion; 1 DDG-51 Arleigh Burke Destroyer - USD2.4 billion; 1 Frigate (FFG(X)) - USD1.3 billion; 1 Fleet Replenishment Oiler (T-AO) - USD853 million; Unmanned Surface Vessels (USV) (Large) - USD203 million; 2 Towing, Salvage, and Rescue Ships (T-ATS) - USD184 million; 1 Ocean Surveillance Ship (T-AGOX(X)) - USD434 million.

Army (USD12.3 billion): 3,799 Joint Light Tactical Vehicles - USD1.1 billion; 70 M-1 Abrams Tank Modifications/Upgrades - USD1 billion; 92 Amphibious Combat Vehicles - USD613 million.

Space and Space-Based Systems (USD20.6 billion): 5 Launch Vehicles - National Security Space Launch (NSSL) and Rocket System Launch Program (RSLP) - USD1.7 billion; Global Positioning System (GPS) Enterprise - USD1.8 billion; Space Based Overhead Persistent Infrared (OPIR) Systems - USD2.6 billion

Cyberspace Activities (USD10.4 billion): cybersecurity, cyberspace operations, and research and development in support of cybersecurity and cyberspace operations.

The FY 2022 Budget builds on current readiness gains and modernises for the future fight across the Services and USSOCOM ($122.1 billion). Investments include:

◆ Army readiness - USD27.8 billion
◆ Navy and Marine Corps readiness - USD48.5 billion
◆ Air Force readiness - USD36.5 billion
◆ Special Operations Command readiness - USD9.4 billion
◆ Driven by divestments and a focus on the future fight, the Department's request of 2.146 million military personnel is a slight decrease in end strength for FY 2022

FY 2022 National Defence Budget Request (Dollars in Billions)

(Source: Office of The Under Secretary of Defence (Comptroller)/Chief Financial Officer, May 2021)

By Department/Agency	FY 2021	FY 2022
Army	174.3	172.7
Navy	207.1	211.7
Air Force	204.0	212.8
Defence-Wide	118.4	117.8
Department of Defence – Total	703.7	715.0
Department of Energy & Other Agencies	37.0	37.9
National Defence – Total	740.7	752.9

DoD Total Budget by Appropriation Title ($ in millions)

(Source: Comptroller Information System, US DoD)

Total Budget	FY 2021	FY 2022
Military Personnel	162,270	167,285
Operation and Maintenance	283,395	290,361
Procurement	141,672	133,640
RDT&E	106,447	111,964
Revolving and Management Funds	1,394	1,902
Defence Bill	695,178	705,153
Military Construction	7,144	8,423
Family Housing	1,401	1,424
Military Construction Bill	8,545	9,847
TOTAL	703,723	715,000

COUNTER-TERRORISM & NATIONAL SECURITY

Terrorist groups such as ISIS, al-Qa'ida, and Hizbullah, etc continue to plot attacks against the United States and its allies and partners. In order to counter terrorism and defend homeland from terrorist activities, the US Dept. of State works with foreign government partners to build the capabilities necessary to prevent, degrade, detect, and respond to terrorist threats. They thus strengthen law enforcement and judicial capabilities, expand aviation and border security, deepen global information sharing, counter terrorist financing, improve crisis response, and counter violent extremism. The State Department also works closely with the Departments of Defence, Homeland Security, Justice, Treasury, and the Intelligence Community to lead an integrated whole-of-government approach to international counterterrorism. As per US Dept's. Country Reports on Terrorism, recently US and its allies made major strides to defeat and degrade international terrorist organisations. Along with the Global Coalition to Defeat ISIS, the US completed the destruction of the so-called "caliphate" in Iraq and Syria. US and its partners also imposed sanctions on Iran and others. The report also stated that, the threat posed by racially or ethnically motivated terrorism (REMT), particularly white supremacist terrorism, remained a serious challenge for the global community. Amid this diverse and dynamic threat landscape, the United States continued its longstanding role as the world's counterterrorism leader, taking decisive action to combat these threats and rallying its allies and partners to contribute to the fight. The United States also played a major role in building our partners' capabilities to detect, disrupt, and dismantle terrorist networks.

Counterinsurgency is any military or political action taken against the activities of guerrillas or revolutionaries and can be considered war by a state against a non-state adversary. Counterinsurgency is done by the country to fight insurgency which is usually violent, armed rebellion against the authority. The US has conducted counterinsurgency campaigns during the Philippine-American War, the Vietnam War, the post-2001 War in Afghanistan, and the Iraq War. They have also been conducting special operations especially the training and development of other states' military and security forces.

The US engaged a host of international partners - from governments to local religious leaders to tech companies - to counter terrorist radicalization and recruitment, both online and offline, and to help develop messaging strategies and counter disinformation and propaganda. These key steps also include information sharing, aviation and border security, countering terrorist radicalisation and recruitment, crisis response capability, countering terrorism finance, repatriating Foreign Terrorist Fighters, countering Iran-backed terrorist groups, and law enforcement "finishes" – arresting, prosecuting and incarcerating terrorists, the 2019 US State Dept. report added.

The **US Bureau of Counterterrorism** in the State Department (CT) continually monitors the activities of terrorist groups active around the world to identify potential targets for designation.

The **FBI's** job is to protect the US from terrorist attacks. The Bureau works closely with its partners to neutralise terrorist cells and operatives here in the United States, to help dismantle extremist networks worldwide, and to cut off financing and other forms of support provided to foreign terrorist organisations.

Domestic terrorism is the unlawful use, or threatened use, of violence by a group or individual based and operating entirely within the United States (or its territories) without foreign direction committed against persons or property to intimidate or coerce a government, the civilian population, or any segment thereof, in furtherance of political or social objectives.

International terrorism involves violent acts or acts dangerous to human life that are a violation of the criminal laws of the United States or any state, or that would be a criminal violation if committed within the jurisdiction of the United States or any state. Acts are intended to intimidate or coerce a civilian population, influence the policy of a government, or affect the conduct of a government.

Cyberterrorism is a computer-based attacks aimed at disabling vital computer systems so as to intimidate, coerce, or harm a government or section of the population. The United States faces persistent and increasingly sophisticated malicious cyber campaigns that threaten the public sector, the private sector, and ultimately the American people's security and privacy. Cyberterrorism ranks among the highest potential security threats in the world. United States Cyber Command (USCYBERCOM) is a military command that operates globally in real time against determined and capable adversaries. USCYBERCOM represents the latest evolution in a series of organisational designs to enable Department of Defense Information Network (DoDIN) and to optimize US military capabilities in cyberspace. The Cybersecurity and Infrastructure Security Agency (CISA) leads the US efforts to understand, manage, and reduce risk to their cyber and physical infrastructure. The Cybersecurity and Infrastructure Security Agency Act amends the Homeland Security Act of 2002 to redesignate the National Protection and Programs Directorate (NPPD) as the Cybersecurity and Infrastructure Security Agency (CISA).

USA's Designated Foreign Terrorist Organisations, as per US State Gov:

Abu Sayyaf Group (ASG), Aum Shinrikyo (AUM), Basque Fatherland and Liberty (ETA), Gama'a al-Islamiyya (Islamic Group – IG), HAMAS, Harakat ul-Mujahidin (HUM), Hizballah Kahane Chai (Kach), Kurdistan Workers Party (PKK, aka Kongra-Gel), Liberation Tigers of Tamil Eelam (LTTE), National Liberation Army (ELN), Palestine Liberation Front (PLF), Palestine Islamic Jihad (PIJ), Popular Front for the Liberation of Palestine (PFLP), PFLP-General Command (PFLP-GC), Revolutionary Armed Forces of Colombia (FARC), Revolutionary People's Liberation Party/Front (DHKP/C), Shining Path (SL), Al-Qa'ida (AQ), Islamic Movement of Uzbekistan (IMU), Real Irish Republican Army (RIRA), Jaish-e-Mohammed (JEM), Lashkar-e Tayyiba (LeT), Al-Aqsa Martyrs Brigade (AAMB) Asbat al-Ansar (AAA), al-Qaida in the Islamic Maghreb (AQIM), Communist Party of the Philippines/New People's Army (CPP/NPA), Jemaah Islamiya (JI), Lashkar i Jhangvi (LJ), Ansar al-Islam (AAI), Continuity Irish Republican Army (CIRA), Islamic State of Iraq and the Levant (formerly al-Qa'ida in Iraq), Islamic Jihad Union (IJU), Harakat ul-Jihad-i-Islami/Bangladesh (HUJI-B), al-Shabaab, Revolutionary Struggle (RS), Kata'ib Hizballah (KH), al-Qa'ida in the Arabian Peninsula (AQAP), Harakat ul-Jihad-i-Islami (HUJI), Tehrik-e Taliban Pakistan (TTP), Jaysh al-Adl (formerly Jundallah), Army of Islam (AOI), Indian Mujahedeen (IM), Jemaah Anshorut Tauhid (JAT), Abdallah Azzam Brigades (AAB), Haqqani Network (HQN), Ansar al-Dine (AAD), Boko Haram, Ansaru, al-Mulathamun Battalion (AMB), Ansar al-Shari'a in Benghazi, Ansar al-Shari'a in Darnah, Ansar al-Shari'a in Tunisia, ISIL Sinai Province (formerly Ansar Bayt al-Maqdis), al-Nusrah Front, Mujahidin Shura Council in the Environs of Jerusalem (MSC), Jaysh Rijal al-Tariq al Naqshabandi (JRTN), ISIL-Khorasan (ISIL-K), Islamic State of Iraq and the Levant's Branch in Libya (ISIL-Libya), Al-Qa'ida in the Indian Subcontinent,

Hizbul Mujahideen (HM), ISIS-Bangladesh, ISIS-Philippines, ISIS-West Africa, ISIS-Greater Sahara, al-Ashtar Brigades (AAB), Jama'at Nusrat al-Islam wal-Muslimin (JNIM), Islamic Revolutionary Guard Corps (IRGC), Asa'ib Ahl al-Haq (AAH), Harakat Sawa'd Misr (HASM), ISIS-DRC, ISIS-Mozambique.

Major Incidents

The terrorist attack of September 11, 2001, marked a dramatic escalation in a trend toward more destructive terrorist attacks which began in the 1980s. Before the September 11 attack, the October 23, 1983 truck bombings of US and French military barracks in Beirut, Lebanon. The September 11 attack also marked the first successful act of international terrorism in the United States since the vehicle bombing of the World Trade Center in February 1993. The September 11 attacks (9/11), a series of four coordinated terrorist attacks by the militant Islamist terrorist group al-Qaeda were the most lethal terrorist attacks in history, taking the lives of 3,000 Americans and international citizens and ultimately leading to far-reaching changes in anti-terror approaches and operations in the US and around the globe, as per FBI.

Between 1978 and 1995, three people die and 23 others are wounded after a string of mail bombings carried out by Ted Kaczynski (The Unabomber).

In Feb 26, 1993, a bomb explodes in the underground parking garage at the World Trade Center in New York.

In April 19, 1995, a bomb rips through the Alfred P. Murrah Federal Building in Oklahoma City, Oklahoma, killing and injuring many innocent people.

In July 27, 1996, a bomb explodes in Centennial Olympic Park in Atlanta during the Summer Olympics.

In Sept 11, 2001, 19 al Qaeda members hijack four US passenger airliners. Two are flown into the World Trade Center towers in New York, one crashes into the Pentagon and another crashes into the Pennsylvania countryside.

In April 15, 2013, twin bomb blasts explode near the finish line of the Boston Marathon. The Boston Marathon bombing was a domestic terrorist attack, carried out by two terrorists, Dzhokhar Tsarnaev and Tamerlan Tsarnaev.

In July 16, 2015, Mohammad Abdulazeez opens fire on a military recruiting center and a Naval reserve facility in Chattanooga, Tennessee, killing four US Marines and a Navy sailor.

In December 2, 2015, Syed Rizwan Farook and Tashfeen Malik open fire on a holiday party taking place at Inland Regional Center in San Bernardino.

In June 12, 2016, Omar Mateen, who'd pledged allegiance to ISIS, kills 49 people and wounds others in a shooting spree at a Pulse nightclub in Orlando.

In August 12, 2017, one person is killed and 19 are injured when a speeding car slams into a throng of counter protesters in Charlottesville, Virginia.

In October 31, 2017, 8 people are killed and almost a dozen injured when a 29-year-old man in a rented pickup truck drives down a busy bicycle path near the World Trade Center in New York.

In Aug 3, 2019, 22 people are killed in El Paso, Texas, after a mass shooting at a Walmart store in a case that's being treated as domestic terrorism.

In December 6, 2019, a gunman opens fire on a Naval air station in Pensacola, Florida, killing three US sailors.

In December 10, 2019, two shooters attack a Kosher grocery store in Jersey City, New Jersey, killing three people inside the shop. These were some of the terrorist attacks on US soil, as per US media reports.

Combating Terrorism

The US intelligence community comprises of **Central Intelligence Agency (CIA), National Security Agency (NSA)**, Defense Intelligence Agency, the **Bureau of Intelligence and Research of the State Department**, intelligence elements of the departments of Defence, Treasury, Energy, and the Drug Enforcement Administration, and intelligence/counterterrorism elements of the **Federal Bureau of Investigation (FBI)**. According to the Office of the Director of **National Intelligence,** the US Intelligence Community is composed of the following 18 organisations: two independent agencies—the Office of the Director of National Intelligence (ODNI) and the Central Intelligence Agency (CIA); Nine Department of Defence elements—the Defence Intelligence Agency (DIA), the National Security Agency (NSA), the National Geospatial- Intelligence Agency (NGA), the National Reconnaissance Office (NRO), and intelligence elements of the five DoD services; the Army, Navy, Marine Corps, Air Force, and Space Force. Seven elements of other departments and agencies—the Department of Energy's Office of Intelligence and Counter-Intelligence; the Department of Homeland Security's Office of Intelligence and Analysis and US Coast Guard Intelligence; the Department of Justice's Federal Bureau of Investigation and the Drug Enforcement Agency's Office of National Security Intelligence; the Department of State's Bureau of Intelligence and Research; and the Department of the Treasury's Office of Intelligence and Analysis. The **National Counter Terrorism Centre (NCTC)** was created from a post-9/11 world in which the United States Government (USG) reorganised and restructured the Intelligence Community (IC) in order to protect and secure our nation from terrorist attacks. NCTC analyses the threat using all available USG information, shares terrorism-related information with US partners across the counterterrorism (CT) enterprise, maintains the single authoritative USG database of known and suspected terrorists, and integrates the national CT effort through effective planning and strategy development. The partners are Central Intelligence Agency, Defense Intelligence Agency, Department of Agriculture, Department of Defense, Department of Energy, Dept. of Health & Human Services, Department of Homeland Security, Department of Justice, Department of State, Department of the Treasury, Drug Enforcement Administration, Federal Bureau of Investigation, Nat'l Geospatial Intelligence Agency, Nuclear Regulatory Commission, National Security Agency, Transportation Security Admin. and US Capitol Police. The **Joint Terrorism Task Forces (JTTF)** are locally-based multi-agency partnerships between various federal, state, and local law enforcement agencies tasked with investigating terrorism and terrorism-related crimes, led by the FBI and US Department of Justice. They are locally based and comprised of investigators, analysts, linguists, Special Weapons and Tactics (SWAT) experts, and other specialists from dozens of US law enforcement and intelligence agencies.

Anti-terrorism legislation are laws with the purpose of fighting terrorism. The September 11, 2001 terrorist attacks prompted the US Department of Justice to redefine its mission, objectives, and priorities to focus its top priority on counterterrorism. The Department of Justice directed the formation or expansion of terrorism task forces and councils (with members from many federal, state, and local agencies and private industry) that coordinate and integrate intelligence and law enforcement functions to achieve the Department's counterterrorism goal. US has Search and seizure method which is governed by the Fourth Amendment to the United States Constitution. The US also passed the **USA PATRIOT Act** after the September 11 attacks, as well as a range of other legislation and executive orders relating to national security. The Department of Homeland Security was established to consolidate domestic security agencies to coordinate anti-terrorism and national response to major natural disasters and accidents. The purpose of the **Uniting and Strengthening America by Providing Appropriate Tools Required to Intercept and Obstruct Terrorism (USA PATRIOT) Act of 200**1 is to deter and punish terrorist acts in the United States and around the world, to enhance law enforcement investigatory tools, and other purposes Some of which include; to strengthen US measures to prevent, detect and prosecute international money laundering and financing of terrorism; to subject to special scrutiny foreign jurisdictions, foreign financial institutions, and classes of international transactions or types of accounts that are susceptible to criminal abuse; to require all appropriate elements of the financial services industry to report potential money laundering; to strengthen measures to prevent use of the US financial system for personal gain by corrupt foreign officials and facilitate repatriation of stolen assets to the citizens of countries to whom such assets belong. The **Foreign Intelligence Surveillance Act of 1978 (FISA)** is a United States federal law that establishes procedures for the physical and electronic surveillance and the collection of foreign intelligence information between foreign powers and agents of foreign powers suspected of espionage or terrorism. The Anti-Terrorism Advisory Council Programme in each United States Attorneys' Office was establish to serve as a conduit for information sharing between federal and state authorities, a coordinating body for carrying out the anti-terrorism plan and an organisational structure for responding to any future terrorist incidents in that district.

Military Intervention

The USA led a global counterterrorism campaign in response to the terrorist attacks of September 11, 2001. The targets of the campaign are primarily extremist groups, with the most prominent groups being Al-Qaeda, the Islamic State and their various franchise groups. The rise of the Islamic State of Iraq and the Levant led to the global Operation Inherent Resolve (Syria and Iraq), and an international campaign to destroy ISIS. US military operations in Afghanistan, Africa, the Philippines, and Colombia were a part of the US-initiated Global War on Terrorism (GWOT). These operations covered a wide variety of combat and non-combat missions ranging from combating insurgents, to civil affairs and reconstruction operations, to training military forces of other nations in counternarcotics, counterterrorism, and counterinsurgency tactics.

Operation JUNIPER SHIELD (OJS) constitutes the Department's support to the US Department of State-led Trans-Sahara Counter Terrorism Program (TSCTP).

Operation Enduring Freedom is the official name used by the Bush administration for the War in Afghanistan.

The US Special Operations Command, Pacific was deployed to the Philippines to advise and assist the Armed Forces of the Philippines in combating Filipino Islamist groups.

Operation NOBLE EAGLE (ONE) is a direct response to the September 11, 2001, terrorist attacks at the World Trade Center in New York City and the Pentagon. It funds the continuing efforts to defend the United States from airborne attacks, maintain air sovereignty, and defend critical US facilities from a potentially hostile threat.

The US has also conducted a series of military strikes on al-Qaeda militants in Yemen since the War on Terror began. Operation Active Endeavour is a naval operation of NATO started in October 2001 in response to the September 11 attacks.

After the wars in Afghanistan and Iraq following 9/11 terror attacks, much of the US armed forces activity has been focused on counterterrorism efforts, either in direct combat, through drone attacks, border patrols, intelligence gathering or training other nations' security forces. The USA has conducted more than 80+ counterterrorism operations around the world. The country has provided training in counterterrorism to many countries, it has engaged in combat (including drone strikes) and conducted military exercises also in many countries.

US Africa Command, with partners, counters transnational threats and malign actors, strengthens security forces and responds to crises in order to advance US national interests and promote regional security, stability and prosperity. Combined Joint Task Force-Horn of Africa (CJTF-HOA) conducts operations in the Combined Joint Operations Area to enhance partner nation capacity, promote regional stability, dissuade conflict, and protect US and coalition interests. CJTF-HOA is critical to US AFRICOM's efforts to build partner capacity to counter violent extremists and address other regional security partnerships.

In Kenya and Somalia, the Department of State continues to build the capacity of border security elements, especially along the Kenya-Somalia border, and strengthen the ability of regulatory agencies, law enforcement, civil aviation authorities, and the criminal justice sector to prevent and respond to terrorist attacks. While military forces have made progress in degrading Boko Haram, governments in the region continue to face challenges in establishing civilian security, handling Boko Haram detainees, and reintegrating fighters. Al-Qaida in the Islamic Maghreb and other terrorist groups have adopted a strategy of asymmetric attacks that increasingly threatens Mali and other West African countries. Tunisian counterterrorism authorities are showing an increasing ability to manage and respond to terrorism threats, yet Tunisia continues to face threats from ISIS in Libya and returning foreign terrorist fighters (FTFs).

All four pictures in the montage are taken by the US Army/Navy.

To counter Iranian influence, the Department of State continues to lead an international initiative focusing on Hizbollah's terrorist and illicit activities, working closely with other US partners, including the Department of Justice, the Federal Bureau of Investigation, the Department of the Treasury, the Department of Homeland Security, and the National Counterterrorism Center.

South and Southeast Asian partner countries, including Bangladesh and India, face ongoing and expanding threats, US State Dept., on its end, implementing new counterterrorism laws, and increasing information sharing and border and aviation security.

In Central Asia and Europe, US is using various methods to counter terrorist travel in and through the region to Western Europe, the conflict zones, and potentially, the United States.

CONCLUSION

The United States has engaged in every type of ground warfare in the last 20 years. No other country comes close to the amount of combat veterans that US have. For decades the United States has been uncontested or dominant in every operating domain. The US could deploy, assemble, and operate its forces in all domains - air, land, sea, space, and cyberspace. United States, after the Cold War, emerged as the world's only remaining superpower and enjoyed a period of military dominance. Operation Desert Storm in 1991, when the US was at the height of its conventional military overmatch and was able to project power with minimal interference, remains a lasting reference point for how many the country view conventional conflict. The defence spending represents about half of the federal government's discretionary spending, and the military's budget has increased by more than 70 percent since 2001. Although the conflicts in Iraq and Afghanistan have cost the Pentagon upward of USD 1 trillion, nearly half of the growth in defence spending in the past decade has been unrelated to the wars. The steady rise of China and her assertiveness in South China Sea, has compelled US declare that she would favour peaceful adjustments in the region. In the Asia-Pacific leaders' summit, President Obama stated his intention to take relations with China to a new level and highlighted the importance of forging a durable strategic partnership with China to ensure its rising power does not destabilise the international system. US is focusing on strategic partnerships with India, Japan, Australia and Vietnam to counter the growing military rise of China. The United States has also been seeking to expand its military cooperation with India as part of the US strategic shift to the Asia-Pacific region. The US also shifted to confront new challenges, particularly insurgent warfare and the threat posed by the rise of violent extremist organisations. USA is working on battles against cyber threats, terrorism around the globe including Iraq, Syria, Afghanistan and to defeat Al Qaeda and Islamic State of Iraq and the Levant (ISIL). US is also taking steps to counter Russia's stance or policies in Eastern Europe and also involving the country's long-term economic and security interests in Asia-Pacific region. Today's security environment is dramatically different from the one the United States has been engaged with for the last 25 years, and it requires new ways of thinking and new ways of acting. This security environment is driving the focus of the Defence Dept.'s planning, budgeting for Armed Forces. As the security environment is evolving. US is currently focusing on rebalancing to the Asia-Pacific, maintaining a strong commitment to security and stability in Europe and the Middle East, sustaining a global approach to countering violent extremists, prioritising and protect key investments in technology and to reinvigorate efforts to build innovative partnerships. The Dept. of Defence is adapting to the constantly changing security environment by adhering to the priorities and approach outlined in the National Defence Strategy. That strategic approach involves building a more lethal force, strengthening alliances and attracting new partners, and reforming existing processes. The country is also strengthening its alliances. The US is continuously working with NATO nations to improve burden sharing to meet common security commitments. They are also enhancing cooperation with Australia, Japan, India and South Korea through ongoing engagements, their procurement of high-end US platforms, and working with some countries to build missile defence systems. The US Armed Forces has significant capabilities in both defence and power projection due to its large budget, resulting in advanced and powerful equipment, and its widespread deployment of force around the world, including about 800 military bases in foreign locations.

CONTACT DETAILS

The Dept. of Defence
Address: 1400 Defence Pentagon
Washington DC 20301-1400
Tel: 703-571-3343
US Army, Navy, Air Force & Marines
Headquarters, The Pentagon
Arlington County, Virginia, US

Joint Staff Public Affairs
9999 Joint Staff Pentagon, Room 2D932
Washington DC, 20318-9999

DARPA
Defence Advanced Research
Projects Agency
3701 North Fairfax Drive
Arlington, VA 22203
DARPA General Information
(703) 526-6630
Contact DPAP
Defence Procurement and Acquisition Policy
3060 Defence Pentagon
Room 3B855
Washington, DC 20301-3060

Missile Defence Agency (MDA)
Office Symbol 5700 18th Street
Bldg 245. Fort Belvoir, Virginia 22060-5573

Defence Security Cooperation
Agency (DSCA)
2800 Defence Pentagon
Washington, DC 20301-2800

The first of two Terminal High Altitude Area Defence (THAAD) interceptors is launched during a successful intercept test. The test, conducted by Missile Defence Agency (MDA), Ballistic Missile Defence System (BMDS) Operational Test Agency, Joint Functional Component Command for Integrated Missile Defence, and US Pacific Command. (Image Credit: US Army)

URUGUAY
(Capital: Montevideo)

INTRODUCTION
Area: 176,215 sq km
Population: 3,398,239 (July 2021 est.)
Coastline: 660 km
Maritime claims: Territorial sea: 12 nm
Contiguous zone: 24 nm
Exclusive Economic Zone: 200 nm
Continental shelf: 200 nm or edge of continental margin

KEY POLITICAL PERSONS

PRESIDENT: Luis Lacalle Pou

VICE PRESIDENT: Beatriz Argimón

KEY DEFENCE PERSONS

DEFENCE MINISTER: Javier Garcia

CHIEF OF DEFENCE STAFF: Gen. Gustavo Fajardo

COMMANDER-IN-CHIEF OF ARMY: Gen. Gerardo Daniel Fregossi Álvarez

COMMANDER-IN-CHIEF OF NAVY: Adm. Jorge Wilson

COMMANDER-IN-CHIEF OF AIR FORCE: Air Gen. Luis Heber de León

ECONOMY
Uruguay's free market economy is characterised by an export-oriented agricultural sector, a well-educated workforce, and high levels of social spending. GDP growth which was 8-9% in 2010 but was reduced in 2012-2016 due to economic slowdown. Growth increased in 2017 due to sound macroeconomic framework. Uruguay belongs to a number of international organisations, including the United Nations, Organisation of American States, International Monetary Fund, World Bank, and the World Trade Organisation. Uruguay's economic growth has remained positive even in 2017 and 2018, in spite of recessions experienced by Argentina and Brazil. Currently, its main trading partners are China (26%) and the European Union (18%). In 2018, bilateral goods trade between the United States and Uruguay was $2 billion. The United States had a USD937 million trade surplus with Uruguay in 2018. Uruguay's main imports from the United States are electrical machinery, machinery, mineral fuels, pharmaceuticals, and cosmetics. The United States was Uruguay's third largest export market and fourth largest importer in 2018, as per US Dept. of State. Uruguay is a member of number of international organisations including United Nations, Organisation of American States, International Monetary Fund, World Bank, and the World Trade Organisation. COVID-19 pandemic has affected the Uruguayan economy badly but the country with funds from World Bank and strong public health system is recovering back its economy to normal and improving the business climate.

GDP (official exchange rate): $75.06 billion (2020 est.), $79.73 billion (2019 est.)
Real Growth Rate (GDP): 2.7% (2017 est.), 1.7% (2016 est.)
Industries: Food processing, electrical machinery, transportation equipment, petroleum products, textiles, chemicals, beverages
Total Exports: $13.55 billion (2020 est.), $16.99 billion (2019 est.)
Export Commodities: Sulfate wood pulp, beef, soybeans, concentrated milk, rice (2019)
Major Markets: China 29%, Brazil 12%, United States 5%, Netherlands 5%, Argentina 5% (2019)
Total Imports: $11.29 billion (2020 est.), $13.31 billion (2019 est.)
Import Commodities: Crude petroleum, packaged medicines, cars, broadcasting equipment, delivery trucks (2019)
Major Suppliers: Brazil 25%, China 15%, United States 11%, Argentina 11% (2019)

INTERNATIONAL DISPUTES
Two uncontested boundary disputes with Brazil over Isla Brasilera at the tripoint with Argentina at the confluence of the Quarai/Cuareim and Uruguay rivers, and, in the 235-square kilometre Invernada River region, over which tributary represents the legitimate source of the Quarai/Cuareim River.

DEFENCE
ARMY
Personnel: 14,500

Equipment

Category	Name	In Service
MBT	T-54/55	10+
	M-24	10+
	M41-A1	30+
APC/MICV/IFV	BMP-1	10+
	M113	20
	Condor	35+
	Gaz 3971 Vodnik	40+
	OT M-64 SKOT	35
	OT M-93	40
	MT-LB	
	Mowag	30+
	EE9 Cascavel	10+
	EE3 Jararaca	10+

...continued

Category	Name	In Service
Artillery	105 mm. M101/M102	35+
	155 mm. M114	
	122 mm. S1	
	122 mm. RM-70	
Mortar	60 mm.	80+
	81 mm.	80+
	120 mm. SL	40+
MRL	122 mm. RM-70	
Anti-Tank GW	Milan	10+
Recoilless rifle	106 mm. M40A1	50+
	75 mm. M-20	2+
AA gun	40 mm. L/60	5+
	20 mm. M167 Vulcan	5
	20 mm. TCM-20	5+

New Procurements/ Upgrades
No major procurement plans are under consideration at present.

NAVY
Personnel: 5,000

Equipment

Category	Name	In Service
Frigate	Uruguay Class	1
Logistics Support	General Artigas	1
Mine Warfare	Audaz Class	1
	Temerario	1
Patrol Vessel	Colonia	1
	Rio Negro Class	1
	Paysandú	1
Amphibious Force	LD-41 Class LCM	2
	LD-45 Class LCVP	2

Naval Aviation

Category	Name	In Service
Aircraft	Beechcraft B-200T	1
	2 Jetstream TM Mk2	1
	T-34C	2
Helicopter	Bo-105	5+
	Wessex HC Mk2	2+
	IH-13 Esquilo	1

New Procurements/ Upgrades
No major procurement plans are under consideration at present.

AIR FORCE
Personnel: 2,500

Equipment

Category	Name	In Service
Fighters/ attack/ Reconnaissance	Cessna A-37 Dragonfly	10+
Transport/ Tanker	C-130 Hercules	1+
	EMB 110 Bandeirante	2+
	Beechcraft Twin Bonanza D50	1
	CASA C-212 Aviocar	1+
	EMB 120 Brasilia	1
Helicopter	Aerospatiale AS 365 Dauphin	1
	Bell 212 Twin Huey	2+
	Bell UH-1 Iroquois	5+
Trainer	Aermacchi SF.260	12
	Pilatus PC-7 Turbo Trainer	3+
	Cessna T-41 Mescalero	5
Utility	Cessna 206 Stationair	5+
	Beechcraft B58 Baron	2

New Procurements/ Upgrades
No major procurement plans are under consideration at present.

Defence Expenditure
Total defence spending: $491 million (approx.)

Estimated defence spending in terms of GDP: 2% of GDP (2020 est.), 2% of GDP (2019)

Major defence suppliers: United States, Brazil, Argentina, Israel, Canada, Russia.

Ministry of National Defence, Uruguay - Budget Execution:
(Source: www.gub.uy/ministerio-defensa-nacional)

Description EU	Current credit	Affected	Committed	Obliged
General Command of the Army	7,533,442,242	575,970,321	527,783,130	500,935,066
General Command of the Navy	3,299,319,700	897,113,747	189,094,243	171,015,161
General Command of the Air Force	2,015,477,297	250,704,161	171,339,336	93,344,078
Defence Staff	95,216,095	8,473,281	8,473,281	6,604,581

Defence Production and R&D
Uruguay has no defence industry, although the navy owns a small shipyard that manufactures small vessel. There is also a small, army-run explosives production facility known as PESMA.

Defence Procurement
The Uruguayan MoD has announced the creation of a new procurement arm as part of its 2010-2014 Defence Budget in a bid to streamline procurement. The Centralised Defence Procurement Unit (UCAD) will be responsible for all future acquisition programmes. It will ultimately have a chief, deputy chief, three department heads, six advisors and five technical staff.

CONTACT DETAILS

Ministry of National Defence
Avenida 8 de octubre, 2628de
Montevideo
Uruguay
Tel: +5982472828
Fax: +5982474425

Army HQ
Avda. General Garibaldi, 2313
Montevideo, Uruguay
Tel: +5982081542, 2081554
Fax: +598-2036600

Navy HQ
Ranbla 25 de Agost s7n esq. Maciel 4.o Piso
Montevideo, Uruguay
Tel: +59829155555
Fax: +598-2-9169048

Air Force HQ
Avenida Don Pedro de Mendoza, 5553
Montevideo, Uruguay
Tel: +5982224401
Fax: +598-2-223830

UZBEKISTAN
(Capital: Tashkent)

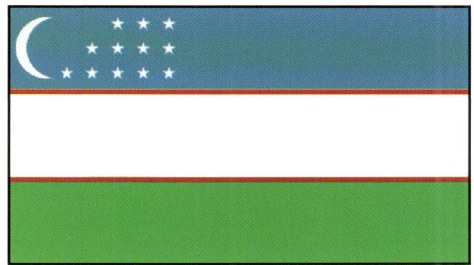

INTRODUCTION
Area: 447,400 sq km
Population: 30,842,796 (July 2021 est.)
Coastline: 0 km (doubly landlocked)
Maritime claims: None

KEY POLITICAL PERSONS

PRESIDENT: Shavkat Mirziyoyev

PRIME MINISTER: Abdulla Aripov

KEY DEFENCE PERSONS

DEFENCE MINISTER: Maj. Gen. Bahodir Qurbonov

CHIEF OF THE GENERAL STAFF: Maj. Gen. Shukhrat Kholmukhamedov

ECONOMY

The landlocked country, Uzbekistan, is transitioning to a more market-oriented economy. The country is a major producer and exporter of cotton and gold with substantial deposits of copper, strategic minerals, gas, and oil. The country's policy goals are: to increase the efficiency of infrastructure, especially of energy, transport, and irrigation; to enhance the competitiveness of specific industries, such as agro-processing, petrochemicals, and textiles; to diversify the economy and thereby reduce its reliance on commodity exports; and to improve access to and the quality and outcomes of education, health and other social services in order to become an industrialised, high middle-income country by around 2050. To mitigate the economic, social, and health consequences of the Covid-19 pandemic, the Government has been taking anti-crisis policy measure. International financial support, including from the World Bank, the International Monetary Fund, the Asian Development Bank, and bilateral donors, is expected to cover the financing needs stemming from the crisis, according to the World Bank.

GDP (official exchange rate): $57.789 billion (2019 est.)

Real Growth Rate (GDP): 5.3% (2017 est.), 7.8% (2016 est.)

Industries: Textiles, food processing, machine building, metallurgy, mining, hydrocarbon extraction, chemicals.

Total Exports: $14.52 billion (2020 est.), $16.99 billion (2019 est.)

Export Commodities: Gold, natural gas, cotton fibers, copper, ethylene polymers (2019)

Major Markets: Switzerland 19%, United Kingdom 17%, Russia 15%, China 14%, Kazakhstan 9%, Turkey 8%, Kyrgyzstan 5% (2019)

Total Imports: $22.56 billion (2020 est.), $26.55 billion (2019 est.)

Import Commodities: Cars and vehicle parts, packaged medicines, refined petroleum, aircraft, construction vehicles (2019)

Major Suppliers: China 23%, Russia 18%, South Korea 11%, Kazakhstan 9%, Turkey 6%, Germany 5% (2019)

INTERNATIONAL DISPUTES

◆ Prolonged drought and cotton monoculture in Uzbekistan and Turkmenistan created water-sharing difficulties for Amu Darya river states.

◆ Field demarcation of the boundaries with Kazakhstan commenced in 2004.

◆ Border delimitation of 130 km of border with Kyrgyzstan is hampered by serious disputes around enclaves and other areas.

DEFENCE

Uzbekistan, known as the best-equipped armed forces in Central Asia has maintained the largest military force in the region. The unified armed forces of Uzbekistan consist of a Ground force, Air and Air Defence forces, National Guard, Frontier Service and a Navy. Tashkent declared national sovereignty and the right to defend its own borders on 31 August 1991 which later saw the creation of a Ministry for Defence Affairs and appointment of the first Defence Minister. In 2018, the government introduced a new military doctrine. The priorities for military reform included rearming the military with modern weapons and equipment, developing a domestic defence industry and reorganising the armed forces.

ARMY

Personnel: 70,000

Equipment

Category	Name	In Service
MBT	T-72	300
	T-62	
	T-64	
	T-80	100
APC	Ejder Yalchin TTZA	
	BTR-60	100
	BTR-70	150
	BTR-80	150
	BMP-2	150
	MRAP	308

New Procurements/Upgrades

◆ Uzbekistan plans to acquire the new Kazakh Arlan 4×4 multi-role armoured wheeled vehicles.

◆ Uzbekistan has reportedly ordered an unspecified number of BTR-82A APCs

NAVY (Riverine Service) operates two Dzaychum class patrol craft (Ukraine-built Gyurza type).

AIR & AIR DEFENCE FORCE

Personnel: 15,000

Equipment

Category	Name	In Service
Fighter	Sukhoi Su-27	6
	Sukhoi Su-25	20
	Sukhoi Su-24	30 (stored)
	Sukhoi Su-17	Unspecified (stored)
	MiG-29	30 (most stored)
Trainer	L-39	20

...continued

Category	Name	In Service
Helicopter	AS532	
	Mi-35	12
	Mi-8	50
	Mi-17	25
	Mi-24	40
Transport	IL-76	6
	An-12	5
	An-24	1
	An-26	15
SAM	SA-2/-3/-5	1 brigade

New Procurements/Upgrades
◆ The Air Force has reportedly placed a second order for AS532 helicopters from Airbus.
◆ Uzbekistan has expressed its interest in purchasing Sopka-2 radar systems.
◆ The government has reportedly entered negotiations with Russia on the potential purchase of the Yak-130 advanced jet trainer.

Defence Expenditure
Total defence spending: $15 billion (2019), $1.6 billion (2018)
Defence spending in terms of GDP: 1.2% (2020)

Defence Production and R&D
The State Committee of Uzbekistan on the defence industry, Goskomoboronprom, reportedly has been making efforts to develop the country's industrial potential in the field of military and dual-use production, as well as equipping the national army with modern weapons and military equipment. It has established military-technical cooperation with twenty leading countries, signed agreements and memorandums of cooperation with foreign partners and modern weapons and military equipment are being acquired. The MoD is working on the modernisation of outdated weapons and military equipment. Currently, a roadmap for the development of military-industrial complex of Uzbekistan for 2020-2025 is being worked out. The country has seen moderate success in establishing a niche industry focused on aerospace. The TAPO plant has manufactured Il-76 military transport aircraft and Il-78 in-flight refuelling aircraft in cooperation with several Russian firms, including the Voronezh aircraft plant.

Defence Procurement
Kazakhstan has reportedly delivered to Uzbekistan SU-30SM aircraft, Mi-35M helicopters, Buk-M2E defence missile systems, BTR-80 and BTR-82A armoured personnel carriers, Orlan-10E UAV, Typhoon-K armoured MRAP vehicles and small arms.

> **CONTACT DETAILS**
> **Ministry of Defence**
> 100, M.Ulugbek str., Tashkent,
> Republic of Uzbekistan, 100000
> Phones: +998 (71) 269-8200,
> +998 (71) 269-8228

STRATEGIC INFORMATION
VENEZUELA
(Capital: Caracas)

INTRODUCTION
Area: 912,050 sq km
Population: 29,069,153 (July 2021 est.)
Coastline: 2,800 km
Maritime claims: Territorial sea: 12 nm
Contiguous zone: 15 nm
Exclusive Economic Zone: 200 nm
Continental shelf: 200 m depth or to the depth of exploitation

GEOPOLITICAL IMPORTANCE
Venezuela, officially called the Bolivarian Republic of Venezuela, is located on the Northern coast of South America. It borders Guyana to the East, Brazil to the South, and Colombia to the West. Venezuela comprises a number of Caribbean islands and archipelagos including Margarita Island, La Blanquilla, La Tortuga, Los Roques, and Los Monjes. The country became the first Spanish American colony to declare independence gaining full independence in 1830. From a relatively poor agrarian society Venezuela developed by exploiting huge petroleum reserves. Venezuela has the world's largest known oil reserves and has been one of the world's leading exporters of oil. The country is a founding member of the Organisation of the Petroleum Exporting Countries (OPEC), Venezuela is also a member of the Union of South American Nations, UNASUR and a key player in establishing the Community of Latin American and Caribbean States (CELAC). Venezuela lies on major sea and air routes linking North and South America

POLITICAL OVERVIEW
Venezuela is a federal republic. Its political system is divided into three groups – Executive, Legislative and Judicial branches. The President is the head of the state. He presides over the Executive branch of the government and is responsible for the appointment of vice-president, members of the cabinet and other important members of the National Assembly. The Legislature is a bicameral legislative assembly, named as the National Assembly or Asamblea Nacional having 167 seats. The members of the house are elected by a popular referendum for a period of five years which can be extended to a two-year term. The Supreme Tribunal of Justice is the highest law court in the judicial system. The magistrates of this court are appointed for a period of 12 years' term. There are lower courts, district courts and municipal courts located at every district.

Venezuela has suffered some coups and military dictatorships. The fall of Marcos Perez Jimenez government in 1958 ended the last dictatorship of the 20th century in Venezuela ushering in a democratic period. The country adopted a new constitution in 1961. Two political parties prevailed during the following decades – the social-democratic Democratic Action (AD) and the Christian-democratic COPEI during the period known as the Fourth Republic. This system came to an end during the 1998 election when Hugo Chavez won thus beginning the Fifth Republic and the left-wing Bolivarian revolution. Under Hugo CHAVEZ, president from 1999 to 2013, the executive branch exercised increasingly authoritarian control over other branches of government.

The current constitution was drafted in 1999 replacing the earlier constitution made in 1961. For the first time since 1999, the opposition was elected to hold the majority in the National Assembly following the 2015 parliamentary election. In 2017, the old legislative body was dismissed and transformed into the New Constituent National Assembly whose President Juan Guaido is recognized by several countries including the United States, the European Union as the interim president, while Mr Maduro is backed by countries such as Russia, China and Cuba. In January 2021, Maduro and his allies took control of the National Assembly after claiming victory in legislative elections.

KEY POLITICAL PERSONS

PRESIDENT & COMMANDER-IN-CHIEF: Nicolas Maduro Moros

EXECUTIVE VICE PRESIDENT: Delcy Rodriguez Gomez

ECONOMY

Venezuela's economy is predominantly based on petroleum sector and manufacturing. The country ranks as one of the ten richest countries in the world in terms of natural resources; approximately $14.3 trillion worth of natural resources, including gold, iron ore, and oil. Oil production has decreased from a peak in 1970 of 3.8 million barrels per day (BPD) in 1970 to its lowest production rate of approximately 13,000 BPD in July 2020, according to a CSIS report. It remains highly dependent on oil revenues which account for almost all export earnings and nearly half of the government's revenue. The country manufactures and exports heavy industry products such as steel, aluminium and cement. Other notable manufacturing includes electronics and auto mobiles as well as beverages and foodstuff. Agriculture accounts for approximately 4.7% of GDP and 7.3% of the labour force. The United States is Venezuela's most important trading partner. Venezuela is one of the top four suppliers of foreign oil to the United States. Falling oil prices have aggravated Venezuela's economic crisis. Insufficient access to dollars, price controls, and rigid labour regulations have led some multinational firms to reduce or shut down their operations in Venezuelan. Sanctions imposed by the United States and other western democracies, shortages of food and medicine have worsened the economic situation, leading to a humanitarian crisis in Venezuela that grew more desperate when the coronavirus SARS-CoV-2 global pandemic reached the country in 2020.

GDP (official exchange rate): $210.1 billion (2017 est.)

Real Growth Rate (GDP): -19.67% (2018 est.), -14% (2017 est.)

Industries: Agricultural products, livestock, raw materials, machinery and equipment, transport equipment, construction materials, medical equipment, pharmaceuticals, chemicals, iron and steel products, crude oil and petroleum products.

Crude oil – proved reserves: 302.3 billion bbl (1 January 2018 est.)

Natural gas – proved reserves: 5.739 trillion cu m (1 January 2018 est.)

Total Exports: $83.401 billion (2018 est.), $93.485 billion (2017 est.)

Export Commodities: Crude petroleum, refined petroleum, industrial alcohols, gold, iron (2019)

Major Markets: India 34%, China 28%, United States 12%, Spain 6% (2019)

Total Imports: $18.432 billion (2018 est.), $18.376 billion (2017 est.)

Import Commodities: Refined petroleum, rice, corn, tires, soybean meal, wheat (2019)

Major Suppliers: China 28%, United States 22%, Brazil 8%, Spain 6%, Mexico 6% (2019)

DEFENCE & SECURITY

The Organic Law of the Armed Forces (LOFAN) approved in September 2005 under the presidency of the late Hugo Chavez legally enshrines three core missions for the Bolivarian armed forces. First, protect the president, his family and his closest associates at all times. Second, maintain internal order against threats to the president. Third, defend Venezuela against external threats. The military doctrine explicitly defines the military's primary mission as defending the stability of the country against internal threats and disruptions and empowers the Bolivarian military to engage in joint actions with the armed forces of other countries. The armed forces have traditionally played a decisive role in the country's politics. Venezuela transition to democracy in 1958 and signed the 'Punto Fijo Pact,' the political agreement aimed at preserving democracy in Venezuela, in the same year. The administration of the late President Hugo Chavez appointed military officers in the state bureaucracy further strengthening the position of the armed forces and implementing large-scale arms modernisation programmes. The military has extended support to the government of President Nicolas Maduro after opposition leader Juan Guaido invoked the constitution in January 2019 to assume the interim presidency arguing that Mr. Maduro's 2018 re-election was illegitimate. The Maduro regime has given the FANB control of a wide array of industries ranging from precious metals to ports and customs. In addition, the FANB also manages military-designated firms in banking, air transport, television, and agriculture.

KEY DEFENCE PERSONS

MINISTER OF DEFENCE & STRATEGIC OPERATIONAL COMMANDER: Gen. Vladimir Padrino Lopez

COMMANDER OF OPERATIONAL STRATEGIC COMMAND: Chief Admiral Remigio Ceballos Ichaso

COMMANDER GENERAL OF NAVY: Adm. Giuseppe Alessandrello Cimadevilla

COMMANDER MILITARY AVIATION: Maj. Gen. Jose Silva Aponte

COMMANDING GENERAL OF THE NATIONAL GUARD: Maj. Gen. Antonio Jose Benavides Torres

COMMANDING GENERAL OF THE NATIONAL MILITIA: Maj. Gen. Carlos Augusto Leal Telleria

Internal conflict

Venezuela continue to face political tensions, economy issues, including expropriations, macroeconomic distortions, physical insecurity, corruption, and a volatile regulatory framework. Tensions mounted when Mr Guaido, leader of the National Assembly, declared himself acting president on 23 January 2019. This was seen as a direct challenge to the power of President Maduro, who had been sworn in to a second six-year term in May 2018. The security forces have remained loyal to Mr Maduro who has rewarded them frequently. Many Venezuelans have blamed Mr Maduro's government as the economy went into free-fall and for the country's decline. Talks were held between representatives from the government and the opposition to resolve the political crisis, however, the government has pulled out of the talks after sweeping sanctions were imposed by the US the governments. Due to hyperinflation and deep recession many Venezuelans have been hit by the shortages of food and home staples such as milk, flour and toiletries, medicine, rising unemployment and soaring violent crimes. According to figures compiled by the United Nations, more than 5.6 million Venezuelans have left the country since the crisis started in 2014 crossing into neighbouring countries such as Colombia, Ecuador, Peru, Chile and Brazil.

External conflict

Venezuela claims most of Guyana west of the Essequibo river. The dispute dates back to the early nineteenth century. Venezuela has a maritime boundary dispute with Colombia in the Gulf of Venezuela and territorial dispute with Dominica over the Isla Aves archipelago located in the Caribbean.

THREAT PERSPECTIVE

Venezuela faces minimal external threat; however, armed guerrilla groups pose the real peril to regional stability. Many of these home-grown guerrilla groups are no longer contained within the confines of their own nation and continue to increase in militancy. Increasing US-led militarisation of Latin America is seen as another threat that appears to be particularly aimed at the country, especially through the US-Colombia agreement for new military bases encircling the country.

STRATEGIC RELATIONS

China: Venezuela and China has good bilateral relations extending support and cooperation in all areas enriching their strategic partnership for common development. The two nations have signed several multi-billion-dollar agreements on investments in oil, energy, construction and high-tech industries. Venezuela has established military-technological ties with China having acquired two squadrons of Chinese-built Karakorum-8 trainer jets and ground radars. They have launched their first joint space satellite, named Venesat-1. China has continued to provide the Nicolas Maduro regime with economic and political support. In October 2019, China helped Venezuela to win a seat on the United Nations Human Rights Council.

Russia: Russia and Venezuela enjoy warm relations and they have agreed to deepen their economic, commercial and investment co-operation in several areas. The leaders of the two nations have reaffirmed their wish for continuing their course towards strategic cooperation in all sectors. Ties between the two countries flourished under Chavez, whose 14-year rule earned Moscow a number of lucrative arms and energy deals and a close ally in South America. They have been building closer military relations and have spoken of their opposition to US global dominance. The Ministry of Defence of both Russia and Venezuela has signed agreements on military cooperation. Venezuela has purchased Rusian S-300 anti-aircraft missiles, Igla-S man-portable air defense systems (MANPADS), and multiuse aircraft, helicopters, and T-72 tanks.

Iran: Iran and Venezuela continue to have strong ties. The two countries are founding members of the Organization of the Petroleum Exporting Countries (OPEC). Venezuela has supported Iran's nuclear programme. They have signed a Memorandum of Understanding pledging full military support and cooperation. Venezuela has also inked six deals on scientific, technological, economic and health cooperation with Iran. Annual bilateral trade between the two countries is estimated to be in the hundreds of millions of US dollars. Amid the Venezuelan economic crisis, Tehran has come to the aid of Caracas sending fuel, refinery parts, and more recently humanitarian aid.

Cuba: Cuba and Venezuela enjoy warm relations and the ideological linkages between the two countries run deep which emerged at the beginning of the Chavez administration. Venezuelan oil and money help to keep the communist-ruled island's troubled economy afloat and the governments have about 30 joint ventures. Venezuela ships thousand barrels of subsidised oil to Cuba daily. In exchange, Venezuela receives thousands of doctors, teachers and some military advisers. Close ties with Cuba has enabled transformation of the Venezuelan military.

Turkey: Bilateral relations between Turkey and Venezuela have gained a new momentum in recent years. President Maduro, as the Chairman of the Non-Aligned Movement (NAM) attended the OIC Extraordinary Summit held on 13 December 2017 in Istanbul. He also participated in the oath-taking ceremony of H.E. President Erdoğan on July 9, 2018. The trade volume between the two countries reportedly was approximately 150 million USD (Turkey's exports: 129,7 million USD, Turkey's imports: 20,3 million USD) by the end of 2019.

DEFENCE CAPABILITIES

The President is the commander-in-chief of the National Bolivarian Armed Forces of Venezuela (Fuerza Armada Nacional Bolivariana, FANB) and has overall supervision and control over it. The armed forces are trained to fight both conventional war and irregular war. The Venezuelan Ministry of the Popular Power for Defence is the federal level organ responsible for maintaining the armed forces. The ministry coordinates numerous counter narcotics operations and oversees the conventional military capabilities. The Army, Navy, Air Force and National Guard serves under the highest organ of command of the national armed forces – the Operational Strategic Command, the National Reserve and the Territorial Guard under the National Militia General Command. According to the official gazette of February 1, 2020, Venezuela has designated its civilian militia as part of the country's military, an administrative change that is intended to expand the armed forces. The militia now stands as a branch of the armed forces alongside the army, navy, air force and national guard. It does not have nuclear, chemical or biological warfare capability. The FANB is a conscript force.

From the time of late president Hugo Chavez, the government has been carrying out a massive military purchase programme to modernise its armed forces. Venezuela purchased billions of dollars in arms and equipment from Russia and China. The United States embargo of military material and equipment to Venezuela has affected its military purchase programme as nations friendly to the US have been pressured to block sales of arms to Venezuela.

ARMY: (Fuerzas Terrestres or Ejército)

The National Army of Venezuela is the largest military branch. It has the responsibility for land-based operations against external, or internal threats. The Army is organised in six operating divisions including the Army

Aviation Command, 6th Corps of Engineers, Army Logistics Command, and Army Education Command.

Personnel: 63,000

Equipment

Category	Name	In Service
MBT	AMX-30V2	80
	AMX-30B	2
	AMX-30D (modernised)	4
	AMX-13C.90 (being withdrawn)	31
	Scorpion 90 (light)	66
	T-72SBIV	100+
IFV/APC	Dragon ASV (90mm gun)	42
	BMP-3	130
	AMX 13VTT	70
	TPz-1 FUCH	10
	V-100/V150- Dragon	115
	BTR-80A	114
Artillery	155 mm. M109 SP (reserved)	5
	155 mm. FMk3 SP (reserved)	20
	155 mm. M114 howitzer (reserved)	24
	105mm M56	80
	105mm M101	40
	2S19 MSTA-S 152mm SP	
Mortar	2S23 Nona-SVK	
	81mm	
	2S12 Sani 120mm towed	
	60mm	
RCL	M40A1 106mm	
MRL	AMX-13/LAR 160mm	12
	BM-30 Smerch	12
	BM-21 Grad 122mm	24
ATK Weapon	Carl Gustaf	
	AT4	
	RPG 7	
ATGW	Mapats 2	
AA Gun	ZSU-23 Zomi twin 23mm towed under CODAI	
SAM	RBS 70 (Giraffe FCS)	
	Mistral	
	Buk-M2	
	Tor-M1	
	IGLA-S (all under CODAI)	1,800
	S-300	four batteries

New Procurements/Upgrades

◆ The Army has reportedly carried out upgrade of 75 of the 78 Scorpion 90, light reconnaissance tracked armoured vehicles.

◆ The TPz-1 FUCH vehicles would be reportedly repaired and updated.

Army Aviation

Category	Name	In Service
Transport	IAI Arava	4
	M-28 Skytruck	12
	Super King Air 200	2
Helicopter	Mi-17V	18
	Mi-35 (attack)	12
	Mi-26	10
	Bell-206	7
	AS-61	3
	Mi-26	10
	AS-61	3

NAVY: (Fueszas Navales or Armada Bolivariana) The Venezuelan Navy carry out the main task of internal security operations in the Exclusive Economic Zone. It is equipped with powerful weapons such as the otomat missiles and several warships. The chain of command of the Venezuelan Navy is: Commanding General in Chief, Inspector General of the Navy and Chief of General Staff of the Navy. There are five major commands: Naval Logistics Command, Naval Personnel Command, Naval Education and Training Command and the Naval Operations Command. The Marine Infantry was reorganised in 2001 into a single division. The country is divided into two naval zone – Western Naval Zone (Hq: Punto Fijo) and Eastern Naval Area (HQ: Carupano) that currently covers the Atlantic coast.

Major naval bases: Puerto Cabello, Puerto Hierro, Punto Fijo

Main naval air stations: Puerto Cabello, La Orchila Island, Caracas, Maiquetia, San Fernando de Apure

Personnel: 23,778 (including 10,000 marines)

Equipment

Category	Name	In Service
Submarine	Sabalo class (Type 209)	2
Frigate	Mariscal Sucre class (Lupo type)	6
Corvette	Guaiquerí class	4
Amphibious Force	Damen Stan Lander 5612	4
	Capana class ex-US LST	2
	Los Frajles class LCU	4
Patrol craft	Guaicamacuto class	4
	Point class	3
	Constitucion Class	6
Auxiliaries	Ciudad Bolivar	1
	Oceanographic ship	1
	Sailing training ship	1
	Fleet tug	1
	Survey vessels	3

New Procurements/Upgrades

No major procurements plans are under consideration at present.

Naval Aviation

Personnel: 2,000

Equipment

Category	Name	In Service
Transport	C-212/200	5
	C-21/400	3
	Super King Air C-200	1
	C-208	1
Helicopter	AB-212 ASW	8
	Bell 412EF	4
	Bell 206L	1
	Mi-17V-5	6
	Bell 206	1
	Cessna C-210	1

New Procurements/Upgrades

No major procurement plans are under consideration at present.

Marine Infantry Division

Personnel: Approximate 12,000

Equipment

Category	Name	In Service
APC/IFV	E-11 Urutus	38
	AAVT	11
Artillery	M-56 105mm pack howitzer	40
Mortar	120mm mortar	18
SAM	RBS-70	12
	Pechora missiles	
AA gun	GAM-BOI 20mm guns	
Patrol vessel	Guardian 25' type	66
	Guardian 22' type	12

New Procurements/Upgrades

No major procurements plans are under consideration at present.

AIR FORCE: (Fuerzas Aérea or Aviación Militar) The Bolivarian National Military Air Force is organised into three major air commands, including a Combat Command, Logistics Command, Air Training Command and a small air defence group. The Air Force is organised into five air zones. Within these air zones the air force deploys three fighter groups, three transport groups, two special operations air groups, one tactical air training group, and one air training group. The aviation component of the National Guard functions as a communications and combat reserve force for the Air Force.

Major air bases: Barcelona, Barquisimeto,

Caracas (La Carlota), Carrizales, Maracaibo, Maracay (Boca de Rio and Palo Negro).

Personnel: 9,580

Equipment

Category	Name	In Service
Fighter/ Light Attack/ Electronic weapon	Su-30 MK2	24
	F-16A/B	21
	CF-5 Freedom Fighter	16
	North American Rockwell OV-10 Bronco	20
	SF-260U	11
	EMB-312 Tucano	24
	Aermacchi SF.260	12
	Tucano (Embraer EMB 312)	19
	K-8 w karakorum	18+12
	Hongdu jl-8	17
Transport/ Tanker/VIP	C-130 Hercules	3
	Boeing 707-320C	2
	Shorts SD3-60-300	2
	A319CJ	1
	Boeing 737-200	1
	Falcon 50/900XL	5
	AS-532UL Cougar	2
	Falcon 20C/50/900	1
	Cessna Citation I/II/X	6
	BE-200 Super King Air	6
Trainer	K-8W	6+^
	Cessna 182R	3
Helicopter	Mi-17	7
	Mi-35	9
Weapon	(SAM) MistraL from France	
	Barak 3 from Israel	
	Breda/Bofors 40/L70 mm	
	TCM-20 Mk.2	
	Thales Reporter	
	Thales Mirador FCS	
	Elta EL/M 2106	
	Westinghouse TPS-63	
	Cetec JLY-3D radar	10
	JY-11B 3D long range radar	3
	Kh-29 (AAM)	
	Kh-59	
	Vympel R-27 (AAM)	
	Vympel R-73 (AAM)	
UAV	Saint Arpia	12+

New Procurements/Upgrades

No major procurements plans are under consideration at present.

NATIONAL GUARD: (Fuerzas Armadas de Cooperacion or Guardia Nacional)

The Bolivarian National Guard of Venezuela founded in 1937 serves as a border patrol, internal and rear-area security function. It was made a branch of the Armed Forces in 2007 and expanded further to include the People's Guards Command in 2011 and the Anti-extortion and Sequestration Command in 2012.

Personnel: 27,720

Equipment

Category	Name	In Service
APC	AUR-416	40+
	Fiat 6646	24
	VN-4 (protected carriers)	111
	WTC-1 (water cannons)	10
	ABV-1 (mobile barriers)	10
Aircraft	M-28 Skystruck	11
	201 Arava	4
	BE-200 Super King Air	2
	BE-90 King Air	1
	BE-95-B.58 Baron	1
	Cessna CE-402	5
	CE-206/U206/U206G	4
	CE-182 Skyline II	3
	CE-152 Aerobat	2
	M-26 Isquierka	6
	DA-42MMP Twin Star	6
Helicopter	Mi-17V-5	6
	Bell 412HP/SP/EP	10
	Bell206L	1
	Bell 206B	12
	A-109A Hirundo	3
	AS-350/AS-355F-2	10
	Enstron F28	2
Patrol craft	23m (Sea Ark)	12
	16.5m (Halter Marine)	10
	US-Protector Class	12
	6.4m Cobra design	10
	5.5m	15
	10.6m	8
	9.1m	25
	7.9 raider	25

New Procurements/Upgrades

No major procurements plans are under consideration at present.

NATIONAL MILITIA

Personnel: 75,000

The Bolivarian Militia is a derivative of the military reserve and has been established as an organ of the Venezuelan armed forces. They are under the immediate command of the President. Unlike the armed forces, which would battle an external enemy, the National Militia's role is to battle with an internal enemy or the regime's opposition. The General Command of the National Militia is divided in two parts:

◆ The National Reserve, consisting of all Venezuelan citizens who are not in active military service, or have completed military service, or who voluntarily join the reserve units.

◆ The Territorial Guard, consisting of all Venezuelan citizens who voluntarily serve to organise local resistance to any external aggression.

DEFENCE PRODUCTION AND R&D

The inventory of the FANB mainly comprised of Chinese and Russian equipment with a mixture of equipment from Western countries such as France, Germany, Italy, the Netherlands, Spain, the UK, and the US. The Venezuelan Defence industry was virtually non-existent until 1975. In recent times, Venezuela has undertaken efforts to establish its own domestic arms industry. The state-owned Venezuelan Military Industries Company (Compania Anonima Venezolana de Industrias Militares – CAVIM) was established to encourage growth of the domestic defence industry and to produce the materiel required by the military. The DIANCA and UCOCAR are involved increasingly in Venezuelan navy's future needs. Today domestic arms production consisted of all-terrain vehicles, trucks, ammunition, rifles, unmanned aircraft, grenades, assembled ships of small and medium-sized ports among other products.

Major Armament Producers

CAVIM: C.A. Venezolana de Industrias Militares is a company dedicated to the production of weapons, explosive munitions as well as various other products.

CENARECA: Centro Nacional de Repotenciacion C.A is the manufacturer of the all-terrain and high mobility (HMMWV) Tiuna vehicles for the Venezuelan armed forces.

MAZVEN: MAZVEN C.A is a joint venture with the Belarusian Company MAZ which manufactures trucks for military use.

DIANCA: Diques y Astilleros Nacionales C.A is the state shipyard created in 1905 in the city of Puerto Cabello, Carabobo state.

UCOCAR: Unidad Naval Coordinadora de

los Servicios de Carenado de la Armada is responsible for the repair, maintenance and construction of ships.

G&F Tecnologia: G&F Tecnologia manufactures unmanned aircraft, communication equipment and other electronic products.

DEFENCE DEALS
Joint Venture Programmes

AK103 assault rifles: Venezuela has signed an agreement with Russia in 2006 to produce AK103 assault rifles. The construction work has been delayed due to international sanctions and the coronavirus pandemic. The production facility is now expected to be completed by the end of this year. Currently, two Kalashnikov plants are under construction in Venezuela which are about 70 per cent completed. The transfer dates for the plants is likely to be postponed until 2022. The plant is expected to manufacture about 25,000 assault rifles annually. Besides, the ammunition production, the plant will reportedly manufacture more than 50 million rounds per year. year, according to a media report.

Arms Export

Venezuela has begun to sell weapons and military vehicles to other Latin American countries within the alliances of ALBA and UNASUR. According to Cavim, other Latin American states have expressed their interest to buy the Venezuelan drone. Ecuador was the largest importer of Venezuelan aircraft parts and missiles.

Arms Import

Venezuela's most imported military hardware comprised of aircraft, missiles and sensors. Due to military embargo imposed by the US, Venezuela bought arms mainly from Russia and China. The European Union has also placed an arms embargo on Venezuela. According to the Stockholm International Peace Research Institute (SIPRI), Venezuela is the largest weapons importer in Latin America. Since 2011, the country spent some $2.6 on weapons, buying the majority of them in Russia.

Venezuela and Russia's state-run arms trader Rosoboronexport have signed more than 30 contracts on arms supplies in 2005-2009. Venezuela has purchased Russia's state-of-the-art S-300 anti-aircraft missiles; imported hundreds of thousands of Kalashnikov rifles and ammunition; and acquired 5,000 Igla-S MANPADS (man-portable air defence systems), Antey-2500, Pechora-2M, Buk as well as T-72M tanks, Grad and Smerch multiple rocket launcher systems, armoured vehicles and artillery. Arms supplies from China include long-range JYL-1 radars. Venezuela has reportedly purchased 24 K-8 Karakorum trainer/light fighter planes from China. Venezuelan arms imports reportedly fell by 83 per cent between 2009–13 and 2014–18.

DEFENCE BUDGET

Total defence spending: $741Million (2017), $218.20 Million (2016)

Defence spending in terms of GDP: 0.35% (2017)

According to the World Bank, defence spending in Venezuela was equivalent to just 0.75% of the country's GDP in 2011 and it has been falling steadily since the 1990s. By this measure, it is two thirds lower than the global average. The report added that Venezuela dedicates an enormous amount to social programmes to guarantee access to essential goods like health care, housing and education. Education spending alone will account for 2.5% of GDP in 2013, and in 2012, Venezuela spent nearly 40 times as much on social investments (USD 115 billion) as on defence.

CONCLUSION

Venezuela with its abundant energy resources continues to be a country of strategic importance. However, the situation in the country is volatile with current concerns such as weakening of democratic institutions, political polarisation, a politicised military, rampant violent crime, over dependence on the petroleum industry with its price fluctuation, foreign exchange controls that discourage private-sector investment, high inflation, a decline in the quality of fundamental human rights, and widespread scarcity of consumer goods forcing many Venezuelans to leave the country.

CONTACT DETAILS
Ministry of National Defence
Fuerte Tiuna-El Valle
Caracas, Venezuela
Tel: +58212-80131104/0296
Website: www.ejercito.mil.ve

Armed Forces HQ
Fuerte Tiuna-El Valle
Caracas, Venezuela
Tel: +58212-692685

CAVIM HQ
Urb Las Mercedes
Calle Jalisco Cavim building
Caracas, Dtto Capital. Venezuela
Tel: +58(212)9934378 – 9935311-9932006; Fax: 9935621

A starboard bow view of the Venzuelan frigates General Salom (F 25) and the Mariscal Sucre (F 21) (both Mariscal Sucre-class) underway. (Image Credit: US Navy)

STRATEGIC INFORMATION
VIETNAM
(Capital: Hanoi)

INTRODUCTION

Area: 331,210 sq km
Population: 102,789,598 (July 2021 est.)
Coastline: 3,444 km (excludes islands)
Maritime claims: Territorial sea: 12 nm
Contiguous zone: 24 nm
Exclusive Economic Zone: 200 nm
Continental shelf: 200 nm or to the edge of the continental margin

GEOPOLITICAL IMPORTANCE

Vietnam's geopolitical significance stems from the fact that the country is located in a strategic playing field. The country has a very long coastline, spanning almost the entire western stretch of the South China Sea (SCS). It is bordered by China to the North, Laos to the Northwest, Cambodia to the Southwest, and the South China Sea to the East. The country consists of two geographic and population cores - the Red River Delta in the North, home to the capital of Hanoi, and the Mekong River Delta in the Southern lowlands, where Ho Chi Minh City sits. The South China Sea is a major shipping route with substantial oil, gas reserves and abundant stock of fish. Vietnam's Cam Ranh Bay, located about 220 miles (354 kilometres) North of Ho Chi Minh City, provide convenient access to the commercially and strategically vital sea lanes which pass through the SCS. Due to its strategic location as well as its particular historical relations with China, Vietnam has emerged as a key player in the Asia-Pacific region. It has a high degree of political and economic influence in Laos and Cambodia. And with its large population, Vietnam has emerged as an attractive destination for foreign investment also for countries seeking influence in South East Asia.

POLITICAL OVERVIEW

Vietnam is a one-party communist state. Political power lies with the Communist Party of Vietnam (CPV). The party's politburo holds authority over the implementation of all major areas of policy. The politburo, headed by a general secretary, is elected by the party's Central Committee. Only political organisations affiliated with or endorsed by the Communist Party are permitted to contest elections in Vietnam.

The unicameral National Assembly is the highest representative of the people – the sole body that has the constitutional and legislative rights. It exercises three main functions: to legislate, to decide on important national issues, to exercise supreme supervision over all activities of the State. The Assembly has 500 members, elected by popular vote to serve a four-year term. The Communist Party provides policy direction and all members of the assembly must be approved by the CPV before being permitted to stand for election.

The President is elected by the National Assembly for a five-year term and acts as the commander-in-chief of the Vietnam People's Armed Forces and Chairman of the Council for Defence and Security. The president declares the promulgation of the constitution, laws and ordinances. He also recommends to the National Assembly the election, removal or dismissal of the Vice President, the Prime Minister, Chief Justice of the Supreme People's Court, and Head of the People's Procuracy. The government, the main executive state power of Vietnam, is headed by the prime minister, who has several deputy prime ministers and several ministers in charge of particular activities.

The Executive Branch is responsible for the implementation of political, economic, cultural, social, national defence, security and external activities of the state. The Supreme People's Court is the highest judicial organ of the Socialist Republic of Vietnam. The National Assembly supervises the work of the Supreme People's Court. In turn it supervises and directs the judicial work of local People's Courts, Military Tribunals, Special Tribunals and other tribunals, unless otherwise prescribed by the National Assembly at the establishment of such Tribunals.

KEY POLITICAL PERSONS

PRESIDENT & COMMANDER-IN-CHIEF: Nguyen Xuan Phuc

PRIME MINISTER: Pham Minh Chinh

ECONOMY

Vietnam is one of the fastest-growing economy in south-east Asia. As a result of economic reforms, the country has enjoyed high economic growth rate, consistently ranked amongst the world's fastest growing economies. Vietnam made a shift from a highly centralised command economy to a mixed economy. Manufacturing, information technology and high-tech industries form a large and fast-growing part of the national economy. Tourism has expanded, manufacturing and export earnings have increased, and the per capita gross domestic product (GDP) has grown rapidly. Though Vietnam is a relative newcomer to the oil industry, it is one of the largest oil producer in Southeast Asia, with an output of about 400,000 barrels per day. The country is a leading agricultural exporter and served as an attractive destination for foreign investment in Southeast Asia. Early in the 21st century, state markets were opened to foreign competition, and Vietnam became a member of the World Trade Organization (WTO).

It is a signatory to the Comprehensive and Progressive Agreement for the Transpacific Partnership and member of the Asia-Pacific Economic Cooperation and Association of Southeast Asian Nations. Vietnam has been named among the Next Eleven and CIVETS countries. The economy although hit by the ongoing COVID-19 pandemic has shown remarkable resilience. According to the World Bank, GDP grew by 2.9 percent in 2020. Vietnam's economy is set to grow 6.6 percent in 2021 on the back of successful control of COVID-19 infections, strong performance by export-oriented manufacturing and robust recovery in domestic demand, it has stated.

GDP (official exchange rate): $259.957 billion (2019 est.)

Real Growth Rate (GDP): 6.8% (2017 est.), 7.16% (2017 est.)

Industries: Food processing, garments, shoes, machine-building; mining, coal, steel; cement, chemical fertilizer, glass, tires, oil, mobile phones.

Oil – proved reserves: 4.4 billion bbl (1 January 2018 est.)

Natural gas – proved reserves: 699.4 billion cu m (1 January 2018 est.)

Total Exports: $248.953 billion (2019 est.), $233.294 billion (2018 est.)

Export Commodities: Broadcasting equipment, telephones, integrated circuits, footwear, furniture (2019).

Major Markets: United States 23%, China 14%, Japan 8%, South Korea 7% (2019)

Total Imports: $266.066 billion (2019 est.), $245.563 billion (2018 est.)

Import Commodities: Integrated circuits, telephones, refined petroleum, textiles, semiconductors (2019)

Major Suppliers: China 35%, South Korea 18%, Japan 6% (2019)

DEFENCE & SECURITY

Vietnam has established a policy to concurrently develop both its socio-economic and defence capabilities and closely coordinate defence-security and diplomatic activities to support the cause of industrialisation and modernisation, and rapid and sustainable economic development. The country faces diversified and complicated security challenges. According to the Ministry of Defence, although the national security has been maintained, there is socio-political instability caused by both internal and external factors. Territorial disputes in the South China Sea, especially with China, constitute Vietnam's main security challenge. It has stationed small military garrisons on the major islands and rocks that it occupies. Other security issues such as illegal trafficking of weapons and drugs; piracy, organised trans-national crimes, terrorism, illegal migration and immigration; environmental degradation, climate change, and epidemics continue to concern the country. Vietnam has stepped up 'defence diplomacy' as a measure to promote military cooperation with partners of interest. It maintains bilateral defence relations with several countries. The defence and security ties between India and Vietnam have witnessed steady expansion. The two countries have deliberated on maritime security cooperation during second maritime security dialogue held in April 2021. Vietnam participates actively in major regional security and defence forums, including the ASEAN Defence Ministers Meeting Plus, the ASEAN Regional Forum, APEC, ASEM, East-Asia summit and the Shangri-La Dialogue.

KEY DEFENCE PERSONS

DEFENCE MINISTER: Sr. Lt. Gen. Phan Van Giang

CHIEF OF GENERAL STAFF OF ARMY: Col. Gen. Nguyen Tan Cuong

COMMANDER OF THE NAVY: Rear Adm. Tran Thanh Nghiem

COMMANDER OF THE AIR FORCE (Acting): Maj. Gen. Vu Van Kha

External Conflict

Vietnam is involved in complex dispute with China, Brunei, Malaysia, the Philippines, and Taiwan over the Paracel and Spratly Islands. The issues in the South China Sea are not only a conflict over the islands, but includes resources of oil, natural gas, underwater archaeology, hydro geothermal energy and fishery. Vietnam and China have demarcated their land border and are currently putting in place mechanisms to resolve local disputes. There is ongoing cooperation between military zones adjacent to the border and between their respective border guards. Its borders with Laos and Cambodia are porous and the main security challenges are transnational. These include trafficking in drugs, weapons and persons; illegal migration; criminal activity and the activities of anti-regime political activists.

THREAT PERSPECTIVE

China has long been the most serious threat to Vietnam's security. In Hanoi's view, the South China Sea relates to almost all aspects of national security and development: protecting territorial integrity and national sovereignty, promoting maritime economic development, maintaining external peaceful environment, especially peaceful relationships with China and other claimants, and safeguarding the regime's legitimacy and internal stability. China claims sovereignty over all islands, rocks, and reefs in the Paracel and Spratly archipelagos. This threat posed by China towards Vietnam is its geographical proximity and also in terms of the size and power between the two countries. China is several times larger than Vietnam, while Vietnam's population stands nowhere near to China in comparison. Economically too China's economic modernisation has caused the power gap between the two countries to become ever wider despite Vietnam's impressive economic performance since the late 1980s. With its economic development, China's military might has grown significantly, posing a formidable threat to Vietnam's security. Its expanding military budget is reportedly concentrated on its air force and navy which makes it particularly worrying for Vietnam as the two nations have competing claims in the South China Sea. Vietnam is dependent on China for some of its major export industries, while Vietnam's exports to China are just a minuscule portion of China's total imports. Damage to Vietnam's economy would be immense if for some reason China decides to discontinue trade with Vietnam.

Cyber threat: Cybercriminal activity has reportedly grown in Vietnam and the government is cracking down on rogue internet usage, blocking its citizens' access to sites it deems to be inappropriate in the name of strengthening cybersecurity.

STRATEGIC RELATIONS

India: India and Vietnam have good bilateral relations. The two nations had upgraded their ties to the level of Comprehensive Strategic partnership in 2016. They share a long-standing tradition of helping each other in difficult times. Both are progressively increasing their defence ties in view of the common approach towards the aggressive Chinese activities. India has offered Vietnam a line of credit worth $500 million to develop its defence industry. Indian Prime Minister Narendra Modi and the then Vietnamese PM Nguyen Xuan Phuc have issued the India-Vietnam Joint Vision for Peace, Prosperity and People containing the guidelines for future development of India – Vietnam Comprehensive Strategic Partnership, on 21st December, 2020, in a virtual meeting. The two countries closely cooperate in various regional forums such as ASEAN, East Asia Summit, Mekong Ganga Cooperation, Asia Europe Meeting (ASEM) besides UN and WTO.

Russia: Russia and Vietnam's friendship has been upgraded to a comprehensive strategic partnership in 2012. The erstwhile Soviet Union helped Vietnam win their war against the United States by offering weapons. Russia also extended financial support to Vietnam for post-war reconstruction and Vietnam reportedly used Russian technology and know-how to reopen an old base at Cam Ranh Bay as a maintenance centre for foreign warships. Cooperation in the military-technical spheres between the two countries have contributed towards strengthening the traditional friendship and facilitating further development of the strategic partnership. Vietnam has become a major customer for Russian weapons, primarily buying submarines and planes. Vietnam has received five Kilo-class submarines from Russia. Bilateral trade and scientific-cultural exchanges are also growing. Russia ranks among the top countries and territories currently investing in Vietnam while Vietnamese companies have invested mainly in Russian oil and gas industry.

United States: Ties between the United States and Vietnam have experienced a significant breakthrough which started with Hillary Clinton's visit to Hanoi in July 2012. The visit paved the way for establishment of the US-Vietnam Comprehensive Partnership. The two former foes are now prepared to downplay their ideological disagreements to focus on common strategic interests. In May 2016, the United States fully lifted its ban on the sale of lethal weapons to Vietnam and continued to provide Vietnam with maritime security assistance – including through the Maritime Security Initiative, the Cooperative Threat Reduction programme, and Foreign Military Financing. In the recent past, several senior US national security officials have visited Vietnam to help reinforce diplomatic and military ties between the two countries. After signing the trade agreement in 2001, the US and Vietnam have concluded a trade and investment framework agreement. They also have signed textile, air transport, customs, and maritime agreements. Their bilateral trade has grown from $451 million in 1995 to over $90 billion in 2020.

Japan: Japan and Vietnam have elevated their strategic partnership to an Extensive Strategic Partnership. The two countries have agreed to a wide-ranging MoU on defence cooperation which included defence exchanges at ministerial, chief of staff and service chief level; naval goodwill visits; annual defence policy dialogue at the deputy defence minister level; cooperation in military aviation and air defence; and personnel training including scholarships for defence personnel to study and train in Japan. Both Japan and Vietnam have territorial and maritime disputes with China in the East China Sea and South China Sea, respectively.

China: China and Vietnam have agreed to deepen their comprehensive strategic co-operation, focusing on maintaining high-ranking contacts through diverse and flexible forms such as bilateral visits, telephone calls via hotline and meetings on the side-lines of multilateral forums to increase strategic exchanges and have a thorough grasp of sound orientations for developing bilateral ties. They have also reached consensus on deepening land and sea border defence co-operation with two joint naval patrols to be carried out in the Tonkin Gulf and comprehensive and effective implementation of the Declaration on Conduct of Parties in the East Sea (DOC) to maintain peace and stability together in the East Sea.

United Kingdom: The UK and Vietnam are strong advocates of global free trade and welcome the signing of the EU – Vietnam Free Trade Agreement (EVFTA) on 30 June 2019. The two nations have agreed to advance defence cooperation which included increased training cooperation, defence industrial cooperation, and maritime cooperation. Both the nations have developed close cooperation at international forums and organisations, especially the United Nations (UN), the Asia-Europe Meeting, and the ASEAN-EU framework. They have committed to ensuring continuity of trade relations even as the UK leaves the EU.

DEFENCE CAPABILITIES

The Armed Forces of the Socialist Republic of Vietnam is known as the People's Army of Vietnam (PAVN). The PAVN comprises of the: Ground Force, Navy, Air Force, Border Guard and the Coast Guard. Vietnam does not have a separate Ground Force or Army branch. All ground troops, army corps, military districts and specialised arms belong to the Ministry of Defence, which is under the direct command of the Central Military Commission, the Minister of Defence, and the General Staff of the Vietnam People's Army.

The Defence Minister oversees operations of the Ministry of Defence, and the Vietnam People's Army (VPA) besides oversees agencies such as the General Staff and the General Logistics Department. Military policy is ultimately directed by the Central Military Commission of the ruling Communist Party of Vietnam. Vietnam's new Defence White Paper released in 2019 is categorised into three parts - the strategic context and national defence policy, building the all-people national defence, and the development of the Vietnam People's Army. However, the two main principles of Vietnam's defence policy remains the same – peace and self-defence.

The country's military modernisation efforts are mostly driven by the threat posed by China over Vietnam's territorial and resource claims in the contested South China Sea. It making efforts to produce its own infantry and artillery weapons. The Vietnamese army are well trained to adopt new weapons and already equipped with submarines, Su-30 MK2 strike fighters, anti-aircraft missile systems, surface-to-shore missiles, radar systems, technical reconnaissance equipment, and armoured tank units.

ARMY

Personnel: 450,000

Equipment

Category	Name	In Service
MBT	T-90S/SK	64
	T-62	60+
	T-54/55	600
	(to be replaced)	100
	M-48	300
	Type-59	80
	(to be replaced)	1,500
Armoured Car	BRDM	80
APC	BTR-40/50/60/152	200
	Type 56	
	K63	
	M113	
	V100 Commando	
Artillery	152mm	100
	130mm	200
	76mm	
	100mm	
	105mm	
	122mm	
	85mm	
Mortar	120mm	
	81mm	
	107mm	

...continued

Category	Name	In Service
Mortar	160mm	
MRL	Type 63 107mm	
	122mm	
	140mm	
SSM	Scud B/C	
ATGW	Sagger	
AA gun	37mm towed	
	23mm towed	
	ZSU-23-4	
	ZSU-57-2 SP	
SAM	SA7	
	SA9	
	IGLA	

New Procurements/Upgrades

No major procurements plans are under consideration at present.

NAVY: Vietnam's Navy (VPN) has transformed into a seagoing, fairly competent, combat-worthy navy from a small coastal patrol force with limited capacity in the 1980s. Vietnam is modernising its maritime capabilities making the protection of maritime sovereignty and the maritime economy a key national security pillar. Vietnam has a 2,000-mile coastline facing the East Sea (South China Sea). The Navy headquarter has the Commander and Vice Commanders, the Commissar and the Deputy Commissar. The Service is divided into five Naval Regions and affiliated units. The force today consists of frigates, corvettes, patrol craft, missile boats, maritime patrol aircraft, submarines and reinforced with equipment for search and rescue. Vietnam plan to develop its surface and submarine fleets, as well as anti-ship batteries, missiles, and other coastal defenses. They are considering purchasing more combat aircraft and naval patrol marine craft.

Major naval bases: Cam Ranh Bay, Can Tho, Chu Lai, Haiphong, Hue, Quang Khe, Qui Nhon, Vinh

Personnel: 40,000 (including 25000 Naval Infantry)

Equipment

Category	Name	In Service
Submarine	Hanoi class (Kilo type)	6
	Midget	2
Frigate	(Gepard 3.9 type) Dinh Tien Hoang, Ly Thai To, Tran Hung Dao, Quang Trung	4
	Petya-II class	5
Corvette	Tarantul-I class	4
	Molniya class	8
	Pauk class	1

...continued

Category	Name	In Service
Corvette	Pohang class	
Missile Boat	Svetlak class	5
	TT400TP gun boat	4
	OSA-II class missile FAC	8
	Turya class	5
	SO-1 class large patrol craft	4
	Zhuk class	11
	Poluchat class	2
Minesweeper	Yurka class	2
	Yevgenya class	2
	Sonya class	4
	Lienyun class	2
Amphibious Force	US LST	3
	US LSM	3
	Ex-USSR T-4 class	12
	LCM & LCU	24
	Truong SA	1
Training Vessel	Shanghai class	6
Weapon	P-5 Shaddock (ASM)	5 batteries
	SSC-5 Bastion (ASM)	2
	Kh-35E	
	Kalibr 3M54	
	3M-14/54 Klub	5+

Naval Aviation

Category	Name	In Service
Helicopter	Ka 27/29 ASW	5
	Mi-4 (SAR)	10
	Beriev Be12	4

New Procurements/Upgrades

◆ The state-owned Z189 shipyard has been commissioned to build the future MSSARS 9316 (multipurpose submarine search-and-rescue ship 9316).

VIETNAM AIR DEFENCE AIR FORCE (VAD-AF)

The Vietnam People's Air Force (VPAF) is one of the main branches in Vietnam People's Army, a part of the Ministry of Defence. The VPAF shoulders the responsibility of both national air defence. The Air Force is organised into the service command, combat units, support units, educational institutions and production units. The service command has the commander and vice commanders, the commissar and the deputy commissar. The main combat units of the Service are air divisions, air defence divisions, and affiliated air units. The Air Force is equipped with various types of modern combat aircraft, missiles, anti-aircraft artillery and other technical means, including multi-purpose fighters, long-range air defence missiles and new generation radars.

Major Air Bases: Bienhoa, Binh Thuy, Cana, Dalat, Da Nang, Dien Bien Phu, Dong Hoi, Gia Lam, Hoa Lae, Phan Rang, Pleiku, Ho Chi Minh City, Vinh

Personnel: 30,000

Equipment

Category	Name	In Service
Fighter/Attack	Su-27SK/UBK	10
	Su-30MK2	36
	Su-22 M4	38
Trainer	L-39	38
Transport	C295	3
	C212	2
	An-26	10
	An-2	15
	An-24	12
	Li-2	30
	Il-18 (V P)	2
Helicopter/Attack/Transport	Mi-24	35
	Mi-8/Mi-17/Mi17l	60
	Ka-32	2
	Mi-6	10
	Mi-4	4
	Mi-2	28
Maritime patrol	PZL M-23 MP	2
AA Gun	37mm	
	57mm	
	85mm	
	100mm	
	ZSU-23-4	75+
	ZSU-57-2	75+
	130mm	
SAM	SA-2	
	SA-7	
	SA-3	
	S-300 PMU-1	10
	2K12 Kub	10
	9K35 Strela-10	
AAM	AA-11, AA-2, AA-8, RVV-AE	
Anti-Ship	AS-13, AS-14, AS-17	

New Procurements/Upgrades

◆ Vietnam has purchased 12 L-39 NG from Czech aircraft manufacturer Aero Vodochody. The aircraft will be delivered between 2023 and 2024 to replace the old L-39 Cs.

◆ Vietnam has signed a $350 million deal to buy at least 12 Russian Yak-130 combat training jets.

◆ The Ministry of National Defence is

reportedly considering to buy either the MiG-35 or Su-35 multi role combat aircraft.

◆ Vietnam has unveiled its new local-made VCM-01 anti-ship cruise missile – a development of the Vietnamese KCT-15, - produced under license in Vietnam.

Vietnamese-made VCM-1 anti-ship cruise missile. (Image credit: Facebook account VietDefense)

BORDER GUARDS

The Border Guard is a component of the VPA, responsible for protecting the national sovereignty, territorial integrity, and security of national borders on land, at sea, and border gates as regulated by law. The Border Guard coordinates with concerned branches and forces in local areas and authorities ensuring implementation of agreements, regulations and laws on border issues, fighting against illegal activities, maintaining contact with concerned agencies of neighbouring countries with a view to fostering peace and friendship.

DEFENCE PRODUCTION AND R&D

Although Vietnam relies on foreign suppliers to meet its demand for advanced military hardware, it has slowly built up a modest naval and maritime air capacity to monitor its territorial waters, continental shelf and Exclusive Economic Zones. It is gradually expanding its national defence industrial base through overseas partnerships and technology transfers. The defence industry is being developed in the direction of mainly self-reliance but at the same time, various forms of associate and co-operative relations with friendly countries are being broadened so as to acquire advanced technologies with a view to bringing the Vietnamese defence industry to a higher level of development. The VPA's Technology General Department is undertaking efforts to improve its capacities in the research, development and application of new technologies. Vietnam has unveiled its new local-made VCM-01 anti-ship cruise missile, a development of the Vietnamese KCT-15. The country has also produced a VTOL twin-boom drone able to scan terrain and loiter above specific areas. Vietnam has pushed for joint production or joint R&D projects to help upgrade its domestic capabilities. The lifting of the US arms embargo has opened the possibility of co-production.

Major Armament Producers

Research Institutes directly attached to the Ministry of National Defence:

◆ The Institute for Military Strategy
◆ The Institute for Military Science & Technology
◆ The Institute for Military History
◆ The Institute for Defence International Relations

Domestic Suppliers: Viettel Mobile, Z111 Factory, Z153 Factory, Precision Engineering 17 Company, Service Flight Corporation, Shipbuilding Industry Corporation, Z189 Shipyard, Vietnam Helicopter Corporation, Vietnam Aerospace Association (VASA), A32 Factory.

Foreign Suppliers: Russia, India, Germany, Israel, Netherlands, Sweden, USA, Turkey, South Korea, UK, Spain, Bulgaria, Portugal.

DEFENCE DEALS

India: In 2016, India extended a US$ 500 million line of credit to Vietnam to develop its defence industry. India has also offered Vietnam, the Akash surface-to-air missile (SAM), which has a range of 27 kilometres and can achieve speeds in excess of Mach 2. Seven agreements were inked during a virtual summit in 2020 which included one on implementing arrangements on defence industry. The summit provided an opportunity to hand over one high speed guard boat to Vietnam and launch two other vessels manufactured in India, and keel-laying of seven vessels being manufactured in Vietnam under the $100 million defence Line of Credit extended by India to that country.

Russia: Russia is Vietnam's major arms supplier. The two countries have established long-term efficient partnership in various industries. Russia's Rostec which has significant research and technological expertise in the space industry has extended support to Vietnam in implementing its Space Technology Research and Application Strategy.

Arms Import

Vietnam is one of the world's most active arms importers. The lack of technology and low domestic defence capability has forced the country to import weapon systems. Vietnam has signed a number of large arms procurement contracts. Ships and aircraft account for majority of the defence imports. The biggest programme is the delivery of six Russian Project 636 (Kilo-class) diesel-electric submarines to Vietnamese Navy and the second is the Molniya-class boat delivery and license production programme. Another large project being implemented with Vietnam is delivery of frigates. The country's defence industry is dominated by the Russians, however, the European suppliers are beginning to make an entry through Foreign Military Sales (FMS). Vietnam has modernised its coastal defences with the purchase of anti-ship batteries and missiles while six fast patrol vessels have been imported from the United States. Vietnam plans to buy Lockheed Martin's (LOCKHE) P-3 Orion maritime patrol aircraft and Raytheon's (RTN) coastal radar systems. Vietnam also plans to boost its maritime security with patrol aircraft, coastal radars and naval craft.

DEFENCE BUDGET

Total defence spending: $5.5 billion (2020), $ 5.1 billion (2019)

Defence spending in terms of GDP: 2.3% (2018)

Vietnam does not publish any data or specifics about tits defence budget or procurements. According to a media report, Vietnam has seen an increase in defence spending, from 2.23 percent of GDP in 2010 to 2.36 percent in 2018, approximately $5.8 billion.

Defence Procurement

Vietnam's Ministry of National Defence (MOND) limits the number of businesses that may import or export defence equipment. General Import-Export Vanxuan Corporation (VAXUCO), a military goods importer owned by the MOND, is the designated importer for MOND for military goods, and is authorized to sign purchases on behalf of the MOND. Other importers of dual-use military goods are GAET, Viettel, Tecapro, Elinco, Hitaco and Thai Son Corporation. It is important to note that these firms are all state-owned enterprises (SOE) under the MOND.

The country relies on foreign suppliers to meet its demand for advanced military hardware. Vietnam has slowly built up a modest naval and maritime air capacity to monitor its territorial waters, continental shelf and Exclusive Economic Zones. The government has taken steps to develop a wider and more diversified procurement network for Soviet-compatible equipment from India, the Ukraine, the Czech Republic and Poland. Vietnam and China have discussed stepping up cooperation in the research and transfer of military technologies. The lifting of the US arms embargo has opened the possibility of co-production.

CONCLUSION

Vietnam's strategic significance has increased dramatically in recent years due to transformations in its economic performance and foreign-policy orientation. Deepening and upgrading relations with leading partners have been prioritised. Vietnam played a pivotal role in helping to establish Asia's emerging security order. Relations with traditional friends and international organisations are being strengthened. Vietnam now has bilateral defence relations with several countries and participates actively in regional security and defence forums such as the Shangri-La Dialogue, the ASEAN Defence Ministers Meeting Plus (ADDM+), and the ASEAN Regional Forum (ARF).

CONTACT DETAILS
Ministry of National Defence
No 7, Nguyen Tri Phuong St.
Ba Dinh Dist.
Hanoi, Vietnam
Tel: 069 534223 - 069 532090
Fax: +84-4-069532090

YEMEN
(Capital: Sanaa)

INTRODUCTION

Area: 527,968 sq km
Population: 30,399,243 (July 2021 est.)
Coastline: 1,906 km
Maritime claims: Territorial sea: 12 nm
Contiguous zone: 24 nm
Exclusive Economic Zone: 200 nm
Continental shelf: 200 nm or to the edge of the continental margin

KEY POLITICAL PERSONS

PRESIDENT & COMMANDER-IN-CHIEF OF THE ARMED FORCES: Fd. Mar. Abd. Rabuh Mansour Hadi

VICE PRESIDENT: Lt. Gen. Ali Muhsin al-Ahmar

PRIME MINISTER: Maeen Abdulmalik Saeed

Note: *Yemen has been in a state of political crisis since 2011 when a fresh wave of protests started, inspired by the Arab Spring. The country has become a base for militant groups like Al-Qaeda and Islamic State and spiralled into civil war in 2014. Yemen is strategically important because it sits on the Bab al-Mandab strait, a narrow waterway linking the Red Sea with the Gulf of Aden, through which much of the world's oil shipments pass.*

The Yemeni Civil War began in 2015 between two factions claiming to constitute the Yemeni government along with their supporters and allies. On 21 March 2015, Abdrabbuh Mansur Al-Hadi rescinded his resignation and declared he was still the legitimate president and called on government institutions to gather in Aden which he proclaimed was Yemen's "economic and temporary capital" while Sanaa remains under Houthi Shiite control.

Meanwhile, a Saudi-led intervention with a coalition of nine Middle Eastern countries was carried out. The conflict is seen as part of a regional power struggle between Shia-ruled Iran and Sunni-ruled Saudi Arabia. In December 2017, ousted leader Ali Abdullah Saleh was killed by Houthi rebels near the capital Sanaa, and the alliance between the Houthis and Ali Abdullah Saleh collapsed in November 2017. On 6 December 2018 the UN-led peace talks aimed at ending nearly four years of civil war in Yemen began in Sweden. The warring parties agreed to a ceasefire at the talks. In July 2019, the United Arab Emirates (UAE), a key ally of Saudi Arabia in the war, announced a withdrawal of its forces from Yemen. There was a sudden escalation in hostilities between the Houthis and coalition-led forces and in April 2020, the Southern Transitional Council (STC) declared self-rule in Aden stating that it would govern the port city and Southern provinces. The conflict has become more complicated with the involvement of other combatants, including an al-Qaeda affiliate and the self-declared Islamic State, as well as the emergence of rival factions within groups. The United States has backed the Saudi-led coalition, as have France, Germany, and the United Kingdom.

The conflict has displaced more than one million people causing the world's worst humanitarian crisis in recent times. Thousands of people have died in fighting and millions have been pushed to the brink of starvation. According to Amnesty International, it is estimated that over 233,000 Yemenis would have been killed as a result of fighting and the humanitarian crisis. The office of the UN High Commissioner for Human Rights has documented more than 20,000 civilians killed and injured by the fighting since March 2015.

KEY DEFENCE PERSONS

DEFENCE MINISTER: Lt. Gen. Muhammad al-Maqdashi

CHIEF OF STAFF: Lt. Gen. Sagheer bin Aziz

ECONOMY

Yemen, one of the world's poorest countries, has been devastated by a civil war. The economy has deteriorated since the escalation of violent conflict in March 2015. According to the World Bank report, "The conflict has caused widespread disruption of economic activities, with substantial reduction in jobs, private sector operations, and business opportunities. Operating costs rose severely due to insecurity and lack of supplies and inputs, leading to massive lay-offs to the country's formal and informal workforce." The war has halted Yemen's exports and accelerated inflation severely limiting food and fuel imports and caused widespread damage to infrastructure. Prior to the start of the political crisis in 2014, Yemen was highly dependent on oil and gas resources for revenue which accounted for roughly 25% of GDP and 65% of government revenue. However, the unrest that began in early 2011 caused the GDP to plunge almost 11% in that year. The conflict has accelerated the country's economic decline and access to food and other critical commodities such as medical equipment is limited across the country. Socio-economic conditions deteriorated further in 2020, affected by low global oil prices and the economic fallout of COVID-19. The ongoing crisis continues to accelerate the country's economic decline. The UN has estimated that 24.3 million people in 2021 were "at risk" of hunger and disease, of whom roughly 14.4 million were in acute need of assistance.

GDP (official exchange rate): $54.356 billion (2018 est.)

Real Growth Rate (GDP): -5.9% (2017 est.), -13.6% (2016 est.)

Industries: Crude oil production and petroleum refining; small-scale production of cotton textiles, leather goods; food processing; handicrafts; aluminum products; cement; commercial ship repair; natural gas production.

Oil – Proved Reserves: 3 billion bbl (1 January 2018 est.)

Natural Gas – Proved Reserves: 4478.5 billion cu m (1 January 2018 est.)

Total Exports: $384.5 million (2017 est.), $940 million (2016 est.)

Export Commodities: Crude petroleum, gold, fish, industrial chemical liquids, scrap iron (2019)

Major Markets: China 53%, Saudi Arabia 10%, United Arab Emirates 7%, Australia 5% (2019)

Total Imports: $4.079 billion (2017 est.), $3.117 billion (2016 est.)

Import Commodities: Wheat, refined petroleum, iron, rice, cars (2019)

Major Suppliers: China 25%, Turkey 10%, United Arab Emirates 9%, Saudi Arabia 8%, India 7% (2019)

INTERNATIONAL DISPUTES

◆ Saudi Arabia has reinforced its concrete-filled security barrier along sections of the fully demarcated border with Yemen to stem illegal cross-border activities.

DEFENCE

The armed forces of Yemen comprised of the Army including the Republican Guard, the Navy including the Marines and the Air Force including the Air Defence Force. Since the Yemen civil war, the armed forces have been divided between loyalists of the former president Ali Abdullah Saleh and pro-government forces of president Abdrabbuh Mansour Hadi. Yemen being in a state of civil war, proper structure of the armed forces no longer exists. Past data of the country's military equipment has been compiled below:

ARMY
Personnel: 45,000 (est.)

Equipment

Category	Name	In Service
MBT	T-72	39
	T-62	200
	T-54	300
	T-55	300
	M-60A1	140
Armoured car	Saladin	60
	BRDM-2	100
	AML-90	125
	Ferret	10+
AIFV/APC	BMP-1/2	150
	BMD-1	
	M-113A1	76
	BTR- 40/60/152	650
	M-577A1	6
	M-578	6
	Walid	
Artillery	76mm	100
	85mm	100
	100mm	100
	105mm	100
	122mm	150
	130mm	75
	M114 155mm towed	12
Mortar	81mm	
	120mm	
	160mm	
MRL	BM-21 122mm	280
	BM-14	11
ATK weapon	LAW	
ATGW	Vigilant	
	Dragon	24 launchers, 1500 missiles
	Tow	

...continued

Category	Name	In Service
AA Gun	ZU-23-2 2mm	50+
	37mm	50+
	57mm	150+
	85mm towed	50+
	ZU-23-4	30+
	Vulcan 20mm	72
SAM	SA-2	21
	SA-6	21
	SA-7	20
SSM	Scud	15+
	Frog-7	12
	Scud-B	6
	SS-21	4

New Procurements/Upgrades

No major procurement plans are under consideration at present.

NAVY
Personnel: 2,500

Equipment

Category	Name	In Service
Patrol craft	P-1022	10
	ex-USSR Tarantul class	2
	Chinese-built Hounan class missile FAC	3
	ex-USSR OSA II class missile FAC	3
	ex-USSR Zhuk class	2
	ex-US patrol boat	7
	Broadsword class	1
	CMN 15-60 fast patrol launches	6
Mine warfare Force	ex-USSR Natya class	2
	ex-USSR Yevgenya class	5
Amphibious Force	Bilquis (modified Polnocny type)	1
	Saba class LCU (modified Deba type)	3
Marine police	Fairey TRACKER Mk2 type coastal patrol craft	5
	Spear type coastal patrol craft	4
Coastal defence	SS-C-3 missile batteries	
	130mm guns & tank turrets	

New Procurements/Upgrades

No major procurement plans are under consideration at present.

AIR FORCE
Personnel: 3,500

Equipment

Category	Name	In Service
Fighter	SU-22	48
	MiG-29 SMT	13
	MiG-29 UBT	5
Transport	An-24	6
	IL-14	8
	An-12	3
	An-26	9
	Fokker F.27	3
	C130H HERCULES	2
	SKYVANS	2
Helicopter	Mi-8/Mi-17	40
	AB-204	2
	AB-205	2
	Mi-24	15
	AB-212	6

...continued

Category	Name	In Service
Helicopter	ALOUETTE	2
	AB-206	6
	Mi-4	4
	Ka-27	2
	HUEY II	4
Trainer	F-5-B	4
	Yak-11	18
	L-39C	12

New Procurements/Upgrades
No major procurement plans are under consideration at present.

Defence Expenditure
Total defence spending: $1.4 billion (2019), $1,222 million (2008)

Estimated defence spending in terms of GDP: 3.97% (2014)

Defence Production and R&D
Yemen currently being affected by war has not undertaken any defence production activities.

Defence Procurement
The Yemen Army/Navy/Air Force has not made any major defence procurements in recent years.

CONTACT DETAILS
Ministry of Defence
P.O. Box 1399,
Sana'a
Tel: 967-1-252-374
Fax: 967-1-252-378

ZAMBIA
(Capital: Lusaka)

INTRODUCTION
Area: 752,618 sq km
Population: 19,077,816 (July 2021 est.)
Coastline: 0 km (landlocked)
Maritime claims: None (landlocked)

KEY POLITICAL PERSONS

PRESIDENT: Hakainde Hichilema

VICE PRESIDENT: Mutale nalumango

KEY DEFENCE PERSONS

MINISTER OF DEFENCE: Ambrose Lwiji Lufuma

COMMANDER OF ARMY: Maj. Gen. Dennis Alibuzwi

COMMANDER OF AIR FORCE: Lt. Gen. Collin Barry

ECONOMY
Zambia had one of the world's fastest growing economies for the ten years up to 2014, with real GDP growth averaging roughly 6.7% per annum, though growth slowed during the period 2015 to 2017, due to falling copper prices as well as domestic pressure. GDP growth picked up in 2017 as mineral prices rose. In 2019, economic growth declined significantly, from 4% (2018) to 1.4%. The services sector remained the country's key driver of growth, growing by 3.5% in 2019. Zambia is Africa's second-largest copper producer. The economy is estimated to have contracted by 1.2% in 2020. A gradual recovery is expected, with

GDP growth projected at 1.8% in 2021, and will average 2.8% over 2021-23, according to the World Bank.

GDP (official exchange rate): $25.71 billion (2017 est.)

Real Growth Rate (GDP): 3.4% (2017 est.), 3.8% (2016 est.)

Industries: Copper mining and processing, emerald mining, construction, foodstuffs, beverages, chemicals, textiles, fertilizer, horticulture.

Total Exports: $8.55 billion (2020 est.), $8.26 billion (2019 est.)

Export Commodities: Copper, gold, gemstones, sulphuric acid, raw sugar, tobacco (2019)

Major Markets: Switzerland 29%, China 16%, Namibia 12%, Democratic Republic of the Congo 9%, Singapore 5% (2019)

Total Imports: $5.92 billion (2020 est.), $8.04 billion (2019 est.)

Import Commodities: Refined petroleum, crude petroleum, delivery trucks, gold, fertilizers (2019)

Major Suppliers: South Africa 29%, China 14%, United Arab Emirates 12%, India 5% (2019)

INTERNATIONAL DISPUTES

◆ In 2004, Zimbabwe dropped objections to plans between Botswana and Zambia to build a bridge over the Zambezi River, thereby de facto recognizing a short, but not clearly delimited, Botswana-Zambia boundary in the river.

DEFENCE

The Zambian Defence Force (ZDF) consists of the Army, the Air Force, and Zambian National Service (ZNS). Being a landlocked country, Zambia has no Navy. The ZDF is designed primarily for internal defence in Zambia, however, it has a commitment to international peacekeeping, specifically on the African continent. The government has committed to making resources available to the ZDF which is equipped with obsolete and outdated equipment to improve their welfare and critical skills.

ARMY
Personnel: 21,500
Equipment

Category	Name	In Service
MBT	Type 59	16
	T54/55	8
	PT-76 light	20
Armoured Car	Ferret	24
	BRDM-1/2	76
	BTR-60	13
	BTR-70	20
Artillery	M1942 76mm	35
	Mod.56 105mm	18
	D-30 122mm	25
	M46 130mm	18
Mortar	81 mm	50
	82mm	24
	120mm	14

...continued

Category	Name	In Service
MRL	BM-21 122mm	50
RCL	M18 57mm	10
	M20 75 mm	10
	Carl Gustav 84 mm	10
ATGW	SAGGER	9
AA gun	M55 20mm	50
	M1939 37mm	40
	S60 57mm	55
	KS-12 85mm	16
SAM	SA-7	9

New Procurements/Upgrades
No major procurement plans are under consideration at present.

AIR FORCE
Personnel: 1,500
Equipment

Category	Name	In Service
Fighter	L-15 Falcon	6
	MiG-21	12
	J-6	12
	K-8P	15
Transport	C-27J	2
	Do-28 Skyservant	9
	DHC-5D Buffalo	5
	Yak-40	3
	An-26	4
	Y-12	9
	MA 60	2
Liasion	MFI-17 Safari	20
Trainer	SF-260MZ	8
	SF-260TW	9
Helicopter	Mi-17	
	AB205As	15
	Z-9	4
UAV		400+

New Procurements/Upgrades
No major procurement plans are under consideration at present.

Defence Expenditure
Total defence spending: $262 million (2020), $292 million (2019)
Defence spending in terms of GDP: 1.2% (2020)

Defence Production and R&D
Zambia does not undertake any defence production activities.

Defence Procurement
Zambia receives military support mainly from China and the United Kingdom. The nation has set up a Defence Procurement Bureau under the Ministry of Defence as part of Zambia's Public Service Reform Programme. The Zambia Defence Force has reportedly displayed new vehicles and weapon systems, many of them Israeli made, during the Defence Force Day parade on 13 June 2021. The equipment included six Elbit ATMOS M46 wheeled self-propelled howitzers (SPHs) and six Elbit Spear MK2 self-propelled mortars, Israeli unmanned aerial vehicles (UAVs) were also on display, with the Zambian Air Force (ZAF) showing three Elbit Hermes 450s: an acquisition it confirmed in 2018. The Army displayed two smaller Elbit Skylark UAVs.

CONTACT DETAILS
Ministry of Defence
Independence Avenue
P/Bag RW 17X, Lusaka
Tel: +260 211 251211
Email: info@MOD.gov.zm

ZIMBABWE
(Capital: Harare)

INTRODUCTION
Area: 390,757 sq km
Population: 14,829,988 (July 2021est.)
Coastline: 0 Km (Landlocked)
Maritime claims: None

KEY POLITICAL PERSONS

PRESIDENT & COMMANDER-IN-CHIEF: Emmerson Mnangagwa

VICE PRESIDENT: Constantine Guveya Chiwenga

KEY DEFENCE PERSONS

DEFENCE MINISTER: Oppah Muchinguri-Kashiri

COMMANDER OF ARMY: Lt. Gen. David Sigauke

COMMANDER OF AIR FORCE: Air Marshal Elson Moyo

ECONOMY

Zimbabwe's economy depends heavily on its mining and agriculture sectors. Following a contraction from 1998 to 2008, the economy recorded real growth of more than 10% per year in the period 2010-13, before falling below 3% in the period 2014-17, due to poor harvests, low diamond revenues, and decreased investment. Lower mineral prices, infrastructure and regulatory deficiencies, a poor investment climate, a large public and external debt burden, and extremely high government wage expenses impede the country's economic performance.

Until early 2009, the Reserve Bank of Zimbabwe (RBZ) routinely printed money to fund the budget deficit, causing hyperinflation. Adoption of a multi-currency basket in early 2009 - which allowed currencies such as the Botswana pula, the South Africa rand, and the US dollar to be used locally - reduced inflation below 10% per year. In January 2015, as part of the government's effort to boost trade and attract foreign investment, the RBZ announced that the Chinese renminbi, Indian rupee, Australian dollar, and Japanese yen would be accepted as legal tender in Zimbabwe, though transactions were predominantly carried out in US dollars and South African rand until 2016, when the rand's devaluation and instability led to near-exclusive use of the US dollar. International financial institutions want Zimbabwe to implement significant fiscal and structural reforms before granting new loans. Foreign and domestic investment continues to be hindered by the lack of land tenure and titling, the inability to repatriate dividends to investors overseas, and the lack of clarity regarding the government's Indigenization and Economic Empowerment Act.

Amidst the Coronavirus health crisis, the Zimbabwean economy shrunk by 8% in 2020, according to World Bank data. The economy is expected to rebound by 2.9% in 2021.

GDP (official exchange rate): $21.44 billion (2019 est.)

Real Growth Rate (GDP): 3.7% (2017 est.); 0.7% (2016 est.)

Industries: Mining (coal, gold, platinum, copper, nickel, tin, diamonds, clay, numerous metallic and non-metallic ores), steel; wood products, cement, chemicals, fertilizer, clothing and footwear, foodstuffs, beverages

Total Exports: $4.42 billion (2018 est.); $6.25 billion (2017 est.)

Export Commodities: Gold, tobacco, iron alloys, nickel, diamonds, jewellery (2019)

Major Markets: United Arab Emirates 40%, South Africa 23%, Mozambique 9% (2019)

Total Imports: $7.21 billion (2018 est.); $9.65 billion (2017 est.)

Import Commodities: Refined petroleum, delivery trucks, packaged medicines, fertilizers, tractors (2019)

Major Suppliers: South Africa 41%, Singapore 23%, China 8% (2019)

INTERNATIONAL DISPUTES

◆ Namibia has supported, and in 2004 Zimbabwe dropped objections to, plans between Botswana and Zambia to build a bridge over the Zambezi River, thereby de facto recognizing a short, but not clearly delimited, Botswana-Zambia boundary in the river.

◆ South Africa has placed military units to assist police operations along the border of Lesotho, Zimbabwe, and Mozambique to control smuggling, poaching, and illegal migration.

DEFENCE

ARMY

Personnel: 25,000

Equipment

Category	Name	In Service
MBT	Type 59	35
	Type 69	10
APC	Type 89	
	UR 416	30+
	BTR 50	40
	MPCV 4x4	100+
Armoured Car	AML-90	20
	Elands Mk7	20
	EE9 CASCAVEL	90
	Panhard AML	30
Artillery	25 pdr 88mm	24
	Type 60 122 mm	18
	Type 54 122mm	12
Mortars	L16 81mm/82mm	600
	2B11 120 mm	140
AA Gun	ZPU1/2/4 14.5mm	200+
	ZU23 23mm	
	M1939 37mm	
SAM	SA-7/SA-18 Igla	30

New Procurements/ Upgrades

No procurement plans are under consideration at present.

AIR FORCE

Personnel: 1,000

Equipment

Category	Name	In Service
Fighter/ Trainer	F-7	6
	MiG-23	3
	SF-260	10+
	K-8 Karakoram	11
Transport, Reconnaissance	Islander	6
	CASA 212-200	10
	An-12	1
Helicopter	Alouette III	
	Mi-17	1
	Mi-35	6

New Procurements/ Upgrades

◆ Negotiations are reportedly going on to procure JF-17 Thunder fighter platforms from China.

Defence Expenditure

Estimated defence spending in terms of GDP: 2.52%

Defence Production and R&D

The Zimbabwe Defence Industries (ZDI), set up by the Government, is the country's only primary defence contractor to meet the requirements of the Armed Forces and the Government. The Defence Ministry has recently announced that the ZDI will enter into strategic partnerships with universities and colleges to provide cutting edge military solutions to the Zimbabwean Armed Forces.

Defence Procurement

No confirmed data or information is available on the current acquisition programmes undertaken by the Zimbabwean military. Defence procurement by the country was affected after the US and EU imposed an arms embargo on the country in 2002. The EU in February 2012 further extended the embargo which continued till 2016 and was partially lifted in 2017. The African nation has eyed military imports from non-EU countries, especially from China in recent times, to modernise its armed forces.

CONTACT DETAILS
Ministry of Defence
Public Relations Office
Ministry of Defence - H/Q
Defence House, cnr Kwame Nkuruma / 3rd Street, Harare
Tel.: +263-4 250042, 252050 – 7, 700155 - 8, 700077 – 8
www.defence.gov.zw

ABBREVIATION

AA Gun	Anti-Aircraft Gun
AAM	Air-to-Air Missile
AAW	Anti-Air Warfare
AB	Airborne
ABM	Anti-Ballistic Missile
ACD	Arms Control & Disarmamanent
ACS	Association of Caribbean States
ACV	Air Cushion Vehicle
ADF	Air Defence Force
AESA	Active Electronically Scanned Array
AEV	Armoured Engineering Vehicle
AEW	Airborne Early Warning
AEW&C	Airborne Early Warning and Control
AFV	Armoured Fighting Vehicle
AGM	Air-to-Ground Missile
AGSS	Auxilliary Research Submarine
AI	Artificial Intelligence
AIFV	Armoured Infantry Fighting Vehicle
AIP	Air Independent Propulsion
ALCM	Air-Launched Cruise Missile
ALH	Advanced Light Helicopter
ALMDS	Airborne Laser Mine Detection System
ALOC	Air Line of Communication
AMRAAM	Advanced Medium-Range Air-to-Air Missile
ANG	Air National Guard
ANZUS	Australia, New Zealand, United States Security
AOI	Arab Organisation for Industrialisation
AOP	Airborne Observation Post
AOPS	Arctic/ Offshore Patrol Ship
APAC	Asia-Pacific
APC	Armoured Personnel Carrier
APEC	Asia-Pacific Economic Cooperation
ASAT	Anti-Satellite
ASBM	Anti-Ship Ballistic Missile System
ASCM	Anti-Ship Cruise Missile
ASEAN	Association of Southeast Asian Nations
ASI	Air-Surface Integration
AShM	Anti-Ship Missile
ASM	Air-to-Surface Missile
ASSW	Anti-Surface Ship Weapon
ASuW	Anti-Surface Warfare
ASW	Anti-Submarine Warfare
ATGM	Anti-Tank Guided Missile
ATGW	Anti-Tank Guided Weapon
Atk	Anti-Tank
ATV	All-Terrain Vehicle
AV	Armoured Vehicle
AWACS	Airborne Warning and Control System
AWD	Air-Warfare Destroyer
AAW	Anti-Air Warfare
BDL	Bharat Dynamics Ltd.
BIMSTEC	Bay of Bengal Initiative for Multi-Sectoral Technical and Economic Cooperation
BISTEC	Bangladesh, India, Sri Lanka, and Thailand Economic Cooperation
BMD	Ballistic Missile Defence
BWC	Biological and Toxin Weapons Convention
C4I	Command, Control, Communications, Computers and Intelligence
C4I2SR	Command, Control, Communications, Computer, Information, Intelligence, Surveillance and Reconnaissance
CATOBAR	Catapult Assisted Take Off but Arrested Recovery
CAEW	Conformal Airborne Early Warning
CAGR	Compound Annual Growth Rate
CDCM	Coastal Defence Cruise Missile
CDF	Chief of Defence Staff
CELAC	Community of Latin American and Caribbean States
CIWS	Close-In Weapon System
CJEF	Combined Joint Expeditionary Force
CMC	Central Military Commission
CN	Chief of Navy
CORPAT	Coordinated Maritime Patrols
CSDP	Common Security and Defence Policy
CTBT	Comprehensive Test Ban Treaty
CTOL	Conventional Takeoff and Landing
CVN	Aircraft Carrier, Nuclear Powered
CWC	Chemical Weapons Convention
DARE	Defence Avionics Research Establishment
DCG	Defence Capability Guide
DCP	Defence Capability Plan
DDG	Guided Missile Destroyer
DECO	Defence Export Control Office
DF	Dong Feng
DMO	Defence Materiel Organisation
DND	Department of National Defence
DPRK	Democratic People's Republic of Korea
DRDO	Defence Research and Development Organisation
DSTO	Defence Science and Technology Organisation
EAC	Eastern Area Command
ECM	Electronic Countermeasures
ELINT	Electronic Intelligence
EMP	Euro-Mediterranean Partnership
ENP	European Neighbourhood Policy
ENPI	European Neighbourhood and Partnership Instrument
EPCO	Equipment Procurement and Construction Office
ESSM	Evolved Sea Sparrow Missile
EU	European Union
EW	Electronic Warfare
FAC	Fast Attack Craft
FASGW-ANL	Future Anti-Surface Guided Weapon - Anti-Navire Leger
FF	Frigate
FFG	Guide Missile Frigate
FGFA	Fifth Generation Fighter Aircraft
FLN	National Liberation Front
FMC	Fast Missile Craft
FMF	Foreign Military Financing
FMS	Foreign Military Sales
FPDA	Five Power Defence Arrangements
G20	Group of Twenty Finance

Brahmand World Defence Update 2022

	Ministers and Central Bank Governors	LCAC	Landing Craft, Air Cushioned	NAM	Non-Aligned Movement
GDP	Gross Domestic Product	LCM	Landing Craft, Mechanised	NATO	North Atlantic Treaty Organisation
GPS	Global Positioning System	LCU	Landing Craft, Utility	NCA	Nuclear Command Authority
GRSE	Garden Reach Ship Builders and Engineers	LCVP	Landing Craft, Vehicle, Personnel	NDHQ	National Defence Headquarters
GW	Guided Weapon	LHA	Landing Helicopter Assault	NEFA	North East Frontier Agency
HAIC	Hongdu Aviation Industry Corporation	LHD	Landing Helicopter Dock	NHQ	Naval Headquarters
HAL	Hindustan Aeronautics Limited	LPD	Landing Platform Dock	NMRH	Naval Multi Role Helicopter
		LRST	Long Range Surveillance and Tracking	NORAD	North American Aerospace Defence Command
HALE	High Altitude Long Endurance	LSM	Landing Ship, Medium	NPC	National People's Congress
IAC	Indigenous Aircraft Carrier	LST	Landing Ship, Tank	NPT	Non-Proliferation Treaty
IAEA	International Atomic Energy Agency	LUH	Light Utility Helicopter	NSFC	Naval Strategic Force Command
		MALE	Medium Altitude Longue Endurance		
IAF	Indian Air Force	MARLANT	Maritime Forces Atlantic	NSPO	National Service Products Organisation
IAI	Israel Aerospace Industries	MBT	Main Battle Tank		
IBSAMAR	India-Brazil-South Africa Maritime	MDIC	Malaysian Defence Industry Council	NTM-A	NATO Training Mission–Afghanistan
ICBM	Intercontinental Ballistic Missile	MDL	Mazagon Dockyards Limited	OAS	Organisation of American States
ICJ	International Court of Justice	MEADS	Medium Extended Air Defence System	OECD	Organisation for Economic Cooperation and Development
IFV	Infantry Fighting Vehicles	MECC	Maritime-Enforcement Co-ordination Centre	OEM	Original Equipment Manufacturer
IGMDP	Integrated Guided Missile Development Programme	MFN	Most Favoured Nation	OIC	Organisation of Islamic Conference
IISS	International Institute for Strategic Studies	MHI	Mitsubishi Heavy Industries		
		MICV	Mechanised Infantry Combat Vehicle	OPEC	Organisation of the Petroleum Exporting Countries
IMB	International Maritime Bureau	MIDES	Malaysian Defence, Security and Enhancement Industry Council		
IMF	International Monetary Fund			OPV	Off Shore Patrol Vessel
IOR	Indian Ocean Region	MINFAR	Ministry of the Revolutionary Armed Forces	PAC-3	Patriot Advanced Capability 3
IRB	Industrial and Regional Benefits			PAK-FA	Perspective Aviation Complex of Frontline Aviation
IRBM	Intermediate-Range Ballistic Missile	MININT	Ministry of Interior		
		MLRS	Multiple Launch Rocket System	PCU	Pre-Commissioning Unit
IRGC	Islamic Revolutionary Guard Corps	MLU	Mid-Life Update	PLA	People's Liberations Army
IRIAF	Islamic Republic of Iranian Air Force	MMA	Multi-Mission Maritime Aircraft	PLO	Palestine Liberation Organisation
ISAF	International Security Assistance Force	MMRCA	Medium Multi-Role Combat Aircraft	PoK	Pak-occupied-Kashmir
				PRC	People's Republic of China
ISC	Integrated Space Cell	MoU	Memorandum of Understanding	QIZ	Qualified Industrial Zone
ISRO	Indian Space Research Organisation			RAM	Rolling Airframe Missile
		MRBM	Medium Range Ballistic Missile	RCL	Recoilless Rifle
JASSM	Joint Air-to-Surface Standoff Missiles			RCN	Royal Canadian Navy
		MRL	Mount Rocket Launcher	RFI	Request for Information
JASSM-ER	Joint Air-to-Surface Standoff Missiles - Extended Range	MRTT	Multi-Role Tanker Transport	RFP	Request for Proposal
				RL	Rocket Launcher
		MTA	Multirole Transport Aircraft	RMA	Revolution in Military Affairs
JSS	Joint Support Ship	MTC	Military-Technical Cooperation		
KMW	Krauss-Maffei Wegmann			RPP	Report on Plans and Priorities
KSEW	Karachi Shipyard and Engineering Works	MTCR	Missile Technology Control Regime		
				SAARC	South Asian Association for Regional Cooperation
LACM	Land Attack Cruise Missile	MTTF	Mission Transition Task Force		
LCA	Light Combat Aircraft			SAATEG	System for Imagery

	Reconnaissance Deep in the Area of Operations	STOVL	Short Takeoff and Vertical Landing
SAC	Southern Area Command	TAPV	Tactical Armoured Patrol Vehicles
SAF	Second Artillery Force	TAR	Tibetan Autonomous Region
SAM	Surface-to-Air Missile	TTH	Tactical Transport Helicopter
SAR	Search and Rescue	TUAV	Tactical Uninhabited Aerial Vehicle
SATCOM	Satellite Communication	UAC-TA	United Aircraft Corporation -Transport Aircraft
SCAF	Supreme Council of the Armed Forces	UAS	Unmanned Aircraft System
SCO	Shanghai Cooperation Organisation	UAV	Unmanned Aerial Vehicle
SIATI	Society of Indian Aerospace and Technologies Industries	UCAV	Unmanned Combat Aerial Vehicle
SIGINT	Signals intelligence	UNASUR	Union of South American Nations
SIMPRO	Simulator Research and Development Centre	UNSC	United Nations Security Council
SIPRI	Stockholm International Peace Research Institute	USS	United States Ship
SLBM	Submarine-Launched Ballistic Missile	VADS	Vulcan Air Defence System
SPD	Strategic Plans Division	VLA	Vertical Launch Anti-Submarine Missile
SRBM	Short-Range Ballistic Missile	VTOL	Vertical Take-off and Landing
SRSAM	Short-Range Surface-to-Air Missile	WAC	Western Area Command
SSBN	Submersible Ship Ballistic, Nuclear / Nuclear-Powered Ballistic Missile-Carrying Submarine	WMD	Weapons of Mass Destruction
SSGN	Cruise Missile Carrying Nuclear Submarine	WPK	Workers' Party of Korea
SSI	Submersible Ship, Conventional with AIP	WTO	World Trade Organisation
SSK	Submersible Ship, Conventional		
SSM	Surface-to-Surface Missile		
SSN	Submersible Ship, Nuclear / Nuclear-Powered Attack Submarine		
STOL	Short Takeoff and Landing		